Professional Commerce Server 2000 Programming

Tim Huckaby
Scott Case
Andreas Eide
Chris Featherstone
Fabio Claudio Ferracchiati
Christopher George
Rodney Guzman
Scott Hanselman
Mark Harrison
Jarrod Marshall
Tim McCarthy
Sophie McQueen
Frank Reashore
Tony Roberts
Mark Seemann
William Sheldon
Joey Smith
Robert Stovenour
Karsten Strøbæk
Lee Whitney

Wrox Press Ltd. ®

Professional Commerce Server 2000 Programming

Published by Wrox Press Ltd,
Arden House, 1102 Warwick Road, Acocks Green,
Birmingham, B27 6BH, UK
Printed in Canada
ISBN 1-861004-64-8

Trademark Acknowledgements

Wrox has endeavored to provide trademark information about all the companies and products mentioned in this book by the appropriate use of capitals. However, Wrox cannot guarantee the accuracy of this information.

Credits

Authors
Tim Huckaby
Scott Case
Andreas Eide
Chris Featherstone
Fabio Claudio Ferracchiati
Christopher George
Rodney Guzman
Scott Hanselman
Mark Harrison
Jarrod Marshall
Tim McCarthy
Sophie McQueen
Frank Reashore
Tony Roberts
Mark Seemann
William Sheldon
Joey Smith
Robert Stovenour
Karsten Strøbæk
Lee Whitney

Technical Architects
Alastair Ewins
Dan Squier

Technical Editors
Claire Brittle
Ewan Buckingham
Howard Davies

Author Agent
Sarah Bowers

Category Manager
Kirsty Reade

Project Administrator
Laura Jones

Technical Reviewers
Russ Basiura
Maxime Bombardier
David Brennan
Steve Celius
Michael Erickson
Cristof Falk
Hope Hatfield
Brian Hickey
Erik Hougaard
Terrence Joubert
Shaun McAravey
Chad Parsons
Scott Robertson
John Roth
Aaron Sloman

Index
Michael Brinkman

Production Manager
Simon Hardware

Production Coordinator
Pip Wonson

Additional Layout
Paul Grove

Illustrations
Shabnam Hussain

Cover
Chris Morris
Dawn Chellingworth

Proof Reader
Fiona Berryman

About the Authors

Tim Huckaby

Tim Huckaby is President of www.InterKnowlogy.com, a software and network engineering firm dedicated to Enterprise, eBusiness, B2C/B2B consulting, application software design and development on the Internet, extranet, and intranet.

As lead author, this is Tim's seventh time with involvements on book projects with Wrox. You can also find Tim's work in magazine columns and regularly published features in the Windows 2000 Magazine family of publications. As Technical Architect and Software Development Lead Tim has over 20 years of industry experience with companies large and small all over the world and worked on the Site Server 3.0 product team for Microsoft.

Tim sits on the Microsoft Commerce Partner Advisory Council and was recently awarded with 'Microsoft Regional Director of the Year' for his work in the Developer Community. MSDN Regional Directors are independent third party advocates of Microsoft technologies whose mission it is to inform, educate and congregate the Windows development community.

You can also expect to see Tim delivering keynotes and technical sessions at developer conferences all over the world. Tim was awarded by Microsoft Corporation for the highest rated Keynote presentations of all the Developer Days held around the world in 1998 and in 1999 and took third in 2000. Tim has done presentations on Microsoft Technologies at developer events like Microsoft Tech Ed, Dev Days, and the PDC, along with Wrox's Devcons and others all over the world getting top 10% ratings in all.

Aside from his dedication to the industry Tim brings balance to his life with activities like mountain climbing, heavy alcoholic consumption, hang gliding, beach volleyball, womanizing, professional skateboarding, extreme surfing, alligator wrestling, gourmet cooking, and haiku poetry. Tim is one of the very first Microsoft Certified Professionals, attaining his first certifications in 1991.

Scott Case

Scott Case is a Principal Software Engineer for www.InterKnowlogy.com. There he provides user interface and architecture services for high volume commerce and content websites. He specializes in web based n-tier applications on the Microsoft platform as well as the targeted user interface design including the use of Macromedia Flash and other dynamic technologies. Previously from The BigStore.com and AltaVista:Shopping.com, he served in making Shopping.com one of PC Magazine's top E-Commerce websites of 1998. His professional experience also includes print and digital media design, outdoor educational media and illustration. In the future, he plans to spend fewer late nights working and more time with his wife Amy.

Andreas Eide

Andreas Eide has a Master of Science degree from the Norwegian Institute of Technology in Trondheim. He has been working as a developer and software architect for the past seven years. He is now principal consultant for Objectware. Objectware is a Norwegian consulting company focusing on component based development using Microsoft and Java based technologies. Andreas is an MCSD, MCT and is also MSDN Regional Director for Microsoft in Norway. When not having fun writing software he likes to dance with his wife Grete and their daughters Kristine and Maria.

Chris Featherstone

Chris Featherstone has been with Microsoft Corporation since early in 1999. Previous to his work at Microsoft, he worked as a consultant for Deloitte Consulting where he had the opportunity to work on many of Compaq's E-Commerce efforts. Currently Chris is on the Microsofts National Technology Team focusing on .NET Servers. Chris is also a husband and father to his beautiful bride Tawny and three wonderful kids; JD, Andersynn, and Grant.

Fabio Claudio Ferracchiati

Fabio Claudio Ferracchiati is a software developer and technical author. In the early years of his ten-year career he worked with classical languages and old Microsoft tools like Visual Basic and Visual C++. After five years he decided to dedicate his attention to the Internet and all the related technologies. In 1998 he started a parallel career writing technical articles for Italian and international magazines. Actually he works in Rome for CPI Progetti Spa (www.cpiprogetti.it) where he develops Internet/Intranet solutions using Microsoft technologies. Fabio would like to say a special thanks to his 'love' Danila for her patience and help. Also to Walter, Brendan and Massimo for their sympathy that alleviates every working day and to Alex Shogren (Microsoft) for his help.

Christopher George

Christopher George's extensive experience in the technology industry has focused on network and systems architecture and implementation in support of Internet businesses. He is currently the Director of Network Services for InterKnowlogy. He is tasked with building the network and systems consulting arm of the business as well as supporting ASP hosting of internally developed web-enabled applications.

Prior to joining InterKnowlogy, Mr. George was the Director of Network and Systems for The BigStore.com. His most notable accomplishments have included the architecting and implementation of reliable global network infrastructures and development of The BigStore.com and its international affiliates. He was heavily involved in supporting investor relations for The BigStore.com, and is responsible for managing the global network and systems support teams. His experience in architecting and implementing network and systems solutions in diverse environments has made him an expert in the creation of stable computing environments necessary for 24/7 technology companies.

Prior to the formation of DevConcepts, Christopher was responsible for the daily operation of the network and systems infrastructure of Shopping.com, making them a winner of PC Magazine's 1999 Top 100 Web Sites. Prior to Shopping.com, he was focused on network design and architecture for Millennium Systems. While studying Computer Engineering at California State University, Long Beach, he was responsible for systems integration and implementation for the university. He has served as primary network and systems architect for many public and private organizations, including several California municipal and county governments.

While away from work, he enjoys flying around Southern California in search of a new airport and a better hamburger with his wife, Jenn. He also enjoys playing hockey, softball and golf, fly-fishing, hiking and camping, snowboarding, jet-skiing, skydiving, and reading.

Christopher George can be reached via e-mail at chrisg@interknowlogy.com.

Rodney Guzman

Rodney Guzman is the Vice President and Chief Technology at InterKnowlogy. Rodney has been an engineer for many years developing many complex applications, including work in E-Commerce and enterprise web security and building complex XML web-based medical solutions and interface systems. His expertise includes a variety of Microsoft technologies and Java. Rodney has written many publications on a variety of topics including IIS and XML.

Scott Hanselman

Scott Hanselman is a Principal Consultant at STEP Technology, Inc. in Portland, Oregon. He's also the MSDN (Microsoft Developer Network) Regional Director for the Portland area. Scott considers himself language agnostic, with skills in C, C++, Visual Basic and Java. He has been developing on the Internet since 1990, and has been involved in designing a number of successful applications spanning the Web, Windows, Unix, as well as various portable devices. Scott was a key member of the development teams that built 800.com and Gear.com. Scott is a specialist in user interface design and human-computer interaction. He authored a successful PalmOS product for diabetics called GlucoPilot, which has won awards for excellence in user interface design. Scott attempts to apply his irrepressible wit as a frequent speaker preaching the gospel of XML and good design at industry conferences. On a more interesting note, Scott and his fiancée Mollar will be married in December 2001 in Zimbabwe.

Scott Hanselman welcomes e-mail and fat checks sent to `scott@hanselman.com`

Mark Harrison

Mark Harrison is a Principal Applications Engineer at Microsoft UK and is responsible for helping customers / partners understand Microsoft Internet technologies and to build business critical web solutions. Mark is also the author of several books on Web Security, ASP and Internet Explorer – all previously written under the pseudonym of Richard Harrison. In his spare time – what spare time – Mark is married with four children (Kirsty, Matthew, Nathan and Danielle) aged eight and under!

Jarrod Marshall

Jarrod Marshall resides in Nashville, Tennessee, where he is a consultant for G.A. Sullivan, a software development company based in St. Louis, Missouri. Jarrod began programming at the age of ten and over the last three years he has worked mostly with Internet-related applications and E-Commerce.

Tim McCarthy

Tim McCarthy is a Principal Engineer at InterKnowlogy, where he architects and builds highly scalable n-tier web applications utilizing the latest Microsoft technologies. He is a regular speaker at Microsoft Developer Days. Tim is also an instructor at the University of California, San Diego, where he teaches Microsoft developer courses.

Tim's hobbies include spending time with his wife, Miriam, his daughter, Jasmine, and his three step kids, Angie, BD, and Chris. He also loves to workout, drink beer, and lives for Notre Dame football and basketball.

Sophie McQueen

Sophie McQueen is a Principle Consultant at Sage Information Consultants Inc. Her role at Sage is to design and lead the implementation of web based solutions. Sophie has implemented Site Server applications for several clients including Panasonic Canada Inc. and the Canadian Automobile Association (CAA). She has been a reviewer on many Wrox books including Beginning Site Server. She can be reached at smcqueen@sageconsultants.com.

Frank Reashore

Frank J. Reashore has a B.Sc. in Physics and an M.Sc. in Mathematics and has done graduate work at Princeton University. He has over ten years experience with Microsoft technologies. He worked in the Visual C++ group at Microsoft where he tested the MFC and ALT wizards for Visual Studio 6.0. He has programmed in a wide range of languages including: Fortran, Lisp (InterLisp, eLisp, CommonLisp), Ada, Pascal, C, C++, Perl, Visual Basic. Recently, he has worked with Commerce Server on the futureshop.ca website. In his spare time he enjoys hiking, creative writing and drawing. He can be reached at reashore@hotmail.com.

Tony Roberts

Tony Roberts has extensive experience in developing technology strategies for start-up operations. Specializing in Application and System Development, he is an expert at creating order from chaos. His experience ranges from front-end systems including order management, product and category administration to back-end systems including database design and EDI. His attention to detail facilitates robust and feature-rich solutions to support complicated and intricate business requirements.

Currently, Tony is employed by InterKnowlogy, – prior to joining InterKnowlogy, he served as Chief Systems Architect for BOSS -TSP. He was responsible for designing and implementing the back-end systems for e-business applications ranging from Order Tracking, Accounting Integration, EDI and Product Management. Before BOSS, he served as Director of Operations Development at Shopping.com. He led a team of developers to create the Order Tracking and Management System, Credit Card Processing, EDI, Product Integration and Accounting Interfaces. These systems shifted the company from a manual operation to an automated solution. Additionally, working in the Health Care industry, he established operational standards and procedures as well as constructed Sales and Marketing Distributed Automation Systems. He also attended the California Polytechnic State University at San Luis Obispo to fulfill a Bachelor of Science in Aeronautical Engineering. This, along with his architectural and design experience, provides him with a unique perspective on developing enterprise class systems.

Mark Seemann

When not reading or embarking on insane (mostly computer-related) hobby projects, Mark Seemann works as a consultant and developer, doing commerce web sites on the Microsoft platform. He has a Master's degree in economics from the University of Copenhagen (Denmark), doesn't have a TV, but owns several computers, which his wife thinks are making too much noise in their Copenhagen apartment.

William Sheldon

William is a software developer and aspiring author originally from Baltimore, Maryland. Holding a degree in Computer Science from the Illinois Institute of Technology (IIT), he has managed to work as a software developer since his departure from the U.S. Navy, following the Gulf War. He has held his Microsoft Certified Solution Developer (MCSD) certification for several years, and is currently employed as a Principal Engineer with InterKnowlogy. As a software engineer, William designs software solutions and develops business components for extranets, intranets and the Internet.

He and his wife live in Southern California where they enjoy beautiful weather and a short commute to the office.

Dedication – This is for those who have gone before. To my Grandfathers, Charles and William, the engineer and the welder who passed on their values of learning and hard work. They would be proud to finally have an author in the family, as I promised so long ago. And of course my sister Lisa; everyone's friend and the best sister ever.

Joey Smith

Joey Smith, MCSE, MCP +I, MCT is currently the Chief Technology Officer for The INJOY Group based in Atlanta GA. Before coming to INJOY; a company dedicated to developing leadership excellence, Joey was the visionary, lead developer and project manager for the project that won the '1999 Microsoft Project of the Year' in the Best Knowledge Management Solution category. As a previous e-business consultant and Internet Evangelist for one of Microsoft's premier Provider Partners, Joey has had the opportunity to envision and build state-of-the-art web applications for fortune top 500 companies including Coca Cola Enterprises and Cox Communications to name a few. Joey's greatest joy comes from challenging business processes and really digging deep into new Microsoft Technologies to see how unions can be made between current business models and future business opportunities through the enablement of technology. Joey's philosophy is comprised of three things, 1) solve business problems, 2) enable business with technology, and 3) deliver technology solutions with excellence. Joey's favorite pastime is visioneering and getting dirty with server and Internet technologies. You can contact Joey at joey@injoy.com. For more information on building leadership skills and seeing Commerce Server in action, go to www.INJOY.com.

I would like to dedicate my portion of this book to my wife Julie and my two sons, Joey and Tommy. Thank you for your patience and support during those weekends I was away at the office.

Robert Stovenour

Robert Stovenour, a Microsoft Certified Solution Developer, is a consultant for Microsoft Consulting Services (MCS) in Dallas. His original goal in life was to become a jet fighter pilot but he was attracted to software development by a computer savvy big brother who is an electrical engineer and part-time programmer. Robert quickly changed his career path and since working on his first software project at 19, he has worked on various solutions including document management and workflow, imaging, electronic commerce, and enterprise integration. Robert has, however, started taking flying lessons in his spare time.

Karsten Strøbæk

Before Karsten turned to IT and became an MCSD and MCDBA he got a Master in Economics and Econometrics. He is currently employed as Chief Solution Developer at Intellix A/S. Here he works with design and development of web based decision support systems that utilize neural network technology. His tools of choice include Visual C++, Visual Basic and Double Espressos. When not working he likes to scuba dive, go to the opera or take his kids to the zoo.

Lee Whitney

Lee Whitney is a Senior Consultant at Micro Endeavors, Inc. Lee has spent the last eight years designing and managing the development of distributed applications utilizing a variety of technologies. Most recently, he has focused on implementing E-Commerce solutions for MEI's dot-com clients. Lee is co-author of *Visual Basic 6 Application Programming*, also from Wrox, and speaks on Visual Basic, E-Commerce and Project Management methodologies at various technical conferences, most recently SQL Connections in Orlando in Spring of 2001.

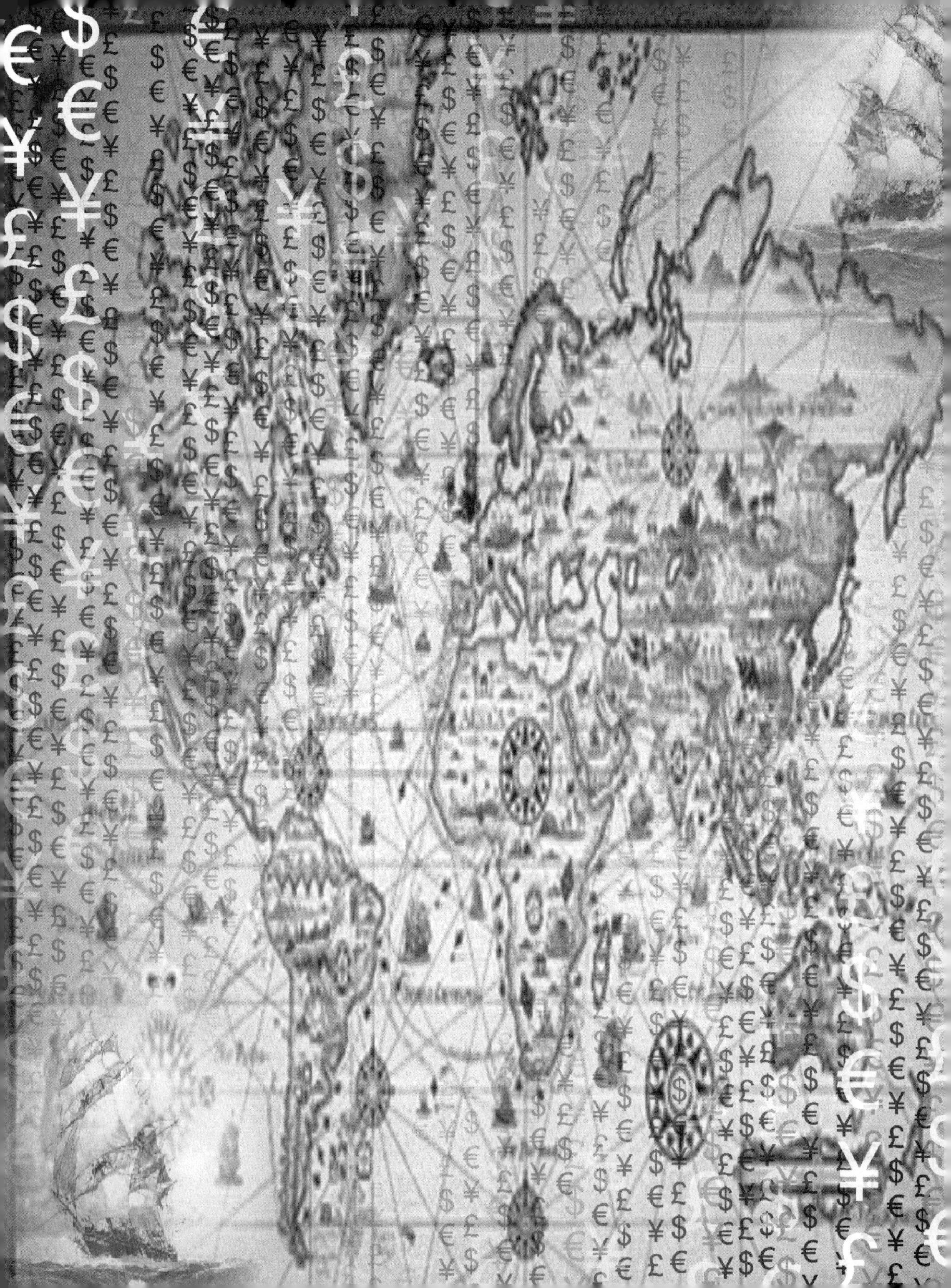

Table of Contents

Table of Contents

Table of Contents

Table of Contents

Table of Contents

Table of Contents

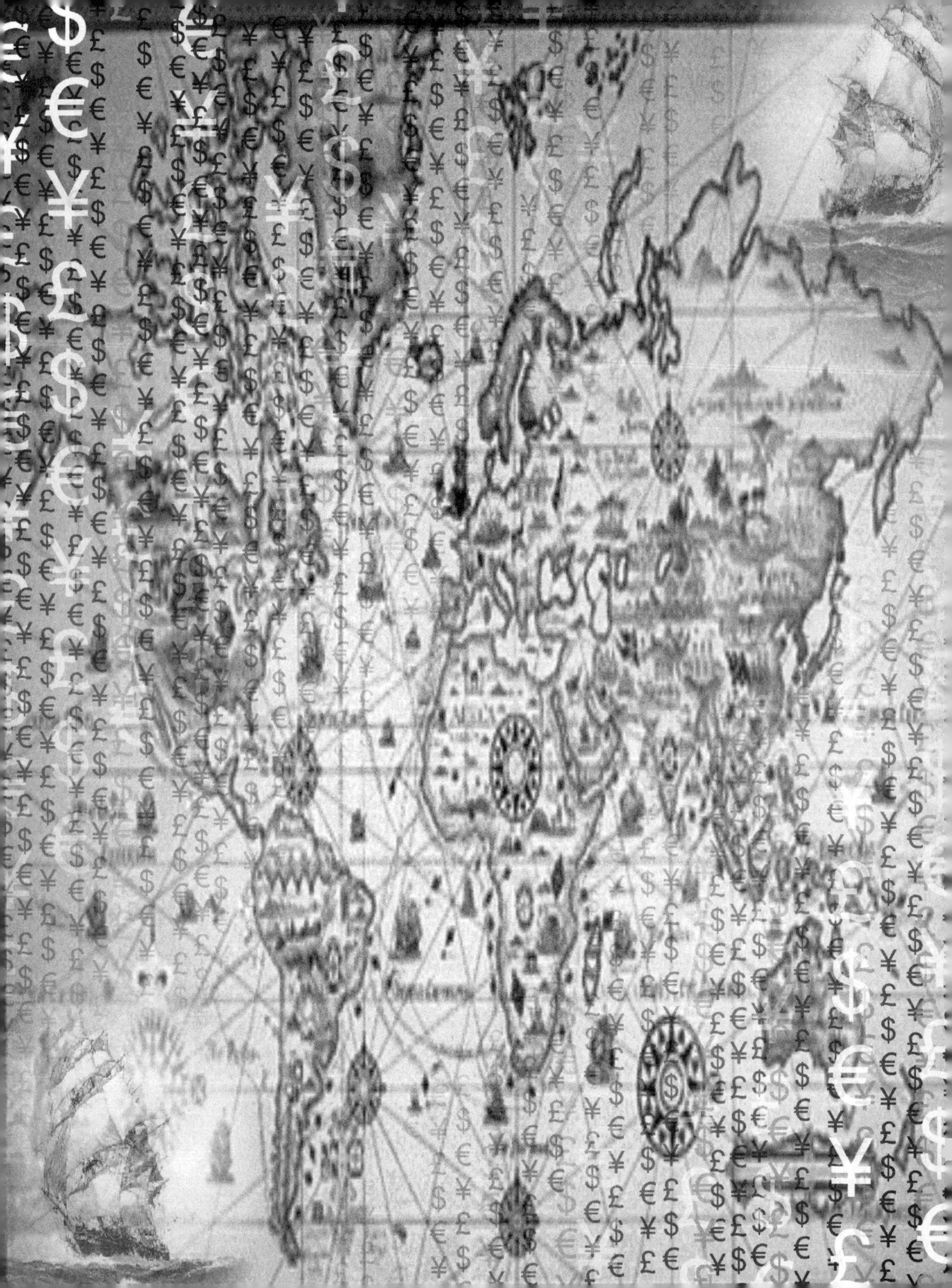

Behind the Scenes on Commerce Server 2000

Less than nine months after the release of Site Server 3.0 Commerce Edition (SSCE), a small team made up of dev and marketing were building the pitch for the new e-commerce business direction to the execs. By this time, specs for the next version were pretty solid. The broad Site Server team had quickly come together as we unified to ship various Internet and intranet technologies in a single package – it was now to be split up again, though at the time no-one knew the full extent to which this would happen.

Nevertheless, it was clear that the intranet team would move in their own direction to do great things in the document publishing and knowledge management space with Tahoe (now SharePoint). That left the Commerce team to build on our existing mission: make it easier to build great B2C and B2B solutions on top of the Microsoft platform.

On March 4, 1999, we revealed our new strategy at the well-attended "Commerce Strategy Day" briefing in San Francisco. Over 300 developers, journalists and analysts listened as Bill Gates and Bob Herbold (Steve B version 2.0 had just been born!) outlined our vision to deliver e-commerce solutions for consumers, small businesses and enterprises. This was the day we announced BizTalk (and BizTalk Server), Hydrogen (then called Small Business Commerce Services), and Commerce Server itself as the next generation of SSCE. Interest was strong – all we now had to do was to deliver on the promise.

To do this, we had to restructure the teams to be successful. We spent a couple of months churning before each product found its final home, but when all was said and done, the Commerce team split in three directions: Hydrogen became the hosted small business e-commerce offering in bCentral; BizTalk Server (BTS) and Commerce Server (CS) formed their own product units and both BTS and CS moved to join the rest of the Enterprise Servers in the 'developer' division. This move turned out to be ideal for everyone concerned, as it put us in a position to really leverage those around us and make smart decisions with the technology. It also gave our team the opportunity to clearly focus on sell-side e-commerce for mid-tier to enterprise customers.

The 3-way team split also left the CS team with some gaps to fill. With this move came a new leadership team and an opportunity to strengthen the vision and goals we had for the product. With only a few months to go before release of the first technical beta, Mike Nappi took the helm as the new Product Unit Manager.

Feedback from customers and partners about the strengths and weaknesses of SSCE gave us the input we needed to clarify and prioritize our goals for the next release. The team jelled very soon, and we were able to quickly reorient ourselves around a new set of release themes for the product, which included:

- ❑ Tighter product integration
- ❑ Broader, more comprehensive functionality
- ❑ Stronger developer tools
- ❑ A central tool for non-technical business users to manage their sites.

When we first previewed the technology to partners in September 2000, the feedback was excellent, with a lot of excitement over the Business Desk, Catalog system, Data Warehouse, and PuP tool. This dev lab made all the difference to the team, giving us invaluable feedback and much-needed incitement to keep plugging away over the holiday season and get a stable build out to partners in early Q1, after a year and a half in the works!

After a couple of months working with close partners, we opened up a broad beta in early July. At this time, our early-adopter customers were well into development and gearing up for test deployment.

Broad beta was a turning point for the Commerce Server 2000 product. We made the decision to test with SQL Server 2000 as the primary database (although still maintaining full support for SQL Server 7.0). We'd also decided to push out the release to make sure we had key sites running in production for a couple of months to get all the unknowns out of the way – all the things you may not catch in lab tests alone. Feedback from the project teams managing our early adopters gave us the direction we needed to reach RC0 – essentially, a restructuring of the Solution Sites for stronger performance and easier development, as well as stronger cube design for the data warehouse/analytics system.

Suffice to say that these quite significant modifications between beta and RC0 were initially rather painful for the project teams – even given the tools we created to make the move simpler. But every site was up and running on the new codebase and went into production without major incident, and the project teams were excited to see their feedback reflected in the product. Yes, this was the green light we were waiting on to get us to RTM! We released Commerce Server 2000 to manufacturing in mid November, two and a half years after shipping SSCE.

But the team couldn't sleep yet! It was now time for the quick fix and support teams to gear up to support these guys over the holidays. As a true testimonial to the product, all accounts ran peak loads over the holiday season, and without raising issues with Commerce Server – even those that were still running RC0! Having pulled long hours (even over nights and weekends) for more than 15 months straight since the first tech preview, this was undoubtedly the best present the team could have received!

We've certainly come a long way since SSCE, and had to make some tough choices along the way, but we hope you'll agree that in the end we delivered a great product. Now that it's available worldwide, and our early adopters have seen it support them through the high-volume holiday season, it's great to see this book hit the shelves, and complement a powerful tool with the expertise of some of the talented developers who use it.

Special thanks to Wrox Press and the whole team who pulled this book together, as it should certainly help to smooth out the learning curve and help you decide when, why, and how to best use Commerce Server. It's sure to be a great resource in helping you to take full advantage of the product's extensive capabilities, so that you can successfully develop e-commerce apps faster and easier.

Rebekkah Kumar
Lead Product Manager
Microsoft Commerce 2000 Development Group

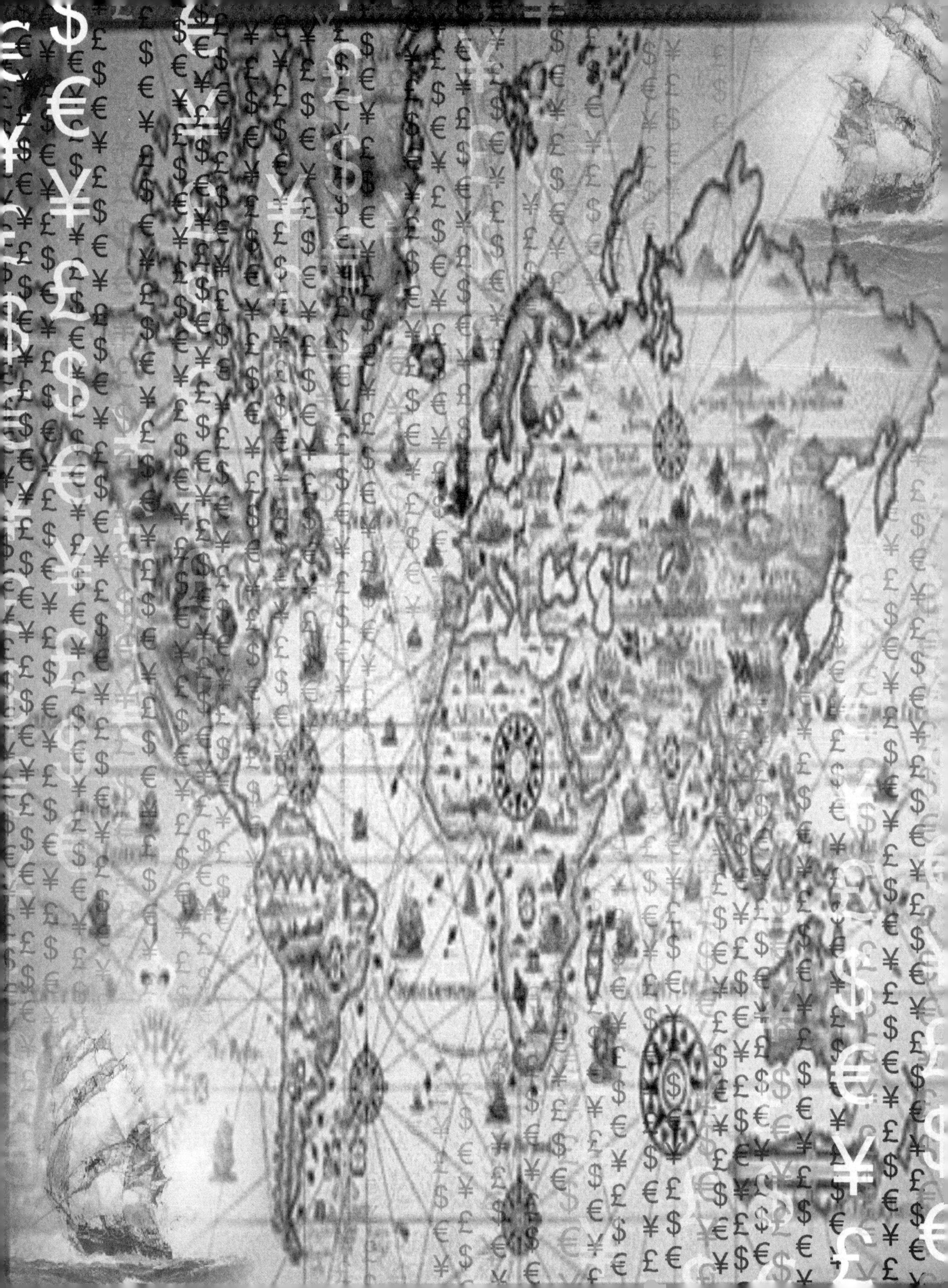

Introduction

Commerce Server 2000 provides a framework and suite of tools for rapidly deploying and managing robust and scalable e-commerce solutions. It enables the developer to roll out complex e-commerce sites in short time spans, implementing functionality to manage product catalogs, authentication and customer profiling, business analysis, complex business logic, including tax, shipping, and internationalization solutions, running campaigns via content targeting, and integrating with supplier catalogs.

In addition to providing a framework for rapidly developing e-commerce solutions, Commerce Server 2000 also provides tools which enable managers to directly manage aspects of the site, including customer and catalog management, selectively targeting customers, analyzing customer behavior, and managing relationships with other businesses (B2B).

In this book, we aim to help you develop a thorough understanding of the architecture and functionality of Commerce Server 2000, and how to get the most out of this exciting new product.

Who Is This Book For?

This book is for developers who are embarking on large e-commerce projects using Commerce Server 2000. It is equally suitable for those familiar with using Site Server 3.0 Commerce Edition and those new to Microsoft's Enterprise Servers. Some familiarity with developing web applications on a Windows environment would be very helpful, if not essential.

What Does This Book Cover?

This book focuses fairly and squarely on utilizing Commerce Server 2000 as effectively as possible. To this end, we'll begin by looking in detail at installation, and implementing and customizing the ready-made solution sites. We'll then burrow a little deeper into the various aspects of Commerce Server 2000: using the user profiling system for authentication and profiling, designing and implementing product catalogs, using the business analytics system, implementing pipelines, constructing pipeline components, using the content targeting system, using Sitelets, and utilizing Active Directory in conjunction with Commerce Server.

We'll then look at ways of utilizing the BizDesk, using third party components, and implementing Business to Business solutions in conjunction with Microsoft's BizTalk Server. Towards the end of the book, for those familiar with Site Server 3.0 Commerce Edition, we'll investigate migration issues.

In common with other books in the Wrox Professional series, this book takes a specifically solutions-oriented approach, demonstrating at all levels how the Commerce Server 2000 product can be used to provide timely solutions to real-world problems. Similarly, an emphasis will be placed on the process of solution development, rather than on issues of administration and management.

Many readers will read this book in sequence, from cover to cover, in order to get up to speed and become familiar with the Commerce Server 2000 product as quickly as possible. Others will wish to dip in on individual chapters, even individual sections therein, effectively using the book as a reference volume. We have aimed to cater as far as possible to both of those groups: each chapter has a clearly defined content that builds on previously discussed material, but does not in any way rely on the material that follows it.

What You Need to Use This Book

At minimum, you'll need a single machine with hardware specifications as follows:

- ❑ 400 MHz or faster Pentium-compatible CPU
- ❑ 128 MB of RAM
- ❑ 100 MB of hard disk space

You will also require the following software prerequisites to install Commerce Server 2000:

- ❑ Microsoft Windows 2000 Server or Advanced Server
- ❑ Windows 2000 Server (with Service Pack 1 and Internet Explorer 5.5)
- ❑ SQL Server 2000 or SQL Server 7.0

The Commerce Server 2000 Evaluation edition is available for download from the Microsoft web site, at http://www.microsoft.com/commerceserver/productinfo/evaluate.htm. This page also features links to download functional versions of the above.

Most of the chapters also assume that you have access to Microsoft Visual Studio 6.0.

Conventions

To help you understand what's going on, and in order to maintain consistency, we've used a number of conventions throughout the book:

When we introduce new terms, we **highlight** them.

Advice, hints, and background information comes in an indented, italicized font like this.

Words that appear on the screen in menus, like the File or Window menu, are in a similar font to what you see on screen. URLs are also displayed in this font.

Keys that you press on the keyboard, like *Ctrl* and *Enter*, are in italics.

We use two font styles for code. If it's a word that we're talking about in the text, for example, when discussing `functionNames()`, `<ELEMENTS>`, and `ATTRIBUTES`, it will be in a fixed width font. File names are also displayed in this font.

If it's a block of code that you can type in and run, or part of such a block, then it's also in a gray box:

```
if HasValue(varSynonym1) then
  varSynonym1 = QuoteSQL(varSynonym1)
  strCondition = " Synonym1 like '" & varSynonym1 & "'"
end if
```

Sometimes you'll see code in a mixture of styles, like this:

```
if HasValue(varSynonym1) then
  varSynonym1 = QuoteSQL(varSynonym1)
  strCondition = " Synonym1 like '" & varSynonym1 & "'"
  if strWhere <> "" then
    strWhere = strWhere & " and "
  end if
  strWhere = strWhere & strCondition
end if
```

In this case, we want you to consider the code with the gray background in particular, for example to modify it. The code with a white background is code we've already looked at, and that we don't wish to examine further.

Downloading the Source Code

As we move through the chapters, there will be copious amounts of sample code available for you, so that you can see exactly how the principles being explained work. The source code for all of the custom examples is available for download from the Wrox website, at the following address:

http://www.wrox.com

Support and Errata

One of the most irritating things about any programming book is when you find that bit of code you've just spent an hour typing simply doesn't work. You check it a hundred times to see if you've set it up correctly and then you notice the spelling mistake in the variable name on the book page. Of course, you can blame the authors for not taking enough care and testing the code, the editors for not doing their job properly, or the proof readers for not being eagle-eyed enough, but this doesn't get around the fact that mistakes do happen.

We try hard to ensure no mistakes sneak out into the real world, but we can't promise that this book is 100% error free. What we can do is offer the next best thing by providing you with immediate support and feedback from experts who have worked on the book, and try to ensure that future editions eliminate these gremlins.

The following section will take you step by step through the process of finding errata on our website to get book-specific help. The sections that follow, therefore, are:

❑   Finding a list of existing errata on the website

❑   Adding your own errata to the existing list

There is also a section covering how to e-mail a question for technical support. This comprises:

❑   What your e-mail should include

❑   What happens to your e-mail once it has been received by us

Finding an Erratum on the Website

Before you send in a query, you might be able to save time by finding the answer to your problem on our website – http:\\www.wrox.com.

Each book we publish has its own page and its own errata sheet. You can get to any book's page by clicking on the Books link on the left hand side of the page.

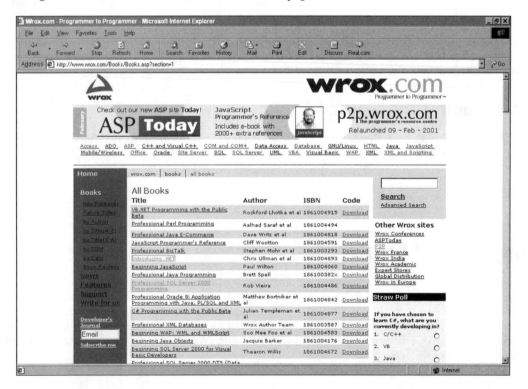

From here, find the book you are interested in and click the link. Towards the bottom of the page, underneath the book information at the right hand side of the central column is a link called Book Errata.

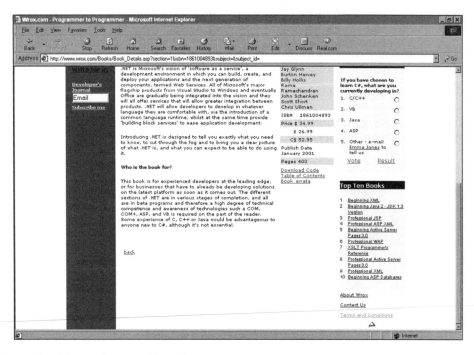

Simply click on this and you will be able to view a list of errata for that book:

Add an Erratum: E-mail Support

If you wish to point out an erratum to put up on the website, or directly query a problem in the book with an expert who knows the book in detail, then e-mail support@wrox.com. A typical e-mail should include the following things:

- The **book name**, **last four digits of the ISBN** and **page number** of the problem in the Subject field
- Your **name**, **contact info** and details of the **problem** in the body of the message

We won't send you junk mail. We need the details to save your time and ours. When you send us an e-mail it will go through the following chain of support.

Customer Support

Your message is delivered to one of our customer support staff, who are the first people to read it. They have files on most frequently asked questions and will answer anything general immediately. They answer general questions about the book and the website.

Editorial

Deeper queries are forwarded to the technical editor responsible for that book. They have experience with the programming language or particular product and are able to answer detailed technical questions on the subject, directly related to the book's contents. Once an issue has been resolved, the editor can post errata to the website or reply directly to your e-mail as appropriate.

The Authors

Finally, in the unlikely event that the editor can't answer your problem, s/he will forward the request to the author. We try to protect the author from any distractions from writing. However, we are quite happy to forward specific requests to them. All Wrox authors help with the support on their books. They'll mail the customer and the editor with their response, and again all readers should benefit.

What We Can't Answer

Obviously with an ever-growing range of books and an ever-changing technology base, there is an increasing volume of data requiring support. While we endeavor to answer all questions about the book, we can't solve bugs in your own programs that you've adapted from our code. However, do tell us if you're especially pleased with the routine you developed with our help.

How to Tell Us Exactly What You Think

We understand that errors can destroy the enjoyment of a book and can cause many wasted and frustrated hours, so we seek to minimize the distress that they can cause.

You might just wish to tell us how much you liked or loathed the book in question. Or you might have ideas about how this whole process could be improved. In which case you should e-mail feedback@wrox.com. You'll always find a sympathetic ear, no matter what the problem is. Above all you should remember that we do care about what you have to say and we will do our utmost to act upon it.

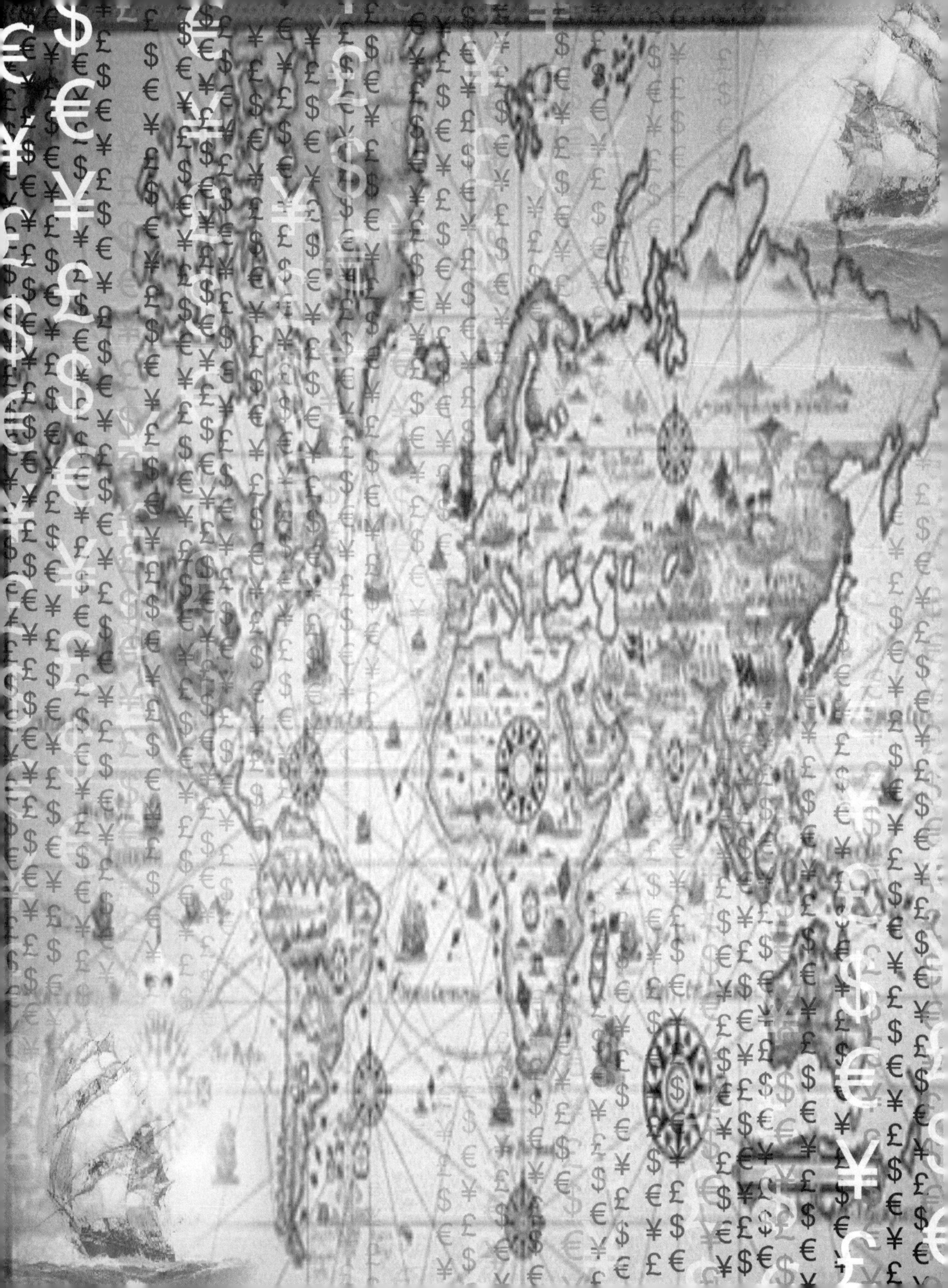

Getting Started with Commerce Server 2000

One of Microsoft's core promises for Commerce Server 2000 (CS2K) is that it can provide you with a rich e-commerce solution 'out of the box'. If you're at all like me, you'll see it just like a new toy, which you'll want to start playing with straight away – before even reading the instruction manual! However, as you will know if you have any prior experience of this sort of application, it's not quite that simple.

Commerce Server 2000 (like its predecessor Site Server 3.0) is an extremely sophisticated system; by design, it provides a broad and flexible framework of tools and components with which to build and administer commercial web sites. By the same token though, it's not the most intuitive of tools to learn how to use, let alone develop for.

Without a little grounding in basic operations and core functionality, you may find that a lot of the discussion in subsequent chapters leaves you a little disorientated. We're therefore going to use this first chapter to give you a crash course in finding your way around Commerce Server 2000.

> *Even if you're familiar with Site Server 3.0 and its underlying architecture, you may wish to read this chapter in order to get a taste of the differences between the two products.*

Developing with Commerce Server

So, given that Commerce Server provides an 'out of the box' solution, why should it be of interest to the Wrox developer community? The answer should be fairly obvious: 'one size fits all' presents you with a very limited scope to work within – even the template Solution Sites (downloadable from http://www.microsoft.com/commerceserver/solsites) are really just 'bare-bone' implementations of quite generic e-commerce solutions. While they're reliably implemented and rich in features, it's quite reasonable to assume you'll want to modify them in some way or other:

- ❏ In many cases, it may be enough to add some custom graphics, tweak a few configuration options and populate the catalog with the relevant products. In this case, you can be online and ready for business in virtually no time, and with minimal effort and cost.

- ❏ For more heavyweight solutions, you may want to differentiate the site from those of your competitors by adding some unique and compelling features of your own design.

- ❏ You may need to integrate your solution with existing applications or databases.

Fortunately, Commerce Server 2000 is a highly component-based product, almost every part of which is designed to be easily extensible. If some part of the standard solution doesn't do exactly what your business requires, then that section can be replaced by custom code – it can then be slotted easily into the project with minimal impact on the rest of the site.

We can start to see that Commerce Server 2000 addresses a broad spectrum of requirements: at one end, a fixed standard e-commerce product, and at the other, a comprehensive e-commerce framework that provides the tools and platform infrastructure with which to rapidly develop a highly customized and unique solution. Of course, in practice, the vast majority of implementations will be somewhere in the middle – mostly using elements of a default solution, and keeping the number of customized areas within manageable limits.

In this opening chapter, we shall put ourselves in the position of a developer whose organization's requirements are near to the 'out of the box' end of this spectrum – our mission will be to implement a standard web-based retail shop. We shall use this task to illustrate a high-level tour of the product, and to investigate some of the basic functionality provided by Commerce Server 2000.

> *Later chapters will explore each of the systems discussed here in much greater depth, and illustrate how developers can implement custom code to address specific business requirements, utilizing the product to its full potential.*

So, in the course of this chapter we shall:

- ❏ Present a high level architectural overview of Commerce Server

- ❏ See the next steps required after installing Commerce Server in order to get an e-commerce shop online and ready for business

- ❏ Learn how to manage the product catalog and user profiles

- ❏ Learn how to target web content and discounts intelligently using known personal information about the site visitor

- ❏ Demonstrate how to populate the data warehouse with the day to day operational data and use this to generate analysis reports about the site

> **We are assuming that the reader has already installed Commerce Server 2000. We have included our own installation notes in Appendix A, to complement the Microsoft installation documentation and provide additional information learnt from our own real world experience of deploying the product.**

Commerce Server – View from 10,000 Feet

We're going to start building up an overall picture of Commerce Server, introducing its constituent components, and looking at how they fit together. We'll do this by studying a simple entry-level configuration, and seeing how we can expand on it to deploy a highly available, scalable site.

Before we begin though, let's briefly consider some important terminology. The following terms will see a great deal of use in the course of the book – while they have quite familiar meanings in a broader context, it's crucial to appreciate their subtleties of meaning when used in reference to CS2K.

There are three terms to which we should give precise definitions. Before proceeding, let's just clarify Commerce Server's exact interpretation of the following terms:

❑ **Site** – a collection of web addresses exposing a unified set of functionality. A CS2K site typically has two such addresses: one for the consumer and one for the business manager. However, there is no inherent restriction, and additional addresses may be associated with a site if we want to further partition functionality (for example, there may be an additional address for use by partner companies).

❑ **Resource** – an item of core functionality, supported by COM objects, which can be utilized by a site's application logic. Examples include Catalog, Authentication and Predictor. A **global resource** is available for use by all local sites, while a **site resource** can only be used by a specified site.

❑ **Web Application** – a collection of ASP and HTML files, components, graphics and pipelines (we'll meet these later) that are associated to a site (by means of its web address) and provide that site with its application logic. The only resources a web application can access are global ones, plus those belonging to its own site.

The Consumer Interface

Let's drill down a bit, and consider a specific web application that will support the part of our site that a consumer will visit. The core elements of this application are illustrated below:

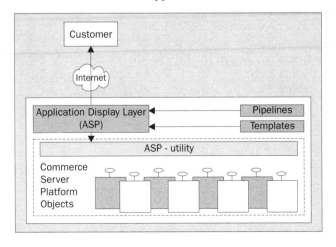

As we'll see in the course of the book, this model can be extended in many ways – however, this core supports the basic functionality we'll be looking at for now.

The web applications that Commerce Server creates are designed with efficiency in mind, ensuring the vast majority of the work is done by compiled COM objects. Likewise, the ASP layer is kept very lean, and for the most part is just used to orchestrate component invocation and to generate the actual presentation layer.

> *Commerce Server does supply a thin layer of ASP utility code, but this is principally to provide a consistent error handling strategy across the components.*

Everything shown within the dashed rectangle is 'core' Commerce Server – these elements will be common to every deployment of the product. The **Application Display Layer** is what will differentiate one site from another, and it's the web developers' responsibility to create and maintain the underlying code.

One way in which Commerce Server 2000 will help you get your site faster to market is by means of the Solution Sites. It will be quite common practice to take one of these and enhance it to fit your own business requirements. However, if you require very specific functionality – whether it's a purely custom feature or something quite generic that's just not implemented in the Solution Site – then the Application Display Layer can be developed from scratch. While all currently available examples are ASP-based, there is no reason why other web technologies can't be used (as long as they support calls to COM components – ISAPI for example).

As we can see, there are two more elements that help to drive our Application Display Layer, namely **templates** and **pipelines**. All static HTML (that is, headers, footers, navigation system, colors, fonts, etc. – the code that defines the site's overall look and feel) is separated from the ASP files, and placed in a number of standard 'Template' files. When required, the Application Display Layer code simply pulls in the appropriate code from these templates for standard rendering. All pages in the site can therefore reference the same piece of header code, the same font specifications, etc. Consequently, if we want to change the overall look and feel of our site, we need only modify a couple of files, and the changes made will automatically ripple through the whole ASP application.

Pipelines are another tremendously useful feature – the 'pipeline framework' environment allows us to link and configure COM components to execute in a specific sequence, so as to perform a particular business task. One example would be to perform the steps needed to handle check-out of a consumer's basket. Both of these elements are central to the flexibility and ease-of-use that CS2K sites are able to offer.

Business Desk

Our site's other web application supports the **Business Desk** (commonly referred to as the BizDesk), which is designed to be your business manager's primary interface with the site. Supported tasks might include updating site content, maintaining and publishing catalogs, controlling campaigns and analyzing the site's effectiveness. The key workings of the application are shown below:

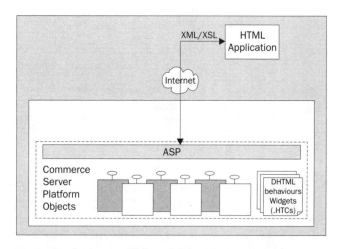

The first thing to point out is that this is an **HTML Application** (HTA), and therefore requires Internet Explorer 5.5 or above. HTAs use a combination of DHTML , XML/XSL and client-side scripting to provide a dynamic and customizable interface for a server-side application, which in this case is our site's web application for business logic processing.

The BizDesk makes full use of the latest web technologies. Information is passed between the web server and the BizDesk as XML data islands, which are rendered using XSL and DHTML behaviors to provide rich UI functionality.

Rather than provide fixed functionality, the BizDesk is supplied as a software framework that enables developers to extend it by developing their own modules that can then be integrated into the navigation system. By using the DHTML behaviors, you can create your own modules quickly and with a consistent look and feel to the rest of the BizDesk.

> *DHTML behaviors are a method for encapsulating web page logic by grouping together HTML tags and script logic and putting it into a single reusable component. We shall look at using HTML Components in Chapters 13, 14 and 15, when we show how to add your own modules into the default Business Desk.*

Commerce Server Manager

The Microsoft Management Console (MMC) framework supports an integrated set of task-specific management tools, enabling various management tools and system status views to be integrated into a single console. These present a simple interface from which you can perform basic administration tasks on specific parts of your system.

In fact, the MMC itself isn't responsible for any of the administration functionality. It simply acts as a container for the various administration programs (written as COM controls), and it's these **snap-ins** that actually perform the tasks. You're almost certainly familiar with MMC snap-ins such as the SQL Server Enterprise Manager and the Internet Service Manager for IIS5.0. All products in the Microsoft .NET Enterprise Server suite make substantial use of them, and Commerce Server is no exception.

The Commerce Server Manager is an MMC snap-in that can be used to manage all available resources (both global and site-specific) and applications. As you can see in the screenshot below, the default console also includes a number of other useful snap-ins, enabling you to manage IIS, Active Directory, SQL Server, Analysis Services, Component Services and the Event Log from the same window. This is very useful, as it's often necessary to administer several systems at the same time. For example, to fully manage a web application, we need to be able to configure both Commerce Server and IIS – with both the relevant snap-ins readily available in a single location, you can get on with shouldn't have to worry about playing 'hunt the window'.

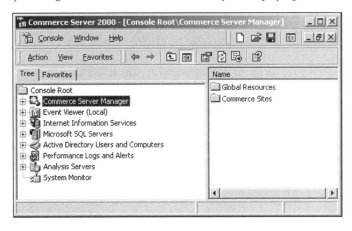

An 'Out Of The Box' Solution

We're now going to make a practical start by setting up one of the Microsoft solution sites on a machine called DANIELS, which has both Commerce Server and SQL Server 2000 installed on it. For our introductory example, we shall use the Retail Solution Site, which provides typical business to consumer functionality.

> At the time of writing, the example solution sites are downloadable from
> http://www.microsoft.com/commerceserver/downloads/solsites.htm. For full
> details of the solution site installation process, refer to Appendix A.

Once the solution sites are installed, double-click on the `retail.pup` file to invoke the Site Packager tool – this will allow you to unpack the complete site onto your machine. We're going to use the default configuration, so select the Quick unpack option and hit Next. The following screen lets us specify an overall name and virtual location for the site we're creating – we're going to call this site Retail, and make it part of the local default web site. The administration database server is located on the machine called DANIELS (clearly, you'll need to substitute the name of your own machine here), and the user credentials you provide should correspond to a valid login for that server. We've created a new user login called `wrox_login` (via the SQL Server Enterprise Manager).

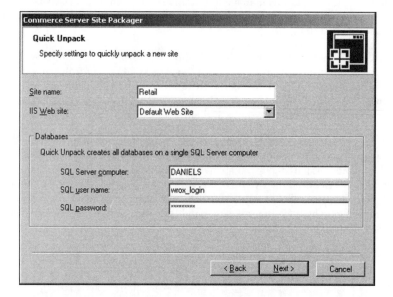

A series of messages will flash up as the PUP files are expanded – after a short period, a screen appears that lets us specify settings for a data warehouse resource. This will be used to store information such as transaction and web click histories for our site's users; business managers can then analyse the data to get an overview of how the site is being used. The requested resource settings include:

❑ Name of the data warehouse (as it will appear in the Commerce Server Manager) – we have set this as Wrox Retail Data Warehouse.

❑ Name of the database server to be used – in this case, we're specifying the same local server as we used for administrative purposes. In a production environment, you would ideally put the data warehouse on a separate machine from the web server; analysis reporting might otherwise impair the performance of the machine serving your customers.

❑ Name of the database to be used.

You can now test your connection to the data warehouse by clicking the **Test Connection** button.

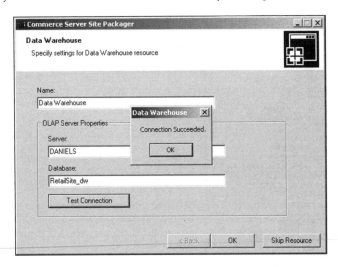

The next two screens let us specify various files with which to define schemas and site terms for the Profiling System, along with a connection string for the data store and any scripts we want to use to populate our resources. We'll take some time to consider their purpose and contents in the course of Chapters 10 and 11, when we take a closer look at the solution sites. For now, we should be fine to accept all the defaults that are supplied within the `retail.pup` file.

Once again, a series of messages flashes past as the unpacking process concludes. Finally, a screen should appear to tell you that the unpacking has completed, and to list the SQL databases and IIS applications created in the process. It will also show any errors that have occurred.

Now that the site is basically set up, let's quickly check out how things look in the Commerce Server Manager. Look in the Start Menu and select **Programs | Microsoft Commerce Server | Commerce Server Manager**. If you browse through some of the branches shown, you should begin to see how the site has been incorporated into the overall tree structure. From here, an administrator can make various low-level configuration changes to the site and its associated resources.

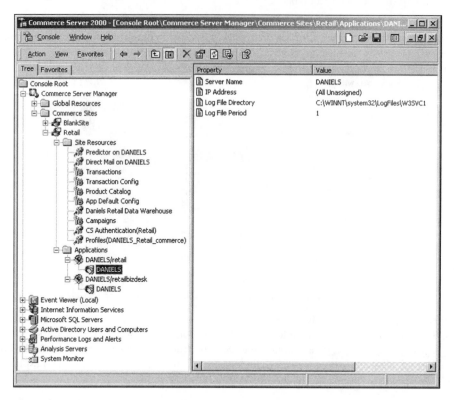

We won't get too bogged down in details at this point, but it's worth taking a quick look at the following for future reference:

- ❏ Console Root | Console Manager | Global Resources
- ❏ Console Root | Console Manager | Site Resources
- ❏ Microsoft SQL Servers | SQL Server Group | *<sql_server_name>* | Databases
- ❏ Analysis Servers | *<analysis_server_name>*
- ❏ Internet Information Services | *<web_server_name>* | Default Web Site

We can use the last of these to call up the two web applications that constitute the site's online interface. Firstly, let's take a quick look at what a consumer will see if they access our site. Right-click on **Default Web Site | Retail** and select **Browse**. Internet Explorer should start up, and load the front page of our new web site's consumer interface.

Okay, it's probably not the most inspiring e-commerce site you've ever seen – it's really rather bland, and (more importantly) there's nothing for sale! We'll see shortly how to resolve these problems by amending the relevant templates files and populating the catalog.

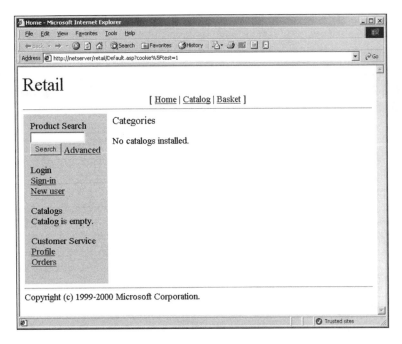

Now, let's take a look at our other new web application – the BizDesk. Remember that this browser-based managerial interface is an HTML Application; it therefore requires some initialization before we can use it. First though, right-click on **Default Web Site | RetailBizDesk** and select **Browse**.

You will shortly be prompted to select a directory in which the application file will be stored – the default is **Program Files | Microsoft Commerce Server**. This will be perfectly acceptable for our purposes, so just hit **OK**.

> *Note that as part of the installation, shortcuts to the Business Desk are placed on both the desktop and the Start menu.*

Eventually the **Business Desk Client Setup** screen should tell you that the Business Desk setup process is complete; select the lower of the two hyperlinks shown to invoke the BizDesk for the first time.

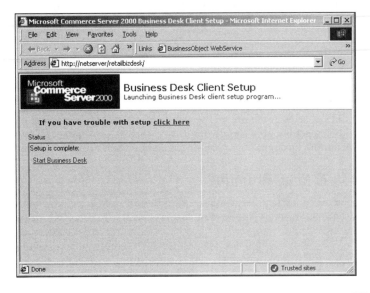

On the left-hand side of the window, you should see a list of module categories, each of which can be expanded to show the various modules of functionality available to the business manager. When a module is selected, a corresponding page is loaded into the main pane on the right.

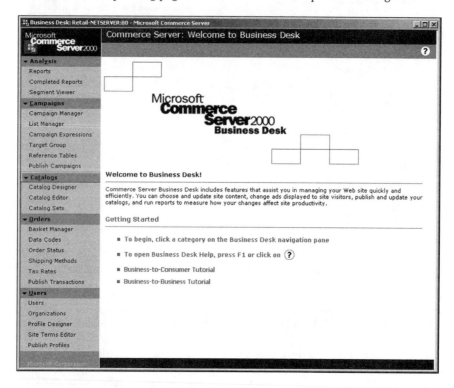

Making the Site Your Own

Now that we have installed the solution site, we're quite close to getting our first e-commerce solution online and ready for business. However, as we saw when we first navigated to the consumer site, we've a few jobs to do before we are likely to attract any customers. We must still:

- ❑ Improve the look of the site
- ❑ Populate the catalog
- ❑ Set up the shipping costs

Let's consider each one of these in turn. In order to demonstrate the changes required, we're going to look at setting up a simple online toy store: 'Dorothy Net's Toyshop'. We'll continue to develop this example throughout the rest of the chapter, so as to illustrate the main features of Commerce Server.

Look & Feel/Branding

As mentioned earlier, static areas of the web site are controlled by means of template files. ASP pages in the solution site's Application Display Layer, are therefore structured as follows:

- ❑ Several initial #includes, which pull in constants and general-purpose utility functions used by the framework.

- ❑ #include setupenv.asp – sets up the environment and invokes the main() function.

- ❑ #include layout1.asp – includes the main template file defining the web page layout.

- ❑ function main() – this programmatically generates the dynamic part of the web page by generating HTML information and assigning it to a variable called htmPageContent.

The order in which files are included is very important – setupenv.asp is included before the template file, so the main() function is actually invoked *before* the templates are rendered. This means that the dynamic part of the web page will already have been determined by the time the templates are processed and so the page rendering can incorporate the dynamic content within the static HTML.

In order to add a logo banner and improve on the dull choice of fonts and colors, we shall replace the main template file (called layout1.asp) with the following version:

```
<HTML>
  <HEAD>
    <TITLE><%= sPageTitle %></TITLE>
    <BASE href='http://<yourservername>/retail/'>
  </HEAD>

<BODY background='images/site/bg.jpg' bgcolor='#FFFFFF'
      text='#000000' link='#006666' vlink='#666666' alink='#FF66CC'>
  <FONT face='Comic Sans MS, Arial, Helvetica'>
  <IMG src='images/site/logo.gif' border='0'
       alt='Dorothy Net's Shop' width='600' height='60'>
  <BR><BR>
  <!-- #INCLUDE FILE='banner.inc' -->
  <!-- #INCLUDE FILE='navbar.inc' -->
  <BR><BR>
  <TABLE BORDER='0' CELLSPACING='1' CELLPADDING='3'>
      <TR VALIGN='TOP'>
        <TD ALIGN='LEFT' BGCOLOR='#6699FF'>
          <!-- #INCLUDE FILE='menu.asp' -->
        </TD><td></td>
        <TD ALIGN='LEFT'><%= htmPageContent %></TD>
      </TR>
  </TABLE>
    <CENTER><%= htmDiscountBannerSlot %></CENTER>
    <BR>
    <IMG src='images/site/horizline.gif' width='600' height='10'>
    <BR>
    <B><FONT size='1'>
      Copyright © 2001 DOROTHY NET Inc. All rights reserved.
    </FONT></B>
  </FONT>
```

Remember to change the reference to *<yourservername>* in line 4 to the name of your own web server.

The files *bg.jpg, logo.gif,* and *horizline.gif* are included along with the code samples for this book, which you can download from *www.wrox.com*. They should be placed in the images/site folder, relative to the retail site's root directory – by default: *C:\Inetpub\wwwroot\retail.*

According to this template, the web page is structured as shown below:

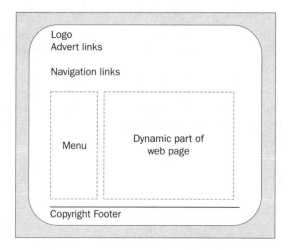

Within the <BODY> tag, we specify colors for the hyperlinks, and an image file bg.jpg to be used for the background – immediately after this we specify our choice of fonts. Working down the screen we have:

- An image – logo.gif – displaying our store's logo.

- An include file – banner.inc – containing the logic to display adverts (if enabled using the campaign management tools).

- An include file – navbar.inc – containing the logic to generate top-level navigation links.

- A two-cell table containing:

  - In the left-hand cell, an include file – menu.inc – containing the logic to generate our store's menu system.

  - In the right-hand cell, the dynamic part of the web page – as generated by the main() function. This is incorporated into the page by outputting the contents of the variable htmPageContent.

- The variable htmDiscountBannerSlot, containing information about any current discounts.

- A horizontal divider line followed by a copyright message at the foot of the page.

The overall result is a page that looks like this. No doubt you can tell I'm not an artist, and you might argue that this is only marginally more attractive than what we started with. However, we can see how a good web designer could use these templates to apply an appealing user interface to our site.

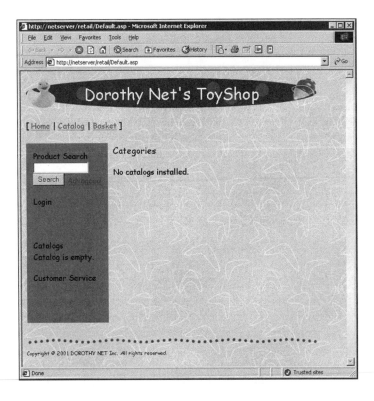

Catalogs

Our next step is to set up a catalog, in which we can store and organize information on the toys we want to sell. A Commerce Server catalog is similar in some respects to a traditional printed catalog – we have a list of products, and associated **properties** (such as name, price, picture, description and so on). However, there's more to it than that: simply presenting a long list of products would make it very difficult for a consumer to locate a particular item.

Catalogs can therefore be subdivided into **categories**, and each product can be associated with one or more of these categories. For example, our toyshop catalog might have categories such as Soft Toys, Construction, Computer Games, Pre-School, Dolls, Bikes, and Models. Some products may reside in more than one category – for example a virtual construction set might sit in both Construction and Computer Games.

A Commerce Server catalog consists of two sets of information: a **schema** (which defines the explicit structure of the catalog – this is stored explicitly in a schema file) and the actual **catalog data**. The catalog proper is simply an arrangement of that data which conforms to the schema. So before we can enter any products into our Toys catalog we must establish how we want to structure it, and define a catalog schema accordingly. In order to do this, we must specify:

❑ **Types of product** (Computer Game, Bike, etc.) and specific **properties** associated with each (such as Name, Price, Platform, Frame Size). A property such as Price would obviously need to be associated with every product; Frame Size, on the other hand, would only be applicable to products of type Bicycle, and certainly wouldn't be associated with a computer game.

Product types Book, CD, Event, Generic Product, Jeans, and Printer are provided by default. You can see them listed in the Catalog Designer module of the BizDesk – select View | Product Definitions from the toolbar, and expand each entry to see its associated properties.

Likewise, to see a full list of available properties, simply select View | Property Definitions from the toolbar – defaults include name, description, and price.

❑ Types of category (Manufacturer, AgeGroup, etc.). Not all our categories will necessarily be based on the same criteria – for example, some may group together all the products manufactured by a single company (possibly including books, videos, models etc.); others may group together products according to the age group at which they're aimed (such as Pre-School). We'll probably want to associate different properties with each of these category types – for example, the category type Manufacturer may well have properties such as Company Name and Contact Details, while AgeGroup would probably require a pair of number properties denoting an appropriate age range.

The generic category type Department is provided by default. You can see this (and any others that you've created) listed in the Catalog Designer module of the BizDesk – select View | Category Definitions from the toolbar and once again expand each entry to see the associated properties.

Creating a Catalog

Now that we've seen a little of how catalogs are structured, we can return to our site and add a catalog for the consumer to browse. We shall create a catalog called 'Toys', a Department type category called 'Soft Toys' and a product called 'Thomas the Teddy Bear'. However, Thomas doesn't really match up with any of the specific default types, and since we want to keep things simple for now (don't worry – we'll look at how to specify custom product types in Chapter 4) we're going to make use of the GenericProduct type. If you take a quick look at the properties associated with this (select View | Product Definitions from the toolbar and expand Generic Product), you'll see that it gives us enough scope to name and describe Thomas, and assign an image to his entry in the catalog.

To create the Toys catalog, select the Catalog Editor module and then select New Catalog from the toolbar. The Catalog Properties edit sheet that appears will allow you to enter properties for the new catalog.

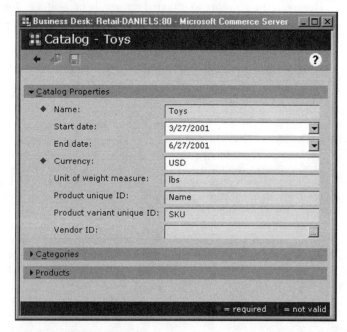

Now save these properties by selecting the **Save** toolbar option. After a short wait, the BizDesk display should automatically refresh.

Expand the **Categories** bar to display the associated categories for the catalog – as this is a brand new catalog, there are no categories listed yet. Select the **New** button to create our new Soft Toys category. The next dialog lists all the available category type definitions – you will probably just see the default entry **Department**. Select this and hit **Continue**.

A **Category Properties** page should now appear, which allows you to enter properties for the new category – the only crucial one we require is a name: 'Soft Toys'. Once this has been entered, select the **Save & Return** toolbar option – this will (eventually) return us back to the **Catalog Properties** sheet, where you will see **Soft Toys** listed in the **Categories** pane.

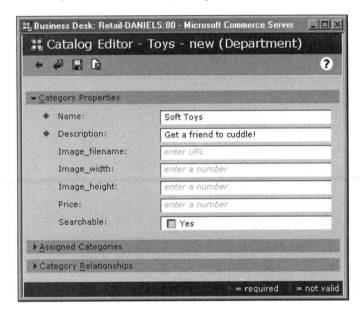

If you now expand the **Products** bar, you should see a list of associated products for the catalog. Select the **New** button to create our 'Teddy' product.

The next dialog lists all the available product type definitions – select **GenericProduct** and hit **OK**.

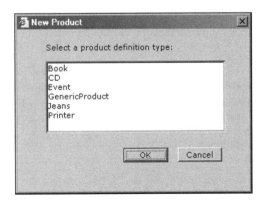

A Product Properties sheet now appears, allowing you to specify properties for the new product:

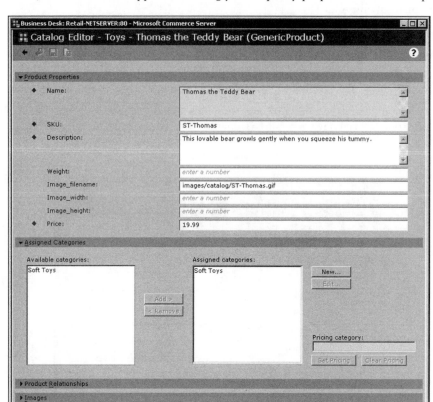

Note that you'll need to place a product image file at the location specified, in this case:

```
images/catalog/ST-Thomas.gif
```

once again, relative to the retail site's root directory – C:\Inetpub\wwwroot\retail by default.

The Assigned Categories displays the categories that have been defined and allows us to select those to which we want to associate our product. You need to choose the Soft Toys category by selecting it and clicking on the Add button. When these details have been entered, select the Save & Return toolbar option and this will return you to the Catalog Properties sheet. You can then Return to the main Catalog Editor page.

To make all these changes available to the site, we must first publish the catalog – select Publish Catalog from the toolbar. Once the usual (and probably rather boring by now) Page Refreshing process completes, your new toy catalog should be live and ready to go – so let's pay another visit to the consumer end of the web site. As you can see, the Soft Toys category is now displayed on the home page. Let's go and buy a Teddy Bear!

Browsing the Catalog

First, select the Soft Toys category – this will take you to a page on which you can see links to and information on all the products assigned to that category – currently just Thomas the Teddy Bear. Select this link and you'll see the product displayed with full details including its description, picture and price.

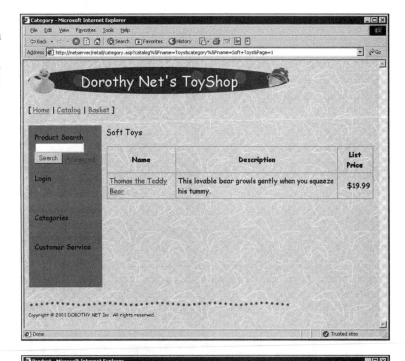

Select the Add to Basket button to indicate that you want to purchase it, and a message is then displayed stating that the item has been added to our basket. To display the contents of the basket, select the Basket link.

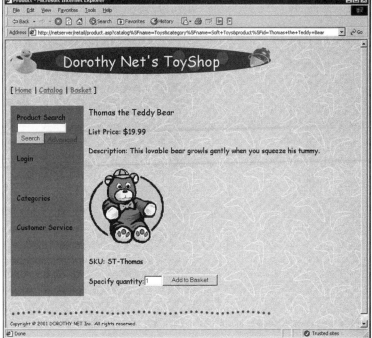

To complete this purchase, select the Check-out button.

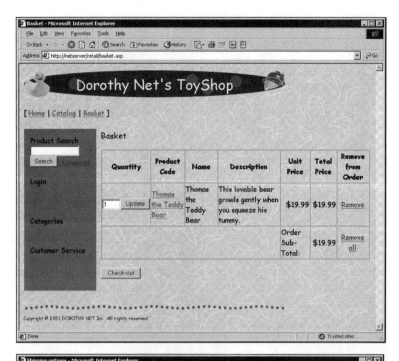

The next screen will prompt you for a Shipping Address – by default, this will also be used as a billing address (the box marked My billing address is the same is automatically checked). Assuming you've entered a valid set of details, click Submit, and you'll continue to the Shipping Options screen. At this stage though, the check-out process hits a problem: we haven't set up any shipping rates.

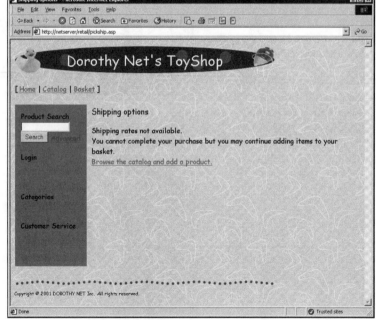

Shipping Rates

The last thing we must do before allowing our customers to make a purchase is to define the shipping rates. These are rules and costs to be applied during the check-out process in order to cover our shipping expenses. Commerce Server provides us with options that enable us to calculate these costs based on:

❑ Weight

❑ Item Quantity

❑ Order Cost

For the sake of our example, we're going to charge a flat fee of $5 if the order value is less than $50; otherwise all shipping costs will be waived. To set this up, you'll need to select the Shipping Methods module from the BizDesk. Select Charge by Subtotal from the toolbar, and you'll soon be presented with page containing the property sheets Shipping Method Properties and Rates.

Start off by setting up the relevant properties – in this case, we're calling the shipping rate Standard. Select New from the Rates property sheet, specify Price, up to: as 50, and Shipping Rate: as 5. Hit Accept and the two entries shown below will appear in the list of rates. Note that you need to manually specify a Shipping Rate of zero for the second entry (select the entry and hit Edit to do so).

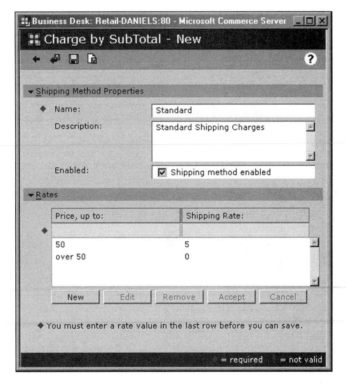

When these details have been entered, select the Save & Return toolbar option and you will be returned to the main page of the Shipping Methods module. In order to finish setting up the Shipping Rate, we now just need to refresh the cache, which is done from the Publish Transactions module. Simply select ShippingManagerCache and hit the Publish Change to Production toolbar option.

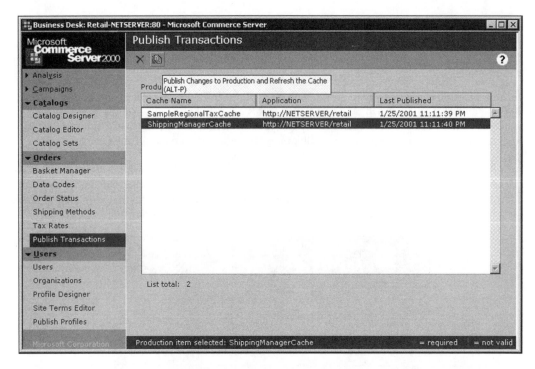

Now let's return to the basket check-out and attempt to complete the purchasing process. This time, when you get to the Shipping costs page, you should see the new Standard shipping rates displayed.

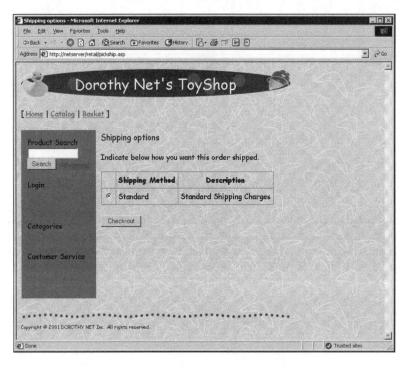

> Note that we're currently just configuring the prerequisites for checking out a basket. In a real world scenario, we would also need to consider other factors, such as tax – this topic is addressed in more detail in Chapter 12.

Now you can select the Check-out button, and you'll be taken on to an Order Summary page – this gives a list of items, billing/shipping addresses, and a complete breakdown of the total order cost.

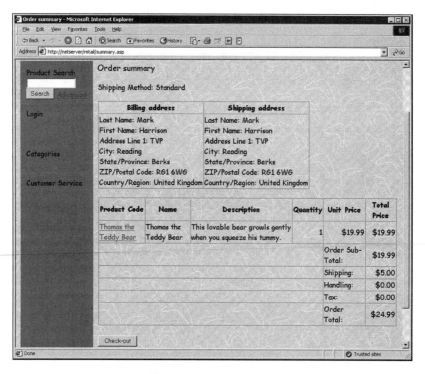

Again, proceed by pressing the Check-out button. The next screen requests our Credit Card details. At this stage, we've not configured the site to do anything with these details; however, you'll still need to put in a valid credit card number to get past Commerce Server's built-in card number validation. You can then proceed by selecting the Submit button. The Order Confirmation screen should now appear, informing you that your order number is 1000 – the first successful purchase on your new site!

If you select the Order Status module in the BizDesk, you can take another look at the details of this transaction – select Find By: Order Date and specify a range of dates including today's – then just hit the Find button and you'll see order number 1000 listed.

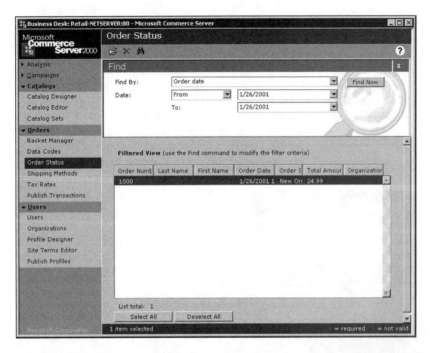

To get more information on this order, you can click on its entry in the list and then select the Open toolbar option – this will display the Order Summary, Order Detail and Addresses edit sheets.

> *Once you have captured a transaction in Commerce Server, you will typically need to integrate with other systems to manage the accountancy and fulfillment of the order. In Chapter 15 we shall see how to use Microsoft BizTalk Server 2000 as part of our overall e-commerce solution, and make the most of its handling of business document interchange (B2B e-commerce) and Enterprise Application Integration (EAI).*

So your site is now working, and you are able to trade with customers. That's only the start of the story though – let's now look at what Commerce Server offers us 'out of the box' to help us to win and keep customers and thus maximize our potential revenues.

Targeting Discounts and Content

We mentioned earlier that it is the business manager's role to apply their business skills to Commerce Server in order to win and keep customers. Winning new customers is crucial, as every one represents instant revenue in the bank. In the long-term though, it's even more important to quickly establish a strong relationship with each customer – make sure that your site is their first choice for all their future needs, and you turn that one sale into an ongoing revenue stream.

As you might expect, it's much easier to make a sale to an existing customer. Some estimates suggest that it costs six to seven times as much to acquire a new customer than to re-solicit an existing one; so once we have a customer we must make an effort to keep them happy and loyal. The last thing we want is to have them roam off to a competitor's site and start adding to their coffers.

Commerce Server provides a set of targeting tools and services, which let us generate personalized web and e-mail content, individually tailored according to a user's preferences and their profile information. With the Web becoming ever-increasingly competitive, personalization is widely recognized as a key technique in maintaining customer loyalty.

For example, consider a site that targets sports fans: it makes sense to quickly ascertain what team a visitor supports, and subsequently target them with announcements/hot news/adverts/promotions that specifically relate to their team. By providing information that they'll be interested in, you can make them much more inclined to think of your site in good terms, and return to it at a later date.

It is important that the business manager puts content on the site that encourages the consumers to volunteer information about themselves. As we shall see shortly, Commerce Server enables us to build up user profiles, storing various pieces of user-specific information. To have a winning online business strategy, it is vital that we build up the fullest possible picture of our customers so that we can realistically attempt to deal with each one in a personalized manner.

Commerce Server provides us with a **data warehouse**, a central repository for all historic information about a site – including profile information about the customer base, their transactions and the web click history. The Business Manager can then use the various analysis tools to gain insights about the effectiveness of the site. Using this intelligence, they can then make educated decisions when determining future site content and the use of the campaign management tools for delivering adverts, personalized e-mail, promotions, and discounts.

In the course of the next couple of sections, we are going to look at putting all of this into action, and show how to apply these techniques to our toy store. We will consider how to profile users, target content and discounts at specific groups of users, and use the analytic tools to examine the effectiveness of our campaigns.

User Management

Any business information required by our Commerce Server applications can be persisted by means of a facility called the **Profile System**. One example of its use is the management of information about our customer base.

Profile information is modeled by means of schemas, which define objects and their associated properties. So, for example, the UserObject might include properties like LogonID, First Name, Last Name, E-mail Address, Age and so on. It can include anything that the business manager wants to know about the users for use as part of the campaign decision logic. Suppose they wanted to display a particular advert for people with blue eyes, they would first add a property called (say) EyeColor to the UserObject, and then add some site content that would enable the user to enter this information so that it could be captured and stored in the profile.

> *Often, the trickiest part is to actually find a method of encouraging a user to provide the correct information about themself – however, this is really more of a business problem than a technical one, so we won't be looking too deeply at it here.*

Instances of the profile schemas are data store agnostic and we can store our profile objects in any data store that is OLE DB or LDAP compliant. Examples include relational databases such as SQL Server, directory services like Active Directory or legacy systems accessed via Host Integration Server.

Commerce Server can also make use of user information stored in Microsoft Passport. This is one of the Microsoft .NET Foundation Services and provides Authentication and Directory Services and enables single sign-on to the Web and facilities for storing Wallet details (credit card numbers, billing/shipping addresses). We shall take a closer look at Passport integration in Chapter 11.

Our web application code is actually insulated from the complexities of where this data is stored thanks to the Aggregation Manager, which is part of the Commerce Server OLE DB provider.

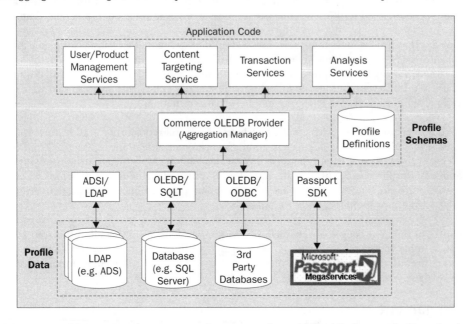

The Aggregation Manager works as a meta-directory and is responsible for marshalling the data to and from the appropriate data store. Nowhere in our code do we specify where the data actually resides.

We shall see how the Aggregation Manager mechanism simplifies our application code in Chapter 3 when we will investigate in detail how to program using the Profile System

Registering Users

So far, you've almost certainly been accessing the Toyshop consumer site as an anonymous guest. Before going any further though, it's well worth registering yourself for a user account – that is, making yourself a registered user on the site. This simply involves selecting the New User link from the front page, and entering a login ID and password (twice, for confirmation purposes). Submit this information, and you'll return to the front page, which will now show your login ID and links to Change Sign-in and Sign-off. Likewise, you can take a look at your profile information and check the status of current orders by clicking on the left-hand column Profile and Orders links respectively. Note that if you register without closing an earlier anonymous session (by restarting the browser and clearing the browser history), any data gathered and orders submitted in that session will be incorporated into your new account.

Extending the User Profile

We're now going to show how we can use the Business Manager to extend the basic user profile schema. We want to add a new property that will store the user's favorite toys – later on we shall use this field to drive personalized content.

To amend the schema, select the **Profile Designer** module (in the **Users** category), click on the **UserObject,** and select the **Open** toolbar option. You should then see all of the Properties associated with the object – notice that they are grouped together for convenience.

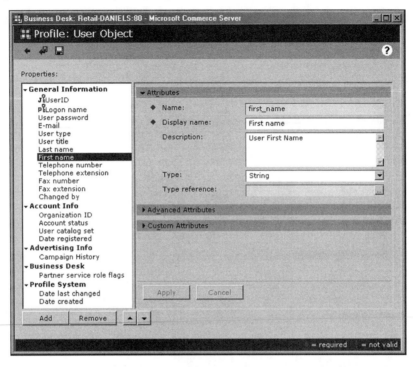

To create a new property, click in the **General Information** group and select the **Add** button. A dialog appears which lets you choose whether to create a new group or a new property. Select the **Add a new property** and hit **OK** – the property's **Attributes** edit sheets should now appear on the right-hand side of the display, into which you should enter the following:

- ❑ Name: FavoriteToy
- ❑ DisplayName: Favorite Toy(s)
- ❑ Type: String

Expand the **Advanced Attributes** sheet and browse for a data source by clicking the button to the right of the **Map to data** entry. The **Data Source Picker** dialog that now appears will let you specify a data store in which the attribute will reside. It lists all potential data stores and any tables that have been configured using the Commerce Manager.

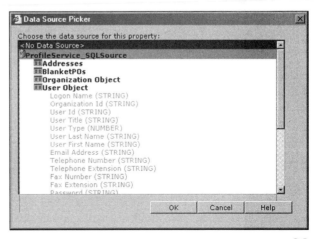

Expand the SQL Server data source ProfileService_SQLSource and the User Object table within. You'll see that a number of spare fields have been set up in this table: select Custom Property 1 – this is where we're going to store the Favorite Toys attribute. Hit OK to confirm your selection.

The next thing to do is to expand the Custom Attributes sheet, and modify the sUserAccess custom attribute. This is used by the solution site to determine whether a field can be viewed and/or edited by a registered user viewing their profile. A setting of 0 hides the property, 1 just shows it, while 2 shows it and allows it to be edited. In this case, we want the user to be able to see *and* edit it, so that they can manually populate the field with appropriate data – so we set it to 2.

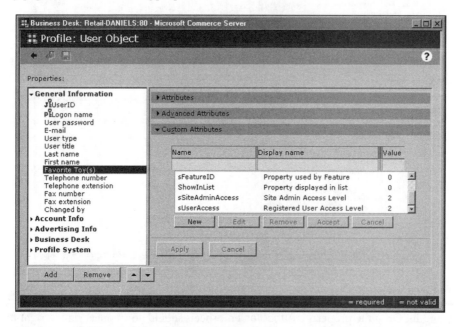

Once you have saved the property, you just need to publish the profile using the Publish Profile module. Click on the Retail entry and select the Publish Changes menu option.

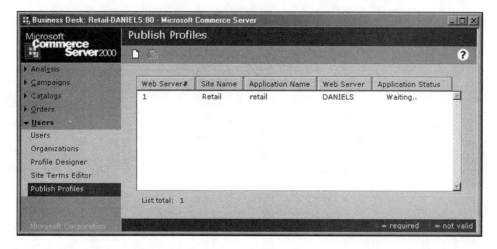

It's time to go and update your profile on the consumer site, so log on and select the Profile link. You'll now see that it includes the option Favorite Toy(s). Enter 'Bikes' and 'Soft Toys' – we shall use these in our later examples.

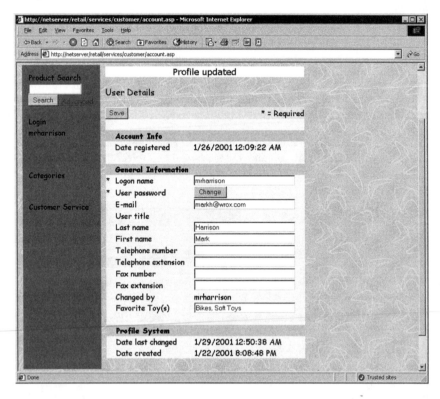

Targeting

One crucial aspect of campaign management is the ability to deliver specific content to specific groups of users, either by displaying it on registered users' web pages or by e-mailing it to them. Commerce Server incorporates two systems by which we can identify these groups:

❑ **Explicit Targeting** – used when we know the profile properties of a customer and can specify rules (called **expressions**) that clearly define the criteria under which certain content can be delivered. Consider a business manager who wants a campaign to address an upcoming Valentines Day. A suitable expression might be: '*Show advert for Pink the Rabbit* when *the visitor likes soft toys* and *the date is between 1st and 14th February*'.

Explicit Targeting is handled by CS2K's **Content Selection Framework**. This is discussed further in Chapter 8, although we touch on it again briefly in the next section, where we show how to provide targeted content and discounts.

❑ **Implicit Targeting** – used when we don't have explicit user information available, but want to make intelligent decisions on what content to deliver based on the aggregate properties of the entire customer base and their transactions. One common use is to segment customers into groups with similar attributes or buying patterns. This can help campaigns to focus more tightly on what is common to all members of the segment.

Implicit Targeting is implemented by way of some very advanced data-mining technology that originated from the boffins at Microsoft Research. We look at this in detail in Chapter 5.

Discount Targeting

Let's return to our Toyshop and see how we can use the properties in a user's profile to determine what discounts we might offer them. In this case, we're going to offer a 25% discount on all products to any customers who are employees of Wrox Press, one of our preferred business partners.

The first thing we must do is set up an expression that detects visitors who work for Wrox. We shall determine this to be true if they have an e-mail address containing @wrox.com, and set this expression up using the BizDesk's Campaign Expressions module. Select New Expression from the tool bar.

A Target Expression dialog appears, which allows you to enter the condition. First of all, name the expression Wrox Employees and add a quick description. Then select the New button to create a new condition – you need to specify 'E-mail contains @wrox.com' within the three adjacent widgets at the center of the dialog:

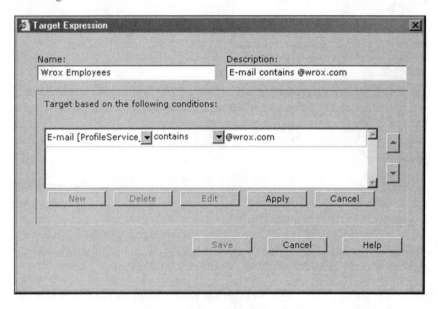

Note that E-mail is listed under User Object | General Information in the left-hand dropdown list – we can in fact set up conditions based on any of the fields in the user's profile object.

Now hit the Save button to store the expression and return us to the main BizDesk interface.

To set up the discount, select the BizDesk Campaign Manager module – this is the module through which business managers can manage all their campaigns, including advertising, e-mail (known as Direct Mail) and discounts. The first thing we must set up is an owner for the campaign – this is done using the New Customer tool bar option.

> **We need to be a little careful with the terminology here – the word 'customer' in this context refers to the campaign owner, and has nothing to do with the consumer who visits our site.**

The Customer Properties and Contact Information edit sheets that should now appear will allow you to enter a series of properties for the campaign owner. We'll call our first campaigns customer 'The Toy Shop'. Note that since this actually refers to the site owner, the Type field (which specifies the relationship between customer and site owner) should be set to Self.

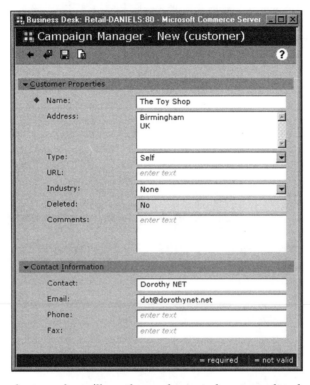

Once you've saved and returned, you'll see the newly created customer listed on the main Campaign Manager list page. We now need to set up the actual campaign, and associate it with this customer, so select them from the list and select New Campaign from the tool bar. On the Campaign Properties edit sheet that now appears, you need to add a Campaign Name (in this case, 'SpringTime'), make sure that Status is set to Active, and check that Start Date and End Date fields are both set – today's date and three months on are used respectively by default.

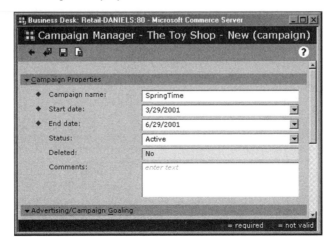

Save this information and return to the main Campaign Manager list screen. Note that our customer entry can now be expanded to show the new SpringTime campaign. Now select this entry and hit **New Discount** on the tool bar. The **Discount Properties** edit sheet that appears lets you enter properties for the discount. Once again, you need to specify a name ('Partner Discount' in this case), start and end dates, and set the status to **Active**.

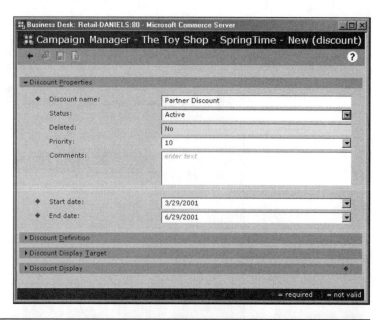

Now expand the **Discount Definition** edit sheet, and set the discount by checking **Buy: Anything** and specifying 25% off unlimited quantities of any product. You also need to add the 'Wrox Employees' expression (which we created earlier) to the list of eligibility requirements.

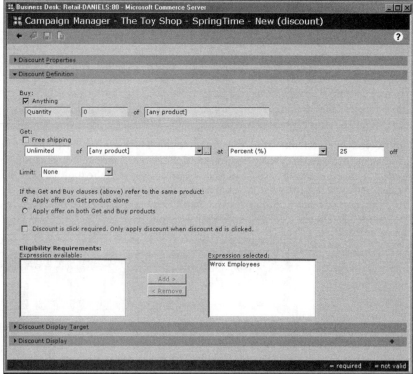

Now expand the **Discount Display** sheet – this is where you can specify the type of content that you want displayed on the relevant web pages when a discount is available. Options include **Text**, **Image**, **HTML** and **Windows Media**. For this example, we'll use **HTML**, and once this has been chosen, you can specify the HTML to be used.

We're going to advertise the SpringTime campaign in a full banner (468x60), with the following text in bold red type:

'Springtime offer – partners are entitled to 25% discount'

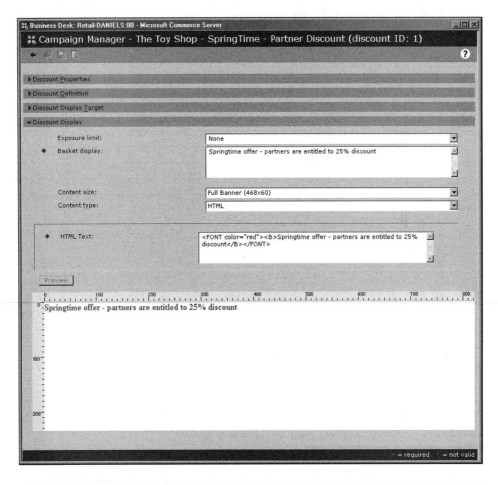

Bear in mind that we have really only touched the surface of the discount facilities available – a full explanation of the various options will be given in Chapter 8.

The last thing we must do is to use the **Publish Campaigns** module to refresh the memory cache that handles the campaign. All we need to do is click on the **Discounts** item and select **Publish Changes** from the toolbar.

That's it! Our discount is now in place ready and is waiting for any Wrox employee to visit the site and make a purchase. To see this in action, logon to the Toyshop site, and access your profile details via the **Profile** link. You must now amend your e-mail address to include the `wrox.com` domain.

Do remember to change it back again afterwards – we're not sending out any targeted mail just yet, but later on when we do, you'll probably want to avoid spamming some poor Wrox editor who happens to share the same name!

Now go and browse the catalog again. Notice the discount message underneath the product details.

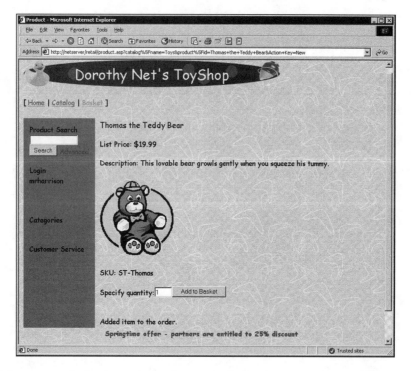

If you add this item to the basket and examine the basket's contents, you'll see that the price shown includes the affiliate discount.

Content Targeting

Let's now take a look at some of the ways in which we can target web content. Three main factors determine the custom content we want to target our users with – these are:

❏ The information we have on a user (from their profile)

❏ Context information (time/date, whereabouts on the web site – we'd probably want to deliver different content on the Computer Games page from that on the Dolls page)

❏ The actual content we have at our disposal

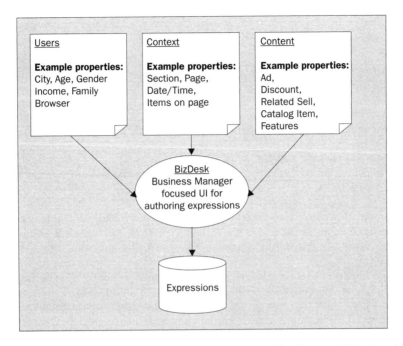

Commerce Server targets web content by means of the server-side **Content Selection** object. When an HTTP request is received, an ASP page is invoked and the Content Selection object instantiated – this object then fires a pipeline. As we mentioned earlier, this invokes a number of components in a well-defined sequence in order to perform a particular task. In this type of pipeline, the components provide filtering and scoring on all of the expressions specified, and return any content that exceeds a particular threshold score.

The ASP layer can handle this scored content in whatever way is appropriate. For example, if it were determining a suitable banner advert, it would probably just display a single content item with the highest score.

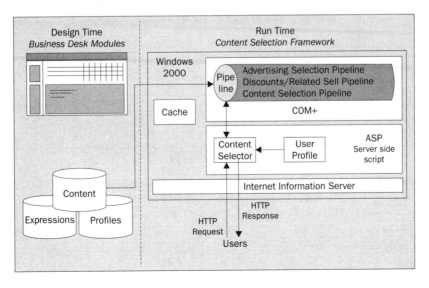

Note that all expressions are compiled into an optimized format and held in a memory cache to enable the content selection to be handled very efficiently.

This may be starting to sound rather complex, particularly if you just want to implement an 'out of the box' e-commerce store and not get involved in developing code. Fortunately, the 'out of the box' solution provides the processing logic to display suitable adverts using the content scoring/targeting described above. This logic is provided in a file called banner.inc, which (as you may recall) was included in our template file, so as to place an advert just below our site's logo – so we're all set to go!

We're going to use our recently added Favorite Toy(s) property from the user profile to determine whether or not to display an advert for bikes. The advert will provide a link to a site providing hot news about the coolest kids' bikes.

First we must set up an expression to detect bike lovers, using the BizDesk Campaign Expressions module (in a similar manner to our earlier expression for Wrox employees). You should call this expression 'Likes Bikes' and specify the condition 'Favorite Toy(s) contains Bike'.

Content targeting requires us to use a **target group**, since you'll generally want to use several expressions to fine-tune the scope of your target audience. We do this using the Target Group module from the Business Desk – create a new group by selecting the New Target Group toolbar option, and name it 'Bike Lover'. To add an expression, hit the New button and select the Likes bikes expression from the list displayed. Set the action to Require, Accept the term, and then save/return.

Now we've defined the group of users at whom we want to target our 'Cool New Bikes' newsflash, the next step is to set up the advert itself. We're going to add this to the SpringTime campaign which we created earlier, so select this campaign in the Campaign Manager and Add New Ad from the toolbar.

Most of the following steps are similar to our earlier Discount Targeting walkthrough, so we won't dwell on them too long – we'll take a much closer look in Chapter 3.

The **Ad Properties** edit sheet appears, which allows us to enter our desired properties for the advert: name, start and end dates, **Active** status and **Paid Ad** type.

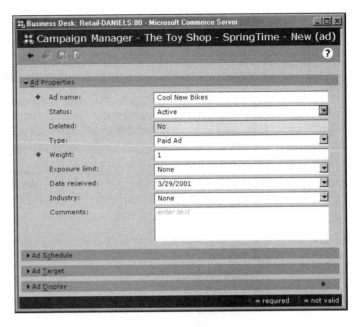

On the **Ad Target** edit sheet, you should specify that this advert be targeted at **Bike Lovers**, the group we set up previously. The **Ad Display** edit sheet lets you specify the advert to be displayed. As with the discount, this can be in any one of several forms, and we shall use the following HTML to display a text hyperlink to the external site featuring the bike newsflash:

```
<A href='http://mikesbikes.net/' target='_blank'>
Click here for the latest Cool Bikes newsflash
</A>
```

Next we must set up the **campaign goaling** – this determines the number of adverts to be delivered, and whether they just need to be displayed or if the user must click on them to count towards the advertiser's paid quota. You can set this information via the **Advertising/Campaign Goaling** edit sheet for our **SpringTime** campaign.

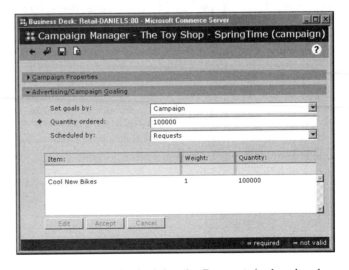

Here we have set the ad quota to one hundred thousand, and scheduling by **Request**, (rather than by click, in which case our system would continue to serve up the ad until 100,000 users had clicked through to the external site). Finally, refresh the campaign memory cache via the **Publish Campaigns** module – click on the **Advertising** item and select **Publish Changes**.

Let's now return to the site and see if our advert is displayed. Log on as a user who has 'Bikes' logged as a favorite toy – if everything's gone according to plan, you'll see a New Bikes newsflash hyperlink displayed just below the main site logo:

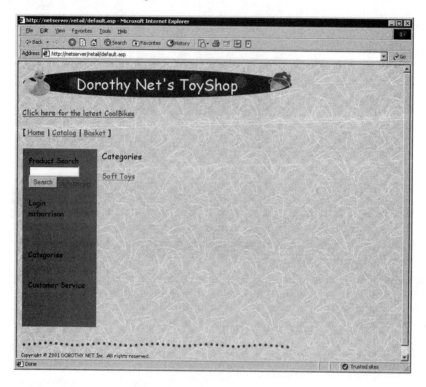

'Out of the Box' – Business Analytics

We discussed earlier how Commerce Server serves to empower business managers by providing them with a near real-time feedback loop on the effectiveness of their site and marketing campaigns. To close this loop we therefore need to consider populating the data warehouse and generating reports.

The Commerce Server data warehouse collects day-to-day operational data about visitors to our site: user profile data, transaction data, and click-history data. This data is gathered from our web server logs and any other data sources we care to specify. Whereas the Commerce Server OLTP database structure is designed for performance and scalability, the data warehouse OLAP database is structured to support complex query and analysis.

Commerce Server provides a set of standard reports, and also comes with a number of OLAP cubes to slice and dice. These reports make use of Excel web controls and ad-hoc pivoting features to make the reports be interactive.

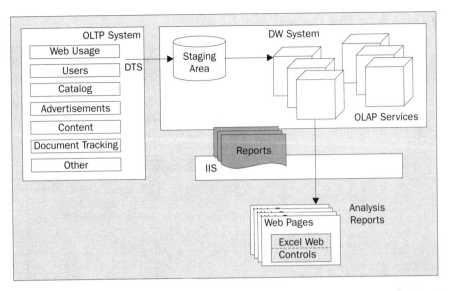

The OLAP features are open (extensible) and built using standard Analysis Services provided with SQL Server 2000. This means that additional reports can easily be created and incorporated in the Reporting module in the BizDesk. Furthermore, there are many business intelligence tools from other vendors that work with Analysis Services, and any of these may be used to analyze our site's data.

Commerce Server also includes a resource called the Predictor, which provides some very clever technology for data mining on the information that has been collected in the data warehouse. This can provide the business manager with indispensable intelligence about their site that would be near on impossible to have ascertained by just inspecting the analysis reports. These can be used to:

- **Cross-sell** products – recommend other products based on (a) what's already in the basket and (b) what other customers typically buy along with those items.

- Group the customer base into **segments** – customers are grouped if they have similar user profile properties or buy similar products; if promotions can be targeted at identifiable user groups, you'll reduce the chance of sending information to someone with no interest in it.

- **Predict** missing user profile attributes by comparing what *is* known about a user with the complete picture of the entire visitor population.

> The use of the Predictor requires a strong understanding of the supported data mining models, how the models are built and viewed, and how this information can be used by the campaign management, and the PredictorClient object within our ASP logic.
> These are advanced topics and beyond the scope of this introductory chapter. We shall however discuss these advanced data mining features in detail in Chapter 5.

Let's return once more to our Toyshop site – first we'll see how to populate the data warehouse and then run a couple of the standard reports.

Importing Data into the Data Warehouse

The **Data Transformation Services** (DTS) is a feature within SQL Server for exporting data from one data store, processing that data (if required) and then importing it into another data store. Commerce Server extends this, providing a number of new DTS tasks for importing data into the Data Warehouse.

In the Commerce Manager, drill down through Microsoft SQL Servers to the Data Transformation Services node, then right-click and select the New Package menu option. A **package** is a group of DTS tasks that collectively perform a complete data migration operation.

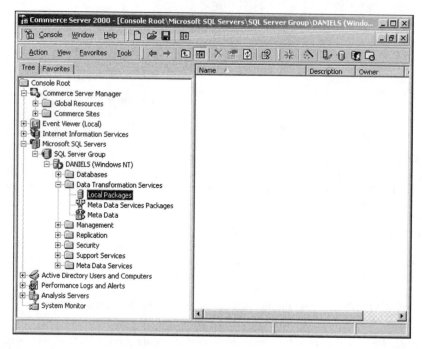

A New Package dialog will now appear – this is where we add icons to represent various individual tasks, and can then connect them graphically to specify the processing order. Each task can be selected from the Task menu option – on selecting each one, a Properties dialog opens. For most of these tasks, all we need do is set the Site Name field to Retail.

We need to add the following tasks:

❑   **Web server log import** (Import Web Server Logs) – transfers a list of web clicks to the data warehouse. The Log file path must be set to wherever the IIS log files are being generated: select the Retail site from the Site name dropdown list, click on the retail,retailbizdesk application, and then click on the square with three dots. The subdirectory W3SVC1 should contain log files for the default web site.

You can choose to import all log files or specify a date range – you may find that the former option doesn't actually result in any logs being imported, particularly if you're setting this up for the first time (select View Log File to check if this is the case). If no files are listed, try specifying a date range beginning a few days ago – this will hopefully include logs that detail your endeavors from earlier on in the chapter. Of course, this all assumes that you have IIS logging turned on – if all else fails, check out the contents of the directory with Windows Explorer, and the Default Web Site Properties under Internet Services Manager.

- **Campaign data import** (Campaign Import) – transfers campaign information (customers, campaigns, ads, discounts, lists) to the data warehouse.

- **User profile data import** (User Import) – transfers user profile information to the data warehouse.

- **Product catalog import** (Catalog Import) – transfers product information to the data warehouse.

- **Transaction data import** (Transaction Import) – transfers order information to the data warehouse.

- **Configuration Synchronization** (Synchronize DW) – transfers site configuration information to the data warehouse.

- **Report Preparation** (Prepare Reports) – populates the OLAP cubes.

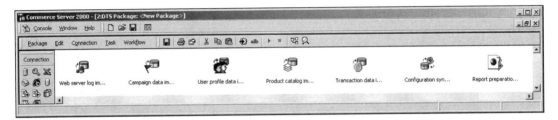

Connect the tasks sequentially by selecting icons two at a time and selecting On Completion from the Workflow menu.

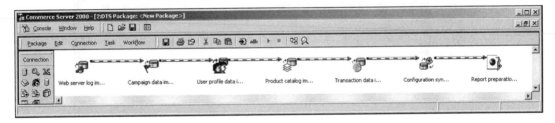

To modify properties for any task, just right-click on the relevant icon and select the Properties menu option. Using the Package menu options, Save the new package as 'RetailLoad' and then Execute it. A dialog will appear showing each task and its execution progress.

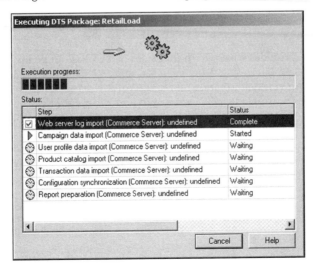

A dialog should eventually appear to signal that the operation has completed successfully. Our data warehouse is now fully up to date and ready for us to analyze its contents.

> **DTS packages can be scheduled to execute automatically on a periodic basis. The frequency with which this is done should weigh the need for current data against the performance impact that execution will have on the live system.**

Standard Reports

Commerce Server 2000 provides 39 standard reports 'out of the box' to address the most common requirements of both Business Managers and Systems Administrators. These can be accessed from the BizDesk Reports module (under the Analysis category). To invoke a report, click on its description and select the Run toolbar option. Let's take a look at a couple of them, starting with the Product Sales report: this shows us how much revenue each of our products is bringing in.

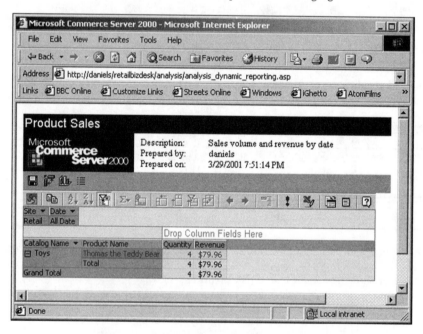

Here we can see that to date there have been four sales of Thomas the Teddy Bear – obviously this report would be a lot more interesting if we had a few more items in our catalog. Let's run the General Activity report, which provides information on requests and visits to our site: there should be rather a lot more to see there.

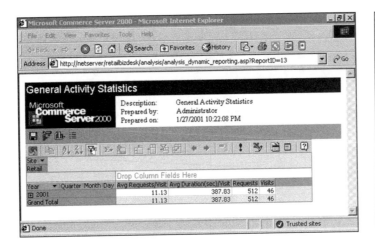

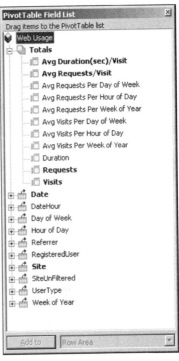

The Pivot Table Field List (which should have appeared alongside the report) lists all the dimensions and measures (in this case from the Web Usage cube) that can be used in the pivot table. This can be toggled on and off from the Field List icon on the report menu bar. If you drag and drop these fields onto the table, the report will update itself accordingly. The information can then be displayed graphically in a number of formats including bar charts, pie charts and doughnuts – click on the Show Chart icon, and a chart appears in the report window below the pivot table:

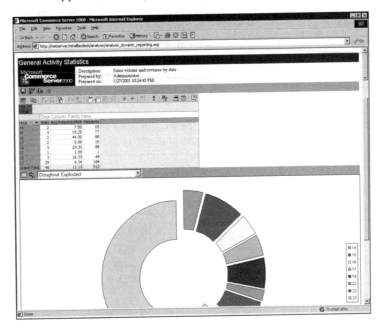

This screen shot shows a table of visits and requests against the hour of the day – beautifully illustrated by an exploded doughnut graph. As you can see, I've been moonlighting lately, and did most of my work on this site after 11:00 pm!

> *Of course it would be impossible for the Commerce Server team to have developed every conceivable report that might be required – there will always be someone wanting something different. However, as we shall see in Chapter 5 it is relatively easy to create custom reports and enable access to them from within the BizDesk.*

Summary

In this opening chapter we have looked at the basic concepts of Commerce Server 2000 and seen the main features that the product provides. You've seen that it really is a huge subject, with many facets for us to explore in more detail in the remainder of the book. Key points covered in this chapter are:

❑ Commerce Server caters for a spectrum of requirements – from those that require an 'out of the box' solution to those that require an e-commerce services platform enabling a highly customized solution. As we shall see, all parts of the product can be extended with custom logic and components if required.

❑ Commerce Server can create highly personalized web solutions by combining the Profile System and the Targeting system.

❑ Commerce Server provides a rich catalog of facilities for defining, organizing and selling products.

❑ In addition to providing all the prerequisites of an e-commerce site (scalability, security, availability, and so on) Commerce Server empowers business managers, giving them the tools to not only monitor the site's performance, but also to take an active, hands-on role in the day-to-day physical management of the site.

❑ Commerce Server enables business agility by providing a platform that can easily adjust to address new business opportunities and threats. It makes heavy use of components (COM and pipeline technology) and XML to enable this flexibility.

❑ Commerce Server enables information about a site's customer base to be combined with the transaction and web click histories; this information is stored in a data warehouse. Various facilities then enable the business manager to gain insights into what is happening across their site – in particular what works and what does not.

Hopefully this chapter has got you excited about the product and the features it can offer. In the next chapter, we're going to take a brief look 'under the hood' of the Blank Solution Site, to start building up a concrete picture of how the bare bones of the system code fit together before we start drilling down into each major area of the product in turn.

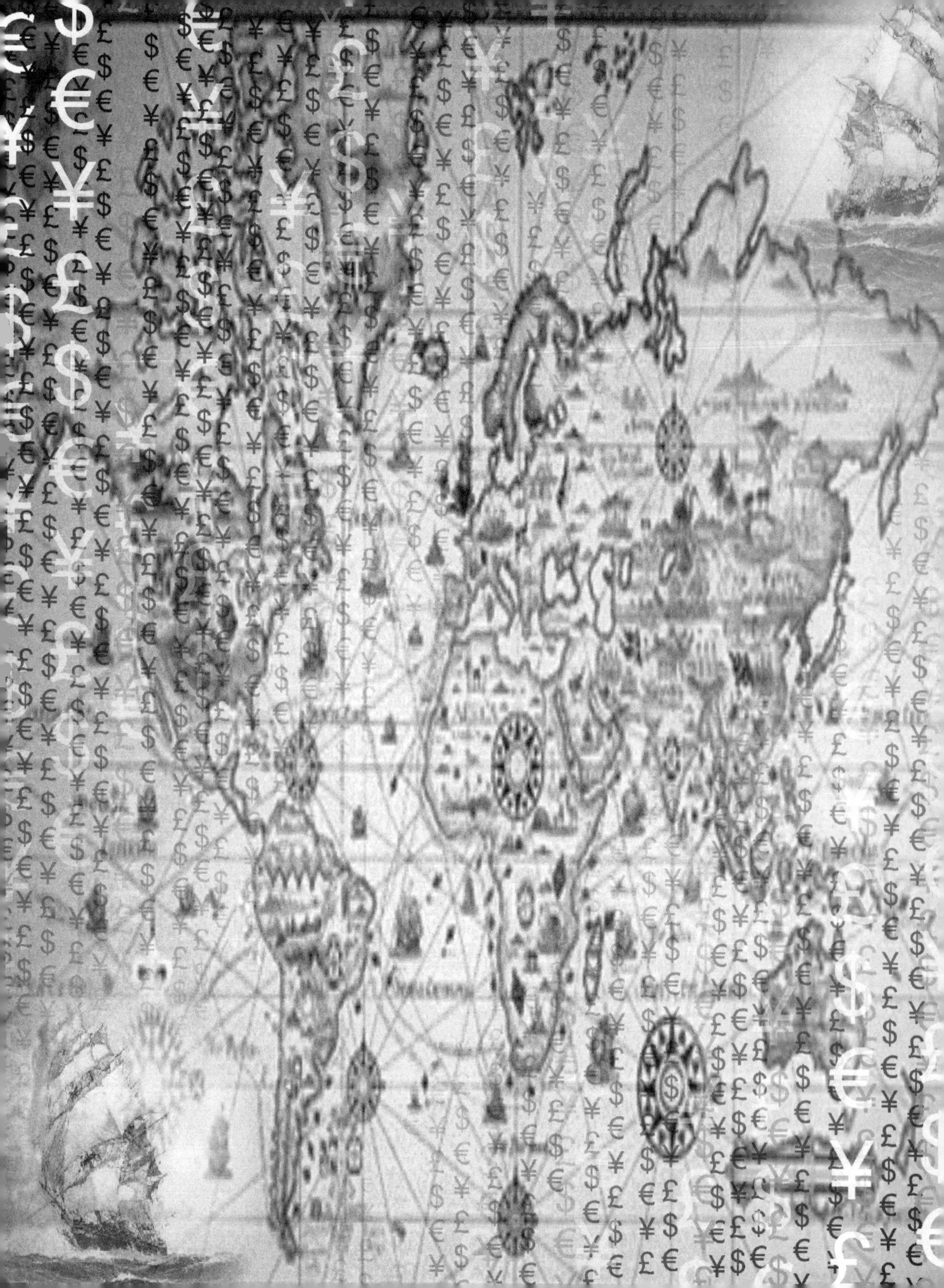

Programming Commerce Server 2000

The previous chapter gave us a whistle-stop tour of Commerce Server 2000 and its main features – we have looked at how to get a site up and running, and ready to attract customers. What we have seen so far should have prepared us to start dabbling with the core functionality provided out of the box.

However, most of what we've considered amounts to little more than configuration and data population. The primary goal of this book is to introduce you, as a software developer, to the underlying framework on which your Commerce Server site will be built, so that you can exploit that framework to the fullest possible extent.

We're now going to dig a bit deeper and start exploring the code, components and database structure that are used to implement the Retail solution site. We shall not try to be in any way comprehensive – subsequent chapters focus on specific features in far greater detail – but rather start to map out a few of the interactions that characterize the CS2K framework.

Solution Site Directory Structure

When we installed our solution site, a huge number of files were installed and distributed over a number of file directories. Let's start by checking out the virtual directory structure of the Retail site.

If we open the Commerce Manager, and find the virtual directory retail under wwwroot in the Internet Information Services branch, we can see that it is structured around the following directories:

Virtual Directory (relative to \retail)	Default Contents
\	Main ASP script logic.
\authfiles	Files used with an ISAPI filter used to **authenticate** site visitors. The default retail site doesn't use this filter or any files in this directory. Authentication options are addressed in Chapter 3.
\error	ASP files responsible for generating error messages.
\images\catalog	Product images used by the catalog.
\images\site	Images that provide the general look and feel, any site branding and the navigation system.
\include	General-purpose library routines – used by many other ASP files.
\login	Files providing user login/logoff functionality. These are applicable when using the **MSCSAuthManager** object, which provides an authentication mechanism using an ISAPI extension.
\pipeline	Pipeline configuration files.
\pipeline\logfiles	Pipeline log files (if enabled).
\services	Files providing 'change user password' functionality and 'help' logic.
\services\customer	Files enabling a user to amend their profile and to view order information – these facilities are known as **Customer Services**.
\services\error	Files that generate **error messages** in Customer and Partner Services.
\services\include	General-purpose library routines – used by many ASP files within Customer and Partner Services.
\services\partner	Files that allow an administrator to amend the profile of their organizations users and to view order information – these facilities are known as **Partner Services**.
\template	Static HTML files that appear on every page. As we saw in the previous chapter, these are responsible for the look and feel of the site.

Now let's take a look at the files that are in the root directory, as shown below:

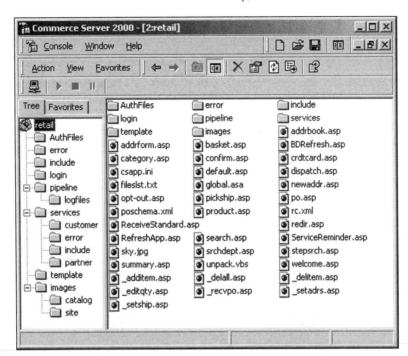

We can see that most of these are ASP files, a few of which have names prefixed by an underscore character. As you may know, this conventionally denotes ASP files that have no user interface – they do not include any template files because they don't generate any HTML. When these ASP scripts have completed their processing, they pass processing (by using a `Response.Redirect` statement) to another ASP file. The following diagram illustrates the sequence of ASP invocations that occurs when a user amends the items in their basket.

csapp.ini

Located in the root directory is a file called `csapp.ini`, which contains basic configuration information. If we open this file, you'll see that it is a text file containing a series of name-value parameter pairs. This data is used by the `global.asa` initialization code to determine which resources the site should be using.

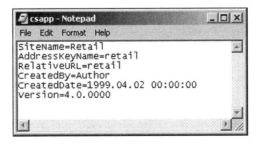

The specified parameters are:

❑ SiteName – the name of the site, which maps onto a node of the same name in the Commerce Server Manager from where the site configuration is handled.

❑ AddressKeyName – not currently used.

❑ RelativeURL – the name of the sites virtual directory / web application in IIS.

❑ CreatedBy – the name of the site Author.

❑ CreatedDate – the intention is that this is the date that the site was created; however this is not implemented and all sites have this value set to 2 April 1999.

❑ Version – the version of Commerce Server (2000 is a branding name – it's actually the fourth generation of Microsoft's Commerce product).

rc.xml

Another file located in the root is rc.xml, which is used to store all the standard text strings displayed on the site. Open this file and examine the strings within – you will see that by default this site only supports English. However, adding support for other languages is very straightforward – we look at doing just this in Chapter 16.

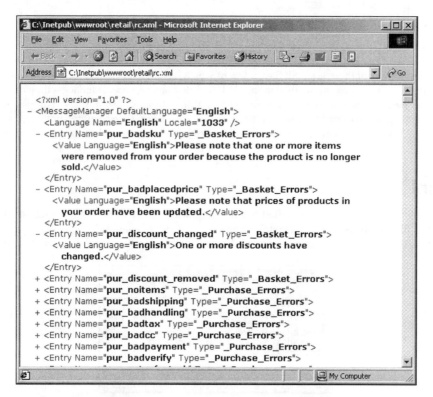

As we'll see, the strings specified in this file are loaded into the MessageManager object when the web application is first started. Whenever a string is to be displayed, the script logic will retrieve the localized version from MessageManager – for example:

```
MSCSMessageManager = Application("MSCSMessageManager")
sPageTitle = MSCSMessageManager.GetMessage("L_Basket_HTMLTitle", "English")
```

We will be addressing matters of internationalization in detail when we consider developing multi-language and multi-currency sites in Chapter 16.

Commerce Server Databases

Before we try piecing together the code that implements the site's front-end, it is well worth perusing the databases that underlie it, in order to understand how each of them is structured. Two databases are created (or referenced, if you're adding servers to a domain) when Commerce Server is initially installed. These are subsequently used by all solution sites installed on that machine (or cluster of machines, in the case of a web farm):

❑ MSCS_Admin – the Administration database containing configuration information for all Commerce Server resources.

❑ DirectMail – the Direct Mail database containing mailing lists and messages that are used to handle e-mail campaigns.

In addition, two more databases are created for each solution site installed. The first is used by the online store to hold its catalogs, campaigns, events, profiles and transactions. The other is our data warehouse, containing the site's day-to-day operational data in a format (OLAP) that's optimized for analysis and data mining. In our example, we've stuck with the default site name 'Retail'; consequently these databases are retail_commerce and retail_dw.

*You can find all of these databases listed under the **Microsoft SQL Servers** node of the Commerce Manager; note that retail_dw also shows up under **Analysis Servers**, which provides interfaces specifically tailored to working with multidimensional data structures.*

As you might imagine, each of these databases is very complex, and it is well worth taking some time to explore the provided tables, views, stored procedures, and cubes for yourself. Obviously, the limited space in this book does not permit us to investigate every one of these in detail. As an example though, let's look at the UserObject table in the retail_commerce database.

The User Profiling system relies heavily on a profile object which is also called UserObject – its properties are mapped onto various fields within the UserObject table. In the previous chapter, we extended this standard object by adding the property FavoriteToys; this was automatically mapped onto a new FavoriteToys field in the UserObject table.

Let's take a look at that table now. Using the Commerce Manager, find the relevant table entry under the Microsoft SQL Servers node, right-click on it, and select Open Table | Return All Rows. This will show us all the records in the UserObject table, and in the process we can see all the fields that make up each record.

As we can see from the following screenshot, at the moment this basically consists of the profile information we entered in the last chapter. Scroll across to the right-hand end of the table, and you should see a field u_Pref1 containing the list of toys that we specified:

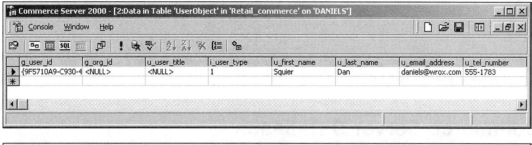

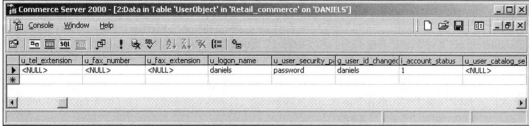

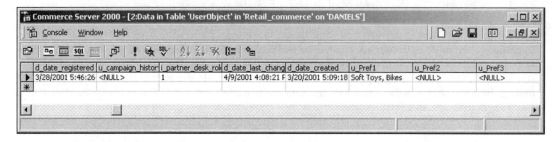

Commerce Server Objects

Commerce Server utilizes a large number of COM components, which form a core part of the product framework. Acquiring a working familiarity with these components and an understanding of the functionality they provide is essential if we are to get the most from Commerce Server. Appendix B provides a complete reference guide to the Commerce Server object model. However, you may also consider the sheer number of components (along with their associated methods and properties) to be quite overwhelming; mastering them completely will be no easy feat.

When we install the retail.pup solution site, we are provided with a series of ASP files that heavily utilize these components. Studying some of these files is an ideal way of identifying the most frequently used components and learning how they can be practically applied. It's certainly not our intention to try to explain every feature of every one of these – that would make for a far larger book than this one! However, the next few sections should give us a reasonably good idea of which ones do what, and prepare us for the more in-depth analysis which follows in later chapters.

> *Installing the BLANK.PUP solution site package installs just basic infrastructure of a solution site. As it provides minimal ASP files, it is really only useful for users developing a site completely from scratch, and developers who are totally up to speed with the full range of Commerce Server objects.*

The Dictionary Object

A Commerce Server `Dictionary` object is a collection object that supports the creation, storage, and retrieval of name/value pairs in memory. You may already be familiar with the `Scripting Dictionary` object – although the Commerce Server `Dictionary` object is very similar in appearance, its internal workings are quite different; for example, a `Commerce.Dictionary` object is actually safe to use as an `Application` level variable in ASP! Every element in a `Dictionary` object is a **variant**, which means you can create a `Dictionary` object that consists of almost any kind of values (including other `Dictionary` objects), and that you can store any combination of variant types in the same `Dictionary` object.

The Commerce Server architecture uses this object for a number of specialized purposes, including the `Site` and `PipeContext` objects. However, because it is designed to be a general-purpose collection, you can use it for almost anything that its internal structure supports. You can create one explicitly (assuming it's not created for you by some other CS2K object), by using the ASP object method `Server.CreateObject()` thus:

```
Set objAddressShip = Server.CreateObject("Commerce.Dictionary")
```

The `Dictionary` object supports three properties: `Count`, `Value`, and `Prefix`. As you might expect, `Count` records the number of elements in the object, while `Value` references a hash of key/value pairs. This enables it to perform fast lookups even when storing a large number of elements is stored. However, it also has the side effect that enumerations of dictionary keys may not be returned in the same order in which they were stored. Suppose we have the following elements in our `objAddressShip` object:

```
first_name = "John"
last_name = "Doe"
_cc_number = "4111-1111-1111-1111"
```

The `Count` property would be 3, and `Value("first_name")` would be `John`.

The property `Prefix` acts as a filter when the contents of the `Commerce.Dictionary` object are saved. It stores a string, and when the key of a name/value pair begins with this string, the key is not saved. The default value of `Prefix` is an underscore, and it is customary to leave it at that and use this character as a prefix. In this example, the keys `FirstName` and `LastName` would be saved, but the key `_cc_number` would not.

By default, the two properties `Value` and `Prefix` are read/write, whereas the property `Count` is read-only.

The SimpleList Object

The `SimpleList` object consists of an array of variants that supports enumeration; as with the `Dictionary` object, you can store any kind of values or objects in it. You should consider using a `SimpleList` object instead of a `Dictionary` object in circumstances where accessing stored content by index is important, and when you do not require the key/value pair structure (or the overhead that entails).

Another difference between the two objects is that at runtime, the `Dictionary` object often operates on a known number of name/value pairs, whereas the `SimpleList` object may contain an arbitrary number of elements. For example, the `Dictionary` object might contain address information, in which case you would probably know in advance how many elements are specified in that address (name, street, city, and so on). The `SimpleList` object might be used to contain the result from a SQL query – you probably wouldn't know, for example, how many products your 'catalog search' query would return before you ran it.

The `SimpleList` object only supports two properties: `Count` and `Item`. As with the `Dictionary` object, the `Count` property is read-only, and stores the number of elements in the `SimpleList` object. The `Item` property stores an element of the `SimpleList` object, and is by nature read/write. The object also has two methods, one for adding items to the `SimpleList`, strangely enough called `Add`, and one for deleting items from it, named `Delete`. To create a `SimpleList` object, use the same method (`Server.CreateObject`) as when creating a `Dictionary` object:

```
Set objListCars = Server.CreateObject("Commerce.SimpleList")
```

So why use the `SimpleList` object and not just an ordinary array? As you probably know, an array is a set of sequentially indexed elements having the same intrinsic data type. Each element of an array has a unique identifying index; hence changes made to one element of an array don't affect the other elements. The `SimpleList`, on the other hand, is a COM object with all the associated niceties. It has methods you can call and properties you can access. It shrinks automatically when items are deleted, so you don't have to re-Dim it yourself. The `count` property of `SimpleList` is defined as a `long` (it can hold up to 2,147,483,648 elements), and it can store elements with *different* data types. It also (just like `Commerce.Dictionary`) implements the `IPersistStreamInit` interface, which means that it can be written and read to and from persistent storage.

Solution Site ASP Processing

As we mentioned earlier, a typical Commerce Server ASP page consists of:

❑   A number of `include` files that pull in constants, utility functions and page templates.

❑   A `Main()` function (and perhaps some other routines) to generate the dynamic part of the page.

We've also seen how the templates are combined with the dynamically generated content to form the complete web page. Shortly, we're going to take a detailed look at the code from a page from the retail solution site, and examine how it uses Commerce Server objects to generate dynamic content. However, the page processing relies on many of these objects having already been instantiated. This happens during initialization of the web application, so we'll look first at this initialization process and then investigate the generation of the home page.

Initializing the Web Application

The first time a request is made to one of the ASP files within the solution site's virtual directory, the web application for that site is started. This invokes the `Application_Onstart` routine, which is located in `global.asa`. This routine takes care of all application initialization.

The `global.asa` file begins with three type library references, which serve to make a number of constants globally available to all ASP files used by the web application. Next, a few constants are defined (specifying standard textbox properties) and global variables are declared. One of these – `MSCSEnv` – is used to identify whether the site is running in a production or development environment; in the latter case, additional debugging diagnostics are enabled.

The `Global.asa` file sets the groundwork for catalog operations, centralized customization, cart mechanics and the order pipeline.

Reinitializing the Web Application

During development, there will be times when we need to reset the application: that is, to reinitialize all objects and restore cache content based on the current content and configuration. To do this, we can call the `RefreshApp.asp` in the root of the application. When this is done, all commerce objects are re-instantiated, as they are initially by the `application_onstart` event in the `global.asa`. During development, when we need a clean slate after changing configuration code, or to refresh content cached at initialization, this technique is much easier than restarting the IIS service.

In the same vein, this can be a big security risk. Not in that it will risk exposing data but in that this file is public knowledge, and with this knowledge an external user with no special tools could actually bring your site to its knees. The same can be said for the `BDRefresh.asp` file, which refreshes the catalog cache.

> You are strongly advised to take action to resolve this issue *before* your site goes live.

This could be done in a number of different ways:

1. By passing a parameter in the query string to validate the requesting call.

2. By locking down user permissions to this file using the ACL or IP constraints.

3. By changing the name of the file entirely.

Let's move on and take a more detailed look at the subroutines that implement the bulk of the functionality contained in `global.asa`.

global.asa – Application_Onstart()

Initialization logic for the web application is actually located in eighteen external files, which are included at the end of `global.asa`. These are accessed via a `Main()` routine in `global_main_lib.asp`:

```
Sub Application_OnStart()
    Application("MSCSEnv") = MSCSEnv
    Call Main()
    Application("MSCSErrorInGlobalASA") = False
End Sub
```

Once the initialization completes successfully, the application scope variable `MSCSErrorInGlobalASA` is set to `False`. All subsequent pages served will begin by checking this flag to ensure that the application was successfully started.

global_main_lib.asp – Main()

This subroutine starts by declaring variables and calling initialization routines in the other `include` files; the instantiated objects are initialized (if necessary) and stored as properties of the ASP `Application` object. They can then be accessed from anywhere within the application.

The first line instantiates the `AppFrameWork` object, which is used to simplify HTML form processing (by extracting form values from an HTTP request message and performing field validation). The next two pairs of lines extract naming information (for the solution site and the web application) from `csapp.ini` and persist the data to the `Application` object:

```
Set appframework = Server.CreateObject("Commerce.AppFrameWork")

MSCSCommerceSiteName = GetINIString(GetINIFileName(), SITE_NAME)
Application("MSCSCommerceSiteName") = MSCSCommerceSiteName

MSCSCommerceAppName = GetINIString(GetINIFileName(), APP_NAME)
Application("MSCSCommerceAppName") = MSCSCommerceAppName
```

The application is synchronized with any other instances of the same site running on other servers in a web farm:

```
Call JoinWebFarm(iWebServerCount)
Application("WebServerCount") = iWebServerCount
```

GetConfigDictionary() is called to instantiate an AppCFG object, and assign it to dictConfig. This is used to access the site configuration, as maintained via the Commerce Manager: hereon, we can access site configuration parameters programmatically via dictConfig:

```
Set dictConfig = GetConfigDictionary()
Application("MSCSPageEncodingCharset") = dictConfig.s_PageEncodingCharset
```

An ExpressionEval object is instantiated, for use by the Content Selection Framework. A communication link between this object and the database storing the configured expressions is established by means of the Connect method. The parameter specified in the Connect method call refers to a database connection string specified during site configuration:

```
Set MSCSExpressionEvaluator = Server.CreateObject("Commerce.ExpressionEvaluator")
MSCSExpressionEvaluator.Connect(dictConfig.s_BizDataStoreConnectionString)
```

The GetSitePages() function is called which instantiates a Dictionary object is created (supporting the storage and retrieval of name/value pairs) and is populated with members that map the name of an operation to the name of the ASP file used to perform it (for example, search → search.asp, login → login/login.asp, and so on):

```
Set MSCSSitePages = GetSitePages()
```

InitProfileService() is called to instantiate and initialize the ProfileService object. This is used to manage ProfileObject objects – instances of the profile schemas we met earlier:

```
Set MSCSProfileService = InitProfileService()
```

An ADOConnection object is instantiated, to connect with Commerce Server's OLE DB provider:

```
Set MSCSAdoConnection = oGetOpenConnectionObject()
```

A Dictionary object is created and populated with PageSets – groups of pages that we wish to relate to one another. Three PageSets are created, for showing product information, checkout details and adverts:

```
Set MSCSPageSets = InitPageSets(MSCSSitePages)
```

`InitSitePipelines()` is called to create and populate a `Dictionary` object that maps pipeline names to PCF filenames (for example, discounts → `pipelines\discount.pcf`):

```
Set MSCSPipelines = InitSitePipelines()
```

`GetSiteStyles()` is called to create and populate a `Dictionary` object that maps style names to HTML fragments (for example, warning → `color='red'`):

```
Set MSCSSiteStyle = GetSiteStyles()
```

A `MessageManager` object is instantiated and populated with data from the `rc.xml` file. As we saw earlier, this is used to provide multi-language support:

```
Set MSCSMessageManager = GetMessageManagerObject()
```

`InitDataFunctions()` is called to instantiate and initialize a `DataFunctions` object. This will provide a number of methods for locale-based data type handling and validation:

```
Set MSCSDataFunctions = InitDataFunctions()
```

`InitCacheManager()` is called to instantiate and initialize a `CacheManager` object. This is used to store items in memory to increase performance:

```
Set MSCSCacheManager = InitCacheManager(MSCSExpressionEvaluator)
```

`InitAltCurrencyDisp()` is called to instantiate and initialize a `EuroDisplay` object. This is used to convert and format various different currencies:

```
Set MSCSAltCurrencyDisp = InitAltCurrencyDisp()
```

`InitCatalogManager()` is called to instantiate and initialize a `CatalogManager` object (used to instantiate various other objects for handling catalogs, categories and products), and `dictGetCatalogAttributes()` to create a `Dictionary` object, which is populated with catalog manager properties:

```
Set MSCSCatalogManager = InitCatalogManager()
Set MSCSCatalogAttribs = dictGetCatalogAttributes(MSCSCatalogManager)
```

`InitPredictor()` is called to instantiate and initialize the `PredictorClient` object – we can load this object with information generated by a data mining model, and use it to display product recommendations:

```
Set MSCSPredictor = InitPredictor()
```

`InitAuthManager()` is called to instantiate an `MSCSAuthManager` object. This is used to authenticate users.

```
Set MSCSAuthManager = InitAuthManager()
```

`InitCatalogSets()` is called to instantiate and initialize the `CatalogSet` object. We can use catalogsets to expose different catalogs to different groups of users:

```
Set MSCSCatalogSets = InitCatalogSets()
```

The site configuration is checked to determine whether Active Directory usage has been enabled – if it has, the domain name is accessed:

```
MSCSProfileServiceUsesActiveDirectory = IsActiveDirectoryPresent()

If MSCSProfileServiceUsesActiveDirectory Then
  MSCSActiveDirectoryDomain = sGetActiveDirectoryDefaultNamingContext()
End If
```

dictGetProfileSchemaForAllProfileTypes() is called in order to create a Dictionary object and populate it with the properties of all Profile schemas:

```
Set MSCSProfileProperties = dictGetProfileSchemaForAllProfileTypes(MSCSProfileService)
```

GetPartnerAndCustomerServicePageAttributes() is called to create a Dictionary object and populate it with a sequence of Dictionary objects; each of these contains information about the ASP pages used in the Customer and Partner services:

```
Set MSCSPageProperties = GetPartnerAndCustomerServicePageAttributes(MSCSSitePages)
```

InitCSF() is called to initialize the Content Selection Framework, specifying the pipeline dictionary, cache manager and the ExpressionEvaluator object initialized earlier:

```
Call InitCSF(MSCSPipelines, MSCSCacheManager, MSCSExpressionEvaluator)
```

Storing Application Properties

Most of the rest of the file is simply concerned with persisting the local object references we've specified as properties of the ASP Application object, so that they can be accessed from any page. There are a few objects left to initialize though, so we'll focus on them:

```
Set Application("MSCSAppConfig") = GetAppConfigObject()
Set Application("MSCSProfileService") = MSCSProfileService
Set Application("MSCSAdoConnection") = MSCSAdoConnection
Set Application("MSCSAltCurrencyDisp") = MSCSAltCurrencyDisp
Set Application("MSCSCacheManager") = MSCSCacheManager
Set Application("MSCSAuthManager") = MSCSAuthManager

Application("MSCSProfileServiceUsesActiveDirectory") = _
                                    MSCSProfileServiceUsesActiveDirectory

If MSCSProfileServiceUsesActiveDirectory Then
          Application("MSCSActiveDirectoryDomain") = MSCSActiveDirectoryDomain
End If

Set Application("MSCSProfileProperties") = MSCSProfileProperties
Set Application("MSCSSitePages") = MSCSSitePages
```

A Dictionary object is created and populated with the addresses of any pages we require to be secure. When running the site in a production environment, the specified pages will be protected by an SSL (Secured Socket Layer) connection:

```
Set Application("MSCSSecurePages") = GetSecurePagesDictionary()
```

Given that we've already called `GetPartnerAndCustomerServicePageAttributes` and assigned the result to `MSCSPageProperties`, this next line seems a little redundant – we could have just assigned this variable to the `Application` object. This is probably nothing more than an oversight, left in from earlier code development.

```
Set Application("MSCSPageProperties") = _
    GetPartnerAndCustomerServicePageAttributes(Application("MSCSSitePages"))
```

Next, we set some more objects in the `Application` object and instantiate the `GenId` object. This is used to generate Globally Unique Identifiers (GUIDs) and manage global counters that work across a web farm:

```
Set Application("MSCSPageSets") = MSCSPageSets
Set Application("MSCSPipelines") = MSCSPipelines
Set Application("MSCSSiteStyle") = MSCSSiteStyle
Set Application("MSCSMessageManager") = MSCSMessageManager
Set Application("MSCSGenID") = oGetGenIDObject()
Set Application("MSCSDataFunctions") = MSCSDataFunctions
Set Application("MSCSCatalogManager") = MSCSCatalogManager
Set Application("MSCSCatalogAttribs") = MSCSCatalogAttribs
Set Application("MSCSExpressionEvaluator") = MSCSExpressionEvaluator
Set Application("MSCSPredictor") = MSCSPredictor
Set Application("MSCSCatalogSets") = MSCSCatalogSets
```

`GetPaymentMethodsForSite()` is then called. This instantiates a `SimpleList` object and populates it with a list of accepted payment methods:

```
Set Application("MSCSSitePaymentMethods") = GetPaymentMethodsForSite()
```

`GetFormDefinitions()` is called. This instantiates a `Dictionary` object and populates it with information about the various forms used by the site:

```
Set Application("MSCSForms") = GetFormDefinitions()
```

`GetObjectInstanceDictionary()` is called to instantiate another `Dictionary` object, which is populated with one `Dictionary` object and one `SimpleList` object – apparently never to be used again. Someone at Microsoft appears to have made another oversight!

```
Set Application("MSCSObjectInstances") = GetObjectInstanceDictionary()
```

Finally, we instantiate the `AppFrameWork` object and assign it to the `Application` object. As mentioned before, this object can be used by the ASP script logic to simplify the task of processing HTML forms:

```
Set Application("MSCSAppFrameWork") = Server.CreateObject("Commerce.AppFrameWork")
End Sub
</SCRIPT>
```

The web application is initialized and ready to process user requests. The `Application` object now contains a whole lot of object references that can be used from anywhere on our site. Next, we'll take a quick look at what we can do with some of them.

Understanding Your Changing Environment

One of the biggest challenges of dissecting and extending an application which we haven't put together ourselves is deriving an understanding of what is occurring on a particular page at a particular time. This can be a real hair pulling experience.

In order to gain a better understanding of the state of the application at any time, it can be very helpful to expose the current working properties of the application environment. To this end, we'll here put together a small function which will display the current state of all the important environment variables.

This function, which we'll call `ExposePageEnvironment()`, loops through a number of arrays and properties that apply to the application, such as Scripting Engine Versions, the complete contents of the `ServerVariable` object, and other Commerce Server specific objects such as `AppConfig`, `SiteStyle` and `MSCSSitePages`.

The section of code provided below is probably most easily placed in the `HTML_lib.asp` file, which resides in the `includes` directory. The `HTML_lib.asp` file is included only on the page level, and of course, already combines several other HTML generating functions.

From here, we will need to place a function call at the base of the template pages. In order that we avoid this function executing in a production environment, we will need to place a condition around it. It is a good idea to use the existing `MSCSEnv` flag in the condition, as this is strictly a development function. In this manner, we do not create unnecessary new flags or operators to keep track of.

```
<% If MSCSEnv = DEVELOPMENT Then Response.Write ExposePageEnvironment() %>
```

Within this code set are several functions that generate HTML tables similar to those that already exist within `HTML_lib.asp` include file. The functions differ in that they handle individual rows, rather than arrays only.

Initially, we perform some stage setting:

```
Function ExposePageEnvironment()
  On Error Resume Next
  dim cnnVersion, oXML
  dim htmContent, tmpContent, tmpContentTable, sKey
  dim sColor1Background, sColor1Foreground, sColor2Background, sColor2Foreground

  sColor1Background = "#EBB923"
  sColor1Foreground = "#000000"
  sColor2Background = "#FFFF80"
  sColor2Foreground = "#000000"

  htmContent = htmContent & htmGenerateEPEHeaderRow("Page Environment for the '" &
MSCSCommerceSiteName & "' site", "#000000", sColor2Background)
  tmpContentTable = ""
  tmpContentTable = tmpContentTable & htmGenerateEPERow("IIS Server",
request.ServerVariables("SERVER_SOFTWARE"), sColor2Foreground, sColor2Background)
  tmpContentTable = tmpContentTable & htmGenerateEPERow("Scripting Engine
Version", ScriptEngineMajorVersion & "." & ScriptEngineMinorVersion,
sColor2Foreground, sColor2Background)
```

We then create a recordset object, and determine its MDAC version:

```
Set cnnVersion = Server.CreateObject("ADODB.Connection")
tmpContentTable = tmpContentTable & htmGenerateEPERow("MDAC Version",
cnnVersion.Version, sColor2Foreground, sColor2Background)
Set cnnVersion = NOTHING

htmContent = htmContent & htmGenerateEPESection("Engine Versions",
tmpContentTable , sColor1Foreground, sColor1Background, sColor2Foreground,
sColor2Background)

htmContent = htmContent & htmGenerateEPESection("MSCSAppConfig",dictConfig,
sColor1Foreground, sColor1Background, sColor2Foreground, sColor2Background)
htmContent = htmContent & htmGenerateEPESection("MSCSSiteStyle",MSCSSiteStyle,
sColor1Foreground, sColor1Background, sColor2Foreground, sColor2Background)
htmContent = htmContent & htmGenerateEPESection("MSCSSitePages",MSCSSitePages,
sColor1Foreground, sColor1Background, sColor2Foreground, sColor2Background)
htmContent = htmContent & htmGenerateEPESection("MSCSPageSets",MSCSPageSets ,
sColor1Foreground, sColor1Background, sColor2Foreground, sColor2Background)
```

Next, we iterate through the collection:

```
tmpContentTable = ""
For Each sKey In Request.ServerVariables
```

And display its contents, and their values:

```
    tmpContentTable = tmpContentTable & htmGenerateEPERow _
      (sKey, Request.ServerVariables(sKey), sColor2Foreground, sColor2Background)
  next

htmContent = htmContent & htmGenerateEPESection _
  ("IIS Server Variables",tmpContentTable , sColor1Foreground, _
  sColor1Background, sColor2Foreground, sColor2Background)

htmContent = RenderTable(htmContent, " border=""0"" cellspacing=""1"" _
  width=""100%"" cellpadding=""2"" bgcolor=""" & sColor1Background & """ ")

htmContent = htmContent & "<STYLE><!-- font.EREKeyFont _
  {color:#000000;font:bold 9pt Arial,Helvetica,sans-serif;}
  font.EREValueFont{color:#000000;font:9pt Arial,Helvetica,sans-serif;}-->
  </STYLE>"

htmContent = "<script>function toggle(e) {if (e.style.display == ""none"")
{e.style.display = """";} else {e.style.display = ""none"";}}
</script>" & htmContent & vbcrlf
htmContent = "<br/>" & htmContent

ExposePageEnvironment = htmContent

end function
```

The htmGenerateEPESection function builds sections which are used by the
ExposePageEnvironment function.

It takes two important parameters: sTitle, and arrTmpArray. sTitle provides the title of the section, and arrTmpArray takes either a string, dictionary, or array. The four other parameters merely allow us to control the colors used in the display.

A table row is returned, which is displayed by the ExposePageEnvironment function:

```
function htmGenerateEPESection(sTitle, arrTmpArray, tmpColor1Foreground,
tmpColor1Background, tmpColor2Foreground, tmpColor2Background)
  dim tmpString, tmpTable, tmpID, tmpLink, sKey
```

Initially, any spaces in the title are removed for use in DHTML ID:

```
tmpID = Replace(sTitle&""," ","")
tmpString = ""
```

A DHTML link is created to open values:

```
tmpLink = "     <span style=""cursor: hand""
onclick=""toggle(document.all." & tmpID & ");""><font size=""2""
color=""#800000""><u>View Properties</u></font></span>" & VBCRLF
```

A section header is created:

```
tmpString = tmpString & htmGenerateEPEHeaderRow(sTitle & tmpLink,
tmpColor1Foreground, tmpColor1Background)

tmpString = tmpString & "<tr>" & vbcrlf & "<td colspan=""2"" bgcolor=""" &
tmpColor2Background & """>" & vbcrlf
```

And a DHTML area is created:

```
tmpString = tmpString & "<span id=""" & tmpID & """ style=""display: none;"">" &
VBCRLF
```

We then iterate through dictionary key/value pairs:

```
    if isobject(arrTmpArray) then

      For Each sKey In arrTmpArray
        Execute "tmpTable = tmpTable & htmGenerateEPERow _
        (sKey, arrTmpArray." & sKey & ", tmpColor2Foreground, tmpColor2Background)"
      Next
    else
      tmpTable = arrTmpArray
    end if

    tmpTable = RenderTable(tmpTable, " border=""0"" cellspacing=""1""
  cellpadding=""2"" bgcolor=""" & tmpColor1Background & """ ")
```

```
    tmpString = tmpString & tmpTable & vbcrlf
    tmpString = tmpString & "</span>" & VBCRLF
    tmpString = tmpString & "</td></tr>" & vbcrlf

    htmGenerateEPESection = tmpString
end function
```

The `htmGenerateEPERow` function builds special rows for the `ExposePageEnvironment` function. The `sKeyCellContent` and `sValueCellContent` parameters accept cell content, and the `sColorForeground` and `sColorBackground` parameters accept color values for the interface.

This function returns a table row with content as a string.

```
function htmGenerateEPERow(byVal sKeyCellContent, byVal sValueCellContent, byVal
sColorForeground, byval sColorBackground)
  dim sRow
  on error resume next
  sRow = sRow & "<tr>" & VBCrLf
  sRow = sRow & "<td width=""20%"" align=""right"" valign=""top"" bgcolor="""&
sColorBackground & """><font class=""EREKeyFont""><b>"
  sRow = sRow & sKeyCellContent
  sRow = sRow & "</td>" & VBCrLf
  sRow = sRow & "<td width=""80%"" bgcolor=""" & sColorBackground & """><font
class=""EREValueFont"">"
  sRow = sRow & sValueCellContent
  sRow = sRow & "</font></td>" & VBCrLf
  sRow = sRow & "</tr>" & VBCrLf
  htmGenerateEPERow = sRow
end function
```

The `htmGenerateEPEHeaderRow` function simply builds header rows for the `ExposePageEnvironment` function. It is passed cell content, and foreground and background color values, and returns a header row with content, as a string.

```
function htmGenerateEPEHeaderRow(byVal sHeaderContent, byVal sColorForeground,
byval sColorBackground)
  dim sRow
  sRow = sRow & "<tr><td colspan=""2"" bgcolor=""" &  sColorBackground & """>" &
VBCrLf
  sRow = sRow & "<font size=""3"" face=""arial"" color=""" & sColorForeground &
"""><b><i>"
  sRow = sRow & sHeaderContent
  sRow = sRow & "</i></b></font>" & VBCrLF
  sRow = sRow & "</td></tr>" & VBCrLf
  htmGenerateEPEHeaderRow = sRow
end function
```

This code is fairly straightforward stuff. However, it should serve serve as a handy little utility when building on Commerce Server features.

When we run this function, we should see something like the following (due to screen size restrictions, we show very few of the exposed environment variables).

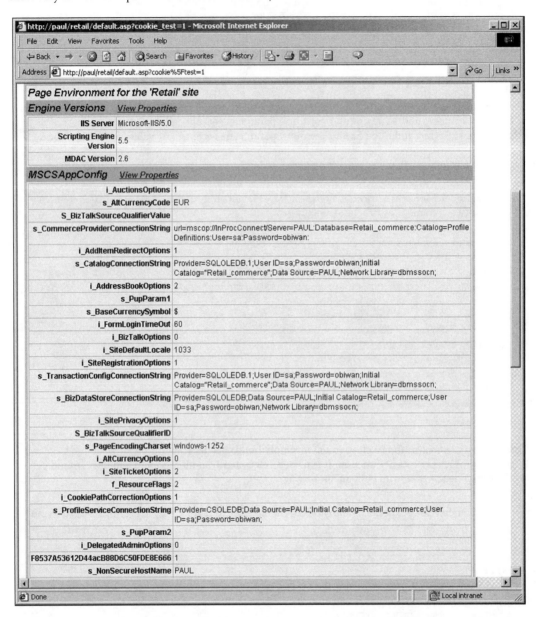

Having such information at hand should enable us to gain far better insights into what is happening within the application background. Customizing it to meet your own needs should be a fairly straightforward matter.

Caching

Caching as a concept is nothing new. By holding on to the results of a complex or resource intensive process, and reusing them at a later time, we can save resources, and thus improve performance.

Very simply this equates to faster websites with less hardware. Many times with content-based sites where only articles are served, this can be done in front of the web servers where complete pages are stored after the first request and remain stored until the article is archived or removed. This same type of scenario is utilized on proxy servers where network bandwidth is conserved by storing commonly viewed pages and served to everyone on a network.

In the case of Commerce Server, resources are cached on two levels, as objects, and as text strings. First, in the Global.asa, reusable objects are generated during the Application_OnStart() event, and are stored in the web server's local application state, thus allowing them to be reused on every page. Second, content blocks in the form of HTML fragments are assembled as strings, and stored in memory via the CacheManager object where they can be called for re-use at anytime.

There are four different areas where fragment caching via the CacheManager is incorporated into the Retail solution site. These include Catalog, Search, Campaign and Pipeline. Basic catalog caching is most simply exemplified in default.asp page.

In the following section of the Default.asp page, we check to see if the page content has been generated and cached. If the cache fragment value is NULL then the content is generated and stored as a cache fragment for use the next time the page is viewed:

```
htmPageContent = LookupCachedFragment("DefaultPageCache", CatalogSetID)
If IsNull(htmPageContent) Then
   Call PrepareDefaultPage(CatalogSetID, rsCatalogs, iCatalogCount, sCatalogName,
                            oCatalog, oCategory, rsProducts, nPageNumber)
   htmPageContent = htmRenderDefaultPage(CatalogSetID, rsCatalogs, iCatalogCount,
                                          sCatalogName, oCatalog, oCategory,
                                          rsProducts, nPageNumber)
End If
```

With this implementation, every cache fragment has a unique name. In this case, we are passing DefaultPageCache as the identifier. The CacheManager object is created during the application initialization process.

Here the LookupCachedFragment() function requests MSCSCacheManager.GetCache() at browse time:

```
Function LookupCachedFragment(ByVal sCacheName, ByVal sCacheItemName)
   Dim oLRUCache, UserIDTag

   Set oLRUCache = MSCSCacheManager.GetCache(sCacheName)

   ' Note that we have to templatize fragments that have been genericized. To
templatize
   ' we replace all token instances with correct userid.

   ' If the ticket is in URL, the fragment must be templatized.
   If m_iTicketLocation = 1 Then
      LookupCachedFragment = oLRUCache.Lookup(sCacheItemName & sLanguage &
"URLMODE")
      If Not IsNull(LookupCachedFragment) Then
         UserIDTag = GetTicketInUrlArg
         LookupCachedFragment = Replace(LookupCachedFragment,
TICKET_REPLACEMENT_TOKEN, UserIDTag)
      End If
```

```
     Else
        ' No need to templatize if the ticket is in the cookie or there is no ticket
(IIS auth).
        LookupCachedFragment = oLRUCache.Lookup(sCacheItemName & sLanguage &
"COOKIEMODE")
     End If

     ' Debug code that will show if a fragment was cached...
     'If Not IsNull(LookupCachedFragment) Then
     '   LookupCachedFragment = "<TABLE BORDER=1><TR><TD>Cached: " & sCacheName & BR &
sCacheItemName& sLanguage & "</TD></TR><TR><TD>" & LookupCachedFragment &
"</TD></TR></TABLE>"
     'End If
End Function
```

Later on in the `Default.asp` page, the generated fragment is placed in the cache by the
`CacheFragment()` function and assigned the id `DefaultPageCache`.

```
Call CacheFragment("DefaultPageCache", CatalogSetID, htmPageContent)
```

Disabling Caching

Now it's not always helpful to have the cache on when in development. This can cause frustrations when you
are expecting content to change, and – mysteriously – nothing happens. Let's take a minute to add a few lines
to allow us to turn this off quickly. Open up the `const.asp` page in the `include` directory. What you
should see here is nothing – nothing but a pair of empty ASP tags. Let's here add a Boolean value to flag our
cache option:

```
' Turn Cache ON or OFF
CONST CacheOn = TRUE
```

In the `std_cache_lib.asp` page, let's add four conditional statements: to `LookupCachedFragment()`,
`CacheFragment()`, `LookupCachedObject()` and finally to `CacheObject()`.

Below is an example of the `LookupCachedFragment()` function. Highlighted here, the conditional
statement has been added to check for the `CacheOn` Boolean that was set in the constants page. When it is
set to `false`, the caching mechanisms are skipped. It is important that the `else` statement contain the
`LookupCachedFragment = NULL`, otherwise the caching tests throughout the site will fail, because they
will expect a `NULL`, not an empty value.

Insert this excerpt in the other functions listed above. You should notice a preexisting function here that
labels a cached fragment. Previously commented out, any deactivating comments have been removed, and a
test to the conditional `if... then` statement, that checks the `MSCSEnv` value that was set in the
`global.asa` – to see if it is set to `PRODUCTION` or `DEVELOPMENT`, has been added. If this is a
`DEVELOPMENT` environment and the cached fragment is `NULL`, then it will create a label displaying the non-
cached status of the fragment.

```
Function LookupCachedFragment(ByVal sCacheName, ByVal sCacheItemName)
   If CacheOn Then
      Dim oLRUCache, UserIDTag
```

```
        Set oLRUCache = MSCSCacheManager.GetCache(sCacheName)

        ' Note that we have to templatize fragments that have been genericized.
        ' To templatize we replace all token instances with correct userid.

        ' If the ticket is in URL, the fragment must be templatized.

    If m_iTicketLocation = 1 Then
      LookupCachedFragment = oLRUCache.Lookup(sCacheItemName & sLanguage & "URLMODE")
      If Not IsNull(LookupCachedFragment) Then
          UserIDTag = GetTicketInUrlArg
          LookupCachedFragment = Replace(LookupCachedFragment, _
                              TICKET_REPLACEMENT_TOKEN, UserIDTag)
      End If
    Else
    ' No need to templatize if the ticket is in the cookie or there is no
    ' ticket (IIS auth).

      LookupCachedFragment = oLRUCache.Lookup _
          (sCacheItemName & sLanguage & "COOKIEMODE")
    End If

      ' Debug code that will show if a fragment was cached...

      If Not IsNull(LookupCachedFragment) AND MSCSEnv = DEVELOPMENT Then
        LookupCachedFragment = "<TABLE BORDER=1><TR><TD>Cached: " & _
          sCacheName & BR & sCacheItemName& sLanguage & _
          "</TD></TR><TR><TD>" & LookupCachedFragment & "</TD></TR></TABLE>"
      End If
    Else
      LookupCachedFragment = NULL
    End If
  End Function
```

We now have two very useful tools to help us in the development of commerce interface functionality. Without these settings, it's very easy to miss these issues when debugging, and can be the source of hours of frustration while looking for updated content. It's also important to point out here that you may wish to move the CacheOn setting to Global.asa, where the MSCSEnv is set, so as to keep these sorts of global settings in one place. You may even wish to add this to the AppConsts 1.0 Type Library. This way, you are sure not to accidentally pass these settings to production by copying a development Global.asa to a production environment.

Cached fragments remain in memory until the application is restarted, the cache is automatically expired on a timed interval, or a catalog update is published. The cache may be manually purged at any time by implementing the RefreshCache method of the cache manager.

Resource requirements for the cache manager will vary drastically based on how many people visit how many pages on your site. Throughout the development stages of a site, and after it is launched, you will want to test and tune your site based on expected volumes. Increasing and decreasing the size of your cache in memory can affect the scalability and speed of your cache dramatically.

Page Execution

We'll now turn to looking at the way in which the Retail site application actually functions. First, we'll look at some general aspects of the Retail site: before looking in detail at the actual functionality of different parts of the site, and how they utilize the Commerce Server 2000 environment.

Coding conventions

When reviewing code, it is worth noting the conventions used. Listed here are the conventions used in the Retail solution site.

In place of standard Hungarian convention, everything used here are all short form prefixes, which is not uncommon for Microsoft's code samples. Most important are the framework prefixes. Capital and lowercase MSCS object prefixes dictate whether an object was created in the Global.asa and stored in the Application scope, or whether these objects were transferred to page level objects for use locally within the execution path. This is important when walking through the page level initialization code and understanding which objects are intended for home use, and which are intended for state storage.

Prefix	Description
arr	Array
b	Boolean
dict	Dictionary
f	Flag
htm	HTML cache string
I	Integer
list	SimpleList
o	Object
s	String (non-HTML)
MSCS	Application scope variables
mscs	Page scope variables

HTML: Everywhere, But Nowhere To Be Found

It is important to mention that we will find little to no HTML within the top-level functions of the site. In this arena, the development team has adopted the maxim that simpler is better, and designed a standard HTML functionality set to generate the interface on the fly, rather than hard coding HTML into the pages.

By binding Commerce Server category and product arrays to functions, Commerce Server allows us to programmatically generate 95% of the site interface without writing a line of HTML by hand. To do this, the site's dynamic content is derived mainly by implementing HTML function calls: these functions generate tables and lists based on server-side styles and parameters which are passed to them.

At least in part, HTML is generated dynamically to utilize Commerce Server's caching mechanisms. These functions spin HTML into variable strings, rather than directly writing them to the page. These strings can be rendered at the appropriate position amongst the static HTML (footers , headers, navigation system), which are stored in just a couple of template files. They can also be stored within the Commerce Server `CacheManager`.

Take some time get to know the functions in the `HTML_lib.asp`, so that they're familiar for when you need them.

One drawback with this type of approach is that it can be very limiting when it comes to detailed interface design.

Initialization

The `setupenv.asp` page is included in nearly every called page within the site. It initializes the page level environment by rehydrating the Commerce Server objects that were created in the `Global.asa`, assigning them to local variables.

After this is done, a call is made to the `SetUpPage()` function, which also resides on the `setupenv.asp` page. As its name suggests, this simply initiates settings related to the page presentation. After the `mscsAuthMgr` is instantiated within the `SetupPage()` function, the absolute path for the website is specified. This allows us to call any page or graphic from anywhere else in the website without regard for the location of the source page.

```
Call SetupPage()

Sub SetupPage()
  ' Setup page variables
  Set mscsAuthMgr = GetAuthManagerObject()
  sThisPage = Request.ServerVariables("SCRIPT_NAME")
  sImagePath = "/images/"
  If Len(MSCSAppFrameWork.VirtualDirectory) = 0 Then
    sThisPage = Mid(sThisPage, 2) 'Site Installed at root, trim off leading \
  Else
    sThisPage = Mid(sThisPage, Len(MSCSAppFrameWork.VirtualDirectory) + 3)
    'Trim off leading vdir
    sImagePath = "/" & MSCSAppFrameWork.VirtualDirectory & sImagePath
  End If
```

After this, the `dictConfig` object is instantiated using the `GetOptionsDictionary()` method of the profile object. This enables us to call specific attributes or loop through the attributes of a dictionary, rather than having to pull the properties of the class one by one.

```
Set dictConfig = Application("MSCSAppConfig").GetOptionsDictionary("")
```

Next, the `CorrectRequest()` function ensures that the case sensitivity issues of some browsers is handled properly by redirecting the user to the appropriate URL, so that a qualified cookie can be set or obtained. This is then followed by several calls which obtain minimal user information and assign the language that the site will use.

```
' Correct the request (handles case-sensitivity issue with cookies)
Call CorrectRequest()
m_iGlobalProfileLookUpOption = 2

  m_iTicketLocation = GetTicketLocation()

Call GetUserInfo()

' Set the language for the user
sLanguage = MSCSMessageManager.DefaultLanguage
```

Finally, a call is made to the `main()` subroutine where the core of the page begins.

```
    Call Main()
End Sub
```

Page Flow

The Retail site is highly modularized. There are a large number of nested functions and subs that are used in rendering `default.asp`. In the following section, we'll look at these functions in turn. This should enable us to build up a picture of how a page operates when a user makes a particular request.

Main

As mentioned already, at this point most of the page level objects we will be using have been set, and we are ready to generate the page itself. This function looks for the home page cache fragment. If found, it displays the fragment without further work. If the fragment is found to be NULL, the two primary functions are called, the first of which generates the arrays to be used in the interface formulation next. This is done by passing in some, as yet unused variables that will later be used as catalog and product arrays.

```
Sub Main()
   Dim CatalogSetID
   Dim rsCatalogs, rsProducts
   Dim iCatalogCount, nPageNumber
   Dim sCatalogName
   Dim oCatalog, oCategory

   Call EnsureAccess()

   CatalogSetID = mscsUserCatalogsetID()
   htmPageContent = LookupCachedFragment("DefaultPageCache", CatalogSetID)
   htmPageContent = NULL
   If IsNull(htmPageContent) Then
      Call PrepareDefaultPage(CatalogSetID, rsCatalogs, iCatalogCount, sCatalogName,
oCatalog, oCategory, rsProducts, nPageNumber)
      htmPageContent = htmRenderDefaultPage(CatalogSetID, rsCatalogs, iCatalogCount,
sCatalogName, oCatalog, oCategory, rsProducts, nPageNumber)
   End If
End Sub
```

PrepareDefaultPage

Below, in the `PrepareDefaultPage()` sub, the data used for the core content area on the page is set. By calling a list of catalogs for the site, we will know how many catalogs we are handling and in turn determine the behavior of the page. This is done via the `iCatalogCount` select statement. If there is a single catalog available, then the catalog itself is used to obtain subcategories and any products that might be available at the current category.

In the case where more than one catalog is available, no more work is done here because the user must choose a catalog before any more information is displayed. When the `PrepareDefaultPage()` sub is complete, we make a quick jump back to the `main()` sub in the `default.asp` page, so that we can continue.

```
Sub PrepareDefaultPage(ByVal CatalogSetID, ByRef rsCatalogs, ByRef iCatalogCount,
ByRef sCatalogName, ByRef oCatalog, ByRef oCategory, ByRef rsProducts, ByRef
nPageNumber)
   Dim sCategoryName
   Dim nRecordsTotal, nOutPagesTotal

   Set rsCatalogs = mscsUserCatalogsFromID(CatalogSetID)
   iCatalogCount = GetRecordCount(rsCatalogs)

   ' Get the page info, depending on the number of catalogs in the system
   Select Case iCatalogCount
     Case 0
     Case 1
        sCatalogName = rsCatalogs.Fields(CATALOG_NAME_PROPERTY_NAME).Value
        sCategoryName = CATALOG_ROOT_CATEGORY_NAME
        Set oCatalog = MSCSCatalogManager.GetCatalog(sCatalogName) 'Catalog Name
comes from trusted source (not url), otherwise we should call GetCatalogForUser or
EnsureUserHasRightsToCatalog
        nPageNumber = 1

        Set oCategory = mscsGetCategoryObject(oCatalog, sCategoryName)
        Set rsProducts = mscsGetProductList(oCatalog, oCategory, nPageNumber,
nRecordsTotal, nOutPagesTotal)
     Case Else
   End Select
End Sub
```

htmRenderDefaultPage

The next command executed in the `main()` subroutine is the `hmtRenderDefaultPage()` sub. This is where the HTML interface is generated from the catalog objects pulled earlier in the `PrepareDefaultPage()`. Here we go through an exercise similar to the one in our previous step where the number of catalogs available is used to determine the behavior of the content area of the page.

Let's examine the highlighted commands below where the behavior for a single catalog takes place. Here a simple call is made to the `MessageManager` to determine the name of the top-level category. This is nested in the `RenderText()` sub which is an HTML function used to render HTML from content. Finally the `HTMLRenderHompage()` sub is called which keys the conversion of our category and product arrays to HTML.

```
Function htmRenderDefaultPage(ByVal CatalogSetID, ByVal rsCatalogs, ByVal
iCatalogCount, ByVal sCatalogName, ByVal oCatalog, ByVal oCategory, ByVal
rsProducts, ByVal nPageNumber)
```

```
        Dim htmTitle, htmContent, htmPageContent
        Dim nPagesTotal


   ' Get the catalog fragment from the cache, or render it
        sPageTitle = mscsMessageManager.GetMessage("L_Home_HTMLTitle", sLanguage)


   ' Render the page, depending on the number of catalogs in the system
        Select Case iCatalogCount
           Case 0
              ' No catalogs available
              htmTitle =
   RenderText(mscsMessageManager.GetMessage("L_MENU_CATEGORIES_SECTION_HTMLTitle",
   sLanguage), MSCSSiteStyle.Title)
              htmContent =
   RenderText(mscsMessageManager.GetMessage("L_No_Catalogs_Installed_ErrorMessage",
   sLanguage), MSCSSiteStyle.Body)
           Case 1
              ' Render the one catalog...
              htmTitle =
   RenderText(mscsMessageManager.GetMessage("L_MENU_CATEGORIES_SECTION_HTMLTitle",
   sLanguage), MSCSSiteStyle.Title)
              htmContent = htmRenderHompage(oCatalog, sCatalogName,
   CATALOG_ROOT_CATEGORY_NAME, oCategory, rsProducts, nPageNumber, nPagesTotal)
           Case Else
              ' Render a list of catalogs
              htmTitle =
   RenderText(mscsMessageManager.GetMessage("L_MENU_CATALOG_SECTION_HTMLTitle",
   sLanguage), MSCSSiteStyle.Title)
              htmContent = htmRenderCatalogList(rsCatalogs, MSCSSiteStyle.Body)
        End Select
        htmPageContent = htmTitle & CRLF & htmContent
        Call CacheFragment("DefaultPageCache", CatalogSetID, htmPageContent)
     htmRenderDefaultPage = htmPageContent
   End Function
```

htmRenderCategoryPage

Here we have left the Default.asp page and have moved to the catalog.asp page, which holds most of the functions used to handle and render product and category navigation on the site. A number of objects and configuration values specific to the context of our execution path are now being passed to each function as we go. Because this function is used throughout the site, there appear to be what may seem like extraneous processes included.

The first process here is a good example, where the code checks to see if there is more than one page of products to be displayed for this category. If there is more than a single page of products to be displayed, a pagination guide is created: where a list of page numbers are shown, and the user can select any page by clicking on the associated number.

From this point, another check is made on the total pages, this time to display sub-categories only if this is the first page in the product pagination. If this is page one, and there are valid sub-categories in the Recordset, then htmRenderCategoryList() function is called. This can be seen highlighted below.

```
Function htmRenderCategoryPage(ByVal oCatalog, ByVal sCatalogName, ByVal
sCategoryName, ByVal oCategory, ByVal rsProducts, ByVal nPageNumber, ByVal
nOutPagesTotal)
    [..]

    ' If the result set is larger than one page, show paging info..
    If (nOutPagesTotal > 1) Then
        htmContent = htmContent & FormatOutput( mscsMessageManager.GetMessage(
"L_Total_Pages_Found_HTMLText", sLanguage), Array(nPageNumber, nOutPagesTotal))
        For i = 1 to nOutPagesTotal
            urlLink = RenderCategoryUrl(sCatalogName, sCategoryName, i)
            htmContent = htmContent & RenderLink(urlLink, i, MSCSSiteStyle.Link) & NBSP
        Next
        htmContent = htmContent & CR & CR
    End If


    ' If on page one, show the subcategories
    If nPageNumber = 1 Then
        Set rsChildCategories = mscsGetSubCategoriesList(oCatalog, oCategory)
        If Not rsChildCategories.EOF Then
            bCategoriesFound = True
            htmContent = htmContent & htmRenderCategoriesList(oCatalog,
rsChildCategories, MSCSSiteStyle.Body) & CR
        End If
    End If

    ' Show any products (using htmRenderProductsTable)
    If Not rsProducts.EOF Then
        htmContent = htmContent & htmRenderProductsTable( _
                                    oCatalog, _
                                    rsProducts, _
                                    sCategoryName _
                                )
    ElseIf Not bCategoriesFound Then
        ' Category didn't contain any products or subcategories
        htmContent = RenderText(
mscsMessageManager.GetMessage("L_Empty_Catalog_Category_HTMLText", sLanguage),
MSCSSiteStyle.Body)
    End If

    htmRenderCategoryPage = htmContent & CR
End Function
```

htmRenderCategoriesList

Here the HTMRenderCategoryList() takes the catalog array, the category Recordset, and body style parameters, and creates the list of categories visible above the product on the homepage, provided you have only one catalog set loaded.

If you should have more than one catalog set loaded, this view is available after you have already selected a particular catalog, after which the category Recordset is checked to ensure that it is not empty, and then loops through the category list to create an HTML string. This is where you would modify the function should you need to display the category list in a different format, such as in multiple columns, to conserve screen space.

The way in which we here loop through the categories is an example of how functions are used to render HTML. The RenderCategoryLink() is customized for creating an anchor tag with specialized style for categories.

```
Function htmRenderCategoriesList(ByVal oCatalog, ByVal rsCategories, ByVal style)
    Dim sProductCategory, sCatalogName
    Dim htmCategory
    Dim lstrTemp

    If (rsCategories.EOF) Then
    lstrTemp = "" & CR
    Else
    sCatalogName = rsCategories.Fields(CATALOG_NAME_PROPERTY_NAME).Value

    lstrTemp = ""
    While Not rsCategories.EOF
      sProductCategory = rsCategories.Fields(CATEGORY_NAME_PROPERTY_NAME).Value
      htmCategory = RenderCategoryLink(sCatalogName, sProductCategory, 1, style)
      lstrTemp = lstrTemp & htmCategory & CR
        rsCategories.MoveNext
    Wend
    End If

  htmRenderCategoriesList = lstrTemp
End Function
```

RenderCategoryLink

Here the RenderCategoryLink() function splits the parameters passed and renders its pieces. IT is specialized for a category link, and uses another specialized function to create a URL back to a category page where the next page in the category level in our pagination can be found, parameters included.

```
Function RenderCategoryLink(sCatalogName, sCategory, nPage, style)
    Dim sURL, HTMLinkText
    sURL = RenderCategoryURL(sCatalogName, sCategory, nPage)
    HTMLinkText = RenderText(sCategory, style)
    RenderCategoryLink = RenderLink(sURL, HTMLinkText, MSCSSiteStyle.Link)
End Function
```

RenderCategoryURL

The RenderCategoryURL function is primarily used as a pass through function to the GenerateURL() function.

```
Function RenderCategoryURL(sCatalogName, sCategory, nPage)
    Dim sURL
    sURL = GenerateURL(MSCSSitePages.Category, Array(CATALOG_NAME_URL_KEY,
CATEGORY_NAME_URL_KEY, PAGENUMBER_URL_KEY), Array(sCatalogName, sCategory, nPage))
    RenderCategoryURL = sURL
End Function
```

GenerateURL

The GenerateURL function is a fairly common function, used throughout the site. It creates a URL to link within the site. Highlighted below, the Commerce Server object method, mscsAuthMgr.GetURL, is used. A great comment in the code here even documents the difference between the mscsAuthMgr method and the depreciated page method. You'll also notice here that this function compensates for HTTPS SSL secured pages.

```
Function GenerateURL(ByVal sPageName, ByRef arrParams, ByRef arrVals)
   Dim bSSLSupport, bCookie

   ' Unlike Page object's URL and SURL methods, whenever the value for a URL
parameter is
   ' Null or Emtpy, the GetURL method of AuthManager object does not include the
parameter
   ' name on the URL. The following work-around forces GetURL method to always
include the
   ' parameter name on the URL regardless of its value. The workaround is disabled
by default.
   'For i = LBound(arrParams) To UBound(arrParams)
   '   If IsNull(arrVals(i)) Or IsEmpty(arrVals(i)) Then
   '      arrVals(i) = ""
   '   End If
   'Next

   bSSLSupport = False
   If Not IsNull(Application("MSCSSecurePages").Value(sPageName)) Then
     bSSLSupport = True
   End If

   ' If the ticket is in URL ...
   If m_iTicketLocation = 1 Then
     bCookie = False
   Else
     bCookie = True
   End If

   GenerateURL = mscsAuthMgr.GetURL(sPageName, bCookie, bSSLSupport, arrParams,
arrVals)
   End Function
```

RenderText

RenderText is a very straightforward function, where we actually encounter some HTML tags. The attribute in the FONT element is a string of element parameters passed as the style string in earlier functions. This function then returns this HTML as a string.

```
Function RenderText(ByVal str, ByVal sAttList)
   RenderText = "<FONT" & sAttList & ">" & str & "</FONT>"
End Function
```

htmRenderProductsTable

The htmRenderProductsTable function takes a simple Recordset and transforms it into an HTML table to be delivered to the homepage. Highlighted here, and based on whether the catalog uses the product name as a unique identifier, an array is built to describe the header cell of each column in the table. From this array, the RenderTableHeaderRow(), a <TH> element row is created and stored for use later when the table is assembled.

Next, as we loop through the Recordset, the values corresponding to header fields are pulled then assigned to fields in an array. A function called GetPriceandCurrency collects the localized price and attaches the appropriate currency symbol to it. At each pass through a product, an HTML table row is generated with the RenderTableDataRow() function, and concatenated to the previously created row. After all the products have been processed, the RenderTable() function is called and wraps table tags around the rows which have just been created.

```
Function htmRenderProductsTable(ByVal oCatalog, ByVal rsProducts, ByVal
sCategoryName)
  Dim sCatalogName, sProductName, sProductDescription, sProductID
  Dim arrRows, arrAttLists
  Dim cyProductPrice, cyCurrency
  Dim htmProduct, htmBody
  Dim bNameIsIdentifyingProperty

  sCatalogName = rsProducts.Fields(CATALOG_NAME_PROPERTY_NAME).Value

  ' Determine if the "name" property is the identifying product property
  bNameIsIdentifyingProperty = StrComp( _
             PRODUCT_NAME_PROPERTY_NAME, _
oCatalog.IdentifyingProductProperty, _
             vbTextCompare _
             ) = 0

  ' Build the column headers depending on if "name" is the identifying property
  If bNameIsIdentifyingProperty Then
        arrRows = Array( _
      mscsMessageManager.GetMessage("L_Product_Name_DisplayName_HTMLText",
sLanguage), _
      mscsMessageManager.GetMessage("L_Product_Description_DisplayName_HTMLText",
sLanguage), _
      mscsMessageManager.GetMessage("L_Product_Price_DisplayName_HTMLText",
sLanguage) _
      )
  Else
    arrRows = Array( _
      oCatalog.IdentifyingProductProperty, _
      mscsMessageManager.GetMessage("L_Product_Name_DisplayName_HTMLText",
sLanguage), _
      mscsMessageManager.GetMessage("L_Product_Description_DisplayName_HTMLText",
sLanguage), _
      mscsMessageManager.GetMessage("L_Product_Price_DisplayName_HTMLText",
sLanguage) _
        )
  End If
  htmBody = RenderTableHeaderRow(arrRows, Array(), MSCSSiteStyle.TRCenter)

  ' Fill out colums for each row in the recordset
  While Not rsProducts.EOF
    ' "name" and "description" are required product properties and cannot have
null values.
    sProductName = rsProducts.Fields(PRODUCT_NAME_PROPERTY_NAME).Value
    sProductDescription =
rsProducts.Fields(PRODUCT_DESCRIPTION_PROPERTY_NAME).Value
    sProductID = rsProducts.Fields(oCatalog.IdentifyingProductProperty).Value

    ' check for price on variant
    Call GetPriceAndCurrency(rsProducts, cyProductPrice, cyCurrency)

    htmProduct = RenderProductLink(sCatalogName, sCategoryName, sProductName,
CStr(sProductID), MSCSSiteStyle.Body)

    ' Build the columns depending on if "name" is the identifying property
```

```
      If bNameIsIdentifyingProperty Then
         arrRows = Array(htmProduct, sProductDescription, cyCurrency)
         arrAttLists = Array(MSCSSiteStyle.TDLeft, MSCSSiteStyle.TDLeft,
MSCSSiteStyle.TDRight)
      Else
         arrRows = Array(sProductID, htmProduct, sProductDescription, cyCurrency)
         arrAttLists = Array(MSCSSiteStyle.TDLeft, MSCSSiteStyle.TDLeft,
MSCSSiteStyle.TDLeft, MSCSSiteStyle.TDRight)
      End If

      htmBody = htmBody & RenderTableDataRow(arrRows, arrAttLists,
MSCSSiteStyle.TRMiddle)
      rsProducts.MoveNext
   Wend

      htmRenderProductsTable = RenderTable(htmBody, MSCSSiteStyle.BorderedTable)
End Function
```

RenderTableDataRow

Nothing more than a pass through function, the RenderTableDataRow function passes the array through to the RenderTableRow() function for processing.

```
Function RenderTableDataRow(arrData, arrDataAttLists, ByVal sRowAttList)
   RenderTableDataRow = RenderTableRow(arrData, arrDataAttLists, sRowAttList,
DATA_ROW)
End Function
```

RenderTableRow

This feature is the finale for all table row generation functions. This nested logic handles both header and data rows, and then loops through the supplied arrays to create an HTML table row. From arrDataAttList() array, built from the global styles dictionary, attributes are applied to the <TD> or <TH> elements in tandem with the data.

```
Function RenderTableRow(arrData, arrDataAttLists, ByVal sRowAttList, ByVal
iRowType)
   Dim i, bErr
   bErr = False

   If UBound(arrDataAttLists) <> -1 Then
     If UBound(arrData) <> UBound(arrDataAttLists) Then
       RenderTableRow = "-1"
       bErr = True
     End If
   End If

   If Not bErr Then
     RenderTableRow = "<TR" & sRowAttList & ">"
     Select Case iRowType
       Case HEADER_ROW
         If UBound(arrDataAttLists) = -1 Then
           For i = 0 To UBound(arrData)
```

```
                If (arrData(i) = "") Or IsNull(arrData(i)) Then arrData(i) = NBSP
                RenderTableRow = RenderTableRow & "<TH>" & arrData(i) & "</TH>"
            Next
        Else
            For i = 0 To UBound(arrData)
                If (arrData(i) = "") Or IsNull(arrData(i)) Then arrData(i) = NBSP
                RenderTableRow = RenderTableRow & "<TH" & arrDataAttLists(i) & ">" &
arrData(i) & "</TH>"
            Next
        End If
    Case DATA_ROW
        If UBound(arrDataAttLists) = -1 Then
            For i = 0 To UBound(arrData)
                If (arrData(i) = "") Or IsNull(arrData(i)) Then arrData(i) = NBSP
                RenderTableRow = RenderTableRow & "<TD>" & arrData(i) & "</TD>"
            Next
        Else
            For i = 0 To UBound(arrData)
                If (arrData(i) = "") Or IsNull(arrData(i)) Then arrData(i) = NBSP
                RenderTableRow = RenderTableRow & "<TD" & arrDataAttLists(i) & ">" &
arrData(i) & "</TD>"
            Next
        End If
    End Select
    RenderTableRow = RenderTableRow & "</TR>"
  End If
End Function
```

RenderTable

From step 6, a string variable storing the body of the table is passed to the `RenderTable()` function, wrapped with `TABLE` tags, and supplied with the appropriate element attributes for the `TABLE`, also from the global site styles dictionary.

```
Function RenderTable(ByVal htmRows, ByVal sAttList)
    RenderTable = "<TABLE" & sAttList & ">" & htmRows & "</TABLE>"
End Function
```

At this point, the content generation is complete. The HTML content strings are passed back up through the nested functions, concatenating them together as they go. When complete, we have a completed HTML fragment to be written to the page and stored within the cache.

Website Interface

The Retail website comes equipped with a particularly uninspiring interface. Fortunately, the Commerce Server 2000 team has made it easy to give it some quick style and branding.

In the interface, links are created by default, as are tables and columns. And the header is empty. Before changing this look, you should be aware that when manipulating the interface, it's probably safe to base estimates on the 80/20 rule. 80% of the website can be changed with 20% of the effort, while the other 20% of the interface will consume the remaining 80% of effort. Fortunately, 80% gets us a long way. In this section, we'll walk through some basic, and not so basic, changes we can make to make the Retail site our own.

Everyone wants to see their company's name writ large, and many see a website as their opportunity to succeed both personally and professionally.

With important issues like these on the table, negotiating everyone to an agreement on one look and feel for branding your site may well be the most stressfull task of all.

If you intend to implement a solution site as the code base for your website, you would be well advised to summarize the basic functionality of Commerce Server as a starting point when planning your online presence. Much of the functionality reviewed throughout this manual should give you a foundation for components to include in your design efforts. Most of the HTML generation features are not difficult to modify, but can prove time consuming when a branding specification is created without consideration for the feature sets provided by Commerce Server.

You should make a list of basic features which are to be included in the interface: a toolbar, navigational features, user profile management, product placement, search features, and cart layout.

Server-Side Styles

To begin adding style to your site, it's important to realize that all attributes from generated HTML elements are predefined in a dictionary list of key/value pairs called `SiteStyles`, defined in the `GetSiteStyle()` function. This is done instead of using normal CSS stylesheets, so that we can have the advantages of styles, but without having to worry whether the browser supports CSS or not.

This list is set into motion when the dictionary is created from the `GetSiteStyle()` function which is assigned to the `MSCSSiteStyle` object in the `Global_main_lib.asp` file:

```
Set MSCSSiteStyle = GetSiteStyles()
```

Before we begin to modify our `SiteStyles` directly, let's make a few additions to make our lives easier as we set up the interface environment.

When a web application is designed and written in a development environment it must eventually be ported to a production environment. When this happens, application paths will probably change. In most cases, sites that were once buried in a development subdirectory may now sit in the root directory of a production web server. When this happens, interfaces that have images mapped statically will magically manifest pages of red X's where images used to be. To avoid this, we'll borrow a Commerce Server technique to provide a dynamic image path. As mentioned, Commerce Server 2000 already provides a virtual path, but in the Retail site there is no real methodology to accommodate images. We'll make a simple modification to deal with this.

On line 21 of `setupenv.asp` in the `include` directory, we will add a single variable to this pre-existing `Dim` line for the new image path variable called `sImagePath`.

```
Dim sPageTitle, sThisPage, mscsUserProfile, sImagePath
```

On what is now line 60 of the same page, the `sThisPage` is defined. `sThisPage` is a generated variable that tells us what the virtual directory path is at start up of the application, and passes this value to the page level. With this, we will create a virtual path to our image folder.

This is done so that, when implementing HTML `<img>` tags, they can call an absolute path to the required image every time, no matter where in the directory structure the link is. This is very handy when calling graphics via HTML from a server-side include file within a nested folder: your execution URL is virtually unpredictable without limiting your source file organizational structure.

We add two simple lines, highlighted here. The first, defining where we store our images with respect to the base website application directory, the second concatenating the website's absolute path to the beginning of the image path when the application is not executed in the root of the website.

```
sThisPage = Request.ServerVariables("SCRIPT_NAME")
sImagePath = "/images/"
If Len(MSCSAppFrameWork.VirtualDirectory) = 0 Then
  sThisPage = Mid(sThisPage, 2) 'Site Installed at root, trim off leading \
Else
  sThisPage = Mid(sThisPage, Len(MSCSAppFrameWork.VirtualDirectory) + 3) 'Trim off
leading vdir
  sImagePath = "/" & MSCSAppFrameWork.VirtualDirectory & sImagePath
End If
```

This code should be available to every page within the application. Once this is done, you should use the `sImagePath` within the path of every image tag you implement on the site. This allows you quite a bit of freedom with your interface server side-includes.

When the `Global.asa` initializes, the `MSCSSiteStyle` object is set by the `GetSiteStyles` function, which resides in `include/global_ui_lib.asp`. These attribute values are laid out by functional HTML elements, first by table, next by font, next by currency, next by form fields, etc. The HTML element itself is not included here. This value or values is passed to the HTML tag when the content is generated in stream. Changing and saving this file resets the global and forces these change to take effect immediately.

One thing that should be conspicuously different is that single quotes have been used to encapsulate all HTML elements defined here. It's important to note that *all* HTML element attribute values handled programmatically in Commerce Server are enclosed in single quotations rather than double quotations.

This technique is not entirely compliant across all browsers. If you plan to use this site in a public arena where users do not solely use Internet Explorer 5.5, then you should consider what impact this will have on your user base. Here I have replaced all single quotations with double quotations.

Next, four lines have been added and four new variables have been included in the `dim` line. This is done to continue the expansion of the `MSCSSiteStyles` dictionary by including new tools to help us implement a more robust interface. In this case, I have added a font face entry as well as three entries for a site color story.

Like the rest of these parameters, this will allow us to reference standard fonts and colors whenever necessary, without consideration for the implemented style, current or future. Times New Roman is fine for print, but screen resolution does not support true readability of a serif font. As discussed earlier, Cascading Style Sheets are a very viable solution for your interface, but they have not been implemented here. If you feel that you can safely implement them, you can do this by adding your style classes to the appropriate elements by appending them in the same manner font face and bgcolor have been added.

```
Function GetSiteStyles ()
    Dim dictStyles, sFontFace, sColorPrimary, sColorSecondary, sColorTertiary

    sFontFace       = "arial, helvetica"
    sColorPrimary   = "#003366"
    sColorSecondary   = "#B3BDD7"
    sColorTertiary    = "#D6DCE9"

    Set dictStyles = GetDictionary()

    ' Table ATTLIST: ALIGN, WIDTH, BORDER, CELLSPACING, CELLPADDING
```

```
    dictStyles.BorderlessTable = " BORDER=""0"" CELLSPACING=""0"" CELLPADDING=""2""
"
    dictStyles.BorderedTable  = " BORDER=""0"" CELLSPACING=""1"" CELLPADDING=""3""
BGCOLOR=""" & sColorPrimary & """"
      dictStyles.AddressTable = " BORDER=""1"" CELLSPACING=""2"" CELLPADDING=""2""
"
    dictStyles.Form = " BORDER=""0"" CELLSPACING=""5"" "
    dictStyles.MenuTable = " BORDER=""0"" CELLSPACING=""5"" "

    ' Basket styles
    dictStyles.BasketTable = " BORDER=""1"" CELLSPACING=""0"" CELLPADDING=""1"""

    ' Interface Colors
    dictStyles.sColorPrimary = sColorPrimary
    dictStyles.sColorSecondary = sColorSecondary
    dictStyles.sColorTertiary = sColorTertiary

    ' Font ATTLIST: SIZE, COLOR
    dictStyles.SiteName    = " SIZE=""+3"" FACE=""" & sFontFace & """"
    dictStyles.Title       = " SIZE=""+1"" FACE=""" & sFontFace & """"
    dictStyles.MenuHead    = " FACE=""" & sFontFace & """"
    dictStyles.MenuBody    = " FACE=""" & sFontFace & """"
    dictStyles.BasketHeader = " FACE=""" & sFontFace & """"
    dictStyles.BasketData  = " FACE=""" & sFontFace & """"
    dictStyles.Body        = " FACE=""" & sFontFace & """"
    dictStyles.Warning     = " COLOR=""Red"" FACE=""" & sFontFace & """"
    dictStyles.Tip         = " COLOR=""Red"" FACE=""" & sFontFace & """"

    dictStyles.BaseCurrency = " FACE=""" & sFontFace & """"
    dictStyles.AltCurrency  = " COLOR=""Red"" FACE=""" & sFontFace & """"

    dictStyles.TextBox     = ""
    dictStyles.PasswordBox = ""
    dictStyles.CheckBox    = ""
    dictStyles.RadioButton = ""
    dictStyles.Button      = ""
    dictStyles.Link        = ""
    dictStyles.ListBox     = ""

    Set dictStyles.Unspecified = GetDictionary()

    ' table ATTLIST: ALIGN, WIDTH, BORDER, CELLSPACING, CELLPADDING
    dictStyles.NoBorderTable = " BORDER=""0"" CELLSPACING=""1"" CELLPADDING=""0"" "

    ' tr ATTLIST: ALIGN, VALIGN
    dictStyles.TRLeft   = " ALIGN=""Left"" VALIGN=""top"""
    dictStyles.TRCenter = " ALIGN=""Center"" VALIGN=""top"""
    dictStyles.TRRight  = " ALIGN=""Right"" VALIGN=""top"""
    dictStyles.TRTop    = " VALIGN=""Top"" "
    dictStyles.TRMiddle = " VALIGN=""Middle"""
    dictStyles.TRBottom = " VALIGN=""Bottom"""

    ' th/td ATTLIST: NOWRAP, ROWSPAN, COLSPAN, WIDTH, HEIGHT, ALIGN, VALIGN,
    dictStyles.TRCenter = " ALIGN=""Center"" VALIGN=""top"" BGCOLOR=""" &
sColorTertiary & """"
    dictStyles.TDLeft   = " ALIGN=""Left"" VALIGN=""top"" BGCOLOR=""#FFFFFF"""
    dictStyles.TDCenter = " ALIGN=""Center"" VALIGN=""top"" BGCOLOR=""#FFFFFF"""
    dictStyles.TDRight  = " ALIGN=""Right"" VALIGN=""top"" BGCOLOR=""#FFFFFF"""

    ' For Partner/Customer service page's styles
    Call AddPartnerAndCustomerServiceStyles(dictStyles)

    Set GetSiteStyles = dictStyles
End Function
```

Tucked away at the bottom of the function is a subroutine called
`AddPartnerAndCustomerServiceStyles()`. This section defines a block of additional styles that are
not included with the original block: they have been included here unchanged, for comparison. You can find
this function in `global_service_lib.asp` in the `include` directory. I recommend making the same
modifications to this set of styles that were made to the primary block in `GetSiteStyles`. A curious
implementation here is that font face and bgcolor is used in this sub, but not the primary
`GetSiteStyles()` function.

```
Sub AddPartnerAndCustomerServiceStyles(ByRef objSiteStyle)
    objSiteStyle.StatusTable = " BGCOLOR='#FFFFFF' border='0' width='100%'
cellspacing='0' cellpadding='0'"

    ' Search box header & body
    objSiteStyle.SearchHeaderTable = " BGCOLOR='#FFFFCC' border='1' cellspacing='5'
cellpadding='0'"
    objSiteStyle.SearchBodyTable = " BGCOLOR='#FFFFCC' width='100%'"

    ' EditSheet grid
    objSiteStyle.ContentsHeaderTable = " BGCOLOR='#CCFFCC' border='0' width='100%'
cellspacing='0' cellpadding='0'"
    ' EditSheet header
    objSiteStyle.ContentsBodyTable = " BGCOLOR='#FFFFCC' border='0' width='100%'
cellspacing='0' cellpadding='0'"
    ' EditSheet Group Divider
    objSiteStyle.ContentsGroupTable = " BGCOLOR='#CCCCFF' border='0' width='100%'
cellspacing='0' cellpadding='0'"

    ' ListSheet grid
    objSiteStyle.ListContentsHeaderTable = " BGCOLOR='#CCCCFF' BORDER='0'
CELLSPACING='0' CELLPADDING='2' WIDTH='100%'" 'For results header
    ' ListSheet header
    objSiteStyle.ListContentsBodyTable = " BGCOLOR='#CCFFCC' BORDER='1'
CELLSPACING='0' CELLPADDING='2' WIDTH='100%'"   'For list results and edit grids

    objSiteStyle.FooterTable = " BORDER='0' WIDTH='100%' CELLSPACING='0'
CELLPADDING='0'"
    objSiteStyle.MsgBoxTitleTable = " BGCOLOR='#CCCCCC' border='0' width='60%'
height='5%' cellspacing='0' cellpadding='0'"
    objSiteStyle.MsgBoxHeadingTable = " BGCOLOR='#CCCCCC' border='0' width='60%'
height='5%' cellspacing='0' cellpadding='0'"
    objSiteStyle.MsgBoxBodyTable = " BGCOLOR='#CCCCCC' border='0' width='60%'
height='15%' cellspacing='0' cellpadding='0'"
    objSiteStyle.MsgBoxFooterTable = " BGCOLOR='#CCCCCC' border='0' width='60%'
height='5%' cellspacing='0' cellpadding='0'"

    objSiteStyle.StatusString = " COLOR='BLACK' FACE='Verdana' SIZE='4'"
    objSiteStyle.SearchHeaderString = " COLOR='BLACK' FACE='Verdana' SIZE='5'"
    objSiteStyle.SearchBodyString = " COLOR='BLACK' FACE='Verdana' SIZE='4'"
    objSiteStyle.ContentsHeaderString = " COLOR='BLACK' FACE='Verdana' SIZE='5'"
    objSiteStyle.ContentsGroupString = " COLOR='BLACK' FACE='Verdana' SIZE='5'"
    objSiteStyle.ContentsBodyString = " COLOR='BLACK' FACE='Verdana' SIZE='4'"
    objSiteStyle.FooterString = " COLOR='BLACK' FACE='Verdana' SIZE='4'"
    objSiteStyle.MsgBoxTitleString = " COLOR='BLACK' FACE='Verdana' SIZE='4'"
    objSiteStyle.MsgBoxHeadingString = " COLOR='BLACK' FACE='Verdana' SIZE='4'"
    objSiteStyle.MsgBoxBodyString = " COLOR='BLACK' FACE='Verdana' SIZE='4'"
    objSiteStyle.MsgBoxFooterString = " COLOR='BLACK' FACE='Verdana' SIZE='4'"
End Sub
```

Now that these additions have been made within the scope of the `Global.asa`, they will need to be implemented at the page level by adding these lines to the `SetupEnv.asp` initialization block, as shown here, on line 53 of that file. This will assign dictionary values for the font face and colors that we created in the `GetSiteStyles()` function to string values.

```
Dim sColorPrimary, sColorSecondary, sColorTertiary

sColorPrimary = MSCSSiteStyle.sColorPrimary
sColorSecondary = MSCSSiteStyle.sColorSecondary
sColorTertiary = MSCSSiteStyle.sColorTertiary
```

At this point, you can save these files and the site will reset because they are nested within the `Global.asa`. Once saved, open up the Retail site in your browser and review your changes. Altough fairly quick and painless these sorts of small changes can have a dramatic effect on the presentation of the site.

Template Pages

There are two major interface template pages in the Retail site. Because the interface is templatized, we can effect major changes to the site with relatively little effort. By opening up the file `layout1.asp` in the template directory of the Retail site, you will find a simple HTML page. This template is the basis for the look of the homepage and all subsequent pages where column navigation is available.

Its sister page, `no_menu.asp`, provides the template for pages with no column navigation available. Included files are as follows:

`Navbar.asp`	This server-side include file lists the toolbar functionality with **Home, Catalog** and **Basket** links across the top of the page.
`Menu.asp`	This include creates and lists your navigation, search and user profile options intended for use in the left side column.
`<%= htmPageContent %>`	This ASP output writes the `htmPageContent` string to the page. This string represents the lion's share of the page where the primary content has been assigned to in the core page called.
`<%= htmDiscountBannerSlot %>`	Followed by a banner output of the variable, this returns generated Campaign content.
`footer.inc`	This include holds copyright information to be placed at the bottom of the page at this point but you may decide to add an additional information here or even an additional tool for convenient access on longer pages.

It would be at this point that we would include meta-tags or Cascading Style Sheets if we planned to support these on our site. Adding a reference here would ensure that it would be included throughout the site.

```
<HTML>
<head>
  <title><%= dictConfig.s_SiteName & " " & sPageTitle %></title>
</head>
<body topmargin="0" leftmargin="0" marginheight="0" marginwidth="0" link="<%=
sColorPrimary %>" vlink="<%= sColorPrimary %>" alink="<%= sColorPrimary %>">
```

```
<basefont face="Arial" size="2">
<table height="100%" width="100%" border="0" cellpadding="0" cellspacing="0">
<tr>
  <td bgcolor="<%= sColorSecondary %>" colspan="3" align="center" width="100%"
height="25">
    <table width="95%" align="center">
    <tr>
      <td valign="bottom">
        <%= RenderText(dictConfig.s_SiteName, MSCSSiteStyle.SiteName) %>
      </td>
      <td align="right" valign="bottom">
        <!-- #INCLUDE FILE="navbar.inc" -->
      </td>
    </tr>
    </table>
    <!-- #INCLUDE FILE="banner.inc" -->
  </td>
</tr>
<tr>
  <td bgcolor="#DBDFE0" colspan="3" align="center" height="25">
    <table width="100%" align="center" cellpadding="0" cellspacing="0" border="0">
    <tr>
      <td width="25" align="left" valign="bottom" bgcolor="<%= sColorPrimary %>">
        <img src="<%= sImagePath %>site/interface_bluecurve_upper_left.gif"
width="25" height="25" alt="" border="0"></td>
      <td align="right" valign="bottom" bgcolor="<%= sColorPrimary %>"> </td>
    </tr>
    </table>
  </td>
</tr>
<tr>
  <td bgcolor="<%= sColorPrimary %>"> </td>
  <td align="left" valign="top">
    <img src="<%= sImagePath %>site/interface_bluecurve_inner_left.gif" width="20"
height="20" border="0"></td>
  <td> </td>
</tr>
<tr>
  <td valign="top" width="200" height="25" bgcolor="<%= sColorPrimary %>">
    <table width="100%" align="center" border="0" cellspacing="0" cellpadding="5">
    <tr>
      <td bgcolor="<%= sColorPrimary %>"></td>
    </tr>
    <tr>
      <td bgcolor="<%= sColorTertiary %>">
        <!-- #INCLUDE FILE="menu.asp" -->
      </td>
    </tr>
    </table>
  </td>
  <td width="10"> </td>
  <td width="90%" valign="top">
    <table width="97%" align="Left">
    <tr>
      <td valign="top">
        <%= htmPageContent %>
        <br>
        <%= htmDiscountBannerSlot %>
      </td>
    </tr>
    </table>
  </td>
```

```
    </tr>
    <tr>
      <td height="2" colspan="3" bgcolor="<%= sColorPrimary %>">
        <img src="<%= sImagePath %>trans.gif" width="600" height="2" border="0"></td>
    </tr>
    <tr>
      <td height="2" colspan="3" bgcolor="<%= sColorTertiary %>">
        <!--#INCLUDE FILE="footer.inc" -->
      </td>
    </tr>
    </table>
    </body>
</HTML>
```

Here is a rewritten interface to replace the `layout1.asp` page. The major architectural elements have not been changed or even moved, but have been adapted in order to present a more polished appearance. You will see here that the new site colors added earlier are used here in table and cell formatting. In addition, image paths include the complete path to the image directory.

With just a few changes, we have completely re-branded our site with no functionality changes at all. The same sorts of changes are made to the `no_menu.asp` template page, omitting the navigational column. It's easy to see what can be done with some simple template overhauls.

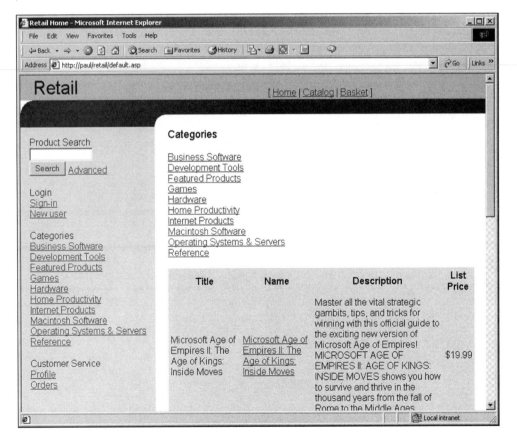

Major Feature Sets

Continuing on the theme of modifying the site interface, we'll next walk through the major feature sets and modify them to our specific needs.

Navigation

We have already looked at many of the core navigation features, but this is a good chance to review the menu.asp page. This page renders the left hand column navigation on the home page, and catalog pages or any page using the layout1.asp template. Let's jump to the core function of the menu, inside the htmRenderMenu() function.

Initially, let's make it a priority to move the categories up to the top of the column. This is valuable real estate, and as a site goal we want our users to find products before anything else. We do this by first taking the LogIn section and moving it down to just above Customer Service. This ends up being a much more logical grouping in that the customer service info is based strictly on the content of the user.

We group these two sections, then wrap them in a bordered table for effect and visual interface cue. It should look something like this:

```
Function htmRenderMenu(ByVal mscsUser, ByVal CatalogSetID)
   Dim htmRow
   Dim bShowPartnerServiceSection
   Dim htmCatalogSection, htmSearchSection, htmPartnerServiceSection,
htmCustomerServiceSection
   Dim rsCatalogs, iCatalogCount, oCatalog, sCatalogName,  rsCategories
   Dim sAuthUser, bFormLoginSupported, sLoginName
   Dim sSearchValue

   ' **************
   ' Search Section
   ' **************

   ' Only cache this fragment if we're not on the search page
   If sThisPage <> MSCSSitePages.Search Then
      htmSearchSection = LookupCachedFragment("StaticSectionsCache", "SearchSection")
      If IsNull(htmSearchSection) Then
         htmSearchSection = htmRenderSearchSection(MSCSSiteStyle.Body,
MSCSSiteStyle.Body, "")
         Call CacheFragment("StaticSectionsCache", "SearchSection", htmSearchSection)
      End If
   Else
      sSearchValue = GetRequestString("keyword", "")
      htmSearchSection = htmRenderSearchSection(MSCSSiteStyle.Body,
MSCSSiteStyle.Body, sSearchValue)
   End If


   ' **************
   ' Catalog section
   ' **************
   htmCatalogSection = LookupCachedFragment("StaticSectionsCache", CatalogSetID)
   If IsNull(htmCatalogSection) Then
```

```
    Call PrepareCatalogSection(rsCatalogs, iCatalogCount, oCatalog, sCatalogName,
rsCategories)
    htmCatalogSection = htmRenderCatalogSection(MSCSSiteStyle.Body, rsCatalogs,
iCatalogCount, oCatalog, sCatalogName,  rsCategories)
    Call CacheFragment("StaticSectionsCache", CatalogSetID, htmCatalogSection)
  End If
  htmRenderMenu = htmRenderMenu & htmCatalogSection

    ' *************************
    ' Partner service section
    ' *************************
    ' shown to user when all following condition are present:
    ' 1) site supports delegated admin
    ' 2) user has a profile
    ' 3) user is authorized to act as administrator for other users
    ' 4) user has been assigned an organization
  bShowPartnerServiceSection = False
  If dictConfig.i_DelegatedAdminOptions = DELEGATED_ADMIN_SUPPORTED Then
    If Not mscsUser Is Nothing Then
        If mscsUser.Fields(GetQualifiedName(BUSINESS_DESK_GROUP,
FIELD_USER_PARTNERDESK_ROLE)).Value = ROLE_ADMIN Then
        If (Not mscsUser.Fields.Item(USER_ORGID).Value = "") Then
          bShowPartnerServiceSection = True
        End If
        End If
    End If
    End If

    If bShowPartnerServiceSection Then
    htmPartnerServiceSection = LookupCachedFragment("StaticSectionsCache",
"PartnerServiceSection")
    If IsNull(htmPartnerServiceSection) Then
      htmPartnerServiceSection =
htmRenderPartnerServiceSection(MSCSSiteStyle.Body)
      Call CacheFragment("StaticSectionsCache", "PartnerServiceSection",
htmPartnerServiceSection)
    End If
    htmRenderMenu = htmRenderMenu & htmPartnerServiceSection
  End If

  htmRenderMenu = htmRenderMenu & "<table width=""100%"" " &
MSCSSiteStyle.BorderedTable & "><tr><td alilgn=""center"" bgcolor=""" &
sColorSecondary & """>"

  ' **************
  ' Login Section
  ' **************
  ' Note: htmRenderLoginSection caches portions of itself as it can
  Call PrepareLoginSection(sAuthUser, bFormLoginSupported, mscsUser, sLoginName)
  htmRenderMenu = htmRenderMenu & htmRenderLoginSection(sAuthUser,
bFormLoginSupported, mscsUser, sLoginName)

    ' *************************
    ' Customer service section
    ' *************************
    ' shown to every user with a profile
```

93

```
   If Not mscsUser Is Nothing Then
      htmCustomerServiceSection = LookupCachedFragment("StaticSectionsCache",
"CustomerServiceSection")
      If IsNull(htmCustomerServiceSection) Then
         htmCustomerServiceSection =
htmRenderCustomerServiceSection(MSCSSiteStyle.Body)
         Call CacheFragment("StaticSectionsCache", "CustomerServiceSection",
htmCustomerServiceSection)
      End If
      htmRenderMenu = htmRenderMenu & htmCustomerServiceSection
   End If
   htmRenderMenu = htmRenderMenu & "</td></tr></table>"
   htmRow = "<TR><TD NOWRAP>" & htmRenderMenu & "</TD></TR>"
   htmRenderMenu = RenderTable(htmRow, MSCSSiteStyle.MenuTable)

End Function
```

This function is very modularized, so moving components around should be easy. Notice here that every section can have its own cache fragment based on the dynamic nature of the piece.

On reviewing our changes, the home page of the retail site should look like this. Note how the list of categories on the left has been moved.

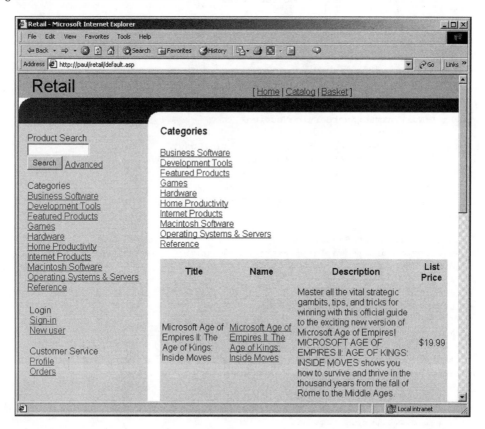

Of Subcategories and Columns

Now the page is better, but still take up quite a bit more screen space than it should. Users with smaller screen resolutions – or short attention spans – may still never get a look at our product. To deal with this, we could take the simple category list in the content area and turn it into columns. This will condense the area needed to list the categories and move the product up higher and closer to the top of the page.

Now, the function that accomplishes this task is `htmRenderCategoryPage()`. This function is used by several other functions which build the left hand navigational column; so if we change this function, it will affect the display of categories in other areas. So rather than altering this function, let's copy it and call it `htmRenderCategoryListColumn()`.

The most reliable way to create columns out of text is by creating a table. The table functions that exist in Commerce Server apply only to arrays and not Recordsets, so the existing HTML table functions will not work for us in this scenario.

The following code implements a very simple looping mechanism that builds an HTML table in place within the function, rather than calling outside functions. You should find that the more complex your interface, the more need there will be to build functions such as these.

```
Function htmRenderCategoriesListColumn(ByVal oCatalog, ByVal rsCategories, ByVal style)
    Dim sProductCategory, sCatalogName
    Dim htmCategory
    Dim lstrTemp
    Dim LoopCount
    If (rsCategories.EOF) Then
    lstrTemp = "" & CR
    Else
    sCatalogName = rsCategories.Fields(CATALOG_NAME_PROPERTY_NAME).Value
    LoopCount = 1
    lstrTemp = ""
    lstrTemp = lstrTemp & "<table" & MSCSSiteStyle.NoBorderTable & ">"
    While Not rsCategories.EOF
      If LoopCount = 1 Then
        lstrTemp = lstrTemp & "<tr><td" & MSCSSiteStyle.TDLeft & ">" & VBCRLF
      Else
        lstrTemp = lstrTemp & "</td><td" & MSCSSiteStyle.TDLeft & "> 
</td><td" & MSCSSiteStyle.TDLeft & ">" & VBCRLF
      End If
      sProductCategory = rsCategories.Fields(CATEGORY_NAME_PROPERTY_NAME).Value
      htmCategory = RenderCategoryLink(sCatalogName, sProductCategory, 1, style)
      lstrTemp = lstrTemp & htmCategory & CR
        rsCategories.MoveNext
      If LoopCount = 1 Then
        LoopCount = 2
      Else
        lstrTemp = lstrTemp & "</td></tr>" & VbCrLf
        LoopCount = 1
      End If

    Wend
    If LoopCount = 2 Then
      lstrTemp = lstrTemp & "</td><td" & MSCSSiteStyle.TDCenter & "> 
</td><td" & MSCSSiteStyle.TDLeft & ">></td></tr>" & VBCRLF
```

```
      End If
      lstrTemp = lstrTemp & "</table>"
      End If

   htmRenderCategoriesListColumn = lstrTemp
   End Function
```

This function is called from within the `htmRenderCategoryPage` function, contained within the same page, and this call will also have to be changed to:

```
   htmContent = htmContent & htmRenderCategoriesListColumn _
       (oCatalog, rsChildCategories, MSCSSiteStyle.Body) & CR
```

This is a very simple script, and you may wish to tackle these sorts of issues in a more complex manner. The results, as you can see here, alleviate that gaping unused white space in the page, givingit back to the product presentation. That's not to say white space is bad, but that this particular patch of white space was using up some of the most valuable space on the page, and could be used more effectively.

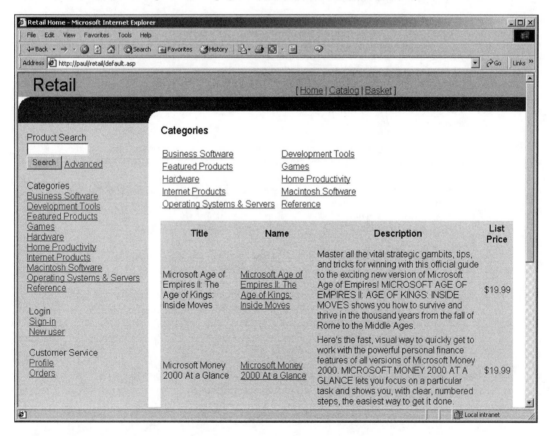

Category Navigation

With all these categories and subcategories around, it would be nice to locate where we are in the category topology at any time. That is, if I were in the Rolling Stones category, it would be nice to know that I am in Music > Rock & Roll > R > Rolling Stones, and then be able to jump to any intermediate level with a mouse click.

This is, of course, a common feature in websites. Users have come to expect this. To illustrate this better, let's say that the Rolling Stones category is a subcategory of both path A: Music > Rock & Roll > R > Rolling Stones, and path B: Music > Top 100 Singers > 60's > Rolling Stones. This kind of multi-homed categorization is to be expected if you have any kind of creative merchandisers on staff. At what point do you decide which path a user travelled down to arrive in the Rolling Stones category?

This matter can become infinitely more complicated as staff become more creative, and you have many multi-homed categories. Given the BizDesk interface, it is easy to conceive of managers creating nested and looping categories that come back on themselves. Where Books > Rolling Stones is a child of Music > Rolling Stones, and Music > Rolling Stones is a child of Books > Rolling Stones. Because of these issues, the Retail solution site does not support this kind of category location feature out of the box.

That is not to say this sort of feature could not be constructed. One answer may be to track the path of a user as they browse to their destination. Tracking a user's path is often troublesome and error prone, in that by providing cross-merchandising and search, you have the ability to jump into the middle of another navigational path. At this point, how do we track where the user came from?

While complicated to manage and track, another solution may be to provide a default path for every category. This would allow the website to assume certain path states though they may not report a uses location with accuracy in all cases. For example, a user who traversed Music > Top 100 Singers > 60's > Rolling Stones to arrive at the Some Girls album would see Music > Rock & Roll > R > Rolling Stones as the reference, if this were the default path to this product.

Either way, techniques to resolve this issue do not exist in the Solution Sites or their companion BizDesk interfaces, so the development here could be fairly complex.

The Shopping Cart

It's difficult to modify anything substantial in the shopping cart without understanding its inner workings, and this requires understanding the `Order` processing pipeline (we look at the order processing pipeline in Chapter 6). However, let's take a look at the life of a product and the cart.

Adding An Item

Laid out here is a sample of the Add to cart form, taken from a product page for a particular book in the sample books catalog. As you would expect, there are a number of hidden fields within the form. The only visible fields are `product_qty` and the Submit button. `catalog_name`, `category_name` and `product_id` are hidden.

It's important to remember that our catalog is dynamic in nature, so that the product could possibly be found anywhere within any catalog navigation category.

```
<table cellpadding="0" cellspacing="0" border="0">
  <tr>
    <td>
```

```
            <FORM ACTION="http://MyServer/retail/_additem.asp" METHOD="POST">
            <INPUT TYPE="HIDDEN" NAME="catalog_name" VALUE="Books">
            <INPUT TYPE="HIDDEN" NAME="category_name" VALUE="Internet &amp; Intranet
  Servers">
            <INPUT TYPE="HIDDEN" NAME="product_id" VALUE="Build Your Own Web Site">
            <FONT FACE="arial, helvetica">
              Specify quantity:
            </FONT>
            <INPUT TYPE="TEXT" NAME="product_qty" VALUE="1" SIZE="3" MAXLENGTH="3">
            <INPUT TYPE="SUBMIT" NAME="btnSubmit" VALUE="Add to Basket">
        </td>
      </tr>
      </FORM>
  </table>
```

At this point, the form is posted to the _additem.asp page where the product is processed. The first real action here is to process the data sent in the form via the GetRequestString() function – even the Request object is not used directly, but rather is also wrapped in a function to process the parameters passed.

This might be a bit cumbersome, but the advantage here lies in moving string handling to a centralized location, and any kind of special operations such as trimming or stripping spaces can be handled in one place.

This code is from the _additem.asp page.

```
Sub Main()
[..]
  sCategoryName = GetRequestString(CATEGORY_NAME_URL_KEY, "")
  sProductID = GetRequestString(PRODUCT_ID_URL_KEY, Null)
  sVariantID = GetRequestString(VARIANT_ID_URL_KEY, Null)
  iProductQty = GetProductQuantity()
[..]
  Set mscsOrderGrp = LoadBasket(m_UserID)

  Set dictItem = Server.CreateObject("Commerce.Dictionary")
  dictItem.product_catalog = sCatalogName
  dictItem.product_catalog_base = mscsCatalog.BaseCatalogName
  dictItem.product_id = sProductID
  dictItem.Quantity = iProductQty
  dictItem.product_category = sCategoryName

  If Not IsNull(sVariantID) Then
      dictItem.product_variant_id = sVariantID
  End If

  ' Add the item to the appropriate OrderForm
  ApplyVendorInfo dictItem, sCatalogName
  Call mscsOrderGrp.AddItem(dictItem)

  ' Note: you may want to run pipeline here if the site is structured not to
  redirect to basket,
```

98

```
     ' for example if you need to keep a total up-to-date, or if you want to notify
users
     ' of basket warnings (e.g. product or discount no longer available) immediately

   Call mscsOrderGrp.SaveAsBasket()

   Call Analysis_LogAddToBasket( _
                                sCatalogName, _
                                sCategoryName, _
                                sProductID, _
                                sVariantID _
                              )
   ' Redirect to desired page
   Select Case (dictConfig.i_AddItemRedirectOptions)
     Case REDIRECT_TO_BASKET
       Call Response.Redirect(GenerateURL(MSCSSitePages.Basket, Array(), Array()))
     Case REDIRECT_TO_PRODUCT
       arrParams = Array(CATALOG_NAME_URL_KEY, PRODUCT_ID_URL_KEY,
PRODUCT_ACTION_KEY)
       arrParamVals = Array(sCatalogName, sProductID, ADD_ACTION)
       Call Response.Redirect(GenerateURL(MSCSSitePages.Product, arrParams,
arrParamVals))
   End Select
End Sub
```

From here, the stored cart is loaded into page scope. At the core of all the pages and pieces that make up the cart feature set is the LoadBasket() function. The basket is a nested property of the Commerce.OrderGroup object. Within the LoadBasket() function, a call for the GetOrderGroup() function is placed, which in turn pulls all pending order information.

Within the LoadOrderGroup() function, we can see the Commerce.OrderGroup object initialize with the current state in place. From this object, we can call the intrinsic LoadBasket() method of OrderGroup object. Once these operations are performed, the object is passed back up to the main() sub of additem.asp.

The LoadBasket and GetOrderGroup functions are in the std_ordergrp_lib.asp include page.

```
   Function LoadBasket(ByVal sUserID)
     Dim mscsOrderGrp

     Set mscsOrderGrp = GetOrderGroup(sUserID)
     Call mscsOrderGrp.LoadBasket()
     Set LoadBasket = mscsOrderGrp
   End Function



   Function GetOrderGroup(ByVal sOrderID)
     Dim mscsOrderGrp

     Set mscsOrderGrp = Server.CreateObject("Commerce.OrderGroup")
```

```
    Call mscsOrderGrp.Initialize(dictConfig.s_TransactionsConnectionString,
   sOrderID)
      Set GetOrderGroup = mscsOrderGrp
   End Function
```

At this point in main(), a Commerce dictionary is created and loaded with the pertinent product information for later storage in the basket. This dictionary, now loaded with all the options, is passed to the OrderGroup object via the AddItem() method. It's important to note here that the AddItem method is designed to handle the commerce dictionary object specifically, and in this format. After it's added to the OrderGroup state, it's then committed to the database via the SaveAsBasket() method. For those who are accustomed to Site Server, it's important to note that instead of just the OrderForm object, we now have the OrderForm and OrderGroup objects.

At the end of this function, you'll find a vbscript SELECT statement which redirects the user to different locations. This is a parameter set in the AppConfig object, and changed via the Commerce Server MMC settings. Note that this value is available within the ExposePageEnvironment() function, which we looked at earlier in the chapter. The value of this setting sends the user back to the product page, or on to the cart. This is behavior that every site team may have a differing opinion on, but in the end, this is usually a business rule determined by a steering team, because it normally ends up being a hot topic for some reason. In whatever manner you get there, your cart is now one item heavier.

Building a Basket

Now that we have an item within the cart, as a user, I want to see it. The basket is initialized by the InitializeBasketPage() function. In its default state, this function does little more than call the fateful LoadBasket() function. The following code comes from the basket.asp page:

```
Sub Main()
   [...]
   Call InitializeBasketPage(mscsOrderGrp, bBasketIsEmpty, bMustSaveBasket,
   oOrderFormDisplayOrder)

   If Not bBasketIsEmpty Then
      ' Run basket pipeline to check for errors; set oOrderFormDisplayOrder
      Call CheckBasket(mscsOrderGrp, bBasketIsEmpty, iErrorCount, bMustSaveBasket,
   oOrderFormDisplayOrder)
   End If

   If Not bBasketIsEmpty Then
      ' Add discount footnote symbols to each lineitem
      Call AddDiscountMessages(mscsOrderGrp)
   End If

   If bMustSaveBasket Then
      ' Save the basket (changes may have occurred when running the pipeline)
      Call mscsOrderGrp.SaveAsBasket()
   End If

   Call RenderBasketPage(mscsOrderGrp, oOrderFormDisplayOrder, bBasketIsEmpty,
   iErrorCount)
End Sub
```

Next, the `CheckBasket()` sub is invoked. Here, all products and attributes are refreshed. This is an extremely important step, in that any attributes that are added, removed or updated in the product catalog after the item was added are now refreshed in the cart. This applies to price changes, variant modifications, availability, and even whether a product is no longer sold.

After the Pipeline runs, any discrepancies between the cart data and the catalog data throws back errors. If errors do occur, then the appropriate explanatory message must be pulled from the message manager, which will describe the actions that have been taken. This occurs only once per error. This means that if an item must be modified or removed from the cart for whatever reason, a message describing this event will be shown once. The next time the cart is viewed or refreshed, the item will have already been modified or removed, and the message will not appear again.

Finally the `RenderBasketPage()` in the `basket.asp` page is called. This is a huge function, too large to list here, but it contains a lot of important processes.

First, the `listAggregatedItems Commerce` a simple list is created. This simple list is populated with each item currently in the basket. It is at this point that a conditional statement determines whether a user has had discounts applied to the product price. This is important, because the number of fields in the generated table will change in order to display the actual discount to the user.

Here an array is created to store header row labels for the basket HTML table. Now the status of the user's discount dictates the dimension and data in the array. After the array is complete, the header row is generated by passing the array to the `RenderTableHeaderRow()` function.

The methodology which is applied to the header array is used here for the body cell styles. It is then that we loop through `mscsOrderForm.Items()`. The line item processing for the basket, which represents the majority of the code in this function, creates a dictionary on each pass, one for each product. The dictionary is then passed to the `RenderTableDataRow()` function at the end of each loop. When the loop is completed, the total and sub-totals are generated, and the table is wrapped and displayed to the user.

This completed basket shows quite a bit of data. In fact, it can be confusing when using the books catalog example where the catalog uses the product name and the unique identifier. This causes the name of the product to show up twice in the row for each product. This confusion is compounded by the fact that the complete product description is also included. This content is much too large for the row, and can force the row to be stretched well beyond the scope of the viewable area within the browser window. This is annoying and superfluous, so let's get rid of it. This will give us a much smaller and easier to read page.

Redesigning the Basket

To change the display of the contents of the basket, we must make several surgical strikes to the arrays, simple lists and dictionaries in the `RenderBasketPage()` function.

Initially, on line 296 we must remove a parameter from the column header array `arrData`. This is done by deleting the fourth parameter: `L_Product_Description_DisplayName_HTMLText`.

This same action must be repeated on line 306, so that this modification is implemented for users with and without discounts.

Once these have been extracted, our calls to `mscsMessageManager.GetMessage` should look like this:

```
If bDiscountApplied Then
    arrData = Array( _
```

```
            mscsMessageManager.GetMessage("L_BASKET_QUANTITY_COLUMN_TEXT", sLanguage), _
            mscsMessageManager.GetMessage("L_ProductCode_HTMLText", sLanguage), _
            mscsMessageManager.GetMessage("L_Product_Name_DisplayName_HTMLText",
    sLanguage),
            mscsMessageManager.GetMessage("L_BASKET_UNITPRICE_COLUMN_TEXT", sLanguage),
    _
            mscsMessageManager.GetMessage("L_BASKET_DISCOUNT_COLUMN_TEXT", sLanguage), _
            mscsMessageManager.GetMessage("L_BASKET_MESSAGES_COLUMN_TEXT", sLanguage), _
            mscsMessageManager.GetMessage("L_BASKET_TOTALPRICE_COLUMN_TEXT", sLanguage),
    _
            mscsMessageManager.GetMessage("L_BASKET_REMOVE_COLUMN_TEXT", sLanguage))
      Else
         arrData = Array( _
            mscsMessageManager.GetMessage("L_BASKET_QUANTITY_COLUMN_TEXT", sLanguage), _
            mscsMessageManager.GetMessage("L_ProductCode_HTMLText", sLanguage), _
            mscsMessageManager.GetMessage("L_Product_Name_DisplayName_HTMLText",
    sLanguage),
            mscsMessageManager.GetMessage("L_BASKET_UNITPRICE_COLUMN_TEXT", sLanguage),
    _
            mscsMessageManager.GetMessage("L_BASKET_TOTALPRICE_COLUMN_TEXT", sLanguage),
    _
            mscsMessageManager.GetMessage("L_BASKET_REMOVE_COLUMN_TEXT", sLanguage))
      End If
```

This removal is performed on the `arrDataAttLists` array where the fourth parameter down is again removed to ensure cells and styles match up properly. When removed, these will look like this:

```
If bDiscountApplied Then
    arrDataAttLists = Array( _
      MSCSSiteStyle.TDCenter, _
      MSCSSiteStyle.TDLeft, _
      MSCSSiteStyle.TDLeft, _
      MSCSSiteStyle.TDRight, _
      MSCSSiteStyle.TDRight, _
      MSCSSiteStyle.TDLeft, _
      MSCSSiteStyle.TDRight, _
      MSCSSiteStyle.TDCenter)
   Else
    arrDataAttLists = Array( _
      MSCSSiteStyle.TDCenter, _
      MSCSSiteStyle.TDLeft, _
      MSCSSiteStyle.TDLeft, _
      MSCSSiteStyle.TDRight, _
      MSCSSiteStyle.TDRight, _
      MSCSSiteStyle.TDCenter)
   End If
```

On line 368, the third parameter – `dictItem.Value("_product_description"), _` – must be removed. The same must also be done to the next section.

Our code should look like this:

```
If bDiscountApplied Then
      ' "name" and "description" are required product properties and cannot have
    null values.
      arrData = Array(_
```

```
            htmQtyCol, _
            htmProdCode, _
            dictItem.Value("_product_name"), _
            htmRenderCurrency(dictItem.Value("_cy_iadjust_currentprice")), _
            htmRenderCurrency(dictItem.Value("_cy_oadjust_discount")), _
            dictItem.Value("_messages"), _
            htmRenderCurrency(dictItem.Value("_cy_oadjust_adjustedprice")), _
            htmRemoveCol)
        Else
            ' "name" and "description" are required product properties and cannot have
    null values.
            arrData = Array(_
            htmQtyCol, _
            htmProdCode, _
            dictItem.Value("_product_name"), _
            htmRenderCurrency(dictItem.Value("_cy_iadjust_currentprice")), _
            htmRenderCurrency(dictItem.Value("_cy_oadjust_adjustedprice")), _
            htmRemoveCol)
        End If
```

Finally, on what should now be line 398, after removing the previous lines, the COLSPANs for the bottom row of the table need to be adjusted so that they appear properly after the spanned columns. This too is done twice:

```
If bDiscountApplied Then
    arrDataAttLists = Array(" COLSPAN='6'", MSCSSiteStyle.TDLeft, _
MSCSSiteStyle.TDRight, MSCSSiteStyle.TDCenter)
    Else
    arrDataAttLists = Array(" COLSPAN='4'", MSCSSiteStyle.TDLeft, _
MSCSSiteStyle.TDRight, MSCSSiteStyle.TDCenter)
    End If
```

We should now have a much cleaner and effective cart presentation:

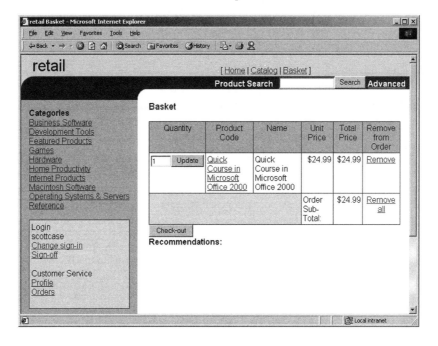

Error Pages

There are two types of error pages within the retail solution site, an IIS error page to handle ASP runtime errors, and response pages to handle predictable application behaviors. IIS custom error pages are normally configured manually via the Microsoft Management Console. In the case of the Retail site, errors 500 and 100, Internal Server errors, are mapped to 500error.asp in the error directory during installation of the solution site. This file handles any http 500 errors encountered by the user by supplying a user-friendly web page with an appropriate message.

Because of the very nature of an error page, it cannot rely on the site's existing infrastructure to be properly functioning when it is executed. In fact, relying on any particular Commerce Server component to be functioning during an error can leave you prone to embarrassing server errors. To this end, this page is extremely self-contained.

To avoid spewing errors to a user while in a production environment, the error page does a check on several application variables to determine behavior later in the page. Here in the first evaluator, it is determined whether we are in a production or development environment by checking the MSCSEnv assigned in the Global.asa. Next, by building upon the environment, it is determined whether to log any errors that occur. Finally, the environment Boolean is passed to another flag which will instruct later code to display errors to the user.

```
' --- Determine if the site was in dev mode... Assume production mode if
unspecified.  Also, take no dependencies on constants being available
bDevelopmentMode = Not IsEmpty(Application("MSCSEnv")) And
(Application("MSCSEnv")=0)

' --- We will log to the eventlog upon first global.asa error, or for any other
error
bLogToEventLog = Not bDevelopmentMode And (Not Application("MSCSErrorInGlobalASA")
Or bFixupGlobalAsa = True)

' --- We will show technical info to browser in DevelopmentMode mode
bShowTechnicalInfo = bDevelopmentMode
```

For the most of the page, the code makes use of the ASPError object, innate to the ASP 3 runtime. This page in many ways simply mimics the functionality of standard IIS 5 error page. By pulling ASP error data, it enables the application data to be used through the page.

Recovering from errors gracefully is all well and good, but it doesn't end there. Best practice requires that we learn from our mistakes. To do this it is necessary to understand what errors are occurring by logging them to a repository for later review. As an added trick, Commerce Server includes the AdminEventLog object, which enables you to safely write messages directly to the Windows event log. By selecting a different method for each type of entry, you can control its importance: whether it's an informative message, or something more critical, for instance.

It's important to mention that the IIS5 metabase property AspErrorsToNTLog can be set to, as you've probably guessed, log all errors encountered by the ASP runtime to the Windows 2000 event log. In the same vein ASPLogErrorRequests performs that same service, but logs errors to the IIS log files. These features completely circumvent the need to log errors manually.

The choice to use the Windows log file or the IIS log file either manually, with an object, or automatically, with one of the above flags, is dependant upon the environment your website is operated in. If your site will be serve from a third party host in a managed environment, you will probably not have access to the windows log files. In this case, you may be better off logging errors to the IIS5 log files, though you will need to determine an effective way to generate reports from these files. Reporting for 'hitlogs' is common, but the intermingled error logs are likely to be overlooked by most reporting software. You will need to determine which is best for your requirements.

Summary

The aim of this chapter was to start building up a picture of how a Commerce Server solution site operates, mapping out a little of the framework architecture in preparation for later, more involved chapters.

We've now walked through most of the primary features of a commerce website, and should have a good idea of the components involved, or at least where to look for them. You may choose to strip certain features from the site, or begin with a blank site, building your site from scratch, but take the time to become familiar with the base classes – these are your bread and butter in this environment, and in most cases will supply you with everything you need within the scope of the Commerce Server base feature set.

We looked at a few of the files involved in configuration, and briefly considered the databases underlying the site. We then stepped through the process of initializing the web application that comprises the consumer interface, and finally looked at the execution of the `default.asp` page itself. Along the way, we saw a little of the interaction that takes place between ASP code, framework COM objects, and the commerce database.

We also looked at customizing the Retail site in various ways.

By the time we've worked through this book, we will have looked in detail at the various aspects of a Commerce Server site. We will have seen how to utilize the main COM objects, and how to exploit the Commerce Server framework to its full potential. We'll start upon this path right away: in the next chapter, we're going to take a close-up look at the User Profiling System.

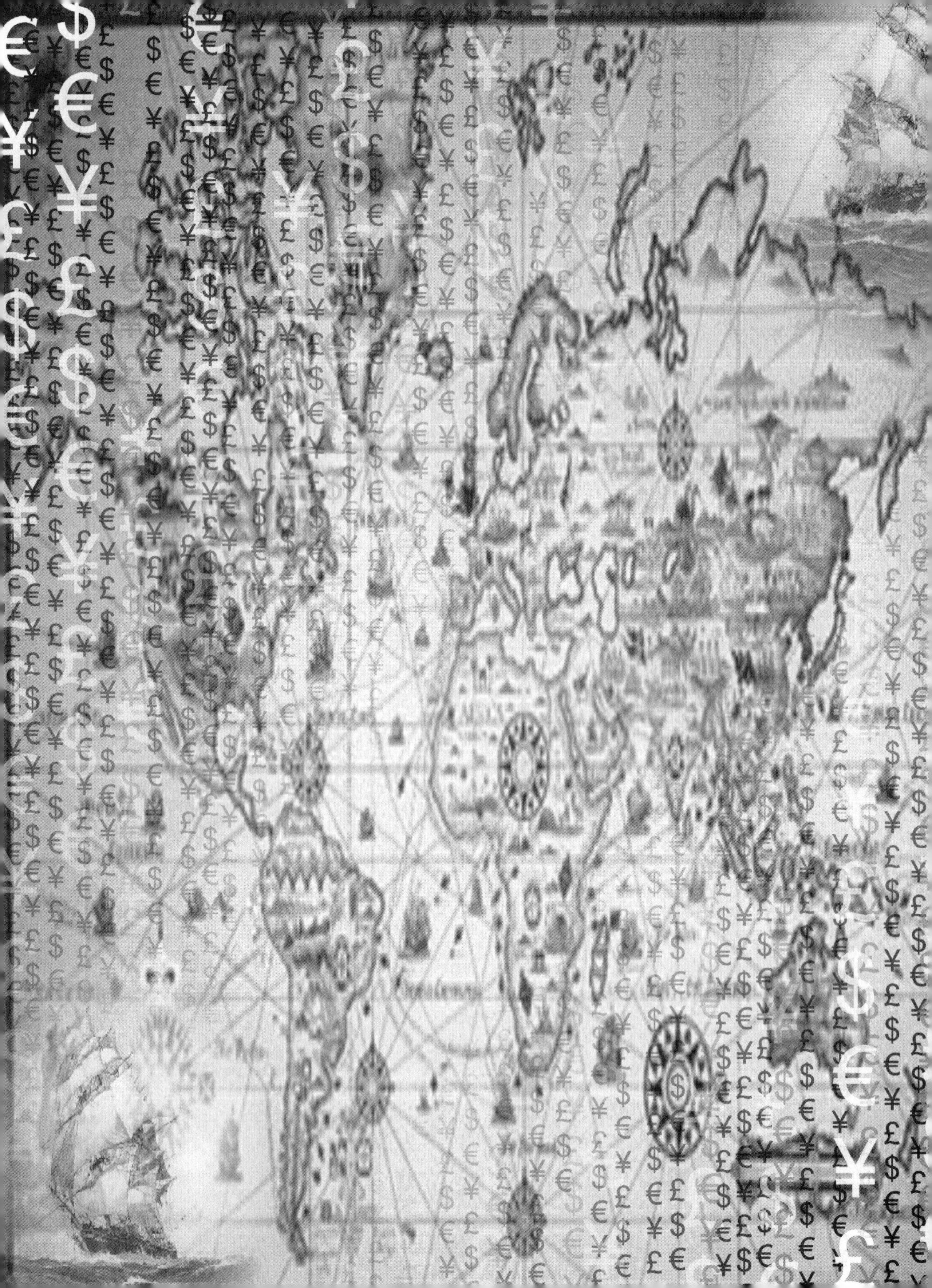

3

User Profiling and Authentication

As we saw in Chapter 1, the Commerce Server 2000 **Profile System** enables us to store persisted information about our site's users. What's more, along with Commerce Server's authentication features, it can actually be used in a wide variety of other solutions. While many of the other product features are targeted specifically at e-commerce sites, the UPS can be useful to any site that needs to authenticate users or provide some kind of user-specific content – consider using it when:

❑   You need to recognize the user.

❑   You need to authenticate the user and limit site access based on user identity.

❑   You need to store information about users, such as their name, address, e-mail and age.

❑   You want to store information about other entities important to your solution, such as organizations.

❑   You have existing data sources with data you want to integrate into the user profile.

Despite its usefulness in isolation, the Profile System is well integrated with other parts of the product. The **Content Targeting System** can use profile information to target content (such as advertisements and discounts) at specific users (or groups of users) and to generate personalized e-mail campaigns. We'll be taking a look at this in Chapters 8 and 9.

Profile data can be fed into the **Business Internet Analytics System** (BIA), which can then derive implicit user data (purchasing trends etc.) and pass that back the Profile System. The Profile System is also used to connect a user to a shopping basket, and collect information about that user during the checkout process.

The CS2K Profile System is the successor to the Personalization and Membership features found in Site Server. While Site Server allowed you to do authentication and to store information about users, Commerce Server is more flexible in several ways:

❑ Authentication is decoupled from user storage, allowing for flexible authentication schemes and integration with different authentication sources.

❑ The Profile System is highly extensible – this allows you to extend predefined profile definitions, create your own profile definitions, and specify where the profile data is stored.

❑ A single profile can span many data sources and present data from all these sources in a single consistent view. If you already have data about your users in other sources, you don't have to move that data over to Commerce Server – as long as they can be accessed via LDAP or OLE DB, the profile system can access them directly. Out of the box, the solution sites provide support for storing profile data in SQL Server and in Active Directory.

So, the Profile System and authentication features can be used separately – nevertheless, in many cases you will want to use them together. The question of what to cover first is a bit like the chicken and egg problem: you need a profile to be authenticated and you need to authenticate to get at your profile.

This chapter deals with authentication *before* profiling, simply because that's the order in which I normally consider them when developing a site. We shall deal with the authentication architecture first – how users are going to identify themselves, how access should be controlled, and so on. We then look at profiling issues, such as which data should be collected about the users, and where is that data going to be stored. Specifically, we will look at:

❑ How to do programmatic authentication using the `AuthManager` object.

❑ How to use the `AuthFilter` ISAPI filter to do automatic authentication using both Custom Authentication mode and Windows Authentication mode.

❑ Differences between authentication modes.

❑ How to program the profiling system to do things such as creating users and retrieve and modify user properties.

❑ How you can modify pre-defined profile definitions and how you can create new profile definitions.

❑ How you can create a profile definition that uses both SQL Server and Active Directory.

Before you can start working with authentication or profiling, you must create a site. Chapter 1 showed how to set up a functional retail site by using the Commerce Server Site Packager tool to perform a default unpacking of the `retail.pup` solution site. This should be enough to get us up and running.

If you didn't choose the default installation (or you haven't yet created a site), I suggest you refer to Appendix A for details. Make sure you select the CS Authentication resource and the Profile resource when unpacking the site, as you'll need them to get the profiling and authentication features enabled for your site. Both resources are selected by default.

For the purposes of this chapter, you can use any of the standard Solution Sites (`Blank.pup`, `retail.pup`, or `supplieractivedirectory.pup`) or the Profile sitelet (`SDK\Samples\Sitelets\Profile\SDK-PROFILE-SITELET.PUP`), which will be discussed in Chapter 14.

Authentication

Authentication is the process of identifying a user. This is closely linked with **authorization**, which is the process of giving that user access to information based on their identity. You can see this all over the web today: many sites provide you with the opportunity to register a user name and password, and store personal information for later use. When you return to the site, you enter your user name and password. The site looks them up in its records to find out who you are (authentication) and on matching your input against its records gives you access to your data (authorization).

An important decision to make when you develop a solution is *when and how* you want to identify the user. Do you want the user to register when entering the site for the first time, or when they complete an order? Do you want to allow both registered and anonymous users access to your site, or require a login for access to all pages? Your choices will depend on *what* your solution is and *who* your users are. On one hand, many users find it hard if they have to register and log in to your site. On the other hand, you can provide registered users with enhanced services because you know who they are.

Commerce Server provides you with a lot of flexibility in this area. You can secure your entire site, mix registered and anonymous user access, and even track anonymous users (in a similar fashion to a site like amazon.com). This flexibility is provided by the `AuthManager` object and by the `AuthFilter`:

❑ `AuthManager` is a Commerce Server COM object that you can use in your site's ASP pages to handle authentication programmatically and manage the `AuthFilter`.

❑ The `AuthFilter` is an ISAPI (Internet Server API) filter – a DLL that's loaded into the IIS web server – which receives notifications from the web server and can modify the handling of requests. It's similar in function to the doorman at a movie theatre: he looks at your ticket to see if it's valid; if it is, you're let in; if not, you are sent back to the ticket booth (login page) to get a valid ticket.

You *must* use the `AuthManager` object in your code when using the `AuthFilter`. For instance you need to use `AuthManager` to get the user name once `AuthFilter` has authenticated a user.

`AuthFilter` has two main modes of operation:

❑ **Windows Authentication mode** uses Active Directory (or a local machine account) to verify the user name and password. You can customize the login page and the ISAPI filter to pass the credentials on to IIS for authentication.

The ASP pages run in the context of the logged on user account. This allows you to do things like protecting content based on NTFS permissions, using COM+-based roles, and propagating credentials down to SQL Server.

❑ **Custom Authentication mode** allows you to customize the login process by adding your own code to validate the user name and password. You can look up the user name and password in a database, read from a password file, or even hardcode values into the login page. Typically though, you would use the user profile stored in the Profile System.

In this mode, pages are run in the context of the anonymous local account `IUSR_<machine name>`. Authentication is performed by `AuthFilter` and your own code – once the user is authenticated, you can retrieve their user id, but they remain anonymous from the perspective of IIS. This means that you lose the ability to use NTFS permissions and COM+-based roles.

`AuthFilter` can also track anonymous users by storing a cookie on their machine. **Autocookie mode** can be used in combination with both Windows Authentication and Custom Authentication modes, allowing a mix of anonymous and authenticated users.

Deciding which mode to use is often quite difficult, so here are a few general rules of thumb:

❑ `AuthFilter` uses cookies – if you need to authenticate without requiring your users to accept cookies, you must use `AuthManager`, which can encode an authentication ticket in the URL.

❑ You can use `AuthFilter` in Custom Authentication mode or Windows Authentication mode if you want to require login for access to all pages. `AuthManager` can only secure individual ASP pages.

❑ If you want to mix authenticated and anonymous access to the same site, you can either use the `AuthManager` object, or `AuthFilter` in Windows Authentication mode.

❑ If you want to use the security context of the logged on user to access system resources you must use `AuthFilter` in Windows Authentication mode.

Authentication Tickets

Commerce Server uses **tickets** to identify users and to store information about them – these are normally stored in cookies. Both registered and anonymous users can be tracked, and two different types of ticket are used to accomplish this:

❑ The **MSCSAuth** ticket is used to track registered users. A cookie is issued when the user authenticates, storing user ID, time of last logon and an expiry period to specify how long the ticket is valid. The ticket will be deleted after this period lapses or when the browser is closed, whichever happens first.

❑ The **MSCSProfile** ticket is used to track anonymous users. A unique ID is generated when the user enters the site for the first time. By default, this cookie is valid until the year 2038, which should be long enough for most sites being built today. You can change the expiry date of the cookie from the Commerce Server Manager.

If the user has disabled cookie support you can store the tickets in the URL string. However, this requires a little more work on your part, as you must ensure that all links contain the URL-encoded ticket. While the `AuthManager` object makes this task easier (it has methods to automatically generate URLs with encoded tickets) it is still important to consider this upfront, since it mean that all your site's URLs must be programmatically generated. Note that tickets are encrypted for increased security.

Managing the CS Authentication Resource

The **CS Authentication** resource is used to manage the authentication settings for your site – for instance, you use it to specify which authentication mode to use. Each server can have multiple authentication resources and several sites can use the same resource – useful if you're running a web farm. The CS Authentication resource can be managed via the Commerce Manager at both global level and at application level.

At the global level you manage settings for all sites using a specific CS Authentication resource. To see the settings, navigate to Global Resources I CS Authentication, right-click the resource, and select Properties. You should see something similar to this:

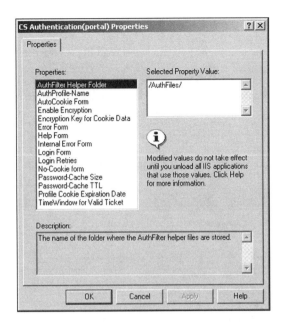

These settings are used by `AuthFilter` and `AuthManager`, and you can use them in your code by means of the `SiteConfigReadOnly` object. In most cases you will probably leave them at their default values.

To manage settings at the application level, navigate to **Commerce Sites** | *<site name>* | **Applications**, right-click the application and select **Properties**. You should now see something like the following:

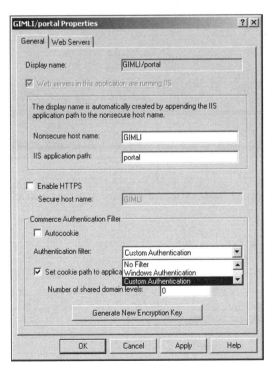

In this dialog you can select the type of authentication you want to use. Selecting Windows Authentication or Custom Authentication will enable the `AuthFilter` for the site. If you check the Autocookie checkbox, you will also enable the `AuthFilter`, even if you select No Filter in the drop-down list.

> **Whenever you change any settings on the CS Authentication resource you must restart IIS before changes will take effect – run `iisreset` at the command prompt.**

Some other authentication settings are stored in the App Default Config resource (under Site Resources in the Commerce Manager), such as a setting that specifies the time window of the AuthTicket.

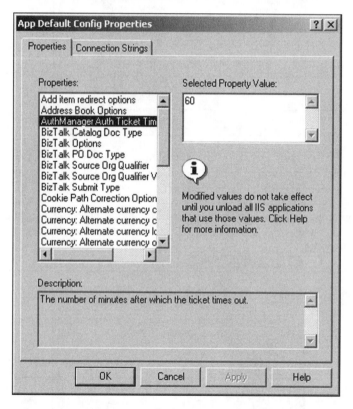

The Solution Sites use these settings in code to control the behavior of the site. Again, you can modify these using the Commerce Manager, or use them in your own code by referencing the `AppConfig` object properties.

The AuthManager Object

If you've ever hand-built a site that incorporated some means by which a user could log in, the chances are that you developed your own authentication scheme, using a session variable or cookie to keep track of the user's status. I have seen many variants of this – in fact, the first ASP site I ever developed used session variables to store a user name and password.

Such a solution would most likely feature a common include file at the start of all its ASP pages. This would check if the user was authenticated, and if not it would redirect them to a login page. When the user logged in, appropriate information would be stored in a session variable or cookie. The code in this include file would probably look something like this:

```
If Not Session("LoggedIn") = True Then
    Response.Redirect("login.asp")
End If
```

The following figure shows the operational flow in such a solution, illustrated as a UML sequence diagram:

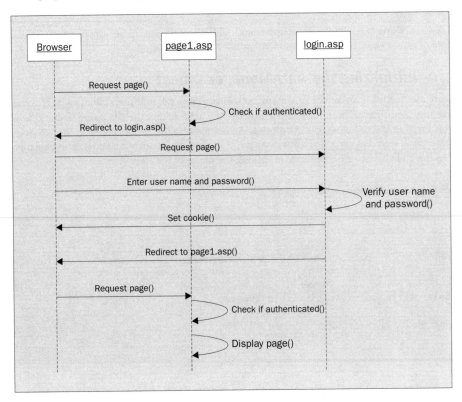

What this actually shows happening is as follows:

- ❏   The user requests a page.
- ❏   The include file checks whether the user is logged in.
- ❏   If not, the user is redirected to a login page.
- ❏   The user enters their user name and password.
- ❏   The login page successfully verifies the user name and password.
- ❏   The login page sets a session variable or cookie to indicate that the user is logged in.
- ❏   The login page redirects the browser to the originally requested page.

❑ The user is successfully authenticated, so this page request also succeeds and the originally requested page is displayed.

You can use the `AuthManager` object in your ASP pages to implement this kind of authentication. The advantage of using this object is that it can handle encryption and decryption of the authentication ticket, storing the ticket in a URL or a cookie, and ticket validation as well as simple user identification.

`AuthManager` depends on ASP objects and can therefore only be used in ASP pages – you cannot use it in your own components. You should also create and destroy instances of the object on each ASP page. It can be used to handle both anonymous users (generating a unique user ID and storing it in an `MSCSProfile` ticket) and registered users (using the `MSCSAuth` ticket).

The following sections describe the most important methods of the `AuthManager` object, finishing off with an example of how to use the object to implement the No Filter mode.

Initialize() – Initializing the AuthManager Object

Before using the `AuthManager` object we must obviously create it, and then initialize it. The following function returns an initialized `AuthManager` object – we assume that the site name is stored as an application variable `MSCSCommerceSiteName`. As we've seen, this is the case with the solution sites, which read the site name into this variable from `csapp.ini` when the application starts. The object is initialized by a call to the `Initialize()` method, specifying the name of the site:

```
Function GetAuthManagerObject()

    Dim oAuthManager
    Dim sSiteName

    sSiteName = Application("MSCSCommerceSiteName")

    Set oAuthManager = Server.CreateObject("Commerce.AuthManager")
    Call oAuthManager.Initialize(sSiteName)

    Set GetAuthManagerObject = oAuthManager

End Function
```

Note that if you are using one of the solution sites, the variable `mscsAuthMgr` *(created in* `setupenv.asp`*) already contains an* `AuthManager` *object initialized in a similar fashion.*

The first time you call `AuthManager` it reads authentication settings from the `MSCS_Admin` database and stores the data in a cache. On subsequent calls, these settings are read directly from the cache.

SetAuthTicket() – Setting the Authentication Ticket

To enable the user to log in, you must provide some sort of login page: they enter their user ID and password; your code then needs to validate them both. Later on, we'll see how to validate such data against entries in the Profile System. Once validated, the user is issued with an `AuthTicket` by means of the `SetAuthTicket()` method. This takes three parameters: the user ID; a Boolean denoting whether the ticket should be issued in a cookie; and the period (in minutes) after which the ticket will expire.

The following code sets `AuthTicket` for a user called `testuser`. The ticket is stored in a cookie and is valid for 90 minutes:

```
Set oAuthManager = GetAuthManagerObject()
Call oAuthManager.SetAuthTicket("testuser", True, 90)
```

IsAuthenticated() – Checking if the User is Logged In

Remember the session approach we mentioned a couple of pages back, where you use a session variable to check whether the user is logged in? The following code does the same thing using `AuthManager`:

```
Set oAuthManager = GetAuthManagerObject()

If Not oAuthManager.IsAuthenticated() Then
    'User is not logged in, redirect to login page
    Response.Redirect("login.asp")
End If
```

The authentication ticket stores the time of last login and a time window specifying how long the ticket is valid. The `IsAuthenticated()` method checks whether the current time is within that time window; if there are less than five minutes until the ticket expires, the last login time is updated with the current time.

> By default, this method uses the time window specified in the call to `SetAuthTicket()`. However, you can set an optional extra parameter to specify a shorter time window. Note that a value of 0 will result in the use of the default time window.

GetUserID() – Getting the ID of the User

Once you have authenticated a user, you may well want to personalize the information displayed next; for that you need the user's ID, which is stored in a ticket. To retrieve the ID you can use the `GetUserId()` method, which takes a parameter specifying if you should get the ID from the `MSCSProfile` ticket or from the `MSCSAuth` ticket. The ID of the authenticated user is stored in the `MSCSAuth` ticket.

To get the user ID from the `MSCSAuthTicket`, use a value of 2 – or better yet, use the `AUTH_TICKET` constant stored in the `Apps Constants` type library. Likewise, if you wanted to get the ID of an anonymous user, you could specify a value of 1 (or `PROFILE_TICKET`).

```
Set oAuthManager = GetAuthManagerObject()
sUserId = oAuthManager.GetUserID(2) 'or use AUTH_TICKET constant
```

SetProfileTicket() – Tracking Anonymous Users

To track anonymous users you use the `MSCSProfile` ticket, which contains a unique ID for the user. To generate the ID you can use the `GenID` object that ships with Commerce Server. This object has a method called `GenGUIDString()` that generates a Globally Unique Identifier (GUID) and returns this as a string. A GUID is 128 bits long and is guaranteed to be unique. The following code shows how to use the `GenID` object to generate a unique ID:

```
Dim oGenId
Dim sGUID
Set oGenId = Server.CreateObject("Commerce.GenID")
sGUID = oGenId.GenGUIDString()
Set oGenId = Nothing
```

You can then call the `SetProfileTicket()` method to issue the ticket:

```
Set oAuthManager = GetAuthManagerObject()
Call oAuthManager.SetProfileTicket(sGUID, True)
Set oAuthManager = Nothing
```

Note that this method does not take a time window – the ticket is valid for the lifetime of the cookie. The expiry date of the profile cookie is set in the CS Authentication resource using the MMC. By default the cookie is valid to the year 2038.

When you use the `AuthFilter` in autocookie mode, the filter routes to a page called `autocookie.asp`. This page uses code similar to that above to generate the profile ticket.

GetProperty(), SetProperty() – Storing Custom Properties in a Ticket

You can use these methods to add custom properties to the authentication ticket and the profile ticket, which are stored as name/value pairs. To store a custom property, use the `SetProperty()` method; to retrieve a property, use `GetProperty()`. Both methods take a parameter specifying the ticket type: 1 for profile ticket and 2 for authentication ticket. Once again, if you include a reference to the `App Constants` type library in `global.asa`, you can use the constants `AUTH_TICKET` and `GUEST_TICKET`.

This functionality should be used with caution, and only to pass small amounts of user data. This data will be passed to and from the browser in a cookie or URL query string, both of which can only store quite limited amounts of data.

The following passage of code retrieves the value of a counter property and increases it by one:

```
Dim oAuthManager
Dim nCount

Set oAuthManager = GetAuthManagerObject()

nCount = oAuthManager.GetProperty(1,"PageCount") 'Or use GUEST_TICKET

If IsNull(nCount) Then
    nCount = 1
Else
    nCount = nCount + 1
End If
```

The counter is then written back to the ticket:

```
Call oAuthManager.SetProperty(1,"PageCount",nCount) 'Or use GUEST_TICKET
```

Example – Authenticating using AuthManager (No Filter mode)

Authentication without using the ISAPI AuthFilter is known as *No Filter mode*. This lets you use the methods of the `AuthManager` object described in this section to handle the authentication programmatically.

By using programmatic authentication you have a lot of flexibility and control over the authentication. You can mix authenticated and anonymous users, you can define at what stage you require the login and where you want to allow the user to be anonymous.

The first thing you need is the include file that checks if the user is logged in. Here is what this include file, called check_login.asp, may look like.

```
<%

Dim m_bIsLoggedIn
Dim m_sUserId

Function CheckLogin(bAnonymousAllowed)

    Dim oAuthManager

    Set oAuthManager = GetAuthManagerObject()
```

I have placed the code to check authentication in a function, which takes a parameter specifying whether anonymous access should be allowed. This code relies on the GetAuthManager() function described earlier in the chapter. In the code download, this function can be found in an include file called profile_lib.asp.

The check_login.asp include file sets two global variables: a Boolean, m_bIsLoggedIn, and a string, m_sUserId. The Boolean is set to True if the user is logged in. The string is set to the username if the user is logged in, and to the unique user ID stored in the profile ticket if we track anonymous users.

```
If oAuthManager.IsAuthenticated() Then
    m_bIsLoggedIn = True
    m_sUserId = oAuthManager.GetUserID(2) 'or use AUTH_TICKET constant
```

The function first checks if the user is authenticated by calling IsAuthenticated(). This function returns True if the user has a valid authentication ticket. Then the GetUserID() function is called with a value of 2 to get the user ID from the authentication ticket.

```
Else 'oAuthManager.IsAuthenticated returns FALSE
    m_bIsLoggedIn = False

    'If we require login we redirect to login.asp
    If Not bAnonymousAllowed Then
        Response.Redirect("login.asp")
    End If
```

If the user does not have a valid authentication ticket, and anonymous access is not allowed, the function redirects the user to the login page.

```
    'If we track anonymous users, the User ID is stored in the sUserID
    If Not IsNull(oAuthManager.GetUserID(1)) Then
        m_sUserId = oAuthManager.GetUserID(1) ' or use_
                          GUEST_TICKET constant
    Else
        m_sUserId = ""
    End If
End If

End Function

%>
```

If anonymous access is allowed, the GetUserID() is called with a value of 1 to get the anonymous user ID stored in the profile ticket. If the user does not have a profile ticket, an empty string is returned in the m_sUserId variable.

Here is an example of a page that uses the check_login.asp, include file. This page allows anonymous access by calling CheckLogin() with a value of True. If the user is logged in, the page greets the user by login name and provides the option to log out. It the user is not logged in the page provides the user with a link to log in.

```asp
<%
OPTION EXPLICIT
%>
<!-- #INCLUDE FILE="profile_lib.asp" -->
<!-- #INCLUDE FILE="check_login.asp" -->

<%

Call Main()

Sub Main()
    'Allows anonymous access if parameter is TRUE
    Call CheckLogin(True)
    Call DisplayPage()
End Sub

Sub DisplayPage()
%>

<HTML>
<BODY>

<P>
    <%
    If  m_bIsLoggedIn Then
    %>
        Hello <%=m_sUserId%>.  You can logout by selecting
        <a href="logout.asp">this</a> link.
    <%
    Else
    %>
        You are not logged in. You can login
        <a href="login.asp">here</a>.
    <%
    End If
    %>

</BODY>
</HTML>
<%
End Sub
%>
```

Here is the login page, `login.asp`:

```
<% OPTION EXPLICIT %>

<!-- #INCLUDE FILE="profile_lib.asp" -->
<!-- #INCLUDE FILE="check_login.asp" -->

<%

Call Main()

Sub Main()

    Dim sMsg
    Dim sUserName
    Dim sPassword

    If Request("realSubmit") = "fromButton" Then
        sUserName = Request("txtUserName")
        sPassword = Request("txtPassword")
        sMsg = Login(sUserName,sPassword)
    End If

    Call DisplayPage(sMsg)

End Sub
```

The `Main()` method checks whether the page was submitted by checking the hidden field `realSubmit`. If the page was submitted, it calls the `Login()` method with the username and password. Then `DisplayPage()` is called to render the page to the user.

```
Function Login(ByVal sUserName, ByVal sPassword)

    Dim sRetAsp
    Dim oAuthManager
    Dim oUserProfile
    Dim sCheckPassword

    Set oAuthManager = GetAuthManagerObject()

    If (Len(sUsername) > 0) Then

        ' Look up user somewhere
        If sUserName <> "billg" Then
            Login = "Unknown user"
            Exit Function
        End If

        ' Retrieve password for user
        sCheckPassword = "password"
```

This method checks if the username is billg and the password is password. In a more realistic example you would look up the username and password in the Profiling System or in some other user store. The Profiling System is a very good place to store information about users. See the section on *Profiling* for more details.

Chapter 3

```
            If sCheckPassword = sPassword Then
                ' Set MSCSAuth ticket with a timeout of 90 minutes
                oAuthManager.SetAuthTicket sUsername, 1, 90
```

If the password is correct, the `Login()` function calls the `SetAuthTicket()` method to set the authentication ticket. The ticket is set with the user name entered and with a time window of 90 minutes.

```
            sRetAsp = oAuthManager.GetURL("default.asp", True, False)
```

To generate the URL of the default page, the `GetURL()` method of the `AuthManager` object is used. The first parameter of this method is the name of the page. The second parameter is set to `True` to indicate that the user supports cookies. The third parameter should be set to `True` too if the URL should be secure (that is, it should use HTTPS). We set this parameter to `False`.

```
            Response.Redirect sRetAsp
```

After logging in, the user is redirected to the default page.

```
        Else ' sCheckPassword <> sPassword
            Login = "Incorrect password"
            Exit Function
        End If
    Else ' Len(sUsername) <= 0
        Login = "Username missing"
    End If
End Function
```

If the login fails, the login page is redisplayed with an error message.

The `DisplayPage()` function renders the login page:

```
Sub DisplayPage(ByVal sMsg)
%>

    <HTML>
    <BODY>
    <P>
    <FORM METHOD="POST" ACTION="login.asp">

    <B><%=sMsg%></B><BR /><BR />

    Username: <INPUT TYPE="text" NAME="txtUsername"> <BR />

    Password: <INPUT TYPE="password" NAME="txtPassword"> <BR />

    <INPUT TYPE="submit" NAME="Login" VALUE="Login">
    <INPUT TYPE="hidden" NAME="realSubmit" VALUE="fromButton">

    </FORM>

    </BODY>
    </HTML>
<%
End Sub
%>
```

Finally we need to provide the user with the capability to log out. To logout the user you need to delete the authentication ticket. This can be accomplished by calling `SetAuthTicket` with a blank user name as shown in the following `logout.asp` page:

```
<%
OPTION EXPLICIT
%>
<!-- #INCLUDE FILE="profile_lib.asp" -->
<%
Call Main()

Sub Main
    Dim oAuthManager

    Set oAuthManager = GetAuthManagerObject()
    Call oAuthManager.SetAuthTicket("",True,0)

    Call DisplayPage()

    Set oAuthManager = Nothing

End Sub

%>

<%
Sub DisplayPage()
%>
    <HTML>
    <BODY>

    You have been logged out. Go back <a href="default.asp">here</a>.

    </BODY>
    </HTML>
<%
End Sub
%>
```

The AuthFilter ISAPI Filter

An ISAPI filter is a DLL that is registered with the web server – it receives events from Internet Information Server and performs appropriate actions. Commerce Server provides the `AuthFilter` ISAPI filter in the form of a file called `SiteAuth.dll`. The `AuthFilter` registers for several IIS events. For instance, the filter is called with a `SF_NOTIFY_AUTHENTICATION` event when authentication occurs. `AuthFilter` uses the events to implement its authentication modes.

By default, the ISAPI filter is registered at the web site with low priority. It is activated for the virtual directories on that site using the Commerce Manager. Settings are stored in the `MSCS_Admin` database, with authentication settings also stored in a local cache to improve performance.

> *The `AuthFilter` is similar to the authentication filter provided by Site Server Membership. With Site Server the filter intercepts requests and checks whether the user is authenticated – if not, they are routed to a custom login page called `formslogin.asp`. Initially, the system looks for this page in the same directory as the page being requested; if it doesn't find it there, it will search back along the URL path to the root directory.*

All of this functionality is carried forward to Commerce Server 2000 – the biggest implementation difference is the separation of the authentication process from the user profiles, allowing much more flexibility in customizing the authentication schemes. The filter now looks for the login page in a special folder named `AuthFiles`.

The functionality of the `AuthFilter` is illustrated in the diagram below, which shows the most important functions performed by the filter using Custom Authentication mode or Windows Authentication mode:

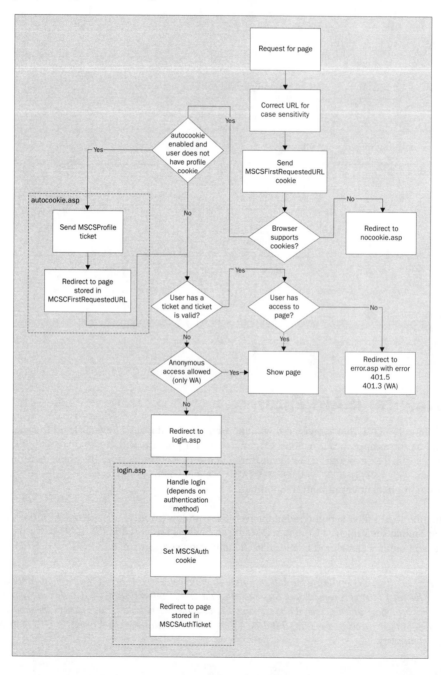

First, the filter corrects the URL for case sensitivity – it then sends the `MSCSFirstRequestedURL` cookie to the browser. Assuming you have your browser set to prompt you before accepting cookies, you will now see something like the screenshot below:

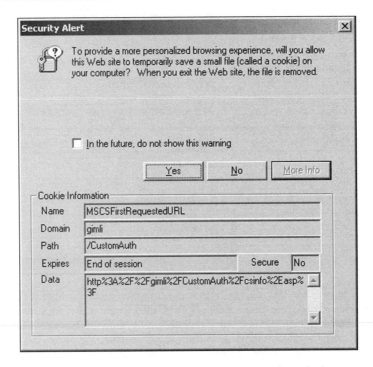

This cookie contains the URL being requested and it is used to remember which page to redirect the user to after the user has logged in. If the browser does not support cookies, the user is redirected to `nocookie.asp`, which displays a message indicating that cookie support is required.

You can actually specify the ASP page used here from within the CS Authentication resource. It's well worth customizing this page with your own design – as you can see, the default page really isn't very user-friendly. You might also choose to specify code in this page that will redirect the user to a version of the site that does not require cookies.

Next, the filter checks to see if the user has a valid authentication ticket – as stored in the `MSCSAuth` cookie. This cookie contains the timestamp and a time window specifying how long the ticket is valid for. If the ticket is good, the requested page is displayed. If the user does not have a valid ticket, they are redirected to the `login.asp` page shown below – again, this page should be customized to your own design. The login page submits to itself and the user name and password are validated.

Of course, authentication is handled differently according to which mode the filter is being used in. If you use Windows Authentication mode, the filter supplies IIS with the user name and password and IIS validates them. If you use Custom Authentication mode it is up to you to verify the user name and password.

In either case, assuming the user name and password supplied are valid, an `MSCSAuth` ticket is set in the `MSCSAuth` cookie. This happens programmatically in the `login.asp` page using the `AuthManager` object. If your browser prompts you to accept cookies you will see a new alert message, much the same as the one below:

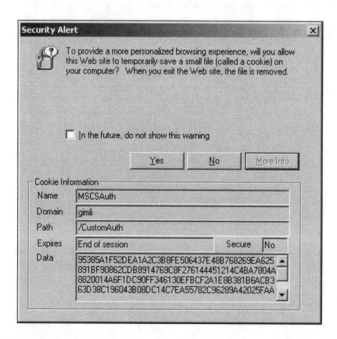

If the user is authenticated but is not authorized to access the page, they are routed to an error page. In Custom Authentication mode this will happen if the anonymous IUSR_<machine name> account does not have permissions to access the file. In Windows Authentication mode this happens if the account of the user does not have access to the file. The default error page is shown below – again, you should modify this page with your own content.

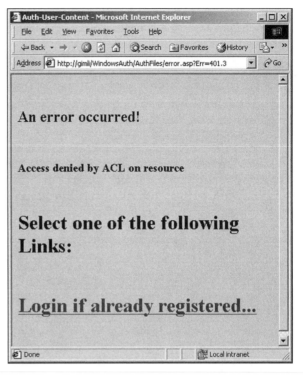

The AuthFilter uses a global cache to store authentication settings. The first time a site is accessed the settings are read from the MSCS_Admin database and stored in the cache. There is one entry for each site and the cache stores the authentication method for the site along with the user names and passwords associated with the tickets.

Custom Authentication Mode

This mode lets you customize how the authentication is performed by letting you write your own code to do it. You can authenticate using the Profiling System, by using ADO to connect to a SQL database, making a call to a mainframe to verify the login, or even use a hard-coded user name and password.

Custom Authentication mode is similar to the forms authentication available in Site Server. One difference is that with Site Server you can control access on a page-by-page basis, while in CS2K Custom Authentication mode all pages are protected. If you use Custom Authentication, you effectively exclude anonymous users from all pages on the site – you either log in and gain access to the whole site, or don't and get access to none of it.

This difference arises because CS2K uses the anonymous account, IUSR_<machine name> to access content on behalf of all users authenticated by custom code, whereas Site Server uses proxy accounts (MemProxyUser), allowing for more configuration flexibility. In this respect, Commerce Server is actually the more limited of the two systems. I can only guess at why the product team chose to do it this way: the most likely explanation seems to be that it simplifies custom authentication – there is a lot of confusion over exactly how Site Server Membership works, and it's particularly important to minimize the potential for security loopholes when implementing custom authentication – perhaps they're just trying to put us off the idea!

If you want one site to feature a mixture of content that can be accessed anonymously and content that requires authentication before access, you can use Windows Authentication mode, which we'll examine shortly.

The following figure shows the control flow using Custom Authentication mode. Note how similar this is to using programmatic authentication (see the figure in the section *The AuthManager Object* earlier in this chapter).

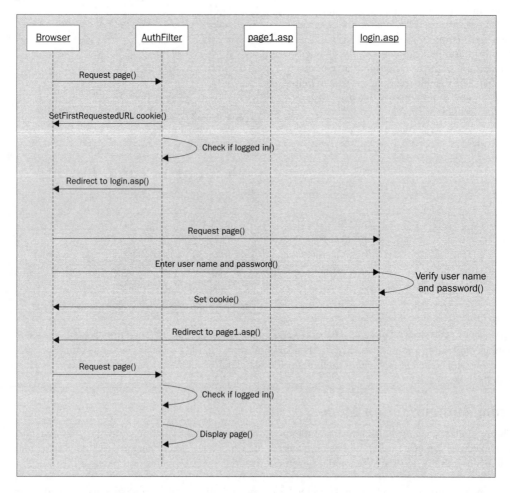

This is clearly very similar to the technique we saw earlier using the `AuthManager` object to customize authentication. The advantage of using the `AuthFilter` is that it handles much of the functionality for you. You don't have to include a file in all your ASP pages, since `AuthFilter` automatically protects all pages, including HTML pages and documents. The `AuthFilter` also takes care of remembering the name of the page you requested.

The actual authentication is customized from within the `login.asp` page. Here is an updated version of our earlier login function, which uses the Profile System to verify user name and password:

```
Function Login(ByVal sUserName, ByVal sPassword)

    Dim oAuthManager
    Dim sRetAsp
    Dim oUserProfile
    Dim sCheckPassword
```

```
     Set oAuthManager = GetAuthManagerObject()

  If (Len(sUsername) > 0) Then

       'Here we use the Profiling System to get the password
       Set oUserProfile = GetUserProfileByLoginName(sUsername)
       If (oUserProfile Is Nothing) Then
          Login = "Unknown user"
          Exit Function
       End If

       'Retrieve password from user profile
       sCheckPassword = _
           oUserProfile.Fields("GeneralInfo.user_security_password").Value

     If (sCheckPassword = sPassword) Then
         ' Set MSCSAuth ticket with a timeout of 90 minutes
         oAuthManager.SetAuthTicket sUsername, 1, 90
         'Redirect to requested page
         sRetAsp = Request.Cookies("MSCSFirstRequestedURL")
         If (sRetAsp = "" Or IsNull(sRetAsp)) Then
            sRetAsp = oAuthManager.GetURL("default.asp", True, False)
         End If
         Response.Redirect sRetAsp
     Else
         ' sCheckPassword <> sPassword
         Login = "Incorrect password"
         Exit Function
     End If
  Else
  Login = "Username missing"
  End If
End Function
```

As you can see, it uses a function called `GetProfileByLoginName()` to retrieve the user profile stored in the Profile System. This looks up a specified user name in the Profile System, and returns a `ProfileObject` object. We then compare the contents of this object's `user_security_password` field with the password entered. We'll look at exactly how this is accomplished later on in the chapter, when we take a proper look at the `ProfileObject` object. Again, you can replace this with any code you want to verify the password. Note that we define the `GetProfileByLoginName()` function in the include file `profile_lib.asp`.

The `AuthFilter` stores the requested page in a cookie called `MSCSFirstRequestedURL` and uses this to redirect the user to the originally requested page. If for some reason the value is not stored in the cookie, the user is redirected to the default page – note that the `AuthManager` method `GetURL()` is used to create the complete URL of the default page.

> The `login.asp` file that is installed (under `AuthFiles`) as part of the blank solution site is not fully functional, and accepts all logins. You must therefore modify it to do the actual authentication. If you uncomment the line to read the password from the profile system you get a runtime error, as the blank solution site doesn't store a profile service object in the `Application` object as `login.asp` expects. The login.asp pages described in this chapter should make this work properly.

Windows Authentication Mode

This mode allows you to use Active Directory or a local machine account to verify a user name and password. The site's ASP pages will then be run in the context of the logged on user account. If you use this mode, the Windows account can be used to verify access to content using Access Control Lists (ACL). You can use role-based security in COM+ or propagate credentials down to SQL Server and use its own security mechanisms.

Typically you will not control access to content for individual users. Instead you create groups and assign users to groups. You then use these groups to control access to pages.

Windows Authentication mode is similar to the Windows NT Authentication mode in Site Server. One notable difference between them is that only Commerce Server allows you to provide your own HTML form for the user to enter their user name and password – you can therefore access the pages with your Windows account using any browser. For security reasons you should enable SSL on the login pages.

The actual authentication is performed by IIS. When authentication occurs, IIS calls the `AuthFilter` with a `SF_NOTIFY_AUTHENTICATION` event. `AuthFilter` supplies the user name and password and IIS verifies them. If they are incorrect, IIS calls `AuthFilter` with a `SF_NOTIFY_ACCESS_DENIED` event.

Using Windows Authentication mode you can control which users have access to which pages by setting NTFS permissions on the files. In the screenshot below, all users who are a member of the Administrators group will get access to the page:

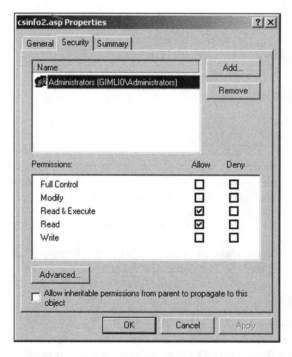

If you now try to access this page as a user who isn't in the Administrators group, you will be routed to an error page (`error.asp`) with an error code of 401.3. Using Windows Authentication mode you can also allow anonymous access to pages, via the Internet Services Manager. Right-click the appropriate file and select Properties | File Security | Edit:

You must also make sure that the anonymous `IUSR_<machine name>` account has access to the file.

With Windows Authentication mode, `AuthFilter` and IIS handle the actual authentication process, although it is still up to you to supply a login form and issue the authentication ticket. The following page is an example of a login page that uses Windows Authentication:

```asp
<%
Option Explicit
%>
<!-- #INCLUDE FILE="profile_lib.asp" -->

<%
Call Main()

Sub Main()

    Dim sMsg
    Dim sUserName
    Dim oAuthManager
    Dim sRetAsp

    If Request.QueryString("realSubmit") = "fromButton" Then

        Set oAuthManager = GetAuthManagerObject()
        sUsername = Request.QueryString("txtUsername")

        oAuthManager.SetAuthTicket sUsername, 1, 90

        sRetAsp = Request.Cookies("MSCSFirstRequestedURL")
        If (sRetAsp = "" Or IsNull(sRetAsp)) Then
            sRetAsp = oAuth.GetURL("default.asp", True, False)
        End If
```

```
        Response.Redirect sRetASP
    End If

    Call DisplayPage()
End Sub

Sub DisplayPage()
%>
    <HTML>
    <BODY>
    <P>
    <FORM METHOD="GET" ACTION="login.asp" >

    Username: <INPUT TYPE="text" NAME="txtUsername"> <BR />
    Password: <INPUT TYPE="password" NAME="txtPassword"> <BR />

    <INPUT TYPE="submit" NAME="Login" VALUE="Login">
    <INPUT TYPE="hidden" NAME="realSubmit" value="fromButton">

    </FORM>

    </BODY>
    </HTML>
<%
End Sub
%>
```

This page is very similar to the one we used for Custom Authentication. However, you should note that this code does *not* check the username and password – these are passed from AuthFilter to IIS for verification. The login page simply checks whether the page was submitted. If it was, an MSCSAuth ticket is issued and the browser is redirected to the originally requested URL

Also note that this code uses GET to submit the form, not POST – when control is first passed from IIS to the AuthFilter, the AuthFilter does not have access to the HTTP body, only to the URL. By using GET, the form variables are submitted in the query string of the URL, so AuthFilter can access the username and password from there.

You *can* use POST, but this requires a bit more work in the login function – control must be given to the login page before user credentials have been verified. You then set the authentication ticket and construct the URL to redirect to. You must then add the username and password, so that the URL you redirect contains a variable called proxyuser (containing the username) and proxypwd (with the password). It should look something like this:

http://mysite/myapp/somepage.asp?proxyuser=username&proxypwd=password

Before the redirect is sent to the browser, control is returned to the AuthFilter. This retrieves the username and password from the query string and stores them in the cache. It then strips off proxyuser and proxypwd before redirecting to the page requested. Once the browser issues the redirect, the username and password are in the cache and can be passed to IIS for verification. If they are correct the page can be displayed – if not, the login page is shown again.

Here is a modified login page that uses HTTP POST to submit the form:

```asp
<%
Option Explicit
%>
<!-- #INCLUDE FILE="profile_lib.asp" -->

<%
Call Main()

Sub Main()

    Dim sUserName
    Dim sPassword
    Dim oAuthManager
    Dim sRetAsp

    If Request("realSubmit") = "fromButton" Then

        Set oAuthManager = GetAuthManagerObject()
        sUsername = Request("txtUsername")
        sPassword = Request("txtPassword")

        oAuthManager.SetAuthTicket sUsername, 1, 90

        sRetAsp = Request.Cookies("MSCSFirstRequestedURL")
        If (sRetAsp = "" Or IsNull(sRetAsp)) Then
            sRetAsp = oAuthManager.GetURL("default.asp", True, False)
        End If

        sRetAsp = sRetAsp + "&proxyuser="
        sRetAsp = sRetAsp + sUsername
        sRetAsp = sRetAsp + "&proxypwd="
        sRetAsp = sRetAsp + sPassword

        Response.Redirect sRetASP
    End If

    Call DisplayPage()
End Sub

Sub DisplayPage()
%>
    <HTML>
    <BODY>
    <P>
    <FORM METHOD="POST" ACTION="login.asp" >

    Username: <INPUT TYPE="text" NAME="txtUsername" > <BR />
    Password: <INPUT TYPE="password" NAME="txtPassword" > <BR />

    <INPUT TYPE="submit" NAME="Login" VALUE="Login">
    <INPUT TYPE="hidden" NAME="realSubmit" value="fromButton">

    </FORM>
```

```
      </BODY>
      </HTML>
<%
End Sub
%>
```

Windows Authentication Mode in a Web Farm

Web farms use multiple web servers in parallel to achieve better system scalability and site availability. Using Network Load Balancing (NLB), requests are automatically distributed over the servers in the farm. In theory, this can play havoc with any system of authentication that makes use of local caching, as each request may well be served by a different machine.

Custom Authentication mode works just fine in a web farm. When the user authenticates, the MSCSAuth ticket is issued. On a subsequent request, when the user hits a new web server, the AuthFilter on this server sees that the user has a valid ticket and grants access.

As provided, Windows Authentication mode does not work in a web farm – the AuthFilter needs to supply IIS with a correct username and password; these are both cached locally when you log in for the first time. As long as you keep hitting the server you logged on to, everything is good: AuthFilter gets the valid user ID from the MSCSAuth ticket, reads the username and password from the cache, and passes them to IIS, which then grants you access to the requested page.

However, if you hit a different server, your username and password will not be in the local cache, so although the AuthFilter sees that you have a valid ticket, it cannot access the corresponding username and password to pass to IIS. We therefore need to give the AuthFilter a helping hand:

❑   When the AuthFilter gets a request, and the username and password are not in the cache, the user is redirected to the login page.

❑   The login page detects that the request for the page was not a Submit. It sees that the user has a valid MSCSAuth ticket and can get the user ID from the auth ticket.

❑   Using this user ID, the login page reads the username and password from the Profile System (or some other user store). It then creates a URL to the requested page, in a similar fashion to the POST example above, where the username and password are appended as query strings:

http://mysite/myapp/somepage.asp?proxyuser=username&proxypwd=password

❑   The login page redirects to this URL; before the redirect is sent to the browser, control is returned to the AuthFilter, which retrieves the username and password from the query string and strips off proxyuser and proxypwd before redirecting to the page requested. The username and password are stored in the local cache.

❑   On receiving the redirect, the AuthFilter can supply IIS with the username and password and access can be granted.

One problem is that if the password is stored in Active Directory it cannot be retrieved in clear text. You need to work around this by creating a property for storing passwords where the password can be read back.

Autocookie Generation Mode

Often you do not want the user to have to log in before giving them access to content. This mode allows you to track anonymous users by automatically generating a cookie that is stored on their machine. You can then personalize the content they see, and even collect information about them – in fact, if they go on to register before that cookie expires, this anonymously gathered data can be stored as part of their user profile.

The user is issued a profile ticket stored in the MSCSProfile cookie. This ticket contains a unique ID, normally a GUID. The profile cookie is persisted across sessions. You can configure the expiration date by setting the Profile Cookie Expiration Date property in the CS Authentication global resource.

When a user enters your site for the first time, without a profile ticket, the AuthFilter redirects them to an ASP file. By default this is named autocookie.asp and it is stored in the AuthFiles folder – the version installed with each of the Solution Sites is appropriate in most cases. Here is a simplified version of that file:

```
Dim oGenId
Dim sGUID
Dim oAuthManager
Dim sRetAsp

Set oGenId = Server.CreateObject("Commerce.GenID")
sGUID = oGenId.GenGUIDString()

Set oAuthManager = GetAuthManagerObject()

Call oAuthManager.SetProfileTicket(sGUID, True)

sRetAsp = Request.Cookies("MSCSFirstRequestedURL")
If (sRetAsp = "" Or IsNull(sRetAsp)) Then
    Response.Redirect "error.asp"
Else
    Response.Redirect sRetAsp
End If
```

The Commerce.GenID object is used to generate a GUID. Then the SetProfileTicket() method is called on the AuthManager object to issue a profile ticket. Finally, the user is redirected to the requested URL.

You can also store profile information in the profiling system about anonymous users. If you want to do this, you should add code to the autocookie.asp page to create the profile. Exercise caution though, as you may end up with a lot of anonymous users in your database.

Autocookie mode can also be combined with both Windows Authentication mode and Custom Authentication mode, allowing you to deal with both anonymous and registered users.

Persisting the Authentication

By design, the MSCSAuth ticket expires at the end of the session. In most cases this is a good thing: for security reasons you don't want the login to be remembered after the user closes the browser. In some cases, however, you may want the user to be automatically logged in again when returning to the site.

All cookies have an expiration date. If this date is not set, the cookie is a **session cookie** and expires at the end of the session. You can programmatically set the expiry date of the MSCSAuth cookie to a date in the future by adding the following line of code to login.asp:

```
Response.Cookies("MSCSAuth").Expires = Date+365
```

This line should be placed before redirecting to the requested page. It sets the expiry date of the cookie 365 days into the future. Note that the time window of the ticket still applies. If you want the login to be valid for one year you should also set the time window to a large value. Alter the line in login.asp that sets the ticket timeout to:

```
objAuth.SetAuthTicket strUserId, True, 60*24*365 'Number of minutes
```

You should also take steps to inform the user of the potential security risk involved in having authentication persisted on the local machine. Other users with access to the machine may enter the site and access personal data. One option is to provide the user with a checkbox to specify whether login details should be persisted, so that they can make their own choice.

Summary of Authentication Modes

As you have now seen, Commerce Server provides a lot of flexibility in its authentication support. The main problem is that it can be very difficult to choose which mode best meets your own specific needs.

It provides four main authentication modes:

❑ **No Filter** mode – allowing you to authenticate by using the AuthManager object alone.

❑ **Windows Authentication**, **Custom Authentication**, and **Autocookie Generation** modes – all of these are implemented by using an ISAPI filter called AuthFilter, which intercepts requests and redirects to ASP pages as appropriate. The AuthManager is also used in these modes, with the ASP pages providing the glue between AuthFilter and AuthManager objects. You can modify these ASP pages.

In Windows Authentication mode, IIS validates the username and password against Active Directory or a local machine account.

In Custom Authentication mode you must check that the username and password are correct.

Autocookie Generation mode can also be combined with Windows Authentication and Custom Authentication modes.

In the table below, we break down each mode by area of functionality, to summarize the main differences:

	No Filter	Windows Authentication	Custom Authentication	Autocookie Generation
Securing pages	Programm atic	Automatic	Automatic	–
Supports cookie-less authentication	Yes	No	No	No

	No Filter	Windows Authentication	Custom Authentication	Autocookie Generation
Can mix anonymous and authenticated pages	Yes	Yes	No	Yes
Single sign-on in web farm	Yes	Yes – requires code in `login.asp`	Yes	Yes
ACL controlled access to files and folders	No	Yes	No	No
Can secure static content (`.html`, `.gif`)	No	Yes	Yes	–
Can integrate with custom authentication	Yes	No	Yes	–
Allows tracking of anonymous users	Yes	No	No	Yes
Account used to access pages	`IUSR` account	User account	`IUSR` account	`IUSR` account

Profiling

A profile is a representation or abstraction of some entity. A user profile, for example, is a representation of a user containing values such as name, e-mail address, and telephone number. A book profile contains values such as title, name of the author, and ISBN number. The Profile System is the part of Commerce Server that deals with profiles – we can use it to store information about entities that are relevant to a site.

Profiles by themselves are not very interesting; it is when we integrate them with other parts of the system that they become useful – as we have seen, user profiles are typically integrated with authentication. We can then use the user profile to collect information about the authenticated user. We can even integrate the Profile System with the Targeting System and use the profile to target relevant content at the user. We'll see how to do this in the next chapter.

Commerce Server makes a distinction between profiles and profile definitions, the same distinction found in object-oriented programming, where we deal with classes and objects. A **profile definition** is the equivalent of a class; it defines the general characteristics of an entity. A **profile** is the equivalent of an object; it is the instance of a profile definition.

Commerce Server ships with a number of predefined profile definitions for typical business entities, such as user and organization profile definitions. We can extend and modify these, and we can also create your own profile definitions from scratch.

You might be inclined to ask why you should use the Profile System at all? Why not just create your own tables in SQL server and store information there? This is, of course, the old 'buy versus build' argument. Sure, you could develop your own tables and write code to deal with the entities, but the Profile System does a lot more than that. Much of the management functionality you're likely to need is provided – you even get a Business Desk for administering users and organizations. If you install the Solution Sites, you get web pages for collecting information about the users, and integration with Targeting and BIA Systems. What's more, the Commerce Server Profile System has a highly flexible architecture – implementing a system with anything like this flexibility on your own will require a great deal of work.

Firstly, a profile can span many data sources. A user profile might use Active Directory to store user ID and password, and keep shipping addresses in SQL Server.

Secondly, Commerce Server separates the logical profile from physical storage. It uses a schema to map logical properties to their physical location. This means that you can modify the physical architecture without having to modify the code that uses the profiles. All you need to do is change the mapping.

There are several ways you can get data into the Profile System. One way is to use the Business Desk. In a business-to-business scenario, an administrator would typically create the organization profiles of the organization they are dealing with. Another way is to use the web site to collect information. In a business-to-consumer scenario, the users will typically register and enter information such as name and e-mail address.

Using the BizDesk and web site to create and modify profiles are examples of **explicit profiling**. You or the users explicitly enter information into the Profile System. You can also use **implicit profiling**, and analyzing web log files to establish information about the users – you might look at how frequently users visit your site, or which products they look at. The Commerce Server Predictor can also use data mining techniques on the user information in your data warehouse to predict likely preferences. Chapter 5 describes the analysis and data mining support available in Commerce Server.

Profile System Architecture

The architecture of the Profile System in Commerce Server provides for a lot of flexibility. Commerce Server separates the physical storage of profile data and the logical schema of the profile and it allows you to span many data sources in a single profile. The main components of the Profile System are shown in the figure opposite.

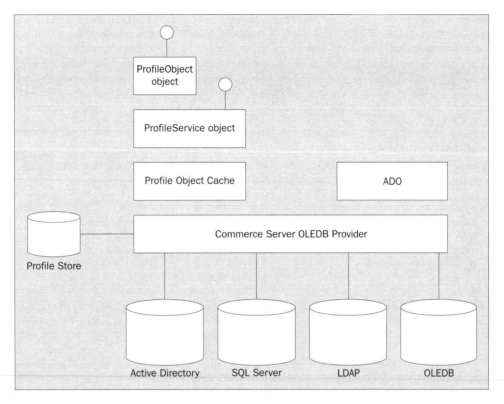

Starting from the bottom, the Profile System supports Active Directory, SQL Server, LDAP and OLE DB data sources.

It should come as no surprise that the Profile System has been optimized for access to Active Directory and SQL Server. To access third party data sources you can use LDAP v3 or an OLE DB provider.

LDAP, or Lightweight Directory Access, is the standard protocol for accessing directory services such as Active Directory, the Windows NT SAM, Novell NDS, and Site Server. Using LDAP to access Site Server Membership is an alternative if you don't want to migrate the Site Server Membership data over to Commerce Server. By keeping the data in the membership database, existing Site Server sites and new Commerce Server sites can access the same user store.

> *You can use OLE DB providers to access third party sources such as Oracle databases.*

The foundation of the Profile System architecture is the Commerce Server **OLE DB provider** (also known as the **Aggregation Manager**). The OLE DB provider supports a subset of the ANSI SQL language. Basically it accepts SELECT, INSERT, UPDATE, and DELETE statements. The OLE DB provider translates the SQL statements into the appropriate format for the physical location of the profile data. When the provider receives a profile request it splits the request up into sub-requests and passes them on to the appropriate source.

The provider aggregates all sources using a profile schema. The profile schema is stored in the Profile Store. When you create a site you specify the location of this store, typically in the main database of the site. To improve performance, the OLE DB provider caches the profile schemas.

If you want to work with many profile instances in bulk mode you can use ADO. Using ADO you can run SQL statements to update, delete or insert profile instances. You could for instance delete all users who have not used your site within the last two years.

Commerce Server provides you with two COM objects you can use in your code to work with the Profile System. The **ProfileService** object is used to connect to the Profile System. You also use this object to create, delete and retrieve `ProfileObject` objects. The **ProfileObject** object is used to work with a single profile instance. Using this object you can access and modify properties in the profile instance.

Also there is a cache that stores profiles, the `ProfileObject` cache. It caches frequently used profile instances on the web server so you don't have to hit the database on each request. Note that the caching of profile instances is in addition to the caching of profile schemas.

> The caching of profile instances on the web server can be a potential problem in a web farm. If you change profile instances, only the cache on the web server used to process the request will contain the correct profile instances. The other web servers may contain invalid profile properties.

This may or may not be a problem, depending on your scenario. If the user is refreshing the Edit Profile page, different data may be displayed each time. One way to overcome this is to always bypass the cache and read from the database. However, this has a negative impact on performance.

The Solution Sites overcome the problem by issuing a cookie whenever a profile is modified. This cookie contains a timestamp specifying when the user profile was modified. This timestamp is also stored in the profile. Whenever the profile is retrieved, the timestamp in the cookie and the timestamp in the profile are compared. If the timestamp in the cookie is newer than the timestamp in the profile, the cache is bypassed. If you want to see how this is done in the Solution Sites, examine the use of the `UserProfileTimeStamp` cookie in the `std_profile_lib.asp` page.

Predefined Profile Definitions

Commerce Server ships with a number of predefined profile definitions. These are profile definitions that are used by the Solution Sites and you can use them in your own code.

The following profile definitions are automatically made available when you create a site:

❑ User Object

❑ Organization

❑ Address

❑ BlanketPOs

❑ Targeting Context

❑ ADGroup (Supplier solution site)

When you create a commerce site, the profile definitions are created and stored in the Profile Store. The data sources are also created. The tables are created in SQL Server for the profile objects. If you unpack the Supplier solution site an organizational unit is created in Active Directory.

The two profile definitions you are most likely to work with are the User Object profile definition and the Organization profile definition. These two profile definitions have Business Desk modules to enter and modify the profile data.

The **User Object** profile definition is used to collect information about both registered users and anonymous users who come to your site. Typically, registered users will create their own profiles and anonymous users will have their profile automatically created.

To see the User Object profile definition in action, open the Users module in the Business Desk. A business administrator uses this module to manage profiles and profile data. In the Users module, select Users again to manage user profiles. Select the icon to enter a new user on the top left. You should now see a page similar to the one below:

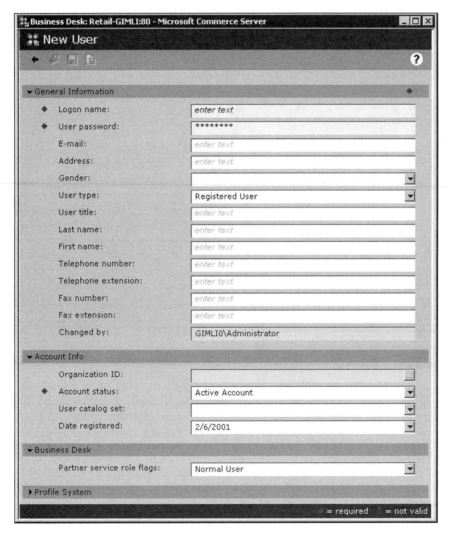

You can see that the properties of the profile definition are grouped and that the User Object profile definition contains many properties predefined. Some of the properties are mandatory, some are read-only, and some have a set of values to choose from. All this is defined in the profile definition.

This page is dynamically created from the profile definition. If you add a new property or a new property group to the User Object profile definition, it will automatically show up in the page. Refer to the Commerce Server documentation for a complete description of all available properties, and see the section *Adding a Property to the User Profile* later in this chapter for details on how to add a property.

The **Organization** profile definition is used to collect information about organizations. Below is the page for entering new organizations.

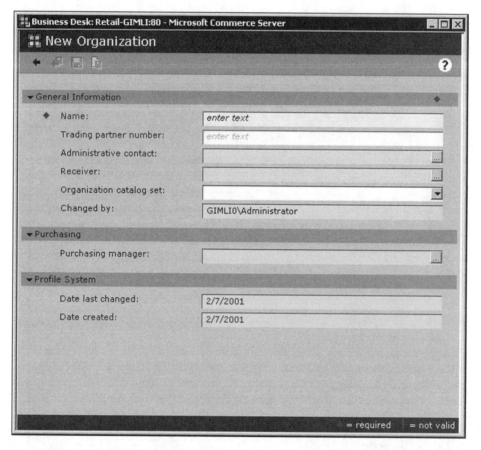

Profiling of organizations is typically used in business-to-business scenarios. We can create organizations and assign users to roles in the organization. In the form above, Administrative contact, Receiver, and Purchasing manager are examples of user roles within the organization. By clicking on the button next to the field, a dialogue for selecting a user appears. As shown in the page to manage users, an organization can also be added to a user. If we enable the partner service module in a solution site, the organizations can administer their own profiles and users.

The **Address** profile definition is used to collect information about addresses. Address profile instances can be linked to other profile definitions (such as user and organization) through the `parent_id` property of the Address profile definition. The Solution Sites use the Address profile definition to store information about shipping and billing addresses. Note that there is no BizDesk module provided for working with this profile definition.

The **BlanketPOs** profile definition is a sample profile definition you can use to collect information about purchase orders. The Solution Sites do not use it. The **Targeting Context** profile definition is used by the Targeting System to create expressions. The **ADGroup** profile definition is used in the Supplier solution site to map to Active Directory groups.

Managing the Profiles Resource

The Profiles resource is a global resource and can therefore be shared between several Commerce Server sites. As you'd expect, it's managed via the Commerce Manager – if you call up the Properties for your site's profile resource, you can modify the connection strings used to connect to various data stores and services.

You can use the Commerce Manager to manage data sources, profile definitions, and site terms. The screenshot below shows the Profiles resource for a Supplier solution site. You can see that the profile is set up with two data sources: one SQL Server source, and one Active Directory source.

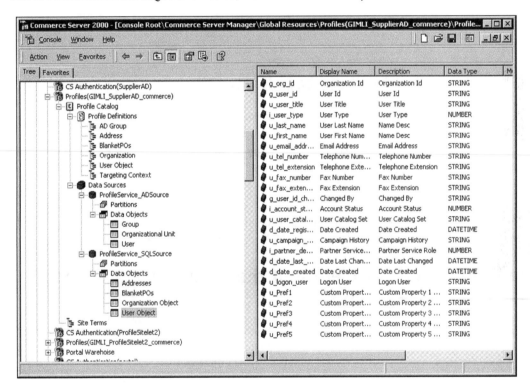

A **profile** actually consists of a number of profile definitions, along with one or more data source. A **profile definition** has several properties – for example, a User Object profile definition has a property called E-mail – which are logically organized into property groups. Each property has several attributes, such as Type (string, Boolean, number etc.), Map To Data, and Required.

A **data source** maps to a database or to an LDAP organizational unit, and consists of several **data objects**, each of which maps to a database table or to an LDAP class. The screenshot above shows three data objects in the Active Directory source, and four in the SQL source.

Finally a data object has a number of **data members**, which correspond to columns in the SQL server table and attributes in the Active Directory class. The following figure summarizes this terminology, using the User Object and its E-mail property as an example:

Mapping a profile property to a data member provides the link between the profile definition and the data source. A property is mapped to a data member by the Map To Data attribute.

The ProfileService Object and the ProfileObject Object

Commerce Server provides two COM objects that you can use to program the Profile System: ProfileService and ProfileObject. You can use these objects in your ASP pages and in your own components.

The ProfileService object is used to create, to get hold of, and to delete ProfileObject objects. The ProfileObject object is used to work with single profile instances.

Site Server has an object called the Active User Object, or AUO for short, to handle user data. The main difference between the AUO and the ProfileObject is that in Site Server the AUO is integrated with the authentication. It's there in the name: the AUO deals with the *active* user. The AUO is initialized automatically with the currently logged on user and you can then query and set properties on the object.

In Commerce Server, authentication is decoupled from the user profiles. You provide the glue that connects the authenticated user with the profile. You use the AuthManager object to get hold of the identity of the user. Then you pass the user identity in a call to the GetProfile() method on the ProfileService object to retrieve a ProfileObject object.

This section describes the profile objects in the context of working with user profiles. The code can easily be adapted to work with other profile definitions such as the Organization profile definition.

Initializing the ProfileService Object

To start using the `ProfileService` object, we must first create it and then initialize it. We initialize the object by calling the `Initialize()` method with the connect string to the profile store. To retrieve the connect string of the profile store, we can use the `AppConfig` object that ships with Commerce Server. The `AppConfig` object is used to retrieve application configuration settings as its name suggests.

The `InitProfileService()` function returns an initialized `ProfileService` object:

```
Function InitProfileService()

    Dim oAppConfig
    Dim sConnString
    Dim oProfileService

    Set oAppConfig = GetAppConfigObject ().GetOptionsDictionary("")
    sConnString = oAppConfig.s_ProfileServiceConnectionString

    Set oProfileService = Server.CreateObject("Commerce.ProfileService")
    Call oProfileService.Initialize(sConnString)

    Set InitProfileService = oProfileService

End Function
```

In the process, it calls `GetAppConfigObject()` – this returns an initialized `AppConfig` object which is used to retrieve the connection string to the profile store. The connection string is then used to initialize the `ProfileService` object. When the `Initialize()` method is called for the first time, the profile schemas are read from the profile store and cached:

```
Function GetAppConfigObject()

    Dim sSiteName
    Dim oAppConfigObject

    sSiteName = Application("MSCSCommerceSiteName")

    Set oAppConfigObject = Server.CreateObject("Commerce.AppConfig")
    Call oAppConfigObject.Initialize(sSiteName)

    Set GetAppConfigObject = oAppConfigObject

End Function
```

You could store a `ProfileService` object in the `Application` object for easy retrieval, as the Solution Sites do. Later examples in this chapter call a function named `GetProfileServiceObject()` to retrieve the `ProfileService` object from the `Application` object. The functions can be found in the `profile_lib.asp` file available as part of the code download for this book from **www.wrox.com**.

Retrieving a ProfileObject Object

To work with profile instances, we use the `ProfileService` object to retrieve `ProfileObject` objects. It has two methods to serve this purpose:

❑ `GetProfile()` uses the primary key specified in the profile definition to find the profile. It takes three parameters:

 ❑ The value used to look up the profile instance – for the user profiles this is the logon name of the user.

 ❑ The name of the profile definition – the name of user profile definition is **UserObject**.

 ❑ An optional parameter specifying if errors should be raised – if this parameter is set to `True`, the object will raise an error if no match is found.

❑ `GetProfileByKey()` takes an additional parameter, in which we specify the name of a key to be used – in case we want to use a key other than the **Logon name**. We cannot use non-key properties to retrieve profile objects. By default, only the **UserID** and **Logon name** properties are keys in the User Object. We can designate other properties as keys by setting the `Key type` attribute. We may, for example, designate the e-mail address field as a key field to be able to look up users by e-mail address.

Here is a function that uses the `GetProfile()` method to retrieve a user profile using the logon name primary key. The example sets the error parameter to `False` to specify that errors should not be raised. If there is no matching profile, the function returns `Nothing`.

```
Function GetUserProfileByLoginName(ByVal sName)

    Dim oProfileService
    Dim oProfileObject

    Set oProfileService = GetProfileServiceObject()
    Set oProfileObject = oProfileService.GetProfile(sName, "UserObject", False)

    Set GetUserProfileByLoginName = oProfileObject

End Function
```

If you want to get error messages, you should set the error parameter to `True`. You need to use `On Error Resume Next` so that the processing of the page continues. You can then read the errors from the `Errors` collection of the `ProfileService` object, as shown in the following example. The example also shows how to use the `GetProfileByKey()` function to explicitly specify the key.

```
On Error Resume Next

Set oProfileService = GetProfileServiceObject()

'Cause error to be raised by passing in wrong user ID
Set oProfileObject =
    oProfileService.GetProfileByKey("logon_name","strangeuser",_
```

```
                                            "UserObject", True)

    If oProfileService.Errors.Count <> 0 then

        For Each oError In oProfileService.Errors
            Response.Write "Error number = " & oError.Number & "<BR />"
            Response.Write "Error description = " & oError.Description & "<BR />"
            Response.Write "Error source = " & oError.Source & "<BR />"
        Next

    End If
```

> When we get a profile object it may be read from the profile object cache. If the
> underlying database has changed you will not see this change. This may happen in a web
> farm scenario or when the profile is modified outside of the site, for example using the
> Business Desk. If we want to by-pass the cache, we can call **GetInfo()** on the
> **ProfileObject** object. This reads the data from the underlying data store. Bypassing
> the cache has a negative impact on performance.

Here is an example that calls GetInfo().

```
    Set oProfileService = GetProfileServiceObject()
    Set oProfileObject = oProfileService.GetProfile(sName, "UserObject", False)

    ' By-pass profile object cache
    Call oProfileObject.GetInfo()

    ' Use profile object
```

Retrieving ProfileObject Properties

The ProfileObject object has a Fields collection with all properties available in the profile. The
Fields collection is similar to the Fields collection in an ADO recordset and supports many of the same
methods and properties. The Fields collection is a collection of groups. Each group, in turn, contains a
collection of properties. Finally, each property has a number of attributes.

There are three ways we can access the properties. Assuming we have a variable called oProfileObject,
the alternatives are:

- ❑ oProfileObject.group_name.property_name

- ❑ oProfileObject.Fields("group_name.property_name")

- ❑ oProfileObject.Fields("group_name").Value("property_name")

Here is an example that greets the user with logon name testuser with his full name. We would use the
AuthManager object to get the logon name of an authenticated user:

145

```
Set oProfileService = GetProfileServiceObject()

Set oProfileObject = oProfileService.GetProfile("testuser","UserObject", False)

If Not oProfileObject Is Nothing Then
   Response.Write "Hello "
   ' Get first name
   Response.Write oProfileObject.Fields("GeneralInfo").Value("first_name")
   Response.Write " "

   ' Get last name using extended dot notation
   Response.Write oProfileObject.Fields("GeneralInfo.last_name")
   Response.Write "<BR/>"
End If
```

Using the `Fields` collection we can enumerate all properties in a profile instance. The function
`DumpProfile()` writes out all property groups, properties and attributes in the profile instance. This
function can be useful for debugging purposes.

```
Function DumpProfile(ByVal sKeyValue, ByVal sProfileName)

   Dim oProfileService
   Dim oProfileObject
   Dim oGroup
   Dim oProperty
   Dim oAttribute

   Set oProfileService = GetProfileServiceObject()
   Set oProfileObject = oProfileService.GetProfile_
                     (sKeyValue, sProfileName, False)

   If Not oProfileObject Is Nothing Then

      Response.Write "<B>Profile Defintion for_
                  " & oProfileObject.Class & " "
      Response.Write sKeyValue & "</B><BR /><BR />"

      'Property groups
      For Each oGroup In oProfileObject.Fields

         Response.Write "<B>Group " & oGroup.Name & "</B><BR />"

         'Properties
         For Each oProperty In oGroup.Value
            Response.Write "Property " & oProperty.Name & "="
            Response.Write oProperty.Value & "<BR />"

            'Attributes
            For Each oAttribute In oProperty.Properties
               Response.Write "---" & oAttribute.Name & "="
               Response.Write oAttribute.Value & "<BR />"
            Next
```

```
            Next
         Next
      End If
   End Function
```

Creating a New User

Creating a new user is fairly simple. You call the `CreateProfile()` method on the `ProfileService` object with the primary key value (the logon name of the new user) and the name of the profile definition (**UserObject**). A `ProfileObject` is returned. We can then set properties on this object and call the `Update()` method on the `ProfileObject` to save the changes.

> When we create a new profile, the profile lives in the Profile object cache. It is not written to the data stores until we call the `Update()` method.

The `CreateUserProfile()` function below creates a new user profile. It takes the username and password as input parameters. The function returns `True` if the user is successfully created. `False` is returned if the user already exists. If an error occurred, an error is raised.

This function is included in the `profile_lib.asp` file, which may be downloaded from the Wrox website. A simple registration page, `newuser.asp`, is also included. This page uses the `CreateUserProfile()` function.

```
Function CreateUserProfile(ByVal sUsername, ByVal sPassword)

    Dim oProfileService
    Dim oProfileObject

    Set oProfileService = GetProfileServiceObject()

    'Verify if user already exists
    Set oProfileObject = oProfileService.GetProfile_
                        (sUserName, "UserObject", False)

    If Not oProfileObject Is Nothing Then
        'User already exists
        CreateUserProfile = False
        Exit Function
    End If
```

There are a few issues to deal with when creating a new user. First of all, if the logon name already exists, we should inform the user. If we call `CreateProfile()` with a primary key that already exists, an error is raised with an error number and error description indicating that the user already exists. The function explicitly checks if a user with the same logon name already exists before creating the user.

```
    On Error Resume Next
    Set oProfileObject = oProfileService.CreateProfile_
```

147

```
                                        (sUsername, "UserObject")

    If Err.number <> 0 then

        Dim nErrNumber, sErrSource, sErrDesc

        nErrNumber  = Err.Number
        sErrSource  = Err.Source
        sErrDesc    = Err.Description

        'If profile already exist an error code of 'C100400B' is returned.
        'In this case we should not delete the profile
        If Hex(Err.number) <> "C100400B" Then
           'If error occured and we have multiple sources in the profile
           'we may need to clean up.
           'The error returned from DeleteProfile should be ignored
           Call oProfileService.DeleteProfile(sUsername, "UserObject")
        End If

        CreateUserProfile = False
        Err.Raise nErrNumber, sErrSource, sErrDesc
    End If
```

Another issue is that if our profile spans several data sources, we may need to manually undo changes if an error occurred when creating a new profile instance. The `CreateUserProfile()` function handles this by calling `DeleteProfile()` if an error occurred.

We can set up a profile definition to be transactional. If our data sources are transactional, the changes will be automatically rolled back. If you have one transactional and one non-transactional store, the non-transactional store will be written to last. If an error occurred when writing to this store, the transactional store will be rolled back. If you have two non-transactional stores, you need to clean up manually.

The profile instance should not be deleted if the error was caused by an already existing profile with the same key or you would inadvertently delete the existing profile. This should not happen, since we check if the user exists before creating it. In theory, however, two requests to create the same user may run at the same time. To be on the safe side, the code explicitly checks if creating a profile with the same key as an existing profile caused the error.

```
    'Set profile properties
    oProfileObject.GeneralInfo.user_type = 1 'REGISTERED_PROFILE
    oProfileObject.GeneralInfo.user_security_password = sPassword
    oProfileObject.AccountInfo.date_registered = Now()
    oProfileObject.AccountInfo.account_status = 1 'ACCOUNT_ACTIVE
    oProfileObject.ProfileSystem.date_last_changed = Now()
    oProfileObject.BusinessDesk.partner_desk_role = 1

    Call oProfileObject.Update()

    If Err.number <> 0 then
       CreateUserProfile = False
    Else
       CreateUserProfile = True
    End If

End Function
```

After creating the profile we populate the profile. Finally, Update() is called on the ProfileObject object to store the data.

Modifying a User

By now, you probably already know that to modify an existing user profile, you retrieve a ProfileObject, set properties on this object, and call Update() on the profile object. Here is an example that changes the first name and the last name of a user with logon name testuser. The date_last_changed property is also set.

```
Set oProfileService = GetProfileServiceObject()

Set oProfileObject = oProfileService.GetProfile("testuser","UserObject", False)

If Not oProfileObject Is Nothing Then
    oProfileObject.GeneralInfo.first_name = "Test2"
    oProfileObject.GeneralInfo.last_name = "User2"
    oProfileObject.ProfileSystem.date_last_changed = Now()
    Call oProfileObject.Update()
End If
```

Available for download is a sample page, modify_user.asp, that enables a logged on user to modify the profile. One thing you should note is that if you allow the user to change the logon name, you should issue a new authentication ticket since the ticket contains the logon name.

Deleting a User

To delete a user, we can call the DeleteProfile() method or the DeleteProfileByKey() method.

The DeleteProfile() method uses the primary key specified in the profile definition to find the profile to delete. It takes two parameters:

❑ The value of the primary key. For the user profiles this is the logon name of the user.

❑ The name of the profile definition. The name of user profile definition is UserObject.

The DeleteProfileByKey() method takes an additional parameter where we specify the name of the key to use. This allows us to use a key other than the primary key.

Here is an example of using the DeleteProfile() method to delete a specified profile.

```
Set oProfileService = GetProfileServiceObject()

Call oProfileService.DeleteProfile("testuser","UserObject")
```

If the profile object is not found, an error is raised by the DeleteProfile() method.

Other Methods

The ProfileService object and the ProfileObject object also implement other methods we have not yet discussed.

The `ProfileService` object has a method named `GetProfileDefXML()` that we can use to retrieve an XML schema representation of the profile definitions. This method takes two parameters:

❑ The name of the profile definition. If this is blank, all profile definitions are returned.

❑ A Boolean indicating if only the name of the profile definitions should be returned (`True`) or if all the properties should be returned (`False`).

The `BindAs()` method can be used to specify the username and password to use to access the underlying data store. Use the `UnBind()` method to revert to using the credentials of the Profile System.

Finally, the `ProfileObject` object also has some XML support. Using the `GetProfileXML()` method we can retrieve an XML representation of a profile instance. The method takes two parameters:

❑ A value specifying if both the XML schema and the XML data should be returned (1), if only the XML data should be returned (2), or if only the XML schema should be returned (3).

❑ A Boolean specifying if the XML should be returned with properties as attributes (`True`) or as elements (`False`).

Here is an example of an XML returned by calling `GetProfileXML(2, True)`. Note that empty fields are not returned.

```
<?xml version="1.0" ?>
<ProfileDocument>
  <UserObject>
  <AccountInfo account_status="1" date_registered="2001- 2-10T 0: 0: 0" />
    <BusinessDesk partner_desk_role="1" />
      <GeneralInfo user_id="{CF0F8CE4-D3B7-431B-8B33-A5190319396A}"
      logon_name="billg" user_security_password="password"
      email_address="billg@microsoft.com" user_type="1" last_name="Gates"
      first_name="Bill" user_id_changed_by="GIMLI0\Administrator"
      Address="One Microsoft Way" />
    <ProfileSystem date_last_changed="2001- 2-17T20:40:33"
    date_created="2001- 2-10T 0: 0: 0" />
  </UserObject>
</ProfileDocument>
```

Working With Other Profile Definitions

The preceding examples have used the **UserObject** profile definition. We can easily use similar code to work with other profile definitions. All we have to do is use the name of the profile definition:

❑ Address

❑ Organization

❑ BlanketPOs

❑ TargetingContext

Here is an example that creates a new organization profile:

```
Set oProfileService = GetProfileServiceObject()
```

```
Set oProfileObject = oProfileService.CreateProfile("Objectware","Organization")

Call oProfileObject.Update()
```

Site Terms

A site term is similar to an enumeration type in many programming languages. It can be used to limit the value of a property to specific values. Typical examples of site terms are Size (S, M, L, and XL) and Color (red, green, blue, and so on).

We can specify the type of a profile property to be a site term. If we want to know the gender of the users, we can create a site term named Gender with the possible values Male and Female. We can then add a property called User Gender to the UserObject profile definition.

The Commerce Server Solution Sites install a few predefined site terms. There are three User Site Terms:

❑   Account Status (Active Account, Inactive Account)

❑   User Role (Normal User, Administrator)

❑   User Type (Guest User, Registered User)

There are also two Calendar Site Terms:

❑   Days (Sunday, Monday, …)

❑   Months (January, February, …)

We can modify existing site terms and add new site terms using the Site Terms Editor. We would probably not add values to the Days and Months site terms, but there is nothing stopping us from doing this. It is always good to be able to add extra days and months when the project deadline is just around the corner!

The Site Terms Editor is available in the Users module in the Business Desk. Using the editor we can create site terms groups to organize the site terms logically. We can create new site terms and add values to existing site terms. Overleaf is a screen shot where a new Gender site term has been added.

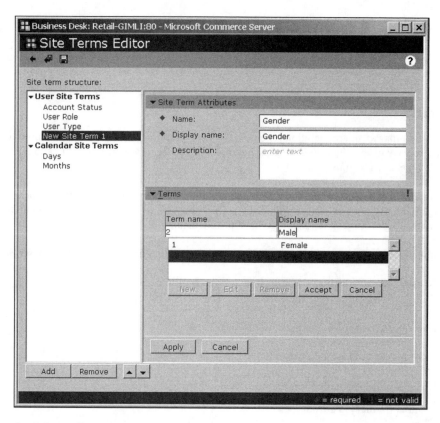

If you use the Solution Sites, site terms added to the user profile are automatically displayed in the Edit Profile page.

If you want to display a site term in a drop-down list in your own code, you can use the following `WriteSiteTermOptions()` function:

```
Public Function WriteSiteTermOptions(ByVal sSiteTerm)

    Dim oAppConfig, oBizData, oSiteTerms
    Dim sConnString, sSearch, sName, sValue
    Dim oXMLProperty, oXMLTerms, oXMLTerm

    'Get connect string to biz data store
    Set oAppConfig = GetAppConfigObject().GetOptionsDictionary("")
    sConnString = oAppConfig.s_BizDataStoreConnectionString

    'Connect to Profile Store
    Set oBizData = CreateObject("Commerce.BusinessDataAdmin")
    Call oBizData.Connect(sConnString)

    'Get all site terms
    Set oSiteTerms = oBizData.GetProfile("Site Terms.MSCommerce")

    'Get specified site term
    sSearch = ".//Property[@name = '" & sSiteTerm & "']"
    Set oXMLProperty = oSiteTerms.documentElement.selectSingleNode(sSearch)
```

```
    If Not oXMLProperty Is Nothing Then

        Response.Write "<SELECT NAME=""" & sSiteTerm & """>"

        'Get all attributes
        Set oXMLTerms = oXMLProperty.selectNodes("./Attribute")

        'Iterate attributes
        For Each oXMLTerm In oXMLTerms
            sName = oXMLTerm.getAttribute("displayName")
            sValue = oXMLTerm.getAttribute("value")
            If IsNull(sValue) Or IsEmpty(sValue) Or (sValue = "") Then
                sValue = oXMLTerm.getAttribute("name")
            End If

            'Write option
            Response.Write "<OPTION VALUE=""" & sValue & """>"
            Response.Write sName & "</OPTION>"

        Next

        Response.Write "</SELECT>"

    End If

End Function
```

The function takes as input the name of the site term to display. The function uses the `GetProfile()` method of the `BusinessDataAdmin` object to retrieve an XML representation of the site terms. This XML contains all the site terms in the profile store. An XPATH query is used to retrieve the XML Property element with a name attribute equal to the name of the site term. The `selectSingleNode()` method returns the XML in a `XMLDOMNode` object. The XML returned looks like this:

```
<Property xmlns="urn:schemas-microsoft-com:bizdata-profile-schema"
  name="Gender" displayName="Gender" propType="STRING">
    <Attribute name="1" displayName="Female" />
    <Attribute name="2" displayName="Male" />
</Property>
```

Finally, all the `Attribute` elements of the site term are enumerated and written to the page.

Adding a Property to the User Profile

Using the Business Desk we can modify the user profile to collect more information about the users. We can remove properties, modify existing properties and add new properties.

Suppose we wanted to add a `Gender` property to the user profile. The following steps may be taken.

1. Modify the commerce database by creating a column named u_user_gender in the `UserObject` table.

2. Add a new User Gender data member to the `UserObject` data object using the Commerce Server Manager.

3. Create a Gender site term with the possible values Male and Female using the Business Desk as described in the previous section.

4. Add the Gender property to the profile definition. This property should be set up to map to the data member created in Step 2. Set the type reference to the Gender site term created in Step 3.

The next section shows how to create new data members. An alternative is to skip Steps 1 and 2, instead using one of the spare data members in the User Object data object. The UserObject has five unused custom property strings.

Assuming we have already created the Gender site term, we can add a Gender property to the User Object profile definition by using the Business Desk. Open the User Object in the profile designer and select Add and then Add new property. Fill out the following attributes:

- ❑ Set the Name attribute to the name you are going to use to refer to the property in code, for example, user-gender.

- ❑ Set Display name and Description.

- ❑ In the Type drop-down list, select Site Term.

- ❑ Click the button next to the Type reference field. In the Site Term Selection dialog, select the Gender site term.

- ❑ Under Advanced Attributes, click the button next to the Map to data field. In the Data Source Picker dialog, select one of the spare custom properties as shown in the screen shot below. Click OK.

- ❑ Click Apply and then click the save icon to save the new property.

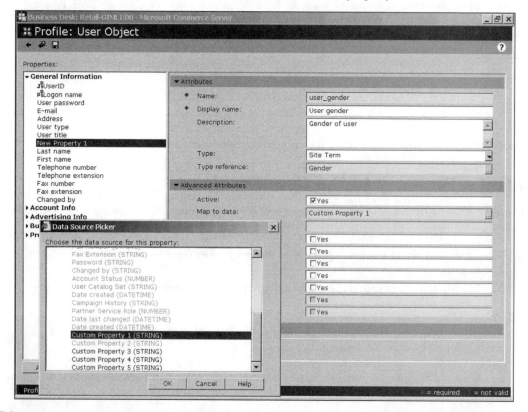

We have now created a new property we can use to store the user's gender.

> If we want the user to be able to view or modify this property in a solution site, it is necessary to set the **sUserAccess** attribute. This attribute is found under Custom Attributes in the profile designer. Set **sUserAccess** to 1 to make the property visible, but read only. Set **sUserAccess** to 2 to allow users to edit the property. Finally, to refresh the profile definition cache, select **Publish Profiles** in the **Users** module in the Business Desk.

We can also create a property that is not mapped to any data member. This type of property only lives in the profile cache. This should be used with caution. If we have a web farm, the property will get out-of-sync. The property will also be lost when the web server is restarted.

Creating a New Profile Definition

Up until now we have seen how we can work with the existing profile definitions in Commerce Server. We have seen examples of programming with the User Object profile definition and the Organization profile definition. We have also seen how to extend the User Object profile definition with new properties.

The Profile System enables us to create our own profile definitions to collect information about entities relevant to a solution. We may ask ourselves why we should want to do this. Why not just create our own tables and then write code and components that use the tables? Before we do this, consider the following:

- ❑ Using the Profile System, we create a layer between our logical profile and the physical location of our profile data. This allows us to change where data is stored, potentially without modifying a single line of code.

- ❑ The Profile System caches profile data. Developing your own caching mechanism is perhaps something you don't fancy doing.

- ❑ A Business Administrator can extend the profile definition. If you plan for extensibility by providing some spare members in your database, this can be done without altering the database or adding code.

On the other hand, there are some things you should be aware of when considering whether to use the Profile System:

- ❑ The Profile System does not support many-to-many relationships. If you want many-to-many relationships between profiles, you need to add your own tables. A user, for instance, can only be member of one organization.

- ❑ Creating the layer between your logical profile and the physical location of the profile data means there is some work to be done. You must create the profile definition in addition to the data structure. In this section, we look at how to do this.

As showed in the figure in the section *Managing the Profiles Resource*, there are many pieces that go into making a profile definition. To create a new profile definition there are several steps we need to complete:

5. Decide where we want to store the data.

6. Create the database structure.

7. Define the data source.

8. Define the data object.

9. Define the data members.

10. Create a profile definition.

11. Add properties to the profile definition.

12. Create site terms and add site terms to the profile definition.

To see how we can create new profile definitions, we will create a Subscription profile. This is a simple profile definition for managing e-mail subscriptions. A subscribed user receives information by e-mail and the profile stores information about the subscription. The Subscription profile is generalized to also handle other delivery channels, such as sending a message to a cell phone.

Typically, we would link the subscription profile to the user profile. The user should be allowed to modify the subscription profile to control the sending of mail. The profile can later be integrated with the Direct Mailer to control the mail campaigns.

The Subscription profile is defined to have the following properties:

❑ Subscription ID.

❑ Subscription channel. The user can select the delivery channel. Examples are e-mail or cell phone.

❑ Subscription address. For e-mail subscriptions, this will be the e-mail address. For cell phone subscriptions, this will be the cell phone number.

❑ E-mail format. This should be the formats supported by the Direct Mailer, which are plain text, MHTML or MIME.

❑ Active flag. The subscription can be activated and deactivated.

By making this a separate profile, and not just including it in the user profile, we increase the potential for re-use. You may want to add more than one Subscription profile for each user, for example one for news items and one for product updates. To add two Subscription profiles, we need to add two properties, each one referencing the Subscription profile.

The Subscription channel and e-mail format properties will be defined as site terms. This allows us to add more channels and formats as they become available.

Step 1: Decide Where to Store the Data

First you need to define where you want to store the data. Commerce Server supports OLE DB database or LDAP sources. For the Subscription profile we use SQL Server.

Step 2: Create the Database Structure

We need a single table to store the subscription data. The table could be stored in the database along with the other tables used by the Profile System. This database is by default called commerce_<sitename>. We could also store it in a different database.

Use whatever tool you prefer to create the new table. You could, for instance, use the SQL Server Enterprise Manager. Using the Enterprise Manager we can right click on the Tables node and select New Table... This brings up a dialog where we can enter the columns. The following screenshot shows the columns for the Subscription profile. Note that the u_subscription_id column is set as primary key.

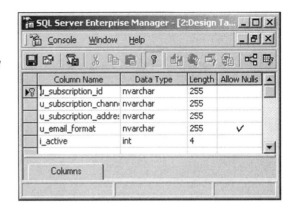

When we save the table we are prompted for a name. Give the table a suitable name, for example. SubscriptionObject.

Step 3: Define the Data Source

If you have decided to use the existing profile database, you don't have to define a new data source: you can use the existing ProfileService_SQLSource, in which case, skip to the next step. If you have stored the table in a different database, you must define the database as a data source in the Commerce Server Manager.

To create a new data source, find the profiles resource for your site in the Commerce Server Manager and navigate down to Data Sources. Right click and select New Data Source... A wizard opens. This wizard has three main screens and some additional screens for defining data source connection strings.

In the first screen, give the source a name and a display name. Use whatever name you like. You can also give the data source a description. Press Next.

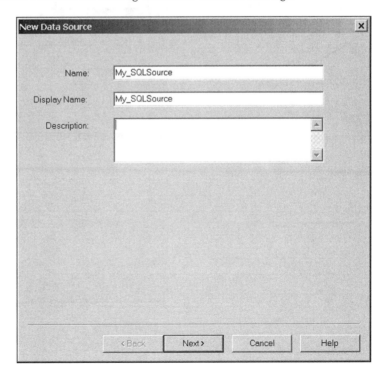

In the second screen select the source type. You can select LDAPv3 compliant source or OLE DB-ANSI Provider. Select the OLE DB-ANSI Provider to use SQL Server as the data source.

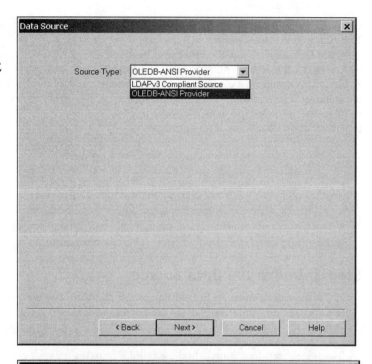

In the third screen, we add a partition to the data source. In most cases, we would add a single partition. The screenshot below shows the dialog after a partition has been added.

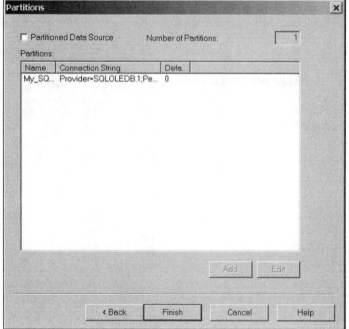

Select Add to add a data source partition. The dialog window, shown here, is then displayed. We can give the data source partition a name. Select Edit to edit the connection string. If you have selected the OLE DB source type, you can now select the OLE DB provider, the database and the credentials to use when accessing the database. If you selected the LDAP source type, you can enter the LDAP server and port number. In both cases, the result is a connection string to the data source.

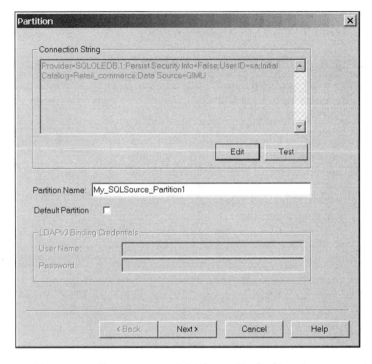

To achieve better scalability, we can partition our profiles over several databases. To do this, it is necessary to create multiple partitions. We must also define one of the profile keys to be a hashing key. For the Subscription profile definition, one data partition is sufficient.

When we select Next in the Partition dialog, we can add custom attributes. Select Finish in the Custom Attributes dialog. Select Finish in the Partitions dialog.

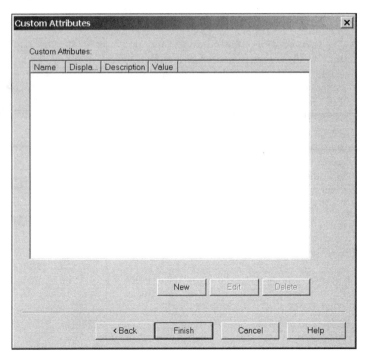

You now have a new SQL Server data source defined. If you select **Properties** on the data source you can modify the settings entered in the wizard.

Step 4: Define the Data Object

Next, we need to define the subscription data object. We do this in the Commerce Server Manager by navigating to **Data Objects** under the data source you created in Step 3. Right-click and select **New Data Object...**

We can now select the database table to use. Select the table you created in Step 2 (in this case, `SubscriptionObject`). You should now see the columns in the table. Enter a **Display Name** and a **Description** for the data object and select **OK**.

Step 5: Define the Data Members

We then need to define data members that map to the columns created in Step 2. Right-click on the data object defined in Step 4 and select **New Data Member**. For each member we want to define, we select the member; give it a display name and a description, and select **Add**. The data type of the column in the database gives the possible data types for the member. The nvarchar types map to String, and the int datatype can be defined as Boolean or Number.

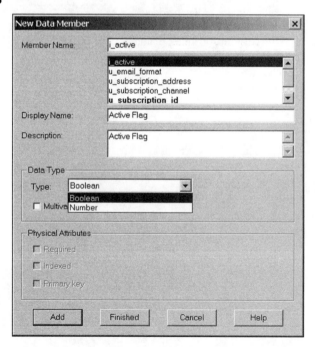

The table below shows the data members needed for the Subscription profile definition.

Name	Display Name	Data Type
i_active	Active Flag	Boolean
u_email_format	Email Format	String
u_subscription_address	Subscription Address	String
u_subscription_channel	Subscription Channel	String
u_subscription_id	Subscription Id	String

Step 6: Add Profile Definition

We have now created the database structure, the data source, the data object, and the data members. We have now completed the lower half of the puzzle illustrated in the figure in the *Managing the Profiles Resource* section.

The next step is to create the profile definition. We do this in the Commerce Server Manager. Navigate to Global Resources | Profiles (Site Name) | Profile Catalog | Profile Definitions. Right-click on Profile Definition and select New Profile... A wizard with two screens opens. In the first screen, give the profile definition a name and a description as shown in the screenshot here. In the second screen, we may add custom attributes. Select Finish.

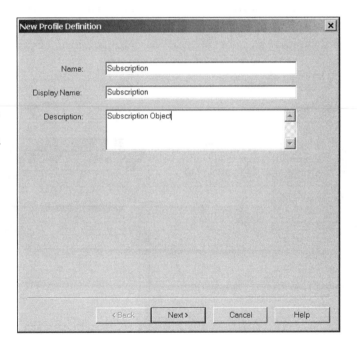

Step 7: Add Properties to a Profile Definition

We are now ready to add properties to the profile definition. This can be done using the Commerce Server Manager or using the Business Desk. In both cases the interface is the same. We encountered this interface when adding a property to a user profile.

Some properties can be designated as key properties. Commerce Server defines the following key types:

❑ **Primary key** – this is the default key used when retrieving profile objects. Set the primary key attribute on the property most often used to reference the profile.

- ❑ **Join key** – a join key is mapped to a data member for each underlying data source. The value of each data member must be the same to be able to join the data source together. If we do not provide a value for the join key when we create a profile instance, a value is automatically generated.

- ❑ **Dual key** – a key that is both a primary key and a join key.

- ❑ **Unique key** – set a property as unique key to be able to retrieve profile objects using the property. The Profile System does not guarantee uniqueness.

Every profile definition must contain a primary key and a join key, or alternatively a dual key.

Open the Profile Designer in the Business Desk. Select Subscription and then Open. We can now add property groups and properties. Create a property group called General Information. Add the following properties:

Name	Display Name	Type	Map to data	Key Type
subscription_id	Subscription Id	String	Subscription Id	Dual key
subscription_channel	Subscription Channel	String	Subscription Channel	
subscription_address	Subscription Address	String	Subscription Address	
email_format	Email Format	String	Email Format	
Active	Active Flag	Boolean	Active Flag	

The following screenshot shows the profile designer after all properties have been added.

Step 8: Create Site Terms and Add Site Terms to the Profile Definition

Finally, we may want to add site terms to limit the values for the Email Format and Subscription Channel properties. This is described in the section *Site Terms* earlier in this chapter. We should also create a site term group to group the site terms for the Subscription profile definition:

❑   Add a new site term group named Subscription Site Terms.

❑   Add a site term named Email Format. Add the values Plain text (1), MIME (2), and MHTML (3).

❑   Add a site term named Delivery Channel. Add the values E-mail (1) and Cell phone (2).

To add the site terms to the Subscription profile, we need to follow these steps:

❑   Open the Profile Designer.

❑   Select the Email Format property and change the type from String to Site Term.

❑   Click the button next to Type Reference and select Email Format from the Site Term Selection dialog box.

❑   Click OK, and then click Apply.

❑   Save the changes.

Do the same to add the Delivery Channel site term to the Subscription Channel property.

Profile Definitions Containing Other Profile Definitions

A profile definition can contain references to other profile definitions. Take the user profile definition as an example. It references the Organization profile definition and can also be modified to reference the address profile definition and the Subscription profile definition we created above.

To add the Subscription profile definition to the User Object profile definition, we simply create a new property in the User Object profile definition. Give this property a name, for example user_subscription. Set the attribute named Type to Profile and the attribute named Type reference to the Subscription profile definition. Finally, we must map the user_subscription property to a data member with the appropriate data type.

The downside of this is that the Business Desk and the Solution Sites do not automatically give us a page to enter Subscription information. If the Gender property is of a string type, a text field will be provided where we can fill in the ID of the Subscription profile. We should modify this and provide a page to enter Subscription information.

Profile Definitions using Multiple Stores – Active Directory and SQL Server

We have seen how we can use SQL Server to store profile data. We have also read that a single profile can span several data sources, and that we can store profile data in Active Directory or an LDAP v3 compliant data source.

The Supplier solution site has Active Directory integration set up for us. We look at the Supplier solution site in detail in Chapter 10. In that chapter, we also look into when we should use Active Directory, and what data we should store in Active Directory.

Typically, we would integrate an Active Directory based user profile with Windows Authentication mode. Windows Authentication mode allows mixing anonymous and registered access to the same site. This is similar to the way that we specify which files and folders to grant anonymous access to using Site Server. In Commerce Server we do this the IIS way: we use the Internet Services Manager to specify which files to allow anonymous access to. Then we use Windows Explorer to grant read access to specific users or groups of users on selected files and directories.

In this section, we will see how to modify a SQL Server based profile definition and place the user credentials in Active Directory. Most of the profile information will still be in SQL Server, but the profile definition spans both SQL Server and Active Directory. To do this, we will:

❑   Define the Active Directory data source in Commerce Server.

❑   Define a new data object in Commerce Server that maps to the user Active Directory class.

❑   Define data members in Commerce Server that maps to Active Directory attributes.

❑   Modify the profile definition to use the defined data members.

For a profile definition to span several data objects, we must define one of the properties as a join key. This property must be mapped to a data member in each of the data objects being joined.

Step 1: Decide Where to Store the Data and Create the Data Structure

This section assumes that you already have Active Directory set up and an unmodified UserObject profile definition based on SQL Server.

Your Active Directory should contain an organizational unit where you want to store your users. The example that follows assumes you have Active Directory with an organizational unit named **Wrox**, which in turn contains an organizational unit named **UK**. The relative distinguished name (RDN) of the container is then OU=UK,OU=Wrox.

Step 2: Define the Data Source

The next thing we must do is to define an Active Directory data source in Commerce Server. This is almost the same as we did in Step 3 in the section *Creating a New Profile Definition*, except we select the LDAP data source and the appropriate connection string and credentials. Do the following (refer to the screenshots in the section *Creating a New Profile Definition*).

1.   Give the data source a name and a display name.

2.   In the Data Source dialog window, select LDAPv3 Compliant Source.

3.   In the Partitions dialog select Add to add a new partition.

4.   In the Partition dialog window, enter the username and password of a user with access to Active Directory.

5.   To edit the connection string; select Edit in the Partition dialog window. In the LDAP Connection String dialog window, enter the name of your domain server, as shown in the following screenshot:

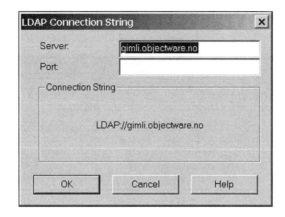

6. In the **System Attributes** dialog, fill in the Parent URL. This is the relative distinguished name (RDN) of the Active Directory container where we want to store the users, for example OU=UK, OU=Wrox. You may also want to check the **Use the same credentials for all users** check-box. The Profile System will then use the username and password you entered in the **Partition** dialog to access Active Directory. Otherwise the credentials of the calling process will be used to access Active Directory. In the **Domain Name** field, enter the name of your Active Directory server.

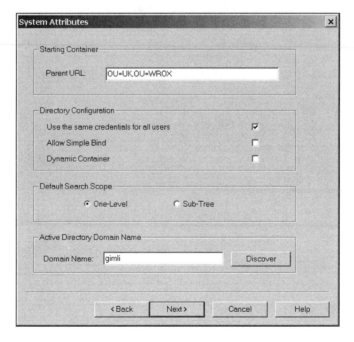

7. In the Custom Attributes dialog, add a custom property named defaultNamingContext and give it the value of the distinguished name (DN) of your Active Directory domain. This attribute is used by the Business Desk application. If you do not intend to use the Business Desk, you do not need to add this property.

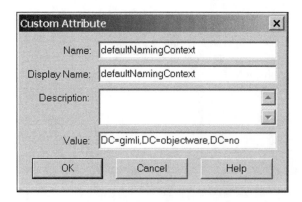

You now have a new Active Directory data source defined. If you select Properties on the data source, you can modify the settings entered in the wizard.

Step 3: Define the Data Object

We next need to create a new data object that maps to the user Active Directory class. This is similar to Step 4 in the section entitled *Creating a New Profile Definition*. Select the user Active Directory class as Object Name and give the data object a display name, for example User, as shown in the following screen shot.

Step 4: Define the Data Members

We then need to define data members that map to Active Directory attributes. We should add the following data members:

Name	Display Name	Data Type
cn	Logon Name	STRING
unicodePwd	User Password	STRING

Name	Display Name	Data Type
sAMAccountName	SAMAccount Name	STRING
userAccountControl	User Account Control	NUMBER

You may also want to map other attributes such as name and telephone number to Active Directory.

Step 5: Modify the Profile Definition

The next step is to modify the profile definition. You can do this using the Profile Designer in the Commerce Server Manager or by using the Business Desk. Select the User Object profile definition. You need to modify the attributes for some of the properties. Do the following:

1. The UserId property is a GUID. Leave it mapped to SQL Server, but make it a unique key instead of a join key.

2. We will join the SQL Server user data and Active Directory user data by using the logon name. Make the Logon name property a dual key. This means that logon name will be both the primary key and the join key. Map the Logon Name property to Logon Name in both the AD source and in the SQL source. You can select multiple data members by holding down the *Ctrl* key.

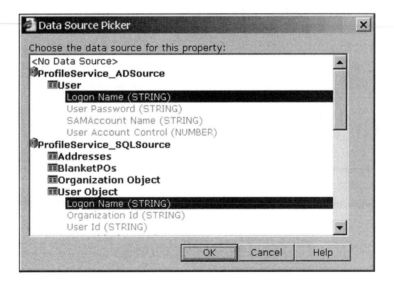

3. Map the User Password property to User Password in Active Directory.

4. Create a new property named sam_account_name and map it to the SAMAccount Name data member in the Active Directory data source. Also, create a new property named user_account_control and map it to the User Account Control data member in the Active Directory source. These properties should be placed in the Profile System group. The user will not control these properties, so you should set them to inactive by unchecking the Active attribute.

5. Create a new property named `ParentDN` with type String. This property should not be mapped to any data member. It should be set to inactive. This property is used by the Business Desk application to check if the profiled definition uses Active Directory.

The following table summarizes the changes in the profile definition. Italics are used to indicate new or changed values.

Display Name	Name	Type	Map to data	Key type	Active
UserID	`user_id`	String	User Id (SQL)	*Unique Key*	No
Logon name	`logon_name`	String	*Logon Name (AD)* *Logon Name (SQL)*	*Dual Key*	Yes
User password	`user_password`	Password	*User Password (AD)*	-	Yes
SAM Account Name	`sam_account_ name`	*String*	*SAMAccount Name (AD)*	-	*No*
User Account Control	`user_account_ control`	*Number*	*User Account Control (AD)*	-	*No*
ParentDN	`ParentDN`	*String*	-	-	*No*

Making the Business Desk Work

If you have followed the steps up to now you have a User Object that spans Active Directory and SQL Server with user credentials stored in Active Directory. This is all we have to do to create the profile definition. It should work fine in your own code. However, if you try to create users in the Business Desk, you will get errors. The Users module in the Business Desk application makes certain assumptions about the UserObject profile definition. The steps so far have already implemented two changes to make the Users module work:

❑ The `defaultNamingContext` custom attribute was added to the Active Directory data source.

❑ The `ParentDN` property was added to the UserObject profile definition.

You need to make one more change to make the Users module work. The Business Desk code assumes there is a profile definition named ADGroup in the Profile System. It uses this profile definition to get the name of the container where the users should be stored. In our case this is OU=UK, OU=Wrox. This is the value we entered in the Parent URL field in the data source definition.

The Supplier solution site installs the ADGroup profile definition. We can create this profile definition using the Commerce Server Manager.

Another alternative is to make the Business Desk code use the UserObject profile definition to read the name of the container. You need to modify line 58 of the common\XMLRoutines.asp file in the business desk application. The line:

```
const AD_PROFILE = "Profile Definitions.ADGroup "
```

should be changed to:

```
const AD_PROFILE = "Profile Definitions.UserObject"
```

Now you should have a fully functional Business Desk. You should be able to use it to create new users and modify existing users.

Making the Retail Solution Site Work

If you have made the changes described above to a profile resource used by a retail solution site, you need to modify the page for registering new users.

When you create new users in Active Directory, you need to set the SAM account name of the user. This name must be unique in your directory, and can be a maximum of 20 characters. For simplicity, we use the login name.

You must also activate the user account in Active Directory by setting the userAccountControl attribute. Setting this to 512 activates the account.

Add the following lines of code to the mscsNewRegisteredUserProfile() function in the login/newuser.asp file.

```
mscsUser.Fields(GetQualifiedName(PROFILE_SYSTEM_GROUP,_
              "sam_account_name")).Value = sLoginName
mscsUser.Fields(GetQualifiedName(PROFILE_SYSTEM_GROUP,_
              "user_account_control")).Value = 512
```

If you get an error when creating a new user or when logging in, this may be caused by insufficient access rights to Active Directory. Set the account used for anonymous access in Internet Services Manager to an account with sufficient rights to access Active Directory.

> **You need to set the anonymous account for the pages accessing the user profile to an account with access to Active Directory. In the Retail Solution Sites this is the login\login.asp page and the login\newuser.asp page.**

Using ADO to Query the Profile System

The ProfileService object and the ProfileObject object can be used to program the Profile System. Using the ProfileObject object, we can work with single profile instances.

To work with many profile instances in bulk mode, we can use ADO and the Commerce Server OLE DB provider. Using ADO, we can run SQL statements to update, delete or insert profile instances. The Commerce Server OLE DB provider supports a subset of the ANSI SQL language. We can run simple SELECT, INSERT, UPDATE, and DELETE statements.

The `QueryProfileSystem()` function below takes a SQL statement as parameter, executes the SQL statement, and returns an ADO recordset.

```
Function QueryProfileSystem(ByVal sQuery)

    Dim rsProfiles
    Dim oAppConfig
    Dim sConnString
    Dim oConnection

    ' Get connect string to Profile System
    Set oAppConfig = GetAppConfigObject().GetOptionsDictionary("")
    sConnString = oAppConfig.s_CommerceProviderConnectionString
    Set oAppConfig = Nothing

    ' Open connection
    Set oConnection = Server.CreateObject("ADODB.Connection")
    oConnection.ConnectionString = sConnString
    Call oConnection.Open

    ' Run query
    Set rsProfiles = CreateObject("ADODB.Recordset")
    rsProfiles.Open sQuery, oConnection

    Set QueryProfileSystem = rsProfiles

End Function
```

This function is provided in the `profile_lib.asp` include file, which can be downloaded along with the rest of the code for this book from `http://www.wrox.com`.

The function reads the connection string to the Profile System using the `AppConfig` object. It then uses straight ADO code to execute the SQL statement. The connection string has the following format:

```
url=mscop://InProcConnect/Server=servername:Database=Retail_commerce:Catalog=Profi
le Definitions:User=userid:Password=pwd:
```

Here is a simple example that lists all users whose first name begins with t. The users are ordered by last name.

```
Dim rsUsers
Dim sQuery

sQuery = "SELECT [GeneralInfo.user_id], [GeneralInfo.logon_name], " &_
    " [GeneralInfo.email_address], [GeneralInfo.last_name], " &_
    " [GeneralInfo.first_name], [ProfileSystem.date_created] " &_
    " FROM UserObject " &_
    " WHERE [GeneralInfo.first_name] like 't%'" &_
    " ORDER BY [GeneralInfo.first_name]"

Set rsUsers = QueryProfileSystem(sQuery)
```

```
Response.Write "User list:<BR />"
While Not rsUsers.EOF

   Response.Write rsUsers("GeneralInfo.logon_name").Value
   Response.Write " "
   Response.Write rsUsers("GeneralInfo.last_name").Value
   Response.Write "<BR/>"

   rsUsers.MoveNext

Wend
```

As you can see, all properties must be specified using their fully qualified name. The FROM clause specifies the name of the profile definition.

Summary

We should have a pretty good understanding of the Profile System and the authentication support in Commerce Server.

The authentication support in Commerce Server provides us with a lot of flexibility. We have seen, for instance:

❑   How to use the AuthManager object to do programmatic authentication.

❑   How the AuthFilter ISAPI filter can be used to do automatic authentication.

❑   How Custom Authentication mode allows us to program how the authentication takes place.

❑   How Windows Authentication mode allows us to use Active Directory to verify user credentials. This allows us to do things such as protect content using NTFS permissions, to use COM+ based roles, and to propagate credentials to SQL server.

❑   How Autocookie mode can be used to track anonymous users.

We have also looked at the Profile System in some detail. Specifically, we have seen:

❑   How physical storage of profile data is separated from the logical schema of the profile.

❑   How a single profile can span many data sources.

❑   The predefined profile definitions in Commerce Server, the most important being the User Object profile definition and the Organization profile definition.

❑   How we can program the profiling system to do things such as create new users and retrieve and modify user properties.

❑   How Site Terms can be used to limit the value of profile properties.

❑   How we can modify existing profile definitions and create new profile definitions.

The Profile System is useful when building any kind of site that requires information about the users and uses that information to authenticate and provide content. In the next chapter, we will see how to target content to users using the Content Targeting System.

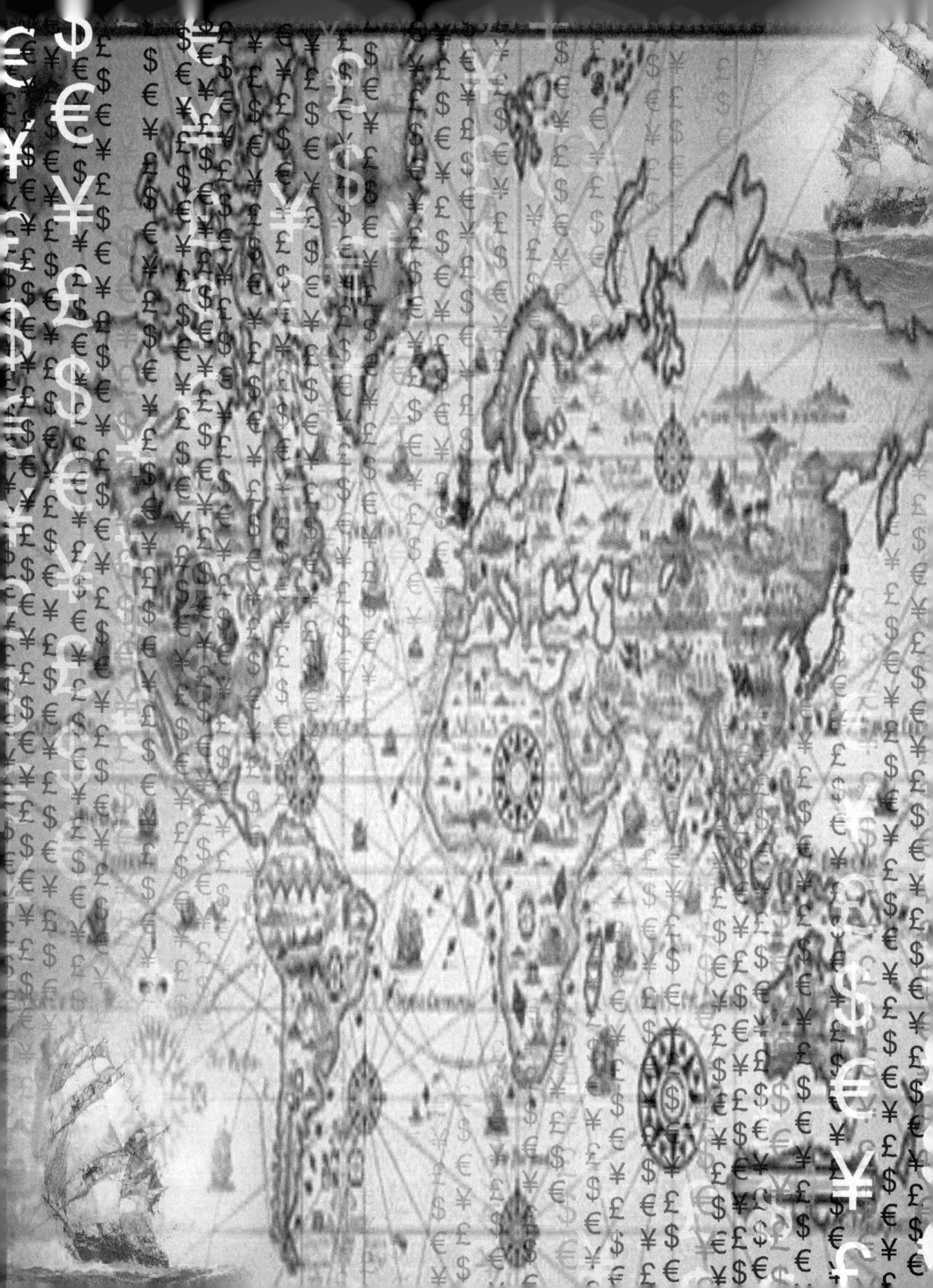

4

Product Catalog System

The Commerce Server 2000 product gives us tremendous flexibility in dealing with product catalogs. Many people found that with Site Server 3.0 Commerce Edition (SSCE), they frequently ended up throwing away the database schema that the site wizard built, and all of the code generated to display and edit the products, and then having to design their own custom database tables and COM objects for product editing, product navigation and product display.

SSCE was just not flexible enough 'out of the box' to handle anything other than a very simple site selling simple products. The good news is that this has all changed with Commerce Server 2000. Now, there is so much more flexibility in dealing with product catalogs. We do not have to build a product catalog from scratch any more.

However, in order to make systems more flexible, there is a trade off involved. The trade off is in complexity. We really need to have a decent understanding of how the product catalog system is architected and implemented before we are able to dive in and start adding products to a site.

This chapter will be split into two areas: the architecture of the Product Catalog System, and implementation of a Product Catalog. First, we will look at the architecture of the product catalog system, and some of the tools that the Business Desk provides for us for changing and editing the catalog. Specifically we will cover the following topics of the architecture and tools:

- ❑   Catalog Creation and Management
- ❑   Catalog Designer
- ❑   Catalog Editor
- ❑   Base Catalogs, Custom Catalogs, and Catalog Sets

Next, we will focus on programmatically manipulating a product catalog, rather than using the tools that Commerce Server 2000 offers. This is important, because we need to do this in the solution sites. In this section, we will look at the implementation of the product catalog. In particular, we are going to cover the following topics:

- ❑ Product Catalog Object Model
- ❑ Import/Export of Catalogs
- ❑ Integrating Third-Party Catalogs
- ❑ Search Support

> *Note that migrating the product catalog data to the data warehouse will not be covered in this chapter. It will be covered in Chapter 5, Business Internet Analytics System.*

Product Catalog Architecture

As previously mentioned, in order to know how to work with the product catalog system, we need to know how it is structured. A Commerce Server catalog has two main parts, the catalog schema and the actual catalog itself. The catalog is just an instance of the catalog schema that contains data. It is structured in the same kind of way as Active Directory, where we have a schema, which consists of attributes and classes, and objects, which are instances of their respective classes in the Active Directory schema.

Another interesting thing to note is that a site can have multiple catalogs in it, and this is also supported by the product catalog architecture. This marks an important difference to SSCE 3.0, where everything had to be integrated into one catalog. We will discuss this in detail later in this chapter.

Catalog Creation and Management

In this section, we'll first take a detailed look at the Catalog structure, before looking at creating and managing catalogs.

Catalog Schema

The catalog schema represents the categories and products for a site. It consists of basic definitions of the categories, products, and properties that are used to define the catalog. Category definitions and product definitions are derived from basic property definitions. This works in very similar way to the way in which classes in Active Directory are defined in terms of attributes, which will have been previously defined.

The following diagram illustrates the way in which category and product definitions are based on basic property definitions. Note how both these definitions may use the same properties: in this case, Name:

Property Definitions

Property	Data Type
Name	Text
Description	Text
Image filename	Text
Manufacturer	Text
Price	Currency

Category Definitions

Category Definitions	Data Type
Name	Text
Description	Text
Image filename	Text

Product Definitions

Product Defintions	Data Type
Name	Text
Manufacturer	Text
Price	Currency

Property Definitions

A property definition represents information about a particular property such as the **data type** of the property (for example, string, number, or money datatypes), the **name** of the property, and a **minimum** or **maximum value** for the property. For example, we can create a property named `Manufacturer` that has a maximum length of 200 characters.

As we would expect, property definitions can be changed. We can edit a property definition even after a catalog has data in it. For example, we could add, remove, or rename property definitions, or change the data type of the property, for example, from a number to a string.

> Note that we cannot change the name or type of property in a catalog schema. We can delete the property, and then add it again using a new name and type.

There are numerous types of attributes at our disposal to define properties. These include such properties as:

❑ `DefaultValue` – As its name suggests, this specifies a default value for intances of a particular property.

❑ `DataType` – This indicates the datatype of a particular property. Datatypes include formats such as `DataTime`, `Money`, `String` and `Number`.

❑ `DisplayOnSite` – This indicates whether a particular property should be displayed on the site when the appropriate part of the catalog is being displayed.

❑ `AssignAll` – This indicates whether a particular property should be automatically assigned to a product definition when it is first created: 1 indicates `true`, and 0 indicates `false`.

❑ `ExportToDW` – This indicates whether a particular property will be exported to the data warehouse. In short, it indicates whether the property will be available for data analysis purposes.

Category Definitions

A category provides a way of grouping products together. This makes it easier for a user to find a particular product. For instance, we might create a category called Laptops, which would have only laptop products associated with it. The **category definition** specifies the properties of a particular category.

For example, a Department category definition might have the following category properties: Name, Description, Image File Name, Image Height, and Image Width. When we create a category based on the Department category definition, we would enter values for the appropriate category properties: for example, the Name category property might be Programming Books. We need to remember that the properties we are talking about are just generic properties, and that we are just assigning them to categories, not to particular products.

Product Definitions

Product definitions specify the characteristics of a particular product by specifying certain product properties. For example, we might create a product definition named Book that would include three product properties: Author, Title, and Name. When we create a product based on the Book product definition, we would enter values for the product properties. For example, the Name product property might be 'Professional ADO 2.5 Programming'. Remember, we can still use the Name property for a category definition as well.

Catalogs, Categories, and Products

A catalog is an instance of a catalog schema that contains data about individual products *and* the categories. A straightforward way to create a catalog is via the Catalog Editor module in the Business Desk.

A catalog would have some particular properties associated with it. These would include such things as:

- ❏   Name – The name of the catalog.

- ❏   Start date – The date on which the catalog is first made available.

- ❏   End date – The date on which the catalog is last available.

- ❏   Currency – The currency type.

- ❏   Unit of weight measure – weight type (imperial or metric).

- ❏   Product unique ID – The property that will be used as a unique identifier for particular products.

Categories are individual instances of a category definition. For example, a category definition named Department might be used to create the category Programming Books.

Products are single items in our catalog, and are defined by a combination of property definitions. For instance, if we had a product definition named Book, which had the properties Name, Title, and Author, we could create particular products by specifying the values of these properties.

Products can be arranged into groups of closely related items, which are called **product families**. For instance, we might have a product family containing all types of shirts. A particular shirt might be differentiated from the other shirts in the family by having a color of blue, and a size of Large. The combination of size and color form one **variant**.

This variant would always have a unique identifier, such as a SKU or ISBN, and a price. So a large, blue shirt may have an SKU of 11315 and a medium, green shirt may have an SKU of 11316. However, both of the shirts would have the same product family identifier.

Catalog Organization: Hierarchies and Relationships

To organize the products in a catalog and make it easier for users to navigate to what they want, we need to create **category hierarchies**, and establish relationships among categories and products. For instance, we could create a **parent category** that includes two different categories, known as **child categories**. When users navigate to the parent category, the child categories are displayed, enabling users to quickly find the products they want.

Catalog Designer

The Catalog Designer is a Business Desk module that enables us to edit the schema of a site's catalogs. With the Catalog Designer, we can find, view, edit, and create property, category, and product *definitions*.

In the following screenshot, we can see the Catalog Designer in Property Definitions mode:

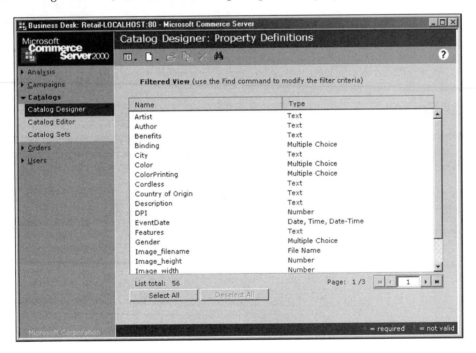

> Note that in order to access the different modes, we just need to click on the far left drop-down of the Catalog Designer toolbar.

Since the Catalog Designer is a very powerful tool, we may want to lock it down a little bit. All we have to do is find the ASP page that corresponds with what we want to lock down, and set an Access Control Entry (ACE) on it.

The files for the Business Desk are by default located in the ...\Inetpub\wwwroot\[site_name]bizdesk folder. The catalog files are in the Catalogs folder of the Business Desk folder. A sensible strategy here would be to lock down what the property definitions are, since everything is based on these. To do this, we just need to find the list_PropertyDefinitions.asp file, which is located in the ..\Inetpub\wwwroot\[site_name]bizdesk\Catalogs\Designer folder, and set its security properties:

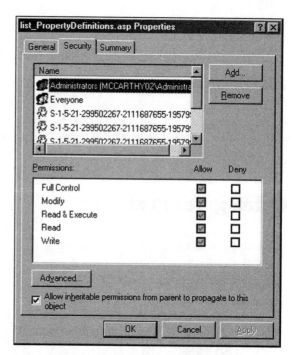

By setting the security on this file, unauthorized users will not be able to edit property definitions.

Catalog Editor

The Catalog Editor is used to create, modify, and delete categories, products, and catalogs. We can also use the Catalog Editor module to import catalogs: either from an XML file or a comma-separated value (.csv) file.

Just as the Catalog Designer is where we edit property, category, and product *definitions*, the Catalog Editor is the module where we edit the actual *instances* of catalogs, categories, and products.

The following screenshot shows the basic Catalog Editor interface in the BizDesk.

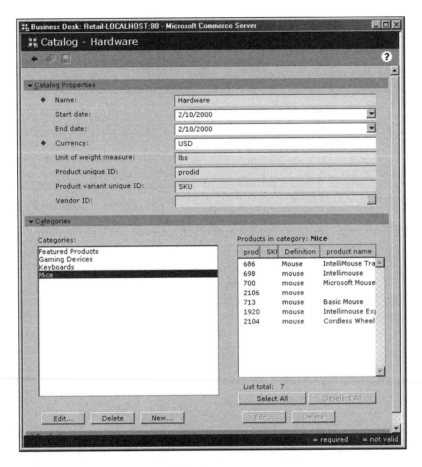

Base Catalogs, Custom Catalogs, and Catalog Sets

Base catalogs contain categories and products, but they do not contain any specific pricing rules. Although they don't have *specific* pricing rules, they do contain prices, but these function as the basic prices, something like manufacturers recommended prices, and are not necessarily the prices displayed on the site.

Custom catalogs are derived from base catalogs, but they contain specific pricing rules for the products in that catalog. The prices in a custom catalog override the prices in a base catalog. We can use custom catalogs in a supplier site, for example, in a situation in which we'd want to give one or more companies custom prices on certain products.

We can also use custom catalogs in a retail site: for example, when we have different membership levels for customers, and want to price products according to the membership level. Or we might want to show different prices to users who shop at our site frequently.

We determine which catalog a user sees on our site by creating **catalog sets**. A catalog set is a group of one or more catalogs that we make available to different users or organizations. For example, we may create one custom catalog, and then combine it with a general catalog, and then display that catalog set to members of a specific organization.

Product Catalog Implementation

Now that we've explored the general architecture of Commerce Server catalogs, we are ready to start looking at the COM object model for product catalogs and how to automate some of the tasks associated with the product catalog.

Product Catalog Object Model

The product catalog objects provide methods to create and manage catalogs, products, and categories in the Product Catalog System. These objects provide an interface for catalog data stored in a SQL Server database. All of these COM objects are threaded, so they are safe to be stored in either an ASP application-level variable or in a session-level variable.

The product catalog object model is hierarchical, and is structured in the following way:

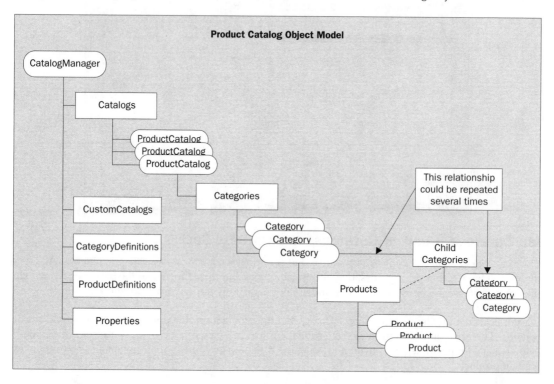

Note that in this figure, the sharp-cornered rectangles represent collections, and the rectangles with rounded corners represent the items in the collections. As we can see, the CatalogManager object is the base object of the product catalog object model. We must use the CatalogManager object in order to create and manage the ProductCatalog, Category, and Product objects in the system.

The CatalogManager contains a set of one or more catalogs, which are represented by ProductCatalog objects. A catalog can be just a simple flat list of products, or it can have one or more further categories in it. And each sub-category in turn can have sub-categories, and so on. Each category object can have a set of product objects associated with it.

The CatalogManager object also contains the property, category, and product definitions that we previously discussed when talking about the catalog schema.

CatalogManager Object

The CatalogManager object is the first object we create when utilizing the Commerce Server 2000 Product Catalog System. Typically, a single CatalogManager object is created in the global.asa file and used throughout an application. This object sets and retrieves properties that apply to all the catalogs in the Product Catalog System. Basically, we use the CatalogManager object to create and manage catalogs. We also need to use the CatalogManager object to create properties, define their attributes, and to create product and category definitions using those properties.

The CatalogManager object also provides methods for queries and free text searches across single or multiple catalogs. We will look at searches later in the chapter.

The CatalogManager.CreateCatalog and CatalogManager.GetCatalog methods return a ProductCatalog object representing a specific catalog. The CatalogManager.Catalogs property is a recordset of all the catalogs in the Product Catalog System. The complete object model may be found in Appendix B.

ProductCatalog Object

The ProductCatalog object represents a single catalog in the Product Catalog System. All of the methods of the ProductCatalog object are executed from the context of a specific catalog. We can use the ProductCatalog object to add new products and categories to a catalog, to create a custom catalog, or to perform a specification search.

The ProductCatalog.RootCategories method returns a recordset of categories that is the starting point for traversing the category hierarchy. These represent the categories collection in the previous figure. This method also returns a recordset of all products, including ones that are not in a category hierarchy.

Category Object

The Category object represents a single category in the catalog. Categories provide a method for organizing products within a catalog. We use this object to perform various operations on a category, such as adding products or other categories, or managing relationships.

The Category.ChildCategories property is a recordset containing the names of categories that exist below this category in the hierarchy. It is a recordset containing all the products that exist directly in this category.

Product Object

The Product object represents a single product or product family in the catalog. A product definition is created using the CatalogManager object and can be used across the Product Catalog System, but a product is always in the context of a single catalog. Use the Product object to perform operations on a product, such as modifying properties, creating product variants, or managing relationships.

CatalogSets Object

The CatalogSets object stores and manages catalog sets, which are arbitrary collections of catalogs. CatalogSets allows us to present different collections of catalogs to different users and organizations. This is not included in the object model diagram because it is a separate object.

CatalogToVendorAssociation Object

The `CatalogToVendorAssociation` object stores and manages associations between catalogs and vendors (suppliers). This is the mechanism by which we can connect what catalogs belong to what vendors. Again, this is not included in the object model diagram because it is a separate object.

Using the Product Catalog System

The following code samples are designed to demonstrate in detail the most interesting properties and methods of the product catalog object model to you. We have tried to pick examples of things that are fairly common operations, yet are not things that we would necessarily find too obvious.

Although we may be able to manage the product catalogs from the Business Desk, there will be situations where we need to manage these properties directly.

> Note that before running the following code, you will need to go to the Catalog Editor module of the Business Desk and import the **WroxHardwareCatalog.xml** file.
>
> Importing this XML file will create the catalog that the code uses to iterate through. This file is available, along with the rest of the source code for this book, at www.wrox.com.

To test the following examples, it will be necessary to create a Visal Basic project with a form containing a ListBox control to display output from the various methods, and option buttons to choose which method to execute.

We have used Visual Basic code for some of the examples simply for the convenience of easy debugging. All of the Visual Basic code can easily be converted to VBScript code for ASP.

The diagram below shows the project's form during run time:

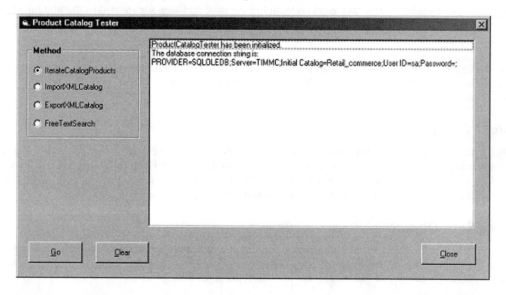

The following code constitutes the `Form_Load` method. `DB_CONNECTION` and `WROX_HW_CATALOG`, are defined in a seperate file called `basConstants.bas` file. All the relevant code may be downloaded from `http://www.wrox.com`.

```
Private Sub Form_Load()

'Handle errors inline
On Error Resume Next

  'Instantiate the CatalogManager
  Set mobjManager = New CATALOGLib.CatalogManager

  'Initialize the CatalogManager. Set the
  'flsADOConnection argument to True, since we
  'are using an ADO connection string.
  mobjManager.Initialize DB_CONNECTION, True

  'Check for errors
  If Err.Number <> 0 Then
    lstOutput.AddItem "Error initializing the CatalogManager. " _
                      & Err.Description
  Else
    'Print out the initialization information
    lstOutput.AddItem App.EXEName & " has been initialized."
    lstOutput.AddItem "The database connection string is: "
    lstOutput.AddItem DB_CONNECTION

  End If

End Sub
```

Note that we are setting the `flsADOConnection` argument to true, since we are using an ADO connection string. If everything is successful after initializing the `CatalogManager` object, we then send a success message to the `lstOutput` ListBox control.

The `mobjManager` variable, which represents our instance of the `CatalogManager` object, is a private, module-level variable.

Navigating through the Product Catalog Object Model

With flexibility can come complexity. Well, it is not too bad finding our way through the hierarchy of the product catalog object model. If you have ever programmed against the Microsoft Excel or Microsoft Word object model, it is very similar. Below is a method that will display all of the products for a given catalog.

For the sake of code brevity, we are not going to bother with the possible sub-categories of each category here. To do that, we would need to create a recursive method to iterate through the categories and call itself each time a category had sub-categories.

```
' Method:    IterateCatalogProducts
'
' Inputs:    None
'
' Output:    text to the lstOutput ListBox control
```

```
'
' Description: This method iterates through all of the root categories and
'          their associated products and properties in a Commerce Server
'          2000 catalog. It uses the Commerce Server 2000 Product Catalog
'          object model to list all of the products in a product catalog.

Sub IterateCatalogProducts()

'Handle all errors inline
On Error Resume Next

    Dim strError As String
    Dim blnError As Boolean
    Dim strCategoryName As String
    Dim objCatalog As CATALOGLib.ProductCatalog
    Dim rstRootCategories As ADODB.Recordset
    Dim rstProducts As ADODB.Recordset
    Dim rstProductProperties As ADODB.Recordset
    Dim objProduct As CATALOGLib.Product
    Dim lngCounter As Long
    Dim lngFieldCount As Long
```

After some initialization, it starts out by using the `CatalogManager` object to get an instance of the `WroxHardware` catalog:

```
'Retrieve a reference to the WroxHardware catalog from
'the CatalogManager object.
Set objCatalog = mobjManager.GetCatalog(WROX_HW_CATALOG)
```

Error checking is performed throughout the method, an appropriate message being returned:

```
'Check for errors
If Err.Number <> 0 Then
 blnError = True
 strError = "Error getting the " & WROX_HW_CATALOG _
      & " ProductCatalog. " & Err.Description
 GoTo ExitProc
End If
```

Once we have the `Catalog` object, we then retrieve all of its root categories in the form of an ADO `Recordset` object:

```
'Get the root categories of the catalog
Set rstRootCategories = objCatalog.RootCategories

'Check for errors
If Err.Number <> 0 Then
 blnError = True
 strError = "Error getting the catalog root categories. " _
                & Err.Description
 GoTo ExitProc
End If
```

Once we have the `categories` recordset, we then need to loop through each one of them and retrieve each category's products. To do this, we first call the `GetCategory` method of the `ProductCatalog` object and pass in the current name of the category that we are on in our loop through the categories. The `GetCategory` method returns a `Category` object, and we then, in the same call, call the `DescendantProducts` property of the `Catalog` object. This will give us all of the products for the category, including all of the sub-categories' products, if there were any sub-categories:

```
With rstRootCategories

'Loop through the Hardware catalog root categories
Do Until .EOF

    'Print the name of the category
    strCategoryName = .Fields("CategoryName").Value
    lstOutput.AddItem strCategoryName

    'Get all of the products in all of the child
    'categories of the current category
    Set rstProducts = _
    objCatalog.GetCategory(strCategoryName).DescendantProducts

    'Check for errors
    If Err.Number <> 0 Then
     blnError = True
     strError = "Error getting the root category products. " _
                    & Err.Description
    GoTo ExitProc
    End If
```

Now, the next step is to loop through the products that we get from the `Category` object, and retrieve all of the properties for every product. This is done by instantiating a `Product` object by calling the `GetProduct` method of the `Catalog` object and passing in the ProdID (the unique identifier for the product), and then calling the `GetProductProperties` method of the `Product` object. This will give us another ADO Recordset that we must loop through to retrieve all of the product's properties:

```
'Loop through the products of the root category
Do Until rstProducts.EOF

    'Get the Product object
    Set objProduct = _
    objCatalog.GetProduct(rstProducts.Fields("prodid").Value)

    'Check for errors
    If Err.Number <> 0 Then
        blnError = True
        strError = "Error getting an instance of the Product " _
                & "object for " & strCategoryName _
                    & ". " & Err.Description
    GoTo ExitProc
    End If
    'Print the name of the product
    lstOutput.AddItem Space(5) _
        & rstProducts.Fields("product name").Value
```

```
      'Get the properties of the product
      Set rstProductProperties = objProduct.GetProductProperties

      'Check for errors
      If Err.Number <> 0 Then
        blnError = True
        strError = "Error getting the product properties for " _
        & "the following ProductID: " & objProduct.ProductID _
                  & ". " & Err.Description
        GoTo ExitProc
      End If

      'Print the properties of the product

      'First, get the count of property fields for the product
      lngFieldCount = rstProductProperties.Fields.Count
```

Once we have the product properties recordset, we then proceed to loop through all of the fields in the product properties recordset to print out all of the property name-value pairs for the product. When it is all said and done, we have three loops nested inside one main loop:

```
      'Loop through the product properties
      Do Until rstProductProperties.EOF

        'Loop through all of the name/value pairs
        'for the property
        For lngCounter = 0 To lngFieldCount - 1

          'Print the name and value of the property
          lstOutput.AddItem Space(10) _
            & rstProductProperties.Fields(lngCounter).Name _
                        & ": " _
            & rstProductProperties.Fields(lngCounter).Value
        Next
        'Get the next product property
        rstProductProperties.MoveNext
      Loop
      'Get the next product
      rstProducts.MoveNext
    Loop
    'Get the next root category
    .MoveNext
  Loop
  End With 'rstRootCategories
ExitProc:

  'Display errors, if applicable
  If blnError = True Then
    lstOutput.AddItem strError
  End If
```

And finally, we do some cleaning up:

```
'Clean up memory
Set rstRootCategories = Nothing
Set rstProductProperties = Nothing
Set rstProducts = Nothing
Set objProduct = Nothing
Set objCatalog = Nothing

End Sub
```

Although this code is a little bit more complex than calling a hypothetical `GetProducts()` method and passing in a connection string, at least now we are able to handle the most complex product catalogs with any custom database tables or custom COM objects.

Importing and Exporting Catalogs

The product catalog import and export features of Commerce Server 2000 are much-needed features that many developers had to previously write on their own. These tasks can be performed through the Business Desk or they can be done programmatically via the product catalog object model. All that is needed is a comma-separated values (CSV) file or an XML file. In this chapter, we will only be working with XML files.

An example of why we would want to do this programmatically is if we need to periodically update a catalog. We could do it manually via the BizDesk, but a more elegant way would be to write a service or a scheduled task that runs periodically to retrieve a catalog file from a vendor, and then update the product catalog. This way, the process is automated, and can be easily duplicated for other vendors.

The nice part of importing and exporting catalogs is that they can be done asynchronously. So, if we have a large catalog, we do not have to wait for the operation to finish; we can continue performing other tasks. If there are errors during the import or export procedures, they will be written to the Application Log of the Event Viewer. If we are importing or exporting via the product catalog object model, we have a choice as to whether or not we want the operation to be asynchronous or synchronous.

Importing and Exporting Programmatically

Let's take a look at how we might use the `ProductCatalog` object to programatically import an XML catalog:

```
'//////////////////////////////////////////////////////////////////////////////
'
' Method:     ImportXMLCatalog
'
' Inputs:     None
'
' Output:     text to the lstOutput ListBox control
'
' Description: This method imports an XML product catalog from a file.
'
'//////////////////////////////////////////////////////////////////////////////

Sub ImportXMLCatalog()
```

```
On Error Resume Next

    Dim strXMLFileName As String
    Dim strError As String
    Dim blnError As Boolean
```

After some preliminaries, we specify the path and name of an XML file:

```
'Get the file name
strXMLFileName = App.Path & "\XML\WroxHardwareCatalog.xml"
```

This is then fed to our instance of the `CatalogManager` object (`mobjManager`) via the `ImportXML` method. The `ImportXML` method has three arguments: `strXMLFilePath`, `fUpdateOnly`, and `fRunSynchronously`. The `fUpdateOnly` argument is a Boolean, and indicates whether or not to update an existing catalog (`True`) or to create a new one (`False`). The `fRunSynchronously` argument is a Boolean and indicates whether or not the import is to be run in synchronous mode or asynchronous mode. When run in asynchronous mode, the `ImportXML` method will be executed on a different thread to the current thread. If it is run synchronously, the method will not return unless the operation has fully completed. There are a few rules to keep in mind with this method. They are:

1. The method cannot be called in a transacted object. This is because this method may create, update, or delete free text indexes and SQL Server does not allow that in a transaction.

2. If your OLEDB connection is lost for more than two minutes (for example the database server goes down, TCP/IP connection breaks, etc.), the operation will fail.

3. The names of catalogs in the source file cannot begin with "#" or consist solely of spaces.

4. During an update, if a property existing in the catalog has one type and the property of the same name existing in the import file has a different type, then the import will fail. For example, if your catalog has a **SKU** property that is a string, and the XML file being imported has a **SKU** property that is an integer, then the import will fail.

```
'Import the file
mobjManager.ImportXML strXMLFileName, False, True

'Check for errors
If Err.Number <> 0 Then
  blnError = True
  strError = "Error importing " & strXMLFileName & ". " _
  & Err.Description
  GoTo ExitProc
End If

'Display the status
lstOutput.AddItem "The catalog was succesfully imported!"

ExitProc:

'Display errors, if applicable
```

```
    If blnError = True Then
      lstOutput.AddItem strError
    End If

End Sub
```

Exporting a catalog to XML is even simpler. Here is an example of exporting a catalog to an XML file:

```
'//////////////////////////////////////////////////////////////////////////////////////////'
' Method:    ExportXMLCatalog
'
' Inputs:    None
'
' Output:    text to the lstOutput ListBox control
'
' Description: This method exports a product catalog as an XML file.
'
'//////////////////////////////////////////////////////////////////////////////////////////

Sub ExportXMLCatalog()

On Error Resume Next

  Dim strXMLFileName As String
  Dim strError As String
  Dim blnError As Boolean

  'Set the file name to export to
  strXMLFileName = App.Path & "\XML\WroxHardwareCatalog.xml"

  'Export the catalog
  mobjManager.ExportXML strXMLFileName, WROX_HW_CATALOG, True

  'Check for errors
  If Err.Number <> 0 Then
   blnError = True
   strError = "Error exporting " & strXMLFileName & ". " _
   & Err.Description
   GoTo ExitProc
  End If

  lstOutput.AddItem "The catalog was succesfully exported!"

ExitProc:

  'Display errors, if applicable
  If blnError = True Then
   lstOutput.AddItem strError
  End If

End Sub
```

This code is essentially the same as the code for the import. The ExportXML method has the following arguments: strXMLFilePath, strCatalogsToExport, and fRunSynchronously. The only different argument is strCatalogsToExport, which takes a comma-delimited string of catalogs to export. If this is left blank or is missing, then all catalogs will be exported.

Product Catalog XML Schema

In order for a catalog import to be successful, we must have the properly formatted XML. By properly formatted, I mean that the XML must conform to the schema of a Commerce Catalog XML file. An easy way to check if our XML file conforms to the schema is to reference the catalog XML Data Reduced (XDR) file (that is, a schema) provided in the Commerce Server root installation folder. An example would be the following:

```
<MSCommerceCatalogCollection xmlns="x-schema:C:\Program Files\Microsoft Commerce
Server\CatalogXMLSchema.xml">
```

After doing that, try to open the XML file in Internet Explorer (IE). If it opens, then everything is OK. Otherwise, IE will show you where the error is in the XML file.

A Commerce Catalog XML file is made up of three main groups:

❑ MSCommerceCatalogCollection

❑ Catalog Schema Elements

❑ Catalog Data Elements

Let's look at the different types of element in more detail.

MSCommerceCatalogCollection

The MSCommerceCatalogCollection is the root node for a Commerce Catalog XML file. Its child elements are CatalogSchema and Catalog. It has no attributes associated with it.

Catalog Schema Elements

The CatalogSchema element is used to extend the catalog, and contains the schema definition elements for the Catalog element: it is made up of the AttributeDefinition, Definition, PropertiesDefinition, Property, and PropertyValue elements. Let's take a look at each of these in turn:

❑ AttributeDefinition Element – this has no child elements and has the following attributes: DataType, id, and name. It defines an attribute that can be used to describe an aspect of a property, such as its display name. This allows additional attributes to be defined on fields on top of the built in ones, such as name, maxSize, and defaultValue.

❑ Definition Elements – this has no child elements, and has the following attributes: DefinitionType, name, properties, and variantProperties. A Definition element defines a type of product or category.

❑ PropertiesDefinition Element – this has one child element: Property; and no attributes. It is used as a container for the individual property definitions.

❑ Property Elements – this has one child element, PropertyValue, and has the following attributes: AssignAll, DefaultValue, DisplayName, ExportToDW, id, IsFreeTextSearchable, MaxValue, MinValue, and name. It is used as a container for the individual property definitions. A Property element defines a property that can be used to describe an aspect of a product or category.

❑ PropertyValue Element – this has no child elements, and has the following attribute: DisplayName. It defines a legal value for a property. The DisplayName attribute is a legal value for the containing property.

- ❏ `Catalog Data` Element – this is used for the actual catalog data. It is made up of the `Category`, `Field`, `Product`, `ProductVariant`, and `Relationship` elements. It has the following attributes: `catalogName`, `currency`, `description`, `endDate`, `locale`, `productIdentifier`, `productVariantIdentifier`, and `startDate`.

- ❏ `Category` Element – this has two child elements, `Field` and `Relationship`, and has the following attributes: `Definition`, `id`, `isSearchable`, `name`, `parentCategories`, and `listPrice`. A `Category` element defines an instance of a type of category.

- ❏ `Field` Element – this has no child elements, and the following attributes: `fieldID` and `fieldValue`. A `Field` element defines a name and value pair for a field. The `fieldID` attribute is the name of a property a value is being supplied for, and the `fieldValue` attribute is the value for the property.

- ❏ `ProductVariant` Element – this defines an instance of a variant of a product. Its child element is the `Field` element and its attribute is the `id` attribute, which is just the XML ID for the variant element.

- ❏ `Relationship` Element – this defines a relationship between one product or category and another product or category. It has no child elements and its attributes are `description`, `name`, and `relation`.

XML Catalog Import Rules

There are two sets of rules to follow when importing an XML product catalog:

- ❏ Catalog Schema Rules
- ❏ Catalog Data Rules

XML Catalog Schema Rules

The main rule for the schema is that the schema defined in the XML file that we are importing cannot conflict with any of the property, category, and product definitions in our existing catalog database. This means that we cannot redefine an existing property to use a different data type and cannot redefine a product or category definition to have a different set of member properties. Schema elements are never deleted during an XML catalog import; only new schema are added, if applicable.

XML Catalog Data Rules

The main rule for the catalog data is that if a catalog we are importing already exists in the database, the existing catalog can be replaced by the imported catalog, or it can just be updated by the imported catalog: this is known as **merge import**.

Exchanging Catalogs with Trading Partners

We have two main choices when it comes to exchanging a product catalog with a trading partner: we can either roll our own solution for managing the catalog exchange, or utilize the power of BizTalk Server. In order to be able to exchange a catalog with trading partners, it is first necessary to associate the vendors with their catalogs using the `CatalogToVendorAssociation` object.

If we decide to roll our own solution, we would have to take into account how we will receive the vendors' catalogs, what the structure of the vendors' catalogs are, and how we will process them and get them into our site. One simple solution is to get the vendor's catalog, transform it to XML (if it is not already in XML format), create an XSL style sheet to transform it into the Commerce Server product catalog XML schema, and then pass it to the `ImportXML` method of the `CatalogManager` object.

This sounds fairly straightforward, but there are lots of things that can go wrong in the process. It could often be very useful to take advantage of BizTalk Server, not only for its XML mapping features, but also for its scheduling, orchestration, and communication features. Although BizTalk seems expensive, the time that it will save in developing quality B2B applications is well worth the money spent. We are not going to talk about BizTalk Server in this chapter, since that forms the focus of Chapter 12.

Integrating a Third-Party Product Catalog

There are two general strategies for using existing product catalog data in Commerce Server 2000. We can migrate the data into the Commerce Server Product Catalog System, or we can integrate our existing, or third-party catalog system with Commerce Server 2000 through its Application Program Interface (API), replacing the Product Catalog System. Choosing between these two approaches depends on a number of factors.

Integrating an existing catalog system with Commerce Server 2000 requires a programming effort to modify or replace components of Commerce Server and possibly components of an existing catalog system.

The most straightforward approach to data migration requires conversion of the existing data to XML or comma separated value (CSV) format. The difficulty of this conversion depends on the format and integrity of our existing data. The size and complexity of a product catalog data will have a direct effect on the length of time needed to process the conversion.

There are other approaches to migrating our existing product catalog data. We may decide to pursue a Microsoft BizTalk Server or Data Transformation Services (DTS) integration solution, or we may decide to transmit a product catalog data via other protocols. We could also write an application that reads existing data and calls all of the appropriate Commerce Server ProductCatalog objects to get the data into the Commerce Server database. The option we choose would depend on our available resources and expertise.

Integrating a third-party catalog with Commerce Server 2000 involves providing a pipeline component (see Chapter 6) that does the work of the Commerce Server `QueryCatalogInfo` pipeline component for our existing catalog, and integration with the following Commerce Server components:

❑ Campaigns

❑ Data Warehouse

❑ Baskets

❑ Applications

❑ Business Desk Catalog Modules

Let's take a look at a data migration example where we have a third-party catalog database and we need to get the data into our new site's product catalog.

Integrating Data from a Third-Party Database

In our example, we'll deal with a hypothetical company called The San Diego Clothing Company (SDCC), purveyors of men's shirts and pants.

As we are merely interested in the mechanics of integrating their product catalog, we can suppose their database structure is very simple. Let's suppose it is structured in the following way:

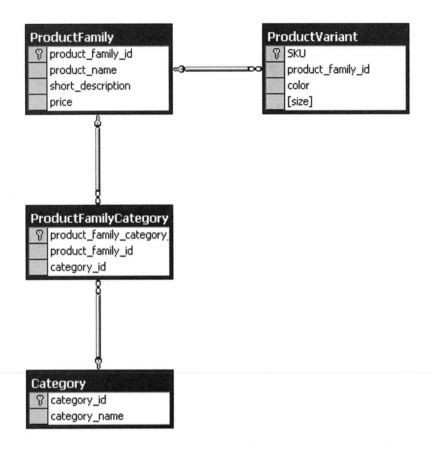

SDCC's product catalog consists only of categories (shirts and pants), product families (a particular style of shirt or pants), and product variants. The product variants are a combination of unique color and size attributes for a particular product family. Individual product variant are represented by SKUs. In the SDCC catalog, product families may or may not be associated with categories.

For the sake of seeing how all of the `ProductCatalog` objects work together, we will build an application that simply reads data from SDCC's database and uses the `ProductCatalog` object model to update the Commerce Server product catalog.

For this demonstration, we are going to build a Visual Basic Standard EXE project that has no user interface. The project name is `CatalogIntegration.vbp`, and all of the code is in the `basMain.bas` and `basConstants.bas` files of this project.

The executable starts by calling `Sub Main()`, and its process is terminated when `Sub Main()` finishes executing.

```
Sub Main()

'Handle errors inline
On Error Resume Next
```

```
'Error-handling variables
Dim blnError As Boolean
Dim strError As String
Dim objFSO As Scripting.FileSystemObject

'Top-level object variables
Dim objManager As CATALOGLib.CatalogManager
Dim objCatalog As CATALOGLib.ProductCatalog

'Category-related variables
Dim rst3PCategories As ADODB.Recordset
Dim str3PCategoryName As String
Dim strCategory As String
Dim objCategory As CATALOGLib.Category

'Product-related variables
Dim rstProductDefinitions As ADODB.Recordset
Dim strProductDefinition As String
Dim blnDefinitionExists As Boolean
Dim rst3PProductFamilies As ADODB.Recordset
Dim rst3PProductVariants As ADODB.Recordset
Dim rstProductVariant As ADODB.Recordset
Dim strProductID As String
Dim objProduct As CATALOGLib.Product
Dim rstProductProperties As ADODB.Recordset

'Instantiate the CatalogManager
Set objManager = New CATALOGLib.CatalogManager

'Initialize the CatalogManager.  Set the
'flsADOConnection argument to True, since we
'are using an ADO connection string.
objManager.Initialize CS2K_DB_CONNECTION, True

'Check for errors
If Err.Number <> 0 Then
    blnError = True
    strError = "Error initializing the CatalogManager.  " _
    & Err.Description
    GoTo ExitProc
End If

'Retrieve a reference to the WroxHardware catalog from
'the CatalogManager object.
Set objCatalog = objManager.GetCatalog(WROX_HW_CATALOG)

'Check for errors
If Err.Number <> 0 Then
    blnError = True
    strError = "Error getting the " & WROX_HW_CATALOG _
    & " ProductCatalog.  " & Err.Description
    GoTo ExitProc
End If
```

This code should look familiar so far, all we have done is declare our variables, instantiate and initialize the CatalogManager object, and retrieve a reference to the WroxHardware catalog. Except for the variable declarations, this code is exactly the same as the previous code that we have looked at.

The rest of the code is broken up into five main stages:

1. Create new product definition

2. Add third-party categories to the Commerce Server product catalog

3. Add third-party product families to the Commerce Server product catalog

4. Add third-party product variants to the Commerce Server product catalog

5. Add third-party product-category associations to the Commerce Server product catalog

Creating a New Product Definition

The first thing we have to do before adding any products to the database is to make sure we have a product definition that is suitable for the products. In this case, we do not have a good enough definition in our catalog for clothing, so we will create one. The following code willl do this.

We first check if the 'Clothing' product definition exists by looping through all of the existing product definitions in the product catalog to see if the DefinitionName field in the ProductDefinitions recordset is equal to Clothing:

```
'Create a new product definition for Clothing
'if it does not exist.

strProductDefinition = "Clothing"
Set rstProductDefinitions = objManager.ProductDefinitions
Do Until rstProductDefinitions.EOF
    If rstProductDefinitions.Fields("DefinitionName").Value = _
    strProductDefinition Then
        blnDefinitionExists = True
        Exit Do
    End If
    rstProductDefinitions.MoveNext
Loop
```

If we cannot find a match, then we go ahead and create the definition. We start by calling the CreateDefinition method of the CatalogManager object. We then proceed to add the following definition properties: Name, product name, and Description. Then we need to also add the variant properties to our definition, since the SDCC catalog's products have variants.

The variant properties that we create are color and size. The Color property already exists, but the Size property does not. Therefore, we must first create the Size property before we can add it as a variant property:

```
If blnDefinitionExists = False Then
    objManager.CreateProductDefinition strProductDefinition
    objManager.AddDefinitionProperty strProductDefinition, _
                                "Name"
    objManager.AddDefinitionProperty strProductDefinition, _
                                "product name"
    objManager.AddDefinitionProperty strProductDefinition, _
                                "Description"
    objManager.AddDefinitionVariantProperty strProductDefinition, _
```

```
                                            "Color"
        objManager.CreateProperty "Size", cscString, 50
        objManager.AddDefinitionVariantProperty _
        strProductDefinition, "Size"
    End If
```

We then conclude this stage by checking for errors:

```
'Check for errors
If Err.Number <> 0 Then
    blnError = True
    strError = "Error creating the new product definition.  " _
    & Err.Description
    GoTo ExitProc
End If
```

Adding Third-Party Categories to the Commerce Server Product Catalog

The second stage is where we add the third-party categories to our product catalog:

```
'Add the 3rd party categories to the catalog.

'Get 3rd party categories.

Set rst3PCategories = GetRSFromSQL("SELECT * FROM Category")
If TypeName(rst3PCategories) <> "Nothing" Then
```

After we get the recordset of SDCC's categories, we then loop through it and check if each category in the recordset is in our product catalog. We do this by calling the GetCategory method of the ProductCatalog object. This method returns a valid Category object if successful; otherwise it will return a null pointer (Nothing):

```
        'Check if any of the 3rd party categories are
        'not in the product catalog.
        With rst3PCategories
            Do Until .EOF
                str3PCategoryName = .Fields("category_name").Value
                Set objCategory = objCatalog.GetCategory( _
                str3PCategoryName)
```

After calling GetCategory, we then check if the category object we got back from the call is valid or not. If it is not valid, we then must add the category to our product catalog. If it is valid, then the category already existed. While adding the new category to our product catalog, we will use the Department category definition, since it is generic enough to handle SDCC's categories of clothing.

```
            If TypeName(objCategory) = "Nothing" Then

                'It is not in the product catalog.
                'Add the new category to the product catalog.
                objCatalog.CreateCategory "Department", _
                                        str3PCategoryName, , True
```

```
                        End If
                        .MoveNext
                Loop
            End With
        End If
```

The first thing we do in this stage is to get a recordset of all of SDCC's categories. This is accomplished through the use of our helper function, `GetRSFromSQL`. Below is the code for this function that returns a recordset when given a valid SQL statement:

```
Private Function GetRSFromSQL(ByRef SQLString As String) As ADODB.Recordset

On Error Resume Next

    Dim rstReturn As ADODB.Recordset
```

This function uses a constant, `THIRDP_DB_CONNECTION`, as its connection string to the SDCC database. It simply takes the SQL string parameter, executes it, and returns a disconnected Recordset object:

```
    Set rstReturn = New ADODB.Recordset
    With rstReturn
        .CursorLocation = adUseClient
        .CursorType = adOpenStatic
        .Open SQLString, THIRDP_DB_CONNECTION
        Set .ActiveConnection = Nothing
    End With

    'Return the recordset
    Set GetRSFromSQL = rstReturn

    'Clean up memory
    Set rstReturn = Nothing
    Err.Clear

End Function
```

We have now completed stage two.

Adding Third-Party Product Families to the Commerce Server Product Catalog

We are now ready to start adding the SDCC products to our catalog:

We start out by using our helper function (`GetRSFromSQL`) again to get a recordset of SDCC's product families. We then begin looping through the recordset. While we are in the loop, on every row in the recordset, we are going to get the SDCC `product_family_id` and prefix it with our `SD_CLOTHING_PROD_ID` string constant. This is to ensure that we do not step on any of the ProductIDs in our product catalog.

```
        'Add the 3rd party product families are to the catalog.
        'Get 3rd party product families.
        Set rst3PProductFamilies = GetRSFromSQL("SELECT * FROM ProductFamily")
        If TypeName(rst3PProductFamilies) <> "Nothing" Then
```

```
    With rst3PProductFamilies

        Do Until .EOF

            'Get the Product ID
            strProductID = SD_CLOTHING_PROD_ID_PREFIX & _
            .Fields("product_family_id").Value
```

The next thing we do is to check if the new ProductID has already been added to our catalog or not. We do this by using the GetProduct method of the ProductCatalog object. This is similar to the GetCategory method; if it returns a valid Product object, then the product exists. If GetProduct does not return a valid Product object (Nothing), then we can add the product family to our product catalog:

```
        'See if the product exists.
        Set objProduct = objCatalog.GetProduct(strProductID)
        If TypeName(objProduct) = "Nothing" Then
```

In order to add the product family, we call the CreateProduct method of the ProductCatalog object, and pass in the name of the product definition that we created earlier (strProductDefinition), the ProductID that we previously created (strProductID), and the price of the product.

```
            'It is not in the product catalog. Add the new
            'product family to the product catalog.
            Set objProduct = objCatalog.CreateProduct( _
                    strProductDefinition, _
                    strProductID, _
                    .Fields("price").Value)
```

The next step, setting the properties of the new product, is a little bit trickier and not quite as obvious. In order to do this, we need a recordset of the product's properties. We get this by calling the GetProductProperties method of our instantiated Product object (objProduct). We then set the Description, Name, and Product Name fields of the disconnected recordset (rstProductProperties), update it, and pass it back to the Product object (objProduct) by calling the Product object's SetProductProperties method.

This method takes the recordset as its argument and iterates through it to update the Product object's properties. We also pass True for the fForceUpdate argument, because we want to force the update of the Product object's properties, even if its property values have changed since we retrieved them.

```
        Set rstProductProperties = _
        objProduct.GetProductProperties
        rstProductProperties.Fields("Description").Value = _
        .Fields("short_description").Value
        rstProductProperties.Fields("Name").Value = _
        .Fields("product_name").Value
        rstProductProperties.Fields("product name").Value = _
        .Fields("product_name").Value
        objProduct.SetProductProperties _
        rstProductProperties, True
```

Adding Third-Party Product Variants to the Commerce Server Product Catalog

Now we are ready for stage four, where we add the product variants to the catalog. This stage is actually wrapped inside of the product families loop.

This code gets the SDCC's product variants recordset, loops through it, and adds them to our product catalog. This is accomplished by calling the `CreateVariant` method of the `Product` object (`objProduct`). We pass in the `ProductVariantID` (SKU) to this method, and it returns a recordset of the product variant properties.

These are what we defined earlier when we created the Clothing product definition for the SDCC catalog in our product catalog (see stage one). Then, similar to setting the properties of the product, we set the field values in the product variant properties recordset, and then pass the recordset back in to the `Product` object via the `SetVariantProperties` method. We also set the `fForceUpdate` argument to `True` here as well.

```
'Get the 3rd party product variants
'and add them to the catalog.

'Get the 3rd party product variants.
Set rst3PProductVariants = GetRSFromSQL("SELECT * " _
& "FROM ProductVariant WHERE product_family_id = " _
& .Fields("product_family_id").Value)

'Add the 3rd party product variants to the
'CS catalog.
Do Until rst3PProductVariants.EOF
        Set rstProductVariant = _
        objProduct.CreateVariant( _
        SD_CLOTHING_SKU_PREFIX _
        & rst3PProductVariants.Fields("SKU").Value)

        rstProductVariant.Fields("Size").Value = _
        rst3PProductVariants.Fields("Size").Value
        rstProductVariant.Fields("Color").Value = _
        rst3PProductVariants.Fields("Color").Value
        rstProductVariant.Update

        objProduct.SetVariantProperties _
        rstProductVariant, True

        rst3PProductVariants.MoveNext
Loop
```

Adding Third-Party Product-Category Associations to the Commerce Server Product Catalog

This stage is also wrapped inside of stage three, and we will also close the product family recordset loop from stage three here as well. This is the last stage of our method, and its purpose is to preserve the product-category associations from the SDCC catalog.

The first thing we do is to get a recordset of all of the categories that the product family in the product family loop belongs to. We do this by querying on the `product_family_id` value that the loop is currently on.

```
'Add the 3rd party product-category
'associations to the catalog.
Set rst3PCategories = GetRSFromSQL("SELECT " _
& "category_name FROM " _
& "Category AS c INNER JOIN " _
& "ProductFamilyCategory AS pfc ON " _
& "c.category_id = pfc.category_id " _
& "WHERE product_family_id = " _
& .Fields("product_family_id").Value)
```

199

Then we loop through the categories and call the `GetCategory` method of the `ProductCatalog` object to get an instance of the current category:

```
Do Until rst3PCategories.EOF
  strCategory = _
  rst3PCategories.Fields("category_name").Value
  Set objCategory = _
  objCatalog.GetCategory(strCategory)
```

We then call the `AddProduct` method of the `Category` object and pass in the `ProductID` that we created in the beginning of the product family loop in order to add the product to the category, and close the loops:

```
        objCategory.AddProduct strProductID
        rst3PCategories.MoveNext
      Loop

    End If

    .MoveNext
  Loop

  End With
End If

ExitProc:
  If blnError = True Then
    Set objFSO = New Scripting.FileSystemObject
    objFSO.OpenTextFile(App.Path & "\IntegrationErrors.txt", _
          ForAppending, True, _
          TristateUseDefault).WriteLine strError
  End If
```

Finally, we do some cleaning up:

```
'Clean up memory
Set objFSO = Nothing
Set objManager = Nothing
Set objCatalog = Nothing
Set rst3PCategories = Nothing
Set objCategory = Nothing
Set rstProductDefinitions = Nothing
Set rst3PProductFamilies = Nothing
Set rst3PProductVariants = Nothing
Set rstProductVariant = Nothing
Set objProduct = Nothing
Set rstProductProperties = Nothing

End Sub
```

There you have it! We have just added the products, product variants, categories, and the product-category associations from our sample third-party catalog into our Commerce Server product catalog.

Search Support

The search support in Commerce Server 2000 is greatly improved over SSCE. In SSCE, there really was not much support at all for searching. Most of the time we had to write our own databases and our own COM objects, and that meant that we had to do our searches as well. It is much different now: the flexibility of the new database schema and the elegant product catalog object model lend themselves well to searching.

There are three main types of searches that can be performed against the product catalog. They are:

- ❏ Free-text Search
- ❏ Query
- ❏ Specification Search

Free-text Search

A free-text search enables us to search on words or phrases in one or more catalogs. It is based on full text indexing in SQL Server 2000, and inherits keywords and operators from SQL Server 2000 to control the search. This means that we can use the CONTAINS and FREETEXT predicates in our search clause, just as we can do in a regular Transact-SQL WHERE clause.

These are much more powerful ways of doing a search than the traditional LIKE predicate in Transact-SQL. This enables us to perform fuzzy matching, and implement weighting in our searches, without having to write any custom COM objects or database tables.

> *For more information on SQL Server 2000 full-text indexing and its associated Transact-SQL predicates, please refer to Wrox's* Professional SQL Server 2000 Programming, *ISBN 1-861004-48-6.*

In order to perform a free-text search, we must use the FreeTextSearch method of the CatalogManager object. We could execute a free-text search in the following way. Note that we here hard code our search parameter into the code.

```
'///////////////////////////////////////////////////////////////////////////////////
'
' Method:    FreeTextSearch
'
' Inputs:    None
'
' Output:    text to the lstOutput ListBox control
'
' Description: This method uses the FreeTextSearch method to search the
'         WroxHardware catalog. We are requesting product data in
'         this search. All products found are sorted by SKU in
'         ascending order and printed out to the screen.
'
'///////////////////////////////////////////////////////////////////////////////////

Private Sub FreeTextSearch()

On Error Resume Next

    Dim rstResults As ADODB.Recordset
```

```
Dim fldCurrent As ADODB.Field
Dim varRecordsReturned As Variant
Dim lngCounter As Long
Dim strError As String
Dim blnError As Boolean
```

After some initial stage setting, we search for all products containing the word 'Dual', returning the Name, prodid, and SKU properties, and sorting the products in ascending order on the SKU property. This uses the FreeTextSearch method of the CatalogManager object. This method returns an ADO Recordset object, and has nine arguments:

Argument	Description
strPhrase	A String that contains the search phrase.
strCatalogsToSearch	(Optional) A Variant that contains all of the catalogs to search in a comma-delimited list. If this is an empty string or is missing, all catalogs will be searched.
eClassTypeRequired	(Optional) A Variant that delineates what type of catalog class to use. The list of valid values comes from the CatalogClassTypeEnum enumeration.
strPropertiesToReturn	(Optional) A Variant that is a comma-delimited list of the properties to return.
strPropertyToSortOn	(Optional) A Variant that indicates what property to sort on. If this is an empty string or is missing, then the results will not be sorted.
fSortAscending	(Optional) A Boolean that indicates if the sort should be in ascending order (True) or descending order (False). The default value is True.
lStartingRecord	(Optional) A Variant that indicates what the starting record number to retrieve should be. For example, if you choose 11, and the method returns 20 records, you will get records 11-20.
lRecordsToRetrieve	(Optional) A Variant that indicates how many records the method should retrieve.
plTotalRecordsInQuery	(Optional) A Variant that is an out parameter. It is used to return the total number of records returned in the search.

Note that we are taking advantage of the full-text indexing by using the CONTAINS keyword.

We set the strPropertiesToReturn argument to Name, prodid, and SKU. These will be the fields that are returned in the resultant recordset.

We set strPropertyToSortOn to SKU, and we then set fSortAscending to True. This will result in all products returned being sorted by SKU in ascending order. We then set lStartingRecord to 1, and finally set lRecordsToRetrieve to 20. We also pass in varRecordsReturned to the plTotalRecordsInQuery. This must be a Variant data type; otherwise, it will return 0 (if it is a Long or Int data type).

```
Set rstResults = mobjManager.FreeTextSearch("CONTAINS (Name, 'Dual')", _
                     WROX_HW_CATALOG, _
                     cscProductClass, _
                     "Name,prodid,SKU", _
                     "SKU", _
                     True, _
                     1, _
                     20, _
                     varRecordsReturned)

'Check for errors
If Err.Number <> 0 Then
 blnError = True
 strError = "Error calling FreeTextSearch. " _
 & Err.Description
 GoTo ExitProc
End If

'Initialize our record counter
lngCounter = 1
```

If there are no errors, then we make sure that we got a valid Recordset object back from the method, and check to see if the total records returned (varRecordsReturned) is more than 0. After that, we simply loop through both the recordset and the fields of the recordset to print out the values:

```
If TypeName(rstResults) <> "Nothing" Then
 With rstResults

   'See if there were any records returned
   If varRecordsReturned > 0 Then

   'Loop through the search results
   Do Until .EOF

     'Print the record number
     lstOutput.AddItem "Record #" & lngCounter & ":"
```

Next, we loop through the fields in the recordset, printing their name and value to the screen:

```
   For Each fldCurrent In .Fields
     lstOutput.AddItem Space(5) & fldCurrent.Name _
     & ": " & fldCurrent.Value
   Next

   'Increment the record counter
   lngCounter = lngCounter + 1

   'Get the next search result record
   .MoveNext

 Loop

 'Print out how many records were returned
 lstOutput.AddItem "(" & varRecordsReturned _
```

```
                      & " records were returned)"

        Else

          'Print out that no records were returned
          lstOutput.AddItem "(No records were found " _
          & "that matched the search criteria)"

        End If

      End With

    Else

      'We did not get a valid Recordset back from the search,
      'so flag it as an error.
      blnError = True
      strError = "Error perfroming search. The method did not return " _
      & "a Recordset object."

    End If

  ExitProc:

    'Display errors, if applicable
    If blnError = True Then
      lstOutput.AddItem strError
    End If

    'Clean up memory
    Set fldCurrent = Nothing
    Set rstResults = Nothing

End Sub
```

When this code is executed from the `ProductCatalogTester.vbp` program, we should see the following results:

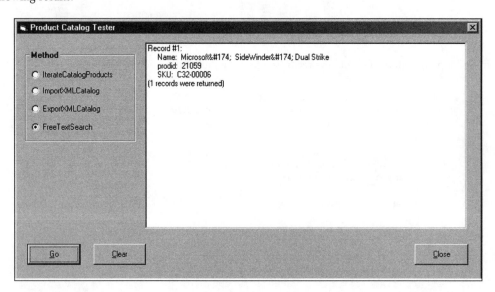

> Note that in order for products to show up using free-text search, the properties that we are searching on must have their `IsFreeTextSearchable` attribute set to 1 (True).

Query

Another method of searching involves calling the `Query` method of the `CatalogManager` object. This method is used to query against `product`, `variant`, and `category` data in one or more catalogs. This method is almost identical to the `FreeTextSearch` method previously discussed. All of the arguments are exactly the same as the `FreeTextSearch` method. The `Query` method returns an ADO Recordset object.

The only difference between the two methods is that with the `Query` method, we are more restricted: we have to treat the `strPhrase` argument just as we would the `Filter` property on an ADO Recordset object. For example, we would have to use the property-operator-value syntax: that is, CONTAINS (Name, 'Dual') instead of just using the word `Dual` for the search phrase. It is interesting to note that the `Query` method does support full-text indexing.

Specification Search

A specification search is an iterative way of performing a search on a particular product catalog. This allows a user to continually refine their searches until they have the results that they want. Specification searches are a great tool when you do not necessarily want to search all of the products in a catalog for a property value. Instead, they are for when you want to identify a particular group of products in a particular category. For example, if you were looking to buy a printer, you may search on pages per minute, then on color, then price, then any other properties, in order to find the printer that best matches your needs.

Specification searches are performed using the `ProductCatalog` object. The methods related to specification searches are `BeginSpecificationSearch`, `AddSpecificationSearchClause`, `GetSpecificationSearchClauses`, `RemoveSpecificationSearchClause`, `PerformSpecificationSearch`, and `GuaranteedSpecificationSearch`.

`BeginSpecificationSearch` is usually the first method we would call when performing a specification search. Its purpose is to specify which category you want to search, and then to return a string that contains the handle of the specification search. The handle is what you must pass in to the `PerformSpecificationSearch` method in order to stay in the context of your search process.

It also has two very useful out parameters, `pRSInitialPropValuesList` (Variant ADO Recordset) and `plTotalRecordsAvailable` (Variant Long). The `pRSInitialPropValuesList` argument is a single-row recordset that contains one field for each searchable property (`IncludeInSpecSearch` attribute of the property = 1) for the given category. The value of each of the fields is a variant array of distinct possible values for the property. This recordset is used to display the properties and possible values to select on for each searchable property for the category.

The `AddSpecificationSearch` method is used to add search clauses to your specification search. Its arguments are the search handle (most likely from the `BeginSpecificationSearch` method), and the actual search clause itself: for example, "Author = 'Tim Huckaby'". You can call this as many times as you need to in order to put all of the constraints you require into your search.

The main method that you will call in order to get the results of your search is `PerformSpecificationSearch`.

I have built a sample ASP application in order to demonstrate one way of doing a specification search. This application is very similar in concept to one of the 'sitelet' applications that come with the Commerce Server 2000 SDK. The sole purpose of this application is to demonstrate the specification search features of Commerce Server 2000.

The first page of the application is the global.asa file. In global.asa, we initialize a CatalogManager object and place it into an Application variable (since it is thread safe). Here is the code for the global.asa file:

```
<SCRIPT LANGUAGE="VBScript" RUNAT="Server">

Option Explicit

  Sub Application_OnStart

  On Error Resume Next

    Dim mobjManager
    Dim mstrConnection

    'Set the connection string
    mstrConnection = "PROVIDER=SQLOLEDB;Server=TIMMC;" _
    & "Initial Catalog=Retail_commerce;User ID=sa;Password=;"

    'Instantiate the Catalog Manager object
    Set mobjManager = Server.CreateObject("Commerce.CatalogManager")

    'Initialize the Catalog Manager
    mobjManager.Initialize mstrConnection, True

    'Put the CatalogManager object in the Application variable
    Set Application("CatalogManager") = mobjManager

    'Clean up
    Set mobjManager = Nothing

  End Sub

  Sub Application_OnEnd

  On Error Resume Next

    Set Application("CatalogManager") = Nothing

  End Sub

</SCRIPT>
```

As you can see, the code here is pretty straightforward and very similar to the Form_Load method in the ProductCatalogTester.vbp project we looked at earlier.

The next page is an include file that gets included on every page in the application. Its purpose is to extract the CatalogManager object from the Application variable and place it in a local variable. Below is the code for initialize_manager.inc:

```
<%

  Dim gobjManager

  Set gobjManager = Application("CatalogManager")

%>
```

Once we have the reference to the `CatalogManager`, we are able to use it to get a reference to the `ProductCatalog` we are searching. The next page, `select_catalog.asp` illustrates this:

```
<%@Language=VBScript%>
<%Option Explicit%>

<!--#INCLUDE file = "initialize_manager.inc"-->

<%

  Dim mstrCatalogSelect
  Dim mrstCatalogs
  Dim mstrCatalog

  'Get all of the available catalogs
  Set mrstCatalogs = gobjManager.Catalogs

  With mrstCatalogs

    'Loop through the catalogs recordset to build the
    'catalogs select box
    Do Until .EOF
      mstrCatalog = .Fields("CatalogName").Value
      mstrCatalogSelect = mstrCatalogSelect & "<option value='" _
      & mstrCatalog & "'>" & mstrCatalog & "</option>"
      .MoveNext
    Loop

  End With

  'Clean up
  Set mrstCatalogs = Nothing
  Set gobjManager = Nothing

%>

<HTML>
<HEAD>
<meta http-equiv="Content-Type" content="text/html; charset=windows-1252">
<TITLE>Specification Search Example - Select Catalog</TITLE>
</HEAD>
<BODY>
<DIV id="Catalogs">
  <FIELDSET>
    <LEGEND><b>Select Catalog</b></LEGEND>
    <FORM name="frmCatalogs" method="POST" action="select_category.asp">
    <SELECT name="cboCatalogs" id="cboCatalogs">
```

```
        <%=mstrCatalogSelect%>
    </SELECT>
    <INPUT type="Submit" name="cmdSubmit" value="Send Catalog">
    </FORM>
    </FIELDSET>
  </DIV>
  </BODY>
  </HTML>
```

This page simply uses the `Catalogs` recordset property of the `CatalogManager` object to build a drop-down list of all of the available catalogs. It then posts the value selected to the `select_category.asp` page.

Here is what the page looks like in action:

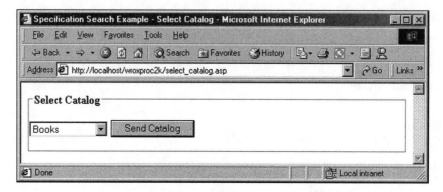

The next page, `select_category.asp`, receives the product catalog posted from the `select_catalog.asp` page, and generates another drop-down list of all of the searchable categories for the product catalog. Here is the code to generate `select_category.asp`:

```
<%@Language=VBScript %>
<%Option Explicit%>

<!--#INCLUDE file = "initialize_manager.inc"-->

<%

    Dim mstrCatalogName
    Dim mstrCategorySelect
    Dim mobjCatalog
    Dim mrstCategories
    Dim mstrCategory
```

After some initial stage setting, we begin by retrieving the product catalog name that was posted from the `select_catalog.asp` page:

```
    'Get the catalog name
    mstrCatalogName = Request.Form("cboCatalogs")
```

Then, we pass in the name of the catalog to the `GetCatalog` method of the `CatalogManager` object, which returns an instance of the `ProductCatalog` object:

```
'Get the catalog object
Set mobjCatalog = gobjManager.GetCatalog(mstrCatalogName)
```

We then get a recordset of all of the categories that are searchable by calling the `SearchableCategories` property of the `ProductCatalog` object:

```
'Get the searchable categories for the catalog
Set mrstCategories = mobjCatalog.SearchableCategories#]
```

We then loop through the recordset to build a drop-down list of all of the searchable categories:

```
With mrstCategories

'Loop through the categories recordset to build the
'categories select box
Do Until .EOF
  mstrCategory = .Fields("Name").Value
  mstrCategorySelect = mstrCategorySelect & "<option value='" _
  & mstrCategory & "'>" & mstrCategory & "</option>"
  .MoveNext
Loop

End With

'Clean up
Set mobjCatalog = Nothing
Set mrstCategories = Nothing
Set gobjManager = Nothing

%>
```

We also put the catalog name into a hidden form field (`catalog_name`), because we will need it on the next page:

```
<HTML>
<HEAD>
<meta http-equiv="Content-Type" content="text/html; charset=windows-1252">
<TITLE>Specification Search Example - Select Category</TITLE>
</HEAD>
<BODY>
<DIV id="Categories">
  <FIELDSET>
  <LEGEND><b>Select Category</b></LEGEND>
  <FORM name="frmCategories" method="POST" action="search_fields.asp">
  <SELECT name="cboCategories" id="cboCategories">
   <%=mstrCategorySelect%>
  </SELECT>
  <INPUT type="Submit" name="cmdSubmit" value="Send Category">
  <INPUT type="hidden" name="catalog_name" value="<%=mstrCatalogName%>">
  </FORM>
  </FIELDSET>
</DIV>
```

This is what our page should now look like:

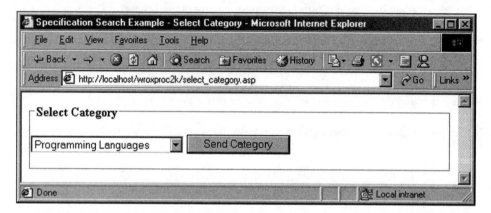

The `select_category.asp` page posts its data to the `search_fields.asp` page. This page is where we begin the specification search and present some drill-down choices to the user. Below is the code for `search_fields.asp`:

```
<%@Language=VBScript %>
<%Option Explicit%>

<!--#INCLUDE file = "initialize_manager.inc"-->

<%

On Error Resume Next

   Dim mstrCatalogName
   Dim mstrCategory
   Dim mrstFields
   Dim mlngFieldCount
   Dim mobjCatalog
   Dim mstrHandle
   Dim mlngRecordsAvailable
   Dim mstrValueSelect()
   Dim mlngFieldCounter
   Dim mlngValueCounter
   Dim mstrFieldName
   Dim marrFieldValues
   Dim mstrSelectBoxesTable
   Dim mstrSelectBoxesTableHeader
   Dim mstrSelectBoxesTableData
```

The first thing we do in this page is to get the name of the product catalog being passed in:

```
'Get the name of the catalog
mstrCatalogName = Request.Form("catalog_name")
```

We then get the category that was selected on the previous page:

```
'Get the category to search on
mstrCategory = CStr(Request.Form("cboCategories"))
```

We then use the catalog name (`mstrCatalogName`) and pass it in to the `GetCatalog` method of the `CatalogManager` object to get an instance of the `ProductCatalog` object:

```
'Get the catalog to search on
Set mobjCatalog = gobjManager.GetCatalog(mstrCatalogName)
```

Next, to get our search handle, we call the `BeginSpecificationSearch` method of the `ProductCatalog` object.

We pass in the category we want to search on (`mstrCategory`), a variant to hold the recordset of property names and their possible values that will be returned to us (`mrstFields`), and also a variant to hold the number of records available that the method will also return to us (`mlngRecordsAvailable`).

We capture the return value of the method in the `mstrHandle` variable.

The recordset that gets returned by reference from the `BeginSpecificationSearch` method is very important. It is a one-row recordset that has a field for every product property in the category, and the name of the field is the name of the property. The interesting part is that the value for the field is a variant array of all of the possible values for the property. This is a clever way to use an ADO Recordset object to return a lot of data packed into one variable.

```
'Call BeginSpecification search to get a search handle.
'This method also returns a recordset of the properties
'(mrstFields) available to search on, and how many
'records are available (mlngRecordsAvailable).
mstrHandle = mobjCatalog.BeginSpecificationSearch(mstrCategory, _
                        mrstFields, _
                   mlngRecordsAvailable)
```

We now have all of the data that we need in order to present to the user the properties and values to select on for their specification search.

The first step is to check to make sure that we have a valid Recordset object reference. We do this by using the `Is Nothing` operator and seeing if it is `True` or not; if it is `True` we stop processing.

```
'If the recordset returned is null, then there are no properties
'available to search on for the category
If mrstFields Is Nothing Then
  Response.Write "There is no criteria available for " _
  & mstrCategory & "."
  Response.End
End If
```

The next step is to loop through the recordset's fields collection and build all of the drop-down lists. To do this, we first get a count of many fields there are (`mlngFieldCount`). Since there will be a drop-down list for every field in the recordset, we then re-dimension our select box array variable (`mstrValueSelect`) to the correct size.

```
'Start building the table for the search criteria form
mstrSelectBoxesTable = "<TABLE>"
mstrSelectBoxesTableHeader = "<TR>"
```

```
mstrSelectBoxesTableData = "<TR>"

With mrstFields

  'Get the count of fields
  mlngFieldCount = .Fields.Count

  'Redimension the select box array
  ReDim mstrValueSelect(mlngFieldCount - 1)
```

We then begin looping through the fields in the recordset. For each field, we collect the name and value of the field. When we get the value of the field, since it is a variant array, we must then loop through the variant array to build the list of values for the drop-down list for the particular field that we are on in the loop.

```
  'Loop through the fields
  For mlngFieldCounter = 0 To mlngFieldCount - 1

    'Get the name of the field
    mstrFieldName = .Fields(mlngFieldCounter).Name

    'Get the value of the field (an array). This is a list
    'of all possible values for the particular property.
    marrFieldValues = .Fields(mlngFieldCounter).Value

    'Only build the select box if it will
    'have possible values to choose from
    If UBound(marrFieldValues) > 0 Then

      'Build the table header
      mstrSelectBoxesTableHeader = mstrSelectBoxesTableHeader _
      & "<TD><B>" & mstrFieldName & "</B></TD>"

      'Build the select
      mstrValueSelect(mlngFieldCounter) = "<SELECT name='cbo" _
      & .Fields(mlngFieldCounter).Name & "'>"

      'Make a default value
      mstrValueSelect(mlngFieldCounter) = _
      mstrValueSelect(mlngFieldCounter) _
      & "<option value=''>Select<option>"

      'Loop through the array value of the field
      For mlngValueCounter = LBound(marrFieldValues) _
      To UBound(marrFieldValues)
        mstrValueSelect(mlngFieldCounter) = _
        mstrValueSelect(mlngFieldCounter) _
        & "<option value='" & _
        marrFieldValues(mlngValueCounter) _
        & "'>" & _
        marrFieldValues(mlngValueCounter) & "</option>"
      Next

      'Finish the select
      mstrValueSelect(mlngFieldCounter) = _
      mstrValueSelect(mlngFieldCounter) _
      & "</SELECT>"

      'Add the select box to the list of select boxes
      mstrSelectBoxesTableData = mstrSelectBoxesTableData _
```

```
         & "<TD>" & mstrValueSelect(mlngFieldCounter) & "</TD>"

     End If

  Next

End With
```

Once we have finished with these loops, we then close up our HTML tags, clean up memory, and then write the HTML out to the client:

```
    'Close the table for the search criteria form
    mstrSelectBoxesTableHeader = mstrSelectBoxesTableHeader & "</TR>"
    mstrSelectBoxesTableData = mstrSelectBoxesTableData & "</TR>"
    mstrSelectBoxesTable = mstrSelectBoxesTable _
      & mstrSelectBoxesTableHeader & mstrSelectBoxesTableData & "</TABLE>"

    'Clean up
    Set mrstFields = Nothing
    Set mobjCatalog = Nothing
    Set gobjManager = Nothing

%>

<HTML>
<HEAD>
<meta http-equiv="Content-Type" content="text/html; charset=windows-1252">
<TITLE>Specification Search Example - Select Filter</TITLE>
</HEAD>
<BODY>
<DIV id="Search">
  <FIELDSET>
    <LEGEND><b>Search Criteria</b></LEGEND>
    <FORM name="frmSearch" method="POST" action="search_results.asp">
    <%=mstrSelectBoxesTable%>
    <INPUT type="Submit" name="cmdSubmit" value="Process Results">
    <INPUT type="hidden" name="search_handle" value="<%=mstrHandle%>">
    <INPUT type="hidden" name="catalog_name" value=<%=mstrCatalogName%>>
    </FORM>
  </FIELDSET>
</DIV>
```

Our page should now look like this:

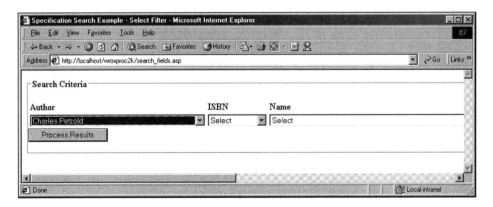

One important thing to note is that we are using two hidden form fields, `search_handle` and `catalog_name`, so we can pass the search handle and the product catalog name on to the next page that we are posting to, which is the `search_results.asp` page.

In the `search_results.asp` page, we take all of the choices that the user made from the `search_fields.asp` page, use them to feed into our search and then display the results of the search. Here is the code for the `search_results.asp` page:

```
<%@Language=VBScript %>
<%Option Explicit%>

<!--#INCLUDE file = "initialize_manager.inc"-->

<%

On Error Resume Next
```

We first start out by defining a constant, `cscProductClass`. This will be used later when we call the `PerformSpecificationSearch` method:

```
Const cscProductClass = 4

Dim mstrCatalogName
Dim mstrHandle
Dim mobjCatalog
Dim mrstResults
Dim mlngFieldCount
Dim mlngFieldCounter
Dim mlngDesiredRecords
Dim mlngRecordsAvailable
Dim mvarField
Dim mstrSearchClause
```

Just like the pages before, the first thing we do again in this page is to get the catalog name and the category name from the posted form. We also get the search handle that was generated from our call to the `BeginSpecificationSearch` method from the `search_fields.asp` page:

```
'Get the search handle
mstrHandle = Request.Form("search_handle")

'Get the catalog name to search
mstrCatalogName = Request.Form("catalog_name")
```

We then proceed to get an instance of the `Catalog` object again.

```
'Get the ProductCatalog object from the CatalogManager object
Set mobjCatalog = gobjManager.GetCatalog(mstrCatalogName)
```

The next step that we take is to loop through all of the items in the `Request.Form` collection, and see which item names begin with the `cbo` prefix. This indicates that the form field is a drop-down list box, and that is what we are after:

```
'Loop through the items in the Request.Form collection
For Each mvarField In Request.Form
```

If the item name begins with cbo, we then check to make sure that a value is associated with it. To do this, we just check to make sure the length of the value is greater than zero. If the item passes these tests, we then build a search clause, in the form of property = value.

```
'If the name of the item starts with "cbo",
'then we know that this is part of our search
'clause
If Mid(mvarField, 1, 3) = "cbo" Then

   'Make sure that the value is not null
   'or an empty string
   If Len(Request.Form(mvarField)) > 0 Then

      'Build the search clause. For example,
      '"Author = 'Tim Huckaby'"
      mstrSearchClause = Mid(mvarField, 4, Len(mvarField) - 3) _
      & " = '" & Request.Form(mvarField) & "'"

      'Write out the search clause
      Response.Write "Search Clause: " & mstrSearchClause & "<BR>"
```

Then we call the AddSpecificationSearchClause method to add the search clause to our specification search under the context of our current search handle:

```
      'Add the specification search clause
      mobjCatalog.AddSpecificationSearchClause _
         CStr(mstrSearchClause), mstrHandle

   End If

End If

Next
```

Once we finish the loop, we then set the mlngDesiredRecords variable to 1; this is to ensure that we only get one record back from our search (that's all that will fit on the screen!):

```
'We only want one record back at a time
mlngDesiredRecords = 1
```

Now we are ready to call the PerformSpecificationSearch method. We pass in our search handle (mstrHandle), the cscProductClass constant, the desired number of records that we want back (mlngDesiredRecords), and we pass in by reference the variant variable mlngRecordsAvailable in order to see how many records the search found. The cscProductClass constant tells the PerformSpecificationSearch method to only return records of the Product class:

```
'Execute the search
Set mrstResults = _
   mobjCatalog.PerformSpecificationSearch(CStr(mstrHandle), _
```

```
          cscProductClass, mlngDesiredRecords, mlngRecordsAvailable)

     'Write out how many records are available
     Response.Write "(" & mlngRecordsAvailable & " Records Total)" _
       & "<BR><BR>"
```

After calling the `PerformSpecificationSearch` method, we then loop through the resultant recordset and its fields to write out the name and value of each field to the page:

```
    With mrstResults

      'Loop through the resultant recordset
      Do Until .EOF

        'Get the number of fields
        mlngFieldCount = .Fields.Count

        'Write out the name of the product
        Response.Write .Fields("product name").Value & "<BR>"

        'Loop through the fields
        For mlngFieldCounter = 0 To mlngFieldCount - 1

        'Write out the name and value of the field
         Response.Write "     " _
         & .Fields(mlngFieldCounter).Name & ": " _
         & .Fields(mlngFieldCounter).Value & "<BR>"

        Next

        'Go to the next record
        .MoveNext

      Loop

    End With

    'Clean up
    Set mrstResults = Nothing
    Set mobjCatalog = Nothing
    Set gobjManager = Nothing

%>

<HTML>
<HEAD>
<meta http-equiv="Content-Type" content="text/html; charset=windows-1252">
<TITLE>Specification Search Example - Results</TITLE>
</HEAD>
<BODY>
</BODY>
</HTML>
```

Our results should look something like this:

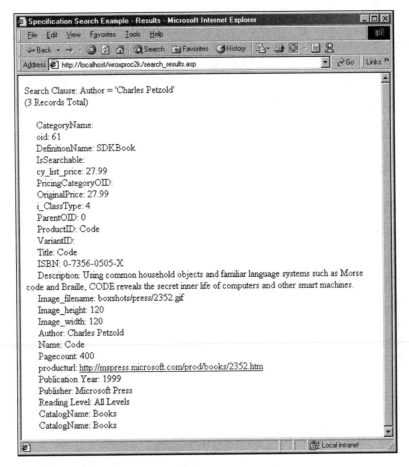

We've now looked in some depth at ways of performing three different types of searches. Such functionality is essential to a well designed e-commerce application.

Summary

In this chapter we covered the architecture of the Commerce Server 2000 product catalog, the product catalog object model, the XML behind the product catalog, and the various methods of searching the product catalog. We also stepped through a good deal of code utilizing the product catalog object model.

The Commerce Server 2000 product catalog's flexibility and extensibility lend themselves to just about any B2C or B2B site. I hope this chapter whets your appetite to think of ways you can programmatically control your own product catalogs, and hopefully integrate your catalog imports and exports with BizTalk Server.

Now that we have some understanding of the architecture of the product catalog, we are ready to start looking at ways of analyzing the data that is contained in the product catalog database. It is to this that we turn in the next chapter.

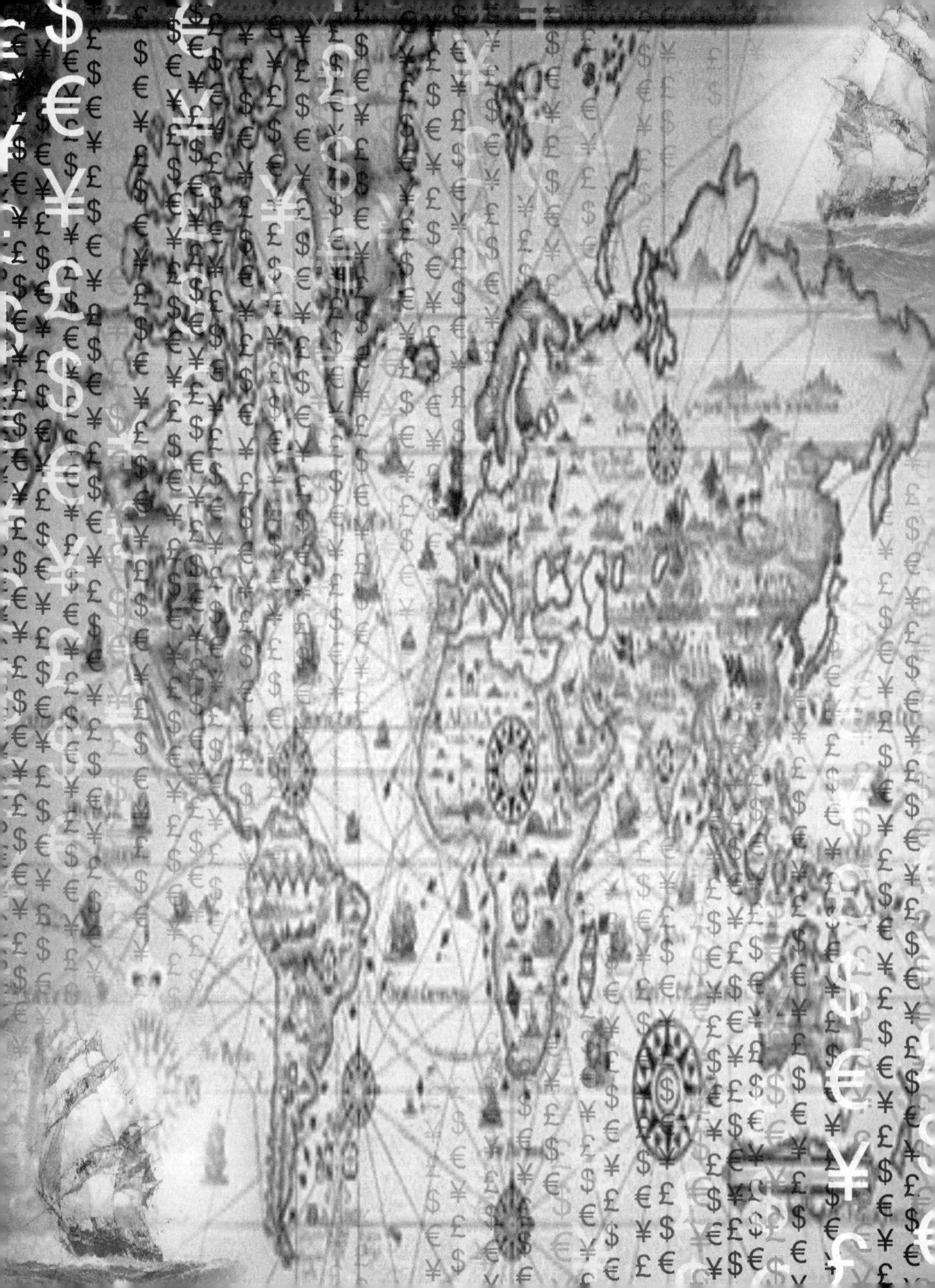

5

Business Analytics

The name of this chapter might cause you to stop and think; after all, how does Business Analytics help you build your website? Business Analytics is web usage analysis and much more, and it is something you usually consider *after* your site is up and running because your marketing department wants to know how your site is being used. However, preparation for Business Analytics is necessary before you bring your site online to ensure that you can take full advantage of all functionality. Before you flip the pages to the next chapter, you must know that Commerce Server gives you a fully featured web usage analysis system with capabilities you cannot find anywhere else. And you can shed all your Site Server 3.0 usage analysis nightmares – Business Analytics does it right and it works.

Typical usage analysis solutions base everything on your Internet Information Server (IIS) logs. If you've looked at these logs then you already know that there's not much more in there than what web resource has been downloaded at what time. This is only a very small piece of the whole puzzle and it is virtually impossible to make good business decisions that will improve your website. If you could use the IIS log, and integrate it with user profiles, how products are selling, how much customers are purchasing, and even your own custom information, then you would have an analysis system that would enable you to make the best business decisions possible to effect change on your website. Business Analytics delivers this functionality.

In this chapter we will be discussing the components of the Business Analytics system, including:

- ❏ **Data Warehouse**. This is the heart and soul of Business Analytics. The Data Warehouse contains all of your data, and all reports are created from this information. We will discuss how to extend the schema of the data warehouse.

- ❏ **Data Import**. This is a discussion on how to get your site's data into the data warehouse, and even your own custom information.

- ❏ **Business Desk Analysis**. Learn how to run reports and create your own custom reports.

Note that this chapter's examples utilize the data warehouse provided with the Retail solution site.

The Commerce Server Data Warehouse

The data warehouse is the heart of Business Analytics. It is a SQL Server database and an Online Analytical Processing (OLAP) database. All of the reports that Business Analytics creates are generated from information in the data warehouse. The data warehouse is designed to support rich query and analysis capabilities, which include robust pivot table views on your data. It is populated with a set of Data Transformation Services (DTS) packages that import all types of information, such as your web usage logs, user profiles, and transaction information. The data warehouse is extensible and allows you to import custom information.

Overview

We'll take a moment to review some basics of the data warehouse. More detailed information is available in the Commerce Server online documentation.

Data Warehouse Structure

We have already mentioned that the data warehouse allows you to extend its schema. All it means is that the data warehouse databases are not closed to you and it does not only support data structures that it came with, such as the ones for web log files created by your web server. However, to allow you to be able to add your own custom information to the data warehouse, and have all the reporting facilities able to use your information, we must follow some rules. The rules give structure to any type of information, and are laid out in the **logical schema** of the data warehouse. The logical schema is a model that maps data to the **physical store**. The physical store is a SQL Server database and an OLAP database. You never modify the structure of the physical store directly: it is done programmatically through the logical schema.

Import Process

Business Analytics allows you to import data from many different data sources. Any data source that you have programmatic access to can be imported into the data warehouse. This includes your web log files, catalog and product information, transaction information, such as which products were placed into the shopping carts, user profiles, and other information. Commerce Server DTS tasks are used to import all of the information (these tasks are further elaborated on later in this section). All imported information is stored in a consistent manner in the data warehouse.

Segment Analysis

Commerce Server allows you to perform analysis on segments of users. Users in the same segment have similar behaviors and properties, such as they are in the same age group. A list of users can be generated from a segment model and fed into the List Manager. The List Manager is the Commerce Server module that allows you to manage lists of user records, such as creating a list of users for a Direct Mail campaign.

Data Analysis

The Business Desk is used to run reports against the data warehouse and analyze segments of user populations. There are two different types of reports: **dynamic reports** and **static reports**. Dynamic reports are built at runtime and are not saved, whereas static reports are stored with the data after they have been run.

Importing Information into the Data Warehouse

The information you use to generate reports does not magically appear in the data warehouse – a conscious effort is made to import the information. Fortunately, you can set it up once and have it scheduled so you don't tie up system administrators with yet another task.

Data Transformation Services

Commerce Server uses DTS tasks (a component of SQL Server) to import data into the data warehouse. When you install Commerce Server, several DTS packages are installed with it. Through these DTS packages, you can perform the following activities:

❑ Data imports, including IIS logs, user profile data for users registered with the User object, catalogs, campaign data, and transactional data, such as what items a user adds and removes from their shopping cart.

❑ Data maintenance, including deletion of data, IP address conversion, and site configuration synchronization.

❑ Report preparation.

The packages are simple to schedule and invoke, but there is an order of execution you should follow to ensure the integrity of the information in your data warehouse. The following diagram shows in what order DTS packages should be run to ensure you have correctly processed your site's information.

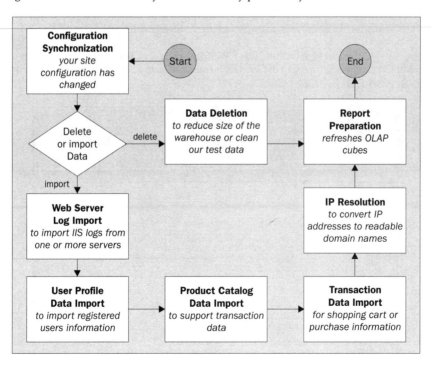

If your site configuration has changed, you must synchronize your site, using the Configuration Synchronization task, before importing or deleting information. After data is deleted or imported, you must refresh your OLAP cubes for report preparation.

To access these DTS tasks, expand the Microsoft SQL Servers snap-in within the Commerce Server Manager. Expand SQL Server Group, and then expand to select the server where your data warehouse was installed. Right-click on Data Transformation Services and select New Package. This is shown here:

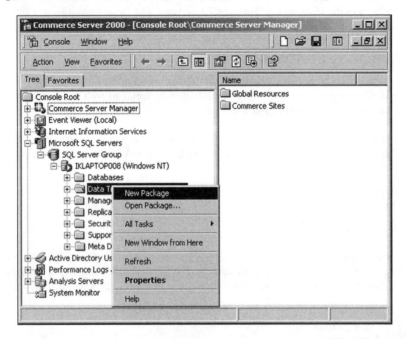

The following is the end result of selecting New Package. Run your cursor over the DTS packages and you will find several Commerce Server specific items. Currently selected is the Web server log import (Commerce Server) DTS package:

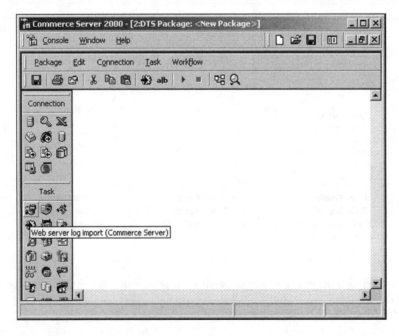

Importing Web Log Files

IIS Configuration

IIS creates log files of user activity on your website; whenever someone hits your website and loads a web page (or image, or other web resource), IIS writes a record to a log file. These files are text files that are recorded in World Wide Web Consortium (W3C) format (a working W3C draft document can be found at http://www.w3.org/TR/WD-logfile). These files become very large and frequently frustrate system administrators, because they have to constantly manage them! It's a worthwhile effort to open a log file and take a look at the structure and understand the type of information that is being recorded. By default, log files are stored in the %SystemRoot%\Winnt\System32\LogFiles\W3SVC%WebSiteInstance% folder where the website instance is created from the instance of the website within the IIS metabase.

The following is a quick example of a sample log file in W3C format obtained from the website and created with the Retail solution site.

```
#Software: Microsoft Internet Information Services 5.0

#Version: 1.0

#Date: 2001-02-06 04:53:13

#Fields: date time c-ip cs-username s-ip s-port cs-method cs-uri-stem cs-uri-query
sc-status sc-bytes cs-bytes cs(User-Agent) cs(Cookie) cs(Referer)

2001-02-06 04:53:13 127.0.0.1 - 127.0.0.1 80 GET /retailsite - 404 3406 332
Mozilla/4.0+(compatible;+MSIE+5.5;+Windows+NT+5.0) - -

2001-02-06 04:53:41 127.0.0.1 - 127.0.0.1 80 GET /retail/ - 302 285 328
Mozilla/4.0+(compatible;+MSIE+5.5;+Windows+NT+5.0) - -
```

As you can see, it is quite painful to look at. Every time someone hits a web page, image, or another resource on your website, IIS will write a single line into these log files. In the Fields line, you see a listing of all the fields that are being recorded in the log. This point is only brought up because you can control which fields are recorded in these logs through the IIS management console, and certain fields are required for proper import into the data warehouse.

IIS needs to be configured correctly in order for you to be able to import your web logs. These three simple configurations include:

❑ Enabling IIS logging

❑ Selecting W3C extended log file format

❑ Selecting (at minimum) Client IP address, URI stem, Date, and Time fields so the logs can be imported

To enable IIS logging and select W3C extended log file format, right click on your website and select properties:

To enable logging and to select the proper format, make sure it is set up as follows:

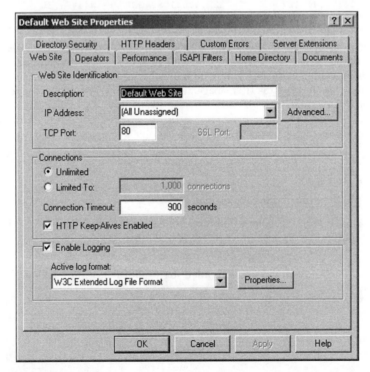

Select the Properties button on the above dialog and select the Extended Properties tab. Then select, at minimum, the Client IP address, URI stem, Date, and Time fields:

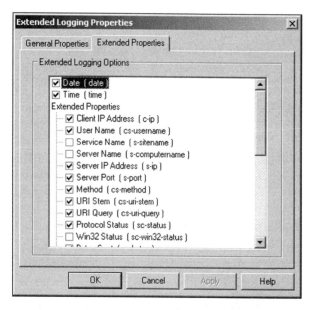

This ensures that your web log files will import into the data warehouse correctly.

Web Log File Import Properties

With every hit to your website being recorded, you can end up with a lot of information that needs to be imported into the data warehouse. However, do you really need all of the information in the web logs? For example, is it important that you track usage on image files? If not, you can dramatically reduce the amount of information imported into the data warehouse. A filtering mechanism is provided by Commerce Server to manage what information is imported into your data warehouse. Additionally, there are import properties that increase the accuracy of the information reported.

To access these properties, select the Web server log import DTS task back on the first screen, and click on the Advanced button. The following dialog will appear:

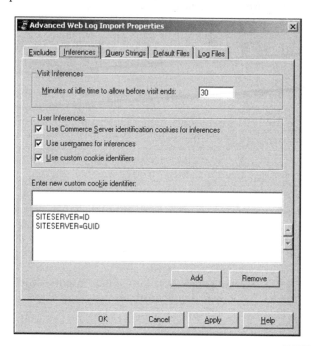

Default files are the web pages users hit when no web page is specified. Sometimes you will set up multiple pages to be your default file for a specific folder, such as `default.htm` and `default.asp`. If a user does specify a file, then a hit on `default.htm` and `default.asp` are considered two separate web page hits.

You can set up **exclusions** based on several factors – for example:

❑ You can exclude users who originated from certain hosts. An example of this feature is to exclude all the in-house users from a website, so only the true usage from external users is recorded.

❑ You can exclude specific file extensions. Most web pages will render several images, so if a web page has ten images on it, then when a user visits the page there will be eleven hits in the IIS log files.

❑ File expressions can be used to exclude different kinds of files where their file names match certain patterns. For example, most likely you will not want to include any file that begins with a "_".

❑ Website crawlers are automatically excluded. You can add or remove new crawlers to the excluded list.

It is often difficult to know what constitutes a unique user visit. If a user is not required to authenticate, for example, what information is available to you to determine a unique visit? Commerce Server uses a set of **inferences** to not only identify a user, but also to determine unique user visits. For example, you can set up Commerce Server to infer a unique user using server cookies, unique user names, or custom cookie identifiers. The beginning of a user visit is easy to determine – when a user visits your site for the first time in that session then a visit begins. However, the end is difficult because you have no idea when the user closed their browser or started viewing another website. The length of time from the last web hit is manipulated to affect the entire length of the visit, which does not absolutely define the length of a visit but provides a best guess.

Many websites use **query strings** to pass parameters into web pages for processing. A query string is the parameters that follow a "?" in a URL (such as in http://wrox.com?x=1&y=2, x=1&y=2), and these parameters are sent with an `HTTP GET` command. This information is stored in your web log files. However, when an `HTTP POST` is used to transmit variables (such as from an HTML form), these variables are not in your web log files and, therefore, cannot be imported into your data warehouse.

You will encounter certain issues with your log files when:

❑ The import process was interrupted or resumed, or you are re-importing logs that someone has already imported.

❑ Web logs files are rotated in the middle of a users session.

The import process detects time overlaps in your log files and, by default, will discard entries in log files that overlap. Also, don't panic if you accidentally re-imported log files – there is a Data Deletion task that will allow you to manage this issue. Finally, web log files are rotated each day, meaning a new log file is created by IIS each day. This will cause some user visits to be distributed between two log files. You can control how the import process handles this condition by:

❑ Storing open visits for the next import, which will produce the most accurate visit account but will increase import time

- Committing all open visits to the database, which will increase visit counts

- Discarding all open visits, which will decrease visit counts (if a visit spans multiple log files)

Importing the Logs

You use the DTS Web server log import task to import web log files. The more activity your site has, the larger your web log files will be. The larger your web log files are, the more frequently you should import your log files into the data warehouse. After running the import task you need to run the Report Preparation task, which organizes the imported data into online analytical processing (OLAP) cubes.

The following figure is the Web server log import task dialog:

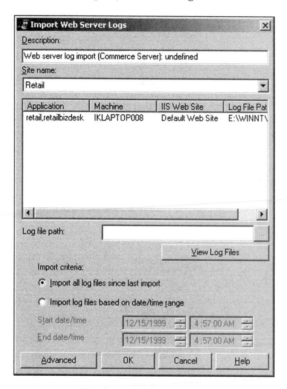

Enter a description of this import task; be certain that it clearly identifies the scope of what you are importing: you don't want to be digging through all your tasks to remember which one you want to execute. Select the website from the Site name drop-down list. This website is where you will be importing log files from. The list box contains the applications, machine names, website name, and log file location information. You can select the Log file path of the web log file you want to import. Choose the data ranges of the log files you want to import, or only import log files since the last import.

Importing Catalog, Campaign, User Profile, and Transaction Data

The process for importing Catalog, Campaign, User Profile, and Transaction Data is much simpler than importing web log files: the DTS tasks handle all the hard work for you. This type of information is where Business Analytics separates itself from the rest of the pack of usage analysis products such as WebTrends. Other products just rely on the web log files. The invaluable business information from your website is integrated into the analysis on your reports.

Setup and execution of the DTS tasks are similar across all of these data types. For example, to import catalog information, run the Product catalog import task. This is what you see for catalog imports:

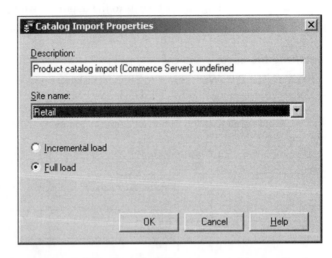

A full load needs to be run for the first time any of these DTS tasks are run. An incremental load will only import the new catalog data since the last import. Before these tasks are run, you must perform a synchronization of the site. After they are run, you must run the Report preparation task to prepare the data for reporting.

Using Non-Commerce Server Sites

You probably already have more than one website, and not all your websites might require Commerce Server, such as a simple company intranet server. You can import your non-Commerce Server sites web logs into the data warehouse.

The following figure shows how to add a non-Commerce application to a website. Expand Commerce Server Manager, expand Commerce Sites, and expand the site you want to administrate. Click Applications, right-click Applications, and click on Add Non-Commerce Application.

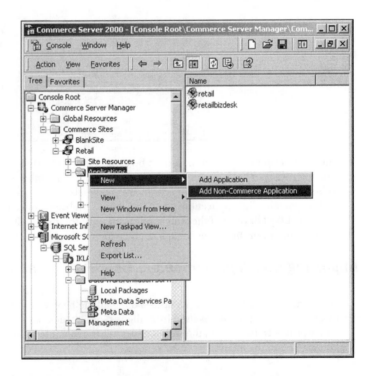

The following dialog will appear after
selecting Add Non-Commerce Application:

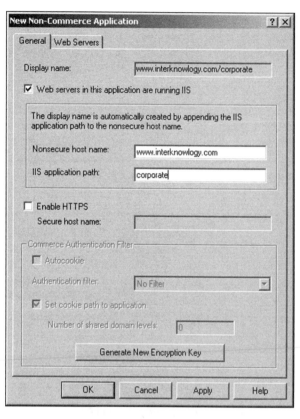

You can use non-IIS websites (even Apache) because the web server log format is a standard (W3C) that is
honored by other web servers. However, you can't use both non-IIS and IIS servers in a single non-
Commerce application. Only check Web servers in this application are running IIS if you are using IIS 5.0.

The following figure
shows how to add a non-
Commerce website to an
application. Expand
Commerce Server
Manager, expand
Commerce Sites, and
then expand the site you
want to administrate.
Expand Applications and
select the non-Commerce
application that you want
to add the web server to.

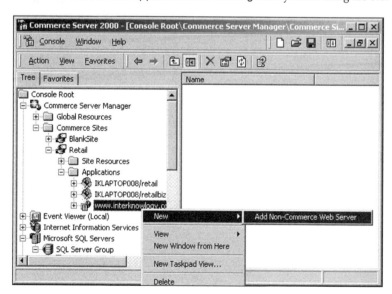

Right-click the application, select New and click on **Add Non-Commerce Web Server**. The following dialog appears:

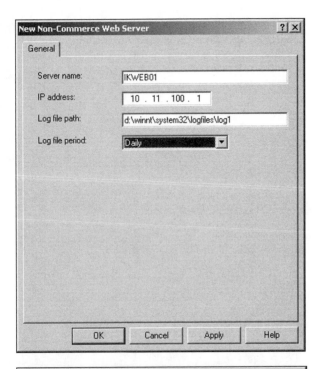

Now that a site is set up, the log files can be imported into the data warehouse. To import these logs, invoke the log import DTS task. For the new site we just added, here's what we now see:

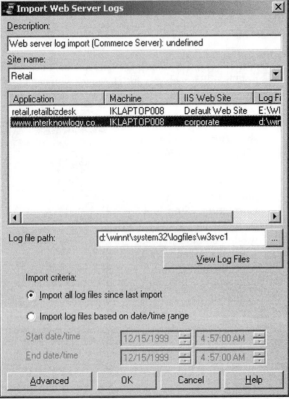

To import your logs click on **OK** then right-click on the task to execute it. Your logs will be imported into your data warehouse.

Data Warehouse Customization

We have seen that there are different types of information that you can import into the data warehouse. What we haven't discussed so far is how to put your own information in. For example, you might have custom information stored in your own databases that is highly related to the usage of your site. If this information was integrated into your reports you might be able to make better decisions on how to change your site to better serve your customers. Using the OLE DB Provider for Commerce Server, you can modify the logical schema of the data warehouse. This OLE DB Provider handles the creation of all the correct relationships in the data warehouse. Standardization within the database is paramount in order to be able to report on the information, because it would be impossible to create a generic reporting mechanism with foreign data sources – there's no way to know the structure. The logical schema enables us to have a standard interface to the data warehouse and not worry about how the information is stored in the database.

Structures in the Data Warehouse

There are several important structures in the data warehouse that you must understand before dealing with the OLE DB Provider for Commerce Server. These structures are how the logical schema organizes information, and include:

- ❑ **Classes**. The class structure is the core of the data warehouse logical schema. It is a collection of data members, and an instance of a class represents data that has been imported. A class definition is analogous to a database design structure. Classes can be set up to inherit the structure from another class. Classes are used to define the structure of the important data in the Data Warehouse.

- ❑ **Data Members**. A data member stores a piece of information. Running with the example, this is similar to a column in a database structure. Generally, multiple data members will be associated with a single class.

- ❑ **Keys**. A key is one or more data members that uniquely define an instance of a class. For example, you might have a class called company where the company name is unique among all companies, so it uniquely identifies an instance of the company. A key might use a data member from an inherited class.

- ❑ **Relationships**. A relationship will tie two classes together in a parent-child association. A relationship allows data members to be shared between classes When a data member is marked as inheritable, it is copied to child classes when the parent-child relation is created. Parent classes can have zero to all of the data members defined as inheritable.

The structures can be very complex. The following is an example of the class structures and relationships that support web topology. This is one of the simpler structures: each box represents a class and the arrows show the relationships between the classes.

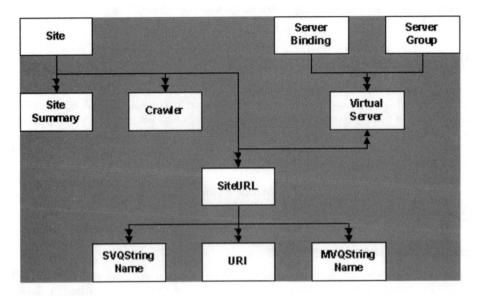

Extending the Schema

When extending the logical schema, there are several steps to follow. The sample application to extend the schema follows this flow. The flow of the application follows these steps:

- ❏ Connect to the data warehouse with the OLE DB Provider for Commerce Server and turn on the schema change mode

- ❏ Create a class definition

- ❏ Add data member definitions to the new class definition

- ❏ If required, create a key definition and key members for the class

- ❏ If required, create relationship definitions for the class

A complete listing of all the fields within each logical schema structure can be found in the Commerce Server online help in the Programmer's Reference section. Now we will look a little more at each step.

Binding to the Data Warehouse

The OLE DB Provider for Commerce Server implements a Binder object. This allows you to bind to the OLE DB Row using the URL naming convention. There are two types of connections string used by the OLE DB Provider for Commerce Server; both are shown below:

```
"URL=mscop://InProcConnect/Server=myserver:Database=dbname:
Catalog=DWSchema:User=sa:Password=:FastLoad=True"
```

The second form is as follows:

```
"Provider=commerce.dso.1;Data Source=mscop://InProcConnect/Server=myserver:
Catalog=DWSchema:Database=dbname:User=sa:
Password=:FastLoad=True"
```

The catalog name must be set to DWSchema, and the Fastload option must be set to True.

Class Definitions

A new class definition is created in the data warehouse by inserting a new instance of a Class Definition into the `ClsDef` table and setting the appropriate attributes. The schema edit mode must be turned on before this operation is attempted. The sample application demonstrates how to do this. The OLE DB Provider for Commerce Server will create a new SQL table in the data warehouse for every new class you add.

Data Member Definitions

A class must exist before a data member can be added to it. A data member is created by inserting a new instance into the `MemDef` table and setting the appropriate attributes. As with all logical schema edits, the schema edit mode must be turned on before this operation is attempted. The OLE DB Provider for Commerce Server will create a new column in the associated SQL table (identified by the class the data member is being added to) for every new data member that is added.

Key and Key Member Definitions

A key is a unique identifier for a class. The class must exist before attempting to create a key for it. A key can have one or more members in it. A key can be created implicitly by setting the `GenerateKeyDef` attribute for a class to `True` and all key members are made into primary keys. Or a key can be explicitly created by inserting a new instance into the `ClsKeyDef` table and creating a class key member in the `KeyMem` table. This is demonstrated in the sample application.

Relationship and Relationship Member Definitions

Parent and child classes need to exist before a relationship is created; the name of the relation must be unique. Due to class inheritance, member names should not be duplicated between parents and children because the parent data members are visible in the child class. The same holds true for one to many relations. Classes should have only one relation between them.

Create a New Data Warehouse

The `csdwschema.sql` script located in the root installation directory of Commerce Server builds the logical schema of the data warehouse. It must be run on an empty database. Create a new database called `test_dw` in SQL Server and execute the script against it.

Logical Schema Extender Sample

A simple web application has been created to easily allow the extending of structures in the data warehouse. This sample application is available for download from http://www.wrox.com, and allows for class, data member, key, and relation creation. With the application we will add new structures to the data warehouse and review the code that makes it all happen. The following figure shows the top level of this sample application, `default.asp`. The application is not intended to be used in production. A single component was created to encapsulate all of the functionality to update the logical schema.

> **Examples in the online Commerce Server help for extending the schema are not always correct. The main issue encountered is the incorrect path when instantiating new records in the logical schema.**

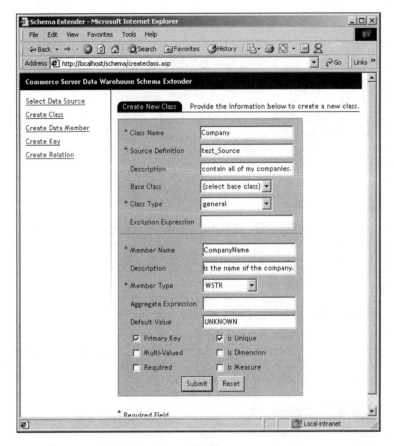

In this section we will create classes for employees and companies and define a one to many relationship between companies and employees (we'll assume no moonlighting for the sake of simplicity!) with the sample application. The test_dw data warehouse created in the previous section will be used to create these new structures.

The Company class will be structured as follows:

```
Class Company
{
   [Key] CompanyName
   PhoneNumber
   WebSite
}
```

The Employee class will be structured as follows:

```
Class Employee
{
   [Key] EmployeeName
   EmailAddress
}
```

A one-to-many relationship will be created between companies and employees.

Select Data Source

In order to make the application a bit more generic, the ability to add your own custom connection information was added. This information is stored in a cookie for the length of your session. We need to connect to the test_dw data warehouse in order to add the two new classes to it.

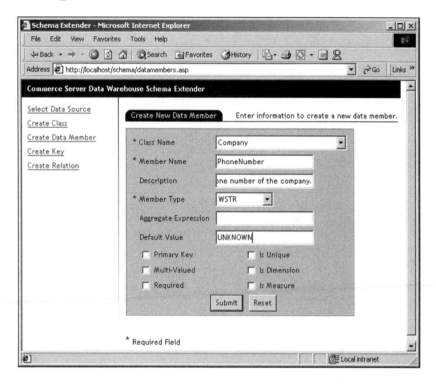

A connection to the data warehouse is attempted to guarantee that correct connection information has been entered. Here's the VBScript that does this:

```
On Error Resume Next

Dim adoConn
Set adoConn = CreateObject("ADODB.Connection")

' just going to do a quick open to make sure connection values are correct
adoConn.Open "URL=mscop://InProcConnect/server=" & strServerName & _
    ":database=" & strDatabase & ":Catalog=DWSchema: user=" &_
    strUsername & ":password=" & strPassword & ":FastLoad=True"

If Err.Number <> 0 Then
    Response.Redirect "datasource.asp?msg=" & Err.Description
Else
    adoConn.Close
    Response.Redirect "default.asp"
End If

set adoConn = nothing
```

This code snippet creates a connection to the data warehouse with the input from the previous screen. The connection string is one of two formats compatible with the OLE DB Provider for Commerce Server:

```
adoConn.Open "URL=mscop://InProcConnect/server=" & strServerName & _
        ":database=" & strDatabase & _ ":Catalog=DWSchema: user=" &_
        strUsername & _ ":password=" & strPassword & _ ":FastLoad=True"
```

Written in the alternative format, the above connection string would be something like the following:

```
"Provider=commerce.dso.1;Data Source=mscop://InProcConnect/" &_
    "Server=" & strServerName & ":Catalog=DWSchema:Database=" &_
    strDatabase & ":User=" & strUsername & ":Password=" & strPassword &_
    ":FastLoad=True"
```

The name of the catalog must be set to DWSchema, and the FastLoad must be set to True. When an error occurs, the user is redirected to the original page.

Create Class

The following web page allows you to create a new class in the data warehouse. Additionally, a member can be added at the same time the class is created. We will be creating the Company class first and the CompanyName primary key, as shown in the following figure.

> This version of the OLE DB Provider for Commerce Server does not support deletion from the logical schema. So type carefully!

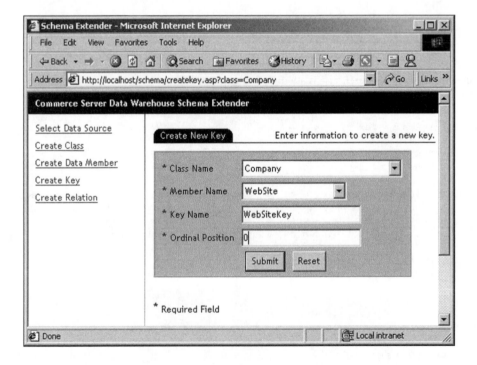

The following tables contain brief descriptions of the fields in the above figure. This table only describes the first set of fields that are used to create a class. The other fields are described in the data members section.

Field	Description
Class Name	This class name uniquely identifies this class in the data warehouse logical schema.
Source Definition	The source definition identifies the data source for storing instances of the class.
Description	This describes this logical class.
Base Class	The name of the base class, which is used for aggregations (which is like inheritance).
Class Type	0 = general, 1 = dimension, 2 = fact, 3 = aggregation
Exclusion Expression	Used as a filter for aggregations. This feature supports the IN and NOT IN operators with this syntax: `BaseClassMemberName IN(value)` This gives you the ability to create a summarization class based on the value of a member of the base class. You might, for example, want to create a class of only the web hits with a HTTP response of 200. With the base class being the Request class, you would add an exclusion expression that would read HttpStatus IN(200).

To create a list of base classes (which is just a list of all the classes in the data warehouse), a method was created to return all of the classes in the data warehouse. The method is invoked from VBScript and put into an HTML drop-down list:

```
Dim objDW, strClasses, arrClasses, cnt, strSel

' instantiate the data warehouse schema object
Set objDW = Server.CreateObject("IKDataWarehouse.Schema")

...' retrieve a list of classes from the data warehouse
strClasses = objDW.GetClasses (strServerName, strDatabase,
    strUsername, strPassword)
```

Once we have the classes, we put them into an array, and then move through this array of classes:

```
...' split the list into an array
    arrClasses = Split(strClasses, "^")

...' iterate through the array of classes
    For cnt = Lbound(arrClasses) to Ubound(arrClasses)
        ' if the base class is found while iterating, then make it the default
        ' selection in the HTML list box
        If strBaseClass = arrClasses(cnt) Then
```

```
         strSel = " SELECTED=""SELECTED"" "
     Else
         strSel = ""
     End If
     ' output an item of the list box
     Response.Write "<OPTION" & strSel & " VALUE=""" & arrClasses(cnt)
         & """>" & arrClasses(cnt) & "</OPTION>"

   Next

   ' the object is destroyed
   Set objDW = Nothing
```

The `IKDataWarehouse.Schema` component contains all of the logic to update the schema. The `GetClasses` method retrieves a list of classes in alphabetical order:

```
' GetClasses: retrieves the list of classes in the data warehouse as a string
' delimited by a ^

Public Function GetClasses(ByVal strServer As String, _
                           ByVal strDatabase As String, _
                           ByVal strUser As String, _
                           ByVal strPassword As String) As String

    ' instantiate variables
    Dim adoConn As Object
    Dim strError As String

    On Error Goto GetClassesErr

    Set adoConn = CreateObject("ADODB.Connection")
```

Once we have the list of classes, we connect to the data warehouse, check to see if an error occurred, then close the connection.

```
...' open a connection to the data warehouse
    Set adoConn = OpenConnection(strServer, strDatabase, strUser, strPassword,_
        strError)

...' check if an error condition occurred
    If Len(strError) Then
        GetClasses = strError ' return the error
    Else
        GetClasses = Sort(BuildClasses (adoConn)) ' sort the list of classes
    End If

...' close the connection to the data warehouse
    CloseConnection adoConn

    Set adoConn = Nothing

GetClassesErr:
```

```
      If Err.Number <> 0 Then
         GetClasses = Err.Description
      End If

      On Error Goto 0

   End Function
```

The `BuildClasses` method starts by opening a connection to the data warehouse.

```
   ' BuildClasses: supports the GetClasses function in retrieving all the classes
   ' in the data warehouse in a string delimited by a ^

   Private Function BuildClasses(ByRef adoConn As ADODB.Connection) As String

      ' instantiate variables
      Dim recClasses As Record
      Dim colRelations As Collection

      Dim strClass
      Dim colClassNames

      ' create an instance of a record ojbect
      Set recClasses = New Record
```

It then retrieves the list of classes, sorting them before closing the connection.

```
      ' retrieves list of classes from the data warehouse
      recClasses.Open "ClassNames", adoConn, adModeReadWrite, _
         adCreateOverwrite
      ' this field has the names of the classes
      colClassNames = recClasses("ClassNames")

      ' iterate through each class, building one huge string delimited by '^'
      For Each strClass In colClassNames
         If Len(BuildClasses) > 0 Then
            BuildClasses = BuildClasses & "^" & strClass
         Else
            BuildClasses = strClass
         End If
      Next

      Set recClasses = Nothing

   End Function
```

The important code from above is the following:

```
      recClasses.Open "ClassNames", adoConn, adModeReadWrite, adCreateOverwrite
      colClassNames = recClasses("ClassNames")
```

A record object is opened on `ClassNames`, and a collection of classes in the `ClassNames` field is returned. The remaining builds a string of classes delimited by a "^".

Once the page has been submitted, it is processed by the action page of the form. Within this ASP page, a method is invoked to create the new class:

```
strError = objDW.CreateClass(strServerName, strDatabase, strUsername,_
    strPassword, strClassName, strDescription, strSourceDefinition,_
    strBaseClass, True, strClassType, strFilter, strMemberName ,_
    strMemberDescription, strMemberType, strAggregateExpression,_
    strDefaultValue , bolPrimaryKey , bolRequired , bolUnique ,_
    bolMeasure , bolDimension , bolMultiValue)
```

Lots of parameters! These are all the values from the HTML form, including all the values necessary to make a connection to the data warehouse. We will discuss all the parameters for creating data members in the next section. The code for `CreateClass` is as follows:

```
' CreateClass: creates a class in the data warehouse; if a data member is
' specified, it will be added at the same time

Public Function CreateClass(ByVal strServer As String, _
                            ByVal strDatabase As String, _
                            ByVal strUser As String, _
                            ByVal strPassword As String, _
                            ByVal strClassName As String, _
                            ByVal strDescription As String, _
                            ByVal strSourceDefinition As String, _
                            ByVal strBaseClassName As String, _
                            ByVal bolGenKey As Boolean, _
                            ByVal strClassType As String, _
                            ByVal strFilter As String, _
                            ByVal strMemberName As String, _
                            ByVal strMemberDescription As String, _
                            ByVal strMemberType As String, _
                            ByVal strAggregateExpression As String, _
                            ByVal strDefaultValue As String, _
                            ByVal bolPrimaryKey As Boolean, _
                            ByVal bolRequired As Boolean, _
                            ByVal bolUnique As Boolean, _
                            ByVal bolMeasure As Boolean, _
                            ByVal bolDimension As Boolean, _
                            ByVal bolMultiValue As Boolean) As String


    ' instantiate variables
    Dim adoConn As Object
    Dim strError As String

    On Error Goto CreateClassErr

    Set adoConn = CreateObject("ADODB.Connection")
```

A connection is established with the data warehouse.

```
    ' create a connection to the data warehouse
    Set adoConn = OpenConnection(strServer, strDatabase, strUser,_
        strPassword, strError)
```

```
    If Len(strError) Then

        CreateClass = strError   ' an error occurred while trying to connect

    Else
        Dim adoCmd As Object
        Dim adoRec As Object

        ' create ADO command object
        Set adoCmd = CreateObject("ADODB.Command")
        Set adoCmd.ActiveConnection = adoConn
```

The schema edit mode must be turned on:

```
        ' turn the schema change mode on
        adoCmd.CommandText = "SchemaMode=1"
        adoCmd.Execute
```

before making any modifications to the logical schema of the data warehouse:

```
        ' create a class definition in the data warehouse
        CreateClassDef strError, adoConn, strClassName, strDescription, _
            strSourceDefinition, strBaseClassName, bolGenKey, strClassType, _
            strFilter

        If Len(strMemberName) Then   ' if a data member has been also specified

            ' create a data member definition in this class
            CreateDataMemberDef strError, adoConn, strClassName, _
                strMemberName, strMemberDescription, strMemberType, _
                strAggregateExpression, strDefaultValue, bolPrimaryKey, _
                bolRequired, bolUnique, bolMeasure, bolDimension, bolMultiValue

        End If
```

Once changes are made, the mode is turned off and the changes are committed to the data warehouse.

```
        ' save the new row
        adoCmd.CommandText = "CommitSchema"
        adoCmd.Execute

        ' turn the schema change mode off
        adoCmd.CommandText = "SchemaMode=0"
        adoCmd.Execute

        Set adoRec = Nothing
        Set adoCmd = Nothing

    End If

    If Len(strError) Then ' check if an error occurred
        CreateClass = strError
    End If
```

The connection is then closed at the end of the method.

```
    ' close connection
    CloseConnection adoConn

CreateClassErr:

    If Err.Number <> 0 Then
        CreateClass = Err.Description
    End If

    On Error Goto 0

    ' if successful, then nothing is returned
    ' (if length, then an error occurred)
End Function
```

From the code sample above, this is how you turn the schema edit mode on:

```
        adoCmd.CommandText = "SchemaMode=1"
        adoCmd.Execute
```

After the schema mode has been turned on, the new class definition is created with the following call:

```
        CreateClassDef strError, adoConn, strClassName, strDescription, _
            strSourceDefinition, strBaseClassName, bolGenKey, strClassType, _
            strFilter
```

The CreateClassDef method creates a class definition (the call to CreateDataMemberDef is documented in the following section):

```
' CreateClassDef: create a new record in the class definition table

Public Sub CreateClassDef(ByRef strError As String, _
                          ByRef adoConn As ADODB.Connection, _
                          ByVal strClassName As String, _
                          ByVal strDescription As String, _
                          ByVal strSourceDefinition As String, _
                          ByVal strBaseClassName As String, _
                          ByVal bolGenKey As Boolean, _
                          ByVal strClassType As String, _
                          ByVal strFilter As String)

    Dim adoRec As Object

    Set adoRec = CreateObject("ADODB.Record")
    strError = ""

    On Error Goto CreateClassDefErr
```

It then creates an instance in the class table:

```
    adoRec.Open "Class/" & strClassName, adoConn, adModeReadWrite,
        adCreateOverwrite

    If Len(strDescription) Then
        adoRec("Description") = strDescription ' class description
    End If

' force the class to be persistent
    adoRec("IsPersistent") = 1
    ' identifies the data source for storing the instances of this class
    adoRec("SourceDefName") = strSourceDefinition
    ' the name of the class identifies the class in the logical schema
    adoRec("ClassDefName") = strClassName
```

Then come a few more definitions:

```
    ' partition definition will be generated automatically
    adoRec("GeneratePartitionDef") = 1

    ' table definition will be generated automatically
    adoRec("GenerateTableDef") = 1

' generate a key definition
    If bolGenKey Then
        adoRec("GenerateKeyDef") = 1
    End If

    ' name of the base class if aggregations are used
    If strBaseClassName <> "" Then
        adoRec("BaseClassName") = strBaseClassName
    End If

    ' the ID of the class will be created automatically
    adoRec("GenerateIdentity") = 1
    ' type of class
    adoRec("ClassType") = strClassType
    adoRec("InstExclusionExpr") = strFilter ' inclusion string
```

Finally, the information is saved:

```
    ' save the new row
    adoRec("__Commit") = 1
    adoRec.Fields.Update

    adoRec.Close

    Set adoRec = Nothing

CreateClassDefErr:

    If Err.Number <> 0 Then
        strError = Err.Description
```

```
    End If

    On Error Goto 0

End Sub
```

The following creates an instance in the class `definition` table of our new class:

```
    adoRec.Open "Class/" & strClassName, adoConn, adModeReadWrite,
  adCreateOverwrite
```

Attributes on the class are set, such as:

```
    adoRec("IsPersistent") = 1
    adoRec("SourceDefName") = strSourceDefinition
    adoRec("ClassDefName") = strClassName
```

There are many attributes that can be set on a class, and they are fully documented in the Commerce Server online help under the metadata sections for the logical schema.

Create Data Member

The following form allows you to add a data member to an existing class:

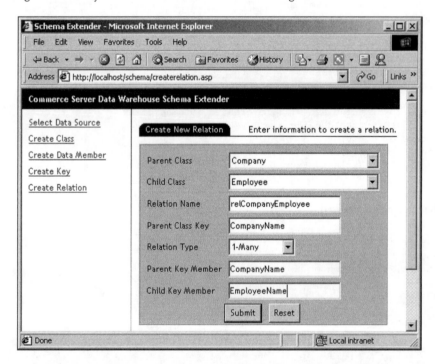

We are using this functionality to build the non-key members of the `Company` class. In the above figure, the `PhoneNumber` data member is added. The `WebSite` data member is added in the same manner. The following table describes the fields in this form:

Field	Description
Class Name	This is the class that this data member is going to be added to.
Member Name	The name of the data member to be added to this class.
Description	This describes the purpose of this data member.
Member Type	The name of the data type for this data member. There are many different types including WSTR (unicode string with a length of 255), LONG, CURRENCY, DATETIME to name just a few. See the Commerce Server documentation for a complete list.
Aggregate Expression	Used by aggregation classes. Stores the expression string using the data member. Can contain any valid base class member or aggregation function.
Default Value	Stores the default value of this data member.
Primary Key	Designates this data member is the primary key for this class.
Multi Valued	Indicates that this data member can contain more than one value.
Required	Indicates this data member requires a value.
Is Unique	Indicates that this data member is part of a unique key for this class.
Is Dimension	Indicates that this data member represents a dimension (in OLAP).
Is Measure	Indicates that this data member represents a measure (in OLAP).

The class names in the above figure are generated with the same method call used in the previous section (GetClasses). After the information is submitted on the form, an ASP page processes the form information and then invokes the following method:

```
strError = objDW.CreateDataMember(strServerName, strDatabase, strUsername,_
    strPassword, strClassName, strMemberName, strDescription, strMemberType,_
    strAggregateExpression, strDefaultValue, bolPrimaryKey, bolRequired,_
    bolUnique, bolMeasure, bolDimension, bolMultiValued)
```

The code for CreateDataMember is as follows, starting off with some definitions:

```
' CreateDataMember: creates a data member for a class in the data warehouse

Public Function CreateDataMember(ByVal strServer As String, _
                                 ByVal strDatabase As String, _
                                 ByVal strUser As String, _
                                 ByVal strPassword As String, _
                                 ByVal strClassName As String, _
                                 ByVal strMemberName As String, _
                                 ByVal strMemberDescription As String, _
                                 ByVal strMemberType As String, _
                                 ByVal strAggregateExpression As String, _
                                 ByVal strDefaultValue As String, _
                                 ByVal bolPrimaryKey As Boolean, _
                                 ByVal bolRequired As Boolean, _
```

245

```
                              ByVal bolUnique As Boolean, _
                              ByVal bolMeasure As Boolean, _
                              ByVal bolDimension As Boolean, _
                              ByVal bolMultiValue As Boolean _
                              ) As String
```

It then creates and opens a connection to the data warehouse.

```
    Dim adoConn As Object ' ado connection object
    Dim strError As String ' will contain the error msg if one occurs

    On Error Goto CreateDataMemberErr

    Set adoConn = CreateObject("ADODB.Connection")

    ' open a connection to the data warehouse
    Set adoConn = OpenConnection(strServer, strDatabase, strUser,_
       strPassword, strError)

    If Len(strError) Then

       CreateDataMember = strError

    Else
       Dim adoCmd As Object
       Dim adoRec As Object
```

Next in line is setting up the command object, and turning on the schema change mode.

```
       ' ado command object
       Set adoCmd = CreateObject("ADODB.Command")
       Set adoCmd.ActiveConnection = adoConn

       ' turn the schema change mode on
       adoCmd.CommandText = "SchemaMode=1"
       adoCmd.Execute
```

The data member definition is created:

```
       ' create a data member definition
       CreateDataMemberDef strError, adoConn, strClassName, strMemberName, _
          strMemberDescription, strMemberType, strAggregateExpression, _
          strDefaultValue, bolPrimaryKey, bolRequired, bolUnique, _
          bolMeasure, bolDimension, bolMultiValue
```

and everything is saved:

```
        ' save the row
        adoCmd.CommandText = "CommitSchema"
        adoCmd.Execute
        ' turn the schema change mode off
        adoCmd.CommandText = "SchemaMode=0"
        adoCmd.Execute

        Set adoRec = Nothing
        Set adoCmd = Nothing

    End If

    If Len(strError) Then ' error occurred
        CreateDataMember = strError
    End If
```

Finally, the connection is closed:

```
    ' close connection
    CloseConnection adoConn

CreateDataMemberErr:

    If Err.Number <> 0 Then
        CreateDataMember = Err.Description
    End If

    On Error Goto 0

End Function
```

Just like in the `CreateClass` method, a connection to the data warehouse is opened and closed upon completion. Additionally, the schema edit mode is turned on and then back off when changes to the logical schema have been completed.

The call to `CreateDataMemberDef` is where it creates the data member of a class; here's the definition part of the code:

```
    ' CreateDataMemberDef: inserts a record into the member table which
    ' represents a new data member for a class

    Public Sub CreateDataMemberDef(ByRef strError As String, _
                                ByRef adoConn As ADODB.Connection, _
                                ByVal strClassName As String, _
                                ByVal strMemberName As String, _
                                ByVal strDescription As String, _
                                ByVal strMemberType As String, _
                                ByVal strAggregateExpression As String, _
                                ByVal strDefaultValue As String, _
```

```
                              ByVal bolPrimaryKey As Boolean, _
                              ByVal bolRequired As Boolean, _
                              ByVal bolUnique As Boolean, _
                              ByVal bolMeasure As Boolean, _
                              ByVal bolDimension As Boolean, _
                              ByVal bolMultiValue As Boolean)

     Dim adoRec As Object

     Set adoRec = CreateObject("ADODB.Record")
     strError = ""

     On Error Goto CreateDataMemberDefErr
```

The data member is created here. Through the OLE DB Provider for Commerce Server, this modifies the logical schema and adds a new data member. Behind the scenes in the SQL data warehouse database, a column has been added to the table supporting this class. A new SQL table will be created for each class you create.

```
     ' create an instance of a data member
     adoRec.Open "Member/" & strClassName & "/" & strMemberName, _
                      adoConn, adModeReadWrite, adCreateOverwrite
```

Several attributes are set on the data member:

```
...' the name of the data member
   adoRec("MemberDefName") = strMemberName
...' table column definition to be generated automatically
   adoRec("GenerateColumnDef") = 1
...' data type of this data member
   adoRec("TypeName") = strMemberType

...' used for filtering
   If Len(strAggregateExpression) > 0 Then
      adoRec("ExpressionStr") = strAggregateExpression
   End If

...' description of the data member (friendly name)
   If Len(strDescription) > 0 Then
      adoRec("Description") = strDescription
   End If

...' default value of this data member
   If Len(strDefaultValue) > 0 Then
      adoRec("DefaultValueAsStr") = strDefaultValue
   End If
```

The following variables should all return Boolean values:

```
...' true of a value is required for this data member
   If bolRequired Then
      adoRec("IsRequired") = 1
   End If

...' true if this data member is multi-valued
   If bolMultiValue Then
      adoRec("IsMultiValued") = 1
   End If

...' true if this data member is part of the primary key
   If bolPrimaryKey Then
      adoRec("IsPrimaryKey") = 1
   End If

...' true if this data member is part of a unique key for the class
   If bolUnique Then
      adoRec("IsUniqueKey") = 1
   End If

...' true if this data member is part of a unique key for the class
   If bolDimension Then
      adoRec("IsDimension") = 1
   End If

...' true if this data member represents a measure
   If bolMeasure Then
      adoRec("IsMeasure") = 1
   End If
```

At the end, the method saves the changes it has made and closes the recordset:

```
' save this row
   adoRec("__Commit") = 1
   adoRec.Fields.Update

   adoRec.Close

   Set adoRec = Nothing

CreateDataMemberDefErr:

   If Err.Number <> 0 Then
      strError = Err.Description
   End If

   On Error Goto 0

End Sub
```

For a detailed description of all the fields in the metadata model for data members, review the online Commerce Server help.

Create Key

The following form allows you to create a new key:

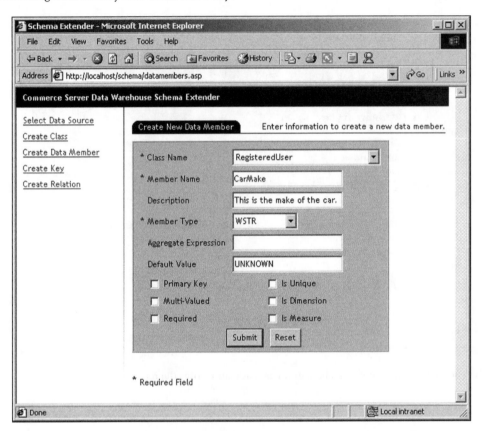

The following table contains a brief description of the fields above.

Field	Description
Class Name	This is the class that this key is going to be made on. A key is one or more data members whose values uniquely identify an instance of a class.
Member Name	This is the data member that is going to be included in this key.
Key Name	This is the name of the key.
Ordinal Position	This is the position in the key where this data member will reside. This starts with 0, and the key is guaranteed unique only when the data members are processed in this order. When evaluating a unique instance of a class, the data members specified in the key are examined in order of their ordinal position.

The same method to create a list of classes is used to build the list box of all the classes. A new method is invoked to obtain all the data members from the selected class. Whenever a new class is selected, this page automatically reloads the new set of data members:

```
<%
        strDataMembers = objDW.GetDataMembers(strServerName, strDatabase,_
            strUsername, strPassword, strClassName)

        arrDataMembers = Split(strDataMembers, "^")

        For cnt = Lbound(arrDataMembers) to Ubound(arrDataMembers)
            Response.Write "<OPTION VALUE=""" & arrDataMembers(cnt) &_
                """>" & arrDataMembers(cnt) & "</OPTION>"
        Next

        Set objDW = Nothing
%>
```

The `GetDataMembers` method retrieves all the data members of a class:

```
' GetDataMembers: returns all the data members for a class as a string
' delimited by a ^

Public Function GetDataMembers(ByVal strServer As String, _
                                ByVal strDatabase As String, _
                                ByVal strUser As String, _
                                ByVal strPassword As String, _
                                ByVal strClassName As String) As String

    Dim adoConn As Object
    Dim strError As String

    On Error Goto GetDataMembersErr

    Set adoConn = CreateObject("ADODB.Connection")
```

The connection to the data warehouse is opened, a list of data members is obtained, and then the connection is closed accordingly.

```
    ' create a connection to the data warehouse
    Set adoConn = OpenConnection(strServer, strDatabase, strUser,_
    strPassword, strError)

    If Len(strError) Then
        GetDataMembers = strError
    Else
        ' retrieve a list of data members for the class
        GetDataMembers = Sort(BuildDataMembers(adoConn, strClassName))
    End If

    CloseConnection adoConn

    Set adoConn = Nothing
```

```
GetDataMembersErr:

   If Err.Number <> 0 Then
      GetDataMembers = Err.Description
   End If

   On Error Goto 0

End Function
```

`BuildDataMembers` retrieves the data members from the data warehouse:

```
' BuildDataMembers: retrieve data members for a class

Public Function BuildDataMembers(ByRef adoConn As ADODB.Connection, _
                                 ByVal strClassName As String) As String

   Dim recClass As Record
   Dim fld As Field
   Dim strVal As String
   Dim strList As String

   On Error Resume Next

   Set recClass = New Record
   recClass.Open "instance/" & strClassName, adoConn, adModeReadWrite, _
      adCreateOverwrite

   If Err.Number <> 0 Then
      BuildDataMembers = Err.Description
   Else

      For Each fld In recClass.Fields
         If Left(fld.Name, 1) <> "_" Then
            If Len(strList) Then
               strList = strList & "^" & fld.Name
            Else
               strList = fld.Name
            End If
         End If
      Next

      BuildDataMembers = strList
   End If
End Function
```

The important code from the above method is the following:

```
recClass.Open "instance/" & strClassName, adoConn, adModeReadWrite,_
   adCreateOverwrite
```

This retrieves the list of data members for the specific class. A string is built from all of these fields delimited by a '^'.

Once the page has been submitted, it is processed by the action page of the form. Within this ASP page, a method is invoked to create the new key:

```
strError = objDW.CreateKey(strServerName, strDatabase, strUsername,_
    strPassword, strClassName, strKeyName, strMemberName, intOrdinalPosition)
```

The code for CreateKey is as follows:

```
' CreateKey: creates or adds a data member of a class to a key

Public Function CreateKey(ByVal strServer As String, _
                          ByVal strDatabase As String, _
                          ByVal strUser As String,
                          ByVal strPassword As String, _
                          ByVal strClassName As String, _
                          ByVal strKeyName As String, _
                          ByVal strMemberName As String, _
                          ByVal intOrdinalPosition As Integer) As String

    Dim adoConn As Object
    Dim strError As String

    On Error Goto CreateKeyErr

    Set adoConn = CreateObject("ADODB.Connection")
```

A connection is established to the data warehouse:

```
    ' opens a connection to the data warehouse
    Set adoConn = OpenConnection(strServer, strDatabase, strUser, strPassword,_
        strError)

    If Len(strError) Then

        CreateKey = strError

    Else
        Dim adoCmd As Object
        Dim adoRec As Object

        Set adoCmd = CreateObject("ADODB.Command")
        Set adoCmd.ActiveConnection = adoConn
```

The schema edit mode is turned on before modifying the logical schema:

```
        ' turns schema change mode on
        adoCmd.CommandText = "SchemaMode=1"
        adoCmd.Execute

        ' create or update the key definition
        CreateKeyDef strError, adoConn, strClassName, strKeyName, _
            strMemberName, intOrdinalPosition

        adoCmd.CommandText = "CommitSchema"
        adoCmd.Execute
```

and turned off once the changes are committed:

```
    ' turns schema change mode off
    adoCmd.CommandText = "SchemaMode=0"
    adoCmd.Execute

    Set adoRec = Nothing
    Set adoCmd = Nothing

  End If

  If Len(strError) Then
     CreateKey = strError
  End If
```

The connection is then closed at the end of the method:

```
    ' close connection
    CloseConnection adoConn

CreateKeyErr:

    If Err.Number <> 0 Then
       CreateKey = Err.Description
    End If

    On Error Goto 0

End Function
```

`CreateKeyDef` is invoked to create a key and key member:

```
' CreateKeyDef: updates the logical schema with the new or updated key
' definition information

Public Function CreateKeyDef(ByRef strError As String, _
                     ByRef adoConn As ADODB.Connection, _
                     ByVal strClassName As String, _
                     ByVal strKeyName As String, _
                     ByVal strMemberName As String, _
                     ByVal intOrdinalPosition As Integer) As String


    On Error Goto CreateKeyDefErr

    Dim adoRec As Object

    Set adoRec = CreateObject("ADODB.Record")
    strError = ""
```

The following creates the key:

```
    ' create a new instance in the class key definition table
    adoRec.Open "Key/" & strKeyName, adoConn, adModeReadWrite, adCreateOverwrite
    adoRec("ClassDefName") = strClassName ' name of the class for this key
    adoRec("__Commit") = 1
    adoRec.Fields.Update
    adoRec.Close
```

And this creates the key member:

```
' create a new instance of a class key member
adoRec.Open "KeyMember/" & strKeyName & "/" & strMemberName, _
   adoConn, adModeReadWrite, adCreateOverwrite
adoRec("KeyDefName") = strKeyName ' name of the key
adoRec("MemDefName") = strMemberName ' data member part of this key
' position of this data member in the key
adoRec("OrdinalPosInKey") = intOrdinalPosition
```

Changes are saved and the recordset closed:

```
adoRec("__Commit") = 1
adoRec.Fields.Update

adoRec.Close

CreateKeyDefErr:

   If Err.Number <> 0 Then
      CreateKeyDef = Err.Description
   End If

   On Error Goto 0

   Set adoRec = Nothing

End Function
```

Create Relation

The following form accepts input to create a new class `relation`:

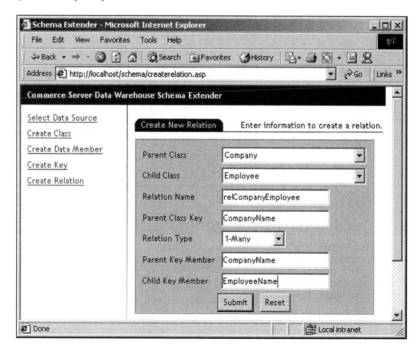

The following table contains an explanation of the fields in the above figure:

Field	Description
Parent Class	This is the name of the parent class.
Child Class	This is the name of the child class.
Relation Name	This is the name of the class relation.
Parent Class Key	This is the name of the key for the parent class.
Relation Type	This is the type of relation. 2 = one to many, 3 = many to many, 194 = one to many with inheritance.
Parent Key Member	This is the name of the data member of the parent class to relate.
Child Key Member	This is the name of the data member of the child class to relate.

Once the page has been submitted, it is processed by the action page of the form. Within this ASP page, a method is invoked to create the new relation:

```
strError = objDW.CreateRelation(strServeName, strDatabase, strUsername,_
    strPassword, strRelationName, strParentClass, strChildClass,_
    strParentClassKey, strRelationType, strParentKeyMember, strChildKeyMember)
```

The call to CreateRelation takes the input from the web page and creates a new relation in the data warehouse. The code follows:

```
' CreateRelation: creates a new relation in the data warehouse

Public Function CreateRelation(ByVal strServer As String, _
                               ByVal strDatabase As String, _
                               ByVal strUser As String, _
                               ByVal strPassword As String, _
                               ByVal strRelationName As String, _
                               ByVal strParentClass As String, _
                               ByVal strChildClass As String, _
                               ByVal strParentClassKey As String, _
                               ByVal strRelationType As String, _
                               ByVal strParentKeyMember As String, _
                               ByVal strChildKeyMember As String) As String

    Dim adoConn As Object
    Dim strError As String

    On Error CreateRelationErr

    Set adoConn = CreateObject("ADODB.Connection")
```

A connection to the data warehouse is made.

```
    ' open a connection to the data warehouse
    Set adoConn = OpenConnection(strServer, strDatabase, strUser, strPassword,_
        strError)

    If Len(strError) Then

        CreateRelation = strError

    Else
        Dim adoCmd As Object
        Dim adoRec As Object

        Set adoCmd = CreateObject("ADODB.Command")
        Set adoCmd.ActiveConnection = adoConn
```

This turns on the schema change mode.

```
        ' turn the schema change mode on
        adoCmd.CommandText = "SchemaMode=1"
        adoCmd.Execute
```

The relation definition is created with the call to `CreateRelationDef`:

```
        ' create the relationship in the data warehouse
        CreateRelationDef strError, adoConn, strRelationName, _
            strParentClass, strChildClass, strParentClassKey, _
            strRelationType, strParentKeyMember, strChildKeyMember
```

Changes are saved and the schema change mode turned off.

```
        adoCmd.CommandText = "CommitSchema"
        adoCmd.Execute

        ' turn the schema change mode off
        adoCmd.CommandText = "SchemaMode=0"
        adoCmd.Execute

        Set adoRec = Nothing
        Set adoCmd = Nothing

    End If

    If Len(strError) Then
        CreateRelation = strError
    End If
```

At the end, the connection is closed.

```
    ' close connection
    CloseConnection adoConn

CreateRelationErr:
```

```
      If Err.Number <> 0 Then
         CreateRelation = Err.Description
      End If

      On Error Goto 0

   End Function
```

Here is the code for the `CreateRelationDef` method:

```
   ' CreateRelationDef: creates a new instance in the relation table in
   ' the data warehouse

   Public Function CreateRelationDef(ByRef strError As String, _
                             ByRef adoConn As ADODB.Connection,
                             ByVal strRelationName As String,
                             ByVal strParentClass As String,
                             ByVal strChildClass As String,
                             ByVal strParentClassKey As String,
                             ByVal strRelationType As String,
                             ByVal strParentKeyMember As String,
                             ByVal strChildKeyMember As String) As String

      Dim adoRec As Object

      Set adoRec = CreateObject("ADODB.Record")
      strError = ""

      On Error Goto CreateRelationDefErr
```

A relation is built:

```
      ' create a new row in the relation table
      adoRec.Open "Relation/" & strRelationName, adoConn, adModeReadWrite,_
         adCreateOverwrite
      adoRec("ParentClassName") = strParentClass ' parent class of relation
      adoRec("ParentClassKey") = strParentClassKey ' key for parent class
      adoRec("ChildClassName") = strChildClass ' child class of relation
      adoRec("RelType") = strRelationType ' type of relation (e.g. 1-many)

      adoRec("__Commit") = 1
      adoRec.Fields.Update
      adoRec.Close
```

A relation member is created:

```
      ' create a new instance in the relation member definition table
      adoRec.Open "RelMember/" & strRelationName & "/" & strParentKeyMember,_
         adoConn, adModeReadWrite, adCreateOverwrite
      adoRec("ChildMemName") = strChildKeyMember ' name of child class member
      adoRec("ParentMemName") = strParentKeyMember ' name of parent class member
```

The changes are saved and the recordset closed.

```
    adoRec("__Commit") = 1
    adoRec.Fields.Update

    adoRec.Close

  CreateRelationDefErr:

    If Err.Number <> 0 Then
       CreateRelationDef = Err.Description
    End If

    On Error Goto 0

    Set adoRec = Nothing

    ' if length is returned, then an error occurred
  End Function
```

So, you can see how the sample application makes extending the data warehouse schema quick, easy and painless; however, there are still issues to consider.

Importing Custom Information

If you are extending the schema of your data warehouse, then you must be planning on importing your own custom information. In the previous section we say how you can create your own custom structures, and now we will discuss the methodology used to import this information into the data warehouse. The most important thing to remember is that you must find a way to line your data up to the business structures already in the data warehouse.

Let us consider the following problem that we would like to solve: There is business data associated with each registered user that needs to be included in reports. This data is not currently in any Commerce Server data structures but it is electronically stored (such as in an Excel worksheet or SQL database). This data has identifying information in it that will allow it to be lined up into the data structures available in the Commerce Server data warehouse. This data is user related, so the schema for registered users needs to be extended. To finish the example, the related user information is what type of cars each user owns, including make, model, year, and color – four distinct pieces of information not already in the data warehouse.

Extend the Schema

We will first extend the RegisteredUser class, using the sample application, with the four additional fields of make, model, year, and color of the cars a user owns. Using the Schema Extender sample application, each field is added. The following figure shows one of the fields being added:

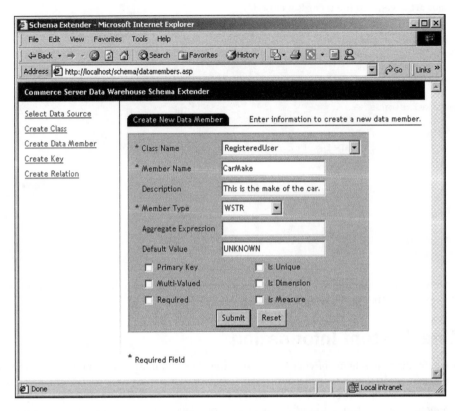

The `CarModel`, `CarYear`, and `CarColor` data members are also added to the `RegisterUser` class following the same procedure.

Data Source

For this example, the data source of the car information is in a SQL Server table called `Members` in a database called `CustomData`. The following figure shows the structure and data of this table:

This table has instances of users and what cars they own. We will insert each of these users into the data warehouse.

Importing the Data

We will now take our custom data and insert it into the data warehouse. Here is the Visual Basic code that does this.

The first section of the code instantiates and creates all the objects being used in this code:

```
Public Sub TestImport()

    Dim adoRec As Object
    Dim adoConnSource As Object
    Dim adoConnTarget As Object
    Dim adoRs As Object
    Dim objGenGUID As Object
    Dim strSource As String
    Dim strTarget As String

    Set adoRec = CreateObject("ADODB.Record")
    Set adoConnSource = CreateObject("ADODB.Connection")
    Set adoConnTarget = CreateObject("ADODB.Connection")
    Set adoRs = CreateObject("ADODB.Recordset")
```

The string to build a DSN-less connection to the SQL database that contains the connection is created:

```
    ' connection to custom data
    strSource = "Provider=SQLOLEDB;Data Source=IKLAPTOP008;Initial_
        Catalog=CustomData;uid=sa;pwd="
```

The string to build a connection to the data warehouse using the OLE DB Provider for Commerce Server is created:

```
    ' connection to Data Warehouse using OLE DB Provider for Commerce Server
    strTarget = "URL=mscop://InProcConnect/Server=IKLAPTOP008:catalog=" _
        dwschema:database=Retail_dw:user=sa:password=:fastload=true:"
```

The database connections are opened to both sources:

```
    adoConnSource.Open strSource ' open SQL table
    adoConnTarget.Open strTarget ' open Data Warehouse
```

A Commerce Server object to create a globally unique identifier (GUID) is instantiated:

```
    ' Commerce Server GUID Generator
    Set objGenGUID = CreateObject("Commerce.GenID")
```

A SQL query is executed to obtain a record set of all the custom data to import:

```
    ' obtain custom data records
    Set adoRs = adoConnSource.Execute("SELECT * FROM Members")

    Do While Not adoRs.EOF
```

261

A new instance of a registered user is created:

```
adoRec.Open "instance/registereduser", adoConnTarget, adModeWrite,_
    adCreateCollection
```

A GUID is generated for this unique user:

```
adoRec("UserID") = objGenGUID.GenGUIDString()
```

The fields of the record are built from data in the SQL Server database and several bookkeeping fields are updated:

```
adoRec("title") = adoRs("MemberTitle")
adoRec("firstname") = adoRs("MemberFirstName")
adoRec("lastname") = adoRs("MemberLastName")

' custom data members
adoRec("CarMake") = adoRs("CarMake")
adoRec("CarModel") = adoRs("CarModel")
adoRec("CarYear") = adoRs("CarYear")
adoRec("CarColor") = adoRs("CarColor")

' bookkeeping
adoRec("UserIDChangedBy") = "Custom Import"
adoRec("DateCreated") = Now()
adoRec("DateLastChanged") = Now()
```

The new record is saved and closed:

```
'Save the new row.
adoRec("__Commit") = 1
adoRec.Fields.Update

'Done with current user.
adoRec.Close

adoRs.MoveNext
Loop
```

A new record has just been added to the data warehouse for this user. This code will loop through the remaining user records in the Members table until all users have been added. All that remains is to clean up.

```
'Close the connection and release the objects.
adoRs.Close
adoConnSource.Close
adoConnTarget.Close

Set objGenGUID = Nothing
Set adoConnSource = Nothing
Set adoConnTarget = Nothing
End Sub
```

Business Desk Analysis

Business Desk Analysis refers to the modules within Business Desk that allow you to analyze activity on your site. It allows access to the reports available to you to run against the data warehouse. Commerce Server comes with several out of the box reports ready to run against your site, and you can also create your own custom reports, which integrate into Business Desk. Finally, it is possible to analyze segments of users (users with similar characteristics or behaviors).

Static and Dynamic Reports

As the header of this section indicates, there are two different kinds of reports: Static and Dynamic. All reports are generated from the information that has been imported into the data warehouse, but you must be aware how each affects your system to understand when to use which type.

Dynamic reports are generated at runtime, which means at the time you are running the report within the Business Desk. Every time you run a dynamic report, the most recent data in the data warehouse is used to build the report. The data displayed in the report is never stored. The results of a dynamic report appear as a PivotTable or PivotChart. Shown below is a PivotTable: to generate the graph of this information select the graph icon to build a PivotChart:

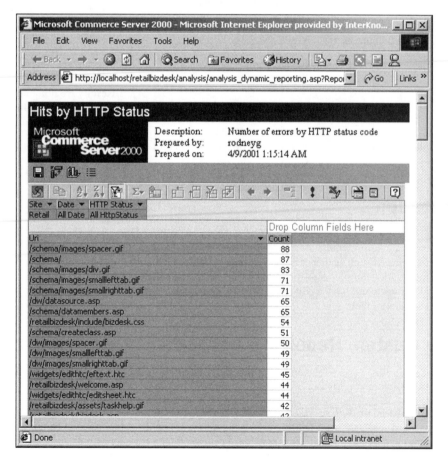

Static reports are run immediately but the data is stored allowing you to view the results later without re-running the report. Static SQL reports run asynchronously so one can be started and then you are free to work within other modules in the Business Desk. However, while running multidimensional expression (MDX) static reports you cannot use the Business Desk until execution is complete. Finally, static reports are able to report on extremely large result sets.

The following table shows some differences between dynamic and static reports:

Feature	Dynamic	Static
Changing report contents	PivotTable features are used to add and remove dimensions and measures from the results.	Contents of the report are modified programmatically.
Exporting to List Manager	Reports cannot be exported to List Manager.	A list is exportable in a dynamic or static form.
Exporting to Excel	Yes.	Yes.
New report definitions	A new dynamic report can be created by making changes to an existing report and then saving the changes to a new report definition.	The report definition can be modified programmatically.
Deleting report definitions	Yes.	Yes.
Save results	Results cannot be saved in Business Desk.	Reports are stored with their data in Completed Reports. Results are not automatically deleted and must be maintained manually.
View results as chart	Reports can be viewed as Pivot Charts.	Reports cannot be viewed as charts.

Segmentation

With Business Analytics, it is possible to perform analysis on groups of users that share the same profile properties and behavior on your site. A group of users is referred to as a segment. Users in the same segment have similar attributes (such as their age). A segment model describes these shared attributes. From a segment model you might, for example, determine that people who purchase a jazz music CD are over age 50, income over $75,000 per year, and have a college education. Using this model you can offer similar products to others in the same segment.

Creating Custom Reports

Commerce Server allows you to customize reports that can be executed through Business Desk Analysis. Both static and dynamic reports can be created.

Static reports are based on SQL or MDX queries (which are queries used for OLAP). Static report definitions consist of this query and parameter definitions into the query. When these reports are executed, the parameters are pushed into the query and HTML documents are generated with the query results. These reports can be opened through the Business Desk or in Internet Explorer. Here is an example of a static report:

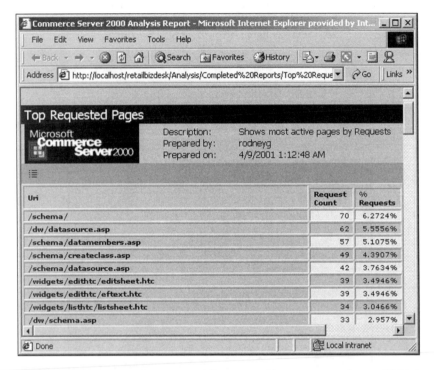

Dynamic report definitions are stored as queries. The pivot table view is stored in an XML document in the data warehouse. Results of these queries are displayed using the Pivot Table component from the Microsoft Office 2000 Web Components.

> **Definitions for the out of the box reports can be found in the `csreports.sql` file located in the Commerce Server installation directory. This file populates the report tables in the data warehouse.**

In this section we will discuss how to create a static SQL report.

Creating Static SQL Reports

You must run through several steps while creating a static SQL report, and they include:

❑ Creating your SQL query

❑ Adding parameter tags to the query

❑ Creating the report definition

❑ Building the report dimensions

❑ Adding the report parameters for the query parameters

❑ Executing the report

Our SQL query will be one that will retrieve the car information we stored from the custom data import in the previous section of this chapter. In the previous section the `RegisteredUser` table was modified with the four car related fields, as shown in the figure below:

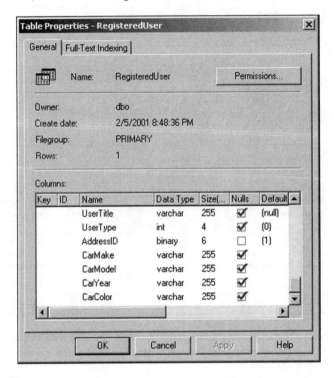

We will use a simple query that will return registered users that like red cars and registered in the month of March of the year 2001:

```
SELECT TOP 50
    FirstName,
    LastName
FROM
    RegisteredUser
WHERE
    (DateRegistered >= '03/01/2001' AND DateRegistered <= '04/01/2001')
    AND CarColor = 'Red'
ORDER BY
    LastName,
    FirstName
```

Parameters are now added to the query. This will allow you to control the query from the Business Desk rather than have one query that produces only one set of results. Parameters are in the form of [$Parameter]. Parameterized, the query looks as follows:

```
SELECT [$TopCount]
    FirstName,
    LastName
INTO
    [$ResultTable]
FROM
```

```
      RegisteredUser
WHERE
    [$DateRange] AND
    [$SingleValue]
ORDER BY
    LastName,
    FirstName
```

Next you must create the base report definition:

```
INSERT INTO
    [dbo].[Report]
        ([DisplayName],
        [Description],
        [ReportType],
        [Category],
        [Query],
        [DmExport],
        [UpmExport],
        [CreatedBy],
        [Protected])
VALUES
    ('Red Car Color',
    'Users Red Car Color',
    2,
    'Users',
    Your Parameterized SQL String,
    1,
    1,
    'a user',
    0)
```

The following table describes the fields on the above SQL command:

Parameter	Description
DisplayName	Name displayed in BizDesk.
Description	Description of the report.
ReportType	0 = dynamic SQL, 1 = dynamic MDX, 2 = static SQL, 3 = static MDX.
Category	Category of the report. Free text such as Web Usage or Sales.
Query	The executable SQL or MDX query.
DmExport	True (1) specifies the report is exportable to Direct Mail.
UpmExport	True (1) specifies the report is exportable to User Personalization via List Manager.
CreatedBy	Creator of the report. Free text so it is the responsibility of the developer to retrieve the username from whatever type of authentication scheme you are using.
Protected	True (1) indicates the report may not be overwritten or deleted. True for all system reports.

The display dimensions of the report now need to be created into the `ReportDimension` table. In this example we will be adding two displayable dimensions for the first name and last name:

```
INSERT INTO
    [dbo].[ReportDimension]
        ([ReportID],
         [DimensionType],
         [DisplayName],
         [FieldName],
         [Ordinal])
VALUES
    (@ReportID,
     0,
     'FirstName',
     'FirstName',
     1)

INSERT INTO
    [dbo].[ReportDimension]
        ([ReportID],
         [DimensionType],
         [DisplayName],
         [FieldName],
         [Ordinal])
VALUES
    (@ReportID,
     0,
     'LastName',
     'LastName',
     2)
```

The following table describes the fields on the above SQL command:

Parameter	Description
ReportID	ID of the report the dimension is associated with.
DimensionType	0 = Column, 1 = Row, 2 = Measure.
DisplayName	Name displayed in BizDesk.
FieldName	Name of the field on the report results.
Ordinal	Used to specify the rendering order in the user interface.

We now need to create the report parameters for this report. Each parameterized item in the query must be defined in the `ReportParams` table. Here we will add the definition of the `$DateRange` parameter:

```
INSERT INTO
    [dbo].[ReportParam]
        (ReportID,
         ParamName,
         ParamDescription,
         ParamType,
         DataType,
```

```
            Opnd1,
            Val1,
            Opnd2,
            Val2,
            FieldName,
            Ordinal)
    VALUES
       (@ReportID,
       '[$DateRange]',
       'User registration date',
       3,
       1,
       1,
       '3/1/2000',
       0,
       '3/30/2000',
         'DateRegistered',
         2)
```

The following table describes the fields on the above SQL command:

Parameter	Description
ReportID	Unique ID of the report with which the parameter is associated.
ParamName	Tag name.
ParamDescription	Text displayed on the clickable bar (shown below).
ParamType	Type of parameter, such as single value, expression, select order, date range, or site name.
DataType	0 = int, 1 = float, 2 = datetime, 3 = char.
Opnd1	First operand.
Val1	First value.
Opnd2	Second operand.
Val2	Second value.
FieldName	Field in query used for expression.
Ordinal	Used to specify the user interface rendering order.

The report can now be run through the Business Desk. After inserting this information into the data warehouse, you will see the report in BizDesk:

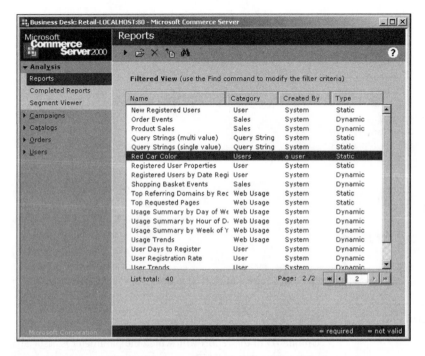

After opening the report, you will see the report definition you defined for it:

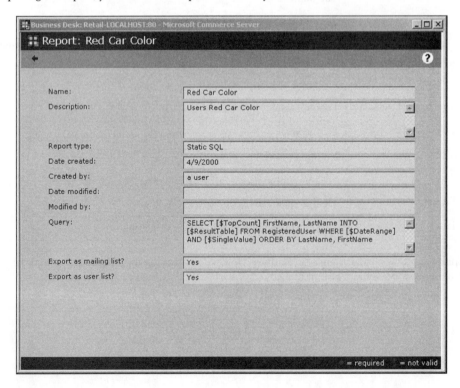

Summary

In this chapter we discussed Business Analytics to the tune of how you could customize the components to better fit the needs of your organization. This topic is huge and could be delivered in a book of its own. The following topics were discussed in this chapter:

❑   Data import into the data warehouse.

❑   Customization of the data warehouse schema.

❑   Building custom reports and importing custom information.

First of all, we discussed how Commerce Server has a whole host of web usage analysis features that we can use to know more about our site – being prepared for how your website will be used is very beneficial in this day and age. However, to use these features, you must have something to analyze, and this comes in the form of web logs. We looked at how to import these into a data warehouse so that we would have something to refer to and work with.

However, we may want functionality from our data warehouse that it does not currently offer – this is where we can customize it to better serve our needs. Perhaps we need new data members, or new classes – we saw all of this in this section. We also looked at an example of how to extend the logical schema and actually create the extra functionality we need.

The latter part of the chapter was devoted to looking at custom information and custom reports, for when the standard options are just not enough. Putting all of this together, you can see how manipulating the data warehouse and analyzing the information we gain from people visiting our site can help us to better target our content and serve our customers' needs.

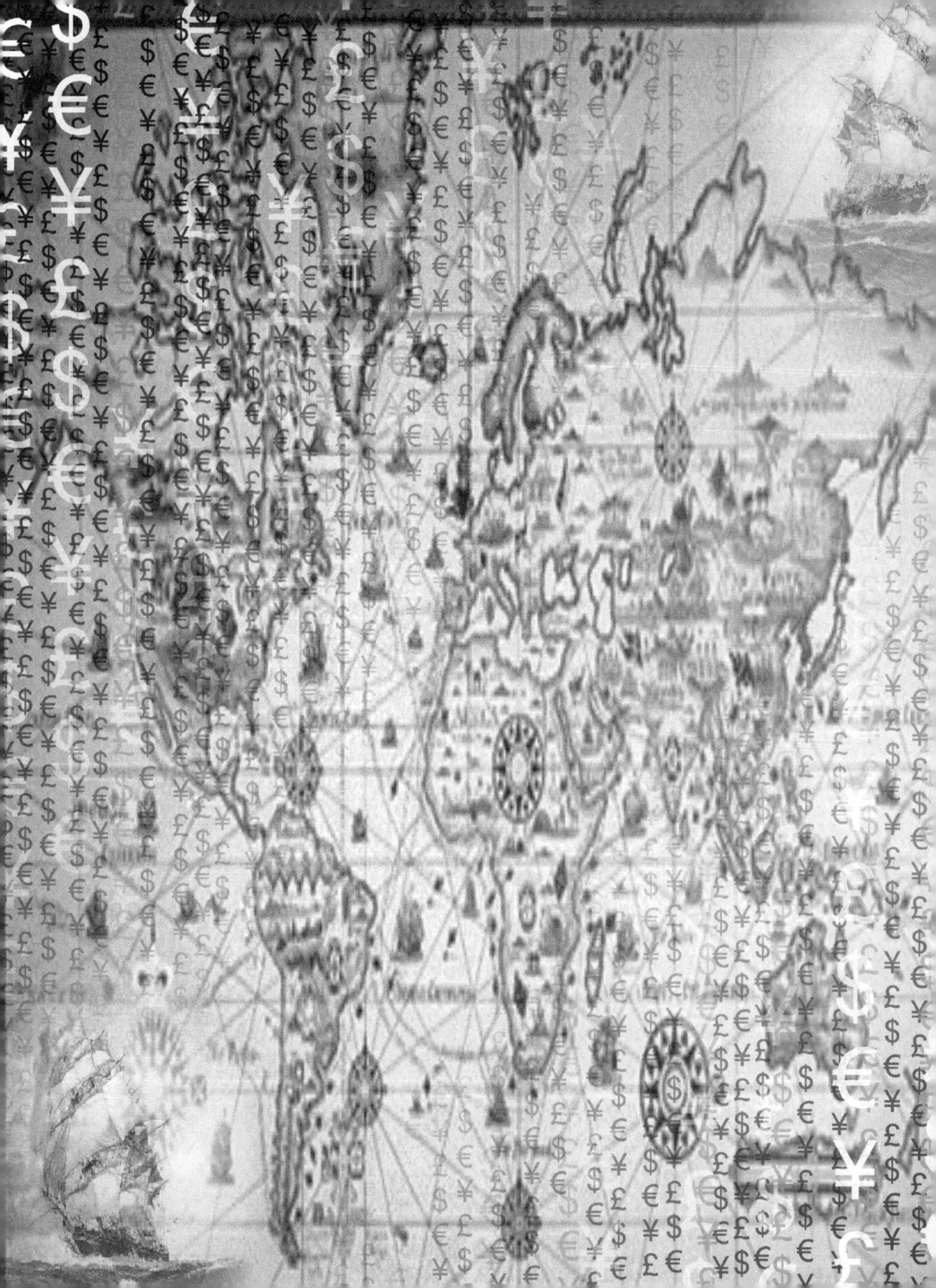

6

Implementing Pipelines

As you will have noticed by now, much of the data access, data modification and computational logic in Commerce Server takes place as a linear sequence of clearly defined and often independent tasks – much of what we're doing involves specifying conditions and processes that need to be tested and executed one after another. What's more, some contexts may require us to apply a single process repeatedly, while others may not be needed at all.

To make such processes as painless as possible, Commerce Server employs a modular (COM-based), sequential flow framework called **pipelines**. This isn't a full-blown flowcharting environment, but is strictly sequential; it can't fork, loop or merge, and can only handle conditional computing to a very limited extent. It does support transactions, though, and while program flow is restricted it is still a robust and flexible tool, as we're now going to see.

In this chapter, we will cover the following topics:

- ❑ An introduction to the pipeline framework
- ❑ The Pipeline Editor
- ❑ An overview of the pipeline components that ship with Commerce Server
- ❑ An in-depth look at some of the more interesting pipeline components
- ❑ A treatment of some of the plain COM components that are essential to the operation of the pipeline framework
- ❑ How to run a pipeline
- ❑ Business-to-business features
- ❑ The new shipment architecture

❏ The new **Currency** data type

❏ An introduction to making our own components

That's a lot of ground to cover, but a good understanding of pipelines is essential if you're to get the most out of Commerce Server, since they are usually responsible for much of a site's business logic.

In the course of the chapter, we will set up and execute a simple 'order confirmation' pipeline, as well as make asides to look at other types of pipeline and component.

The Pipeline Framework

As described briefly in the introduction to this chapter, the pipeline framework is a transactional environment for the sequential execution of components, and it is used to handle much of the business logic of a commerce site. Let's take a look at a very simple example of what this means in practice.

Suppose we want to display a 'shopping basket' page, but all we have to work with is a list of product SKUs (Stock Keeping Units) and the relevant quantities of each. Obviously, we'd like to display some rather more helpful information to the user – but we also want to ensure that any relevant business rules (such as those associated with a discount campaign) are applied. This is what the server needs to do:

1. Get values for the product name, product description, and price for each SKU listed.

2. Determine whether any of the current price campaigns apply to any of the products in the basket – if necessary, modify the price associated with a particular product.

3. Multiply the 'price per item' for each product by the quantity of that product in the basket.

4. Add all the prices together to calculate the total price of selected products.

This is obviously very simple business logic – in particular, we have skipped very lightly over Step 2: at this point we don't really know what business logic is involved in modifying prices. (In fact, the minute we implement a 'buy one get one free' campaign, our model simply can't cope!) Nevertheless, it should give you a feel for the kind of task the pipeline framework is designed to solve. By the time you have completed this chapter, you should have a good idea of how to go about effectively implementing business logic (such as campaign discounts) using the pipeline framework.

Before we look at the details, we need to examine the framework itself: what exactly is a pipeline? Well, to start with, let's take a look at a representation of our example pipeline in the **Pipeline Editor**, which you can access under Programs | Commerce Server 2000 on the Start menu. Pipelines are stored as files with a .pcf (Pipeline Configuration File) extension, and we'll take a closer look at these files in the next section. The pipeline shown below is called Plan.pcf, and is one that you will be shown how to create for yourself during the course of this chapter.

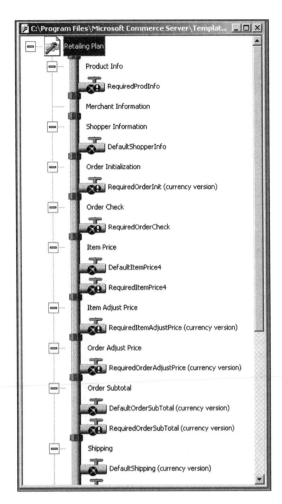

As you can see, the folks at Microsoft take the pipeline metaphor very seriously! However, it is worth keeping in mind that pipelines are *only* used as a metaphor – it's useful just as long as it helps you to visualize what's going on – it could just as easily be a railway line with stations, or pearls on a string. Let's consider how this pipeline might be used:

❑   Two data-carrying objects are sent to the top of the pipeline: an OrderForm object and a Context object.

For the moment, we can simply think of the OrderForm object as a representation of a shopping basket, and the Context object as a representation of the surrounding framework (databases, global resources, etc.). The Context object is never manipulated during this process – it is only queried for values. You can therefore consider it as being applied to the pipeline as a whole. On the other hand, the OrderForm object undergoes a transformation; usually coming out of the bottom end of the pipeline much larger than it was when it entered. This is what we're actually passing *through* the pipeline.

❑   Soon the OrderForm encounters the first tap, which represents a **Pipeline Component**. This component takes the OrderForm object as input, usually reads one or more of its attributes, modifies them (or possibly even creates new attributes), and returns the modified OrderForm to the pipeline, where it continues down until meeting the next object.

❑   This process continues for each pipeline component, until an object emerges from the bottom of the pipeline, fully processed and ready for subsequent use.

Executing the Pipeline

So how exactly is a pipeline executed? Well, assuming it is called from ASP code, it's executed using one of six COM objects. Each one is slightly different, each one serving a distinct purpose:

❑   **MtsPipeline** – the basic pipeline execution component.

❑   **MtsTxPipeline** – allows the pipeline execution to run as a single transaction. This is obviously an advantage if a pipeline contains one or more steps that write to a database, such as a purchase pipeline.

❑   **PooledPipeline** – like MtsPipeline, but enhanced to take advantage of COM+ object pooling. Pipeline objects to be pooled must adhere to certain restrictions. Chief amongst these restrictions is that they must be free-threaded.

Visual Basic (6 and below) components are apartment threaded, and therefore can't be pooled, but can still be used in a pooled pipeline along with poolable objects – they are simply instantiated each time they are called, just as with MtsPipeline and MtsTxPipeline.

Although object pooling can provide us with performance benefits, we should use it only in production sites, as the pipeline configurations are cached in memory. Thus, every time a pipeline is reconfigured during development, the object pool must be refreshed – in this case, by restarting IIS Admin and all related services. This could be quite an impediment during project development, as it would have to happen rather frequently. Therefore, it can be simpler to use MtsPipelines during development and PooledPipelines in production.

❑   **PooledTxPipeline** – allows the pipeline execution to run as a single transaction, and takes advantage of COM+ object pooling.

❑   **OrderGroup** – an object for handling multiple order forms at the same time. Apart from many other functions, the OrderGroup object can also load a pipeline and execute it for a group of OrderForms in one step, providing additional grand totals across all orders in the group.

❑   **OrderPipeline** – a special pipeline execution object designed for use as a global application object. As it is not transacted, it is not recommended that we use this for order processing pipelines. However, pipelines for content selection can utilize the OrderPipeline effectively, as it can be created once in global.asa and referenced indefinitely thereafter without loading and unloading.

Apart from the OrderGroup object, which uses a slightly different syntax, all these components use similar method invocations to load and run pipelines. Using MtsPipeline as an example, we create the object in the following way:

```
'Create a pipeline execution object
Set objPipeline = Server.CreateObject("Commerce.MtsPipeline")

'Load the pipeline configuration file
objPipeline.LoadPipe "C:\Inetpub\wwwroot\ProfCS2kBook\sample.pcf"

'Run the pipeline
objPipeline.Execute 1, objOrderform, objContext, 0
```

where `objOrderform` is the order form and `objContext` the site context, and both would have been defined earlier in the script.

The Pipeline Editor

In this section we will take a detailed look at the **Pipeline Editor**, the tool that we can use to create, modify and review pipelines. It is actually little more than a Win32 program for editing `.pcf` files. As we have already seen, it looks like this:

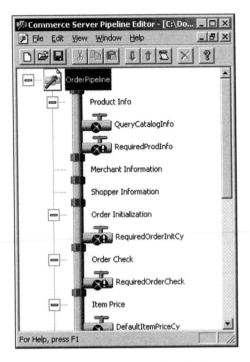

Each pipeline begins with the document root object (here, it's called `OrderPipeline`) representing the entire pipeline. Setting properties on this level, you can edit transaction levels, currency settings and a description for the pipeline.

A pipeline consists of zero or more **stages**, each containing zero or more **pipeline components**. Stages can be collapsed and expanded by using the minus or plus signs to their left, but serve mostly to organize the pipeline into conceptual sections. Stages do possess some properties, though. The `error level` property is the only one with a serious impact on program execution – this property defines a threshold for errors, where execution stops if the threshold is exceeded. Apart from the `error level` property, other stage level properties are mostly of an informational nature, such as label and description.

In the picture above, some stages (*Merchant Information, Shopper Information*) are left empty, which can be seen because they have no tap and no plus sign to their left – if they had had a plus sign, it would mean that the stage view had just been collapsed, but that components were present in the stage although out of view. The picture shows a so-called pipeline template, so some empty stages are included and should either be filled out with components or deleted. Empty stages have no impact on performance or logic progression. Pipelines with zero stages or only empty stages don't do anything at all, so there's no reason to have them around (but they actually report success if you try to run them).

Each tap on the pipeline represents a pipeline component, and this is where all the program execution actually takes place. Pipeline components are called in sequence with the topmost going first. Components have properties too, and some of these may be very significant for program execution.

Pipeline component property pages can contain two or three tabs, two of which are always present: **Component Properties** and **Values Read and Written**. Both tabs mainly contain information, and the only editable properties are the usual `Label` and `Description`. The `Values Read and Written` tab can be informative, as it states (in theory) the names of all attributes read and written from both the order form and the site context objects. It's nice for a quick glance, but nine out of ten times you'll find yourself having to look the component up in the documentation anyway to determine what it does.

The third tab is optional and can contain any number of text and controls the programmer of the component could think of putting there. This is where you can edit custom properties for the component, if applicable.

Values Read and Written

As described above, the `Values Read and Written` tab contains information about which values are read and written during execution of a component. If you need an overview of what happens in a pipeline, it can soon become tedious to open the property page for each component in the pipeline. For that reason, the pipeline editor comes with a functionality to save all values read and written to a file.

On the File menu, click **Save Values Read and Written** and specify a file in which to save the information. The result will be a text file you can open in the text editor of your choice. The file states the values read and written for every component in the pipeline.

It is important to notice that both `Values Read and Written` functionalities are based on an implementation of the `IPipelineComponentDescription` interface. This implementation is written by the programmer responsible for developing the component, and is not a feature that automatically 'scans' the component for all values that it reads or writes – thus, if the programmer forgets to inform about a value read or written, you will not be informed about it. And these omissions do occur, also in the pipeline components shipping with CS2K.

This is why, although the `Values Read and Written` functionalities can provide a nice overview, the pipeline log files still provide a more accurate picture of what actually gets read and written during execution.

The Pipeline Configuration File

When editing and troubleshooting pipelines, it may be useful to know a little bit about the file format. The file format itself belongs to Microsoft and is not public domain, so we can't cover the details of it here. However, one observation (which can be very quickly confirmed) is that it's a binary format.

Although we can't explore the exact structure, we *can* ascertain what gets saved to the file and what doesn't. A PCF file contains information on:

❑ Stages and their properties

❑ Pipeline structure: the order of stages and components, plus properties of the overall pipeline

❑ Pipeline component properties

While this may seem pretty inclusive, one very important class of information is left out: namely, the components themselves! In a pipeline, a component is only defined as a set of properties – two of these properties are the `Class ID` and `Program ID` of the real component.

When saving a component into a pipeline, only these two pieces of data are actually saved to the file. To execute the pipeline, the calling component extracts information about which objects to instantiate, and then references them like ordinary COM components. So don't think you save the component in the pipeline – if you modify or delete the component from the server, all pipelines containing this component are affected too – which also means that you can edit and recompile your own components without having to edit the pipeline (if you're using Visual Basic, be sure to remember to use binary compatibility).

Setting up a Pipeline

Let's take a look at an example. We want to be able to create a basket confirmation page, based on product ID's, quantities and a few other user-selections such as shipping methods. In fact, the only information we need from the user for this example is:

❑   SKU (Stock Keeping Unit) – this is the unique product ID

❑   Quantity – the quantity of each product ordered

❑   Shipping Method – the user's selection of shipping method for each item

Later in the chapter, we'll see how these selections are entered on the order using CS2K's order objects. For now, let's take a look at actually setting up the pipeline, and later we will also return to trace what's actually going on in the pipeline.

To give you an idea of what we're trying to accomplish, here is a preview of what we intend to finish up with:

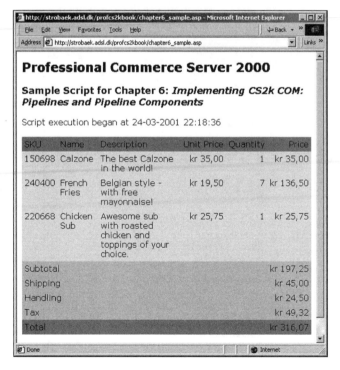

You may notice that prices seem somewhat unfamiliar: this is because the locale chosen for this example (and this chapter as a whole) is Danish. Prices, currency and formatting will be in Danish throughout – don't worry though, the explanations and site text will remain in English, so it shouldn't pose too much of a problem, even if your Danish language skills are a little rusty!

To begin creating the pipeline, open the CS2K Pipeline Editor – initially, no pipeline is loaded so the main pane is empty. Click File | New and the Choose a Pipeline Template dialog appears:

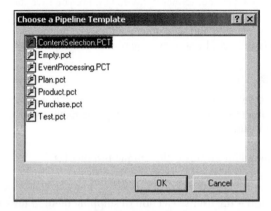

This presents a list of installed pipeline templates, including `Empty.pct`, which you can use to create your own custom template from scratch. We're going to work from the `Plan.pct` template, so select this entry and click OK.

As you can see, this pipeline template is already quite large and confusing, especially when you can only see a few components on the screen at once. In order to get a better overall view of the pipeline, click View | Icon Size | Small Icon, and it should now look more like the screenshot below:

To begin with, right-click on the pipeline root, currently named Retailing Plan, and select Properties. In the Pipeline Properties dialog box we can edit the overall properties of this particular pipeline. In the Label edit field, enter a descriptive text such as Basket confirmation pipeline, and optionally write a description for the pipeline in the Description field.

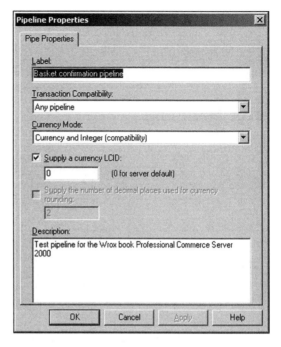

In the Transaction Compatibility drop-down control you can control whether this pipeline should run as transacted, non-transacted or if it doesn't matter. In the case of our example, it doesn't matter, so we'll just leave it as Any pipeline.

We can also set the Currency Mode to inform the pipeline framework about what sort of currency we are going to use in this pipeline. Later in the chapter we'll talk more about the new Currency data type; for now let's just say that we are going to use both types in this pipeline, so we should choose Currency and Integer (compatibility).

When using currencies, a currency locale ID is required. On an international site, the locale ID (and other currency information set on this property page) can be supplied by the order itself, using the following OrderForm keys:

❑ _currency_compatibility

❑ _currency_lcid

❑ _currency_decimal_places

For now though, we'll just create a simple pipeline configured for a single locale, so we can just use the server default, as shown above. As we are satisfied with these properties, click OK to return to the pipeline.

> **At this point we should save the pipeline for the first time. Take care though, and be sure to select File | Save As. It's worth noting that the Pipeline Editor has a not-so-useful little feature, which means that if we were to click Save at this point, we would overwrite the original template file!**

Give the file a descriptive name such as `sample.pcf`, and save it to a place where your ASP script can get to it, for example in a subfolder of the web application you're coding. In order to actually use this pipeline for something practical, we shall need to modify it further –but we'll leave our example for now, and come back to it repeatedly throughout the chapter, showing you how to set it up and run it, and explaining what happens inside it.

Error Handling

The pipeline framework also contains facilities for handling errors. Ideally, this sort of system should be totally self-contained, allowing errors to be trapped and friendly messages displayed on appropriate web pages – but just like all programs, pipeline executions sometimes crash. The error-handling environment essentially builds on error handling in the individual components – it is therefore the responsibility of the *component developer* to provide a robust error handling process.

In essence, error handling in pipelines works like this:

❑ If an error occurs during object processing within a pipeline component, an error message is written to the `OrderForm` by that pipeline component; in fact it is added to a `SimpleList` on the order form. Standard error lists in Commerce Server are named `_basket_errors` and `_purchase_errors`, and the value written is usually a string taken from an application-level `MessageManager` object.

❑ In addition to the error message, the pipeline component returns an error level value, which can be one of the following:

❑ **1** – all is well; the pipeline executed without problems.

❑ **2** – warning; there were some problems, but pipeline execution still completed; you should examine any errors reported and possibly let the user decide upon further action.

❑ **3** – error; the pipeline didn't execute as planned; errors should definitely be handled.

❑ The highest reported error level is returned by the calling component after pipeline execution ends.

❑ Wherever possible, errors should be trapped and handled by the pipeline components in which they occur.

Each pipeline stage has an error level threshold; a stage will not execute if that threshold is reached. This is especially useful if later components in a pipeline are supposed to write modifications to a database. Although such changes will be rolled back if the pipeline is running as part of a transaction, it would be preferable not to write the changes at all, if the earlier components were in error. The typical error level threshold is 2, indicating that the stage will run on, excepting direct failure.

Pipeline Logging

When developing and troubleshooting pipelines, it can sometimes be rather difficult to determine exactly what happens where, and what values are assigned at what times. Pipeline logging can be a tremendous help in this case.

Logs are stored in a specified file on the local hard disk. We can assign a separate log file for each pipeline, or use one common file for all pipelines in a site.

> **Pipeline logging should only ever take place on production systems in extreme cases –
> normally, it should be strictly confined to development systems, as it degrades
> performance, may compromise security, and frequently results in file lock situations when
> two or more sessions try to write to the same file simultaneously.**

Turning logging on and off is easy – just use the `SetLogFile` method of the pipeline execution object,
like this:

```
'Create a pipeline execution object
Set objPipeline = Server.CreateObject("Commerce.MtsPipeline")

'Load the pipeline configuration file
objPipeline.LoadPipe "C:\Inetpub\wwwroot\ProfCS2kBook\sample.pcf"

'Set log file
objPipeline.SetLogFile "C:\Inetpub\wwwroot\ProfCS2kBook\sample_log.txt"

'Run the pipeline
objPipeline.Execute 1, objOrderform, objContext, 0
```

Calling the `SetLogFile` method with an empty string turns off logging.

*Remember to set the appropriate permissions for the `IUSR` account to view log files – however, be aware
that this should only take place in a development environment, never in the outside world!*

Pipeline log files can quickly become very large and complex, and it takes some practice to get used to
reading them. Here's an excerpt from a typical log:

```
...lots of log text comes before this...

MICROPIPELINE:++ 2001/02/10 13:14:08.0876  Micro Pipeline Execution starts
(lFlags==0x0)

RootObject:ReadValue _cy_tax_total VT_I2 300 VT_EMPTY __empty__
RootObject:WriteValue saved_cy_tax_total VT_EMPTY __empty__ VT_I2 300

...more text goes here...

Items: ReadItem 0 VT_DISPATCH PV=[0x1717d18] VT_EMPTY __empty__
: ReadValue_product_VariantID VT_I2 5 VT_EMPTY __empty__
: WriteValue saved_product_VariantID VT_EMPTY __empty__ VT_I2 5

...yet more text goes here...

MICROPIPELINE:-- component returned hr: 0x0 in 30 milliseconds

...and it just keeps on going...
```

Not the most readable format, you'd probably agree. Microsoft recommends that we import the log into
Excel or some other tool that can help us arrange things better, but with Notepad (or your favorite text
editor), it's not too difficult to find the information you might be looking for.

The first thing a log will tell you is when it begins; likewise, the last thing it tells you is when it stops again.
For each component in the pipeline there's an entry delimited by information about when component
execution began and ended, which component it was, and what the return value was.

Between the begin and end information for each component, all values read and written are reported – both for the order form dictionary itself (called the RootObject) and for each item in the Items dictionary (marked by Items). The logging format for both dictionary objects is the same:

1. We're told first whether a particular operation was a *read* or *write* operation:

2. Next, we're given the name of the attribute on which the operation takes place. Note that if the entry concerns the item itself, this will be the index number of the item: 0, 1, 2, etc.

3. We're then told the data type of the attribute to be read, if any. Note that for dictionary items themselves, the data type is VT_DISPATCH, as the item is a COM object in its own right. If nothing was read, the data type is reported as VT_EMPTY. Actually, all data types are reported as COM data types, which will probably be most familiar to Visual C++ programmers.

   Programmers not familiar with these data types can find information about them on MSDN – at http://msdn.microsoft.com/library/psdk/automat/chap6_7zdz.htm there's a nice overview of the VARIANT subtypes.

4. After stating the data type, the log states the value of the attribute.

5. The last two columns match the two just described. The first contains the data type of the attribute written...

6. ...while the last contains its value.

It may take some patience and creative use of *Ctrl-F* to navigate successfully through a log to extract the information you need, but in troubleshooting situations, these logs can mean the difference between success and failure.

Pipeline logs can grow very large very quickly. A useful alternative is to use the sample VBScript DumpOrder.vbs (for use with the Scriptor component, which we cover later on in the chapter). It can be found under SDK\Samples\Sitelets\Order\source\pipeline\, and can be inserted into a pipeline as a Scriptor component in one or more places. It provides a snapshot of the OrderForm object at the time it was executed, writing the result to a file specified by entering filename=MyFilename (where MyFilename is the full path and filename to the output file) in the Scriptor component's Config edit box.

Inserted at critical points in a pipeline, the DumpOrder Scriptor sample can provide some information about the state of the OrderForm object, but in detail level it's no match for a real pipeline log file, which provides information about *every* value read and written during execution, including the correct sequence of events, which component does what, and the data types of the values.

COM Components for Pipelines

In this section we will take a detailed look at the COM components most often used in conjunction with pipelines. As we saw in Chapter 2, the Dictionary object is one of the most important COM components used by Commerce Server as a whole, as it supports the creation, storage, and retrieval of name/value pairs in memory. Likewise, the SimpleList object consists of an array of variants, and can be compared to a normal array, except that it offers greater functionality.

The pipeline framework relies heavily on both of these objects – in particular, we're now going to see how they form the foundation of the OrderForm object, as used by an Order Processing Pipeline.

> The Order Processing Pipeline (OPP) is one of several pipeline types provided with CS2K, and is used to process orders or lists of products to enable product display, basket display, order placement, etc. It handles most of a site's product-related business logic and is the most important type of pipeline by far – in fact a Commerce Server site can't really do much without one.

Another significant instance of the Dictionary object is the PipeContext object. This is a read-only dictionary that provides the pipeline with information about the execution environment – for example, it might contain the connection string for a database.

The last two objects we'll discuss are the ProfileObject and ProfileService objects. As we saw in Chapter 3, the first of these is used to represent business entities such as customers, companies, products, purchase orders, and accounts – a profile contains properties of the business entity. For example, Joe User is a specific customer, and the data concerning Joe User is stored as an instance of a customer profile. The ProfileService object is used to create, delete, and retrieve ProfileObject objects.

We will wrap up the section by looking at some of the naming conventions used when assigning keys to a Dictionary object.

The OrderForm Object

The pipeline framework requires that data being passed from the site to the pipeline (and likewise from the pipeline to the site) be in a Dictionary object. In the case of the default OPP, this must be an OrderForm object: a Dictionary containing a mixture of simple key/value elements, Dictionary and SimpleList objects.

This structure makes it possible to present a detailed summary of all (or part) of one or more shopping sessions to the user (or to the pipeline). This summary includes user data such as name, address, and credit-card information, as well as product information related to the purchase.

The following figure shows some of the key elements of the OrderForm object:

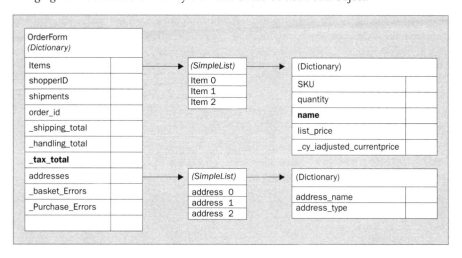

The first element in the top-level `Dictionary` object is the `Items` list; this is a reference to a `SimpleList` object containing the items that make up the order. Each of these items is another `Dictionary` object, containing details about the product (such as name, price, and quantity).

A vital key in this product information `Dictionary` is the **Stock Keeping Unit** or **SKU**. In CS2K, the SKU is a unique identifier for a product; it can be a number or a combination of numbers and letters. The SKU allows a product to be tracked, for example, for inventory purposes, and can be associated with any item that can be purchased.

As mentioned previously, the `OrderForm` object can be looked at as inheriting from the `Dictionary` object and as such is made up of the same elements, consisting of a key, or name, and a value. Each component that you include in the Order Processing Pipeline for your site is designed to operate on one or more of these keys and values. Operations include the creation and initialization, modification, verification and calculation of keys and values.

A number of the elements in the root `Dictionary` object of the `OrderForm` object include underscore characters. The appearance of an underscore character as the first character of an element name indicates that these items are not persisted: that is, they are not saved to the `OrderForm` storage for the site.

To manage the order form, the `OrderForm` object supports a number of methods: `AddItem`, `ClearItem`, and `ClearOrderForm`. While the last two clear the items collection and the entire `OrderForm` object respectively, the `AddItem` method adds a specified item to the `Items` collection. As we shall see shortly, the method takes three arguments: the SKU, the quantity, and one last parameter, reserved for future use. (Until this future arrives, the parameter must be set to 0.)

Let's now continue our sample script by creating an `OrderForm` and adding some items to it:

```
'Add base elements
objOrderForm.cc_type = "VISA"
objOrderForm.[_cc_expmonth] = "08"
objOrderForm.[_cc_expyear] = "02"
objOrderForm.customer_name = "Anders Kirkeby"
```

Note the special syntax used when adding the base elements. When referring to keys prefixed by an underscore character, you need to enclose the key in square brackets. You may also enclose keys that are not prefixed by an underscore in brackets, as it makes no difference. Note however, that the use of square brackets is related to the use of VB Scripting Edition and can not be used in regular VB, where you have to use the alternative syntax `objOrderForm.Value("_cy_tax_total") = 300`.

After creating the `OrderForm` object itself and adding some elements to the root object, let's add some products to the order:

```
'Add items
Set dictItem = objOrderForm.AddItem(150698, 1, 0)
dictItem.[_product_VariantID] = 5
dictItem.shipping_address_id = "My shipping address"

Set dictItem = objOrderForm.AddItem(240400, 7, 0)
dictItem.[_product_VariantID] = 4
dictItem.shipping_address_id = "My shipping address"
```

```
Set dictItem = objOrderForm.AddItem(220668, 1, 0)
dictItem.[_product_VariantID] = 3
dictItem.shipping_address_id = "My shipping address"
```

And last add the `addresses SimpleList` created previously.

```
'Add addresses SimpleList
Set objOrderForm.addresses = objAddresses
```

The PipeContext Dictionary

As we mentioned earlier, two objects enter the pipeline as input: an `OrderForm` object and a `Context` object. The `PipeContext` object is a `Dictionary` object functioning as a container of properties needed by pipeline components.

> *Where the `OrderForm` object undergoes a transformation during its path through the pipeline, the `PipeContext` object is almost never manipulated. Think of it as a read-only object, queried for information.*

Each specific pipeline may require different contextual information. Some information, however, is often supplied:

❑ Reference to the `MessageManager` object. The `MessageManager` object stores error messages in multiple languages used by the OPP to describe error conditions generated during order processing.

❑ Reference to the `DataFunctions` object. The `DataFunctions` object is used to perform locale-based formatting, parsing, etc., and includes a variety of utilities useful for site development.

❑ String value containing the Language (for example, English).

❑ Reference to the `CatalogManager`. Allows access to the entire Product Catalog System.

❑ Reference to the `CacheManager`. Used to establish and use a collection of data caches.

❑ Reference to the `ProfileService`. The `ProfileService` object is used to create, delete, and retrieve `ProfileObject` objects. We will cover these two objects in the next section.

Let us now create a `Context Dictionary`, and add some items to it. More specifically, we will add a `CacheManager` object and a string containing a connection string to a database.

```
'Constants
'This string should actually be written on the same line
Const conTransactionConfigConnectionString = _
    "Provider=SQLOLEDB;User ID=sa;Password=password;
    Initial Catalog=""Retail_commerce"";Data Source=LOKE;
    Network Library=dbmssocn;"

'Create Context Dictionary
Set objContext = Server.CreateObject("Commerce.Dictionary")
```

```
'Create a CacheManager object.
Set objCM = Server.CreateObject("Commerce.CacheManager")

'Do something interesting with the CacheManager object here...

'Add elements to Context
Set objContext.CacheManager = objCM
objContext.TransactionConfigConnectionString = _
          conTransactionConfigConnectionString
```

OrderGroup

To avoid any confusion or misunderstanding about the OrderGroup object in connection with the other data-carrying objects we've just been looking at, let's take a closer look at it. The OrderGroup object does not contain or carry data in a structured way – instead, it's an object that collects a set of methods for manipulation of OrderForm objects, including database access and pipeline execution.

Instead of providing the developer with a set of new functionality, OrderGroup provides a different angle of attack on a lot of functionality provided by other components in CS2K. The focus of the component is, of course, the order.

As OrderGroup provides functionality for streaming OrderForms in and out of a database, it must first be initialized with a connection string.

```
'Create the OrderGroup object
Set objOrderGrp = Server.CreateObject("Commerce.OrderGroup")

'Initialize the object
objOrderGrp.Initialize(conTransactionConfigConnectionString, strUserID)
```

Besides providing OrderGroup with a connection string, initialization also requires a user ID GUID, ensuring that all operations performed with the object affects only the specified user.

Methods provided by the object include functionality for:

- ❑ Reading and writing OrderForm objects from and to a database
- ❑ Manipulating attributes on the OrderForm, including subordinate objects such as Items or Addresses
- ❑ Running OrderForms through a pipeline and aggregating values from several OrderForms on the OrderGroup level (such as aggregating order totals into one grand total)

The object can handle several OrderForms at the same time and perform operations on the whole group at the same time. In spite of this, OrderGroup does not actually provide any functionality that's not available through other components – it simply collects a number of frequently used methods into one convenient package.

Besides providing one object for order manipulation, the OrderGroup is also convenient because it allows the handling of separate orders as one. This could come in handy if the site handles products from several different suppliers, and each supplier should receive an order containing only their products, but the site still want to present this grouping as a unit to the user.

To add several orders to the same `OrderGroup` object, you can use code like the following:

```
'objOrder1 and objOrder2 are 2 Orderform objects
objOrderGrp.AddOrderform objOrder1, "Food"
objOrderGrp.AddOrderform objOrder2, "Movies"
```

The individual orders can be extracted again by accessing the `OrderGroup` collection `Orderforms`:

```
Set objOrder1 = objOrderGrp.Value("Orderforms").Value("Food")
```

It even supports extended dot notation, so you can reference the orders like this:

```
'cyMovieTotal is an uninitialized currency variable
cyMovieTotal = _
    objOrderGrp.Value("Orderforms").Value("Movies").[_cy_total_total]
```

In some cases, handling the order as several logical units may provide an advantage. If the site handles orders which are supposed to go out to subcontractors, using the `OrderGroup` object in this way may be a good idea, as each order is still treated as a separate entity. When performing the final purchase, you don't have to split the order up into several pieces to send each order to the correct subcontractor – `OrderGroup` runs a pipeline for each `OrderForm`, so each would in this case run through the purchase pipeline.

Values can be aggregated across orders, by defining attributes to aggregate. Summing all the totals for each order into a grand total could be done like this:

```
objOrderGrp.AggregateOrderFormValues "_cy_total_total", "_cy_grand_total"
```

This grand total could again be referenced like this:

```
'cyGrandTotal is an unitialized currency variable
cyGrandTotal = objOrderGrp.Value("_cy_grand_total")
```

If you just need to split the order up into multiple shipments, the new shipment architecture (explained later in this chapter) may be a better match for the job than having multiple orders in the `OrderGroup` object. In that case, the `OrderGroup` object can be used with its default `OrderForm`.

```
'objOrder is an Orderform object
objOrderGrp.AddOrderform objOrder
```

Omitting the second name parameter to the method call adds the order to the `OrderGroup`'s *default* `OrderForm`, and it can be referenced like this:

```
Set objOrder = objOrderGrp.Value("Orderforms").Value("Default")
```

Profiles

As we know, profiles represent business entities such as customers, companies, products, purchase orders, and accounts. In the following section we shall concentrate on the `UserObject` profile, which is used to hold information about registered and anonymous users. Properties of each of the business entities mentioned above are stored in a profile, and these profiles are persisted to the **Profile Store**. This store is made up of a group of data sources (such as tables in a SQL Server database), which store items such as named expressions and site terms, as well as the profile definitions.

The structure of each profile is defined by an XML schema, which can be modified at design-time by means of the BizDesk's **Profile Designer** module and the **Profiles** resource in the Commerce Server Manager. At run-time, you don't work on the `ProfileObject` object directly – instead, you use the `ProfileService` object to create, maintain, and delete profiles. Now let's look more closely at this construction.

The ProfileService Object

The `ProfileService` object gives us run-time access to `ProfileObject` objects. In a web-based application context, it should be created and initialized in the application's `global.asa` file – as opposed to `ProfileObject` objects, which should always be created within page scope.

You should always start by initializing the `ProfileService` object. This initialization is used to establish a connection to the CS2K `Profile Store`, and populate the schema cache with all the schemas from the specified catalog. A `ProfileService` object must connect to only *one* Profile Store. In case you need access to multiple stores, you must create multiple instances of the `ProfileService` object.

Let's now create the `ProfileService` object and initialize it:

```
'Connection string
'This string should actually be written on the same line
Const conConnectionString = _
    "Provider=CSOLEDB;Data Source=LOKE;Initial Catalog=Retail_commerce;
    User ID=sa;Password=password;PsSchemaCacheSize=128;
    PsObjectAgeoutPeriod=8;"

'Connect using an explicit connection string.
Set objPS = Server.CreateObject("Commerce.ProfileService")
objPS.Initialize conConnectionString, "Profile Definitions"
```

As you can see, the `Initialize` method takes two arguments: a connection string, and a string specifying the catalog. This last argument is actually optional, but if specified, must have the value of `Profile Definitions`. Of the tokens in the connection string, only the `Data Source`, `Initial Catalog`, and `User ID` are mandatory; the rest are optional.

Having successfully established a connection to the Profile Store, we can now create a new `ProfileObject` object:

```
'Create User Profile
Set objUser = objPS.CreateProfile("JaneUser", "UserObject")
```

The first argument contains the primary key for the new `ProfileObject` object, and the second the schema type – of course, one must correspond to the other, so, for example, when working with the `UserObject`, the primary key might specify the user's logon name. When creating a new `Address` profile, the primary key is a globally unique identifier (GUID), normally obtained through a `GenID` object.

Having first created an empty `ProfileObject` object, you can now populate and save it to the underlying data store. This is done by calls directly to the `ProfileObject` object, as we shall see shortly.

The following piece of code would retrieve an existing profile by using the primary key and schema type:

```
'Retrieve User
Set objUserR = objPS.GetProfile("JaneUser", "UserObject")
```

It is also possible to retrieve a user profile by specifying a name/value pair and schema type. To do this, you must use the method GetProfileByKey:

```
'Retrieve User Profile using name/value pair
Set objUserR = objPS.GetProfileByKey("user_id", _
    "{E533A8B7-7CB0-4A3D-A26A-DAA9AF52A792}", _
    "UserObject")
```

To delete a profile, you would make a call to either DeleteProfile or DeleteProfileByKey on the ProfileService object. The two methods correspond to their Get counterparts.

The ProfileObject Object

This object is used to retrieve data from a specific profile and to modify its properties. Let's populate the ProfileObject instance just created, and save it to the underlying Profile Store:

```
'Populate profile
objUser.GeneralInfo.first_name = "Jane"
objUser.GeneralInfo.last_name = "User"
objUser.GeneralInfo.email_address = "Jane.User@wrox.com"
objUser.AccountInfo.account_status = 1

'Save the profile to the underlying Profile Store
objUser.Update
```

If you are observant, you may have noticed references to GeneralInfo and AccountInfo in the above example. These are in reference to the **group** in which each property belongs – as defined in the profile schema.

Now we have spent a little time creating profiles and putting data into them, how about getting some of that data out again? This is done using the Fields method on the ProfileObject object:

```
strLastName = objUser.Fields("GeneralInfo.last_name")
```

Once again, we can use the shorthand notation, and write:

```
strLastName = objUser.GeneralInfo.last_name
```

Naming Conventions

We will conclude this section by looking at some of the conventions used when naming keys:

❑   Any order form keys with names that begin with an underscore character will not be saved along with the rest of the object. Remember that the OrderForm operates in a similar way to a Dictionary object; effectively its prefix property is set to the underscore character. For obvious reasons of security, you don't usually want to save data such as a user's credit card details – by naming the relevant key "_cc", you can ensure that it's not persisted any longer than necessary.

❑ The names of most (if not all) keys containing price information begin with "cy_", showing that the value is a high precision currency value, represented by a 64-bit integer. This feature is new to CS2K, as Site Server 3.0 Commerce Edition only supported 32-bit integers. For example, the high precision currency version of the key _oadjust_adjustedprice is _cy_oadjust_adjustedprice.

❑ You may have noticed that some keys' names begin with an i, while others begin with an o. These two letters are used to distinguish between prices on *individual* items, and prices on aggregated values – o standing for *order*. For example, _cy_iadjust_currentprice holds the current price of an item (regular price minus any promotional discounts) whereas the _cy_oadjust_adjustedprice key contains the total price of this item – that is, the current price times the quantity (minus any discounts).

Overview of Available Pipeline Components

As we will see in the next chapter, you can quite easily develop your own custom pipeline components for Commerce Server 2000. Before doing this though, you might wish to look at some of the various components that are already available to you.

This section is not intended to present an encyclopaedic discourse on all the components supplied with CS2K. A complete list of over 77 components can be found in the documentation, under the item Programmer's Reference | Pipeline Component Reference. Instead, we shall take an overview of the standard pipeline types and available components, and look at how they naturally group together.

These are the standard pipeline categories distinguished in CS2K:

❑ **Order Processing Pipeline** (OPP) – this type of pipeline processes an order or list of products to enable product display, basket display, order placement, etc. It is by far the most important type of pipeline (you can't have a CS2K site without it). Virtually all CS2K sites have at least one (and very often more than one) of these. They handle most business logic concerned with products.

❑ **Content Selection Pipeline** (CSP) – this type of pipeline processes a list of items that may be relevant to show to the user. They may be used to manage advertisement campaigns, including examining the user with respect to the target group, balancing the display frequency of competing campaigns, etc. They handle business logic concerned with marketing.

❑ **Event Processing Pipeline** (EPP) – this type of pipeline is used to record events taking place on the site. If the user clicks on a specific ad, an Event Processing Pipeline can be used to record this event for further analysis. They are often used in conjunction with Content Selection Pipelines to record, for example, which ads were clicked.

❑ **Direct Mailer Pipeline** – this type of pipeline is used for direct mail campaigns. It can be used to construct personalized e-mails from a template, or send static (non-personalized) messages.

We can group components in various ways, such as where they are used and how they are used. Some of the components are provided simply as samples – we will mention which these are and look briefly at what they do. Others are supplied for purposes of backward compatibility with Site Server 3.0 Commerce Edition (SS3CE). These components should only be used if legacy issues demand it, like upgrading or maintaining a site based on SS3CE – again, a short list will be supplied.

Location

Let's start with *where* the pipeline components can be used – most will be used exclusively in one type of pipeline, while three can be used in more than one type:

- ❏ The `ExecuteProcess` component runs an external executable file – an action you might find a use for in any of the pipelines.

- ❏ The `RecordEvent` component is used in Content Selection and Event Processing pipelines to record events, such as an ad click or an image download.

- ❏ The `Scriptor` component will run any script you ask it to – as with `ExecuteProcess`, you might wish to do this in any pipeline type.

If you look in the list of the available pipeline components you will see four components mentioned, even though they are not real pipeline components. Firstly, we are talking about the `CSFLoadAdvertisements`, `CSFLoadDiscounts`, and `CSFWriteEvents` components. Although they all implement two pipeline component interfaces, they are not real pipelines: they will not appear in the list of available components inside the Pipeline Editor, and therefore, cannot be used or configured. All three are used in connection with the `CacheManager` object. The fourth component of this type is the `StepWiseShipping` component, which is used to calculate shipping costs for shipments in the new multi-shipment shipping architecture. This component should never be inserted directly into a pipeline, but is executed by the `ShippingMethodRouter`.

Purpose

So *what* do the different pipeline components do? While the various different components accomplish a lot of different tasks, these tasks ultimately boil down to the following:

- ❏ You can **extract** product data from a number of data sources, but most likely you will use the new CS2K catalog structure. `QueryCatalogInfo` retrieves catalog information for every item in the order form.

- ❏ Most components shipping with CS2K **manipulate** items on the order form. Some add new items to the order form – for example, `DefaultItemPriceCy`, which is used to set the regular price of an item. This regular price is often the list price, as returned by a component like `QueryCatalogInfo`.

   Other components modify existing key values, like adding a handling cost to the total cost or giving a discount. Others will delete items – for example, if a product in the basket is no longer available. Perhaps a user selects an item on Monday, and instead of checking out, saves their shopping basket. On Tuesday, the shop removes that item from their catalog. On Wednesday, the user returns and tries to check out. Since it's now impossible to purchase the removed item, the component `RequiredProdInfo` might be used to remove that item from the order form.

- ❏ The last group of components consists of those that **return** data. This could be either to a data source, a file or some other backend system.

Samples

Five *sample* components are supplied with Commerce Server 2000, all of which deal with calculation of tax. These are provided for evaluation and testing purposes only – in fact, Microsoft strongly recommends that you have an independent tax professional verify all applicable tax rates and data generated by these components before using such information for personal or business purposes – in other words, *you* are responsible for ensuring that the tax calculation is correct. The five components are:

❑ **SimpleCanadaTax** – calculate the Canadian Goods and Services Tax (GST) and Provincial Sales Tax (PST).

❑ **SimpleJapanTax** – compute taxes according to the Japanese tax model.

❑ **SimpleUSTax** – apply taxes on any order sent to a specified state in the United States.

❑ **SimpleVATTax** – calculate a Value Added Tax (VAT).

❑ **SampleRegionalTax** – calculate taxes in pipelines using the multiple shipment features of CS2K.

`SimpleCanadaTax`, `SimpleJapanTax`, `SimpleUSTax` and `SimpleVATTax` are all Site Server 3.0 Commerce Edition sample tax components, and are not capable of utilizing the new shipment architecture of CS2K. The new shipping architecture will be covered later in the chapter.

Legacy

Strictly speaking there are a lot more than 77 components. The main reason for this is that some of the components are supplied in two versions: a legacy version for SS3CE, and a new one for CS2K.

As we shall see later in the chapter, CS2K gives you the option of using a **high-precision currency value** representation. It goes without saying that only the 'pure' CS2K components utilize this new representation, and if you were to build a new site, you would naturally use these.

The way you can distinguish between the two versions is that Cy is appended to all the names of the high-precision components – let's look at an example. The component `DefaultTotal` calculates the order total from the subtotals. It is supplied for backward compatibility only, and you should use its younger sibling `DefaultTotalCy`. Apart from the name of the component, they also perform on different keys. High-precision values are stored in keys prefixed with _cy. The `DefaultTotal` components will store the total in the key _total_total, and the `DefaultTotalCy` components will use the key _cy_total_total to store the total of the order.

> *As you can see, there should not be any problem keeping the components apart – just remember Cy for high precision.*

So, what if you have an existing site – can you use the new components in your old pipelines? The answer is yes, you can. However, if you mix legacy components and CS2K components within a single stage, you will need to surround the former components with the `MoneyConverter` component. This will ensure that the dictionary values, for example _total_total and _cy_total_total, are kept current for both types of components.

Six other components are supplied for backward compatibility. `DBOrderPromoADO` and `ItemPromo` are used in connection with price promotions on individual items. The Discount objects of the Content Selection pipeline provide a much more powerful and general instrument for applying discounts. We'll look at these some more in Chapter 8.

The components `FixedHandling`, `FixedShipping`, `LinearHandling`, and `LinearShipping` add shipping and handling charges to the order. None of them supports the new high-precision currency.

`QueryProdInfoADO` is the last component we should mention in this brief look at the available legacy components. In contrast with its younger cousin `QueryCatalogInfo`, it obtains product information directly from a database, and not from the new CS2K catalog structure.

Components in our Example

When we introduced the Pipeline Editor earlier on, we began creating an example pipeline based on the standard template `Plan.pct`. So far, we have not made any modifications to its components – in order to make it work though, we'll now need to apply a few tweaks. We'll look at each component in turn, examine what it does, and consider whether we need to delete or modify it, or (as we're just about to see) add another component.

QueryProdInfoADO

Yes, the first component we need is not yet in our pipeline, so the first thing you must do is to add it. Currently, the pipeline's first stage is the Product Info stage, and this is where we populate the `Items` list with more information about the products. As you may remember, we added three different products to the `OrderForm`:

```
Set dictItem = objOrderForm.AddItem(150698, 1, 0)
dictItem.[_product_VariantID] = 5
dictItem.shipping_address_id = "My shipping address"

Set dictItem = objOrderForm.AddItem(240400, 7, 0)
dictItem.[_product_VariantID] = 4
dictItem.shipping_address_id = "My shipping address"

Set dictItem = objOrderForm.AddItem(220668, 1, 0)
dictItem.[_product_VariantID] = 3
dictItem.shipping_address_id = "My shipping address"
```

To demonstrate what's going to happen if we add a product that doesn't exist, we'll try that. We haven't really defined what's in the database, but we'll get to that in a minute.

```
'Add an item that doesn't exist in the database
Set dictItem = objOrderForm.AddItem(241598, 1, 0)
dictItem.[_product_VariantID] = 3
dictItem.shipping_address_id = "My shipping address"
```

We need more information, such as product name, description and price. There are more ways of doing this in CS2K, but the simplest component to understand is probably `QueryProdInfoADO` – normally, product information population should be done by the `QueryCatalogInfo` component, which uses the new CS2K catalog structure. For clarity we'll use `QueryProdInfoADO`, as we don't need to set up a complete *catalog* to demonstrate product information population.

At this stage we need to look at the data source of this information. Let's assume that we've set up a `Products` table in our database:

SKU	Name	Description	cy_list_price	taxID
1506 98	Calzone	The best Calzone in the world!	35.0000	1
1925 73	Bacon & Cheese Burger	Boring, dry burger with too much fat...	60.0000	1

SKU	Name	Description	cy_list_price	taxID
2206 68	Chicken Sub	Awesome sub with roasted chicken and toppings of your choice.	25.7500	1
2404 00	French Fries	Belgian style – with free mayonnaise!	19.5000	1

The `taxID` column is a foreign key pointing to the `TaxRates` table, which currently only contains a single row containing the Danish value-added tax (yes, it really is 25 percent!):

TaxID	tax_rate
1	25

Now that we know about the data, we can insert the `QueryProdInfoADO` component into the pipeline. Right-click on the **Product Info** stage and select **Insert Component** – the **Choose a component** dialog box appears:

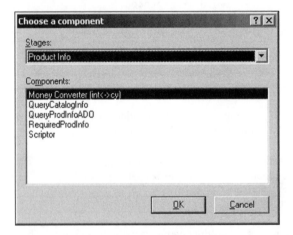

As you can see, only a few components are immediately available to the **Product Info** stage. If you click on the **Stages** drop-down control, you will be able to select **All** to see all pipeline components installed on the system. However, we don't need to do this, as the **QueryProdInfoADO** component is right there where we need it.

This arrangement is called **Stage Affinity**, with most components naturally fitting into one or more specific stages (as defined by their GUID). Note that a few components (such as the `Scriptor` component) are available in all stages. Stage Affinity doesn't imply that you can't use a component in another stage than the one with which it fits, but it is mostly there to help you select among the components that best fit the task at hand. For our example, select **QueryProdInfoADO** and click **OK**.

Before we can use the `QueryProdInfoADO` component, it needs to be configured. Right-click on the component in the pipeline and select **Properties**. The **Component Properties** dialog box appears:

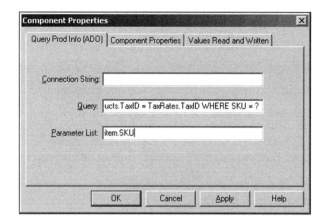

When we first open this dialog box, **Connection String** and **Parameter List** are empty, and in the **Query** edit field it only says query. In this case, we don't need to assign a connection string, because `QueryProdInfoADO` will use the `DefaultConnectionString` of the context if no connection string is stated.

To work, the component must be supplied with a SQL query for the product information. We define it as:

```
SELECT Products.[Name], Products.[Description],_
                    Products.cy_list_price, TaxRates.tax_rate
FROM Products INNER JOIN TaxRates ON Products.TaxID = TaxRates.TaxID
WHERE SKU = ?
```

The string inserted in the component should be one line without line breaks, but here we've formatted it a little for clarity. As you have probably already noticed, the WHERE clause is defined with a question mark. This question mark is replaced at run time with the parameter defined in the **Parameter List** input field: item.SKU, meaning that each item's SKU should be used in this place. If more parameters were needed, a space-separated list could have been provided here, and more question marks used in the SQL query. Click OK to close the dialog box, and save the pipeline.

Running QueryProdInfoADO

Let's look at what actually happens when the component runs as a part of executing the pipeline.

First, the component starts iterating through the Items list. As we have defined our single SQL input parameter to be each item's SKU, this value is read. For the first item, the value is 150698, as we originally defined it when we added the product:

```
Set dictItem = objOrderForm.AddItem(150698, 1, 0)
```

This value is inserted into the SQL query we defined, replacing the question mark. The query is then executed, returning a recordset of one record, containing the values:

Name	Description	cy_list_price	tax_rate
Calzone	The best Calzone in the world!	35.0000	25

297

These values are then written to the item by prefixing the string _product_ to each column name:

- ❑ item._product_Name gets the string value "Calzone"
- ❑ item._product_Description gets the string value "The best Calzone in the world!"
- ❑ item._product_cy_list_price gets the currency value 35
- ❑ item._product_tax_rate gets the integer value 25

The component then loops back to the next item (240400) and repeats the process, and then does it one more time for the third item. Each of the first three items is now equipped with a name, description, price and tax rate.

Upon reaching the fourth item, the component again reads the SKU from the item to find a value of 241598. Inserting this value into the query and executing it, an empty recordset is returned, as the product doesn't exist in our database.

QueryProdInfoADO then creates an attribute called delete on the item, and sets the value to 1, thus marking the item for deletion.

RequiredProdInfo

The next component in our pipeline is a standard pipeline component included with the **Plan** template that we used to create the pipeline. RequiredProdInfo ensures the integrity of the order at this point. If QueryProdInfoADO finds any items not available in the database, it will set an attribute called delete on the item to the value 1. RequiredProdInfo looks at all the items on the order to check if this attribute exists. If it does, and the value is one, it writes an error message to the OrderForm's _Basket_Errors list and deletes the item. There is no configuration to be done with this component, so like so many other pipeline components it's pretty easy to use – just plug it in and ensure that it has all the information that it needs. That last element proves to be the tricky part, but in this case it's not so bad.

As long as everything is all right (all products exist at the data source), RequiredProdInfo does nothing. If an item is to be deleted, the component adds a message to the _Basket_Errors list. This message is extracted from the MessageManager object, which is part of the pipeline context. Let's take a look at how to set the MessageManager up for this specific purpose.

```
'Create the MessageManager object
Set objMessageMgr = Server.CreateObject("Commerce.MessageManager")

'Add a language
objMessageMgr.AddLanguage "US English", 1033

'Add a message
objMessageMgr.AddMessage "pur_badsku", _
                "One or more items were deleted from the basket!"
```

Setting up the MessageManager object usually happens in global.asa. After setting up the message manager, it must be added to the pipeline context before running the pipeline.

```
Set objContext.MessageManager = objMessageMgr
```

The message we added is called pur_badsku, which is the message RequiredProdInfo reads and adds to _Basket_Errrors if one or more items are deleted.

Running RequiredProdInfo

In our example, `RequiredProdInfo` iterates through the items, looking for the `delete` attribute. As it iterates from end to beginning, it immediately hits the fourth item and finds its `delete` attribute to be 1. It deletes the item from the `Items` list and continues on.

The three other items don't even have a `delete` key, so they are left untouched.

After iterating through the items, `RequiredProdInfo` extract the value of the `pur_badsku` message from the `MessageManager` object in the pipe context, and adds this message (One or more items were deleted from the basket) to the `OrderForm`'s `_Basket_Errors` list.

Merchant Information Stage

At this moment, we still have an empty Merchant Information stage in our sample pipeline. This stage can be used to insert information about the seller, but we are not going to use it, so it should be deleted, which is easily done by highlighting the stage and hitting the *Delete* button. Remember to save the pipeline after deleting the stage.

Shopper Information Stage

The next stage in our pipeline is the Shopper Information stage. It can be used to extract information about the user. User information will normally be available in the context as a `ProfileObject` object, but it may be necessary to extract extra information about the user. This can be done and placed on the `OrderForm` in this stage, but like the previous stage, we are not going to use it for this example, so this stage should be deleted too, even though it already contains a component.

RequiredOrderInitCy

This component does attribute initialization. First, it reads the `order_id` attribute from the `OrderForm` to check if it has a value. If not, it creates a value and saves it back to the order.

It then initializes a lot of price fields on the `OrderForm` by setting them to `Null`:

- ❏ `_cy_total_total` – stores the total price of the whole order.
- ❏ `_cy_oadjust_subtotal` – stores the price of all the items.
- ❏ `_cy_shipping_total` – stores the total shipping fee.
- ❏ `_cy_tax_total` – stores the total tax amount.
- ❏ `_cy_handling_total` – stores the total handling fee.
- ❏ `_cy_tax_included` – stores the amount of tax already included in the order.
- ❏ `_payment_auth_code` – stores a code for payment authorization. When validating payment, this attribute must be set to something other than `Null` as part of the validation.

In addition to initializing these fields on the order level, the component also initializes values on each item:

- ❏ `_n_unadjusted` – this attribute is set to the value of the `quantity` attribute.
- ❏ `_cy_oadjust_adjustedprice` – this attribute is initialized to 0 .

Running RequiredOrderInitCy

The component begins by reading the currency compatibility mode of the order. As we've decided to run in compatibility mode, it initializes not only those attributes stated above, but also all the price fields in their Site Server 3 Commerce Edition equivalents, which means that all the fields with the _cy prefix also gets saved without the _cy prefix as a Long integer scaled by 100 or initialized as Null where applicable. For more information about _cy and running the pipeline in compatibility mode, please refer to later in the chapter.

Not wanting to take a look at all values, let's take a look at selected attributes.

The order_id attribute is examined and found to be nonexistent on the order. RequiredOrderInitCy generates an ID of 9H6D5W5JQK818PV5X4AXW10A16 and sets it to the order_id attribute on the order.

As we're running in compatibility mode, the component sets both the _total_total and _cy_total_total attributes to Null.

The _payment_auth_code is not a price field, so it's only created once and set to Null.

On the first item, _n_unadjusted is set to 1, which is the value of the item's quantity attribute. Both the item's _oadjust_adjustedprice and _cy_oadjust_adjustedprice attributes are set to 0.

The second item has its _n_unadjusted attribute set to 7, as that is the value of its quantity attribute. Both price fields are again set to 0.

The third item has _n_unadjusted set to 1 and both price fields set to 0.

RequiredOrderCheck

The RequiredOrderCheck component checks whether there's at least one item on the order. If not, it extracts the pur_noitems message from the MessageManager object and writes it to the _Purchase_Errors list on the OrderForm.

Running RequiredOrderCheck

In our example, there are three items in the order, so the component exits without doing anything.

DefaultItemPriceCy

The DefaultItemPriceCy component initializes price values on each item. It reads the _product_cy_list_price and writes the _cy_iadjust_regularprice with the same value. The _cy_iadjust_regularprice is used later on by other pipeline components.

Running DefaultItemPriceCy

In our example, the component first reads the currency settings for the pipeline to determine the currency mode. Finding that we are running in compatibility mode, both the _cy prefixed values and the SS3CE-compatible attributes must be created and set.

For the first item the component reads the value of _product_cy_list_price to be 35. As the component has determined that it is running in compatibility mode, it also tries to read the _product_list_price and, finding it non-existent, sets it to 3500. It then copies these values, setting _cy_iadjust_regularprice to 35 and _iadjust_regularprice to 3500.

For the next item, _cy_iadjust_regularprice is set to 19.5 and _iadjust_regularprice to 1950.

The third item gets _cy_iadjust_regularprice as 25.75 and _iadjust_regularprice as 2575.

RequiredItemPriceCy

The RequiredItemPriceCy component checks whether the _cy_iadjust_regularprice key exists and contains a value for each item. If this is not the case, it raises an error.

Running RequiredItemPriceCy

In our example, the component first reads the currency settings for the pipeline to determine the currency mode. Finding that we are running in compatibility mode, both the _cy_iadjust_regularprice and _iadjust_regularprice fields for each item are to be checked.

As we just set these values in the component before, RequiredItemPriceCy finds _cy_iadjust_regularprice as 35 and _iadjust_regularprice as 3500 for the first component, and equivalently for the next components, so the component exits without making any trouble.

RequiredItemAdjustPriceCy

This component has affinity with the **Item Adjust Price** stage. In this stage, components to modify the regular price based on business logic (such as campaign prices) can be placed. In the case of our example, we've tried to keep things simple, so we're not doing any of this.

The RequiredItemAdjustPriceCy component is intended to verify that all proper attributes are present after this stage. It checks for the existence of the _cy_iadjust_currentprice, and if that doesn't exist, assumes that no price modification logic has been applicable, and sets the attribute to the value of _cy_iadjust_regularprice.

Running RequiredItemAdjustPriceCy

In our example, the component first reads the currency settings for the pipeline to determine the currency mode (this sentence is beginning to sound like a mantra!).

For the first item, the component finds that _cy_iadjust_currentprice doesn't exist, so it sets it to 35, which is the value of _cy_iadjust_regularprice. Equivalently, it sets _iadjust_currentprice to 3500.

Values are similarly copied for the two other items.

RequiredOrderAdjustPriceCy

The RequiredOrderAdjustPriceCy component calculates the total cost for each item. It takes the _cy_iadjust_currentprice and multiplies it with quantity. The quantity of the item could have been modified previously, so it also multiplies _cy_iadjust_currentprice with _n_unadjusted to calculate any potential discount. The total price is written to the _cy_oadjust_adjustedprice attribute, and the discount to the _cy_oadjust_discount attribute.

Running RequiredOrderAdjustPriceCy

In our example, the component first reads the currency settings to determine the currency mode.

For the first item, the component reads _cy_oadjust_adjustedprice and _oadjust_adjustedprice, finding them both to be 0, which is the value they were initialized to by the RequiredOrderInitCy component. It then reads _cy_iadjust_currentprice to be 35, and _iadjust_currentprice to be 3500. Both quantity and _n_unadjusted are 1. Multiplying 35 by 1 gives 35, which is written to cy_oadjust_adjustedprice. Similarly, 3500 is written to _oadjust_adjustedprice. As quantity and _n_unadjusted are both equal, no discount is in effect here, and _cy_oadjust_discount and _oadjust_discount are both set to 0.

For the next item, the component reads _cy_iadjust_currentprice to be 19.5 and quantity to 7. Multiplying 19.5 with 7 gives 136.5, which is written to _cy_oadjust_adjustedprice. Similar numbers are written to the SS3CE-fields, scaled by 100, and both discounts are still 0.

The thirds item is as trivial as the first, as it only contains one item, so _cy_oadjust_adjustedprice is set to 25.75.

DefaultOrderSubtotalCy

The DefaultOrderSubtotalCy component calculates the total cost of all the items by adding the total cost for each item together. The result is written to _cy_oadjust_subtotal.

Running DefaultOrderSubtotalCy

The component reads _cy_oadjust_adjustedprice for each item in the order, getting 35, 136.5, and 25.75. Adding these together gives 197.25, which is written to the _cy_oadjust_subtotal attribute on the OrderForm.

RequiredOrderSubTotalCy

This component is, like so many others, intended for checking the integrity of the order at this point. It checks whether the _cy_oadjust_subtotal key is set.

Running RequiredOrderSubTotalCy

In our example, the component first reads the currency settings to determine the currency mode.

It reads the _cy_oadjust_subtotal attribute to be 197.25, so all is good. As we are running in currency compatibility mode, this value is scaled by 100 and written to _oadjust_subtotal as 19725.

Continuing the Example

At this point we are going to leave our example for now. We've calculated the total cost for each item, as well as the total cost for all items. Although it may seem an overly complex way of doing this, two points should be remembered here: we didn't write any code to perform these calculations, and the example should hopefully have given you a vague idea about how extensible this framework is, when it comes to price calculation and such.

The work done so far would have been enough to show a simple basket page. In the case of this example, we also want to calculate shipping, handling and tax to show an order confirmation page. Later in the chapter we will continue looking at our example to see how this is implemented.

Standard Pipelines

As you know, a set of standard pipeline templates is provided with CS2K to enable the developer to quickly create a pipeline for a specific purpose. In this section, we'll examine some of the standard pipeline templates and explain the purpose of each.

Order Processing Pipelines

A site will typically have several Order Processing Pipelines, and there are actually three different OPP pipeline templates:

❏   Product – use this pipeline type to calculate information such as price and discount for a product. This is very useful for a product information page.

❏   Plan – use this pipeline type to verify the integrity of an order. A Plan pipeline can also be used to display a basket or order summary page, as it contains many stages from the initial product information all the way to subtotal, shipping, handling, tax and total cost calculation stages.

❏   Purchase – use this pipeline type to place the actual order. This type of pipeline contains components for writing the order to a database, or may contain components delivering the order to a back-end system or another computer such as a BizTalk Server.

It is, of course, entirely possible to create pipelines from scratch (using the Empty template), but the templates provide good starting points for building your own pipeline. Let's now take a closer look at each of these.

Product Pipeline

The Product pipeline is typically used to compute and display information about a single product, although it can also be used to display a list of products. What distinguishes a Product pipeline is its focus on the single product. Even if more than one product is displayed, no subtotals or other aggregate values are computed – each product in the Items list is treated as an autonomous unit.

For display of subtotals and other aggregate values, a Plan pipeline would typically be used instead of a Product pipeline.

The first stage in a Product pipeline will typically be the Product Info stage. Here, components extract detailed data for each product and write it to attributes on each Item Dictionary. When entering the pipeline, each item is equipped only with the sparse information we've deigned to put on it. Before performing other business logic on the item, we need to know more about it, such as its price.

In the Product Info stage, a component will query the catalog data source (whether it be a database or the CS2K product catalog system) and create attributes on the Item Dictionary corresponding to fields in the data source. These attributes are named _product_<field name>; for example, if the data source contains the description field, an attribute called _product_description will be created. If the product could not be found in the data source, the item.delete attribute is created and set to 1.

The RequiredProdInfo component then deletes any item with the delete key set to 1.

The next stage in a Product pipeline is the Shopper Information stage. Here, shopper information is extracted – usually from the Context Dictionary – and added to the OrderForm object as attributes. These attributes may be necessary to calculate customer-specific discounts later on.

In the Item Price stage, the _iadjust_regularprice key is set on each item – typically to the value found in item._product_cy_list_price. This stage is mostly for validation purposes, ensuring that the correct price key exists for components further down the pipeline.

In the Item Adjust stage, each item is examined for discounts, campaigns, customer-specific prices, etc. The end result of the stage is the item._iadjust_currentprice key.

This stage contains all business logic potentially affecting the price of a single item – quantity discounts or discounts based on a combination of products are not implemented in the Product pipeline, as the focus is on the single product. Such price modification logic would typically be implemented in a Plan pipeline. In our continuing example in this chapter, we would have had a Product pipeline if we had stopped at the RequiredOrderAdjustPriceCy component.

The last standard stage in the `Product` pipeline is the `Inventory` stage, containing components ensuring that products are in stock and can be delivered.

Plan Pipeline

Continuing our example, we've already calculated the total of all the items. To display shipping, handling and tax information, we need to continue. The inclusion of these calculations (including the items total) conceptually makes this pipeline a plan pipeline, although it's only a question of semantics – there's no difference in functionality just because you choose to call it something else.

We *are* going to be calculating shipping cost in our example, but we are going to save it till later in the chapter, where the new shipping architecture has its own section. Here we will be examining handling, tax, and order totals.

Handling

In our example we have a simple business logic that dictates that we should always add DKK 24,5 in a handling fee. This can be implemented by using a few standard components a little creatively.

In the Pipeline Editor, first delete the DefaultHandlingCy component, as we're not going to use it.

Next, in the Handling stage, insert a FixedHandling component before the RequiredHandling component, and open its property pages. Choose Always in the Apply when drop-down control to indicate that this rule should always be in effect, and write 2450 in the Cost edit field.

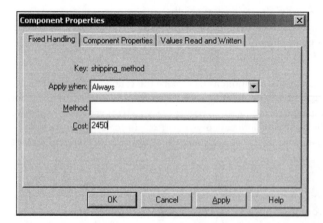

This component is actually only intended to provide backwards compatibility with Site Server 3 Commerce Edition, but as CS2K doesn't really ship with any specific handling components using the `Currency` data type, this can be used in a bind. In reality, the new shipping components could be used to calculate handling as well, but a little tweaking would be necessary.

Running the FixedHandling component sets the `_handling_total` attribute on the `OrderForm` to 2450, as we've defined that it should always do that.

As this is not a `Currency` data type, but a `Long` integer, we need to convert the value. For this purpose, CS2K ships with the Money Converter components. In the Pipeline Editor, insert the Money Converter (int<->cy) component between FixedHandling and RequiredHandling, and open its property pages.

On the property page, select the Convert int to currency radio button, and in the Currency Fields: (space seperated) input field, write order._cy_handling_total, which is the name of the attribute we want to convert to.

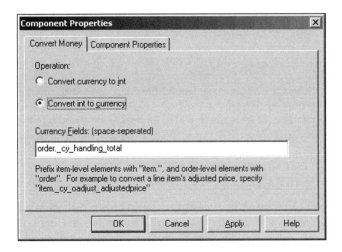

When the component runs, it knows to throw away the _cy prefix in the field we've defined, and goes looking for the _handling_total attribute, finding it to be 2450. This value is then converted to a Currency value and written to the OrderForm as _cy_handling_total with a value of 24.5.

Remember to save the pipeline.

RequiredHandlingCy checks for the existence of the _cy_handling_total and _handling_total keys, and finding them both present, exits peacefully.

Tax

Microsoft actually recommends that you develop tax components yourself, or buy a third party component, which has been checked by a tax professional. What this really means, of course, is that Microsoft doesn't want to be held responsible for the use you put their components to. Nonetheless, CS2K ships with some rather usable components for tax calculation.

In Denmark it's pretty simple, because almost all goods have a value added tax of 25% (yes, ouch!), and this is what we want to model in our example.

In the Pipeline Editor, first delete the DefaultTax component, as we are not going to use it.

Then, insert the SimpleVATTax before the RequiredTaxCy component, and open its property pages. In the Apply when drop-down box, select Always, and in the Rate Item Key input field, write _product_tax_rate – this is the field holding the tax rate for the product.

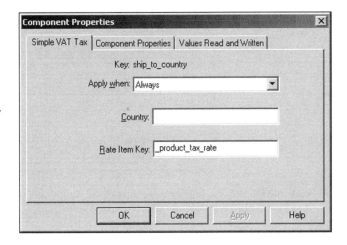

Running this component in our example, it reads the _product_tax_rate attribute to be 25 for the first item – remember this was set back when running the QueryProdInfoADO component. It also reads the _oadjust_adjustedprice attribute to be 3500. Multiplying these two values together and dividing by 100 yields 875, which is written to both the _tax_vat_item and _tax_included fields for the item.

Similar calculations happen for the other two items, and the sum of the item._tax_included fields are written to the order._tax_included field as 4932. We really need a _cy_tax_total field, but as this component is mainly provided for backwards compatibility with SS3CE, it doesn't support Currency fields. It *does* write a _tax_total field, though, but unfortunately it is always set to 0.

There are ways around this problem. One is to write a very simple Scriptor component that copies the value of _tax_included into _tax_total, but another possibility exists.

With all the attributes with underscores living their short lives on the order, you may find that some of these values may be desirable to persist – remember that any key that begins with an underscore is not saved to the data store when the order is saved. After having written a lot of attribute-copying Scriptor components, Microsoft decided to include a pipeline component for this purpose into one of their best practices projects.

If you visit the **Reference Architecture for Commerce: Business-to-Consumer** sample application on the **MSDN Code Center** (http://msdn.microsoft.com/code/default.asp?URL=/code/sample.asp?url=/MSDN-FILES/026/002/195/msdncompositedoc.xml), you can find the source code for a component called PersistUtility, which will prove very useful in any case. Download the whole package, unzip it to your hard drive, then run the installation file. The default folder is C:\Program Files\B2C Reference Architecture. Within this folder, you will have to register the DLLs using Regsvr32.

Insert the PersistUtility component between the **SimpleVATTax** and **RequiredTaxCy** components, and open its property pages. Fill it out by writing _tax_total = _tax_included in both boxes, as both the items and the order have zero-valued _tax_total attributes that we want to copy. PersistUtility was actually created to copy a non-persisted attribute to one that could be persisted in a database, but it luckily is so generic that it just copies whatever you ask it to. In this case we've asked it to copy the value of the _tax_included attributes to the _tax_total attributes.

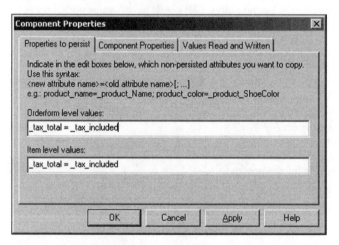

Remember to save the pipeline. Running it, the component reads 4932 from the OrderForm's _tax_included attribute and inserts the value into _tax_total. It does equivalent operations on each item.

We now have the total tax, but only in SS3CE-format. Using the Money Converter component again, we insert it between PersistUtility and RequiredTaxCy and instruct it to convert from Int to Currency into the order._cy_tax_total field. Remember to save the pipeline.

Running the pipeline in our example, the component converts the value of _tax_total (4932) to 49.32, which is written to the _cy_tax_total key.

Lastly in the Tax stage we have the RequiredTaxCy component, which checks that all keys are present and have values. As we are running in currency compatibility mode, all appropriate combinations of _cy_tax_total, _tax_total, _cy_tax_included, and _tax_included are read and/or written on both the order and the item level in the pattern, which should be familiar by now.

Order Total

We've now reached the stage where we can calculate the total price of the order. The DefaultTotal component takes the values of _cy_oadjust_subtotal, _cy_shipping_total, _cy_tax_total, and _cy_handling_total and adds them together to form the _cy_total_total.

Running the pipeline in our example, we read _cy_oadjust_subtotal to be 197.25, _cy_shipping_total to be 45 (and why this is you can read further down in this chapter), _cy_tax_total to 49.32, and _cy_handling_total to 24.5. Adding these four values together, we get 316.07, which is written to the _cy_total_total key.

The last component (RequiredTotalCy) of the pipeline reads 316.07 from _cy_total_total and writes it to the _total_total fields as 31607, and performs some integrity checking in the hopefully now very familiar pattern.

The pipeline is now done, as we don't want to do the Inventory stage in this example. Delete the stage and save the pipeline.

We still need to set up shipping, but apart from that, we've now been running successfully through a complete Plan pipeline, and we can now write the order confirmation out on a web page.

Printing the Result on a Web Page

When writing the result of the pipeline execution on a web page, we should somehow handle errors. This can be done in ASP like this:

```
PrintErrors objOrderForm.[_Basket_Errors]
PrintErrors objOrderForm.[_Purchase_Errors]
```

PrintErrors is a function defined on the page or in an include file:

```
Sub PrintErrors(objErrorList)
    Dim strErrorMessage

    If objErrorList.Count > 0 Then
        For Each strErrorMessage In objErrorList
            Response.Write "<font color=""red""><b>" _
                              & strErrorMessage _
                & "</b></font><br>" & vbNewLine
        Next
        Response.Write "<br>" & vbNewLine
    End If
End Sub
```

As we had one error in our pipeline (we had tried to add a non-existent item), we will get the error message **One or more items were deleted from the basket!** which is written at the top of the page.

After setting up the table and writing the table headers (which we are not going to show here, as it is pure HTML), we can output the items of the order:

```
For Each dictItem in objOrderform.Items
%>
    <tr bgcolor="gainsboro" valign="top">
        <td>
           <%= dictItem.SKU%>
        </td>
        <td>
           <%= dictItem.[_product_Name]%>
        </td>
        <td>
           <%= dictItem.[_product_Description]%>
        </td>
        <td align="right" nowrap="true">
           <%= FormatCurrency(dictItem.[_cy_iadjust_currentprice])%>
        </td>
        <td align="right" nowrap="true">
           <%= dictItem.quantity%>
        </td>
        <td align="right" nowrap="true">
           <%= FormatCurrency(dictItem.[_cy_oadjust_adjustedprice])%>
        </td>
    </tr>
<%
Next
```

This will write each item, but we still need to write the subtotal, shipping fee, and so on. All these are highly similar, so we'll just show how to do one of them – the total:

```
    <tr bgcolor="gray">
        <td colspan="5">
           Total
        </td>
        <td align="right" nowrap="true">
           <%= FormatCurrency(objOrderform.[_cy_total_total])%>
        </td>
    </tr>
```

That's all there is to outputting the results of pipeline execution. The resulting page will look something like this (depending on your locale settings, of course!):

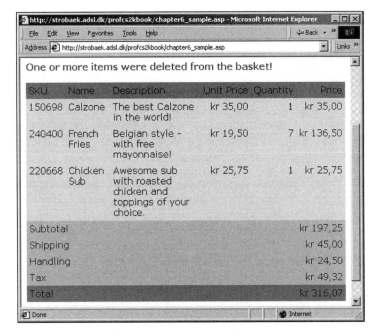

Although it may seem a complex operation, once you get the hang of setting up a pipeline, it can be done surprisingly fast, is very reusable, and maybe most noteworthy: although we made a few shortcuts on our way (such as using components mostly intended for backwards compatibility), we've managed to implement our business logic by *writing no code* at the pipeline level apart from a SQL statement, and only minimal code to set up and run the pipeline, and a little, very simple ASP code to display the result!

Purchase Pipeline

Whereas the `Product` and `Plan` pipelines are used to calculate prices and other information about the individual items and the order in its entirety, a `Purchase` pipeline places the actual order. As this is where the order is actually written to the database, or delivered to some external system, this type of pipeline is of course more sensitive to errors and should always be transacted, ensuring that no order is lost, but reported to the user as having been placed.

A `Purchase` pipeline typically takes an order with values created by a `Plan` pipeline – thus, most applicable attributes are already present on the order when it enters the `Purchase` pipeline.

The first stage in a standard `Purchase` pipeline is the `Purchase Check` stage, validating that information such as billing addresses or credit card numbers are present and conform to whatever guidelines the business logic dictates.

The `Payment` stage is for validating the payment itself. This mostly applies for credit card purchases, as purchases made on invoice are usually based on faith. The `DefaultPayment` component initialises the `_payment_auth_code` key. If subsequent components fail to validate the payment, the key value is set to `DENIED`, and the error level is set to 2, causing the pipeline to fail (and, if transacted, roll back).

The final stage of a `Purchase` pipeline is the `Accept` stage, where the actual order is entered into whatever system is set up to receive it. Many different components exist to perform the actions required in this stage, to accommodate a wide range of data transport methods. The trivial action is using ADO to save the order to a database, but the purchase order can also be saved to a file, dropped on an MSMQ queue, or sent as an e-mail.

Purchase Pipeline Example

Let's look at an example of a purchase pipeline. We've already looked at creating a `Plan` pipeline in our big example for the chapter, so let's take a partial look at how to create a `Purchase` pipeline for that order. In this example, we are going to focus on saving the order to the database. Payment, which is supposed to be set up using custom or third-party components anyway, we will look at only briefly.

To create a `Purchase` pipeline, open the **Pipeline Editor** and click **File**, then **New**. In the **Choose a Pipeline Template** dialog box, select **Purchase.pct** and click **OK**. Save the file by clicking **File**, and **Save As** and give the file an appropriate name, such as **Purchase.pcf** – remember that if you just click **Save**, you overwrite the template file.

Delete the **Purchase Check** stage, as we are not going to use it in this example. We are not going to touch the components in the **Payment** stage for this example, but in a real-world scenario, the **DefaultPayment** component should be replaced with a component implementing payment-checking business logic.

In the **Accept** stage, insert a **SaveReceipt** component. We are not going to touch its property pages for this example – the default will do just fine. Remember to save the pipeline.

The **SaveReceipt** component saves the order to a database table. Before being able to use the `Purchase` pipeline, we must set up the table where the order should be saved.

We set up the table by using this DDL (Data Definition Language) SQL statement:

```
CREATE TABLE [dbo].[PlacedOrders] (
    [order_id] [varchar] (50) NOT NULL ,
    [customer_name] [varchar] (100) NULL ,
    [marshalled_order] [image] NOT NULL ,
    [date_changed] [datetime] NOT NULL
) ON [PRIMARY] TEXTIMAGE_ON [PRIMARY]
GO

ALTER TABLE [dbo].[PlacedOrders] WITH NOCHECK ADD
    CONSTRAINT [PK_PlacedOrders] PRIMARY KEY  CLUSTERED
    (
        [order_id]
    )  ON [PRIMARY]
GO
```

As we can see, we create a table called `PlacedOrders` with a primary key of `order_id`, and three other columns called `customer_name`, `marshalled_order`, and `date_changed`. The `order_id` column will be stored with the `order_id` of the order, and `marshalled_order` is used to save the `OrderForm` object in a binary format. The `date_changed` field is used to track the time the order was entered into the table, and `customer_name` is a table for duplication of the `order.customer_name` attribute directly on the table level – it will also be persisted into `marshalled_column` together with all the other persisted attributes (remember that attributes with the underscore prefix are not saved to the database).

The **SaveReceipt** component uses the `DBStorage` object to save orders to the table, so we must add the `ReceiptStorage` object to the pipeline context.

```
'Create the DBStorage object
Set objDBStorage = Server.CreateObject("Commerce.DBStorage")
```

```
'Initialize the object
objDBStorage.InitStorage conTransactionConfigConnectionString, _
    "PlacedOrders", "order_id", "Commerce.OrderForm", _
    "marshalled_order", "date_changed"

'Add the DBStorage object to the pipe context
Set objContext.ReceiptStorage = objDBStorage
```

When **SaveReceipt** runs, it reads all attributes not prefixed with an underscore and saves the `OrderForm` object to the `PlacedOrders` table's `marshalled_order` column as a binary object. It additionally writes the value of `order.customer_name` to the `customer_name` column, as there are two names equal to each other. Thus, saving an order results in a table entry like this:

order_id	customer_name	marshalled_order	date_changed
JCG5NB3W8W6X9GNNVB36LUDST7	Anders Kirkeby	0x01001000800B0000...	2001-03-25 16:31:39.000

The `marshalled_column` really contains a lot more binary values than shown in this table, but this should give you an idea about what it looks like.

If you want to retrieve and show the order at a later date, you can first retrieve the relevant order ID from the table by using a simple `Select` SQL statement. With the order ID, you can then retrieve the order from storage using the `DBStorage` object.

```
'Get the orderform object from storage
Set objOrderForm = objDBStorage.GetData(Null, strOrderID)
```

`strOrderID` contains the value of the order ID you want to see (for example, `JCG5NB3W8W6X9GNNVB36LUDST7`).

Content Selection Pipeline

Although the pipeline framework was originally designed to handle Order Processing Pipelines (OPPs) – in fact, that was all pipelines did in Site Server 3 Commerce Edition – in CS2K, pipelines are now also employed for other uses, such as marketing. Where OPPs implement business logic with relation to the actual shopping process, **Content Selection Pipelines** (CSPs), together with the Event Processing and Direct Mailer pipelines, implement business logic related to marketing.

A CSP is used to deliver content, as its name suggests – not content in the form of a catalog (which is the realm of OPPs), but content in the form of ads, information about complementary products, or other information drawing the user's attention to something he might not otherwise have discovered. In its most pure form, the CSP is used to deliver ads to the site.

A very detailed description of CSPs (or the other marketing pipelines) is beyond the scope of this chapter, but a general overview of how they perform their magic is still in order.

It is worth noting that the data flowing through a CSP is differently structured to the data entering an OPP. In an OPP, an `OrderForm` object represents the data to be manipulated, and the `Context` object provides additional information about the environment. In a CSP, all data originates from the `Context` object, and only an empty `Dictionary` object is passed as the `OrderForm`.

Initially, the CSP copies some information from the Context to the Order object. A part of this information is a list of all applicable content items (ads) for the site, and the purpose of the CSP is to select a small amount of items from this potentially large list, applying marketing business rules as it is going along.

Selection is accomplished by applying a **score** – a floating point number – to each content item, and then manipulating this score during pipeline execution. Typically, scores are initialized to the **Need of Delivery** of the item – increasing the score of a content item increases its chance of selection, and decreasing the score decreases the selection probability. A score of 0 indicates that the item should not be selected under any circumstances.

Part of initialization is the loading of user-specific history: this is a list of content items already displayed to the user, and is represented as a comma-separated string.

After initialization, filters (specified outside the pipeline, typically in the BizDesk campaign module) are applied to narrow down the list of applicable ads. The filtering done at this stage is only initial and unsophisticated, but efficient, and should be used to perform a basic separation of warranted and unwarranted ads. After filtering, only a subset of the original content list survives, and having the pipeline only apply business rules to a smaller collection of items thus ensures efficiency.

The pipeline then calculates the Need of Delivery for each surviving content item. Need of Delivery is a term describing how desirable it is to show the particular item at this particular time. The formula takes into account the obligation the site may have to show the item a particular number of times, but also tries to ensure an even distribution of content display during the desired time period – actually, the formula is pretty simple:

```
NoD = (Events Scheduled / Time Total) / (Events Served / Time Elapsed)
```

For example, let's assume that we want to show the content item 100 times over a week, and that we currently – three days into that week – have displayed it 23 times. The Need of Delivery then becomes:

```
(100 / 7) / (23 / 3) = 1.86
```

indicating that we're somewhat behind schedule, and that it is thus desirable to display this item.

The Need of Delivery usually serves as the initialization value of the content item's score – only if the Need of Delivery is not calculated at all, the item score will be initialized to 1.

After having initialized the score of each content item, further modifications to the score are applied. Score modification can be based on:

❑   **User History** – the user history is a comma-separated string of the items already shown to the user. The most recent item has the most drastic score reduction applied, ensuring that items are not shown to the user repeatedly if alternatives exist.

❑   **Target Groups** – the content item will often be associated with a target audience, and scoring can be modified by how well the current user fits the target expressions.

❑   **Discounts** – some discounts apply to a combination of products, for example, *Buy one pair of shoes and get a 50% discount on socks*, but it may be more desirable to display the discount information in some contexts rather than others: if the user already placed shoes in his basket, it may be more desirable to show the discount ad than if he's looking at a product page for shirts.

Custom components to apply other score modification business logic can of course be developed, just like with any other type of pipeline.

Having adjusted scores according to business rules, the pipeline then performs the actual selection. A specified number of items can be chosen, or if no number has been specified, a single item is chosen. Items are selected based on scores, with the highest scores winning, but with a few restrictions, such as not selecting an item again if already just selected, and not selecting competing ads.

At this stage, the selection can then be recorded to a number of places, updating the history for the user, saving the information to a data warehouse, and so on.

Finally, the list of selected items is formatted according to a template to create a string immediately usable on an ASP page.

As can be seen from this overview, Content Selection Pipelines can be at least as complex as OPPs, but with just as many possibilities to implement whatever business rules may be desirable. This section has just provided you with the notion of a CSP – to learn more, there's a lot of information in the CS2K documentation, and by installing the `AdSitelet` you can see CSPs in action.

Event Processing Pipelines

Compared to CSPs, **Event Processing Pipelines** (EPPs) are simple. They are used to record events (typically click events) on a site. Your marketing people may want to know which ads were actually clicked, or you may have scoring logic dictating that all ads users actually bothered to click on should have their score drastically decreased, as the ad should now be considered exhausted for that user. Whatever the reason, the EPP is there to do the work for you.

An EPP is usually invoked on a redirection page referenced by the URL supplied. Ad links supplied by a CSP will usually point to a redirection page, which runs the EPP and redirects the user to the actual target.

The EPP is simple, and typically just consists of the data recording stage also found in the CSP.

Direct Mailer Pipelines

Unlike all the other pipelines described so far, **Direct Mailer Pipelines** don't run in the context of Internet Information Server (IIS), but are instead executed by the **Direct Mailer** service.

`Direct Mailer` is a service that ships with CS2K, making use of SQL Server as its database, ADO for database connection, and CDO (Collaboration Data Objects) for e-mail creation and delivery. The service is used to deliver e-mail messages in either personalized or static form to users, typically as part of a large direct mail campaign targeting many users. `Direct Mailer` runs as a SQL Server job, which means that it is running in the context of the SQL Server Agent, and that again means that the service must be installed and running on the same box as SQL Server.

`Direct Mailer` works from a list of recipients and invokes a `Direct Mailer` Pipeline once for each recipient in the list. As a very large amount of recipients can pose a problem to the SMTP server, the first stage in the pipeline provides an option for imposing a delay on each pipeline execution, giving the SMTP server time to send out each message without overloading.

The pipeline then validates recipient data and may apply a filter, in effect stopping mail delivery for that particular recipient and proceeding to the next. Typically, more efficient program execution can be achieved by filtering the `Direct Mailer` recipients list before invoking the pipeline.

313

As personalized content is typically provided to the pipeline by requesting a template ASP page from IIS, a user cookie may be required, and can be created from the recipient data on the `Order` object before the page is requested. Attachments can also be added at this stage.

IIS returns the personalized page to the pipeline; the content is verified and added to the CDO e-mail object as the message body; other fields such as recipient and subject are set on the e-mail, which is then finally sent.

Setting up and running `Direct Mailer` can be done from the CS2K BizDesk.

Shipping Architecture

CS2K employs a very flexible, albeit somewhat complex, architecture for dealing with shipping calculations of one or multiple shipments per order. In this section we will be looking at the architecture itself, and its purpose, as well as an example.

Shipping Architecture Purpose

Those readers familiar with Site Server 3 Commerce Edition will remember that in this product, shipment calculation was dealt with once per order. Several methods for calculating shipping costs existed, enabling the site developer to perform the calculations based on a simple percentage of weight, price or any other applicable attribute, as well as based on fixed prices per unit of product, weight, price, etc. Although providing a rich range of opportunities for the developer, that architecture's main limitation was that it couldn't easily accommodate multiple shipments included in the same order.

Let's say that a customer assembles a shopping basket on a site acting as a shopping center for several different suppliers. The customer orders a power drill, two books on home improvement, a brush, and three buckets of paint. Although the site acts as The Home Improvement Shopping Center, it's actually just a front for many different stores, each selling a range of products related to home improvement.

For this example, the power drill will actually be shipped from a hardware store, the brush and paint from a painter's shop, and the books from a bookstore. So, one order contains several different shipments, but it should still be possible for the site to display the shipping costs to the customer when he places his order.

Other scenarios involve the customer himself choosing certain items in an order to be shipped using a different shipping company, or letting the site ship items in an order as they become available.

CS2K's shipping architecture is designed to accommodate scenarios such as these, as well as the standard scenario with one shipment per order. It is well worth noting that this architecture does not address the question about how shipments are distributed to the items on the order – for this purpose the site developer will have to program or adapt the applicable business logic. What the shipping architecture *does* support is calculation of shipping costs given the knowledge of the shipping method of every item.

Context

The shipping components, which are implemented as pipeline components, make some use of the site context for information about shipping methods, etc. More specifically, the `ShippingManagerCache` object is used to provide information about available shipment methods, and how to calculate costs for these methods.

ShippingManagerCache

The `ShippingManagerCache` object caches information from the `ShippingConfig` database table. This table contains configuration information about the available shipping methods. This information is read from the table and cached, usually in `global.asa`. It might look something like this:

```
'Constants
'This string should actually be written on the same line
Const conTransactionConfigConnectionString = _
    "Provider=SQLOLEDB;User ID=sa;Password=password;
    Initial Catalog=""Retail_commerce"";Data Source=LOKE;
    Network Library=dbmssocn;"

'Create a CacheManager object.
Set objCM = Server.CreateObject("Commerce.CacheManager")

'Create a dictionary object to hold the configuration information.
Set dictShipConfig = Server.CreateObject("Commerce.Dictionary")

'Add the connection string to the configuration dictionary.
dictShipConfig.ConnectionString = conTransactionConfigConnectionString

'Set the ProgID of the loader for the cache.
objCM.LoaderProgId("ShippingManagerCache") = "Commerce.ShippingManagerCache"

'Set the loader's configuration dictionary.
Set objCM.LoaderConfig("ShippingManagerCache") = dictShipConfig
```

Later, the `ShippingManagerCache` should be added to the site context prior to running the pipeline:

```
Set objContext.CacheManager = objCM
```

where `objContext` is the site context `Dictionary` object.

As described, the `ShippingManagerCache` holds information from the `ShippingConfig` table, but it might be worth taking a close look at that information. More specifically, the `ShippingManagerCache` contains a list of available shipping methods. Each shipping method is represented as a `Dictionary`, corresponding to each row in the `ShippingConfig` table. Later in this section, when we look at the `ShippingMethodRouter` component, we will examine this data in even more detail.

Components

Like everything else concerning order processing in CS2K, the shipping architecture is implemented as pipeline components, although with some modifications, as some of the components are actually not supposed to be inserted directly into a pipeline – but they are pipeline components nonetheless.

Confused? With the shipping architecture, there's ample opportunity for that, and it may seem overly complex for simple shipping cost calculation. It does offer a great deal of flexibility, however, and when examined closely, turns out to be quite logical after all. So keep cool and read on.

Basically, the Shipping stage of a pipeline should contain two mandatory objects and one optional: `Splitter`, `ShippingMethodRouter` and the optional `ShippingDiscountAdjust`.

In short, the `Splitter` component examines the order and creates a shipping dictionary for each separate shipment present on the order. The `ShippingMethodRouter` then examines these shipping dictionaries and apply business logic to calculate the shipping cost for each shipment, as well as the total shipping cost for the order. The optional `ShippingDiscountAdjust` applies any discounts on shipping if so specified on the order.

That didn't sound so bad, did it? OK, let's look at one component at a time and examine what it does to the `OrderForm` object.

Splitter

The `Splitter` component is a rather generic component for examining each item in the order for information about how to group the items into one or more groupings, for example, shipments. It takes a few input parameters:

- ❏ Output Structure – a string containing the name of the `SimpleList` object to be created as the result of the component execution. This object will be appended to the `OrderForm` object.

- ❏ Input Distinguishers – a string specifying names of keys on an item, which will be used to distinguish the different groupings. If more than one key is to be specified, the string should contain a space-separated list. The default is `shipping_method_id shipping_address_id`, indicating that both the shipping method and the shipping address will be used to distinguish separate shipments.

The input distinguishers can alternatively be defined using the site context.

The output of the component is a `SimpleList` on the order form. This list will contain a `Dictionary` for each distinct grouping found among the items.

Let's look at our running example and the case where the only input distinguisher is `shipping_method_id`.

The `Splitter` component examines the items on the order to determine which shipments are present on the order. One of the many key/value pairs on each item specifies in which shipment this particular item should be shipped. This information is a string contained in the `shipping_method_id` key, and it would typically look something like this:

```
dictItem.shipping_method_id = "{00000000-0000-0000-0000-003548006355}"
```

where `dictItem` is an `Item` `Dictionary` object in the `Items` `SimpleList`. As described before, this information would have been placed on the `Items` before the `OrderForm` object enters the `Shipping` stage, maybe letting the user choose from a list of available shipping methods and setting the value as shown above based on that choice. Of course the user will be presented with a more readable representation of the shipping method, but the GUID is the value getting written to the item.

For each distinct `shipping_method_id` found among the items, a `Dictionary` is appended to the `Shipments` `SimpleList` (the Output Structure) on the order. Each `Shipment` `Dictionary` contains information about this particular shipment – its method ID (the GUID) and yet another `SimpleList` called `ItemIndexes`. This is a list of the items (in the order's `Items` `SimpleList`) that belongs to this particular shipment – for example, if item number 0, 3, and 4 all had a `shipping_method_id` of `{00000000-0000-0000-0000-003548006355}`, the `ItemIndexes` `SimpleList` would contain the elements 0, 3, and 4 only.

The structure of the Shipments SimpleList (and incidentally the more general SimpleList defined by the Output Structure property of the Splitter component itself) looks something like this:

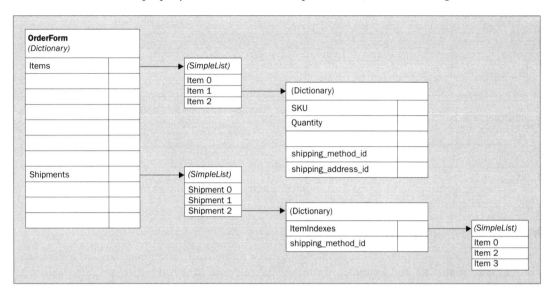

As can be seen from the diagram, Shipments is a SimpleList of Dictionaries. Each Dictionary represents a distinct shipment. One attribute of the shipment is the shipping_method_id of the shipment; another is the list of items contained in this shipment. This list is again a SimpleList called ItemIndexes, and it contains the indexes of the items from the Items list which should be shipped with this shipment – thus, if the particular shipment contains the first, third and fourth item of the Items list, the ItemIndexes will contain the values 0 (first), 2 (third), and 3 (fourth), as SimpleList indexing begins with zero.

Let's take an even closer look at the Splitter component in action. You may remember from earlier that we added items to the order like this:

```
'Add items
Set dictItem = objOrderForm.AddItem(150698, 1, 0)
dictItem.[_product_VariantID] = 5
dictItem.shipping_address_id = "My shipping address"
dictItem.shipping_method_id = "{00000000-0000-0000-0000-003548006355}"

Set dictItem = objOrderForm.AddItem(240400, 7, 0)
dictItem.[_product_VariantID] = 4
dictItem.shipping_address_id = "My shipping address"
dictItem.shipping_method_id = "{00000000-0000-0000-0000-003896000938}"

Set dictItem = objOrderForm.AddItem(220668, 1, 0)
dictItem.[_product_VariantID] = 3
dictItem.shipping_address_id = "My shipping address"
dictItem.shipping_method_id = "{00000000-0000-0000-0000-003548006355}"
```

As you may have noticed, we're assigning a shipping method (in the form of a GUID) to each item. When we run these items through a pipeline containing the Splitter component with its default configuration, the component reads the values off the shipping_method_id and shipping_address_id of each item and creates a SimpleList called Shipments of distinct shipments. In this case there are only two distinct shipments, so the Shipments list contains two elements.

Each element is a `Dictionary`, and their values will be defined like this:

Shipment 0	shipping_method_id	{00000000-0000-0000-0000-003548006355}
	ItemIndexes	0
		2
Shipment 1	shipping_method_id	{00000000-0000-0000-0000-003896000938}
	ItemIndexes	1

As we can see, `ItemIndexes` of the first shipment (shipment 0) contains 0 and 2 pointing back to the first (index 0) and third (index 2) items of the `Items` list.

ShippingMethodRouter

The `Splitter` component is always the first component in the standard Shipping stage of a pipeline, and the **ShippingMethodRouter** is normally the second. In many ways, the `ShippingMethodRouter` component is more difficult to understand than the `Splitter` component, but now that we have prepared the ground so thoroughly in the previous section, we should have come a long way already.

The `ShippingMethodRouter` component oversees the calculation of shipping costs, but does not perform these calculations itself. Instead, it calls other shipping pipeline components to do the actual calculation for it. All the component actually does itself is examine the `Shipments SimpleList` for shipping methods and then calls the relevant components for each method. Many shipping methods are set up to use the `StepwiseShipping` component for shipping cost calculation, but other pipeline components can be custom developed and put to use in this framework.

The component doesn't take any configuration values, but reads values from the order and site context.

❑   From the order form, it reads the `Shipments SimpleList`

❑   From the site context, it reads the `CacheManager` for shipping method configuration information

We've already looked at the `Shipments SimpleList` in detail, so let's turn our attention to the shipping method configuration.

Each shipping method is represented as a `Dictionary` object containing a few attributes:

❑   `progid` – this is the Prog ID of the component that should perform the actual shipping cost calculation. `ShippingMethodRouter` will use this Prog ID to instantiate and call the component. In many cases, this value will be `commerce.stepwiseshipping`, the Prog ID of the `StepwiseShipping` component, but other, custom-developed pipeline components could be referenced here.

❑   `config` – this is a `Dictionary` object holding configuration information for the component defined by the `progid` attribute. When `ShippingMethodRouter` instantiates the object defined by `progid`, it passes the `config Dictionary` to the object before calling it.

The `progid` and `config` attributes together define a component to be called, and a configuration `Dictionary` to be passed to it before execution. Although the component to be called must be a pipeline component, it should only ever be instantiated and called by `ShippingMethodRouter`, and never placed directly in the pipeline.

`ShippingMethodRouter` instantiates and executes a pipeline component for each shipping method defined in the `Shipments SimpleList`. These components write the attribute `_cy_shipping_total` to each shipment `Dictionary`, and `ShippingMethodRouter` then adds these values together to get the total shipping cost for the order. This value is written to the `_cy_shipping_total` attribute on the order itself.

It would be nice to continue our example from before, but before that, we need to take a close look at the `StepwiseShipping` component.

StepwiseShipping

`StepwiseShipping` is actually the only shipping cost component in CS2K that implements the multiple shipments shipping architecture. Other shipping cost components in CS2K are provided for backwards compatibility only.

Designed to be called by `ShippingMethodRouter`, `StepwiseShipping` is nonetheless a pipeline component. It calculates shipping cost in steps based on subtotal, quantity or weight, and is configured by `ShippingMethodRouter` by setting its configuration dictionary.

In effect, the configuration dictionary for `StepwiseShipping` is very simple, as it contains only a single attribute, `mode`, which is an integer with one of these values:

❑ **0** – use the subtotals (`item._cy_oadjust_adjustedprice`) for the items to calculate shipping cost

❑ **1** – use the quantity (`item.quantity`) for the items to calculate shipping cost

❑ **2** – use the weight (`item._product_weight`) for the items to calculate shipping cost

Irrespective of the `mode`, the component reads a database connection string from the site context, connects to the database and extracts shipping cost data for the specified shipping method from the `TableShippingRates` table.

Using this information, it calculates the shipping cost for each shipment and writes the result to the `Shipment Dictionary` in an attribute called `_cy_shipping_total`. This is the value that `ShippingMethodRouter` then reads off each shipment and adds to get the total shipping cost for the order.

Now that we know how `StepwiseShipping` works, let's continue looking at our example from before. `ShippingMethodRouter` begins by examining the `shipping_method_id` of each shipment in the `Shipments SimpleList`, and finds two distinct shipments each with a `shipping_method_id` – {00000000-0000-0000-0000-003548006355} and {00000000-0000-0000-0000-003896000938} – a GUID representing each shipping method, with more data available in the `ShippingConfig` table.

Before going any further with the `StepwiseShipping` component, we'll need to take a detour around the database to see how the data is set up. In our `ShippingConfig` table, we have the following values (this view shows only a partial view of the table – some columns have been left out, as they don't apply directly to the topic at hand):

shipping_method _id	shipping_method _name	description	progid	config	enabled
00000000-0000-0000-0000-003548006355	Vigor Airlines	We'll ship anything	commerce. stepwiseship ping	...	1
00000000-0000-0000-0000-003896000938	US Snail	The best of US Mail and the Russian Postal Agency	commerce. stepwiseship ping	...	1

The `config` column requires a little extra explanation, as it contains a `Commerce.Dictionary` in XML representation. The first `Dictionary` defines the configuration of `StepwiseShipping` for Vigor Airlines:

```
<DICTIONARY xmlns:dt="uuid:304FB305-29A4-11d3-B0D4-00C04F8ED7A2" version="1.0">
    <DICTITEM key="mode">
        <VALUE dt:dt="i2">
            0
        </VALUE>
    </DICTITEM>
</DICTIONARY>
```

These values are actually defined in the CS2K BizDesk under **Orders | Shipping Methods**.

Taking one shipping method at a time, it reads shipping method configuration values from the site context (but it originates from the `ShippingConfig` table) and finds that we've defined the first shipping method to use the `progid` commerce. `stepwiseshipping` with a `mode` of 0 (taken from the `config` `Dictionary`), meaning that we want to calculate shipping cost based on the subtotals of that shipment. `ShippingMethodRouter` instantiates the `StepwiseShipping` object and passes the configuration dictionary (containing the sole attribute `mode = 0`) to it.

`StepwiseShipping` reads `ItemIndexes` and initially gets a 0, meaning item 0 in the `Items` list. Examining item 0, it reads `_cy_oadjust_adjustedprice = 35`, as you may remember was the price set by the `RequiredOrderAdjustPriceCy` component.

Moving further on in `ItemIndexes`, the next value we get is a 2, and examining item 2 we see that `_cy_oadjust_adjustedprice = 25.75`. Still no surprises, as this is the price for the third item.

We now have a subtotal for the shipment of $35 + 25.75 = 60.75$, but now we need to take a look at the `TableShippingRates` (defined in the BizDesk):

shipping_method_id	maxval	cy_price
00000000-0000-0000-0000-003548006355	-1.0	15.0000
00000000-0000-0000-0000-003548006355	10.0	5.0000
00000000-0000-0000-0000-003548006355	20.0	10.5000
00000000-0000-0000-0000-003896000938	-1.0	30.0000
00000000-0000-0000-0000-003896000938	1.0	10.0000
00000000-0000-0000-0000-003896000938	5.0	20.0000

We have a subtotal for this shipment of 60.75, which is well above the highest maxval for that shipping method. The value of -1 is a special case meaning everything above what is explicitly defined, so this is the row we need, and we find that the shipping cost is 15, which we write to the _cy_shipping_total attribute of the shipment Dictionary.

Moving on to the next shipping method, we find that we should again use the StepwiseShipping component – this time, the config Dictionary is defined like this:

```
<DICTIONARY xmlns:dt="uuid:304FB305-29A4-11d3-B0D4-00C04F8ED7A2" version="1.0">
    <DICTITEM key="mode">
        <VALUE dt:dt="i2">
          1
        </VALUE>
    </DICTITEM>
</DICTIONARY>
```

We see that now the mode is 1, indicating that for this shipment we should use the quantity of the shipment to determine cost.

Reading ItemIndexes we find that there's only one element – a 1, and looking at item 1 we get quantity = 7. Again, querying the TableShippingRates we find that we should apply a shipping cost of 30 to the _cy_shipping_total attribute.

No more shipments are present on the order, so ShippingMethodRouter pulls _cy_shipping_total values off both shipments, getting 15 and 30. Adding those together, we get 45, which is written to the OrderForm's _cy_shipping_total attribute as the shipping fee for the order. The observant reader will remember that we earlier in our example had a total shipping cost (_cy_shipping_total) *of precisely 45.*

That's it – now we've got shipping cost per shipment and for the order as a whole.

ShippingDiscountAdjust

The third, optional component of a normal shipping stage, ShippingDiscountAdjust is very simple compared to Splitter and ShippingMethodRouter. It is intended for calculation of a discount on shipping, should such a feature be applicable.

The ShippingDiscountAdjust component takes no configuration values, but reads these keys from the order:

❏ _cy_shipping_total – the total shipping cost for the order. This value is of course needed to calculate a new shipping cost and apply the discount

❏ _shipping_discount_type – the type of discount to apply:

  ❏ 1 – discount by the amount defined by _cy_shipping_discount_value

  ❏ 2 – discount by the percentage defined by _cy_shipping_discount_value

  ❏ [Blank] – do nothing (apply no discount)

❏ _cy_shipping_discount_value – either the amount or percentage with which to discount

The component very simply reads the values from the order, performs the calculation and writes the new value (if applicable) of _cy_shipping_total back to the order.

B2B Features

When discussing e-Commerce sites, we normally distinguish between two types: Business-to-Consumer and Business-to-Business.

Business-to-Consumer (B2C) sites are your regular shopping sites, where Mr. Johnson can buy his books, electronics and home groceries. Contrary to this, Business-to-Business (B2B) sites are designed for exchange between two businesses, and as such often contain a number of features not needed in the B2C site.

In this section, we will concentrate on how to enable a `Purchase` pipeline to deliver an order to a separate business entity: the ability to e-mail the contents of an `OrderForm` to a given recipient, and the ability to place an `OrderForm` on an MSMQ (MicroSoft Message Queue) queue. Both features are obtained by using a designated pipeline component.

Another way of integrating two businesses is by using BizTalk Server. As a whole chapter is dedicated to this subject, we will only mention that it is possible, and then pass the reader on.

Component Availability

The two components we will describe here are not part of CS2K, but can be found on Microsoft's MSDN Code Center, where they are readily available at the time of writing.

The particular placement for the components is called **Reference Architecture for Commerce: Business-to-Consumer**, but don't let that fool you – the components are well suited for B2B.

At the time of writing, the address of the application is:
http://msdn.microsoft.com/code/default.asp?URL=/code/sample.asp?url=/MSDN-FILES/026/002/195/msdncompositedoc.xml
However, this may change at a later time. If not available when you read this, try going to the MSDN Code Center (http://msdn.microsoft.com/code) and look for Reference Architecture for Commerce: Business-to-Consumer under Sample Applications, or you can try to search for PipelineEmail or PipelineMSMQ using the site's search facility.

PipelineMSMQ is available as source code only, in which case you'll need Visual C++ version 6.0 to compile it. PipelineEmail, however, comes as part of the previously mentioned downloadable package.

Common Technology

Both components make use of the `DictionaryXMLTransforms` component for converting the `OrderForm` object to an XML string using a specified schema.

The `DictionaryXMLTransforms` object is a CS2K object for converting `Dictionary` objects to XML and the other way around. To enable conversion, an XML schema must be supplied.

Using the `OrderForm` object as input, both `PipelineEmail` (found under **Commerce Server**) and `PipelineMSMQ` (found under **BizTalk Server**)use `DictionaryXMLTransforms` to convert the order to an XML string. The difference between the two pipeline components lies in how this XML string is afterwards transported.

The PipelineEmail Component

At the end of our Purchase Pipeline example we would like to mail a purchase order to the customer. To do this, we use the `PipelineEmail` component.

In short, `PipelineEmail` transforms the order to XML and applies an XSLT style sheet to the XML representation of the order, and sends it via SMTP.

Besides `DictionaryXMLTransforms`, `PipelineEmail` also uses the `XMLEmail` component to send the message.

Like `PipelineEmail` and `PipelineMSMQ`, `XMLEmail` doesn't ship with CS2K, but can be found at the same place in the MSDN Code Center as the two other components. It's a helper component for `PipelineEmail`, but can also be used as independent COM component for use outside a pipeline.

After you have inserted the PipelineEmail.OrderEmail component, you need to set a few properties. Open the property page and go to the last tab (Custom Properties). As you can see in the figure below, you are not presented with the normal properties, but instead with the option to open a Custom User Interface.

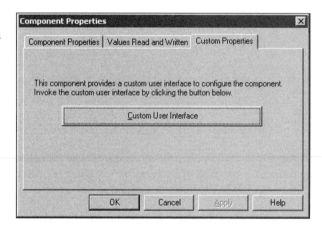

This is a new feature in CS2K that lets you design your own dialogs, fully equipped with tabs, etc.

If you click the button, the property page will open.

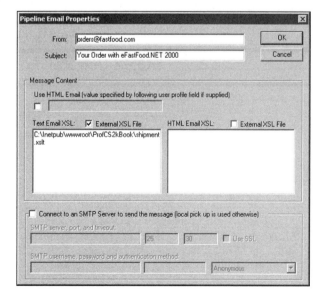

The properties do the following:

- ❏ **From:** The e-mail address of the sender of the e-mail.
- ❏ **Subject:** Write the subject of the e-mail here.
- ❏ **Use HTML Email:** Use this check box to indicate that the message body of the e-mail should be sent in HTML format. If this check box is checked, use the **HTML Email XSL** edit box to the right; otherwise, use the **Text Email XSL** edit box to the left.

  The unnamed edit box to the right of this check box requires a little extra explanation. If the check-box is checked, the edit box provides the option to specify a field in the **user profile**, defining the e-mail format for the particular user. Let's assume that the **user profile** contains a boolean field named **UseHTMLEmail**, where the user can store his choice of e-mail formatting. In other words, if this field contains a value of False, the format of the e-mail will be overwritten to plain text.

- ❏ **Text Email XSL:** Defines an XSLT style sheet. If the check box **External XSL File** is checked, specify the path to the XSLT file; otherwise, write the style sheet directly in the edit box.
- ❏ **HTML Email XSL:** Defines an XSLT style sheet. If the check box **External XSL File** is checked, specify the path to the XSLT file; otherwise, write the style sheet directly in the edit box.
- ❏ **Connect to an SMTP Server to send the message:** If you are not going to use the SMTP service on the local machine, you can use this control group to define SMTP server settings, by checking this check box.

In our example we have filled in orders@fastfood.com as the sender (**From**). The subject of the e-mail will be **Your Order with eFastFood.NET 2000**. We do not wish the mail to be in HTML format, so we leave the **Use HTML Email** check box unchecked, and fill in the **Text Email XSL** part of the properties.

As we have our style sheet in an external file, we check **External XSL file** and supply the path `C:\Inetput\wwwroot\ProfCS2kBook\shipment.xslt`.

The beginning of the style sheet looks like the following:

```
<?xml version="1.0"?>
<xsl:stylesheet xmlns:xsl="http://www.w3.org/1999/XSL/Transform" version="1.0"
xmlns:msxsl="urn:schemas-microsoft-com:xslt" xmlns:local="#local-functions"
xmlns:xql="#xql-functions">
<xsl:output method="text"/>
<xsl:template match="/" >
<xsl:for-each select="orderform">
Hello <xsl:value-of select="@customer_name"/>.

Thank you for shopping at eFastFood.NET 2000.  Your order (order id <xsl:value-of
select="@order_id" />)
is currently in processing.  We will notify you as soon as it ships.
```

As you can see this is actually the layout of our order e-mail and written in regular XSLT/XPath syntax. More information about XSLT can be found in the MSDN Library under the item **Platform SDK | Data Services | XML (Extensible Markup Language) | XSLT Developer's Guide** or the documentation for MSXML 3.0 SDK.

When the component is executed the following tasks occur:

The recipient e-mail address is read from the key `user_email_address` on the order form.

The schema defining the XML representation of the order form is read from the `po_schema_path` key on the `Context` object. It is the XML representation that defines which attributes from the order form are converted to XML. In other words, if your schema is not correct, your XML will not be either. In our example, we have added this key to the context, using the line:

```
'Add path to po schema
 objContext.po_schema_path = "c:\Inetpub\wwwroot\ProfCS2kBook\poschema.xml"
```

The following shows the XML for the items collection in the schema (this is only a small part of the schema).

```
<ElementType name="Items" content="empty" model="open">
   <attribute type="sku"/>
   <attribute type="_product_name"/>
   <attribute type="quantity"/>
   <attribute type="_product_description"/>
   <attribute type="_cy_iadjust_currentprice"/>
   <attribute type="_cy_oadjust_adjustedprice"/>
</ElementType>
```

To help build the schema you can use the method `GenerateSampleXMLInstanceFromDictionary` on the `DictionaryXMLTransforms` object. This will generate an XML schema, which can be used as a fundament and manipulated manually.

Using the just loaded schema, we then transform the order to XML.

The last action before the mail is actually sent (using `XMLEmail`) is that we apply the style sheet to our order form XML. Having done this, the mail is sent off giving the following result (only the top part of the e-mail is shown):

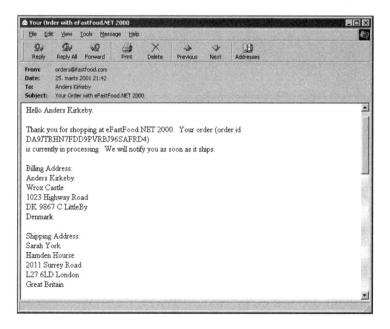

The PipelineMSMQ Component

PipelineMSMQ converts the OrderForm object to XML and drops it on an MSMQ queue. The component takes three properties on its property page:

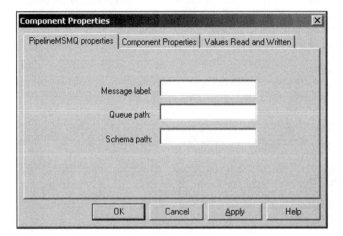

- ❏ **Message label:** This field defines a prefix for the MSMQ message label. This prefix is appended with the order_id key of the OrderForm. If the field is left empty, the message label will be identical to the order_id key.

- ❏ **Queue path:** Defines a path to the target queue. The queue can be on the local machine or a remote server. Use the ordinary MSMQ syntax for specifying queue paths.

- ❏ **Schema path:** The path to a file containing a schema definition used by DictionaryXMLTransforms.

PipelineMSMQ Example

PipelineMSMQ is probably best illustrated by an example. Let's assume that our purchase pipeline from before is supposed to deliver the order to some external system, and that saving the order to the CS2K database was just for use with displaying order history, etc. on the site – a rather normal way of doing things, in fact.

The order should be delivered to some outside system, and the solution architect has decided to implement this by dropping the order in XML format on an MSMQ queue, where the other system can then lift it off and do whatever it needs to do with it.

PipelineMSMQ works similarly to PipelineEmail by using CS2K's DictionaryXMLTransforms object to convert the OrderForm object into XML. It then drops the XML string representation of the order on an MSMQ queue.

To set up PipelineMSMQ, we must first create an MSMQ queue, where the component can place the order. If Message Queuing Services are not installed (which they aren't in a default Windows 2000 Server installation), you must first install the service by using the Windows Components Wizard in Add/Remove Programs.

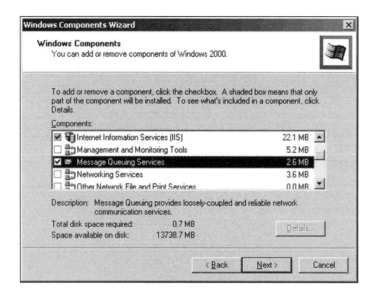

With MSMQ installed, we need to create a queue where the order can be placed. This doesn't have to be on the same computer as the one where the pipeline is running, but for simplicity it will be on the local machine in this example. To set up the queue, open Computer Management under Administrative Tools, and drill down to Message Queuing:

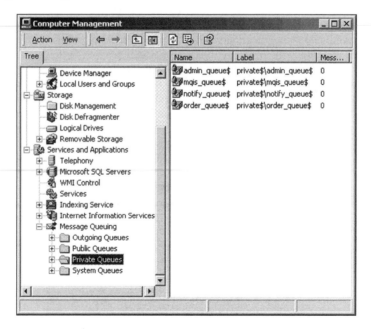

Right-click on Private Queues, select New, then Private Queue to set up a new MSMQ queue. The Queue Name dialog box appears. Enter order_drop$ into the input field, and make sure that the Transactional check box is checked – this last part is by far the most important. You can call the queue whatever you want, but if you don't mark it as Transactional, PipelineMSMQ will not work.

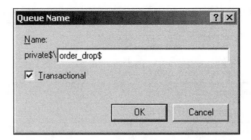

When you click **OK**, the queue is ready to receive orders.

Before you can set up and use `PipelineMSMQ` you must download the component source code from the URL listed above and compile it using Visual C++. If the server where you want to run the component is not the machine where you compiled the component, you need to install it by going to the directory where it is placed and enter:

```
regsvr32 PipelineMSMQ.dll
```

at the command line.

Now open the **Pipeline Editor** and open the `Purchase` pipeline from our continuing example. Insert `PipelineMSMQ` before **SaveReceipt**, as this component represents the actual delivery of the order out of the system, and we shouldn't do secondary things like saving a copy of the order in our own database or sending out an e-mail, before we know that the order has been placed.

After inserting the component, open its property pages. In the **Message label** input field, write **Order**, with a trailing space – although not overly important, this will constitute a prefix for the message label; if you don't want any message label prefix, you can just leave this field blank.

In the **Queue path** input field, enter the name of the queue we just created: .\private$\order_drop$ – the dot before the queue name is a short hand notation for the local machine.

In the **Schema path** input field, enter the full path to and name of the schema file for the order – this is the same `poschema.xml` file used before in the **PipelineEmail** example.

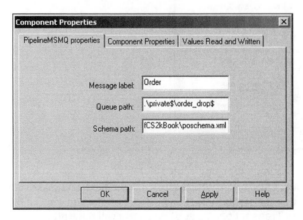

Click OK and remember to save the pipeline. We run the pipeline by calling the page where it gets executed and return to Computer Management to take a look at the queue to see if anything happened. You may need to refresh the view to see any additions, but then you should be able to confirm that one message has indeed been placed on the queue, and that the label has been prefixed by Order (including the space), as we defined earlier.

Double-clicking on the message we are able to see a preview of the message body, and we can see that it is indeed the order in XML format.

This may not be the most human-readable format, but just as we used a component to place the order on the queue, so can another developer write another program to lift the order from the queue and import it into whatever system it is needed.

Currency

By now you will more than once have heard about the new currency data type, and that a currency value can be high precision. What does all this mean?

This section will focus on two subjects: the new 64-bit currency data type and the relationship between the currency data type and the SQL money data type.

The Currency Data Type

Back in the old days, where Site Server 3.0 Commerce Edition ruled the world, money values were represented by long (32-bit) integers, in the base monetary unit of a locale. The base monetary unit is the smallest denomination of a currency, for example US cents or Indian paise. The problem with this representation is that it allows for a relatively low limit on the maximum value that can be represented.

The example mentioned previously was that in pre-CS2K days, you would not be able to go to your favorite site and buy your spouse (or yourself) a new Ferrari – at least not if you were paying in Italian lira. OK, you might say, a nice example, but how realistic is it really? Not that far out, when you think about it. The maximum value that can be represented by a 32-bit integer is 2,147,483,647. If this were dollars, I guess you would be set, but not everything is traded in dollars!

Adding to the problem, however, is the fact that SS3CE used an integer representation when storing numbers, for example, $4.45 was actually stored as 445. So instead of the aforementioned value, you now had a maximum of 21,474,836 (if we round down). Again, in dollars this would probably by sufficient in most cases. However, if this value were actually lira, it would be just over $10,000 or £7,000 given the current exchange rate.

CS2K now supports the OLE automation currency data type for monetary values. Internally the data type is a 64-bit integer, allowing for larger values, as well as allowing up to four decimal places. In other words, CS2K no longer stores a value of $4.45 as 445, but as 4.45.

Before you fall off the chair in excitement about this new data type, note that it is nothing more than the good old `Currency` type, known from Visual Basic and Visual C++.

Pipeline Currency Modes

For legacy purposes, CS2K retains the SS3CE representation, so you can choose if you wish to use the old representation or the new higher-precision representation. By default, the Order Processing Pipelines work in something called **compatibility mode**. In this mode, monetary values are maintained in both formats, though under different `Dictionary` keys.

For example, as we have seen a couple of times, the high-precision currency version of the key `_oadjust_adjustedprice` is `_cy_oadjust_adjustedprice`. The compatibility mode allows SS3CE pipelines to run without change under CS2K, and it also allows for mixing components from SS3CE and CS2K. Note, however, that if you mix components from the two versions in the same stage, you will need to surround the SS3CE components with the `MoneyConverter` component to ensure that the `Dictionary` values are kept in sync for both types of components.

The other available mode is **high precision mode**. In this mode, only the high-precision currency type is used. There are two other advantages from using this mode, apart from the ability to store larger monetary values. It avoids possible loss of precision in converting the values to and from lower-precision integer format, and it provides better performance, because the pipeline maintains only one set of keys. If you decide for the high precision mode, all the components in the pipeline must support the high precision currency type.

To change the mode of a pipeline, use the Pipeline Editor. Open the pipeline and go to the pipeline properties – not the properties of an individual component, but the whole pipeline, so you need to activate the 'root' of the pipeline. Select Edit I Properties or press *Alt+Enter*. In the drop-down list labeled Currency Mode you can select between Currency and Integer (compatibility) or Currency (high-precision).

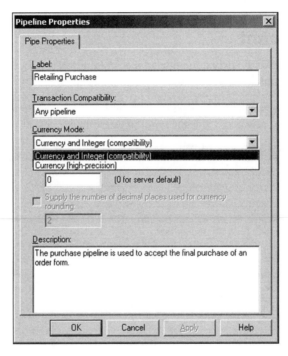

So, to summarize the above: use the new high precision currency type to avoid overflow problems, obtain a higher degree of accuracy, and increase performance.

Currency and the SQL Money Data Type

When designing a new e-Commerce site using CS2K, you would in most circumstances use the new currency type to obtain the aforementioned advantage. Using the high precision currency type would be of little use, however, if the underlying data store did not support this high degree of precision, as all persisted values would lose some of their accuracy. Lucky for us, it does.

SQL Server 2000 represents monetary and currency values by using two monetary data types – money and smallmoney. We will concentrate on the money data type. The money data type is represented as a 64-bit integer with accuracy to a ten-thousandth of a monetary unit, making it possible to store four decimal points. Where have we heard this before?

As you can see, there is a very close relationship between the two data types used to store monetary values.

Baking your own Pipeline Components (Light)

As this chapter has demonstrated, CS2K presents a very strong and versatile framework for modeling business logic as pipelines, but no matter how great the number of standard pipeline components, or the adaptability of the structure, sooner or later you will find yourself in a situation where you need to develop your own pipeline components.

In many cases, building a full-fledged pipeline component in Visual Basic or Visual C++ may not be worth the effort. Often, you'll only need to perform some small, although vital operation. For these cases, CS2K provides the `Scriptor` component.

Scriptor Component

The `Scriptor` component is a pipeline component that will run whatever script you ask it to. The component accepts VBScript, JScript and XML as a scripting language, the default being VBScript.

When first added to a pipeline, the component is empty and does nothing. Opening its property pages allows you to configure the component and define the script to be executed.

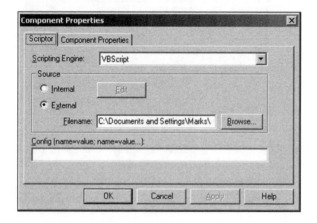

On the property page you can choose the scripting engine, set configuration parameters, and determine whether the script should be internal or external to the component. Internal means that you get to edit your script in everyone's favorite editor, Notepad, and that the script code is saved with the component in the pipeline configuration file, and thus not reusable anywhere else (except by cut and paste). External means that you point the component to a file where you then place your script – in this case, the script is available to other pipelines, and you can use the editor of your choice.

No matter if an internal or external source is used, the script must conform to certain standards – incidentally resembling a part of the `IPipelineComponent` interface. There are three entry points into the script:

```
Sub MSCSOpen(config)
End Sub

Function MSCSExecute(config, orderform, context, flags)
End Function

Sub MSCSClose()
End Sub
```

The `Scriptor` component calls these three functions in the sequence shown here.

❏ `MSCSOpen` is the first procedure to get called. Here, you can place any initialization code, but you might as well put that code in the next function as well. Only one input parameter can be used in this procedure: The configuration `Dictionary` representing the name/value pairs entered in the **Config** edit box on the property page. The procedure may be omitted.

❏ `MSCSExecute` is the main function of the `Scriptor` component. It must appear in the script, and this is where you put the main part (if not all) of your script. It takes four arguments:

  ❏ `config` is the configuration `Dictionary`, as just described.

  ❏ `orderform` represents the `OrderForm` of the pipeline. This object can be referenced for attributes and subordinate objects, and you can modify these attributes and put them back to the pipeline.

  ❏ `context` represents the pipeline context and is, as always, read only.

  ❏ `flags` are typically never used.

  The `MSCSExecute` function must return a success code corresponding to the standard pipeline error levels: 1 for success, 2 for warning, and 3 for failure.

❏ `MSCSClose` runs after the `MSCSExecute` function has returned, and as the component is destroyed. You may place any exit code here, but you might just as well put that in the `MSCSExecute` function and omit this procedure too.

As the next section will show, developing scripts for simple components is not very hard, but the `Scriptor` component quite naturally does have its limitations. In essence, you should only use it for small scripts doing nothing much more than reading or writing a few attributes on the `OrderForm` or `Items` list, making a single query to a database, or other such simple actions. Complex business logic should be developed as fully-fledged pipeline components.

Maybe the most important limitation of the `Scriptor` component is its performance. Inherently, by having to execute script code, a `Scriptor`-based component would be no match for a well-designed pipeline component (although it's easier to update).

When developing a pipeline component containing complex business logic, you may also wish to use the extra facilities for debugging, and so on, provided by Visual Studio or your other preferred development tool that supports COM component creation.

The `Scriptor` component also presents severe limitations in object design. It allows you to implement code only in the `Execute` method of the `IPipelineComponent` interface, as well as initialization and exit code. For a simple component, this is not a big drawback, as you can even set configuration values on the `Scriptor` component's property page. For a more complex component, this may present the difference between a well-designed pipeline component, and one not really up to the task.

With a real pipeline component, you can develop custom property pages, which can be accessed through the **Pipeline Editor** – these property pages are developed by implementing other pipeline COM interfaces, such as `ISpecifyPropertyPages` and `IPersistStreamInit`. This isn't possible using the `Scriptor` component.

The SpecialProduct Sample

To better describe how to use the `Scriptor` component, let's look at an example. Imagine that in the catalog, some products are in some ways special compared to others – maybe these products should have a warning shown whenever they appear; or maybe the `Purchase` pipeline should perform a special action (such as sending an e-mail) if a special product is present in the order. In any case, a component counting the number of special products in an order will be useful.

Beginning the script, we start with the function declaration and some variables:

```
Option Explicit

Function MSCSExecute(config, orderform, context, flags)
    Dim dictItem
    Dim connCommerce
    Dim rsSpecialProduct
    Dim strSQL
    Dim intSpecialProductCount
```

As you may notice, the function declaration is like previously described. In this script, we'll only use the `MSCSExecute` entry point, as we can just as well place initialization and exit code in this single function.

In this example, we assume that information defining the special product status is defined in a database table. Because of this, we first need to create a database connection.

```
'Connect to the database
Set connCommerce = CreateObject("ADODB.Connection")
connCommerce.ConnectionString = context.DefaultConnectionString
connCommerce.Open
```

Next, we initialize some variables.

```
'Initialize variables
strSQL = ""
'This variable tracks the number of special
'products on the orderform. As a default, there are none.
intSpecialProductCount = 0
```

As we want to count the number of special products present in the order, we need to iterate through all the items. The `Items` list is a `SimpleList` object, so we can iterate through it using the `For Each` syntax.

```
'Iterate through the items in the orderform
For Each dictItem In orderform.Items
```

For each item we need to examine whether it is marked as a special product in the database table, so we initialize an attribute, construct the SQL text, and execute the query:

```
'This attribute tracks whether the product is a special
'product or not. The default is that it isn't.
dictItem.SpecialProduct = False
'Define query - is this product a special
```

```
    'product?
    strSQL = "SELECT bSpecialProduct FROM Products " _
        & "WHERE SKU = '" & dictItem.SKU & "'"
    Set rsSpecialProduct = connCommerce.Execute(strSQL)
```

Examining the returned data, we set the `SpecialProduct` attribute on the item to `True`, allowing us to easily recognize any special products later in the pipeline or on an ASP page. We also increase the counter of special products by one.

```
    If Not rsSpecialProduct.EOF Then
        If rsSpecialProduct("bSpecialProduct") Then
            'This product is special, so set the
            'tracking attribute to True.
            dictItem.SpecialProduct = True
            'We've found a special product.
            intSpecialProductCount = intSpecialProductCount + 1
        End If
    End If
```

Done with one product we perform a little garbage collection and end the `For` statement (looping on to the next product in the items list until all are done):

```
    'A little garbage collection
    rsSpecialProduct.Close
    Set rsSpecialProduct = Nothing
Next
```

Almost done, we set the counter of special products as an attribute on the `OrderForm` object, so that we easily can reference this value later.

```
    'This attribute tracks whether at least one special
    'product exists on the orderform.
    orderform.SpecialProductCount = intSpecialProductCount
```

Then we do a little more garbage collection. This code we could have placed in the `MSCSClose` procedure, but then we would have had to define `connCommerce` as a global variable, so it would only have made life more difficult for us.

```
    'Garbage collection
    connCommerce.Close
    Set connCommerce = Nothing
```

Finally, we set the return code for the function. Remember that the function must return one of the three error levels of pipelines: 1 for success, 2 for warning, or 3 for failure. For clarity we haven't really implemented any error handling in this script, so we just assume success no matter what.

```
    MSCSExecute = 1
End Function
```

That's it – one custom pipeline component ready to use! It's pretty simple to do, but as we've already described, the `Scriptor` component has its limitations. In the next chapter, we turn our focus towards programming real components using Visual Basic and Visual C++.

Summary

In this chapter we have demonstrated the CS2K pipeline framework. The pipeline framework is a modular framework for modelling and executing business logic.

The most basic type of pipeline is the Order Processing Pipeline, which implements business logic on orders, but other pipeline types also exist: Content Selection Pipelines, Event Processing Pipelines and Direct Mail Pipelines – and you can also create your very own custom pipeline type if you can think of a situation where none of the standard pipelines apply.

Using Order Processing Pipelines as examples, we saw Plan and Purchase pipelines in action. During our examples, we learned how to use the Pipeline Editor, how the new shipment architecture works, and how to implement business-to-business logic.

We also reviewed how to set up the environment for running pipelines, and how to execute them. The Currency data type was explained and also used extensively during our examples, and at the end of the chapter, we demonstrated how to use the Scriptor component.

All of this goes towards an introduction to the pipelines in Commerce Server 2000; in the next chapter, we will look more in depth at building pipeline components.

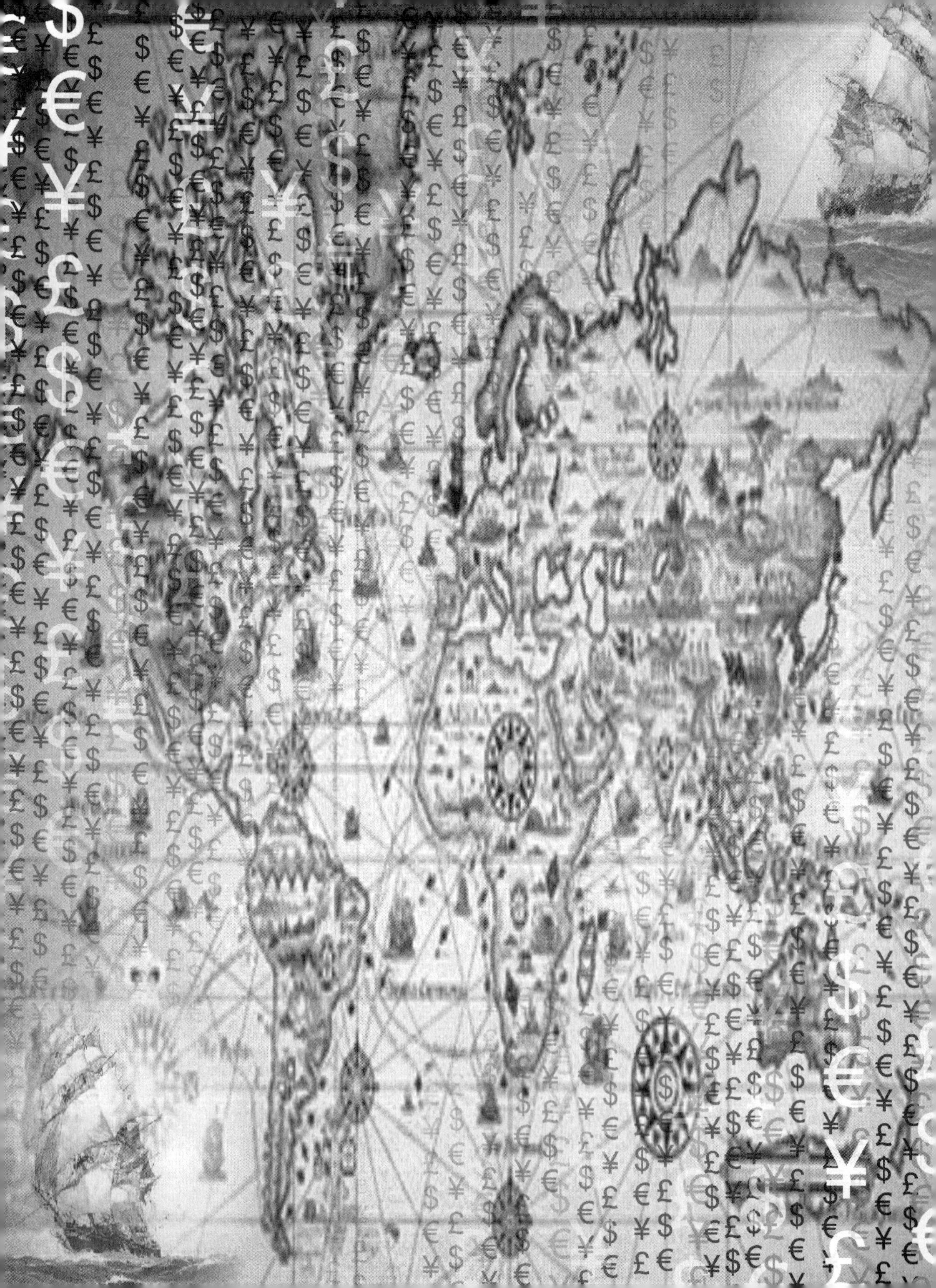

Building Pipeline Components

In the previous chapter, we investigated Pipelines and Scriptor Components. We saw how a pipeline is a series of components defined in a `.pcf` file, and that these components support a common set of interfaces. We also looked at how to script custom additions to the pipeline. In this chapter, we're going to look at actually building pipeline components.

We'll investigate the following topics:

- ❑ Different types of pipeline components.
- ❑ Factors we should consider when choosing between Visual Basic 6.0 and the Visual C++ ActiveX Template Library (ATL).
- ❑ Installing the Visual Basic Pipeline Component Wizard, and using it to create a component that sends a basic order confirmation e-mail.
- ❑ Unit testing a stand alone component.
- ❑ Using the Pipeline Registry Wizard, which will make our Visual Basic component available in the Pipeline Editor.
- ❑ Debugging pipeline components.
- ❑ The basic `IPipeline`, and related interfaces, that are supported by pipeline components.
- ❑ Registering and using the ATL wizard to create a simple component that will track some product related data.

This chapter is aimed primarily at developers with minimal experience of using COM+. A minimal familiarity with Visual Studio and developing and debugging components will be sufficient in order to follow this chapter. No C++ experience is presupposed, so those without C++ experience needn't shy away from the section in which we create a component using the ATL framework.

To really show the power of the pipeline architecture we're going to go through the creation of a component, test it, and then look at ways of enhancing its functionality. In doing this, we'll also look at debugging and rebuilding the component. By the time we reach the end of this chapter, we'll have constructed three Pipeline Components, two using Visual Basic, and one using ATL.

Pipeline Component Overview

As we'll see later in this chapter, pipeline components need to support a defined set of interfaces. These will vary slightly, depending on their implementation.

Pipeline components may be compiled or merely scripted. The main advantages of compiled components over scripted components are performance, scalability and their ability to support transactions. Because scriptor components reside in the interpreted environment of the pipeline configuration file, at execution, the pipeline object first needs to look at what engine to use with the component, this being based on the scripting language used. The script engine then executes the commands in the script. These might include commands which are part of whether those commands are physically part of the configuration file or in a separate file that must be opened.

All of this takes processor time. While scriptor components provide an excellent way to test the functionality of a component, they do not have access to the MTS or COM+ context. The result is that they cannot explicitly participate in a transaction, which can limit their use in a production environment.

Once we have decided to use a compiled pipeline component over a scripted component, we still face the question of what language to use. This, of course, is a question that faces us whenever we want to implement a component.

In most cases, using Visual Basic may prove to be the fastest and most maintainable strategy. While it is possible to squeeze a little more performance out of any component by using the C++ ATL library to create it, the difference in runtime performance alone generally doesn't justify a C++ implementation.

These slight differences in performance between VB and C++ will diminish further as the .NET runtime environment becomes prevalent. However, until this happens, C++ has a specific advantage for performance in the COM+ environment involving pooled components. The critical issue is whether the pipeline object runs under COM+.

In Commerce Server 2000, there are six pipeline objects, and four of them run under COM+. The two that do not, OrderGroup and OrderPipeline, are kept out of COM+ primarily because it allows them to be fully reentrant by multiple threads. Of the four objects that run under COM+, two have become obsolete with Commerce Server 2000: MtsPipeline and MtsTxPipeline. If you are working with these objects from Site Server 3.0 Commerce Edition, you should consider changing your site to take advantage of the new PooledPipeline and PooledTxPipeline objects respectively.

These pooled versions are an improvement in two areas. The first is that under Site Server 3.0 Commerce Edition, it was not always possible to use components built using Visual Basic in pipelines that run under MtsPipeline or MtsTxPipeline. Visual Basic has a limitation in that it does not create components that support the free-threading model. Visual Basic components do support apartment threading and are safe for use in any pipeline executed strictly on a per page basis. However, in part because the MtsPipeline and MtsTxPipeline objects did not check the threading model of components in a pipeline, these components could not be used if the pipeline was kept in memory using either session or application scope: at least, not without implementing complex workarounds. The result was that if the MtsPipeline or MtsTxPipeline objects included Visual Basic components that did not support the free threading model, where different threads may call the same instance of a component, forms of 'unexpected behavior' could be expected.

The good news is that the new `PooledPipeline` and `PooledTxPipeline` resolve this issue, and do check for the threading model of objects that make up the pipeline.

Additionally, the second improvement is that the new `PooledPipeline` and `PooledTxPipeline` take advantage of the COM+ object pooling to retain them in memory. This means that after a copy of the object has been created in memory, COM+ will keep the instance of the pipeline object active and attach the next thread which requests a copy of the same object to the existing instance. This gives a nice performance improvement. However, we can expand on this by having the objects that make up the pipeline remain in the pool as well.

Unfortunately, this is only available to components implemented in C++. This ability to flag C++ components with the `CATID_POOLABLE` category would possibly be the key reason why we would want to create a pipeline component using C++. The good news is that once we move to .NET, this limitation on Visual Basic should disappear. Unfortunately the bad news is that .NET will also require us to change much of our existing code.

Although Commerce Server is called a .NET server, it does not operate within the Common Runtime Library (CRL) of .NET. However, it will work alongside the .NET framework, so the components we create today will not become obsolete: they, like Commerce Server 2000 itself, simply will not run within the CRL.

Visual Basic Pipeline Wizard

Commerce Server 2000 ships with an easy to use wizard that handles much of the difficult work when creating a new pipeline component. The pipeline wizard is one of the tools that is included as part of the SDK.

> *Note that the pipeline wizard requires that other elements associated with Commerce Server and its SDK be installed on the same machine, so it isn't possible to simply copy the SDK onto a development machine box.*

After installing Commerce Server 2000, we need to register the actual wizard component. Run `regsvr32` on the `PipelineComWizard.dll` located in the `SDK\Tools\VB Pipe Wizard` folder.

The pipeline wizard is useful because it takes away the need for a developer to spend time concentrating on implementing interfaces and instead the developer can focus on the business problems that needs to be solved. Once the wizard is complete, we are given a project group that contains the structure and interfaces of a pipeline component as well as the accompanying user interface for the component's dictionary data. Amongst other things, the wizard prompts us to define the names and types of the values in the object's dictionary. We'll discuss the actual pipeline component interfaces in detail later, when we prepare to build a component using ATL.

Creating a Pipeline Component in VB

In this section, we will create a pipeline component which will send e-mail messages that confirm completed orders. One portion of the retail site that seems somewhat lacking is sending an e-mail message confirming to the user that their order has been accepted by the system, and is being processed. Of course a useful message not only identifies the order and perhaps its contents, but also allows the user to easily follow up and track their order.

This is not an uncommon design element. In fact, Microsoft even proposes a solution in the Commerce 2000 help that uses the Message Manager Object. The component we are going to build has a couple of advantages over the solution that is presented in the help files: the first is that we send a blind carbon copy of the message to a third party representing our supplier, internal sales, or other similar organization; the second is that the component we finish with is actually going to send an order number that the system will later recognize for tracking purposes.

It will become apparent as we work through our example why it is that most pipeline components that send a confirmation message fail to provide a value that can be used to follow up on the order status. The basic problem that these solutions fail to address is that the database entries that reflect the order have not been created by the time the order processing pipeline is complete, and it is not until the creation of these entries that the order number exists.

In this section we will create a new pipeline component called `IKEmailConfirmation`, which will send a very simple message to both the customer and, via blind carbon copy, the supplier. In order to go through all the steps of creating a valid pipeline component, we will walk through creating the pipeline component's framework using the component wizard. We will then look at customizing the component user interface and creating the code to actually send the confirmation message.

Once complete, the new component will be tested, and then registered for use in the order pipeline. This carries into the next section of this chapter, which looks at modifying the initial component, debugging the pipeline and rectifying any problems that we might discover.

Starting with a Wizard

So, let's create a new Commerce Server Order Pipeline Component in Visual Basic. Once the PipelineComWizard component is installed, on starting up Visual Basic, we will be presented with the option of creating a new Commerce Server Order Pipeline Component.

Selecting this will start the Visual Basic Pipeline Component Wizard.

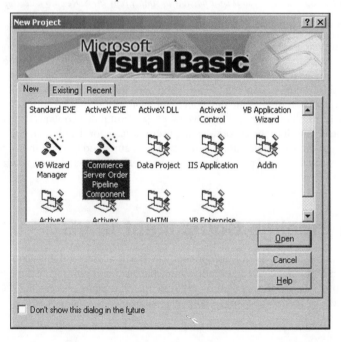

On the second screen, we are given the opportunity to select whether or not our component will support transactions. If the component is going to make any updates to a database, this should be set to default to **Yes**. This causes the wizard to add the COM+ Services Type Library to the pipeline component project's references. By adding the project reference the wizard can, and does, add the implementation of the `ObjectControl` COM interface to our pipeline component.

The additional code associated with making the component transactional may be found in the generated `pipecomp.cls` file, under the comment `'Implement IObjectControl for COM+ transaction support`.

In addition to the `Implements` declaration, the wizard also generates basic stubs to support the `IObjectControl` interfaces. For those of you not familiar with interfacing to COM+, the object control interfaces allow the component to obtain a reference to the current context. This is required if the component is to participate in a transaction. The object context allows the object that references it to actually participate in starting, completing or canceling a transaction, among other things.

The next screen asks if this component will be part of the multiple-shipment shipping architecture. The shipping stage has an architecture that relies on three primary components. New to Commerce 2000, these components, the `Splitter`, `ShippingMethodRouter` and `ShippingDiscountAdjust`, take the order and split it into separate shipments. The default for this is **No**, and in most cases this is the appropriate option, when not building a component which will interoperate with the multiple-shipment shipping architecture.

However, if we select this option, the wizard will modify the execute module of our pipeline component to contain the following code:

```
' Shipping components iterate over a list of shipments to process

Dim objShipment As CDictionary
Dim objShipmentsToProcess As CSimpleList
Dim objAddresses As CDictionary 'Ship-to addresses

Set objShipmentsToProcess = objPipeCtx.Value("shipments_to_process")

For Each objShipment In objShipmentsToProcess
 ' Your code for handling shipping addresses goes here

Next
```

We'll take a brief glance at this, just to note how the multiple-shipment shipping architecture functions. Note how code gets the 'shipments_to_process' container from the object context. This container is new with Commerce Server 2000, and holds a series of shipments associated with a single order. Components that will operate as part of this architecture need to work with the `Splitter` Component that ships with Commerce Server 2000.

Working with the shipping components is beyond the scope of this chapter and our example does not contain this code.

The fourth screen in the wizard allows us to define the properties that are part of our component:

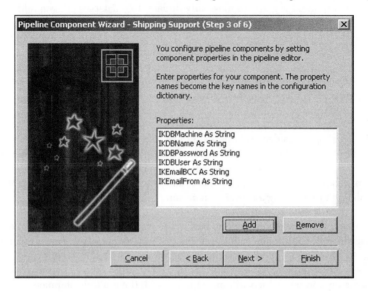

For the `IKEmailConfirmation` component we're building in this section, we'll add six string properties:

❑ The values needed for a DSN-less connection:

Machine Name

Database

Account

Password

❑ The blind carbon copy recipient that can be used by a supplier or sales and marketing

❑ The account from which e-mail confirmation messages will be sent from

To do this, we click the add button and the dialog box below opens. After entering the property name and selecting the data type, the OK button saves this entry.

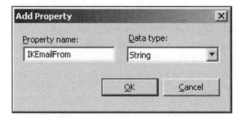

After we have entered the properties that we would like to have available as part of our pipeline component, we use the Next button to move to the next screen.

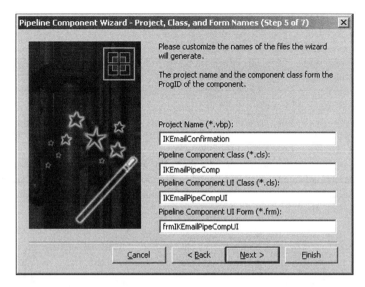

Here we can provide a project name: for our example, we'll use **IKEmailConfirmation**, and name the components that will be created. The wizard actually creates a project group containing the pipeline component (`IKEmailPipeComp.cls`) in one project, and the user interface class and form (`IKEmailPipeCompUI.cls` and `frmIKEmailPipeCompUI.frm` respectively), which are used to edit the component's dictionary data, in the second project.

Bear in mind that the project name concatenated with the Pipeline Component Class represents the `progid` that references this component.

The next step in the wizard is the designation of the directory in which to create the new project. After this, we can complete the wizard.

What is still needed is the custom business code to implement the task that our component is designed to fulfill. In our case, that is the code to gather the order data and send a confirmation message to the customer.

Customizing the Component

After the wizard completes it's a good idea to examine the project information. As this window shows there are two projects, the first is for the new pipeline component, while the second contains the class and form that manage the component's properties:

345

The next thing to review briefly is the project properties for the newly created pipeline component. The screen below shows the project properties for the IKEmailConfirmation project. The two items that I want to specifically note are the **Unattended Execution** and **Retained in Memory** check boxes. The wizard has automatically selected these two. However, if you were building these components manually, you would need to set these values.

The first, **Unattended Execution** ensures that if an unexpected error is encountered, the VB Runtime Library doesn't try to open a dialog box to expose the error. Not checking this has the potential to hang the server as it waits for a response to a local dialog.

The second item is something of a poor man's pooling. The **Retained in Memory** check box essentially tells the VB Runtime library that once this object's source files have been accessed to create this object, the object should remain in memory even if it appears that it's no longer being accessed. This isn't as efficient as the caching used by COM+, but will at least minimize the cost of recreating the object.

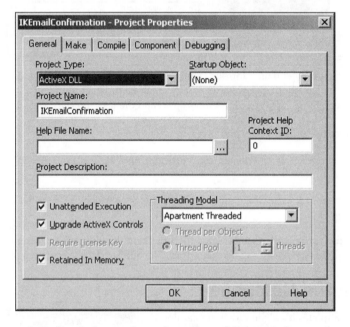

The next thing we need to adjust before we leave the variety of dialog windows and move to actually writing some code is the list of references for the new project. By default, the wizard automatically includes the Microsoft Commerce 2000 Default Pipeline Component Type Library and Microsoft Commerce 2000 Core Components Type Library. Additionally, by indicating that we wanted a transacted component, the COM+ Service Type Library is also included in the project by the wizard. The final two references support the custom functions this component will provide. The first, Microsoft ActiveX Data Objects 2.6 Library provides the tools to access the site database. The other, Microsoft CDO for Windows 2000 Library, allows access to the Collaboration Data Objects that support programmatic e-mail generation.

Since these references aren't generated as part of the wizard, you need to scroll down the list of available references to select them.

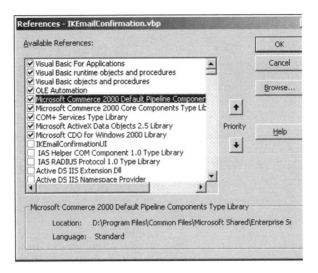

Setting Default Properties

Before we start customizing the code in the actual component, we should take a short trip through the user interface component that supports the generated component dictionary. The wizard generates a basic user interface to allow entry of the associated values.

For our IKEmailConfirmation component, you can see a copy of this dialog window pictured below. The user interface has been edited slightly, to change the order of the input boxes to correspond to their logical order instead of their alphabetical order. You'll see each of the different property values mentioned while stepping through the wizard. The machine specific information needed for the ADO Connection string, the source of our confirmation e-mail and an optional Blind Carbon Copy to our supplier, sales organization, or other address that might monitor sales.

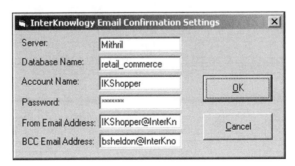

The other difference in the user interface from the default is that I have added the default values seen in the text boxes. As the component is modified and recompiled for testing, previously saved dictionary values are often lost. To get around this, it can be helpful, while testing, to have a ready set of default values. My preference is to add this code to the start of the user interface component.

In looking at the generated IKEmailPipeCompUI class in the IKEmailConfirmationUI project there is really only one module that has a significant amount of code. Included below is the implementation of the IPipelineComponentUI_ShowProperties subroutine in the IKEmailPipeCompUI class. The component wizard, to implement the IPipelineComponentUI interface, generates the subroutine shown

below. The Pipeline Editor normally accesses the interface when it calls the
`IPipelineComponentUI_ShowProperties` method on the user interface component
`IKEmailConfirmationUI.IKEmailPipeCompUI`. Calls to the `IpipelineComponentUI` interface are
made when the custom properties of a VB Pipeline Component are accessed in the Pipeline Editor.

```
Private Sub IPipelineComponentUI_ShowProperties(ByVal pdispComponent As Object)
On Error GoTo HandleError

'Use IPipelineComponentAdmin Interface to get configuration information
Dim pdispPCA As IPipelineComponentAdmin
Set pdispPCA = pdispComponent

'Populate a dictionary with component configuration
Dim dictConfig As CDictionary
Set dictConfig = pdispPCA.GetConfigData
```

After the initial setup of local variables the generated code instantiates a copy of the display form associated
with the `IPipelineComponentUI` project. The various text fields from the form are associated with the
current dictionary values that are retrieved from the reference to the current object's
`IPipelineComponentAdmin` interface. The `pdispComponent` reference that is passed as a parameter to
this `ShowProperties` subroutine is the pipeline component object for which the properties are being set.
Thus, in conjunction with generating the `ComponentUI` class, the component wizard generates the custom
properties and the implementation of `IPipelineComponentAdmin` interface as part of the pipeline
component's implementation file (`IKEmailPipeComp.cls`). It is this interface on the
`IKEmailConfirmation` component that the `IKEmailConfirmationUI` component uses to get the
current values, and later to save the new dictionary values associated with the object. The code below takes
advantage of the properties that were generated to get the current values assigned to the pipeline component.

```
Dim frmIKEmailPipeCompUIObj As New frmIKEmailPipeCompUI
'Display the properties for the user to edit
With frmIKEmailPipeCompUIObj
    .txtIKDBAcct.Text = dictConfig.Value("IKDBAcct")
    .txtIKDBMachine.Text = dictConfig.Value("IKDBMachine")
    .txtIKDBName.Text = dictConfig.Value("IKDBName")
    .txtIKDBPwd.Text = dictConfig.Value("IKDBPwd")
    .txtIKEmailBCC.Text = dictConfig.Value("IKEmailBCC")
    .txtIKEmailFrom.Text = dictConfig.Value("IKEmailFrom")
```

The code below is a custom modification made to set the values for the property display. We have simply
hard coded some system specific values for testing, so that when debugging the pipeline, uninstalling, and
rebuilding the `IKEmailConfirmation` component, it's possible to quickly reestablish the test values.

```
' Provide some default values if the database machine isn't defined.
If .txtIKDBMachine.Text = "" Then
    .txtIKDBMachine.Text = "Mithril"
    .txtIKDBName.Text = "retail_commerce"
    .txtIKDBAcct.Text = "IKShopper"
    .txtIKDBPwd.Text = "C2KRulz"
    .txtIKEmailBCC.Text = "bsheldon@InterKnowlogy.com"
    .txtIKEmailFrom.Text = "IKStore@InterKnowlogy.com"
End If
```

Following the custom code, there is code that shows the form to the user. When the user presses the **OK** button; the new property values are saved to the pipeline component's dictionary properties. After it updates the values in the dictionary, it calls the `SetConfigData` method to permanently save the updated property values.

The `SetConfigData` method is part of the `IPipelineComponentAdmin` interface that is implemented in the `IKEmailConrimation` component. This is passed as the `pdispComponent` parameter to the `ShowProperties` sub routine. Finally, in the event of an error, the component UI includes some basic error handling to prevent crashing the host application.

```
.Show 1

If .fOk Then
  'Save entered values into the dictionary
  dictConfig.Value("IKDBAcct") = CStr(.txtIKDBAcct.Text)
  dictConfig.Value("IKDBMachine") =
CStr(frmIKEmailPipeCompUIObj.txtIKDBMachine.Text)
  dictConfig.Value("IKDBName") = CStr(.txtIKDBName.Text)
  dictConfig.Value("IKDBPwd") = CStr(.txtIKDBPwd.Text)
  dictConfig.Value("IKEmailBCC") = CStr(.txtIKEmailBCC.Text)
  dictConfig.Value("IKEmailFrom") = CStr(.txtIKEmailFrom.Text)
  'Update the component with new configuration information
  pdispPCA.SetConfigData dictConfig
End If
End With

Set pdispPCA = Nothing
Set dictConfig = Nothing
Exit Sub

HandleError:
MsgBox Err.Description & " " & Err.Number
End Sub
```

The generated `IKEmailPipeCompUI` component is easily maintainable and supports the addition of properties to our component with only a limited amount of work. Of course adding new properties doesn't just involve updating the `showproperties` sub routine of the `IKEmailPipeCompUI` class. Any new properties must actually be added to the `IKEmailPipeComp` class, in particular, to those portions of the pipeline component that support the implementation of the `IPipelineComponentAdmin` interface.

To better illustrate this, let's look at a section of the property management code from the `IKEmailPipeComp` class. This section of code provides an example of how the wizard generates a `Property Let` and `Get` combination for each property that is defined. It also shows the wizard-generated implementation of just one of the methods on the `IPipelineComponentAdmin`, the `GetConfigData`:

```
Public Property Let IKEmailFrom(ByVal strValue As String)
  m_strIKEmailFrom = strValue
End Property

Public Property Get IKEmailFrom() As String
  IKEmailFrom = m_strIKEmailFrom
End Property

Private Function IPipelineComponentAdmin_GetConfigData() As Object
```

```
    Dim objDict As MSCSCoreLib.CDictionary
    Set objDict = CreateObject("Commerce.Dictionary")

    objDict.Value("IKDBAcct") = m_strIKDBAcct
    objDict.Value("IKDBMachine") = m_strIKDBMachine
    objDict.Value("IKDBName") = m_strIKDBName
    objDict.Value("IKDBPwd") = m_strIKDBPwd
    objDict.Value("IKEmailBCC") = m_strIKEmailBCC
    objDict.Value("IKEmailFrom") = m_strIKEmailFrom


    Set IPipelineComponentAdmin_GetConfigData = objDict

End Function
```

The GetConfigData function, shown above, first creates a Commerce Server 2000 dictionary object. It then populates this object with the property values associated with the pipeline component. This communication of object properties via a dictionary of properties is another facet of the standard interface used to communicate with pipeline objects. As the sample code from the IKEmailPipeComp class that implements the actual pipeline component illustrates, the pipeline component wizard took a great deal of the underlying work to create a solid framework. Having reviewed part of the framework that supports our new component, let's take a closer look at the heart of that portion of the IKEmailConfirmation component code that requires customization to accomplish our primary task of sending the user an e-mail confirmation message.

Implementing the Component Code

The next step is to start customizing the code in the execute module of the IPipeline interface. This interface, as we saw in Chapter 6, is the primary interface for a pipeline component, and, thanks to the wizard, the only code that we need to customize in order to get the IKEmailConfirmation component operational. We will step through both the generated and custom code for our IKEmailConfirmation component's Execute function, and review both the code generated by the Pipeline Wizard and the custom software added to meet our business requirement.

The first customization to the generated wizard code was to comment out those objects which the wizard provided that we don't require. The IKEmailConfirmation implementation will not be referencing the objItems list and objMsgMgr objects that the wizard automatically included in the generated code. In order to maintain an edit trail on the component being developed, we will comment out these generated declarations, rather than delete them, as we would in a production component.

In addition to these two objects, the only time that objPipeCtx was used was to initialize the objMsgMgr, so it has also been commented out. The real customization of the component starts by defining the ADO connection and recordset objects used to retrieve data about the customer. The definition of the local variables to hold the user's e-mail address and the order number is followed by some error handling.

```
    Private Function IPipelineComponent_Execute(ByVal objOrderForm As Object, ByVal
    objContext As Object, ByVal lFlags As Long) As Long

     'Dim objPipeCtx As CDictionary 'Pipe Context
     'Dim objItems As CSimpleList 'Items
     'Dim objMsgMgr As Object 'Message Manager
     Dim objAdoConn as ADODB.Connection
```

```
Dim objAdoRS as ADODB.RecordSet
Dim objCdoMsg as CDO.Message
Dim strSQLQry As String
Dim strUserEmail As String
Dim strOrderNumber As String

On Error GoTo ErrCatch
```

The function continues by setting a default return value for the function. The value 1 indicates that a pipeline component implemented in VB has returned successfully. Additionally, the following code copies the orderform to itself and the objContext to a local variable. The generated code then goes on to set up the objItems list and objMsgMgr objects.

However, since these generated lines aren't needed, they were removed from the execution path of the variable, and could be deleted from the source file. The remaining line in this block of code assigns the order id from the current order form to the custom variable. This will be used when creating the confirmation message.

```
' Return 1 for Success
IPipelineComponent_Execute = 1

' Initialize the Pipe Context and Order Form
' The 2 lines below were not needed and were removed.
'Set objPipeCtx = objContext
'Set objOrderForm = objOrderForm

' Initialize the Message Manager and get the Items from the Order Form
' The 2 lines below were not needed and were removed.
'Set objMsgMgr = objPipeCtx.Value("MessageManager")
'Set objItems = objOrderForm.Value("Items")
strOrderNumber = objOrderForm.order_id
```

The next step is to define and initialize the objects. Using the newly initialized ADO connection object, a connection with the data source is established. In this case, after defining the provider as being the SQL Server OLE DB component, the connection string is created using the component dictionary values that we defined in the wizard. As noted earlier, the wizard generated all of the Let functions and subroutines so the code can directly reference the values that make up the component's properties.

```
Set objAdoConn = CreateObject("ADODB.Connection")
Set objCdoMsg = CreateObject("CDO.Message")

With objAdoConn
  .Provider = "SQLOLEDB"
  .ConnectionString = "User ID=" & IKDBAcct & ";Password=" & _
     IKDBPwd & ";Data Source=" & IKDBMachine & _
     ";Initial Catalog=" & IKDBName
  .Open
End With
```

Once the connection to the database has been prepared, the code prepares a SQL statement. This call retrieves the e-mail address associated with the current user. If this value isn't valid, then the user won't be able to be notified, so, when defining the site, it is a good idea to make this a required data element if not (as in Microsoft Passport) the name of the user's account.

```
strSQLQry = "Select u_email_address FROM UserObject WHERE g_user_id = '" _
   & objOrderForm.user_id & "'"

Set objAdoRS = objAdoConn.Execute(strSQLQry)

If Not objAdoRS.EOF Then
 strUserEmail = objAdoRS("u_email_address")
Else
 strUserEmail = ""
End If

objAdoRS.Close
Set objAdoRS = Nothing
```

The code then checks for a valid e-mail address before attempting to send the purchase confirmation message. This is simply a basic check to make certain that it will be using something that at least has the appearance of an e-mail address. The code then associates the message text and addressees before calling the CDO send method to transmit the message.

```
If Not strUserEmail = "" And InStr(strUserEmail, "@") Then
 With objCdoMsg
 .TextBody = "Your order has been validated and processing has begun." _
    & vbCrLf & "For tracking purposes please refer to order number: " _
    & strOrderNumber & vbCrLf
 .To = strUserEmail
 .From = IKEmailFrom
 .BCC = IKEmailBCC
 .Subject = "Your order number: " & strOrderNumber
 .Send
 End With
End If
```

In most cases, we would want to create a separate SendMail() function to localize all CDO functionality. This would provide encapsulation, and facilitate reuse. However, for simplicity, we haven't done this here.

The final steps involve cleaning up the objects that were created as part of the custom code, and the handling errors.

The IKEmailConfirmation component is designed to send a confirmation message to the user when the system has accepted their order. The final stage of the ordering process is the Checkout pipeline. Using the Pipeline Editor to open the .pcf file for the checkout pipeline, we see that the last step in checking out is the Accept stage. Since this component is about providing the user with a way to track an accepted order, the IKEmail Confirmation component will be part of the Accept stage of the Checkout pipeline:

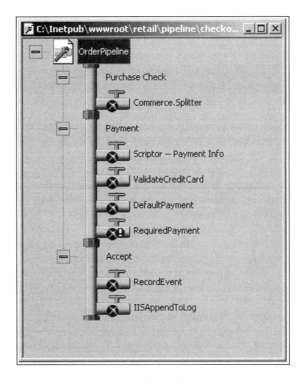

As a pipeline processes the various components that make up its configuration, it will stop when it receives an error or, if so configured, a warning. The `Checkout` pipeline fails when one of the components returns either an error or warning condition. In some cases, you would want to decide what to return from your component, depending upon whether the issue should stop the ordering process. However, since the checkout pipeline is halted whether an error or warning is returned, we will return a warning if the message fails.

```
Cleanup:
  Set objAdoConn = Nothing
  Set objAdoRS = Nothing
  Set objCdoMsg = Nothing
  Set objPipeCtx = Nothing
  Set objOrderForm = Nothing

  Exit Function
ErrCatch:
  ' Return 2 for Warning, or 3 to indicate a fatal error.
  IPipelineComponent_Execute = 2
  Resume Cleanup

End Function
```

The highlighted code that we looked at in this section is the only custom code required in order to create a fully operational pipeline component. As noted earlier, the pipeline wizard took care of implementing the necessary interfaces for our component to interact as part of a pipeline. At this point, we are almost ready to try to run the new component.

Unit Testing the Component

Even the best software engineers run into errors, and early discovery means easier repair. As you will see later in the chapter, attempting to determine why your component failed while it's running inside a pipeline is a painful process, slowed even more by the need to execute all of the steps required to trigger a specific pipeline.

Being able to step into the code of an executing pipeline component normally requires setting up your web server and Visual Interdev development environment for debugging. Preparing to step into components that are executing on your web server is not a simple task, and is not generally a favored approach to debugging.

Let's create a simple test form that will enable the creation and execution of our new pipeline component. The IKEmailConfirmation component is at its core just another ActiveX component, and we can create a test form in the same project group to allow us to test its operation.

Add another standard executable project to the current project group. The added project has a single form that is used to instantiate the component(s) being created, acting like a test form. Generally the files associated with the test form are saved in a sub directory of the project directory. The main advantage of a test form is that it can be set to start up and, using the Visual Studio debuggers, we can step line by line through the code that makes up our new component.

However, in the case of pipeline components, we run into a unique problem. Specifically, in order to call the IPipeline_Execute function, the form needs to have the appropriate parameters and call from within a pipeline context. This could be quite a challenge if it wasn't possible to utilize some of the components that ship with Commerce Server 2000 to build a framework in which to run the component.

By taking advantage of the Micropipe component that ships with Commerce Server 2000, we can create the pipeline framework in our test form, and debug it using the native Visual Basic debugger. The Micropipe component provides a way to call a single pipeline component without requiring a pipeline configuration file or executing a full pipeline. While it will be using this from within a Visual Basic form, it can just as easily be used as part of an ASP page on your Commerce Server 2000 site.

The test form we create will establish the necessary dictionary parameters to allow it to execute a custom pipeline component using the Micropipe. Obviously, this will require a little manipulation of the data, since we won't have all of the environment variables available. Fortunately, the IKEmailConfirmation component only references a couple of properties from the order form, allowing for the creation of a manageable test form project. Additionally, the test form will demonstrate some interface programming so that we can call the property page associated with our object and set the property values.

Creating a Test Form

Add a new Standard EXE project to the group. Right-click on the project name in the **Project Group** window (pictured earlier), and select the **Set as Startup Project** option from the context menu. While here, it's a good idea to go to the **Properties** window and change the project name to something such as **IKEmailTest**.

Next, it's good practice to change the default Form1 name and caption. Something such as IKEmailTestForm, this provides a distinct name and caption. Then go to the **Project** menu and select the **Project References** menu item, to open the references dialog pictured earlier.

The IKEmailConfirmation and IKEmailConfirmationUI should be visible near the top of the list of components; since these are the components to test, add references to them. Next, since we are working with Commerce Components, add project references to the same commerce libraries that are in the pipeline components. Both the Microsoft Commerce 2000 Core Components Type Library and the Microsoft Commerce 2000 Default Pipeline Components Type Library should be visible in the window. Then it's time to scroll down through the list of available References and find the Microsoft Commerce 2000 Micropipe Type Library. Add a reference for this component to your Test Form project and select OK.

Trigger the form editor, and place one big button named something like cmdStart and give it a simple caption:

Open the code window associated with the form and place the focus inside a newly created module called cmdStart_Click(). The newly created Sub is empty, but we will step through the highlights of what to add to test the IKEmailPipeComponent.

```
Private Sub cmdStart_Click()
 Dim dOrder As CDictionary
 Dim dContext As CDictionary
 Dim lngFlags As Long
 Dim objMicro As CMicroPipeline
 Dim objTest As IKEmailPipeComp
 Dim objTestUI as IKEmailPipeCompUI
 Dim ojbIFaceUI as IPipelineComponentUI
 Dim lngErrVal As Long

 Set dOrder = CreateObject ("Commerce.Dictionary")
 Set dContext = CreateObject("Commerce.Dictionary")
 lngFlags = 0
```

The dOrder and dContext variables are Commerce Dictionary components used to provide the environment data to the Micro Pipe, along with the lngFlags variable. The next step is to create the values in the dictionary object that the IKEmailConfirmation component uses. Since there are only a couple of values, manually add them to this code. Copy a valid user id and order id from the appropriate database columns and set the appropriate dictionary values to these static values.

> The values copied were from the **retail_commerce** database using the same table that the **IKEmail** component will use. However, by adding a reference to the ADO library, the Test Form could use a database call to collect and populate a large number of historical order data elements for a component requiring a more robust test environment.

```
dOrder("user_id") = "{9D19044B-116A-43D3-9B3E-00011A743E65}"
dOrder("order_id") = "{F4EF7C8C-D80D-46DD-8B16-51FFC167F5B9}"
Set objTest = CreateObject("IKEmailConfirmation.IKEmailPipeComp")

Set objTestUI = CreateObject("IKEmailConfirmationUI.IKEmailPipeCompUI")
Set objIFaceUI = objTestUI

ObjIFaceUI.ShowProperties objTest
```

After the test frame creates an instance of the IKEmailConfirmation component it creates an instance of the IKEmailConfirmationUI component. The user interface component is then associated with the IpipelineUI type and the ShowProperties method of this interface is called to set the properties of the IKEmailConfirmation component to be tested.

After the user interface has been tested, and the component properties initialised, a micropipe is created. The micropipe has three possible methods, of which this code uses two. The first is SetComponent. This method associates the instance of the pipeline component to execute with the micropipe.

The second method that is used is the Execute method. This method is passed the environment variables so that the component is run with the appropriate data. In the event that the micropipe is on an ASP page on the production site, it could be passed the actual environment variables that would be present for any other pipeline. However, this test form passes the variables created and populated above.

The third method available to a micropipe SetLogFile, sets the logging file, which isn't something we need as part of a test form.

```
Set objMicro = CreateObject ("Commerce.MicroPipe")

obyMicro.SetComponent objTest
lngErrVal = obyMicro.Execute(dOrder, dContext, lngFlags)
```

The Execute method returns the status of the component following execution. Since we are primarily looking to use this test form for debugging we aren't going to examine this value. However, the return value is the same one that in a production pipeline is used to determine if the component was successful.

Following the execution of the component, it is possible to examine the various environment variables such as the order form and context value for updated values. Depending upon the task associated with the custom component being tested, it is possible that additional code to examine or echo dictionary values could be quite valuable. Once the values have been examined the test form completes its run by cleaning up the variables that were instantiated by the test form and returns control to the form display.

Using a test form is a great way to confirm that your component should operate as expected when you finally install it as part of a pipeline. Keep in mind however, that running as part of a pipeline called by a remote user under IIS changes the security environment, and there is no guarantee that everything will work. If you think the security context is an issue, it is possible to install the component under COM+, and have it run as a server component in the security context of your choice. In general however, if you can get through some successful examples using this test form it will reduce the odds of facing that generic error page after the first test run.

Unlike the Micropipe that has almost no required configuration, a full pipeline requires additional configuration in the form of a .pcf file. As was shown in Chapter 6, the Pipeline Editor allows components to be associated with each stage of a pipeline in a graphical environment. However, before the Pipeline editor will recognize your component, it needs to be registered as a pipeline component.

One last thing before we finish our component: you will want to return to the Project Properties dialog, and access the **component** tab. This tab is where you indicate that the future builds of the project should use binary compatibility for deployment. Binary compatibility tells Visual Studio not to generate a new GUID for your project on future compilations, which is important once a component has been registered since each GUID gets its own entry in the registry. Once binary compatibility is set, other items such as the Order Pipeline can rely on the registered GUID for your component remaining unchanged.

Registering the Component for a Pipeline

To recognize a component as being compatible with a pipeline requires registering it as such. In Site Server 3.0 Commerce Edition, this involved a custom solution. Thankfully, in addition to providing a VB component wizard, Commerce Server 2000 provides a Pipeline Registry Wizard. The great thing about this wizard is that you don't need to manually work with a single GUID or registry entry. To access the tool navigate to the SDK folder under your Commerce Server 2000 installation directory, there you will find the Tools folder. Within the Tools folder is the Registration Tool directory containing the complete C++ project for the Registry Tool. To start the tool, run `PipeReg.exe`, located in this directory. The first screen, pictured below, shows the entry of the ProgID for the IKEmailConfirmation project. It is possible to select a component by its ProgID or by the entire set of component interfaces identified by a given Type Library or DLL.

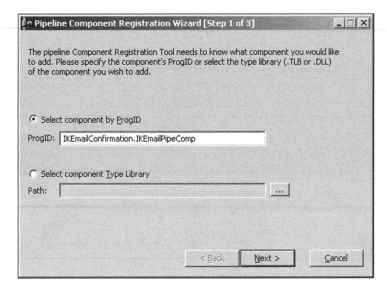

After selecting the component, you use the next screen to identify the stage or stages to use the component. In order to recognize pipeline components, the system looks for a set of keys associated with each component's Clsid registry key. The **Implements Category** key holds the set of key GUIDs that indicate how a component should be associated with the Commerce Server pipelines. Rather than needing to work with values such as: {cf7536d0-43c5-11d0-b85d-00c04fd7a0fa} the wizard manipulates the known values using commonly recognizable names. For those that still need to manipulate these values directly, you will recognize the preceding GUID as the generic definition of a pipeline component.

For example, the IKEmailConfirmation project relies on certain values being present in the database. However, this data will not be present for most pipeline stages. This knowledge is something that as component authors we can be very familiar with. However, others attempting to use our component would find it very difficult to discover. Additionally, the wizard allows for the specification of a custom stage. This opens a dialog box where we can provide a recognizable stage name and GUID for that stage. In this way, if developing custom pipelines, in addition to the components used in them, you can still minimize the amount of time spent working with GUIDs.

Finally, you'll notice the All Stages entry highlighted from the list of Available Categories. Selecting this category is the equivalent of selecting a wildcard category name. The best example of a component that takes advantage of this category is the component used to implement the scriptor functionality (Commerce.Scriptor).

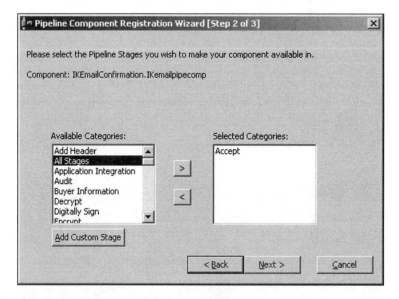

Having used the first two screens to determine which GUIDs need to be associated with the component, the final screen determines where to save the information. We might immediately assume that this should be saved in the registry. Certainly, this is the end target, but what if we are running the wizard on a development box with plans to deploy the component to a production server. In this case, instead or along with the creation of the registry entries, the wizard will create a .reg file for packaging with the component. The generated file contains the registry values that associate the component with the selected pipeline stages.

As part of the installation on the development server, the install package can add these values to the registry. To examine the entries that are associated with the selections made in the wizard, open the file using Notepad or a similar text editor. Additionally, although there is no visual cue in the wizard screen after selecting either of the options that involves exporting the registration data you can change the target path and filename for the registry data. Just remember to include the .reg file extension since the wizard does not automatically append it to the edited filename.

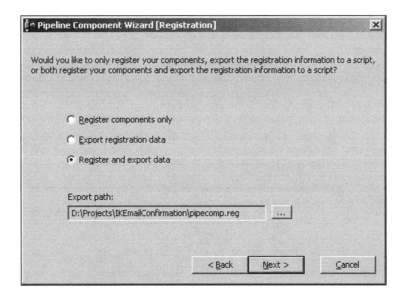

After successfully navigating the registration wizard, you are ready to add your new component to the appropriate pipeline stage as shown in Chapter 6. If, when you first open the Choose a Component dialog box, you don't see the Progid of your new component in the pick list, review the registry entries for your component, perhaps rerunning the registration tool.

Debugging the Pipeline

Now that the component has been unit tested and registered, it can be added to the pipeline. Using the Pipeline Editor, add the newly compiled `IKEmailConfirmation` to the `Accept` stage of the `Checkout` pipeline. Then fire up the browser. Navigate through the site, pick up a few items for the basket, start the checkout process, get to the last screen and submit the order. If everything is configured correctly, you should see an e-mail message in the inbox of the customer account you are using. Of course, this presumes that you actually entered an e-mail account for the user you are using to test with on your server.

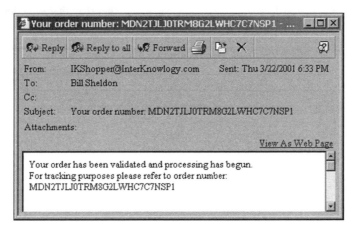

The good news is that you have a functioning pipeline component. The bad news is that the order number you are sending doesn't match the order number that appears on the customer screen after the order is entered. In fact, the order number in this message wasn't even saved into the retail database. This means our `IKEmailConfirmation` component doesn't meet it's business requirement of providing the user with an order number they can use to track their order status. The reason has to do with the order number in the form vs. the order number that is generated in the retail database. So what we are now going to do is change our component to get its order number from the database. The code to do this is below and can be inserted just after the ADO connections that we added to the `IKEmailConfirmation`.

```
strSQLQry= "Select order_number FROM OrderGroup WHERE ordergroup_id = '" _
      & objOrderForm.order_id & "'"

Set objAdoRS = objAdoConn.Execute(strSQLQry)
If Not objAdoRS.EOF Then
  strOrderNumber = objAdoRS("order_number")
Else
  strOrderNumber = ""
End If

objAdoRS.Close
objAdoConn.Close
```

> **Note the section of code above will not work. This code is presented to support going through the debugging and modification of this component presented in the following portions of this chapter.**

Changing and recompiling our object may reveal a feature of the PooledPipeline. Since the pipeline has loaded the `IKEmailConfirmation` component, and in turn been loaded by COM+, the component DLL cannot be immediately replaced on the system. If you run into a problem compiling the source code after you have run the component, you probably need to force COM+ to release its reference. The way to do this is to use either the command line function `IISReset`, or the context menu on the server in the Internet Information Services MMC Snap-in, to stop and restart IIS, thus unloading the pipeline from the retail site application.

So now what? The default page doesn't give much information, other than that something bad happened. You can get a little more detail from IE by going to the Internet Options dialog, and on the advanced tab, deselecting the Show Friendly HTTP error messages check-box. But we need to get beyond the fairly generic messages. To this end, we're going to look at some of the resources with which we can debug errors that occur once we install our component in a pipeline. We will cover the following tools that can help you isolate and resolve an issue.

❑ The Application Event Log and the default site type.

❑ The `DumpOrder.vbs` script and what it can reveal.

❑ Setting up and using a pipeline log file.

After we cover the debugging, this section is going to briefly cover creating a new component based on the original component designed with the VB Component wizard. As noted, attempting to set up ASP debugging is a little beyond the scope of this chapter; however, a good reference that addresses some of the steps and problems with trying to use the debugging tools is in Microsoft Knowledge Base article Q244272 (http://support.microsoft.com/support/kb/articles/Q244/2/72.asp).

The Application Event Log

So, the first place to check is the application event log. This is a native utility provided as part of the Windows 2000 operating system. The event logs, like many other system utilities, are accessible programmatically from the Windows Management Instrumentation (WMI) interface. The WMI interface is beyond the scope of this chapter, but basically, it is a set of script compatible objects that can be used to support web based management of your enterprise servers. Later in this section, when we change the site definition, Commerce Server will provide the same error information we are about to review directly to your web browser using the WMI interface.

To access the windows event logs from your desktop you use the Event Viewer that is part of the Administrative Tools. The Event viewer allows you to review any of the event logs that are being created on your system. The common logs include System, Security and Application. In this case we are interested in the Application event log that is used by a variety of applications, including Commerce Server 2000. If a pipeline error has occurred, you will see an entry in this log associated with Commerce Server 2000.

This means that when you are monitoring a production site, the application error log should be regularly monitored. If your customers are consistently getting errors during the order process, the information in the application event log will potentially be your first indication of a problem. To get more information than the single line provided by the Event Viewer's display, double click on the event to get a detailed view of the event information. As we can see in the following screenshot, the log entry doesn't have much in the way of error information. However, it does tell us a couple of valuable things. The first is that the error occurred on line 156 of the `retail/include/payment.asp` page. It also suggests a good way to get additional information by changing the site environment to DEVELOPMENT. Which, since this is a development site, is a useful suggestion.

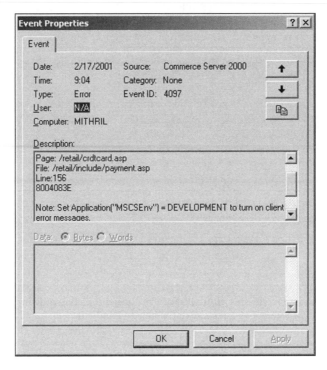

Changing the environment to indicate it is being used for development involves editing the `global.asa` file for the site. Below is a snip from the top portion of this file where the application variable is set up. The line comes with the default of PRODUCTION, changing this to DEVELOPMENT has at least two important changes to the way your site works.

```
' *** Global variables ***
Dim MSCSCommerceSiteName, MSCSCommerceAppName
Dim MSCSEnv, dictConfig, appframework

'Set the environment to PRODUCTION or DEVELOPMENT
MSCSEnv = DEVELOPMENT

Sub Application_OnStart()
 Application("MSCSEnv") = MSCSEnv
 Call Main()
 Application("MSCSErrorInGlobalASA") = False
End Sub
```

The first, although not advertised in the error message, is that instead of trying to force you to enter a valid credit card, flipping this switch triggers a change that inserts a dummy value into the credit card number field, thus speeding up the testing of the `checkout` pipeline.

The second is that, as advertised, this switch sends the error message to the client browser instead of the event log. This change works very well. In fact, after making the switch and rerunning the pipeline, the same error message that was previously in the Application Event Log was now displayed on the page.

So to dig a little deeper, open the file referenced by the error message and look at the code that was on the page. What becomes immediately apparent is that the error thrown wasn't from the `IKEmailConfirmation` component, but rather one generated by the ASP page in the code shown below.

```
iErrorLevel = RunMtsPipeline(MSCSPipelines.Checkout,
GetPipelineLogFile("Checkout"), mscsOrderGrp)

  If iErrorLevel > 1 Then
   If GetErrorCount(mscsOrderGrp, BASKET_ERRORS) > 0 Then
                Err.Raise vbObjectError + 2111, ,
mscsMessageManager.GetMessage("L_Bad_Pipeline_Warning_ErrorMessage", sLanguage)
   ElseIf GetErrorCount(mscsOrderGrp, PURCHASE_ERRORS) > 0 Then
                CheckOut = iErrorLevel
   Else
                Err.Raise vbObjectError + 2110, ,
mscsMessageManager.GetMessage("L_Unspecified_Pipeline_Warning_ErrorMessage",
sLanguage)
   End If
  End If
```

> **This illustrates an important rule of thumb for attempting to debug pipeline components: never catch an error unless you have a plan for how to handle it.**

In order to get more information regarding our error, we need to follow one of two paths. The first is to add a significant amount of code to recognize an unexpected error, and then raise the error again from the handler. The second option is to just comment out the error handling in the component forcing the system to raise the error when it occurs. Since error handling is a generally good practice I am not going to remove the error handler from this component; however, in order to get meaningful information, while in development I will temporarily comment out the On Error statement forcing errors to appear in the correct state.

Rebuild the component with error handling disabled. Navigate through the retail site, until the error again occurs. This time the displayed error message is from the IKEmailConfirmation component, and thanks to setting this as a development environment, the error message is returned to your browser. As the following screenshot shows, this made the error message much more applicable to the IKEmailConfirmation component that caused the problem.

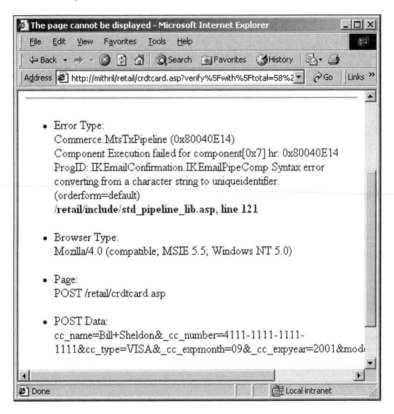

The preceding message made it apparent that the error occurred because of a problem with the one of the values associated with the Order Form. But notice what else is in the error. Right there in both the ASP page, and accordingly in the application event log, is the customer credit card number. By not catching the error, we have potentially placed some important customer data in a very unsecure location. That's why every pipeline component needs an active error handler before it is deployed to production. So go back now, remove the comment from the On Error statement, and recompile the IKEmailConfirmation component.

Remembering that the pipeline components are executing several layers deep within the commerce server architecture is important when debugging. While this error message may not pinpoint the problem with the data that is causing the error, it does indicate that the problem is associated with one of the data elements. The next step is to look at the data in the order form to see if the problem is readily apparent.

Using Dumporder.vbs

The `Dumporder.vbs` script is included as part of the Commerce 2000 SDK. This script is a very powerful debugging tool in that, when properly installed in a pipeline, it creates a text file containing the elements that make up the `OrderForm` object. As a scriptor component, it's available for installation on any section of the order pipeline, and can provide excellent insight into the values that are actually available.

The scriptor component gets installed under the SDK folder associated with your Commerce Server installation. To find it follow this path from the SDK folder:
`SDK\Samples\Sitelets\Order\source\pipeline\dumporder.vbs`.

The second important customization for this script to work is that it requires a configuration value. It needs to know where to write the file of order data. An important thing to know about this file is that the component does not append subsequent order forms with each call. Instead, it opens and truncates any existing data in the file for each call. Thus, if, for example, you would like to capture the state of the order form data both before and after a call to a specific pipeline component, be certain to provide a separate output file for each instance. The format of the configuration is:

```
filename=C:\path\file.txt
```

Where the path on the right hand side of the equal sign might read something like:

```
D:\DumpingGround\Accept.txt
```

if the component were being installed in the `Accept` stage.

Installing this component so that it executes in the accept stage, just prior to the `IKEmailConfirmation` component, will provide a snapshot of the order data just prior to the execution of our component. So again, open the site and go through the steps of creating and submitting an order until an error occurs. The result is that the dumporder scriptor will create a file of orderform data.

Here is an excerpt of some captured data, containing `order_id` value that the `IKEmailConfirmation` component is designed to use:

```
Order Key [saved_cy_total_total] {String} Value [78.96] {Currency}
Order Key [billing_address_id] {String} Value [{245EE006-73F1-4FAF-8E5D-
485C897B32F2}] {String}
Order Key [order_id] {String} Value [6L297266LDW09H57SNCN5C73P1] {String}
```

Using the order form data captured in our most recent attempt to insert this order we can see the value for the `order_id` is a string. The reason we are getting an error stating that there is a string to GUID conversion issue is that instead of the `order_id` that is in the order form being a GUID, which is the key to the order group table in the retail site SQL Server database, we are attempting to use a string in our SQL statement. If we were attempting to determine what was wrong with our component, this information would probably be enough to resolve our issue.

This example proves not only how powerful the `dumporder.vbs` script is as a debugging tool, but also as a planning tool. By using this tool before you build your component you can recognize if data elements you are depending on to serve a function are actually available, and have meaningful values. However, for now we need to examine the final debugging tool for Commerce Server 2000 pipeline components: pipeline logging.

Pipeline Logging

Pipeline logging provides information such as:

- ❏ The number of components configured for execution as part of the pipeline
- ❏ The status of each component as it executes in the pipeline
- ❏ A history of any dictionary values read and written
- ❏ A final status on when the pipeline completes

In addition, the log file will display a component error in the context of where in the pipeline it occurs. The key, however, is enabling the logging and selecting an appropriate target directory.

Commerce Server documentation on pipeline logging is oriented around the `SetLogFile` method. This is important when you are directly accessing a pipeline object as we do in the case of the Micropipe. Calls require a single parameter, the string of the filename and path where the log should be written. However, in working with the retail site, the actual calls to the various pipelines have been encapsulated.

This code that controls logging for all the various pipelines in contained in the page called `global_siteconfig_lib.asp`. This is the top portion of the `InitSitePipelines` function from that page:

```
Function InitSitePipelines()
Dim objPage, dictPipeline
Dim MSCSEnv

Set dictPipeline = GetDictionary()

dictPipeline.Folder     = GetRootPath() & "pipeline\"

' You must grant Internet Guest Account (IUSER_machinename)
' write permission on the following directory to enable logging
dictPipeline.LogFolder = GetRootPath() & "pipeline\logfiles\"

    If MSCSEnv = DEVELOPMENT Then
        dictPipeline.LoggingEnabled = False
        dictPipeline.LogsCycled    = False
    ElseIf MSCSEnv = PRODUCTION Then
        dictPipeline.LoggingEnabled = False
        dictPipeline.LogsCycled    = False
    End If
```

The highlighted section of this function indicates where we need to make changes in order to adjust pipeline logging on the retail site. You may notice that by default logging is turned off. The first item has to do with file permissions. By default, the code will attempt to place the log files in a subfolder of the retail site, `pipeline\logfiles\`. However, the default permissions on this directory do not include write permission for the anonymous user account `IUSR_machinename`. Because, when logging, an IIS application has to write data to a file, pipeline logging should only be used in development.

If you are tempted to run pipeline logging on your production site, bear in mind that having IIS write to a text file entails writing between 10-20K for each pipeline that a customer executes, and this is not going to go unnoticed. In fact, note that, in the above code, the development settings are separate from the production settings, so that if a developer accidentally shipped a copy of this file with logging turned on, the production site would ignore the development setting.

Note that the way in which pipeline logging operates is very different to the way IIS keeps a running log of HTTP information. The IIS log is built in memory in 64K chunks, and then a thread that is not handling user requests writes the data out to the actual log file. When you turn on pipeline logging, the thread handling your IIS request is now forced to wait while the file I/O required to log a pipeline is placed on the disk, and this, of course, will have a big impact on performance.

Similar to the dumporder.vbs or explicit error messages, pipeline logging isn't available to review what is occurring on your production site, but the good news is that to turn on logging, we just need to change the two Booleans under the Development branch from False to True. The first setting turns on logging, and the second item determines whether to truncate the log files with each execution of a selected pipeline, or whether they accumulate entries from one call to the next. This is a very useful setting to use if you are doing serious debugging.

Not only does the retail site automatically create the log files for each pipeline with the pipeline name as part of the filename, it appends the user GUID to the filename. If you have ever experienced a bug where it works for user A but not for user B, the value of this naming will be obvious. Pipeline logging supports capturing data from each user in clearly identified files, based on a naming convention that, as previously mentioned, uses the pipeline name and user id, to maintain separate data for each pipeline in a common directory structure.

An excerpt from the start of a typical log file is shown below. Executing the Checkout pipeline generated this file, which starts by showing the date and time of the execution. The reason the name of the pipeline isn't in this data is that it is part of the filename.

```
Sink started at 2001/08/10 20:35:06.0040
PIPELINE:++ 2001/08/10 20:35:06.0040 Pipeline Execution starts (lMode==0x1,
lFlags==0x0)  8 components in the list (MTS is enabled)
PIPELINE:++ component[0x0] about to be called ProgID: Commerce.Splitter.1
RootObject:ReadValue    items VT_DISPATCH        PV=[0x967d678] VT_EMPTY
    __empty__
Items:        ReadItem    0      VT_DISPATCH     PV=[0x7273bc8] VT_EMPTY
    __empty__
:     ReadValue    vendorid    VT_BSTR    MyBooks VT_EMPTY        __empty__
:     ReadValue    vendorid    VT_BSTR    MyBooks VT_EMPTY        __empty__
RootObject:WriteValue  _vendorsVT_EMPTY        __empty__        VT_DISPATCH
        PV=[0x72735c8]
PIPELINE:-- component [0x0] returned hr: 0x0, IErrorLevel=1 in 0 milliseconds
```

The third line indicates how many components are in the pipeline, and that MTS is enabled. Logging relating to a specific component, in this case, the Commerce.Splitter, begins on the next line. The subsequent lines list the specific dictionary items read or written by this component.

With the three tools described in this section, and the unit testing in Visual Basic, we can debug most any pipeline without ever attempting to set up a web-based debugging session. Attempting to set up such an environment generally adds more complexity and requires more time, cost and effort than the problem being solved. On the other hand, in virtue of their simplicity, the debugging tools we've looked at in this section provide a very manageable and cost effective way to get to a solution in a short amount of time.

Sending the Real Order Number

Unfortunately, while the IKEmailConfirmation component doesn't produce an error, it doesn't work quite as we might like, since it isn't providing the customer with information that can be used to track their order. Let's make the appropriate enhancements to it, and make it into a new component: IKEmailConfirmation2.

Creating a new component has several advantages, the first of which is that it follows the basic goal of COM which states that you shouldn't change an interface, you should create a new one. The interface of IKEmailConfirmation supported six properties, and was designed to run as part of the Accept stage of the Checkout pipeline. The new IKEmailConfirmation2 component will have only two properties and be designed to run in a Micropipe object. Additionally the IKEmailConfirmation2 component will implement an additional business requirement to send the user a confirmation message with an order number that can be tracked.

The basic problem with the IKEmailConfirmation component is that Commerce Server won't have created the real order number until after the checkout pipeline is complete. In fact, in looking at the file crdtcard.asp, it's possible to see where the call to insert the order group table entry for the order, and generate the GUID and order number, doesn't occur until after the checkout pipeline has completed.

There are three main options to solve this problem:

❑ Move the database transaction in relation to the pipeline

❑ Change the data saved as part of the transaction

❑ Change where the message is triggered

Each of these options, in theory, has advantages and disadvantages and a quick review is in order to help clarify the selection.

The first, which involves creating a transaction containing both the pipeline and the database update has so many risks and involves such a key portion of the ordering process that given the simplicity of the other options we can quickly discard it.

The second option, adding the order_id value from the form to a new column in the database is in some ways a version of the first option. However, in this case we avoid all of the issues with attempting to manage a transaction or changing a major portion of the order update logic. The disadvantages of this solution include the fact that it adds a secondary key value to a table which already has a key, requires updates to the search logic to support finding values based on this new value, and requires changes to the order update logic. Part of the reason why the IKEmailConfirmation component is included as part of the book's source code is to allow those of you who may have already implemented this to take advantage of that component. However, the changes to implement this are not component based and as such we will look at the third option.

The third option changes the point in the process to trigger the message. The disadvantage of this option is that the component won't be part of the checkout pipeline, and that, since there isn't a pipeline associated with true post order processing, a new pipeline would need to be created. An alternative to creating a new pipeline would be to use a micropipe. Micropipes provides a simple, robust way to take advantage of a pipeline component in a situation where a full pipeline does not exist.

Where in the process would we add the micropipe?

The ASP function to trigger our new pipeline may be encapsulated in a new function ConfirmMsg. We'll return to this function later in this chapter. This will be called from the htmRenderCreditCardPage function.

The following code is from the crdtcard.asp page's htmRenderCreditCardPage function. We have made a couple of changes to support the new call to ConfirmMsg.

```
If bSuccess Then
    arrParams = Array("ID")
    arrParamVals = Array(iOrderGroupID) 'mscsOrderGrp.Value(ORDERGROUP_ID)
    ConfirmMsg iOrderGroupID, GenerateURL(MSCSSitePages.ViewUserOrder,
arrParams, arrParamVals)
    arrParams = Array(ORDER_ID)
    Response.Redirect(GenerateURL(MSCSSitePages.Confirm, arrParams,
arrParamVals))
End If
```

One change was the addition of an additional call to create the `arrParams` value. The new call involves the string `"ID"`. Note the call to the `GenerateURL` function. This function automatically generates the URL for a page. It is by taking advantage of a call to `GenerateURL` that the `IKEmailConfirmation2` component can include a link to the order status page in the message, along with the order number.

Creating a New Pipeline Component

Let's now construct the `IKEmailConfirmation2` component. Use the VBPipeline Component Wizard to create a new pipeline component called `IKEmailConfirmation2`. Define two properties: `IKEmailBCC` and `IKEmailFrom`.

Let's look at the `IKEmailConfirmation2` component's `Execute` method.

```
Private Function IPipelineComponent_Execute(ByVal objOrderForm As Object, ByVal
objContext As Object, ByVal lFlags As Long) As Long

 Dim objPipeCtx As CDictionary 'Pipe Context
 'Dim objItems As CSimpleList 'Items
 'Dim objMsgMgr As Object 'Message Manager
 Dim objAdoConn As ADODB.Connection
 Dim objAdoRS As ADODB.Recordset
 Dim objCdoMsg As CDO.Message
 Dim strSQLQry As String
 Dim strUserEmail As String
 Dim strOrderNumber As String


 On Error GoTo ErrCatch

 ' Return 1 for Success
 IPipelineComponent_Execute = 1

 ' Initialize the Pipe Context and Order Form

 Set objPipeCtx = objContext
 'Set objOrderForm = objOrderForm

 Set objAdoConn = CreateObject("ADODB.Connection")
 Set objCdoMsg = CreateObject("CDO.Message")
```

The code to this point is only marginally different to that in the `IKEmailConfirmation` component: the line that sets up the local `objPipeCtx` has not been removed. However, from this point on, we do encounter some significant differences.

Instead of setting the provider and connection information using individual component properties as was done in IKEmailConfirmation, the IKEmailConfirmation2 uses a dictionary value that contains this information:

```
With objAdoConn
   .ConnectionString = objPipeCtx("connection")
   .Open
End With
```

The next lines query the retail site database to find the information related to the order_id. Since the IKEmailConfirmation2 component runs after the retail site has created the ordergroup_id, the query succeeds. In addition to the original order_number, this query also obtains the user_id. For this reason the calling code does not define the customer as part of the order form dictionary used for this micropipe.

The result is that the query to get the user's e-mail address, highlighted below, uses the first query's user_id value instead of a the user_id value from the order form (as was the case in our old component).

```
strSQLQry = "Select order_number, user_id FROM OrderGroup WHERE ordergroup_id =
'" _
    & objOrderForm.order_id & "'"

Set objAdoRS = objAdoConn.Execute(strSQLQry)
If Not objAdoRS.EOF Then
  strOrderNumber = objAdoRS("order_number")
  strUserEmail = objAdoRS("user_id")
Else
  strOrderNumber = ""
End If

objAdoRS.Close
Set objAdoRS = Nothing
'Use the user id from the first query to find the user e-mail address.

strSQLQry = "Select u_email_address FROM UserObject WHERE g_user_id = '" _
    & strUserEmail & "'"
```
```
Set objAdoRS = objAdoConn.Execute(strSQLQry)

If Not objAdoRS.EOF Then
  strUserEmail = objAdoRS("u_email_address")
Else
  strUserEmail = ""
End If

objAdoRS.Close
objAdoConn.Close

If Not strUserEmail = "" And InStr(strUserEmail, "@") > 1 Then
With objCdoMsg
  .TextBody = "Your order has been validated and processing has begun." _
     & vbCrLf & "For tracking purposes please refer to order number: " _
     & strOrderNumber & vbCrLf
```

A local variable for the e-mail address is assigned, and message functionality is initiated.

Next, a link to the order status page is created. This requires adding a couple lines to the confirmation e-mail message, and referencing the custom dictionary value: `order_url`. We will see how this value is placed in the dictionary a little later.

```
    .TextBody = .TextBody & "In order to check your order feel free to return to our
site, and use the following link for additional information:"
    .TextBody = .TextBody & vbCrLf & objOrderForm("order_url")
  .To = strUserEmail
  .From = IKEmailFrom
  .BCC = IKEmailBCC
  .Subject = "Your order number: " & strOrderNumber
  .Send
End With
End If
Cleanup:
  Set objAdoConn = Nothing
  Set objAdoRS = Nothing
  Set objCdoMsg = Nothing
  Set objPipeCtx = Nothing
  Set objOrderForm = Nothing
  Exit Function

ErrCatch:
  ' Return 2 for Warning, or 3 for a fatal error
  IPipelineComponent_Execute = 3
  Resume Cleanup

End Function
```

The new `IKEmailConfirmation2` component is very similar to the original component with the exception that now it requires fewer parameters, is not associated with a specific pipeline stage of the order pipeline, and sends a URL to retrieve order data.

One of the key differences is that the `IKEmailConfirmation2` component will be called by a custom function utilizing a micropipe object. The following code shows the `ConfirmMsg` function which was added to `crdtcard.asp` in order to call the new pipeline. The first parameter is the `OrderGroupID` and the second is the URL to use as part of the confirmation e-mail:

```
Sub ConfirmMsg (ByVal iOrderGroupID, ByVal strUrl)
  Dim dOrder
  Dim dContext
  Dim lngFlags
  Dim oMicro
  Dim objComp
  Dim errVal

  Set dOrder = CreateObject("Commerce.Dictionary")
  Set dContext = CreateObject("Commerce.Dictionary")
  lngFlags = 0
```

The input parameters are assigned to the appropriate order form variables. The string URL is the generated URL to get to the order status page for the user, while the `iOrderGroupID` is the primary key on the Order Group table in the `retail_commerce` database. The third line takes the system wide variable that holds the Catalog Connection String and loads it into the Context dictionary for the call to the `IKEmailConfirmation2` component.

```
dOrder("order_url") = strUrl
dOrder("order_id") = iOrderGroupID
dContext("connection") = dictConfig.s_CatalogConnectionString

Set oMicro = CreateObject("Commerce.MicroPipe")

Set objComp = CreateObject("IKEmailConfirmation2.IKEmailPipeComp2")

objComp.IKEmailBCC = "BSheldon@interknowlogy.com"
objComp.IKEmailFrom = "IKStore@InterKnowlogy.com"

oMicro.SetComponent objComp
errVal = oMicro.Execute(dOrder, dContext, lngFlags)

Set dOrder = Nothing
Set dContext = Nothing
Set oMicro = Nothing
Set objComp = Nothing

End Sub
```

All told, there really wasn't that much custom code necessary in order to build this component. With a few additional modifications, this e-mail confirmation component could include the list of items ordered.

For the time being, our new component will send the following message to the user:

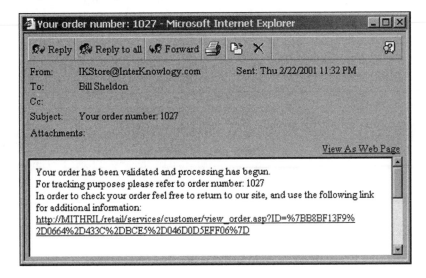

Pipeline Interfaces

The Visual Basic Pipeline Component Wizard abstracts many of the details of pipeline component implementation. For the majority of custom components, this is just fine: these details don't need to play a role in the development of the component. However, as we attempt to do more, and in particular, if we want to create an ATL component, knowledge of the interfaces becomes a necessity. The wizard demands that we pick out capabilities by interface type.

The table below describes some of the common interfaces related to pipelines. The first five interfaces are used by components created with the Visual Basic Pipeline interface, with the sixth being present in the UI component created in conjunction with a Visual Basic component.

Interface Name	Description
IPipelineComponent	The basic interface required to create a pipeline component, it is automatically present whenever the component is created with one of the two pipeline wizards (ATL or Visual basic).
IPersistDictionary	This interface persists dictionary information from Visual Basic components. This is an optional interface that allows the component to save values to its dictionary.
ISpecifyPipeline ComponentUI	This Visual Basic interface provides the Pipeline editor with the progid of the object to create when a component needs to support administrative modification of a component's dictionary.
IPipelineComponent Description	This interface creates a SAFEARRAY that defines the names of the external dictionary elements this component uses. While optional, a commercial component might consider this the pipeline equivalent of providing an interface definition.
IPipelineComponentAdmin	This interface reads and writes values to the component dictionary. In addition to the component itself, the PipelineComponentUI object specified by the ISpecifiyPipelineComponentUI uses this interface.
IPipelineComponentUI	Visual Basic objects normally support this interface in a separate component from the actual pipeline component. Having an object support this interface requires that the actual pipeline component support the IpersisDictionary, IPipelineComponentAdmin, and ISpecifyPipelineComponentUI interfaces.
IObjectControl	This standard COM interface, used in both ATL and Visual Basic, determines if the object can be pooled by COM+. Components created by the Visual Basic Pipeline wizard implement this interface with the setting of false. Using ATL it is possible to create components where this interface call returns true.
IPersistStreamInit	This is a standard COM interface used by ATL to persist the data associated with the object via a stream.
ISpecifyPropertyPages	This is another standard COM interface use by ATL when an object supports property pages.

There is only one required interface in order to support a pipeline component, IPipelineComponent. While the remaining interfaces are all optional, a few of them, especially on the Visual Basic side of things, have some logical dependencies.

For example, unless a dictionary is persisted, there is little reason to provide a user interface to edit it. One Visual Basic interface that is independent of others is the IpipelineComponentDescription interface. This interface is used to describe the dictionary items that are accessed by a pipeline component.

For example, in the case of the `IKEmailConfirmation` component, we could use this interface to describe the two order form dictionary items in the following way:

```
Private Function IPipelineComponentDescription_ValuesRead() As Variant

  IPipelineComponentDescription_ValuesRead = Array("order.order_id",
"order.user_id")

End Function
```

The implementation is very simple in VB since, by simply putting the names of the values read into an array that is then returned to the Pipeline Editor, users of the component can see what elements of the order form we will expect to access. Additionally, it indicates that the access is for reading, as in the case shown, or for writing, or any special context values the component expects to access. If a value is optional, this can be indicated as part of the free text string used to list the value.

Notice some of the interfaces specified above are ATL or VB specific. Because of the way the language implementations vary, the optional interfaces supported by components with different language implementations vary. In some cases, even though the interfaces are the same, the different language implementations appear quite different.

While the `IPipelineComponent` interface is the same for both Visual Basic and Visual C++ ATL, the implementation varies between the two languages. For example, let's look at the `Execute` function prototype for both Visual Basic and ATL.

In C++ ATL, it will look something like this:

```
HRESULT Execute(..IDispatch* pDispOrder,..IDispatch* pDispContext,..long
lFlags,..long* plErrorLevel);
```

And in VB:

```
Function Execute(pdispOrder As Object,pdispContext As Object,lFlags As Long) As
Long
```

In Visual Basic, the `Execute` function has three parameters: the order form dictionary, the context dictionary, and any flags. It returns a 1 for success, a 2 for warning or a 3 for a fatal error. In ATL, the implementation for the same `Execute` function of the `IPipelineComponent` interface has four parameters, and returns an HResult.

An HResult is a 32-bit value indicating the result of a COM call. A simple way to think of it is an index into a table of possible results. Some HResult return values indicate success, most notably 0x00000000. Other values indicate a failure status. A good listing of some of the hundreds of possible errors is located in the file `winerror.h`.

While the first three parameters of the execute `Function` for ATL are the same as those used in Visual Basic, the fourth parameter replaces the return value. It's not exactly the same, however, since while the Visual Basic return values go from 1 to 3 to indicate success, warning, or failure, in ATL those values start at 0 for success and go through 2 for failure.

The values are the same: it's just that in Visual Basic the error object is provided as part of the environment, whereas, the ATL function needs to return an HRESULT to indicate if an error has occurred in the component in addition to the error level.

The good news is that we have at our disposal what the Commerce Server documentation calls an ATL wizard. In this case, however, it isn't so much a wizard as a framework accessed from within a new ATL project.

Creating a Pipeline Component using C++ and ATL

Earlier in the chapter it was mentioned that in order to create a poolable component, the implementation needed to use C++. Specifically, the simplest way to carry out such an implementation is to use the Active Template Library (ATL) component wizard that ships with Commerce Server.

ATL was introduced to help simplify the C++ interface to COM. Unlike the older Microsoft Foundation Classes that were designed to wrap windows operating system functions, ATL was designed to be a lightweight high performance toolkit that would simplify interfaces for C++ developers. This section is going to look at setting up and using the ATL Wizard to create a simple component based on the scriptor component that we designed and implemented in Chapter 6.

As a component that is potentially called repeatedly during a session, and may be called from different pipelines – allowing it to take advantage of both faster execution and COM+ object pooling – the scriptor component introduced in Chapter 6 is a good candidate for implementation in ATL.

Additionally since this component goes to the database to determine the specific basket items that are special products, it is an excellent candidate to demonstrate accessing the database using ATL and OLE DB. The addition of a simple OLE DB query provides a reusable sample for other ATL components that goes beyond the sample provided as part of Commerce Server.

Unlike the Visual Basic wizard, the ATL pipeline component wizard isn't involved as part of the process of creating an ATL project. What the ATL wizard really provides is a set of source files containing support code providing support for the Commerce Server pipeline architecture. This chapter will look at some of the steps to customize these baseline files in order to create a component using ATL.

> *Note that while building an ATL component does involve using C++, we will be going through the sample in enough detail that even those who primarily work with Visual Basic should be able to follow and repeat the required steps in order to create custom ATL components.*

> *If you need more information on working with ATL I highly recommend Wrox's* Beginning ATL 3 Programming, *ISBN 1-861001-20-7.*

The ATL Pipeline Component Wizard

We must register the ATL wizard before we can use it. The DLL is located under the Commerce Server installation directory at `..\SDK\Tools\ATL Pipe Wizard\CommerceDLG.dll`. Perform the registration with the Visual C++ 6.0 development environment closed.

Prior to working with the ATL wizard it's important to note that due to the way that ATL works, using the ATL wizard is a two step process. Unlike VB where the wizard is tied in with the creation of the project, for ATL, the project creation is done separately before using the ATL pipeline component wizard.

So, first open the Visual C++ development environment. Select **New** from the file menu to start the **ATL COM AppWizard**. After entering the name of the project (let's call it `IKSpecialProduct`) and selecting the project folder, press the **OK** button to display the one and only screen of the ATL Wizard.

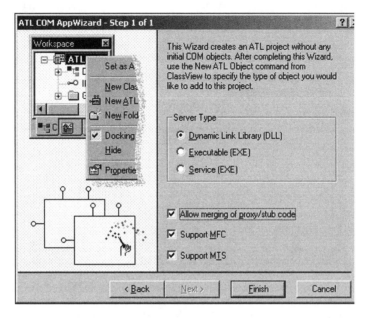

In the only step of the ATL wizard, allow the merging of proxy/stub code for the DLL, as this simplifies the generated project by not requiring a second DLL for marshaling information. Select support for the Microsoft Foundation Class (MFC) library to allow for many of the more programmer friendly classes and conventions, and choose to use the Microsoft Transaction Server (MTS) that provides the necessary include files to support COM+.

Click the **Finish** button to bring up the confirmation screen, and finish the generation of an ATL project.

After the creation of the files, the workspace display contains a class and set of global functions:

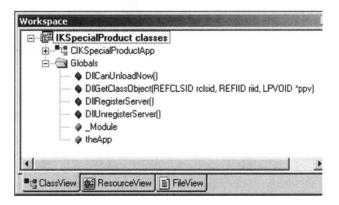

The `CIKSpecialProductApp` class is the primary class associated with the project while the **Globals** are functions and variables that can be accessed through traditional DLL calls. In looking around this project, notice that while there are some structures in place, it doesn't really do anything.

By going to the Build menu, it is possible to compile the project in its current state. The way to make the project useful is to add an interface and code to support the pipeline. The first step in this process is to use the ATL wizard to add some additional source files, along with their interfaces and functions to the project. In order to do this, go to the Insert menu and select New ATL Object... Once selected, this will trigger a dialog box:

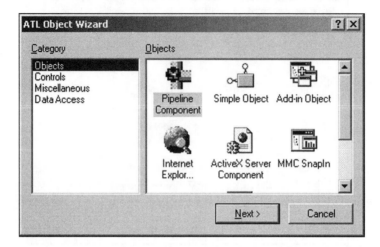

The actual order of the items in the object window of the ATL Object Wizard screen may vary, but the Pipeline Component icon should be available, so long as CommerceDLG.dll has been registered. This is the ATL Pipeline Wizard. Selecting it and hitting the Next button triggers the start of the wizard:

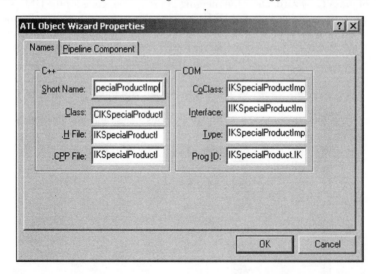

The entry of the Short Name triggers the creation of derived names for the other text boxes shown. For this project, the name IKSpecialProductImpl is used. This creates an interface called IIKSpecialProductImpl and a C++ class of CIKSpecialProductImpl. However, before the OK button on this screen is pressed, select the second tab to customize the pipeline settings.

The Pipeline settings tab allows for customization of the types of interfaces that the component will support:

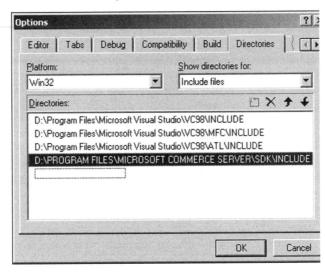

Since the `IPipelineComponent` interface is mandatory, it is not included in the list of interfaces. The list contains all of the available optional interfaces. For this example, the selected `IObjectControl` interface allows the object to expose itself as a pooled component. Additionally, this tab contains two sets of radio buttons. The first set indicates if this component is to support the Content Selection Framework. This framework allows for the targeting of advertisements to customers on our site. The second set of radio buttons deals with whether or not this component will be involved in the shipment process, which it is not.

After clicking **OK**, the development environment is populated with a large set of new classes, the new interface, and new globally accessible functions. The next step is to save your work and go to the build menu to build the project.

If it fails to build, and reports a problem finding the reference to `commerce.h`, you have a minor include file issue. The `commerce.h` file is one of several include files that the ATL components generated by the ATL Component Wizard rely on. To resolve the problem you need to map the directory where this file is located. We need to open the **Tools** menu and select the **Options** item. This triggers the opening of the **Options** dialog. Once this dialog is open, select the **Directories** tab. On this screen, add a new reference to the Commerce Server SDK include files directory:

Copying the `commerce.h` file to the project directory will not work. It will only result in other files from this same directory showing up as compile errors. To add a new entry, either double-click the empty square or use the new button that is just above the display windows. When selected, the accompanying browse button supports navigation to the appropriate directory. After selecting the correct directory, click the **OK** button to close the windows. Then attempt to build your project.

Another possible build problem occurs at the linking stage and involves the error message:

```
LINK fatal error LNK1104: cannot open file mfc42ud.lib.
```

This error is associated with the UNICODE version of the MFC libraries. It turns out that the default installation of Visual Studio doesn't always include the UNICODE library files. The solution is to go to the **Add/Remove Programs** dialog within the **Control Panel** and use the **Change/Remove** button to start the Visual Studio installer. Then go into the detail libraries for Visual C++ and select to install the Unicode libraries (shared and static) on your system. After doing this you should be able to successfully make the ATL project.

Registering the ATL Component

Now that the wizard has completed its task of getting the basic project set up, it's time to start customizing the code to do something. The first step is to add the code that will register this component as a pipeline component. To do this, first go to the project window and double-click on the function called `DLLRegisterServer()`. This is one of the original project functions shown earlier in this section as part of the project window. Double-clicking this will cause Visual Studio to open the `IKSpecialProjects.cpp` file, so that the start of the function is in the middle of the screen.

Inside the function you will see the following code.

```
// registers the object. typelib and all interfaces in typelib.
return _Module.RegisterServer(TRUE);
```

Unlike Visual Basic, ATL components are self registering. Since they don't use the Registration wizard it is necessary to add the code to conduct the registration in place of the lines above. However, it is necessary to continue to carry out the current registration of the object and its typelib. The code above is replaced in the `DLLRegisterServer` function with the following:

```
    HRESULT hr = S_OK;
// registers object, typelib and all interfaces in typelib
hr = _Module.RegisterServer(TRUE);

    if (FAILED(hr)) return hr;

    hr = RegisterCATID(CLSID_IKSpecialProductImpl,
                       CATID_MSCSPIPELINE_COMPONENT);

    if (FAILED(hr)) return hr;

    hr = RegisterCATID(CLSID_IKSpecialProductImpl,
                       CATID_MSCSPIPELINE_ANYSTAGE);

    if (FAILED(hr)) return hr;

    hr = RegisterName(CLSID_IKSpecialProductImpl,
                      L"IKSpecialProduct.IKSpecialProductImpl");

    return hr;
```

What this code does is first declare a variable `hr` to hold the return value from other functions. It then calls the original registration function to register the component on the system. If that is successful, then the next step is to call the function `RegisterCATID` to begin to set up the Implemented Categories keys that the registration wizard creates for VB components. The ATL Pipeline Wizard provides the function `RegisterCATID` to simplify the registration. The first parameter is the GUID of the interface. The second parameter needs to be one of the constant GUIDs associated with either pipeline identification, or with one of the stages that are part of the pipeline.

These values are available in the file `Pipe_stages.h`. In this case, the component is being register as a pipeline component, and for simplicity, since the possible stages that the scriptor version of this component has been associated with is unknown, the 'any stage' identifier.

Finally, the code calls the `RegisterName` function to set a recognizable `prog_id` for the component. The ATL wizard also creates this function and, like the `RegisterCATID` function, it's in the list of global functions in the Workspace window.

Once the registration is complete, the function returns the final status. Now that the coding is complete, save the project and attempt to build. If entry of the code was correct, the project will build without error. Instead of moving to the next stage of implementation, take a moment to open the pipeline editor. Select any pipeline and attempt to add a new component. When the dialog opens to select a component the `IKSpecialProduct.IKSPecialProductImpl` component should be present in the list. This means that the registration code works successfully and it's time to look at implementing the component logic.

Implementing the Component Logic

The goal of this object is to determine, using information contained in the database, how many of the current basket items are special products. The steps to do this involve connecting to the database, cycling through each item currently in the basket, and retrieving its status from the database. The best way of doing this involves using a stored procedure to access the SQL Server database.

Below is a stored procedure created for SQL Server, which dynamically builds a query against the appropriate catalog for the current product to determine if the associated product id has been flagged as a special product.

```
CREATE PROCEDURE usp_CheckSpecial
        @catalog as nvarchar(128),
        @productid as nvarchar(128),
        @specialproduct as int OUTPUT

  AS

Set Nocount on
-- default to not special
set @specialproduct = 0

DECLARE
        @query as nvarchar(500),
        @param as nvarchar(128)

Set @query = N'Select @temp = specialproduct from ' + @catalog +
N'_CatalogProducts where ProductID = @value and specialproduct = 1'
Set @param = N'@value nvarchar(128), @temp int'

execute sp_executesql @query, @param, @value=@productid, @temp=0
```

```
    if @@ROWCOUNT = 1
    BEGIN
        set @specialproduct = 1
    END

    return @@ERROR
```

This stored procedure accepts the catalog name and product id as input, and sets up an integer value to indicate the product's special status. It sets up a default for the output as false and then checks the database. The @temp value is used because we wish to return a single result, and not a recordset. When the query executes, it looks for the row with the selected product id and with the special product indicator set. Finding a match indicates a special product, and the output value is changed to reflect this. Finally the procedure returns with an error code if an error occurs. Of course, this particular procedure relies on the specialproduct column existing in each catalog that is part of our site.

The easy part is accessing this stored procedure from our ATL project. Rather then attempt to write the class to access the database by hand we are going to use another wizard. Just as above, when we used the ATL Pipeline wizard, open the Insert menu and select the New ATL Object... menu option. This time, when the dialog opens, use the list box on the left to select the Data Access category. This category contains two basic object templates that can be added to our component. The first is the data provider template that is used by those writing new OLE DB interfaces, and the other is the consumer object that we will select. Selecting the consumer object will start the ATL Object Wizard to edit the properties of our new object:

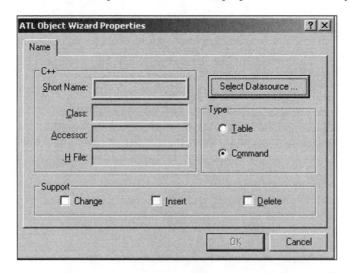

The class name is not immediately editable in this dialog because the Client Data Consumer wizard first requires the definition of a data source and data object. The class name will be automatically generated, based on the name of the database object that will be coupled to this class. The next step is to click the Select Datasource button and open the dialog shown below where the appropriate OLE DB provider is selected.

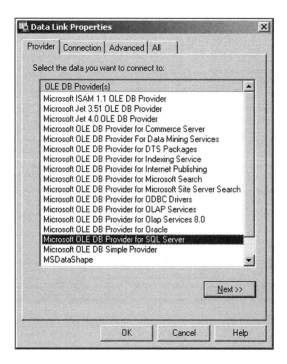

Clicking the Next or OK button, you are brought to the next tab in the Data Link properties dialog. This tab collects the parameters to create a database connection. You may recognize these parameters as the same properties that are part of the IKEmailConfirmation component property list. First enter the server machine name and then provide a valid database account. After a valid account is entered the dialog will connect to the database and allow you to select the database of choice from the drop-down box. Finally, it's always a good idea to test your new connection before clicking the OK button to continue.

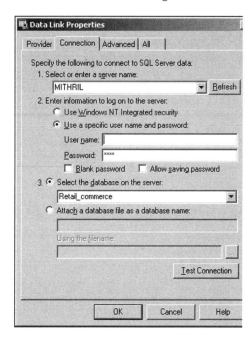

381

After selecting OK from the Data Link Properties dialog, the wizard brings up the Select Database Table dialog. This dialog allows for the selection of the table, stored procedure or other database object that will be coupled to the ATL class we are generating. The display below shows the usp_CheckSpecial stored procedure that was created earlier, already selected. Clicking OK will return us to the ATL Object Wizard Property dialog.

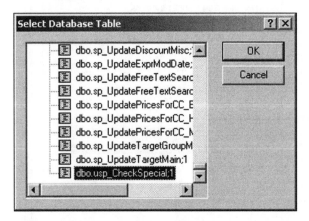

On our return to the ATL Object Wizard Property dialog, all of the data fields will be active and have default values. Clicking OK triggers Visual Studio to create the header (.h) file for our class with the name shown in ATL Object Wizard Property dialog and adds the new file to your project.

The code for the classes we have created in our wizard-generated file is below. The first section defines the accessor class used to access the data involved in using the stored procedure. This generated code is used to map the C++ variables to their comparative values in the selected database object. It includes a member variable to hold product SKU, the special product indicator and the return value. These variables are then associated with placeholders in the database command that executes the stored procedure, as shown in the DEFINE_COMMAND statement:

```
// dbouspCheckSpecial1.H : Declaration of the CdbouspCheckSpecial1 class

#ifndef __DBOUSPCHECKSPECIAL1_H_
#define __DBOUSPCHECKSPECIAL1_H_

class CdbouspCheckSpecial1Accessor
{
public:
    LONG m_RETURNVALUE;
    TCHAR m_catalog[129];
    TCHAR m_productid[129];
    LONG m_specialproduct;

BEGIN_PARAM_MAP(CdbouspCheckSpecial1Accessor)
    SET_PARAM_TYPE(DBPARAMIO_OUTPUT)
    COLUMN_ENTRY(1, m_RETURNVALUE)
    SET_PARAM_TYPE(DBPARAMIO_INPUT)
    COLUMN_ENTRY(2, m_catalog)
    COLUMN_ENTRY(3, m_productid)
    SET_PARAM_TYPE(DBPARAMIO_INPUT | DBPARAMIO_OUTPUT)
    COLUMN_ENTRY(4, m_specialproduct)
END_PARAM_MAP()
```

```
DEFINE_COMMAND(CdbouspCheckSpecial1Accessor, _T("{ ? = CALL dbo.usp_CheckSpecial;1
(?,?,?) }"))

    // You may wish to call this function if you are inserting a record and wish
to
    // initialize all the fields, if you are not going to explicitly set all of
them.
    void ClearRecord()
    {
        memset(this, 0, sizeof(*this));
    }
};
```

The next section of the generated code contains the functions that will be called to execute actions against the database. The first function, Open, while very useful, actually does a bit more than we probably want. It first calls the function OpenDataSource to open a connection to the database, and then calls OpenRowset to actually execute the command against the database. While this type of one stop shop function can be great, in our situation, where we will be calling the database in a loop, a function that repeatedly opens a connection to the datasource would require that we both close the connection between calls, and pay a price to reestablish our relationship with the existing connection (COM+ could cache the connection).

As a result, the OpenDataSource function provides a public interface where we can create the connection and return control to our application. Of course, this implies that we are going to actually access the database separately using the OpenRowset function, but first let's look at what the OpenDataSource function does.

It first creates local datasource and property set objects. It then begins to populate the database property set object with the specific values we defined for our connection. If we wanted to integrate this component to automatically use our site's database connection settings, we would want to modify this function to accept these values as parameters, and pass in the actual connection information at run time.

Once the parameters have been set, the function makes a call using the datasource object to actually create a connection to the database. If this call succeeds, then the goal of this function can be met on its last line, where it makes a call to associate an open database connection with the class's session object. The session member used in the last line of this function is actually defined on the last line in the class's implementation.

If you intend to do several different database calls, you should actually consider moving the OpenDataSource function's capabilities to a class other then the individual connection. Creating a session object that is separate from the individual database objects allows you to instantiate the connection and then modify the OpenRowset code to accept a session parameter, thus providing more complete reuse of your database connection.

The OpenRowset method is the trigger to actually access the stored procedure with the DEFINE_COMMAND statement. The execute method of our pipeline component calls the OpenRowset function to execute the stored procedure. In addition to having a valid session (either the member variable as shown or one that is provided as a parameter) this function relies on the calling object to have set each parameter (which were defined earlier as part of the accessor).

Finally, keep in mind that since the stored procedure does not return a recordset, this function will not return one. Instead, the execution of the stored procedure loads the stored procedure output parameter value in the m_specialproduct variable defined as part of the accessor.

```
class CdbouspCheckSpecial1 : public
CCommand<CAccessor<CdbouspCheckSpecial1Accessor> >
{
public:
    HRESULT Open()
    {
        HRESULT              hr;

        hr = OpenDataSource();
        if (FAILED(hr))
              return hr;

        return OpenRowset();
    }
    HRESULT OpenDataSource()
    {
        HRESULT              hr;
        CDataSource db;
        CDBPropSet  dbinit(DBPROPSET_DBINIT);

        dbinit.AddProperty(DBPROP_AUTH_PASSWORD, OLESTR("C2KRulz"));
        dbinit.AddProperty(DBPROP_AUTH_USERID, OLESTR("IKShopper"));
        dbinit.AddProperty(DBPROP_INIT_CATALOG, OLESTR("Retail_commerce"));
        dbinit.AddProperty(DBPROP_INIT_DATASOURCE, OLESTR("MITHRIL"));
        dbinit.AddProperty(DBPROP_INIT_LCID, (long)1033);
        dbinit.AddProperty(DBPROP_INIT_PROMPT, (short)4);
        hr = db.Open(_T("SQLOLEDB.1"), &dbinit);
        if (FAILED(hr))
              return hr;

        return m_session.Open(db);
    }
    HRESULT OpenRowset()
    {
        return CCommand<CAccessor<CdbouspCheckSpecial1Accessor>
>::Open(m_session);
    }
    CSession    m_session;
};

#endif // __DBOUSPCHECKSPECIAL1_H_
```

There is really only one more step in order to start using the class. A reference to the definition of CdbouspCheckSpecial1 class is required as part of the source code where it is used. To do this, add the following line to the top of the file containing the IPipelineComponent Execute method.

```
#include "dbouspCheckSpecial1.h"
```

Since this line goes with the execute method, and since the IpipelineComponent was defined in the IKSpecialProductImpl object, expand that object in the workspace window and double-click the execute method which is part of that object. Once again, Visual Studio will bring the desired function up in the middle of the screen. Scroll to the top of the function and add the include statement so that the code in this file will reference the new database object.

In order to have the component call the database class that we generated, we need to customize the Execute function.

The code for the Execute function starts with the basic function header, followed by the declaration of all the variables that are used in the function. Many of the variables, such as MoneyInfo, Orderform, and Item are defined based on type information created in the project by the ATL Component Wizard. Without the wizard generated classes and definitions, much of the dictionary manipulation would require us to spend hours writing the code to support custom structures such as the Commerce Server Dictionary object. Instead, we have been able to use a wizard to generate the framework necessary to interact with Commerce Server 2000.

```
STDMETHODIMP CIKSpecialProductImpl::Execute (
    IDispatch* pdispOrder,
    IDispatch* pdispContext,
    LONG  lFlags,
    LONG*  plErrorLevel)
{
    HRESULT hRes = S_OK;
    CdbouspCheckSpecial1 objDBConn;
    CMoneyInfo MoneyInfo;
    CSmartDict Orderform;
    CSmartList OrderformItems;
    CSmartDict Item;
    CComVariant vtItem;
    CComBSTR bstrProduct;
    CComBSTR bstrCatalog;
    LONG  lIndx;
    LONG  lLimit;
    LONG  lngSpecial = 0;

    // Initialize for success.
    *plErrorLevel = 0;
```

Unlike the VB Wizard, the ATL wizard really expects us to create the implementation on our own. While many of the variables declared, such as HRESULT and the Money, Dictionary and List classes will be discussed later, we should note a few things. Note that objDBConn is defined as a CdbouspCheckSpecial1 class. For those more familiar with VB, this is the equivalent of using 'Dim objDBConn as New CdbouspCheckSpecial1', in that it both defines the variable type and assigns it a value: in this case, an object reference.

It is possible to make a declaration that defines only the object type by using the CdbouspCheckSPecial1 * objDBConn; syntax. This type of pointer declaration then requires a later statement to assign an actual object reference to the variable using the objDBConn = new CdbouspCheckSpecial1; syntax, which should be recognizable to experienced VB programmers.

Just as with VB, ATL must free objects created using the new statement. ATL uses the delete keyword to accomplish the same role that Set obj = nothing does in VB.

To simplify working with COM from C++, the ATL library provides the CComVariant and CComBSTR classes. Those of you with at least some C++ experience have undoubtedly heard about needing to count references and allocate memory. It is possible as a C++ developer to get very wrapped up in the seemingly simple tasks of ensuring that all paths release references and memory correctly when developing your components. However, the CComVariant class was designed to automatically manage reference counting in conjunction with the CComBSTR class managing string memory.

By creating an instance of the CComVariant class and then using it to hold a reference to a COM component the developer does not need to worry about the reference count. Instead, the class manages this for the developer. The CComBSTR class is very similar in that it manages the allocation, deallocation and reallocation of memory associated with a BSTR. By using these classes a C++ developer can allow the framework to manage resources while concentrating on the business logic of the problem to be solved.

Following the initialization of the variables and the result, it is necessary to put in some code to support the dictionary framework. The dictionaries that store related data in the Commerce Server 2000 architecture are very customizable. However, this means that there is a certain amount of code required to related values. In the case of getting an order form, the first thing to do is to initialize a helper class. These are provided by the ATL Pipeline Component wizard. The CmoneyInfo class is used to manage the currency data associated with an order form. It is initialized from the currency settings that are present in the pdispOrder dictionary object that is passed to the execute function.

Once the current currency has been initialized, another ATL Pipeline Component wizard generated helper class, the Orderform class, can be initialized with the pdispOrder dictionary, a string for its identifier and the MoneyInfo object. Once initialized, this object contains the list of order form items that the code will iterate through to determine if any are special items. In order to support that, we create a CSmartList object and pass it to the order form object to populate it with the list of elements. The CSmartList object is another helper class that was automatically generated by the ATL Pipeline Component Wizard. The code then gets the number of items that were placed into the smart list object, and then attempts to open a connection to the database.

Each of the preceding tasks includes the possibility of failure. If a failure occurs, rather then throwing an error that the calling program may not be able to handle, COM components in C++ return an Hresult. While there are thousands of Hresults, those that indicate failure can be recognized by the FAILED macro. As we will see later, there is an accompanying SUCCEEDED macro that will check to see if the associated Hresult indicates success instead of failure. For our purposes, if any of the functions to set up our list of order items or open the data source fail, the object returns the failed Hresult, so that the calling code can examine the problem, and an error condition is returned for the calling pipeline.

```
hRes = MoneyInfo.Init(pdispOrder, L"");
if (FAILED(hRes))
{
        *plErrorLevel = 2;
        return hRes;
}


hRes = Orderform.Init(pdispOrder, L"orderform", &MoneyInfo);
if (FAILED(hRes))
{
        *plErrorLevel = 2;
        return hRes;
}

hRes = Orderform.GetValue(L"Items", OrderformItems);
if (FAILED(hRes))
{
        *plErrorLevel = 2;
        return hRes;
}

hRes = OrderformItems.GetCount(&lLimit);
```

```
    if (FAILED(hRes))
    {
        *plErrorLevel = 2;
        return hRes;
    }

    hRes = objDBConn.OpenDataSource();
    if (FAILED(hRes))
    {
        // Return an error if the database connection failed.
        *plErrorLevel = 2;
        return hRes;
    }
```

Next, the number of products in the list is used as the control value to limit the number of passes to retrieve each value in the list. For each item in the list, the code attempts to get that item, using a generic variant to hold the data. If the data is returned from the list, then the item data is formatted with the assistance of the MoneyInfo class using the Init method of the smart dictionary object.

As long as the items values can be initialized correctly in the Item instance of the smart dictionary object, the Product_id and product_catalog values associated with the current item are retrieved and passed to the database class we created earlier. Finally, if the object is flagged in the database as being a special product, the count of special products is incremented by one.

If any of these steps fails, then a warning is flagged for Commerce Server, and the break command is used to exit the loop and halt processing. Regardless of how the loop ends, we need to close the connection to the database as soon as it is no longer needed, so the first command following the end of the for loop takes care of closing the connection.

After the connection has been closed the final step – so long as the loop was not exited due to a failed Hresult – is to update the order form with the count of special products that have been included on the order form. This is done by using the PutValue method to add the new value to the order form dictionary using the string provided as the name of the value. The PutValue method will either add a new dictionary value or overwrite an existing value.

```
    for (lIndx = 0; lIndx<lLimit; lIndx++)
    {
        hRes = OrderformItems.GetItem(lIndx,&vtItem);
        if (FAILED(hRes))
        {
            *plErrorLevel = 1;
            break;
        }

        hRes = Item.Init(&vtItem, L"item", &MoneyInfo);
        if (FAILED(hRes))
        {
            *plErrorLevel = 1;
            break;
        }
        hRes = Item.GetValue(L"product_id", &bstrProduct);
        if(FAILED(hRes))
        {
```

```
                        *plErrorLevel = 1;
                        break;
                }
                hRes = Item.GetValue(L"product_catalog", &bstrCatalog);
                if(FAILED(hRes))
                {
                        *plErrorLevel = 1;
                        break;
                }

                wcscpy(objDBConn.m_productid, bstrProduct);
                wcscpy(objDBConn.m_catalog, bstrCatalog);
                hRes = objDBConn.OpenRowset();
                if(FAILED(hRes))
                {
                        *plErrorLevel = 1;
                        break;
                }

                if (objDBConn.m_specialproduct == 1)
                        lngSpecial++;
        }
        objDBConn.Close();

        if (SUCCEEDED(hRes))
        {
                // update the order form.
                Orderform.PutValue(L"SpecialProductCount", lngSpecial);
        }

    return hRes;
}
```

Finally, although the component was initially created to be able to support pooling, the settings associated with pooling were not modified. It is a very straightforward task to open the IsPoolable method call and modify it to let COM+ know that this object can be retained in memory, by setting the return value to 1 for true.

```
BOOL CIKSpecialProductImpl::CanBePooled()
{
     return 1;
}
```

That's it! At this point, compile the component again. Once compiled, not only is it visible from the Pipeline Editor, it is possible to insert it into a pipeline. Using the Pipeline Editor, open the basket pipeline and add the component in place of the Scriptor component which implements the same function.

Summary

We have covered a lot of ground in this chapter. Specifically, we have investigated:

❑   The different types of pipelines and which components work best with them.

❑   Installing and using the Visual Basic Component Wizard.

❑   Editing Visual Basic components.

❑   Testing using the Micropipe component.

❑   The Visual Basic Pipeline Component Registration Wizard.

❑   Using the Commerce Server 2000 tools for debugging.

❑   Pipeline Component Interfaces.

❑   Creating an ATL project, and using the ATL Pipeline Component Wizard to extend the project.

❑   Creating a simple stored procedure and its accompanying C++ classes for simple database access.

❑   Editing the generated ATL code to create a Pooled Component.

Any of the components that were part of this chapter will provide an excellent starting point for custom components. Take advantage of the code to improve the user experience on your site.

In the next chapter, we're going to change tack and look at the Commerce Server 2000 Content Targeting System.

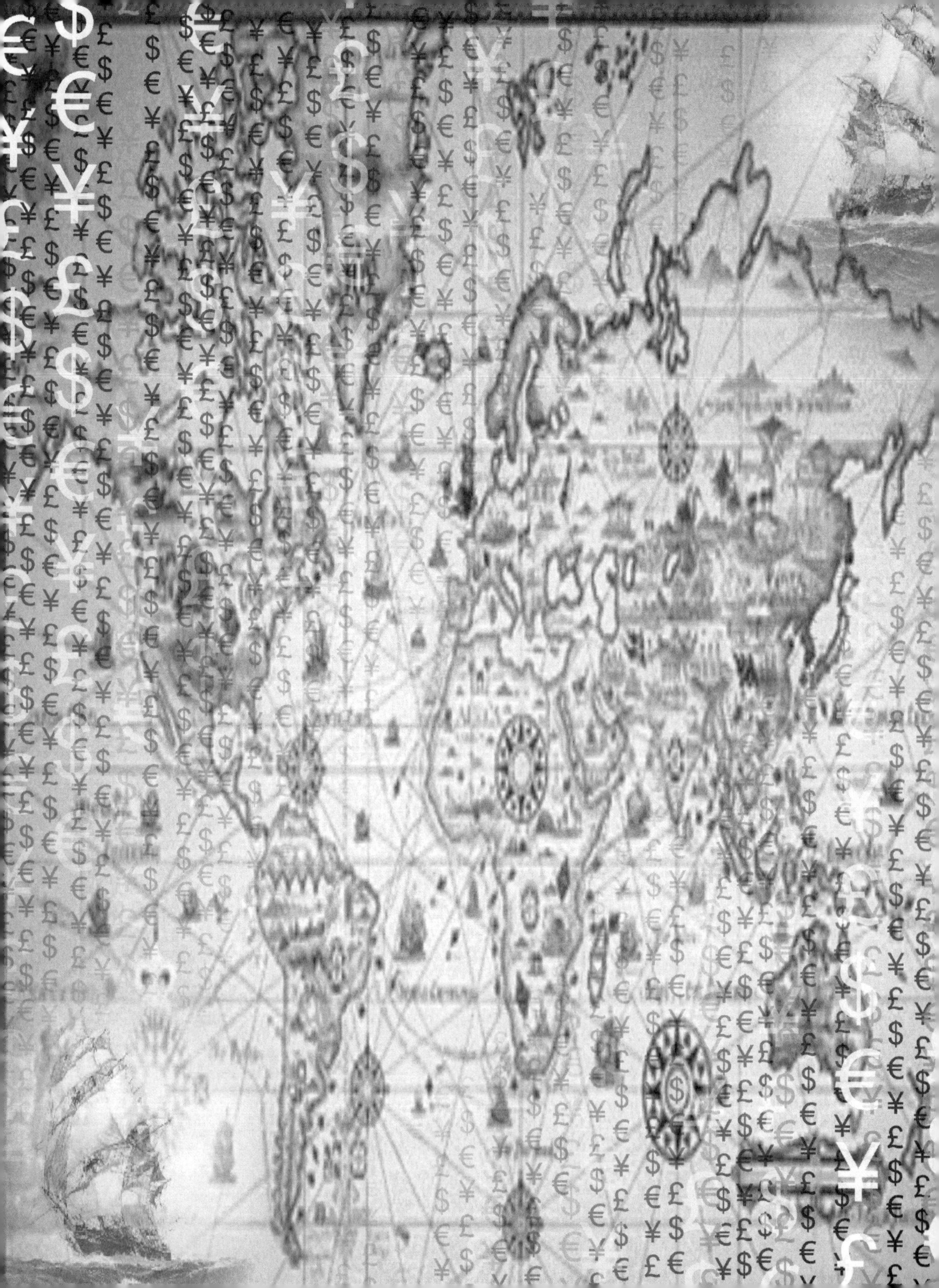

8

Campaigns and Content Selection

Introduction

As you may have noticed in the last few years, the Internet has become one of the largest ever sources of information. While this has many positive aspects, it can also lead to information overload, making it increasingly difficult to find specific information that's relevant to your needs. As a result of this, the ability to populate a website with informative content that's relevant to individual users (or well-defined groups of users) is extremely desirable to any sort of business with an online presence.

A website typically consists of a variety of **content elements**, each of which provides information to users in a consistent format. This can take many forms, such as ads, discounts, promotions, available services, general information, and streaming media.

Each of these will pass through a number of stages as it is produced, managed, integrated, and made available to appropriate users. For example, a typical content element will be produced by the site's creative team, then handed over to the development team for incorporation into a set of web pages (which may or may not use scripting to place it dynamically) on a development server. A site manager will then want to ensure that the content is valid and correctly presented – this process will be repeated until the content has been ensured for quality. This finally leads to a publication process, which probably consists of uploading the files to a production server for display on the public website. This can be both costly and time consuming; it can also limit your site's ability to react to market changes and provide relevant content on a timely, consistent basis.

Your task as a technical specialist is to provide a way for your organization to rapidly develop, deploy, and manage website content, and maximize the effectiveness of that content. That means building a flexible and dynamic content delivery system that doesn't require low-level recoding every time a new marketing strategy comes into your manager's sights. You'll probably find yourself being asked to tailor the site in one (or more) of the following ways:

❑ Personalize the buying experience with targeted merchandising.

❑ Deliver optimal content for a given user in a given context.

❑ Create, analyze, and manage personalized and targeted discounts, and direct marketing and advertising campaigns.

❑ Add predictive capabilities to your website.

❑ Target ads or discounts to users of a specific profile. For example, you can target ads to female users who visit your site three times a week, and who have purchased three or more products.

❑ Create and schedule campaigns for customers who compete within the same industry. The competing ads are never shown on the same page.

❑ Charge your advertising customers based on the number of ad requests or clicks they want their ads to receive.

❑ Charge your advertising customers based upon the page on which they want their ad to display.

In fact, this is precisely what the Commerce Server 2000 Targeting System sets out to help you do – as you'll see if you've checked out the documentation (see 'Commerce Server Features at a Glance'). As we've seen, these tasks can also be broken down into **explicit** and **implicit** targeting, according to the origin of the information being used to specify the target audience.

In many respects, the 'backbone' of the Targeting System is the **Content Selection Framework** (CSF), a self-contained platform on which you can build systems for delivering targeted content. It effectively allows you to modularize your site's content delivery process, separating it from the static architecture in the same way that the Profile and Product Catalog systems do with user profiles and product catalogs respectively. As we'll see later on in the chapter, it consists of various components that can be used to score, cache, filter, and format elements of content.

One simple custom application of the CSF might be to manage the presentation of a DVD catalog on the front page of an online DVD store. Perhaps you want to show all titles due for release in the next seven days – by specifying an appropriate data store (the DVD catalog database) and a validation term (release date is 0-7 days from now), we might use the CSF to provide appropriate titles for display each time that page is requested. As soon as we hit tomorrow, the list of titles will be updated accordingly; likewise when the catalog is updated with new titles – with no intervention at all required from the site manager or administrator, let alone the developer.

Of course, examples such as ad placements and product discounts may require active intervention from the business manager – as we'll see later on, the BizDesk can be closely integrated with the CSF to enable the easy configuration of content source and delivery terms – this puts business users in a good position to deliver a rapid response to the ever-changing behavioral habits of their customers.

So, the CSF can be used to programmatically handle many of the day-to-day processes that might otherwise require developer or administrator intervention, and put the power in the hands of the business decision makers while maintaining a high rate of performance. It can also help you to:

❏   Specify content ranking, prioritizing one element over another

❏   Schedule content delivery for specific dates and times

❏   Score content based on its relevance

❏   Format content in a meaningful and consistent fashion

❏   Track the performance and effectiveness of content

❏   Target content to specific users and to specific locations on a website

❏   Prevent similar content being displayed more than once on a single web page

❏   Add plug-in components to extend the processes involved during content selection

Thanks to the BizDesk interface, most of the specific configuration details (choice of campaign, identification of segmentation criteria, and so on) can be left to managers; but you'll still benefit from an understanding of the mechanisms by which Commerce Server implements this functionality, and that's what we shall look at in this and the next chapter.

Campaigns

Campaigns are effectively marketing programs that use various content channels (such as web pages, e-mail) to deliver specific content to selected users. They serve a multitude of different purposes, and might well be used to help increase your market share, or introduce new products, as well as their more pedestrian (though no less important) role in personalizing the site. As we saw back in Chapter 1, it's not hard to set up a campaign that will play to your users' tastes, and encourage them to come back for more – it can literally be as simple as giving them news or discounts on their favorite toys.

Each campaign can hold multiple **campaign items** (individual ads, discounts, etc.). Each of these is based on a pre-defined 'template', a **campaign item type**, which specifies a generic structure for each type of campaign item. CS2K is provided with a few standard item types for online campaigning, namely:

❏   Advertising – embedding advertisements in the pages of the website

❏   Discounts – selling specific items at discounted rates

❏   Direct Mail – send news, ads, or other site content directly to a user's registered e-mail account

Other campaign item types you might implement using the CSF include:

❏   Cross-selling – displaying catalog items that complement the user's current selection

❏   Up-selling – suggesting possible upgrades to the user's current selection; for example, a deluxe version or special edition of the product they have selected

❏   Coupons – rewarded to a user on product purchase and redeemable against future purchases

❏   Headlines – latest product releases or news items

So, for example, a campaign for a new product promotion might include three campaign items: an ad banner on the home page; a personalized direct mail message announcing the new product; and a discount campaign item offering 15 percent off all orders received during April.

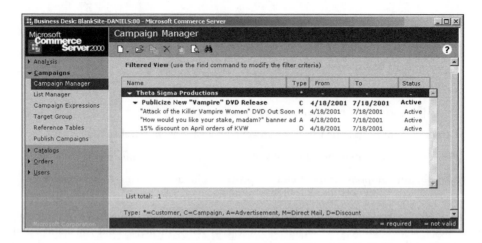

By defining specific *types* of campaign item, CS2K separates the nuts and bolts of campaign implementation from the definition of specific content targeting rules, which we really want to leave in the hands of a business manager. They can then target and re-target campaigns items at specific user groups, or at specific pages on the site, and respond quickly to changing trends and up-to-the-minute BIA reports. BizDesk's Campaign Manager module lets managers implement and configure specific campaigns (based on the pre-defined campaign item types) so as to maximize their day-to-day usefulness.

Campaigns (and their constituent items) are grouped by **customer** – for example, other companies to whom we've sold ad space. All campaigns created for a particular customer can make use of a single set of information defined for that customer.

All campaign items within a campaign have a common customer and schedule. For instance, in the sports section of a Newspaper site, an advertiser might purchase 10,000 ad requests within a week to users from the South. The advertiser might decide to run three different ads to fill those 10,000 requests and then see which one of the three ads creates the highest click rate. Each ad is a campaign item within the overall campaign.

By default, the Content Targeting System supports the following functionality:

❑ Targeting content according to specific profile attributes. Each data element in the current user's profile can be tested against a specified **expression** to determine whether that user should be considered for a specific element of targeted content.

❑ Ensuring that competing content elements are never shown on the same page. Each item has an **industry** property, which is used to determine whether one conflicts with another.

❑ Charging campaign **customers** based on the number of times their content appears. In the case of ads, we can also count how many times users have actually clicked-through to the customer's site. As we'll see, the Content Selection Framework considers these counts in **ranking** content elements.

Content Selection Framework

As we saw demonstrated in Chapter 1, the CSF is principally used to help manage campaigns (the delivery of ads, promotions, and so on), but it can also be used to rank, select, and schedule *any* type of content, whether it's an element in a displayed web page or part of a mail shot.

- **Scoring** – each item is assigned a floating-point value that is used to reflect how well suited it is to a particular context and user – a sequence of pipeline components will test specific targeting criteria and modify this value accordingly. High-ranking items are most likely to show up on the user's system.

- **Filtering** – systematic elimination of specific content items, which can be filtered on any string, integral, or array column. A filter can either require that content items have a particular column value, or may *exclude* content items in which the column contains particular values. Filters can also use sets of values, so that content items with any one of the values in the set will meet the filter requirements and will be passed through.

- **Selecting** – winning content is picked from the ranked items. This may simply involve selecting the item with the highest score. Alternatively, the scores are used to weight a random selection.

- **Formatting** – the winning content item(s) must be appropriately formatted as strings before being sent to the user. The end result is a SimpleList object of string values, with each list entry containing the string that represents a particular content item.

- **Recording** – in order to compute the score of an advertisement, it's necessary to record all instances of that ad being served or clicked upon.

You should note right away that CSF is *not* a content management system – it does not have workflow and does not understand the concepts of content approval. If you require this sort of functionality, then you may want to consider certain third-party solutions that integrate well with Commerce Server 2000 to provide this capability.

In order to understand how CSF works, we must first consider each of its main components:

- The **ContentSelector** object provides a single point of access to the content selection process. By hiding the messy details from the ASP developer, it allows them to focus on providing data on the current page context. It invokes an appropriate Content Selection pipeline and returns the modified content as a SimpleList of formatted content strings.

The CSF combines these strings with predefined **content templates** (with different templates used by each campaign item type) to provide consistent style and formatting for each type. These consist of a mixture of static text and template variables into which the selected content can be placed.

The rest of the framework consists of objects made specifically for content caching, filtering, scoring, and formatting:

- **CacheManager** – This object provides simple cache management services. It can periodically invoke COM components to fill a cache object (usually a Dictionary component) with information used in the content delivery process. It can also be used to invoke components that write out information collected during the content delivery process, such as ad request counts.

- **CacheLoader** – This loads information from external content sources into local memory, so as to provide scaleable access to data that would otherwise require high resource utilization. Cache loaders in combination with the CacheManager are critical to any website for providing a scaleable way to access data and to ensure that the data is not outdated.

❏ **ContentListFactory** – Used by the CSF to store a complete list of available content elements, with each element in the list corresponding to a specific element. When a web page is viewed, the CSF can select items from this content pool that are likely to be relevant to the current user and context. This serves as a container for creating and storing ContentList objects in memory.

❏ **ContentListSchema** – Used to hold a schema that describes the layout of a content list. This allows the CSF to correctly interpret the listed content data, and usefully perform tasks such as filtering and scoring on each of the elements.

❏ **ContentList** – This object is instantiated by the ContentListFactory to serve as a dedicated content pool for each specific request.

These objects can be used to build entirely new content decision applications and extend existing ones. The diagram below illustrates how they interact with one another:

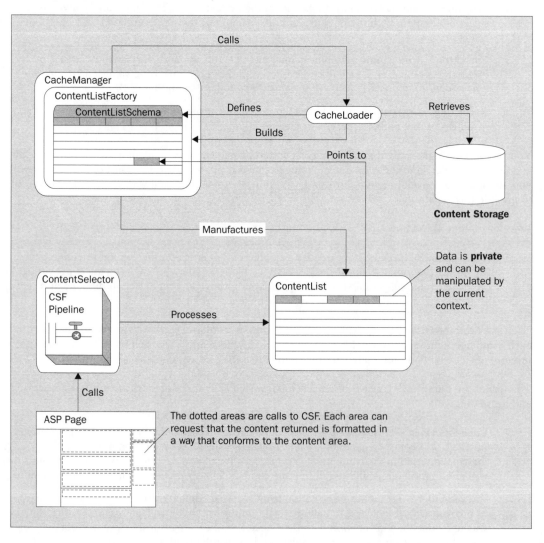

Consider what might happen when a user requests one of the ASP pages on your site:

1. The server executes the code in the requested page, which sets page context properties and requests content from the CSF.

2. The CSF initializes cached content for use by the current request, with a filtering routine ensuring that only relevant content is selected.

3. A method of scoring is applied to each content item by a specialized process (which will be specific to each type of content).

4. An event recording mechanism records the request event in memory.

5. CSF formats the selected content items using a template that brings together content properties, page context, and global context.

6. The formatted items are returned to the ASP page, which sends this content to the user's browser.

Let's assume that the user now clicks on a content item:

1. The user is sent to a special 'event recording' page, which invokes a content event recording process.

2. The user is redirected to the URL that the content points to, and the content is rendered.

After a specified refresh interval expires, a background process will fire:

1. An event writing process flushes the recorded events that are in memory to a database for analysis.

2. New content is loaded into memory for use by CSF.

Content Pipelines

In many situations, the Content Selection Framework needs a flexible, extensible, linear processing engine to do its job. Consider the delivery of ads and discounts – the CSF must take a collection of content elements, then filter, score, and format them according to a static (user-specific) context. Sound familiar? It should come as no great surprise to learn that pipelines are used as the main driving force behind many applications of the CSF. More specifically, both ads and discounts are served up by the CSF via pipelines.

Content Selection Pipeline

As you can see if you create a new pipeline based on ContentSelection.pct, content pipelines are really defined by no more than a particular sequence of stages. Given the wide range of possible applications it may be put to, the design of this template wisely makes no assumptions about the actual pipeline components that might be used. Instead, we're presented with a list of generic tasks, and left to add functionality ourselves.

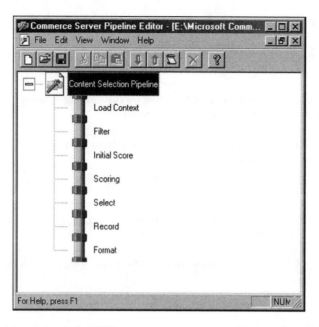

When a page request is received, the CSF `ContentSelector` object will send the pipeline a specially generated `ContentList`. The default stages through which this object then pass are as follows:

Stage	Purpose	Components Provided
Load Context	Initialize context values based on data from a user profile, ASP session, or cookie.	`InitCSFPipeline` `LoadHistory`
Filter	Apply specified filters to the ContentList	`FilterContent`
Initial Score	Set initial ad scores to ensure required delivery frequency	`AdvertisingNeedOfDelivery` (ads only)
Scoring	Adjust content scores according to targeting criteria	`ScoreDiscounts` (discounts only) `HistoryPenalty` `EvalTargetGroups`
Select	Pick highest scoring content	`SelectWinners`
Record	Store selection information in database, server log file, or history string	`RecordHistory` `SaveHistory` `RecordEvent` `IISAppendToLog`
Format	Format remaining content elements as HTML or XML for return to the web page	`FormatTemplate`

Bear in mind that while the Content Selection pipeline can be used to *select* discounts, the actual discounts are applied by the **OrderDiscount** pipeline component in an Order Processing pipeline.

Event Processing Pipeline

There are actually two pipelines associated with each CSF application. As well as a content selection pipeline for handling content delivery, an **event processing** pipeline (based on `EventProcessing.pct`) is responsible for handling events such as ad clicks, which don't involve any content retrieval.

By default, this consists of three stages: LoadContext, Record, and Format. At present though, Microsoft are only supporting the second of these (with components `IISAppendToLog` and `RecordEvent`). The other stages are provided for 'custom extensions and future enhancements'

Advertisements

Ads consist of a number of components that are specifically geared towards dealing with advertising scenarios such as **industry conflict prevention** (ensuring that conflicting ads don't appear on the same page) and **Need Of Delivery** (NOD – used to determine scheduling frequency from the number of purchased ads outstanding and the time remaining in the schedule). If you're familiar with Site Server 3.0 Commerce Edition you may like to note that this item type is essentially a component-based implementation of the old Ad Server. It supports two types of ad:

- ❑ **Paid ads** – Third-party content that's served according to the NOD formula.

- ❑ **House ads** – Native content that can be served in the event that there are no paid ads available (or if all the paid ads that *are* available are ahead of their delivery schedules).

House ad content can consist of just about anything you choose – Microsoft suggests using them to sell off old stock at discount rates, but this is just one of many possible options. Note that if there were no house ads on hand, you might find your pages served with an empty ad banner – the CSF would return an empty `list` – so it's important to have at least one or two of them on your site.

Let's explore some of this functionality via the BizDesk, which we can use to determine *when* an ad is displayed, *where* it is displayed, and to *whom*. On creating an ad, we can specify the following:

- ❑ Exposure limit – The number of times the ad can be shown per user session.

- ❑ Weight – A way to specify how frequently an ad is displayed, relative to all of the campaign items for a given customer. Note that weight only applies to ads that are goaled at the campaign-level; if a paid ad is goaled at the item level (that is, a fixed number of ads is to be served in a given period) then weighting will not be applied.

- ❑ Page Groups – A set of related web pages is tagged with a particular page group name and used for targeting ads. For example, if you are running a newspaper site, you might create a page group for Sports, one for the Top Story, and another for Local News. You can then target ads to display only on pages in certain page groups.

- ❑ Target Groups – A collection of targets to which content should be displayed. For example, you can target ads to users who have specific profile properties.

Let's look at a simple example of how weighting works. Assume three paid ads have been created in a single campaign to sell books, and the weight for each ad is assigned as follows:

Ad	Weight	Percentage of times serviced
Professional .NET	1	20%
Professional BizTalk	1	20%
Professional Commerce Server	3	60%
Total Weight	5	100%

The combined weight of the ads is 5 (1+1+3 = 5). The 'Professional .NET' ad has a weight of 1 so it should be displayed once every five ad requests. The 'Professional Commerce Server' ad has a weight of 3, so it ought to show up three times in every five requests. Ad weights can take any value between 1 and 999999999.

> **A campaign-level paid ad is served according to the ratio of its weight to the sum of all item weights in that campaign – as we see above. For a house ad, the frequency is relative to its weight ratio to the sum of all other house ads (for all customers and all campaigns).**

Page groups can be defined in the BizDesk **Reference Tables** module, while Target groups are defined in the **Target Group** module. They can both be applied to an ad using the BizDesk's **Campaign Manager** module.

Need of Delivery

The CSF processes each part of an ad (including campaign goaling, exposure limit, schedule, weight, page groups, and target groups) using the Advertising pipeline. Each time a user visits the site, the CSF runs through a decision process to ensure the content meets the applied rules for display.

It uses a formula called Need of Delivery (NOD) to assign initial scores to each advertisement, based on how far behind schedule it is. This formula takes into account the total quantity of content to be delivered, and the length of time over which that content must be delivered. For each ad request, the CSF calculates the NOD after it has processed the ad request.

> **Need of Delivery is applied to paid ads only; it is not applied to house ads.**

If you plan to run many campaigns simultaneously using the same target group and the same priority, the Content Selection Framework selects which ad to display based on the ad type. If the ads are both house ads, an ad is selected at random using the weights as relative probabilities. If the ads are paid ads, an ad is selected for display based on the Need Of Delivery calculation, which takes into account the following parameters:

- ❑ Start date (dtStart) – date when the ad is available for display
- ❑ End date (dtEnd) – date when the ad is no longer valid for display
- ❑ Number of events scheduled (evtSched) – number of times the ad can be requested or clicked
- ❑ Number of events served to date (evtSrvd) – number of times the ad has been requested or clicked

To arrive at the calculated NOD, these values are applied to the following formula:

```
NOD = (evtSched / (dtEnd - dtStart)) / (evtSrvd / (Now - dtStart))
```

The resulting value is assigned as the initial score of the ad, with the following implications:

Need Of Delivery (NOD)	Meaning
> 1.0	The ad is behind schedule and will be given a higher priority.
1.0	The ad is on schedule.
< 1.0	The ad is ahead of schedule and will be given a lower priority.

The farther behind of schedule an ad is, the higher the value of the NOD. Ads that are ahead of schedule will have a NOD that is less than 1.0.

Another component provided for score modification is `HistoryPenalty`, which penalizes ads according to how recently they have been served to a user – this has the effect of 'rotating' ads so that the same ones don't appear time after time.

Discounts

The Discounts campaign item type is an open discounting architecture for displaying and applying discounts. As such, it serves two important roles: deciding where and when to show content pertaining to the discount; and detecting a user's shopping basket to actually issue the discount. These roles are actually performed by separate components, both working on the same information:

❑   `ScoreDiscounts` in the Content Selection pipeline – this adjusts the scores in a list of available discounts so as to prioritize the most relevant ones.

❑   `OrderDiscount` in the Order Processing pipeline – this applies the selected discounts to the relevant items in the users shopping basket.

Discounts can be applied at **item-level** (discounting specific items in the basket) or at **order-level** (discounting the entire contents of a shopping basket). Free shipping is implemented as an order-level discount – in fact it is the only order-level discount provided with Commerce Server. If you want to offer another type of order-level discount besides free shipping (for example, a 15% reduction for preferred users) you must develop a custom pipeline component that will make appropriate changes to the order as it is processed.

Note that if you apply a discount to an entire order, the relevant pipeline component will effectively apply that discount to each item individually. Only one discount can be applied to any given line item, because of the way the information is stored in the data warehouse, so you cannot apply item-level discounts and order-level discounts within the same basket.

Discount Types

There are several standard discount types available:

❑   Click-required – discounted product available via a special discount URL

❑   Leverage – based on other products purchased (for example, a free bookmark with each book order)

❑   Percentage-off – reduce a product's price by a fixed percentage, rather than a fixed sum

❑   Dollar-off – reduce a product's price by a fixed sum

❑   Happy Hour – reduce a product's price on certain dates and at certain times

Each of these discounts can be applied to individual products, all the products in a category, or to all products that meet a specific expression criterion – as defined via the BizDesk Campaign Manager module:

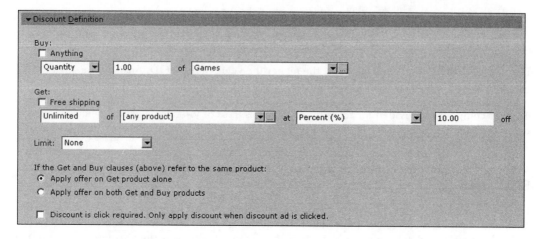

You cannot apply multiple discounts simultaneously, though they can be applied sequentially.

Parts of a Discount

A discount campaign item type consists of discount **properties** (name, priority, start/end dates), a discount **definition** (target expression, context requirements, award condition), discount **targets** (which pages will be used to advertise the discount), and a discount **display** (how, where, and how many times a discount will be displayed). The Campaign Manager can be used to define these components when creating a discount.

Priority

We assign discounts a priority value to help the CSF determine whether one should be applied in place of another on a single product. This can range between 10 and 200 (where 10 is the highest priority and 200 the lowest). For example, if we created three discounts, and assigned them priorities as follows:

Discount	Priority
30 percent discount for preferred customers who buy batteries, software, or books.	10
10 percent discount for books.	20
Free shipping.	30

If a preferred customer shops at the site and purchases some books, the 30% discount will be applied – neither the 10% discount nor the free shipping would apply, because they have a lower priority specified. If a non-preferred customer was to add the same items to their basket, only the 10% discount will be applied to their books because the 30% discount doesn't meet the preferred customer criteria, while the free shipping discount has a lower priority.

> If two discounts have the same priority, the first to appear in the database will be applied.

Limiting Discounts

If a discount condition is met multiple times in a single basket, that discount will also be applicable multiple times. However, we can specify a limit to the number of discounts that can be applied to the items in a single shopping basket. If we specify a value of zero, the discounts are unlimited. This limit is basket-specific and will not apply beyond a single user session.

Applying Discounts

We can apply discounts based on **quantity** (the number of items in the user's basket, for example 'buy one, get the second half-price') or **value** (the total value of the user's basket, for example 'spend $30 or more and get 10% off the total').

Once again, we can only apply one type or another to any given item. Consider an online bookstore, which is running a 'buy one, get the second half price' discount, alongside another '10% off on all titles' discount. The discounts are prioritized as follows:

Discount	Priority
Buy one book, get the second at half-price	10
10% off all books	20

If a user buys four books, the discounts will be applied as follows:

- ❏ First book: 10 percent discount
- ❏ Second book: 50 percent discount
- ❏ Third book: 10 percent discount
- ❏ Fourth book: 50 percent discount

Of course, this assumes that the first discount has not been limited to one instance per basket.

Processing Discounts

Discounts are processed by the Discounts content selection pipeline and the `OrderDiscount` pipeline component. The `OrderDiscount` component in the Basket pipeline is used to apply discounts to the shopping basket. The discounts CSF pipeline can be used to advertise the most appropriate discount to a particular user.

- ❏ Discount pipeline – checks the start date and end date of the discounts, and then adjusts the scores in the content list of possible discounts. It also ensures that the discounts that are most relevant to the current user receive the highest priority.

❏ OrderDiscount pipeline component – first applies the requirements to the available discounts. Depending on the discount involved, it uses the user profile and context profile information to evaluate target expressions. In addition, if a discount is click-required, it checks a list of campaign item IDs of every item clicked. Next, the Order pipeline processes each item, testing the conditions and awards. Discounts are applied from highest to lowest priority. If two discounts have the same priority, the priority setting will not be used. The other factors involved will be used to determine the order in which the discounts are applied.

Applying the Content Selection Framework

Throughout the rest of the chapter, we're going to look at piecing together the various parts of the framework discussed above. In the course of implementing a simple content selection application, we'll explore each of them in greater detail, and hopefully give you some ideas for how you might use them in your own custom systems.

Content Selection Objects

We're going to start with a detailed look at some typical code using each of the objects that make up the CSF, and put them together in a working application that supports a 'news headline' campaign item type. Each of our site's main pages will incorporate an area that lists current news headlines that might be of interest to the user. In this section, we'll see how to use the CSF objects to extract these lists of headlines from the content data store. For a full list of properties, methods, and required library references for these objects, you should refer to Appendix B.

We'll start by defining a **schema** for our 'news headline' elements, and then create and populate a content list **factory**, which will be responsible for generating request-specific **content lists**. These are the collections of news elements that we'll ultimately feed to the content selection pipeline via the **content selector**. So without further ado, let's get stuck in!

ContentListSchema

Before loading a list of content elements into memory, we must define a schema to describe some essential elements of their data structure. The contents of the ContentListSchema object we create will eventually be used to define the content schema for a ContentListFactory object. This can be thought of as being similar to a database table schema: a specified sequence of table fields with a number of attributes associated with each. A content list schema works in a similar fashion, except that it is persisted in memory, and is built and programmatically configured at run-time.

The first field we need to specify is **Score** – this is common to all ContentListSchema objects, letting us assign each item a score value. Values stored in this field will be *private* to each ContentList object, held locally and available for later modification by the content selection pipeline.

The remaining fields we're going to specify here are all **public** – data is persisted in the content factory and is *shared* by all ContentList objects created by that factory; it will be referenced, but *not* duplicated in each new one:

❏ Target_groups is an array of the target groups at which a content item will be targeted.

❏ Pagegroups is an array of page groups at which a content item will be targeted.

❏ Values is a dictionary containing properties specific to each content template (such as imgUrl, clickUrl, html, text, asfUrl).

These shared fields are all **read-only**, and their contents will effectively serve as context data for the content selection pipeline.

We instantiate the ContentListSchema object oSchema and use its Add method to add columns as follows:

Column	Type	Flags
Score	CLCOL_R4	CLCOL_SCORE_COLUMN + CLCOL_PRIVATE
Target_groups	CLCOL_VARIANTARRAY	CLCOL_READONLY
Pagegroups	CLCOL_VARIANTARRAY	CLCOL_READONLY
Values	CLCOL_DISPATCH	CLCOL_READONLY

The following code can be used to build a schema for a content list using the ContentListSchema object:

```
Const CLCOL_READONLY      As Integer = 1
Const CLCOL_PRIVATE       As Integer = 2
Const CLCOL_SCORE_COLUMN As Integer = 4

Set oSchema = New CacheCompLib.ContentListSchema
oSchema.Add 'Score',           CLCOL_R4,          CLCOL_SCORE_COLUMN + CLCOL_PRIVATE
oSchema.Add 'Target_groups',CLCOL_VARIANTARRAY, CLCOL_READONLY
oSchema.Add 'Pagegroups',     CLCOL_VARIANTARRAY, CLCOL_READONLY
oSchema.Add 'Values',          CLCOL_DISPATCH,    CLCOL_READONLY
```

ContentListFactory

Now that we have defined a schema, we are ready to create and populate a ContentListFactory object with the full set of content elements we wish to make available. The first part's simple:

```
Dim oFactory As CacheCompLib.ContentListFactory
Set oFactory = New CacheCompLib.ContentListFactory
```

Now let's assume our content elements can be accessed from an ADO Recordset object. We might use the following subroutine to populate the new factory:

```
Sub PopulateFactory(ByRef Factory As CacheCompLib.ContentListFactory, _
                ByRef Data As ADODB.Recordset)

  Dim fld As ADODB.Field

  Do Until Data.EOF
    With Factory.Fields(Data.AbsolutePosition - 1)
      For Each fld In Data.Fields
        .Item(fld.Name) = fld.Value
      Next fld
    End With
```

```
        Data.MoveNext
    Loop

      Set fld = Nothing
  End Sub
```

Of course, for this to succeed, the data structure of the recordset would need to conform exactly to the schema we defined earlier. Since this schema is defined implicitly by the structure of the recordset, it seems like rather a waste of effort to be specifying it all twice. Fortunately, the factory method `ConstructFromRecordset` saves us this extra effort: it automatically creates and initializes a ContentListSchema object for us, basing its contents on the structure of a specified recordset; it then uses this schema to initialize the factory itself, and uses the recordset contents to populate it:

```
oFactory.ConstructFromRecordset rstContent
```

So, the recordset object `rstContent` contains rows of consistently structured data, which the content factory uses it in two ways:

❑ To describe schema information for the content list. Each field in the recordset's `Fields` collection is used to specify a corresponding field in the factory's content list – even data type is carried over.

❑ To provide a source of population data. The purpose of the factory is to store data – the factory will loop through each row of data in the `recordset` object, and make a copy of that data for its own use.

We can optionally specify two more parameters: the first is a SimpleList of field names to **skip** – fields from the recordset that should not be copied across to the factory; the second can reference a ContentListSchema containing information to **add** to the automatically generated schema – additional columns or new flags for existing columns. For example:

```
oFactory.ConstructFromRecordset rstContent, Null, oSchema
```

We'll create and initialize the factory with the schema oSchema, which describes how the factory must structure itself and the content lists it produces:

Of course, there's nothing to prevent us from manually populating the factory, by simply looping through the records and copying each one across. In this way, we can populate the factory from *any* data source to which the code has access.

ContentList

The CSF uses this object to store particular subsets of the overall list of content elements (as held by the ContentListFactory object). It is a dependent object – the only way to create a new one is to call the method `CreateNewContentList` on the factory object. Whenever the ContentSelector requests content from a factory, the factory creates a new ContentList object for use by *that request only*.

The beauty of the ContentList object is that it allows a single process to work with (and, where appropriate, modify) data that's specific to the executing context, while providing access to data that all processes can see. When the ContentList object is created, only private data is actually copied to its memory space – public data is referenced for read-only access.

The function of a `ContentList` object is:

❑ To aggregate private data with the publicly shared data in the `ContentListFactory` object.

❑ To provide functionality for scoring, searching, and filtering the list of contents.

> **The ContentList and the ContentListFactory objects are designed to be run in-process with their clients. GetData and SetData methods assume direct memory access for reasons of performance.**

ContentSelector

This object serves a dual role, as the main interface to CSF content selection, and a property bag for the context properties used by targeting expressions and filters. It provides the means to pass extensible sets of global and page level properties to the Content Selection pipelines by invoking the appropriate pipeline object and returning the resulting content as a `SimpleList` of formatted content strings (typically HTML or XML).

At design time you can manage and extend the properties available in the profiles using the Profile Designer module available in the BizDesk and Commerce Manager.

The `ContentSelector` object inherits from the `Dictionary` object and therefore supports the functionality of custom properties.

It uses the method `GetContent` to initiate the content selection process. This takes a `Dictionary` object, whose only required element must contain a loaded pipeline object – this ensures that it knows which pipeline to execute. The Dictionary may also contain configuration information for the CSF application (including global objects and settings – for example, the `CacheManager` object, configuration settings, and so on – used by the `ContentSelector` object). Let's take a look at a simple example:

```
Dim listItems    'As Commerce.SimpleList
Dim sHeadline    'As String
Dim oCSO         'As Commerce.ContentSelector

Set oCSO = CreateObject('Commerce.ContentSelector')
```

Set the context values on the selector object. These values are accessible in the `ContextProfile` element of the OrderForm object in the pipeline components.

```
With oCSO
  .Size = 'Headline'
  .PageGroup = 'Home'
  .NumRequested = 5
  Set .UserProfile = oUserProfile

  Set listItems = .GetContent(Application('CSFHeadlinesContext'))
End With

For Each sHeadline In listItems
  Response.Write sHeadline
Next sHeadline
```

The ContentSelector allows the desired number of returned content items to be programmatically set at run-time by specifying `NumRequested`. In this example, the CSF will return a maximum of five content items. If the number of items returned is less than five, only these items will be valid for the current context – we therefore guarantee that 0-5 items will be returned by the selection process.

> *It is good practice to ensure that the selection process returns at least one item – this can be achieved by specifying default content within the ASP page. Alternatively, you can create a custom CSF pipeline component that checks for results after the selection process and supplies default content if the list is empty. As you'll recall, Advertising campaigns utilize house ads to serve precisely this purpose.*

The last call made on the ContentSelector object is to `GetContent` – this method does the work of executing the CSF pipeline and unifying the content. The parameter `Application('CSFHeadlinesContext')` is a dictionary-type application variable, which (for performance purposes) is ideally set up at application startup. At the very least, it must contain the pipeline object that is to be used for the content selection process.

Configuring a CSF Context

Below we can see an example of configuring a CSF context for a 'headlines' cache:

```
Sub InitCSFHeadlines(ByRef oCacheManager, ByRef oExpressionEvaluator)

    Dim sRedirectUrl
    Dim oPipe
```

We set the **redirect URL** to the full http path to `redir.asp`, and create Global Context for CSF Headlines:

```
    sRedirectUrl = GetBaseUrl() & '/redir.asp'

    Set CSFHeadlinesContext = CreateObject('Commerce.Dictionary')
    With CSFHeadlinesContext
        Set .Value('CacheManager') = oCacheManager
        .Value('CacheName') = 'Headlines'
        Set .Value('Evaluator') = oExpressionEvaluator
        .Value('RedirectUrl') = sRedirectUrl
```

The first line sets a string variable to the value of the base URL with the ASP page `redir.asp` appended to the end. The base URL will be the name of the website, while `redir.asp` page is specific to the CSF – it is used to tell the CSF where to send the user when click tracking is desired. If our site is www.wrox.com, then the final value of `sRedirectUrl` will be http://www.wrox.com/redir.asp.

The CSF also relies on references to `CacheManager` and `ExpressionEvaluator`. The `CacheManager` serves as a source of cached information for the selection process. Because of this, we must supply the CSF with an object reference to a pre-configured `CacheManager` object. We also need to supply a *name* for the current context's cache to use within the `CacheManager` – in this case 'Headlines'. Very shortly, we shall take a more detailed look at how the `CacheManager` works.

Now, we need to provide the CSF with a pipeline for content selection:

```
    Set oPipe = CreateObject('Commerce.OrderPipeline')

    oPipe.LoadPipe(Server.MapPath('/pipelines/headlines.pcf'))
    Set .Value('Pipeline') = oPipe
End With
```

The last step is to cache the context into the Application object:

```
    Set Application('CSFHeadlinesContext') = CSFHeadlinesContext

    Set oPipe = Nothing
End Sub
```

Cache Management

In order to maintain a high level of scalability, the web server must keep requests to external resources and processor intensive operations to an absolute minimum. If we start out by retrieving all the data we need from a database, web service, or other external resource, and putting it into local memory, we subsequently let the web server get on with processing data and serving requests – instead of hanging around wasting clock cycles while it waits for information to download.

Commerce Server 2000 has built-in mechanisms to help make the process of storing information in memory quite straightforward. In the past, you may well have used the Application object to cache data – while this is still a valid cache store, certain situations require a more advanced, automated system to ensure that the information contained remains valid.

For instance, if we chose to cache advertising information in the Application object, we would probably have to restart the web application every time we wanted to refresh values – otherwise, we would need to create a background mechanism to de-reference the values in the application object and then reload them; if we wanted to do this on a timed basis, we would also have to create a mechanism with an internal clock. Fortunately, the caching mechanisms provided with Commerce Server provide us with all of this functionality.

CacheManager

The CacheManager provides simple cache management services – Microsoft recommends its use for all CSF content caching requirements. It can periodically invoke COM components to fill a cache object, usually a Dictionary object, with information used in the content delivery process. It can also invoke components to write out information collected during the content delivery process, for example, performance numbers of advertising events such as number of ad requests and ad clicks.
The first thing that we need to look at is configuring CacheManager for use. There are a few controllable variables that we must provide to CacheManager before we do anything else:

```
    sMachineBaseURL = GetMachineBaseURL()

    'Create a CacheManager object
    Set oCacheManager = CreateObject('Commerce.CacheManager')
    With oCacheManager
        .AppUrl = sMachineBaseUrl

    'Configure CacheManager for headlines
        .RefreshInterval('Headlines') = (5 * 60) '5 minutes
        .RetryInterval('Headlines') = 60 '60 seconds
        .LoaderProgId('Headlines') = 'WROX.LoadHeadlines'
        .WriterProgId('Headlines') = 'Commerce.CSFWriteEvents'
        Set .LoaderConfig('Headlines') = dictCampaignConfig
        Set .WriterConfig('Headlines') = dictCampaignConfig
    End With
```

The first thing we do is to build a cache identifier – in this example, we use the URL of the machine on which the cache resides. By using the *machine's* base URL (rather than the application's base URL), we allow the cache to be refreshed from BizDesk on a per machine basis. The GetMachineBaseURL() function returns a string of the form http://*<machinename>*/*<vdirname>*. For instance, if the machine executing this code was named WROXSERVER and the IIS virtual directory running the application was Retail, the value stored in sMachineBaseURL would be http://WROXSERVER/Retail. When a manual cache refresh is required, the value held in this variable will be used to give external applications a pointer to where a cache refresh resource resides.

The next few lines set intervals for cache refresh and retry. In this example, we tell CacheManager to refresh the cache every five minutes. If the refresh fails (due to network or other problems) then CacheManager will continue to use the current cache and make an attempt to refresh the cache every 60 seconds.

> *CacheManager will log an event to the Event Log for every failed attempt to refresh its cache. This is typically done when the cache loader component raises an error.*

Now we tell the CacheManager which object to use for loading the cache, by specifying the ProgID of a valid cache loader component:

```
.LoaderProgId('Headlines') = 'WROX.LoadHeadlines'
```

When CacheManager needs to load or refresh its cache, this component will be instantiated and a call to the Execute method of the IPipelineComponent interface will be made. The loader configuration dictionary is set with the LoaderConfig property:

```
Set .LoaderConfig('Headlines') = dictCampaignConfig
```

This dictionary contains elements specific to the object that was specified by the LoaderProgId property (in this case WROX.LoadHeadlines). The following code fragment demonstrates how we can create such a dictionary:

```
Set dictCampaignConfig = CreateObject('Commerce.Dictionary')

dictCampaignConfig('ConnectionString') = sCampaignConnectionString
Set dictCampaignConfig('Evaluator') = oEvaluator
```

WriterProgId and WriterConfig are used in the same way as the loader properties, except that the CacheManager calls the set writer component *before* the loader component, in case information has been cached that needs to be worked on before it is flushed:

```
.WriterProgId('Headlines') = 'Commerce.CSFWriteEvents'
```

```
Set .WriterConfig('Headlines') = dictCampaignConfig
```

For example, during the content selection process of advertisements, certain performance information is tracked for each ad selected for display. Before the cache is flushed, CacheManager sends this performance information to a 'cache writer' component that persists the each of associated performance numbers to the data warehouse for analysis.

LRUCache (Least-Recently-Used Cache)

This object can be used to support the creation, storage, and retrieval of name/value elements from a cache in memory. It functions in a similar fashion to the `Dictionary` object, except that it only stores a small number of elements and internally ranks them according to use. When the cache is full and new elements must be added, the *least-recently* used elements are removed from the cache to make room for the new ones.

In actual fact, the replacement algorithm used is an approximate method that allows the cache size to grow to 110% of its maximum size setting. When the limit has been exceeded, the least recently used 10% of items are removed from the cache. This prevents the server from thrashing due to constant cache dumping if the cache becomes full.

When an element is added to a cache object, that object checks for an existing element with the same key. If one exists, it is removed from cache. A new element is created and the key and data is then copied into it. If the cache has reached its maximum size then the least-recently-used element in the cache (the one at the tail of the linked list) is removed. The new element is then inserted into the hash table and added to the head of the linked list.

When a request for an element in cache is made, if the given key is found then it is retrieved and the data associated with it is returned to the caller. The element is then moved to the front of the internally stored linked list. If the key is not found in the cache, the `Lookup` method returns a `Null` value and the `LookupObject` method returns a value of `Nothing`.

> The `Lookup` method is intended to retrieve variants that do not contain object references. To retrieve an object reference, use the `LookupObject` method instead.

The `Set` statement must be used with the `LookupObject` method as shown in the following example:

```
'Create the cache object and set a maximum size for it
Set oLRUCache = CreateObject('Commerce.LRUCache')
oLRUCache.SetSize 10

'Create an object to store in cache
Set dictObject = CreateObject('Commerce.Dictionary')
dictObject.Value('Test') = 'Test'

'Store the object in cache
oLRUCache.Insert 'Object', dictObject

'Store a value in cache
oLRUCache.Insert 'NotAnObject', 'Test'

'Retrieve the object from cache
Set dictObject = oLRUCache.LookupObject('Object')

'Retrieve the value from cache
Response.Write oLRUCache.Lookup('NotAnObject')
```

The above sample sets the cache size to a maximum of ten entries, though because of the internal caching algorithms, it will actually hold eleven. If we add a twelfth, then the least recently used 10 percent of items (that'll be two items) will be removed from cache and the new one will be inserted. There will then be a total of ten items in the cache.

411

Cache Synchronization

The Content Selection Framework depends heavily on caching data into the web server's memory. Although the `CacheManager` provides an automated mechanism to ensure the cached data is not stale, sometimes the cache needs to be refreshed manually at the request of a user.

For instance, if a campaign has been created with a cache refresh interval of 24 hours, and a business user (working via the BizDesk) decides to add a new ad to the campaign, they need to be able to refresh the cache on demand in order to display the ad on the website immediately. Otherwise, they might have to wait until the next day.

Thanks to the integration of the `CacheManager` with the BizDesk, the user can simply select which cache to refresh and at the click of a button, issue a cache refresh on the website to introduce the new ad.

We discussed earlier the `AppUrl` property of the `CacheManager`. When `CacheManager` needs to refresh its cache it will execute the cache loader component.

> *It is the responsibility of the cache loader component to update the virtual_directory table upon a successful refresh. Business Desk has knowledge of this table and will query it for the available caches so that the user can select which one to refresh.*

For example, if there are three web servers in a farm then there will be three times the number of configured caches in the table. A configured cache is identified by the name given to the cache (such as advertising, or discounts) and the value given to the `AppUrl` property of the `CacheManger`. The screenshot below shows a list of caches that are currently in use:

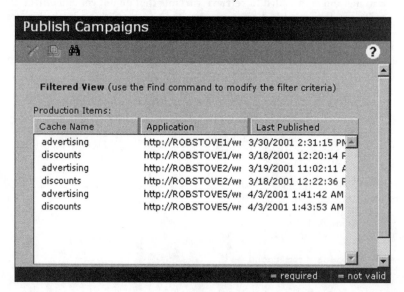

Altogether, there are six items in the list, and three unique host names shown in the Application column. Each application has two different caches available for refresh ('advertising' and 'discounts'). When the BizDesk user clicks the refresh button for a specific cache, the file name `BDRefresh.asp` is appended to the URL in the Application column, and a page request is made – the cache name is also appended as a `query string`. The `BDRefresh.asp` file uses this to identify the required cache, and calls the `Refresh` method on that cache.

CSFLoadCampaignsCommon

Very shortly, we shall look at implementing our own cache loader component. Before we do though, we must introduce a specialized component that we can use to load all campaign item metadata (including target groups and page groups) from an independent source. It's named `Commerce.CSFLoadCampaignsCommon` and is intended for use by cache loader components requiring access to elements of campaign data that are common to all CSF campaign item types.

> *Components that make use of* `CSFLoadCampaignsCommon` *include both* `Commerce.CSFLoadAdvertisements` *and* `Commerce.CSFLoadDiscounts`.

In order to use this object, it must be provided with the following items of information:

`ConnectionString`	A valid connection string for the campaigns database.
`TempTable`	The name of the temporary table created and used by the cache loader to hold the content information. Rows in this table must be in the same order as the rows in the factory. The temporary table includes an integer column `idx`, which serves to uniquely identify each table entry – values therein can be used to index into the factory by subtracting 1.
`factory`	A `ContentListFactory` object containing the content items. The factory must contain the following columns in an uninitialized state: ❏ pagegroups (CLCOL_VARIANTARRAY) – a list of page groups each item is targeted to for display ❏ target_groups (CLCOL_VARIANTARRAY) – a list of target groups for each item ❏ Values (CLCOL_DISPATCH) – a list of template substitution values

In addition, the following columns must exist in the factory's schema and must be initialized using the following settings:

❏   template (CLCOL_STRING) – the template name for each content item.

❏   item_id (CLCOL_I4) – the campaign item id for each content item.

Internally, this component performs the following steps:

1. Reads the `ConnectionString` and `TempTable` entries from the `Order` dictionary.

2. Opens a connection as specified by `ConnectionString`.

3. Gets a reference to the `ContentListFactory` object from the `factory` entry of the `Order` dictionary.

4. Reads the `ContentListSchema` from the factory and queries for the column names used by the schema from the temporary table.

5. Adds an `Idx` column to the temporary table. This table holds the index of the content item in the factory plus one. This means that the rows in the temporary table must be in the same order as the rows in the factory.

6. Builds a dictionary that maps page group tags to page group ids. Puts the dictionary in the Order dictionary using the key TargetGroups.

7. Builds a dictionary containing format templates and associated properties. The keys in the dictionary are template names. The values are sub-dictionaries for the given template that contain various template properties. It then inserts the dictionary into the Order dictionary using the key Templates.

8. Loads the creative property values for all rows in the creative table referenced by a content item in the temporary table. The Dictionary object returned uses the key creative_id.

9. Queries for the rows in the creative table to use for each item in the temporary table and inserts a reference to the appropriate Values dictionary into the row for that item.

10. Queries for the list of page groups each item in the temporary table is targeted for. It then inserts a safearray list into the pagegroups column in the content list.

11. Queries for the list of target groups each item in the temporary table is targeted for. It then inserts a safearray list into the target_groups column in the content list.

12. If a template exists that contains no template text and if a content item on schedule uses that template, then an entry in the Order dictionary is inserted with a key of NoDisplayTemplate. The value of this key is set to the name of the template. If more than one template has no template text, the first one found in the dictionary of templates (Templates) is used.

Building a Cache Loader Component

We are now ready to go through the steps involved in creating a custom cache loader component:

1. Define the content list schema to describe the cache.

2. Load the content factory.

3. Add code to update the cache entry table for manual cache refresh.

4. Configure CacheManager to use the loader.

In order to make these values available to the component, we must first build a content factory with the appropriate columns, and add the values to the original Order dictionary object. We need to build the content factory in a specific way, and can do this with a specialized SQL query. As an example, let's take a look at the query used by the Commerce.CSFLoadAdvertisements component. We can use a simple VB program to access the query:

```
Debug.Print GetSQL()

Private Function GetSQL() As String
    Dim oAdLoader  As Commerce.LoadDiscounts
    Dim dictConfig As MSCSCoreLib.Dictionary
```

```
      Set oAdLoader = New Commerce.LoadAdvertisements
      Set dictConfig = oAdLoader.GetConfigData()

      GetSQL = dictConfig.Query
   End Function
```

Upon viewing the `Query` key of the `dictConfig` object, we see the following SQL query:

```
SET NOCOUNT ON
SELECT      cs.u_size_tag                 AS size,
            cs.i_size_width               AS width,
            cs.i_size_height              AS height,
            et.u_event_name               AS event_name,
            pt.i_perftot_served           AS events_served,
            ci.u_campitem_name            AS name,
            ci.i_campitem_id              AS item_id,
            ci.i_campitem_exposure_limit  AS exposure_limit,
            ci.dt_campitem_start          AS date_start,
            ci.dt_campitem_end            AS date_end,
            ci.i_camp_id                  AS campaign_id,
            ad.i_aditem_events_scheduled  AS events_scheduled,
            ad.i_aditem_days_of_week_mask AS days_of_week,
            ad.i_aditem_time_of_day_start AS time_of_day_start,
            ad.i_aditem_time_of_day_end   AS time_of_day_end,
            ad.i_aditem_type              AS ad_type,
            ad.i_aditem_prev_served       AS prev_events_served,
            ad.dt_aditem_eff_start        AS eff_date_start,
            ic.u_industry_code            AS industry,
            ad.i_aditem_weight            AS ad_weight,
            ct.u_ct_name                  AS template,
            cr.i_creative_id              AS creative_id,
            cu.i_customer_id              AS customer_id
INTO        ##GUIDGUIDGUIDGUIDGUIDGUIDGUIDGUIDGUID
FROM        campaign_item AS ci
INNER JOIN campaign AS ca
ON          ci.i_camp_id = ca.i_camp_id
INNER JOIN creative AS cr
ON          ci.i_creative_id = cr.i_creative_id
INNER JOIN creative_size AS cs
ON          cr.i_creative_size_id = cs.i_creative_size_id
INNER JOIN event_type AS et
ON          ca.i_event_type_id = et.i_event_type_id
INNER JOIN creative_type AS ct
ON          cr.i_creative_type_id = ct.i_creative_type_id
INNER JOIN ad_item AS ad ON ci.i_campitem_id = ad.i_campitem_id
INNER JOIN customer AS cu on cu.i_customer_id = ca.i_customer_id
LEFT OUTER JOIN industry_code AS ic
ON          ad.i_industry_id = ic.i_industry_id
LEFT OUTER JOIN performance_total AS pt
ON          ci.i_campitem_id = pt.i_campitem_id
AND         pt.u_perftot_event_name = et.u_event_name
WHERE       ci.b_campitem_active = 1 AND
            ci.dt_campitem_archived IS NULL AND
            ca.b_camp_active = 1 AND
            ca.dt_camp_archived IS NULL AND
```

415

```
            cu.dt_customer_archived IS NULL AND
            DATEADD(minute, -15, ci.dt_campitem_start) <= ? AND
            ci.dt_campitem_end >= ? AND
            ci.guid_campitem_type = '82851f92-48d9-11d2-9c52-00c04fc29cc1'
SELECT * FROM ##GUIDGUIDGUIDGUIDGUIDGUIDGUIDGUIDGUID
```

Notice the SELECT columns shown in bold – these are the two required by the
CSFLoadCampaignsCommon component. Most of the details behind the query are specific to the
Advertising campaign item type. When building new cache loader components, we can use this query as
a starting point, deleting and adding columns, tables, and joins where appropriate. We now need to form
a ContentListSchema object that describes the columns we want to appear in the
ContentListFactory. This is just the same schema definition code that we saw earlier in the chapter,
formulated as a function:

```
Private Const CLCOL_READONLY       As Integer = 1
Private Const CLCOL_PRIVATE        As Integer = 2
Private Const CLCOL_SCORE_COLUMN As Integer = 4

Private Function GetSchema() As CacheCompLib.ContentListSchema
   Set oSchema = New CacheCompLib.ContentListSchema
   oSchema.Add 'score', CLCOL_R4, CLCOL_SCORE_COLUMN + CLCOL_PRIVATE
   oSchema.Add 'target_groups', CLCOL_VARIANTARRAY, CLCOL_READONLY
   oSchema.Add 'pagegroups', CLCOL_VARIANTARRAY, CLCOL_READONLY
   oSchema.Add 'Values', CLCOL_DISPATCH, CLCOL_READONLY
   Set GetSchema = oSchema
End Function
```

With the resulting Recordset object built from the query mentioned above we can use the
ContentListFactory method ConstructFromRecordset to complete the process. We create and
initialize the factory with the recordset containing the content data and the schema describing the
content list:

```
Private Function GetFactory(ByRef Content As ADODB.Recordset) _
   As CacheCompLib.ContentListFactory

   Dim oSchema     As CacheCompLib.ContentListSchema
   Dim oFactory    As CacheCompLib.ContentListFactory

   Set oSchema = GetSchema()
   Set oFactory = New CacheCompLib.ContentListFactory

   oFactory.ConstructFromRecordset Content, Null, oSchema

   Set GetFactory = oFactory
End Function
```

*Once the factory has been loaded it becomes locked and ready for use. No other modifications can be
made subsequently. Any attempt to modify or extend the factory will result in an error.*

We can now call the Execute method of the IPipelineComponent interface of the
CSFLoadCampaignsCommon object passing in the Order and Context objects. This allows the
component to add the common information to the Order dictionary object that is being used for
caching purposes:

```
Private Sub LoadCommonData(ByRef Order As MSCSCoreLib.CDictionary, _
                          ByRef Context As MSCSCoreLib.CDictionary, _
                          ByRef TempTable As String)

    Dim oLoadCampCommon As IPipelineComponent

    Set oLoadCampCommon = CreateObject('Commerce.CSFLoadCampaignsCommon')

    'Pass it the required information through the Order dictionary
    Order.Value('ConnectionString') = m_sConnStr
    Order.Value('TempTable') = TempTable

    'Execute it!
    oLoadCampCommon.Execute Order, Context, 0
End Sub
```

When executed, the component will add the following entries to the Order dictionary passed in:

❑ size – Dictionary object with name/value pairs for all available content sizes. This data is loaded from the creative_size table.

❑ Templates – Dictionary object containing Dictionary objects that provide information about each content template.

❑ TargetGroups – Dictionary object with name/value pairs for all configured target groups.

❑ PageGroups – Dictionary object with name/value pairs for all configured page groups.

Each time a cache loader component refreshes its data, it should update a known database table in order to allow users of BizDesk to manually invoke a cache refresh. If we register our application with the virtual_directory table in the campaigns database, we can enable BizDesk 'production refresh' functionality using the site's BDRefresh.asp page.

```
Private Sub UpdateVDir(ByRef Conn As ADODB.Connection, _
                       ByRef Dict As MSCSCoreLib.CDictionary)

    Dim sCacheName As Variant
    Dim sAppUrl    As Variant
    Dim sQuery     As String
    Dim sParams    As String

    'These values are written into the cache by the CacheManager object.
    sCacheName = Dict('_CacheName')
    sAppUrl = Dict('_AppUrl')

    sParams = 'N'' & sAppUrl & '', N'' & sCacheName & '''
    sQuery = '{ call sp_update_vdir (' & sParams & ') }'

    Conn.Execute sQuery
End Sub
```

Note that we invoke the stored procedure sp_update_vdir on the campaigns database. This procedure is installed with the Solution Sites as part of the Campaign resource.

Configuration information is supplied to our component by CacheManager, via the SetConfigData method of the IPipelineComponentAdmin interface. We use a module-level variable to store the connection string to the campaign database in which the content we want to cache is stored.

```
Private m_sConnStr As String

Private Sub IPipelineComponentAdmin_SetConfigData(ByVal pDict As Object)
    Dim vData As Variant

    vData = pDict.Value('ConnectionString')
    If Not IsNull(vData) Then
        m_sConnStr = vData
    End If
End Sub
```

The last thing we need to do is add code to the `Execute` method of the `IPipelineComponent` interface of our cache loader component:

```
Private Function IPipelineComponent_Execute( ByVal objOrderForm As Object, _
                                             ByVal objContext As Object, _
                                             ByVal lFlags As Long) As Long

    Dim oOrder      As MSCSCoreLib.CDictionary
    Dim oContext    As MSCSCoreLib.CDictionary
    Dim oFactory    As CacheCompLib.ContentListFactory
    Dim rstContent  As ADODB.Recordset
    Dim oGenID      As GENIDLib.GenID
    Dim oConn       As ADODB.Connection
    Dim sTempTable  As String
    Dim sFinalSQL   As String

    Const GUID_REPLACE As String = 'GUIDGUIDGUIDGUIDGUIDGUIDGUIDGUIDGUID'

    On Error GoTo ProcErr

    'Return 1 for success
    IPipelineComponent_Execute = PIPECOMP_STATUS_OK

    Set oConn = New ADODB.Connection
    oConn.Open m_sConnStr

    'We need a name for our temporary table. We can use a GUID and replace
    'the dashes '-' with underscores '_'.
    Set oGenID = New GENIDLib.GenID
    sTempTable = Replace(oGenID.GenGuidString, '-', '_')

    'We will also cut off the beginning and ending brakets '{}'.
    sTempTable = Mid$(sTempTable, 2, Len(sTempTable) - 2)

    'Get the SQL text returned from the GetSQL function and replace the
    'GUID_REPLACE string with the value of the sTempTable variable.
    sFinalSQL = Replace(GetSQL(),GUID_REPLACE, sTempTable)

    Set rstContent = oConn.Execute(sFinalSQL)

    'Load the returned content into the factory.
    Set objOrderForm.Value('factory') = GetFactory(rstContent)

    'Load the common campaign data into the Order dictionary.
```

```
   Call LoadCommonData(objOrderForm, objContext, sTempTable)

   Call UpdateVDir(oConn, objOrderForm)

ProcDone:
  Exit Function

ProcErr:
  IPipelineComponent_Execute = PIPECOMP_STATUS_FAIL
  Resume ProcDone

End Function
```

Now that we've completed the cache loader component, we can configure a new cache to use it. We should do this at application startup in the `global.asa` file:

```
'Configure CacheManager for headlines
With oCacheManager
  .RefreshInterval('Headlines') = (5 * 60) '5 minutes
  .RetryInterval('Headlines') = 60 '60 seconds
  .LoaderProgId('Headlines') = 'WROX.LoadHeadlines'
  .WriterProgId('Headlines') = 'Commerce.CSFWriteEvents'
  Set .LoaderConfig('Headlines') = dictCampaignConfig
  Set .WriterConfig('Headlines') = dictCampaignConfig
End With
```

In this example, the ProgID of the component is `WROX.LoadHeadlines`. As shown in the example, we set the property of the cache entry `'Headlines'` of the `CacheManager` property `LoaderProgId` to that value. When a request for the cache `'Headlines'` is made `CacheManager` will recognize that the cache has not been loaded and instantiate the `WROX.LoadHeadlines` component using the `IPipelineComponent` interface. `CacheManager` will then call the `Execute` method, passing in an `Order` and `Context` dictionary object. The cache loader component can expect to receive the following entries in the passed in `Order` dictionary object provided by the `CacheManager`:

❑   `_CacheName` – a string indicating the name that has been given to the current cache.

❑   `_CacheRefreshInterval` – a long indicating the interval in seconds that has been set as the amount of time in between cache refresh calls.

❑   `_CacheFirstRefresh` – a long indicating whether or not the current cache load call is the first time the cache has been loaded. Possible return values are 0 (current call *is not* the first refresh) and 1 (current call *is* the first refresh).

In order to retrieve the cache that is loaded by the cache loader into `CacheManager`, we need to call the `GetCache` method as shown in the following code:

```
Dim dictCache 'As Commerce.Dictionary
Set dictCache = MSCSCacheManager.GetCache('Headlines')
```

> *The default cache object is a Dictionary object. In order to use a store other than a Dictionary you can set the `CacheObjectProgID` property of the CacheManager to any valid cache object.*

At any point in the `CacheManager` object's lifetime we can access the cache and its contained data, which includes the `ContentListFactory` (as initialized and loaded by the CacheLoader) and any other data added to the `Order` dictionary during the cache load process.

Initializing the Content Selection Pipeline

When a request for content is made, we must first load the content into the pipeline from cache in a well-known format so that other components can access the data. This process is typically done by the first component in the pipeline at the Load Context stage. In this stage there are a few things we want to accomplish.

1. Retrieve cached data from the `CacheManager`

2. Put the retrieved cache into the `Order` dictionary using a well-known key (_content)

3. Set up any additional dictionary keys for use by other components

Typically the `InitCSFPipeline` component is used for initializing content for the pipeline. In order to understand what the component does, let's take a look at a simple example of the `Execute` method of an initialization component.

```
Private Function IPipelineComponent_Execute( _
    ByVal objOrderForm As Object, _
    ByVal objContext As Object, _
    ByVal lFlags As Long) As Long

    Dim oOrder      As MSCSCoreLib.CDictionary
    Dim oContext    As MSCSCoreLib.CDictionary
    Dim dictCache   As MSCSCoreLib.CDictionary
    Dim oCacheMgr   As CacheCompLib.CacheManager
    Dim sCacheName  As String

    On Error GoTo ProcErr

    'Return 1 for success
    IPipelineComponent_Execute = PIPECOMP_STATUS_OK

    'Early bind to the pipeline OrderForm and Context
    Set oOrder = objOrderForm
    Set oContext = objContext

    'Get the cache name and a reference to the CacheManager object.
    sCacheName = oContext.Value('CacheName')
    Set oCacheMgr = oContext.Value('CacheManager')
```

The default cache object is a Dictionary object. In order to use a store other than a Dictionary you can set the CacheObjectProgID property of the CacheManager.

```
    Set dictCache = oCacheMgr.GetCache(sCacheName)
```

We can now get a reference to the cached `ContentListFactory` object – this was created and loaded by the cache loader component specified by the CacheManager's `LoaderProgId` property.

```
    Set oFactory = dictCache.Value('factory')
```

Now we need to get a private copy of the cached data for use by the selection process. Default components use the key name _content and for sake of consistency, so shall we:

```
        Set oOrder.Value('_content') = oFactory.CreateNewContentList()

    ProcDone:
        Set oOrder = Nothing
        Set oContext = Nothing
        Set oCacheMgr = Nothing
        Set oFactory = Nothing
        Set dictCache = Nothing
        Exit Function

    ProcErr:
        IPipelineComponent_Execute = PIPECOMP_STATUS_FAIL
        Resume ProcDone

    End Function
```

When we configured the cache in `CacheManager`, we set a few properties that will be used by this component. The `CacheManager` and the `CacheName` dictionary elements will be sent into the component via the context object. We can reference these entries with the same keys that we used to set them. We need these keys because in this example we are using the `CacheManager` object for our cache storage.

The first step we need to do is reference the `CacheManager` and the `CacheName`. We need the `CacheName` value in order to know which cache within `CacheManager` to use.

```
    sCacheName = oContext.Value('CacheName')
    Set oCacheMgr = oContext.Value('CacheManager')
```

With a reference to the `CacheManager`, we can now call the `GetCache` method to get the cache.

```
    Set dictCache = oCacheMgr.GetCache(sCacheName)
```

In this example we are using the default cache object which is a Dictionary object. The component that loaded the cache specified by the CacheObjectProgID property on the CacheManager is responsible for ensuring that the cache is loaded properly.

We can retrieve the `ContentListFactory` by referencing the 'factory' key within the `Dictionary` cache. The `ContentListFactory` was created and loaded by the cache loader object.

```
    Set oFactory = dictCache.Value('factory')
```

The object returned is the `ContentListFactory` object. We can now make a private copy of the data so that other components can make adjustments to the data and score it based on the current context. The value '_content' is a well-known value that all content selection objects use to gain access to the content as it flows through the pipeline.

```
    Set oOrder.Value('_content') = oFactory.CreateNewContentList()
```

Certain implementations may require that other elements be pre-created at the Load Context stage. An example of this is to copy the `ContextProfile` elements into the `Order` dictionary in order to improve performance of other components. We can do this by simply adding the following code within the implementation:

```
Set oCtxProfile = oContext.Value('ContextProfile')

For Each vItem In oCtxProfile
    If IsObject(oCtxProfile.Value(vItem)) Then
        Set oOrder.Value(vItem) = oCtxProfile.Value(vItem)
    Else
        oOrder.Value(vItem) = oCtxProfile.Value(vItem)
    End If
Next
```

The dictionary entry `ContextProfile` contains the values provided to the `ContentSelector` object at run-time. Since the `ContentSelector` object inherits from `Dictionary`, it has the same capabilities. Therefore, we can set any custom property to any value. In the example below the property `FirstName` is given the value `'Rob'`.

```
oCSO.FirstName = 'Rob'
Set listContent = oCSO.GetContent(Application('CSFContentContext')
```

When we loop through the `ContextProfile` dictionary we will find that there is an entry with a key of `FirstName` that has a value of `Rob`. This means that data can be programmatically provided by CSF at run-time. The retrieval of the items and the associated data can be retrieved within a component that initially retrieves the cache or can be another component that is executed afterwards by inserting it into the pipeline accordingly.

If we take a look at the values written by the `InitCSFPipeline` component, we can see that multiple items have been written to the OrderForm:

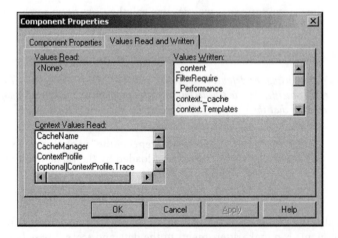

Although the InitCSFPipeline component writes values to the context Dictionary, indicated by entries shown with a preceding 'context' value, it is typically a bad practice and should not be done by custom components.

Filtering Content

Content filtering is basically a process of logical elimination – using content list indexes to efficiently exclude specific pieces of content. Since these indexes have been previously built, it's considerably more efficient than expression evaluation. For example, in the content selection pipelines for ads and discounts, filters are used on the `PageGroup` and content `Size`. These can be extended to filter on any string, integral, or array column in the `ContentList` object.

A filter can either require that content items have a particular column value, or it may exclude content items where the column contains particular values. Filters can also use sets of values, so that content items with any one of the values in the set will meet the filter requirements and will be passed through.

The `FilterContent` pipeline component can be used for most content filtering requirements. We can use it to extend the filtering process by adding items to the `FilterRequire` and `FilterExlude` dictionary objects of the `Order` dictionary.

In order to understand how the component works, let's look at a simple example of a component that utilizes the filtering capabilities of the `ContentList` object. For clarity, we've highlighted the lines that pertain specifically to filtering processes:

```
Private Function IPipelineComponent_Execute( _
    ByVal objOrderForm As Object, _
    ByVal objContext As Object, _
    ByVal lFlags As Long) As Long

    Dim oOrder  As MSCSCoreLib.CDictionary
    Dim oFilter As MSCSCoreLib.CDictionary
    Dim vItem   As Variant

    On Error GoTo ProcErr

    IPipelineComponent_Execute = PIPECOMP_STATUS_OK

    Set oOrder = objOrderForm
```

We now get a reference to the ContentList object initialized in the earlier **LoadContext** pipeline stage:

```
    With oOrder.Value('_content')
        'Filter all the non required items
        Set oFilter = oOrder.Value('FilterRequire')
        For Each vItem In oFilter
            .Filter vItem, oFilter.Value(vItem), FILTER_REQUIRE
        Next

        'Filter all the excluded items out of the content list
        Set oFilter = oOrder.Value('FilterExclude')
        For Each vItem In oFilter
            .Filter vItem, oFilter.Value(vItem), FILTER_EXCLUDE
        Next
    End With

ProcDone:
    Set oFilter = Nothing
    Set oOrder = Nothing
    Exit Function

ProcErr:
    IPipelineComponent_Execute = PIPECOMP_STATUS_FAIL
    Resume ProcDone

End Function
```

Scoring Content

The CSF content selection process is a process of scoring content items and then using those scores to select winners. The score for each content item is managed by the `ContentList` object and is a floating-point number. A content item score of zero means that the content item will not be selected under any circumstances – so if you need to rule out a specific item for selection, simply set its score value to 0. Scores are adjusted using a multiplier, so any later adjustment to the score will continue to result in 0, and still exclude the content item from selection.

There are two stages in a CSF pipeline that manipulate the scores of content items:

1. Assign an initial score to each item

2. Adjust the score based on targeting criteria

If content is not scored in the Initial Score stage, then all content items receive an initial score of 1.0. Score adjustments made in the scoring stage should apply multipliers. A multiplier less than 1.0 can be used to reduce the score of a content item. A multiplier greater than 1.0 can be used to increase the score of a content item. A multiplier of 0.0 can be used to eliminate a content item from further consideration.

```
'Score headline given its priorty, publish date, and today's date/time
'Score will always be between 0.0 and 1.0
Private Function GetHeadlineScore(ByRef Priority As Integer, _
                                  ByRef DatePublished As Date, _
                                  ByRef Today As Double) As Double

    Dim dblMaxScore As Double
    Dim dblDaysOld  As Double
    Dim dblScore    As Double

    'This algorithm will give a score between
    '0 and (m_lLowestPriority * m_dblMaxDaysToShowHeadlines)
    dblMaxScore = m_lLowestPriority * m_dblMaxDaysToShowHeadlines

    'Compute age in days
    dblDaysOld = Today - DatePublished
    dblScore = dblMaxScore - (Priority * dblDaysOld)
    If (dblScore < 0.0) Then
        dblScore = 0.0
    End If

    GetHeadlineScore = dblScore / dblMaxScore
End Function
```

Here's the corresponding execution code for a scoring pipeline component:

```
Private Function IPipelineComponent_Execute( _
    ByVal objOrderForm As Object, _
    ByVal objContext As Object, _
    ByVal lFlags As Long) As Long

    Dim oOrder         As MSCSCoreLib.CDictionary
    Dim vItem          As Variant
    Dim iPriority      As Integer
```

```
        Dim dtDatePublished As Date
        Dim dblToday       As Double
        Dim lRow           As Long
        Dim dblScore       As Single

        On Error GoTo ProcErr

        IPipelineComponent_Execute = PIPECOMP_STATUS_OK

        Set oOrder = objOrderForm
```

We reference the ContentList object initialized in the Load Context stage:

```
        With oOrder.Value('_content')
            For lRow = 0 To .Count
                iPriority = .Fields(lRow).Item('priority').Value
                dtDatePublished = .Fields(lRow).Item('date_published').Value
                dblToday = Now()

                dblScore = GetHeadlineScore(iPriority, _
                                            dtDatePublished, _
                                            dblToday)

                .SetScore(lRow, dblScore)
            Next lRow
        End With

    ProcDone:
        Set oOrder = Nothing
        Exit Function

    ProcErr:
        IPipelineComponent_Execute = PIPECOMP_STATUS_FAIL
        Resume ProcDone

    End Function
```

Selecting Content

Once score adjustments have been made, the content selection pipeline must select the winners – to this end, Commerce Server features the SelectWinners component. For generic content items, this simply picks the items with the highest score. For advertisements, it must first decide whether to show a house ad or a paid ad (using the ad weights and NOD formula to determine whether a paid ad is appropriate at the current time. If a paid ad *is* selected, it presents the ad with the highest score – if a house ad is selected, it uses the weights of all house ads as probabilities and selects one at random.

The SelectWinners component also prevents competing ads from running on the same page and can use a PageHistory string to prevent multiple selection of the same content item on a single page.

Formatting Content

Content items that have been selected for display need to be formatted as strings before they are returned to the page. The formatting process brings the properties of the content item and the global-level and page-level context properties together and uses them as replacement variables for an Active Content Template. The end result of formatting is a SimpleList object of string values, with each list entry containing the string representing a content item.

425

```
Private Function IPipelineComponent_Execute( _
    ByVal objOrderForm As Object, _
    ByVal objContext As Object, _
    ByVal lFlags As Long) As Long

    Dim oOrder        As MSCSCoreLib.CDictionary
    Dim dictValues    As MSCSCoreLib.CDitionary
    Dim listFormatted As MSCSCoreLib.CSimpleList
    Dim vItem         As Variant
    Dim sOpenId       As String
    Dim sCloseId      As String
    Dim sFormatted    As String
    Dim lRow          As String

    On Error GoTo ProcErr

    IPipelineComponent_Execute = PIPECOMP_STATUS_OK

    Set oOrder = objOrderForm
    sOpenId = oOrder.Value('OpenId')
    sCloseId = oOrder.Value('CloseId')

    Set listFormatted = New MSCSCoreLib.CSimpleList
```

Again, we need to get a reference to the ContentList object initialized in the Load Context stage:

```
    With oOrder.Value('_content')
        For lRow = 0 To .ActiveRows.Count
            sFormatted = .Fields(lRow).Item('template').Value

            Set dictValues = .Fields(lRow).Item('Values').Value

            For Each vItem In dictValues
                sFormatted = Replace$(sFormatted, _
                                      sOpenId & vItem & sCloseId, _
                                      dictValues.Value(vItem))
            Next vItem

            listFormatted.Add sFormatted
        Next lRow
    End With

    Set oOrder.Value('_formatted') = listFormatted

ProcDone:
    Set oOrder = Nothing
    Set listFormatted = Nothing
    Exit Function

ProcErr:
    IPipelineComponent_Execute = PIPECOMP_STATUS_FAIL
    Resume ProcDone

End Function
```

Recording Events

Whenever content is served or clicked, the event can be recorded. The `RecordEvent` component can be used to record events to an in-memory `Dictionary` object, called the **Performance Dictionary**. When the cache is next refreshed, all events accumulated up until the refresh time can be written to a database by the CSFWriteEvents component.

Additionally, the `IISAppendToLog` component can also record these events to the IIS web log so that the data can be imported into the Commerce Server Data Warehouse.

Active Content Templates

As we've observed, templates are used substantially by the CSF (and Commerce Server as a whole) to help ensure that dynamically generated content is consistently formatted and displayed. A content template consists of a mix of static text and template variables (recognizable by their opening {% and closing %} tags). Let's take a look at an example of a simple content template:

```
<A HREF='{%ClickUrl%}'>{%Text%}</A>
```

Since `ClickUrl` is enclosed by the tags {% and %}, the CSF knows that it must look for a key with this name in the incoming `Order` dictionary. Assuming it finds one, it then replaces the template's tagged element with the associated value defined in the dictionary. When the page is output, it features the CSF-provided content in place of the template variables – for example, the output generated from this template might be:

```
<A HREF='http://www.wrox.com'>Professional Commerce Server 2000</A>
```

In this case, we have a string that denotes the URL in an HTML link, a typical use of CSF in a website. Let's look at another example that includes a call to the `ContentSelector` object for a given content item. Consider the following content template:

```
Welcome back {%FirstName%} {%LastName%}.
<A HREF='{%ClickUrl%}?user_id={%UserId%}'>Click here</A>
 for a special gift just for you.
```

This is evidently designed to serve as the template for a welcome message to greet registered users. We can use the following ASP code to provide the CSF with the dynamic data it will use to replace the content variable items used in the template:

```
Dim oCSO
Dim sMessage

Set oCSO = CreateObject('Commerce.ContentSelector')
With oCSO
    .Size = 'StandardMessage'
    .PageGroup = 'WelcomePage'
    .NumRequested = 1

    If Not oUserProfile Is Nothing Then
        Set .UserProfile = oUserProfile
        .FirstName = oUserProfile.GeneralInfo.first_name
```

427

```
            .LastName = oUserProfile.GeneralInfo.last_name
            .UserId = oUserProfile.GeneralInfo.user_id
        End If

        Set listItems = .GetContent(Application('CSFContentContext'))
    End With

    For Each sMessage In listItems
        Response.Write sMessage
    Next sMessage
```

Assuming that `oUserProfile` is a valid registered UserProfile reference and that the content item was previously configured in BizDesk with a click URL of http://www.wrox.com/gift.asp, the resulting HTML would be as follows:

```
Welcome back Rob Stovenour.
<A HREF='http://www.wrox.com/gift.asp?user_id=robstove'>Click here</A>
 for a special gift just for you.
```

The power and integration capabilities of the Content Selection Framework become very clear in this example. Keep in mind that the text of a content template does not necessarily need to be formatted using HTML. In fact, it does not need to be in any particular format. The only requirement is that template variables must be enclosed within {% and %} tags.

In fact, even this requirement is not absolute – it is imposed by the default `FormatTemplate` component. If, for some reason, you need to specify a different variable identification format, you can build a new formatting component to handle your custom requirements.

Content Event Tracking

In the previous section we defined a content template with template text as shown below:

```
<A HREF='{%ClickUrl%}'>{%Text%}</A>
```

This is a very simple example and will work, but in order to track the event of a user clicking on the item and fully utilize the framework, we must take our example a few steps further. Let's take a look at a modified version of the template that has been extended to allow CSF to track the usage of this content item:

```
<A HREF='{%RedirectUrl%}?
    ciid={%item_id%}&
    cachename={%CacheName%}&
    PageGroupId={%PageGroupId%}&
    url={%ClickUrl%}'>{%Text%}</A>
```

By changing the template text, CSF now has the ability to know whether the end user clicked on a given piece of content and track the performance of the content on the website. We've extended the HREF tag to include some identifying QueryString parameters. These include:

❑ ciid – the Campaign Item ID of the campaign item associated with the content

❑ cachename – the name of the cache that CacheManager should use to store the event in-memory

❑ PageGroupId – used to track the performance of page groups

❑ url – the URL to which the user should be redirected once the event has been recorded

Notice also that the HREF is now using a replacement variable named RedirectUrl. This variable is inserted by CSF from the value specified when the content configuration was specified earlier as indicated below:

```
'The RedirectURL should be set to the full http path to 'redir.asp'
sRedirectUrl = GetBaseUrl() & '/redir.asp'
...
With CSFHeadlinesContext
...
    .Value('RedirectUrl') = sRedirectUrl
...
End With
...
```

The CSF will use the value specified here as a replacement for the template variable in the template text. This value should be the URL of a resource that can accept QueryString parameters and do some intelligent recording of the event. The values recorded can then be imported into the data warehouse for reporting and analysis, and be used to track the performance of the content in real-time. The number of scheduled content items will also be decremented if the scheduling is based on content clicks.

Notice in the example above that we have specified that redir.asp will be what CSF uses to redirect users back to for event tracking. Once the page has recorded all relevant information, the page redirects the user to the URL specified in the ClickUrl template variable.

As another example, let's look at a content template that contains an image for the given content:

```
<A HREF='{%RedirectUrl%}?ciid={%item_id%}&
                    cachename={%CacheName%}&
                    PageGroupId={%PageGroupId%}&
                    url={%ClickUrl%}'>
    <IMG SRC='{%ImgUrl%}?
        CEVT={T=CAMP,CI={%item_id%},PG={%PageGroupId%},EVT=DOWNLOAD}'
        WIDTH={%Width%}
        HEIGHT={%Height%}
        ALT='{%AltText%}'>
</A>
```

For clarity, we've formatted this example quite unconventionally; but you should be able to see that when we specify the IMG tag for the content, there are extra template variables associated to the template including:

❏   ImgUrl – a URL from which the image associated with the content comes

❏   item_id – CSF will use the ID of the content item for tracking performance

❏   Width – the width of the content specified by the size parameter

❏   Height – the height of the content specified by the size parameter

❏   Alt – the alternate text that will be used in case the image download fails

Also notice the HTML SRC attribute. It contains some specific information associated with the image. This information is for analysis within the data warehouse. When a browser downloads an image the web server will log the fact that the request has been made using a GET method. The extended information is also stored in the web log – this allows the Web Log Import process to capture the fact that the image for the associated campaign item was requested. You can then view reports on this information to better understand the effect and performance that the content had on the site.

Here's what the CSF might make of this content template:

```
<A HREF='http://www.wrox.com/redir.asp?ciid=1&
                        cachename=advertising&
                        PageGroupId=All&
                        url=/books/cs2k.asp'>
    <IMG SRC='http://www.wrox.com/images/cs2k.gif?
        CEVT={T=CAMP,CI=1,PG=All,EVT=DOWNLOAD}'
        WIDTH=150
        HEIGHT=75
        ALT='Professional Commerce Server 2000'>
</A>
```

Content Template Management

The logical structure of a template consists of three items:

❏ **Template** – the main item that represents the object. The template contains the name of the template and the template text. The template text is the content that will be formatted by CSF by outputting all static content in the template text combined with the template variables.

❏ **Property** – the items associated with a template that represents dynamic data. A template can contain multiple properties. Each property provides CSF with information about the data associated with the template and is used by CSF during the formatting process.

❏ **Campaign Item Type** – a category that is specific to a CSF application (Advertising, Discounts, DirectMail).

The following diagram depicts the logical relationships between these items:

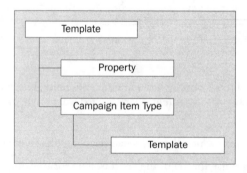

Each template consists of multiple properties and can also be related to multiple campaign item types. Campaign item types are the supported types of campaigns that are running on the system. The campaign item types that are shipped with Commerce Server are Advertising, Discounts, and DirectMail. Whenever a new template is created, it must be associated with an available campaign item type. This will allow the template to be available in the Campaigns module of Business Desk for the related campaign item type.

Now that we have covered the items that make a content template, we can take a look at the underlying data structure for building new content templates. The following diagram shows the tables, and the relationships between them, that hold information about a specific template:

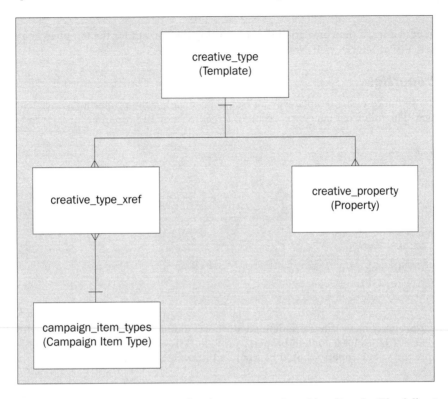

We can retrieve information about a template by accessing the tables directly. The following query will return information about all available templates:

```
SELECT     i_creative_id,
           u_ct_name,
           text_ct_template
FROM       creative_type
```

Content Template Text

Behind every content template is the template text. The template text can be thought of as the body of all content templates. The template doesn't become useful until relevant text is provided to serve a specific purpose.

As mentioned earlier, template text consists of static text and template variables. With the data in the `text_ct_template` field, the template author can modify the contents of the template text by editing the contents returned from the recordset. By updating the contents the modified text will be published to the database to be consumed by CSF.

To make things easier, it may be a good idea to develop the content for the template in an editor such as FrontPage, Visual InterDev, or Notepad.

Content Properties

For each row in the resulting templates recordset, we can gather the properties associated to each template item. The following query will result in a recordset of all properties for a given template:

```
SELECT      i_cp_id,
            u_cp_name,
            i_cp_type,
            u_cp_label,
            i_cp_order,
            b_cp_required,
            u_cp_default,
            i_cp_source,
            i_cp_encoding,
            i_creative_type_id
FROM        creative_property
WHERE       i_creative_type_id = ?
```

Each content property has various pre-defined attributes defined by the columns of the resulting recordset. The attributes for a content property provide CSF with information about the property so that it can interpret how the property should be used by the content template.

The attributes are as follows:

Attribute (Field)	Explanation
Name (u_cp_name)	Name of the template property. If the property will be used as a template variable, this is the value that CSF will look for in the template text.
Label (u_cp_label)	This label is for identification purposed within the Business Desk. Typically, if the property is not user definable, the label is left blank.
Default (u_cp_default)	When the template is being consumed by CSF, if no value for the property has been found, this value will be used.
Type (i_cp_type)	This property type is used for display purposes within the Business Desk. The current implementation supports three different values.
	Text (1) – Free-form text box.
	Text Area (2) – Free-form multi-line text box.
	Number (3) – Text box that allows numeric values only.

Attribute (Field)	Explanation
Source (i_cp_source)	Content Item (1) – CSF Looks for a value in the content item. First, the `Values` dictionary in the `ContentList` object is used, if it is present. Next, the columns of the `ContentList` object are examined.
	Intrinsic Value (2) – CSF will use an intrinsic value if one matches. The only currently supported intrinsic value is 'unique', which causes a unique number to be generated.
	Context Profile (3) – CSF looks for a value in the `Context` dictionary. First the `ContextProfile` entry (the CSO) in that dictionary is examined for a matching entry name, and then the `Context` dictionary is examined for a matching entry name.
	Null or zero (0) – CSF examines all of the above sources in the order shown, stopping when the first match is found.
Encoding (i_cp_encoding)	A number indicating the type of HTML encoding, if any, to apply to the value.
	Null (0) – No encoding.
	Full (1) – Performs full URL-encoding. An example of when this encoding is required would be a `ClickUrl` entry passed to the redirector.
	Limited (2) – Limits encoding in which space characters are encoded as plus characters. As an example, this type of encoding is useful in would-be URLs that do not go through the redirector, such as image URLs.
Required (b_cp_required)	When set to true (checked), the property value must be specified within Business Desk. The Business Desk user cannot save the campaign item without entering a value when this is set to true.

Content Property Ordering

When creating content that uses a particular content template, it is possible to specify the order in which the properties are displayed within Business Desk and whether or not the property is displayed at all. This can be done by updating the i_cp_order column of the creative_property table. The values are numeric and are displayed in Business Desk in ascending order.

Campaign Item Type Associations

For a content template to be used, an association must be made to a campaign item type. This can be accomplished by inserting a row in the creative_type_xref table.

To discover which campaign item types are supported by the system we can run the following query:

```
SELECT      u_campitem_type_name,
            u_campitem_type_table,
            guid_campitem_type
FROM        campaign_item_types
```

The resulting recordset will provide information about the supported applications. By looking at the cross-reference table (`creative_type_xref`) we can discover which templates are available for use by the available applications. The following query will result in a recordset containing the campaign item types that a given template is available in:

```
SELECT      guid_campitem_type,
            i_creative_type_id
FROM        creative_type_xref
WHERE       i_creative_type_id = ?
```

Making an Ad Work

Now that we have an understanding of CSF and the Advertising campaign item types, we can relax a little, and look at how we'll link these back-end concepts to our front-end user interface.

First thing we'll do, is create a new ad item by going into the Campaigns module of the BizDesk and working through the steps outlined, below. When we configure the ad item we'll need to set a few properties on it to allow CSF to understand how to process its contents. In this example we will focus on the display properties so we can relate them to what we've already learned about CSF.

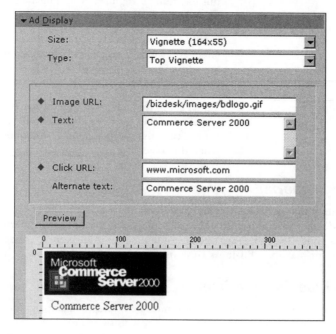

In the illustration above we see that the Size property specified is **Vignette**. This is a key concept in the content selection process. When requesting content from CSF using the `ContentSelector` object, which we have seen in previous examples, we specified to the CSO a value for the property `Size`. This property is essentially a filter that CSF will use to ensure that all content that doesn't have the size specified by the property will be excluded from the content list.

A vignette ad is composed of text that is displayed adjacent to the image where the ad is shown.

For CSF to select the ad in the illustration above, the value 'Vignette' would have to be applied to the Size property of the CSO before the call to GetContent, as follows:

```
oCSO.Size = 'Vignette'
Set listContent = oCSO.GetContent(Application('CSFContentContext'))
```

The available values for the Size filter are managed using Business Desk in the Reference Tables module of the Campaigns category:

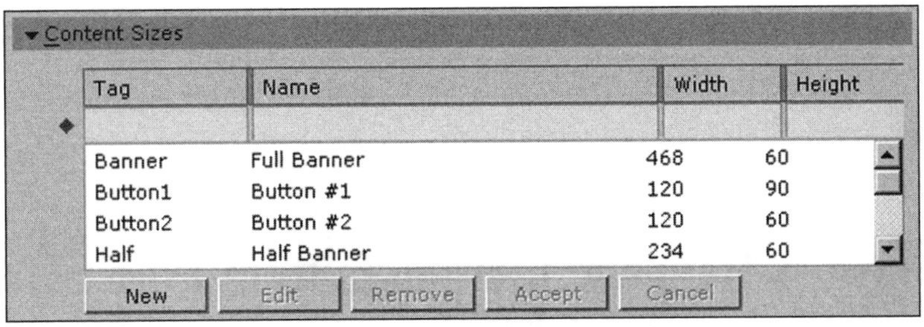

Tag	Name	Width	Height
Banner	Full Banner	468	60
Button1	Button #1	120	90
Button2	Button #2	120	60
Half	Half Banner	234	60

New | Edit | Remove | Accept | Cancel

Another setting we see is that the Type specified is **Top Vignette**. When we select this option Business Desk queries the campaigns database for the definition information of the content template. It has found that the **Top Vignette** type has the properties imageUrl, Text, clickUrl, and altText. The properties are displayed in the order specified in the database. This can be managed using Template Creator.

Troubleshooting

Included with Commerce Server is an Active Server Page named TraceScores.asp that can be used to trace the content selection process. TraceScores.asp can be used to help understand how the internal content decision process works. The page works with the ContentSelector object in order to get the processed items that CSF has effectively scored.

> You must ensure that the oCSO.Trace property is set to **True** before calling the GetContent method in order for the TracesScores procedure to work properly.

Following is the contents of the TraceScores procedure:

```
Sub TraceScores(ByRef oCSO)
    Dim dictContext, dictOrder
    Dim oContentList
    Dim listTrace
    Dim sTrace, sName, sOutput
    Dim lCount, lRow
    Dim ciid

    Set dictOrder = oCSO.Order
    Set dictContext = oCSO.Context
    Set oContentList = dictOrder('_content')

    lCount = oContentList.Count
```

```
      For lRow = 0 to lCount - 1
          ciid = oContentList.Fields(lRow).Item('item_id').Value
          sName = oContentList.Fields(lRow).Item('name').Value

          sOutput = '<B>' & _
                    'ad: ' & sName & _
                    ' (item_id=' & ciid & ') ' & _
                    ' score: ' & oContentList.GetScore(lRow) & _
                  '</B><BR>' & vbCrLf

          Response.Write sOutput

          Set listTrace = oContentList.TraceMessages(lRow)
          For Each sTrace In listTrace
              Response.write(sTrace & '<BR>' & vbCrLf)
          Next sTrace
      Next lRow
  End Sub
```

Building a News Headline Campaign Item Type

Now that we have seen a couple of the campaign types provide with Commerce Server, let's look at the steps involved to create a new campaign item type by using some of the skills we've learned in the previous sections:

1. Create a new table with a foreign key from the creative_type table.

The first task we need accomplish is to create a table to hold our campaign item specific information.

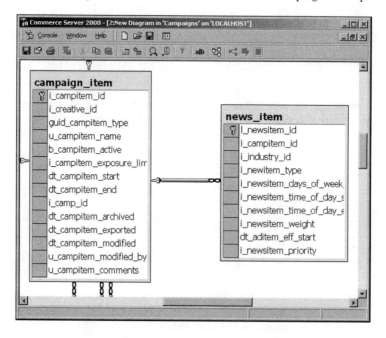

2. Add a row to the campaign_item_types table specifying the new campaign type.

We can use the following SQL INSERT statement:

```
INSERT INTO campaign_item_types(guid_campitem_type,
                                u_campitem_type_name,
                                u_campitem_type_table)
VALUES                          ('82851F92-48D9-11D2-9C52-00C04FC29CC2',
                                'WROX Headline',
                                'headline')
```

In SQL Server Enterprise Manager we can see that the row has been added:

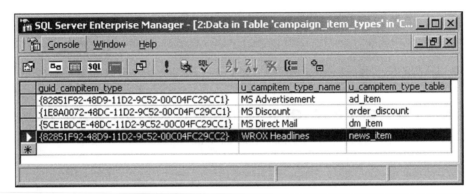

3. Associate creative types with the new campaign type using the Template Creator tool.

We also need to associate a content template with the new campaign item type. We can do this using Template Creator by opening the properties dialog for the desired template and ensuring that the WROX Headlines type is checked as illustrated below:

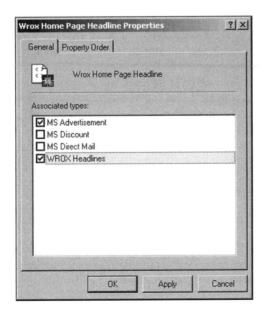

4. Create a cache loader component to store the content specific to the campaign – our cache loader needs to query information from the news_items table for caching.

5. Create any needed pipeline components to work with the content – it would be useful to create a score pipeline component to score the new items by date and priority.

6. Create a Business Desk module for maintaining the campaign:

   ❑ Add search meta element (/marketing/cmanager.asp)

   ❑ Create page for management (/marketing/newsitem.asp)

   ❑ Add config element for adding (/config/marketing_cmanager.xml)

7. Configure the ASP pages to use the campaign item type.

8. Create the campaign and campaign items with Campaign Manager in Business Desk.

9. Run the campaign.

Lifecycle of a Request for a Targeted Advertisement

Let's examine the steps that take place for a simple content request.

1. A user accesses an ASP web page.

2. The code in the ASP page creates a ContentSelector object (CSO).

3. The code in the ASP page sets the CSO page context properties.

4. The code in the ASP page calls the GetContent method of the CSO.

5. Internally, the CSO calls the Execute method of the Advertising pipeline.

6. The InitCSFPipeline component calls the GetCache method of the CacheManager.

7. The CacheManager invokes the CSFLoadAdvertisements component (only the first time).

8. The InitCSFPipeline component copies some page and global context properties into the pipeline Context dictionary.

9. The InitCSFPipeline component creates filters for the size and PageGroups dictionary entries.

10. The LoadHistory component loads the user-specific history string.

11. The FilterContent component applies the filters specified in the FilterRequire and FilterExclude dictionaries.

12. The AdvertisingNeedOfDelivery component assigns each ad an initial score based on the start date and end date of the ad, the duration of the ad run, and how many events have been served to date.

13. The HistoryPenalty component applies penalties for ads that have already been shown to the current user and enforces exposure limits.

14. The EvalTargetGroups component evaluates target groups and adjusts content item scores.

15. The SelectWinners component selects the winning advertisement(s). It prevents industry collision and uses the PageHistory string to avoid showing the same ad multiple times on the same page.

16. The RecordEvent component records the event into an in-memory performance Dictionary object.

17. The IISAppendToLog component records the event to the IIS log file.

18. The RecordHistory component records the event to the user-specific history string.

19. The SaveHistory component saves the user-specific history string.

20. The FormatTemplate component formats the selected advertisements using a template that brings together ad properties, page context, and global context and puts the resulting strings into a SimpleList object.

21. The CSO returns a SimpleList object of formatted advertisements.

22. The content is rendered onto the ASP page.

23. A user clicks an ad.

24. The redir.asp page is called.

25. The redir.asp page invokes the RecordEvent component.

26. The RecordEvent and IISAppendToLog components are called.

27. The content is rendered onto the ASP page.

28. The CacheManager background thread fires after the refresh interval expires.

29. The CSFWriteEvents component flushes events in the in-memory performance Dictionary object to the database.

30. The CSFLoadAdvertisements component loads new advertising information, including the updated aggregate event counts used for the Need Of Delivery (NOD) calculation.

Summary

To recap then, the Content Selection Framework (CSF) is one of the most powerful features Commerce Server 2000 offers you to facilitate building highly scaleable, robust, and intelligent content targeting applications. It allows the site developer to concentrate on architecture and functionality rather than day-to-day content issues, which can be administered almost exclusively by the site's business manager.

The main lesson you take from this chapter should be that the CSF is a powerful platform on which to build applications where content has to be dynamically linked to the user.

You learned about content lists, factories, schemas, and the components that process these objects to intelligently select content. There are many working parts involved with CSF and trying to absorb them all at once can be a little overwhelming at first. Once you begin working with the objects and start connecting the pieces together, you will start to become familiar with the `ContentListFactory` and the processes involved in manufacturing `ContentList` objects.

You learned how to use the building caching mechanisms provided by `CacheManager`. Performance is key, and the site that makes information available the fastest wins. By building cache loader components you can enable your website to pull from external resources on a timed interval rather than accessing them for every request. The `LRUCache` object gives you the ability to remove unused information from memory to make room for data that is more relevant and more frequently used. This provides the web server with the biggest bang for the buck.

The Internet is all about display and personalization. After being consumed by CSF, we examined the before and after shots of a content template. At this point we began to understand how CSF brings personalization to a website. Targeting content that is relevant to the user and then customizing it provides a means to grab their attention and keep them coming back.

Advertisements and discounts are two content decision applications provided by Commerce Server to allow you to use CSF straight off the shelf. These tools alone provide solutions for a major part of the information overload problems that are consistently causing user satisfaction to decline. Even if you never build applications using CSF you will undoubtedly be able to utilize these to provide critical information about the content on your website and to help ensure that the content that you do provide is relevant to the user who sees it.

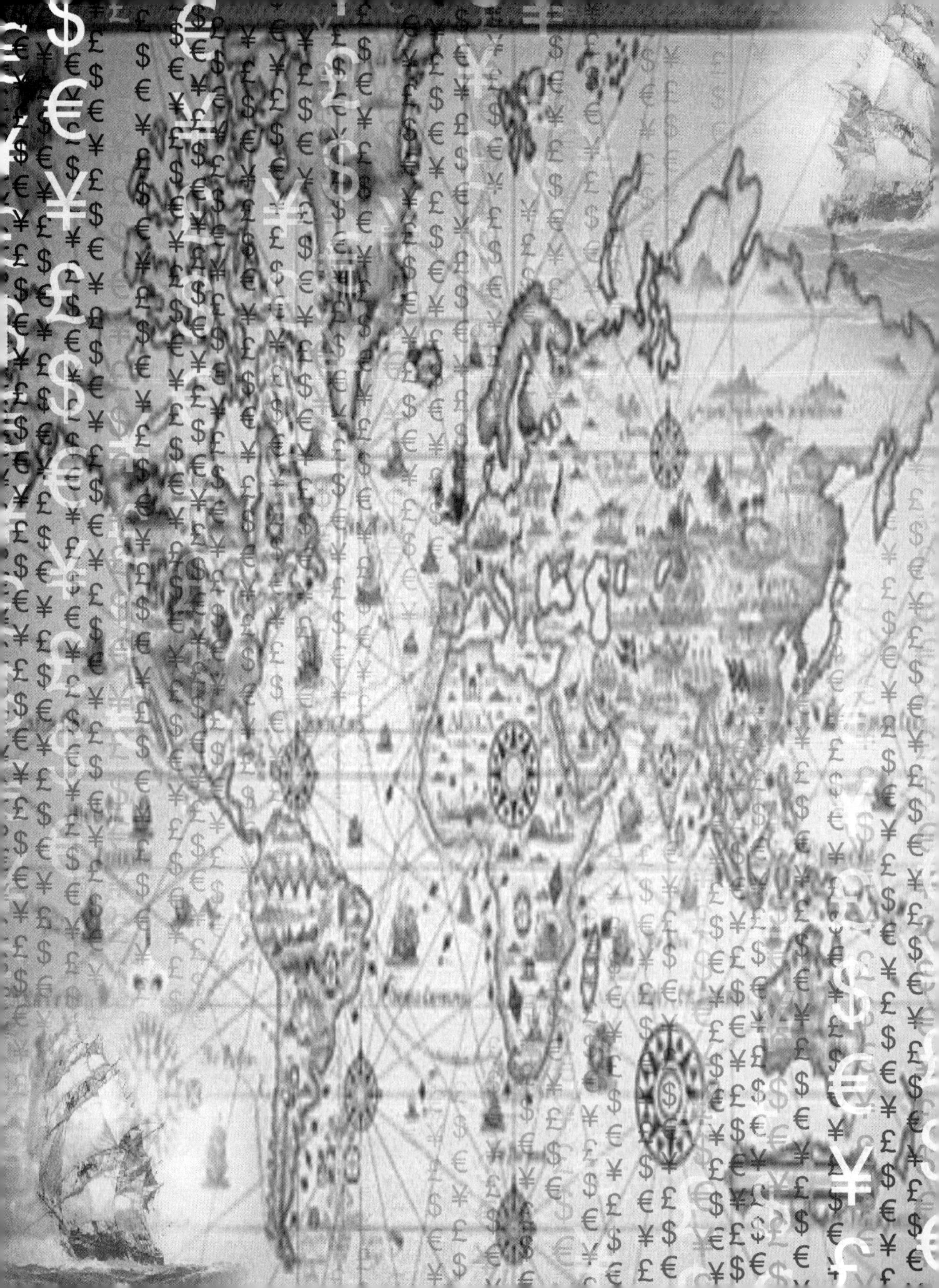

9

Applying the Content Targeting System

An e-commerce site, by virtue of its electronic nature, is able to collect information about its users that a traditional store cannot. For example, it can record the frequency a user visits your site, and a complete history of the items that they buy. Commerce Server 2000 acknowledges this important difference, and provides a sophisticated prediction engine to help you examine the relationships between your users and their purchases, to help you better promote and select your stock.

E-mail is a powerful weapon in the e-commerce site's armory. Within CS2K, if you implement a database to store user profiles, you can use ListManager and DirectMailer to collate and handle your customer information, allowing you to create targeted advertising, and mail it out to your customer base.

In this chapter we'll consider the following services:

❑ **Prediction Resource**. Using this tool we can create complex analysis models showing our site history (for example, user purchases and click history). We'll analyze prediction and segment models. The first one consists of a set of data used by the Predictor Engine to create a Dependency Network populated by decision trees showing statistical dependencies of the attributes. The second, groups users into segments based on similar attributes. We'll use this to export a list from List Manager in order to create a specific advertising campaign based on user flavors.

❑ **List Manager System**. The List Manager is a useful tool for creating lists of user records from data stored in a database, or a file. You can use this service to retrieve either mailing lists for use in a Direct Mail advertisement campaign or to obtain a list of users that have registered. In this section you'll learn how to create, delete, export, copy and merge lists of user records. Moreover you'll see how create these lists programmatically using the ListManager Objects.

❑ **Direct Mailer**. At the end of this chapter you'll find a section dedicated to the Direct Mailer service. It's a great tool allowing you to send e-mails to users previously stored in a mailing list by List Manager. In this section you'll learn how use Direct Mailer, both in its standalone mode, and inside a Direct Mail Campaign. Moreover, you'll see how to send e-mail messages to recipients, how to construct personalized and non-personalized message bodies and, finally, how to convert message bodies to the correct message type such as MIME Encapsulation of Aggregate HTML (MHTML), Multipurpose Internet Mail Extensions (MIME) or plain text.

The Prediction Engine Resource

Decision Support Systems (DSS) and OLAP databases have provided a new tool for technical and commercial analysts to analyze the financial balances and related information stored by companies. In Microsoft Commerce Server 2000 it is possible to create a data warehouse where OLAP cubes are used to create analysis models for predicting user purchases and preferences.

It would be preferable for you to have a basic knowledge of OLAP systems and data warehousing, so you can get the most from this section. However CS2K offers a selection of visual tools and facilities allowing others to make use of the predictor resources as well.

Below is a list of a few key terms and concepts that you would be well advised to review thoroughly before proceeding, as they are used extensively in discussions of the Predictor Resource:

❑ **Cases**: A case usually indicates a single user buying at least one object from our e-commerce site. Sometimes a case may include a user's click and purchase histories, and their user profile, as well. A good analysis model will normally use at least 50,000 such cases to produce a representative sample of the data. All of these will be extracted from the relevant data warehouse that you will have previously populated using SQL Server Data Transformation Services packages.

❑ **Decision trees**: These are a graphical representation of prediction rules allowing the analysis of probability values. They are used primarily to determine the likelihood of a user buying an item, based on previous purchases they have made.

❑ **Dependency Network**: This is a graphical representation of the predictive rules that bind the various articles.

❑ **Arc**: A graphical representation of the statistical relationship between various articles.

❑ **Segments**: Represent groups of users who share similar attributes. An example of a segment would be all the users buying a particular Rock music CD. A second segment would be those users purchasing Classical music, and so on.

❑ **Segment hierarchy**: Similar segments are grouped into a segment hierarchy representation where the topmost level includes 100% of the possible segments.

Prediction Models

You'll probably find it useful to analyze the behavior of users on your site. Their activities can tell you a great deal about the profitability of your e-company. If you can determine, for example, which items are most frequently purchased, and which customers purchase from you most often, you can then use this information to tailor your sites stock and advertising. For a prediction tool to be able to do this, you first have to create a proper model, after which you can review the results in the Prediction Model Viewer.

We're going look to at predicting the purchasing behavior of a client with respect to two products: Pants and Hats. Specifically, we want to see how likely it is that clients will buy both Hats and Pants (indicating that our cross selling is effective) versus a Hat or Pants singly. We'd also like to know how likely it is that a customer will buy more than one of a specific product.

Create a New Prediction Model

A Prediction model takes data from the data warehouse associated with your e-commerce site, so the first thing to do is import the user's data, transactions, and clicks into the database. This is accomplished by particular Data Transformation Services (DTS) packages added during the Microsoft Commerce Server 2000 installation. You can reach the DTS service from the Commerce Server Manager, by selecting the Microsoft SQL Servers node, then selecting the SQL Server that you are working on. The Data Transformation Services folder will now be visible.

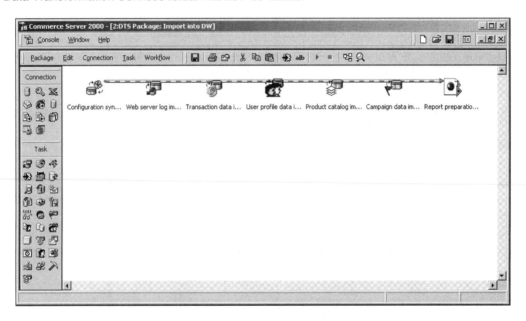

Above there is an example of a DTS package called Import into DW that takes web server log files, transaction data, user profile data, product catalog, and campaign information and imports them into the data warehouse. Usually, to create a prediction model using transaction data and user profile data is sufficient. However, including more data, like this, means that the analysis reports you prepare are also useful for reviewing the complete site. From the Task menu you begin to insert the necessary packages, setting their properties from the relative dialog boxes. Finally you could choose to select all the packages inserted and pick a rule from the Workflow menu. For example, with the On Success option you can decide that a package executes its task only if the previous package has completed without errors.

Now we have all the data stored into the data warehouse, we can add a new prediction model to our site. From the tables option in your data warehouse, follow these steps:

❏ In the SiteName column of the PredictorModelCfgs table, you have to insert the template name that will be used to build the final model (for example, Selling predictions).

❏ In the PredictorDataTables you have to specify more than one value:

❏ In the ModelCfgName column you have to repeat the previous template name given.

❑ In TableName you have to specify either the table or view you'll use to take the data.

❑ In the Type column you have to insert 0 if the table is going to be dense, 1 when it is sparse and 2 for an attributes table. A dense table is characterized by a one-to-one tie between rows and table primary keys, so for each unique identifier, a single row will be received. While, a sparse table has a one-to-many tie between rows and table primary key, so for each unique identifier more than one row could be received. Finally, specifying the attribute table will create a table where you have to indicate the properties and the distribution type for each attribute used in the model.

❑ The CaseColumn column usually contains the UserID value but generally it indicates the column that contains the case ID's.

❑ You'll use PivotColumn only when the Type column is equal to 1. This column usually stores the column that contains product names.

❑ You'll use AggregateColumn only when the Type column is equal to 1. You use it to specify on which column the aggregate operation will be accomplished.

❑ The AggregateOperation column identifies the aggregate operation type. Insert 0 for the SUM, 1 for MAX, 2 for MIN, 3 for AVG and 4 is equal to COUNT.

Now you can launch the Commerce Server Manager and go to the Prediction node under the root node labeled Commerce Server Manager.

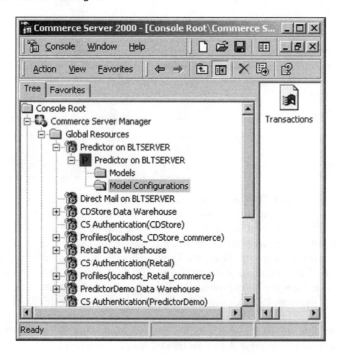

Here you'll find a new model configuration item that you'll use to build your prediction model. You should right-click on it, and choose Build from the menu. The following dialog box will appear:

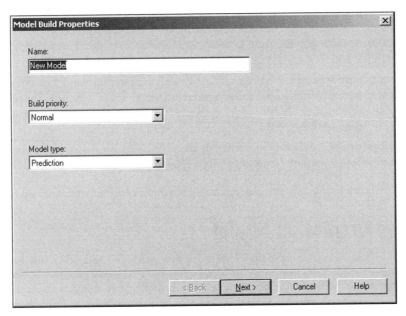

You should enter the model Name, choose the Build priority for this model and set the Model type to Prediction.

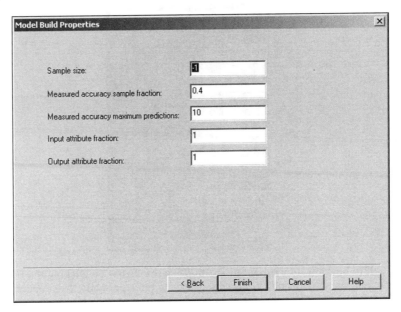

In the next window you have to specify a series of values:

❑ **Sample size:** Here you have to insert the number of cases that you want to use in the prediction model. The default value is -1, which corresponds to 20,000 rows.

❑ **Measured accuracy sample fraction:** You can specify the fraction of the sample data that you want to use in order to score the accuracy of the model. The range of this field is between 0.0 and 1.0. The default value of 0.4 indicates that 40% of the data will be used to score the model while the remaining 60% will be used to build the model.

❑ **Measured accuracy maximum predictions:** Specify how many recommendations will be inserted into your site when you use the prediction engine programmatically.

❑ **Input attribute fraction:** You can specify a value between 0.0 and 1.0. This field indicates how many attributes the model will use to create the prediction model. The topmost value indicates that all the attributes will be used while 0.1 indicates that only the most significant 10% of attributes will be used.

❑ **Output attribute fraction:** Here you can specify how many attributes will be predicted. The range of values is the same as we have seen above.

On pressing the Finish button a prediction model will be built and then inserted into the Models folder.

Analyze the Prediction Model

Selecting View Model from the context menu that appears when you right-click the model's name inside the Models list view, will cause the Predictor Model Viewer to appear in a separate window. It will contain a Dependency Networking diagram where every node, represented with a colored oval, will be tied with one or more edges to other nodes, showing various dependencies. At the beginning, connected nodes are quite close to each other, so press the Improve Layout button to space them out (the button is shown in the next screenshot).

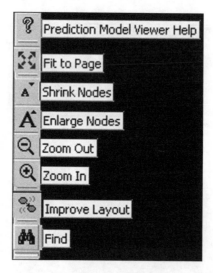

The nodes are still in position, so we can further improve the layout by clicking the Fit to Page button, which fits the Dependency Networking diagram inside the page perfectly. If you click on a node its dependencies will be highlighted in order to show all the nodes involved in the prediction relationship. If you want to predict a particular product, you have to double click on its node and the relative arc will be shown:

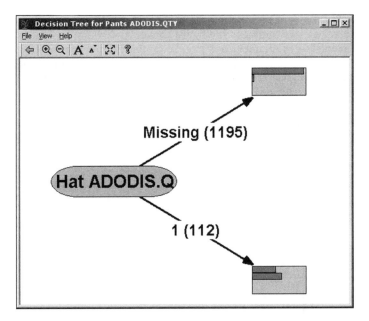

The figure, above, shows a relationship between two types of clothes: Pants and Hats. In the example, I have double clicked the Pants node, as I would like to know its predicted sales based on the number of hat purchases. The Missing label tells me that 1195 cases have bought Pants without buying a Hat while the 1 tells me that a Hat has been bought 112 times with or without a corresponding Pants purchase. To view the Predictor Resource predicted purchases, click on the corresponding square (called a *leaf*, and defined as a node with no outgoing link).

Each leaf expresses an IF condition THEN prediction formula with its predictions summarized in the Details dialog box (see an example in the figure above). The character p stands for *purchase* and the number in brackets indicates the number of items. So, in this example shown on the previous pages, if a client doesn't buy a Hat, then 95.4% of the time, they won't buy Pants, either. There is a very small (4.4%) chance that a user will buy Pants without buying a Hat, and an even more remote possibility that he buys either two or three pairs of Pants.

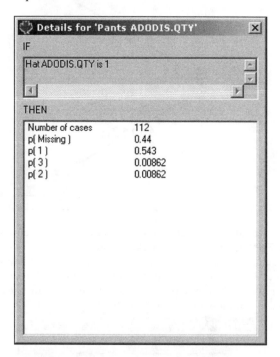

Examining the predictions where someone first purchases a Hat, the Predictor Resource predicts that 54.3% of customers will subsequently purchase Pants as well. Moreover the detail says that 44% of users will buy a Hat without purchasing any Pants and a small percentage of clients will buy more than one Pants together with the Hat.

This is a relatively simple case but the rules characterizing it are equally applicable to more complex situations.

Adding Prediction Capabilities to Our Site

A Prediction Model is not only useful to analysts and commercial experts, but could also be very useful for predicting users' preferences during their purchases. In fact it's quite simple to add a few lines of code in order to display correlated goods to those inserted into the customer's basket. It means we can advise our purchasers of more products that may be of interest to them, while they shop.

PredictorClient is the main object to use when adding prediction functionality to our site. Thanks to its methods we can load the prediction model from our basket page and use it to predict user preferences by calling the relative method. Let's see a snippet of code showing that (we've cut less important lines of code to improve readability).

At the beginning of the code we've defined the model name and retrieved the connection string to the data warehouse database.

It's very important to specify the same name given to the model during its construction.

```
Function InitPredictor()
   Dim objPredictor
   Dim connstr_db_dw
   Const strModelName = "Fashion Transactions"

   On Error Resume Next

   ' Retrieve connection string
   . . .
```

After `PredictorClient` creation the `LoadModuleFromDB` method is called in order to load the corresponding prediction model stored in the data warehouse database.

```
Set objPredictor = Server.CreateObject("Commerce.PredictorClient")

' Load the model from the data warehouse

objPredictor.LoadModelFromDB strModelName, connectionString
If Err.Number <> 0 Then
   ' No model found.
   Set objPredictor = Nothing
   Set InitPredictor = Nothing
   Exit Function
End If

On Error Goto 0
```

The script terminates setting values for `fpPopularityPenalty` and `fpDefaultConfidence` properties respectively.

```
' The popularity penalty weights the predictions
' against always recommending the most popular products.
'
' The higher the value, the greater the penalty.
' 0.0 = No penalty.
' 1.0 = Maximum penalty.

objPredictor.fpPopularityPenalty = 0.8

. . .

' The confidence threshold sets a lower bound on how
' confident the predictor needs to be in order to return
' a recommendation.
' 0.0 = Do not restrict based on confidence.
' 100.0 = Don't return any predictions.

objPredictor.fpDefaultConfidence = 10

. . .
End Function
```

In the `PredictorClient` object, everything revolves around the `Predict()` method. It must be called providing one Dictionary object, and one SimpleList object.

```
Function htmRenderPredictions(mscsOrderGrp, oOrderFormDisplayOrder)
    Dim sOrderFormName, oOrderForm, htmContent, dItem,_
                     strPropName, varValue, lQuantity
    Dim slToPredict, dCase
    Dim arPredictedProps, arPredictedVals
    Dim lMaxPredictions, i, lPredictionCount
    Dim strHREF

    ...
```

We construct the input case from the items in the basket. The constructed property name in the input dictionary is of the form: *[Catalog Name].[Product ID]*. This must correspond to the format used for SKU in the Trans_Predictor view in the data warehouse. This means that we treat all variants of a product equally for the purposes of prediction.

```
    Set dCase = Server.CreateObject("Commerce.Dictionary")
    Set slToPredict = Server.CreateObject("Commerce.SimpleList")
```

`Dictionary` must contain all the cases you want to participate in the prediction model while `SimpleList` must contain the properties to be predicted. To predict for the `SimpleList` object we simply have to add the column to be predicted (for example, `slToPredict.Add "SKU"`). To predict for the `Dictionary` object the story is a bit more complex. The `Predict()` method waits for a precise dictionary entry syntax, with the following structure:

```
<AggregateColumnName>(<PivotColumnContent>) = <value>
```

Let's see a couple of examples:

```
dCase("QTY([Clothes].[Pants_Adodis_Blue])") = 2
```

or

```
dCase("Hits(www.fashionstore.com/spring2001)") = 1
```

In the first case, as with the code above, `QTY` stands for the aggregate column name while, between the brackets, there is the content of the SKU pivot column name. Here we are asking the Prediction Engine to return recommendations relative to two pairs of blue pants.

```
    ' Add list of properties to predict. For product recommendations,
    ' we give the name of the PivotColumn defined in PredictorDataTables.
    slToPredict.Add "SKU"

    For Each sOrderFormName in oOrderFormDisplayOrder
        Set oOrderForm = mscsOrderGrp.value.OrderForms.Value(sOrderFormName)
        For Each dItem in oOrderForm.Items
            strPropName = "QTY" & "([" & dItem.product_catalog & "]._
                               [" & dItem.product_id & "])"
            lQuantity = CLng(dItem.quantity)
```

```
            dCase(strPropName) = lQuantity
        Next
    Next
```

Rereading the example code, we can now understand what happens inside the `For...Next` cycle. Each item inside the order form will be used to create a dictionary entry. The third and fourth `Predict()` parameters will contain the method's predictions after its execution. The last parameter indicates how many predictions the method will have to return.

```
    ' Call the predictor.
    lMaxPredictions = 5 'Display no more than this many predictions.
    oPredictor.Predict dCase, slToPredict, arPredictedProps,_
                       arPredictedVals, lMaxPredictions

    . . .
End Function
```

After the `Predict()` method is called, two `SucureArrays` will be filled with the recommendations. All that remains is to go through the array and show the recommendations on the site page.

Segment Models

The second model offered by the Prediction Engine system is the Segment Model. In this case, using the same data warehouse structure created for the Prediction Model, all the users with similar purchase preferences will be grouped into *segments*. Commerce Server uses data stored in the data warehouse to calculate segments and groups of segments. For instance, if you create a specific segment model that retrieves users' preferences tied to their age and salary, then you could compare that data to take advantage of common characteristics and offer similar products previously bought by these users.

Creating a segment model is similar to creating a Prediction model, with just a couple of differences:

In the Model Type field you should change the value to Prediction with Segment. Another two fields will then appear in the following property sheet. They are:

❑ **Number of Segments**: Here you can specify the maximum number used to partition the users.

❑ **Buffer size**: Specify the buffer size used by the Prediction Engine when it builds the segment model. If you have a lot of users, consider increasing this value from the 1-megabyte default to a more considerable one.

Pressing the Finish button causes a new segment model to be inserted in the Models list view. You use it by opening the BizDesk application and navigating to the Analysis I Segment Viewer menu.

Analyze the Segment Model

The first time you launch the Segment Viewer tool from the BizDesk application you'll see the segment hierarchy on the left, showing the global population of users. Segment Viewer shows the users' percentage for that segment between the brackets. So, for the root node you'll see a 100% value representing the entire population. Expanding the segment hierarchy, by clicking on the little arrow on the left of the segment label, means that you can navigate between segments in order to analyze them in more detail. After creating the segment model for the first time, each segment label will have totally unrelated names, like Segment 1, Segment 8 and so on. You will need to rename them with more meaningful alternatives – you could take inspiration from the analysis of users' tendencies for that segment!

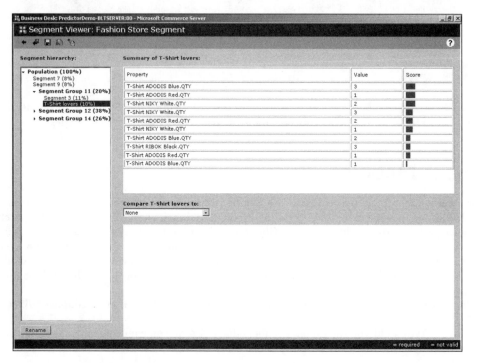

As you can see from the figure above, the generic Segment x has been substituted with a T-Shirt lovers label, because analyzing the segment summary shows it contains customers that bought a T-Shirt. You can accomplish this operation by clicking on the Rename button in the bottom left corner of the window. The Property/Value pairs will change their contents based upon the query you have used to create the model configuration template. For instance, if you retrieve records by hair color you'll see that the Property will contain Hair while the value could contain Blonde, Red and so on. The Score column will be more or less lengthy based upon the Property/value matches with records in the database. In the figure above I have retrieved data and created a view that contains the following SQL instruction:

```
SELECT RU.UserId, OFLI.product_id AS SKU, OFLI.quantity AS QTY
FROM dbo.OrderGroup OG INNER JOIN
    dbo.OrderFormLineItems OFLI ON OG.ordergroup_id = _
        OFLI.OrderGroup_id INNER JOIN
        dbo.RegisteredUser RU ON OG.RegisteredUserID = RU.RegisteredUserID
```

I specified a new row, following the instructions already seen above, inside `PredictorDataTables` to populate the previous SQL Server view.

```
INSERT INTO PredictorDataTables VALUES
('Fashion_Transactions','FashionUsers',1,'UserID','SKU','QTY',4)
```

So, in my case, the Property/Value pairs stand for the quantity of a particular product bought by a single user, compared to how many products have been sold.

Your analysts will be excited when they see the Compare combo box and its features. It contains a list of all the segments forming the segment model and you can choose a value to compare with the previously selected segment. Intelligent segment models will allow you to understand why a particular segment of users purchase particular kinds of products rather than others, or which is the common item bought by the two segments. A yellow bar indicates the level to which the Property/Value pairs correspond for the selected segment rather than the comparison one. While a blue bar indicates the level to which the Property/Value pairs correspond for the comparison segment as opposed to the selected one.

List Manager System

How many times you have bought a book or a CD from an e-commerce site? On some sites you will find that you have to enter your personal information into a form, whereas on other sites you have to register yourself in order to obtain a username and password to use when you want to buy from that site. Whatever solution you choose to implement in your e-commerce site you have to know that user information will be stored in a database. You may be asking "Why is this information not used on the fly? Why is it inserted into a storage space?" This is because user information is very powerful! Imagine what you can do with this data – interrogating the database to retrieve new users, or selecting the most loyal customers for discounts and promotions. Microsoft Commerce Server 2000 offers the List Manager System to accomplish this. With the List Manager you can create lists of user records to use in your site.

> *Remember that you can use this tool only if you create your site using a Solution Site (see more on solution sites in Chapter 10).*

In this section we'll see:

- ❑ How to create a list of registered users from the Reports module, the Segment Viewer module, an ASCII text file and a SQL query.

- ❑ How to delete an existing list.

- ❑ How to export lists as an ASCII file, or in other formats.

- ❑ How to create a new list by copying from another one.

- ❑ How to merge two lists.

- ❑ How to subtract two lists.

- ❑ Finally we'll analyze the ListManager Objects that allow us to manage user lists programmatically.

Creating Lists

We can create a user list with the List Manager Service, either to just keep as a users list, or to turn into a mailing list (if the user's information contains e-mail addresses). A mailing list is necessary to implement a **Direct Mail campaign** – a great feature of Microsoft Commerce Server 2000 that allows you to contact users by e-mail to propose goods and promotions. Additionally, a user list can be used with the BizDesk application in order to manage user profiles.

Using the Report Module to Create Lists of User Records

The first method we'll look at to create a list of user records is by launching reports from the Reports module contained in the BizDesk application. There are many precompiled reports we can use in order to obtain lists of user records based upon certain conditions. As an example, imagine we want know which users have most recently registered on our site. Expanding the Analysis menu in the BizDesk application gives us access to the Reports submenu. After selecting it, the BizDesk will show a list of preformatted reports to choose from (for further explanations on the Reports module see Chapter 5).

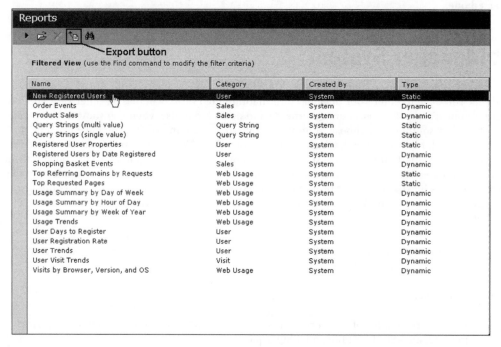

When you click the right arrow near the bottom of the page, the second page of reports will be shown, which contains the New Registered Users report. When you click the Run button, the Report module will produce a list of the new users just registered on our site, showing them as an HTML page inside Internet Explorer. Now, we want to export that list in order to create an element in the List Manager Service list. To accomplish this we have to use the Export button located on the toolbar (indicated in the figure above)

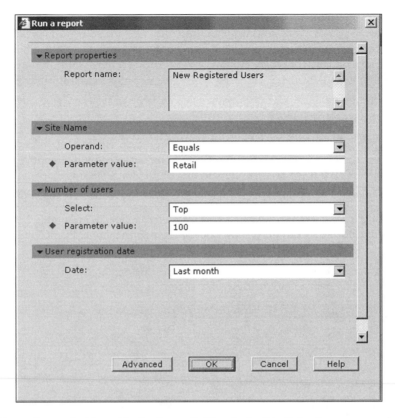

The figure above shows the **Export** button's result. Thanks to this dialog box we can change the final report result by selecting various attribute combinations.

The available fields are:

❏ **Report** Name: This is a disabled field that shows the report name.

❏ **Operand**: This field allows you to set the operand value to one of the following:

   ❏ All. In cases where we have more than one e-commerce site installed on our Internet Information Server, we can choose this value in order to search for users through all the available sites.

   ❏ Equals. Choosing this option, we can specify, in the **Parameter Value** field, which is the site from where the Reports module has to get user lists.

   ❏ Not equal to. If we have more than one e-commerce site installed on our Internet Information Server we can choose this value in order to search for users through all the available sites, excluding the one specified in the **Parameter Value** field.

   ❏ Like. Choosing this option, we can specify, in the **Parameter Value** field, which is the site from where the Reports module has to get user lists. We can use the percent character (%) to retrieve a user list from more than just one site. For example, we can insert a `Ret%` value into the field, and so obtain all the users registered in sites whose name begins with the `Ret` string.

- ❑ Not Like. With more than one e-commerce site installed on our Internet Information Server we can choose this value in order to search for users through all the available sites, excluding the ones specified into the **Parameter Value** field and retrieved using the percent character (%). For example, we can insert a `Ret%` value into the field, so excluding all the users registered in sites whose name begins with the `Ret` string.

❑ **Select**. In this field we can specify how many users to retrieve. We can select one value from the three possible values:

- ❑ All. Choose this option if you want to retrieve all the users available.

- ❑ Top. If you want to limit the number of users retrieved by the report you can specify a number (100 is the default value) in the **Parameter Value** field.

- ❑ Distinct. With this option you can avoid retrieving more than one record per user.

❑ **Date**. This is a combo-box field where we can select a value representing a date's range. This value is included between the Today value and the selected one. Possible values include `Last Month`, `Last Week`, `Yesterday`, and `Today`.

Pressing the **OK** button will make the following dialog box appear:

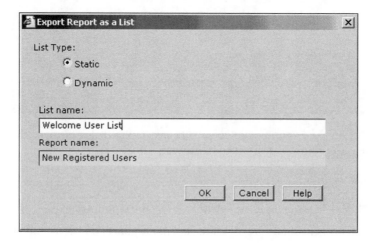

As well as the **List** name field, where we have to insert the list name, there are two much more important choices:

- ❑ Static. The list produced will contain a 'snapshot' of the users registered in the Microsoft Commerce Server 2000 site at the exact instant of pressing the OK button. Subsequent new customers who meet the criteria will not be included, as the information is never refreshed.

- ❑ Dynamic. Choosing this option means that a dynamic list of users will be produced. In this way every time that the report is executed, an updated list of customers will be included.

- ❑ We'll choose the Static option and press the OK button – the Welcome User List will be inserted into the List Manager submenu of the Campaigns menu.

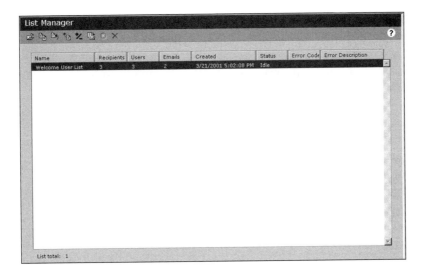

As you can see from the figure above, a new row has been inserted into the List Manager table. You can access the List Manager service by clicking on the List Manager submenu of the Campaigns menu.

Using the Segment Viewer Model to Produce Lists of User Records

As we have seen previously a Segment model groups users by a specific characteristic, such as their purchases or their age. By analyzing your model, you could find that a particular category of customers have purchased a particular item and might be interested in additional products as well. For example, you could retrieve a list of Stephen King readers and propose Clive Barker's books to them. The Segment Viewer offers the Export segment to list option that generates a user list, complete with corresponding e-mail addresses that you can use it in your Direct Mailer ad campaign.

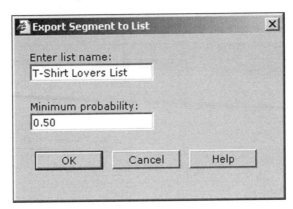

In the figure above you have to enter the list name you want to generate and a probability number indicating how close a user must be to the segment criteria for admission (range 0.0 to 1.0). A value close to zero will result in only a small number of users being accepted, while a value closer to one will result in a correspondingly larger number fitting the probability criteria.

Using an ASCII Text File to Create Lists of User Records

Now we'll look at how to import an ASCII text file to create a list of user records. There are a few rules to follow to ensure we do this successfully. Each row of the ASCII file will be assumed by the service to correspond to a recipient, and all the parameters on that line must be recorded as a series of comma-separated values:

Parameter (Required/Optional)	Description
Username or e-mail address *Required*	The user's name or e-mail address.
GUID *Optional*	The user's global unique identifier. It must be the same GUID value as that stored in the `UserObject` table of the database.
Message format *Optional*	The message format type used by the CDO libraries when the Direct Mail service contacts the users contained in the list. Possible values are `text`, `MIME` and `MHTML`.
Language *Optional*	E-mail messages can be created in multiple languages based on the user's nationality and language. This field specifies the locale code to use for the recipient.
URL *Optional*	Here we can specify a URL for the CDO libraries when the Direct Mail service contacts users contained in the list.

So, as we can see from the table, we could provide an ASCII text file containing only the users' e-mail addresses. If we did this we'd not be able to filter users using the BizDesk Users menu as it relies upon the GUID key to perform this operation. However for a list of users to use with the Direct Mail service (explained in more detail later) this is not an issue, and the e-mail addresses alone would be more than sufficient.

```
boh@perserv.com
qwerty@qwerty.com,,MIME
JillUser@Microsoft.com,{31296787-1E0E-4712-9582-B26B15062DEC}
```

The first row, of the code above, contains only an e-mail address, the second row an e-mail address and message format, the third row an e-mail address and a GUID key.

If you wish to omit an optional parameter, but specify one of those following it, you must insert a comma-separator for each value you are omitting, otherwise the service will assume the value is for the earlier – missing – parameter.

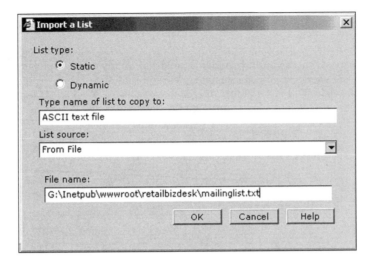

Pressing the import button, located on the toolbar, the BizDesk will show the above dialog box.

❏ Since a text file's content is always static, we must select the Static option for the List Type.

❏ In the Type name of list to copy to field you should insert the name of the list to be copied to.

❏ The List Source combo-box allows us to choose either From File or From SQL Database. To import an ASCII text file we must select the first option.

❏ The File Name text field will contain the complete path and filename of the ASCII text file.

After clicking the OK button, the file will be processed and a mailing list produced and included in the List Manager table.

Using a SQL Query to Create Lists of User Records

This method is very useful when we have to create dynamic lists of users. We can specify a SQL command that retrieves records from the UserObject table of our database so that every new user will be extracted each time the command is executed. We have to follow just a few rules:

Field name	Description
rcp_email – *Required*	Retrieves either the user name or e-mail address.
rcp_guid – *Optional*	Obtains the *User ID* expressed in GUID format.
rcp_fmt – *Optional*	Retrieves the format message type. Possible values are text, MIME and MHTML.
rcp_locale – *Optional*	Obtains the locale code used by CDO in the Direct Mail campaign service.
rcp_url – *Optional*	Retrieve individual URLs associated with each user.

Our query must contain at least the rcp_email field in order to produce a valid List Manager list. Let's see a real situation where we would use a SQL query method:

```
SELECT u_email_address AS rcp_email, g_user_id AS rcp_guid FROM UserObject WHERE
u_Pref1='Male'
```

This could be employed where you have added a gender property to the user's profile and want to retrieve only the male users. As you can see, you have to insert alias values for the column names in order to provide the right field names to the List Manager service. We have inserted the SQL query inside the **SQL Query** text field of the **Import a List** dialog box:

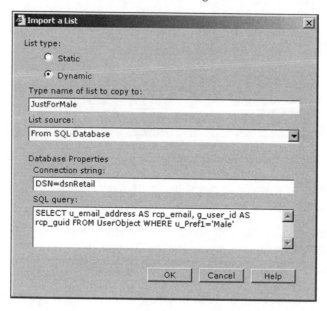

In the **Connection** string text field you need to specify a valid string containing either a previously created DSN name or a valid OLE-DB provider.

You can validate the SQL query using the **Users** submenu located under the **Users** menu in the left panel of the BizDesk application.

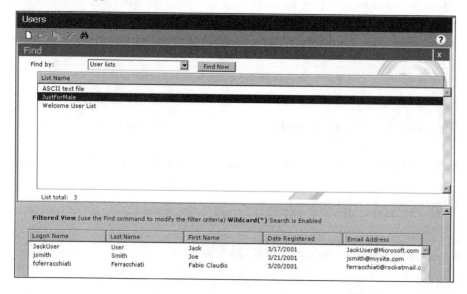

In the upper panel of the Users window we select User lists criteria in order to commit our searching. If the SQL query doesn't contain errors, the bottom panel will show the final result of the query execution.

Deleting a List

This is a simple operation for when we have generated a non-working list or when a specific list is no longer required. All we have to do is select the name of the list we want to delete and press the Delete button on the toolbar.

After we confirm our intention, the list will be removed from the List Manager listbox and the database.

Exporting a List to an ASCII Text File and a SQL Server Table

The BizDesk application gives us the possibility of exporting either a mailing list or a generic list from List Manager to either an ASCII text file or a SQL Server table. A common example of using the export functionality is when we have to import a user list from another e-commerce application. Imagine that our company has opened a new e-commerce site, and would like to use all the clients already registered on its other sites. The site administrator can export all the lists from each BizDesk application and use them to create a new list on the new e-commerce site. Exporting a list is an easy operation. You simply select the name of the list you want to export in the List Manager listbox and then press the Export button on the toolbar.

The following dialog box will appear asking for the path, where you want create the file:

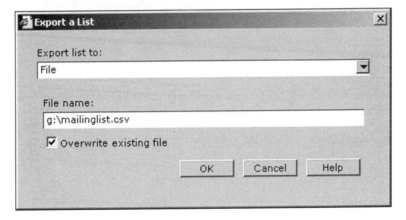

Another option offered by the List Manager Export functionality is to export users into a new SQL Server table. The steps are the same, we just have to select SQL database from the Export list to combo box.

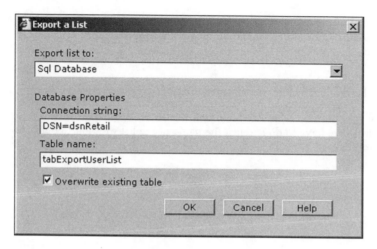

Instead of the file path field, we have to specify a connection string to a SQL Server database and the name of the new table. Also, we can decide to overwrite the table if it already exists.

Copying a List

Select a list from the List Manager and press the Copy button.

on the toolbar; you can duplicate the selected list by specifying a new list name. This operation can be useful in cases where you want to manipulate a list without losing the original.

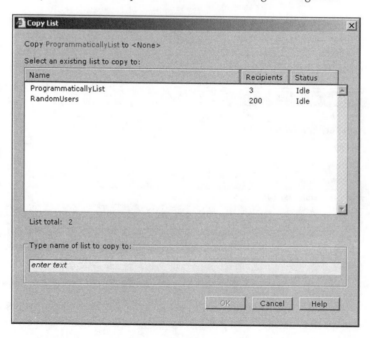

In the above dialog box we can choose either to append the selected list to an existing one, choosing its name from the Select an existing list to copy to: list box, or copy a new one, specifying a new list name in the Type name of list to copy to: field.

Merging and Subtracting Two Lists

Imagine you have an entire site's customers divided into two lists, each grouped by a different gender. It might be the case that you need a unique user list in order to manipulate all the users registered on your site. Certainly, this can be accomplished by creating a new list but it's easier and faster to merge two existing lists. By selecting a list from the List Manager list box and pressing the Add/Subtract list button.

you could merge the list with another, and save yourself time and effort.

Add/Subtract Lists		x
Current list:	ProgrammaticallyList	
Operation:	Add to ...	▼
Target list:	RandomUsers	▼
Save list as		
Name for new list:	MergeList	
Description:	*enter text*	
	OK Cancel Help	

After pressing the OK button, a new list called MergeList will be generated. We can use the same procedure even when we have to subtract a list from another one. Just select the Subtract from... option from the Operation: combo box and the list of where to remove records from.

The ListManager Object

All the operations we have seen so far in this section can be done programmatically using the ListManager methods and properties. Now, we'll analyze two easy examples, developed using Visual Basic 6.0, to explore this in more detail.

- ❏ In the first example we'll open an Excel spreadsheet file containing a few users and then create a mailing list using their e-mail addresses.

- ❏ In the second example we'll generate up to two hundred virtual users, creating a SQL table in which to store them. This table will be used to populate the UserObject table in order to increase the number of users of the site.

Importing a Mailing List from an Excel Spreadsheet File

Imagine we have an Excel spreadsheet file filled with raw information and we'd like to produce a mailing list from that information. We can't export this information as a comma-separated text file because it isn't formatted the right way. But, fortunately, we can use ListManager object methods and properties.

First of all we have to add the List Manager Type library and ADO 2.5 Type library to our Visual Basic project in order to be able to instantiate and use these objects. This can be accomplished from the Project | References menu of the Visual Basic IDE. Now we can insert our code into the Form_Load event of the Form1 form. In the first few lines of the example an ADO Recordset is used to retrieve all the e-mail addresses from the Excel spreadsheet file. The Open() method of the Recordset object uses a SQL instruction and an OLE-DB provider to connect to the data source. In order to retrieve data from an Excel file using ADO we have to name the spreadsheet.

To do this, open the Excel.xls file, select all the columns and rows, point to the Insert | Name | Define menu and specify a name; this will be used by ADO just like a table name. For my file, I have specified rcp_email as the name, so the line "SELECT * FROM rcp_email" appears in the code. You should substitute this with whatever name you choose to use.

```
On Error GoTo err_
    Dim dbRec As New ADODB.Recordset

    'Retrieve all records from Excel file
    dbRec.Open "SELECT * FROM rcp_email", "DSN=Excel_Files;DBQ=G:\mailinglist.xls;
    DefaultDir=G:;DriverId=790;FIL=excel_
        8.0;MaxBufferSize=2048;PageTimeout=5;"

    'Create List Manager Object
    Dim lm As New LISTMANAGERLib.ListManager

    Dim id As Variant
    Dim retId As Variant
```

Going on with our code explanation, we now need to create and initialize some of the ListManager objects. Here we have to specify either an OLE-DB provider or a data source name pointing to the <sitename>_commerce database (or the database where the lm_master table is stored).

```
    'Connection to the database and object initialization
    lm.Initialize "Provider=sqloledb;Data Source=BLTSERVER;
    Initial_
        Catalog=Retail_Commerce;User ID=sa;Password="
```

After that the CreateEmpty() function is called. It allows the creation of an empty list to populate with the AddUserToMailingList() method. The parameters are in the form of :

```
CreateEmpty (Name As String, Description As String, Flags As Long, userFlag As
Long) As Variant.
```

Name is the new list name, Description is the list description, Flags defines the list type to create, (userFlags is not used and is always equal to zero). The entire function returns a Variant variable that identifies the new list ID.

Once the empty list is created, new users need to be added. This is achieved with the AddUserToMailingList function. It takes the following parameters:

```
AddUserToMailingList (listID As Variant, e-mail As Variant,
Optional userID As Variant, Optional userFMT As Variant,
Optional userLocale As Variant,
Optional userURL As Variant) As Variant.
```

Where, listID represents the new list identifier returned by the CreateEmpty() function, e-mail is the user e-mail address, userID the user identifier, userFMT is the format message type to use with the CDO library, userLocale indicates the user locale and, finally, userURL specifies a URL associated with the user.

The code to apply these functions could look like the following:

```
'Create list from file
retId = lm.CreateEmpty("ProgrammaticallyList", "List created by_
   VB6 code", 0, 0)

'Populate the list
Do While dbRec.EOF = False
   lm.AddUserToMailingList retId, dbRec(0)
   dbRec.MoveNext
Loop

'Remove all objects from memory
dbRec.Close
Set dbRec = Nothing
Set lm = Nothing


Exit Sub

err_:
 Set dbRec = Nothing
Set lm = Nothing

MsgBox Err.Description
```

The final result of the code is shown in the figure overleaf.

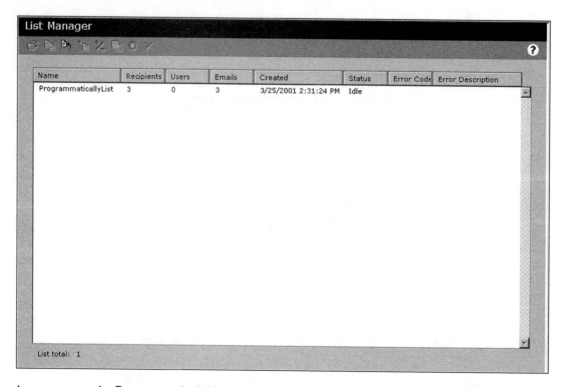

As you can see the ProgrammaticallyList list has been added to the ListManager container in the BizDesk application.

Using the ListManager Object to Export Users to the UserObject Table

The next example uses the ListManager object to export a mailing list to a SQL Server table. Visual Basic 6 was used to generate a comma-separated file containing up to two hundred users and the ListManager object to create a mailing list to export to a SQL Server table. The code for this is:

```
Option Explicit
Private Sub Form_Load()
    Dim lm As New LISTMANAGERLib.ListManager
    Dim retID As Variant
    Dim connString As String
    Dim sql As String
    Dim dbCon As New ADODB.Connection
```

The GenerateRandomUsers() subroutine creates a comma-separated file and saves it to the hard disk. The file respects List Manager directives, so in the first column there is an e-mail address, while the second contains a GUID user identifier. Attached to it, *but not separated by a comma*, there is a string we'll use for the logon name column of the UserObject table. The next step is to initialize the ListManager object. This is accomplished by the Initialize() method, which we pass a database connection string.

```
    On Error GoTo err_
    'Set connection string to the commerce database
    connString = "Provider=sqloledb;Data Source=BLTSERVER;
Initial_
```

```
        Catalog=Retail_Commerce;User ID=sa;Password="

    'Generate up to two hundreds users
    GenerateRandomUsers

    'Initialize ListManager object
    lm.Initialize connString
```

The `CreateFromFile()` and `ExportToSQL()` methods represent the main functions of this algorithm. They allow the creation of a mailing list from a comma-separated file and its export to a SQL Server table.

```
    Function CreateFromFile(listName As String, listDesc As String, lFlags As Long,
    userFlags As Long, fileName As String, errLimit As Long, bAsync As Boolean,
    Optional pvarOpID As Variant) As Variant.
```

`listName` is the new list name, `listDesc` the new list description, `lFlags` specifies the type of the list (generic list, mailing list and so on), (*userFlags is not used and is always zero*), `fileName` is the path plus the name of the comma-separated file, `errLimit` specifies how many errors can occur before the operation is terminated, `bAsync` is a Boolean that indicates if the operation has to be asynchronous and, `pvarOpID` is the operation ID necessary to other functions.

The parameter format for `ExporttoSql` is :

```
    Sub ExportToSql(listID As Variant, connStr As String, resTable As String,
    bOverwrite As Boolean, lOptions As Long, bAsync As Boolean, Optional pvarOpID As
    Variant).
```

`listID` represents the list identifier returned by the `CreateFromFile()` function, `connStr` is the connection string to the database, `resTable` is the name of the table that will contain the exported data (if it doesn't already exist it will be created), `bOverwrite` specifies whether to overwrite the data already stored in the table, `lOptions` determines the exporting method, 0 to export like a generic list, 1 to export for Direct Mail use `bAsync` is a Boolean that indicates if the operation has to be asynchronous and, finally, `pvarOpID` is the operation ID.

```
    'Create a mailing list from comma-separated file
    retID = lm.CreateFromFile("RandomUsers", "RandomUsers List", 20, 0,_
        "G:\mailinglist.csv", 0, False)

    'Export the mailing list to a temporary table
    lm.ExportToSql retID, connString, "RandomUsers", False, 0, False
```

Finally the routine inserts records from the exported table into the `UserObject` table, as shown below.

```
    'Insert new record into UserObject table
    dbCon.Open connString

    'Set SQL command and execute it
    sql = "INSERT INTO UserObject (g_user_id, u_email_address, u_logon_name,_
        u_user_security_password, i_account_status) SELECT LEFT(rcp_guid,38),_
```

```
      rcp_email, SUBSTRING(rcp_guid,39,LEN(rcp_guid)),'wroxrules',1 FROM_
      RandomUsers"

   dbCon.Execute sql

   'Remove exported table
   sql = "DROP TABLE RandomUsers"
   dbCon.Execute sql

   'Remove List Manager mailing list
   lm.Delete retID

   'Remove objects from memory
   Set lm = Nothing
   Set dbCon = Nothing

   Exit Sub

   err_:
   Set lm = Nothing
   Set dbCon = Nothing

   MsgBox Err.Description

End Sub

Sub GenerateRandomUsers()
   Dim I As Integer
   Dim Guid As New GENIDLib.GenID

   'Create and open the comma-separated file
   Open "G:\mailinglist.csv" For Output As #1

   'Insert up to two hundreds generated users with GUID identifier
   For I = 1 To 200
      Print #1, "User" & I & "@microsoft.com," & Guid.GenGUIDString &_
         "User" & I
   Next I

   'Close the file
   Close #1

End Sub
```

Direct Mailer System

One of the greatest advantages offered by an e-commerce site is its capacity for directed advertising. By implementing a good advertisement campaign you can inform your clients about new articles, discounts, and promotions, without wasting resources. I know of a merchant in my city that knows my dress preferences and phones me when there's something new in his shop: "Come here; I have new stuff to show you". However, I have to take my car and go to his store, then I have to find a parking space and finally I can see the new goods, only to exclaim, "Well, I don't like pink jeans...!". The moral of this story is that I have lost a lot of time. Consider the difference if it was an e-commerce operation:

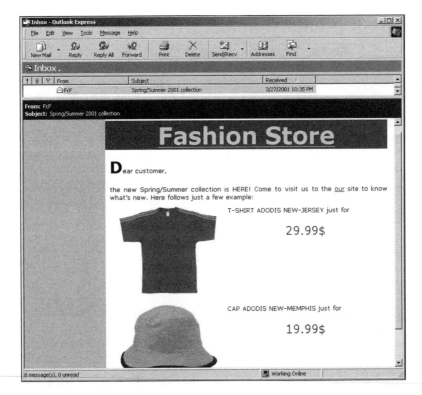

The figure above shows an e-mail sent by a hypothetical store informing me about their new Spring/Summer 2001 collection. As I comfortably sit in my chair, I can read news about my favorite store, visit it virtually and buy that cap that looks so pretty! Microsoft Commerce Server 2000 offers the Direct Mailer service allowing the sending of personalized e-mails to customers informing them of new arrivals and promotions. Direct Mailer uses a mailing list previously created by the List Manager service.

At the end of this section you'll understand:

- ❏ **How to use the BizDesk application to create a Direct Mailer campaign**. In this section we'll see how to use the Direct Mail tool, accessible from the BizDesk application under the Campaigns | Campaign Manager menu, in order to contact clients and keep them informed.

- ❏ **What a Direct Mailer Pipeline is**. The Direct Mailer Pipeline is an important part of the Direct Mailer service. It determines how information has to be processed and what to do when we encounter unexpected errors. We can customize its behavior by both adding and removing objects from the logical flow to which the information is subjected.

- ❏ **How to use Direct Mailer in standalone mode**. The Direct Mailer service offers a command line interface in order to create and manage a Direct Mailer job. You can use it in standalone mode, by supplying a mailing list or SQL Server query and allowing it to launch a job without necessarily associating it with a campaign.

Create a Direct Mailer Campaign

The first method we'll look at creates a Direct Mailing campaign based on a mailing list previously created by the List Manager service. If you installed Microsoft Commerce Server 2000 as a complete installation on your system, a new Windows 2000 service called **Commerce Server Direct Mailer** will have been installed (during a Custom install, select the Direct Mailer check box). This service operates at the Commerce Server global resource level. That means there will be just one Direct Mailer global service on the Windows 2000 Server and every site created using Commerce Server, will utilize an instance of it. From the Commerce Server Manager you can configure the service choosing the attributes that every site will utilize when they implement the Direct Mailer functionality.

> *The Direct Mailer service depends on the SQL Server Agent working correctly. This implies that SQL Server and Direct Mailer must reside on the same server because SQL Server Agent has not been created to work remotely.*

To create a Direct Mailer Campaign you're advised to follow these few steps:

❑   Import the user information into a data warehouse.

❑   Create a mailing list using reports.

❑   Add a customer and a campaign using the BizDesk's **Campaigns** tool.

❑   Create the Direct Mailer campaign.

❑   Test it.

From the **Campaigns** menu on the left panel of the BizDesk we can access the Campaign Manager. Here there will be a list of all the campaigns each e-commerce site already has installed on our web server. We need to insert the customer name and campaign attributes.

We do this by pressing the **New Campaign Item** button:

and choosing the **New Customer** option; the BizDesk displays the following form:

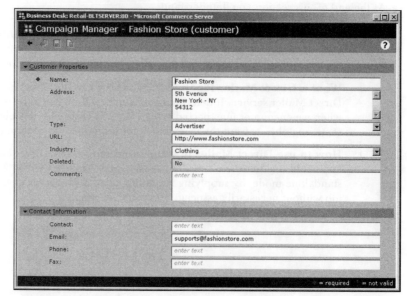

As you can see from the figure above, in order to create a new customer, we must at least specify their name. Optionally, other information such as e-mail addresses and home addresses can be included. After clicking the **Save and Back** button, we can insert our new campaign by selecting the **New Campaign** option from the menu.

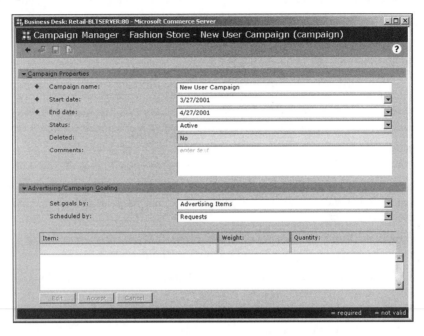

Next, we have to specify a campaign name, initial campaign date and final campaign date. Also we have to change **Set goals by** to the **Advertising Items** option. Lastly, we have to expand all the new voices inserted into the Campaign Manager list box and selecting the campaign name. If you've followed the previous steps, you'll now find that the **New Direct Mail** sub-menu is highlighted and selectable.

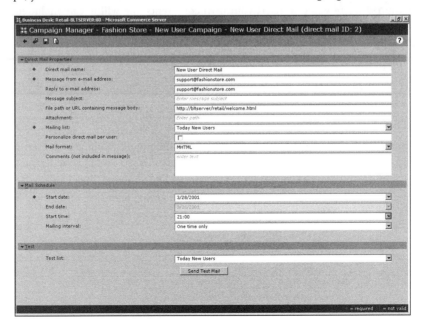

473

Now, we'll review each field in detail:

- ❑ **Direct Mail name**: Here you have to insert the new direct mail name.

- ❑ **Message from e-mail address**: This field represents the e-mail's sender address.

- ❑ **Reply to e-mail address**: If you need to indicate an e-mail address different to the sender's address, you can specify it in this field.

- ❑ **Message subject**: Write here what you want to appear in the e-mail subject line.

- ❑ **File path or URL containing message body**: In this field you have to specify either a path to a text file or a URL to an ASP/HTML page containing the text of the message. If you prefer to send a generic message to the users you can create a text file or an HTML page with generic text inside; otherwise you can create dynamic messages specifying ASP files.

- ❑ **Attachment**: Here you can specify a path to a file that will be attached to the message. For example, this could be very useful when you want to send a full catalog of your products.

- ❑ **Mailing List**: From this combo box you have to select the mailing list that will be used by the Direct Mailer service to contact your clients. You have to create at least one mailing list before arriving at this step.

- ❑ **Personalize Direct Mail per user**: If you want to implement a personalized e-mail system you have to select this check box; otherwise leave it unchecked.

- ❑ **Mail format**: From this combo box you can choose between three e-mail message types.

  - ❑ *Text*. The file name specified in the File path or URL containing message body field will be used like a message body. Even if it contains special text like tags or commands they will not be processed.

  - ❑ *MHTML*. The message body will be processed like a multilingual HTML format.

  - ❑ *MIME*. The message body will be processed like a Multipurpose Internet Mail Extensions format.

- ❑ **Comments**: Here you can insert your own comments that will not be included in any e-mail messages.

- ❑ **Start date**: Choose the initial date of the direct mail campaign from this date calendar control.

- ❑ **End date**: Choose the final date of the direct mail campaign from this date calendar control.

- ❑ **Start time**: Here you can choose the starting time from a combo box filled with full hour values.

- ❑ **Mailing interval**: From this combo box you can define the mailing interval for when every mail will be sent.

A good example of the Direct Mailer campaign could be sending welcome e-mail messages to new users who just registered on our site.

The figure above shows the e-mail message, in MHTML format, sent by the Direct Mailer service. Now we'll look at how to accomplish this end result.

Sending Generic E-mail

In order to create a Direct Mailer campaign pointing to new users, we first have to import a mailing list into the List Manager service using either a SQL Server query or the **New Registered Users** report (see the List Manager section in this chapter). The next step consists of preparing the e-mail message body using either an ASCII text file or an HTML file. For this example I've used a simple HTML page that you can download from Wrox Internet site (**www.wrox.com**).

The next operation in the Direct Mailer campaign creation consists of inserting the HTML file name into the **File path or URL containing message body** field of the **Campaign Manager** form. Here we have to compile all the required fields, too. Put a name into the **Direct mail name** field, an e-mail address into the next field, choose the right mailing list from the combo box, uncheck **personal direct mail per user** check box and, finally, choose the MHTML option from the **Mail format** combo box. You are now ready to test the new Direct Mailer campaign. Expand the **Test** section in the BizDesk application form, to show the **Send Test Mail** button, select the correct mailing list and press the button. After confirming your intention to run the test, the following message box will appear.

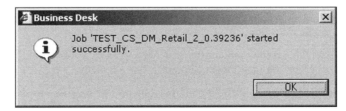

After that, nothing seems to happen! This is because the Direct Mailer job reads the information in the configuration module inside Commerce Server Manager. Default attributes tell the job to create a local e-mail and store it in the <commerce server path>\DML_drop directory.

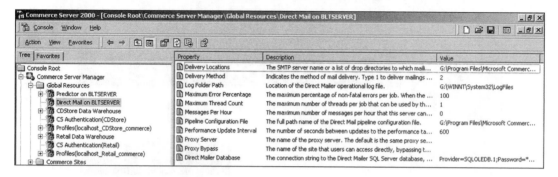

In order to implement a real sending service we need to change the generic configuration parameters in the SMTP server to send real e-mail messages to the customers. These parameters are accessible from the Commerce Server Manager shown in the figure above. Clicking the Direct Mail on <server name> node of the Global Resources tree, a list of all parameters will appear on the right-hand side of the screen:

- **Delivery location**s: This value will contain either a path to store e-mail messages locally or the SMTP server address.

- **Delivery Method**: The 1 value represents the intention to use an SMTP server; otherwise a 2 value indicates we want to use an 'e-mail drop locally' method.

- **Log Folder Path**: This value will contain a path to where the Direct Mailer service will create a log file to trace every job's operation.

- **Maximum Error Percentage**: In this field we have to insert a maximum percentage of fatal errors, beyond which the job will be stopped. Inserting a 100 value will indicate the intention to stop a Direct Mailer job as soon as any error occurs.

- **Maximum Thread Count**: This value will contain the thread number that you want to associate with each Direct Mailer job.

- **Message Per Hour**: This field indicates how many messages the SMTP server has to send per hour. If you specify a zero value, Direct Mailer will try to be as fast as it can during the process stage.

- **Pipeline Configuration File**: Here you have to specify the full path name of the Direct Mail pipeline configuration file. Default installation places DMLPipe.pcf file under the <Drive Letter:\>Program Files\Microsoft Commerce Server directory.

- **Performance Update Interval**: This field is expressed in seconds and indicates how often the Direct Mailer has to update the performance table with the number of e-mails sent.

- **Proxy Server**: Here you have to insert the name of the Proxy server, if there is one present on your Internet connection LAN.

- **Proxy Bypass**: This is the name of the site that users can access directly without passing through a Proxy site you may have installed.

- **Direct Mailer Database**: This field contains the connection string to the Direct Mailer SQL Server database.

From these parameters we only need to change the Delivery Locations and Delivery Method options, specifying the SMTP server name (usually equal to the name of your machine) and '1' as their values respectively. If you have a network configuration where there are proxy systems installed you should enter the Proxy settings, too.

Sending Personalized E-mail Messages

As we've just seen, in the Direct Mail campaign form there is a Personalize direct mail per user check box. Check this when you want to send personalized e-mail messages to the user. A personalized message means either an e-mail with personal customer information or an e-mail proposing articles specific to the user preferences. We have just covered the second case so all that remains is to look at e-mail messages with personal customer information.

The figure above shows an example of a personalized e-mail message where the Dear Customer phrase has been replaced with Dear <first name>. There are a few rules to follow to implement a fully working personalized e-mail message:

❑   You have to create a mailing list, using List Manager, where the e-mail address and user identification key must both appear.

❑   You have to create an ASP page containing the code to retrieve the user's personal profile.

❑   You have to create a new Direct Mail campaign where you have checked the Personalize direct mail per user item and specified the ASP page just created.

We've already covered everything except the ASP page creation, so we'll only cover that point here. As you can see from the code the AuthManager object is instantiated and initialized using the Application global variable that contains the site's name. It's imperative to put the ASP page into the site's virtual directory, managed by Internet Information Server, otherwise it will not be able to read global variable contents. AuthManager is essential to retrieve user information like the UserID.

```
' Create and initialize AuthManager object
Set objAuthManager = Server.CreateObject("Commerce.AuthManager")
objAuthManager.Initialize(Application("MSCSCommerceSiteName"))

If Err.number <> 0 Then
   Response.End
End If

' If we had to create a direct mailer campaign
' a cookie with its ID has been created
If Request.Cookies("CampaignItemID") <> "" Then
   UserID = objAuthManager.GetUserID(1)
   If Err.number <> 0 Then
      Response.End
   End If
Else
   Response.End
End If
```

The next snippet of code checks whether the Direct Mailer pipeline component has created a cookie with the campaign item id – if this is the case we can retrieve the user identification string. Otherwise there was an error in campaign creation, and the code has to exit.

The next step is the Profile object creation. This object contains all the necessary methods and properties associated with a specific user. In fact, thanks to the GetProfileByKey() method we can retrieve the profile of the user specified by the method parameters. The code, below, shows how to retrieve the information.

```
' Create the Profile Object
Set objUserProfile = Application("MSCSProfileService")

If Err.Number <> 0 Then
   Response.End
End If

Set objProfile = objUserProfile.GetProfileByKey(_
   "User_ID", UserID, "UserObject")

If Err.Number <> 0 Then
   Response.End
End If
```

The profile is then formatted using an XML schema defined during the e-commerce site creation:

```
<%' Here we get user first name using GeneralInfo
   ' collection.
%>
<P><FONT SIZE="-1" FACE="Verdana,Tahoma,Arial,Helvetica,sans-serif">_
   Dear <% = objProfile.GeneralInfo.First_Name %>,</FONT></P>
```

Direct Mailer Pipeline

The Direct Mailer service is based upon the `DMLpipe.pcf` pipeline configuration file, from where it gathers all the necessary information to send e-mail messages. As you'll learn in both Chapter 6 and Chapter 7, a pipeline configuration file contains all the information necessary for the Pipeline Editor to build a pipeline graphical representation. In the pipeline, all the steps involved in an e-mail message sending operation are specified. Like the other pipelines, you can configure it for your own scope, by adding, editing and removing pipeline stages. In the next section you'll find the method to add an opt-out list used to filter recipients in a Direct Mailer campaign. For the moment, though, we'll concentrate on the pipeline steps:

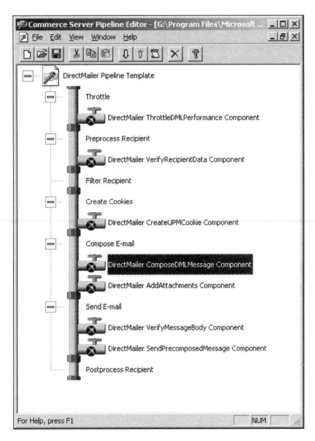

Each node of the pipeline's tree represents a stage. As you can see from the figure above, a stage can be either expanded or collapsed by clicking on the plus/minus square near to it. Every mail sent by the Direct Mailer is designed to pass through each stage from the previous one. Inside a stage there can be one or more components running to accomplish a particular task. In the Pipeline Editor a component is represented by a tap that you can open and close in order to execute it or not. Let's analyze each pipeline stage:

❑ **Throttle**: Inside this stage there is the DirectMailer ThrottleDMLPerformance Component that reads from the global resource how many seconds it has to wait before sending a message. That value is contained inside the **context** dictionary in the `delay_msec` key.

❑ **Preprocess Recipient**: Inside this stage there is the DirectMailer VerifyRecipientData Component that preprocesses Direct Mailer data in order to check consistency. If an error is found the `rcp_bypass` Boolean field is set to `True` avoiding the other stages in the pipeline process. The check operation foresees that our application verifies personalization information by itself.

❑ **Filter Recipient**: This is an empty stage where you can add your own objects. We'll see in the next section how to add a component here, to manage an opt-out list.

❑ **Create Cookies**: In this stage the DirectMailer CreateUPMCookie Component combines information from both the context and order dictionaries to create a cookie dictionary that will be used in the next stage.

❑ **Compose E-mail**: This stage has two objects inside it. The first one, DirectMailer ComposeDMLMessage Component, represents the core of the entire pipeline. It prepares e-mail messages, both personalized and non-personalized. In the first case it creates a cookie using information taken by the CreateUPMCookie object while, in the second case, the `precomposed_body` key will be used to write the message body. The second object included in this stage is the DirectMailer AddAttachments Component, used when you have to send attachments in your e-mail messages. Both components are based upon the CDO for Windows 2000 library.

❑ **Send E-mail**: This stage has two objects. The DirectMailer VerifyMessageBody Component verifies message body integrity checking it is not empty. At last, the DirectMailer SendPrecomposedMessage component sends the final messages using the CDO for Windows 2000 library.

❑ **Postprocess Recipient**: This is an empty stage. You can use it to do final operations like writing to a database or a log file.

Each component inside a stage manages two objects: `Context` and `Order`. The first object, `Context`, is a read-only Dictionary object filled through each pipeline stage with the following values:

Key	Description
Campaign_item	The campaign item identifier.
Campaign_item_name	The campaign item name.
cdo_config	Contains a reference to `CDO.Configuration` object.
cdo_message	Contains a reference to `CDO.Message` object.
css_site	Contains the e-commerce site name.
default_formatting	The default message format.
default_url	The default message URL.
default_url_content	Contains the path to a file if `default_url_isfile` is equal to `True`, otherwise it will contain the URL to use for the message body.
default_url_isfile	If `True` it indicates that `default_url_content` contains a path to a file.
delay_msec	This value will contain the delay between messages, expressed in milliseconds.

The second, Order, is a read/write dictionary object used through the stages to retrieve the necessary information.

Key	Description
Attachments	Contains a SimpleList object with a list of URLs pointing to attachment files.
cdo_error	Contains the most recent CDO error. A null value indicates that no errors occurred.
cdo_result	Contains the HRESULT handle returned from the most CDO operations.
Cookie	Contains the Cookie dictionary created in the Create Cookies stage.
default_locale	Contains the default locale code used by CDO when no entry is specified in rcp_locale key.
from_field	Contains the sender e-mail address.
messages_sent	Contains the 'message sent' number in a pipeline cycle.
precomposed_body	Contains the plain-text message body when the use_precomposed_body flag is set to True.
rcp_bypass	This flag is set to true when a previous operation generated an error. In this case the other stages will skip their message building task.
rcp_email	Contains the e-mail address of the user.
rcp_formatting	Contains the e-mail message type format.
rcp_guid	Contains the user's identification string.
rcp_locale	Contains the user's locale code-page.
rcp_personalize	This value contains a number indicating whether or not to personalize the message.
rcp_url	This value could contain the URL pointing to the message body content. If specified the default_url key will be ignored.
rcp_url_content	This field could contain file content when rcp_url_isfile is set to True.
rcp_url_isfile	When this flag is equal to True the rcp_url_content field will point to a file and not to an http address.
replyto_field	Contains the reply-to e-mail address.
subj_field	Contains the e-mail message subject.
use_precomposed_body	This flag, when set to True, indicates that the message will be created using the plain-text body stored in precomposed_body key.
user_flags	This value will contain a bit mask indicating elements of the message to check. At the moment only the rightmost bit is used. If set to 1 the component ensures that the body message text is not empty.

Using these two objects we can create our pipeline objects in order both to improve and personalize pipeline behavior. In the next section we'll see how to create a pipeline component, using Visual Basic 6.0, in order to manage an opt-out users list.

Using an Opt-out List to Filter Users

A respectable ad campaign has to offer the user the choice of whether or not to continue to receive e-mail messages from the site. In Commerce Server 2000 sites, this can be accomplished by creating an opt-out user list.

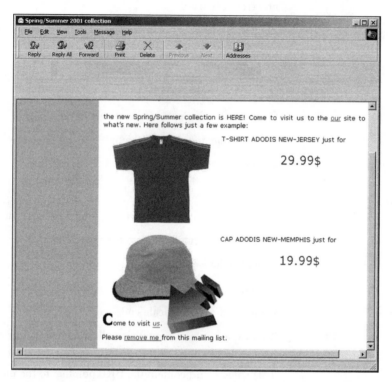

After that, either the site administrator or the advert campaign manager can subtract the content of the opt-out list from the mailing list and send e-mail messages to the resulting recipients. In this way, anyone who removes themselves from the mailing list will not be contacted anymore. Here follows a snippet of code that illustrates how add to this functionality to our site:

```
Please <A HREF="http://bltserver/retail/opt-out.asp?rcp_email=<% =
objProfile.GeneralInfo.email_address
%>&campitem_id=<%=Request.Cookies("CampaignItemID")%>&campitem_name=<%=Request.Coo
kies("CampaignItemName")%>"> remove me </A> from this mailing list.
```

All we have to do here is create a link to the opt-out.asp page, providing an e-mail address, a campaign item identifier, and, optionally, a campaign item name. Inside opt-out.asp is the code that inserts the e-mail address into the opt-out table contained inside the site's database created using the connection string specified into Commerce Server Manager attributes. The following snippet of code is an extract from the opt-out.asp file that comes with the Solution Site. There are two focal points in the Main() subroutine: first the code stores the query string parameters inside local variables and then calls the OptOut() method.

The less important code has been removed to clarify the example. It can be found in complete form in the Solution Site.

```
Sub Main()
    . . .
    . . .

    ' Get Query Strings
    rcp_email = Request.Querystring("rcp_email")
    campitem_id = Request.QueryString("campitem_id")
    campitem_name = Request.QueryString("campitem_name")

    . . .

    ' do the work of opting-out
    Call OptOut(rcp_email, campitem_id)
    If Err.Number <> 0 Then Call ErrorOut

    g_operatorMessage = "SUCCESS"

    . . .
End Sub
```

In the next section of code a connection to the database is operated together with the List Manager object creation:

```
Sub OptOut(rcp_email, campitem_id)
    Dim listmanager, list_id, conn_campaigns, campaigns_connstr

    . . .
    . . .

    ' get connection strings from Site Config
    campaigns_connstr = dictConfig.s_CampaignsConnectionString
    If Err.number <> 0 Then Call ErrorOut

    ' open DB connection
    Set conn_campaigns = CreateObject("ADODB.Connection")
    conn_campaigns.open campaigns_connstr
    If Err.number <> 0 Then Call ErrorOut
```

GetOptOutList carries out a query to the dm_item database table in order to retrieve the list_id; otherwise a null value will be returned. This value will be checked to create a new opt-out list using the CreateOptOutList() and SetOptOutList() methods.

```
    ' create and initialize the ListManager
    Set listmanager = CreateObject("Commerce.ListManager")
    listmanager.Initialize(campaigns_connstr)

    ' Get List ID
    list_id = GetOptOutList(conn_campaigns, listmanager, campitem_id)
    If Err.number <> 0 then call ErrorOut

    ' If the list doesn't exist, create a new one
```

```
    If isNull(list_id) Then
        list_id = CreateOptOutList(listmanager, campitem_id)
    If Err.number <> 0 Then Call ErrorOut

        ' Set Opt out list
        Call SetOptOutList(conn_campaigns, campitem_id, list_id)
    If Err.number <> 0 Then Call ErrorOut
    End If
```

The final step is to add the user to the opt-out mailing list using the `AddUserToMailList()` method of the `ListManager` object.

```
    ' add user to the list
    listmanager.AddUserToMailingList CStr(list_id), rcp_email
    If Err.number <> 0 Then Call ErrorOut
End Sub
```

The figure below shows the results after clicking on **remove me** from the ad campaign.

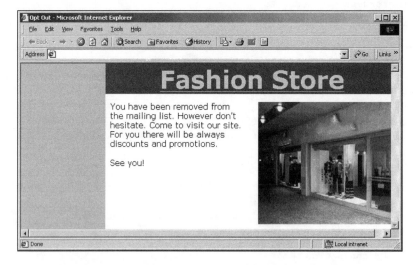

By opening the BizDesk application and pointing to the **List Manager** menu, you'll see the new opt-out list inside the list box. Before scheduling a new Direct Mailer campaign we can subtract its content from the mailing list. Also, we can create a pipeline component that filters messages, excluding the recipients from the opt-out list.

Opt-out Pipeline Component

As we have seen earlier there is a stage called **Filter Recipient** where we can insert objects to skip the message-sending process when the user has opted out of the mailing list. Using the **Pipeline Wizard Creation** tool, the Visual Basic pipeline object creation is a piece of cake. It creates all the necessary code to manage a pipeline component by adding code and classes to a Visual Basic project.

```
    Private Function IPipelineComponent_Execute(ByVal objOrderForm As Object, ByVal
    objContext As Object, ByVal lFlags As Long) As Long

        Dim objOptOutCtx  As CDictionary 'Pipe Context
```

```
    Dim objItems As CSimpleList 'Items
    Dim dbRec As New ADODB.Recordset
    Dim strEMailAdd As String, strConnectionString As String, SQL As String
    Dim lCampaignID As Long, strOptOutTable As String

    ' Return 1 for Success
    IPipelineComponent_Execute = 1

    ' Initialize the Pipe Context and Order Form
    Set objOptOutCtx = objContext
    Set objOrderForm = objOrderForm

    ' Retrieve e-mail address
    strEMailAdd = objOrderForm.Value("rcp_email")

    ' Retrieve campaign ID
    lCampaignID = objContext.Value("campaign_item")

    ' Format SQL string in order to retrieve Opt out list's presence
    SQL = "SELECT list_location From lm_master WHERE list_name = 'Opt Out_
        (" & lCampaignID & ")'"

    ' Connection String
    strConnectionString = "Provider=SQLOLEDB.1;User ID=sa;Password=;_
        Initial Catalog=Retail_commerce;Data Source=localhost;Network_
        Library=dbmssocn;"

    'Execute query
    dbRec.Open SQL, strConnectionString

    'if a opt out table exists
    If dbRec.EOF = False Then
        ' store its table name
        strOptOutTable = dbRec("list_location")
        dbRec.Close

        ' Looking for the processing user in list
        SQL = "SELECT rcp_email FROM " & strOptOutTable & " WHERE_
            rcp_email='" & strEMailAdd & "'"
        dbRec.Open SQL, strConnectionString

        If dbRec.EOF = False Then
            'Yes, user is in the list.
            'Stop the sending process
            IPipelineComponent_Execute = 3
        End If
    End If

    'Clean memory
    Set dbRec = Nothing
    Set objOptOutCtx = Nothing
    Set objOrderForm = Nothing

End Function
```

The core of the object resides in the `IPipelineComponent_Execute()` event that is called every time the pipeline flow passes through the **Filter Recipient** stage. Inside this event we can retrieve a user's e-mail address and campaign item identifier and query the database to see if the user e-mail is stored inside the `opt-out` table. From the event parameter we receive `Order` and `Context` dictionaries so we can use their keys to retrieve the fields we're interested in.

To find out whether the user is included in the `opt-out` list we have to interrogate the database by looking inside the `lm_master` table. This table contains two really useful columns: Firstly, there's `list_name`, that contains the name assigned to the mailing list, and secondly, `list_location`, which contains the opt-out list table name.

The first part of code calls the `Open()` method of an ADO Recordset to query the table name from the `lm_master` table. Using the name returned we launch another query to look for the user. If we find at least one row in the recordset then the user is inserted into the opt-out list and we stop the mailing execution by setting `IPipelineComponent_Execute` equal to 3 (error).

All that remains is to use the `PipeReg.exe` registration tool to insert pipeline component information into the Windows registry and to include the new component in the **Filter Recipient** stage.

Direct Mailer in Standalone Mode

Sometimes, we may want to send e-mail messages to those users who ignore any communication from the application using the Direct Mailer service. In order to obtain this, Commerce Server 2000 offers the Direct Mailer service in standalone mode. We can use the `DMLRUN.EXE` file with a few parameters to create and manage a job.

```
G:\WINNT\System32\cmd.exe                                              _ | □ | x |
Microsoft Windows 2000 [Version 5.00.2195]
(C) Copyright 1985-2000 Microsoft Corp.

G:\>dmlrun

 Microsoft DirectMailer Runtime Executable

Usage: dmlrun <command>, where <command> can take one of the following values:

/h or /? or /help       Displays this help screen
/create:<parameters>    Creates a new mailing job
    <parameters> can be one of the following:
        filename=<job data file> or
        type=css;dml_item=<item id>;css_site=<site id>
/run:<job id>           Executes or resumes the mailing job.
/pause:<job id>         Suspends the mailing job; it can be resumed later
/term:<job id>          Terminates the mailing job
/delete:<job id>        Permanently deletes the mailing job from the database
/del_old:<max age>      Permanently removes completed jobs with
                        age more than <max age> days
/list                   Types a list of all mailing jobs on the screen
/list:<options>         Lists all the mailing jobs accordingly to the <options>
    <options> can be either one (or both) of the following:
        css_site=<site id>;    Lists all the jobs for the given site
                               All the jobs for all the sites will be listed
                               if this parameter is omitted
        filename=<file name>;  All the output will be stored to the file
                               instead of the system console


The following modifiers can be appended to the command line:

/server:<computer>      Redirects the command to the DirectMailer service
                        on the given computer. Can be combined with any
                        other option
/execute                Can be combined with /create ONLY. Causes the new job
                        to start immediately
/wait                   Causes the Executable to wait on the command completion.

                        Can be combined with /execute, /run, /term options
```

As you can see from the figure above, DMLRUN has a lot of command line parameters to completely manage a job. Let's look at the more important ones:

❑ **/create:<parameters>** allows the creation of either a new job, taking its parameters from a job data file, or the launch of an existing job, specifying the direct mail campaign identifier and site name.

❑ **/run:<job id>** runs an existing job. You can retrieve a job identifier by launching the DMLRUN command with the /list command. Moreover you can specify either the job data file name or site name after the /list command in order to retrieve just the job identifiers for that site.

In cases where you want to use a job data file, you have to create a Windows .INI file containing a Job Data section, a Job Attachments section (optional) and a Results section:

```
[Job Data]
MailFrom=support@fashionstore.com
MailSubject="Standalone mode"
MailingListType=1
MailingListLocation=G:\mailinglist.csv
TemplateURL=http://bltserver/retail/welcomeuser.asp
DefaultFmt=3

[Results]
ErrorCode=0
JobID={86923AED-A8C4-4CF8-AF11-3BEC27BCCE22}
ErrorString=
```

To understand each of section's attributes you should consult the following table:

Parameter	Description
Job Data Section	
JobDesc (128 characters max)	The description associated with the job.
TemplateURL (2048 characters max)	Set this field with either URL source or file path.
MailFrom (256 characters max)	**Required.** Set this field with sender e-mail address.
MailSubject (256 characters max)	Set this field to e-mail message's subject.
MailReplyTo (256 characters max)	Set this field with e-mail message receiver.
DefaultFmt (Number)	1 – Text
	2 – MIME
	3 – MHTML
JobLocale (255 characters max)	Set this field with the default locale code-page for the job.

Table continued on following page

Parameter	Description
MailPersonalize (Number)	0 – You are not delivering personalized content.
	1 – You are delivering personal content.
MailingListType (Number)	**Required.**
	1 – Flat file
	2 – List Manager mailing list
	3 – SQL Server query
MailingListLocation (256 characters max)	**Required**. Set this field specifying the location of mailing list.
	- *File*: you have to specify the path pointing to the file containing mailing list.
	- *List Manager*: You have to specify the list identification number.
	- *SQL query*: You have to specify connection string to database.
MailingListSQL (256 characters max)	Set this field with SQL query content only when MailingListType is equal to 3.
OptoutListType (Number)	1 – Flat file
	2 – List Manager mailing list
	3 – SQL Server query
OptoutListLocation (256 characters max)	**Required**. Set this field to specify the location of your mailing list.
	- *File*: you have to specify the path pointing to the file containing the mailing list.
	- *List Manager*: You have to specify the list identification number.
	- *SQL query*: You have to specify connection string to database.
OptoutListSQL (256 characters max)	Set this field with SQL query content only when MailingListType is equal to 3.
UserFlags (Number)	Set this field with user-defined flags associated with the direct mailer job.
Job Attachments Section	
AttachmentCount (Number)	Set this field with the number of attachments you'll add to message.
Attachment_*n* (2048 characters max)	Set every field with either a URL or file system path pointing to the n attachments specified in the previous field.

Results Section	
ErrorCode (HRESULT)	Direct Mailer job fills this field with return error code. 0 if no errors occurred.
ErrorString (256 characters max)	Direct Mailer job fills this field with return error description. Empty if no errors occurred.
JobID (GUID)	Direct Mailer job fills this field with the new job identifier.

Summary

Every competent e-commerce site should be implementing advertisement campaigns to inform its users about the latest news and offers from their store. In this chapter we've discussed how you can go about making these campaigns more effective by tailoring them to your customers.

We saw how Microsoft Commerce Server 2000's Prediction Engine could be used to analyze dependency network diagrams, decision trees and probability percentages to assist you in understanding and predicting your users' preferences and settings. We then went on to look at how Prediction Objects could be used to insert tailored product links for each individual customer based on their previous purchases.

Then we went on to consider the powerful advertising tool of e-mail, and how the Commerce Server 2000 tools of Direct Mailer and List Manager can be implemented together to create tailored, fully functional, advertising campaigns. Finally we reviewed the procedures for creating an opt-out list, something required by every responsible e-company, as it allows you to stop sending mail to disinterested customers.

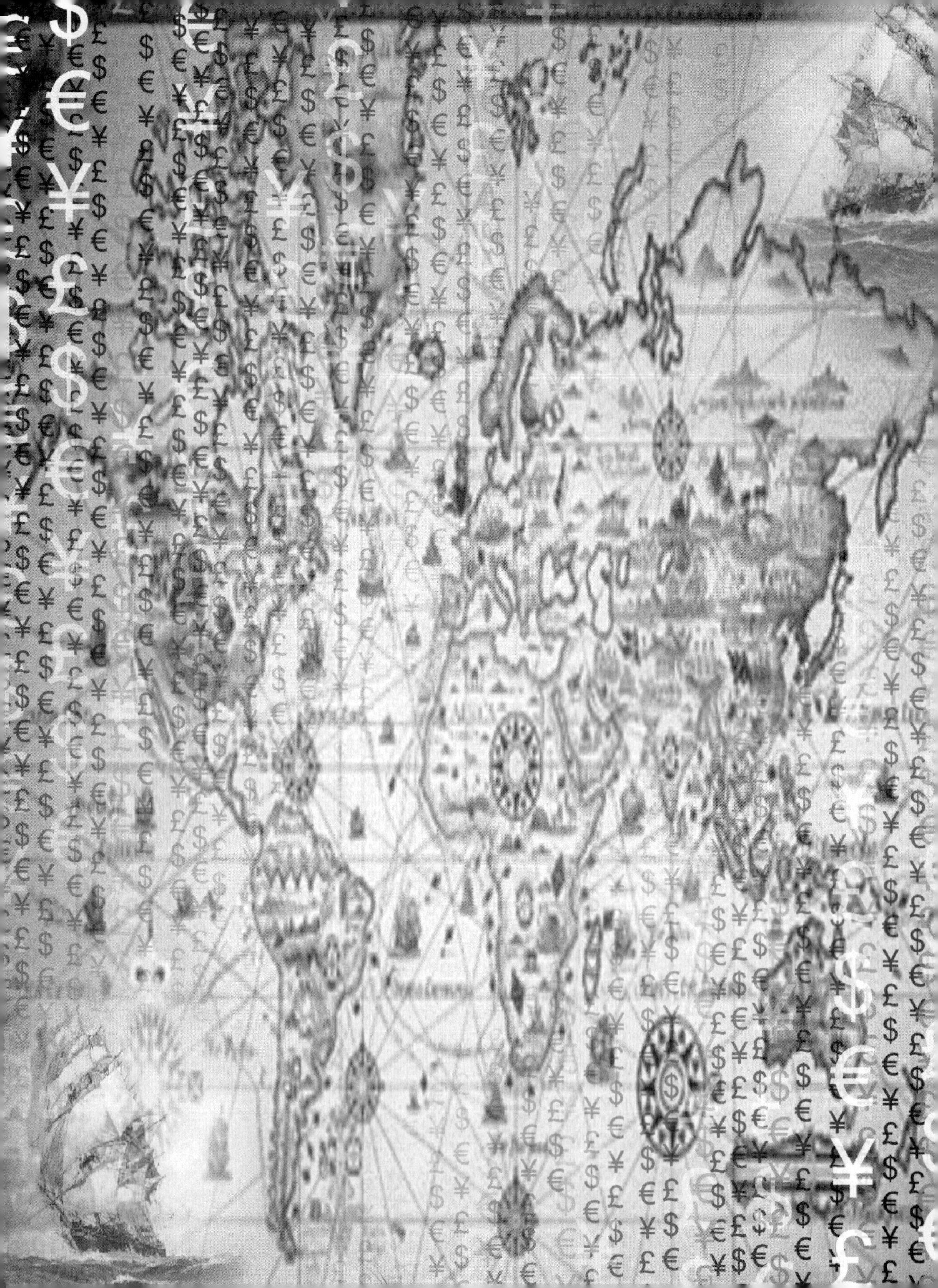

Active Directory and the Supplier Solution Site

In this chapter, we're going to turn our attention to the Supplier Solution Site. Specifically, we will be looking at the following topics:

❑ Active Directory – and why it's important for the Supplier Site.

❑ Installing and Configuring the Supplier Site.

❑ Adding users, product catalogs, catalog sets, and organisations to a Supplier Site.

❑ Authentication – using the authentication filter.

❑ SQL Server fields and Active Directory attributes.

Initially, we should note that the Supplier Solution Site and the Retail Solution Site are largely based on the same code. Differences in the applications' behavior stem mainly from configuration information – the **App Default Config**, stored in the Commerce Server Administration database – and not from differences in the code base.

If you have a Retail Solution Site and a Supplier Solution Site at your disposal, you can examine the minor configuration differences by navigating to the Commerce Server Manager. The Properties form of the App Default Config under, the Site Resources folder within the Commerce Site Folder, is the user interface by which we can change or examine the Application Default Configuration Settings:

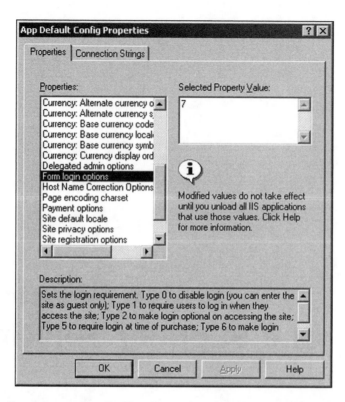

As we've seen, the Retail site installs a Profiling System based exclusively on SQL Server. However, the solution site's profiling system utilizes Active Directory – we'll be concentrating on this throughout the bulk of this chapter. Furthermore, there are some interesting quirks, road mines, and a few strangely architected components within the Supplier Site, which we'll look at in the course of this chapter.

So, what is the Supplier Solution Site, and when would we use it? According to Microsoft, we should:

> "Use the Supplier Solution Site as a starting point for building a business-to-business site. It uses Microsoft Windows 2000 Active Directory to provide secure user authentication and group access permissions. It provides purchase order and requisition handling, eXtensible Markup Language (XML)-based catalog updates and exchange, and trading partner self-service. It includes the Partner Desk that enables a delegated administrator, a contact at the supplier company, to manage organizational information, purchase orders, and order status for that supplier company."

So that's the Supplier Site as defined by Microsoft's marketing team. We know that it's almost identical to the Retail Solution Site, but for some key differences, which will be outlined shortly. The Supplier Solution Site is a feature-rich combination of two web applications: the retail and the supplier site. In the configuration recommended in this chapter, a significant amount of Active Directory design will be required before implementation in production. And, of course, it will require a skin (look and feel). Short of this, the Supplier Solution Site is ready for production on the Internet or on your Intranet / Extranet.

Once installed, we'll wind up with 1042 total files spread over 50 folders, in two virtual directories: the Supplier Site itself contains 151 files (in 15 folders) and its associated BizDesk application contains 891 files (in 35 folders) – that's an awful lot of content! In addition, we will end up with two SQL Server Databases containing 223 tables (93 for the application database and 130 for the data warehouse).

My purpose in this chapter isn't to steer through every line of code. In fact, compared to the prior chapter, we will look at very little code in this chapter, as the two sites are so similar. However, we will cover the following topics:

❑   Installation and configuration of the Supplier Solution Site.

❑   Enhancing the Supplier Solution Site.

❑   Contrasting the Supplier Site with the Retail Site.

Background on Active Directory

It is important to have an understanding of Directory Services (and Directory Services in general) prior to installing the Supplier Site. Directory Services are one of the most misunderstood (and under-utilized) technologies around, and grasping the way in which the Supplier Site depends on Active Directory will be essential.

The software development community has been talking about encapsulating Directory Server Access into the middle tier for a long time, but in many cases, this has yet to be done adequately. Most software developers writing web applications have bought into the idea of a set of standard data access COM components; it makes sense to encapsulate all directory service access in the very same way. Thankfully, the Commerce Server 2000 User Profile System gives us a rich set of COM components to do exactly that.

The Supplier solution site configuration that we design and configure in this chapter has a dependency on Active Directory. However, if you do not have Active Directory available on your network, you should still be able to get an understanding of Active Directory integration from this chapter.

Directory Services Defined

The directory service stores information about entities on a network. 'Entities' would include things such as users, groups of users, and printers. Software developers can make information about these entities available to users and network administrators. The Microsoft Windows 2000 Active Directory provides user access to permitted resources anywhere on the network, using a single logon process, such as a shared file. It provides network administrators with an intuitive hierarchical view of the network, and a single point of administration for all network objects.

As developers, there are two particular aspects of Active Directory that we'll utilize:

❑   **Authentication** – the Windows 2000 Active Directory provides a framework for secure authentication within the operating system.

❑   **Attributes** – it also provides a data store to persist data. Active Directory entities may have *attributes*, which may be thought of, in the first instance, as being akin to the fields of a database table. Every entity in the Active Directory is an instance of a class, and every entity is defined by a set of attributes. The classes determine what attributes particular entities can have, and all possible attributes are defined in the Active Directory schema. The attribute definition includes its syntax, which specifies the type of value it can have.

Why do we need another data storage mechanism and API when we have SQL Server and ADO? And why do we need another authentication mechanism when the operating system already provides such a mechanism for us? The answers to these questions should emerge over the subsequent sections.

The Authentication Features of the Directory Service

Active Directory supplies flexible and secure authentication and authorization services, which provide protection for data while minimizing barriers to doing business over the Internet, an intranet or an extranet. Active Directory supports multiple authentication protocols including:

❑   Kerboros V5 protocol

❑   Secure Sockets Layer v3

❑   Transport Layer Security using X.509v3 certificates

Active Directory also supports security groups that can span domains efficiently, and provides a way of overcoming the domain authentication restrictions of Windows NT 4.0. (which will generally not allow more than 2000 users at the same time).

With Active Directory, we can, in principle, have millions of concurrently authenticated users. User authentication in Windows 2000 Active Directory gives users the ability to log on to a system to access network resources, whether the access is from the local LAN, intranet, extranet or from the Internet. Within this authentication model, the security system provides two types of authentication:

❑   **Interactive logon** – confirms the user's identification to the user's local computer or Active Directory account.

❑   **Network authentication** – validates the user's identification and consequent authorization to any network service that the user is attempting to access.

In addition to authentication, Active Directory provides a mechanism for **access control**. This allows software developers to write tools, which allow administrators to control access to resources, or objects, on the network. Windows 2000 implements access control by allowing administrators to assign **security descriptors** to objects stored in Active Directory. A security descriptor lists the users and groups that are granted access to an object, and the specific permissions assigned to those users and groups. A security descriptor also specifies the various access events to be audited for an object. By managing properties on objects, administrators can set permissions, assign ownership, and monitor user access.

Not only can software developers write tools for administrators to control access to a specific object, but we can also control access to a specific *attribute* of that object. For example, through proper configuration of an object's security descriptor, a user could be programmatically allowed to access a subset of information, such as an employee's e-mail address, but not their social security number.

Active Directory allows administrators to create **group accounts** so that they can more efficiently manage system security. For example, by adjusting a file's security properties, an administrator can permit all users in a group to have read access to that file. Groups also let us control access to resources in the directory. In this way, access to objects in Active Directory is based on group membership and thereby much easier to manage than by individual user.

The Attribute Features of the Directory Service

Attributes describe objects within the Active Directory. The types of object stored within the Active Directory fall into three main categories:

❑   User information

❑ Application information

❑ Enterprise information

Attributes in a Directory Service are synonymous with columns in a database table, but organized much more rigidly. Attributes are organized into classes: the User class in the Active Directory, for instance, contains attributes specific to a user, such as name and address. Attributes are stored in the directory service as name/value pairs. For instance, if the value of a user's e-mail address is persisted in the Active Directory, the attribute name, mail and the value of the attribute, TimHuck@InterKnowlogy.com are persisted together. Unlike a relational database like Microsoft SQL Server, where table columns exist whether or not they are null, if an attribute in a directory service is not persisted, then the space for the attributes name is not persisted either, therefore bypassing the wasted space.

Also, the attributes in a directory service can be single-valued *or* multi-valued. An example of a multi-valued attribute is userGroups: this attribute is multi-valued because it contains several values – the names of the multiple groups that a user belongs to.

As with a relational database like Microsoft SQL Server, all attributes have a **syntax** that determines the kind of data that the attribute can store. There are a fixed number of syntaxes allowed in the Active Directory Schema; we cannot add additional or custom-made syntaxes to the Active Directory. This is beneficial because, as software developers, we don't have to worry about casting to user-defined types. Some examples of attribute syntaxes are:

❑ Boolean – true or false

❑ Integer – a number between 0 (zero) and 4,294,967,295

❑ NumericString – a character string that contains only numbers

Similarly, attributes can have length or range **constraints**: for attributes with numeric syntax, the range specifies the minimum and maximum value; for attributes with string syntax, the range specifies the minimum and maximum length.

Again, like data in a relational database, Active Directory attributes can be **indexed**. Indexing attributes helps queries more quickly find objects having data persisted in that attribute.

Attributes can also be included in the **global catalog**. The Active Directory global catalog contains a subset of attributes for every object in the Active Directory. Applications can use the global catalog to locate objects within the Active Directory. The global catalog holds a replica of every object in Active Directory but with only a small number of their attributes. The attributes that exist in the global catalog are those most frequently used in search operations (such as a user's first and last names, e-mail addresses, login names, and so on). The global catalog facilitates quickly locating Active Directory objects without having to know what domain they reside in.

Attributes that may be appropriate to include in the global catalog have the following characteristics:

❑ **Globally useful** – the attribute is needed for locating objects that may occur anywhere on the network that the active directory is available to, or read access to the attribute is valuable even when the object itself is not accessible.

❑ **Not volatile** (in order words, it doesn't change often) – attributes in a global catalog are replicated to all other global catalogs in the enterprise. If an attribute changes often, significant replication traffic on the network will result.

❑   **Small persisted footprint** – for attributes which do change, the smaller the attribute, the lower the network traffic impact of that replication. This is a tough scenario to pin down – if the attribute is large but very seldom changes, it will have a smaller replication impact than a small attribute that changes frequently.

Attributes that are frequently queried and referenced by users across the enterprise, such as employee names, e-mail addresses, and phone numbers, are good candidates for inclusion in the Active Directory global catalog. Attributes that are rarely queried (home addresses, for example) are not good candidates for inclusion in the Active Directory Global Catalog.

Directory Service Structure

The biggest difference between a database and a directory service is that a directory service is not relational. Directory Services, like the Active Directory, are hierarchical and support **object inheritance**. As we have seen, every object in Active Directory is an instance of a particular class. A class defines the attributes available to an instance of that particular class. A class, such as User, defines properties such as first and last name. An instance of a class, such as TimHuck, has Active Directory properties called attributes: firstName=Tim lastname=Huckaby.

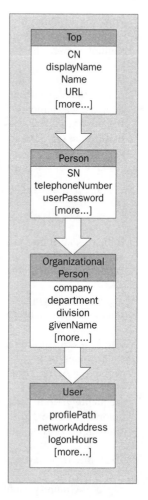

Classes follow a simple inheritance model. When defining a class, we must declare a parent class. This class defines what attributes are *implicitly* inherited from their parent class. The figure below shows an example of the class hierarchy for the User class. Notice that the class at the peak of the hierarchy tree is an object called Top, and that this class is the only one without a parent class.

The Active Directory **Schema** is a description of the object classes and attributes stored in the Active Directory. For each object class, the schema defines the attributes an object class must have, the additional attributes it may have, and the object class that can be its parent. For instance, the Person class has one attribute that is mandatory: this is cn. The Person class has four attributes that are optional: seeAlso, sn, telephoneNumber, and userPassword. And, as we can see, the parent for the Person class is the Top class.

The Active Directory schema is extensible and can be updated dynamically. For example, software developers can write applications that extend the schema with new attributes and classes, and use the extensions immediately in their applications. Schema updates are accomplished by creating or modifying the schema objects stored in the Active Directory. Like every object in the Active Directory, schema objects have an **access control list** (**ACL**), so only authorized users may alter the schema. Of course, this doesn't mean we are limited to modifications when accessing the schema programmatically: we can write code to read which attributes a particular class instance should have without making modifications.

Each class definition within the Active Directory specifies the following:

- ❏ The structure rules that determine the class's super-class or parent class. This is necessary to determine where to implicitly inherit from.

- ❏ The list of attributes that can be present in an instance of that class. For instance, the User class where domain users exist, has attributes available that are specific to a user, like an e-mail address. An attribute that determines the color printing capabilities of a printer, for instance, would not be applicable in the User class.

- ❏ Which of the attributes are mandatory (mustContain). Examples of mustContain attributes in the User class are Username and Password. Those two attributes are mandatory (there are others) for each instance of a user. A user cannot be created without persisting mustContain attributes.

- ❏ Which of the attributes are optional (mayContain). Examples of mayContain attributes in the User class are attributes relating to the home address of the user. Attributes like the home address are not mandatory, and hence it's optional whether they are persisted or not.

Active Directory uses entities, often called objects (which should not be confused with COM Objects) to represent network resources such as users, groups, machines, devices, and application settings. Like all directory services, the Active Directory uses **containers** to represent organizations, such as the marketing department, or collections of related objects, such as printers. It organizes information in a hierarchical, tree-like structure made up of these objects and containers; similar to the way we use folders and files to organize information on our computer.

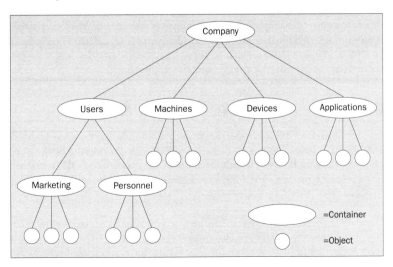

The Active Directory hierarchy is flexible and configurable, supporting the organization of resources in a way that optimizes usability and manageability. In the picture above, containers are used to represent collections of users, machines, devices, and applications. Containers can be nested (as in the case of the Marketing and Personnel containers being nested within the Users container) to reflect accurately a company's organizational structure. Nesting objects in the Active Directory facilitates the manageability of objects on a macro-level (as collections) rather than one-by-one. This, of course, increases Active Directory's management efficiency because it means we can manage sets of objects by managing groups.

All classes in an Active Directory schema are ultimately derived from the special class called Top. With the exception of Top, which is often called the top-level container, all classes are subclasses of some other class. Inheritance enables us to build new classes from existing classes. The original class becomes a super-class or parent of the new class. A subclass inherits the attributes of the parent, including structure rules and content rules. A class can inherit attributes from more than one parent.

Structure rules define the possible hierarchical relationships between objects in the Active Directory. The structure rules are completely expressed by each Class Schema object's Poss Superiors (Possible Superiors) attribute. This attribute lists all of the possible super-class (parent) objects from which that particular object can inherit attributes.

For example, we could create a new Extranet User class that defines information about the domain users who are partners of a company, who don't specifically work in the home office or corporate headquarters and who are not even employees. We will use a specific instance of this example to explain how to configure and customize Active Directory to fit the needs of the Supplier Site. Attributes specific to these extranet users might include the location of where they work, and any network specific information regarding how they connect to the corporate LAN.

We could specify that the Extranet User class is a subclass of the User class. As the Extranet User class would inherit all the Must Contain and May Contain attributes of the User class, as well as the attributes of all of the super-classes (parent classes) of the User class, we would not have to define these attributes for the Extranet User class. The only attributes we would need to define would be the attributes specific to location and network connectivity, which would be unique for all instances of the Extranet User class.

Directory Services scale horizontally through partitioning over machines and multi-node replication. Availability in this case doesn't mean 24/7, which of course is a feature of Windows 2000: what is meant by availability is an enterprise available data store for user and application data. The Active Directory is completely integrated in Windows 2000 which means we get the security for free – no longer is a user database and security coding necessary for our enterprise applications.

What Goes in SQL and What Goes in AD?

Determining what data goes into the relational database and what data goes into the directory service is a frequent source of heated debate. There is no clear-cut formula for making the distinction, but there are some concepts that can make it easier for us to decide. Relational databases like SQL Server are designed to spread performance evenly over the process of writing and reading data. For the sake of explanation, let's call this the 'relational database 50-50 rule'.

Enormous amounts of engineering are done to ensure that writes to the database are accomplished just as quickly as reads. Those of us in the Software Development community who have been programming relational databases for a long time have taken the '50-50 rule' for granted; that is, until we start programming directory services.

A directory service like the Windows 2000 Active Directory is designed quite differently. The hierarchical structure isn't simply architected to attain object-oriented properties: hierarchical structures are designed for lightning-quick reads. The Windows 2000 Internet Information Server (IIS) metabase and the Windows 2000 registry are good examples of structures that were designed hierarchically to support fast access through reads.

The drawback (or in this case, the by-product) is that the lightning fast reads accomplished with the hierarchical structure of a directory service are accomplished at the expense of some latency in the writes. For the sake of explanation, let's call this the 'Directory Service 80-20 rule' which implies that reads are four times faster than writes – although the actual performance numbers between reads and writes is going to depend on a number of factors, such as the type of Directory Service, the resources available, the format of the hierarchical structure, and so on.

Additionally, LDAP servers have features that facilitate hosting directory services completely in memory – similar, if not identical, to the concept of in-memory databases. Obviously, we will see dramatic speed increases in reads and writes from directory services that are hosted completely in memory.

We can now draw up a few general rules about what type of data should be persisted as an *attribute* in the Directory Service, and what type of data should be persisted as a *field* in SQL Server:

❑ Data that is not frequently changed, and that benefits from being enterprise available, such as data specific to the user (username, password, e-mail address, home address, etc.) is more aptly placed in the directory service.

❑ Data such as network resources (printers, computers, etc.) is more aptly placed in the directory service.

❑ Data such as software application settings (such as language settings, look and feel, settings) is more aptly placed in the directory service.

❑ Data that changes very frequently and does not gain benefit from being available to all software applications in the enterprise is more aptly placed in a table in a relational database such as SQL Server.

Let's consider the example of designing a business-to-business (B2B) electronic commerce web application such as the Supplier Solution Site. We would want to profile users, when possible, after authentication. We could *explicitly* force the user to give data about themselves when they register on the web site: name, address, gender, partner affiliation, role. This type of data, which is entered once and is rarely ever changed, is appropriately kept in Active Directory.

In the other hand, in a business to consumer (B2C) web application such as the Retail Solution Site, we would also want to *implicitly* profile the users. Behind the scenes in the web application, we would want to track the URLs and other resources on our web site that the user accesses. We may also want to track the frequency with which a user on our web site looks at particular products. Additionally, we may want to implicitly track referrals – where a visitor, or user, on our web site comes from, or where they go after leaving our site. Since the frequency of this type of implicitly-profiled data is not controllable, and has the potential for a massive amount of writes, it is perfect for a relational database like SQL Server.

So, in summary, we are not advocating either using SQL Server or Active Directory only: we would rarely write a web application that only uses a directory service like Active Directory, without also using a relational database like SQL Server. Most likely, we would use them both, and persist data where it seems most applicable.

The Commerce 2000 User Profile System allows us to distribute data over the Active Directory and SQL Server in a fashion that makes sense. As we saw in Chapter 3, The User Profile System embodies a set of COM components that isolates us from what source the data actually lives in (Active Directory or SQL Server) so that we code to one simple interface, and the COM components handle the complexity of actually accessing the data. Additionally, we can write providers for other disparate data sources such as Oracle or other directory services.

Having said all that, there is a generic design flaw in the Supplier Solution Site. Out of the box the Supplier site does not fully use Active Directory for authentication, nor does it persist any attributes in the Active Directory: all data goes to SQL Server. Yet the Supplier Site still requires a dependency on Active Directory.

We will see later in this chapter how to overcome this by fully utilizing Active Directory in our Supplier Site. To do this, though, we will explore in some detail reconfiguring the Supplier Site.

I encourage you to walk through a Supplier Site installation on your own development server, which includes a development Active Directory in the next section with the full intention of removing it when you are done, because there are a large number of design issues that you will need to consider before installing a Supplier Site that you intend to use for your business.

> *When installing the Supplier site, it can be a good idea to use NTFS partition copying software such as Symantec's Ghost, http://www.ghost.com, so that you can restore your Commerce Server 2000 environment to a pristine state once you've been through an installation of the Supplier Site.*

Unpacking, Configuring and Installing the Supplier Site

You may have already installed a Supplier Solution Site successfully on your Commerce Server 2000 machine. Even if you have, I suggest following through the next section, because I will identify some design issues and undocumented configuration tips and tricks that will help you dramatically in the long run with your Supplier Site.

More often than not, we are forced to run wizards 'blind', only discovering what actually happened after it has happened. This phenomenon undermines the whole idea behind 'plan and design before doing'. The Supplier solution site makes significant changes to your servers, not the least of which are the creation of Organizational Units, and Schema modifications in the Active Directory. It also creates two SQL Server Databases, one of which is an OLAP data warehouse.

By unpacking the Supplier site, we:

❑ Create two virtual directories that host two web applications on IIS Web Server.

❑ Create two Organizational Units (OUs) to host users of the web applications in Active Directory (an Organizational Unit is an Active Directory container object used within domains).

❑ Create two SQL Server Databases, which host much of the data for the web applications.

The Supplier Site wizard will create an OU off the main tree of Active Directory called **MCS_40_ROOT**. Most users find this lack of control over the naming of the OU, not only annoying, but totally unacceptable – especially since Directory Services objects can never be deleted (or renamed, as in this case). I have heard of numerous complaints about the 'hard-coded' Organizational Unit, although undocumented. We will see later in the chapter how to control the location and name of the OU where users are stored in Active Directory.

Installation

Download the solution sites from http://www.microsoft.com/commerceserver/downloads/solsites.htm, and then execute it.

> *Note that this won't install the solution sites – it simply installs the relevant PuP files to the local folder. It's therefore advisable to execute the file in the location from which you plan to unpack the solution site PuPs (Packager/UnPackager format), probably* \Program Files\Microsoft Commerce Server\PuP Packages*.*

The InstallShield Wizard is self-explanatory, and although the status screens say the process may take a few minutes, it will generally just take a few seconds. Once the Wizard is complete, click the Finish button to acknowledge the completion of the process. We are now ready to unpack the Supplier Solution Site.

> *If you've already installed the Solution Site Pups on your server, you'll be presented with options to repair or remove your installation. Note that if you choose to remove it, you'll be required to reboot your machine.*

Unpacking and Configuring the Supplier Solution Site

As mentioned earlier, we're going to look at a few techniques that should help us set up a well-designed installation of the Supplier Solution Site. First, we'll need to decide where we want the Organizational Unit to be created in our Active Directory, and decide on a name for it.

> **As we've seen, the default is an Organizational Unit called SupplierAD within an Organizational Unit called MSCS_40_ROOT on the root of our Active Directory.**

Okay, now let's unpack the Supplier Solution Site. From the Start Menu, select Programs | Microsoft Commerce Server 2000 | Solution Sites to open the PuP Packages folder.

Double-click on the supplieractivedirectory.pup file to start the unpacking process.

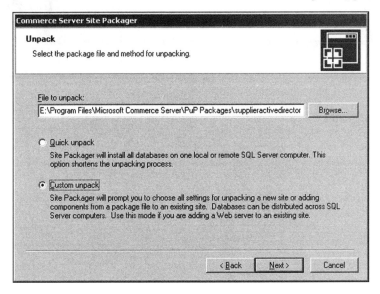

Custom unpack gives us control over the distribution of SQL Databases, and is practically mandatory for adding web servers to a farm – that is, unless we create custom PuP files for our site.

Ironically, we'll be able to control the name and placing of the Organizational Unit in Active Directory under either method. Since the Custom unpack default settings are identical to those used by Quick unpack, we have nothing to lose by choosing the Custom route. Hit Next to continue.

If this is the first Supplier Solution Site you have chosen to install, then the following options will all be disabled:

❑ **Add resources in the package to an existing site** – you might use this to add the Direct Mail resource to your Supplier Site. The Commerce Server Direct Mailer requires local instance of SQL server on the Commerce Server Web Server. This is a good example of where we'd use the Commerce Server 2000 CD to install the Direct Mailer components, and then use the Add Resources option to add support for Direct Mail in the site itself.

❑ **Add an application in the package to an existing site** – the Supplier Site PuP consists of two applications: the Supplier Site itself and the corresponding BizDesk management site.

❑ **Add a Web server to an existing application in an existing site** – to add another server in a web farm.

The remaining option – **Create new site** – will be highlighted (otherwise, select it yourself); click Next to continue.

We can now choose a name for our site – the name SupplierAD is chosen for us by default, and if any sites were previously installed, they would appear in the Existing sites list. For purposes of example and explanation, let's imagine we're setting up the customer extranet for the distributors of Wrox Press Ltd. Under this example site, B2B partner companies like Barnes and Noble, Amazon.com, and Crown Books could securely order copies to sell on their B2C sites and in their stores.

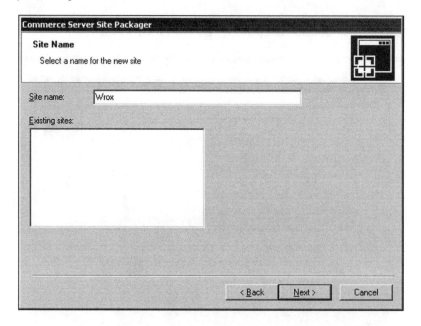

On the Site Name screen, call the site Wrox, then move to the next screen. Next we have to choose which resources to install into the site – by default, all resources are selected.

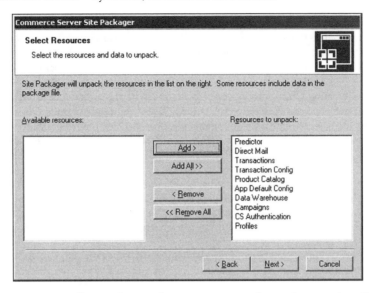

It is not a requirement to install everything at this point, you can always choose to install them later. Either way, when you have decided on which resources to install, choose Next to continue. Also, we can choose to remove resources at a later date without breaking the site, so I suggest you install them all at this point.

At this stage of the wizard, we map global resource pointers to global resources. On the very first site installation, there will be no choices other than the defaults. The Predictor and Direct Mail will already exist as a result of simply installing Commerce Server 2000. However, the Data Warehouse, CS Authentication and Profiles will need to be created as a process of unpacking the site. This is important because the next time we run the Supplier Site, the Retail Site, or any PuP for that matter, we can choose to use an existing Data Warehouse, CS Authentication or Profiles resource. In that case, two completely different sites could share the same authentication and profiling resource.

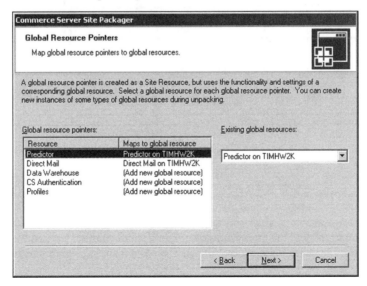

On the Global Resource Pointers screen, just click next to accept the dafult and move on to the next stage of the process.

We next need to choose the database and connection strings you will use in your site. We have quite a few options and can manipulate the configuration of the database to a fair extent. In our case, the Product Catalogs, Campaigns, Transactions, Transaction Configurations, and the Profiles will be stored in a database called wrox_commerce by default; however, this isn't really very descriptive.

Technically, we are creating a B2B site, so we are going to create a new database from this wizard and call it wrox_b2b. Additionally, we can choose to create this SQL Server database on another server, which, of course, is the most likely scenario in a production environment. Click the New Database... button to create a new SQL Server database. We will need to name the database and provide credentials with enough privilege to create a database. Click Create Database when you have filled out the form.

Now, we are ready to change from the default database names to the name of the database that was just created. Click on the Product Catalog resource to give it focus, and then click the Modify button. The Data Link Properties form will appear. This is the form where we can change from the defaults to the SQL Server database we just created (or a pre-existing SQL Server database, if we have one which we want to use).

Choose the SQL Server, enter, the User name and Password, select the database and then click the Test Connection button.

Click the OK button when the connection succeeds.

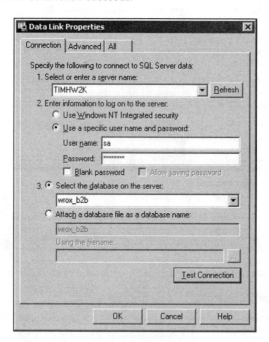

Notice, that the database and server name only changed for the Product Catalog resource. This can allow us to easily distribute the different database functionalities over multiple SQL Servers. In large sites, we would most definitely want to split out the transactions databases from the more infrequently updated databases such as the product catalogue or campaigns. Obviously, a bit of planning and design goes a long way here.

Consider also that with SQL Server 2000 Distributed Partition Views, we are provided with Federated Database Servers, which provides a means for horizontal scaling over multiple SQL Server Machines. So technically, we could distribute the transactions database over a number of SQL servers. SQL Server 2000 Distributed Partition Views allow us to treat a distributed table as one.

Since we are creating our Supplier Site in a Developer environment, we want to use the same wrox_b2b database for our Product Catalogue, Campaigns, Transactions, Transaction Configurations, and Profiles. Thankfully, the Commerce Server 2000 Product team incorporated a little time saving functionality in this wizard: we don't have to go through the process of using the Modify button to change each resource manually in the Data Link Properties form: we can use the Copy button and the Paste button to apply the new database name uniformly for all the resources.

Click on the Product Catalog resource, then use the Copy button to apply the database name to the Campaigns, Transactions, Transaction Config, and Profiles resources.

Lastly, notice that the Data Warehouse resource has it's own SQL Server Database dedicated to it by default. In my case it is named wrox_dw, which is a naming convention that suits my site just fine so I won't change it. As we saw in Chapter 5 – Commerce Server 2000 has rich and robust data warehouse capabilities. The Supplier Site PuP will build the data warehouse and the OLAP cube for us in SQL Server.

Click Next when you have completed the configuration of the SQL Server Database strings.

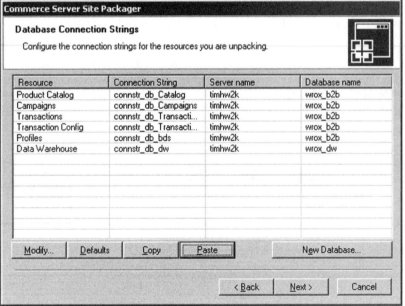

Now we choose which of the applications to unpack in the Supplier Site PuP. In the Supplier Site's case there are two applications: the Supplier Site itself (called SupplierAD), and the Business Desk application (called SupplierADBizDesk). In a production scenario, we would most likely not unpack the BizDesk application for the Supplier Site on the production web server itself: we would more probably install the BizDesk in locations on your intranet behind the firewall.

Accept the default on the Select Applications screen and move on to the next screen:

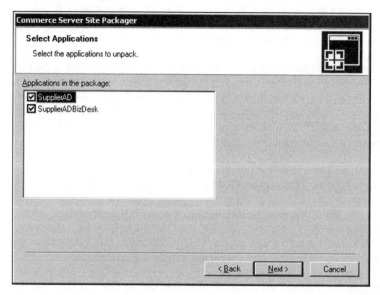

Next we will select the Web Site and Virtual Directories on which you are going to install the application. Again, by default, the Supplier Site PuP has selected supplierad as the name of the Virtual Directory. Because, probably, this will not be descriptive in your environment, I suggest changing it to WroxB2B and WroxB2BBizDesk.

To do this, you'll need to select each application separately (the site itself and the BizDesk) and change the name of the IIS Virtual Directory for each. If you create a new website on your server (as opposed to installing it on Default Web) then you can switch over to the Internet Services Manager, create the site, then come back to the wizard and click the Refresh Web Sites button. The new web site will appear so that you can select it.

We will install our sites on Default Web.

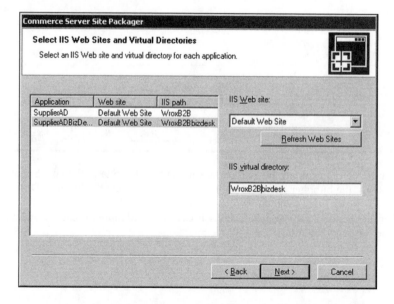

Before clicking Next, it's important to know that there is no going back after this point. There is no Back button after this, and an uninstall is required if any mistakes have been made.

On clicking Next, we will then move to a form in which we specify some settings for the Data Warehouse resource. At this point, we can name the data warehouse. The default is **Data Warehouse 1**, if this is the first solution site created. However, let's change ours to **Wrox Data Warehouse**, and then click the **Test Connection** button to ensure connectivity.

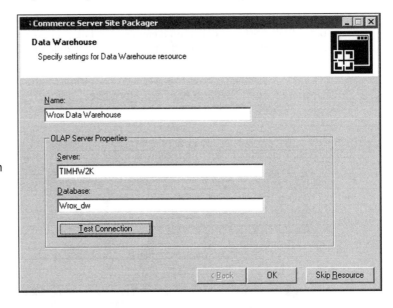

Click the OK button to continue.

After a short time a Commerce Server Site Packager form will appear with some descriptive details of what is currently being configured and installed. Eventually the wizard will stop at the Profiling System from where XML data stores for the Profile Schema, the Site Terms, and the Expression Definition may be navigated.

Notice that the Profile Schema Definition is highlighted.

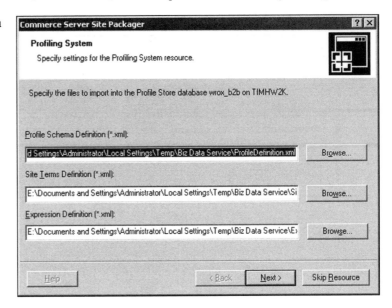

ProfileDefinition.xml

First take a look at the XML data file that contains the profile schema definitions. We can do that by making a copy of the Profile Schema definition filename. The PuP process creates the XML data files and places them in a temporary directory under the current windows 2000 profile. If you are logged on as the Domain Administrator, the path to the Profile Schema Definition file will be:

E:\Documents and Settings\Administrator\Local Settings\Temp\Biz Data Service\ProfileDefinition.xml

Open the file. Internet Explorer is a great tool to view XML. As it is a fairly large file, collapse the it down to its third level by clicking on the minus signs in order to view the major categories of data.

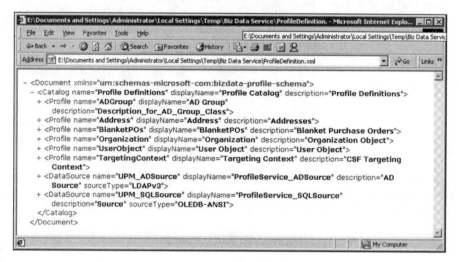

As we can see, there are six Profile elements, named:

- ❏   ADGroup
- ❏   Address
- ❏   BlanketPOs
- ❏   Organization
- ❏   UserObject
- ❏   TargetingContext

These are followed by two DataSource elements, named:

❑ UPM_ADSource

❑ UPM_SQLSource

Within the six Profile Name branches is the data that defines the attributes that are used within the Supplier Site.

Expand each of these eight branches and peruse the contents of the profile name branches. There's a great deal of data here, so don't try wading through it all; just have a casual look at what's there. The important point to recognize is that each attribute used in the site is defined within this file. If we were to build our own PuP file we would define our profile schema and attributes within this file.

Do a search on "city". You should find the first match within the GeneralInfo Group name branch within the Address Profile name. Take careful notice of the attribute properties defined on the city property itself.

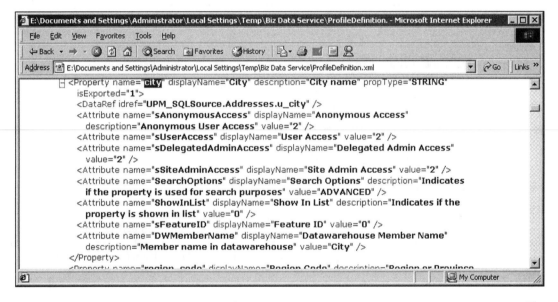

Of special note is the DataRef idref attribute property – UPM_SQLSource.Addresses.u_city. This defines where the actual data is persisted.

Continue searching for instances of "city" until you pass through the "Address" Profile name. Your next match will be close to the end of the XML file, under the UPM_SQLSource DataSource name branch.

Within this branch the SQL Server connection parameters are defined in the "SourceInfo name" branch and then each attribute is defined (including u_city) in a "DataMember name" branch.

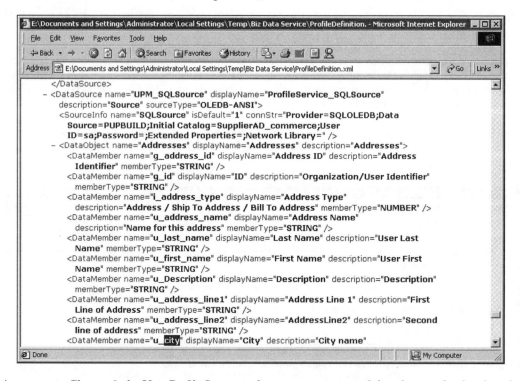

As we saw in Chapter 3, the User Profile System is data store agnostic, and therefore can be distributed against multiple data stores. The Supplier Site User Profile System is distributed between Active Directory and SQL Server. This particular piece of data, City, is persisted by default in SQL Server. As we saw earlier in the chapter, User data such as demographic data is perfect for the Active Directory. By design, the Commerce Server 2000 team who developed the Supplier Site used Active Directory solely for authentication and SQL Server solely for the storage of data. I would suggest that we distribute data which is written once and read frequently, such as city, to Active Directory.

We can set things up to do this at this point by making appropriate alterations to the profile schema definition file. However, it is important to realise that tinkering with the data here in its raw format is a tricky business.

As discussed earlier in this chapter, there is one piece of data that you absolutely need to change up front in this file before proceeding, because not only can it not be changed after the installation of the Supplier Site, but it can never be removed from the Active Directory once it has been installed. That is the location and creation of the Organizational Units.

In Active Directory, like any directory service, schema data like Organizational Units are 'marked as deleted' but never actually removed. The Supplier Site Creates two Organizational Units by default: MSCS_40_Root and ADSite. For our site, we will create an Organizational Unit called Extranet_Users and another Organizational Unit called Wrox_B2B.

To do this, we open the Profile Schema Definition file, and change the two appropriate values:

We'll change MSCS_40_Root to Extranet_Users and ADSite to Wrox_B2B.

Once these are changed, save the file.

Upon completion, the UPM_ADSource DataSource name branch will now look like this:

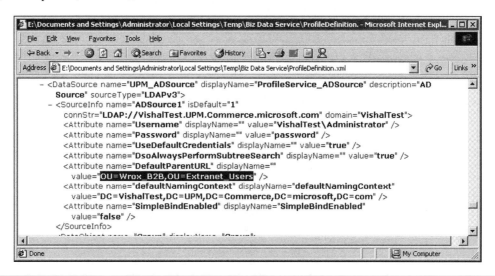

SiteTerms.xml

Now, back to the Supplier Site PuP wizard. The next XML data file that the Profiling System uses for the creation and configuration of the site is SiteTerms.xml. Site Terms are metadata items that the Supplier Site uses. For instance, there is a site term called UserType and its valid values are Guest User and Registered User. If you are logged in as the Domain Administrator, the path to the Site Terms Definition file will be:

```
E:\Documents and Settings\Administrator\Local Settings\Temp\
                        Biz Data Service\SiteTerms.xml
```

Open the Site Terms XML file in Internet Explorer exactly as you did in the prior step (with the Profile Schema Definition File) – notice that the file is organized into two main branches.

The first of these – UserSiteTerms – has three properties defined:

❑ AccountStatus – with valid values of Active Account and Inactive Account

❑ UserRole – with valid values of Normal User and Administrator

❑ UserType – with valid values of Guest User and Registered User

The second branch – CalendarSiteTerms – has two properties defined: Days and Months.

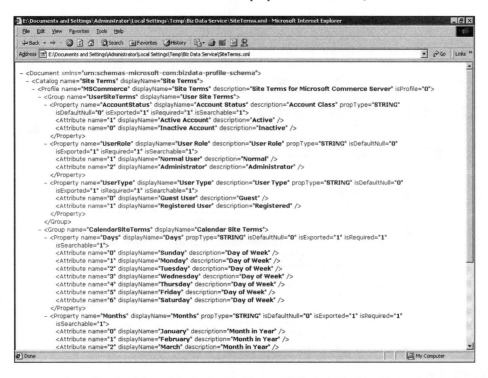

There is no need to edit any of the values in the Site Terms XML data file, but this is where we would define site terms if we created our own PuP package.

ExpressionDefinition.xml

Finally, let's take a look at the Expression Definition XML data file:

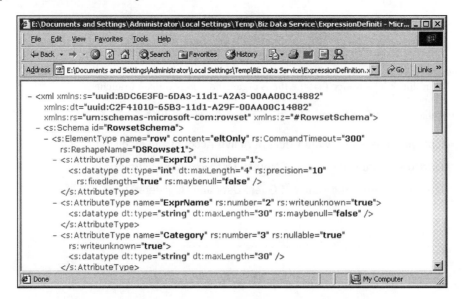

The Expression Definition File contains the properties by which expressions can be defined. The structure defined for expressions in this file is the basis for campaign expressions created in the BizDesk. Items (properties) such as Expression ID, Name, Category, Description, Date Created, Date Modified are all examples of the type of Expression Structure data, defined in the Expression Definition XML file. There is no need to edit any of the values in the Expression Definition XML data file.

Active Directory Profiling System Resources

We are now ready to continue with the Supplier Site PuP wizard. Click Next to continue and you will move to the Active Directory Profiling System resource form. This is an important stage of the process because there is a well-documented bug at this stage. The bug has to do with authentication in the Active Directory. The Supplier Site wizard may seem to have the right credentials, because the verification button provided in the wizard falsely reports success. However, although we receive this report, we do not necessarily have a successful connection.

In the `Readme_Solution_Sites.htm` (extracted as part of the original installation of the PuP files) you'll find a topic called 'Supplier Solution Site: Must use domain name and user name'. Read it carefully before proceeding. It warns us that even though the Test Connection button may report a successful connection to the Active Directory, in actuality we have to follow one of two very specific naming conventions for the UserID. From the documentation:

> *In the UserID box, type the domain name and user name using one of the following formats:*
>
> ```
> <domain_name>\<username>
> <username>@<fully_qualified_domain_name>
> ```
>
> *Example*
>
> ```
> testdomain\administrator
> ```
> *or*
> ```
> administrator@testdomain.microsoft.com
> ```

In my case, the domain name is TIMHUCK, so my username becomes TIMHUCK\Administrator. I would also need to change the Parent URL from OU=Wrox,OU=MSCS_40_Root to OU=Wrox_B2B,OU=Extranet_Users.

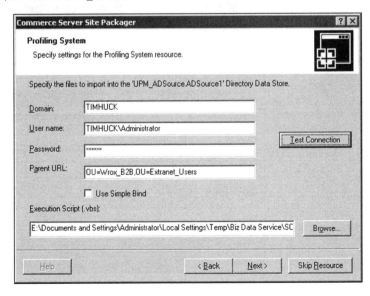

Click the **Test Connection** button when ready – it should report **Connection Succeeded**. If not, determine the problem and test again. If you do have a problem getting a successful connection, it will most likely be a result of a mistake in the credentials, such as an incorrectly typed password. If not, it may well be a connectivity or DNS problem.

If you open the Execution Script, `SCHEMAUPM_ADSource.ADSource1.vbs` (which may be found in the `\Documents and Settings\Administrator\Local Settings\Temp\Biz Data Service` folder), you will see a WSH script containing a small amount of ADSI. This creates the two Organizational Units in Active Directory by passing names, properties and credential parameters.

This WSH script, along with some other configuration scripts, are created during the unpacking of ta site, and are consequently executed.

We could add functionality to this in order to create a number of users within the Organizational Unit, or maybe to move users from the default **Users** container of the Active Directory to any new Organizational Units we create. A good approach to doing this would be writing the ADSI necessary for interaction with Active Directory, and Designing an XML Data file with the User Data. In any event, this is a good example of how we can extend the functionality of this Pup with an open interface – the ability to enhance a standalone WSH in the form of a `.vbs` file.

Click **Next** to proceed to the SQL Server Profiling System resource form.

SQL Server Profiling System Resources

The value for the Profiling System Connection String to the SQL Server can be edited with the **Modify** button. However, we entered the parameters for this connection in a prior step of the wizard.

Next, we encounter the Schema definition scripts.

By default, the file name for the `SCHEMAUPM_SQLSource.sql` file is populated for us. If we open the file, you will see the SQL statements that the Supplier Site Pup uses to create the four tables: `Addresses`, `BlanketPOs`, `UserObject`, and `OrganizationalObject`, and their associated indexes in SQL Server. There is no need to edit this file (though we would if we were creating a Pup for our own site).

Next in this SQL Server Profiling System resource form is the Data population scripts. It's slightly disappointing that the Commerce Server 2000 product team did not supply these, but one can understand leaving these out because of the complexity involved (because each user profile system is extensible by nature, a generic data population script, in this case, would be made obsolete (and consequently break the site) by any modification to the user profile system).

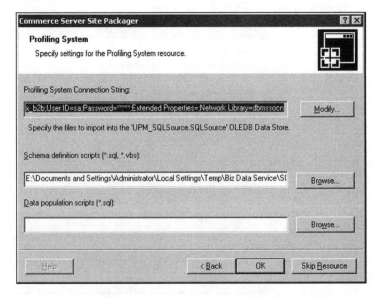

Now we are ready for the actual installation of the two applications within the Supplier Site Pup. Click the OK button. Status messages on all the tasks that are being performed will alert us to what's going on.

When the process is complete, we will end up with a form similar to this one:

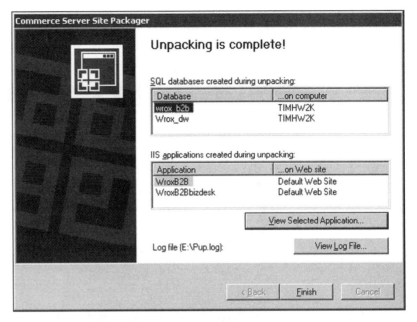

Before we Finish, we'll click the View Log File button – by default, the log file is written to the root of the file system in which Windows 2000 is installed, and it is called Pup.log. Many of the details of the unpacking, installation, and configuration process of the Supplier Site are contained in this file. If there were any errors during the process, they would also be reported in this file.

The View Selected Application... button will instantiate a browser and run the Supplier Site or its associated Business Desk, if selected. Before we run either of these applications, let's take a brief look at what the wizard actually did – so click the Finish button to complete the process.

A First Look at the Installed Site

Open up the Active Directory Users and Computers tool from Start | Programs | Administrative Tools. In here, we can see the OUs that were created. Assuming you made the Organizational Unit changes as described above, your Active Directory should look like this:

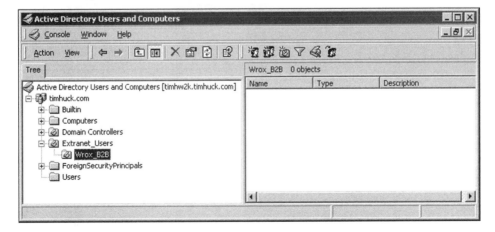

Additionally, two virtual directories were created on your IIS 5.0 web server. View them by running the Internet Services Manager tool from Start | Programs | Administrative Tools. Navigate to the Web Server on which you installed the Supplier Site applications to view the virtual directories and their folders and content:

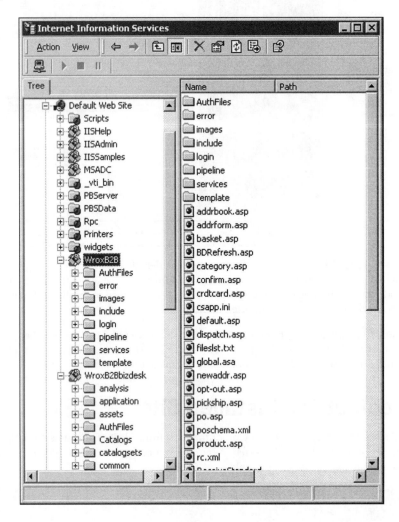

Now run the SQL Server Enterprise Manager by clicking Start | Programs | Microsoft SQL Server | Enterprise Manager. Note the two databases that the Supplier Site Pup created:

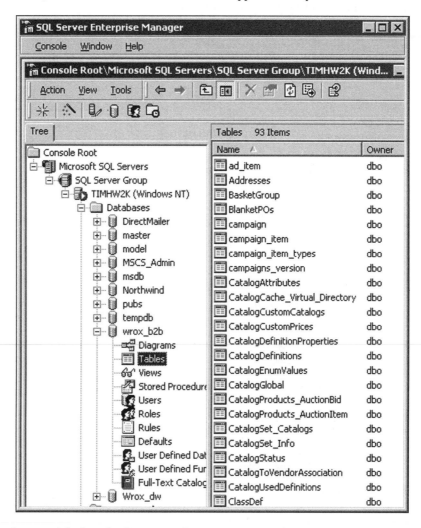

Now, let's take a quick look at the Commerce Server Manager tool. Run it by clicking Start | Programs | Microsoft Commerce Server 2000 | Commerce Server Manager. The first thing you should notice is that the Commerce Server 2000 Product team embedded the Active Directory Users and Computers snap-in, the Internet Information Services snap-in, and the SQL Server snap-in (amongst other tools) into the Commerce Server Manager.

This gives you, as the Site administrator, a 'one-stop shop' (so to speak) when it comes to managing your Supplier Solution Site. Also, notice how the tool breaks out Global Resources from Commerce Sites resources. This will be important later in this chapter when we make some configuration changes.

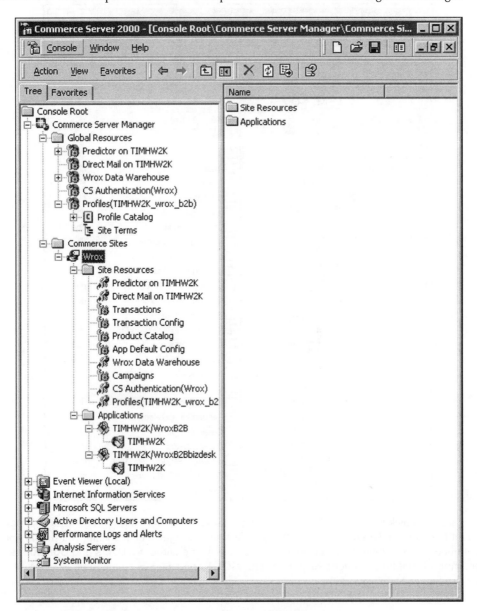

Standard Supplier Site Configurations

Before we start navigating our way around the Supplier Site in order to test its functionality, the logical first step is to create a user in whose name we can roam. We can do this quite simply from the Supplier Site BizDesk.

As you know, the BizDesk is an HTML Application (HTA), which requires Internet 5.5 (and higher). HTAs are web applications where much of the HTML, code, and components are installed locally, as opposed to most web applications where the code lives on a web server. If you want to install the BizDesk on the server running the Supplier Site itself (as in the scenario of a development server), then proceed as follows:

❑   Run the Commerce Server Manager.

❑   Navigate down to the Internet Information Services snap-in.

❑   Right-click on the virtual directory of your Supplier Site BizDesk application, and choose Browse. The address in your browser should resemble http://localhost/WroxB2Bbizdesk.

If you want to install the BizDesk on another computer, then:

❑   Run IE5.5, and navigate to http://servername/BizdeskSiteName.

❑   Once you've successfully navigated to the BizDesk Virtual directory (and assuming you haven't changed IE's default security settings) you will be prompted with a security warning that a component is being downloaded to your computer. Click Yes to download and run the component.

Upon completion, you will receive a status update that the Setup is complete and a link to the BizDesk will be provided for you. Additionally, a shortcut to the BizDesk application will be created on your desktop and in your start menu. Click the Start Business Desk link and a new instance of a browser will appear and run the BizDesk. There's not a enormous amount to say about the Supplier Site BizDesk – most of the functionality has already been discussed, as it's largely the same as its equivalent in the Retail Site. However, there are a few points of interest, and creating a user to browse the site with is one of them.

Adding a User

From the front page of the BizDesk, give your user a Logon Name and Password and fill out all the rest of the General Information properties for the user. Additionally click the Business Desk section and change the Partner service role flags drop-down to Administrator. This will make your new user an Administrator on the site.

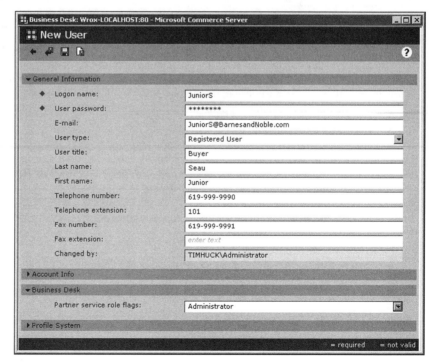

Click the Save and back button to save the user and return to the Users List.

Now, that we have created a user, let's look at something relatively interesting. Open up the Active Directory Users and Computers tool (either standalone via the Administrative Tools menu, or from within the Commerce Server Manager). Now navigate to the Organizational Unit created in the Pup unpacking process – you should find the user you've just created! This illustrates an important feature that you should be aware of:

> **Site users created in the BizDesk of this custom configured Supplier Site are, in fact, domain users within the Active Directory.**

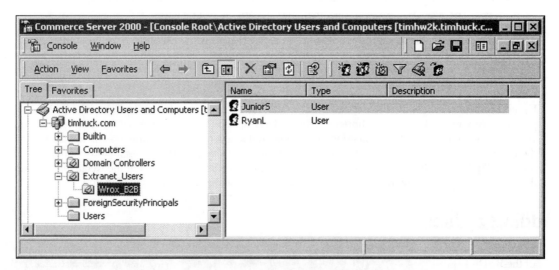

If you double-click the user from within the Active Directory Users and Computers tool, you will see very few attributes set with a value; however, if you click on the member of tab, you'll see that the user we created is an actual domain user. Later in this chapter, we will see how to actually map the user profile data from elements in SQL Server to attributes in the Active Directory. For now, though, we have a user to authenticate with, so let's use it to navigate the Supplier Site.

A particular problem that is frequently encountered is that users created within the Supplier Site BizDesk will fail to authenticate. To overcome this, it is necessary to add Log on locally privilege to the domain users within the User Rights Assignments branch of the Local Policies for the Domain Controller Security Policy tool. This is mandatory.

Before you authenticate a user on the Supplier Site, you must set the Security Mode on the Domain Controller, as follows:

1. Select Start | Programs | Administrative Tools | Domain Controller Security Policy.

2. In the Security Settings option, select Local Policies | User Rights Assignment | Log on Locally.

3. In the Security dialog box, add Domain\Users to this policy, and then click OK.

Navigate to the Supplier Site; authenticate the user we just created. As with the Retail solution site, there is a lot of functionality, but the look and feel is quite plain. If we chose to, we could brighten it up, just as we did the Retail Site – however, let's concentrate this time on the functionality.

Having been authenticated, you'll see that there is no product catalog, as one has yet to be created.

Adding a Product Catalog

In this section, we'll import a product catalog: contained in the file called `booksfull.xml` which comes as part of the Commerce Server 2000 SDK.

From the Catalogs section of the business desk, click Catalog Editor | Import Catalog | Import XML. Unfortunately there is no navigation button, so we will need to type the full name of the XML catalog. Pay careful attention to the Delete existing data in this catalog check box if you already have data in your catalog. Click the OK button when ready to import.

A dialog box will immediately appear alerting us to the fact that a Catalog Import process has been started successfully and we will need to click OK to clear the message. Unfortunately, we do not get the same luxury of a dialog box when the import is completed. We need to carefully monitor disk activity and the status messages at the bottom of the BizDesk screen to determine when the import process has completed.

Once the catalog has been imported, we will need to select the Update Catalog button (in the Catalog Editor) to refresh and publish the catalog to the web site. We will not receive any status on the updating of the catalog and the page will not automatically refresh when it is complete. You will receive no acknowledgement as to whether or not the catalog publishing process was successful.

Creating a Catalog Set

As we saw in Chapter 4, **catalog sets** are subsets of product catalogs. Using the BizDesk, we can create catalog sets and assign them to a specific group of users according to their profile. In our sample scenario, we will create a catalog set for buyers from 'Barnes and Noble'. To do so from the BizDesk, click Catalog Sets. On the top of the Catalog Sets screen, click the Add Catalog Set button (or *Alt-N*). Give the Catalog set a name and description, click the available catalog that you want to assign to this catalog set (in this case, this is Books) and click Add.

Once complete it should look like this:

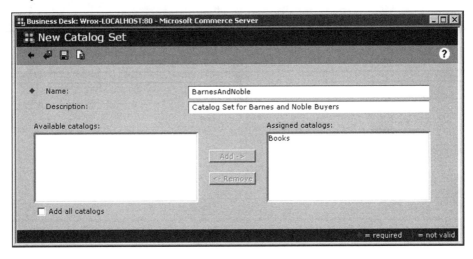

Click Save and Back to Catalog Sets Lists (or press *Alt-K*) to save and return when you are ready.

Creating an Organization

We can use the Organizations Module of the BizDesk to add a B2B partner on your Supplier Site. The Organizations Module also facilitates entering demographic and business rule data about your B2B partners such as:

❑   Contact Information

❑   Address Information

❑   Phone Numbers

❑   Purchase Order Information

❑   Cost Center Information

❑   Discounts

From the main navigation menu of the BizDesk choose Users. Click the Organizations button. Then click the New Organization button (or press *Alt-N*). Give the Organization a name (BarnesAndNoble), a trading partner number (02) and pick a catalog set (BarnesAndNoble). Click Save and Back to Organizations List (or press *Alt-K*) when completed.

Now, switch over to the Active Directory Users and Computers tool from within the Commerce Server Manager. Check closely what happened as a result of creating an Organization. An Organization Unit was created in the Active Directory beneath the site OU. Additionally, two security groups (AdminGroup and UserGroup) are created and placed in the OU. Also, if you check the security properties of the new OU, you'll see that the Supplier Site BizDesk automatically delegates the appropriate permissions to these two groups.

From the View menu of the Active Directory Users and Computer tool choose Advanced Features. Right-click on the BarnesAndNoble OU you created and choose Properties. Click the Security tab. Notice the Administrators group that was created has delegated permissions.

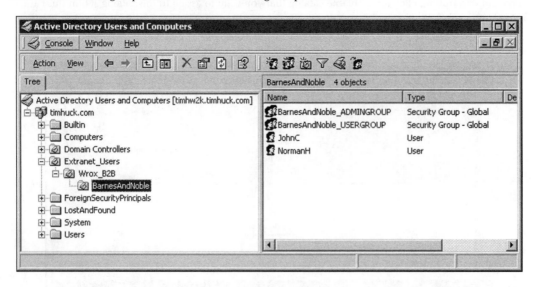

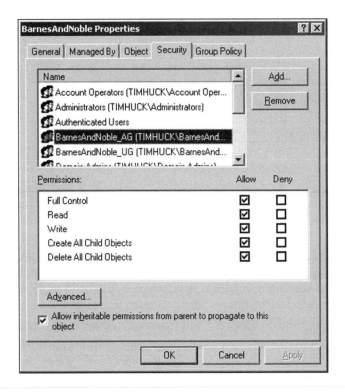

Make sure that you Publish Profiles from the Users menu of the BizDesk after making user-related changes in the BizDesk.

Other BizDesk Configurations

Now that we have a catalog, a catalog set, and an Organization, we can go back to the users module and create some more users for testing scenarios. Use the Account Info section of the user to assign them to an Organization and a Catalog Set.

Additionally, it would be a good idea to create Shipping methods and Tax Rates from within the Orders Module of the BizDesk so that we can place test orders in our development environment.

Advanced Supplier Site Configurations

Using the Authentication Filter

When using the Commerce Server 2000 Authentication Filter, a user can log into our site, then Commerce Server 2000, in combination with Windows 2000, authenticates the user by verifying the login and password against the login and password stored in the Profiles database, which, in this case, is the Active Directory.

After Commerce Server verifies the user information, it creates a non-persisted cookie and stores it in an ISAPI filter cache for the application. The cookie specifies that the user is authenticated and is allowed to see secured pages on our site.

When we use `AuthFilter`, we can choose the following authentication modes:

❑ Windows Authentication mode – Anonymous and registered users can access the site, depending on the ACLs applied to the site resources. The `AuthFilter` uses Windows Authentication to control authorization access to the site.

❑ Custom Authentication mode – A custom authentication process is designed and implemented to control authorization access to the site while still using the base services of the `AuthFilter` for Authentication.

❑ Autocookie mode – The `AuthFilter` permits anonymous user access to the site if a persisted cookie is written to allow tracking of the user.

❑ Windows Authentication with Autocookie mode – A mixed mode that permits both registered and anonymous users access and authorization to the site. Additionally, it allows tracking of the anonymous users through persisted cookies.

❑ Custom Authentication with Autocookie mode – A mixed mode that permits both registered and anonymous users access and authorization to the site. Additionally it allows tracking of the anonymous users through persistent cookies. Instead of controlling access through Windows ACLs, a custom authentication process is designed and implemented to control authorization access to the site.

To enable the Authentication Filter for Windows Authentication on our Supplier Site, perform the following steps to ensure that the AuthFiles subfolder and all pages within it have anonymous access enabled:

1. Using the Internet Information Services snap-in, navigate to the AuthFiles Folder, and select Properties from its context menu.

2. Select the Directory Security tab and click the Edit... button within the Anonymous access and authentication Control section. Check the Anonymous box, and click OK twice to apply the change.

Let's assume for a moment that our domain controller and Web server are installed on different computers within the same domain – which is, of course, a quite legitimate production scenario. `AuthFilter` must then have an anonymous account on the server in order to execute `ProfileService.GetUserProfileByKey()` on the login page for any authenticated user.

By default, an anonymous user account is named `IUSR_<servername>`. In Internet Services Manager, `IUSR_<servername>` does not have enough permissions to execute the method. Additionally, we must add a user account from that domain as the anonymous account.

To do this, we first create a user account on the domain that has access to read the user properties from Active Directory. Then, on the Web server, use IIS Manager to set up the same user account as the anonymous account for the `AuthFiles` subfolder and all the files in that subfolder.

3. Within Commerce Server Manager, expand Commerce Sites, and click on the site you want to administer.

4. Expand Applications, and select Properties from the context menu of the application you want to work with. In our example, this will be TIMHW2K/WroxB2B.

5. On the General tab of the Properties dialog, set the Authentication Filter to Windows Authentication, and click OK.

You may find that the first time you do this, after a flurry of disk activity, the entire Commerce Server Manager MMC will abort. Nevertheless, when you restarted the MMC, you should find that the change has been applied.

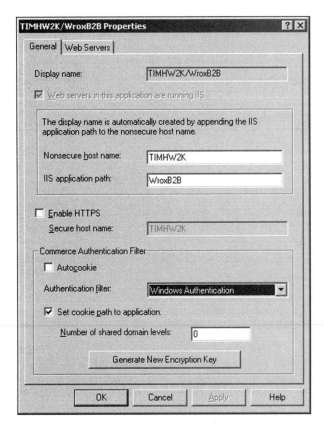

6. Expand **Internet Information Services** within the Commerce Server Manager, right-click the Supplier Site (in my case it's the virtual directory **WroxB2B** off default Web), and then click **Properties**.

7. On the **Directory Security** tab of the **Properties** dialog, in the Anonymous access and authentication control section, click **Edit**. In the **Authentication Methods** dialog box, clear the Integrated Windows authentication box, if it is checked. By default, Basic Authentication is enabled on a Supplier Solution Site – do not change it to any other security settings for this supplier site configuration.

8. If you are using a Web farm, or require proxy account support, you will need to update the code in `Login.asp`. **If you are working on a development server or a single server requiring no such proxy account support, you don't need to update login.asp, so you can skip the rest of this step) and move to step 9.** In a web farm scenario where non-sticky load balancing is used, the information in the HTTP header that the AuthFilter uses will be lost, and the user will be forced to re-authenticate if redirected to a new server in the farm. Microsoft has developed a special login.asp for this scenario, where a proxied user account is used to authenticate between non-sticky load balanced, or other cross domain single sign-on scenarios where a proxied user account is necessary to authenticate.

9. The code is available to copy and paste in the Commerce Server Help File under the topic 'Enabling Auth Filter for the Supplier Solution Site'. Alternatively, you can download an adapted version of the login.asp from the Wrox web site at: http://www.wrox.com.

Of particular interest in this special version of login.asp is the scenario where a user is already authenticated. When a user moves to a new page in the site, he is bounced to a new server. Since the HTTP header information that the AuthFilter uses is lost upon a non-sticky load-balanced scenario, the user is redirected to login.asp. A valid Authentication Ticket exists, but it is no longer cached in the AuthFilter:

```
If objAuth.IsAuthenticated(30) Then
```

This is the scenario where a user is already authenticated, but since they have landed here in the authentication (login) page, the HTTP header information has been lost – A valid AuthTicket Exists, but it is not cached in the AuthFilter.

```
strUserName = objAuth.GetUserID(2)
```

Next the LoginID is retrieved:

```
sAuthUser = LoginName(strUserName)
```

Next the domain information is added to strUserName. It is converted to the format: Domain\UserLoginID.

```
Set objMSCSProfileObj = GetUserProfileByLoginName(sAuthUser)
```

Next, the profile is retrieved with the user profile object and the password is retrieved.

```
strPassword =
objMSCSProfileObj.Fields.Item("GeneralInfo").Value.Item("user_security_password")
Set objMSCSProfileObj = Nothing
```

The user profile object is cleaned up and the user's cookie is retrieved. The authentication information is added to the data in the cookie. And then the user is redirected back to the page he requested with the authentication information.

```
strRetAsp = Request.Cookies("MSCSFirstRequestedURL")
strRetAsp = strRetAsp + "&proxyuser="
strRetAsp = strRetAsp + strUserName
strRetAsp = strRetAsp + "&proxypwd="
strRetAsp = strRetAsp + strPassword

Response.Redirect strRetAsp
```

10. Now open up \include\Std_access_lib.asp for the Supplier Site. You will need to change the GetUserInfo() method and add the LoginName() method in Std_access_lib.asp. The code is available to copy and paste in the Commerce Server Help File under the topic 'Enabling Auth Filter for the Supplier Solution Site'. Alternatively, you can download a version of the GetUserInfo() method and

`LoginName()` method from the Wrox web site.

`GetUserInfo` is called from the setupenv include file. `GetUserInfo` derives the following information:

❑   m_userID – The User ID

❑   m_UserAccessType – IIS_AUTH or TICKET_AUTH or GUEST_VISIT or ANON_VISIT

❑   m_UserType – AUTH_USER or GUEST_USER or ANON_USER

Before you make the proper edits to the `GetUserInfo` function, you may notice that the only difference of significance between the original function and the new one is the way that the authenticated user is retrieved and processed. Since the user in the supplier site is truly authenticated in the OS, the user name is retrieved with the LOGON_USER Server Variable:

```
sAuthUser = LoginName(Request.ServerVariables("LOGON_USER"))
```

Once the user is identified, the user profile is retrieved accordingly:

```
Set mscsUser = GetUserProfileByLoginName(sAuthUser)
```

The LoginName Function is a simple little string manipulation and parsing function that uses the Split command to remove the domain information from the username.

```
aName = Split (sUserName, "\")
LoginName = aName(UBound(aName))
```

11. Open up `\SupplierAD\template\menu.asp` for the Supplier Site. In the `PrepareLoginSection()` method, change the `Request.ServerVariables()` string that refers to the AUTH_USER server variable so that it refers instead to LOGON_USER. A user that is authenticated in the OS is retrieved with the LOGON_USER server variable. Therefore:

```
sAuthUser = Request.ServerVariables("AUTH_USER")
```

becomes:

```
sAuthUser = Request.ServerVariables("LOGON_USER")
```

You may notice other instances of AUTH_USER in the function used as a constant in the code. You do not need to change the constant, only the one line pointed out above.

You should now be ready to test the Supplier Site with the Authentication Filter running. If you have trouble authenticating, you may want to check the application log within the event viewer for syntax error reports.

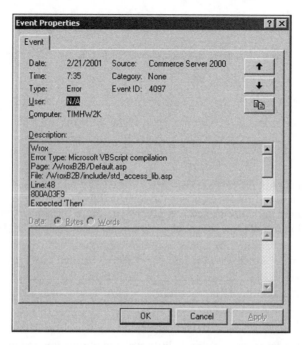

Additionally, you can turn on client error messages in the `global.asa` file. By default, the Application Variable MSCSEnv is set to PRODUCTION.

```
Set Application("MSCSEnv") = DEVELOPMENT
```

Additionally, you can customize client error messages in `error\500error.asp`. Of course, you can always set up (indeed, you're encouraged to do so) a complete debugging environment.

The first thing to notice about using the Authentication filter is the HTML form that is now used to authenticate with. The Site Server 3.0 Membership Directory Service was the first Microsoft technology to include this feature – that uses HTML forms to authenticate seamlessly in the OS. Being able to customize the HTML form that is used for Authentication provides for some great control over the look and feel of a site. Additionally, you will quite probably spend a little time parsing in the domain name so that your users can authenticate simply with their user name.

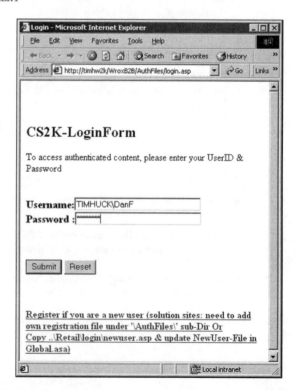

Mapping the SQL Fields to Active Directory Attributes.

As mentioned earlier in the chapter, data which is written once, but accessed many times, such as that pertaining to users, is perfect for the Active Directory. By default, data like this is persisted to SQL Server in the Supplier Solution Site. As we saw in Chapter 3, the User Profile System is data store agnostic.

The following steps will show you in painstaking detail how you would change a user attribute from one data store (SQL Server) to another (Active Directory) through the BizDesk Application. For this exercise, we will change the e-mail field/attribute of registered users to persist in Active Directory instead of SQL Server.

- ❑ Run the BizDesk for the Supplier Site. Click on Users in the left navigation, and then click on Profile Designer.

- ❑ Choose User Object by clicking on it, then click the View button (or press *Alt-O*).

- ❑ Click the arrow next to General Information to drop down the specific attributes. Note that if you simply click on the words General Information you will not be presented with the list of attributes – only a form allowing you to change the display name and description of the General Information category of the User Object.

- ❑ Click E-mail, then click the Advanced Attributes Section.

- ❑ Click the ellipsis (...) in the Map to data: field. Notice that the e-mail address is mapped to a field in SQL Server (ProfileService_SQLSource) called Email Address (STRING).

- ❑ Click ProfileService_ADSource, then click Group to list the available attributes from the Active Directory.

529

❑ Click on mail (STRING) to choose the mail attribute from the Active Directory, and then click the OK button. Click Apply to apply the change. Then click the Save and Close button (*Alt-K*) to complete the operation.

Unfortunately, you will now encounter an error message:

> The profile property 'email_address' is mapped to a data member in a source which is not referenced by the join key.

The reason for this is that the logon name is used as the join key between SQL Server and Active Directory. The Logon name field in the SQL Server data source lives in the User Object Data Member. The Logon name attribute in the Active Directory data source lives in the User Data Member. The limitation of the design of the User Object in this case is that only the data elements common between data members can be mapped. If you examine a little further, the mail attribute from Active Directory lives in the Group data member. Additionally, the User Profile System is limited to a one-to-one join, and only one join per data member.

Why has this happened. Well, it is due to a problem in the design of the `ProfileDefinition.xml`, which was used in the creation of the profile when we installed the site earlier in the chapter. A few small fixes to that XML file will prevent this problem in design and limitation when we install another Supplier Site. We would simply have to move the Active Directory Mail attribute out of the Group data member and into the User Data Member. Additionally, we might want to add the first name, last name, address details, etc. to the Active Directory User Data Member at the very bottom of the `ProfileDefinition.xml`. These Active Directory attributes are not even included in the profile definition file.

A profile definition XML file (`ProfileAD_SQL.xml`), which has been configured to be more appropriate for distributing data between SQL Server and Active Directory, is available in the download from the Wrox website. Use this XML data file when you build the solution site in the Unpacking process.

Now that you have seen how easy it is to switch data elements with the Map to Data button from SQL Server to Active Directory, it makes sense to go back to a ghosted image and install the solution site again (or install another version of the site). You would do this, of course, only after some adequate planning on which data elements you want to persist in SQL and which ones you want to persist in Active Directory.

The table below summarizes the attributes of the Active Directory that we would most typically want to utilize in our supplier Solution Site. Note that the mail attribute cannot simply be added to the User Profile System: it would need to be moved from the Group Data Object to the User Data Object.

Attribute	Display Name
GivenName	First Name
Sn	Last Name
streetAddress	Street Address
l	City
st	State/Province
postalCode	ZIP/Postal Code
mail	E-Mail Address

Believe it or not, there are no easy to use tools available in a standard Windows 2000 Server installation that allow us to navigate the Active Directory to view the actual attribute names, their properties, and values. Because of this, we've supplied a simple ASP page, ADGet.asp, with the example code for this book, which enables us to do this.

Let's take a quick look at how it works.

The first part of the ASP page uses the ADSI Get() method to retrieve the multi-valued attribute, attributeDisplayNames. This is the location of the name/value pairs that are used in the Tab controls of the **Active Directory Users and Computers MMC**. The data is returned in a Variant Array, so it must be iterated to display the values:

```
'use the ADSI Get method on the IADs interface to retrieve attribs from AD
strObject = "LDAP://CN=user-Display,CN=409,CN=DisplaySpecifiers,"
strObject = strObject & "CN=Configuration,DC=timhuck,DC=com"

Response.Write("AD Object: <STRONG>" & strObject & "</STRONG><BR><BR>")

Set objADs = GetObject(strObject)

varAttribute = objADs.Get("attributeDisplayNames")
Response.Write("Type: " & TypeName(varAttribute) & "<BR>")

Response.Write("<STRONG>attributeDisplayNames: </STRONG><BR>")
For Each varElement In varAttribute
  Response.Write(varElement) & "<BR>"
Next
```

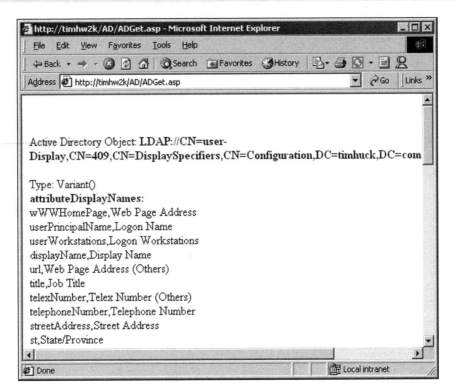

The same ADSI `Get()` method is then used on the Mail attribute of the user within Active Directory. In this case, we have added a user called "DanF". This is how we can use ADSI in simple Active Server Pages to view the values of the attributes we are using in our Commerce Server 2000 User Profile System in Active Directory.

```
strObject = "LDAP://CN=DanF,OU=BarnesAndNoble,OU=Wrox_B2B,OU=Extranet_Users,"
strObject = strObject & DC=timhuck,DC=com"          'AD Users Container
Response.Write("AD Object: <STRONG>" & strObject & "</STRONG><br><BR>")

Set objADs = GetObject(strObject)
Response.Write("Email: " & objADs.Get("mail"))
```

As we saw in Chapter 3, we can choose to modify SQL or Active Directory data without using the object model of the User Profile System, but in most cases, it isn't recommended. I have included a small amount of code in the same ASP page, to show how you might use ADSI to modify the data of your Active Directory that is used on the User Profile System of your Supplier Site.

The ADSI `Put()` method is the opposite of `Get()`, and writes data. The only other major difference is that each `Put()` is cached, and committed to the Active Directory with the `Setinfo` method.

```
bSuccess = objADs.Put("mail", "TimF@BarnesAndNoble.com")
bSuccess = objADs.Setinfo
```

To make the necessary configurations once the Supplier Site has been installed, run the Commerce Server Manager Tool (Programs | Microsoft Commerce Server 2000 | Commerce Server Manager from the Start Menu). Navigate to Global Resources and then choose Profiles for your Supplier Site. A profile will be listed for each Supplier Site that you have installed. Navigate to Profile Catalog, then to Data Sources. Choose the ProfileService_ADSource. Navigate to the Data Objects and then to the Group Data Object. Locate the Email Address attribute and delete it from the Group Object by right-clicking and choosing Delete. It will ask you for confirmation before deleting it. Now, choose the User Data Object. Add the email attribute (and every attribute listed in the previous table) by right-clicking on the User Data Object and choosing New Data Member...

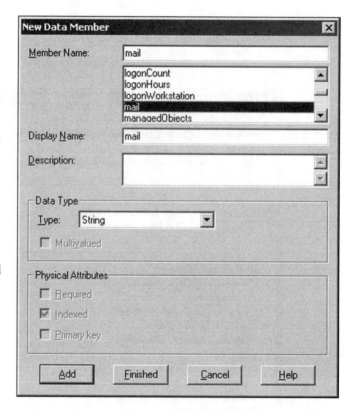

You will need to select each attribute from a long list, which are available to the Active Directory Users Class (either directly or by inheritance). The New Data Member Wizard will not read the Display Name and Description properties from each attribute in the Active Directory allowing some flexibility for you to use your own. Unfortunately, the New Data Member Wizard will not read the Data Type property for each attribute either – one mistake in applying the wrong data type and you will break the entire profile system, which will break the entire site.

Every attribute from the table above that we have chosen to add to the Supplier Site is of String Data type.

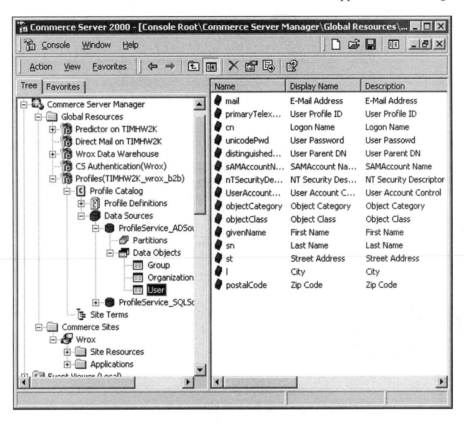

Now we can go back to the BizDesk to map the fields/attributes of registered users to persist in Active Directory instead of SQL Server, as we did earlier in this section. Map the e-mail address, the first name and the last name attributes within the General Information Section of the User Object. Once you have completed the task of mapping the Active Directory attributes to the User Data Objects, publish the profile from the Publish Profiles link in the User section of the BizDesk.

Once the profiles have been successfully published, run the Supplier Site and authenticate as one of the Users we created earlier. Click the profile link within the Customer Service section in the left-hand navigation bar. Update the e-mail address, first name and last name and then click the Save button. Now, go back to the Active Directory Users and Computers snap-in within the Commerce Server Manager tool. Navigate to the user you were working on in the Organizational Unit. Double-click on the user to verify that the Supplier Site User Profile System did, in fact, update the data in Active Directory.

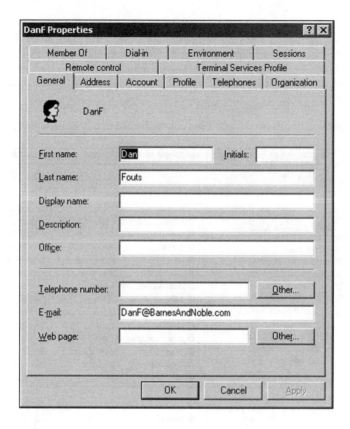

Navigating the Supplier Site

Since we've seen quite a lot of the Retail Site in earlier chapters, it doesn't make sense to do it again here since the two sites are almost identical in site navigation, but it is important to view the areas in which the Retail and Supplier Sites are different.

The Supplier Site differs from the Retail site in the following respects:

❑ Partner Services are enabled in the Supplier Site – as indicated by a setting of 1 for the i_DelegatedAdminOptions property of App Default Config. The Partner Service is a functional area of the site, which provides trading partners access to their accounts. This management area of the site facilitates editing profile, user and order data.

❑ Logging in is required in the Supplier Site, and authentication is provided through Internet Information Services (IIS) using Basic or Integrated Windows authentication – specified by a setting of 7 for the i_FormLoginOptions property of App Default Config.

❑ Both credit cards and purchase order billing are allowed as payment options in the Supplier Site – specified by a setting of 5 for the i_PaymentOptions property of App Default Config.

❑ Self-registration is not allowed in the Supplier Site – specified by a setting of 0 for the i_SiteRegistrationOptions property of App Default Config.

Authenticate on the Supplier Site as a **Delegate Admin**. A delegate Admin is a user whose role is set by changing the Partner service role flags from **User** to **Delegate Admin**. Upon authentication, first notice that the home page includes a new area in the left navigation called **Partner Service**. It is within this section that the B2B partner can maintain the user accounts, the orders, and other details generic to the entire organization.

The Partner Service is only activated in the Supplier Site. It is only available to Delegated Admins who have administrative privilege for their organization. The code that determines whether to display the Partner Service Section or not can be found in `template\menu.asp`:

```
bShowPartnerServiceSection = False
If dictConfig.i_DelegatedAdminOptions = DELEGATED_ADMIN_SUPPORTED Then
  If Not mscsUser Is Nothing Then
    If mscsUser.Fields(GetQualifiedName(BUSINESS_DESK_GROUP,
FIELD_USER_PARTNERDESK_ROLE)).Value = ROLE_ADMIN Then
      If (Not mscsUser.Fields.Item(USER_ORGID).Value = "") Then
        bShowPartnerServiceSection = True
      End If
    End If
  End If
End If

If bShowPartnerServiceSection Then
  htmPartnerServiceSection = LookupCachedFragment("StaticSectionsCache",
"PartnerServiceSection")
  If IsNull(htmPartnerServiceSection) Then
    htmPartnerServiceSection =
    htmRenderPartnerServiceSection(MSCSSiteStyle.Body)
     Call CacheFragment("StaticSectionsCache", "PartnerServiceSection",
htmPartnerServiceSection)
  End If
  htmRenderMenu = htmRenderMenu & htmPartnerServiceSection
End If
```

Now, add something to a basket and make a purchase. When you get to the payment information, notice that you can pay with a purchase order. This is accomplished with `PO.asp`. PO integration can be the basis of numerous effective biztalk implementation architectures.

Summary

In this chapter, we've looked at the installation, configuration and operation of the Supplier Solution Site. We covered simple configurations, all the way through to some very advanced topics. We made a fairly detailed exploration of Active Directory, why directory services are useful, and authentication and authorization within Active Directory.

We also looked at some advanced Supplier Site configurations, such as applying the Authentication Filter and the mapping of SQL Sever and Active Directory Data elements.

In the last few chapters, we've looked systematically at the various aspects of Commerce Server 2000, and considered the Retail and Supplier solution sites. We should now be in a position to implement and customize a Commerce Server 2000 solution based on utilizing the solution sites.

In the next chapter, we'll change tack slightly, by looking at the BizDesk in some more detail.

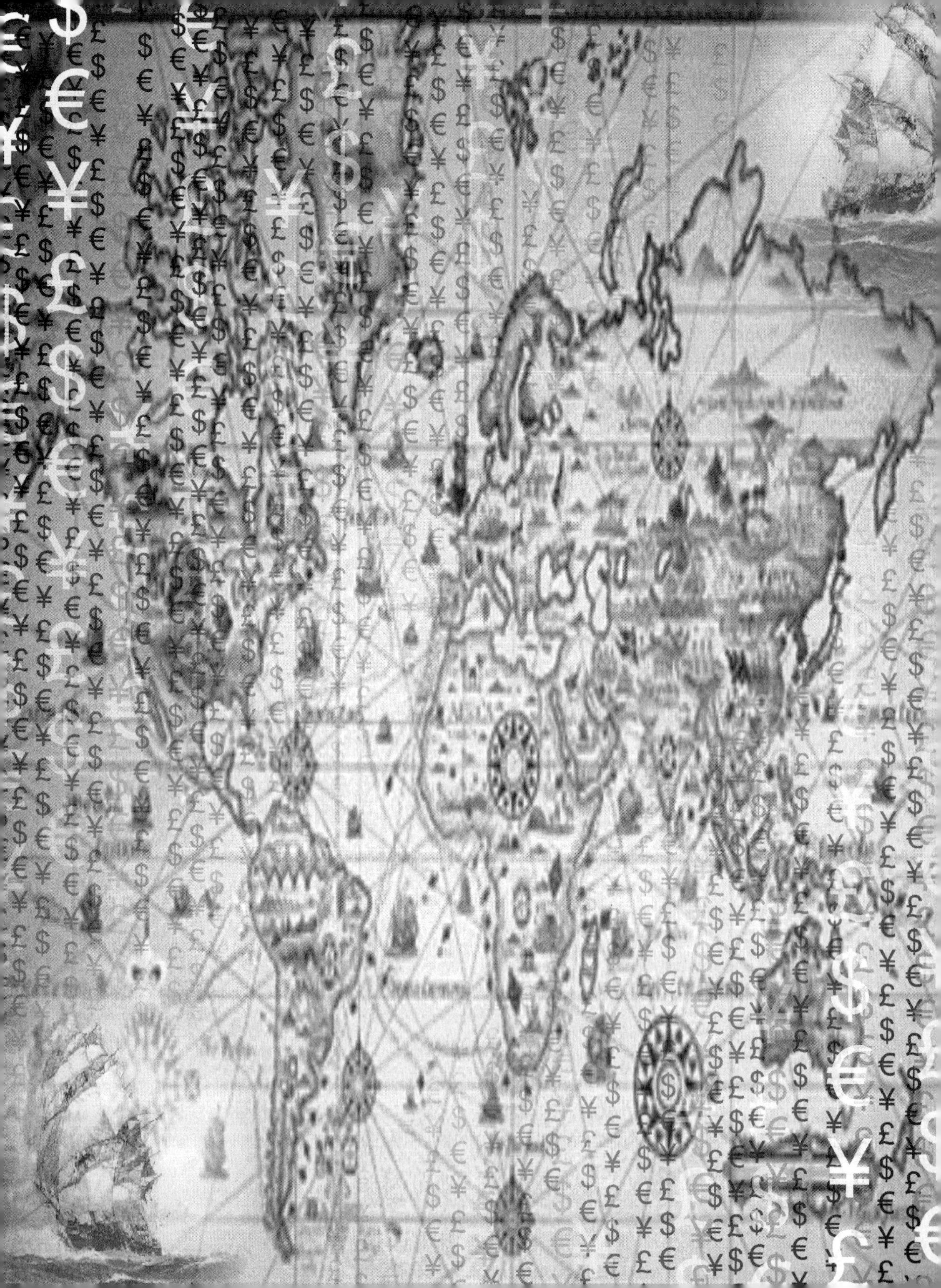

11

Sitelets

Sitelets are more than source code, but less than full Commerce Server 2000 applications – they are literally mini-sites. There are seven Sitelets included with Commerce Server 2000 and each of them covers a functional area that you might want to add to your existing applications. Each Sitelet includes ASP source code, and additionally the Order Sitelet includes pipeline files, and the Auction Sitelet includes an add-on BizDesk module.

Originally Microsoft most likely intended Sitelets to be used as a tool for testing the various components of Commerce Server 2000, but somewhere along the line they became included with the product, which for us is a great thing. Let's hope that Microsoft may some day make more Sitelets available.

If you've spent any large amount of time with the included Retail site, you've probably noticed that there is a great deal to it. The Sitelets demonstrate how to use the Commerce Server API sets without having to manually look through extraneous code of an entire site that you're not interested in. If the Retail site has more functionality than you need, perhaps the Sitelets are a better starting point for your Commerce Server 2000 implementation.

From the point of view of education, Sitelets demonstrate how to implement the APIs for the major features of Commerce Server 2000 in ASP. You may find Sitelets useful when adding features to a site, when creating a site that only uses a subset of features of Commerce Server 2000, or for studying how various components of Commerce Server work. Each of them stands alone, which makes it easy to ignore the extraneous code that would be in a sample of a full site. They're certainly more useful than just example source code, since each Sitelet not only exercises a specific Commerce Server 2000 feature, but each can also be integrated into your existing sites fairly easily. As with all Commerce Server 2000 implementations, there are always details to remember and steps to follow, but once you begin to understand each feature and how it exists within the total system, the Sitelets can jump start the development of new functionality.

To maximize the use of them, this chapter will be looking at the philosophy of Sitelets, or how and why they were designed. First we will focus on a few of the more interesting Sitelets, exploring their source code, what components they use, and the functionality that can be easily added to your Commerce Server site. Sitelets are offered as a convenience, but we should take full advantage of the convenience. It's beyond the scope of this chapter to look at all seven Sitelets in excruciating detail, so we'll pick the ones that you are likely to find most useful, and in the process, give you the tools to explore the remaining Sitelets.

In this chapter, we will show you which Sitelets are the most useful to kickstart development, and which are just good source code to reference. The following seven Sitelets, are installed with Commerce Server 2000 when you select to install the Commerce Server SDK:

- ❏ **Discount Sitelet** – Demonstrates how to create group discounts in the order capture process.

- ❏ **Advertising Sitelet** –Demonstrates how to a use the Profiling System in combination with the Targeting System to display targeted advertisements.

- ❏ **Catalog Sitelet** – Demonstrates how to use the Product Catalog System to offer catalog browsing and search functionality.

- ❏ **Order Sitelet** – Demonstrates how to implement the order capture process, as well as shipping one order to multiple addresses.

- ❏ **Profile Sitelet** – Demonstrates how to use the Profiling System to register and authenticate users.

- ❏ **Passport Sitelet** – Demonstrates how to integrate with Microsoft Passport, Microsoft's single-sign-in authentication service.

- ❏ **Auction Sitelet** – Demonstrates how to use the auction component to implement winning bid auctions. It also includes a custom BizDesk module for managing auctions.

These Sitelets give a fairly broad view of the kinds of functionality that you might want added to a Commerce Server site. With the knowledge that you take from examining these Sitelets, you'll have a fairly clear view about how the original developers of Commerce Server 2000 think, as well as some insights into how you might create and improve Commerce Server implementations of your own.

We'll take a brief look at each of the Sitelets that ship with Commerce Server, highlighting the most interesting parts of the code and pointing out what's useful and what's not. We'll explore how to install a Sitelet, looking specifically at the Discount Sitelet and how the code you write interacts with the business rules you set up in BizDesk. We'll look at how to integrate Microsoft's Passport single sign-in service, allowing sign-in, sign-out, and sign-up forms to be hosted by a Microsoft centrally located server. And finally we'll spend some time on the Auction Sitelet, looking at the source code in some detail, examining how to integrate it with an existing retail site and how to allow our users to bid on products in any existing product catalogs.

Integrating Sitelets

Sitelets are installed in the SDK Samples directory, typically in `C:\Program Files\Microsoft Commerce Server\SDK\Samples\Sitelets`. Each Sitelet includes both source code and a PUP (Packager/Unpackager archive) file that encapsulates that particular Sitelet. Each Sitelet can be installed by unpacking its associated PUP file, which creates an application within an existing site.

For example, if you have unpacked the Commerce Server 2000 Retail Site, you would see two distinct Applications when you run the Commerce Server Manager: one for the site itself and one for that site's Business Desk. Each logical Commerce Server site can consist of multiple IIS applications, which share that site's shared resources. From within the Commerce Server Manager, if you expand the tree and right-click on the Applications folder, the New context menu will present you with an option to Add Application. If you select Add Application, you can select a PUP file to be unpacked and added to your existing Commerce Server site.

There are pros and cons to the convenience of packaging up everything that makes up a Commerce Server site. At deployment time, when you decide to package your site, all the applications that make up the site will be included in the package. When unpacking, any newly added Sitelet applications will exist as their own IIS application with their own `global.asa`, and if you like, their own memory space. This can present problems when sharing cookies between sites, since most authentications to the profile system are typically handled with cookies. While cookies are usually assigned on a machine-by-machine basis, Commerce Server has an option to include a site's virtual root in the cookie. We will look at the pros and cons of installing a Sitelet as its own sub-application, as well as how to install a site manually into an existing Commerce Server application by integrating source code. Neither one of these techniques is right or wrong; it's really all up to you to determine what will work best for your Commerce Server 2000 implementation.

The Sitelets

Now that we've covered a little background, here is an important disclaimer: expect that most of the Sitelets will not run perfectly out of the box. The Commerce Server team has packaged up some useful source code, but these are not to be thought of as full and complete sites. Be prepared to spend some time building onto the source code as well as changing various settings to make sure that the Sitelets work alongside your existing sites. Of course, that's why you bought this book, so we'll do our best to give you some insight into the Sitelets.

Preparing your Commerce Server Installation for the Sitelets

This chapter assumes that you will have already installed Commerce Server 2000 on the same system you are planning to install the Sitelets, and have all the same information used for the Commerce Server install (for example, SQL login, Administrator account, etc.). We also assume that you have unpacked the Retail Solution Site and have it working on your system with a product catalog imported. Quick installation of the Retail site is covered in Chapter 1. If you don't have the Retail site installed, you can find it either in `C:\Program Files\Microsoft Commerce Server\Pup Packages` or on the Web at http://www.microsoft.com/commerceserver/productinfo/solsites.htm. If you haven't done so already, go ahead and unpack the Retail site's PUP.

If you attempt to view the Retail site in your browser immediately after unpacking it, you'll be informed that there are no catalogs installed. We mentioned this in Chapter 1, but we'll mention it again; the packages included with Commerce Server 2000 don't include an already imported product catalog. Some product definitions are included, but the actual product data isn't. However there are multiple copies of the `booksfull.xml` sample catalog in the SDK folders within your Commerce Server 2000 installation. You'll want to import this catalog to better follow the examples in this chapter – we've imported and used it for most of the examples. If you have already made or imported a catalog of your own, feel free to use it for this chapter.

You may recall that there is no navigation button to facilitate browsing to an XML file when importing a catalog, but if you have a Share on your system called CommerceCatalogs, BizDesk will look there first. This means you don't have to type a full path. I made a directory called C:\commercecatalogs and shared it as CommerceCatalogs.

Having the CommerceCatalog share doesn't just make importing catalogs into BizDesk easier; the BizDesk also looks for that folder when exporting catalogs. Additionally the BizDesk will look for this share whether you are importing CSV or XML. Also, philosophically it's just good to have a standard, and Microsoft has given us one in this instance.

Once you have the working Retail site on your system, you're ready to continue and start playing with the Sitelets. Of course the Sitelets work with any existing Commerce Server site, but we're using the Retail site for ease and consistency.

The Discount Sitelet

The Discount Sitelet demonstrates how to leverage targeted discounts during the order capture process of your website. When this Sitelet runs, you will be able to login as a 'Premier User' or a 'Standard User'. Premier Users will receive different product pricing to Standard Users.

You may think that another section describing how to install a PUP is excessive, but you are wrong! Unpacking a PUP as its own Commerce Server Site is a fairly simple exercise, but adding a PUP as a sub-application of an existing Site is different. Take a look at the differences now, and you'll thank me later. Failing to follow these instructions will cause your Sitelets to exist as separate sites with their own resources; instead we want these Sitelets to share resources with a current site.

Installation of a PUP as a Sub-application

To install the Discount Sitelet you will need to use its Packager/Unpackager file (PUP), which can be found in the C:\Program Files\Microsoft Commerce Server\SDK\Samples\Sitelets\Discount directory. Bring up the Commerce Server Manager, open up the tree of your existing Retail site, and open up the Applications folder. Right-click on the Applications folder, and from the context menu Select New | Add Application. This same technique will be used for almost any Sitelet that you want to add as an application under an existing Commerce Server site. We'll only go over this in detail for the Discount Sitelet and a little later for the Auction Sitelet. For the rest of the Sitelets the installation steps are the same.

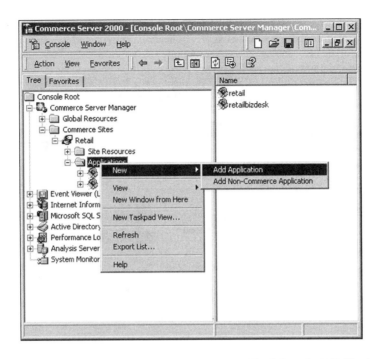

Note: this is an important and subtle extra step. If we simply double-click on the PUP file, the Sitelet will be unpacked as its own Commerce Server site, and won't use any of the resources our existing site uses such as the database and the profile system. What we want to do is add this Sitelet as an application to an existing site. Don't forget, a logical Commerce Server 2000 Site can contain multiple physical IIS applications.

Navigate into the Sitelets directory and select the Discount PUP. The filename is SDK-DISCOUNT-SITELET.PUP. When you double-click on the PUP, the Commerce Server Site Packager will pop up and show you the applications that are included in the package. As we can see from the screen shot only the Discount Sitelet is included in this particular package. None of the seven Sitelets include multiple applications in a single PUP, but if multiple applications were included, you'd see all of them in this list box, and be able to check just the ones you want to install.

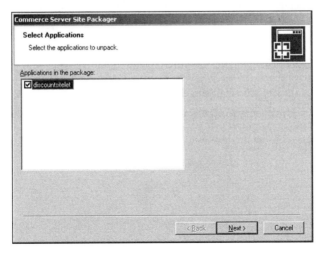

Click Next and we will be prompted to choose the IIS website and virtual directory for our discount Sitelet. Remember, we're adding the Discount Sitelet as an application underneath our existing retail site, rather than integrating the code manually. The Retail site is a separate IIS Application, as is our Discount Sitelet. However, a site from the point of view of Commerce Server is different to what we may think is a site in IIS. Commerce Server 2000 allows multiple IIS Applications to be grouped together as a logical Site. Therefore, our Retail site consists of two Applications, *Retail* and *DiscountSitelet*.

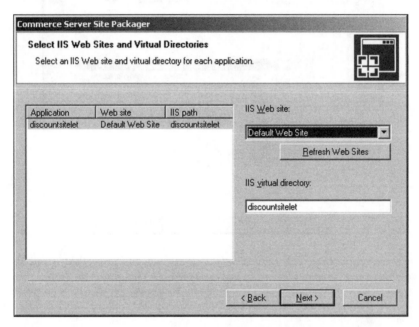

Click Next, the site is unpacked, and we arrived at the final screen that says unpacking is complete. If any errors occur you'll be informed on the final screen. View the log file to check for any errors that may have happened. If everything went well, and you accepted all the defaults, the Discount Sitelet will be unpacked in `C:\inetpub\wwwroot\discountsitelet`.

Since our Sitelet is now a member of the same Commerce Server site and a peer application to our existing Retail site, it can use all the same global resources as our existing site. This includes the Global Resource Pointer, Database Connection, Product Catalog, Campaign Management system, and Profiles resources.

Now, if you go to the Commerce Server 2000 Manager, you should see a screen that looks something like the following screenshot. I've named my site retail, but you may have renamed yours. You can see in the Commerce Server Manager below that the Commerce Sites folder contains three applications:

- ❑ **Retail** – This is the default retail site that ships with Commerce Server 2000
- ❑ **RetailBizDesk** – This is the Business Management Desk for my retail site.
- ❑ **DiscountSitelet** – This is the Discount Sitelet we've just unpacked.

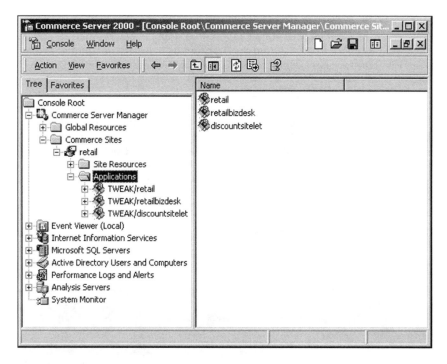

Additional Setup

Once the Commerce Server Site Packager/Unpackager is done setting up the Discount Sitelet, you can browse to the application, usually found at http://<computername>/discountsitelet, if you accepted the defaults. If you visit the Sitelet just after unpacking you'll get an error indicating a UserProfile cannot be loaded.

Of course, as with many of the Sitelets, the Discount Sitelet is not ready to go out of the box. There are a number of places in the code where values are hard coded and you'll need to plug-in code that is appropriate for your site. The Discount Sitelet as it sits is just example code, and counts on two specific users to exist in your site. There is a SQL file that is included with the source code called PopulateDiscountSitelet.SQL. This file creates two test users named PremierUser and StandardUser. Run the SQL file against your Commerce Database, using the SQL Server Query Analyzer, to create these two user profiles.

Be sure to choose the correct Commerce Server 2000 database for your site from the pull-down menu in Query Analyzer; in my case it was called Retail_commerce. Run the Query Analyzer and open up the `PopulateDiscountSitelet.SQL` file from the Discount directory of the Commerce Server SDK. Execute the query and the two users will be added to your site, one called StandardUser and one called PremierUser.

> Note: if you have a database named DiscountSitelet_Commerce then you have made a mistake. We want the Discount Sitelet to share the resources, namely the Product Catalog and User Profiles, of the existing Retail Site. If the Discount Sitelet isn't added as a sub-application of the Retail Site, it will create its own database as if it were a site all by itself. If you've made this error, delete your DiscountSitelet site from Commerce Server Manager and start over from the beginning of the installation instructions.

Now, return to BizDesk and open up the Users module, do a search for all active accounts. In my example, since I'm not looking at a production site, there aren't a lot of users, just the two that were added programmatically with Query Analyzer.

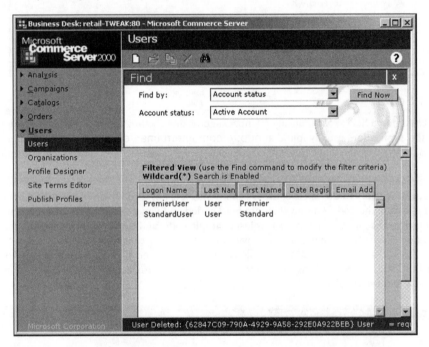

BizDesk Business Logic Setup

Now that we have the Discount Sitelet hooked up, and the two test users added to our Profile System, to get anything useful to happen we'll need to add a discount. If you don't have the discount, and you visit the Sitelet you'll be able to shop for a few items, add them to your basket, and place an order. However, the product prices will be the same no matter who you are logged in as. Of course, that doesn't exactly show how to implement discounts. Our goal here is to offer different users different prices for the same products. So, for this example we'll add a discount of 10 percent off all products for Premier users, while Standard users will not receive a discount.

Campaign Target Expressions

A campaign in Commerce Server 2000, regardless of whether it's a discount, an advertisement, or a direct-mail campaign, needs target expressions. A target expression describes exactly the kind of user that we're going to target. In this case we need a target expression that's tailored for Premier users. Since in our example the Premier User is a just one specific user, and not a group of users, our expression will be fairly simple. Our user's logon name is PremierUser so our expression will be as simple as 'the condition where the logon name is equal to PremierUser'.

Launch your site's BizDesk, navigate to the Campaigns module and select the Campaign Expressions module. From the toolbar, select Target Expressions. Click New Target Expressions, and the Target Expressions Builder will launch. Various BizDesk modules use the **Target Expression** dialog. It's a flexible dialog that allows you to build fairly advanced expressions using any aspect of Profile System or the context of what you're targeting. Once you've built an expression and given it a name, you can use that expression throughout the BizDesk.

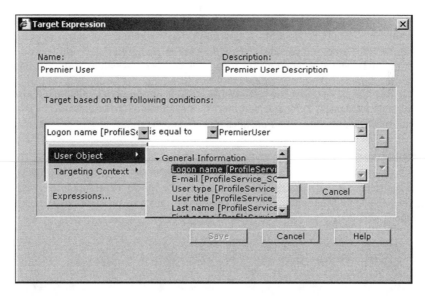

From this dialog, build a target expression with the condition that the login name is equal to PremierUser.

What's so exciting about target expressions is that when they are used in campaigns your expressions can be as complicated or simple as you'd like. Our example is very simple but it could just as easily be something like, 'men named John who are five foot 10 inches and have not visited the site in a week' assuming we have that information in the profile service. This allows you to tailor your discounts to any group using any target expressions using all the information you have available to you. You might also want to keep track of different groups of pages, supplying discounts for only those people who are visiting particular pages. Be sure to save the target expression, and return to the previous screen.

Create the Customer, Campaign, and Discount

In Commerce Server 2000, a targeted advertising or discount campaign must have an associated customer. Perhaps *Sponsor* would have been a less confusing word, but Customer is the terminology used in Commerce Server 2000. They are the interested party who requested the campaign. In this example, I am the creator of the Retail site, and the party responsible for the discount, so the *Customer*, or *Advertiser,* in this example is me and my organization.

Go to the **Campaign Manager** and select **New Customer** from the toolbar. The customer in this case is going to be ourselves. Campaigns can apply to advertising campaigns we sell to vendors, discount campaigns we run internally, or direct-mail campaigns to generate spam. Since the discount is ours, I am the customer. If I was selling advertising space to a third party, the customer would be that third party.

> *The* New *button that pulls down in the toolbar changes contextually based on what you have selected from the grid. I find this fairly irritating because I never seem to have what I think I've selected actually selected. Once you get used to it, the BizDesk user interface isn't all that bad, but remember that, since right-clicking isn't available to us in the BizDesk, the toolbar buttons will change contextually as kind of a poor man's right-click.*

Create a new customer, and give it a proper name. I've named my customer **Self**. You can also keep contact information and other customer specific details if it pleases you. Save your new Customer and return to the main Campaign Manager screen, and, with this new customer highlighted, from the **New** pull down menu select **New Campaign**. I gave my campaign the very creative name of **Discounts**, but you might name yours something like **New Fall Fashions**, as long is it differentiates this grouping of Discounts. Make sure that the **Start date** and the **End date** are set far enough in the past and far enough in the future that the discount will be effective when it runs today. Leave the other values at their defaults.

After you've created the campaign, return to the main Campaign Manager screen, make sure that the new campaign is highlighted, and select **New Discount** from the **New** pull down menu. The **Discount** screen is a lot more complicated than the others and includes four separate sections.

Discount Properties

The Discount Property section is just about the same as we saw before. Make sure that the status is set to active and that the start and end dates are set appropriately. I've given a fairly descriptive name, but the actual name really isn't that important, it's for your reference, and how the discount will be referred to elsewhere in the application.

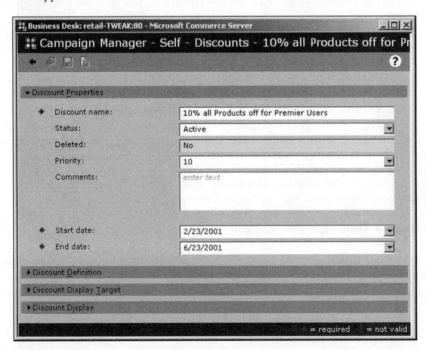

Discount Definition

The Discount Definition screen is where the actual building of the discount occurs. It allows for a great deal of flexibility in designing your discounts. Users can buy something and get free shipping, or buy two of a particular thing and get 10 percent off on another thing.

As you can see in the screenshot, I've decided that Premier users can buy anything and receive 10 percent off the order total. If you leave the eligibility requirements list box empty, shown below, all users will be eligible for this discount. I've taken the Premier User campaign target that we built earlier and added it to the eligibility requirements dialogue, so this discount will only apply to users that match my target expression. The eligibility requirements for a particular discount can take any target expression.

Discounts may also be associated with a banner advertisement, and the discount will only be applied when the user clicks on the discount's banner. The discount being created in this chapter will not have this requirement.

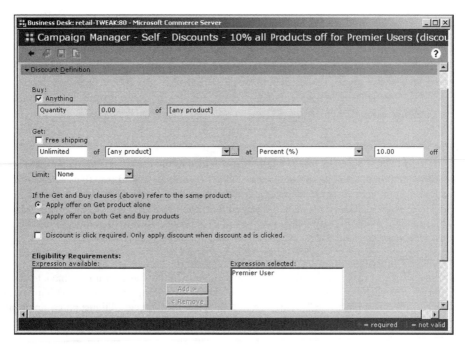

Discount Display Target

The Discount Display Target section allows you to target a specific discount to a specific page group. You can decide that a discount campaign item appears on all the pages of the site, or only on specific pages. Pages can be groups, such as Support Pages, or Portal Pages. For example, if you run an online electronics store you might only want DVD discounts to appear in the DVD portion of your site. For the purposes of this chapter, leave this section as it is.

Discount Display

The Discount Display section describes what this discount will look like. Discounts can include text that appears in the basket when the discount is applied. You can also have content associated with the discount, like images for banner ads. From here you can also set a limit to the exposures that this discount receives on your site.

For my example, I'm going to leave the Image URL and Click URL text boxes with garbage values, opting only to add a string in the Basket Display box. We'll display this string when the user visits the basket and the discount is applied. Other than this string, our discount won't have a banner ad or graphic associated with it. If a discount item has an associated page and graphics, they would be entered in the Image URL and Click URL text boxes.

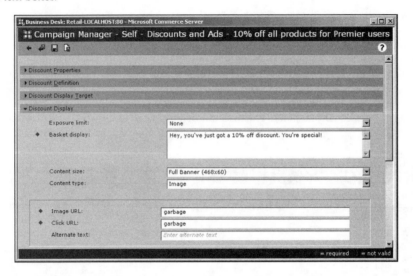

Publishing the Discount Campaign

Click the Save and Back button from the toolbar, and return to the Campaign Manager main screen. You should see something that looks like the screenshot, with a combination grid-tree that, when unfolded, displays your customer, your discount campaign and the Premier User discount we just added. Since Commerce Server 2000 includes a caching component and caches most objects aggressively, when making a change to a campaign, or adding any items, you'll need to publish that campaign. Publishing the campaign refreshes and clears any relevant caches.

Go to the Publish Campaigns module and publish the campaign changes to your sites. If you have trouble publishing the campaigns or find that one of your site's caches will not clear, you may have to restart that specific application as caches are often loaded in the `global.asa`. Hopefully this won't happen to you to in a production environment, but when I want to restart an application quickly I'll just add a single space to the end of my application's `global.asa`, thereby causing it to restart automatically.

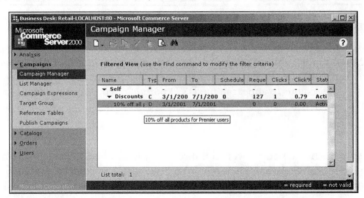

So, to review the steps involved in creating a discount from the BizDesk:

1. Create a new target expression, targeting the users who we want to receive the discount

2. Create a new customer

3. Create a new campaign

4. Create a new discount

5. Ensure the discount is active and that the effective dates are valid

6. Ensure the discount applies to valid products

7. Ensure our new target expression is added to the eligibility requirements for that discount

8. Publish the campaign

9. Refresh or reload any cached copies of the campaign (or restart the application)

The Pipeline

When you visit the Discount Sitelet's default page, probably at http://<computername>/discountsitelet, you are given the choice to login as either a Premier or Standard user. When you login as a Premier User, select a product, and click Buy Now, you're sent to the `basket.asp` page. `Basket.asp` calls `AddItemToBasket`, which runs the basket pipeline stored in the `basket.pcf` pipeline file. All the pipeline files for this Sitelet are in the `discountsitelet\pipeline` directory of your Sitelet installation.

> *Note that the discount is applied to anyone who meets the requirements of the Target Expression created earlier. The discount can be easily expanded to include groups of users by changing the Target Expression.*

The basket pipeline takes all the products in the user's `OrderForm`, looks up the details of that product in the product catalog and applies any appropriate discounts that might adjust the price of the order. Pipelines are covered in detail in Chapter 6.

When you open the Discount Sitelet's `Basket.pcf` in the Commerce Server Pipeline Editor, take note of the **OrderDiscount** component in the Order Adjust Price section. Without getting into the gory details, the `OrderDiscount` component writes out a number of values to the `OrderForm`, the most significant being `_discount` and `discounts_applied`. The Discount Sitelet will use these values in the source code when displaying the basket to determine for which items discounts are applied. If you removed the **OrderDiscount** component from the basket pipeline everything would run exactly as if no discounts were ever applied.

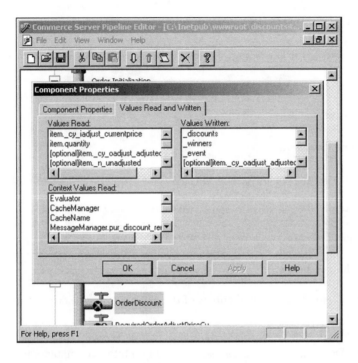

The Code

The code in the Discount Sitelet is interesting, but fairly straightforward. The work really happens inside the basket pipeline, but even then it's handled by a built-in Commerce Server 2000 component. The example code we find in `basket.asp` is there to show us how to present the discount once it has occurred. There are a couple of important things to note in the code if you're planning on retooling it for use in a production site.

User Profiles

In the Include directory there is a file called `siteletconst.asp` that contains a hard coded user profile.

```
'Hard coded user id for the purposes of this sample
Const GENERIC_USER_ID = "857A42EE-BD0A-46ad-A83E-28BF897CDDD2"
```

This constant is used throughout the Discount Sitelet code like this:

```
'Load a basket. Note that we've hardcoded the user id for the purposes of
'this sample. Normally you would retrieve the user's profile (or create
'one if necessary) and load the basket based on the GeneralInfo.userid
'property.
Set g_oBasket = LoadBasket(GENERIC_USER_ID)
```

This code is inside the `setupenv.asp` file and loads the global variable called `g_oBasket` with a hard coded user id. You'll want to change this to load baskets like the Retail site does. In the Retail site's `setupenv.asp` the basket is loaded from the page variable called `m_UserID`. This variable is set by the authentication manager's `EnsureAccess` function in the Retail site's `include/std_access_lib.asp`. However you set up authentication in your site you want to make sure that you're loading the correct basket for the correct user.

The Basket and the Basket Pipeline

Most of the work of the Discount Sitelet is done in the pipeline. The most significant addition to the discount Sitelet pipeline is the `OrderDiscount` component. As discussed in Chapter 6, the order discount component acts on individual items. You can use this component to apply discounts defined and scheduled in the **Campaign Manager** module of the Commerce Server BizDesk. The component reads the values `_cy_iadjust_currentprice`, examines discounts that apply and if necessary, assigns the adjusted price to the key `_cy_oadjust_adjustedprice`. The basket code included with this Sitelet illustrates detecting the discounts that have been applied, and generates a string listing out each item with discounts.

This line of code means to check if there is anything in the basket. There appears to be a bug here, so more on this line later.

```
'if no items exist in the basket, then there are no discount messages to display.
'THIS NEXT LINE IS A BUG, WE WILL FIX IT LATER
If (g_oBasket.Value("total_line_items") > 0) Then
```

Then we retrieve a `Content List` dictionary of discounts.

```
    Set oDiscounts =
g_oBasket.Value("orderForms").Value("default").Value("_discounts")
```

Then for each item in the basket that has an applied discount, we'll concatenate the description of the item to a string that is displayed at the end of the basket page.

```
    For Each oItem In g_oBasket.Value("orderForms").Value("default").Items
        For Each strVal In oItem
            If strVal = "discounts_applied" Then
                For Each i In oItem.Value(strVal)
                    If Not arrDiscounts(i) Then
                        strDiscounts = strDiscounts & "<b>"
                        strDiscounts = strDiscounts & oDiscounts.Fields_
                            (i-1).Item("description").Value & "</b><br>"
                        arrDiscounts(i) = True
                    End If
                Next
            End If
        Next
    Next
End If
```

Now if any discounts have occurred, we'll output a string letting the user know what a great deal they got on our site.

```
If strDiscounts <> "" Then
    %>
    <div>The following discounts have been applied to your
        order:<br><%=strDiscounts%></div>
    <%
End If
```

Bugs

There appears to be a bug in the basket code that comes with the Discount Sitelet. On line 186 of `basket.asp`, the Basket Order Form dictionary is checked for the value `total_line_items`. It's really just to check if the basket has anything in it. This value doesn't appear to be set anywhere in the pipeline or in the code. So I changed this line of code: the original is shown below.

```
'if no items exist in the basket, then there are no discount messages to display.
If (g_oBasket.Value("total_line_items") > 0) Then
```

You could certainly set this value yourself, either in the pipeline or earlier in the ASP code. Instead we can fix this easily by checking the number of items in the order form using the count property of the items collection. So our new line of code translates to 'if there's anything in the basket then continue', and I commented out the old line.

```
If (g_oBasket.Value("orderForms").Value("default").Items.count > 0) Then
'If (g_oBasket.Value("total_line_items") > 0) Then
```

You may find other minor bugs like this in the Sitelets' sample code, but we all know that's just the nature of sample code. It certainly doesn't diminish the usefulness of the samples, and it sure keeps us on our toes.

The Result

Now that we've installed the Sitelet, configured the appropriate targets and discount in BizDesk, fixed the bug in the basket, and examined the pipeline, let's see what we have. If we bring up the discount Sitelet's default page using http://<computername>/discountsitelet, we can login as the Premier or Standard User. If we login and add a few things to our basket, we'll see different results depending on which user we are.

According to our discount business rules, Premier Users get a 10% discount off the total. This can be confirmed by comparing the totals of our baskets. I picked four books that will cost the Standard User $114.96. However the total for the Premier User is only $103.46, resulting in a saving of $11.50. Since we are logged in as the Premier User, discounts were applied to the Premier User's order and the `_discount` value was set in the `OrderForm`, our ASP code has also output an additional personalized message to the Premier User indicating that they've received the discount and that they're very special. Notice that the text of the message is the exact text that we set earlier in the BizDesk under Discount Display in the Basket Display text box.

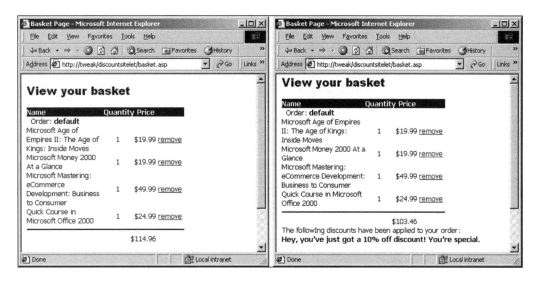

This is what makes Commerce Server 2000 framework and the BizDesk such a compelling story. The BizDesk is meant to enable non-technical people to describe whatever goofy business rules or crazy marketing campaigns they can dream up. When marketers want a particular message to go to the user and they're not interested in putting a change order to an engineer, they can make that change directly from the BizDesk without breaking the order process. It's this difficult separation between business rules and technical work that makes marketing on the Web such a frustrating proposition, and frameworks such as Commerce Server 2000 such a compelling solution.

The power of this example is that now, using only the default Retail site and the Discount Sitelet, we've assembled a framework for adding complicated pricing schemes and group discounts without adding additional code or complexity to our site. At this point you might want to use this functionality in a production site.

Now we will take a break and look at the next four Sitelets: Advertising, Catalog, Order, and Profile. Then we'll talk about the Passport Sitelet, and dive into the Auction Sitelet.

The Advertising Sitelet

The Advertising Sitelet demonstrates how to show targeted advertisements using the Profiling System in conjunction with the Targeting System. It's very similar to the Discount Sitelet in that it uses Target Expressions to describe users and through the campaign manager decides what content to display. The Advertising Sitelet uses the **ContentSelector** object to invoke the Content Selection Framework pipelines. These pipelines take various inputs and pieces of context and evaluate target expressions to select the appropriate advertisement to show that user. This Sitelet uses **ProfileService** and the `ContentSelector` objects to generate a list of ads based on if the current user is Anonymous, or if logged in to the site, if the user is a male (John Doe) or a female (Jane Doe).

The Advertising Sitelet also demonstrates the concept of redirecting users. If an advertiser who has purchased ad impressions from our site supplies us with an ad and requests that when that ad is clicked the browser should navigate to that advertiser's site, we need a mechanism to know that the user clicked on the ad. This is seen all over the Web when the URL of a banner ad doesn't point to the final destination, but rather to a `redir.asp` file that records the click then redirects the user to his final destination. We'll look at the redirection of users after we've installed the Advertising Sitelet.

553

Installation

To install the Advertising Sitelet you will need to use the site pack file (PUP), which can be found in the `C:\Program Files\Microsoft Commerce Server\SDK\Samples\Sitelets\Ad` directory. Using the Commerce Server Manager, right-click on the **Applications** folder of your existing retail commerce site and select **Add Application**. Follow the same procedure to install the Advertising Sitelet as we did for the Discount Sitelet. The **adsitelet** application will be unpacked as a separate IIS website, but will still use the site resources of your existing retail site. If all goes well you should see something in Commerce Server Manager like this screenshot.

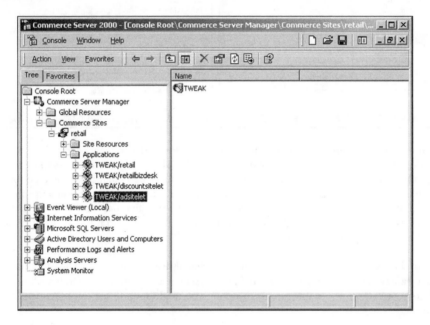

Additional Setup

Once the Commerce Server Site Packager/Unpackager is done setting up the Advertising Sitelet, you can browse to the application, usually http://<computername>/adsitelet, if you've accepted the defaults. If you visit the Sitelet just after unpacking you'll get an error indicating an array value is out of range.

Once again, there are additional steps to set up the Sitelet. You'll need to run SQL Server Query Analyzer again, and this time load the `adSiteletProfileData.sql` file that you'll find in the `C:\Program Files\Microsoft Commerce Server\SDK\Samples\Sitelets\Ad` directory. This SQL file will load two Demo users into the user profile system. Be sure to select the right database when you run this query. Since you installed the Advertising Sitelet as an application underneath your retail Commerce Server site they will each share the same database. The name of my database is still **Retail_commerce**. For this Sitelet the demo users that are added are named John and Jane Doe. You can confirm that the users were added correctly by returning to the Commerce Server BizDesk for your site and searching for all active users. In this screenshot you can see John and Jane Doe living alongside Standard and Premier from the previous site.

It bears repeating that these instructions are meant to get these sites working for you so that you can immediately become productive with them. Feel free to do whatever works for you for these examples, whether it's changing names of users profiles, site names, Sitelets or virtual directories.

Now that you've added your two sample users, here are the steps necessary to get the Ad Sitelet working and serving targeted banner advertisements:

1. **Target Expressions:** From the BizDesk Campaign Expressions module create two target expressions:
   One targeting "Men named John with a rule like where loginid contains John
   One targeting Women named Jane with a rule like where loginid contains Jane

2. **Target Groups:** From the BizDesk Target Group module, create two target groups:
   One named Men that requires the target expression Men named John and excludes the target expression Women named Jane
   One named Women that requires the target expression Women named Jane and excludes the target expression Men named John

3. **Graphical Content:** Create two banner ad GIFs that are 468x60 (standard banner ad size) named `male.gif` and `female.gif` and put them in your `C:\inetpub\wwwroot\adsitelet` directory.

4. **Create the Male Ad:** From the BizDesk Campaign Manager, create a new ad under your existing campaign and customer. Make the ad a House Ad. Make certain it's set to active. Leave the Ad Schedule alone, but in the Ad Target section you should have two available target groups, Men and Women. Assign *Men* as the target group for this ad.
   In the Ad Display section set the Image URL to http://<computername>/adsitelet/male.gif. The Click URL is the target destination for this ad; it might be a product category, another site or a particular product. I set mine to http://www.wrox.com.

5. **Create the Female Ad:** Repeat Step 4, but create an ad for women.

If we return to the Campaign Manager module we can see our ads for men and our ads for women. The Campaign Manager will also display what dates an advertisement is available, how many times an advertisement has been requested, as well as how many people have clicked on an ad. We can see from the screenshot that my ads have never been clicked on, so maybe I need a new marketing manager!

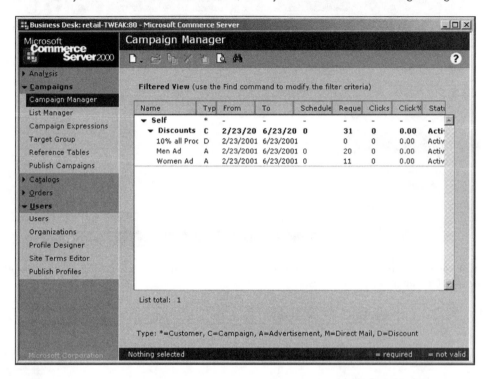

The Pipeline

Once you publish your campaign and refresh your caches, your ads will be scheduled for requests. When you visit your Ad Sitelet now you can choose to load the **Male** or **Female** profiles, or load **no profile**. The pipeline directory of the advertising Sitelet includes two content selection pipelines:

❏ **Advertising.PCF** – this pipeline runs within the context of the content selection framework for choosing the appropriate piece of content, in our case a banner ad.

❏ **RecordEvent.PCF** – This pipeline records the click event in the database and appends details to the IIS log.

These pipeline files are loaded in the `global.asa` in the `InitSitePipeline` helper function and stored in the application object as `Application('MSCSPipelines')`. The Content Selection Framework is also initialized and prepared in an `InitCSF` helper function.

```
'Note that dictPipeline.Folder includes a trailing "\"
dictPipeline.Advertising = dictPipeline.Folder & "advertising.pcf"
dictPipeline.RecordEvent = dictPipeline.Folder & "RecordEvent.pcf"
```

The Code

Going deeply into the content selection framework is beyond the scope of this chapter, but the two important functions to note are in include/advertlib.asp.

GetAdContent takes a User's Profile as a parameter and optionally, a Page Group, and the number of advertisements selected, since some pages might have multiple banner ads. It returns a SimpleList of the ads generated by that User Profile. The work of getting an advertisement is abstracted by this helper function; all you have to do is provide a valid User Profile.

```
<%
Set lstAds = GetAdContent(oProfile, Empty, Empty)

If (IsValid(lstAds, VALIDATE_OBJECT)) Then
    'Now you have a SimpleList in lstAds of Advertisements
%>
    Advertisement for this page:<BR>
<%
    Response.Write lstAds(0)
End If
%>
```

When an ad is clicked on, rather than being directed to the target URL, the user is sent instead to redir.asp, which records the click event first. Remember, if the user was simply sent to the target URL directly, our servers would have no way to capture the event. The RecordEvent function (which is identical in both the Retail Solution site and in the Advertising Sitelet) launches the RecordEvent.pcf pipeline, which is crucial to the Campaign Manager keeping track of ongoing campaign item performance. This function also handles any click-related discounts that may be associated with this ad, and discounts that need to be added to the user's basket. The URL for the final destination is stored in the query string. After the click is recorded, the user is sent to their final destination.

```
<% 'Redir.asp is called like "/redir.asp?url=http://www.wrox.com"
Call RecordEvent()
Call Response.Redirect(Request.QueryString("url"))
%>
```

The Result

I didn't create a default ad for the no profile option, that is left as an exercise for you! Integrating this Sitelet with your existing code could happen a few ways. You could certainly leave it as is, and just hook up the profiles to your profile system. However, rather than having a separate IIS application handling your advertisements, you might want to simply leverage the existing helper functions in the advertlib.asp file. I would recommend using the Advertising Sitelet primarily as source code to guide you in integrating advertising and content selection in your existing Commerce Server implementation.

The Catalog Sitelet

The Catalog Sitelet shows us an alternate navigation style from the Retail site. It illustrates how to use the Product Catalog System to offer catalog browsing, but more importantly full-text search and property search functionality. The Browse the Catalog option gives a two-level deep structure of the catalog.

Installation

To install the Catalog Sitelet you will need to use the site pack file (PUP), which can be found in the `C:\Program Files\Microsoft Commerce Server\SDK\Samples\Sitelets\Catalog` directory. Using the Commerce Server Manager, right-click on the Applications folder of your existing Retail commerce site and select Add Application. Follow the same procedure to install the Catalog Sitelet as we did for the Discount Sitelet. The `catalogsitelet` application will be unpacked as a separate IIS website, but will still use the site resources of your existing Commerce Server Retail site. When the Catalog Sitelet queries Commerce Server for the Catalog Database, if the Sitelet has been installed as a sub-application of the Retail site, Commerce Server will point the Sitelet to the Retail Database. If all goes well you should see the Catalog Sitelet in the Commerce Server Manager as a sub-application of the retail site.

Additional Setup

The Catalog Sitelet works immediately after unpacking. Assuming you have the Retail site installed and a valid product catalog, you should be able to browse your product catalog. The Sitelet will also browse existing product catalogs on other Commerce Server sites if you've installed the Catalog Sitelet as a sub application of those sites.

The Code

The Catalog Sitelet code is full of examples on how to navigate through an existing product catalog. Since the Retail site contains much of the same code, we'll only take a quick look at the code in the Catalog Sitelet.

Browsing

The powerhouse file in the catalog Sitelet is `browse.asp`. It allows the user to drill down through many levels of categories and child categories. Since the Commerce Server Product Catalog is flexible enough to allow products within categories as well as subcategories within categories `browse.asp` has to be able to handle those situations.

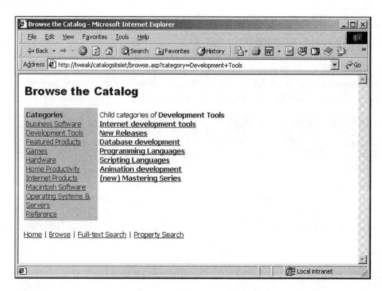

`Browse.asp` first stores a cached copy of the catalog root categories in a page global variable called `g_rsCategories`.

```
Set rsCategories = GetCategoriesRs(oCatalog, Empty, False)

If (rsCategories.RecordCount > 0) Then
   rsCategories.MoveFirst()
   Set g_rsCategories = rsCategories
End If
```

Then we output the root categories on the left-hand side of the page, creating a navigation tree against a silver background. First we make sure the categories object is valid, then, for as many categories as there are, we output a link to `browse.asp`, passing in the next category as a parameter. By calling itself recursively, `browse.asp` is able to handle a great depth of categories, limited only by the data in the product catalog.

```
<TD VALIGN=TOP BGCOLOR="silver" WIDTH=130>
<B>Categories</B><BR>
<%
 'Write out the list of available categories.
If IsValid(g_rsCategories, VALIDATE_OBJECT) Then
   Do While Not g_rsCategories.EOF
      %>
      <a href="browse.asp?category=
      <%=Server.URLEncode(g_rsCategories(CATALOG_PROP_NAME)) %>">
      <%= g_rsCategories(CATALOG_PROP_NAME) %>
      </a>
      <br>
<%
      g_rsCategories.MoveNext()
   Loop
End If 'IsValid
%>
</TD>
```

Finally, we retrieve all the products for the current category, by calling the helper function `GetProductRs` located in `cataloglib.asp`. `GetProductsRs` is just a wrapper function around the Product Catalog Object Model with additional error handling. We pass in the name of the current catalog, pulled from the query string, along with a reference to the current product catalog.

```
'Elements from the GET request that we care about
Const QSTRING_CATEGORY_KEY   = "category"

'De-ref the Request.QueryString collection and make it friendly.
Set colQString = Request.QueryString

'Now get the products
Set rsProducts = GetProductsRs(_
                        oCatalog, _
                        colQString(QSTRING_CATEGORY_KEY) _
                        )
```

`GetProductsRs` returns the records that it gets by navigating the product catalog's object model using the passed-in category name. From that point it's a simple effort to spin through the recordset of products, outputting the names and details for each product.

```
Function GetProductsRs ( _
   ByVal oCatalog, _
   ByVal strName)
On Error Resume Next
   Dim rsProducts

'Some error handling code removed for clarity

   Set rsProducts = oCatalog.GetCategory(strName).Products
   Set GetProductsRs = rsProducts
End Function
```

Full-Text Search

You need to have added the Full-Text Search option during your installation of SQL Server 2000 for the Catalog Sitelet full-text search example to work. The Commerce Server Catalog Manager object is initialized in the global.asa, and a reference to it is stored in the Application object. We let the manager object know where the database is by pulling the connection string from our shared site resources.

```
Function InitCatalogManager()
   Dim mscsCatalogMgr

   Set mscsCatalogMgr = Server.CreateObject("Commerce.CatalogManager")
   Call mscsCatalogMgr.Initialize(dictConfig.s_CatalogConnectionString,_
      ADO_CONNECTION_STRING)

   Set InitCatalogManager = mscsCatalogMgr
End Function
```

The Commerce Server Catalog Manager has a function called FreeTextSearch that takes a fairly large number of optional parameters. This function abstracts the complexities of the FreeTextSearch and allows us to think about things in terms of searching a Product Catalog, rather than the sordid details of the underlying database tables and columns. Only the first parameter is required, but including the optional parameters adds a lot of flexibility.

```
Set oCatMgr = Application("MSCSCatalogManager")

   'Note that calling this method (or any of the lookup methods for that
   'matter) is extremely inefficient and we only do this in this sample
   'to demonstrate how to use the objects.  A best practice approach to this
   'would be to cache each result set in a Commerce.CacheManager cache, and
   'use the contents of the GET request (query string) as the key.  Then
   'lookup each request in the cache before deciding to actually do a lookup
   'using the catalog objects.

   Set rsResults = oCatMgr.FreeTextSearch( _
      colQString(QSTRING_SEARCHTERM_KEY), _      'Search Phrase
      CATALOG_NAME, _                            'What Catalogs to Search
      CLASS_VARIANT Or CLASS_PRODUCT, _          'Search Products and Variants
      , _                                        'Properties to Return
      PRODUCT_PROP_TITLE, _                      'Property to sort on
      True, _                                    'Sort Ascending
      intStartPos, _                             'What record to start with
      intMaxRecords, _                           'Max records to retrieve
      intCount _                                 'Total records returned
      )
```

In BizDesk's **Property Definitions** module the Catalog Designer allows you to set whether a particular product's property is free text searchable. For example, in the Books Catalog, Books have their `name`, `description`, `author`, and `publisher` properties set to be free text searchable, while `publication_year` and `image_width` are not strings and therefore not searchable via free text. If you set up property definitions that are used internally by your system make sure not to set them to free text searchable.

Property Search

The Catalog Manager object also has a `Query` function that abstracts some of the complexities of generating dynamic SQL queries. It's always a hassle to concatenate string after string when generating a `WHERE` clause, and it can often introduce uncomfortable bugs into your system.

The Catalog Sitelet includes some helper functions like `BuildPropSearchClause` that takes a name and a value and returns a string with a correctly formatted `WHERE` clause. When passing in a `WHERE` clause to the Commerce Manager Object's `Query` function the search term for a property search must be formatted as `sku='1324' and title='something' or this='that'`. This clause needs to conform to SQL Server format for `WHERE` clauses.

For example, if a Form GET occurs that passes in an URL like propsearch.asp?searchtype=propsearch&title=access&cmdSearch=Search, we check the validity of the query string, and if we have a valid query we pass in our title to the helper function along with the current where clause. We can chain together as many where clauses as there are properties to search.

```
If (IsValid(colQString(QSTRING_TITLE_KEY), VALIDATE_STRING)) Then
    fValidQuery = True
    strClause = BuildPropSearchClause( _
                strClause, _
                QSTRING_TITLE_KEY, _
                colQString(QSTRING_TITLE_KEY) _
                )
End If
```

Take the resulting `WHERE` clause and pass it into the `Query` function, which takes most of the same parameters as the `FreeTextSearch` function.

```
Set rsResults = oCatMgr.Query( _
                strClause, _
                CATALOG_NAME, _
                CLASS_VARIANT Or CLASS_PRODUCT, _
                , _
                PRODUCT_PROP_TITLE, _
                True, _
                intStartPos, _
                intMaxRecords, _
                intCount _
                )
```

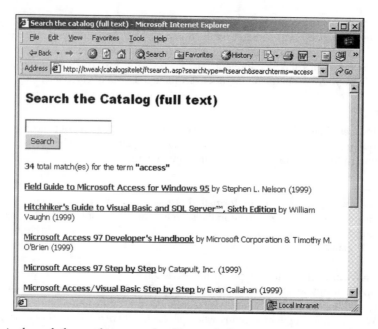

Then we can spin through the resulting recordset like we do for any other list of products. Pretty slick, huh?

The Result

The Catalog Sitelet provides lots of source code to refer to, and is a bit easier to study than the complete Retail Site since it only includes those functions that are significant to browsing or searching a catalog. If you're putting together a site that doesn't involve ordering products or you just want to view a read-only catalog, the Catalog Site may be a good place to start.

The Order Sitelet

The Order Sitelet shows how to use Commerce Server to implement a simple order capture process on your website. The Sitelet implements a simple order site that allows purchases to be made then allows for the viewing of all details of the past orders. The Sitelet shows how to maintain multiple shipping addresses for a single user as well as multiple billing methods. In my opinion, it's considerably easier to look at the source code from the Order Sitelet than digging through source code in the Retail Solution Site. The Order Sitelet is simple, straightforward, and lends itself to extension.

Installation

To install the Order Sitelet you will need to use the site pack file (PUP), which can be found in the `C:\Program Files\Microsoft Commerce Server\SDK\Samples\Sitelets\Order` directory. Using the Commerce Server Manager, right-click on the **Applications** folder of your existing retail commerce site and select **Add Application**. Follow the same procedure to install the Order Sitelet as we did for the Discount Sitelet. The `ordersitelet` application will be unpacked as a separate IIS website, but will still use the site resources of your existing Commerce Server Retail site. If all goes well you should see the Order Sitelet in Commerce Server Manager as a sub-application of the retail site.

Additional Setup

Once the Commerce Server Site Packager/Unpackager is done setting up the Order Sitelet, you can browse to the application, usually http://<computername>/ordersitelet, if you've accepted the defaults. If you visit the Order Sitelet just after unpacking you'll immediately get an error indicating a call to `GetProfile` failed.

Once again, there are some additional steps to set up the Sitelet, in addition to unpacking. You'll need to load the SQL Server Query Analyzer again, and this time to load up `PopulateOrderProfileSitelet.sql`, which you'll find in the `C:\Program Files\Microsoft Commerce server\SDK\Samples\Sitelets\Order` directory. This SQL file will load a demo user named joeuser with the e-mail address someone@microsoft.com into the user profile system. You can confirm that the user was added correctly by returning to the Commerce Server BizDesk and searching for Joe User. Be sure to select the right Commerce Server site database when you run this query. Since you installed the Order Sitelet as an application underneath your Retail site it will share the same database. The name of my site's database is Retail_commerce.

> *As with most of the Sitelets there's a number of things in the Order Sitelet that are hard coded, the User just being one of them. When you're pulling code from any Sitelet's source code for your development work be sure to look in every nook and cranny to make sure that there are no additional hard coded values.*

You'll also need to go into the BizDesk Orders Module and visit Shipping Methods. The Order Sitelet requires at least one shipping method to be set up ahead of time or you'll get an error when you visit `shipping.asp`. Go ahead and set up a shipping method based on quantity. Perhaps you'll offer your users shipping for a dollar!

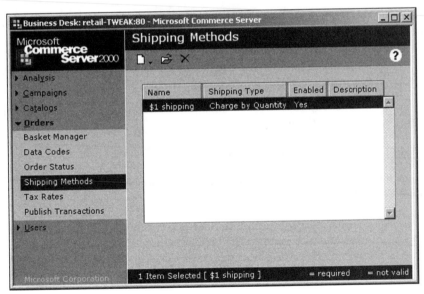

The Pipeline

The Order Sitelet consists of a number of pipelines but the most interesting one is the checkout pipeline. It's located in `checkout.pcf` in the `C:\inetpub\wwwroot\ordersitelet\pipelines` directory. The checkout pipeline validates the user's credit card, splits up orders that are being shipped to multiple addresses, and commits the `OrderForm` to the Database. It's an all or nothing proposition, if this pipeline fails with an error the order doesn't go through.

DumpOrder.vbs

Microsoft has seen fit to include a very useful pipeline utility script called `DumpOrder.vbs`, and it does literally that. It takes an `OrderForm` at any stage of a pipeline and dumps it to a file of your choice. Let's make the Order Sitelet more useful by adding this component to the checkout pipeline. As we saw in Chapter 6, when scripts are used as pipeline components they have to implement the `mscsexecute` function, so the pipeline framework can call them.

```
Function mscsexecute(config, orderform, context, flags)
```

There are a few easy steps needed to add the `DumpOrder` script to your checkout pipeline.

1. Open up the `checkout.pcf` file in the Commerce Server 2000 Pipeline Editor.

2. Insert a component at the end of the pipeline. Be sure to select a `Scriptor` Component.

3. Right-click on your new Scriptor component to bring up its property pages. The source of the Scriptor will be the external `dumporder.vbs` in your `C:\inetpub\wwwroot\ordersitelet` directory.

4. In the config text box make sure to add filename=c:\ orderdump.log so the component knows where to put the log file. When you write components with script you can pass in additional context via this config line as name/value pairs. Also remember to name your component something other than Scriptor.

5. The user your IIS is running as should have *write* access to the directory to which the log file will be written. Since my computer's name is TWEAK, IIS is running on my system as the user IUSR_TWEAK. Of course I wouldn't recommend giving write access to the root directory of a production system, so be warned! Feel free to put your log files wherever you want.

6. Save the pipeline, and restart your web application to reload the changes. (Make sure your `.PCF` file is *NOT* read-only.)

`DumpOrder.vbs` knows how to dump order forms, lists of items and the items themselves to a text file. It dumps all the contents of the dictionary and also logs any errors it finds in the dictionary, including items it does not dump. Pipelines are notoriously difficult to debug, and it's nice to have a clear log of what is occurring during execution.

```
Function mscsexecute(config, orderform, context, flags)
    Set fs = CreateObject("Scripting.FileSystemObject")
    Set a = fs.CreateTextFile(config.filename, True) 'Create the log file here!
    DumpOrderForm orderform, a
    a.Close
    mscsexecute = 1
End Function
```

The `DumpOrderForm` function spins through each key in the order form calling `DumpItem`, `DumpItems` or `DumpList` depending on what it encounters. If you store objects in the dictionary that it doesn't handle you can easily modify the `DumpOrderForm` function to handle any new type conversions you need.

```
' code snipped for clarity...
' Some object, assume it is a list.  This code could be expanded to handle
' other kinds of objects to
   a.WriteLine(" ")
   a.WriteLine("Order Key is [" + key + "]" + " Start List")
   On Error Resume Next
   DumpList orderForm.Value(key), a
   If err.number > 0 then
       If err.number = 438 Then 'can't handle this object
           If TypeName(orderForm.Value(key)) = "IContentList" then
               a.writeline " *** unable to write the contents of a " & _
                   TypeName(orderForm.Value(key)) & " with " &_
                   orderForm.Value(key).Count & " rows."
           End If
       Else
           a.writeline " *** ERROR in DumpOrderForm # " & CStr(Err.Number) &_
               " " & Err.Description
       End If
   End If
   a.WriteLine("End of List")
   a.WriteLine(" ")
```

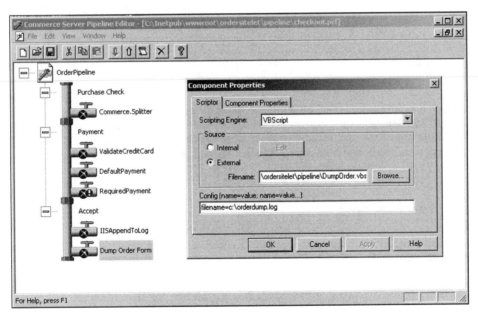

Now when the pipeline runs, `orderdump.log` is created with all the excruciating details that you need to debug your order process. You can move the position of your new Dump Order Form component up or down the pipeline, or duplicate it, depending on where debugging is needed. When you have the component in the pipeline multiple times, put in a different name in the config text box for your log file, like `startorder.log` and `endorder.log` to debug the changes that occur to your `OrderForm` during the purchase process. If you give the same filename twice it will overwrite your order form log file! It might be useful to put in a filename generation function that creates log file names based on the current date and time and the `order_id`.

Example OrderDump.log

```
Order Key [user_id] {String} Value [{857A42EE-BD0A-46ad-A83E-28BF897CDDD2}]
{String}
Order Key [user_org_id] {String} Value [{590858E1-08A7-11D3-B8C4-00104B95AE0E}]
{String}
Order Key [_oadjust_subtotal] {String} Value [1999] {Long}
Order Key [shipping_method_name] {String} Value [$1 shipping] {String}

...

Order Key [order_id] {String} Value [SVBV71ND26RH8G93MXHPTVUST5] {String}
Order Key [billing_address_id] {String} Value [Home] {String}
Order Key [_payment_auth_code] {String} Value [FAITH] {String}
Order Key [d_DateCreated] {String} Value [3/24/2001 9:16:57 PM] {Date}

...

Order Key [user_e-mail_address] {String} Value [someone@microsoft.com] {String}
Order Key [_tax_total] {String} Value [0] {Long}
** End of Orderform Contents *
```

The Code

The code in the Order Sitelet is fairly clear by Commerce Server standards, and rather well organized. The `orderlib.asp` file in the include directory contains some very useful helper functions that abstract a great deal of work from us.

> Although we all know it's very difficult to abstract the presentation layer from business logic, the well thought out functions in the `<siteletname>lib.asp` files are worth your time exploring. They include `cataloglib.asp`, `orderlib.asp`, and `profilelib.asp`, as well as `advertlib.asp`, and `auctionlib.asp`.

Purchase and Order Summary

The Order Sitelet has some great code on how to handle multiple orders within a single basket, and multiple shipments with a single order. Here's a pared-down version of the code in the Order Sitelet's `summary.asp`, with the HTML and display generation code removed, and comments added for clarity.

Just as we get ready to confirm an order the `Totals` pipeline is run. The `Totals` pipeline splits the order into multiple shipments (if multiple shipments exist), adjusts for any shipping discounts, sets the tax and totals the order. Think of it as a little more than the shopping cart but not quite a confirmed order.

When we display the summary page, asking for confirmation, we first spin through each order in our baskets or forms collection.

```
For Each sOrderFormName in m_oBasket.Value("orderforms")
    Set oOrder = m_oBasket.Value("orderforms").Value(sOrderFormName)
    intShipmentIndex = 0
```

For each order that we find, we spin through that order shipments collection. Each new shipment has a subtotal of 0.

```
'* For each Shipment in an Order *
For Each dictShipment In oOrder.shipments
    intShipmentSubTotal = 0
```

Then for each item in a shipment, we output the details about the product/item.

```
'* For each Product/Item in this Shipment *
For Each intIndex in dictShipment.ItemIndexes
    Set dictItem = oOrder.Items(intIndex)
    '* Output details each product in this order
```

We add up the subtotal for this shipment.

```
'* Calculate the Subtotal for this shipment*
intShipmentSubtotal = intShipmentSubtotal +_
    oOrder.Items(intIndex).Value(ITEM_TOTAL)
Next
```

We retrieve the shipping total from our shipment dictionary and add that to the total shipping for the entire order, then repeat the process until we run out of shipments and orders.

```
'* Add in Shipping Charges *
intShipping = dictShipment.Value(SHIPMENT_SHIPPING_TOTAL)
intShippingTotal = intShippingTotal + intShipping
intShipmentIndex = intShipmentIndex + 1
    Next
Next
```

If the order is confirmed from the Order Summary Page the user is given a GUID as their OrderID.

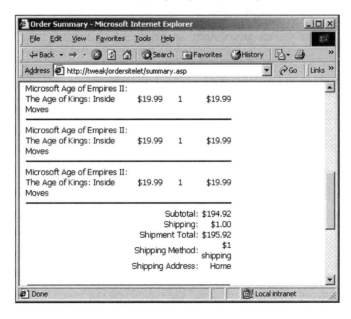

Order History

If the user visits our site again they may wish to view their order history as well as the details about a specific order. The `history.asp` page uses the **OrderGroupManager** object to search for that user's ID and retrieve a record set of their order history. The `OrderGroupManager` object manages any situation where there are multiple `OrderForms`, whether multiple `OrderForms` are being searched, or a Shopping Cart contains multiple `OrderForms`. In this snippet of code from the Order Sitelet we use a hard-coded User ID. You can provide multiple ways to search for order history using either the `Find` or `SimpleFind` functions of the `OrderGroupManager` object. You could let the user search for an order that occured during the last few weeks or only those orders that are currently active.

```
Dim oOrderMgr
Dim rsOrderHistory
Set oOrderMgr = GetOrderGroupManager()
Set rsOrderHistory = oOrderMgr.Find( _
   Array("user_id = '" & GENERIC_USER_ID & "'"), _
   Array(), _
   Array() _
   )
Set g_rsOrderHistory = rsOrderHistory
```

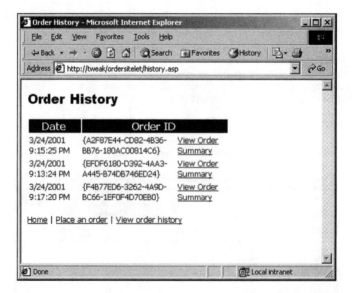

It's then a simple task to spin through the Order History recordset and output a list of all the user's orders.

```
<%
Do While Not g_rsOrderHistory.EOF
%>
   <tr>
      <td><%=g_rsOrderHistory(ORDER_DATE)%></td>
      <td><%=g_rsOrderHistory(ORDER_ID)%></td>
      <td><a href="<%=PAGE_SUMMARY%>?<%=ORDER_ID%>=_
         <%=Server.URLEncode(g_rsOrderHistory(ORDER_ID))%>">View Order_
         Summary</a></td>
```

```
    </tr>
    <%
    g_rsOrderHistory.MoveNext
Loop
%>
```

We then take the `OrderID` out of the Order History recordset and build a URL that can send the user back to the Order Detail Page for any historical order.

The Result

Now that we've completed a few orders successfully, we can return to the Order Status Module in BizDesk to do a little order analysis. I can see that I've received three new orders in the last two days, and I can see that Joe User placed each of those orders. I can also open any specific order and drill down to the detail level.

From this point we could hook up existing user profiles and log in as a few different users for variety. The Order Sitelet is a great tool for seeing how Commerce Server 2000 manages multiple addresses for single user, multiple shipping methods, and having one order split and sent to multiple shipping addresses.

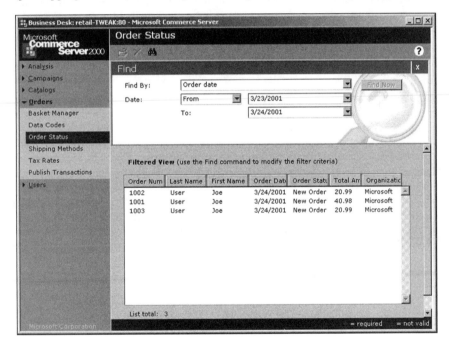

The Profile Sitelet

The Profile Sitelet provides source code to demonstrate how to use the Profiling System to let users register and authenticate on a site. This Sitelet shows how to create a new profile, login using that profile, then make modifications to it. The Retail Site includes this functionality also, but you may find the source code of the Profile Sitelet easier to reference and learn from, as it's not in the context of a complete solution.

Installation

To install the Profile Sitelet you will need to use the site pack file (PUP), which can be found in the `C:\Program Files\Microsoft Commerce Server\SDK\Samples\Sitelets\Profile` directory. Using the Commerce Server Manager, right-click on the **Applications** folder of your existing retail commerce site and select **Add Application**. Follow the same procedure to install the Profile Sitelet as we did for the Discount Sitelet. The `profilesitelet` application will be unpacked as a separate IIS website, but will still use the site resources of your existing Commerce Server retail site. If all goes well you should see the Profile Sitelet in Commerce Server Manager as a sub–application of the retail site.

The Code

The Profile Sitelet only shows the very basics of creating and editing a User Profile, but at least it's simple right? Most of the useful functions are in `include/profilelib.asp`, which does the useful job of hiding the complexities from us.

Logging In

`Login.asp` has a simple HTML form on it that posts to itself. After this form posts back to `Login.asp` we call the helper function `LogOnUser` with the contents of the form along with a bunch of magic numbers. Not only is this a horrible thing to do, but Microsoft knows it. So much so that they were pleasant enough to mark that line with `BUGBUG` – pity that it didn't get fixed before they shipped, though!

```
'BUGBUG: Lots of magic numbers used.  Must move to using constants.
If (Not LogOnUser(CStr(colForm(FORM_USER_ID)), CStr(colForm(FORM_USER_PWD)), 1,
90, 2)) Then
    'Deal with the errors...
Else
    'Logon Success
End If
```

`LogOnUser` is defined in `include/profilelib.asp`. Now we can see what those unnecessary and evil magic numbers were for. We passed in a 1 for `fCookieSupport`, which is a Boolean `TRUE`. We passed in 90 seconds for `strTimeout` and a 2 for `fTicketType`. An `fTicketType` with a value of 2 corresponds to the enumerated value `enumMSCS_AuthTicketType`, which is the MSCSAuth ticket used for a registered user. We're telling the profile system that we are trying to authenticate a registered user, as opposed to an anonymous one. More on this in the Bugs section below.

I've removed the error handling code from the following listing of `LogOnUser` in the interest of brevity. I've added comments in the interest of long-windedness.

```
Function LogOnUser(ByVal strUserName, ByVal strUserPwd, ByVal fCookieSupport, _
    ByVal strTimeout, ByVal fTicketType)
On Error Resume Next

    Dim objAuthMgr
    Dim objProfile
```

Here we'll initialize the authentication manager for the site.

```
    Set objAuthMgr = InitAuthMgr(Application("MSCSSiteName"))
```

We then try to get a profile with this user name, which is hard coded in this example.

```
Set objProfile = GetProfile(USER_LOGON_NAME, strUserName, PROFILE_TYPE_USER)
```

It's important to ensure that the retrieved profile's password matches the supplied password.

```
If (objProfile.Fields(USER_PASSWORD).Value = strUserPwd) Then
    'if the password matches, issue an authentication ticket
    objAuthMgr.SetAuthTicket strUserName, fCookieSupport, strTimeout
    objAuthMgr.SetUserID 1, objProfile.Fields(USER_ID). Value
    Set objAuthMgr = nothing
Else
    'this was a bad logon, bail
    LogOnUser = False
    Exit Function
End If
LogOnUser = True
End Function
```

Creating a User

`Create.asp` also consists of a simple HTML form to create a new user. When this form posts back to `create.asp` we do some cursory validation then call the `CreateProfile` helper function defined in `include/profilelib.asp`.

```
'Now that we've made it through validation, create the new
'profile instance.
'CreateProfile() function defined in include/profilelib.asp
Set objProfile = CreateProfile( _
    CStr(GetGUID()), _
    PROFILE_TYPE_USER _
    )
```

After creating a new profile we have a reference to the new User Profile Object in the `objProfile` variable. We load up an array specific to the `SetMultipleAttributes` helper function. This is just one way to hide the complexities of setting multiple attributes in a user profile; loading up arrays is not how user profiles are typically set up. It works very well for what it does.

```
'The SetMultipleAttributes() function expects a specially formatted
'array containing the attribute names, and values you wish to update.
'The format for the array is attribute names are in the even elements
'and attribute values are the odd elements.  So you get an array that
'looks like:
'rgAttrs(0) = "GeneralInfo.user_security_password"
'rgAttrs(1) = "mypassword"
'rgAttrs(2) = "GeneralInfo.user_firstname"
'rgAttrs(3) = "John"
'See the function header for SetMultipleAttributes for more info.

'Load up the array with all information from our posted form
rgAttrs = Array( _
    USER_LOGON_NAME, CStr(colForm(FORM_USER_ID)), _
    USER_PASSWORD, CStr(colForm(FORM_USER_PWD)), _
    USER_FIRST_NAME, CStr(colForm(FORM_USER_FIRST_NAME)), _
    USER_LAST_NAME, CStr(colForm(FORM_USER_LAST_NAME)), _
    USER_E-MAIL, CStr(colForm(FORM_USER_E-MAIL)), _
```

571

```
            USER_ACCOUNT_STATUS, 1, _
            USER_DATE_REGISTERED, CDate(Date()), _
            USER_DATE_UPDATED, CDate(Date()), _
            USER_TYPE, 1 _
            )

    'Pass the loaded array along with the profile object
    Call SetMultipleAttributes(objProfile, rgAttrs)
```

SetMultipleAttributes is a fairly clever helper function, spinning through the array of attributes we passed in, and updating the profile object.

```
    Dim intItr
    intItr = LBound(rgAttrs)

    Do While intItr < UBound(rgAttrs)

        'Update the specified attribute.  For example:
        'objProfile("GeneralInfo.user_security_password") = "password"

        objProfile.Fields(CStr(rgAttrs(intItr))).Value = rgAttrs(intItr + 1)

        'we have to skip TWO in this array, to skip over the next name value pair
        intItr = intItr + 2
    Loop

    objProfile.Update()
```

Editing a user works the same way: we get a reference to that user's profile, and then call SetMultipleAttributes. In the sample code, all the attributes get set regardless of whether they've been changed or not. If you were going to use this code in a production site, it would be more efficient to only set those attributes that have actually been changed. That would be a fairly simple but fairly powerful optimization.

Bugs

There appears to be a bug in the Profile Sitelet sample code that allows you to modify an existing profile. On line 161 of edit.asp we use the authentication manager to retrieve a user ID that is stored in a ticket. You can see in the code that the Microsoft engineers actually put BUGBUG lamenting the fact that they use the magic number in the GetUserID function.

```
    'Now that we have the Auth Manager, retrieve the profile stored for the
    'logged on user.
    'BUGBUG: More magic numbers to get rid of
    g_strUser = objAuthMgr.GetUserID(1)
    Set objUser = GetProfile(USER_LOGON_NAME, g_strUser, PROFILE_TYPE_USER)
```

If you refer to the Commerce Server documentation the GetUserID function takes a ticket type as a parameter. Here's a table defining the possible values for the EnumMSCS_TicketType that can be passed into GetUserID.

Name	Value	Description
enumMSCS_ProfileTicketType	1	A MSCSProfile ticket used for an anonymous user.
enumMSCS_AuthTicketType	2	A MSCSAuth ticket used for a registered user.

We can see that he's passing in a ticket value for an anonymous user, not a registered user. This means that if you login as a registered user and then visit the edit page, rather than editing the registered user you are currently logged in as, the profile system will pass back a GUID representing a new anonymous user for you. Then when we call `GetProfile` passing in the new Anonymous GUID, a reference to an Anonymous UserObject is returned. We don't want that; suddenly we are editing an Anonymous User!

If we change this line of code to pass in the `enumMSCS_AuthTicketType`, everything works as expected.

```
Const enumMSCS_ProfileTicketType = 1
Const enumMSCS_AuthTicketType = 2
g_strUser = objAuthMgr.GetUserID(enumMSCS_AuthTicketType)
```

The Result

The Profile Sitelet gives you a framework and a few convenient ASP functions to assist in creating, editing, and deleting user profiles. It's a little primitive, but it's a useful starting point, and a good reference to the Profiling System.

The Passport Sitelet

The Passport Sitelet shows how to use Passport single sign-on capability with the Profiling System. The Microsoft Passport Service is a single sign-in service that you can authenticate your users against. The Commerce Server 2000 Profiling System can still be used for targeting users, managing user data, and so on, even though Passport is used for sign-on to the site. Since its introduction, the Passport service has become more and more popular; there are now more than 130 million Passport accounts! By allowing Passport to manage your authentication services, it theoretically gives you one less thing to worry about on your site. Passport also includes an option for an express purchase service that allows users to store credit card and shipping information in their Passport Wallets that are stored on Microsoft's servers.

Installation

In order to use the Passport Sitelet you will have to install the Passport SDK, which can be found at http://www.passport.com/devinfo. Microsoft Passport uses a pre-production environment (PREP) for testing with different user databases and you'll need a Passport on these Test Servers to develop with the Passport Sitelet and the Passport SDK. If you're working against one of the Passport test environments, you'll find your regular Passport does not work.

You'll need to visit http://www.passport.com/devinfo and perform the following steps before setting up the Passport Sitelet:

1. Get a Preproduction (PREP) Passport Account.

2. Download and install the Passport SDK 1.4 or greater.

3. Get a PREP Site ID. Whenever your servers make a call to the Passport servers, Passport uses your Site ID to access the values specific to your site. You could skip this step and the system will use a SiteID of 1. This will prevent you from performing any customizations to the Passport Login screens.

After installing the Passport SDK, to install the Passport Sitelet you will need to use the site pack file (PUP), which can be found in the `C:\Program Files\Microsoft Commerce Server\SDK\Samples\Sitelets\Passport` directory. Using the Commerce Server Manager, right-click on the Applications folder of your existing retail site and select Add Application. Follow the same procedure to install the Passport Sitelet as we did for the Discount Sitelet. The `passportsitelet` application will be unpacked as a separate IIS website, but will still use the site resources of your existing Commerce Server retail site. If all goes well, the Passport Sitelet will appear in Commerce Server Manager as a sub-application of the retail site.

Additional Setup

The most important component of the Passport SDK running on your server is the **Passport Manager** object. According to their documentation, the Passport Manager is a dual-interfaced COM object you can script to or directly invoke via ISAPI. Passport Manager uses your Site ID to decrypt ticket and profile information sent by the Passport login servers and to encrypt information stored in your website domain cookies.

More importantly, it handles all the Passport cookie setting, parsing, and expiration logic so you don't have to access them via `Request.Cookies`. Microsoft Passport doesn't involve any server-to-server communication; it handles everything via standard redirection technology.

Microsoft says that future versions of Commerce Server will directly integrate with Passport, so sites created with Commerce Server will support single sign-in right out of the box.

The Code

Passport and the Passport Manager take care of the mundane tasks of user login and authentication. The code to check if the user is authenticated and greet them by name is straightforward:

```
<%
    Dim objMgr
    Set objMgr = Server.CreateObject("Passport.Manager")
    If (oMgr.IsAuthenticated) Then
        Response.Write "Hello <b>" & CStr(oMgr.Profile("nickname")) & "</b>"
    Else
        Response.Write "You need a Passport, my friend!"
    End If
%>
```

Passport Manager

The Passport Manager has a lot of methods and properties, and a complete discussion of its capabilities is beyond the scope of this book. Complete documentation for the Passport SDK 1.4 can be found at http://www.passport.com/SDKDocuments/SDK14; there are however a few important things to keep in mind when using the Passport Manager:

❑ The Passport Manager object should only be created once per page in page scope. The object is responsible for reading and writing cookies on page start.

❑ Do not create the Passport Manager object in application or session scope.

❑ Use the Passport Manager methods exclusively to create the URLs that are used to redirect a member to the appropriate server. Remember that all the code and pages used for Passport Sign-In are contained on the Passport authenticating domain login server, not your server.

❑ Always use Passport Manager functions to create graphics like the Passport sign-in logo GIF, rather than hard coding.

For example, here's the homepage of the Passport Sitelet installed on a system. Right now the URL for the Login using Passport link is generated by the code below. The synchronization page is the page to which Passport will redirect the authenticated user – note that this URL is encoded and passed into the Passport Manager. Additional parameters are also passed in, such as the time window for the user's sign and if the site should be secured under SSL.

```
<%
Dim strSynchPage
strSynchPage = "http://<<computername>>/passportsitelet/synchprofile.asp"
%>


  . . .

<A HREF="<%= oMgr.AuthURL(Server.URLEncode(strSynchPage), 300, True, False, 0,
False) %>">Login using Passport</A>
```

The HTML generated by this code looks like this. Note that the return URL has been encoded inside the Passport URL.

```
<A HREF="http://current-
login.passporttest.com/login.asp?id=1&ru=http%3A%2F%2Ftweak%2Fpassportsitelet%2Fsy
nchprofile%2Easp&tw=300&fs=1&kv=1&ct=985763091&cb=0&ns=0&ver=1.400.0981.1">Login
using Passport</A>
```

Now, to change the Login using Passport link to a friendlier Passport Sign-In graphic is a simple function call.

```
<%
Dim strSynchPage
strSynchPage = "http://<<computername>>/passportsitelet/synchprofile.asp"
%>


  . . .

<%= oMgr.LogoTag2(Server.URLEncode(strSynchPage), 300, True,False,0,False) %>
```

The resulting HTML includes an image tag we didn't have to worry about.

```
<IMG SRC="http://current-www.passportimages.org/signin.gif" WIDTH="66" HEIGHT="19"
CLASS="PassportSignIn" BORDER="0" ALT="Sign in with your Passport"/>
```

Signing in to Passport and Creating a New Profile in Commerce Server

```
<A HREF="http://current-
login.passporttest.com/login.asp?id=1&ru=http%3A%2F%2Ftweak%2Fpassportsitelet%2Fsy
nchprofile%2Easp&tw=300&fs=1&kv=1&ct=985763091&cb=0&ns=0&ver=1.400.0981.1">Login
using Passport</A>
```

When the user clicks Login Using Passport from your site, they are sent to the Passport servers with the return URL for your site encoded in the request. When authentication succeeds, the user is then redirected back to the page you specified. In our example above, the user will be redirected back to http://<<localcomputer>>/passportsitelet/synchprofile.asp. The Passport Sitelet uses synchprofile.asp to copy information from the newly authenticated Passport user into the Commerce Server 2000 Profile System.

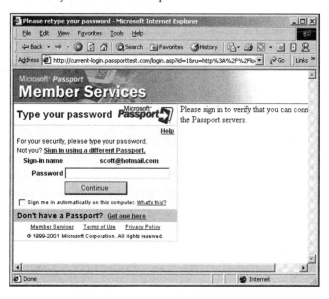

When the user returns to synchprofile.asp, we initialize the Passport Manager, as well as the Commerce Server Authentication Manager. GetPassportPuid is called to generate a unique number that will be used internally as an ID. Microsoft Passport calls their Unique ID a **PUID**. Even though the user's sign-in name is a guaranteed unique identifier, Passport recommends using a PUID so sign-in names themselves are not stored in a database other than Passport's. Even though sign-in names might potentially be recycled in the future, PUID are never reused. This code creates a unique identifier that will be used as the user's loginid in the local Commerce Server Profile System.

```
Function GetPassportPuid(ByRef oPassportMgr)
    GetPassportPuid = CStr(oPassportMgr("MemberIDHigh")) & _
                      CStr(oPassportMgr("MemberIDLow"))
End Function
```

If the Passport Manager authenticates the user, GetProfile is called to look up the user via their PUID. If the user does not already exist in the database, we'll create a profile for them.

```
Set oPassportMgr = InitPassportMgr()
    Set oAuthMgr = InitAuthMgr(Application("MSCSSiteName"))
    strPuid = GetPassportPuid(oPassportMgr)
If (oPassportMgr.IsAuthenticated()) Then

    On Error Resume Next
    Set oUser = GetProfile(USER_LOGON_NAME, strPuid, PROFILE_TYPE_USER)

    'GetProfile() will generate an error if the profile doesn't exist
    'in this case, we don't care about the error and should get rid of it
    Err.Clear

    On Error GoTo 0

    If (oUser Is Nothing) Then
        Dim rgAttrs

        'User has never been here before, so we need create a profile for them
        Set oUser = CreateProfile(strPuid, PROFILE_TYPE_USER)

        'Note that this is a "dumb" way of doing this.  We're updating each
        'attribute instead of only updating those attributes that have changed.
        'But this is done in the interest of simplicity and brevity.
        rgAttrs = Array( _
            USER_ACCOUNT_STATUS, 1, _
            USER_DATE_REGISTERED, CDate(Date()), _
            USER_DATE_UPDATED, CDate(Date()), _
            USER_TYPE, 1 _
            )

        Call SetMultipleAttributes(oUser, rgAttrs)
    End If
```

Regardless of whether the user's profile existed already, or was created, at this point oUser holds a reference to a valid user profile. A call to CopyPassportToLocalProfile updates the information from the user's Passport into the local Commerce Server 2000 Profile System.

```
    'Synch the local profile with the passport profile
    Call CopyPassportToLocalProfile(oPassportMgr, oUser)
    Response.Redirect PAGE_DEFAULT
    Exit Sub
Else
    Call LogOnPassportUser(oPassportMgr, strSynchPage, 300)
    Exit Sub
End If
```

The code that comes with the Passport Sitelet only synchronizes the preferred e-mail attribute of the User's Passport with the local profile. It's a simple matter to pull additional core attributes from the passport manager. The Passport Manager holds such information as the user's birthday (if supplied), their city, country, their gender, and their preferred language. Using some or all of these attributes gives the user more a personalized experience and leverages the information users have already entered into their Passport elsewhere.

```
Function CopyPassportToLocalProfile( _
    ByRef oPassportMgr, _
    ByRef oUserProfile _
    )
    'copy additional user attributes here...
    oUserProfile.Fields(USER_E-MAIL).Value = oPassportMgr.Profile(PASSPORT_E-MAIL)
    oUserProfile.Update()
End Function
```

The Result

After signing into Passport from the Passport Sitelet, the newly created user is visible from the User module in BizDesk. The User that was created via the Microsoft Passport system is the one that has a PUID as his login name.

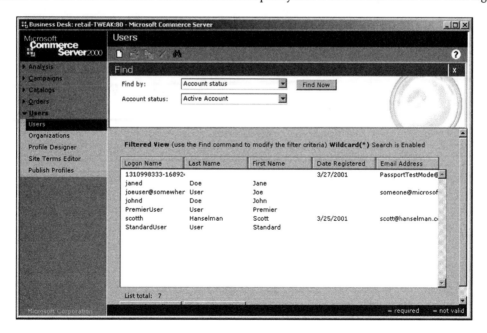

The Auction Sitelet

The Auction Sitelet demonstrates how the Auction component can be used to implement Winning Bid auctions (simple highest bid wins). The Auction component enables a site to auction products, accept bids, and determine winners, using rules ranging from simple to sophisticated. It can also allow the participants of an auction to be notified of important auction-related events via e-mail. The Auction Sitelet also includes a custom Business Desk module. This is an excellent example of how a commerce site and its accompanying BizDesk site can work together.

Installation

The Auction Sitelet is little more complicated to set up than the other Sitelets. The steps are as follows.

❑ Unpack the Auction Sitelet as a sub–application of an existing Commerce Server Site

❑ Ensure the new database tables are created

❑ Ensure the Profile System is populated with test users

❑ Manually integrate the custom Auction BizDesk module with our existing Retail BizDesk

To install the Auction Sitelet you will need to use the site pack file (PUP), which can be found in the `C:\Program Files\Microsoft Commerce Server\SDK\Samples\Sitelets\Auction` directory. Using the Commerce Server Manager, right-click on the **Applications** folder of your existing Retail Commerce Site and select **Add Application**. Follow the same procedure to install the Auction Sitelet as we did for all the Sitelets. The `'auctionsitelet'` application will be unpacked as a separate IIS website, but will still use the site resources of your existing Commerce Server Retail site. If all goes well you should see the Auction Sitelet in Commerce Server Manager as a sub-application of the Retail site.

The Auction Sitelet is dependent upon an existing valid product catalog, and it does not include any auctions out of the box. Once the BizDesk module is installed, it will allow the creation of auctions based on products in your product catalog.

Database Setup

The Auction Sitelet uses two database tables in our Retail Site database. This is the same database referred to by the Transaction site resource. The default name of the retail site is Retail so the default database name is Retail_commerce. These tables should be created during the unpacking of the retail site, but it's worth confirming that they exist after unpacking the Auction Sitelet.

Table Name	Description
CatalogProducts_AuctionItem	Describes the items being auctioned
CatalogProducts_AuctionBid	Holds the bids for each auction item

As an interesting side note, these two tables were created when you unpacked the Retail Solution Site, NOT when you unpacked the auction site. Why is this interesting you say? Because it appears that Microsoft meant to include the Auction Sitelet with the Retail Solution Site and the decision was made the last minute to pull the Auction functionality out and included instead as a separate Sitelet. Be aware of this fact if you intend to use the Auction Sitelet with a Commerce Server Site that is not based on the Retail Solution Site; you'll need to create these two tables manually.

CatalogProducts_AuctionItem Table

Here's a table describing the details of each column in the two tables. The Auction object abstracts 90% of this information from the developer, but it's useful to be familiar with these tables anyway.

Column Name	Description
auction_id	The unique ID assigned to the auction
product_id	The unique ID assigned to the product, often the title
identifier_name	The name of the attribute used for the product_id. for example, Title
product_name	The name of the product
catalog_name	The name of the catalog of the product came from
sku	The particular SKU of the product
reserve_price	How much we'd like to sell the product for
available	How many we have available
bid_increment	The amount each bid must increment by
auction_type	An enumeration of the type of auction, 0 for Winning Price, 1 for Clear Price, 2 for Second Price
minimum_bid	The minimum bid
sealed_bid	Whether or not check the bid against the minimum bid
sealed_inventory	Whether or not check the number of wanted items against the inventory
active	Whether the auction is active

Table continued on following page

Column Name	Description
processed	Whether or not the auction has been processed/resolved
start_date	When bids will be accepted on the item
end_date	When the auction disclosed the items can be purchased
auto_close_seconds	The number of seconds to wait after the last bid to close the auction; 0 indicates to ignore the time of the last bid and close on the end date
modified_date	The date the auction was last month
bid_date	The date of the last bid
auto_close_date	The date the auction will be automatically close
created_date	The date the auction was created
resolve_date	Date the auction was resolved
number_sold	The number of items sold
number_updates	Number of bids has been updated
number_desired	The number of products that are desired
number_bids	The number of bids for this item
number_bidders	The number of different bidders (people) bidding on this item
clear_price	The lowest winning price bidders receive the item they bid on during a clear price auction
bid_price	The current bid price
current_minimum_bid	The current minimum bid
second_price	Winning bidders pay the lowest of the following: The highest losing bid plus the bid increment, the lowest winning bid, or the reserve price, assuming the number of bids above the reserve price is less than the number of available items
client_status	Status changes are due to bid updates or calculated field updates

CatalogProducts_AuctionBid Table

Each bid the user places on an auction item will have an associated row in this table:

Column Name	Description
auction_id	The ID of the auction this bid relates to
shopper_id	The Shopper ID of the user who bid on this auction; this is their ID in the profile system.
bid_name	The name of the person who bid
bid_e-mail	The e-mail of the person who bid

Column Name	Description
bid_price	The amount of their bid
desired	The amount of product they desire
take_less	Whether the user will take less than the wanted number of items
number_updates	Number of times it has been updated
number_bids	The current number of bids
created_date	The date his record was created
modified_date	The date his record was modified
status_date	The date the status of this bid was modified
number_won	The number of products is that one
win_price	The winning price
notified_date	The date the user was notified
client_status	The client current status

Additional Setup

You'll need to load the SQL Server Query Analyzer again, and this time to load up the `PopulateOrderProfileSitelet.sql` file that you'll find in the `C:\Program Files\Microsoft Commerce Server\SDK\Samples\Sitelets\Auction` directory. This SQL file will load a demo user named joeuser with the e-mail address someone@microsoft.com into the User Profile System. You can confirm that the user was added correctly by returning to the Commerce Server BizDesk and searching for Joe User. Be sure to select the right Commerce Server site database when you run this query. Since you installed the Order Sitelet as an application underneath your Retail Commerce Server site it will share the same database. The name of my site's database is Retail_commerce.

Adding test users to the Profile System is the same as the step that was performed during the setup of the Order Sitelet. If you have already run this SQL file against your commerce site's database, you can skip running the `PopulateOrderProfileSitelet.sql` file.

BizDesk Module Setup

Before Auctions can be added, the Auction BizDesk module has to be integrated with the Retail site's BizDesk. Here's a list of the required steps; a detailed breakdown follows this summary.

1. Copy the Auction Sitelet's `auction.xml` BizDesk module configuration file to the Retail site's `retailbizdesk/config` directory, which is usually `C:\inetpub\wwwroot\retailbizdesk\config`.

2. Create an entry in `bizdesk.xml` for the Auction module.

3. Create an Auction directory below your BizDesk directory. The newly created directory will usually be `C:\inetpub\wwwroot\retailbizdesk\auction`.

4. Copy the Auction Sitelet's ASP files from the `SDK/Sitelets/Auction/BizDesk` directory to the newly created Auction directory under the root of your BizDesk website. Usually this means copying files from

```
C:\Program Files\Microsoft Commerce Server\SDK\Samples\Sitelets\Auction\BizDesk
```
to
```
C:\inetpub\wwwroot\retailbizdesk\auction.
```

Be sure to copy the include directory as well.

5. Restart the BizDesk IIS Application.

Auction.xml Module Configuration File

If the Auction BizDesk Module is being added to the BizDesk of an *unmodified* (since installation) Commerce Server 2000 Retail Solution Site, `auction.xml` and `bizdesk.xml` can be safely copied to the Retail site's `retailbizdesk/config` directory, overwriting any existing files.

If the Retail Site's BizDesk *has* been modified, it's best to perform the installation of the Auction BizDesk Module manually. Start by copying *only* the `auction.xml` file to the `retailbizdesk/config` directory. If you have made any modifications to your BizDesk while reading the BizDesk chapter, it would be best for you to integrate the Auction module manually.

> A lot of people use XMLSpy (**http://www.xmlspy.com**) to edit their XML files. XMLSpy Version 3.5 reports a validation error when loading `BizDesk.xml` and configuration files like it. The XML Data Reduced (XDR) schema for the Product Catalog describes what elements and attributes are allowed in a BizDesk configuration file but doesn't mark the element type as having a certain kind of 'content'. For example some elements may only contain other elements, or some elements may only contain attributes. This schema doesn't say either way, and that adds up to a validation error. Rest assured that the BizDesk schema does work within the context of Commerce Server, and if you choose 'Save Anyway' (assuming other than this error your files are valid) you can still use XMLSpy.

The `config` directory of any BizDesk installation consists of one XML file for each primary module that is installed. The `auction.xml` file is the module that describes all the components of the Auction BizDesk module. It lists the two menus that will appear when our auction module is integrated with BizDesk. Each `<module>` element in the XML file corresponds to one menu in the left-hand side navigational tree of the BizDesk. BizDesk looks to this XML file to know which ASP pages make up each module.

In this code snippet from the `auction.xml` file, the first module is called Auction Manager and its functionality is handled by the `auction_list.asp`. The second module is the Bids Manager and it is handled by `bids_list.asp`. The `<name>` element and `<tooltip>` element control the text that appears for that menu item in the menu item's tool tip.

```xml
<modules>
    <module id="auction/auction_list.asp">
        <name>Auction Manager</name>
        <tooltip>Manage Auctions</tooltip>
    </module>
```

```
        <module id="auction/bids_list.asp">
           <name>Bids Manager</name>
           <tooltip>Manage Auction Bids</tooltip>
        </module>
     </modules>
```

The `auction.xml` file also lists a number of actions and tasks that each page has available to it. The BizDesk's built-in toolbar is provided to each page via an include ASP page, and it is configured in this section of the XML file.

The vocabulary chosen here is interesting and possibly not intuitive.

BizDesk modules are grouped in BizDesk by parent categories.

A BizDesk module is one large functional area, like the User's Module.

An action is either going to a page or posting information to a page.

A task describes actions to the BizDesk, instructing it to display a save button.

This code listing not only shows the tasks available from a list of auctions but also the relationship between pages. Additionally, the appearance of a Task's icons and hotkeys can be controlled via the module configuration files. The `<task>` element is where the magic happens. Tasks explain to BizDesk which ASP page relates to which tool bar button. Tasks also define how data moves between pages. Refer to Chapters 13 and 14 for the details on how BizDesk passes information from model to module.

For example, the code listing shows that the main page for the Auction Bid Manager is `bids_list.asp`. When a user clicks **Delete Auction Bid**, the data from the form named `selectform` is posted to the `bids_list.asp` page.

```
<actions>

...
```

(Other actions removed in the interests of brevity.)

```
...

   <action id="auction/bids_list.asp" helptopic="cs_ft_auctions_VJMH.htm">
      <name>Auction Bid Manager</name>
      <tooltip>Manage Auction Bids</tooltip>
      <tasks>
         <task icon="taskdelete.gif" id="delete">
            <postto action="auction/bids_list.asp" formname="selectform"/>
            <name>&lt;U&gt;D&lt;/U&gt;elete</name>
            <key>d</key>
            <tooltip>Delete Auction Bid</tooltip>
         </task>
         <task icon="taskfind.gif" id="find">
            <goto action="auction/bids_list.asp">Find Auctions</goto>
```

```
              <name>&lt;U&gt;F&lt;/U&gt;ind</name>
              <key>f</key>
              <tooltip>Find Auction Bids</tooltip>
          </task>
       </tasks>
    </action>
</actions>
```

BizDesk.xml Master Module Configuration File

The `auction.xml` module configuration file is a child file of the `bizdesk.xml` Master configuration file. BizDesk doesn't know to load the auction module unless it is told by an entry in `bizdesk.xml`. `Bizdesk.xml` is also located in the `config` directory of your Retail Site's BizDesk installation.

There is a category element for each menu item. To add a menu item for auctions, add the code highlighted below to the `bizdesk.xml` file. The ID of the category element must be unique within the file, in this case it's `'auction'`.

```
      <category id="users">
         <name>&lt;U&gt;U&lt;/U&gt;sers</name>
         <key>u</key>
         <tooltip>Manage Users and Organizations</tooltip>
      </category>
      <category id="auction">
         <name>&lt;U&gt;A&lt;/U&gt;uction</name>
         <key>A</key>
         <tooltip>Manage Auctions</tooltip>
      </category>
      <category id="framework">
         <name>do not delete</name>
         <key>|</key>
         <tooltip>do not delete - used by framework</tooltip>
      </category>
```

BizDesk associates the ID of the category with the category attribute of a `<moduleconfig>` element. The `moduleconfig` element tells BizDesk which child module configuration file to load. The highlighted `moduleconfig` element in the code below tells BizDesk to look in the `auction.xml` file for configuration information and the locations of the ASP files for the Auction Module.

Make sure to add the following line

```
      <moduleconfig id="auction.xml" category="auction"/>
```

to the bizdesk.xml file. The complete `moduleconfig` section as it should look when finished is shown below.

```
   <moduleconfigs>
      <moduleconfig id="analysis.xml" category="analysis"/>
      <moduleconfig id="marketing_cmanager.xml" category="campaigns"/>
      <moduleconfig id="catalogs_designer.xml" category="catalogs"/>
      <moduleconfig id="catalogs_editor.xml" category="catalogs"/>
      <moduleconfig id="catalog_sets.xml" category="catalogs"/>
      <moduleconfig id="baskets.xml" category="orders"/>
```

```
    <moduleconfig id="application.xml" category="orders"/>
    <moduleconfig id="orders.xml" category="orders"/>
    <moduleconfig id="shipping_methods.xml" category="orders"/>
    <moduleconfig id="tax.xml" category="orders"/>
    <moduleconfig id="refreshcache.xml" category="orders"/>
    <moduleconfig id="users.xml" category="users"/>
    <moduleconfig id="organizations.xml" category="users"/>
    <moduleconfig id="profiles.xml" category="users"/>
    <moduleconfig id="auction.xml" category="auction"/>
    <moduleconfig id="bdmaster.xml" category="framework"/>
  </moduleconfigs>
```

When the BizDesk launches for the first time it checks the `BizDesk.XML` *file for the list of modules to load. Then it looks at each module's XML file checking for the existence of action files the module refers to. If the BizDesk doesn't find all the proper directory and ASP files listed in the XML files the menu item just won't appear. Since we have not created an auction directory and copied the ASP files for the auction module, BizDesk will not show the Auction menu yet and will not report an error.*

The Auction Task BizDesk ASP Files

Create a directory named **auction** underneath the directory or retail site BizDesk is installed in. Copy all of the ASP files from `C:\Program Files\Microsoft Commerce Server\SDK\Samples\Sitelets\Auction\BizDesk` as well as the entire `include` directory. Don't copy the `config` directory, as it holds the configuration files that were used earlier.

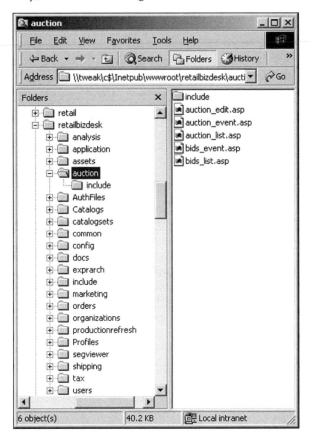

It bears restating that the Auction main menu item in BizDesk is generated by the `<category>` element in `BizDesk.xml`. The Auction Manager and Bids Manager sub-menu items are generated by the `<module>` elements in `auction.xml` and its functionality is handled by the `auction_list.asp` and `bids_list.asp` respectively.

Each ASP file in the `auction` directory is an action. They are either the `id` attribute of an `<action>` or the `action` attribute of a `<task>` element. The look and functionality of each module's toolbar is managed by the `<task>`.

For example, the Auction Manager is referenced in `auction.xml` in the `<id>` attribute of the `<action>` element and appears as a menu on the left side navigation of BizDesk.

```
<action id="auction/auction_list.asp" helptopic="cs_ft_auctions_FFBK.htm">
    <name>Auction Manager</name>
    <tooltip>Manage Auctions</tooltip>
    <tasks>
        <task icon="tasknew.gif" id="new">
```

The Auction Edit screen is referenced in the `action` attribute of the `<postto>` element beneath the task `<element>`. When the New or Open icons are clicked, the BizDesk framework looks at the `<task>` element to find what ASP page to post the data to. The BizDesk framework uses the data from the HTML form referenced by the `formname` attribute to execute a Form POST.

```
            <postto action="auction/auction_edit.asp" formname="newform"/>
            <name>&lt;U&gt;N&lt;/U&gt;ew</name>
            <key>n</key>
            <tooltip>New Auction</tooltip>
        </task>
        <task icon="taskopen.gif" id="open">
            <postto action="auction/auction_edit.asp" formname="openform"/>
            <name>&lt;U&gt;O&lt;/U&gt;pen</name>
            <key>o</key>
            <tooltip>Open Auction</tooltip>
        </task>
    </action>
```

Note: if BizDesk is running in debug mode and the BizDesk Framework can't find the associated ASP files, BizDesk will display the offending menu items in yellow.

After the changes have been integrated into the XML configuration files and the ASP files, the next time the Retail BizDesk Application starts up after the `global.asa` executes the changes will be reflected. An easy way to ensure BizDesk starts up fresh is to completely restart IIS from the Internet Services Manager.

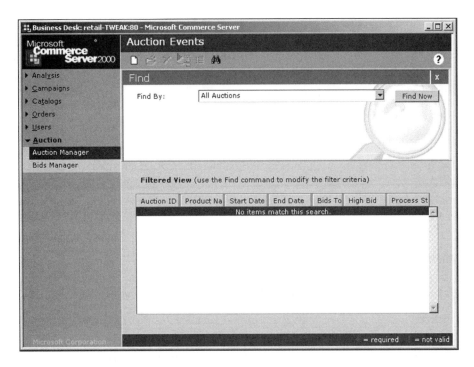

The Auction Component and the Auction Sitelet Code

Commerce Server 2000 ships with the Auction COM component, which abstracts the complexities of the Auction database tables, and the subtle differences in business rules between the various kinds of auction. This object is dual-interfaced, and can therefore be used by C++, Visual Basic, or scripting environments like ASP.

Auction Object Methods

Method	Description
AuctionAddBid	Adds or updates a bid on an auction.
AuctionAddItem	Adds a new auction item to the Auction tables.
AuctionBidNormalize	Normalizes a bid to the bid increment amount.
AuctionDeleteBid	Deletes a bid in an auction.
AuctionDeleteBids	Deletes all bids in a particular auction.
AuctionDeleteItem	Deletes an item and all bids on the item in a particular auction.
AuctionGetBid	Returns a recordset containing a bid from a specific user for a specific auction item.
AuctionGetBids	Returns a recordset containing all bids for an auction item.
AuctionGetItem	Returns a recordset for the item up for auction.

Table continued on following page

Method	Description
AuctionGetStatus	Returns a Dictionary object containing recordsets for the item up for auction.
AuctionInit	Initializes the Auction object.
AuctionRandomBids	Adds random bids to an auction to aid testing.
AuctionResolve	Resolves the auction based on the current settings and rules.
AuctionUpdateItem	Updates an auction item in the Auction tables.

Through the use of these functions the Auction object completely hides the inner workings of the business logic of an auction. The BizDesk module adds the ability to reference to products in the Product Catalog and users in the Profile System.

Adding an Auction

Auctions can be programmatically added with the Auction object, although much like the CatalogProducts_AuctionItem table, the parameter list is fairly flat and unruly.

```
'Function AuctionAddItem(szSKU As String,cyReservePrice As Currency,
'    nAvailable As Long,cyBidIncrement As Currency,nAuctionType As Long,
'    cyMinimumBid As Currency,fSealedBid As Boolean,fSealedInventory As Boolean,
'    fActive As Boolean,dtStartDate As Date,dtEndDate As Date,
'    nAutoCloseSeconds As Long,objErrorList As Object) As Long

'These lines are added by Microsoft for educational context
'lNumErrStrings is a Long
'dtStartDate is a Date
'dtEndDate is a Date
'oErrors is a list object

lNumErrStrings = oAuction.AuctionAddItem("123456", 2.50, 2, 0.50, 1, 1.50, False,
False, True, dtStartDate, dtEndDate, 0, oErrors)
```

It's much simpler to add an auction using the custom BizDesk Auction module than programmatically. The BizDesk module includes a product 'picker' that interfaces auctions with the Commerce Server Product Catalog. The BizDesk module uses the ASP helper function AddAuctionItem in auction_edit.asp to handle the dirty work. It uses the Auction object to manage the database tables, but then uses a combination of custom dynamic SQL and Commerce Server Objects to handle the relationships between the Auction tables and the rest of Commerce Server.

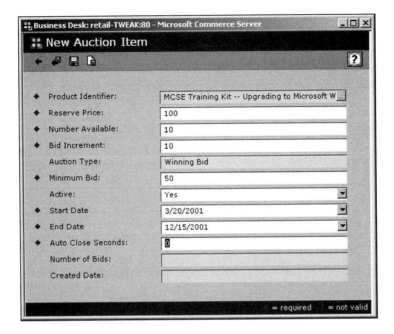

Listing Available Auctions

Surprisingly, the Auction object does not include a function for enumerating active auctions. Instead, the `auctionlib.asp` uses another ASP helper function `GetActiveAuctionList` that goes directly to the database with SQL.

```
Function GetActiveAuctionList()
On Error Resume Next
    Dim rsAuctionList
    Dim strAuctionQry
    Dim dteNow

    Set rsAuctionList = Server.CreateObject("ADODB.Recordset")

    'Disconnected recordsets require a client-side cursor
    rsAuctionList.CursorLocation = adUseClient

    dteNow = CDate(Now())
    strAuctionQry = "SELECT auction_id,product_id," _
                & "product_name,catalog_name,auto_close_date " _
                & "FROM CatalogProducts_AuctionItem " _
                & "WHERE active = 1 and end_date > '" & dteNow & "' " _
                & "AND auto_close_date > '" & dteNow & "'"

    'Retrieve the list of auctions in the database
    Call rsAuctionList.Open( _
                strAuctionQry, _
                GetTxConnectString(), _
                adOpenForwardOnly, _
                adLockReadOnly _
                )
    'Disconnect the recordset
    Set rsAuctionList.ActiveConnection = Nothing
    Set GetActiveAuctionList = rsAuctionList
End If
```

Once the disconnected ADO recordset has been returned, the `auctions.asp` page spins through the recordset creating an HTML table of available auctions.

```
<%
Do While Not g_rsAuctionList.EOF
    Dim strDetailUrl

    'For viewing product details
    strDetailUrl = PAGE_DETAIL

    'BuildGetRequest is a helper function to aid in the creation of URLs
    strDetailUrl = BuildGetRequest( strDetailUrl, QSTRING_AUCTION_KEY, _
        g_rsAuctionList.Fields(AUCTION_ID).Value _
        )
%>
<tr>
    <td>
        <%= g_rsAuctionList.Fields(AUCTION_PRODUCT_NAME).Value %><br/>
    </td>
    <td>
        <%= g_rsAuctionList.Fields(AUCTION_CLOSE).Value %><br/>
    </td>
    <td>
        <a href="<%= strDetailUrl %>">Details</a><br/>
    </td>
<%
    g_rsAuctionList.MoveNext()
Loop
%>
```

The Details link is appended to the auction ID in the URL as `auctiondetail.asp?auctionid=102` to be caught by the auction detail page later.

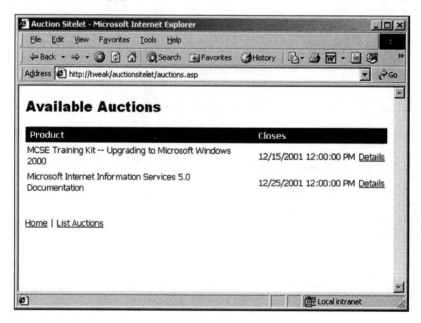

Auction Details

The unique identifier for an auction is passed into `auctiondetail.asp` and subsequently passed into the `AuctionGetStatus` method of the Auction object. `AuctionGetStatus` returns a dictionary with two Recordsets. One recordset is for the auction detail, the other for the bid detail.

```
oAuctions = InitAuctions()
'Retrieve the status dictionary
Set oStatus = oAuctions.AuctionGetStatus(Request.QueryString("auctionid"))
```

Once the auction status dictionary has been retrieved, the two disconnected recordsets are pulled out and their information is displayed using ASP.

```
<%
    Set rsAuction = oStatus.rsAuctionItem
%>
Detail for auction of <br/>
<b><%= rsAuction.Fields(AUCTION_PRODUCT_NAME).Value %></b><br/>
```

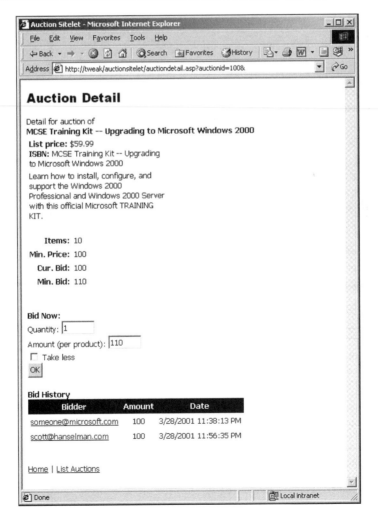

Listing Auction Bidders

Using the same dictionary retrieved from `AuctionGetStatus` above, a record set containing the bid history is retrieved.

```
'Retrieve the status dictionary
oAuctions.AuctionGetStatus(Request.QueryString("auctionid"))

'Now look at the bid details
Set rsBids = oStatus.rsAuctionBids
```

Then again, it's an easy matter to spin through the recordset of bids, listing the users that have bid on a particular auction.

```
<%
    Do While Not rsBids.EOF
%>
        <tr>
            <td>
                <a href="mailto:<%= rsBids.Fields(BID_E-MAIL).Value %>">
                <%= rsBids.Fields(BID_E-MAIL).Value %></a><br/>
            </td>
            <td align="center">
                <%= rsBids.Fields(BID_PRICE).Value %><br/>
            </td>
            <td align="center">
                <%= rsBids.Fields(BID_CREATED).Value %><br/>
            </td>
        </tr>
<%
        rsBids.MoveNext()
    Loop
%>
```

Bidding on Auctions

The `auctiondetail.asp` page posts its HTML form to `auctionbid.asp` for handling. The status of the current auction is retrieved as well as the user's e-mail address from their profile. If the auction and user are both valid, a bid on an auction is added by calling `AuctionAddBid`.

```
<%  Set oAuction = InitAuctions()
    Set oStatus = oAuction.AuctionGetStatus(CStr(colQString(FORM_AUCTION_ID)))

    'Some lines removed for brevity

    'dereference the query string collection for convenience
    colQString = Request.QueryString

    'Lookup the user's e-mail address
    Set oShopper = GetProfile(USER_ID, oAuthMgr.GetUserID(1), PROFILE_TYPE_USER)

    If (Not oShopper Is Nothing) Then

        Call oAuction.AuctionAddBid(  _
```

```
            CStr(colQString(FORM_AUCTION_ID)), _
            CStr(colQString(FORM_SHOPPER_ID)), _
            CStr(colQString(FORM_SHOPPER_ID)), _
            CStr(oShopper.Fields(USER_E-MAIL).Value), _
            CCur(colQString(FORM_BID)), _
            CLng(colQString(FORM_QUANTITY)), _
            CBool(fTakeLess), _
            CCur(oStatus.rsAuctionItem.Fields(AUCTION_CURRENT_MIN_BID).Value), _
            g_lstErrors _
            )
    End If
%>
    Your bid has been placed.
```

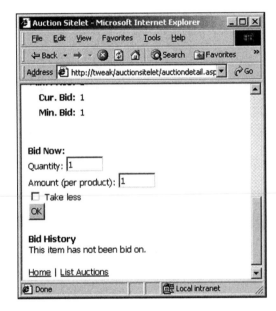

This sitelet does not come automatically hooked into the profile system. In `auctionsitelet/login.asp` there is a line of code with the name of the UserProfile hard coded as `GENERIC_LOGON_NAME`.

```
Call LogOnUser(GENERIC_LOGON_NAME, "password", 1, 90, 2)
```

Until the Auction Sitelet is hooked into your login screens, all bids will appear as if a single anonymous user was the bidder. For the purposes of getting the Auction Sitelet to work quickly for your own exploration, you can certainly hard code this line to load an authenticated user. For example:

```
Call LogOnUser("scotth", "password", true, 90, 1)
```

Resolving Auctions

When an auction is closed and a winner must be determined and notified, the auction's Process State changes in the BizDesk to awaiting process. An auction administrator can select the auctions from the Auction Manager in BizDesk and choose Process Auction from the BizDesk toolbar. The auctions are processed by the Auction BizDesk Module's `auction_util.asp`. Mail is sent to the winners of each resolved auction and they are marked closed and no longer appear in the list of active auctions.

```
'Loop through selected auctions to resolve, then send mail to winner(s)
nCount = 0
Set fdProcessed = rs("process_state")
Set fdAuctionID  = rs("auction_id")
Set fdBids = rs("number_bids")

Do While not rs.EOF
    ' Only process auctions with process state = "awaiting process"
    If fdProcessed.value = L_AwaitProcess_Text Then
        g_oAuction.AuctionResolve fdAuctionID, False

        'Send mail to notify winners
        Call MailBidWinners(fdAuctionID)
    End If
    rs.MoveNext
Loop
```

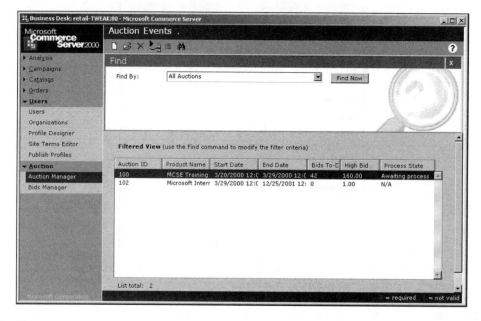

Notifying Users

The `ResolveAuction` method of the Auction object takes care of modifying the database tables to mark the winners. However, determining who won after the fact, and sending a notification e-mail to that user, is a bit more complicated.

```
Function MailBidWinners(sAuctionID)
    Dim sBidTable, sItemTable, sQuery, rs, dMail
    Dim sBidName, nWon, sProductName, cWinPrice, sMailText, sE-mail

    On Error Resume Next
    With g_oAuction 'passed the auction object the name of each database table
        sItemTable = .szItemTableName
        sBidTable = .szBidTableName
    End With
```

A dynamic SQL query is created and run to select the winning bids in the variable `rs`.

```
' Get bid winner information
sQuery = "SELECT a1.*, a2.product_name FROM " & sBidTable & _
    " a1," & sItemTable & " a2 " _
    & "WHERE a1.auction_id = '" & CStr(sAuctionID) _
    & "' AND a1.auction_id = a2.auction_id and a1.number_won > 0"
Set rs = Server.CreateObject("ADODB.Recordset")
rs.Open sQuery, g_MSCSAuctionConnStr, AD_OPEN_STATIC, AD_LOCK_READ_ONLY
```

A Commerce Dictionary is created that comprises the parameters passed to the `Commerce.SendSMTP` Component. Each entry in the dictionary is pulled out of the record set and comprises all the dynamic text that will be used to generate notification e-mails.

```
' Send e-mail notification to all winners
Set dMail = CreateObject("Commerce.Dictionary")
Do Until rs.EOF
    sBidName = rs("bid_name")
    nWon = rs("number_won")
    sProductName = rs("Product_Name")
    cWinPrice = g_MSCSDatafunctions.LocalizeCurrency(rs("win_price"),_
        g_MSCSCurrencyLocale)
    sMailText = sFormatString(L_GREETING_TEXT, Array(sBidName)) & vbCRLF _
        & sFormatString(L_MailBody_Text, Array(nWon, sProductName, cWinPrice))
    sE-mail = rs("bid_e-mail")
```

The commerce dictionary is loaded with the e-mail address and the full body of the notification e-mail.

```
With dMail
    .TO = sE-mail
    .Body = sMailText
    .Subject = sFormatString(L_MAILSUBJECT_TEXT, Array(sProductName))
End With
```

A reference to an instance of a `Commerce.SendSMTP` Component is stored in `g_oSMTP`. A Commerce Server 2000 MicroPipe executes against this component to send mail to each winner.

```
Dim oMPipe
Set oMPipe = Server.CreateObject("Commerce.MicroPipe")
Call oMPipe.SetComponent(g_oSMTP)
Call oMPipe.Execute(dMail, dMail, 1)


    rs.MoveNext
Loop
Set rs = Nothing
ProcessBidWinners = True
End Function
```

Be sure to set up your default SMTP Server under Site Resources in the Commerce Server Manager or users won't be notified of their winning bids via e-mail when an auction has been processed.

The name of the SMTP server that will send the notification e-mail is pulled from the Site Resources of the current site using `GetOptionsDictionary`. This is good coding practice and typical of Commerce Server 2000 sites. Always try to get configuration options from Commerce Server Configuration rather than using a constant.

```
Sub ConfigMailServer()
'Set up mail (SMTP) component object with configuration data.
   Dim sSMTPServer, dMailConfig
   sSMTPServer = g_MSCSAppConfig.GetOptionsDictionary("")_
      .Value("s_SMTPServerName")
   Set g_oSMTP = CreateObject("Commerce.SendSMTP")
   Set dMailConfig = CreateObject("Commerce.Dictionary")
   With dMailConfig
      .SMTPhost = sSMTPServer
      .From = SITE_ADMIN
      .ToField = "to"
      .SubjectField = "subject"
      .BodyField = "Body"
       .BodyType = 1
   End With
   g_oSMTP.SetConfigData(dMailConfig)
End Sub
```

Integrating with the Retail Site's Profile System

The first step to integrating the Profile Systems of the Retail Solution Site and a Sitelet is to get them to share cookies. The currently logged-in user's authentication ticket is stored in a cookie, but by default Commerce Server applications are set to have their own unique cookies.

In order to share cookies between Commerce Server applications, bring up the Properties Dialog for each Application and *uncheck* Set cookie path to application. When this is checked, each site receives its own cookie, which can be evidenced by viewing your browser's cookies. If you are running IE5 on Windows 2000 they are usually in `C:\Documents and Settings\<UserName>\Cookies`.

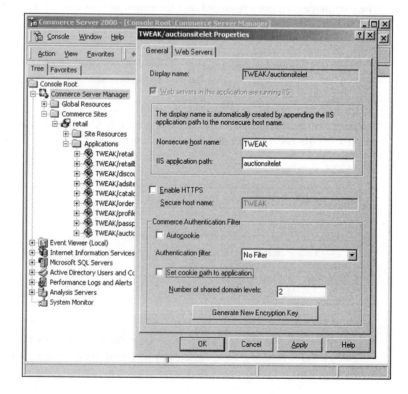

After turning off Set cookie path to application for both the Retail and AuctionSitelet Applications, user logins will be shared between apps.

Comment out the hard coded login line in `auctionsitelet/login.asp` to prevent continually logging in as Joe User.

```
'Comment the line below line out or you'll always login as this guy!
'Call LogOnUser(GENERIC_LOGON_NAME, "password", 1, 90, 2)
```

Now, login as whoever you like at http://<computername>/retail and then visit http://<computername>/auctionsitelet to place bids as that user. Now, when the Bid History is viewed, the effects of multiple users biding on the same item can be seen.

Bid History

Bidder	Amount	Date
someone@microsoft.com	100	3/28/2001 11:38:13 PM
scott@hanselman.com	100	3/28/2001 11:56:35 PM

Summary

The basis of this chapter was to help you get as much as you possibly can out of the source code Microsoft provides you with. We covered each of the seven Sitelets in increasing detail from the very basic Catalog and Advertising Sitelet, to the much more complicated Passport and Auction Sitelets. You learned that even Microsoft isn't perfect and that their sample code sometime ships with bugs. You learned some workarounds and gotchas to watch out for in the Sitelets sample code. You learned how to unpack, configure and install each of the seven Sitelets, and the additional set up needed to get them to work on the first try. You learned how powerful and easy Commerce Server 2000 can be when ASP, COM objects, SQL server, and the BizDesk framework all work together to solve a specific business problem.

Armed with this knowledge, and the knowledge you obtained from previous chapters, you're ready to go and create additional pieces of functionality yourself – extending and expanding on the framework and tools that Commerce Server has provided.

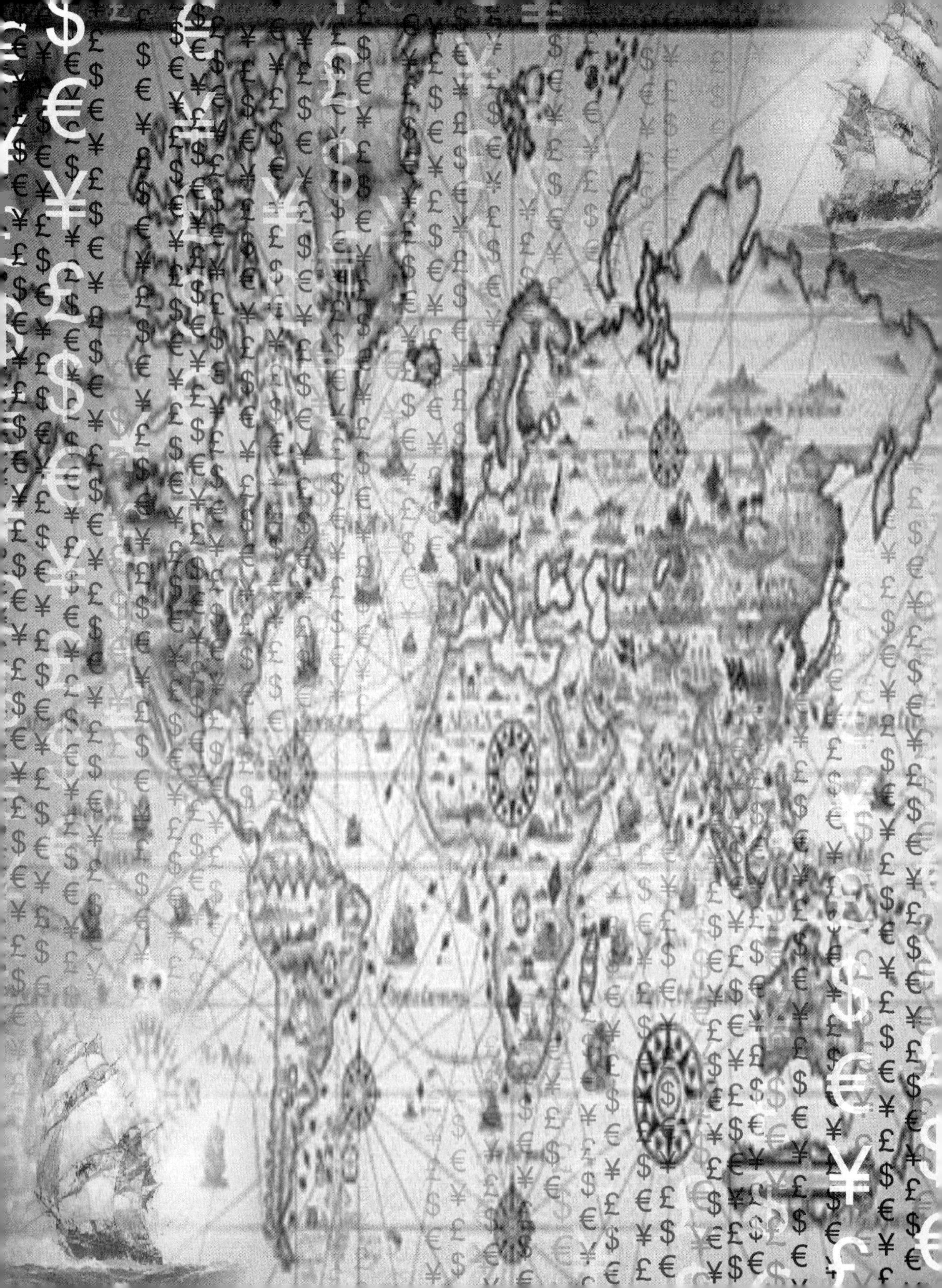

12

Third-Party Solutions for Payment, Tax & Shipping

One of the great benefits of using Commerce Server 2000 is that it enables us to integrate third party components into our pipeline architecture with relative ease. By now, we should be quite familiar with the plug-in functionality of components for Commerce Server. In this chapter, we will discuss extending the pipeline architecture for additional payment processing, tax calculation, and shipping calculation functionality through the use of third party components, in conjunction functionality exposed by a service provider.

Why do we need to extend the pipeline for payment, tax and shipping functionality? The out of the box components were never designed for production use in these areas. The Default Payment Component in Commerce Server only sets values that are needed by some of the other components to complete transactions. It never connects to a banking institution; therefore a live authorization does not take place. Tax components are similar. These components calculate tax rates based on values set, but they do not take tax calculation to the appropriate level of 'precision' that is needed by most businesses. The same goes for shipping calculation. The cost of shipping can vary between carriers, weight, the type of products shipped, the size of the packaging and the shipping method used; therefore the components included with Commerce Server only scratch the surface. These may work fine in certain instances, but when calculation need to be very precise, and may be quite complex, it is best to look into third party components and services.

We will look at a few of the companies that provide these services, and see how to incorporate their components into a Commerce Server 2000 solution site. We will see the ease of setting up this type of functionality with Commerce Server, and will gain an understanding of how these components and services differ from each other. By the end of this chapter, we should have a good understanding of how to implement each one of the components. We will discuss the following services:

❑   Credit Card Payment – considering **CyberSource** and **CyberCash** solutions

❑   Tax Calculation – considering **CyberSource** and **ClearCommerce** solutions

❑   Shipping Calculation – considering the **ClearCommerce** solution

There is also relevant information in Appendix D to aid you in your selection of a service provider and your implementation of the component/service with Commerce Server 2000.

Credit Card Payment Solutions

You've created an e-commerce site with Commerce Server 2000, and you have a large product catalog that you're sure will attract a lot of customers. Now there's just one catch: right now, you don't have any way to take their money. Commerce Server 2000 ships with a default 'out of the box' payment component that really does nothing more than fill a place in the pipeline until you choose to add a more functional component. The default payment component writes to the order._payment_auth_code name/value pair so that the required payment component will not fail. This component doesn't actually implement any credit card pre-authorization; there is no true billing of a customer's credit card, and no type of fraud screening taking place. The reason this component lacks this functionality is because there are so many different credit card providers available with many different rates, connections, banks and services. It would be impossible for Microsoft to supply a component to fit everyone's needs; therefore they provide us with a starting point and enable us to expand and move forward choosing exactly what you need from other service providers. If you want to process live transactions you *must* select a payment service that handles these things for you.

However, before we look at the implementation of services and components, it's important to understand just how these services work, the different types of services, and what we need to have already in place.

How Payment Processing Solutions Work

There are three types of payment processing solutions available today. There are many other solutions that can be customized to be integrated with existing payment solutions, but we will focus on those readily available for Commerce Server 2000.

❑   Real-time payment via the Internet

❑   Real-time/batched payment with in-house systems

❑   Redirection based payment solutions

We will discuss each of these individually, enabling you to determine which is best for your own situation.

Real-Time Payment Via the Internet

Okay, let's imagine this scenario: a customer is sitting at their computer with a full shopping cart, looking at the total cost of their order. They click the Purchase button after entering their credit card information, and a few seconds later get a message on the screen informing them that the specified credit card is over its limit.

This is an example of real time credit verification – so what exactly happened? Let's break it down a little:

1. First, the user clicked the Purchase button, sending credit card information to the e-commerce web server.

2. The e-commerce web server then opened a connection across the Internet to a payment service provider and sent the customer's credit card information (and, very probably, their billing address information as well).

3. The payment service provider (which is connected to the banking network) sent that information on to the bank where the e-commerce business holds its merchant account.

4. The bank ran a pre-authorization on the card number, along with an AVS (Address Verification Service) check, to make sure the billing address given matched that of the card being used.

5. Once this was complete, the banking processor sent back 'card over its limit' information to the payment service. This in turn handed the information back to the e-commerce site's web server, which used it to generate a message for display on the customer's browser.

To expand on why someone would use this type of service, we'll cover some of the advantages:

❏ Ease of implementation.

❏ Low maintenance, because the payment system is a service and another company's responsibility.

❏ Low cost.

The adjacent diagram shows the interaction between the systems involved:

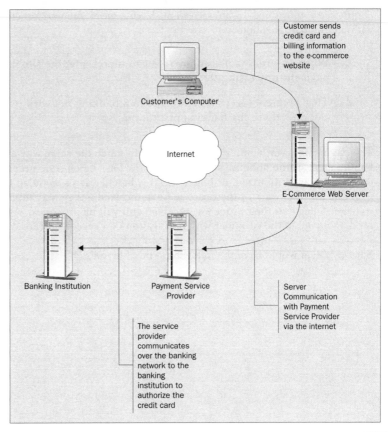

However, there are some disadvantages to this type of system:

❑ In most cases there must be a constant Internet connection between the payment provider and the web server. If this connection fails, it will result in lost sales. Some providers do offer a dial up link or leased line into their external systems to alleviate that possibility.

❑ We must deal with latency over the Internet service provider's server and the service's network – response times can increase and decrease depending on congestion levels; ultimately, we have no control over the speed of the connections. Remember, this is also a service – check into the uptimes of the services, because if they go down, so does your website if you do not have another form of payment or telephone ordering system in place.

Real-time/Batched Payment with In-house Systems

There are some types of systems that that do not send information via the Internet to process payments. Some of the third party solutions available are sold as packages that handle all of the processing in-house. With these systems, the communication is much faster because the system is running on the same network as the web server.

What might be another benefit to a system that runs in-house? The payment processors that transmit data on the Internet usually charge a fee per transaction. For a large enterprise that processes many transactions it will be more cost effective to pay a larger initial fee and bring the payment processing inside the company. Also, with in-house systems, it is potentially easier to tie in customer service call centers, phone operators who take orders, the e-commerce site, and point of purchase systems. Many of the Internet based payment solutions are designed for server use only and for integration with e-commerce applications. In-house systems have a more open architecture, allowing them to be used within custom applications.

1. When an order is placed on an e-commerce site, the site's web server will contact the payment-processing server.

2. This payment server is connected to a banking network (via a leased line) and makes a call directly to the banking institution.

The payment server handles the transactions in much the same way as the payment service providers handle them. Some in-house systems also allow for a batch-style processing architecture, whereby the credit cards are authorized (or billed) in large batches at a scheduled time. In this case, the customer won't be asked to wait for their card to be authorized – they may just receive a message from the website stating that their order was received and will be processed. At a later time, the system might send an e-mail to the customer with notification of a successful card authorization (or failure).

Such a system would have the following type of layout:

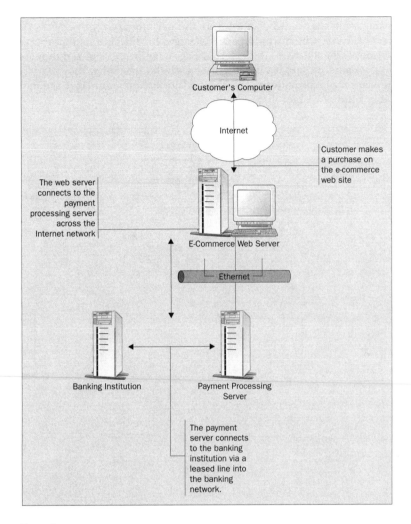

Customer's Computer

Internet

Customer makes
a purchase on
the e-commerce
web site

The web server
connects to the
payment
processing server
across the
Internet network

E-Commerce Web Server

Ethernet

Banking Institution

Payment Processing
Server

The payment
server connects
to the banking
institution via a
leased line into
the banking
network.

Redirection Services

Some companies offer services that allow us to post data or link to their page for payment services. They then handle all the payment processing, and can even return a success/failure message to the customer. This type of service is usually cheaper on per-transaction rates, monthly fees and development time. However, one of the drawbacks is that the user may get a sense of leaving the website, which will make some users feel the transaction is not secure.

> *This type of service requires no direct component integration with Commerce Server, so we're not going to go into detail here on how to implement the service. However, it is important for developers to know that this type of service exists and how it works in order to make informed design decisions.*

Using the same scenario given in the previous two payment type solutions, we can begin to understand where this type of service would come into play:

1. While the customer is looking at the total for their order, they click the Purchase button to proceed.

2. At this stage, the site would post information pertaining to the order to the service provider's website, which would generate pages for the submission of credit card information. In many cases, the external pages can be customized to match the look of the original e-commerce site, leaving the user with the sense that they are just accessing one system. The service provider processes the transaction and places the money in the e-commerce company's merchant account.

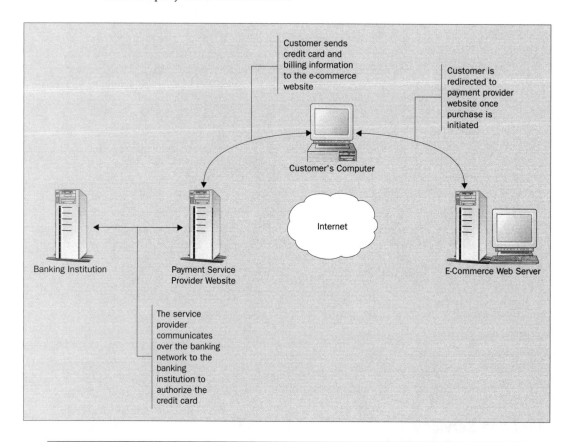

A very important concern with this type of service, as with all payment services, is security. If the system is designed poorly, a person could potentially manipulate URL strings and trick the merchant's site into thinking that the payment was successful.

Commerce Server 2000 Payment Integration

At this point, we will cover the implementation of two major payment service providers that supply components that easily integrate into Commerce Server 2000. There is very little development involved with these components, as the implementations are fairly straightforward.

The first component we will start with is a component developed by the CyberSource Corporation. This component is simple to implement and provides a wide range of services.

CyberSource Commerce Component

The CyberSource payment solution is an Internet-based solution that transmits information to the CyberSource servers for processing using an RSA and DES public key encryption scheme they call Simple Commerce Messaging Protocol (SCMP). The component then takes the returned information and puts it back into the `OrderForm` object.

The CyberSource Commerce Component is a single Commerce Server 2000 pipeline component that can be placed in a number of different pipeline templates. The property page of the component configures the services that the component will perform.

You will need:

❑   The CyberSource Commerce Component – download from http://www.cybersource.com/CS2000/.

❑   A merchant account with CyberSource – register at http://www.cybersource.com/register.

❑   A live Internet connection.

❑   A live implementation for actual billing and payment of credit cards/checks will *require* you to have a banking merchant account for processing credit cards. CyberSource will work with you to set this up and they have a large amount of useful documents on their website to help you.

Finally, the examples will make use of the Retail Solution site, so this must be installed and configured.

Setup and Configuration

Once we have downloaded the CyberSource Commerce component, we can execute the install program and install it to the directory of our choice. You should find three executables in the Start Menu under Programs | CyberSource Commerce Component.

❑   Register Component

❑   Test a SCMP Transaction

❑   Test the Commerce Component

You must first register the component – this sets the necessary values in the registry for the component to be seen as a pipeline component. Once you have registered the component, you will be able to add the component to a pipeline template using the Pipeline Editor (as demonstrated in Chapter 6).

In order to test your connectivity to the CyberSource server, you can execute the Test a SCMP Transaction program to make a test transaction. This is useful in determining whether the component can communicate with the server.

> *The* Test Commerce Component *program actually creates an* OrderForm *object and executes the CyberSource component inside a pipeline object. This is useful in testing the component itself after initial install.*

Creating the Public/Private Keys

Once you have registered as a CyberSource merchant, you should receive a merchant ID. This will be used as your login to the CyberSource support websites as well as in configuring your component. One of the most important uses of your ID is that it ties your encryption keys to your CyberSource merchant account.

A CyberSource merchant account is quite different to a banking merchant account. A banking merchant account involves your company's relationship with the banking institution that handles the actual payment of credit card transactions. A CyberSource merchant account, on the other hand, is your account with CyberSource to access their system.

At this stage, you will need to create your new keys using the program provided by CyberSource. These keys are used to encrypt the data as it travels the Internet to the payment servers. This will require your CyberSource merchant ID.

1. Open a command prompt window and navigate to the directory in which you installed the CyberSource component.

2. In the keys subdirectory, you'll find the file ecert.exe which you should execute with your merchant ID as the argument – so if your merchant ID happened to be WROX_COMMERCE, you would enter:

```
C:\...\keys> ecert.exe WROX_COMMERCE
```

This will generate your new keys, place them in the keys subdirectory, and automatically update the CyberSource server with your key.

Once you have completed this task, you're ready to start the integration with the Retail Solution Site.

If you would like more information on the security used, it would be a good idea to read over CyberSource's security overview at http://www.cybersource.com/technology/security.html.

The Retail Solution Site

This section of the chapter deals with implementation of the CyberSource component within the Retail Solution site. For a detailed discussion of the Retail Solution Site, please see Chapter 10. The CyberSource implementation does not require any changes to the actual ASP code, but does require changes to the purchase pipeline. This will allow payment processing to occur.

Due to the nature of third party components, they cannot accommodate every possible usage and custom code written. Service providers try to be as general as possible in their component design, so it's sometimes necessary to make changes in the ASP code to facilitate integration of the component into the site.

Adding the Component to the Retail Site Pipeline

For the payment service CyberSource offers, we will be working with the checkout.pcf file found in the pipelines directory of the Retail site. Open the file using the Commerce Server Pipeline Editor (see Chapter 6 for details) – now delete the Default Payment component provided by Commerce Server, and add the CyberSource Commerce Component in its place.

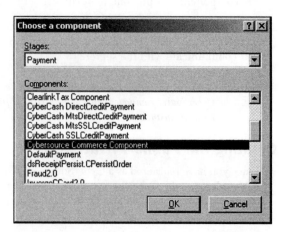

Once we have the component in place we can now set up the service it will use. Double-click the component and the property page will open. The page first displayed allows us to select services.

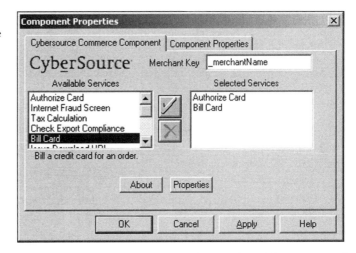

One of the other important fields on this property page is the **Merchant Key** text box. This must match the merchant ID used when the key set was created. This is how the CyberSource servers identify the account the transactions are being passed to.

Once we select a service from the available services, the check (the tick) will become green. We can then click the check to move the service to the selected services box. For payment there are normally two services that are selected:

- ❑ Authorize Card
- ❑ Bill Card – the Bill Card service actually processes the payment and initiates the transfer of funds from the card to the merchant account

The authorize card service performs a pre-authorization on the credit card before actually settling the payment amount. This checks for funds available and also performs AVS (Address Verification Service) to make sure the billing address for the card matches the address given by the user. Once you set the service, the components properties will be displayed.

This is another tabbed dialog box that is accessible from the main property page via the **Properties** button. The Bill Card service requires that the Auth Request ID be filled in. Therefore, we need to check the box **Auth Request ID Filled by Authorize Card**.

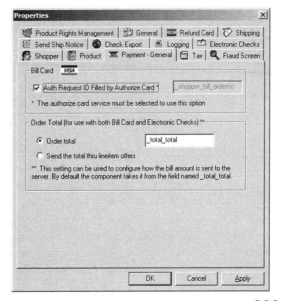

At this point, we must configure the address keys the component will read from the `OrderForm`. To do this, select the **Shopper** tab. This will allow the component to know which values are read for the billing address of the customer and are required for the payment services.

The values from the `OrderForm` that we are concerned with are as follows:

CyberSource Component Fields	Commerce Server 2000 Address Dictionary Keys
First Name	first_name
Last Name	last_name
Bill Address1	address_line1
Bill Address2	address_line2
Bill City	city
Bill State	region_code
Bill Zip	postal_code
Bill Country	country_code
Bill Phone	tel_number
Bill Email	email

These must be filled in for the values on the **Shopper Properties** page. The retail site does not have the e-mail information in the form, so we need to enter a value. Even though CyberSource requires an e-mail address to be present, the component itself will fill in this value for the billing and shipping e-mail address if one is not present. If you change the name/value pairs in the address dictionary to something else, you will need to make sure that these match what you enter in the component. The values are based on a packaged retail solution site only.

Once the property page is correctly filled in, it should look like this:

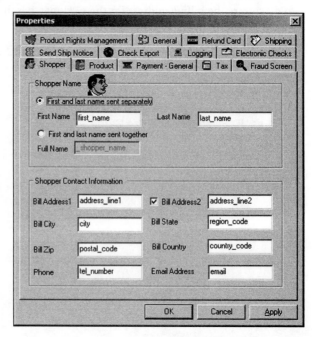

Once this configuration is complete, you can execute a transaction with CyberSource.

One sure way to verify the transaction is to check the logging tab on the component and have it log to a file on the server. This will allow you to see the actual information the component sends to the service.

The next step is to add a scriptor component just after the CyberSource component. This will check the code returned from CyberSource, and will indicate a failure if the transaction was not completed successfully.

Remember, a credit card that will exceed its limit with the purchase is not an error, but a condition in which the pipeline should stop execution and relay the message back to the customer. The CyberSource component writes a reply code value to a key in the `OrderForm` depending upon which service was called. This value contains the success or failure the transaction.

Adding the Scriptor to the Pipeline

With the `Checkout` pipeline, we need to be able to roll back the transaction if the returned code is not successful. The simplest way to handle this is to use a scriptor component and write script to check the value and return a success or failure value. For this, we will be looking at two values the `CyberSource` component adds to the `OrderForm` object. Why two? Because we call two services in our example: `Authorize Card` and `Bill Card`.

The first step is to add the scriptor component just after the **CyberSource Commerce Component**.

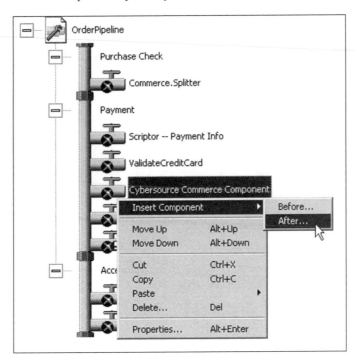

Now, the two values we are validating are `auth_rflag` and `bill_rflag`. The values returned could each be one of the following:

❑ `S` – indicating a successful call to the service.

❏   E – indicating an error during call to service (error is returned in `auth_rmsg*` or `bill_rmsg*`).

An example of an error message returned is: "The request data was either invalid or missing: The following database input fields are either invalid or missing: customer_cc_number". This message would be returned if the credit card field was not correctly populated.

❏   D – indicating that the call was declined (reason is returned in `auth_rmsg*` or `bill_rmsg*`).

> **Do not use the returned error messages to write responses to the users. These responses are system based and might confuse the users or give the user too much information about their transaction (particularly if the user is attempting to make a fraudulent purchase).**

Let's put the following code into the scriptor, so as to validate these messages.

```
Function MSCSExecute(config, orderform, context, flags)
    Dim iOutput
    Dim strAuthRFlag
    Dim strBillRFlag

    strAuthRFlag = UCase(orderform.value("auth_rflag"))
    strBillRFLag = UCase(orderform.value("bill_rflag"))

    Select Case strAuthRFlag
        Case "S"
            iOutput = 1
        Case "E"
            iOutput = 3
        Case "D"
            iOutput = 2
    End Select

    Select Case strBillRFlag
        Case "S"
            iOutput = 1
        Case "E"
            iOutput = 3
        Case "D"
            iOutput = 2
    End Select

    MSCSExecute =iOutput
End Function
```

The following screenshot shows the raw data output for an invalid card number for the CyberSource payment component:

Retail_CYBS

[Home | Catalog | Basket]

Product Search

Search | Advanced

Login
Sign-in
New user

Categories
Business Software
Development Tools
Featured Products
Games
Hardware
Home Productivity
Internet Products
Macintosh Software
Operating Systems & Servers
Reference

Other Payment Options: Credit Card ▼ Submit

Credit card

The following request field(s) is either invalid or missing: customer_cc_number
The following request field(s) is either invalid or missing: customer_cc_number
DINVALIDCARD

Name on card: Marshall Jarrod
Card number: 4111111111111112
Type: VISA ▼
Expiration month: April ▼
Expiration year: 2004 ▼

Reset Submit

Copyright (c) 1999-2000 Microsoft Corporation.

Behind the Scenes

The site should now be able to complete test transactions using the CyberSource component.

The component itself connects to the CyberSource servers once this transaction begins. The user's address and credit card information is read from the component and an 'offer' is created. An offer is a string that contains all of the necessary information about the user, which services are to be called and the credit card information. This string is then encrypted using the keys generated to secure the data, and is then transferred over the Internet to the CyberSource servers. Once the data is received it is decrypted and passed on to the banking networks. They will either authorize the card or bill the card depending on the services called, so long as the card is valid and funds are available. Once the banking networks have finished processing the payment, they send information back to CyberSource, where the transaction is logged, and which returns the pass/fail message back to the component, along with any relevant messages.

You're now ready to start using the payment services from CyberSource. However, we'd strongly suggest that you consult the CyberSource support site at http://www.cybersource.com/support/ for their documentation. They go into much more detail explaining how to optimize the components, provide a checklist for development procedures, and many other things that will aid you in your implementation.

CyberCash Component for Commerce Server 2000

The CyberCash component for Commerce Server 2000 is very easily implemented. This component allows for payment processing over the Internet using a pipeline component customized for their services.

The CyberCash service also allows for a fraud check service, which we will not discuss implementing with Commerce Server 2000.

What you will need:

❑ The CyberCash Commerce Component – download from www.cybercash.com
❑ A live Internet connection

Once again, our examples are based on the Retail Solution site, so that must be installed and configured.

In order to process actual live credit card transactions, you must register for the CyberCash cash register service at www.cybercash.com. If this is not done, no exchange of funds will take place.

Setup and Configuration

Once you have the component downloaded, execute the setup program and accept the defaults. This will install the necessary components for the CyberCash service.

From this point you may be able to insert the component into a pipeline template to allow for your site's communication with the CyberCash service. The documentation for the component is downloadable but is not part of the setup package.

The Retail Solution Site

The CyberCash component is one of the easiest components to implement. There are no code changes in the ASP pages required, and the integration is fast and painless.

Before we add the component to a pipeline for the site, it's important to understand the two different components that can be chosen. These are:

❑ MTSDirectCreditPayment
❑ DirectCreditPayment

The MTSDirectCreditPayment should only be used with pipelines that will run under the MTSTxPipeline or the PooledTxPipeline. This component supports transactions and will not function properly in a pipeline that is executed using another pipeline type.

The DirectCreditCardPayment component is not transaction-enabled; therefore it should be used with the MTSPipeline and PooledPipeline objects.

> It is highly recommended that when dealing with payment software the component is transaction enabled. One thing to note however: the banking network is not wrapped within the same transaction context as the pipeline. Once a transaction has completed in the banking network, an error in a later pipeline component only rolls back changes the local system has made; it does not void the transaction with the banking institution.

Adding the Component to the Retail Site Pipeline

To add the CyberCash component to the retail site, open the `checkout.pcf` file using the Pipeline Editor. You must delete the DefaultPayment component from the payment stage. Once this is done, it's time to add the CyberCash component to the pipeline.

Right-click on the Required Payment Component and select Insert Component│Before. This will allow us to insert the component before the Required Payment Component. Select the CyberCash MTSDirectCreditPayment Component.

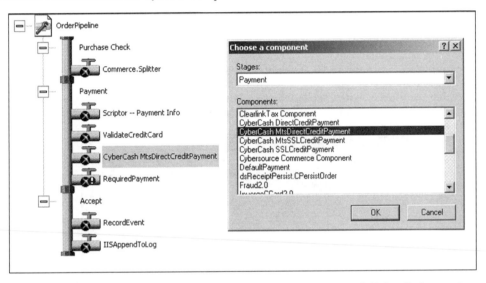

The CyberCash component does not require that you have a registered CyberCash merchant to test. The default settings on the component will allow you to complete test transactions with the CyberCash service.

Once you have a merchant account established with CyberCash, you will need to make a few changes to allow the component to process live transactions.

The CCID (an identification number assigned by CyberCash to identify merchants) and Merchant Key fields are required; these fields will be changed once you have your own merchant account from CyberCash. The host location will not change.

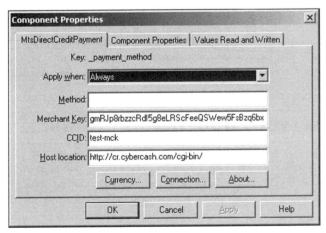

The next property page we will discuss is the Currency property page that may be accessed from the main property page. This will allow you to set the currency type you will be working with. You may select the currency via the drop down list or you may specify your own currency, currency code and the number of digits after the decimal place. This is useful when you do not wish to use one of the currencies listed.

The next property page enables us to configure the connection the component makes to the CyberCash service. Due to varying network infrastructures, the web server may or may not be behind a proxy server. With this feature you may select the proxy server the component should communicate through and also you may allow the component to use a specific access account.

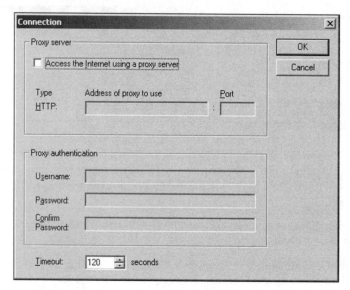

Once you have configured your connection support (if needed), you may perform test transactions with the CyberCash component until you are ready to use your own merchant account. During testing it is a good idea to log the execution of your pipelines to validate that the component is reading and writing the correct values. Some things to look for in the log are the payment_auth_code and _payment_pop.error-message name/value pairs. If the transaction is successful, you should have an auth code and if an error occurred the error will be written to the error message name/value pair.

Commerce Server 2000 Tax Integration

The next topic we'll look at is the use of third party components to calculate tax on products and services being sold over the Internet. These components, like the payment processing components, use the Commerce Server 2000 Pipeline functionality and are fairly easy to implement.

When discussing the payment components we started with an understanding of how they worked. The tax components function in much the same way, although there are no redirect services available for tax calculation alone. Many times, with the redirection services, tax calculation is part of the payment process or that value is handed off to the site handling the payment service and is not calculated by the service at all.

We will discuss two types of tax calculation services within this chapter – real time over the Internet and real time in-house. CyberSource provides these services and components for the tax calculation over the Internet and ClearCommerce for in house tax calculation. There are many other tax calculation services available but these two companies had readily available Commerce 2000 Server solutions.

Before we begin with the technical implementation it is important to understand that a tax expert for your business should be consulted. There are many different tax laws from state to state, country to country and sometimes even postal code to postal code. We will not discuss what these laws are or how they may affect your business because they are too numerous and out of the scope of this chapter. We will only be discussing the technical implementation of the services provided by these two vendors.

CyberSource Commerce Component

CyberSource Tax Services provide tax calculation for the United States, Canada, and the main European countries. These services can be applied down to the line-item level of the product price, product type, and the physical location of the company (Tax Nexus).

This section of the chapter will discuss a basic implementation of the CyberSource component to calculate tax on products in the Retail Solution Site. As stated previously, there are so many factors that go into calculating taxes, it is advised to consult a tax professional and plan the implementation with the features needed.

This section will not follow the previous section format due to the fact that this chapter has already gone through the installation process of the CyberSource component in the payment section. It will cover only the new specifics of configuring the component for use in the tax calculation service.

Adding the CyberSource Component to the Retail Site for Tax Calculation

Tax calculation takes place in the Total pipeline (total.pcf), in the tax calculation stage. The Total pipeline is configured with the Regional Tax component that uses information supplied through the BizDesk to calculate sales tax. The first step is to replace the Regional Tax Component with the CyberSource Commerce Component.

If the Regional Tax component is in place, there will be problems, as one will overwrite the values the other has calculated depending on which of the two components is executed last.

The next step is to configure the component to call the Calculate Tax service. This will tell the CyberSource service what action needs to be performed with the data being sent to the their servers. This is done by selecting the Calculate Tax service from the left side of the available services box and clicking the blue check mark button.

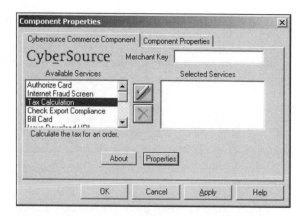

Once the service is selected, it will bring up the tax configuration property page. With this property page you can configure the component to look for certain values in the OrderForm object. Not all of these keys will be used; depending on your business and how you need to calculate taxes it is possible you may not use any at all.

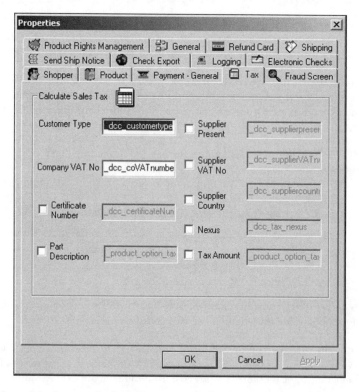

We'll discuss a few of the keys and what they are used for but will not go into great detail on these because it will vary from business to business as to which keys are used.

CyberSource Key Name	Definition
Customer Type	This is used for calculation of VAT taxes. This is a required field for VAT.
Company VAT number	Field required for VAT calculation.
Certificate Number	Field that is optional for VAT calculation. This is the VAT certificate number.
Part Description	Optional field contains product information.
Supplier Present	Optional field for VAT if the supplier is different to the e-commerce merchant.
Supplier VAT Number	Optional field for VAT calculation.
Supplier Country	Optional field for VAT calculation.
Nexus	Optional field for listing areas to compute tax in.
Tax Amount	Optional field. Overwrites CyberSource calculated tax and adds the amount of the value listed to the product.

The following values also need to be set for the component to function properly. This is again review of some of the implementation of values used for the payment processing service. The **Shopper** tab of the properties page must contain values that are present in the `Address Dictionary`. This is needed to determine the appropriate tax rates to apply to the product price.

CyberSource Component Fields	Commerce Server 2000 Address Dictionary Keys
First Name	first_name
Last Name	last_name
Bill Address1	address_line1
Bill Address2	address_line2
Bill City	city
Bill State	region_code
Bill Zip	postal_code
Bill Country	country_code
Bill Phone	tel_number
Bill Email	email

Once these are configured you can test the component by running through a purchase on the Retail site.

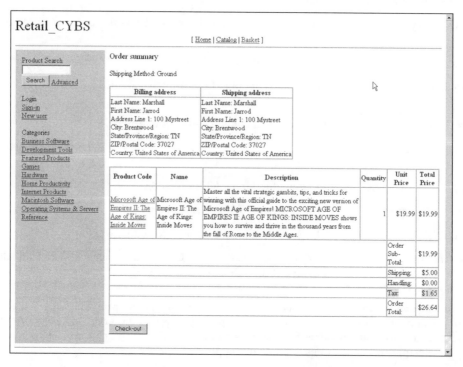

Within the figure above, we can see that for the address shown, there is a $1.65 tax calculated. Prior to this page, the `basket.pcf` and `total.pcf` pipelines were executed. Within the `total.pcf` file, the CyberSource component read the necessary information from the `orderform` then created an 'offer'. An offer is the information sent to CyberSource in the format their servers expect. Once this offer is generated, it is encrypted using the keys created and sent across the Internet to the CyberSource server. The CyberSource system calculates the tax then sends the information back to the component. The component then writes the data back to the `orderform` object. The page above displays the data that has been returned.

The following figure shows a different address and tax figure.

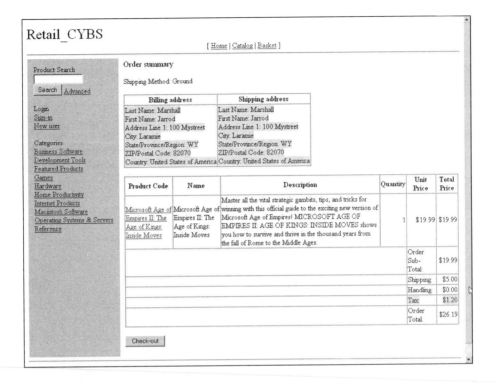

ClearCommerce Clearlink Component

The next component we will discuss in the tax calculation area is the **ClearCommerce Clearlink** component for Commerce Server 2000. The ClearCommerce tax component is part of a package of several components for Commerce Server 2000. The package consists of tax calculation, shipping calculation and payment services. This component is the first in-house service payment, tax and shipping component we have discussed. This component connects to an in-house engine to perform its calculation or to a ClearCommerce Service Provider that hosts the ClearCommerce engine at their location.

We will only be discussing the integration with Commerce Server 2000 in detail and keep the ClearCommerce engine to a minimum. As this system requires an in-house or hosted engine to perform its tasks, ClearCommerce has provided a test server that is accessible via the Internet for testing and trial purposes. We will focus mostly on what they offer as a test solution.

Within the downloaded package, there is extensive documentation on implementing this component and also the APIs for the Clearlink 3.8 engine. It is highly recommended that the Clearlink APIs be read for the service you need to implement. For work with the ClearCommerce Clearlink engine, a C or C++ compiler is required.

We will cover a few things needed to set up a Retail Solution site to use the Clearlink Commerce Server 2000 component. What you will need:

❑   Download the Clearlink Component from http://www.clearcommerce.com/cs2000/

❑   A functioning Retail Solution Site

❑   An Internet connection that allows communication on port 1139

For a live implementation of this component, the Clearlink Engine is required. If only tax or shipping calculation is used, a leased line to the banking network is not required.

Setup and Configuration

Once the component has been downloaded, the first thing is to execute the setup application `Setup.exe`. This will install the ClearCommerce components. The default installation location is `C:\Program Files\clearcommerce corporation\Clearlink\`. Within this directory you will find all of the documentation as well as the component `.dll` files, the test encryption certificate, a sample ASP page and sample pipeline configuration files (`.pcf` files). The `readme.doc` file included with the download includes all of the information needed to integrate with the retail solution site. We will be working with the sample `checkout.pcf` and `total.pcf` files within this section of the chapter.

The first thing we need to do is create the COM+ applications in which these components will reside:

1. Open up the **Component Services MMC**, and select the computer, expanding down to **COM+ Applications**.

2. Right-click on **COM+ Applications** and select **New | Application**. This will start the wizard to create a new application. Click **Next**.

3. Choose to **Create an empty application**, and click **Next**.

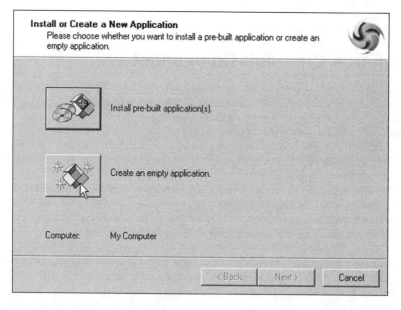

4. Enter the name **ClearCommerce Tax** and verify that the activation type is **Server**. Click **Next**.

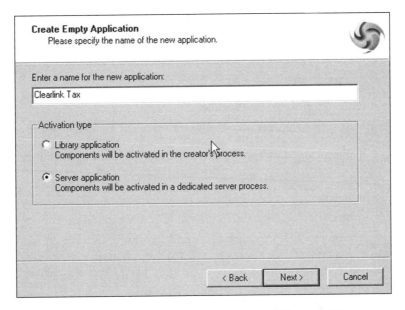

The Application Identity screen sets what user the component will run as. The components will function fine if set to 'interactive user' while someone is logged onto the server, but most servers should be locked and a user should not be logged on constantly.

5. Create a user called ClearCommerce, make sure password does not expire is checked and user must change password on next login is unchecked when creating this user.

6. Add this user to the Administrators group.

Note that this is for testing purposes only and should not be used in a production environment. Security is a delicate matter and a user with only the *needed* access rights should be used on a production server.

7. Move back to the COM+ wizard and select This User. Set the user name and password for the user just created. Click Next, and then Finish.

At this point we must add the component to the application:

8. Expand the application, click on Components and select New | Component. This will launch the COM+ New Component wizard. Click Next.

9. Select to Import components that are already registered.

10. Find `Commerce.ClearlinkTax.1` and then select it. Click Next and Finish.

Once the component is imported into the application we can begin integrating it into the website.

The Retail Solution Site

The Retail Solution Site with the ClearCommerce component *must* be modified for this component to perform its task. The ClearCommerce documentation goes into detail and even the download supplies code to replace existing Commerce Server 2000 files. Therefore, we will not cover the same ground that the documentation goes into.

The download consists of a file called _setadrs.asp – this file sets shipping and billing address information in the OrderForm once a user selects an address from the address book. ClearCommerce supplying the example code for this is very helpful, but we need to make changes to allow for the anonymous users that wish to make a purchase. This is not covered within the ClearCommerce documentation, and that is what we will discuss in this section.

Adding the Component to the Retail Site Pipeline

With the ClearCommerce download, two .pcf files are supplied. These files are exact duplicates of the files unpackaged with the retail solution site except the ClearCommerce components have been added. To begin with our implementation we should copy these files over to the pipeline directory under our store directory.

As the component is already part of the pipeline and adding components to a pipeline has already been covered earlier in this chapter, we will not walk through adding it to an empty pipeline.

Open the total.pcf file with the Pipeline Editor once you have copied the file over. We will be working with the tax component first, therefore we will need to remove the shipping component from the pipeline so that we do not get any errors associated with having that component in the pipeline.

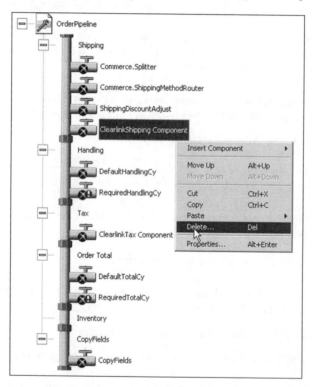

At this point, let's focus on the property page of the Clearlink Tax component and understand the fields that are set – properties that may be set are as follows:

❑ Key File Name – This is the path to the encryption key used by the component to communicate with the server. For testing purposes, ClearCommerce supplies a file called cs2k.pem, which is found within the directory of the documentation. Make sure the path on the component property page matches the patch to this file.

❑   Host Name – This is the hostname of the server that will process the requests.

❑   Port – This is the port on which communications to the server will be handled. It must match the port on which the server is listening for requests.

❑   ConfigFile – This property is the name of the file residing on the server hosting the Clearlink engine. This file is used to configure the services. For testing purposes ClearCommerce has a file set up specifically for the downloaded components called cs2k.

❑   Process Mode – This property allows you to configure the behavior of the component and has four possible values. These values are very important for payment processing but during shipping calculation they do not provide much value – possible values are:

   ❑   Live – This sets the component to process all transactions as if they were live. Failures, declines, successes will all be processed. During production this should be the value used.

   ❑   Good – All service calls return successfully.

   ❑   Decline – This will force the component to return a transaction declined (useful for payment processing testing).

   ❑   Duplicate – The final value allows you to simulate that a duplicate order has just occurred and the component returns accordingly. (Useful for payment processing testing.)

❑   Debug – The debug value is a string path. The component will create a debug file at this path with the file name specified. If no debugging is needed, set the value to zero.

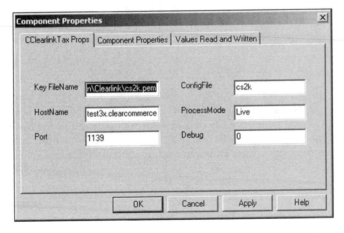

For our purposes these values will not change through the course of our implementation. You may wish to set the debug value so that you may see what is taking place.

Executing the site at this point will return errors because the ASP code has not been modified to support the component at this time.

Modifying the Active Server Pages

The ClearCommerce component requires values from the OrderForm that are present but found in different areas of the OrderForm or with different key names. One of the downsides to this component is that you cannot configure where it looks for its values; you must supply it with the values it needs. Another downside to this component is the broad implementation: not only are you maintaining your web server/commerce site but also the ClearCommerce Clearlink system. This can be a double-edged sword: it allows for a great amount of control but added development time and maintenance.

The `Tax Calculation` component needs two values not found in the `OrderForm`: `order.ship_to_state` and `order.ship_to_zip`. Since these keys don't exist in the `OrderForm` we must make sure they are available ourselves. The `_setadrs.asp` file included with the download of the `ClearCommerce` component adds these keys with the corresponding values to the `OrderForm` by copying them over. We will be doing the same thing, but in a different active server page – `addrform.asp`.

This is a self-referencing file that retrieves user information through an HTML form when the user is anonymous and does not have an address book within the database. Another file we will be working with is `const.asp` for setting up our constants and following the coding conventions used in Commerce Server 2000.

To begin, let's make the necessary additions to `const.asp`, which is found within the include directory of the retail solution site. This file will be empty if you have unpackaged the site and made no modifications to it.

We need to define the key names that will be used as follows:

```
<%
'=====================================
'File: Const.asp
'=====================================
Dim ROOT_SHIPPING_STATE,ROOT_SHIPPING_ZIP
'Root key names
ROOT_SHIPPING_STATE="ship_to_state"
ROOT_SHIPPING_ZIP = "ship_to_zip"

%>
```

These constants will give us a section of code for easier editing should these names change. Once we have defined our constants, we can go back and write the code to add the keys and values to the `OrderForm`. Within `addrform.asp`, I added a new subroutine to allow for this called `SetRootAddrValues`. This takes the `ship to address` dictionary and the `OrderGroup` object as arguments and sets the new key names and values using the function `SetKeyOnOrderForms()`, which is defined in `std_ordergrp_lib.asp`.

```
'=================================================================================
' File: addrform.asp
' Purpose: Add required name/value pairs to the orderform for the ClearCommerce
component
'=================================================================================
Sub SetRootAddrValues(byval dictShipAddr,byval objOrderGroup)
    Call SetKeyOnOrderForms(objOrderGroup, _
    ROOT_SHIPPING_STATE,dictShipAddr.value("region_code"))

    Call SetKeyOnOrderForms(objOrderGroup, ROOT_SHIPPING_ZIP, _
    dictShipAddr.value("postal_code"))
End Sub
```

After this modification you should be able to connect to the ClearCommerce component and receive a calculated tax value back.

> You should refer to the Clearlink 3.8 API documentation and understand the tax configuration file that is used on the server to calculate taxes. This allows you to customize the level of calculation necessary for your business.

Integrating Clearlink Shipping

Calculation of shipping can be handled in many different ways and Commerce Server ships with some nice out of the box features for shipping calculation as well as integration into the Biz Desk application. If Commerce Server has out of the box components why would you not use the shipped components?

One scenario would be a situation in which you had many different systems calculating shipping for customers that ran on separate platforms. You would need a central shipping calculation service. Another situation would be that you might want real time shipping calculation based on rates available from major shipping companies. These services provide the rate with more detailed information than just weight – sometimes package size and contents provide a role in determining the cost of a package as well as the different shipping methods (next day air, international shipping, etc) provided by the different carriers.

We will only be discussing one shipping service within this chapter due to the fact that Commerce Server 2000 specific components for shipping are only available from ClearCommerce at the time of this writing. It only makes sense to tie directly into this section because we will be working with the same pipelines and files – adding the shipping component to them so that our site calculates shipping.

Setup and Configuration

We will begin by configuring the component for use in COM+ services. This is exactly what we did when we set up the tax component except we will be using the shipping component.

1. Open up the Component Services MMC and select the computer, expanding to COM+ applications.

2. Right-click on COM+ Applications and select New | Application. This will start the wizard to create a new application. Click Next.

3. Choose to Create an empty application and click Next.

4. Enter the name ClearCommerce Shipping and verify that the activation type is Server. Click Next.

5. On the Application Identity screen, select This User. Set the user name and password for the user created when configuring the tax COM+ application. Click Next and Finish.

Now, to add the component, follow these steps:

6. Expand the application, choose Components and select New | Component.

7. This will launch the COM+ New Component wizard. Click Next.

8. Select Import components that are already registered.

9. Find `Commerce.ClearlinkShipping.1` in the list of components and then select it. Click Next.

10. Click Finish.

The Shipping Component in the Pipeline

The `ClearCommerce` shipping component has exactly the same property page as the `Tax` component and functions in much the same way. At the beginning of the ClearCommerce section, we removed the shipping component from the `total.pcf` file. This was to break everything out and focus only on tax at that time. If this had not been done, we would not have been able to complete tax calculations because the code was not present in the Active Server Pages to support the shipping component.

Let's go ahead and add this component back to the pipeline at the end of the shipping stage. The component will show up within the applicable components as ClearlinkShipping Component.

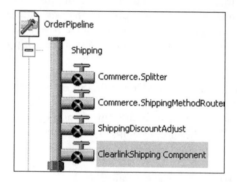

A few things to be aware of with the shipping component, before we begin modifying the Active Server Pages to support the component, are the values read. Some of these values will need to be filled into the `OrderForm` via the Active Server Pages, but there is one in particular that will not. The component requires that `Orderform.shipping_weight` be present to handle calculation. This means two things:

❑ Every item in the catalog must have a weight property with a valid value.

❑ We must total this weight and save the calculated total in the root of the `OrderForm` object in the pipeline before the shipping component is executed.

If you do not have a weight property in your catalog, you must add this along with a valid weight through the Biz Desk. The key name does not matter as we will be totaling this value ourselves and you will be able to accommodate for your own naming conventions.

The simplest solution to calculating the total weight is to add a scriptor component to the pipeline just before the Clearlink Shipping Component. The code will loop through the items in the basket and total up the weight – placing the total in the key `shipping_weight`. The `QueryCatalog` component in the `basket.pcf` file will take care of adding the product weight to the `OrderForm` object once it executes. The key in the `OrderForm` is as follows for a product attribute called 'weight' – `_product_weight`.

The following is sample code to show the calculation of weight total within a scriptor pipeline component running just before the Clearlink Shipping component:

```
Function MSCSExecute(config, orderform, context, flags)
Dim nItems
Dim items
Dim lWeight
Dim iLineItem
Dim lineitem

Set items = orderform.value("items")
nItems = items.count
lWeight = 0
For iLineItem = 0 To nItems - 1
    Set lineItem = items(iLineItem)
    lWeight = lWeight+ lineItem.value("_product_weight")
Next

orderform.shipping_weight    = lWeight

MSCSExecute = 1
End Function
```

This will complete the tasks needed on the pipeline side of the integration. We must now modify the
Active Server Pages to support the component.

Modifying the Active Server Pages

To integrate the ClearCommerce shipping component we will be working with the functions we have
already created. As with the tax component, _setadrs.asp has been modified and is part of the
download of the component; therefore we do not need to worry about this file. We will modify the ASP
pages that only affect the shoppers that wish to buy without having an account (anonymous shoppers).

We will be writing code to add the following name/value pair to the OrderForm object
Ship_to_country. Ship_to_state and ship_to_zip are also required fields, but this is also
required for the tax component and we have already made the necessary changes to support this.

Following the coding conventions used earlier, we should first edit the const.asp file to add the
constants to support these key names.

```
<%
'========================================
'File:Const.asp
'========================================
Dim ROOT_SHIPPING_STATE,ROOT_SHIPPING_ZIP, ROOT_SHIPPING_COUNTRY
'Root key names
ROOT_SHIPPING_STATE="ship_to_state"
ROOT_SHIPPING_ZIP = "ship_to_zip"
ROOT_SHIPPING_COUNTRY="ship_to_country"
%>
```

The next step is to edit our custom function that we had written for the tax component in
addrform.asp.

This will add the value of the country to the root of the OrderForm object.

```
' ========================================================================
' File: addrform.asp
' Purpose: Add required name/value pairs to the orderform for the ClearCommerce
' component
' ========================================================================
Sub SetRootAddrValues(byval dictShipAddr,byval objOrderGroup)
    Call SetKeyOnOrderForms(objOrderGroup, _
        ROOT_SHIPPING_STATE,dictShipAddr.value("region_code"))
    Call SetKeyOnOrderForms(objOrderGroup, ROOT_SHIPPING_ZIP, _
        dictShipAddr.value("postal_code"))
    Call SetKeyOnOrderForms(objOrderGroup, ROOT_SHIPPING_COUNTRY, _
        dictShipAddr.value("country_code"))
End Sub
```

At this point you should be able to execute test transactions with the component.

Let's walk through what happens here with the shipping component. The user selects the shipping method they would like to have their product shipped with. Once this happens, the basket and total pipelines are executed.

The total pipeline executes the shipping component and passes the orderform to it. The shipping component reads in the information necessary for making a calculation on shipping cost. The component then connects to the Clearlink Engine server using SSL. This server contains configuration files that are used to calculate the shipping rate based on the information the engine just received. Once this information is calculated the server returns the cost back to the calling server (our e-commerce web server). The component then sets values in the orderform based on the data it just received from the engine server.

> An important thing to note since this chapter did not go into detail about the ClearCommerce engine itself: the **shipping** method must map to the shipping methods listed in the ClearCommerce shipping file. This is described within the Clearlink 3.8 API documentation.

Summary

With this chapter, we have covered payment processing components and services, tax calculation services and also one of the shipping component services available for Commerce Server 2000. This chapter should prove as an example to the extensible architecture of Commerce Server 2000 and show how it is easy to add on features and services to the solution sites. The design of the pipeline architecture allows for such easy implementation and also allows developers to write their own components if the software does not ship with a needed component or if there is not a third party solution available.

The components and services discussed in this chapter also extend beyond what was discussed and it would be a very good idea to look into all of the different services offered from each provider. Another such provider within the payment industry that was not discussed is Paylinx. Paylinx offers an in-house-based system only; therefore we have not explained its integration. If you have noticed with the examples provided in this chapter, the Internet-based systems are usually the easiest to integrate but they do not offer the speed and enterprise-wide integration potential of the in-house solutions.

When considering these types of services for your e-commerce site consider three factors:

- **Cost of ownership** – This will be a very important consideration as it does cut into your profits as an e-tailer. Along with this, you must look at:

  - Cost per transaction – does the service charge per transaction?

  - Monthly service fee – does the service charge on a monthly basis?

  - Customer support – is customer support free or do you have to pay?

- **Speed** – One of the most important aspects of site design now is performance. With these types of services being either Internet-based, or even in-house, the time it takes to communicate between the site and the service provider can vary greatly. With Internet-based systems it is hard to judge the amount of transactions the service provider is processing and you must have faith that they will scale appropriately. With in-house systems it's easier because you can monitor the system's performance yourself.

- **Ease of implementation** – Does your company need to focus on time to market? Are the resources available with the correct skills to implement the solution? There are times when a solution must be implemented no matter what the cost, but many companies do have concerns when choosing a solution if they will be able to support, administer and extend the initial roll outs. The ease of development must be balanced with the features that are required.

There will be many new versions of these types of services and components arising for Commerce Server 2000. Microsoft keeps a frequently updated list of the third party ISVs that have written components for it on their website at http://www.microsoft.com/commerceserver/thirdparty/partners.htm. Clearly this list will continue to grow as other companies move into the market. Many of the companies that offered products and services for Microsoft Site Server 3.0 Commerce edition have yet to release components for Commerce Server at the time of writing, but since we're right at the beginning of the product's life, I am sure we can expect many great new components and services for Commerce Server 2000.

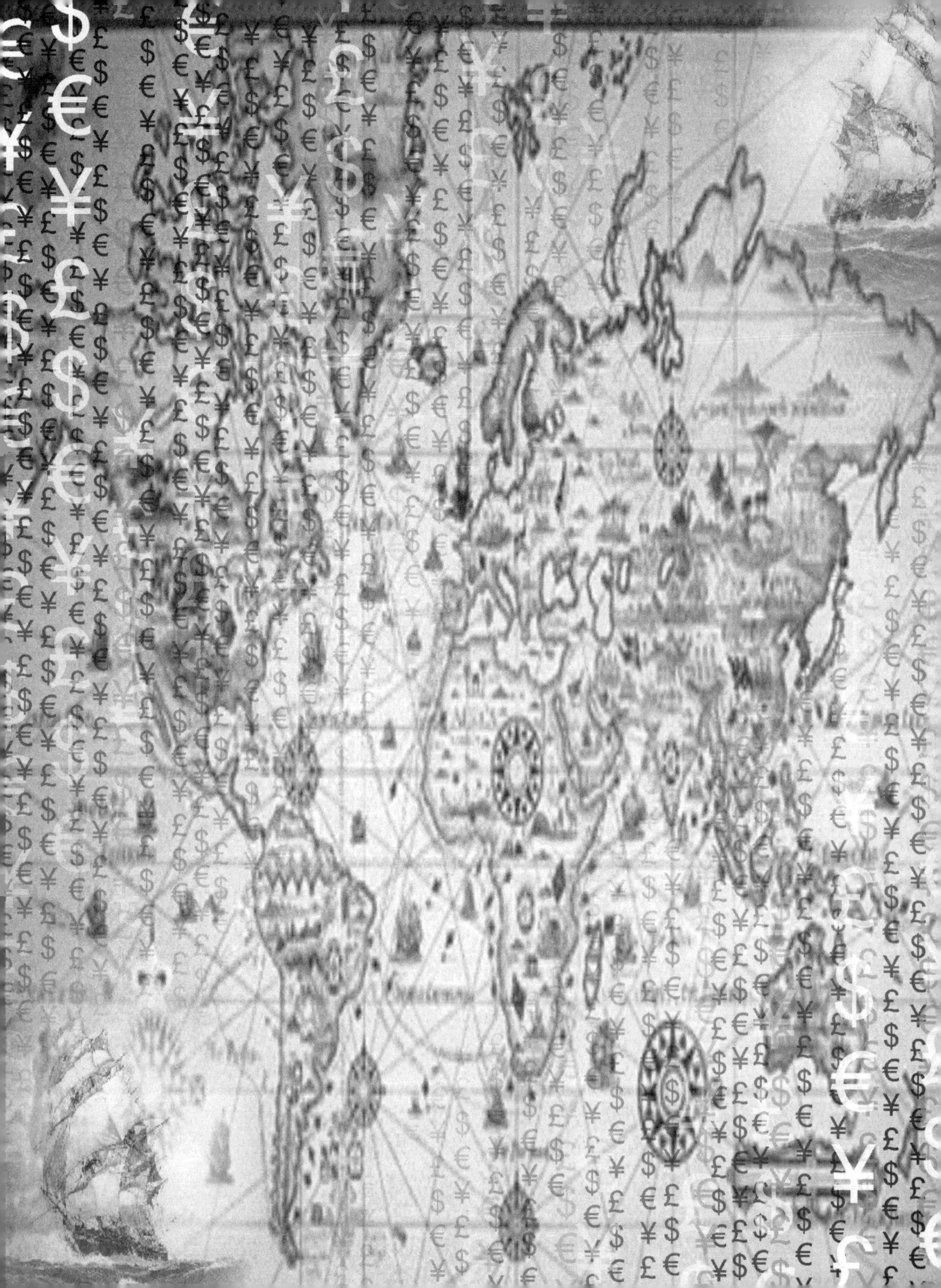

BizDesk Architecture

BizDesk is a powerful new web application provided with Commerce Server 2000 for administering e-commerce websites. In addition to providing extensive built-in functionality, its highly modular design means that it's quite straightforward to extend and customize.

In particular, it makes use of two new browser-based technologies, which are currently only supported by Internet Explorer 5.5 and above – **HTML Applications** (HTAs) and **HTML Components** (HTCs). An HTA allows tighter control over navigation than a conventional web application, while HTCs are web components containing properties, methods, and events. They allow component-based web development, which has the benefits of providing code reuse and a uniform look and feel for administration interfaces.

The primary goal of this chapter and the next is to show you how to create and integrate custom BizDesk modules for your server. Once we have explored the overall architecture of the BizDesk, we will take a detailed look at integrating a custom module called 'Synonyms'. This module provides quite generic functionality and demonstrates a user interface for basic database operations such as creating, editing, and deleting records. In addition, it illustrates searching, scrolling and sorting of recordsets. The techniques we present can be easily adapted to construct other modules.

BizDesk makes extensive use of HTCs, so much of the rest of this chapter will focus on a detailed examination of the HTCs provided by default with Commerce Server 2000. We shall consider their properties, methods, and events, and present a sample application to demonstrate each one.

HTML Applications

Let's begin with a quick look at HTML Applications (HTAs). The screenshot below shows a sample HTA in action, based on code from a file named HTMLApp.hta, which you can find in the sample download for this chapter.

As we've observed, HTAs are a special type of web application supported by recent versions of Internet Explorer. A key feature of HTAs is that they restrict navigation to the content area of the web page by not displaying the standard menu and tool bars. This gives the application complete control over what navigation controls are made available to the user, and it must provide these controls within its content area. The example shown above uses simple buttons for navigation. Note that this HTA is configured to have thick borders and its own icon (in this case, the BizDesk icon).

The HTML for the body of this page is quite standard:

```
<body scroll='no'>
  Address:
  <input id='txtURL' type='text' value='http://www.wrox.com'>
  <input id='cmdGo' type='button' value='Go'>
  <iframe id='fraMain'></iframe>
  <input id='cmdClose' type='button' value='Close'>
</body>
```

The DHTML script block contains some simple functionality for the two buttons on the page. The first navigates to the target address, while the second closes the application:

```
sub cmdGo_onClick()
  document.all.fraMain.src = txtURL.value
end sub
'******************************************
sub cmdClose_OnClick()
  window.close
end sub
```

The HTA properties of the above page are obtained by simply adding the following element to the header block:

```
<hta:application
  applicationName='HTMLApplication'
  border='thick'
  borderStyle='sunken'
  caption='yes'
```

```
        contextMenu='yes'
        icon='HTMLApp.ico'
        innerBorder='yes'
        maximizeButton='yes'
        minimizeButton='yes'
        navigable='yes'
        scroll='yes'
        scrollFlat='no'
        selection='yes'
        showInTaskbar='yes'
        singleInstance='no'
        sysMenu='yes'
        version='1.0.0.0'
        windowState='normal'>
    </hta:application>
```

The attributes used in the `<hta:application>` element are described in the following table:

Property	Description
ApplicationName	Name of application
Border	Border style of the window (thick|dialog|thin|none)
BorderStyle	Border style of the content area (normal|complex|raised|static|sunken)
Caption	Determines if title bar is displayed (yes|no)
ContextMenu	Determines if context menu is displayed (yes|no)
Icon	File name of application icon
InnerBorder	Determines if 3–D inner border is displayed (yes|no)
MinimizeButton	Determines if minimize button is displayed (yes|no)
MaximizeButton	Determines if maximize button is displayed (yes|no)
Navigable	Determines if links are displayed in a new window (yes|no)
Scroll	Determines if scroll bars are displayed (yes|no)
ScrollFlat	Determines if scroll bars are flat or 3–D (yes|no)
Selection	Determines if content can be selected (yes|no)
ShowInTaskbar	Determines if application is displayed in taskbar (yes|no)
SingleInstance	Determines if only one instance of the application can run (yes|no)
SysMenu	Determines if the system menu is displayed (yes|no)
Version	String defining application version
WindowState	(normal|minimize|maximize)

Unlike conventional HTML pages, HTAs are trusted applications and consequently have read/write access to the file system and the registry on the client machine.

Although an HTA is trusted, it may contain a `<frame>` or `<iframe>` element that is not trusted. To explicitly mark a `<frame>` or `<iframe>` element within an HTA as safe or unsafe, use the `application` attribute. The allowable values of the `application` attribute are 'yes' and 'no'. Below, an `<iframe>` is explicitly marked as unsafe.

```
<iframe id='fraMain' application='no'></iframe>
```

The above concepts can be applied to BizDesk by noting that the target of the BizDesk shortcut contains the following HTA file:

```
<html>
  <head>
    <title>Retail BizDesk</title>
    <hta:application
      applicationname='Retail'
      border='thick'
      caption='yes'
      icon='Retail.ico'
      showintaskbar='yes'
      singleinstance='yes'
      sysmenu='yes'
      windowstate='maximize'
      version='1.0'>
    </hta:application>
  <script language='VBScript'>
    option explicit
    '*************************************************
    sub document_onContextMenu()
      with window.event
        .returnValue = (.srcElement.tagName = "INPUT" or _
                        .srcElement.tagName = "TEXTAREA")
      end with
    end sub
    '*************************************************
    sub document_onKeyDown()
      window.event.returnValue = false
    end sub
    '*************************************************
  </script>
  </head>
  <body>
    <frameset>
      <frame
        src='http://localhost/retailbizdesk/bizdesk.asp'
        scrolling='no'
        application='yes'
        style='height: 100%; width: 100%; border: none' border='0'
        frameborder='0'
        framespacing='0'>
      </frame>
    </frameset>
  <body>
</html>
```

The `header` block contains an `<hta:application>` element. In addition, it uses the application attribute to mark the contained `<frame>` element as safe. The `script` block further limits user interaction by restricting context menus and disabling keyboard input. It is worth noting for later that the URL of the page displayed in the body of BizDesk is http://localhost/retailbizdesk/bizdesk.asp. This observation will be used when creating a Visual InterDev project for debugging.

BizDesk Overview

This section presents an overview of the BizDesk installation, navigation, and configuration files. In addition, it defines some terms used within BizDesk.

Client Installer

The first time BizDesk is started, via the URL http://localhost/RetailBizDesk/ the file `default.asp` is run. This checks that the browser is of version IE5.5 or later and then transfers control to `ClientSetup.asp`. (If the browser version is **not** IE5.5 or later, it simply exits with a warning to upgrade your browser.) `ClientSetup.asp` downloads the file `ClientSetup.cab`. If you examine this `.cab` file in WinZip you will notice that it contains `ClientSetup.ocx` and several other files. The OCX is instantiated by `ClientSetup.asp` and passed four parameters:

- ❑ Server name (localhost)
- ❑ Port (80)
- ❑ Application name (RetailBizDesk)
- ❑ Protocol (http or https)

When the hyperlink Start Business Desk, displayed by the OCX file, is clicked the above parameters are used to create the BizDesk HTA file, in this case called Retail `LOCALHOST 80.hta`. A File Save dialog pops up for you to save the HTA file. Once you have saved, shortcuts to the HTA file are created, and BizDesk started for the first time.

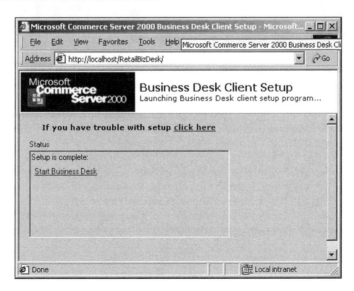

The purpose of this rather unusual installation procedure is to ensure that BizDesk runs as an HTA and that the correct files are downloaded. BizDesk can be placed in debug mode by setting the variable MSCSEnv in global.asa to DEVELOPMENT. In debug mode BizDesk can be run as a regular web application.

Note that in production mode BizDesk will not start unless it is run as an HTA.

Navigation

Since BizDesk is implemented as an HTA, it has to provide navigation within the content area of the page. It does this through a vertical menu bar (on the left side of the screen) and a taskbar (near the top of the page).

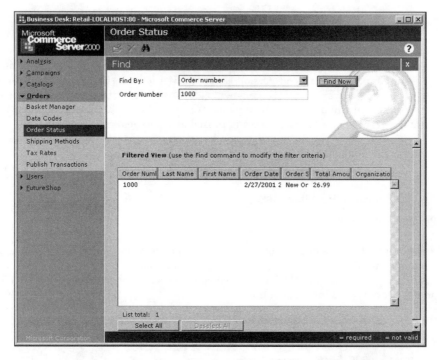

The expandable headings in the navigation bar are called **categories**. Items listed under a category represent **modules**. A module consists of a collection of ASP pages together with a configuration file. Modules contain two types of pages: **list pages** and **edit pages**. List pages are read–only pages that either display a list of items (allowing the user to select one for editing) or perform a search to find a specific item. Edit pages are used to modify data. The entry point to a module is usually a list page. (The Tax Rates module is an exception to this rule.)

List pages and edit pages both contain a taskbar at the top of the page. There are two types of taskbar buttons: those requiring a selection from the list and those requiring no selection. BizDesk pages are implemented in DHTML, so the taskbar buttons can be enabled and disabled by events within the page. Taskbar buttons can also implement drop-down menus. List pages generally implement a Find pane to facilitate searches. Both list pages and edit pages contain a status line at the bottom of the page.

When an item is selected and opened (via a taskbar button) control is transferred to an edit page where data can be entered or modified.

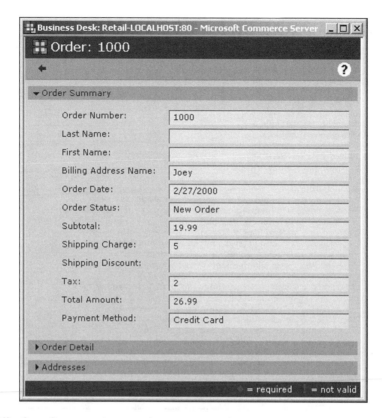

Edit pages differ from list pages in several respects:

❑   Edit pages use the entire screen and never display a navigation bar

❑   The taskbar of an edit page generally consists of four buttons: Back, SaveBack, Save and
     SaveNew

❑   Edit pages record whether the page has been modified and enable and disable the taskbar
     buttons accordingly

❑   Edit pages use a different color scheme from list pages

*Note that since edit pages do not have a navigation bar, it is impossible to transfer directly from an
edit page in one module to an edit page in another without returning to list page.*

Configuration Files

The BizDesk vertical menu bar and the taskbar are customizable by means of XML configuration files.
The vertical menu bar is configured through a single master configuration file, called `bizdesk.xml`. In
addition, each module has a module configuration file that defines the taskbar for all pages within the
module. All configuration files are located in the `config` directory under the application root.

The master configuration file defines the categories that exist, and specifies the parent category for each
module. Note that the framework category is used by BizDesk and should not be altered or deleted.

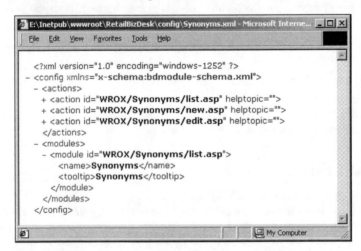

Module configuration files define an `<action>` setting for the entry page and all task target pages. The module configuration file for the Synonyms module, `Synonyms.xml`, defines three ASP pages. The entry page is `List.asp`. The module configuration file also defines the module name and tooltip.

Action elements define the properties of the taskbar buttons on a specific module page, such as: the internal name, display name, icon, access key, and tooltip. In addition, it determines whether data is posted between pages. Action elements of module configuration files will be examined later in the chapter.

Adding a Category and Module to BizDesk

The default installation of BizDesk contains a fixed set of categories and modules. The first step towards extending BizDesk is to create a new category and add an existing module to it. The sample code for the chapter contains two modules, Synonyms and Test. These samples are contained in the `Modules\Synonyms` and `Modules\Test` directory. In this section we will present a detailed procedure for adding the Synonyms module to BizDesk. The end result of this procedure will appear as follows:

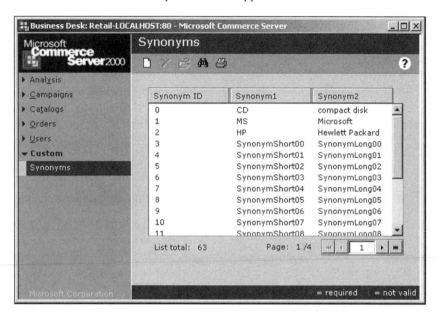

Note that a new category Custom *has been added to the navigation bar and that this category contains the Synonyms module.*

In order to simplify the installation procedure below, the root application name of BizDesk will be assumed to be `RetailBizDesk`. This saves having to qualify the instructions with a variable root. Therefore, if you are using a different application name, please make the appropriate adjustments.

To create a new category Custom and add the existing module Synonyms to it, proceed as follows:

1. Create a new directory under `RetailBizDesk`. In order, to keep our modules separate from the rest of BizDesk, create a directory called `WROX` with a subdirectory `Synonyms`. Thus create the following directory structure.

`C:\inetpub\wwwroot\RetailBizDesk\WROX\Synonyms`

2. Copy all the files from `Chapter13\Modules\Synonyms` to the new `WROX\Synonyms` directory.

3. Move the module configuration file, `Synonyms.xml`, from `RetailBizDesk\WROX\Synonyms` to `RetailBizDesk\config`.

4. Edit the master configuration file, `bizdesk.xml`, and add the following `<category>` element to the body of the `<categories>` element:

```
<category id="custom">
  <name>Custom</name>
  <key>m</key>
  <tooltip>Custom</tooltip>
</category>
```

This defines the new category 'Custom'.

5. Now add the following <moduleconfig> element to the body of <moduleconfigs>:

```
<moduleconfig id="Synonyms.xml" category="custom"/>
```

This assigns the Synonyms module to the 'Custom' category.

6. Check that the paths used in the module configuration file, Synonyms.xml, are correct. If you have followed the suggestions above then no changes should be necessary. (Otherwise, adjust the paths so that they are valid paths relative to the root of the RetailBizDesk application.) The path used by our module is WROX/Synonyms/.

Note that the paths used in include files assume two directory levels.

7. Restart IIS or unload the application so that the configuration changes will take effect.

8. Start RetailBizDesk and note that the Synonyms module is now installed under the Custom category.

Before running the Synonyms module, the database used by the Synonyms application must be created and populated with data. The sample code for the chapter contains a SQL directory with the following two SQL Server scripts:

Script	Description
SynonymsDB.sql	Creates the table and stored procedures for the Synonyms module
SynonymsData.sql	Populates the table used by the Synonyms module

These two scripts should be run in the retail_commerce database using SQL Query Analyzer.

The Synonyms Module

The purpose of the Synonyms module is to provide a simple utility for managing abbreviations used in site searches of product data. For example, the abbreviation CD could be mapped to 'compact disc'. Thus, when a user performs a search both terms would be used in the keyword list, enhancing the search.

The Synonym module uses the three ASP files: List.asp, New.asp and Edit.asp. List.asp, the entry point for the module, was shown above in the previous section.

Edit.asp is used for modifying records. The field values below have not been modified and therefore the save buttons are disabled. Note that the primary key, SynonymID, is greyed since it is read–only. The red diamonds indicate required fields. A record cannot be saved if any required field is missing a value.

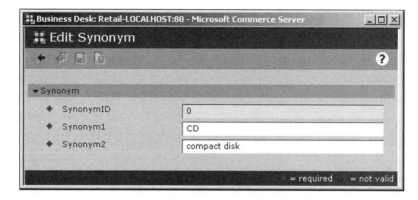

New.asp is used for creating new records. The fields below have been modified and therefore the save buttons are now enabled.

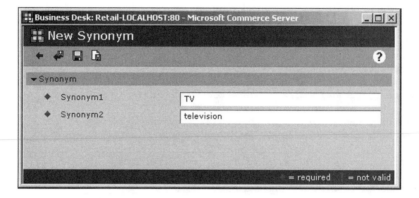

HTML Components

Notice from the screen shots of the Synonyms module, that the controls used are not conventional HTML controls. Instead they are HTML components (HTCs) installed by Commerce Server. Therefore, before proceeding with a detailed examination of the Synonyms module we need to take a detailed look at HTCs. First we will look at HTCs in general and then we will focus on the specific properties of the HTCs shipped with Commerce Server.

HTC Overview

HTCs are web components – they have properties, methods, and events. The role of HTCs within web development is exactly analogous to that of ActiveX controls in Visual Basic development. Microsoft has submitted a proposed specification for HTCs to the W3C – for more information, you may wish to check out http://www.w3.org/TR/1998/NOTE–HTMLComponents–19981023).

When Commerce Server is installed, it creates a virtual directory, Widgets, containing the following HTCs:

❑   EditField

❑   EditSheet

- ❏ ListSheet
- ❏ ListEditor
- ❏ DynamicTable
- ❏ TreeView
- ❏ ListBox
- ❏ ExpressionBuilder
- ❏ QueryBuilder
- ❏ ProfileDesigner

HTCs are text files with an `.htc` extension. HTCs are implemented via a combination of XML and scripting. They contain an interface section and an implementation section. The interface section defined by the `<public>` element declares the properties, methods, and events of the component. The implementation section is defined via a `<script>` block. The code for the `EditSheet` HTC is shown below with the body of the `<script>` block omitted:

```
<public:component urn='Commerce.EditSheet' tagName='editsheet'>
  <public>
    <property name='DataXML'/>
    <property name='MetaXML'/>
    <property name='required'  get='bGetRequired'/>
    <property name='valid'     get='bGetValid'/>
    <property name='dirty'     get='bGetDirty'/>
    <property name='xmlRecord' get='xmlGetRecord' put='SetRecord'/>

    <method name='field'  internalname='elGetField'/>
    <method name='hidden' internalname='bGetHide'/>
    <method name='hide'   internalname='Hide'/>
    <method name='show'   internalname='Show'/>
    <method name='focus'/>
    <method name='resetDefault' internalname='ResetDefault'/>
    <method name='resetDirty'   internalname='ResetDirty'/>
    <method name='disableAll'/>
    <method name='clearAll'/>

    <event name='onError'    id='evtError'></event>
    <event name='onChange'   id='evtChange'></event>
    <event name='onRequire'  id='evtRequired'></event>
    <event name='onValid'    id='evtValid'></event>

    <attach event='oncontentready' OnEvent='Initialize()'/>
  </public>

  <script language='VBScript'>
    ' code omitted here.
  </script>
</public:component>
```

Each of the Commerce Server HTCs contain the following line in their `<script>` block:

```
m_bDebug = false
```

Setting this variable to `true` puts the HTC into debug mode. In this mode more user–friendly messages are generated when an HTC fails to load, or encounters an error.

The `ListSheet` and `TreeView` HTCs support special operations called **XMLHTTP** operations. These will be discussed in detail later in the chapter. When the variable m_bDebugXMLHTTP is set to `true`, XMLHTTP operations are set to debug mode. In this mode dialog boxes appear showing what data is being posted to and received from the server.

HTCs are made available to an HTML page by including the BizDesk cascading style sheet, as each HTC defines a class in `bizdesk.css`. For example, the following entry defines the EditSheet class:

```
.editSheet
{
  behavior: url(/widgets/editHTC/EditSheet.htc);
}
```

(Currently `bizdesk.css` does not include classes defining behaviors for `ExpressionBuilder`, `QueryBuilder` and `ProfileDesigner`. Therefore, these HTCs require either a declaration in a local `<style>` or a `style` attribution using `<div>`. The sample code for these HTCs contains examples of such declarations.)

Below is a typical instantiation of an HTC – here an `EditField`.

```
<xml id='xmlMeta'>
  <editfields>
    <text id='Password' required='yes'
      minlen='3' maxlen='15' subtype='password'>
      <prompt>Password</prompt>
      <error>Password must be between 3 and 15 characters</error>
    </text>
  </editfields>
</xml>

<xml id='xmlData'>
  <document>
    <record>
      <Password>pass</Password>
    </record>
  </document>
</xml>

<div id='efPassword'
  class='editField'
  metaXML='xmlMeta'
  dataXML='xmlData'
  onchange='OnChange'
  onrequire='OnRequire'
  onvalid='OnValid'>
  Loading EditField...
</div>
```

It is important to make several observations from this instantiation. First, the <div> represents the actual HTC and the class attribute assigns the EditField behavior to the <div>. The properties of the HTC are separated into presentation and data as represented by the two XML islands. The first XML island, the meta XML island, defines the presentation properties of the HTC, such as minlen and maxlen. The second XML island, the data XML island, defines the data value (or values) that the control will display. The metaXML and dataXML attributes of the <div> associate the XML islands with the HTC. Note that the value of the id attribute (Password) in the meta XML must be equal to the field element <Password> in the data XML. Finally, the <div> defines event handlers for events fired by the HTC.

Each HTC has a unique XML syntax for specifying its meta XML. Examples of meta XML for the various HTCs are given in the following sections.

> *For complete definitions of the meta XML for an HTC, see the following section in the Commerce Server documentation:* Programmer's Reference | XML Reference | Business Desk XML Structures.

The most common form of data XML island has the following format:

```
<document recordcount='m'>
  <record>
    <name1>Value11</name1>
    <name2>Value12</name2>
    ...
    <namen>Value1n</namen>
  </record>
  ...
  <record>
    <name1>Valuem1</name1>
    <name2>Valuem2</name2>
    ...
    <namen>Valuemn</namen>
  </record>
</document>
```

This format represents tabular data. In addition, there are two-tier and three-tier formats for representing hierarchical data. These formats are only used by the ListSheet and are described under that section below.

The table below indicates which HTCs require data XML and meta XML.

Control	dataXML	metaXML
DynamicTable	Yes	Yes
EditField	Yes	Yes
EditSheet	Yes	Yes
ExpressionBuilder	No	Yes
ListBox	No	No
ListEditor	Yes	Yes

Control	dataXML	metaXML
ListSheet	Yes	Yes
ProfileDesigner	Yes	No
QueryBuilder	No	Yes
TreeView	Yes	No

Note that HTCs can fail to instantiate if either the data XML or meta XML is not well–formed and valid. (Recall that an XML document is well-formed if it conforms to the XML syntax. An XML document is valid if it is a valid instance of its schema or DTD.) The following message will appear Control could not load. Please contact system administrator. When a control fails to load check that the data XML and meta XML islands are well-formed and valid using an XML validator.

The sample code for the chapter contains a directory called XMLValidator with a simple XML validator. It will validate XML either from a file or a text fragment. Create a bookmark for this file, XMLValidator.htm, so that it is easily accessible.

To check that an XML fragment is well–formed, paste the fragment into the input field labelled XML: and click Validate. Here the meta XML for the password EditField has been tested and found to be well-formed.

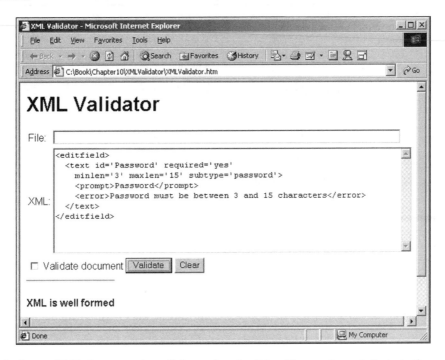

To check that an XML document is well-formed and valid, add an xmlns attribute to the root element containing the name of the schema file as shown, below. Ensure that the Validate document check box is checked. This simple check for validity reveals a bug in the EFschema.xml, since minlen is a valid HTC attribute but it does not exist in the schema. The schema fails to validate until the minlen attribute is removed.

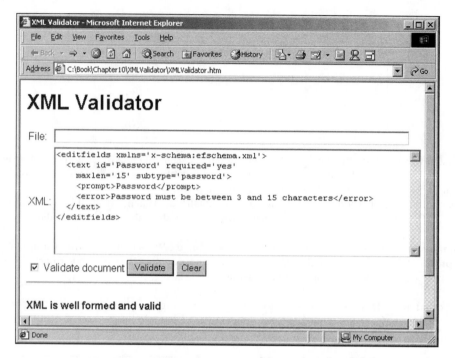

Schemas for common HTCs are listed below:

HTC	Schema
EditField	EFschema.xml
EditSheet	ESschema.xml
ListSheet	LSschema.xml
ListEditor	LEschema.xml
DynamicTable	DTschema.xml

These schemas can be found under `\SDK\Samples\Management\Widgets` in the Commerce Server root directory. They are included in the same directory as the XML validator, which saves having to type a path for the schema file.

> `TreeView` *and* `ListBox` *are not included in the above table, as they do not use meta XML.*

A limitation of HTCs is that they do not support event handlers via the conventional DHTML syntax:

```
Sub efPassword_OnChange()

End Sub
```

Therefore, unlike conventional controls, event handlers for HTCs must be attached outside the `<script>` block.

For further information on HTCs refer to the following two topics under Programmer's Reference in the Commerce Server documentation:

❑ Business Desk Reference | HTML Components

❑ XML Reference | Business Desk XML Reference

The following sections will examine each HTC listed above. The sample code for the chapter includes a directory HTCSamples that contains sample HTML pages that demonstrates each HTC. The HTC samples have been intentionally kept simple in order to highlight the basic features of these components. Therefore these samples do not use any ASP.

> Since these samples require **bizdesk.css**, it is essential that a new virtual directory be created for HTCSamples in order to access them. If these samples are accessed without using a virtual path then the HTCs will simply fail to load since **bizdesk.css** will not be located.

The most commonly used HTCs are EditField, EditSheet, and ListSheet. In addition, these are the only HTCs used in the Synonyms module. Therefore, on a first pass of the HTCs below you may want to focus on these specific components.

EditField

The EditField HTC is an input control for simple datatypes. The big advantage of this component is that it provides extensive data validation. It supports the following datatypes:

❑ Boolean

❑ Date

❑ Numeric (currency, float, integer)

❑ Select (for example, drop-down list box)

❑ Text (long, password, short)

❑ Time

The properties, methods, and events supported by the EditField are outlined below.

Property	Description
Dirty	Indicates whether the field value has changed (read-only)
Disabled	Disables control such that text is dimmed and input is not accepted (read-write)
DisplayValue	(select only) Indicates display value for current selection (read-only)
Options	(select only) Read-only collection of option elements (read-only)
Prompt	Text string displayed when field value is empty (read-write)

Table continued on following page

649

Property	Description
ReadOnly	Indicates whether field value is read-only (read-write)
Required	Indicates whether field requires non–empty value (read-only)
Selected	(select only) returns the currently selected option (read-only)
Valid	Indicates if the field value satisfies field constraints (read-only)
Value	Current field value (read-write)

Method	Description
AddItem	(select only) Adds new option to drop-down list
Focus	Sets focus to the field
Reload	(select only) Loads a different set of enumerated values in drop-down list
RemoveItem	(select only) Removes option from drop-down list
ResetDefault	Sets field value to default

Event	Description
OnBrowse	Fires when the browse button to the right of the edit field is clicked
OnChange	Fires when the field value changes and the field loses focus
OnError	Fires when a developer error occurs
OnRequire	Fires when a required field becomes empty or becomes non-empty
OnValid	Fires when a field value changes from valid to invalid or vice versa

The previous section gave an example of instantiating an EditField. The EditField.htm sample below demonstrates input fields for each of the datatypes listed opposite.

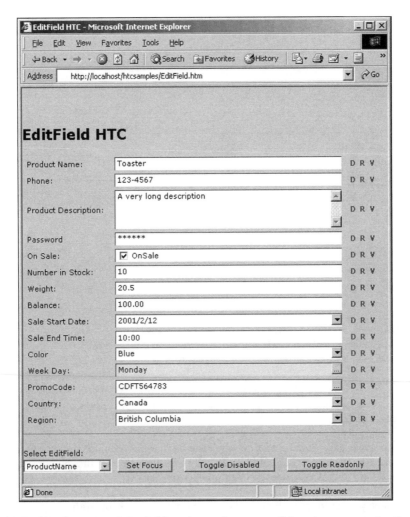

The letters (**D R V**) to the right of the fields indicate the status of the Dirty, Required and Valid properties of the field. A red value indicates True and a green value indicates False. When one of these properties changes, an event fires that sets the letter's color. The event handler for the OnChange, OnRequire and OnValid events are:

```
sub OnChange()
  dim strField

  strField = "Changed" & window.event.srcElement.id
  document.all(strField).style.color = "red"
end sub
'*******************************************************************************
sub OnRequire()
  dim strField

  strField = "Required" & window.event.srcElement.id

  with document.all(strField)
```

```
      if window.event.required then
        .style.color = "red"
      else
        .style.color = "green"
      end if
    end with
  end sub
  '**********************************************************************
  sub OnValid()
    dim strField

    strField = "Valid" & window.event.srcElement.id

    with document.all(strField)
      if window.event.valid then
        .style.color = "red"
      else
        .style.color = "green"
      end if
    end with
  end sub
```

*Note that the name of the status field is derived from the control name by pre-pending "Changed".
In addition, note that the current values of the Required and Valid properties are obtained
from the window.event object.*

The Dirty, Required and Valid properties are important in BizDesk, as we will see later, since they
determine when data can be saved. Therefore, let us examine how these properties are set in the
EditField.htm example.

The Dirty property is easy. It is set to true when the field value is changed. Therefore, if any field is
changed then the Dirty property should be set to true (red). Note that the event does not fire until the
HTC loses focus. The only way to set the Dirty property back to false is to reload the page.

The Valid property is set to true when the field value satisfies the constraints of the field, and false
otherwise. For example, the password field is defined by the following meta XML.

```
<editfield>
  <text id='efPassword' required='yes'
    minlen='3' maxlen='15' subtype='password'>
    <prompt>Password</prompt>
    <error>Password must be between 3 and 15 characters</error>
  </text>
</editfield>
```

The minlen and maxlen attributes constrain the password length to be between 3 and 15 characters. If
the initial value of the password is 'foobar', the constraint will be satisfied and the Valid property will
be true (red). If the password field is shortened so that it does not satisfy this constraint then the Valid
property will change to false (green). In addition, the field background is set to yellow when a field
value is invalid or missing.

The `Required` property is set to `True` when a field marked as required is missing data and `False` otherwise. Note that meta XML for the password field (above) has a required attribute with a value of `'yes'` indicating the field should not be empty. The password's `Required` property appears initially `False` (green) since it has a value (`'foobar'`). If the password field value is deleted then the `Required` field will change to `True` (red) indicating that a value is required.

A typical instantiation of an `EditField` was given in the previous section. In that example a password `EditField` is created (with a data type of `text` and a subtype of `password`). The field is required and has no initial value. When initially displayed, it will contain the prompt **Password** and will appear in yellow indicating that the current value is invalid. When a valid value of between 3 and 15 characters is entered the field will change to white. Event handlers are defined for the `onchange`, `onrequire` and `onvalid` events. If the field loses focus when it contains an invalid value, a dialog box will appear containing the text of the `<error>` element.

The `<charmask>` element can be used with the text field to force it to match a specific VBScript regular expression. For example, the following.

```
<charmask>^\d{3}-\d{4}$</charmask>
```

will match a simple telephone number of the form nnn-nnnn. Here, `'\d'` means match a digit and `'\d{3}'` means match exactly three digits.

The `<format>` element can be used with date and numeric fields. Valid numeric formats are:

- ❏ "1.1" – do not display negative sign
- ❏ "-1.1" – display negative sign before number
- ❏ "1.1-" – display negative sign after number
- ❏ "(1.1)" – display number in parentheses

Note that the decimal syntax is used even for integers. Valid date formats are:

- ❏ "m/d/yyyy" (default)
- ❏ "d/m/yyyy"
- ❏ "yyyy/m/d"

The separator can be a forward slash (`'/'`), hyphen (`'-'`), or period (`'.'`).

A browse button can be displayed to the right of an `EditField` by including the `onbrowse` attribute. The value of this attribute is the event handler to be called when the browse button is clicked.

```
<text id='WeekDay' required='yes' subtype='short'
      onbrowse='ShowWeekdayDialog' browsereadonly='yes'>
  <prompt>Week day</prompt>
  <browsetooltip>Browse for a week day</browsetooltip>
</text>
```

When the browse button is clicked, the following event handler will display a dialog box.

```
sub ShowWeekdayDialog()
  dim strValue
  dim strURL

  with window
    strURL = "Dialog.htm"
    strValue = .showModalDialog(strURL, , _
            "dialogHeight:260px;dialogWidth:400px; status:no; help:no")
    if strValue <> "" then
      .event.srcElement.value = strValue
    end if
  end with
end sub
```

The meta XML for a drop-down list box is:

```
<select id='Color'>
  <prompt>choose one</prompt>
  <select>
    <option value='Red'>Red</option>
    <option value='Yellow'>Yellow</option>
    <option value='Blue'>Blue</option>
  </select>
</select>
```

The final example shows how dependencies can be set up between drop-down list boxes. In the EditField.htm sample, the Region drop-down will display states if the Country is USA and provinces if the Country is Canada. The meta XML is:

```
<select id='Country' onchange='PopulateRegion'>
  <prompt>choose one</prompt>
  <select>
    <option value='Canada'>Canada</option>
    <option value='USA'>USA</option>
  </select>
</select>

<select id='Region'>
  <prompt>choose one</prompt>
  <select id='Canada'>
    <option value='BC'>British Columbia</option>
    <option value='On'>Ontario</option>
    <option value='QC'>Quebec</option>
  </select>
  <select id='USA'>
    <option value='CA'>California</option>
    <option value='NY'>New York</option>
    <option value='WA'>Washington</option>
  </select>
</select>
```

Note that the Region drop-down contains two distinct sets of values. When the value in the Country drop-down is changed, the onchange event reloads the values of the Region drop-down list as follows:

```
sub PopulateRegion()
  onChange()
  Region.reload(Country.value)
end sub
```

EditSheet

An `EditSheet` acts as a control container and is used primarily on edit pages. `EditSheets` are grouped into collapsible sections and use a pre-defined format for laying out controls contained in the meta XML island. The pre-defined layout can be over-ridden using the `<template>` mechanism to define a custom HTML layout.

The properties, methods, and events supported by the `EditSheet` are outlined below.

Property	Description
Dirty	Indicates whether an embedded field value has changed (read-only)
Required	Indicates whether an embedded required field needs a non-empty value (rea-only)
Valid	Indicates whether an embedded field contains an invalid value (rea-only)

Method	Description
Field	Retrieves a particular field element
Focus	Sets the focus to a field
Hidden	Indicates if a field is hidden
Hide	Hides a field and its label
ResetDefault	Sets all fields to their default values
ResetDirty	Sets the Dirty property to false
Show	Makes a hidden field and its label visible

Event	Description
OnChange	Fires when the field value changes and the field loses focus
OnError	Fires when a developer error occurs
OnRequire	Fires when a required field becomes empty or becomes no-empty
OnValid	Fires when a field value changes from valid to invalid or vice versa

Required fields in an `EditSheet` are marked with a red diamond. `EditSheet` sections containing a required field with a missing value display a red diamond in the section header. Similarly, an exclamation mark in a section header indicates a section with an invalid field.

The `EditSheet.htm` sample below demonstrates a typical `EditSheet`.

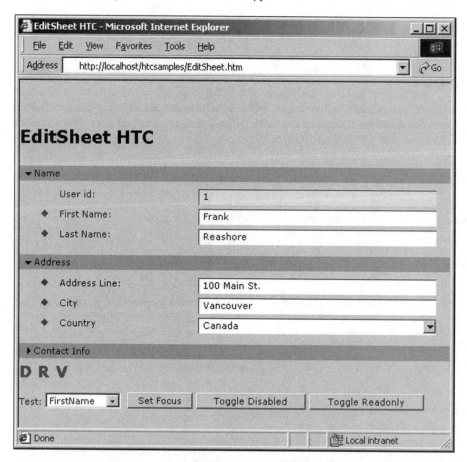

The `EditSheet` is instantiated within the HTML body using a data XML and meta XML islands as shown below. Each section of the `EditSheet` is given a name and an access key in the `<global>` element.

```
<xml id='esData'>
  <document>
    <record>
      <UserID>1</UserID>
      <FirstName>Frank</FirstName>
      <LastName>Reashore</LastName>
      <AddressLine>100 Main St.</AddressLine>
      <City>Vancouver</City>
      <Country>Canada</Country>
      <Phone1>111-1111</Phone1>
      <Phone2>222-2222</Phone2>
      <Email1>foo1@bar.com</Email1>
      <Email2>foo2@bar.com</Email2>
    </record>
  </document>
</xml>
```

```xml
<xml id='esMeta'>
  <editsheets>
    <editsheet>
      <global expanded='yes'>
        <name>Name</name>
        <key>n</key>
      </global>
      <fields>
        <numeric id='UserID' subtype='integer' readonly='yes'>
          <name>User id:</name>
        </numeric>
        <text id='FirstName' required='yes'
          maxlen='15' subtype='short'>
          <name>First Name:</name>
          <prompt>First name</prompt>
        </text>
        <text id='LastName' required='yes'
          maxlen='20' subtype='short'>
          <name>Last Name:</name>
          <prompt>Last name</prompt>
        </text>
      </fields>
    </editsheet>

    <editsheet>
      <global expanded='yes'>
        <name>Address</name>
        <key>a</key>
      </global>
      <fields>
        <text id='AddressLine' required='yes'
          maxlen='100' subtype='short'>
          <name>Address Line:</name>
          <error>Address line is too long</error>
          <prompt>Address line</prompt>
        </text>
        <text id='City' required='yes' maxlen='20' subtype='short'>
          <name>City</name>
          <error>City must be less than 20 characters</error>
          <prompt>City</prompt>
        </text>
        <select id='Country' required='yes'>
          <name>Country</name>
          <prompt>Country</prompt>
          <select>
            <option value='Canada'>Canada</option>
            <option value='UK'>UK</option>
            <option value='USA'>USA</option>
          </select>
        </select>
      </fields>
    </editsheet>
```

Note that the following EditSheet section is initially collapsed since the meta XML contains an expanded='no' attribute:

```
      <editsheet>
        <global expanded='no'>
          <name>Contact Info</name>
          <key>c</key>
        </global>
        <fields>
          <text id="Phone1" subtype='short' required='yes'>
            <name>Phone1</name>
            <charmask>^\d{3}-\d{4}$</charmask>
            <prompt>Phone1</prompt>
          </text>
          <text id="Phone2" subtype='short'>
            <name>Phone2</name>
            <charmask>^\d{3}-\d{4}$</charmask>
            <prompt>Phone2</prompt>
          </text>

          <text id="Email1" subtype='short' required='yes'>
            <name>Email1</name>
            <prompt>Email1</prompt>
          </text>
          <text id="Email2" subtype='short'>
            <name>Email2</name>
            <prompt>Email2</prompt>
          </text>
        </fields>
      </editsheet>
    </editsheets>
</xml>

<div id='esMain'
  class='editSheet'
  MetaXML='esMeta'
  DataXML='esData'
  language='VBScript'
  onrequire='OnRequire()'
  onchange='OnChange()'
  onvalid='OnValid()'>
  Loading EditSheet...
</div>
```

The EditSheet defines event handlers for the OnChange, OnRequire and OnValid events; these set the color of the (**D R V**) variables (red=True and green=False) on the page to indicate control state. Unlike the previous example, which used individual (**D R V**) flags for each field, the EditSheet uses a single set of (**D R V**) flags that represents the state of all the HTCs that it contains. The event handler for the OnRequire event is shown below:

```
sub OnRequire()
  with document.all("Required")
    if window.event.required then
      .style.color = "red"
    else
      .style.color = "green"
    end if
  end with
end sub
```

Where the id of the required status field (**R**) is 'Required'. Note that within the event handler the current value of the Required property is given by window.event.required.

The Focus Set button sets the focus to the EditField currently selected in the drop-down list box.

```
sub cmdSetFocus_OnClick()
  dim strField
  strField = GetSelectedField()
  esMain.field(strField).focus()
end
'****************************************************************
sub function GetSelectedField()
  with optSelect
    GetSelectedField = .options(.selectedIndex).innerText
  end with
end function
```

Here the field() method of the EditSheet is used to access an embedded HTC.

ListSheet

The ListSheet HTC is used to display data on list pages. It supports five modes:

- ❑ Flat list
- ❑ Two-level homogeneous grouped list
- ❑ Three-level homogeneous grouped list
- ❑ List-style heterogeneous grouped list
- ❑ Properties-style heterogeneous grouped list

The flat list mode is used to represent tabular data and is by far the most commonly used mode. The extended modes are used to represent hierarchical data. Examples of the data format used by these modes are given below.

The properties, methods, and events supported by the ListSheet are outlined below.

Property	Description
Page	The page number displayed in the page control (read-write)
RecordCount	The current number of records (read-write)
XMLlist	Returns a standard XML list format of the current list values (read-only)

Method	Description
Reload	Reloads the ListSheet using an XMLHTTP operation
SelectAllRows	Selects all rows
UnselectAllRows	Unselects all rows

Table continued on following page

Events	Description
`OnAllRowsSelect`	Fires when all rows are selected
`OnAllRowsUnselect`	Fires when all rows are unselected
`OnError`	Fires when a developer error occurs
`OnGroupOpen`	Fires when a row is opened to display sub-items
`OnHeaderClick`	Fires when a column heading is clicked
`OnNewPage`	Fires when one of the page navigation buttons is clicked
`OnRowSelect`	Fires when a row is selected
`OnRowUnselect`	Fires when a row is unselected

Flat List

`ListSheet1.htm` shows the `ListSheet` operating in flat list mode. `ListSheet1.htm` is a simple sample designed only to show the firing of events. Paging and sorting of data in a `ListSheet` can be handled easier using XMLHTTP (see *XMLHTTP Operations* later in Chapter 14).

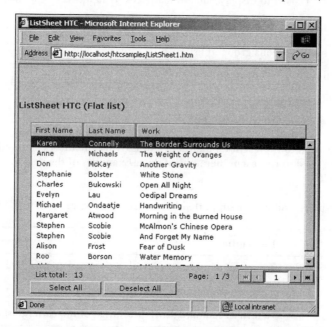

This `ListSheet` is instantiated with the code below. Note that the `Select All` and `Deselect All` buttons are only displayed when the attribute `selection` of the `<global>` element has the value `'multi'`.

```
<xml id='xmlMeta'>
  <listsheet>
    <global selection='multi' pagecontrols='yes' pagesize='5'/>
    <columns>
      <column id='UserID' hide='yes'>User ID</column>
      <column id='FirstName' width='10'>First Name</column>
```

```
              <column id='LastName' width='10'>Last Name</column>
              <column id='Work'>Work</column>
          </columns>
      </listsheet>
  </xml>

  <xml id='xmlData' src='ListData.xml'></xml>

  <div
      id='lsMain'
      class='listSheet'
      MetaXML='xmlMeta'
      DataXML='xmlData'
      language='VBScript'
      OnRowSelect='OnRowSelect()'
      OnRowUnselect='OnRowUnselect()'
      OnAllRowsSelect='OnAllRowsSelect()'
      OnAllRowsUnselect='OnAllRowsUnselect()'
      OnHeaderClick='OnHeaderClick()'
      OnNewPage='OnNewPage()'
      OnError='OnError()'>
      Loading ListSheet...
  </div>
```

The data XML island uses an `src` attribute to obtain the XML from a file. Here the data XML uses the standard tabular or rectangular format:

```
<document>
  <record>
    <UserID>1</UserID>
    <FirstName>Karen</FirstName>
    <LastName>Connelly</LastName>
    <Work>The Border Surrounds Us</Work>
  </record>
  <record>
    <UserID>2</UserID>
    <FirstName>Anne</FirstName>
    <LastName>Michaels</LastName>
    <Work>The Weight of Oranges</Work>
  </record>
          ...
</document>
```

The `OnRowSelect` event fires when a row is selected. Within the handler for this event, the variable `window.event.XMLrecord` contains the XML for the current record.

```
sub OnRowSelect()
  dim strMsg
  strMsg = "OnRowSelect" & vbCRLF
  strMsg = strmsg & "XMLRecord = " & window.event.XMLrecord.xml
  LogEvent(strMsg)
end sub
'****************************************************************
sub LogEvent(strMsg)
  with txtLog
    .value = strMsg & vbCRLF & .value
  end with
end sub
```

This simple handler merely logs the event to a `<textarea>`.

Two-Level Homogeneous Grouped List

`ListSheet2.htm` demonstrates the `ListSheet` in two-level homogeneous mode. Note that clicking the arrow on the left side of the row can expand each row in the table.

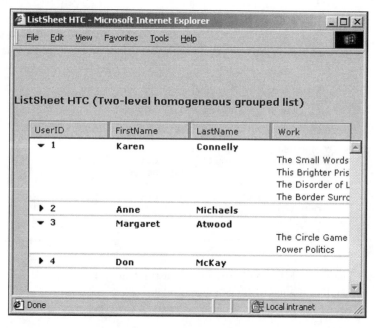

The two-level homogeneous grouped list is instantiated with the code below. There are two principal differences with the instantiation of the flat list. First the data has a two-level format which we will see shortly and the Work column uses an `id2` attribute to indicate which field in the data XML contains the `detail` field.

```
<xml id='xmlMeta'>
  <listsheet>
    <global pagecontrols='no'/>
    <columns>
      <column id='UserID'>UserID</column>
      <column id='FirstName'>FirstName</column>
      <column id='LastName'>LastName</column>
      <column id2='Work'>Work</column>
    </columns>
  </listsheet>
</xml>

<xml id='xmlData' src='ListData2.xml'>
</xml>

<div
  id='lsMain'
  class='listSheet'
  MetaXML='xmlMeta'
  DataXML='xmlData'
  language='VBScript'
  OnRowSelect='OnRowSelect()'
  OnRowUnselect='OnRowUnselect()'
  OnGroupOpen='OnGroupOpen()'>
  Loading ListSheet...
</div>
```

The data XML uses the following two-level format:

```
<document>
  <record>
    <UserID>1</UserID>
    <FirstName>Karen</FirstName>
    <LastName>Connelly</LastName>
    <record>
      <Work>The Small Words in My Body</Work>
    </record>
    <record>
      <Work>This Brighter Prison</Work>
    </record>
    <record>
      <Work>The Disorder of Love</Work>
    </record>
    <record>
      <Work>The Border Surrounds Us</Work>
    </record>
  </record>
  ...
</document>
```

Note that the `<Work>` sub-records contain the detail rows, as indicated in the meta XML.

Three Level Homogeneous Grouped List

The three-level homogeneous grouped list is a simple extension of the previous example to three levels. It is demonstrated in the `ListSheet3.htm` sample.

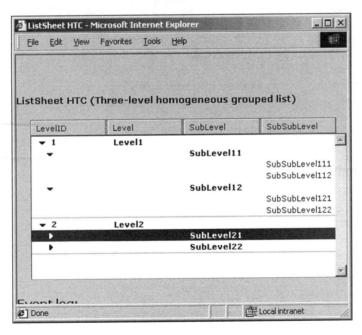

The instantiation is quite similar to the two-level except that the meta XML (shown below) uses an `id2` and an `id3` attribute to identify the `detail` fields in the data.

```
<xml id='xmlMeta'>
  <listsheet>
    <global pagecontrols='no'/>
    <columns>
      <column id='LevelID'>LevelID</column>
      <column id='Level'>Level</column>
      <column id2='SubLevel'>SubLevel</column>
      <column id3='SubSubLevel'>SubSubLevel</column>
    </columns>
  </listsheet>
</xml>
```

The data XML uses a three-level format:

```
<document>
  <record>
    <LevelID>1</LevelID>
    <Level>Level1</Level>
    <record>
      <SubLevel>SubLevel11</SubLevel>
      <record>
        <SubSubLevel>SubSubLevel111</SubSubLevel>
      </record>
      <record>
        <SubSubLevel>SubSubLevel112</SubSubLevel>
      </record>
    </record>
    <record>
      <SubLevel>SubLevel12</SubLevel>
      <record>
        <SubSubLevel>SubSubLevel121</SubSubLevel>
      </record>
      <record>
        <SubSubLevel>SubSubLevel122</SubSubLevel>
      </record>
    </record>
  </record>
    ...
</document>
```

List-Style Heterogeneous Grouped List

The list-style heterogeneous grouped list is demonstrated by the `ListSheet4.htm` sample.

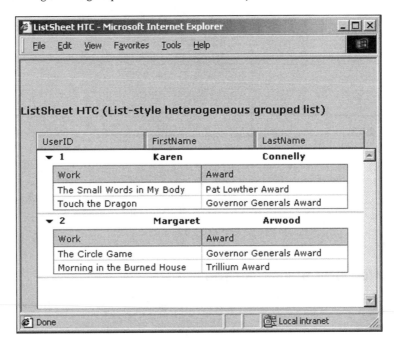

This instantiation differs from the previous two homogeneous grouped list examples because it introduces a `<subobject>` element in the meta XML and only uses a two–level data format. This particular format is characterized by a `type='list'` attribute in the `<subobject>`.

```
<xml id='xmlMeta'>
  <listsheet>
    <global pagecontrols='no'/>
    <columns>
      <column id='UserID'>UserID</column>
      <column id='FirstName'>FirstName</column>
      <column id='LastName'>LastName</column>
      <subobject type='list'>
        <column id='Work'>Work</column>
        <column id='Award'>Award</column>
      </subobject>
    </columns>
  </listsheet>
</xml>

<xml id='xmlData' src='ListData4.xml'>
</xml>

<div
  id='lsMain'
  class='listSheet'
  MetaXML='xmlMeta'
  DataXML='xmlData'
  language='VBScript'
```

```
      OnRowSelect='OnRowSelect()'
      OnRowUnselect='OnRowUnselect()'
      OnGroupOpen='OnGroupOpen()'>
      Loading ListSheet...
  </div>
```

The data XML has the following two-level format:

```
<document>
  <record>
    <UserID>1</UserID>
    <FirstName>Karen</FirstName>
    <LastName>Connelly</LastName>
    <record>
      <Work>The Small Words in My Body</Work>
      <Award>Pat Lowther Award</Award>
    </record>
    <record>
      <Work>Touch the Dragon</Work>
      <Award>Governor Generals Award</Award>
    </record>
  </record>
      ...
</document>
```

Properties–Style Heterogeneous Grouped List

ListSheet5.htm demonstrates the properties-style heterogeneous grouped list. It is essentially identical to the previous example except that the `<subobject>` element uses a `type='properties'` attribute as shown below:

```
<subobject type='properties'>
  <column id='Work'>Work</column>
  <column id='Award'>Award</column>
</subobject>
```

The data XML used in the last two examples is identical.

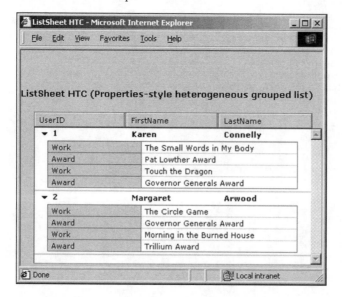

The extended modes of the ListSheet support the event, OnGroupOpen(), that fires when a row is expanded. XMLHTTP operations (discussed later in the chapter) can be used to request detail data when a row is expanded.

ListEditor

The ListEditor displays a list similar to the ListSheet; however, it allows editing of rows by means of a form below the list. In addition, it provides a New button for creating new rows and a Remove button for deleting existing rows.

The properties, methods, and events supported by the ListEditor are outlined below.

Property	Description
Dirty	Indicates if a row has been added, edited or deleted (read-only)
XMLlist	Returns a standard XML list format of the current list values (read-only)

Method	Description
Field	Retrieves a particular field element

Event	Description
OnCancel	Fires when the Cancel button is clicked.
OnChange	Fires when the Done or remove button is clicked.
OnEdit	Fires when a row is selected and its values placed in the edit area.
OnError	Fires when a developer error occurs.
OnNew	Fires when the New button is pressed.
OnValid	Fires when editing begins and when editing ends. This ensures that a save cannot occur during an edit.

The ListEditor.htm sample overleaf demonstrates the ListEditor

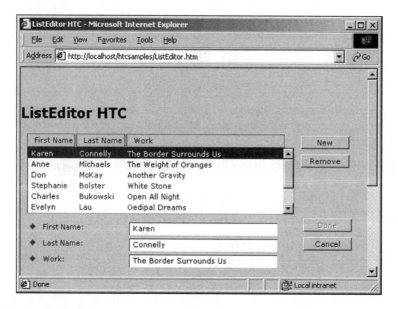

The meta XML for the ListEditor is:

```
<listeditor>
  <columns>
    <column id='FirstName' width='10'>First Name</column>
    <column id='LastName' width='10'>Last Name</column>
    <column id='Work'>Work</column>
  </columns>
  <fields>
    <text id='FirstName' maxlen='20'
      subtype='short' required='yes'>
      <name>First Name:</name>
      <tooltip>First Name</tooltip>
      <error>First Name error</error>
    </text>
    <text id='LastName' maxlen='30'
      subtype='short' required='yes'>
      <name>Last Name:</name>
      <tooltip>Last Name</tooltip>
      <error>Last Name error</error>
    </text>
    <text id='Work' subtype='short' required='yes'>
      <name>Work:</name>
      <tooltip>Work</tooltip>
      <error>Work error</error>
    </text>
  </fields>
</listeditor>
```

DynamicTable

This is actually quite similar to the `ListEditor`, but it presents the record to be edited as the top line of the table. The properties, methods, and events supported by the `DynamicTable` are outlined below.

Property	Description
Dirty	Indicates if a row has been added, edited or removed (read-only)
Required	Returns true if the global required attribute is set and the table has no row data, otherwise false (read-only)
XMLlist	Returns a standard XML list format of the current list values (read-only)

Method	Description
CleanUp	Removes all records with a state attribute of "deleted" and clears the state attribute for all remaining records
Field	Retrieves a particular field element

Event	Description
OnChange	Fires when the Done or Remove button is clicked.
OnError	Fires when a developer error occurs.
OnRequire	Fires when the global required element is set and the table data changes from having rows to not having, or vice versa.
OnValid	Fires when editing begins and when editing ends. This ensures that a save cannot occur during an edit.

The `DynamicTable.htm` sample below demonstrates the `DynamicTable` HTC.

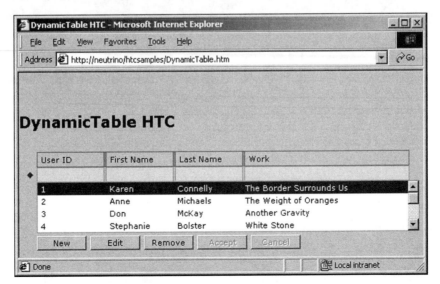

The meta XML for this `DynamicTable` is:

```xml
<dynamictable>
  <global keycol='UserID' required='yes' uniquekey='yes'/>
  <fields>
    <numeric id='UserID' subtype='integer'
      required='yes' min='1' width='10'>
      <name>User ID</name>
      <prompt>User ID</prompt>
    </numeric>
    <text id='FirstName' subtype='short' required='yes' width='10'>
      <name>First Name</name>
      <tooltip>First Name</tooltip>
      <prompt>First Name</prompt>
    </text>
    <text id='LastName' subtype='short' required='yes' width='10'>
      <name>Last Name</name>
      <tooltip>Last Name</tooltip>
      <prompt>Last Name</prompt>
    </text>
    <text id='Work' subtype='short' required='yes'>
      <name>Work</name>
      <tooltip>Work</tooltip>
      <prompt>Work</prompt>
    </text>
  </fields>
</dynamictable>
```

The DynamicTable is used in BizDesk for editing shipping rates. It has a highly specialized feature called `overx` for editing values associated with contiguous ranges. A typical usage from BizDesk is shown below:

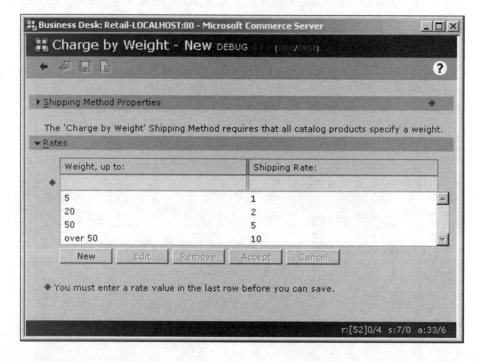

Note that the upper bound of the ranges is named **over 50**. The XML corresponding to a row is obtained from `window.event.XMLList`. The row implementing `overx` will contain a key of –1. The following DHTML code demonstrates how a key field is extracted from an XML record.

```
set nodKey = window.event.XMLrecord.selectSingleNode("MyKey")
intKey = Cint(nodKey.text)
```

TreeView

The `TreeView` differs slightly from the other HTCs we have seen up to this point as it only uses the data XML island. The methods and events supported by the `TreeView` are outlined below. Note that `TreeView` has no properties.

Method	Description
AreRelated	Indicates if two tree items are descendents of each other
EnableActive	Expands or collapses the active item
ExpandAll	Expands or collapses all items
HideActive	Hide or show the active item and its children
ReLoad	Reloads the TreeView data using an XMLHTTP operation

Event	Description
OnError	Fires when a developer error occurs
OnItemClose	Fires when a container item in the tree is closed
OnItemExecute	Fires when an item is double-clicked
OnItemOpen	Fires when a container item is opened
OnItemSelect	Fires when an item is selected
OnItemUnselect	Fires when an item is unselected

`TreeView.htm` demonstrates basic functionality of the `TreeView` HTC.

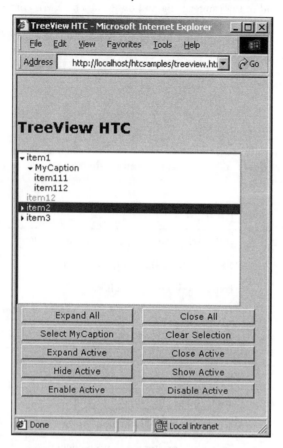

The following HTML instantiates the TreeView above:

```
<xml id='xmlData' src='TreeData.xml'></xml>

<div id='divContainer'>
  <div id='treeView'
    class='treeView
    class = 'Treeview'
    DataXML='xmlData'
    language='VBScript'
    OnItemSelect='OnItemSelect()'
    OnItemUnselect='OnItemUnselect()'
    OnItemExecute='OnItemExecute()'
    OnItemOpen='OnItemOpen()'
    OnItemClose='OnItemClose'>
    Loading TreeView...
  </div>
</div>
```

where the XML data source, `TreeData.xml`, is defined as follows:

```
<document skip='yes'>
  <item1>
    <item11 caption='MyCaption'>
      <item111/>
      <item112/>
    </item11>
    <item12 enabled='no'>
      <item121/>
      <item122/>
    </item12>
  </item1>
  <item2 closed='yes' selected='yes'>
    <item21>
      <item211/>
      <item212/>
    </item21>
    <item22>
      <item221/>
      <item222/>
    </item22>
  </item2>
  <item3 closed='yes'>
    <item31>
      <item311/>
      <item312/>
    </item31>
    <item32 hidden='yes'>
      <item321/>
      <item322/>
    </item32>
  </item3>
</document>
```

The attributes of the XML data affect the data display as follows:

❑ The skip attribute on the root element excludes it from the display.

❑ The caption attribute on item11 overrides the default node name.

❑ The enabled attribute makes item12 appear disabled.

❑ The closed attribute makes nodes item2 and item3 appear closed initially.

❑ The selected attribute makes item2 appear selected.

❑ The hidden attribute on item32 causes it, and its child nodes, to be hidden.

The event handlers for this application merely log events in the <textarea> at the bottom of the screen. For example, when an item is selected, the following event handler fires:

```
sub OnItemSelect()
  dim strMsg
  strMsg = "OnItemSelect" & vbCRLF
  strMsg = strMsg & "XMLItem = " & window.event.XMLitem.xml
  LogEvent(strMsg)
end sub
```

The command buttons on the page are implemented by calling TreeView methods. For example, the 'Select My Caption' and 'Clear Selection' buttons are implemented as follows:

```
sub cmdSelectNode_OnClick()
  treeView.SelectNode("MyCaption")
end sub
'*****************************************
sub cmdUnSelectAll_OnClick()
  treeView.UnselectAll()
end sub
```

The TreeView supports an XMLHTTP operation, expand, that allows data retrieval for a node to be deferred until the node is expanded. Such an operation is useful if a tree contains an exceptionally large amount of information or if retrieving the information is time-consuming. For these cases the expand operation allows the data retrieved to be done on an as-needed basis. The operation is initiated as follows:

```
TreeView.Reload("expand")
```

ListBox

The ListBox HTC provides standard list box functionality. It does not use data or meta XML islands.

The properties, methods, and events supported by the ListBox are outlined below.

Property	Description
Disabled	Disables control such that text is dimmed and not selectable (read-write)
Selected	Returns HTML definition of currently selected item (read-only)
Text	Displays name of the currently selected item (read-write)
Value	Value associated with the currently selected item (read-write)

Method	Description
Add	Adds one or more items from an XML node
AddItem	Adds an item
MoveDown	Moves the selected item down the list
MoveUp	Moves the selected item up the list
Remove	Removes all selected items and returns them as XML
Select	Selects the first item with a specified value
SelectAll	Selects all items in the list
UnSelect	Unselects the first item with a specified value
UnSelectAll	Unselects all items in the list

Event	Description
OnChange	Fires when an item is added or removed
OnSelect	Fires when one or more items is selected
OnSelectAll	Fires when all items are selected via the SelectAll() method
OnUnselect	Fires when an item is selected
OnUnselectAll	Fires when all items are unselected via the UnselectAll() method

ListBox.htm demonstrates a typical usage scenario:

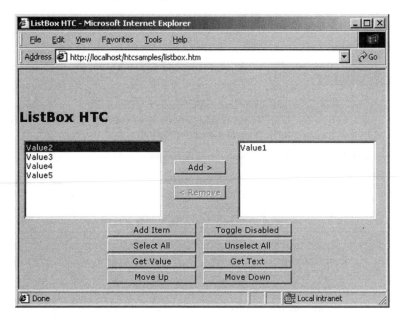

The left ListBox is instantiated with the code below. Note that the initial values are set in the body of the declaration.

```
<div id='lstLeft'
  class='listBox'
  selection='multi'
  onselect='lstLeft_OnSelect()'
  onunselect='lstLeft_OnUnselect()'
  onchange='lstLeft_OnChange()'
  onselectall='lstLeft_OnSelectAll()'
  onunselectall='lstLeft_OnUnselectAll()'>
  <div value='val1'>Value1</div>
  <div value='val2'>Value2</div>
  <div value='val3'>Value3</div>
  <div value='val4'>Value4</div>
  <div value='val5'>Value5</div>
</div>
```

The sample code demonstrates standard operation on a ListBox. For example, the Add and Remove buttons are implemented as follows:

```
sub btnAddItem_OnClick()
  dim strValue
  dim strDisplayValue

  strValue = "Val" & gintValue
  strDisplayValue = "Value" & gintValue
  lstLeft.AddItem strValue, strDisplayValue
  gintValue = gintValue + 1
end sub
'******************************************************
sub btnRemove_OnClick()
  lstLeft.add(lstRight.remove())
  btnRemove.disabled = true
end sub
```

ExpressionBuilder

ExpressionBuilder creates targeting expressions and saves them to the expression store. The expressions are expressed in XML and consist of a sequence of clauses. The properties, methods, and events supported by the ExpressionBuilder are outlined below.

Property	Description
IsActive	Indicates if the control is ready for user input (read-only)
IsReady	Indicates if the control is ready to use (read-only)

Method	Description
Activate	Activates the control with a mode of create, createfrom, edit or view
Deactivate	Deactivates the control
GetResults	Returns a dictionary containing the expression ID, name and value
Save	Saves the current expression
Cancel	Discards any unsaved editing and disables the control

Event	Description
OnComplete	Fires when successfully terminated (via Save or Cancel button)
OnError	Fires when activation fails
OnReady	Fires when fully loaded and initialized

Note that the Activate(strMode, intExpressionID) method requires a numeric expression ID of an existing expression for the "createfrom", "edit" and "view" modes. For "create" mode the expression ID is ignored and can be given a value of −1.

The `ExpressionBuilder.htm` sample below demonstrates a simple query with two clauses. The **New** button adds a new clause to the expression. When a new clause is completed, it is committed by clicking the **Apply** button. Clicking the **Save** button saves the entire expression to the expression store.

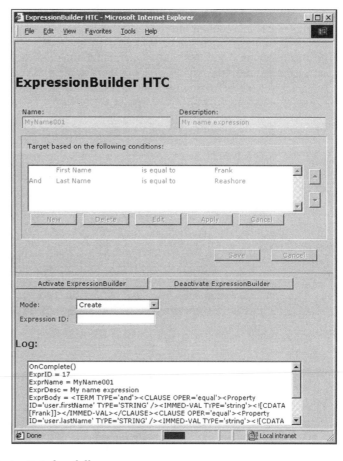

The `ExpressionBuilder` HTC is instantiated as follows:

```
<XML id='xmlConfig'>
  <EBCONFIG>
    <DEBUG/>
    <EXPR-ASP>/retailbizdesk/exprarch</EXPR-ASP>
    <SITE-TERMS URL='SiteTerms.xml'/>
    <PROFILE-LIST>
      <PROFILE SRC='ProfileDefs.xml'/>
    </PROFILE-LIST>
    <EEE-INTRINSICS/>
    <ADVANCED/>
  </EBCONFIG>
</XML>

<div id='ebExpressionBuilder'
     class='clsExprBldr'
     style='behavior:url(/widgets/exprbldrhtc/ExprBldr.htc)'
     XMLCfgID='xmlConfig'
     onready='OnReady()'
     oncomplete='OnComplete()'
     onerror='OnError()'>
  Loading ExpressionBuilder...
</div>
```

Note that the configuration XML for `ExpressionBuilder` requires upper case unlike the previous examples that all required lower case. In addition, note that a `style` attribute is used to attach the `ExpressionBuilder` behavior to the `<div>` since `bizdesk.css` does not include a predefined class for this behavior. The `<EXPR-ASP>` element defines a directory containing ASP files that are used to save expressions to the expression store. For example, if you examine the file `ExprSave.asp` in that directory you will see that it uses the ExpressionStore object (ProgID = 'Commerce.ExpressionStore') to save expressions.

The `OnComplete` event fires after a save operation has executed successfully.

```
sub OnComplete()
  Dim objResults
  Dim strMsg

  Set objResults = ebExpressionBuilder.GetResults()
  with objResults
    strMsg = "OnComplete()" & vbCRLF & _
             "ExprID = " & .Item("ExprID") & vbCRLF & _
             "ExprName = " & .Item("ExprName") & vbCRLF & _
             "ExprDesc = " & .Item("ExprDesc") & vbCRLF & _
             "ExprBody = " & .Item("ExprBody") & vbCRLF & _
             "SavedExpr = " & .Item("SavedExpr")
  end with
  set objResults = nothing

  LogEvent(strMsg)
end sub
```

The `GetResults()` method extracts the results from the `ExpressionBuilder` HTC. The properties of the result object are then appended to the event log at the bottom of the page. When the expression XML from the event log is reformatted it appears as follows:

```
<TERM TYPE='and'>
  <CLAUSE OPER='equal'>
    <Property ID='user.firstName' TYPE='STRING' />
    <IMMED-VAL TYPE='string'>
      <![CDATA[Frank]]>
    </IMMED-VAL></CLAUSE>
  <CLAUSE OPER='equal'>
    <Property ID='user.lastName' TYPE='STRING' />
    <IMMED-VAL TYPE='string'>
      <![CDATA[Reashore]]>
    </IMMED-VAL>
  </CLAUSE>
</TERM>
```

QueryBuilder

`QueryBuilder` is a sub-component of `ExpressionBuilder`. `QueryBuilder` differs from `ExpressionBuilder` in that it does not have the ability to save expressions to the expression store. Other than that, the expressions created by `QueryBuilder` are identical to those created by `ExpressionBuilder` – they are XML expressions consisting of a sequence of clauses.

The properties, methods, and events supported by the QueryBuilder are outlined below.

Property	Description
IsActive	Indicates if the control is ready for user input (read-only)
IsReady	Indicates if the control is ready to use (read-only)

Method	Description
Activate	Activate the control read-only or read-write
Deactivate	Deactivate the control
GetExprBody	Returns the current query as an XML string
GetExprBodyXML	Returns the current query as an XML document
GetProfileList	Returns a safe array containing the loaded profiles
SetExprBody	Sets the current query via an XML string
SetExprBodyXML	Sets the current query via an XML document
SetExprListXML	Allows ExpressionBuilder to provide a list of named expressions

Event	Description
OnActive	Fires when the Activate() method successfully completes
OnError	Fires when activation fails
OnQueryChange	Fires when the current query changes
OnReady	Fires when the control is loaded and initialized

The QueryBuilder.htm sample below shows a query and the XML it generates.

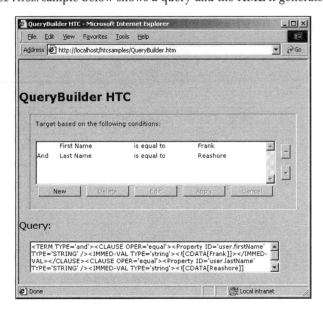

QueryBuilder is instantiated as follows:

```
<XML id='xmlConfig'>
  <EBCONFIG>
    <DEBUG/>
    <EXPR-ASP/>
    <SITE-TERMS URL='SiteTerms.xml'/>
    <PROFILE-LIST>
      <PROFILE SRC='ProfileDefs.xml'/>
    </PROFILE-LIST>
    <EEE-INTRINSICS/>
    <ADVANCED/>
  </EBCONFIG>
</XML>

<div id='qbQueryBuilder'
  class='clsQueryBldr'
  style='behavior:url(/widgets/exprbldrhtc/QueryBuilder.htc)'
  XMLCfgID='xmlConfig'
  AutoActivate='True'
  onready='OnReady()'
  onquerychange='OnQueryChange()'
  onactive='OnActive()'
  onerror='OnError()'>
  Loading QueryBuilder...
</div>
```

This instantiation is quite similar to that for ExpressionBuilder. QueryBuilder uses a different style attribute to attach the behavior to the <div>. Note however that QueryBuilder does not use the <EXPR-ASP> element since it does not save expressions to the expression store. In addition, QueryBuilder uses the AutoActivate attribute to avoid having to explicitly activate the control.

The OnQueryChange event fires when each clause is added by clicking the Apply button.

```
sub OnQueryChange()
  dim strMsg

  strMsg = "OnQueryChange()" & vbCRLF
  strmsg = strMsg & "ExprBody = " & qbQueryBuilder.GetExprBody()
  LogEvent(strMsg)
end sub
'**************************************************************
sub LogEvent(strMsg)
  with txtLog
    .value = strMsg & vbCRLF & .value
  end with
end sub
```

This extracts the current value of the expression and logs it to the <textarea> at the bottom of the page.

The ConvertExprToSqlFltrStr() method of the ExprFltrQueryBldr object can be used to convert an XML query into a SQL where expression. Conversion of the above query yields the more familiar string:

```
user.firstName = 'Frank' and user.lastName = 'Reashore'
```

ProfileDesigner

The ProfileDesigner HTC allows editing of profile schemas. It is not officially documented with the other BizDesk HTCs, therefore its status is unclear. Hence, we will limit ourselves here to showing a screen shot and a typical instantiation.

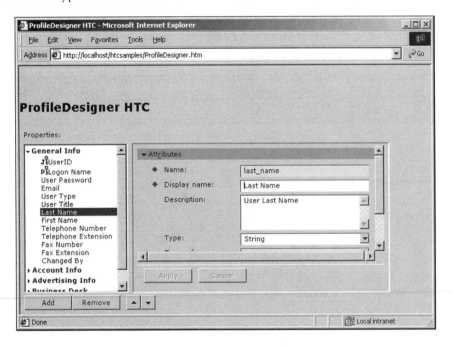

ProfileDesigner is instantiated as follows:

```
<xml id='xmlConfig'>
  <profiledesigner
      docid='xmlProfData'
      sitetermsid='xmlSiteTerms'
      catalogid='xmlCatalogData'>
  </profiledesigner>
</xml>

<xml id='xmlCatalogData'></xml>
<xml ID='xmlSiteTerms'></xml>
<xml id='xmlProfData' src='ProfileData.xml'></xml>

<div id='pbProfileDesigner' ConfigXML='xmlConfig'>
  Loading ProfileDesigner...
</div>
```

Summary

In the course of this chapter, we've examined the architecture that underlies the BizDesk management interface. BizDesk is an HTML application, which provides easily configurable navigation controls: by default, a combination of a vertical navigation bar, and a taskbar. We saw how BizDesk divides pages into list pages (that display data) and edit pages (that allow data to be updated).

Our first step in extending BizDesk was to add an existing module, Synonyms, to the default configuration. This module provides a good example of how we can manipulate database records. The user interface demonstrates how records are created, updated, and deleted. In addition, it illustrates searching, sorting, and scrolling of recordsets.

All BizDesk modules make extensive use of HTML Components (HTCs), and we went on to examine these in detail. HTCs are web components with properties, methods, and events, which use XML islands to configure their data and presentation properties.

In this chapter, we have looked at all the HTCs that are installed with Commerce Server 2000. A sample application was provided with each one to demonstrate typical usage. We examined the sample code to see how each HTC was instantiated and we have looked at representative DHTML to see how certain properties, methods and events are used.

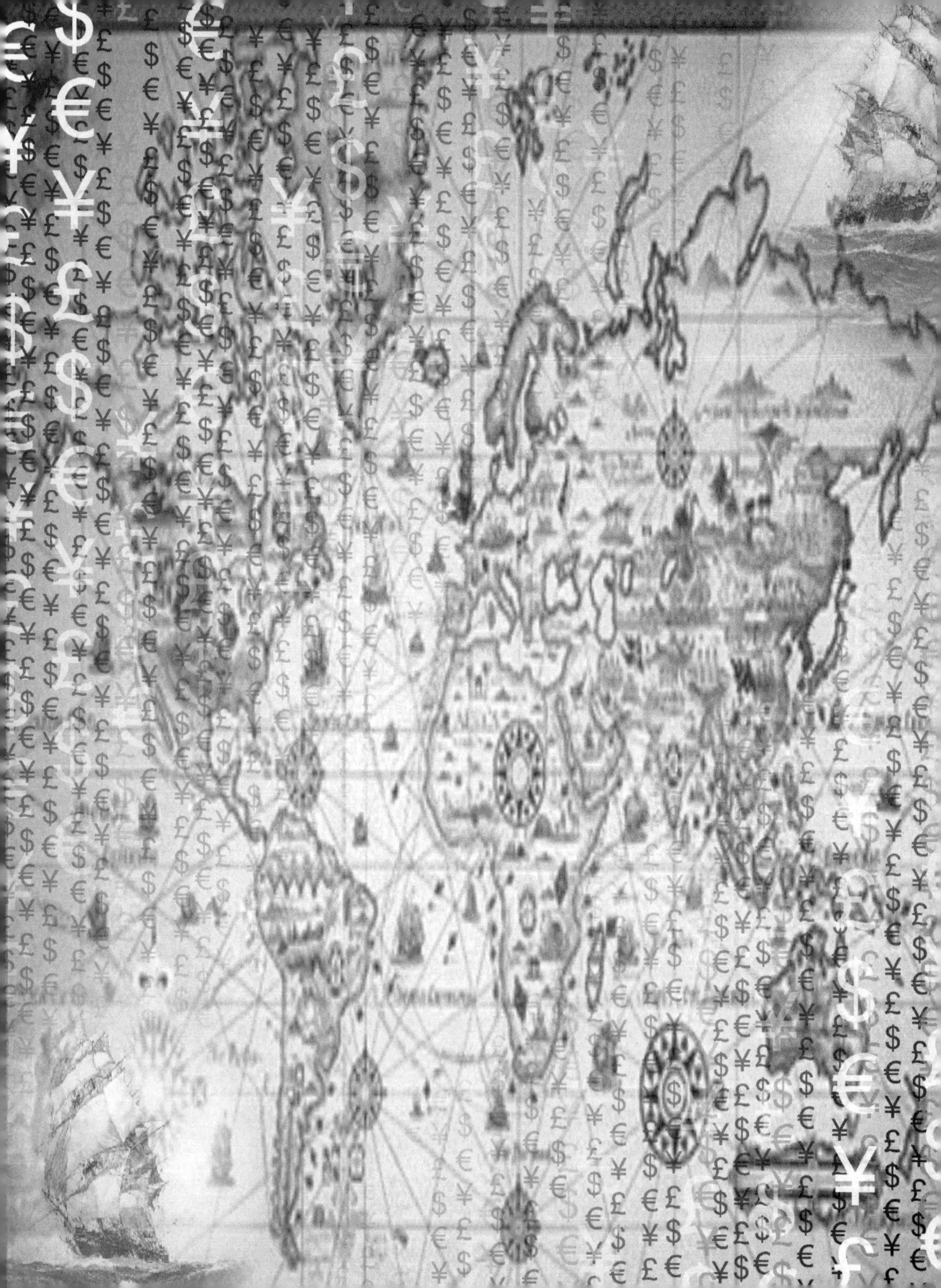

14

Extending the BizDesk

In this chapter, we're going to take a look at how the various elements that make up our custom 'Synonyms' module fit together. This won't be an exhaustive account of the potential capabilities of a BizDesk module; nevertheless, it should give you a good idea of the structure and resources made available to you by the standard BizDesk. This should provide a good head start when you come to build your own modules.

Before we look at the mechanics of BizDesk module development, we're going to briefly look at setting up a debugging environment in which to build the module. As you'll appreciate, the importance of being able to properly debug your code cannot be overemphasized – being able to set breakpoints and examine the immediate development environment will save you an enormous amount of time and effort if your module starts playing up.

These sort of debugging capabilities are supported by many applications, but for demonstration purposes, we're going to use Visual Interdev (VID). We will start by describing how to create a VID project for `RetailBizDesk`, the BizDesk application provided with the Retail Solution Site. By working in this environment, we will have access to full debugging capabilities – and not just for the `Synonyms` application we're adding, but for the RetailBizDesk as a whole.

> *As in the previous chapter, we shall assume that the BizDesk's root application name is* `RetailBizDesk`. *Of course, if you are using a different application name, you should make the appropriate adjustments to the following instructions.*
>
> *Also, make sure that VID's server-side (`VID_SS`) and remote debugging (`SCRPT_SS`) components are installed. You can install these from disk 2 of the **Professional** and **Enterprise** editions of Visual Studio 6.0. If you are installing these components after running the latest Visual Studio Service Pack (which you may well require to get much joy out of VID), you should re-run the service pack on completing the install.*

The procedure outlined below for creating a VID project from an existing RetailBizDesk site rests on two observations:

❑ VID uses FrontPage Extensions and HTTP to read and write files to and from the web server.

❑ It is safest to reuse the existing virtual directory name (RetailBizDesk) in case there are any hard-coded dependences.

Our strategy will therefore be to backup the contents of the existing RetailBizDesk directory, delete the corresponding virtual directory, recreate that virtual directory as a VID project, and add the copied files into that project. The detailed steps involved in this procedure are as follows:

1. Backup the existing RetailBizDesk virtual directory by copying the contents of the directory C:\inetpub\wwwroot\RetailBizDesk to C:\RetailBizDeskSave.

2. Delete the RetailBizDesk application from IIS Manager.

3. Create a new VID project named RetailBizDesk – specify your web server name (or localhost) and choose Master mode, then choose Create a new Web application and uncheck the full-text search checkbox. The remaining options simply define the theme and layout, so we can ignore them.

4. Delete all files and folders from the new project except for _private.

5. Add the contents of RetailBizDeskSave to the new project, along with the files provided in the code download for this chapter – these support the modules Synonyms and Test.

6. Set BizDesk.asp as the default start page for the project – we don't want to use Default.asp, as this will run the client installer.

7. Right-click on the root directory and select Get Working Copy to move all project files from IIS into your local project directory. All the project's file icons should now change from a lock to a pencil.

8. Edit global.asa and put the project into debug mode by changing the line:

```
MSCSEnv = PRODUCTION
```
to
```
MSCSEnv = DEVELOPMENT
```

9. From IIS Manager, modify the site's custom errors according to the table below:

HTML Error	Error File	Type
401;1	C:\Inetpub\wwwroot\retailbizdesk\bdaccesserror.htm	File
401;2	C:\Inetpub\wwwroot\retailbizdesk\bdaccesserror.htm	File
401;3	C:\Inetpub\wwwroot\retailbizdesk\bdaccesserror.htm	File
401;4	C:\Inetpub\wwwroot\retailbizdesk\bdaccesserror.htm	File

HTML Error	Error File	Type
401;5	C:\Inetpub\wwwroot\retailbizdesk\bdaccesserror.htm	File
404	C:\Inetpub\wwwroot\retailbizdesk\bdaccesserror.htm	File
500;100	/retailbizdesk/500error.asp	URL

The screenshot below shows the RetailBizDesk loaded as a Visual InterDev project:

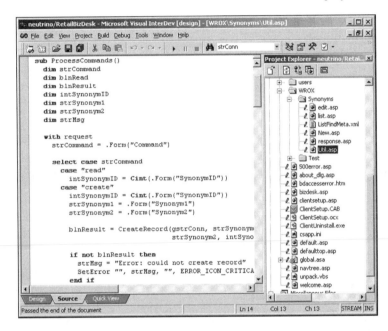

When you start the project, a dialog box will appear requesting authentication for debugging. Enter your user name and password, and the BizDesk should appear as shown below. Note that it is running in BizDesk debug mode and not as an HTA:

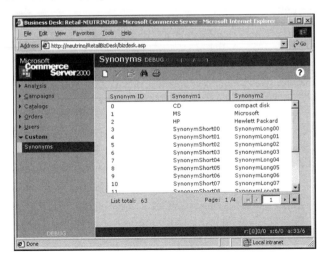

Debug mode actually has two interpretations here – any ASP application can be run from VID in debug mode, while BizDesk can also be run in its own debug mode by changing the debug flag in `global.asa` (as we've just done). For clarity, these will be referred to as VID debug mode and BizDesk debug mode.

BizDesk will insist on running as an HTA unless it is run in BizDesk debug mode, which has the following notable features:

❑ Errors in configuration files are reported.

❑ Page status (dirty/required/valid) is displayed as "d r v (TRUE/FALSE)" where true is green and false is red.

❑ Menus (main and context) are enabled, allowing operations such as View Source.

❑ Modules for which the user lacks access permissions appear in yellow. (In production mode such modules are simply not displayed.)

❑ Application, session, and response info is displayed in the lower right-hand corner.

Integrating HTCs with the Taskbar on Edit Pages

As you will have gathered by now, BizDesk uses two types of pages: list pages (read-only pages based on a `ListSheet` HTC) and edit pages (which accept input and use an EditSheet as a control container for EditFields and other HTCs). Since edit pages accept input, their state is determined by whether the page is **saveable**. An edit page is saveable when:

❑ The page has been modified since last having been saved (the page is **dirty**)

❑ All required fields contain values

❑ All fields contain valid values

The advantage of using an EditSheet on an edit page is that it monitors the state of all embedded HTCs through its `Dirty`, `Required` and `Valid` properties. Each edit page has a taskbar with the following buttons for saving data on the page:

Button	Icon	Action
Back		Return to previous page – if page is dirty then it will first provide a Yes/No/Cancel dialog to let you save the page.
SaveBack		Save page and return to previous page.
Save		Save page.
SaveNew		Save page and create new record.

If a page is dirty and the **Back** button is hit, a dialog will appear, which asks the user whether they want to save the page – if **Yes** is selected, a call is made to the **Save** button's `OnClick()` method.

Of course, some mechanism is required to enable the taskbar buttons only when an edit page is saveable. BizDesk accomplishes this by means of three special event handlers:

❑ `SetDirty()`

❑ `SetRequired()`

❑ `SetValid()`

These are all defined in the include file `ASPActionUtil.asp`, so when an EditSheet is instantiated on an edit page, these functions should be used as the event handlers. Below is an example from `Edit.asp` of these event handlers being used in the EditSheet instantiation:

```
<div id='esMain'
   class='editSheet'
   metaXML='xmlMeta'
   dataXML='xmlData'
   language='VBScript'
   onchange='SetDirty("")'
   onrequire='SetRequired("")'
   onvalid='SetValid("")'>
   Loading EditSheet...
</div>
```

Note that each of these handlers accepts a string argument that defines a confirmation message to be displayed before exiting – for example, "**Save data before exiting**". If an empty string is set, as above, then standard predefined messages will be used.

This simple mechanism allows the edit page taskbar buttons to be kept in sync with the state of the page.

State Transitions

The Synonyms module contains three ASP pages, each of which has a number of buttons on the taskbar – let's try and summarize what each of them actually does in any given situation. A state transition diagram for these pages is shown below:

Origin	Button	Condition/Action	Operation	Target
`List.asp`	New			`New.asp`
	Edit		Read	`Edit.asp`
`New.asp`	Back	Page not dirty		`List.asp`
		Page dirty / user selects Yes	Create	`List.asp`
		Page dirty / user selects No		`List.asp`
		Page dirty / user selects Cancel		`New.asp`

Table continued on following page

Origin	Button	Condition/Action	Operation	Target	
New.asp	SaveBack		Create	List.asp	
	Save		Create	Edit.asp	*
	SaveNew		Create	New.asp	
Edit.asp	Back	Page not dirty		List.asp	
		Page dirty / user selects Yes	Update	List.asp	
		Page dirty / user selects No		List.asp	
		Page dirty / user selects Cancel		Edit.asp	
	SaveBack		Update	List.asp	
	Save		Update	Edit.asp	
	SaveNew		Update	New.asp	*

As an example, the fourth entry on this table is interpreted as follows:

❑ Starting on the New.asp page, the Back button is pressed.

❑ The page is dirty, so a Yes/No/Cancel dialog pops up.

❑ The user selects Yes.

❑ The data on the page is then posted to List.asp along with a hidden field indicating a Create operation.

❑ List.asp reads the posted data, creates a record, and displays the updated list of records.

Most of this table is quite straightforward – however, the two lines marked by asterisks warrant special consideration. In the first case, we are adding a new record. The table, tblSynonyms, is implemented with an IDENTITY key. Therefore, the new record is assigned a key the first time it is saved. Consequently, the New.asp page does not display the primary key field. If a Save operation is performed from a New.asp page, a primary key will be generated, so the record must be displayed on an Edit page with a read-only primary key. In the second case we are editing a record in Edit.asp, when the SaveNew button is clicked; this takes us directly to New.asp.

We'll see shortly how these conditional transitions are coded into each of our ASP pages.

List Pages and Edit Pages

We're now going to examine the general structure of list pages and edit pages by taking a look at List.asp and Edit.asp from the Synonyms module. All list pages and edit pages must include:

❑ BDHeader.asp – this header specifies character set and content type, and features an Option Explicit line.

❑ BizDeskUtils.asp – this header includes four other include files containing required utility code.

❑ BizDesk cascading style sheet (CSS) – specifying styles used to render the BizDesk interface.

List.asp

`List.asp` demonstrates a typical list page. List pages have the following general properties:

- ❏ Read-only
- ❏ `InsertTaskBar()` is placed immediately after the `<body>` tag
- ❏ The ListSheet HTC is used
- ❏ A Find pane is often featured

`List.asp` begins by including the two standard BizDesk header files and the BizDesk CSS. All ASP processing is neatly relegated to a single call to `ProcessCommands()` which is included in `Util.asp`. `ProcessCommands()` is responsible for reading any commands (such as create or update) and their arguments and processing them by reading and writing to the database.

```
<!-- #include file='../../include/BDHeader.asp' -->
<!-- #include file='../../include/BizDeskUtil.asp' -->
<!-- #include file='Util.asp' -->
<% ProcessCommands() %>
<html>
  <head>
    <title>Synonym List</title>
    <link rel='stylesheet'
      type='text/css'
      href='../../include/bizdesk.css'>
    </link>
    <style>
      .hide {
        display:  none;
      }
      div.esContainer, .esEditgroup div.esContainer
      {
        background-color: transparent;
      }
      #divMain {
        height:   80%;
        margin:   20px;
      }
    </style>
```

The `<script>` block contains all the client-side processing for the page. The `window_OnLoad()` handler is responsible for initially populating the ListSheet HTC and enabling the taskbar buttons:

```
<script language='VBScript'>
  Option Explicit
  '*************************************************************
  sub window_OnLoad()
    divMain.ReLoad("newpage")
    EnableNonselectionTasks()
    SetFindByHeight(100)
  end sub
  '*************************************************************
  sub EnableNonselectionTasks()
```

```
            ' these task buttons do not require a selection
            ' and are always enabled
            EnableTask("New")
            EnableTask("Find")
            EnableTask("Print")
        end sub
        '**************************************************************
```

`OnRowSelect()` and `OnRowUnselect()` keep track of which items are selected in the ListSheet:

```
        sub OnRowUnselect()
          DisableTask("Edit")
          DisableTask("Delete")

          frmEdit.SynonymID.value = "-1"
          SetStatusText "No items selected"
        end sub
        '**************************************************************
        sub OnRowSelect()
          dim strSynonymID
          dim nodSynonymID

          ClearStatusText()
          with window.event
            set nodSynonymID = .XMLrecord.selectSingleNode("SynonymID")
          end with

          if not nodSynonymID is nothing then
            EnableTask("Edit")
            EnableTask("Delete")

            strSynonymID = nodSynonymID.text
            frmEdit.SynonymID.value = strSynonymID
            SetStatusText "Selected SynonymID = " & strSynonymID
          end if
        end sub
        '**************************************************************
```

We'll examine the functions `OnFindChange()` and `cmdFind_OnClick()` later on, when we look at implementing a **Find** pane:

```
        sub OnFindChange()
          ...
        end sub
        '**************************************************************
        sub cmdFind_OnClick()
          divMain.reload("findby")
        end sub
        '**************************************************************
```

`OnDelete()` and `OnPrint()` implement additional toolbar functionality:

```
    sub OnDelete()
      dim strMsg
      dim strSynonymID

      strSynonymID = frmEdit.SynonymID.value
      frmDelete.SynonymID.value = strSynonymID
      strMsg = "Delete SynonymID = " & strSynonymID

      if confirm(strMsg) then
        if not divMain.Reload("delete") then
          msgbox "Error deleting SynonymID = " & strSynonymID
        end if
      end if

      EnableNonselectionTasks()
    end sub
    '***************************************************************
    sub OnPrint()
      window.print()
      EnableNonselectionTasks()
    end sub
    '***************************************************************
  </script>
</head>
```

`InsertTaskbar()` is called immediately after the `<body>` tag to insert the taskbar. The next two XML islands and the following HTML form implement the Find pane:

```
<body>
  <% InsertTaskBar "Synonyms", "" %>

  <xml id='xmlFindMeta' src='ListFindMeta.xml'>
  </xml>

  <xml id='xmlFindData'>
    <document>
      <record/>
    </document>
  </xml>

  <form id='frmFind' action='response.asp'>
    <div id='bdfindbycontent' class='findByContent'>
      <div id='fbtypepicker'
        class='editSheet'
        metaXML='xmlFindMeta'
        dataXML='xmlFindData'>
        Loading EditSheet...
      </div>
    </div>
  </form>
```

We continue with two more XML islands and a `<div>`, which instantiate the ListSheet. The ListSheet is placed within a `<div>` container so that the task buttons remain at the top of the screen when the page is scrolled:

693

```
<xml id='xmlMeta'>
  <listsheet>
    <global pagecontrols='yes'/>
    <columns>
      <column id='SynonymID'>Synonym ID</column>
      <column id='Synonym1'>Synonym1</column>
      <column id='Synonym2'>Synonym2</column>
    </columns>
    <operations>
      <newpage  formid='frmNextPage'/>
      <sort     formid='frmSort'/>
      <findby   formid='frmFind'/>
      <delete   formid='frmDelete'/>
    </operations>
  </listsheet>
</xml>

<xml id='xmlData'>
  <document>
    <record/>
  </document>
</xml>

<div id='bdcontentarea'>
  <div id='divMain'
    class='listSheet'
    dataXML='xmlData'
    metaXML='xmlMeta'
    language='VBScript'
    onrowselect='OnRowSelect()'
    onrowunselect='OnRowUnselect()'
    onallrowsunselect='OnRowUnselect()'>
    Loading ListSheet...
  </div>
</div>
```

The page finishes off with a collection of HTML forms that are used by the taskbar for posting commands to pages and performing XMLHTTP operations (which again, we describe later).

```
    ...
  </body>
</html>
```

Edit.asp

Edit pages have the following general properties:

❑ Features an editing taskbar with buttons: Back, SaveBack, Save, and SaveNew

❑ `InsertEditTaskBar()` is placed immediately after the `<body>` tag

❑ The EditSheet HTC is used as a control container

❑ Standard BizDesk event handlers `SetChange()`, `SetRequire()` and `SetValid()` are used

`Edit.asp` begins by including the two standard BizDesk header files and the BizDesk CSS. It also uses the same function `ProcessCommands()` as `List.asp`, to handle commands posted to the page:

```
<!-- #include file='../../include/BDHeader.asp' -->
<!-- #include file='../../include/BizDeskUtil.asp' -->
<!-- #include file='Util.asp' -->
<% ProcessCommands() %>
<html>
  <head>
    <title>Synonym Edit</title>
    <link rel='stylesheet'
      type='text/css'
      href='../../include/bizdesk.css'>
    </link>
```

The following script block calls the `focus()` method of the EditSheet, which sets the focus to the first control in the EditSheet:

```
<script language='VBScript'>
  option explicit
  sub window_onload()
    esMain.focus()
  end sub
</script>
</head>
```

The edit taskbar is inserted immediately after the body tag. Next are the meta XML and data XML islands. Note that the contents of the data XML island are generated dynamically via ASP code:

```
<body>
  <% InsertEditTaskBar "Edit Synonym", "" %>

  <xml id='xmlMeta'>
    <editsheets>
      <editsheet>
        <global expanded='yes'>
          <name>Synonym</name>
          <key>s</key>
        </global>
        <fields>
          <numeric id='SynonymID' required='yes'
                readonly='yes' subtype='integer'>
            <name>SynonymID</name>
            <tooltip>SynonymID</tooltip>
            <error>SynonymID error</error>
            <prompt>SynonymID</prompt>
          </numeric>

          <text id='Synonym1' required='yes' subtype='short'>
            <name>Synonym1</name>
            <tooltip>Synonym1</tooltip>
            <error>Synonym1 error</error>
            <prompt>Synonym1</prompt>
          </text>
```

```
            <text id='Synonym2' required='yes' subtype='short'>
              <name>Synonym2</name>
              <tooltip>Synonym2</tooltip>
              <error>Synonym2 error</error>
              <prompt>Synonym2</prompt>
            </text>
          </fields>
        </editsheet>
      </editsheets>
    </xml>

    <xml id='xmlData'>
      <% = gstrRecordXML %>
    </xml>
```

The HTC is instantiated using the data and meta XML islands together with the standard BizDesk event handlers `SetDirty()`, `SetRequired()` and `SetValid()` that connect it to the taskbar. The HTC is placed within a `<form>` together with a hidden field. When a save operation is performed from the taskbar, the fields contained within the HTC, and the hidden field, will be posted to a target page.

The EditSheet is placed within a `<div>` container so that once again, the task buttons remain at the top of the screen when the page is scrolled:

```
    <div id='bdcontentarea' class='editPageContainer'>
      <form id='frmUpdate'>
        <input type='hidden' name='Command'
              id='Command' value='update'>
        <div id='esMain'
          class='editSheet'
          metaXML='xmlMeta'
          dataXML='xmlData'
          language='VBScript'
          onchange='SetDirty("")'
          onrequire='SetRequired("")'
          onvalid='SetValid("")'>
          Loading EditSheet...
        </div>
      </form>
    </div>
  </body>
</html>
```

Implementing TaskBar Functionality

Let us now look at how we can attach functionality to taskbar buttons. In particular, we shall examine how the New and Edit taskbar buttons are enabled in `List.asp`.

The module configuration file, `Synonyms.xml`, contains the following `<task>` elements.

```
<task icon='TaskNew.gif' id='New'>
  <goto action='WROX/Synonyms/New.asp'/>
```

```
      <name>New</name>
      <key>n</key>
      <tooltip>New</tooltip>
   </task>

   <task icon='taskopen.gif' id='Edit'>
      <postto action='WROX/Synonyms/edit.asp' formname='frmEdit'/>
      <name>Edit</name>
      <key>e</key>
      <tooltip>Edit</tooltip>
   </task>
```

These XML fragments illustrate the two possible ways of attaching an action to a taskbar button, namely via a `<goto>` or a `<postto>`. The `<goto>` element acts as a hyperlink, and no data is posted to the target page, while the `<postto>` element is used when data must be posted. A taskbar button implemented with `<postto>` is essentially a **Submit** button on the form specified by the element's `formname` attribute. In the case of the **Edit** button in the example above, this will be `frmEdit`, which is defined near the button of `List.asp` as follows:

```
   <form id='frmEdit'>
     <input type='hidden' name='Command' id='Command' value='read'>
     <input type='hidden' name='SynonymID' id='SynonymID' value='-1'>
   </form>
```

The posted parameters are defined as hidden fields; in this case they define a command (`read`) and its argument.

Note that the `<input>` elements have been given duplicate names via the `id` and `name` attributes. The `id` attribute is used for DHTML access. The `name` attribute is used for non-DHTML access.

There are two types of taskbar buttons, those that require a current selection (**Edit**) and those that do not (**New**, **Find**, and **Print**). Task bar buttons requiring a selection must be enabled and disabled by the ListSheet event handlers `OnRowSelect()` and `OnRowUnselect()`:

```
sub OnRowUnselect()
  DisableTask("Edit")
  DisableTask("Delete")

  frmEdit.SynonymID.value = "-1"
  SetStatusText "No items selected"
end sub
'*********************************************************************
sub OnRowSelect()
  dim strSynonymID
  dim nodSynonymID

  ClearStatusText()
  with window.event
    set nodSynonymID = .XMLrecord.selectSingleNode("SynonymID")
  end with

  if not nodSynonymID is nothing then
```

```
      EnableTask("Edit")
      EnableTask("Delete")

      strSynonymID = nodSynonymID.text
      frmEdit.SynonymID.value = strSynonymID
      SetStatusText "Selected SynonymID = " & strSynonymID
   end if
end sub
```

Note that in the `OnRowSelect()` event handler, the XML for the selected ListSheet record is extracted from the window event. The `SynonymID` of this record is then extracted from the XML node and assigned to the `SynonymID` hidden variable of `frmEdit`.

Similarly, note that in the `OnRowUnselect()` event handler, the `SynonymID` hidden variable of the `frmEdit` is assigned a flag of -1, indicating no current selection. The taskbar buttons are also enabled and disabled by the event handlers.

Consequently, when the **Edit** task bar button is pressed, the `SynonymID` of the currently selected record is posted to `Edit.asp`.

All the `<task>` elements we have considered so far use a single `<goto>` or `<postto>` element. These `<task>` elements implement a single button on the taskbar. However it is possible to include multiple `<goto>` or multiple `<postto>` elements in a single `<task>` element, so long as you do not mix the two together: a `<task>` element must either contain all `<goto>` elements or all `<postto>` elements.

As you've probably guessed, a `<task>` that contains multiple `<goto>` or multiple `<postto>` elements will implement a drop-down menu. As you can see below, you must also remember to include the attribute `type='menu'`:

```
<task icon='TaskNewMenu.gif' id='NewMenu' type='menu'>
  <goto action='MyModule/NewItem1.asp'>New Item1</goto>
  <goto action='MyModule/NewItem2.asp'>New Item2</goto>
  <goto action='MyModule/NewItem3.asp'>New Item3</goto>
  <name>NewMenu</name>
  <key>n</key>
  <tooltip>NewMenu</tooltip>
</task>
```

The `Assets` subdirectory contains a number of icons for use in building taskbars. Each icon's filename is based on a corresponding task name (as shown in the table below), constructed as: `Task<name>.gif`. For example, the icon for the **Open** command is `TaskOpen.gif`.

AddSub		Print		Convert	
ExportMenu		Stop		Legend	
Open		Cancel		Restore	

SaveBack		Help		ViewDetails	
Approve		ProcessAuction		Copy	
Find		Unarchive		New	
Pivot		Chart		Run	
SaveNew		Import		ViewMenu	
Archive		Publish		Delete	
FindMenu		Update		NewMenu	
Preview		Compose		Save	
Send		ImportMenu		ViewProperties	
Back		Refresh		Export	
FlipSeries		View			

Note that the <task> name element has been slightly over-simplified above for readability. The name should contain an underlined access key and the resulting string must be HTML encoded. Hence the proper form of the <name> element for the New taskbar button is, for example, New with an underlined N:

```
<name>&lt;u&gt;N&lt;u&gt;ew</name>
```

The final enhancement to the dispatching model for taskbar buttons with <postto> elements is to allow an event handler to run before the form is submitted. The Print button uses this feature. The <task> element for the print command is:

```
<task icon='taskprint.gif' id='Print'>
   <postto action='WROX/Synonyms/list.asp' formname='frmPrint'/>
   <name>Print</name>
   <key>p</key>
   <tooltip>Print</tooltip>
</task>
```

An event handler is attached by the `ontask` attribute in `frmPrint`:

```
<form id='frmPrint' ontask='OnPrint()'>
</form>
```

and here is how that event handler is defined:

```
sub OnPrint()
  window.print()
  EnableNonselectionTasks()
end sub
```

The `window.print()` method creates a standard print dialog box – since this changes the focus, the taskbar buttons must be explicitly re-enabled once `window.print()` completes, with a call to the routine `EnableNonselectionTasks()`. Note that this technique can be used *whenever* an edit page loses focus to a dialog box.

The print command is a not an ideal example since it only involves client-side processing. The more general case uses the `ontask` attribute to perform some client-side processing and then explicitly call the `Submit()` method of the associated form to perform some server-side processing:

```
frmSomeForm.Submit()
```

For example, the Back button checks if the form is dirty and if so displays a yes/no/cancel dialog. If yes is selected the save operation is submitted to the server.

Command Processing

Recall when we looked at the state transition diagram for the Synonyms module, that when transitioning between specific pages it was necessary to perform certain operations. For example, if a selected item is opened on a list page then the record for the item must be read from the database so that it can be displayed on the edit page. Similarly, if a modified record on an edit page is saved then the record must be updated in the database before the saved record is displayed on an edit page. These operations are key to the functionality of the Synonyms module and this section will show how they are implemented.

The Synonyms module posts the following three commands and their arguments between pages:

Command	Arguments
Read	SynonymID
Create	Synonym1, Synonym2
Update	SynonymID, Synonym1, Synonym2

These commands are processed by adding the following lines of ASP code to the top of `List.asp`, `New.asp` and `Edit.asp`:

```
<!-- #include file='Util.asp' -->
<% ProcessCommands() %>
```

The command processing is performed by the following function:

```
sub ProcessCommands()
  dim strCommand
  dim blnRead
  dim blnResult
  dim intSynonymID
  dim strSynonym1
  dim strSynonym2
  dim strMsg

  with request
    strCommand = .Form("Command")

    select case strCommand
      case "read"
        intSynonymID = Cint(.Form("SynonymID"))
      case "create"
        intSynonymID = Cint(.Form("SynonymID"))
        strSynonym1 = .Form("Synonym1")
        strSynonym2 = .Form("Synonym2")

        blnResult = CreateRecord(gstrConn, strSynonym1, _
                                 strSynonym2, intSynonymID)

        if not blnResult then
          strMsg = "Error: could not create record"
          SetError "", strMsg, "", ERROR_ICON_CRITICAL
        end if
      case "update"
        intSynonymID = CInt(.Form("SynonymID"))
        strSynonym1 = .Form("Synonym1")
        strSynonym2 = .Form("Synonym2")

        blnResult = UpdateRecord(gstrConn, intSynonymID, _
                                 strSynonym1, strSynonym2)

        if not blnResult then
          strMsg = "Error: could not update record"
          SetError "", strMsg, "", ERROR_ICON_CRITICAL
        end if
    end select
  end with

  blnRead = (strCommand = "read") or _
            (strCommand = "create") or _
            (strCommand = "update")

  if blnRead then
    if not ReadRecord(gstrConn, intSynonymID, gstrRecordXML) then
      strMsg = "Error: could not read record"
      SetError "", strMsg, "", ERROR_ICON_CRITICAL
    end if
  end if
end sub
```

This function reads the command and then branches into a `select` statement. The command arguments are read within the three `case` statements, and the `create` and `update` commands call the corresponding functions `CreateRecord()` and `UpdateRecord()`, as required. Finally the record is read and converted to standard XML format for display with `ReadRecord()`. The XML returned is saved in the global variable `gstrRecordXML` and later inserted into a data XML island in `Edit.asp` as follows:

```
<xml id='xmlData'>
  <% = gstrRecordXML %>
</xml>
```

Database Access

All database access in the Synonyms module is performed by three functions, defined in `Util.asp`:

- ❏ ReadRecord()
- ❏ CreateRecord()
- ❏ UpdateRecord()

In this section we will examine these functions and other issues related to database access.

The functions `CreateRecord()` and `UpdateRecord()` are quite similar and involve basic ADO functionality. We'll examine the first, since it is slightly more complex, using both input and output arguments and thus requiring an ADO parameters object:

```
function CreateRecord( _
  byval strConn, _
  byval strSynonym1, _
  byval strSynonym2, _
  byref intSynonymID)

  dim objConn
  dim objCommand
  dim objParameter
  dim intRecordsAffected

  CreateRecord = false
  set objConn = oGetADOConnection(strConn)
  set objCommand = oGetADOCommand(objConn, AD_CMD_STORED_PROC)
  strSynonym1 = QuoteSQL(strSynonym1)
  strSynonym2 = QuoteSQL(strSynonym2)

  with objCommand
    .CommandText = "sp_SynonymCreate"
    set objParameter = .CreateParameter("Synonym1", _
                        AD_VAR_CHAR, AD_PARAM_INPUT, 20, strSynonym1)
    .Parameters.Append objParameter
    set objParameter = .CreateParameter("Synonym2", _
                        AD_VAR_CHAR, AD_PARAM_INPUT, 20, strSynonym2)
    .Parameters.Append objParameter
    set objParameter = .CreateParameter("SynonymID", _
```

```
                              AD_INTEGER, AD_PARAM_OUTPUT)
       .Parameters.Append objParameter

       .execute intRecordsAffected, , AD_EXECUTE_NO_RECORDS
    end with

    if intRecordsAffected = 1 then
      intSynonymID = objCommand.Parameters("SynonymID")
    end if

    CreateRecord = (intRecordsAffected = 1)

    set objCommand = nothing
    set objConn= nothing
    set objParameter = nothing
  end function
```

The above function involves standard ADO coding. Note that BizDesk defines two ADO helper functions oGetADOConnection() and oGetADOCommand() that return ADO connection and command objects respectively. The SQL input arguments have been protected against embedded single quotes by QuoteSQL(). The stored procedure sp_CreateSynonym is given by:

```
CREATE PROCEDURE sp_SynonymCreate
  @Synonym1  varchar(20),
  @Synonym2  varchar(20),
  @SynonymID  int output
AS
BEGIN
  INSERT INTO tblSynonyms(Synonym1, Synonym2)
  VALUES(@Synonym1, @Synonym2)

  SELECT @SynonymID = @@IDENTITY
END
```

Note that the key of the created record is returned from the stored procedure.

The other function worth examining is ReadRecord().

```
function ReadRecord( byval strConn, byval intSynonymID, byref strRecordXML)

  dim objConn
  dim objCommand
  dim strSQL
  dim rstQuery

  ReadRecord = false
  set objConn = oGetADOConnection(strConn)
  set objCommand = oGetADOCommand(objConn, AD_CMD_STORED_PROC)

  with objCommand
    .CommandText = "sp_SynonymSelectWhere"
    set rstQuery = .Execute(, Array(intSynonymID))
  end with
```

```
    strRecordXML = xmlGetXMLFromRS(rstQuery).xml
    ReadRecord = true

    rstQuery.Close()
    set objConn = nothing
    set objCommand = nothing
    set rstQuery = nothing
end function
```

Again the ADO coding is quite standard, but note that since only input arguments are being used, the ADO `parameters` object is not used and the calling sequence is much simpler. The function worth noting here is `xmlGetXMLFromRS()` that converts a recordset to the standard XML data format used in data XML islands in BizDesk. The XML is converted to a string and returned via the `byref` argument. A typical call to `ReadRecord()` might return the following XML:

```
<document>
  <record>
    <SynonymID>1</SynonymID>
    <Synonym1>CD</Synonym2>
    <Synonym2>Compact Disk</Synonym2>
  </record>
</document>
```

This would be used to populate `Edit.asp`, below:

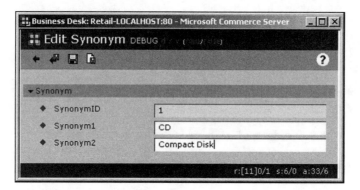

The stored procedure used in `ReadRecord()` is:

```
CREATE PROCEDURE sp_SynonymSelect
WHERE @SynonymID int
AS
SELECT SynonymID, Synonym1, Synonym2
FROM tblSynonyms
WHERE SynonymID = @SynonymID
```

It is worth pointing out that the BizDesk headers re-define the ADO constants. For example, the `CreateRecord()` uses `AD_EXECUTE_NO_RECORDS` rather than the usual `adExecuteNoRecords`. Such redefinitions are contrary to the principles of code reuse and Microsoft's motivation for this is unclear. Perhaps it was due to the fact that BizDesk uses only a small subset of ADO. The recommended way of accessing ADO definitions is either by an include file:

```
<!-- #include file='adovbs.inc' -->
```

or by referencing a type library:

```
<!-- metadata type='typelib' file='msado15.dll' -->
```

Finally, note that the connection string is obtained in a site independent manner at the top of `Util.asp` as follows:

```
gstrConn = GetSiteConfigField("Product Catalog", "connstr_db_Catalog")
```

Each site defines site resources that can be viewed in the **Commerce Manager**:

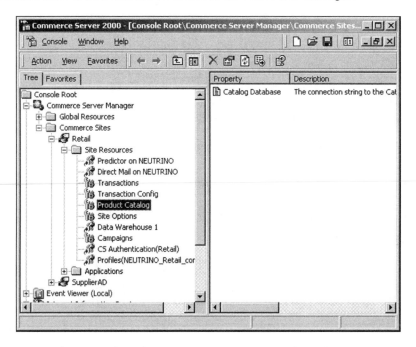

These resources can be accessed via the `SiteConfigReadOnly` object that is created in `global.asa`. The table used in the Synonyms module, `tblSynonyms`, is stored in the `retail_commerce` database, the same place as the product catalog files. Therefore, `GetSiteConfigField()` uses the `SiteConfigReadonly` object to read the product catalog connection string. This eliminates hard-coding connection strings in our module.

XMLHTTP Operations

Using what we have learned to this point, it would be possible to implement scrolling by posting `List.asp` to itself and using hidden fields to indicate that a new page was required. The only problem with this approach is that it causes the entire page to reload. XMLHTTP operations provide a more elegant solution by posting XML requests on an independent HTTP connection. The responses are then used to update the HTC in place. This eliminates having to repaint the entire page. Instead, only the HTC is repainted with the updated data. Thus, using XMLHTTP operations results in a higher quality user interface. Both ListSheet and TreeView support XMLHTTP operations.

ListSheet XMLHTTP operations can be used for:

❑ Paging through recordsets (newpage)

❑ Sorting on a column (sort)

❑ Finding data (findby)

❑ Expanding and collapsing hierarchical data (sublist)

❑ Deleting records (custom operation)

In this section we will take a look at how ListSheet scrolling is implemented. XMLHTTP operations are declared in the <operations> element of the meta XML of an HTC, for example:

```
<listsheet>
  <global pagecontrols='yes'/>
  <columns>
    <column id='SynonymID'>Synonym ID</column>
    <column id='Synonym1'>Synonym1</column>
    <column id='Synonym2'>Synonym2</column>
  </columns>
  <operations>
    <newpage  formid='frmNextPage'/>
    <sort      formid='frmSort'/>
    <findby    formid='frmFind'/>
    <delete    formid='frmDelete'/>
  </operations>
</listsheet>
```

Each operation declares a corresponding form that it uses to post the data. Below are two such forms from List.asp.

```
<form id='frmNextPage' action='response.asp'>
</form>

<form id='frmDelete' action='response.asp'>
  <input type='hidden' name='SynonymID'>
</form>
```

The newpage operation defined in the <operations> element of the meta XML for the ListSheet above is a standard operation. It has predefined arguments that it posts namely: page, prevpage, column and direction. The last two arguments are used for scrolling recordsets that have a sort order defined.

The delete operation is a custom operation and hence the form includes a hidden field, with data specific to that operation. Here the primary key, SynonymID is posted.

Both operations use the same ASP page, Response.asp, to service requests.

Clicking the ListSheet navigation bar generates a newpage XMLHTTP request. Note that it is important to include the pagecontrols='yes' attribute in the <global> element otherwise the navigation bar will not appear. Similarly, clicking a column header of the ListSheet generates a sort XMLHTTP request.

It is also possible to initiate an XMLHTTP operation programmatically by calling the
Reload(strOperation) method of the HTC. For example, List.asp uses XMLHTTP operations
for scrolling the ListSheet. When the page loads the control is empty and an explicit request is made to
populate the control in the OnLoad event:

```
sub window_OnLoad()
  divMain.ReLoad("newpage")
  EnableNonselectionTasks()
  SetFindByHeight(100)
end sub
```

When HTCs are placed in XMLHTTP debug mode (by setting m_bDebugHTTPXML to True), the XML
requests and responses are displayed in dialog boxes – these can prove extremely useful when debugging:

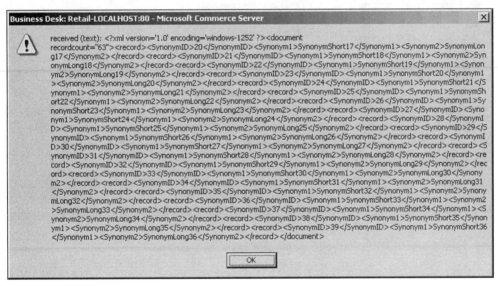

In the Synonyms module Response.asp services all XMLHTTP requests.

Servicing XMLHTTP Requests

In the previous section we saw how an XMLHTTP operation posts an XML request to the server. This
XML request is essentially a dictionary of name-value pairs – as can be seen from the XML request debug
dialog shown above. Servicing such a request requires parsing the command and its parameters from the
XML request, and then generating an XML response. In this section we will see how XMLHTTP requests
are serviced.

Response.asp

XMLHTTP processing in the Synonyms module provides a good example of typical XMLHTTP processing. The header files and main entry point for `Response.asp` is shown below:

```
<!-- #include file='../../include/BDXMLHeader.asp' -->
<!-- #include file='../../include/ASPUtil.asp' -->
<!-- #include file='../../include/DBUtil.asp' -->
<!-- #include file='../../include/HTTPXMLUtil.asp' -->
<!-- #include file='Util.asp' -->
<%
ServiceXMLRequest()
'********************************************************************
```

ASP pages servicing XMLHTTP operations must use a content type of `text/xml` and return only XML. Including any headers – even one returning HTML – will invalidate the response. Note that the regular BizDesk header has been replaced with `BDXMLHeader.asp`. This header sets the content type to `text/xml`.

ServiceXMLRequest()

All XMLHTTP requests are serviced by `ServiceXMLRequest()`. The structure of this function is quite simple. It starts by determining which operation is requested:

```
sub ServiceXMLRequest()
  dim dicRequest
  dim strOperation
  dim intSynonymID
  dim intPage
  dim intRecordCount
  dim strColumn
  dim strDirection
  dim varSynonym1
  dim varSynonym2
  dim varSynonymID
  dim strID
  dim strSource
  dim strMsg
  dim strXML
  const intPageSize = 20

  set dicRequest = dGetRequestXMLAsDict()
  strOperation = dicRequest("op")
```

The function `dGetRequestXMLAsDict()` is used to convert the XML request that was posted to `Response.asp` into a dictionary – the specific operation is then extracted from that dictionary.

Then a `select` statement branches to the specific code to read any command arguments and generates an XML response string:

```
select case strOperation
  case "newpage"
    intPage = Cint(dicRequest("page"))
    strDirection = dicRequest("Direction")
```

```
        strColumn = dicRequest("Column")

        strXML = GetPage(gstrConn, intPage, intPageSize, strColumn, strDirection)
      case "sort"
        intPage = Cint(dicRequest("page"))
        strDirection = dicRequest("Direction")
        strColumn = dicRequest("Column")

        strXML = Sort(gstrConn, intPage, strColumn, strDirection, intPageSize)
      case "findby"
        varSynonymID = dicRequest("SynonymID")
        varSynonym1 = dicRequest("Synonym1")
        varSynonym2 = dicRequest("Synonym2")
        strXML = Find(gstrConn, varSynonymID, varSynonym1, varSynonym2)
      case "delete"
        intPage = Cint(dicRequest("page"))
        strDirection = dicRequest("Direction")
        strColumn = dicRequest("Column")
        intSynonymID = Cint(dicRequest("SynonymID"))

        if DeleteRecord(gstrConn, intSynonymID, intRecordCount) then
          ' if deleting last record on last page then decrement intPage
          if (intRecordCount mod intPageSize) = 0 then
            intPage = intPage - 1
          end if

          strXML = GetPage(gstrConn, intPage, intPageSize, _
                        strColumn, strDirection)
        else
          strID = 2
          strSource = "response.asp"
          strMsg = "Error: could not delete synonym"
          strXML = CreateError(strID, strSource, strMsg)
        end if
      case else
        strID = 1
        strSource = "response.asp"
        strMsg = "Error: XMLHTTP operation not found"
        strXML = CreateError(strID, strSource, strMsg)
    end select
```

The last statement of the function writes to the ASP `Response` object:

```
  response.write strXML
end sub
```

GetPage()

The `newpage` operation uses `GetPage()`, shown below, to generate a response. This function creates a recordset, extracts the page requested, and converts it to XML:

```
function GetPage(byval strConn, byval intPage, byval intPageSize, _
                        byval strColumn, byval strDirection)
  dim objConn
```

```
   dim objCommand
   dim rstQuery
   dim intStartRecord
   dim strSQL
   dim strXML

   set objConn = oGetADOConnection(strConn)
   set objCommand = oGetADOCommand(objConn, AD_CMD_TEXT)

   strSQL = "select SynonymID, Synonym1, Synonym2 from tblSynonyms "

   if strColumn <> "" and strDirection <> "" Then
     strSQL = strSQL & "order by " & strColumn & " " & strDirection
   end if

   with objCommand
     .CommandText = strSQL
     set rstQuery = .Execute
   end with

   intStartRecord = (intPage - 1) * intPageSize
   strXML = xmlGetXMLFromRSEx(rstQuery, intStartRecord, _
                              intPageSize, -1, null).xml
   GetPage = strXML

   set rstQuery = nothing
   set objConn = nothing
   set objCommand = nothing
end function
```

The functions used to generate responses for the other XMLHTTP operations follow an exactly analogous pattern.

CreateError()

If an error occurs during an XMLHTTP operation, an XML error must be returned – this function creates such an error response:

```
function CreateError(byval strID, byval strSource, byval strMsg)
   dim docError

   set docError = xmlGetXMLDOMDoc()
   AddErrorNode docError, strID, strSource, strMsg
   CreateError = docError.xml
end function
```

> **XMLHTTP operations do not work with Visual InterDev debugging because the debugger inserts a comment element before the XML header that creates an invalid XML format.**

Implementing a Find Pane

A Find pane is a standard feature of most list pages. In this section we will implement the screen shown below:

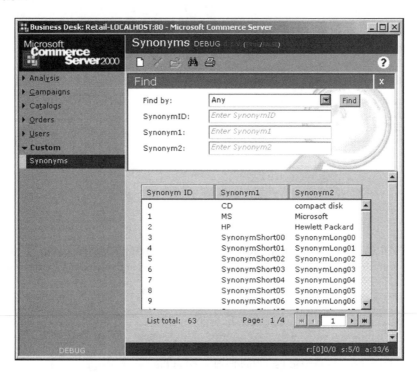

Find panes are implemented using an XMLHTTP operation. When the Find button is clicked, an XML request containing the Find parameters and their values is sent to the server. As in the previous section, an ASP page processes the request and returns an XML response. The processing involves creating a recordset that satisfies the search parameters and then converting the recordset to the standard XML data format.

ActionPageUtil.asp

BizDesk contains built-in functionality for Find panes, defined in `ActionPageUtil.asp`. In particular, this `include` file contains the following `<div>`:

```
<div id='bdfindby'>…</div>
```

together with the function, shown below, (attached to the Find taskbar button) for toggling the visibility of the Find pane:

```
sub ToggleFindBy()
  if bdfindby.style.display <> "none" then
    HideFindBy()
  else
    ShowFindBy()
  end if
end sub
```

The Find pane is instantiated as follows:

```
<xml id='xmlFindMeta' src='ListFindMeta.xml'>
</xml>

<xml id='xmlFindData'>
  <document>
    <record/>
  </document>
</xml>

<form id='frmFind' action='response.asp'>
  <div id='bdfindbycontent' class='findByContent'>
    <div id='fbtypepicker'
      class='editSheet'
      metaXML='xmlFindMeta'
      dataXML='xmlFindData'>
      Loading EditSheet...
    </div>
  </div>
</form>
```

It defines an EditSheet together with the associated data XML and meta XML islands. It also defines the form used to post the find criteria and the ASP page used to service the XMLHTTP request.

ListFindMeta.xml

The meta XML that defines the Find pane is shown below. Note that it uses a `<template>` element to override the default layout defined by the EditSheet. This element provides an HTML code fragment in a CDATA section, which defines the custom layout of the table. The `fields` attribute of the `<template>` element contains a space-delimited list of field `ids` used in the `<template>`:

```
<editsheet>
  <global title='no'/>
  <fields>
    <select id='selFindBy' onchange='OnFindChange()'>
      <prompt>Choose one</prompt>
      <select id='selFindBy'>
        <option value="SynonymID">Synonym ID</option>
        <option value="Synonym1">Synonym 1</option>
        <option value="Synonym2">Synonym 2</option>
        <option value="Any">Any</option>
      </select>
    </select>
    <numeric id="SynonymID" subtype='integer' min='0'>
      <name>Synonym ID</name>
      <prompt>Enter SynonymID</prompt>
      <tooltip>Synonym ID</tooltip>
      <error>SynonymID error</error>
    </numeric>
    <text id="Synonym1" subtype='short' maxlen='20'>
      <name>Synonym1</name>
      <prompt>Enter Synonym1</prompt>
      <tooltip>Synonym1</tooltip>
      <error>Synonym1 error</error>
```

```
          </text>
          <text id="Synonym2" subtype='short' maxlen='20'>
            <name>Synonym2</name>
            <prompt>Enter Synonym2</prompt>
            <tooltip>Synonym2</tooltip>
            <error>Synonym2 error</error>
          </text>
      </fields>
      <template fields='selFindBy SynonymID Synonym1 Synonym2'>
        <![CDATA[
          <table width='100%' style='table-layout: fixed'>
            <colgroup>
              <col width='100'>
              <col width='200'>
              <col>
            </colgroup>
            <tr>
              <td><span>Find by:</span></td>
              <td><div id='selFindBy'>Loading...</div></td>
              <td>
                <button id='cmdFind' diabled class='dbbutton'>
                  Find
                </button>
              </td>
            </tr>

            <tr id='SynonymIDRow' class='hide'>
              <td><span>SynonymID:</span></td>
              <td><div id='SynonymID'>Loading...</div></td>
            </tr>

            <tr id='Synonym1Row' class='hide'>
              <td><span>Synonym1:</span></td>
              <td><div id='Synonym1'>Loading...</div></td>
            </tr>

            <tr id='Synonym2Row' class='hide'>
              <td><span>Synonym2:</span></td>
              <td><div id='Synonym2'>Loading...</div></td>
            </tr>
          </table>
        ]]>
      </template>
  </editsheet>
```

Here the `<template>` defines an HTML `<table>` layout for the search fields. Each table row is given an `id` that is used in the `<script>` block to control the visibility of the search fields. It also defines a `<button>`, `cmdFind`, that is used to initiate a search.

When the Find pane is visible, the search type can be selected from the drop-down list box. Changing the list box values, fires the `OnChange()` event which toggles the visibility of the rows in the table as follows:

```
sub OnFindChange()
  document.all.cmdFind.disabled = true
  SynonymIDRow.className = "hide"
  Synonym1Row.className = "hide"
  Synonym2Row.className = "hide"
  SetFindByHeight(100)
```

```
select case selfindby.value
  case "SynonymID":
    SynonymIDRow.className = ""
  case "Synonym1":
    Synonym1Row.className = ""
  case "Synonym2":
    Synonym2Row.className = ""
  case "Any":
    SetFindByHeight(150)
    SynonymIDRow.className = ""
    Synonym1Row.className = ""
    Synonym2Row.className = ""
end select
```

The `Field()` method of the EditSheet is used to assign values to EditFields within the EditSheet:

```
' clear previous find values
with fbtypepicker
  .Field("SynonymID").value = ""
  .Field("Synonym1").value = ""
  .Field("Synonym2").value = ""
end with

document.all.cmdFind.disabled = false
ShowFindBy()
end sub
```

Finally, a search is initiated by pressing the Find button in the search pane:

```
sub cmdFind_OnClick()
  divMain.reload("findby")
end sub
```

where `divMain` is a ListSheet that supports the XMLHTTP operation `findby`:

```
<xml id='xmlMeta'>
  <listsheet>
    <global pagecontrols='yes'/>
    <columns>
      <column id='SynonymID'>Synonym ID</column>
      <column id='Synonym1'>Synonym1</column>
      <column id='Synonym2'>Synonym2</column>
    </columns>
    <operations>
      <newpage  formid='frmNextPage'/>
      <sort     formid='frmSort'/>
      <findby   formid='frmFind'/>
      <delete   formid='frmDelete'/>
    </operations>
  </listsheet>
</xml>
```

The `ReLoad()` method on the ListSheet performs this `findby` operation using `frmFind` to post to `Response.asp`. The criteria from the Find pane (`SynonymID`, `Synonym1` and `Synonym2`) are posted in the request.

Find()

The XMLHTTP `findby` request is serviced by the `Find()` function below – parameters are the values posted in the XMLHTTP request. The find query is executed and the recordset returned is converted into XML. Note that the SQL statement is constructed dynamically, rather than using a stored procedure:

```
function Find(byval strConn, byval varSynonymID,
              byval varSynonym1, byval varSynonym2)
  dim strSQL
  dim strCondition
  dim strWhere
  dim varArg
  dim objConn
  dim objCommand
  dim rstQuery
  dim strXML

  if HasValue(varSynonymID) then
    strWhere = "SynonymID = " & Cint(varSynonymID)
  end if

  if HasValue(varSynonym1) then
    varSynonym1 = QuoteSQL(varSynonym1)
    strCondition = " Synonym1 like '" & varSynonym1 & "'"
    if strWhere <> "" then
      strWhere = strWhere & " and "
    end if
    strWhere = strWhere & strCondition
  end if

  if HasValue(varSynonym2) then
    varSynonym2 = QuoteSQL(varSynonym2)
    strCondition = " Synonym2 like '" & varSynonym2 & "'"
    if strWhere <> "" then
      strWhere = strWhere & " and "
    end if
    strWhere = strWhere & strCondition
  end if

  if strWhere <> "" then
    strSQL = "select SynonymID, Synonym1, Synonym2 "
    strSQL = strSQL & "from tblSynonyms "
    strSQL = strSQL & "where " & strWhere
  else
    strXML = "<document><record/></document>"
    Find = strXML
    exit function
  end if

  set objConn = oGetADOConnection(strConn)
  set objCommand = oGetADOCommand(objConn, AD_CMD_TEXT)

  with objCommand
    .CommandText = strSQL
    set rstQuery = .Execute
  end with
```

```
      strXML = xmlGetXMLFromRS(rstQuery).xml
      Find = strXML

      set rstQuery = nothing
      set objConn = nothing
      set objCommand = nothing
   end function
```

Three-Tier Design Issues

The design used in the Synonyms module was essentially a heuristic design chosen in the interests of simplicity and visibility. For a production environment it is better to use a three-tier design. This section will give a brief overview of converting the current design to this structure.

The problem with the current design is that it uses ASP code exclusively, and ASP code is weakly typed, interpreted, and has poor error handling (at least if you limit yourself to VBScript). Therefore, a solution is to simply convert the following ASP functions from the Synonyms module into methods on a Visual Basic COM object:

❑   ReadRecord(strConn, intSynonymID, strRecordXML)

❑   CreateRecord(strConn, strSynonym1, strSynonym2, intSynonymID)

❑   UpdateRecord(strConn, intSynonymID, strSynonym1, strSynonym2)

❑   DeleteRecord(strConn, intSynonymID, intRecordCount)

❑   GetPage(strConn, intPage, intPageSize, strColumn, strDirection)

❑   Sort(strConn, intPage, strColumn, strDirection, intPageSize)

❑   Find(strConn, varSynonymID, varSynonym1, varSynonym2)

For example, UpdateRecord() can be converted to a Visual Basic object method as follows:

```
Function UpdateRecord( _
  ByVal strConn As String, _
  ByVal intSynonymID As Long, _
  ByVal strSynonym1 As String, _
  ByVal strSynonym2 As String) As Boolean

  On Error GoTo ErrorHandler

  Dim strSQL              As String
  Dim strMsg              As String
  Dim objConn             As ADODB.Connection
  Dim objCommand          As ADODB.Command
  Dim varArgs             As Variant
  Dim intRecordsAffected  As Long

  UpdateRecord = False
  Set objConn = New Connection
```

```
      objConn.Open strConn
      Set objCommand = New Command
      strSynonym1 = QuoteSQL(strSynonym1)
      strSynonym2 = QuoteSQL(strSynonym2)

      With objCommand
        .CommandType = adCmdStoredProc
        .CommandText = "sp_SynonymUpdate"
        varArgs = Array(intSynonymID, strSynonym1, strSynonym2)
        .Execute intRecordsAffected, varArgs, adExecuteNoRecords
      End With

      UpdateRecord = (intRecordsAffected = 1)

  Cleanup:
    Set objCommand = Nothing
    Set objConn = Nothing

    Exit Function
  ErrorHandler:
    strMsg = "Synonyms: " & Err.Description
    App.LogEvent strMsg, vbLogEventTypeError
    Resume Cleanup:
  End Function
```

This code now has the advantage of being strongly typed and compiled. In addition, the error handler allows all unexpected errors to be trapped and logged to the windows error log with App.LogEvent().

You should bear in mind that it is bad programming practice to raise an error out of a COM object. It violates the principle of information hiding since the caller is given internal details of the callee. Instead, methods on COM objects should trap all errors and return a Boolean (or enumerated type) variable to indicate if the method has succeeded or failed. Further the callee should log errors.

Finally, note that the Synonyms COM object with the above methods is stateless. The object has no properties and all information required to execute a method is passed as arguments in the call. This allows the Synonyms COM object to be registered as a COM+ application.

The Synonyms COM object would be used from an ASP page as follows:

```
  set objSynonyms = Server.CreateObject("Synonyms.Synonyms")

  blnResult = objSynonyms.UpdateRecord(strConn, intSynonymID, _
                                        strSynonym1, strSynonym2)

  set objSynonyms = nothing
```

Here the creation function would request an object from COM+. The (stateless) method would be executed and then the object would be released back to COM+.

Programming Techniques

The following sections cover some additional programming topics.

The sample code also contains a module, Test, which provides a simple shell for testing. Several of the programming features discussed below are demonstrated in the Test module. The Test module is installed in the same manner as the Synonyms module. An investigation of this module will be left to the interested reader.

Localization

The code used in this chapter has intentionally not been localized in order to simplify the code and improve readability. Localizing the Synonym module would involve the following steps:

1. Set the correct code page in the include files BDHeader.asp and BDXMLHeader.asp.

2. Replace hard-coded strings with string constants in ASP blocks. For example, a hard-coded string such as "Line of text", would be replaced with a localized equivalent <% = LINE_OF_TEXT %>.

3. Create an include file for each localized file, defining the file's string constants – for example, List.asp would have an associated include file, called ListStrings.asp, that would define all its string constants.

4. Since the subject/verb/object order can vary between languages, you may need to use the function sFormatString(strFormat, strArg1, strArg2, ...) to substitute values into a format string.

We'll consider these processes in much more detail in Chapter 16, when we look specifically at Commerce Server's support for localized and internationalized sites.

Error Handling

Errors can occur in server-side ASP code or in client-side DHTML code. There are four possible types of server-side errors:

❑   ASP errors

❑   ADO errors

❑   XML errors

❑   Script errors

Only the last pair of these can appear on the client-side.

When a server-side error occurs, BizDesk cannot simply return an error page, because one was not defined as a task target in the module configuration file. Instead, it sets an error flag with the following call in server-side script:

```
strTitle = "MyTitle"
strError = "MyError"
strDetails = "MyDetails"
SetError strTitle, strError, strDetails, ERROR_ICON_CRITICAL
```

This flag is subsequently tested by `InsertTaskbar()` on list pages and `InsertEditTaskbar()` on edit pages – on detecting the raised flag, these will both create the following dialog:

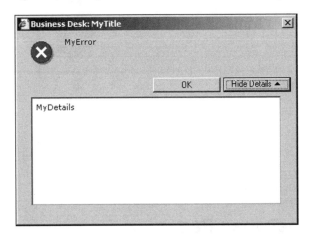

They will also log the error to the **Application** section of the Windows Event Log.

Each of the four errors listed above has an associated error object, as shown in the table below. Functions listed in the right-hand column are used to convert the information in the corresponding error object into a string for use as the third argument of the `SetError()` function:

Error Type	Error Object	Details Function
ASP	`Server.GetLastError()`	`sGetASPError()`
ADO	`objConnection.Errors(0)`	`sGetADOError()`
XML	`xlDocument.ParseError()`	`sGetXMLError()`
Script	`Err`	`sGetScriptError()`

An error dialog identical to the one above can be created from a client-side script block as follows:

```
strTitle = "MyTitle"
strError = "MyError"
strDetail = "MyDetail"
ShowErrorDlg strTitle, strError, strDetail, ERROR_ICON_QUESTION
```

The default error icons are as shown below:

Name	Icon
ERROR_ICON_ALERT	
ERROR_ICON_CRITICAL	
ERROR_ICON_INFORMATION	
ERROR_ICON_QUESTION	

The Test module contains examples of these routines.

Passing Data between Pages

In the Synonym module, we passed data between pages by posting a form that contained hidden fields. This section presents two additional methods for passing data between pages.

The first method saves values in a dictionary object attached to a hidden frame on the client. All BizDesk pages share the same dictionary, so we prefix each of the variable names with an appropriate module name, to prevent data from being overwritten. We use the following functions:

❑   `SetTemp(strName, varValue)`

❑   `GetTemp(strName)`

❑   `ClearTemp()`

These are designed to be called from client-side script, after the taskbar has been inserted, by calling either `InsertTaskBar()` or `InsertEditTaskBar()`. For example, to pass the variable `Name` between pages, you might set the data on the source page as follows:

```
SetTemp "Test_Name", "Frank J. Reashore"
```

On the target page read the value as:

```
strName = GetTemp("Test_Name")
```

The second method involves saving the dictionary on the server as an ASP Session variable – you must:

1. Save the value to a dictionary

2. Convert the dictionary to XML

3. Post the XML to the server

4. Convert the XML back to a dictionary

5. Save the dictionary in a Session variable

This method uses the following functions:

- ❏ dSetServerState(strSessionVariable, dicNew)
- ❏ dGetServerState(strSessionVariable)
- ❏ dClearServerState()

For example, to pass the Name variable between pages, set the data on the source page as follows:

```
set dicNew = CreateObject("Scripting.Dictionary")
dicNew.Add "Test_Name", "Frank J. Reashore"
set dicOld = dSetServerState("MySessionVariable", dicNew)
```

On the target page read the value as:

```
set dicValues = dGetServerState("MySessionVariable")
strName = dicValues.Item("Test_Name")
```

The Test module contains examples of each of these routines.

Dialog Boxes

DHTML dialog boxes provide a valuable means of prompting the user for additional information. Dialog boxes can be displayed when a taskbar button is clicked, or when a field's **Browse** button is selected. The novel feature of the approach here is that the dialog pages are constructed using HTCs. This allows dialog boxes to take advantage of the powerful data validation features of HTCs.

Dialog boxes are displayed with either of the following DHTML methods:

```
varValue = window.showModalDialog(strURL, varArgs, strFeatures)
varValue = window.showModelessDialog(strURL, varArgs, strFeatures)
```

where the arguments are defined as follows:

Parameter	Description
strURL	HTML file defining the dialog page layout
varArgs	(optional) variant input value
strFeatures	(optional) semi-colon delimited string of name-value pairs
varValue	Return value

The `strFeatures` argument specifies windows ornaments according to the following table:

Name	Value	Description
dialogHeight	Integer	Height in pixels
dialogWidth	Integer	Width in pixels
dialogLeft	Integer	Dialog left relative to desktop top left
dialogTop	Integer	Dialog top relative to desktop top left
center	yes|no	Specifies whether to center dialog.
help	yes|no	Specifies whether to display help icon.
resizable	yes|no	Specifies if dialog has set dimensions
status	yes|no	Specifies whether dialog has a status bar

A typical value for `strFeatures` is:

```
status: false; dialogWidth: 300; dialogHeight: 300
```

The arguments that we pass into a dialog box call – `varArgs` – can be accessed from a DHTML script using `window.dialogArguments`. Similarly, the return value is set using `window.returnValue` from DHTML script.

The code used to implement the HTML of the following dialog box is shown below.

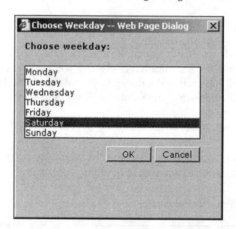

Here a TreeView HTC is instantiated and populated from a data XML island:

```
<html>
  <head>
    <title>Choose Weekday</title>
    <link rel='stylesheet' type='text/css' href='/widgets/bizdesk.css'>
    <style>
      body {
        margin:          0px;
```

```
        padding:       10px;
        height:        200px;
    }
    #btnOK, #btnCancel{
        width:         60px;
    }
    #tvList {
        width:         100%;
        height:        90px;
        background:    white;
        border:        solid;
        border-width: 1;
    }
    #divButtons {
        padding-top:   10px;
    }
</style>
<script language='VBScript'>
    Option  Explicit
    dim nodSelected
    '****************************************
    sub window_onload()
        nodSelected = null
    end sub
    '****************************************
```

The HTC defines event handlers for selection and execution (double-clicking). When a node is selected, the XML value of the node is extracted from the window event. The OK button returns the name of the currently selected node.

```
    sub btnOK_OnClick()
        with window
            .returnValue = nodSelected.nodeName
            .close()
        end with
    end sub
    '****************************************
    sub btnCancel_OnClick()
        with window
            .returnValue = empty
            .close()
        end with
    end sub
    '****************************************
    sub OnItemSelect()
        set nodSelected = window.event.xmlItem
        btnOK.disabled = isNull(nodSelected)
    end sub
    '****************************************
    sub OnItemExecute()
        OnItemSelect()
        btnOK_OnClick()
    end sub
    '****************************************
</script>
```

723

```
    </head>
    <body>
      <h5>Choose weekday:</h5>

      <xml id='xmlValues'>
        <document skip='yes'>
          <Monday/>
          <Tuesday/>
          <Wednesday/>
          <Thursday/>
          <Friday/>
          <Saturday/>
          <Sunday/>
        </document>
      </xml>

      <div id='tvList'
        class='treeView'
        DataXML='xmlValues'
        language='VBScript'
        onitemselect='OnItemSelect()'
        onitemexecute='OnItemExecute()'>
        Loading...
      </div>

      <div id='divButtons' align='right'>
        <button id='btnOK' disabled>OK</button> 
        <button id='btnCancel'>Cancel</button>
      </div>
    </body>
</html>
```

The technique shown above can easily be modified to create an input dialog as shown below – here we use an EditField, the big advantage of which is that it lets us validate input values. This dialog is attached to the **Browse** button of the PromoCode field in the `EditField.htm` sample:

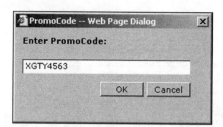

When working with dialog boxes, ensure that your browser is not caching pages – otherwise, refreshing the calling page will not automatically refresh the dialog page, and this can lead to very confusing browser behavior. To turn off caching in IE5, select **Tools | Internet Options,** and from the **General** tab choose **Settings.** The dialog box shown below will now be displayed – make sure that the radio button "**Every visit to the page**" is selected:

BizDesk uses some custom dialog boxes defined in the `include` directory. The variable `g_sBDIncludeRoot` is used to specify the path to the dialog file as follows:

```
strIncludeRoot = "<%= g_sBDIncludeRoot %>"
strURL = strIncludeRoot & "Dlg_warn.asp"
```

Security

You can restrict network-authenticated access to modules by simply setting access permissions on the module entry point using the security tab of the file property dialog:

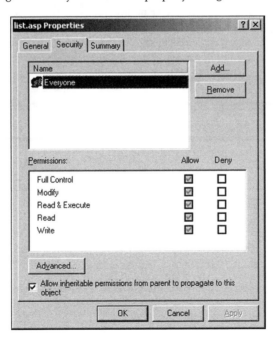

To assign permissions to a specific user (such as **Administrator** or **System**) or group (such as **BizDeskUsers**) click the **Add...** button and specify appropriate permissions using the check boxes. Once these have been assigned, remove the **Everyone** entry. You'll first need to uncheck the **Allow inheritable permissions** check box – the following dialog box will appear:

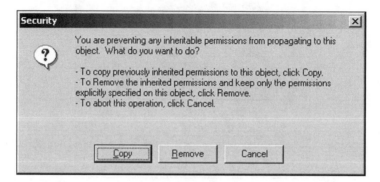

Click **Remove** to keep only the permissions explicitly specified on the object.

Once specific access permissions have been set on a module entry point, the module will only be displayed in the navigation bar (in production mode) if the user has access permissions. In debug mode the module entry point will be displayed in yellow but will not be accessible.

Client-side DHTML Functions

Some common DHTML functions used on both list and edit pages are shown below:

Function	Description
SetStatusText(strText)	Sets the status line text
ClearStatusText()	Clears status line
SetWaitDisplayText(strText)	Sets the text within the wait box
ShowWaitDisplay()	Displays the wait box
HideWaitDisplay()	Hides the wait box
SetPageTitleText(strText)	Sets the title text at the top of page
DisableTask(strTask)	Disables a task button
EnableTask(strTask)	Enables a task button
EnableAllTasks(blnEnable)	Enables or disables all tasks depending on blnEnable
ToggleTask(strTask)	Toggles a task button between enabled and disabled states

Function	Description
`DisableTaskMenuItem(strItem, intPosition)`	Disables a menu button
`EnableTaskMenuItem(strItem, intPosition)`	Enables a menu button
`EnableAllTaskMenuItems(strID, blnEnable)`	Enables or disables all menu items depending on blnEnable

Before we finish off, let's take a quick look at elGetTaskBtn(`strButton`).

Consider a group of taskbar buttons that share the same event handler. As you may recall, this will happen if each task button defines the same `formname` attribute (say `frmAction`) in its `<task>` element, and `frmAction` contains an `OnTask` attribute defining a common event handler. `elGetTaskBtn()` can be used to determine which task bar button was pressed within the event handler, as follows:

```
sub EventHandler()
  dim elSource

  set elSource = window.event.srcElement

  if elSource = elGetTaskBtn("button1") then
    ' handle button1
  elseif elSource = elGetTaskBtn("button2") then
    ' handle button2
    ...
  end if
end if
```

Once again, the Test module contains examples of these routines.

Summary

This chapter began with a quick walkthrough of how to set up a configured BizDesk application as an integrated project in Visual InterDev – most of the steps being equally applicable to your own IDE of choice – in order to facilitate any necessary debugging.

We continued with a detailed analysis of the custom module 'Synonyms', and saw how BizDesk defines special event handlers to allow the events fired by HTCs to enable and disable the taskbar buttons. We then examined in detail the structure of the listpages and editpages contained within the Synonym module.

We looked at how taskbar functionality (such as saving data) can be implemented by posting data between pages. We also saw how the module performs command processing, and examined XMLHTTP operations, seeing how they can be used to implement scrolling and searching.

Finally we considered some other useful tweaks, such as localization, error handling, other techniques for passing data between pages, dialog box construction using HTCs, and security.

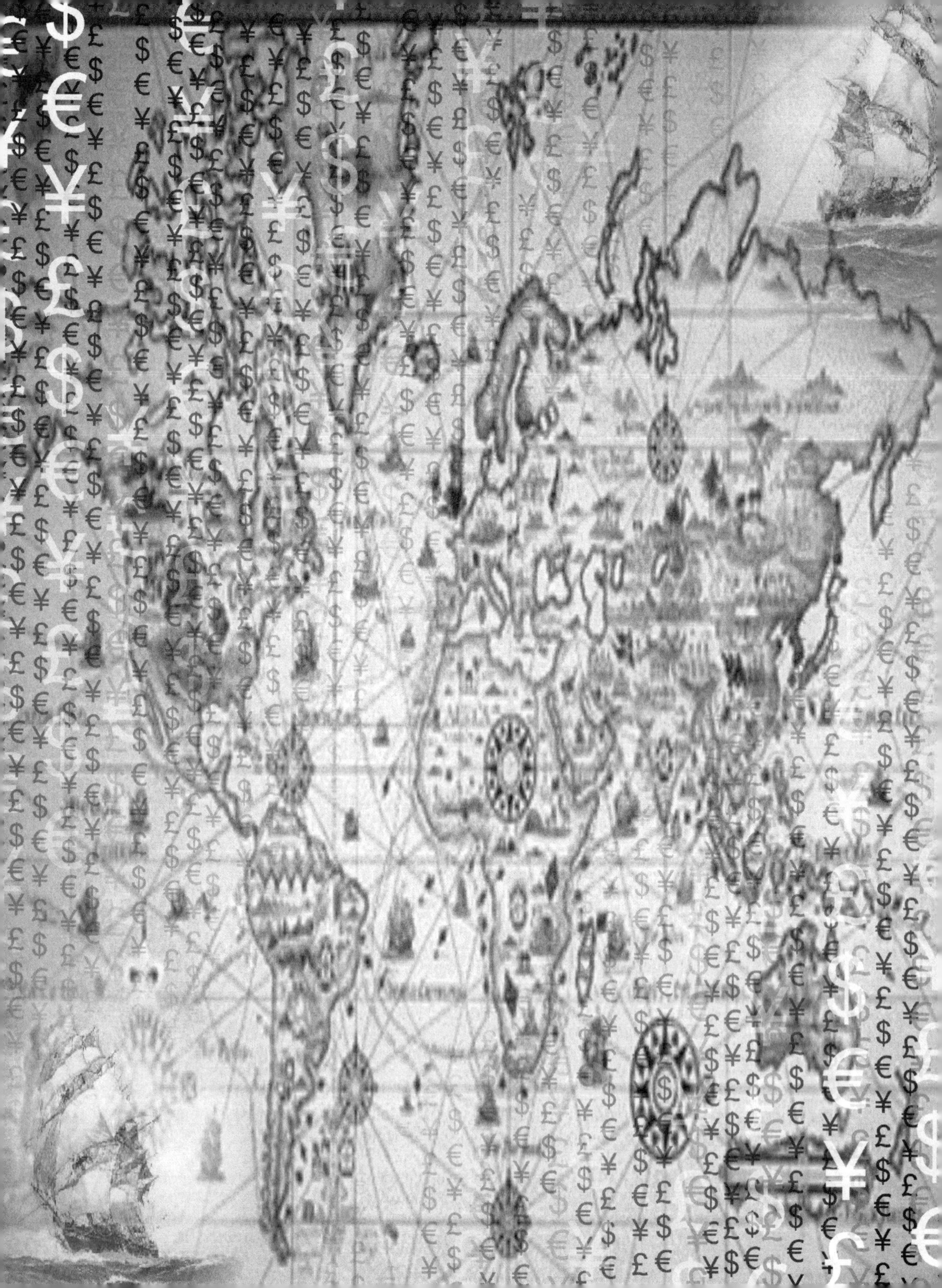

15

BizTalk Integration

Microsoft's BizTalk Server provides a framework for Business to Business (B2B) application integration, and as such, promises to make a big impact on the way in which B2B and E-Commerce solutions will be implemented. As a sister product of Commerce Server 2000, we would expect BizTalk Server to integrate well with e-commerce solutions based on Commerce Server. After an introduction to BizTalk Server, this is precisely what we'll be looking at in this chapter. Specifically, we'll investigate the following topics:

- ❑ The BizTalk Initiative
- ❑ Using the BizTalk Editor
- ❑ Using the BizTalk Mapper to specify data transformations
- ❑ Using the BizTalk Messaging Manager
- ❑ Administering BizTalk Server Groups
- ❑ BizTalk Document Tracking
- ❑ Using the BizTalk Orchestration Designer
- ❑ Exchanging catalogs
- ❑ Generating catalogs in the Commerce Server XML format
- ❑ Importing catalogs from other sources
- ❑ Importing a catalog to Commerce Server using BizTalk
- ❑ Order management using BizTalk

Without further ado, we'll look at what the BizTalk Initiative actually is.

The BizTalk Initiative

Site Server 3.0 Commerce Edition implemented **Commerce Interchange Piplines** (**CIP**), a series of pipeline components that enabled businesses to create COM based business logic that would enable Business to Business (B2B) solutions. From this came the idea of creating a set of standards for B2B interaction.

A steering committee made up of representatives from Microsoft and host of other industry leading hardware, software, and ISVs created an initiative based on XML and B2B called the **BizTalk Initiative**. This can be broken down into three components:

❑ The BizTalk Framework – based on XML and SOAP, the BizTalk Framework supports application integration and electronic commerce. SOAP – the Simple Object Access Protocol – provides a simple and lightweight mechanism for exchanging structured and typed information between peers using XML.

The BizTalk framework is designed for implementing an XML schema and a set of XML tags in messages sent between applicatons. It is not a specification yet, but has been submitted to the W3C for review as an XML schema standard.

❑ The second part of the initiative is to maintain a community and a repository for the storage of these schemas. The community address is http://www.BizTalk.org. At this site, we can access all the different document schemas that have been uploaded from various companies. After registration, we may download these schemas for use in our own implementations, or upload other schemas.

❑ The third and last piece of the BizTalk initiative is a server product that encapsultate the ideas created for the BizTalk Framework document specification: a server product that makes it easier to create, route, translate, store, and track data from one system to another system. Microsoft's implementation of this is called **BizTalk Server**.

BizTalk Server provides ways of integrating multiple data sources and different types of document exchanges. In this chapter, we will focus on how Commerce Server 2000 integrates with BizTalk, looking at ways of implementing integrated solutions.

BizTalk Server 2000

Let's take a look at BizTalk Server, setting the stage for exploring the integration of BizTalk Server with Commercer Server.

BizTalk Server is built upon two distinct technologies:

❑ **BizTalk Messaging Services**: BizTalk provides tools and technologies for routing documents and data to and from applications and organizations.

BizTalk Orchestration: BizTalk Orchestration designer is a tool and technology for building Business process applications out of Visio based diagrams.

Installing BizTalk Server

We'll install BizTalk Server on the same machine as Commerce Server. It is possible to install BizTalk on a different machine, but for some of the examples, it will be helpful to install it on the same machine.

> *A 120 day evaluation edition of BizTalk server may be downloaded from* http://www.microsoft.com/BizTalk/downloads/default.htm.

Ideally, starting with a fresh machine, we would follow the following sequence in order to install BizTalk:

- ❑ Install Windows 2000 SP1.
- ❑ Make sure that MSMQ is installed on the machine.
- ❑ Install Visio SR-1 for the BizTalk Orchestration.
- ❑ Install SQL server 7.0 or SQL 2000.
- ❑ Install Commerce Server 2000.
- ❑ Install the Commerce Server Retail solution site.
- ❑ Install BizTalk Server 2000.

BizTalk Server will install three databases for the messaging services, and one for BizTalk orchestration.

Before moving on to Commerce Server integration, we will take a look at **Messaging Service**s.

Overview of BizTalk Messaging Services

The BizTalk Messaging Services is an environment for automating XML data exchange both within and between companies. It enables us to receive, deliver and track documents, transfer data from one source to another, analyze document transaction, generate document receipts, and utilize reliable secure messaging.

There is a great deal of flexibility as to how or in what way we can set up our server to send or receive documents. BizTalk can be set up to receive from specific sources, or multiple sources. It can be set up to send to multiple destinations through distribution lists, or to specific locations. It also provides us with the flexibility to utilize loosely coupled or queued component type models using **Microsoft Message Queue** (**MSMQ**).

BizTalk can also speak to different organizations or applications over a host of different protocols. Flexibility on multiple standards based protocols is a fundamental part of the core design of BizTalk Messaging services. Once the core infrastructure is in place, documents can then be sent via these transports to BizTalk.

BizTalk Server Tools

In order for BizTalk Server (BTS) to communicate with other systems, it first needs to be given a description of the data that will be sent or received. This is provided by an XML representation of the data: this document tells BTS how to parse the data when it is received.

There are five main tools in BizTalk Server which provide ways of utilizing its functionality. In the following sections, we'll look at these.

The BizTalk Editor

In order to send and receive documents, BizTalk has to know what the data being sent or received will look like, so we need to create a **Document Specification** or **Document Definition** for BizTalk to reference for parsing out the relevant data from the document sent to it. This specification is like a template in XML that describes the structure of our data. The BizTalk Editor enables us to create or revise these document specifications.

We may have existing documents that we want to utilize. In the BTS Editor, we can import other documents which are based on XML standards. These other documents might include:

❑ DTDs - (Document Type Definitions)

❑ XML schemas

❑ Electronic Data Interchange (EDI) specifications such as:

  ❑ ANSI X12

  ❑ EDI for administration, commerce, and transport (EDIFACT)

❑ Flat files

❑ Well-formed XML

❑ Structured document formats

❑ XML-based templates

As we can see, there are quite a few different types of documents that can be utilized to format data. All we do with the BizTalk Editor is create a framework for what the data structure looks like. For instance, let's look at a simple flat file.

Suppose we have a simple flat file that we want to send to a different location. In order for BTS to know what to send, or how to send it, we need to create a document specification for it. Suppose also that the file is a delimited flat file, and that any parsing routine that we write will have to know what the elements of the file are: whether it is positional or delimited, what the delimiters are, and so on.

Lets take a look at a flat file. Copy the information below and paste it into notepad, saving the file as po.csv.

```
HD112345
HD2mySupplier
ITEMbook,Developing BizTalk applications,15243,2,34.95
ITEMoffice,Spiral Notebook,4231,10,1.29
ITEMoffice,Pen,6789,5,0.10
```

Notice that there are two header elements, and that each of the other elements is separated via commas. This is a delimited flat file, or a comma separated value file. For us to send this to BTS, we need to create a BizTalk document that represents the structure of this data. A core aspect of BTS is transforming a document from one format to another.

To get data in and out if BTS, we need to know both the structure of the input data, and the structure of the output data. So not only do we use the BizTalk Editor to create the document template for receiving data, but also to create document specification for the output data.

The following XML determines the desired structure of the output data (this file, `output.xml`, can be downloaded with the other code from the Wrox website):

```xml
<?xml version="1.0" ?>
<!-- Generated by using BizTalk Editor on Wed, Feb 07 2001 02:51:25 PM -->
<!-- Microsoft Corporation (c) 2000 (http://www.microsoft.com)  -->
<Schema name="SupplierOutput" b:BizTalkServerEditorTool_Version="1.0"
b:root_reference="SupplierOutput" b:standard="XML" xmlns="urn:schemas-microsoft-
com:xml-data" xmlns:b="urn:schemas-microsoft-com:BizTalkServer"
xmlns:d="urn:schemas-microsoft-com:datatypes">
  <b:SelectionFields />
  <ElementType name="TotalCost" content="textOnly" model="closed" d:type="float">
  <b:FieldInfo />
  </ElementType>
  <ElementType name="SupplierOutput" content="eltOnly">
  <b:RecordInfo />
  <element type="Supplier" maxOccurs="1" minOccurs="1" />
  <element type="ItemCount" maxOccurs="1" minOccurs="1" />
  <element type="TotalCost" maxOccurs="1" minOccurs="1" />
  </ElementType>
  <ElementType name="Supplier" content="textOnly" model="closed" d:maxLength="50"
d:minLength="1" d:type="string">
  <b:FieldInfo />
  </ElementType>
  <ElementType name="ItemCount" content="textOnly" model="closed" d:type="int">
  <b:FieldInfo />
  </ElementType>
  </Schema>
```

The BizTalk Editor provides us with five tabs for helping us create such documents. They help us with things such as setting the data type, determining whether the file is positional, or delimited and so on.

Let's open the editor from **Start | programs | Microsoft biztalk server 2000 | BizTalk Editor**, and look at a document specification of the flat file above.

Open the file `BasicPO.xml` (this is downloadable from the Wrox website).

The five tabs for the BizTalk Editor are:

- **Declaration Tab** – This handles information such as **Name**, **Description**, and **Data Type** information about a specific element in a structure.

- **Reference Tab** – This tab lets us specify the name of the document and what type of document it is.

- **Parse Tab** – Structure of data: if a flat file, then how the file is delimited, such as how the field order is structured (**prefix**, **infix**, and **postfix**), and what the delimiters are.

- **Namespace Tab** – This tab is specifically for namespace information of the XML documents, usually defined as URNs (Uniform Resource Name).

- **Dictionary Tab** – This is for source type information as well as document types and version information.

- **Code List Tab** – For EDI (Electronic Data Interchange) implementations: the information contained in this tab specifies X12 (Standard implementation of EDI) or EDIFACT (European EDI specification) code values, and their descriptions.

Once the document is completed, we then store the information in a WebDAV for reference and retrieval. **WebDAV (Web Distributed Authoring and Versioning)** is an extension to the HTTP 1.1 standard that exposes a hierarchical file storage media – such as a file system – over an HTTP connection. It locks documents to prevent users from accidentally overwriting each other's changes. It also enables users to share and work with server-based documents, regardless of their authoring tools, platforms, or the type of web servers on which the files are stored.

The BizTalk Editor provides the first steps in creating the documents we need to reference. It provides flexible ways of describing our data and creating XML representations or templates for BTS to understand what we are sending it. We will see examples of building document specifications later when we look at specific implementation scenarios.

Once a document has been defined in the BizTalk Editor, we store each of the files listed above to the WebDAV for use later; the next step is to get the data from one format, such as a flat file, to another format, such as XML, as the output. We need to create another document specification or template: this is a **mapped document** specification. We do that by using the BizTalk Mapper.

BizTalk Mapper

A BizTalk Map represents a set of data transformations between two specifications: the source specification and the destination specification. BizTalk Mapper is a translation design tool that utilizes XSL. XSL is a style sheet format for XML documents. It is used to define the display of XML in the same way that Cascading Style Sheets (CSS) are used to define the display of HTML. BizTalk Server uses XSL as the translation language between two specifications. XSL is utilized by BizTalk Mapper as an output engine, which enables us to determine how fields and records in one specification will correspond to fields and records in another.

BizTalk Mapper supports a variety of mapping scenarios, ranging from simple, parent-child tree relationships, to detailed, complex looping of records and hierarchies. This is done by means of **links** and **functoids**. A link simply specifies a **copy operation** from the value in one field to the value in another field, whereas a functoid is an **object** that facilitates complex structural manipulation operations between source elements and destination elements. These operations can range from simple calculations to elaborate script functionality.

> *As soon as we've defined a specification in the BizTalk Editor, it can be used in BizTalk Mapper, which supports EDI, flat files, XML files, schemas, and even ADO recordsets – it can also create XSL stylesheets for mapping.*

When the mapping process is complete, a **serializer** component uses the specification to create a file format that can be recognized by a trading partner or internal application. BizTalk Mapper also includes a style sheet compiler component that takes the visual representation of the map and creates an XSL style sheet.

Creating a Map

Let's retrieve the basicpo.xml document that we saved in the WebDAV. Click on Start | programs | Mirosoft biztalk server 2000 | BizTalk Mapper. Once the BizTalk Mapper is opened, click on File | New. The WebDAV window will now open.

We now double-click on the WebDAV files folder, find the BasicPO.xml file, and double-click on it. The window will automatically open again for the destination specification. Find the supplieroutput.xml file. Once we have both files open, the interface should look like this:

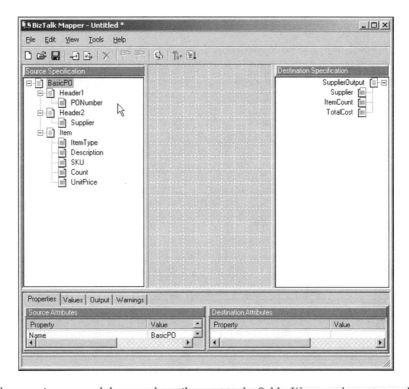

Let's start the mapping; expand the records until we get to the fields. We map elements together by clicking on a source node, and dragging across to a destination node.

We'll start the mapping by connecting the Supplier name to the Supplier.

The ouput that we need will typically be different to the input, so we need a way of specifying different types of transformations. The BizTalk Mapper supports complex structural transformations from records and fields in the source specification tree to records and fields in the destination specification tree. By selecting a **functoid** from the Functoid Palette, dragging it to the mapping grid, and linking it to elements in the source specification and destination specification trees, data can be added together, date or time information can be modified, data can be concatenated, or other operations can be performed.

The Functoid Palette should appear like this:

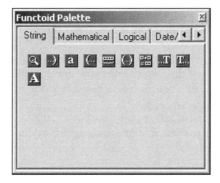

It includes the following functoids:

- ❏ String – these functoids manipulate data strings by using string functions; for example, the String Find functoid finds one text string within another text string, and returns the position of the first character of the found string.

- ❏ Mathematical – these functoids perform calculations by using arguments in a particular order, or structure; for example, the Addition functoid adds the values of the designated fields or records.

- ❏ Logical – these functoids perform specific logical tests; for example, a logical functoid can evaluate a value from the source specification against a set argument. If the value meets the argument, the logical functoid produces a value and places it in a record or field in the destination specification.

- ❏ Date/Time – these functoids manipulate date and time data or add current date, time, or date and time data to a record or field in the destination specification.

- ❏ Conversion – these functoids closely match functions such as DEC2HEX, which returns a hexadecimal value given a decimal value. They can also be used to convert a character to its ASCII value or a value to the corresponding ASCII character.

- ❏ Scientific – these functoids convert a numeric value to a scientific value; for example, the Cosine functoid takes a value from a field or record and returns the cosine.

- ❏ Cumulative – these functoids return the sum, average, or minimum or maximum input of a looping record.

- ❏ Database – these functoids extract data from a database.

- ❏ Advanced – this tab has a functoid that can use custom Microsoft VB script, functoids for value mapping, and functoids for managing and extracting information like record looping.

We can also use cascading functoids which enable us to create maps for which we must link fields or records to multiple functoids to produce the necessary output in a field or record in the destination specification. Cascading functoids make it easy to create multiple, consecutive transformations in the mapping grid. Functoids are cascaded when one functoid is linked to another functoid before it is linked to a record or field in the destination specification. For example, we can create cascading functoids in which two concatenated strings are used to produce a third string, which will be fed into a field in the destination specification. There is no limit to the number of functoids we can cascade together in the mapping grid. However, complex cascading scenarios might result in poor performance.

Open up the functoid palette by clicking on View | Functoid Palette. Navigate to the Cumulative Functoids and drag a Sum functoid to the map area. Next, in our output, we need the sum of the count in the data be the item count of our output. Drag Count on the Source to the Sum Functoid and drag a connection from the Functiod to the Item Count on the Destination.

To get the total cost in the output, we are going to cascade some functions. On the Functoid Palette, navigate to the Mathematical Functoids, and drag a multiplication functoid onto the map area. Next, drag a connection from Count to the Multiply functoid, then drag Unitprice to the Multiply functoid.

We are after the sum of these two quantities, so navigate back to the Cumulative functoid and drag a Sum functoid to the map area. Connect the Multiply functoid to the Sum functoid and the Sum functoid to the TotalCost in the destination spec.

Our map should look like this:

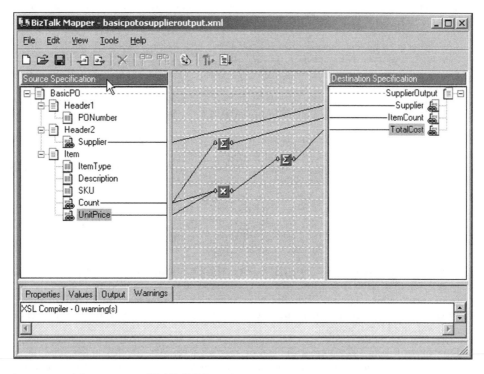

Save the map, and the store it to WebDAV for reference as `BasicPOtoSupplierOutput.xml`.

To look at what the mapper created in the form of XML, we can open and view the document in Internet Explorer.

We should see a node called `<links>`. This handles all of the linkage information that we created in the mapper.

This tool really provides us with a lot of flexibility in mapping documents. Once we have created all of our document definitions, we are now ready to look at setting up the plumbing and framework for sending and receiving documents.

BizTalk Messaging Manager

BizTalk Messaging Manager is a graphical user interface (GUI) with which we can manage the exchange of documents by configuring **BizTalk Messaging Services**. BizTalk Messaging Services can also be configured programmatically.

BizTalk Messaging Manager is an application that stores all the data for setting up configurations of documents being received for applications or oganizations. This enables system administrators to retain security and central control of the server, while enabling remote users to access BizTalk Messaging Manager.

There are some key pieces to the BizTalk Messaging Manager that we should look at.

737

- ❑ **Channels** – The purpose of all other BizTalk Messaging Manager objects is to either create channels or support the operation of channels. Channels identify the source of documents, which can be an organization or an application within a business. Channels also identify inbound and outbound documents by using document definitions.

- ❑ **Messaging ports** – Messaging ports identify a destination for the documents that are processed by a channel. The destination can be an organization or an application within your business. A messaging port specifies a destination address to which the documents are sent, how they are transported to that address, and if and how they are secured and/or enveloped. You must create at least one channel for an individual messaging port.

- ❑ **Organizations** – Organizations represent other trading partners with which we exchange documents. A special organization type, called the home organization, represents your business. We can create applications for the home organization that represent the internal applications that our business might use. Organizations and applications serve as the source for a channel or the destination for a messaging port.

- ❑ **Document definitions** – The document definitions represent a specific type of document that is processed by BizTalk Server 2000. A document definition provides a pointer to a document specification. A document definition can be used in any number of channels.

- ❑ **Envelopes** – Envelopes provide BizTalk Server 2000 with the information that the server needs to either open inbound or create outbound interchanges. Envelopes can be selected from within a messaging port to direct the server in creating outbound interchanges. Envelopes, which are independent of a messaging port, can be used by BizTalk Server 2000 to open inbound interchanges.

- ❑ **Distribution lists** – these are groups of messaging ports with which you can send the same document to a group of different trading partner organizations or internal applications. You must create at least one channel for a distribution list, just as you do for an individual messaging port.

Let's create channels and ports for BTS to send our document. Open the BizTalk Messaging Manager: Start | Programs| Microsoft BizTalk Server 2000 | BizTalk Messaging Manager. Once we've opened the Messaging manager, the first thing we need to do is to create our **Document Definitions**.

From the console, click on the Document Definitions, and then click search. From the file menu, click on File | New | Document Definition. Name the first document `BasicPO.xml`, click on browse, and find the `BasicPO.XML`. Create another Document Definition for our `Supplieroutput.xml` Document:

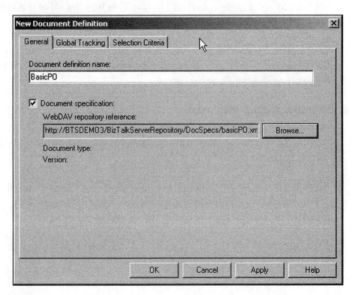

Since we are sending a flat file, we also need to declare it as an envelope in the Messaging manager: go to **File | New | Envelopes,** and an enevelope dialog should popup. Name the envelope BasicPO, select the envelope format as flatfile and click ok.

We set up our flat file format in an envelope format so that we can have header and footer information, like this:

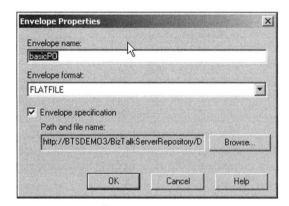

Now lets create the messaging ports needed for our simple scenario. From the Messaging Manager, click on **Messaging Ports** and click **Search.** From the File menu, click on File| New | Messaging Port| To An Application. Name this messaging port SupplierMessagingPort.

In the Destination Application screen, select New XLANG schedule and enter the file path C:\Supplieroutput\po.skx.

We are going to create a file in a tool called **BizTalk Orchestration**. We'll take a more detailed look at this tool later in the chapter. Enter StartPOPort as the port name and click Next:

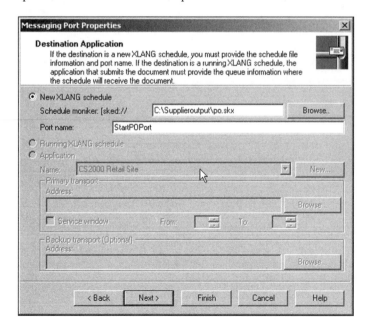

We need to leave the envelope information as the default, and click Next. In the Security Information screen, we would configure the encoding or encryption of our documents. In this instance, we'll keep the defaults, and click Finish.

The New Channel Wizard will pop up, asking us for an organization name. Click New. Name the new organization Supplier. Back on the defaults for the organization name, click Next.

On the Inbound Document screen, browse and click on BasicPO.xml, and click OK. We should see the file path updated with the file in the BizTalk Repository.

Click Next to the Outbound Document screen. Browse to find the suppliertooutput.xml file, select this, and click OK. Select the check box on the mapped outbound document, and select Browse. Another window will pop up, and you should see the WebDAV basicpotosupplierouput.xml. Select this and click OK.

On the document logging screen, click Next on the defaults. At thus point, we could, if we wished, choose to log information about inbound and outbound documents being sent. On the Advanced Configuration screen, click Finish. The advance configurations are for setting overriding properties of a channel.

Let me explain what we just created. In the scope of receiving our document, we set up the properties for our base plumbing in receiving and translating our document. What we need to do now set up the properties in BTS to send the documents out to the destination.

Let's create another messaging port for a place to send our documents out. In the messaging manager, click on File | New| Messaging Port |To An Organization. Name the messaging port FileMessagingPort and click Next:

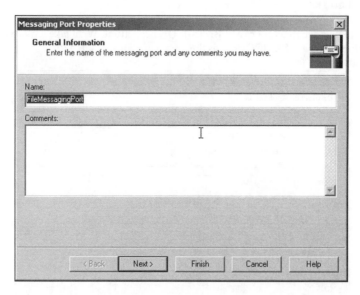

On the Destination Organization, click New on the organization, name the new organization Supplier, and click OK. Click on the primary address, and for the transport type click the drop-down menu, and select File. For the path of the file, use file://c:\supplieroutput\output.xml, making sure that you create a file directory for the supplier output in the C directory. Then and click OK.

Back on the destination organization, page click **Next**. We don't have any envelope information, so click **Next**. In the Security Information screen make sure that **Create A Channel For This Messaging Port** is checked, and make sure that it's **From an Application**. Then click Finish.

The new Channel wizard should pop up. Name this channel **FileMessagingChannel**, and click **Next**.

In the Source Application screen select the **XLANG schedule** and click **Next**.

In the Inbound Document screen, click **Browse**, select the `supplieroutput.xml` document, and click Ok. Since the output document is already in a state that is useful to us – we have already created the output – we can define the inbound and outbound document as the same.

In the Outbound Document screen click **Browse**, select the `supplieroutput.xml` document, and click OK. In the Document Logging screen click **Next.** In the Advanced Configuration screen click **Finish.**

We have now created all the necessary pieces in the BizTalk Messaging Manager for sending and receiving the flat file to an organization. The BizTalk Messaging Manager stores all the information in a SQL server database called **InterchangeBTM**. Since all this information is stored in a data store, the flexibility of extending the messaging manager is relatively simple. Also, the messaging services are all exposed, and we can, if we wish, configure these properties programmatically. We will look at how to do this a little later in the chapter, when we look at application integration components.

The BizTalk messaging Manager has quite a few different components, and so it's easy to get lost when creating the different ports and channels. Remember that we cannot have a port without a channel, and that the channel is a representation of the path to the document, and we will be well on our way to understanding this tool.

We now need to set up BTS to receive documents from a server, and ensure that the server is up and running. We can do this through the BizTalk Server Administration.

BizTalk Server Administration

BizTalk Server Administration – also called the **Administration Console** – is a Microsoft Management Console (MMC) snap-in that provides a visual representation of the BizTalk Server components. The left side of the administration console is called the console tree, and consists of folders and subfolders that represent different items, such as **server groups**. The right side of the administration console is called the details pane and contains information about the item that is selected in the console tree:

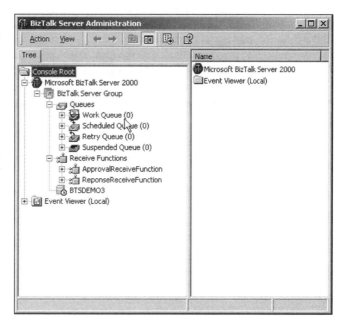

Microsoft BizTalk Server 2000 is displayed as a sub-item of the Console Root on the left side of the administration console. Each server group configured in BizTalk Server is displayed in a separate subfolder and consists of the Queues and Receive Functions for that group, as well as the names of servers in the group. Expand any item in the console tree to display additional details about the item in the details pane of the administration console. We can right-click on any item to configure it, or to create new items.

BizTalk Server Groups

A server group is the key organizing principle in BizTalk Server Administration. Server groups are collections of individual servers that are centrally managed, configured, and monitored. All servers in a BizTalk server group have in common:

❑ **Shared Queues**: The Shared Queue database stores all checkpoint information related to documents processed by BizTalk Server. If a server fails, other computers that use the same Shared Queue database can continue to retrieve messages from and post messages to the **Work Queue**. This provides redundancy and process load balancing. The Shared Queue database is presented in BizTalk Server Administration as a series of distinct queues. There are four queues in the Shared Queue enviroment:

Work Queue: The Work queue contains documents that are currently being processed by BizTalk Server. Transactions in the Work queue do not remain in the queue very long because they are processed upon arrival. BizTalk Server Administrators can select any document in this queue and move it to the Suspended queue.

Scheduled Queue: The Scheduled queue contains work items that have been processed by BizTalk Server and are waiting for transmission. BizTalk Server Administrators can select any document in this queue and move it to the Suspended queue.

Retry Queue: The Retry queue contains documents that are being resubmitted for delivery and documents that are waiting for reliable messaging receipts. It is not possible to tell the difference between the two types of transmissions. By default, failed transmissions are retried every five minutes for a maximum of three tries before they are moved to the **Suspended Queue**. These numbers can be changed through BizTalk Messaging Manager or programmatically. This is done in the scope of the specific machine. BizTalk Server Administrators can select any document in this queue and move it to the Suspended queue.

Suspended Queue: The Suspended queue contains work items that have failed processing for a variety of reasons, including parsing errors, serialization errors, failed transmissions, or the inability to find a channel configuration. BizTalk Administrators can right-click any document in this queue to choose any of the following options:

    a. **View Error Description:** Enables BizTalk Administrators to view error descriptions that indicate why the document was sent to the Suspended queue.

    b. **View Interchange:** Enables BizTalk Administrators to view the contents of an interchange that has failed processing for a variety of reasons, including parsing errors or failed transmissions.

    c. **View Document:** Enables BizTalk Administrators to view the contents of a document that has failed processing for a variety of reasons, including serialization errors or the inability to find a channel.

    d. **Delete:** Enables BizTalk Administrators to completely remove an entry from the Suspended queue. This action is not recoverable. After a document has been deleted from the Suspended queue, we cannot retrieve it.

   e. **Resubmit: Enables BizTalk Administrators to resubmit interchanges and documents to BizTalk Server for processing.**

❑ **Receive functions**: Functionality that enables any BizTalk server to monitor directories and submit documents to BizTalk Server for processing. BizTalk Server 2000 supports File and Message Queuing receive functions.

We need to set up some receive functions for our document. So, open the BizTalk Administrator at Start I Programs I Microsoft BizTalk Server 2000I BizTalk Server Administration. Once we have it opened, click on the BizTalk Server Group and expand the group.

On the Receive Functions, right-click and select New I File Receive Function. The Add A File Receive Function window will appear, and the name of the function will be POReceive. In the Types Of Files To Poll For enter PO.csv.

Create a folder in your C: drive called PODrop. Back on the receive function page, add the newly created directory in the polling location as c:\podrop. Click on the Advanced tab: this is where you can determine if the sourse is open, or if it's specified by organization. In this instance, we'll leave the default: Not open.

We need to set the envelope properties. The drop-down menu under Envelope name should contain basicPO. Select this, and then select the drop-down menu for the channel. Select the SupplierMessagingChannel and click OK:

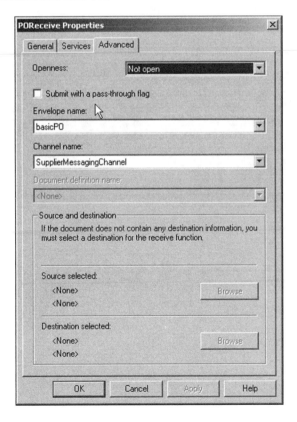

We now have the plumbing set up to receive our document and process it to a different format. There is just one more step we need to take: this will be covered in our discussion of BizTalk Orchestration.

Now that we've looked at using BizTalk Administration, let's move on to the last tool of the BizTalk messaging services: **BizTalk Document Tracking**.

BizTalk Document Tracking

BizTalk Document Tracking is a standalone web application that we can use to view interchanges and documents that are configured to be tracked in Microsoft BizTalk Server. At install, BizTalk Server installs a database in SQL Server called Interchange DTA (where DTA is an acronym for Document Tracking and Analysis).

The tracking tool will track all document exhanges on the BizTalk servers that we set up. It's also useful to see if any problems are occuring with transmission of documents.

The main page allows us to manage six main aspects of document tracking:

Date Range

Source Selection

Destination Selection

Advanced Query

Sort Control

Document Type Selection

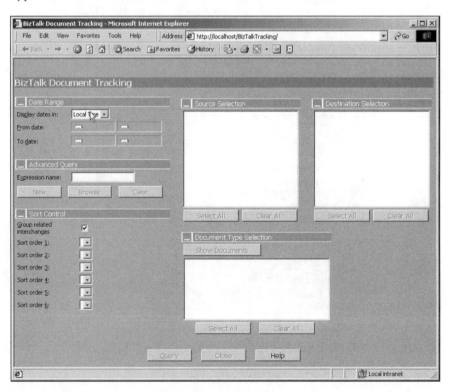

We can configure query parameters in the Date Range, Source Selection, Destination Selection, and Document Type Selection areas. The lower-left side of the page contains the Advanced Query and Sort Control areas.

We would configure the parameters in the Advanced Query area to find specific information or custom search fields. Options in the Sort Control area enable us to specify the sort order on the Query Results page.

When we click the Query button on the main page, the Query Results page appears. If any records in the Interchange DTA database match our query parameters, interchange records appear in a list.

The BizTalk Document Tracking application can be used remotely and can be customized to meet the needs of the business issues.

BizTalk Server 2000 provides a set of tools that enables us to create, store, track, route, and specify document exhanges internal to a company and between companies. Enabling systems to share information through BTS provides a flexible way to share information.

We will return to our simple scenario, but there is one more piece that we need to put in place: **BizTalk Orchestration**.

Overview of BizTalk Orchestration

Orchestration is about **integrating** and **automating business interactions** that span applications, people, and organizations, either behind a firewall, or across the Internet. It's an entirely new aspect of Commerce Server 2000, and is completely separate from BizTalk messaging services.

Orchestration is about connecting the dots that comprise the business model, ensuring that they are performed in sequence, and that information from one step is passed to the next. Each stage (or **action**) in the business process will be implemented in some way – possibly by calling a method in a COM component, posting a message to a queue, invoking a Windows scripting component, or sending a request via BizTalk messaging to another orchestration.

A key point about successful modeling and design (not just business processes) is that, as far as possible, the scheme produced should be language independent. This leaves the developer free to implement a model in whatever way is most suited to the individual. Indeed, each action could be implemented in a different manner.

It is also worth considering that we may already have a number of pieces already written that implement parts of this process in a less integrated way – maybe even some legacy environments. Companies want to protect their investments if at all possible, and reuse them. Again, separating the definition of the business process from its implementation will help. We can identify where we can retain existing code, and discover opportunities for building new optimized components.

A Business Process is a series of logical actions, and each action must be implemented in some way. An action is linked to its implementation by a **port**. The port provides the definition of the communication method between the implementation and the action (where this could be a message queue or a COM method call) and the direction of travel of messages (does the implementation send data to the action, or does the action invoke the implementation?) Additionally, security information regarding the origin or destination of messages can be specified.

745

The act of tying an Action to its Implementation is referred to as **binding**. The **Application Designer** has **Binding Wizards** for each type of implementation available.

The data that passes through the port between the action and the implementation is referred to simply as a **message**. The definition of a message depends upon the implementation. If the implementation is a message queue, the message will be an XML document, if it is a COM component, the message will be a method call (with parameters), and so on.

Let's get back to our example of sending our flat file through BTS for the XML output. In this example, we will tie our BTS messaging services to fire an event that will pick up our document and send it through the process that we defined in the BizTalk messaging manager.

Using the BizTalk Orchestration Designer

Open the **BizTalk Orchestration Designer**: Start | Programs| Microsoft BizTalk Server 2000 | BizTalk Orchestration Designer.

Drag an Action shape from the left stencil to somewhere below the begin shape in the section entitled Use Flowchart Shapes to Draw a Business Process. Right-click on Action1, select Properties… and then set the Name property to ReceivePO. Then click OK.

Drag one more Action shape from the left stencil to the Use Flowchart Shapes to Draw a Business Process section of the design surface. Right-click the Action2 shape, select Properties… and change the name of the shape to SendtoSupplier.

Click OK when finished.

Connect the shapes up, so that our drawing looks like this:

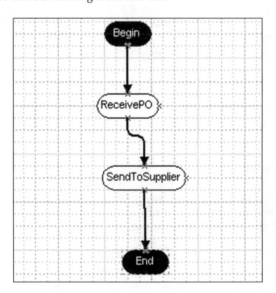

Drag and drop a BizTalk Messaging shape onto the right side of the design surface – where the pane is labeled Use Implementation Shapes to Implement Ports. In the BizTalk Messaging Binding Wizard Welcome screen, name the new port StartPOPort. Click Next to proceed.

On the Communication Direction screen, set the port to receive by choosing the Receive option button. Click Next. On the XLANG Schedule Activation Information screen, select Yes to indicate that this schedule will be activated by a messaging port.

Click Finish to complete creation of the orchestration port. Select the ReceivePO action, and connect the port binding output (green on right side of shape) with the input (red, on left) of the newly created StartPOPort port. This will bring up the **XML Communications Wizard**.

Click Next to accept the default to receive messages from the port. On the Message Information screen, enter the name SupplierOutput in the Message name: text box.

Click Next to proceed. Accept the default values on the XML Transformation Information screen by clicking Next. On the Message Type Information screen, enter SupplierOutput as the Message Type. Then click Next.

On the Message Specification Information screen, for the Messaging Specifications field, click Browse and browse to C:\SupplierOutput\Supplieroutput.xml in the dialog box. Click OK to close the dialog box.

Check Validate Messages Against The Specification.

Drag and drop a BizTalk Messaging shape onto the right side of the design surface. The (now familiar) port binding wizard dialog appears.

Name the port ToSupplierPort and click Next. Accept the default (Send) for the Communication Direction screen and click Next to proceed. On the Static or Dynamic Channel Information screen, select the Static channel option button.

Enter the name FileMessagingChannel for the name of a known, pre-existing channel. Click Finish. Connect the binding output of the SendToSupplier action to the input of the ToSupplierPort port. This will open the XML Communication Wizard.

Accept the defaults on the first screen and click Next. On the Message Information screen, click the Add A Reference To An Existing Message button.

Select SupplierOutput, and click Next to proceed. Accept the defaults on the XML Translation Information screen, and click Next. Accept the defaults on the Message Type Information screen and click Next, and then accept the defaults on the Message Specification Information screen, and click Finish to complete the message creation.

Our final drawing with all the implementations should look like this:

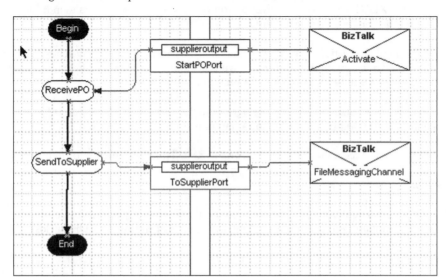

Once we are done with our drawing, we need save it. Save it at the following location with the following filename: C:\supplieroutput\ PO.skv. Once it is saved, we need to compile it to XLANG.

> *XLANG is a mathematical language that can define flow control, messaging, and binding. It supports constructs similar to most programming languages such as conditionals and loops. However, unlike many traditional programming languages, it can determine whether a given sequence of actions and flow control will terminate correctly or result in possible deadlock situations.*

We may write COM+ applications that act as hosts for XLANG schedule instances. Once BizTalk has been installed, all server applications (as opposed to library applications) are configured with the XLANG tab in their property sheets. If the various management interfaces have been implemented, we can check the This application is a host for XLANG Schedule instances box in order to make it XLANG compliant.

Typically, we would invoke an XLANG schedule by calling the **Scheduler Engine**. The easiest way to do this programmatically is to call the COM function GetObject, passing it the moniker of the schedule. The moniker is the string sked: followed by the URL of the compiled schedule file (which may be over the Web).

It is possible to obtain a handle on a specific port in a schedule using the moniker syntax. In this way we can write code that sends messages directly to a particular port in a schedule or invokes methods on that port. This could be done in the following way:

```
Dim objExec as Object
Dim strURL as String
strURL = "sked://localhost/c:\Po.skx"
Set objExec = GetObject(strURL)
```

Returning to our scenario, we'll compile this to XLANG by clicking on File| Make Xlang Po.Skx and saving it to the C:\supplieroutput folder. You will see it compile and finish. We should now be able to run our scenario.

To run it, open two explorer windows. Open one of the directories to `c:\supplieroutput` and the other one to `c:\podrop`. Copy and paste the `PO.csv` file into the `c:\podrop` folder and wait for it to disappear. Once it disappears, the `out.xml` file that we specified within the channel should appear in the `c:\supplieroutput` folder.

Open `myPO.csv` and then open the `out.xml` file so you can see the source for both files.

`MyPO.csv` should look like this:

```
HD112345
HD2mySupplier
ITEMbook,Developing BizTalk applications,15243,2,34.95
ITEMoffice,Spiral Notebook,4231,10,1.29
ITEMoffice,Pen,6789,5,0.10
```

And `Out.xml` should look like this:

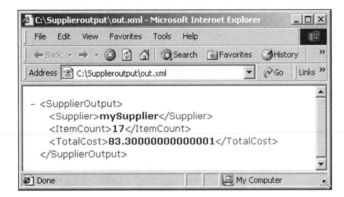

We have seen how all the tools fit in to receive documents, and translate them into the necessary output format.

In the next sections, we are going to spend some time looking into how Commerce Server can integrate with BizTalk Server to provide a robust and seamless solution for Commerce applications.

> *A more thorough investigation of BizTalk Server may be found in* Professional BizTalk, ISBN 1-861003-29-3, *also by Wrox Press.*

Integration (B2B) Scenarios

Now that we have covered the key elements of BizTalk Server, we can move on to focus on integrating it with Commerce Server. We will discuss a couple of different integration scenarios. Although each business-to-business (B2B) scenario is different, many requirements are common to all sites. These include the following:

- ❑ Integration of existing business applications
- ❑ Secure exchange of business documents
- ❑ Catalog exchange and management
- ❑ Order management

BizTalk Server and Commerce Server offer a number of core features that can help companies satisfy these requirements in a timely, cost-effective manner.

Catalog Management and Catalog Exchange

The catalog stores the products and services that a company procures through a B2B application. It must be accurate, current, complete, extensible, and flexible. In many scenarios, the catalog also has to support multiple vendors. Commerce Server and BizTalk Server offer a number of features that can help us manage our catalogs.

Suppose a B2B site hosts catalogs from a number of suppliers. Buyers can purchase products and services from the supplier catalogs through the B2B site. Catalog exchange and management are major issues in this situation. For example, the B2B application might host catalogs for hundreds of suppliers. It is likely that each supplier will send catalog data to the B2B application in a different file format, and this poses a significant challenge to the system administrator of the B2B site, who must convert the various formats into a single one that can be used on the site.

BizTalk Server and Commerce Server can facilitate catalog management. Both products include features that specifically address common B2B catalog management challenges, such as the following:

❑ Catalog mapping tools

❑ Commerce Server XML format for catalogs

❑ Catalog import, export, and exchange tools

❑ Application Integration Components (AIC)

We can use these tools to streamline the process of aggregating catalog data in various formats into a single, consistent format, thereby eliminating the need to write costly mapping scripts for each supplier that hosts a catalog on our B2B site. In addition to lowering catalog management costs, these tools can also significantly reduce the time it takes to bring a new supplier online.

Catalog Mapping Tools

The BizTalk editing and mapping tools provide easy-to-use, drag-and-drop interfaces that we can use to define and map catalog formats. These tools can greatly reduce the time it takes to define the structure of various supplier catalogs, and also to graphically define maps between different catalog schemas.

Mapping from a Commerce Server Catalog to a Flat Schema

Commerce Server site managers need the ability to map data from a Commerce Server catalog to a flat schema. We can use the **Value Mapping (Flattening)** functoid to do this.

For example, suppose we had the following XML code, containing three records in a particular format:

```
<Root>
 <Record>
  <Field Name="X" Value="1"/>
  <Field Name="Y" Value="2"/>
  <Field Name="Z" Value="3"/>
 </Record>
 <Record>
  <Field Name="X" Value="4"/>
  <Field Name="Y" Value="5"/>
```

```
    <Field Name="Z" Value="6"/>
   </Record>
   <Record>
    <Field Name="X" Value="7"/>
    <Field Name="Y" Value="8"/>
    <Field Name="Z" Value="9"/>
   </Record>
  </Root>
```

We could transform this to the following:

```
  <Root>
   <Record X="1" Y="2" Z="3"/>
   <Record X="4" Y="5" Z="6"/>
   <Record X="7" Y="8" Z="9"/>
  </Root>
```

We use the Value Mapping Functoid, included with in the Functoid Palette of the BizTalk Mapper to create a flat version of the XML document. Obviously, in this type of mapping scenario, it is important to maintain the one-to-one correspondence between the three records in the catalog, and the three records in the flat schema.

Mapping from a Flat Schema to a Commerce Server Catalog

This is just the reverse of the above scenario, except that in the BizTalk mapper, we would utilize the Looping Functoid to extract the data, and loop through to create a Commerce Server catalog. Once we have specified the location, Commerce Server will provide us with the catalog in a flat file, even if you imported it as an XML file.

Generating Catalogs in the Commerce Server XML Format

A product catalog must exist in the XML or CSV format in order that we can import it into Commerce Server. If the vendor supplying the catalog is using Commerce Server to produce the catalog, and BizTalk Server to deliver the catalog, the process is simple.

However, if the vendor doesn't use Commerce Server to produce the catalog, we can still use BizTalk Server to import the catalog to Commerce Server. We can take advantage of the Mapper tool in BizTalk Server, using the Looping functoid, to convert the product catalog from its native format to the XML format required by Commerce Server.

If a vendor doesn't use BizTalk Server, a proprietary solution must be devised to convert their catalog format to the XML format required by Commerce Server.

Importing Catalogs from Other Data Sources

We would normally use the Catalog Editor module of Business Desk to import a catalog. However, we can also use the ImportXML method of the CatalogManager object to programmatically import a catalog that is already in XML format into the Commerce Server Catalogs database.

To verify that your catalog XML file is in the right format, it is necessary to edit the root element in the catalog XML file, so that it references the catalog XML Data Reduced (XDR) file provided in the Commerce Server root installation folder:

```
  <MSCommerceCatalogCollection xmlns="x-schema:C:\Program Files\Microsoft Commerce
  Server\CatalogXMLSchema.xml">
```

On opening the catalog XML file in Internet Explorer, Internet Explorer will verify that the XML file conforms to the specified schema, and provides diagnostic errors if it doesn't.

Importing a Catalog to Commerce Server via BizTalk Server

Let's take a look at a real scenario of importing a Catalog into Commerce Server via BizTalk Server.

To keep things simple, we'll work on the assumption that two sites are unpacked on a single computer. One site is named Supplier, and represents the supplier who has generated a catalog that needs to be sent. The supplier sends the catalog through BizTalk Server to a retail site. The Retail site represents the retailer who receives the catalog.

Initially, we'll need to make sure we have the Retail and Supplier solution sites installed.

For this example, we will use a catalog from the Catalog sitelet called booksfull.xml, but it doesn't really matter what particular catalog you use to follow through the example.

We'll need to configure the site options on the Supplier Site. To do this we'll use the **App Default Config** resource. This will enable us to set properties that enable Commerce Server and BizTalk Server to work together.

A Commerce Server resource with site-level properties can be managed through Commerce Server Manager. Use App Default Config to set properties that determine site functionality in areas such as currency options, billing options, and BizTalk Server integration.

To open and configure these resources, click Start | Programs | Microsoft Commerce Server 2000 | Commerce Server Manager.

Once opened expand the Commerce Sites | Retail | Site Resources. Right-click on App Default Config | Properties:

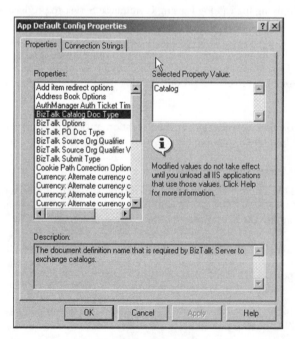

Set the following five properties:

- ❏ **BizTalk Catalog Doc Type = Catalog** (the document definition name that is required by BizTalk Server to exchange catalogs).

- ❏ **BizTalk Options = 1** (**Type 1** to enable integration with BizTalk Server to exchange documents; **Type 0** to disable this feature).

- ❏ **BizTalk Source Org Qualifier = OrganizationName** (this is literally the word OrganizationName, the alias qualifier for this site in BizTalk Server: for example, **BizTalk**).

- ❏ **BizTalk Source Org Qualifier Value = MyOrganization** (the alias value for this site in BizTalk Server: for example, **MySite**).

- ❏ **BizTalk Submit Type = 1** (**Type 0** to submit documents to BizTalk Server synchronously; **Type 1** to submit them asynchronously).

If BizTalk Server is not installed on the same computer as Commerce Server, on the **Connection Strings** tab, click **Modify**. In the **Data Link Properties** dialog box, specify the connection string to the BizTalk server.

After we've modified the BizTalk Server properties in the previous table, we should unload the application from memory. We can do this from **Start | Run**, typing **iisreset** in the text box, and clicking **OK**. The caches created by the Commerce Server `global.asa` are released, so when the next user visits the site, the resource properties are read again and loaded into the cache.

We need to copy `CatalogXmlSchema.xml` to theWebDAV for reference. The schema of the XML document we are transferring must be available through WebDAV to BizTalk Server through the repository. To make the XML document schema available to BizTalk Server, we need to do the following:

1. Open the BizTalk Editor, click on **Tools | Import** and select the **XDR** icon.

2. Specify the path to the `catalogxmlschema.xml` file in `<drive>:\Program Files\Microsoft Commerce Server`.

3. Click **File | Store the file to WebDAV**, and then save the file in the `Microsoft` folder.

Now that we have the catalog schema ready to reference a BizTalk messaging port, we need to open the BizTalk messaging services and set up a new Document Definition:

1. In BizTalk Messaging Manager, click **File | New | Document Definition**. The name will be Catalog. Click **Browse**, and navigate to the `Catalogxmlschema.xml` file in WebDAV.

2. The next step we need to configure is on the Retail site. The `Receivestandard.asp` file receives XML documents and calls an interchange submit. We must modify this file (on the Retail site, because it receives the catalog) to call a specific channel.

The name of the channel called by `Receivestandard.asp` must match the name of an existing channel. To ensure that the name matches, we must modify line 89 of `Receivestandard.asp`:

```
SubmissionHandle = interchange.submit(1, PostedDocument)
to
SubmissionHandle =
interchange.submit(1,PostedDocument,,,,,,"catalogimportchannel")
```

3. This takes the `PostedDocument` object, which is the exported catalog, and submits it to the `catalogimportchannel` object.

The next step is to modify the organizations that we create, using BizTalk Messaging Manager. These represent the vendors with whom we want to exchange documents. A special organization type, called the **Home Organization**, represents our own company. BizTalk Messaging Manager creates the home organization for us automatically. We need to modify the Home Organization to reflect the supplier information and the key identifiers:

1. Open the BizTalk Messaging Manager.

2. On the left hand navigation, click on Organizations and then click Search. A list of organizations will show up.

3. Right click on the Home Organization and click Edit.

4. On the popup window click Identifiers Tab, and then click Add.

5. In the Custom field, enter Catalog, in the Qualifier field, enter Catalog, and in the Value field, enter Supplier:

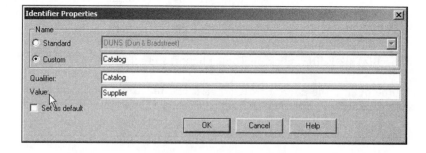

We need to create a new organization other than the home organization. We will call this Retail. This represents an external vendor, or a business unit of a vendor. We can create any number of organizations. We can designate a vendor organization either as a source organization in a channel or as a destination organization in a messaging port.

1. Click File| New | Organization.

2. On the pop-up window in the org name type Retail, click Identifiers Tab and click Add. In the Custom field, enter Catalog, in the Qualifier field, enter Catalog, and in the Value field, enter Retail.

We next need to create the **Supplier Messaging Port** and **Supplier Messaging Channel** to the Retail site. We use the **New Messaging Port Wizard** to create a new port for sending a catalog from the Supplier to the Retailer.

1. In the BizTalk Messaging Console, click File | New | Messaging Port | To An Organization. Name the Messaging Port CatalogPort. Then click Next.

2. In the Destination Organization click Browse, select Retail, and click on the Browse on the primary transport. In the po-pup window set the Transport Type as HTTP.

3. In the address, add the appropriate URL: http://<computer name>/Retail/receivestandard.asp and click OK.

4. Click Next, and accept the defaults for the Envelope Information screen.

5. Click Next, accept the defaults for the Security Information screen, and then click Finish.

6. At this point, the new channel dialog will pop up. Add the channel name as CatalogApplication and click Next.

7. In the Source Organization screen, click Browse, select the Supplier, click OK, and then click Next.

8. On the Inbound Document Definition screen click Browse, click on Catalog, and then click Next.

9. On the Outbound Document Definition screen click Browse, click on Catalog, and then click Next.

10. Keep the defaults on the Log Inbound Document screen, and click Next.

11. On the Advance Configuration screen, click on the Advanced Tab and the 'Override Messaging Port Defaults' window will pop up.

12. Since the Supplier site is based on Active Directory for authentication, we need to add the URL for the receivestandard.asp and the username and password. On the Primary Transport click Properties. Enter http://<computer name>/Retail/receivestandard.asp for the URL and the associated username: <domain>/<username> and password: <user password>. Click OK:

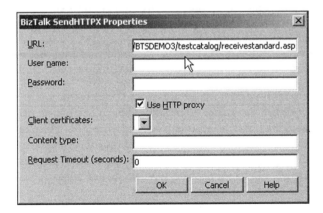

Next we'll need to create the **Catalog Import Channel** and the **Retail Receive Port**. This time we will do things a little different and submit the document to the channel and implement an **AIC** component.

Application Integration Components are COM objects that the BizTalk Server state engine calls to deliver data to an application. If a messaging port is configured in BizTalk Server 2000 to include the use of an AIC for application integration, this component is automatically instantiated and passed the requisite data. The component then determines how to handle communicating this data back to the application. This can be done using private API calls, invoking other COM objects, using database writes, and so on.

1. In the BizTalk Messaging Manager, click on File | New | Messaging Port to Organization and name the messaging port RetailReceivePort.

2. In the Destination Organization screen click Browse and select Retail.

3. In the primary trasport click Browse, leave Application Integration Component as the default, and on the component name, click Browse, select the BizTalk Scriptor, and click OK.

The BizTalk Scriptor enables us to write an AIC in VBScript or JScript, which gives us more flexibility in routing documents. We can specify whether we want to run them internally or externally. With internal running, we have to write and utilize a script when the document is sent through the channel. With external, we can set the path to call a script file.

1. Click OK and click Next for the Envelope screen, making sure that the Organizational Identifier is set to Catalog/Retail. Then click Next.

2. On the security screen click Finish. The new channel window should appear. Name this channel CatalogImportChannel, and click Next.

3. Click Browse for the Organization and select Retail and Organization Identifier as Catalog/Retail. Click Next.

4. On the Inbound Document screen click Browse, select Catalog, and click OK.

5. On the Outbound Document screen click Browse and select Catalog. Click OK, and then Next.

6. In the Log Inbound screen keep the defaults, and click Next.

7. On the Advanced Configuration Properties screen, click on the Advanced button to reveal the Overrides Messaging Port dialog box. Since we declared that we wanted to use a BizTalk AIC component, the default is set to BizTalk Scriptor. To add VBScript, click on the Properties button.

The BizTalk Scriptor Screen should look like this:

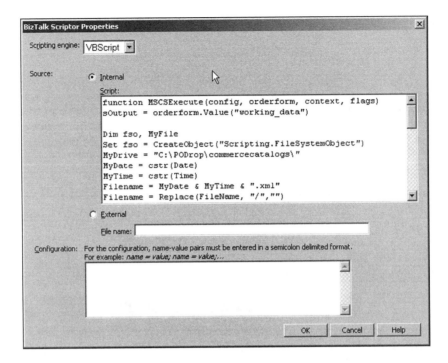

8. In a BizTalk Scriptor, the `OrderForm` object is used to pass in the contents of the XML document. Use the `scripting.filesystemobject` object to write out the XML document to a file. To modify the scriptor, use the following code:

```
function MSCSExecute(config, orderform, context, flags)
sOutput = orderform.Value("working_data")
Dim fso, MyFile
Set fso = CreateObject("Scripting.FileSystemObject")
Mydrive = "c:\commercecatalogs\"
MyDate = cstr(Date)
MyTime = cstr(Time)
Filename = MyDate & MyTime & ".xml"
FileName = Replace(FileName, "/", "")
FileName = Replace(FileName, ":", "")
Filename = Mydrive & FileName
Filename = Replace(Filename, " ", "")
Set MyFile = fso.CreateTextFile(Filename, True)
MyFile.WriteLine(soutput)
MyFile.Close
set appcfg = createobject("commerce.appconfig")
set catalogmanager = createobject("commerce.catalogmanager")
appcfg.initialize("Retail")
set optdict = appcfg.getoptionsdictionary("")
connstr = optdict.s_CatalogConnectionString
catalogmanager.initialize connstr, true
catalogmanager.importxml Filename, TRUE, FALSE
  MSCSExecute = 1  'set function return value to 1
end function
sub MSCSOpen(config)
```

```
  'optional open routine
end sub
sub MSCSClose()
  'optional close routine
end sub
```

9. This code will take the file that we send, and initialize the `Catalogmanager` object to import the catalog to the specific site. We can use the Catalog Editor module in Business Desk to send a catalog from the Supplier site. We tell it which site to send the document to with `appcfg.initialize("Retail")`. BizTalk Server then automatically imports the catalog into the Retail site.

To send a catalog to the Retail site, we do the following:

1. Open the Commerce Server Business Desk for the Supplier site.

2. On the right hand side, click on **Catalogs**, and then **Catalog Editor**. On the menu bar of the Catalog Editor, click on the **Export** icon, select the **Retail Vendor**, and click **OK**.

The process will fire off to BizTalk Server, which in turn will send the catalog to the AIC BizTalk Scriptor. The Scriptor will then fire off the Catalog manager object, which will import our catalog file into the retail site:

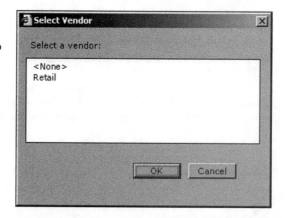

This is just a simple way to import a catalog using the BizTalk messaging services. This strategy works very well for an application that needs to update catalog information frequently.

Another way that we might look at integrating or updating a catalog would be to write the database directly, using an ADO connection string to connect directly to SQL Server. To do this, we would initialize the code in the following way:

```
Const DB_Connection As String = "PROVIDER=SQLOLEDB;Server=<your server name>;" _
  & "Initial Catalog=Retail;User ID=sa;Password=;"

'Instantiate the CatalogManager
Set mobjManager = New CATALOGLib.CatalogManager

'since we are using an ADO connection string
mobjManager.Initialize DB_Connection, True
```

Once compiled, we can encapsulate this object within the scope of BizTalk Orchestration Designer to pull the catalog information from files, MSMQ, or BizTalk, and implement a connection to the database to update the catalog information.

If we were to adopt this strategy, our BizTalk Orchestration Designer diagram could look something like this:

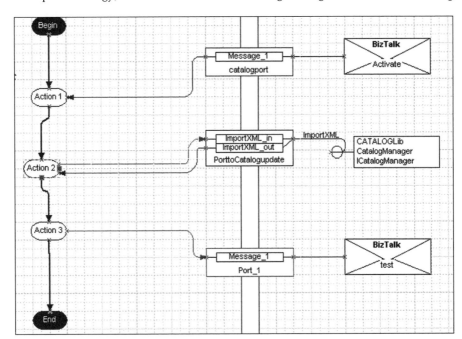

Order Management Using BizTalk

Our order fulfillment process might be managed by an internal order management system within a private network, a remote distribution and fulfillment center, or a vendor that provides an outsourced fulfillment service. It can be important to integrate web order-capture processes with order fulfillment process.

Commerce Server enables us to submit orders to BizTalk Server flexibly, depending on our needs. We can use mapping to submit orders, or a variety of different protocols. Alternatively, a trading partner could create a Commerce Server site or a non-Commerce Server site to receive the submitted orders.

Commerce Server can integrate seamlessly with BizTalk to pass a document to an application. It can use the same protocols, such as HTTP, FTP, and MSMQ, but from a COM object instead. However, we may want to provide more complex business processing as we pass the document.

A Commerce Server application accepts an order from a consumer or business buyer. The order is then passed to BizTalk Server. Let's create a solution for this type of scenario.

Some Preliminaries

We will utilize the catalog from the last section on integrating catalogs from the Retail site. One thing to keep in mind is that we need to purchase a product within our Retail site, so we need to make sure that our site has a catalog installed, and tax and shipping information.

Once Commerce Server has sent the purchase out, we need some way of capturing the data that has been sent. To simulate this on one machine, we have created a simple ASP file that opens a file system object and writes the file to disk. This, called Upload.asp, is included in the code download. Place the file in the root of your web server.

Creating a Purchase Order XML Schema

Before we can exchange documents with suppliers, we must first agree on the format in which we will exchange documents. BizTalk supports a variety of document formats including XML, CSV, and EDI. We will exchange purchase order data in XML format.

Commerce Server 2000 ships with a standard purchase order schema named `poschema.xml`. This schema can be modified to add or remove attributes as needed. We will add a custom attribute to the standard `poschema.xml` file. The custom attribute will be called **order_number**, which will be used by the supplier as a tracking number. We will use the BizTalk Editor to add the **order_number** attribute to the Commerce Server purchase order schema.

1. Open the BizTalk Editor, and select **Tools | Import**. This will allow us to import the Commerce Server purchase order schema definition.

2. Select **Well-Formed XML Instance** as the type, then navigate to c:\inetpub\wwwroot\retail, or wherever the root of your web server is located, and select `poschema.xml`.

3. We will add the **order_number** attribute at the order level. To do this, right-click the element named **orderform** and select **New Field**.

4. Name the new attribute **order_number**. This is what the extended schema should look like in the BizTalk Editor:

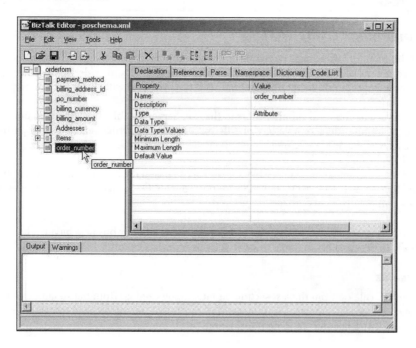

5. Click the save icon to commit the changes. If prompted, overwrite the existing file.

6. We must now publish this new document specification to BizTalk Server. To do this, select **File | Store to WebDAV**, and save as `poschema.xml`, which will allow us to save a copy of this specification to the BizTalk document repository.

We have now created the purchase order reference file needed to send a document through BizTalk Server, and also modified the XML schema for Commerce Server and BizTalk, so that a tracking number can be placed within the purchase order document.

The next step in configuring BizTalk is to provide an organization profile for each supplier. An organization profile allows us to make BizTalk aware of all of the companies with which we will exchange documents.

1. Launch the BizTalk Messaging Manager. A dialog box will appear asking us to create a new port. Click Cancel.

2. Expand File | New | Organization. In the New Organization Dialog box, enter <Your Organization Name> as the organization name:

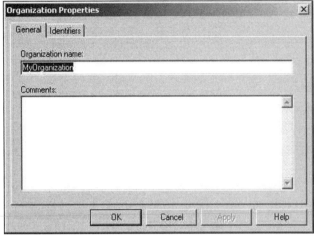

3. Select OK to save the information.

4. Create the Document Definition to tell BizTalk what type of data we will exchange. In this case, we will exchange purchase order documents. Click File | New Document Definition, then enter CS2000 as the document definition name.

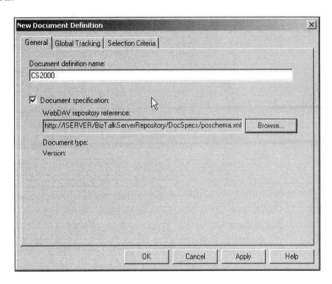

5. Check the Document Specification check box, click the Browse button, and open the poschema.xml specification. This is the specification that we modified above. It defines the structure of a Commerce Server purchase order.

6. Select Apply and then OK to save this information.

We will now need to create a Messaging Port to tell BizTalk how to get the data to our supplier, and when to send it:

1. Click File | New | Port | To an Organization. Enter Port to < Your Organization Name > as the name in the New Port dialog box.

2. Select Next to get to the Destination Organization screen. We now need to select the company that this port refers to. Click Browse and select < Your Organization Name > as the organization:

We now need to tell BizTalk how to transport our purchase orders to our supplier. In this case, we will send the POs via HTTP.

1. Click Browse for the Primary Transport and select HTTP as the Transport type.

2. Enter http://localhost/upload.asp as the Address:

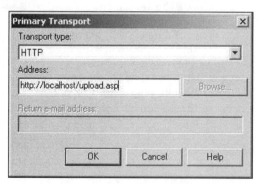

3. Select OK to save this and select Next until the end of the wizard (we will accept all the default values).

When we click the Finish button at the end, it will invoke the BizTalk Channel wizard, which will allow us to complete our BizTalk messaging configuration. We'll now configure the messaging channel.

1. We need create the channel to tell BizTalk which documents we will exchange with our supplier and what processing needs to occur on the document prior to transmission.

2. Enter Channel to < Your Organization Name > as the name in the New Channel dialog box.

3. Click Next, which brings us to the Source Application screen.

4. Click the Application radio button and select New to add the name of the application that submits the purchase orders to BizTalk. In our case, the Commerce Server Retail site is the application that submits the purchase orders to BizTalk.

5. Click Add and name the application CS2000 Retail Site.

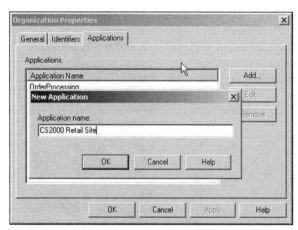

6. Click OK to return to the Source Application screen and select Next.

7. In the Inbound Document dialog box, click Browse and select CS2000 PO as the inbound document definition name. Then select Next.

8. In the Outbound Document dialog box, click Browse to select CS2000 PO as the outbound document definition name.

9. Accept all other defaults by selecting Next until the end of the wizard.

At this point, BizTalk is configured to transport purchase order documents to our supplier. Next, we need to configure Commerce Server so that it will send purchase orders to BizTalk for transmission. Commerce Server can be configured so that it will automatically convert orders into XML, and then submit them to BizTalk for transmission.

1. Open the Commerce Server Manager and drill down to Commerce Sites I Retail I Site Resources. Right-click on the App Default Config node and select Properties. Set the following parameters:

BizTalk Options = 1 (this instructs Commerce Server to submit documents to BizTalk)

BizTalk PO Doc Type = CS2000 PO (this tells Commerce Server the name of the BizTalk document definition that defines the structure of a purchase order document)

BizTalk Source Org Qualifier = OrganizationName (this is literally the word OrganizationName)

BizTalk Source Org Qualifier Value = Home Organization (this is literally the words Home Organization)

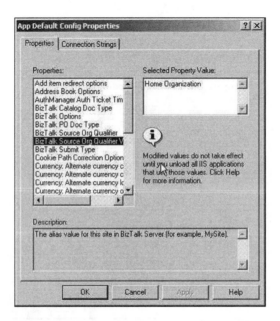

The final step in configuring the integration is to associate BizTalk suppliers with the Commerce Server catalogs. This step is needed so that Commerce Server knows which suppliers actually supply a particular product. For example, if a customer adds a product named 'Microsoft Windows 2000 Server' to the basket, Commerce Server needs to know that Microsoft owns this product. In this way, Commerce Server can direct the order to Microsoft via BizTalk Server.

To make this association, we need to restart IIS by running the `iisreset` command, and then launch the Commerce Server Business Desk.

1. Expand the Catalog module of the Business Desk to get to the Catalog Editor.

2. Open the Books catalog and select the Vendor ID ellipsis in the Catalog Properties section.

3. Select < Your Organization Name >. This tells Commerce Server to send all purchases from this catalog to < Your Organization Name >. Select OK.

4. Click the save icon to save these changes, and then exit to the main BizDesk page.

5. Publish your catalog to make your changes take effect in production. It should look like this:

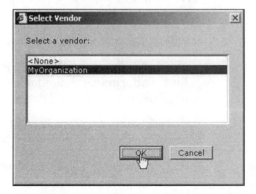

Now we can test the Retail site by doing some shopping on it. Open the Retail site in Internet Explorer. Make sure BizTalk Server is not started, so that it is possible to catch the file and see the interchange happen.

Buy a product from an associated catalog, launch the BizTalk Administrator, and navigate to BizTalk Server. Expand our Work Queue. Verify that the document there is the one just sent by viewing the XML and checking for the order number, as it was displayed at the completion of ordering and purchasing your items from the catalog on the Retail site:

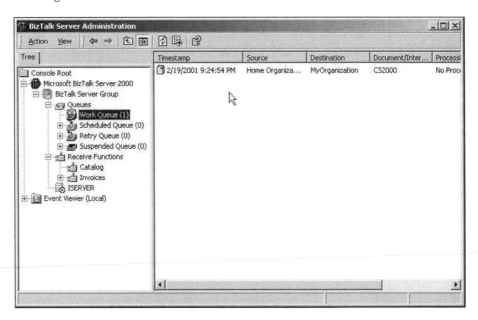

Start BizTalk Server, and the item should disappear from the Work Queue. We should be able to find the uploaded XML file on the C drive:

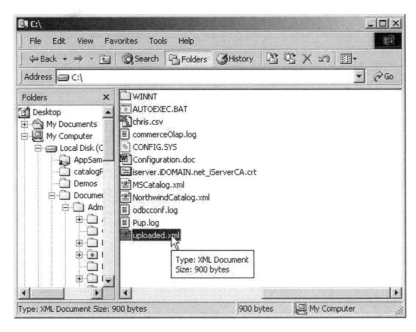

We should be able to open the file and find the specified VendorID:

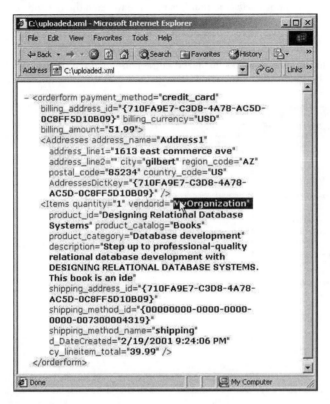

BizTalk will send the data to the supplier. In our example, the supplier will receive the data at `http://localhost/upload.asp`. This file simply takes the PO and writes it out to disk (at `c:\supplier_po.xml`). We should be able to find this file here.

Of course, in practice we could have sent this document to a web site anywhere on the Internet.

BizTalk Integration and Pipelines

Other ways in which we might integrate Commerce Server and BizTalk Server is in the Pipeline Components. If BizTalk Server is on the same machine as a commerce server, we can write AICs; we can also programmatically set up pipelines to handle the multiple supplier solution.

The `Splitter` is a pipeline component that creates a collection of **Shipment Dictionaries** (each pointing to a collection of references to line items). We can configure the `Splitter` to create the required data structures by taking the Shipping method and vendor ID properties as input. The required data or input distinguishers (for example, shipping_method_id and shipping_address_id) are the keys in the required data structure or dictionary.

We can also use the `Splitter` to specify the input distinguishers, and then use the associated dictionary item as the input. By specifying the input distinguishers, we effectively add a column to the product catalog indicating the source of the product. At this point, we need to use the associated dictionary item as the input distinguisher, which we configure on the `Splitter` component. The **Splitter** creates multiple dictionaries (one for each source of the product).

We can implement the `Splitter` using the **Catalog Vendor Id** feature, which is based on the product type. If we do this, we must create a separate catalog for each source, and then assign each catalog a vendor ID to specify the source for the catalog products. Commerce Server then automatically places the items into separate order forms when a customer adds them to the shopping cart (order group). This splits the order into groups of items, which we can then send to different back-end systems.

A common e-commerce scenario is to collect a group of catalogs from various drop-ship vendors and present them to users as one catalog. When users place orders on our site, the `Splitter` component separates the line items in any given order (basket) into logical groups, so that each line item can be routed to the appropriate vendor for fulfillment. This logical separation of an order should be completely transparent to the users.

The `Splitter` identifies the fulfillment vendor for each line item in an order, and then groups vendors with the appropriate `OrderForm` objects. As the existing pipelines (`Plan`, `Product`, `Purchase`, and so forth) are operating against the `OrderForm` object, the order processing happens on a subset of the `OrderGroup` object (based on how the order will be routed internally).

When a customer adds an item to a basket, it must be added to the default `OrderForm` object to ensure that there is only one `OrderForm` object within each `OrderGroup` object.

Other components might involve the `ShippingMethodRouter`. This is a run-time component that iterates through the Order Routing dictionaries to invoke the components specified by the `ShippingMethodManager` object.

Summary

Integrating BizTalk Server and Commerce Server 2000 is a vast topic, as the possibilities and scope for novel and innovative solutions are so very broad. In this chapter, we've looked at the basics of BizTalk Server, and have investigated some of the fundamental aspects of integrating this with Commerce Server.

In the next chapter, we will take a closer look at the complexities of internationalization.

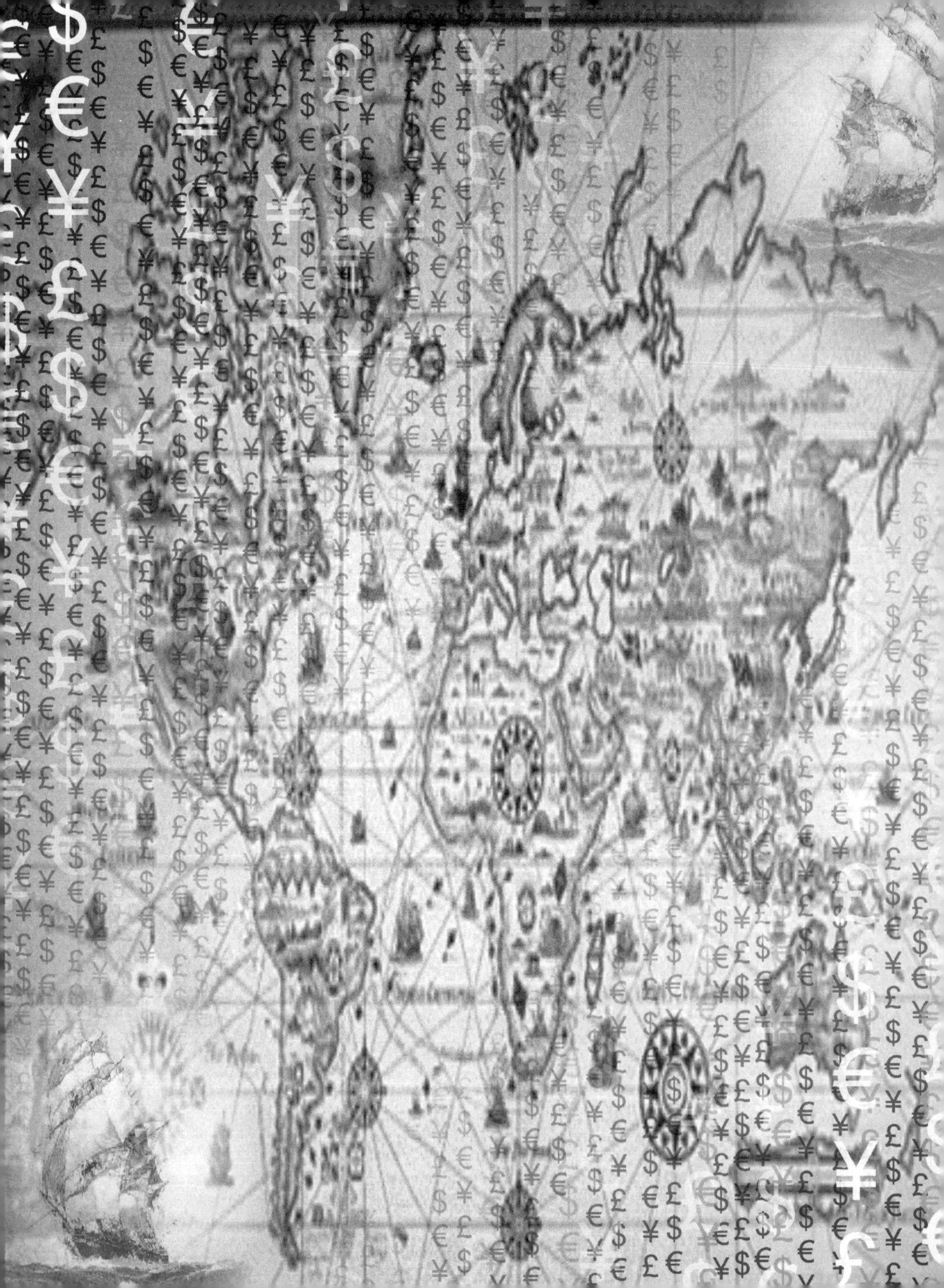

16

Internationalization

Once we've spent a lot of time designing a product catalog and various categories, planning a checkout process and integrating our site with existing systems, it's time to think about going global. Actually, it's well past time to start thinking about it. The topics we discuss in this chapter can have far reaching effects across the entire design of a site. Depending on the level of internationalization, you could end up redesigning every system in your application. Your site needs to be designed with flexibility in mind. It's much easier (and much less costly) to plan the integration from the beginning of your design process.

In this chapter, we'll look at the various processes involved in expanding a site to accommodate an international audience. Initially, we'll concentrate on general internationalization principles: the differences between internationalization and localization, language variations, date formats, currency issues, taxes, and shipping issues.

We'll then look at ways of enhancing the Retail site to incorporate international design principles and techniques. We'll enhance the product catalog and the web code to display multiple languages and allow the user to switch between them, and show how to convert the currency information associated with the products and order processing. By the end of the chapter, we'll be in a position to convert the entire site between English and French.

Internationalization vs. Localization

In discussions of global e-commerce, the terms internationalization (or I18N), and localization are frequently encountered. Localization is the process of rolling out an application (or website) into a specific locale or geopolitical region. Internationalization, however, is the practice of designing an application to function appropriately in a specific locales: accommodating additional languages and locale specific data elements.

Note the use of the word locale. Localization covers more than just language issues: it also covers sets of rules and data that is specific to a given geographic area and language. These rules and data generally include (but are not limited to) information on:

❑ Character classification

❑ Sorting or collation rules

❑ Date and time formats

❑ Number, currency, weight and measurement conventions

❑ Paper and envelope sizes

For example, supposing we have a site up and running selling women's shoes. The product data and user interface are all in English, and we're targeting the US market. At some point, we decide to target the French market: we'll need to localize the site. Product data needs to be translated into French, as well as the user interface (UI). There needs to be some mechanism for our customer to switch between the English and French versions. We will need to be able to display the product prices in French Francs (FF) and accept orders in that currency. And we'll also need to accept French addresses, and calculate shipping charges and tariffs on orders. Additionally, many of the graphics on the site will have to be redone.

Internationalization issues should come into play from the very beginning of the design process. The database needs to be able to store multiple character sets: schemas need to be expanded in appropriate ways. For instance, the addresses need to include a field for country, as well as an expanded telephone field.

We'd need to design a mechanism into the product catalog to store descriptions in many languages, and prices in many currencies. This mechanism should be easy to reference for the web designers. The user interface needs to be flexible enough to allow multiple languages to be displayed. If you ever think you're going to expand into the global market, start thinking about these issues from the beginning. Waiting to change the design whenever you're ready to move to your second market can be extremely costly and time consuming.

Language Variations

First, let's take a look at how languages vary and ways of accomodating these variations. For a start, on average, it can take from 10% to 100% more room to display information in a language other than English, and this can have far reaching implications for the design of our site. In fact, it's usually the shorter strings that increase by a higher percentage in other languages. This will certainly have an effect on our database schema design. We may need to increase the size of many of our fields.

This fact will also have a tremendous effect on our web design. If we have a busy web page, changing to another language will exacerbate the problem. Although this should go without saying, we should make every effort to design a clean site. We shouldn't try to fit too much information across a single line: for example, if we have a horizontal menu, we should make sure that it will accommodate longer words.

Another major factor that will affect your website is the direction of the language. English, of course, is written left to right. That's not the case for all languages. Arabic, Hebrew and Yiddish are examples of right to left languages. Not only will readers of these languages expect the text to be flipped, they will expect the functionality of the user interface to be reversed as well. You will need to come up with a method that gracefully flips the interface. This means that we would have to pay special attention to graphics. If we have a graphic that adds a swoop to the right of a title bar, how will it look when displayed to the left of the other graphics? A browser won't switch the direction of the graphic automatically, so your swoop will end up going the wrong way.

Another major hurdle to overcome is the collate order. Although we sort our lists by alphabetical order within an individual language, the individual words will be in different positions in lists for different languages. This could really become a problem if you don't speak a particular language, and you're trying to find a particular item on your website.

Also, we should make sure we don't try to use the English sort order when displaying a Spanish site. This sounds obvious, but it does happen. More difficult still is dealing with languages like Chinese. There is no alphabetical order in Chinese: the most common way Chinese words are sorted is first by a key part of the character, and then by the number of strokes in the rest of the character. To confuse matters, sometimes you'll see Chinese words sorted alphabetically, according to their translation in Roman letters. Microsoft SQL Server 2000 provides a few different methods of sorting these types of character sets.

Something else to consider are local customs. For example, maybe your site is selling glasses, and our mascot is an owl. A US audience would understand the symbolism. However, in many parts of the world, owls have ambiguous associations. For instance, in Poland owls are associated with impending death.

More common, however, are more mundane symbols that seem universal to one culture, but might not necessarily be understood by other cultures around the world. Suppose you used an American mailbox with a flag on the top to indicate a message. This symbol is not universal, and won't be readily recognized by people in much of the world. We may consider using an envelope instead, which is more universal.

Make certain that you understand the nuances of each language before attempting to localize your site. The last thing you want to happen is to roll out to a region and look like you don't belong there.

Standard Practices

Many other considerations need to be taken into account besides the variation in languages. From a usability and business perspective, a local presence is just as important. As a matter of fact, many could-be international customers are scared away by (more or less justified) stories of missing goods, or problems returning or replacing damaged goods. A local presence reassures the customer. In this section, we'll look at many standard practice conventions that change with different regions.

Date and Time

We encountered an example of different date formats earlier in the book in Chapter 13. However, in addition to the basic format of a date, there are also differences in the separators used. Some countries use periods between the month, days and year, instead of slashes and hyphens. Also, some countries state the months and days in a two-digit format only. Long date formats have even more varieties.

To avoid confusion, it's best to spell out a date as October 11, 2000 or Oct-11-00, instead of abbreviating with only numbers. This should minimize the risk of misunderstanding.

Time considerations need to be taken into account as well. Some countries use the am/pm convention while others use a 24-hour clock. There are regions that put the am/pm in front of the time. The period can also replace the colon to separate hours from minutes. It may be convenient to use the 24-hour clock exclusively. Most countries will understand this convention.

Also, when expressing times, be sure to indicate the time zone in a way that will be understood by everyone. If you use the acronym PST (Pacific Standard Time) to make it easy to understand for a US audience, be sure to include the international standard of GMT (Greenwich Mean Time).

Currency and Numbers

Currency and number formats can cause all manner of problems on an international website. For display purposes, there are many local symbols to denote the different currencies. The other alternative is to use some internationally recognized acronyms such as USD (United States Dollar) and GBP (Sterling).

People will want to see prices in their own currency. However, most people are aware, at least generally, of the exchange rate between their local currency and US dollars. Because of that, you should make an effort to provide the converted price in US dollars as well as the local price.

This may well be a fairly complex undertaking. We'll have to let our customer know in which currency they are actually buying the product. Since conversion rates change, the price at time of checkout may be different to the price at the time the credit card is charged. If the customer expects a certain price in their currency, they'll likely complain if they are charged more. As operators of the site, we might think of absorbing any differences: if we pass savings on, we will be rewarded with future business. Also, a disclaimer referencing fluctuating exchange rates will do a lot to alleviate surprise or anger if prices change.

Address Structure

Internationally, the structures addresses don't really vary too much. The main issue is space. Address conventions in some countries will mean that addresses generally occupy more lines than in other countries.

The key to taking address on the web is flexibility. One of the most obvious changes we'd want to implement when making our site international is the addition of a field for the country.

> *Note that you should also consider your back-end systems when designing your order pages for shipping addresses. If you are sending orders to your vendors via EDI, you must consider the provided fields in your data transfer schema. Many times, the EDI specification is not appropriate to submit an international address. If this is a limitation that you have to live with, one possible solution is to force the customer to conform their address to the limited fields. Otherwise, the product may not be able to be delivered.*

For developers, probably the most difficult part of internationalizing the address fields will be in data validation. Normally, in the US, you would check the length and validity of the zip code and have drop-down lists for all possible states. For addresses for other countries, other forms of validation will be required. Some countries don't have states or provinces, nor are postal codes all the same length. Because of these differences, it's extremely difficult to provide any meaningful data validation if you're trying to support many locales. However, if you're trying to roll out to a few specific regions, you can find out the specific rules for each region, and validate based on the value in the country field. There are also some third party solutions available to achieve this.

While addresses can differ greatly across locales, phone numbers are fairly standard.

Units of Measurement

Almost every country except the US has now standardized on the metric system. If you are doing business with an international audience, be sure to provide measurements in both the metric and imperial systems. In fact, you can probably standardize across the board by providing the metric units first, and then the imperial units in parentheses:

```
23 mm x 55 mm x 100 mm (0.92" x 2.2" x 4")
```

Also, remember that temperature should be provided in Celsius as well as Fahrenheit.

Shipping Charges

Calculating shipping charges within a single country is fairly straightforward. However, international shipping is far more complex.

Shipping charges can vary widely across the world. Not only might weight be taken into consideration, but the dimensions of a package can affect the cost as well. And finally, import and export tariffs have to be calculated, and these will be based on the type of goods being shipped. Luckily, more and more carriers are providing online rate calculations and software tools for small businesses.

We have a few options for dealing with international shipping on a website. The first option is to try to maintain a matrix of shipping costs. However, maintaining such records could be very labor intensive, although keeping the number of carriers to a minimum will help keep costs down.

Another option is to use some third-party tools in your checkout process to calculate shipping in real time. You can get some of these tools directly from the shipping companies. Many carriers have finally recognized that e-business is going to bring them a tremendous amount of revenue and are trying to make it easier to use their services for on-line businesses. If your preferred carrier does not provide any tools, you should be able to purchase them from a third party.

With either of these options, there's one critical point that you need to consider. Almost all of the shipping companies will handle calculating and paying duty charges for shipping products across borders. You could possibly have the customer charged directly, but this may not be possible. The key problem is, what do you do with this charge? You will have to decide if you're going to eat the charge, or pass it back to your customer. If you're going to pass it to the customer, you need to make sure that you disclose this charge at the time of checkout. You may not be able to give a firm amount, but your customer needs to be aware that the charge will come later.

This leads to the final option for calculating shipping charges on your website: don't. Some sites simply tell the customer that they can't calculate the shipping cost until after they place the order. Once the order is placed, we would have to contact the shipping company to determine the shipping and duty charges. Once we have these figures, we can contact the customer to get their approval. Only after we get the approval do we send the product. This method may be more labor intensive, but it's definitely safer. You won't have to worry about undercharging for an item that was more expensive to ship than could be calculated.

One final note, be sure to put in place procedures so that you don't ship to embargoed countries. If you are shipping from the United States, for instance, certain types of shipments to certain countries are banned for political reasons. An updated list of such restrictions may be obtained from the Office of Foreign Assets Control on the US Treasury Department's web page at http://www.treas.gov/ofac/index.html.

Taxes

Probably the most difficult part about designing an e-commerce website is figuring out how to charge sales tax, not because it's technically difficult to implement, or involves difficult concepts to grasp, but because some laws are so unclear. Just within the continental United States, it's often unclear what sales tax to charge.

Building an International Website

In this section, we'll discuss some of the nuts and bolts of building a website that supports an international audience. We'll discuss the character sets that allow us to display the variety of languages that we'll need to display. We'll talk about the methods used to get the browser to display the correct character set and switch gracefully between them. We'll also look at some of the back-end considerations for supplying products to the rest of the world.

First, let's discuss the character sets that Windows uses for displaying the different languages.

ANSI

The ANSI (American National Standards Institute) character set has been used in every Microsoft Operating System prior to Windows NT 4.0 and Windows 95. The ANSI character set maps all of the letter and number symbols needed for displaying the English language, and many symbols and control characters, to numbers between 0 and 255. Since the character set used 8-bits to determine the character, there are only 256 positions available. In general, the first 31 characters are control characters that provide functionality such as carriage return and line feed. ANSI characters 32 to 127 contain punctuation, lower and upper case characters as well as numbers. Characters from 128 to 255 include additional characters that extend the basic character set. These include many currency symbols and accented letters.

All the Windows fonts use this character set as their base. In order to support multiple languages, they used codepages. Each locale would use a different codepage in order to have the characters needed to display the appropriate language. The ANSI character set is split into two sections, the lower 128 and the upper 128. Every different codepage contains the same lower 128 characters. The upper 128, however, is replaced with characters appropriate for the language being displayed. Windows uses codepages to display all 8-bit languages, but this is insufficient to display far east languages such as Chinese which require from 3,000 to 15,000 characters.

Double-Byte Character Sets (DBCS)

Double-Byte Character Sets extend the 8-bit codepages into 16-bits. They're actually multi-byte encodings, a mixture of 8-bit and 16-bit characters, and there are several to support the 16-bit languages. Since an 8-bit character can exist right beside a 16-bit character, there has to be a mechanism to indicate that a 16-bit character is being displayed rather than an 8-bit character. This mechanism exists as a leadbyte. The leadbyte signals that the next byte will be the trailbyte of the 16-bit character unit. The leadbyte is never in the lower 128 range, but the trailbyte may be. The leadbyte tells the operating system which codepage to use to lookup the character indicated in the trailbyte. The combination of a leadbyte and trailbyte then extends the 8-bit codepages to span 16-bit character sets.

Unicode

The Unicode character set was created in order to solve the problem of switching between multiple codepages. In Unicode, all of the most common characters from every supported language are represented with a unique 16-bit code. This provides space for over 64,000 characters (65,536 minus control and compatibility codes). In fact, as of this writing, nearly a third of the space is still open for future use.

It's this sharing of characters among different languages that leads us to the most significant difference between Unicode and earlier character sets using codepages. For the double-byte character sets and ANSI, the sort order was defined by the position of each glyph within the codepage. That's not true of the Unicode character set. Since any one character could possibly be used in multiple languages, it would be impossible to keep the sort order within the set. This means that the operating system or application is responsible for performing the sort.

UTF-8

The last topic to discuss in this section is UTF-8. UTF-8 is not another character set. The UTF stands for UCS (Universal Character Set) Transformation Format. Basically, what it does is transform the Unicode character encoding into a format that can be better handled by certain operating system, especially Unix.

To really explain, we need to look at the bit patterns for the character codes. First let's look at the letter 'a'. Standard ANSI would give us hex value 0x61 or, in binary, 0110 0001. To portray this character in Unicode, you would simply append two zero bytes to the beginning, giving you U+0061, or binary, 0000 0000 0110 0001.

This wouldn't necessarily be a problem, although I've seen some applications on a Unix system that would interpret the two bytes of zeros as the end of a record. When it really becomes a problem is when the first 8 bits of a 16-bit character could be translated into a valid 8-bit character, such as '/'. A slash has a very specific connotation, and could cause a lot of problems: if used in a filename, for instance. So let's explore the mechanism that UTF-8 uses to prevent that problem.

The following chart details the byte sequences used to represent Unicode characters in various ranges:

```
U+00000000 to U+0000007F:    0xxxxxxx

U+00000080 to U+000007FF:    110xxxxx 10xxxxxx

U+00000800 to U+0000FFFF:    1110xxxx 10xxxxxx 10xxxxxx

U+00010000 to U+001FFFFF:    11110xxx 10xxxxxx 10xxxxxx 10xxxxxx

U+00200000 to U+03FFFFFF:    111110xx 10xxxxxx 10xxxxxx 10xxxxxx 10xxxxxx

U+04000000 to U+7FFFFFFF:    1111110x 10xxxxxx 10xxxxxx 10xxxxxx 10xxxxxx 10xxxxxx
```

The xxx positions represent the bits that are used to determine the Unicode value of the character. It's fairly easy to translate, as well. The number of 1 bits before the first 0 bit tell us how many total bytes to expect to complete the character.

Notice that if we translated the 'a' character we were talking about earlier from Unicode (U+0061) to UTF-8, we would end up with the standard ANSI value of 0110 0001 or 0x61. This is a very convenient byproduct of the UTF-8 system, especially for operating systems that already rely on the ANSI character set. To further clarify, let's look at another example. U+2260 points to the not equal sign. In UTF-8, the binary value would be 1110 0010 1000 1001 1010 0000 or 0xE289A0 in hex.

This information may help you decide which character set to use in order to store information in the database. Make sure that the chosen character set can support all of the languages that are being stored. If you don't choose the correct character set, you may need to store the information in multiple databases, which could complicate your design.

HTML Coding Techniques

We've explored the standard character sets which can be used to store data. Now you need to be able to display that data on your site so that your customers can view those pages in the language of their choice. In this section we'll explore some design ideas for switching between languages, plus some coding techniques to tell the browser which character set to display.

Web Design Considerations

As we've seen, the design for our website will probably need to change in order to support an international audience. For instance, we will have to come up with some method to allow the user to select the desired language in which to view the pages. Although there are many methods to accomplish this task, we'll discuss a few of the most common.

Manual Selection

A simple approach to this would be to implement manual selection. We could have a drop-down box containing all the possible languages that our site can display. Another possibility would be to have a link to a page that lists each of the possible languages where each language name is written in the language itself. This can be a more elegant solution, although both methods are adequate.

Lookups

Two other methods can help determine the language of choice for your customers. One is to use a DNS reverse lookup, to try to determine the locale from their provider. However, this method can be inaccurate in many areas of the world.

Another method to determine the language that needs to be displayed is to use the HTTP_ACCEPT_LANGUAGE server variable. This variable tells you to what language the user has set their operating system.

These methods are a great way to give you a starting point; however, they should not be used alone. Once you've attempted to automatically find out the locale, ask your user if it's correct and allow them to change the default setting.

Storing the Language Selection

Once you've determined the language of choice, you need to be able to use that language choice to provide the user with pages in their chosen language. Essentially, you have four choices.

The first choice is to use static HTML pages. For this to work, you would have to generate static pages in every language that you offer, and update the links on each page to go to the appropriate page in the correct language. The biggest advantage to this solution is the speed at which the pages are presented. On the other hand, maintenance can quickly become unmanageable as you add pages and additional languages.

The second option is to store the language preference in the browser's cookie. This is probably the easiest way to track the language choice. However, it is dependent on whether or not the user has enabled cookies within the browser settings. By storing an appropriate string in a language variable, you can query the cookie to determine what language, currency, and date format to display.

You could also pass the language selection through the URL query strings. This method would require you to adapt the AuthManager object's GetURL method to include a language variable and value in every link. The variable could then be extracted from the query string and used to dynamically alter the page's locale settings.

The final method would be to store the language setting in the user's profile. Simply adding a property to the profile and initializing that property when the user chooses a language is all that's required. This approach has many advantages. All settings are stored locally on the server and can be quickly accessed through the user profile objects. It still uses a cookie, but the value will be saved for future visits.

Commerce Server Modifications

In this section, we'll leave the theory behind, and look at the internationalization features included in Commerce Server 2000, and design modification to be integrated into our solution.

First, we'll look at the user interface and the modifications needed to convert the various interfaces into the language of choice. Next, we'll cover the product catalog, and how to allow for multiple languages and currencies. Finally, we'll explore modifications needed to your pipelines to allow for currency settings and appropriate changes.

User Interface

First, let's look at modifying the web interface. In this chapter, we'll be using the Retail solution site.

We'll assume that we are a US site, expanding our e-commerce activities into other parts of the world. In particular, we want to capture the French market. We'll only add support for the one country, but we do need to design our modifications with the thought that we'll be expanding to more countries down the road.

XML Data Store

All of the strings associated with the user interface are stored in an XML file called `rc.xml`. This file is located in the root directory of the retail site. The format of this file is fairly simple. The root element `<MessageManager>` has an attribute that defines the default language for the site to use. Underneath the root node, there can be multiple nodes that define the supported languages for the site. Finally, there are hundreds of nodes that define name/value pairs for all of the strings used in the site. This file is loaded in the `global.asa`, and populates the `MSCSMessageManager` object with the appropriate values.

On a side note, the method of storing the site values in an XML file was changed just prior to releasing the final version of Commerce Server 2000. While a case can be made for not using an XML file for a database, this design does have some advantages. The XML may now be passed around with the code for the site, and can easily be sent to a third party to be translated. Plus, when updating the website to a new version, we can easily include a new XML data store with modifications. This would be more difficult to synchronize if the data were in SQL. One major disadvantage is when adding a new value; there is no validation to make sure that we don't enter the same entry name twice.

In the file that comes with the retail site, the default language is set to English:

```
<MessageManager DefaultLanguage="English">
    <Language Name="English" Locale="1033"/>
```

If you wanted your default language to be different, you could update this value, but for our purposes we'll leave it unchanged. The next line in the file defines the only language currently supported by this site: English.

On the language node, we can define both the language name as well as the locale to be used. A list of valid Windows locale values can be found in the Commerce Server 2000 documentation. The documentation shows that United States English has a locale value of 0x0409. Translating the hex value to decimal yields 1033.

Languages List

Since we're going to add the French language, let's add a language node now. The French (Standard) locale value is 0x040c or 1036. Add the following line in the `rc.xml` file, below the English language node:

```
<Language Name="French (Standard) " Locale="1036"/>
```

By adding this node, you will be able to use the `MSCSMessageManager.GetLocale` method to return the French locale setting. Unfortunately, there is no support in the `Commerce.MessageManager` object for listing the available languages via the settings in this file. However, we'll need this list in order to allow the user to select the appropriate language.

To store the list, we'll use a commerce dictionary object and store it in an application variable. In `global.asa`, add the following line to the global variables section:

```
Dim dictLanguages
```

Next, open up `include\global_messagemanager_lib.asp` and find the `For...Next` loop that goes through the language nodes. Modify the code as follows:

```
Set LanguageNodes = SchemaNode.selectNodes("Language")
Set dictLanguages = Server.CreateObject("Commerce.Dictionary")
For Each LanguageNode In LanguageNodes
    LanguageName = LanguageNode.Attributes.getNamedItem("Name").Text
    Locale = LanguageNode.Attributes.getNamedItem("Locale").Text
    Call MsgMgr.AddLanguage(LanguageName, Locale)
    dictLanguages.Value(LanguageName) = Locale
Next
```

Finally, store the dictionary object in an application variable. Add the following line to the end of the `Main()` subroutine in `include\global_main_lib.asp`:

```
Set Application("dictLanguages") = dictLanguages
```

Now that we have a list of the languages that are available in the `rc.xml` data store, let's update the entry values with some French text.

Entry Values

To finish with the XML Data Store, we need to add some French values. Here's a list of the values used on the retail home page:

```
<Entry Name="L_Home_HTMLTitle" Type="Page titles">
    <Value Language="French">Accueil</Value>
</Entry>
<Entry Name="L_Catalog_HTMLTitle" Type="Page titles">
    <Value Language="French">Catalogue</Value>
</Entry>
<Entry Name="L_Basket_HTMLTitle" Type="Page titles">
    <Value Language="French">Panier</Value>
</Entry>
<Entry Name="L_Search_Section_Head_HTMLText" Type="Menu">
    <Value Language="French">Recherche de produit </Value>
</Entry>
<Entry Name="L_Search_Button" Type="Buttons">
    <Value Language="French">Rechercher</Value>
</Entry>
<Entry Name="L_Advanced_Search_Link_HTMLText" Type="Menu">
    <Value Language="French">Options avancées</Value>
</Entry>
<Entry Name="L_MENU_CATALOG_SECTION_HTMLTitle" Type="Menu">
    <Value Language="French">Catalogues</Value>
</Entry>
<Entry Name="L_Empty_Catalog_Root_HTMLText" Type="Site Error messages">
    <Value Language="French">Le catalogue est vide.</Value>
</Entry>
<Entry Name="L_CustomerService_Section_Head_HTMLText" Type="Menu">
    <Value Language="French">Service clientèle</Value>
</Entry>
<Entry Name="L_MENU_MANAGEMENT_USER_TEXT" Type="Menu">
    <Value Language="French">Profil</Value>
</Entry>
<Entry Name="L_MENU_MANAGEMENT_ORDERS_TEXT" Type="Menu">
    <Value Language="French">Commandes</Value>
</Entry>
<Entry Name="L_MENU_CATEGORIES_SECTION_HTMLTitle" Type="Menu">
    <Value Language="French">Catégories</Value>
</Entry>
<Entry Name="L_No_Catalogs_Installed_ErrorMessage" Type="Site Error messages">
    <Value Language="French">Aucun catalogue installé.</Value>
</Entry>
<Entry Name="L_FOOTER_COPYRIGHT_NOTICE_TEXT" Type="Menu">
    <Value Language="French">Copyright (c) 1999-2000 Microsoft
Corporation.</Value>
</Entry>
```

Normally, we would have to integrate them into the existing rc.xml file by matching up the Entry tags and copying the value element to the correct position. However, we'll write some code to do this task automatically.

Microsoft provides the French and Japanese versions of the Commerce Server Solution Sites on its Commerce Server downloads page. However, the installation file provided will not install to an English version of Windows. On a Windows 2000 server, in order to install the product, we can go into Regional Options in the Control Panel and change your locale setting to French (France). The installation file should now proceed without problems.

Once we have the French `rc.xml`, we can use the code below to integrate it with the English version. This code will work in Visual Basic or as a VB Script file.

```
Dim domEnglish 'As DOMDocument
Dim domFrench 'As DOMDocument
Dim nodTo 'As IXMLDOMNode
Dim nodFrom 'As IXMLDOMNode
Dim nodFromList 'As IXMLDOMNodeList

Set domEnglish = CreateObject("MSXML.DOMDocument")
domEnglish.Load "%path_to_English_rc%\rc.xml"
domEnglish.preserveWhiteSpace = True

Set domFrench = CreateObject("MSXML.DOMDocument")
domFrench.Load "%path_to_French_rc%\rc.xml"

Set nodFromList = domFrench.selectNodes(".//Entry")

For Each nodFrom In nodFromList
    Set nodTo = domEnglish.selectSingleNode(".//Entry[@Name='" & _
nodFrom.Attributes(0).Text & "']")
        nodTo.appendChild nodFrom.childNodes(0)
Next nodFrom
domEnglish.save ("%path_to_English_rc%\rcnew.xml")
```

Remember to replace `%path_to_French_rc%` and `%path_to_English_rc%` with the actual file paths for the appropriate files.

At this point we can test the modifications we've made. The language of the site is determined by the `MSCSMessageManager.DefaultLanguage` property. During the processing of `global.asa`, this property is populated with the default language attribute stored in the root level of the data store. Edit the `rc.xml` root node and replace the `DefaultLanguage` attribute with the value `'French'`. Now go to the retail site's home page and refresh. Note that you may need to reset `global.asa` by opening it in Notepad and saving it without modifications. We now have a Commerce site in French.

Adding Language Selection

But, since we won't allow the user to edit the data store directly, we need to allow them to change the language from the website. We'll place the selection functionality in the menu on the left side of the page.

Open the file `template\menu.asp`. We'll be making our changes in the `htmRenderMenu()` function. I've decided to place the language selection just below the Search section. Add the following code right before the Login section:

```
' ****************
' Language Section
' ****************
Call PrepareLanguageSection(dictLanguages)
If dictLanguages.Count = 0 Then
    htmLanguageSection = ""
Else
    htmLanguageSection = htmRenderLanguageSection(dictLanguages,
MSCSSiteStyle.Body, MSCSSiteStyle.Body, "")
End If

htmRenderMenu = htmRenderMenu & htmLanguageSection & BR
```

Also, remember to declare the `dictLanguage` variable in the declarations section of the `htmRenderMenu()` function by adding the following line:

```
Dim dictLanguages
```

Of course, this code doesn't do much except call the function that does all the work: the `htmRenderLanguageSection()` function. It does determine if there is more than one language to choose from, and only displays the list if there is.

Now, in order to write the rest of the code, we need to determine where we will be storing the results of the language selection. Earlier in the chapter, we discussed the four ways in which we can store this information. We'll here store the language in the user profile. To implement this method, we have four main tasks. First, we'll add a field in the user profile to store the language selection. Next, we'll create a tween page to save the selection in the user profile. After that, we'll create the `htmRenderLanguage()` function in `template\menu.asp` to call the new tween page. And finally, we'll modify the code that sets the `sLanguage` variable to pull the information from the user profile.

Adding the field to the user profile is straightforward. Open the BizDesk for the retail site and open the Users section to get to the Profile Designer. Open the User Object and double-click on **General Information**. When you click the **Add** button, you can enter the attributes for this property. Modify the values as follows, leaving the rest to the default values:

❑   Attributes

   `Name: language`

   `Display Name: Chosen Language`

   `Description: Chosen Language`

❑   Advanced Attributes

   `Active: Yes`

   `Map to data: Custom Property 1`

❑   Custom Attributes

   `sAnonymousAccess: 2`

   `sDelegatedAdminAccess: 2`

   `sUserAccess: 2`

When finished adding the property, remember to publish the profile.

The code to update this profile property is a little more complex, but we'll keep it as simple as possible. Create a file in the root retail directory called `_setlang.asp`. I found it easiest to copy one of the existing `_set.asp` files and edit that. Here's the code:

```
<!-- #INCLUDE FILE="include/header.asp" -->
<!-- #INCLUDE FILE="include/const.asp" -->
<!-- #INCLUDE FILE="include/addr_lib.asp" -->
<!-- #INCLUDE FILE="include/catalog.asp" -->
<!-- #INCLUDE FILE="include/std_access_lib.asp" -->
<!-- #INCLUDE FILE="include/std_cache_lib.asp" -->
<!-- #INCLUDE FILE="include/std_cookie_lib.asp" -->
```

```
<!-- #INCLUDE FILE="include/std_ordergrp_lib.asp" -->
<!-- #INCLUDE FILE="include/std_pipeline_lib.asp" -->
<!-- #INCLUDE FILE="include/std_profile_lib.asp" -->
<!-- #INCLUDE FILE="include/std_url_lib.asp" -->
<!-- #INCLUDE FILE="include/std_util_lib.asp" -->
<!-- #INCLUDE FILE="include/setupenv.asp" -->
<%
' ============================================================================
' _setlang.asp
' Tween page for setting the chosen language in the user profile.
'
' Commerce Server 2000 Solution Sites 1.0
' ----------------------------------------------------------------------------

Sub Main()
    Dim rsUser, sNewLanguage, sCurrentPage

  sNewLanguage = Request.QueryString("language")
  sCurrentPage = Request.QueryString("currentPage")

  'Set the language in the user profile
  Set rsUser = GetCurrentUserProfile()
  rsUser.Fields("GeneralInfo.language").Value = sNewLanguage
  Call UpdateUserProfile(rsUser)

  'Remove the beginning of the url
  sCurrentPage = Mid(sCurrentPage, InStr(2, sCurrentPage, "/")+1)

  Response.Redirect(GenerateURL(sCurrentPage, Array(), Array()))
End Sub
%>
```

When called, this code will update the user profile with the new language setting, then refresh the calling page with the new language.

Now that we've created the tween page and know what variables to pass in the query string, let's return to the template\menu.asp page and create the htmRenderLanguageSection() function. This function will need to create a link for every possible language that passes the requested language and the current page to the tween page. Add the following code to the bottom of the retail\menu.asp file:

```
' ----------------------------------------------------------------------------
' htmRenderLanguageSection
'
' Description: Provides a list of languages from which to choose.
' ----------------------------------------------------------------------------

Function htmRenderLanguageSection(ByVal dictLanguages, ByVal
dictSectionTitleStyle, ByVal dictSectionBodyStyle, sSearchValue)
    Dim htmBody, htmText, urlAction, urlLink, htmLinkText
    Dim elLanguage, arrParams, arrParamValues

    htmBody =
RenderText(MSCSMessageManager.GetMessage("L_Language_Section_Head_HTMLText",
sLanguage), dictSectionTitleStyle) & BR
```

```
        arrParams = Array("language","currentPage")

    For Each elLanguage in dictLanguages
        If elLanguage = sLanguage Then
            htmText = RenderText("-" & elLanguage, dictSectionBodyStyle)
            htmBody = htmBody & htmText & BR
        Else
            sCurrentPage = Request.ServerVariables("URL")
            sQueryString = Request.ServerVariables("QUERY_STRING")
            If Not IsNull(sQueryString) Then
                sCurrentPage = sCurrentPage & "?" & sQueryString
            End If
            arrParamValues = Array(elLanguage, sCurrentPage)
            urlLink = GenerateURL(MSCSSitePages.SetLanguage, arrParams, _
                        arrParamValues)
            htmLinkText = RenderText(elLanguage, dictSectionBodyStyle)
            htmBody = htmBody & RenderLink(urlLink, htmLinkText, _
                        MSCSSiteStyle.Link) & BR
        End If
    Next
    htmRenderLanguageSection = htmBody
End Function
```

You also need to add a line to `include\global_siteconfig_lib.asp` to set the
`MSCSSitePages.SetLanguage` property.

```
' Language pages
dictPages.SetLanguage = "_setlang.asp"
```

The last thing to do is to change the code that sets the `sLanguage` variable and a new `nLocale` global
variable to read from the user profile. The code that does this is found in the `include\setupenv.asp`
file almost at the end of the file. Modify the code as follows:

```
' Place in the global variable section of the include/setupenv.asp file
Dim nLocale

' Placed in the declarations section of the SetupPage subroutine.
' Don't put the declaration with the other declarations or the variable will
'  be global
Dim rsUser

' Set the language for the user
Dim dictLanguages
Set rsUser = GetCurrentUserProfile()
sLanguage = rsUser.Fields("GeneralInfo.language").Value
If IsNull(sLanguage) Then
    sLanguage = MSCSMessageManager.DefaultLanguage
End If
Set dictLanguages = Application("dictLanguages")
nLocale = dictLanguages.Value(sLanguage)
```

That's it. The site can now be changed between English and French by clicking on the appropriate link
in the menu bar. Try navigating the site and you'll see that each page is translated.

Notice that on the login pages, you won't be able to change the language directly because those pages don't use the `template\menu.asp` code. This is one of those design decisions that you need to consider when adding multilingual support to your website. For this reason, it would probably have been better to place the language selection in own area and included it in appropriate areas of the template files. For the purposes of this demonstration, however, we've kept things simple.

Product Catalog

In this section, we'll discuss how to incorporate multiple languages in the product catalog. We'll continue with the modifications discussed in the previous section, but, again, these techniques could easily be applied to an existing application, or an example from another part of this book.

There are two main topics to discuss. The first is a method to translate the descriptions of the product such as the name and long description. The second is a method to translate the numeric values associated with a product, including dimension values and currency fields. The main difference between these methods is that the former relies on the language selection, while the latter relies on the locale. To illustrate, two users in Canada may want to see the site in different languages, English and French. However, these same two users would probably use the same currency. Dimension fields will probably be calculated from a base unit instead of being stored in a separate field. Because of this difference, the methods of translation will be radically different.

Descriptions Translation

In order to display certain description fields in multiple languages, we'll need to come up with a storage mechanism that is easily expandable and maintainable.

One method would be to expand the schema by adding properties with the language name appended to the end of the property name. For example, we would edit the `name` property to `name_English`, and add a new property called `name_French`. This would allow us to dynamically display the name of the product in the correct language by appending the sLanguage variable to the required field name.

This method has a couple of advantages. It's easy to implement by updating just a few sections of code. Additionally, administration of the product catalog can still be done from the BizDesk. The biggest disadvantage will be the maintenance requirements and performance issues when adding new languages. Each additional language adds an additional set of property definitions: this could get very complex if you plan to support many languages.

So what are the alternatives? Really, the only alternative is to create your own database structure, stored procedures, and COM objects to manage a custom product catalog. You would also need to create maintenance tools to allow the product schema to be updated as well as the products themselves. Finally, you would need to incorporate your new COM objects into the site code. Depending on your implementation, you may need to consider this path.

Some of the major roadblocks will be ensuring that the appropriate sorting techniques for different languages are implemeted, as well as product variants.

This custom option is well beyond the scope of this chapter: we'll look at the first method.

Initially, for our example, we need to obtain an xml catalog in both English and French. Download the sample product catalogs from http://www.microsoft.com/commerceserver/downloads/tutorial.htm. Make sure you download both the English and the French versions.

The file that we're interested in is `hardwarefull.xml`. Rename the English version `hardwarefull_English.xml` and the French version `hardwarefull_French.xml`.

We'll use the import catalog feature of BizDesk to get these sample products into our system. But first, we'll need to modify the schema and combine the files into one.

Note that the French version of hardwarefull.xml will not display properly in Internet Explorer unless you change intances of '®' with '&reg;'.

The steps that we need to take in order to combine the XML files are generally the same steps we would take if we were changing the catalog in BizDesk. They are:

- ❏ Edit existing property definitions to include English.
- ❏ Add matching property definitions for French.
- ❏ Add new properties to the Definition groups.
- ❏ Copy matching French Categories into English xml file using new properties.
- ❏ Copy matching French Products into English xml file using new properties.
- ❏ Modify the site code to switch between the multiple languages.

Updating the Schema

To update the product catalog schema, we'll edit the English property definitions and rename them to include the English indicator. Next, we'll add the French counterpart of each English property definition. Finally, we'll update the Definition groups to include the new French property definitions that we've added. To do this, we'll construct a small function. This can be run as an ASP page, or as VB6.

We need to decide on which fields we want to see in multiple languages. As we said earlier, many of the numeric fields will be calculated from a base value, so we don't need to add new fields for those. The description fields will definitely need to be updated, as will any enumeration fields.

Here's a list of those properties that will be displayed in multiple languages:

Benefits	Gender	Product name
Color	Licencetype	Productcount
ColorPrinting	Manufacturer	ScrollWheel
Cordless	Mediatype	System Requirements
Country of Origin	Name	Unit of Measure
Description	Os	Venue
DPI	PPM	Versioncd
Features	PrintingTechnology	Voltage

Some of these fields, such as DPI, may contain the same value in English as well as French. The reason we need to add another field is actually for the display name. In French, DPI is abbreviated PPP.

Before we continue, we'll need to update some of the values in the French data. The enumeration field that is used to indicate a variant, Color, needs some special treatment. I'll explain in more detail below. For now, update the Color property definition in the French file to read:

```
<PropertyValue displayName="Aubergine|Aubergine"/>
<PropertyValue displayName="Beige|Beige"/>
<PropertyValue displayName="Black|Noir"/>
<PropertyValue displayName="Blue|Bleu"/>
<PropertyValue displayName="Red|Rouge"/>
<PropertyValue displayName="Silver|Gris clair"/>
<PropertyValue displayName="White|Blanc"/>
```

The reason behind this will become clearer when we write the code to display the variants.

As we write the code that updates these property definitions, we need to understand how the code that displays the page works. As the code is written in the solution site, the label for each property is pulled from either the `DisplayName` attribute, if it exists, or the property name attribute if the `DisplayName` attribute is missing.

Since we'll be replacing all of the property name attributes, we must ensure that a `DisplayName` attribute is included in each of these fields.
The following code will update our schema in appropriate ways:

```
Private Sub UpdateEnglishProperties()
    Dim domEnglish As DOMDocument
    Dim domFrench As DOMDocument
    Dim nodPropDef As IXMLDOMNode
    Dim nodProps As IXMLDOMNodeList
    Dim nodPropsFrench As IXMLDOMNodeList
    Dim nodProp As IXMLDOMNode
    Dim nodPropFrench As IXMLDOMNode
    Dim attName As IXMLDOMAttribute
    Dim strProperties As String
    Dim strName As String
    Dim strID As String
    Dim strNewID As String
    Dim lngCatProp As Long
    Dim lngCatPropTemp As Long
    Dim strQuery As String
    Dim strFrenchName As String
    Dim dictIDs As Object
    Dim strProps As String
    Dim varNewProp As Variant
    Dim strNewProps As String
    Dim arProps() As String
    Dim x As Long

    Set dictIDs = CreateObject("Commerce.Dictionary")

    strProperties = GetAffectedProperties()

    Set domFrench = CreateObject("MSXML3.DOMDocument")
    domFrench.Load "%path_to_tutorial_files%\hardwarefull_french.xml"
```

```
Set nodPropsFrench = domFrench.selectNodes(".//Property")

Set domEnglish = CreateObject("MSXML3.DOMDocument")
domEnglish.Load "%path_to_tutorial_files%\hardwarefull_english.xml"
Set nodPropDef = domEnglish.selectSingleNode(".//PropertiesDefinition")
Set nodProps = nodPropDef.selectNodes("./Property")
```

After some initialization, we determine the maximum CategoryProperty number:

```
For Each nodProp In nodProps
    strID = nodProp.Attributes.getNamedItem("id").Text
    lngCatPropTemp = Mid(strID, 16)
    If lngCatPropTemp > lngCatProp Then
        lngCatProp = lngCatPropTemp
    End If
Next nodProp
```

We then edit the English properties, and add the French ones: In the code below, notice the two underscores before English and French being appended to the property names. The reason we do this will be clear when we modify the site code.

```
For Each nodProp In nodProps
    Set attName = nodProp.Attributes.getNamedItem("name")
    If InStr(strProperties, attName.Text) Then
        'Verify and create displayName attribute unless type enumeration
        EditDisplayName nodProp

        'Edit name attribute
        strFrenchName = attName.Text & "__French"
        attName.Text = attName.Text & "__English"

        'Add matching French property definition
        strID = nodProp.Attributes.getNamedItem("id").Text
        strQuery = ".//Property[@id='" & strID & "']"
        Set nodPropFrench = domFrench.selectSingleNode(strQuery)
        lngCatProp = lngCatProp + 1
        strNewID = "CatalogProperty" & lngCatProp
        dictIDs.Value(strID) = strNewID
        nodPropFrench.Attributes.getNamedItem("id").Text = strNewID
        EditDisplayName nodPropFrench
        nodPropFrench.Attributes.getNamedItem("name").Text = strFrenchName
        nodPropDef.appendChild nodPropFrench
        Set nodPropFrench = Nothing
    End If
    Set attName = Nothing
Next nodProp
Set nodProp = Nothing
Set nodProps = Nothing
```

Next, we update the definition groups to include the new French properties:

```
        Set nodProps = domEnglish.selectNodes(".//Definition")
    For Each nodProp In nodProps
        strNewProps = ""
        strProps = nodProp.Attributes.getNamedItem("properties").Text
        'Special code to add name to the categories
        If nodProp.Attributes.getNamedItem("name").Text = "Department" Then
            strProps = strProps & " CatalogProperty24"
        End If
        arProps = Split(strProps, " ")
        For x = LBound(arProps) To UBound(arProps)
            varNewProp = dictIDs.Value(arProps(x))
            strNewProps = strNewProps & " " & arProps(x)
            If Not IsNull(varNewProp) Then
                strNewProps = strNewProps & " " & varNewProp
            End If
        Next
        strNewProps = Trim(strNewProps)
        nodProp.Attributes.getNamedItem("properties").Text = strNewProps
    Next nodProp

    Set nodProp = Nothing
    Set nodProps = Nothing
```

We then update matching French items in the English file:

```
    domEnglish.save "%path_to_tutorial_files%\hardwarefull_english_new.xml"

    Set domEnglish = Nothing
End Sub

Public Function EditDisplayName(ByRef nodProp As IXMLDOMNode) As Boolean
    Dim attName As IXMLDOMAttribute
    Dim attDisplayName As IXMLDOMAttribute
    Dim strDisplayName As String
    Dim attNew As IXMLDOMAttribute

    EditDisplayName = False
```

And then verify and create the `displayName` attribute:

```
    Set attName = nodProp.Attributes.getNamedItem("name")
    Set attDisplayName = nodProp.Attributes.getNamedItem("DisplayName")
    If attDisplayName Is Nothing Then
        strDisplayName = attName.Text
        Set attNew = nodProp.ownerDocument.createAttribute("DisplayName")
        attNew.Text = strDisplayName
        nodProp.Attributes.setNamedItem attNew
        Set attNew = Nothing
        EditDisplayName = True
        Set attDisplayName = Nothing
    End If

End Function
```

```
Function GetAffectedProperties() As String
    Dim strProperties As String

    strProperties = "Description, Country of Origin, Manufacturer, " & _
        "Voltage, Color, Gender, PrintingTechnology, Unit of Measure, " & _
        "DPI, Venue, Name, PPM, ColorPrinting, Os, Product name, " & _
        "System Requirements, Benefits, Licencetype, Productcount, " & _
        "ScrollWheel, Mediatype, Versioncd, Features, Cordless"

    GetAffectedProperties = strProperties
End Function
```

Copy Matching Items

The next two steps are to update the existing English categories and products to include the properties from the French categories and products. The code listed below should be added to the above code below the appropriate comment:

```
'Code to update matching French items to the English document
'Update the categories and products
Dim nodItems As IXMLDOMNodeList
Dim nodItem As IXMLDOMNode
Dim nodFields As IXMLDOMNodeList
Dim nodField As IXMLDOMNode
Dim nodItemFrench As IXMLDOMNode
Dim nodFieldFrench As IXMLDOMNode
Dim strFieldID As String
Dim varNewFieldID As Variant
Dim nodNewItem As IXMLDOMNode
Dim nodNewAtt As IXMLDOMAttribute

Set nodItems = domEnglish.selectNodes(".//Catalog/*")
For Each nodItem In nodItems
    strID = nodItem.Attributes.getNamedItem("id").Text
    Set nodItemFrench = domFrench.selectSingleNode(".//*[@id = '" & _
                        strID & "']")
    If Not (nodItemFrench Is Nothing) Then
        Set nodFields = nodItem.selectNodes("./Field")
        For Each nodField In nodFields
            strFieldID = nodField.Attributes.getNamedItem("fieldID").Text
            Set nodFieldFrench = nodItemFrench.selectSingleNode _
                        ("Field[@fieldID = '" & strFieldID & "']")
            varNewFieldID = dictIDs.Value(strFieldID)
            If Not IsNull(varNewFieldID) Then
                nodFieldFrench.Attributes.getNamedItem("fieldID").Text = _
                        varNewFieldID
                nodItem.insertBefore nodFieldFrench, nodField.nextSibling
            End If
            Set nodFieldFrench = Nothing
        Next

        If nodItem.nodeName = "Category" Then
            strFieldID = "CatalogProperty24"
            Set nodField = domEnglish.createNode(NODE_ELEMENT, _
```

```
                                   "Field", "")
                Set nodNewAtt = domEnglish.createAttribute("fieldID")
                nodNewAtt.Text = strFieldID
                nodField.Attributes.setNamedItem nodNewAtt
                Set nodNewAtt = domEnglish.createAttribute("fieldValue")
                nodNewAtt.Text = nodItem.Attributes.getNamedItem("name").Text
                nodField.Attributes.setNamedItem nodNewAtt
                nodItem.appendChild nodField
                Set nodField = domEnglish.createNode(NODE_ELEMENT, _
                                   "Field", "")
                varNewFieldID = dictIDs.Value(strFieldID)
                Set nodNewAtt = domEnglish.createAttribute("fieldID")
                nodNewAtt.Text = varNewFieldID
                nodField.Attributes.setNamedItem nodNewAtt
                Set nodNewAtt = domEnglish.createAttribute("fieldValue")
                nodNewAtt.Text = nodItemFrench.Attributes.getNamedItem _
                                   ("name").Text
                nodField.Attributes.setNamedItem nodNewAtt
                nodItem.appendChild nodField
                Set nodNewAtt = Nothing
            End If
            Set nodField = Nothing
            Set nodFields = Nothing
        End If
        Set nodItemFrench = Nothing
    Next nodProp
    Set nodItem = Nothing
    Set nodItems = Nothing
```

That's it. Run the program and take a look at the resulting file. You'll see that the French properties have copied over and the products and categories include the French values. Try importing this file into the product catalog from BizDesk and take a look at the results.

One thing you may notice, especially if you've loaded the English version separately before, is that not all the products have been imported. If you take a look at your event log, you'll see that a few of the products got errors during the import process. This is due to an error in the SQL OLE DB that only allows certain size queries. The combination of English and French data is a little too much for the OLE DB drivers. Obviously, we'd have to deal with this situation if we try to import our data and have strings that are long. It's enough for our purposes to have a subset of products loaded into the system.

Another thing to take note of are the products with variants. The Hardware and Mouse definitions both use a property in their variants that has both English and French values. However, if we tried to add the French property to the variant, we would have a three dimensional variant list, which is not what we want. There really is no way to represent the variant in multiple languages properly from within BizDesk, so we'll have to take care of it in code.

Modify the Site Code

The final step is to modify the site code to incorporate the changes we made to the product catalog. The steps include:

❑ Updating the category.asp page

❑ Updating the product.asp page

790

We'll start with the `category.asp` page. The category page uses a few functions in the `include\catalog.asp` file. The main function is `htmRenderCategoryPage()`, which calls `htmRenderCategoriesList()` and `htmRenderProductsTable()`.

Starting with `htmRenderCategoriesList()`, we'll change the line that gets the category names to include the current language. Change the function to the following:

```
' --------------------------------------------------------------------------
' htmRenderCategoriesList
'
' Description:
'   This function renders a recordset containing categories.
'   It provides links to each of the contained categories.
' --------------------------------------------------------------------------

Function htmRenderCategoriesList(ByVal oCatalog, ByVal rsCategories, ByVal style)
    Dim sProductCategory, sProductCategoryText, sCatalogName
    Dim htmCategory
    Dim lstrTemp
    Dim rsCategoryDetails

    If (rsCategories.EOF) Then
            lstrTemp = "" & CR
    Else
            sCatalogName = rsCategories.Fields _
                        (CATALOG_NAME_PROPERTY_NAME).Value

            lstrTemp = ""
            Do While Not rsCategories.EOF
                sProductCategory = rsCategories.Fields _
                                    (CATEGORY_NAME_PROPERTY_NAME).Value
                Set rsCategoryDetails = oCatalog.GetCategory _
                                    (sProductCategory).GetCategoryProperties
                sProductCategoryText = rsCategoryDetails.Fields("Name__" & _
                                    sLanguage).Value
                htmCategory = RenderCategoryLink(sCatalogName, _
                            sProductCategory, sProductCategoryText, 1, style)
                lstrTemp = lstrTemp & htmCategory & CR
                rsCategories.MoveNext
            Loop
    End If

    htmRenderCategoriesList = lstrTemp
End Function
```

It is necesssary to change the `RenderCategoryLink()` function in order to view the category's French text, but still link to the English value. Change that function as follows:

```
Function RenderCategoryLink(sCatalogName, sCategory, sCategoryText, nPage, style)
    Dim sURL, htmLinkText
    sURL = RenderCategoryURL(sCatalogName, sCategory, nPage)
    htmLinkText =  RenderText(sCategoryText, style)
    RenderCategoryLink = RenderLink(sURL, htmLinkText, MSCSSiteStyle.Link)
End Function
```

Next, we'll edit the `htmRenderProductsTable()`. There are a couple of lines to edit in this function. The line that checks to see if the name property is the identifying product property should be changed as follows:

```
bNameIsIdentifyingProperty = StrComp( _
                                      PRODUCT_NAME_PROPERTY_NAME & _
                                      "__" & sLanguage, _
                                      oCatalog.IdentifyingProductProperty, _
                                      vbTextCompare _
                             ) = 0
```

Next, change the two lines that collect the name and description properties as follows:

```
sProductName = rsProducts.Fields(PRODUCT_NAME_PROPERTY_NAME & _
                   "__" & sLanguage).Value
sProductDescription = rsProducts.Fields(PRODUCT_DESCRIPTION_PROPERTY_NAME & _
                   "__" & sLanguage).Value
```

That does it for the category page. Now let's look at the `product.asp` page. In the `Main()` function, line 90 looks for the name property. Since we got rid of the original name property and added language related properties, we need to edit this line as follows:

```
sProductName = rsProperties.Fields(PRODUCT_NAME_PROPERTY_NAME & _
                   "__" & sLanguage).Value
```

We need to edit the code that displays the user-defined properties. If we left the code as it is, we will display all the properties for each product no matter which language is selected. Let's fix this now. The function that we need to start with is `htmRenderUserDefinedProductProperties()`, and is in the `product.asp` page. The first thing we'll do is filter out the properties that are not in the language that we're looking for. This is where the double underscores that we talked about earlier in the chapter come into play. That string tells us that this is a property that has multiple values.

Update the appropriate code in the function with:

```
' Find out if the property can be shown. Do not display empty properties.
bShowProperty = False
If Not IsNull(fldProperty.Value) Then
    ' Filter out built-in properties. Built-in properties do not have
    ' attributes.
    If Not IsNull(MSCSCatalogAttribs.Value(fldProperty.Name)) Then
        If MSCSCatalogAttribs.Value(fldProperty.Name).Value _
                        (DISPLAY_ON_SITE_ATTRIBUTE) = True Then
            bShowProperty = True
        End If
    End If
    'Filter out properties that are in the wrong language
    nPos = InStr(fldProperty.Name, "__")
    If nPos > 0 Then
        If Not (InStr(nPos, fldProperty.name, sLanguage) > 0) Then
            bShowProperty = False
        End If
    End If
End If
```

The last line we need to change in this function is where we check the property name to see if it's the name field. The select case statement should be changed to read:

```
Select Case UCase(fldProperty.Name)
    Case UCase(IMAGE_FILENAME_PROPERTY_NAME)
        nWidth = PeekField(rsProperties, IMAGE_WIDTH_PROPERTY_NAME)
        nHeight = PeekField(rsProperties, IMAGE_HEIGHT_PROPERTY_NAME)
        htmProperty = BR & RenderImage(rsProperties.Fields _
                            (IMAGE_FILENAME_PROPERTY_NAME).Value, nWidth, _
                            nHeight, mscsMessageManager.GetMessage _
                            ("L_Standard_Image_Description_Text", _
                            sLanguage), "") & CRLF

    Case UCase(PRODUCT_NAME_PROPERTY_NAME & "__" & sLanguage), _
        UCase(IMAGE_WIDTH_PROPERTY_NAME), _
        UCase(IMAGE_HEIGHT_PROPERTY_NAME)
        htmProperty = ""

    Case Else
        ' Use DisplayName attribute if it is set, otherwise use PropertyName
        sPropertyName = sGetPropertyDisplayName(fldProperty.Name)
        htmProperty = RenderText(FormatOutput(LABEL_TEMPLATE, _
                        Array(sPropertyName)) & fldProperty.Value, _
                        MSCSSiteStyle.Body) & BR
End Select
```

So, the last thing to change is the code that renders the variant table. This will require a little more complicated code since we're not reading the information directly from the property. We'll have to look up the proper value from the related property in the correct language. First let's update the code that displays the table headers. You'll find it at the bottom of the page in function sGetPropertyDisplayName().

Update the function to read:

```
Function sGetPropertyDisplayName(ByVal sPropName)
    Dim nPos
    ' Check to see if the property is a multilingual property
    nPos = InStr(sPropName, "__")
    If nPos > 0 Then
        ' If so, replace the language with the current language
        sPropName = Left(sPropName, nPos + 1) & sLanguage
    End If
    ' Use property's display name attribute if it is set
    If Not IsNull(MSCSCatalogAttribs.Value(sPropName).Value _
                    (DISPLAY_NAME_ATTRIBUTE)) Then
        sGetPropertyDisplayName = MSCSCatalogAttribs.Value _
                    (sPropName).Value(DISPLAY_NAME_ATTRIBUTE)
    Else
        ' Otherwise, use property name
        sGetPropertyDisplayName = MSCSCatalogAttribs.Value _
                    (sPropName).Value(PROPERTY_NAME_ATTRIBUTE)
    End If
End Function
```

And finally, we need to change the code that gets the variant values and displays them on the page. The function is called `htmRenderVariantsList()`. Add the following line to the declarations section:

```
Dim nPos, sOrigVal, sLangName, rsLangVariant, rsLangProps, arVals
```

Then change the iteration code to:

```
' Note that we assume a user-defined variant property has a data type of
' string.
'       If you have assigned a different data type to a such a property, you may
'       need to perform additional transformation on the property value (such as
'       calling htmRenderCurrency() for currency values) prior to displaying it.
For i = 0 to listProps.Count - 2
        ' Check if this is a multilingual property
        nPos = InStr(listProps(i), "__")
        sOrigVal = rsVariants.Fields(listProps(i)).Value
        If nPos > 0 Then
                'Make sure we have the correct language
            If Not (InStr(nPos, listProps(i), sLanguage) > 0) Then
                    sLangName = Left(listProps(i), nPos + 1) & sLanguage
                    Set rsLangVariant =
MSCSCatalogManager.GetPropertyAttributes(sLangName)
                    If rsLangVariant.Fields("DataType").Value = 9 Then
                        Set rsLangProps =
MSCSCatalogManager.GetPropertyValues(sLangName)
                        Do While Not rsLangProps.EOF
                            arVals = Split _
                                    (rsLangProps.Fields("Value").Value, "|")
                            If arVals(0) = sOrigVal Then
                                sOrigVal = arVals(1)
                            End If
                            rsLangProps.MoveNext
                        Loop
                    End If
            End If
        End If
        arrDataCols(i + 1) = sOrigVal
Next
```

That does it for the description data. Now when we view the site, we should be able to switch back and forth between English and French and the product and category values will change appropriately.

Note that we will see missing data when viewing the Featured Products and Gaming Devices in French. The reason for this is that Microsoft did not provide the French data for these products in the appropriate `hardwarefull.xml` file. The code is working, but not finding any French data.

The last piece of the puzzle that we need to put in place is translating the numeric values.

Numeric Values

The data that came with the solution site only included a weight and a price that we'll have to convert. In your application, you'll probably have dimensions, and possibly some other fields to work with. The techniques we discuss in this section will be easily extensible to include your custom fields. Let's discuss the specific method we're going to use.

In order to convert the weight property, we'll write a function that accepts the weight value in the default catalog's weight unit of measure, and the destination locale's weight unit of measure. We'll look up the conversion factor between the different units of measure and return the converted value with the correct unit of measure. We'll keep the code fairly simplistic and place the conversion factors directly in the function. In a production environment, we would most likely data drive these conversion values instead.

Weight Calculation

First, we'll go back to the `product.asp` page and update the `htmRenderUserDefinedProductProperties()` page again. We need to add a few lines that detect the weight property and convert it to the right value. This action is performed in the `Select...Case` statement.

Replace the `Case Else` segment with the following:

```
Case Else
    Rem Use DisplayName attribute if it is set, otherwise use PropertyName
    sPropertyName = sGetPropertyDisplayName(fldProperty.Name)
    vFieldValue = fldProperty.Value
    'If weight, translate to correct locale
    If sPropertyName = "Weight" Then
        vFieldValue = TranslateWeight(vFieldValue, nLocale)
    End If
    htmProperty = RenderText(FormatOutput(LABEL_TEMPLATE, _
                    Array(sPropertyName)) & vFieldValue, _
                    MSCSSiteStyle.Body) & BR
```

Now we need to write the new function that we introduced in the previous code, `TranslateWeight()`. We'll add this to the `include\catalog.asp` page at the bottom. The function will look up the default weight unit of measure, and the destination unit of measure based on the passed locale value, find the conversion factor, and calculate the new value including the new unit of measure.

Add the following code to the bottom of the page:

```
Function TranslateWeight(vValue, nNewLocale)
    Dim sDefaultUnit
    Dim sNewUnit
    Dim nConversion

    sDefaultUnit = dictConfig.s_WeightMeasure

    Select Case nNewLocale
        Case 1033
            sNewUnit = "lbs"
        Case 1036
            sNewUnit = "kg"
        Case Else
            sNewUnit = sDefaultUnit
    End Select

    Select Case nNewUnit
        Case "lbs"
            nConversion = 1
        Case "kg"
```

```
                  nConversion = 1 / 2.204
         Case Else
                  nConversion = 1
      End Select

      TranslateWeight = CStr(vValue * nConversion) & " " & sNewUnit
End Function
```

Obviously, we've made this function extremely simple. In a production environment, we would want to have data driven the conversion table, and included a record for every locale. In your site, you can easily update this function to provide the functionality that you require.

In order to test the functionality, you will need to add a weight to one or more of the products, as weight wasn't included in the sample files from Microsoft. Go into BizDesk and add the property to your product definitions, then add a value to the weight property for one of the products and view it on the site. You should now be able to switch between French and English, and watch the weight change from kilograms to pounds.

Currency Conversion

So finally, we get to the last piece of the puzzle as far as the website user interface is concerned. Converting the currency field shouldn't be too different from the weight conversion, with the exception of some helper functions provided by Microsoft Commerce Server 2000. Again, in a production environment, we would want to put the conversion factors in a database, especially since it will need to be updated on a daily basis. However, for this demonstration, we'll keep all the values in the code. The price values come up on two of the main pages, `category.asp` and `product.asp`. They also show up on `basket.asp` and in the checkout process, but we'll save those for the next section.

First, let's look at the `category.asp`.

The work to display the `category.asp` page is actually done in the `include\catalog.asp` page, so we'll first open this. We'll add a single line to convert the currency in the `ConvertCurrency` function that we'll create. After the function `GetPriceAndCurrency()` that retrieves the price and currency of each product in the list, add the following lines:

```
'Convert currency to current locale
Call ConvertCurrency(cyProductPrice, cyCurrency)
```

The real work is done in the new `ConvertCurrency` function. Let's add this to the bottom of the `include\catalog.asp` page.

```
Sub  ConvertCurrency(ByRef cyPrice, ByRef cyCurrency)
     Dim oEuro
     Dim nBaseLocale
     Dim sBaseSymbol
     Dim sConvertSymbol

     'Only convert if the currency locale is different from the base locale
     nBaseLocale = dictConfig.i_BaseCurrencyLocale
     If Not (IsNull(cyPrice) Or Trim(cyPrice & "") = "") Then
          If CInt(nBaseLocale) = CInt(nLocale) Then
               sConvertSymbol = dictConfig.s_BaseCurrencySymbol
```

```
                 Else
                         sBaseSymbol = dictConfig.s_BaseCurrencySymbol
                         Set oEuro = Server.CreateObject("Commerce.EuroDisplay")
                         Select Case nLocale
                             Case 1036
                                     sConvertSymbol = "FF"
                                     Call oEuro.Initialize(sBaseSymbol, nBaseLocale, _
                                                           "FF", nLocale, 7.293)
                         End Select
                         cyPrice = oEuro.ConvertMoney(cyPrice)
                         Set oEuro = Nothing
                 End If
                 cyCurrency = MSCSDataFunctions.LocalizeCurrency(cyPrice, _
                                                 nLocale, sConvertSymbol)
         End If
End Function
```

That should take care of the category page. Next, let's update the product.asp page. First, we need to edit the code that renders the non-variant price, then work on the variant prices. The code to display the non-variant pricing is in the htmRenderBuiltInProperties() function in the product.asp page.

Replace the existing code with the following:

```
Function htmRenderBuiltInProperties(ByVal rsProperties, ByVal sPropertyName, ByVal
style)
    Dim sText
    Dim cyPrice
    Dim cyCurrency
    Dim nDefaultLocale

    sText = mscsMessageManager.GetMessage _
               ("L_Product_Price_DisplayName_HTMLText", sLanguage)
    nDefaultLocale = dictConfig.i_BaseCurrencyLocale
    cyPrice = rsProperties.Fields(sPropertyName).Value
    cyCurrency = MSCSDataFunctions.LocalizeCurrency(cyPrice, nDefaultLocale)
    Call ConvertCurrency(cyPrice, cyCurrency)
    sText = sText & ": " & cyCurrency
    htmRenderBuiltInProperties = RenderText(sText, style)
End Function
```

Notice that we replaced the htmRenderCurrency() function with the output from our new ConvertCurrency() function. You may want to study the htmRenderCurrency() function to see if there is any functionality you will need on your site.

Next, we'll update the code that displays the variant pricing on the product page.

The code that we're looking for is in the htmRenderVariantsList() function in the product.asp page. We'll do the same thing we did for the non-variant pricing display. Replace the one line near the end of the function using the htmRenderCurrency() function with the following:

```
'Update the price column
Dim cyPrice
Dim cyCurrency
```

```
Dim nDefaultLocale

nDefaultLocale = dictConfig.i_BaseCurrencyLocale
cyPrice = rsVariants.Fields("cy_list_price").Value
cyCurrency = MSCSDataFunctions.LocalizeCurrency(cyPrice, nDefaultLocale)
Call ConvertCurrency(cyPrice, cyCurrency)
arrDataCols(listProps.Count) = cyCurrency
```

That should do it. Except for pipeline components on the basket page and checkout, we can now convert the site between English and French. We haven't updated the search pages, but we could apply the same techniques to update those pages. In the next section, we'll update the rest of the site to complete the process.

Pipeline Modifications

In this section, let's look at what's required to change the pipeline processes to support our international website. We'll start with the basket pipeline and finish with the checkout process. We'll be discussing both modifications to the pipeline components themselves as well as updating the web pages that support them.

Basket

The basket pipeline component takes input from the product page when someone presses the Add to Cart button, and stores the information about the product in the Items dictionary. Luckily for us, it is already written to store all of the information about the product in the dictionary, so we won't have to rewrite any of the pipeline components or change the pipeline. The only thing we have to do is select the proper fields to display on the basket page and convert the currency.

The code that we want to change is on the basket.asp page in the htmRenderBasket() function. The section that we're looking for is near the middle of the function within the For...Next loop, iterating through the listAggregatedItems() list. The values are being placed in the arrData array to be processed by the RenderTableDataRow() function. The changes will be very similar to the changes we made in the previous section.

Replace the entire If statement with:

```
Dim cyCurrentPrice, cyCurrentCurrency
Dim cyAdjustPrice, cyAdjustCurrency
cyCurrentPrice = dictItem.Value("_cy_iadjust_currentprice")
cyAdjustPrice = dictItem.Value("_cy_oadjust_adjustedprice")
Call ConvertCurrency(cyCurrentPrice, cyCurrentCurrency)
Call ConvertCurrency(cyAdjustPrice, cyAdjustCurrency)
If bDiscountApplied Then
      ' "name" and "description" are required product properties and
      '  cannot have null values.
      arrData = Array(_
            htmQtyCol, _
            htmProdCode, _
            dictItem.Value("_product_name" & "__" & sLanguage), _
            dictItem.Value("_product_description" & "__" & sLanguage), _
            cyCurrentCurrency, _
            cyAdjustCurrency, _
```

```
            dictItem.Value("_messages"), _
            htmRenderCurrency(dictItem.Value("_cy_oadjust_adjustedprice")), _
            htmRemoveCol)
    Else
        ' "name" and "description" are required product properties and
        '  cannot have null values.
        arrData = Array(_
            htmQtyCol, _
            htmProdCode, _
            dictItem.Value("_product_name" & "__" & sLanguage), _
            dictItem.Value("_product_description" & "__" & sLanguage), _
            cyCurrentCurrency, _
            cyAdjustCurrency, _
            htmRemoveCol)
    End If
```

The other change to make is to the order subtotal. The code for that is just a few lines further down the page where we next set the arrData array. Replace that one line with:

```
Dim cySubtotal, cySubtotalCurrency
cySubtotal = mscsOrderGrp.value.saved_cy_oadjust_subtotal
Call ConvertCurrency(cySubtotal, cySubtotalCurrency)
arrData = Array(_
    NBSP, _
    mscsMessageManager.GetMessage("L_BASKET_SUBTOTAL_COLUMN_TEXT", _
    sLanguage), _
    cySubtotalCurrency, _
    RenderLink(urlLink, htmLinkText, MSCSSiteStyle.Link))
```

Check out the basket page now. The name and description have shown up again and they, along with the prices, change back and forth between languages. Unfortunately, the checkout process won't be quite as easy to implement.

Check-out

Let's go through the check-out process one page at a time. First, we'll start with the shipping address form. You'll notice, if you look at that site, that none of the form labels are translated. This might seem strange, since the modifications we made earlier have affected everything else. However, when we delve into the code, we quickly discover why.

The entire address form is stored in an application variable. The application variable is set in global.asa, so it's not dynamic, and won't change when we change the sLanguage variable. The actual function that sets up the form is GetAddressFieldDefinitions(), located in the include\global_addressbook_lib.asp page. We can see, in this function, that the Label property of the dictionary is set at the application startup with a value using the default language. This is where the problem resides.

Luckily, it's easily fixed. Instead of storing the value in the Label property, let's change it so the constant is stored there instead. This will allow us to look up the value on the display page and use our sLanguage variable to get the correct language. To make the change, replace every line in the function that looks like this:

```
dictFld.Label = MSCSMessageManager.GetMessage("L_LastName_HTMLText", _
                                              sLanguage)
```

with this:

```
dictFld.Label = "L_LastName_HTMLText"
```

using the correct constant, of course. We'll need to do the same with the `ErrorMessage` property as well. Replace all lines that look like this:

```
dictFld.ErrorMessage = MSCSMessageManager.GetMessage _
                    ("L_BadLastName_ErrorMessage", sLanguage)
```

with this:

```
dictFld.ErrorMessage = "L_BadLastName_ErrorMessage"
```

We will also have to repeat this process in the `GetShipToAddressFieldDefinitions()` function.

Now, to complete the transformation, we need to update the code that displays the form on the web page. The code is located in the `include\form_lib.asp` page in function `htmRenderFillOutForm()`. This couldn't be simpler. At the top of the `For...Next` loop, the variable `sLabel` is assigned from the dictionary object. Simply replace that line with the following:

```
sLabel = MSCSMessageManager.GetMessage(dictField.Label, sLanguage)
```

and we're done. The address pages should now convert.

> *Note that you'll have to add shipping options in BizDesk before you'll be able to complete the checkout process.*

Once you've got one or more shipping options, browse through the check-out process until you reach the shipping selection page. Notice, when you switch languages on this page, the text for the shipping option does not change. In fact, there's no way to use the technique we used in the rest of this chapter to provide the translated values. We don't have any additional properties that we could set to represent each language.

One possible solution to the problem would be to create your own shipping component that accepts the language variable to display the correct option. In a real international website, building a custom shipping component could well be the most viable option. The main reason for doing this is that Commerce Server 2000 does not offer enough flexibility in their shipping methods to support the types of shipping methods and charges that would be required.

We saw an example of creating our own shipping component in Chapter 12. Here we'll see an alternative method of providing the localized language, that will work in the shipping functionality provided by Commerce Server 2000, as well as a custom component.

The method we'll be using is similar to what we did in the shipping and billing address. Instead of storing the language to be displayed on the site within BizDesk, we'll store a constant lookup string in the name and description attributes of each shipping item. We'll store the actual text in the `MessageManager.xml` file. This is the first time we've had to manually add records to `MessageManager.xml`, but it'll illustrate how simple this process is, and how easy it is to implement and maintain.

Go into BizDesk and edit the shipping options. If you're implementing this solution on your own site, you'll need to update all shipping options, or you'll receive an error when the MessageManager can't find the constant string in the database.

We'll use one shipping option to make things simple, replacing the name attribute with custom_Shipping_Fast_Method_Text, and the description attribute with custom_Shipping_Fast_Description_Text.

Next, we'll need to add the values to the rc.xml file. Open it up and add the following to the end, or wherever you would like:

```
<Entry Name="custom_Shipping_Fast_Method_Text" Type="custom Fast shipping method
text">
      <Value Language="English">Fast</Value>
      <Value Language="French">Rapide</Value>
</Entry>
<Entry Name="custom_Shipping_Fast_Description_Text" Type="custom Fast shipping
method description">
      <Value Language="English">UPS Express Saver</Value>
      <Value Language="French">UPS Express Saver</Value>
</Entry>
```

Finally, we'll edit the pickship.asp page to use the new values. We'll make our changes to the htmRenderShippingMethods() function in the While...Wend loop. Replace the line that assigns data to the arrData array with:

```
arrData = Array(htmRadioBtn, mscsMessageManager.GetMessage _
                    (rs.Fields("shipping_method_name").Value, sLanguage), _
                mscsMessageManager.GetMessage _
                    (rs.Fields("description").Value, sLanguage))
```

Now, we'll move on to the Order Summary page. Here, we simply need to fix the code that displays the shipping method and add our ConvertCurrency function to the item and order totals. Open the summary.asp file. First, we'll edit the htmRenderSummaryPage() function. We simply need to replace the line:

```
htmContent = htmContent & ": " & dictAnyItem.Value("shipping_method_name") & _
                                    CRLF
```

with:

```
htmContent = htmContent & ": " & mscsMessageManager.GetMessage _
                    (dictAnyItem.Value("shipping_method_name"), sLanguage) & CRLF
```

The next piece of code we need to update is in the htmRenderOrderForm() function. This is almost identical to the change that we made when rendering the basket totals. Inside the For...Next loop is the code that assigns the product information to the arrData() array.

Replace that code with the following:

```
Dim cyCurrentPrice, cyCurrentCurrency
Dim cyAdjustPrice, cyAdjustCurrency
cyCurrentPrice = dictItem.Value("_cy_iadjust_currentprice")
```

```
cyAdjustPrice = dictItem.Value("_cy_oadjust_adjustedprice")
Call ConvertCurrency(cyCurrentPrice, cyCurrentCurrency)
Call ConvertCurrency(cyAdjustPrice, cyAdjustCurrency)
If bDiscountApplied Then
      ' "name" and "description" are required product properties and cannot
      ' have null values.
      arrData = Array(_
            htmProdCode, _
            dictItem.Value("_product_name" & "__" & sLanguage), _
            dictItem.Value("_product_description" & "__" & sLanguage), _
            dictItem.Value("quantity"), _
            cyCurrentCurrency, _
            cyAdjustCurrency, _
            dictItem.Value("_messages"), _
            htmRenderCurrency(dictItem.Value("_cy_oadjust_adjustedprice")))
Else
      ' "name" and "description" are required product properties and cannot
      ' have null values.
      arrData = Array(_
            htmProdCode, _
            dictItem.Value("_product_name" & "__" & sLanguage), _
            dictItem.Value("_product_description" & "__" & sLanguage), _
            dictItem.Value("quantity"), _
            cyCurrentCurrency, _
            cyAdjustCurrency)
End If
```

Also in that function, we need to update the code that renders the sub-totals. This is found right at the end of the function, so replace the bottom of the function with the following code:

```
cyCurrentPrice = mscsOrderForm.Value(SUBTOTAL)
Call ConvertCurrency(cyCurrentPrice, cyCurrentCurrency)
arrData = Array(NBSP, mscsMessageManager.GetMessage _
      ("L_BASKET_SUBTOTAL_COLUMN_TEXT", sLanguage), _
      cyCurrentCurrency)
htmRenderOrderForm = htmRenderOrderForm & RenderTableDataRow(arrData, _
                     arrDataAttLists, MSCSSiteStyle.TRMiddle)

htmShipTotal = mscsMessageManager.GetMessage _
                     ("L_BASKET_SHIPPING_COLUMN_TEXT", sLanguage)
If Not IsNull(mscsOrderForm.Value("_shipping_discount_description")) Then
      cyCurrentPrice = mscsOrderForm.Value _
                                 ("_shipping_discount_description")
      Call ConvertCurrency(cyCurrentPrice, cyCurrentCurrency)
      htmShipTotal = htmShipTotal & " (" & cyCurrentCurrency & ")"
End If

cyCurrentPrice = mscsOrderForm.Value(SHIPPING_TOTAL)
Call ConvertCurrency(cyCurrentPrice, cyCurrentCurrency)
arrData = Array(NBSP, htmShipTotal, _
      cyCurrentCurrency)
htmRenderOrderForm = htmRenderOrderForm & RenderTableDataRow(arrData, _
                     arrDataAttLists, MSCSSiteStyle.TRMiddle)

cyCurrentPrice = mscsOrderForm.Value(HANDLING_TOTAL)
```

```
        Call ConvertCurrency(cyCurrentPrice, cyCurrentCurrency)
        arrData = Array(NBSP, mscsMessageManager.GetMessage _
            ("L_BASKET_HANDLING_COLUMN_TEXT", sLanguage), _
            cyCurrentCurrency)
        htmRenderOrderForm = htmRenderOrderForm & RenderTableDataRow(arrData, _
                              arrDataAttLists, MSCSSiteStyle.TRMiddle)

        cyCurrentPrice = mscsOrderForm.Value(TAX_TOTAL)
        Call ConvertCurrency(cyCurrentPrice, cyCurrentCurrency)
        arrData = Array(NBSP, mscsMessageManager.GetMessage _
            ("L_BASKET_TAX_COLUMN_TEXT", sLanguage), _
            cyCurrentCurrency)
        htmRenderOrderForm = htmRenderOrderForm & RenderTableDataRow(arrData, _
                              arrDataAttLists, MSCSSiteStyle.TRMiddle)

        cyCurrentPrice = mscsOrderForm.Value(TOTAL_TOTAL)
        Call ConvertCurrency(cyCurrentPrice, cyCurrentCurrency)
        arrData = Array(NBSP, mscsMessageManager.GetMessage _
            ("L_BASKET_ORDERTOTAL_COLUMN_TEXT", sLanguage), _
            cyCurrentCurrency)
        htmRenderOrderForm = htmRenderOrderForm & RenderTableDataRow(arrData, _
                              arrDataAttLists, MSCSSiteStyle.TRMiddle)

        htmRenderOrderForm = RenderTable(htmRenderOrderForm, _
                                  MSCSSiteStyle.BasketTable)

        htmRenderOrderForm = htmRenderOrderForm & RenderText _
                (mscsOrderForm.Value("_shipping_discount_description"), _
                MSCSSiteStyle.Body) & BR
End Function
```

The next task to complete is the rendering of the order totals. That code is found in the
htmRenderGrandTotals() function. Replace the entire function with the following:

```
Function htmRenderGrandTotals(mscsOrderGrp)
    Dim arrData, arrDataAttLists, cyPrice, cyCurrency

    Call mscsOrderGrp.AggregateOrderFormValues(SHIPPING_TOTAL, _
            SHIPPING_TOTAL)
    Call mscsOrderGrp.AggregateOrderFormValues(HANDLING_TOTAL, _
            HANDLING_TOTAL)
    Call mscsOrderGrp.AggregateOrderFormValues(TAX_TOTAL, TAX_TOTAL)
    arrDataAttLists = Array(MSCSSiteStyle.TDLeft, MSCSSiteStyle.TDRight)
    cyPrice = mscsOrderGrp.Value(SAVED_SUBTOTAL)
    Call ConvertCurrency(cyPrice, cyCurrency)
    arrData = Array(mscsMessageManager.GetMessage _
        ("L_BASKET_SUBTOTAL_COLUMN_TEXT", sLanguage), cyCurrency)
    htmRenderGrandTotals = htmRenderGrandTotals & RenderTableDataRow _
        (arrData, arrDataAttLists, MSCSSiteStyle.TRMiddle)
    cyPrice = mscsOrderGrp.Value(SAVED_SHIPPING_TOTAL)
    Call ConvertCurrency(cyPrice, cyCurrency)
    arrData = Array(mscsMessageManager.GetMessage _
        ("L_BASKET_SHIPPING_COLUMN_TEXT", sLanguage), cyCurrency)
    htmRenderGrandTotals = htmRenderGrandTotals & RenderTableDataRow _
        (arrData, arrDataAttLists, MSCSSiteStyle.TRMiddle)
```

```
            cyPrice = mscsOrderGrp.Value(SAVED_HANDLING_TOTAL)
            Call ConvertCurrency(cyPrice, cyCurrency)
            arrData = Array("A" & mscsMessageManager.GetMessage _
                ("L_BASKET_HANDLING_COLUMN_TEXT", sLanguage), cyCurrency)
            htmRenderGrandTotals = htmRenderGrandTotals & RenderTableDataRow _
                (arrData, arrDataAttLists, MSCSSiteStyle.TRMiddle)
            cyPrice = mscsOrderGrp.Value(SAVED_TAX_TOTAL)
            Call ConvertCurrency(cyPrice, cyCurrency)
            arrData = Array(mscsMessageManager.GetMessage _
                ("L_BASKET_TAX_COLUMN_TEXT", sLanguage), cyCurrency)
            htmRenderGrandTotals = htmRenderGrandTotals & RenderTableDataRow _
                (arrData, arrDataAttLists, MSCSSiteStyle.TRMiddle)
            cyPrice = mscsOrderGrp.Value(SAVED_TOTAL_TOTAL)
            Call ConvertCurrency(cyPrice, cyCurrency)
            arrData = Array(mscsMessageManager.GetMessage _
                ("L_BASKET_ORDERTOTAL_COLUMN_TEXT", sLanguage), cyCurrency)
            htmRenderGrandTotals = htmRenderGrandTotals & RenderTableDataRow _
                (arrData, arrDataAttLists, MSCSSiteStyle.TRMiddle)
    End Function
```

The next page gathers the credit card information. The form is built in the same way that the address form was built so we need to edit the correct function in exactly the same way. The function referenced is the `GetCreditCardFieldDefinitions()` in the `include\global_creditcards_lib.asp` page.

Again, simply replace all lines that look like this:

```
    dictFld.Label = MSCSMessageManager.GetMessage("L_CreditCardName_HTMLText", _
                    sLanguage)
```

with this:

```
    dictFld.Label = "L_CreditCardName_HTMLText"
```

Also replace all lines that look like this:

```
    dictFld.ErrorMessage = MSCSMessageManager.GetMessage _
                    ("L_Bad_CreditCard_Name_ErrorMessage", sLanguage)
```

with this:

```
    dictFld.ErrorMessage = "L_Bad_CreditCard_Name_ErrorMessage"
```

And that should do it. We can now go all the way through viewing products, adding them to our basket, and checking out in French as well as English. As you can see, the modular design of the solution site makes it possible to internationalize a site with a minimum of code changes. While we wouldn't be ready to go to production, the techniques that we used can be applied on most of a site without much modification.

Summary

While Commerce Server 2000 makes updating an existing site much less difficult, it is still a non-trivial matter to globalize a site. As we discussed, you have many tough design decisions to make in order to support customers from across the world. Your database design needs special consideration to support multiple languages and allow for increased data lengths. You need to consider locale specific elements such as date and time formats, currency types, units of measure and address structures. You will also need to spend time researching the overseas shipping methods that you'll use as well as deciding what to charge your customers. Finally, you need to keep on top of tax laws in the various parts of the countries where you plan to do business.

Commerce Server 2000 provides us with many tools that can be used to more easily implement an international site. We showed how to use the `MessageManager` object and its supporting xml file to quickly convert much of the site's verbiage. To implement this solution, we simply needed to provide the correct language value in the `sLanguage` variable and be able to associate the chosen language with each user. We discussed a couple ways of doing this, including passing the variable in the query string, as well as storing the value in the users' cookie.

We chose to store the language preference in the user profile. Since we needed to look up the language preference when each page was rendered, this method allowed us to keep all of the processing on the server side, without having to query information stored on the user's computer.

The product catalog can be especially difficult to convert into a multilingual entity. Without building a custom catalog, we were able to portray product information in two languages. However, as discussed, the method we used could get unwieldy as we increase the number of languages supported. But, for only a few languages, such an approach works quite well, and only requires minimal modifications to the solution site code.

Currency conversion can be especially difficult to implement. You'll need to create a custom object to provide the conversion ratio between the default currency to the currency requested by the user. You'll also need to provide a way to store the history of the conversion rates so they can be used later on when you need to communicate the sale price in the user's currency of choice.

The most important rule to remember when globalizing your site is to plan early. While Commerce Server 2000 makes upgrading easier, it can still cost quite a bit of time and money to introduce these concepts after a site has gone live. Incorporating the lessons learned in this chapter early in the design process will provide a higher level of integration and allow you to expand your site much more easily.

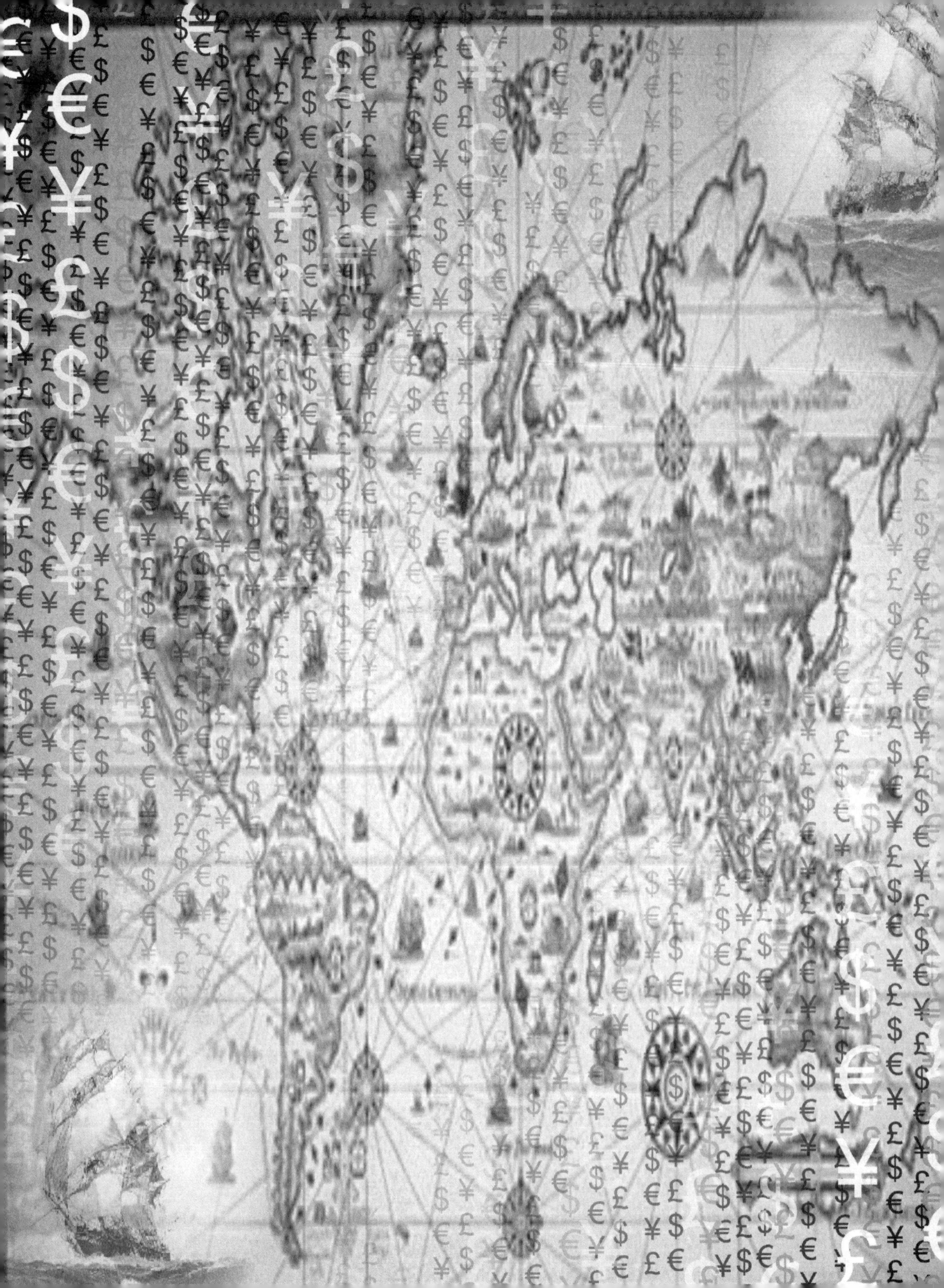

17

Migrating Your Membership Directory

It may be the case that you're currently using Site Server 3.0. In this case you're not going to want to lose your membership details. The next two chapters look at the practical business of migrating these Site Server 3.0 applications to Commerce Server 2000.

This first chapter will deal with the intensive task of migrating the membership directory. It has been structured so that the user who simply wants to gather enough information to migrate their members can simply peruse the first half of the chapter. While, the more advanced programmer, who may want a more in-depth understanding of the migration tools and how to customize them for their specific application, will be able to get the relevant details, from subsequent sections specific to those tools, in the second half.

The next chapter will delve into the migration of the different elements of your e-commerce store, such as AdServer, catalog, analysis and web pages. So, any discussion of those topics will be reserved until then.

Microsoft has put a fair amount of time and effort into providing tools to perform the membership directory migration. This makes sense, since they have made it virtually impossible to use the existing membership directory structure in the new Commerce Server 2000 platform, and there is no seamless upgrade from the Site Server 3.0 Membership Directory to the Commerce Server 2000 User Profile System. So, Microsoft provides the Solution Developer Kit (SDK), along with the standard Commerce Server 2000 installation. This provides the tools to migrate your Site Server 3.0 membership directory. Along with these tools, you will have to perform a number of manual tasks to ensure that your members are migrated with all of the necessary attributes.

The chapter will cover the following topics, in order:

❑   Migration in General

❑   Data Structure

❑   Coding Modifications

❑   Migration – Quick Reference Guide

❑   Migration Tools – In Depth View

By the end of the chapter, you should have a real appreciation for the work involved and the complexity of migrating your Site Server 3.0 Membership Directory to Commerce Server 2000 Profile System.

Migration – An Overview

Commerce Server 2000 offers a number of new features to its users. As we've seen, the more prominent ones include the User Profile System, Business Internet Analytics, the Site Packager (Packer-UnPacker), the Management Desk and the Content Targeting System. All of these are take-off ideas from existing Site Server features and all good reasons to migrate to the next platform.

However, there are other features in Site Server 3.0 that have not been carried forward to Commerce Server 2000 – some have been transferred to other products, while others have been discontinued altogether. This section will explore some of these issues in more detail. A feature-by-feature comparison table is also included.

A number of the major modifications that must be implemented before migrating to CS2K derive from the fact that CS2K is specifically built upon the functionality of Windows 2000 – it requires Windows 2000 Server Edition as its operating system. This will be the first hurdle to cross for most users, who will probably have implemented their original site on an NT 4.0 platform. Having said that, Site Server 3 can be migrated to Windows 2000 if the appropriate service packs and hotfixes are applied.

The installation on Windows 2000 must be performed in the correct order, just like the installation on NT4.0. A hotfix, SS3W2K.EXE must be applied before Site Server can be installed on Windows 2000. Also, Site Server Service Pack 4 must be applied **after** the installation. You must not overwrite any existing files on your system, as this would affect some of the system files that Windows 2000 and IIS 5.0 have already installed. There are also some known errors that can be encountered during the installation of Site Server Commerce Edition:

❑   File(s) failed to self-register. D:\Microsoft Site Server\Bin\Xenroll.dll

❑   Cannot set attribute description. Details: Error: 80071392

These errors can be ignored and the installation will complete properly.

Since Windows 2000 utilizes Active Directory for its user base to store login information, user properties, Active Directory Sites, user groups, and so on, CS2K can use the same Active Directory technology for membership and authentication. However, CS2K also offers the option of using any other data source just as long as it is permits OLE-DB connectivity. This means that you can use SQL Server 7.0, SQL Server 2000, Oracle or any other OLE-DB Data Source to store information such as member attributes In fact, if you are already using a catalog in a SQL Server or Oracle datastore, you can use this same database to store your member attributes as long as you create the necessary tables in your database and add the database as a data source in the User Profile System.

Also, CS2K utilizes ADO 2.6 and integrates with Windows 2000 technology that includes BizTalk Server (replacing the Commerce Interchange Pipeline) and Application Center 2000 (replacing the content deployment and knowledge management). Therefore the Commerce Server 2000 platform offers functionality and scalability improvements over the Site Server 3.0 platform.

However, you will find that you need to make some code modifications in order to make your application compatible with the new platform's tools. These modifications will come in the form of ASP coding modifications, coding modifications in your DLL to incorporate and integrate with the Windows 2000 technology.

Even the installation procedure (which is covered in Appendix A) has been greatly simplified in CS2K, when compared to the 5-page instruction booklet that Microsoft publishes in their Knowledge Base for the installation of Site Server 3!

To Migrate or Not to Migrate

Aside from the new features, Commerce Server also offers some improvements and business benefits:

❑ Better predictor capabilities, which can be translated into better advertising campaigns.

❑ More tightly integrated with Windows 2000 than Site Server 3.0 is with NT 4.0. The user can therefore benefit from some of the advancements that Windows 2000 offers over NT 4.0, such as the integration of COM+, and easier integration with other Windows 2000 technology. Also the tighter interface with the operating system translates into a more stable platform for your e-commerce site.

❑ The Business Desk offers both the developer and the site manager a management platform that simplifies the management of the e-commerce site, right through from the least complex of tasks (such as user management and rule creation), to those that are traditionally more arduous (such as the creation and management of catalogs and campaigns).

❑ Site Server Rules are replaced by Expressions, which resemble the business logic much more than the old rule structure. This means that you spend less time on coding and more on the business logic and management of your site.

❑ When a site is totally configured and ready for deployment, the Site Packager's `Packer-UnPacker` utility enables rapid cloning of the store for deployment. So goodbye to deployment projects which only transfer the files and don't register components! The Site Packager feature is further enhanced by the use of Application Center, which not only provides content replication functionality but can also automate content synchronization.

Note: the Business Desk is a very dynamic application, but it does have drawbacks, such as the level of complexity for new feature development and poor performance in its default format.

Migration does include some drawbacks; amongst these is the fact that some of the old Site Server 3.0 functionalities are not carried forward. These features are probably the least used and least beneficial of the Site Server 3.0 feature set – they include:

❑ Active Channel Multi-Caster

❑ Active Channel Server (push)

❑ Content Analysis

❑ Content Deployment

Content Deployment is included in the list because the concept of the Site Packager is totally different to that of the old Content Deployment. The content replication feature has been moved to Application Center 2000.

Some other functionality is carried forward but in a different application, Microsoft SharePoint. These features include:

❑ Content Management

❑ Knowledge Management

❑ Search

The remaining features **are** carried forward, but with major modifications, which, in some cases, will require significant recoding.

The following table is a feature comparison chart with a list of all of the features of Site Server 3.0 and, where applicable, which feature in Commerce Server 2000 has taken over the role or whether the feature is available in another Microsoft Product.

Site Server 3.0 Features	CS2K Features	Other Microsoft Products
Ad Server/Manager	Content Selection Framework / Campaign Manager	
Analysis: Report Writer, Custom Import, Usage Import, Content Analyzer	Analysis: Reports, Custom Import, Data Warehouse	Microsoft SQL Server
Direct Mail	Direct Mail	
Pipelines	Pipelines	
Personalization and Membership	User Profiles	LDAP, as part of the Operating System
Site Vocabulary	Site Terms	
Rule Builder	Expressions – Builder / Evaluator	
Predictor	Predictor Resource	
Starter Site	Solution Site	
Transactions	Transactions	
Content Deployment and Content Replication System	Site Packager	Application Center 2000
Commerce Interchange Pipeline		Microsoft BizTalk Server 2000

Site Server 3.0 Features	CS2K Features	Other Microsoft Products
Internet Locator Service (ILS) / Dynamic Directory		Microsoft Windows 2000
Search: Index, Crawl, Scripts		
Knowledge Manager		Microsoft SharePoint

Migrating the Directory

The structure of the Site Server 3.0 membership directory is not supported in the new Commerce Server 2000. Instead, it incorporates the User Profile System, which creates a virtual mapping of all attributes to the relevant data stores, making it appear to the user as if all attributes were stored in a single database. The User Profile System not only manages the location of the attributes, but also provides an interface to the data for the application. Further, it supports the caching of frequently used data, and enables the structure of the database (or other data store such as Active Directory – see Chapter 10 for details) to be designed for optimum read/write functionality. This can be crucial in situations where efficiency and performance are paramount.

So what does this all mean? Well, it means that all the data in your current membership directory must be migrated to the new User Profile System. You must also decide whether to store the attributes in an Active Directory or in a SQL database (or in both for a distributed system). You should also decide whether or not it is beneficial for you to migrate your membership directory, considering the amount of work that it entails.

> *If you do not plan on using the new functionality in Commerce Server 2000, then it would not be advisable for you to migrate your users.*

The rest of the chapter will look specifically at the migration of your membership directory: how to map attributes from the Membership Directory to the User Profile System and how to customize the import process to meet your needs.

Data Storage/Structure

Between Site Server 3.0 and Commerce Server 2000, data storage for the membership base has changed drastically with the introduction of a different data storage format. In SS3.0, the two default formats for the membership directory were MS Access and MS SQL Server. You could use other types of database as membership directories – but not without a lot of programming time and effort – and against the recommendation from Microsoft not to use other types of data store. Commerce Server 2000 includes the ability to link to other data storage types out of the box – this offers you the freedom to design a datastore that meets your need for the information stored in it, for example, one which is optimized for read/write when member properties need to be frequently accessed and changed, but optimized for read when member properties only need to be frequently read.

Site Server 3.0 Data Structure

In Site Server 3.0, the membership directory format is pre-defined for the user, and closely resembles that of a directory. The low-level table structure is difficult for the average developer to comprehend, let alone modify, or update. There has been precious little documentation on the structure of the membership directory database and poor information in error messages, so if something went wrong in the membership directory, and the MMC (Microsoft Management Console) or WebAdmin (Web Based Administrative Tool of Site Server 3.0) couldn't fix the problem, a developer would generally find it very difficult to make sense of the issue on the basis of the raw data in the database. Even the simple backup and restore operation could prove to be quite challenging and frustrating for both the developer and the system administrator.

If the developer or system administrator is trying to remove an attribute from the membership schema, in order to successfully remove it, the attribute must firstly be removed from all class-level objects. If you don't do this then you will be forced to query the raw database in order to determine which class objects still contain the attribute. This query is not straightforward, as you'll see, from the example below. SAPNumber is the example attribute's common name.

```
SELECT vc_Val
FROM object_attributes
WHERE i_aid = 502 AND
   i_Dsid in ( SELECT i_Dsid
      FROM   object_attributes
      WHERE i_Aid in (SELECT i_aid
         FROM attributes
         WHERE vc_Name = 'SAPNumber'))

SELECT vc_Name
FROM classes
WHERE i_Clsid in ( SELECT  i_Container_Clsid
   FROM attribute_containers
   WHERE i_Aid in
      (SELECT i_aid
      FROM attributes
      WHERE vc_Name = 'SAPNumber'))
```

Although any data manipulation in the raw data format is strongly discouraged, sometimes querying the raw data is much more efficient than leafing through the different levels of the membership directory in the MMC.

So, the membership directory in Site Server 3.0 is cumbersome. Each object, each attribute of each object, and so on, represents an entry in one table of the database. Understanding the relationship between objects and their attributes is really a matter of understanding the relationship between the tables. However, even the naming conventions used with the tables and their fields are far from intuitive.

For example, configuration information regarding the LDAP service configuration is stored in a table called DsConfiguration – this includes the name of the server and the membership server instance. However, membership database configuration information is stored in DsoGrid – this includes the name of the database, the SQL Server name, the username and password.

The organization name is again stored in another table called `SubRefs`, while the list of attributes is store in the `Attributes` table. The relationship between the attributes and the classes is stored in the `Attribute_Containers` table (with a flag indicating whether or not the attribute is required). The objects themselves (members, groups, etc.) are stored in the `Object_Lookup` table with a reference to the type of object (member, group, tagterm, etc.) Each attribute for each object is stored in the `Object_Attributes` as separate recordsets.

You've probably got the message by now – the overall database structure makes it very hard to usefully peruse the information, or perform any kind of quick query. Fortunately, Commerce Server 2000 will not give you nearly so many headaches.

Commerce Server 2000 Data Structure

As Commerce Server 2000 leaves the data store format entirely up to the developer, it necessarily opens up the data structure to the user. It is very easy for the developer to peruse the raw data in the database to find the user information, as it is all stored in the `UserObject` table. Each user is represented by one entry in the database and each field in the database contains the user's attributes. The attribute definitions are then stored in a few other tables but these are still arranged intuitively enough for the user to peruse and understand. Even the table names make sense!

Furthermore, any custom data store that the user wishes to include will naturally conform to whatever design and structure the user sees fit. Say they simply want to add one data store, containing one table with five fields that represent 'username' along with four properties (such as 'password reminder', 'hair color', 'default background color' and 'default homepage'). This would be perfectly acceptable, just as long as the user adds the data store and configures the User Profile System accordingly.

The CS2K Data Structure is also much easier to peruse and understand. For example, configuration information for the data store is located in the `SourceDef` table. As you'd expect, this table contains the name of the data store, its display name, the catalog name in which the attributes will be stored, and so on. The `SourceAttrib` table contains more information for the connection string. The table called `ColDef` stores details for custom attributes, such as the table definition, attribute name, display name of the attribute, description, etc. The members are listed in the `UserObject` table – attributes are organized as fields in this table, which makes it much easier to peruse. Of course, the attributes listed are those associated with the `UserObject` in the Profile Definition.

Coding Modification

Unfortunately, migrating data is not the only task involved in migrating a membership directory; some code modification will be necessary as well. This will be the most time consuming portion of the membership directory migration, since every call to the membership directory for membership data will have to be modified. In this section, we will discuss removal of the Active User Object (AUO) and the incorporation of the User Profile System into the commerce store application.

There are a few coding modifications that you will have to perform on your ASP application in order to start utilizing the User Profile System. Microsoft no longer supports the Active User Object (AUO), so any `Server.CreateObject` calls to the AUO must be modified in order to work under the Commerce Server 2000 platform.

As a first step, Microsoft recommends extracting all AUO `Server.CreateObject` calls from the individual web pages and centralizing them in a single include file. Therefore, even if you don't plan to start your e-commerce site on CS2K (or you're still in the early planning phase of the migration process), it would be wise for you to perform this centralization, in preparation, so that you will have only one location to modify your AUO call. Microsoft also recommends that User Profile System instantiation be performed from within `global.asa`, so that it is available whenever required.

Consequently, the Site Server 3.0 AUO `Server.CreateObject` call format in the include file:

```
Dim objAUO
Set objAUO = Server.CreateObject("Membership.UserObjects.1")

If Err.Number<>0 Then
   Response.Write "Unable to create AUO."
   Response.End
End If
```

should be replaced with the following User Profile System instantiation:

```
Dim mscsProfileService
Dim oUser
Dim dictConfig
Dim strUserID
Dim objAuthManager
Set objAuthManager = Server.CreateObject("Commerce.AuthManager")
objAuthManager.Initialize(Application("MSCSCommerceSiteName"))

If( Err.number <> 0 ) Then
   Response.Write "AuthManager Failed to initialize"
End If

strUserID = objAuthManager.GetUserID(1)
Set dictConfig = Application("MSCSAppConfig").GetOptionsDictionary("")
Set mscsProfileService = server.CreateObject("Commerce.ProfileService")

Call mscsProfileService.Initialize_
              (dictConfig.s_ProfileServiceConnectionString,_
              "Profile Definitions")

Set oUser = mscsProfileService.GetProfilebyKey_
              ("User_ID", strUserID, "UserObject")

If Err.Number <> 0 Then
   Response.Write "Failed to set User Object"
End If
```

The retrieval of the member's attribute is slightly different on both platforms. For example, to retrieve the member's full name and display it on the welcome screen, the AUO call would look like this:

```
Dim strFullNameAUO
StrFullNameAUO = ObjAUO.firstname & " " & objAUO.lastname
```

However, in the case of the User Profile System, the code would have to include not only the attribute name but also the profile definition class. Therefore, to obtain the member's full name, the following code would have to be executed:

```
Dim strFullNameUPS
StrFullNameUPS = oUser.GeneralInfo.First_Name & " " & _
                oUser.GeneralInfo.Last_Name
```

This code represents one of many ways to obtain the user's profile from the User Profile System. The Solution Sites have been configured so that any given page is implemented by means of include files, making it particularly easy to implement a new page by reusing code from existing pages. If you stick with this structure, you can achieve exactly the same result with the following code:

```
<!--#include file="include/std_profile_lib.asp"-->
<!--#include file="include/std_access_lib.asp"-->
<!--#include file="include/setupenv.asp"-->
<!--#include file="include/std_cookie_lib.asp"-->
<!--#include file="include/std_url_lib.asp"-->

Sub Main()
    dim rsUser
    dim strUserName2
    set rsUser = GetCurrentUserProfile()
    If Err.Number <> 0 Then
        Response.Write "Failed to set Current User Profile"
    End If
    strUserName2 = rsUser.GeneralInfo.First_name & " " & _
        rsUser.GeneralInfo.last_name
    If Err.Number <> 0 Then
        Response.Write "Failed to set Username "
    End If
    Response.Write "<h2>" & strUsername2 & " Welcome to the Wrox " & _
                        "Conference"Store </h2>"
End Sub
```

Also note that all interfaces that the AUO object utilizes are also not supported. This means that if you are using AUO in your code, you will have to modify it to use the User Profile Object instead. This could have serious ramifications if you use AUO frequently in your code and you've not extracted the calls to an include file, as suggested earlier. The only interface that will remain is the iADS interface, but this will be used with a different base object, the User Profile Object, and may also require recoding.

Quick Reference Guide to the Migration Tools

In order to migrate the membership directory, you must follow several steps:

❑   the generation of attribute mapping between the two platforms

❑   Membership Directory Group migration to the Active Directory Groups, optional step

❑   finally migration of the actual data

The only optional step is that of the group migration, and then only if your Site Server 3.0 Membership Directory does **not** utilize groups, or if you do not wish to migrate your group structure to the Active Directory.

We'll now take a look at some of the tools that are provided to help simplify these tasks.

Profile Builder Tool

This tool maps Site Server 3.0 membership attributes to the attributes found in the User Profile System in Commerce Server 2000. The tool performs three essential tasks:

❏ Reads the user attributes from the Site Server 3.0 Membership Directory

❏ Reads the user attributes from Commerce Server 2000

❏ Generates an XML Configuration File for the migration objects

This tool requires that the user provide a username that has administrative rights on the domain so that all of the domain in the Active Directory Forest can be read. If you are not using Active Directory as a data source in your User Profile Configuration, this administrative username is not required.

Before running the Profile Builder Tool, you will have to create, either via the Business Desk or the Commerce Server MMC, any custom attributes that are not included in the default User Profile System profile definition. For example, the default User Profile System profile does not include an attribute for 'password reminder' and therefore, if you are using that attribute in your e-commerce site, you will have to create a similar attribute in the User Profile System before running this tool.

The default User Profile System has five extra attributes that can be used for your custom attributes. If you require more than five additional attributes, you will have to create custom attributes, either by modifying the default SQL Server Database or adding another data store to the User Profile System profile for your attributes.

> *If you have installed the Beta release of Commerce Server 2000 and have tried to run the executable version of this tool, you probably encountered some errors. These errors have been fixed in the final release of Commerce Server 2000.*

Running the Profile Builder Tool

To run the Profile Builder tool, select **Programs | Microsoft Commerce Server 2000 | Software Development Kit** from the **Start Menu**. In the **Tools** folder, navigate to **Membership Migration | ProfileBuilder** and double-click on `ProfileBuilder.exe`. On starting, the following screen will appear:

> *If the SDK did not install properly with Commerce Server 2000, you will be able to find the* `ProfileBuilder` *file on your system in the following location: C:/Program Files/Microsoft Commerce Server/SDK/Tools/MembershipMigration/ProfileBuilder.*

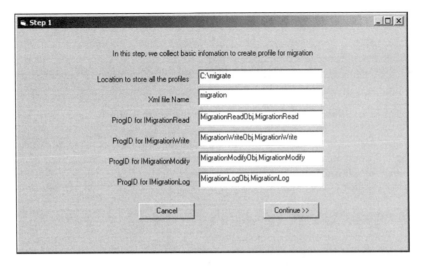

This first screen gathers information relating to the destination of the generated XML Configuration File, the filename of the Configuration File and the program ID of the migration objects that will be used during the membership data migration. The values offered are default for the migration process, and only need to be changed if you intend to change the migration object. In this case it would be wise to change the name of the migration object so that the original objects are left intact. The profile ID, added in Step 3, will also be appended to the filename. The next screen will then be accessed.

This screen requires the configuration information for both the Site Server 3.0 Membership Directory and the Commerce Server 2000 User Profile System information. The Membership Directory information required includes: the server name of the server where the membership directory resides, the LDAP port, and the administrative username and password.

Note that the username must be entered using the full ADSI path.

As for the Commerce Server 2000 information, you will need to have the following ready:

- ❏ The server name of the Commerce Server 2000
- ❏ The Commerce Server site database where the User Profile System resides
- ❏ The administrative username and password of the database
- ❏ Whether or not the commerce site is an Active Directory site

If you do not wish to use Active Directory to store membership information, then you must answer No to the Is this an AD site? question and you are not required to enter the administrative username and password. Before continuing onto the next step, you will be required to create a DSN name of BizDataStore, which points to the User Profile System datastore.

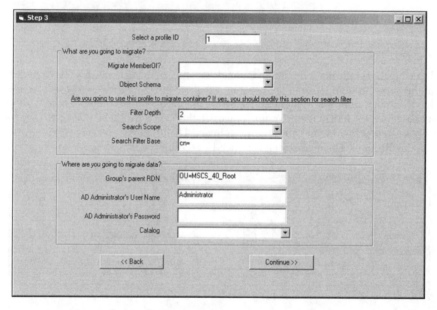

The first item on the page is the profile ID. This profile ID should be a numeric integer that has not previously been used. Please note that if there is an existing profile with the same ID you will be prompted to change the profile ID upon submission of the form.

The Migrate MemberOf question asks the user whether or not they wish to migrate the users to Active Directory Groups; this is the case where you already using groups in your Site Server 3.0 Membership Directory and you wish to migrate the groups and the member of the groups. If left blank, your Site Server 3.0 members will not be allocated to groups under the Commerce Server 2000 platform.

Then the object Schema is requested; in most cases the default 'member' will suffice. However, if you wish to migrate a custom class, you would need to enter the class as the Object Schema.

The filter concept is probably the most confusing part of the ProfileBuilder tool. However, it provides a way to limit the number of timeouts obtained when performing LDAP queries. It consists of three items: filter depth, filter scope and filter base. The filter depth indicates how many wildcard characters will be added to the filter base. For example, if you indicate a filter depth of 3 then the migration tools will add three wildcard characters at the end of the filter for the search criteria.

The filter scope indicates whether or not the search should indicate subcontainers; a Base Search will just do the container indicated, whereas a SubTree search will search all subtrees in that container.

The filter base is essentially that: a base for the search. In the case of migration of members, the filter base would be the usernames to migrate. For example, if you wish to migrate all of your `test` accounts, you would enter the filter base as `cn=test`. The wildcards from the filter depth would then be added to the filter base to construct the search as `cn=test**`.

The administrative account for the Active Directory must be provided if you are using the Active Directory to store membership information. Although you have answered the question in the previous form, you must enter the credential here to access the Active Directory. If you are not using Active Directory, you may bypass the username and password fields. Finally you must select the catalog to which the user attributes will be mapped. In the case of basic migration, the user profile catalog will be the catalog of choice.

The final step will look like this:

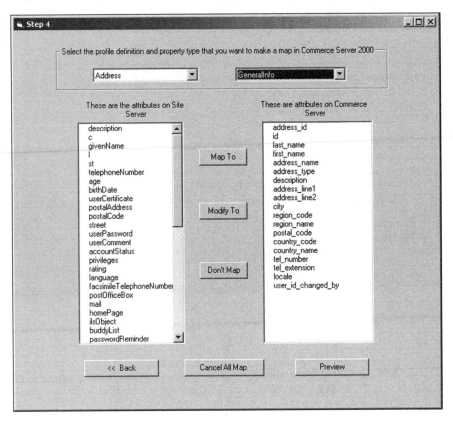

The attribute list in the bottom left hand window is the list of user attributes in the Site Server 3.0 Membership Directory. The bottom right-hand window will list the attributes of the profile definitions set by the top pair of drop-down list boxes. To map a user attribute, select the user attribute from the Site Server Membership Directory, select the user attribute from the Commerce Server user attribute, then click on the Map To button. The `ProfileBuilder` tool will then indicate by number the mapping between the attributes. Once all of the attributes are mapped, click on the Preview button. The preview screen will appear and you will be prompted to save the XML configuration file.

XML Configuration File

The XML Configuration File generated has two main sections, the configuration information and the member attribute mapping.

The first of these sections retains all the information that was entered during the Profile Building process. It looks like this:

```
<MIGRATION-PROFILE>
    <ProfileID>8</ProfileID>
</MIGRATION-PROFILE>

    <MigrationObjects>
        <ReadObj>MigrationReadObj.MigrationRead</ReadObj>
        <WriteObj>MigrationWriteObj.MigrationWrite</WriteObj>
        <ModifyObj>MigrationModifyObj.MigrationModify</ModifyObj>
        <LogObj>MigrationLogObj.MigrationLog</LogObj>
    </MigrationObjects>

    <MembershipDirectory>
        <MConnectionString>LDAP://laptop:1003</MConnectionString>
        <MigrateMemberOf>True</MigrateMemberOf>
       <MDUserName>cn=Administrator,ou=members,o=wroxconference</MDUserName>
        <MDPassword>password</MDPassword>
    </MembershipDirectory>

    <SearchFilterInfo>
        <FilterDepth>2</FilterDepth>
        <ADsSearchScope>0</ADsSearchScope>
        <SearchFilterBase>cn=*</SearchFilterBase>
    </SearchFilterInfo>

    <UserProfileService>
        <ADSite>FALSE</ADSite>
        <UConfigStore>Server=laptop;DataBase=Retail_commerce;_
                             UID=sa;PWD=</UConfigStore>
        <UCatalog>Profile Definitions</UCatalog>
        <GroupOUToDC>OU=MSCS_40_Root</GroupOUToDC>
        <CSUserName>Administrator</CSUserName>
        <CSPassword></CSPassword>
    </UserProfileService>
```

The second portion of the XML configuration file establishes the mapping of the attribute. It provides the name of the Site Server 3.0 attribute, the name of the attribute in the User Profile System, along with the profile definitions. This portion is wrapped around with `<mapping>` XML tags. The following is an example:

```
<Mapping>
    <FromMembership>cn</FromMembership>
    <ToUps>GeneralInfo.logon_name</ToUps>
    <WProfileType>UserObject</WProfileType>
    <WTypes>VT_BSTR</WTypes>

    <FromMembership>userPassword</FromMembership>
```

```
            <ToUps>GeneralInfo.user_security_password</ToUps>
            <WProfileType>UserObject</WProfileType>
            <WTypes>VT_BSTR</WTypes>

            <FromMembership>mail</FromMembership>
            <ToUps>GeneralInfo.email_address</ToUps>
            <WProfileType>UserObject</WProfileType>
            <WTypes>VT_BSTR</WTypes>

            <FromMembership>sn</FromMembership>
            <ToUps>GeneralInfo.last_name</ToUps>
            <WProfileType>UserObject</WProfileType>
            <WTypes>VT_BSTR</WTypes>
        </Mapping>
```

Group Pre-population Tool

Group Migration is an optional step, mandatory only if your current site uses groups in its installation and you wish to keep the current structure. Clearly, if you want to assign members to groups, those groups must already exist; therefore this step must be performed prior to migrating users.

You must also ensure that the Active Directory has been activated in your Profile data store, because the group structure is only supported if the Active Directory is used as part of the User Profile System. Other than Active Directory, the User Profile System does not have the architecture necessary to support groups without customization.

Also, the implementation of groups via Active Directory in Commerce Server 2000 is different (and perhaps not as compatible with certain sites) to the implementation in the Site Server 3.0 Membership Directory. Active Directory will limit the groups to 5000 objects – to maintain a group structure with over 5000 members subgroups must be created. The performance of Active Directory also degrades as the size of the database increases, which only serves to enhance the limitation mentioned above. Another difference to note is that the sitename_groupname security account for authentication is not generated when the group is created under the Active Directory platform as it is in Site Server 3.0. Also, your development environment will require its own domain, if you are using the Active Directory.

Microsoft is assuring users that the group size limitation will be rectified in later versions of Active Directory – for now though, a workaround is necessary. The groups are still created with this tool, but the Directory Migration Tool handles the creation of subgroups and the assignment of users to those subgroups.

In order to be able to run the Group Pre-population tool, the credentials must be provided with which the tool will be able to access the Site Server 3.0 Membership Directory via LDAP and the Commerce Server computer.

The group migration tool is located in Tools | MembershipMigration | GroupMigration under the SDK directory linked to from the Start menu. Once again, both the source code and the compiled executable for the tool are provided – simply double-click on GroupMigration.exe. The following screen will appear, containing the default values:

821

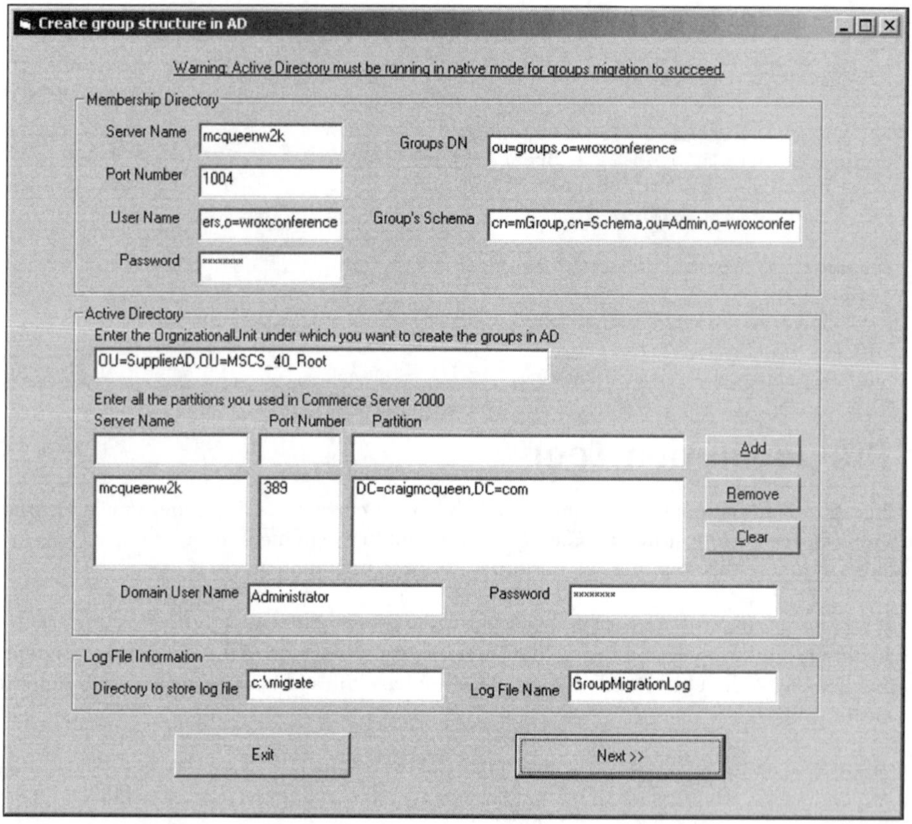

The top portion of the window gathers the Site Server 3.0 Membership Directory information – most of the fields are self-explanatory.

> A notable exception is the field **User name** – according to the CS2K Help file this must be entered in the form **domain\user**. However, the tool will not work unless the username is entered using the ADsPath format, like the **cn=administrator, ou=members, o=wroxConference** form shown above.

Also, do not forget to modify the Groups DN and the Group's Schema to reflect the correct organization.

The lower portion of the window is the configuration detail of the Active Directory. The important setting in this section is the Active Directory Partitions that will contain the groups. The partitions must be entered using the correct ADsPath DN, shown above.

The next screen provides the mapping configuration for the group attribute. The attributes from the Site Server Membership Directory will appear in the left column in the upper drop-down combo box. The default attribute values, description and mbsTokenID will appear in the drop-down combo box along with any additional attributes that have been added to the Group Class in the Membership Directory.

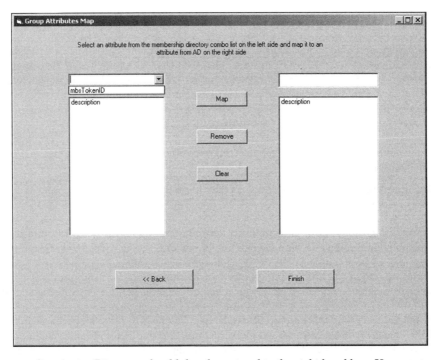

The corresponding Active Directory should then be entered in the right-hand box. You must ensure that the attribute exists in the Active Directory and that it is associated with the **Group Class** before running the Group Migration Tool. Then click on **Map** to register the mapping. Once the mapping is completed, click on the **Next** button to proceed with the migration.

The following screen will now appear, detailing the progress of the migration. The process can be very lengthy if there are a lot of groups to migrate. Any errors and events are logged to the log file (that you specified on the first screen of the group migration tool).

Directory Migration Tool

The Directory Migration Tool is the final step in the migration of the membership directory, and utilizes the configuration that was set up in the previous steps. The `ProfileBuilder` created the mapping of the attributes between both platforms. The `GroupMigration` Tool migrated the groups from Site Server 3.0 to the Active Directory. This tool will migrate your members and their attributes. It will use the XML Configuration file to migrate the users and the groups created by the GroupMigration Tool to migrate the `memberof` attribute. This tool can be run in two modes:

❑ **Batch mode** – this performs sequential migration based on the filter criteria in the XML Configuration file.

❑ **Real-time mode** – this migrates users as they log into the e-commerce application, that is, on an as-needed basis.

The tool can be run in either one of these modes, or even both simultaneously – this would allow for all the users to be migrated in batch mode, with the real-time mode only taking effect if a user attempted to log in *before* their profile had been migrated. For the first phase of the migration, it would be recommended that you perform a batch migration and then as you get ready to put the migrated site into production, you could run both in batch and real-time mode to migrate your membership base without jeopardizing your data integrity.

The Directory Migration Tool is composed of six objects, five of which play an active role in the migration; the sixth is the `Utility` object, which holds global settings. A client tool is also provided to perform migration in batch mode. A detailed description of the relationship between the objects will be given in the next section, along with details on the registration of the component.

The Migration tool adds an attribute called `Migration` to the `members` class in the Site Server 3.0 Membership Directory and therefore, to each member being migrated. If there are no errors in the migration, this attribute will be set to `True` for the member; however if a problem occurred during migration the attribute will be set to `False`. If no migration attribute exists, the migration components will assume that no migration has yet been attempted. This migration attribute is valuable when testing the success of your migration. The goal should be that all members in your membership directory have a migration attribute with a value of `True`.

SubGroup Manager

The SubGroup Manager is a tool that is utilized to determine where a user is stored in the Active Directory in order to determine the group membership. The tool does have an executable program that takes as input the user's DN and the parent group. The tool will create the subgroup to the parent group and assign 4500 objects to the group to allow for growth. The subgroup name will take on the parent name along with an underscore and a numeric index (that is, `ParentName_0001`). There are four methods in the SubGroup Manager:

❑ SubGroupMembership – retrieves the DN of the subgroup into which the user profile is placed

❑ AddUserToMasterGroup – writes the user profile to subgroup

❑ RemoveUserFromMasterGroup – removes the user profile from subgroup

❑ IsUserOfMasterGroup – tests the subgroup for whether or not the user profile is a member

However, the tool does have a hard-coded user name and password that it uses to connect to Active Directory. For example, the code sample below is taken from the `SubGroupManager` Class Module of the VB Project and you can see that the administrative account and password has been hardcoded into the program.

```
'This Function binds to the specified group
Private Function GetDirectoryGroupFast(GroupDN As String) As IADs
Dim openDS As IADsOpenDSObject
Dim Admin As String
Dim DomainName As String

DomainName = GetDomainNameFromDN(GroupDN)
Admin = DomainName & "\" & "Administrator"

Set openDS = GetObject("LDAP:")
Set GetDirectoryGroupFast = openDS.OpenDSObject("LDAP://" & DomainName & _
                    "/" & GroupDN, Admin, "password", _
                    ADS_SECURE_AUTHENTICATION Or ADS_FAST_BIND)

End Function
```

There are three functions that have the hardcoded administrative account and password: `GetDirectoryContainer`, `GetDirectoryGroup` and `GetDirectoryGroupFast`. You will have to change the username and password at all three locations to reflect an administrative username in the Profile System. Once you have changed the username, you will have to recompile the SubGroup Manager component and register again before utilizing.

Contrary to what the documentation indicates, this tool is not used in the migration of your members. Instead, the subgroup management is handled within the `MigrationWriteObj`. This tool almost appears to be a bonus and will allow you to check the Active Directory Subgroup that the member has been assigned to and also if you wish to add members to the group, you will be able to use this tool.

Batch Mode

The Directory Migration Tool also comes with a client tool that can be used to migrate the users in batch mode. The batch mode client tool utilizes the XML Configuration file to migrate the users. The client tool and the source code are all available as part of the Commerce Server 2000 SDK. The filter base, filter scope and filter depth are only used in the batch mode when you are migrating a container of information. See the later section on Real-Time Mode for more information as to how this is used.

To run the client tool for the batch mode migration simply open a command prompt window and navigate to the location of the client tool: `C:>\Program Files\Microsoft Commerce Server\SDK\Tools\MembershipMigration\bin\Release`. To invoke the client tool you must provide the following parameters:

- ❏ **S1** – the location of the XML Configuration profile
- ❏ **S2** – ADsPath of the user to be migrated
- ❏ **N3** – the XML Configuration profile number

The command line should look something like this if you are migrating a single user :

```
Client.exe c:\migrate ldap://mcqueenw2k:1004/cn=jdoe,_
                              ou=members,o=wroxconference 2
```

or as follows for a container.

```
Client.exe c:\migrate ldap://mcqueenw2k:1004/ou=members,o=wroxconference 2
```

There will be two log files created, one for the initialization of the objects, `migrationInitLog` and one for the migration process, `migrationLog`. Both can be found in the main root directory of the Operating System Disk. If any errors have occurred during the migration process, the details will be logged in these files.

Real-Time Mode

For clarity, the code displayed in this section is a series of extracts from a larger body contained in `login.asp` *and the include files it references.*

Microsoft has provided an ASP page to help in the setup of the real-time migration mode. This is located in **Tools | MembershipMigration | Client** (under the SDK directory) and is accessed through `login.asp`. The following excerpts of code are necessary for the migration.

The first step is to initialize the migration object, `MigrationMainObj`, which occurs in the include file `global_main_lib.asp`, referenced by `global.asa`:

```
Function InitMigration()
   Dim mscsMigration

   Set mscsMigration = _
           Server.CreateObject("MigrationMainObj.MigrationProfile")
   Call mscsMigration.Initialize ("c:\migrate\xml")

   Set InitMigration = mscsMigration
End Function
```

Once the object is initialized, the user's common name is passed to the object for migration:

```
Dim strLDAPDN
Dim strLoginName

strLDAPDN = "LDAP://Laptop:1003/cn=" & strLoginName & _
"/ou=members/o=wroxconference"
call MSCSMigration.MigrateObject(LDAPDN,2)
if Err.Number <> 0 Then
   Response.Write "An error has occurred during the migration of the" & _ "user
profile.<BR>"
   Response.Write Err.Number & ": " & Err.Description
   Err.Clear
   Response.End
End If
```

Please note that this component will load the **first** XML file that it encounters, assuming it to be the XML configuration file. Therefore, in order for the component to work properly, ensure that the only XML file in the directory specified in the `InitMigration` Function is the XML Configuration File.

The user may be well advised to consider additional code around the migration call for two reasons:

❏   To check if the migration has already occurred.

❏   To ensure that the user is an authenticated user.

This is achieved by surrounding the code with the following logic (in Login.asp).

```
Set mscsLoginUser = GetUserProfileByLoginName(dictFldVals.Value(LOGON_NAME))
If mscsLoginUser Is Nothing Then

    'migration
    Dim LDAPDN
    On Error Resume Next
    err.clear
strLDAPDN = "LDAP://Laptop:1003/cn=" & strLoginName & _
                 "/ou=members/o=wroxconference"
Call MSCSMigration.MigrateObject(LDAPDN,2)
    If Err.Number = 0 Then
    Set mscsLoginUser = _ SetUserProfileByLoginName(dictFldVals.Value(LOGON_NAME))
    End If
    If mscsLoginuser is Nothing Then
    Err.Clear
    Set dictFldErrs = GetDictionary()
       dictFldErrs.Value(LOGON_NAME) = _
mscsMessageManager.GetMessage("L_Invalid_Login_UserName_ErrorMessage", _sLanguage)
    iErrorLevel = 1
    End If
End If


If iErrorLevel = 0 Then
    If StrComp(dictFldVals.Value(LOGON_PASSWORD), _
               mscsLoginUser.Fields(GetQualifiedName(GENERAL_INFO_GROUP, _
               LOGON_PASSWORD)).Value, vbBinaryCompare) <> 0 Then
        Set dictFldErrs = GetDictionary()
        dictFldErrs.Value(LOGON_PASSWORD) = _
               mscsMessageManager.GetMessage_
               ("L_Invalid_Login_Password_ErrorMessage", _ sLanguage)
        iErrorLevel = 1
    End If
End If
```

The first portion of the code verifies attempts to log the user into the membership base in the User Profile System base. If GetUserProfileByLoginName() fails to return the user as an object, then the migration will be attempted. If the user object is created then the user has already been migrated, and no further action is necessary. If no error is returned from the migration, then the creation of the user object will be attempted again. This time, if no object is created then the user did not provide the right credentials – either an incorrect login name (which would fail to migrate users) or the wrong password (therefore failing the authentication). If no error is encountered and the user object is successfully created, then the user profile is loaded into memory. Otherwise, an error is raised to the user.

Modifying the Migration Tools

Profile Builder Tool

The Profile Builder Tool is a VB6.0 application, with source code made available for modification and recompilation. Although the tool is well designed, the chance of repeated use is high; so a little customization would quite probably be quite beneficial. Modifying the default text in all textboxes to reflect your own environment (for example, changing the default **servername** entry to the actual server name) would save you a great deal of time. Once these modifications are made (along with any others desired), the user can then recompile the application.

Note that the application must be recompiled using Visual Basic 6, with Service Pack 3 and above.

Group Pre-Population Tool

The Group Pre-Population tool is also a VB6.0 application, once again with the source code available for modification and recompilation. As with the Profile Builder Tool, this migration tool also has a high probability of repeated use. Therefore, the same customization as the Profile Builder Tool would be beneficial for this tool, as well. The other modification I'd suggest is to enable a drop-down box listing of the attributes for the group class in the Active Directory. This eliminates the need to type in the attribute, and minimizes the risk of typing errors. Additionally the user is provided with a listing of the attributes available for mapping.

Once these, and any further modifications, are done the user can then recompile the application.

Again, compilation must take place using Visual Basic 6 with Service Pack 3 or higher.

Directory Migration Tool

The Directory Migration Tool is the most complex of the membership migration tools, as it has the task of taking all the data from the old Site Server 3.0 Membership Directory, modifying it as required, and then inserting it into the User Profile System. In order to perform these tasks effectively, the tool makes use of five objects:

- ❑ MigrationMainObj
- ❑ MigrationReadObj
- ❑ MigrationWriteObj
- ❑ MigrationModifyObj
- ❑ MigrationLogObj.

An additional object, MigrationUtil, is used during the recompilation process.

Once again, the tool can either be run in batch mode, in real-time mode, or in both modes at once, so that if a user whose profile hasn't been migrated tries to log in, their profile will be transferred there and then. This ensures that all members use the same directory/user profile system at all times.

The migration tools are intertwined with the `MigrationMainObj` as the primary object in the process. The following figure illustrates this point.

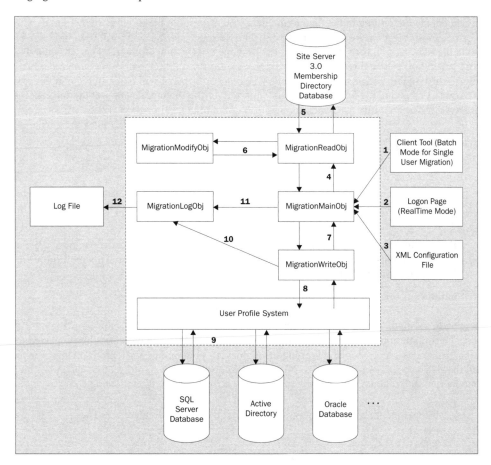

`MigrationMainObj` takes requests for migration either from the `client.exe` tool (marked 1 on the previous figure) or the ASP page (2), as explained previously. It calls the migration XML Configuration File generated by the Profile Builder tool (3), then passes the Site Server 3.0 Membership Directory Connection String to the `MigrationReadObj` along with a list of the attributes to be migrated and any modifications that are required (4). If no migration attribute is set for the member, `MigrationReadObj` will add the migration attribute and set it to `True` so that no other instances of the Directory Migration tool will attempt to migrate the user. The `MigrationReadObj` will then retrieve the user profile from the Membership Directory (5).

If the XML Configuration File has marked the attribute for modification, the attribute value will be passed to the `MigrationModifyObj` along with the modification required (6). This object will perform the modification and return the modified value to the read object. Once the modification has been performed, the member's profile is returned to the `MigrationReadObj` (6). The `MigrationReadObj` will then pass to the `MigrationMainObj` (4) a pointer to the profile buffer. If an error has occurred during the retrieval or modification of the profile, the `MigrationReadObj` will return a failure, the `MigrationMainObj` will log the failure through the `MigrationLogObj` (11) and call the `MigrationReadObj` to set the migration attribute to `False` (4).

If no errors occurred, the profile buffer is then sent to the MigrationWriteObj along with the connection string to the User Profile System and the corresponding mapping for the attributes (7). The MigrationWriteObj will then send the request to the User Profile System object (8). The User Profile System will handle the writing of the data to the data store (9). Again the MigrationWriteObj will return a failure or success to the MigrationMainObj (7). The MigrationMainObj will then write the errors to the log file via the migrationlogobj (11), then the process repeats until all members are migrated. The MigrationWriteObj can directly call the MigrationLogObj if the error is encountered while returning the status to the MigrationMainObj (10). The MigrationLogObj will enter all log entries into the MigrationInitLog log file for any errors encountered during the initialization of the migration process and MigrationLog for any errors encountered during the migration process (12).

MigrationMainObj

The MigrationMainObj object has three methods:

❑   **Initialize** – this initializes all of the components for the migration process; the input to this method is the ProfileDirectory that holds the XML Configuration File. This method will parse the file and supply the other components.

❑   **MigrateObject** – this is called either from an ASP page (like login.asp), or a VB project, to migrate a member based on a particular ADsPath; the two inputs to this method are the ADsPath and the migration profile ID.

❑   **Shutdown** – this releases all the resources that have been initialized.

The Initialize method calls the ParseProfile method, which then calls the LoadFromXML method, that loads the configuration information from the configuration XML file based on the ID passed to the object. The parsing is simply done by looping through every node in the XML file. The initialize function will then call the MigrateObject method to migrate the information. This information can either be a member or a container; to differentiate between the two MigrateObjects use the following code:

```
If ( getCNFromDN(bstrKeyName, pwszCN, NULL))
{
    // doesn't make sense checking errors here
    hr = MigrateUser(bstrKeyName, lprofile_id, bufIndex,_
                    dwSafeArrayIndex, TRUE);

}
Else
    {
    hr = MigrateContainer(bstrKeyName, lprofile_id, bufIndex,_
                        dwSafeArrayIndex);

}
```

The getCNFromDN method (from the MigrateUtil object) strips off the common name from the distinguished name submitted to the MigrateObject. If this method fails – for example if you entered a container (ou) not a common name (cn) – then the MigrateObject assumes that you are in batch mode and calls the method to migrate the container, and not the user.

In batch mode, the MigrateContainer method is called. It will perform the search based on the filter information you entered in the XML Configuration File and will call MigrateUser for each individual member that meets the filter criteria. This is done by first constructing the search filter using the GetNextFilter method, and then using the iDirectorySearch ADSI interface to perform the search, as follows:

```
                tStatus = GetNextFilter(&m_pProfileBuffers[bufIndex]._
                        pwszFilters[dwSafeArrayIndex], bufIndex);
        While (tStatus == tSUCCEEDED)
        {
        COMCALL(pIDirSearch->ExecuteSearch(m_pProfileBuffers[bufIndex]._
                pwszFilters[dwSafeArrayIndex], pszAttr, dwCount, &hSearch ));

        COMCALL(pIDirSearch->GetFirstRow(hSearch));
        While(  hr  != S_ADS_NOMORE_ROWS )
            {
            COMCALL(pIDirSearch->GetColumn(hSearch, pszAttr[0], &cl ));
            // we don't log info based on container but user.
            // so we don't care about the return result here.
            // when we try to migrate a container, all the users
            // in the container must use the same xml file as profile.
            MigrateUser(cl.pADsValues->CaseIgnoreString, lprofile_id,_
                               bufIndex, dwSafeArrayIndex, FALSE);
            COMCALL(pIDirSearch->FreeColumn (&cl));
            COMCALL(pIDirSearch->GetNextRow(hSearch));
            }
        COMCALL(pIDirSearch->CloseSearchHandle(hSearch));
        tStatus = GetNextFilter(&m_pProfileBuffers[bufIndex]._
                pwszFilters[dwSafeArrayIndex], bufIndex);
        }
```

If you are migrating a member, the `migrateUser` method is called. This method is the central nervous system for the migration, meaning that it is the main method for all calls to all other objects, to read and write the membership information. The first call it performs is to the read object to retrieve the member's attributes based on the profile information that it retrieved from the XML file:

```
// Read the values to be migrated from MD
hr = m_spIMigrationRead->ReadAttributes(bstrKeyName, lprofile_id,_
        &m_pProfileBuffers[bufIndex].rgAttVal[dwSafeArrayIndex].parray,_
        &m_pProfileBuffers[bufIndex].varValueIndex[dwSafeArrayIndex],_
        &m_pProfileBuffers[bufIndex].vMemberOfs[dwSafeArrayIndex]);
// 0x80072030 is the error code that the user does not exist in MD
if (FAILED(hr) && E_ADS_OBJECT_EXISTS != hr && 0x80072030 != hr)
{
// backoff
if (m_dwInitalPeriodToWait)
    {
    dwTries = 0;
    while(dwTries < m_dwRepeatTimes)
        {
        Sleep(m_dwInitalPeriodToWait * (dwTries+1));
        hr = m_spIMigrationRead->ReadAttributes(bstrKeyName,_
                                    lprofile_id,_
            &m_pProfileBuffers[bufIndex].rgAttVal[dwSafeArrayIndex].parray,_
            &m_pProfileBuffers[bufIndex].varValueIndex[dwSafeArrayIndex],_
            &m_pProfileBuffers[bufIndex].vMemberOfs[dwSafeArrayIndex]);
        if (SUCCEEDED(hr))
            break;
            dwTries++;
        }
    }
}
```

As you can see, it will attempt to connect several times before finally admitting defeat. The default value of m_dwRepeatTimes is set to the default value DEFAULT_BACKOFF_TIMES, which can be found in the MigUtil.h file. Out of the box, this value is set to 0, and should be modified to fit your situation.

If successful, the MigrateUser method will then pass the buffer with the member's attributes to the MigrationWriteObject.

```
hr = m_spIMigrationWrite->WriteUserAttributes(bstrKeyName, lprofile_id,_
        &m_pProfileBuffers[bufIndex].rgAttVal[dwSafeArrayIndex].parray,_
        &m_pProfileBuffers[bufIndex].varValueIndex[dwSafeArrayIndex],_
        &m_pProfileBuffers[bufIndex].vMemberOfs[dwSafeArrayIndex]);
If (FAILED(hr))
{
    LogInfoToFile(typeWRITE, hr, bstrKeyName, lprofile_id);
    If ( 0x80071392 != hr && -1056948213 != hr )
    {
        dwTries = 0;
        do
        {
            Sleep(m_dwInitalPeriodToWait * dwTries);
            hres = m_spIMigrationRead->MigrationFailed(bstrKeyName);
            If (SUCCEEDED(hres))
                break;
                dwTries++;
        } While (m_dwInitalPeriodToWait && FAILED(hres) &&_
            dwTries < m_dwRepeatTimes);
            If (FAILED(hres))
            {
                fMigrationFailed = TRUE;
            }
    }
}
Else If (m_dwLogLevel & SUCCESSPLUS )
{
    m_spIMigrationLog->LogSuccess(bstrKeyName, lprofile_id);
}
```

You can see from this code snippet that the MigrationMainObject will log the information to the file via the LogInfoToFile method to register the corresponding error and also call the MigrationReadObject to set the Migration attribute to False. If the migration is successful it will log the success directly with the MigrationLogObject.

MigrationReadObj

The MigrationReadObj object has four methods:

❑ **Initialize** – this takes an array of attributes for input along with the connection string to use.

❑ **ReadAttributes** – this is called for each migration and uses the ProfileID to determine which attribute to retrieve and store in the array.

❑ **MigrationFailed** – this is used to set the migration attribute to false if the migration failed; the required input is the ProfileID.

❑ **Shutdown** – this is called to free the connection pools.

The important method in this object is `ReadAttributes`, it performs the retrieval of the member's attribute from the Site Server 3.0 Membership Directory. The first step, however, is to check if the member has been migrated previously.

```
hr = ADsOpenObject(bstrKeyName, m_pwszUser, m_pwszPassword,_
        m_nFirstChoiceOfAuthentication, IID_IDirectoryObject,_
        (void**)(&pIDirObject));
// this number is obtained by passed a new user to the above function.
If ( 0x80072030 == hr ) // -2147016656)
{
    WCHAR wszBuf[MAX_STRING_BUF_SIZE];
    LoadString(_Module.GetResourceInstance(), IDS_NEWUSER, wszBuf,_
                                            MAX_STRING_BUF_SIZE);
    Error(wszBuf, IID_IMigrationRead);
    goto Error;
}
Else If (FAILED(hr))
{
    // try secure authentication
    COMCALL(ADsOpenObject(bstrKeyName, m_pwszUser, m_pwszPassword,_
                                m_nSecondChoiceOfAuthentication,_
                    IID_IDirectoryObject, (void**)(&pIDirObject)));
}
// check to see if this object has been migrated
COMCALL(pIDirObject->GetObjectAttributes(pM, 1, &pMigC, &dwMig));
If (dwMig && (4 == pMigC->pADsValues->OctetString.dwLength))
// wcslen(L"TRUE") == 4
{
    // check to see if this object has been migrated
    hr = E_ADS_OBJECT_EXISTS;
    WCHAR wszBuf[MAX_STRING_BUF_SIZE];
    LoadString(_Module.GetResourceInstance(), IDS_OBJMIGRATED, wszBuf,_
                                            MAX_STRING_BUF_SIZE);
    Error(wszBuf, IID_IMigrationRead);
    goto Error;
}
Else If ( (0 == dwMig) || (5 == pMigC->pADsValues->OctetString.dwLength) )
    // wcslen(L"FALSE")==5
{
    // set migration attributes   lock MD???
    COMCALL(pIDirObject->SetObjectAttributes(pMigInfo, 1, &dwMig));
}
```

This portion of the code checks to see if the member has a `Migration` attribute and whether or not it is set to `True`, or `1`. If not, then it proceeds to set the `Migration` attribute to `1`, ensuring that the member will not be migrated by another instance of the object.

The next step is to retrieve the attributes for that member. The code must loop through all the attributes that were mapped in the XML Configuration file and fetch the attributes individually for the member being migrated. This is done in the following code snippet:

```
If ( nAttributesToFetch)
{
// variable pAttrNames is ugly. But we need this in GetObjectAttributes()
    pAttrNames = new LPWSTR[nAttributesToFetch];
    VALIDPOINTER(pAttrNames);
```

```
   For ( i = 0; i < nAttributesToFetch; i++)
   {
      pAttrNames[i] = m_prprfProfiles[dwIdIndex].prgAttributes[i +_
                                        nAttributesMigrated];
   }
   COMCALL(pIDirObject->GetObjectAttributes(pAttrNames,_
                     nAttributesToFetch, &pAttrInfo, &dwReturn ));
}
Else
{
   pAttrNames = new LPWSTR[m_pdwNumAttributes[dwIdIndex]];
   VALIDPOINTER(pAttrNames);
   For ( i = 0; i < m_pdwNumAttributes[dwIdIndex]; i++)
   {
      pAttrNames[i] = m_prprfProfiles[dwIdIndex].prgAttributes[i];
   }
   COMCALL(pIDirObject->GetObjectAttributes(NULL, -1, &pAttrInfo,_
                                        &dwReturn ));
}
```

The rest of the method transfers the data into a buffer for the rest of the objects to use. As it is writing the attributes to the buffer, ReadAttributes also checks to see if the attribute has been marked for modification; if so, it passes the attribute and the ProfileID to MigrationModifyObj. This is done as follows:

```
// go to modify object even though no attibute valuse was feteched.
For ( i = 0; i < m_prprfProfiles[dwIdIndex].lNumModifies; i++)
{
   long j = m_prprfProfiles[dwIdIndex].rgnModIndex[i];
   If (bModAttHasValues[j] == FALSE)
   {
      // modify object need to alloc space for pvarAttrValues[i] when the
      //source type is VT_EMPTY
      COMCALL(m_pIMModify->ModifyAttributes(lProfile_id,_
         CComBSTR(m_prprfProfiles[dwIdIndex].prgAttributes[j]),_
         m_pvarAttributeTypes[dwIdIndex][j], VT_EMPTY,_
         &pvarAttrValues[j]));
   }
}
```

MigrationWriteObj

The MigrationWriteObj object has three methods:

❑ **Initialize** – the Initialize method takes the profile array for each profile ID to migrate, in a similar manner to MigrationReadObj.

❑ **WriteUserAttributes** – called for each profile to migrate. The method will transfer the data from the profile array to the User Profile System data store.

❑ **Shutdown** – the Shutdown method is called to free the connection pool.

It is not surprising here that the core of the object resides in the WriteUserAttributes method. This method uses the User Profile System to write the information to the data store. The tool will first verify whether or not the member exists in the User Profile System, and if not, create an account.

```
COMCALL(m_pIProfileServices[m_pprwProfiles[dwIdIndex].lProfileServiceID]_
    CreateProfile(CComVariant(pwszCN),_
    CComBSTR(g_pwszUserObject), &pIProfileObject));
```

Once you have created the account, you must activate the member.

```
// activate user account
If (m_pprwProfiles[dwIdIndex].bADSite )
{
    COMCALL(pFields->get_Item_
        (CComVariant(L"ProfileSystem.user_account_control"), &pField));
    COMCALL(pField->get_Value (&varAccountStatus));
    If (VT_NULL == V_VT(&varAccountStatus))
    {
        V_VT(&varAccountStatus) = VT_I4;
        V_I4(&varAccountStatus) = AD_USER_ACTIVE;
    }
    Else
    {
        V_I4(&varAccountStatus) |= AD_USER_ACTIVE;
    }
    COMCALL(pField->put_Value (varAccountStatus));
    pField = NULL;
}
// commit
hr = pIProfileObject->Update();
```

It is while trying to update that the method will check to see if the member already exists. If it does, the migration will fail, WriteUserAttributes will exit, and the error will be logged. If the migration is successful, the next step will be to migrate the MemberOf attribute of the member, if it is an Active Directory site, and if the MemberOf attribute was selected during the ProfileBuilder step.

It is during the MemberOf migration that the object will deal with the subgroup management. A call will be made to the AddMemberToGroup method which handles the subgroups and the membership.

```
// next add member to groups
If (VT_EMPTY != V_VT(vMemberOfs))
{
    If (m_dwLogLevel & PERFPLUS)
    {
        clkStart = clock();
    }
    dwTries = 0;
    do
    {
        Sleep(m_dwInitalPeriodToWait * dwTries);
        hr = AddMemberToGroups(vMemberOfs, vADsPath.bstrVal, dwIdIndex);
        dwTries ++;
    } While (FAILED(hr) && m_dwInitalPeriodToWait_
        && dwTries < m_dwRepeatTimes && 0x80072030 != hr);
        // record the time
        If (m_dwLogLevel & PERFPLUS)
        {
        clkEnd = clock();
        dbMemberOfTime = (double) (clkEnd - clkStart)/CLOCKS_PER_SEC;
        }
}
```

835

The detail of the subgroup management will be left for you to peruse at your leisure; the code is not complicated just very lengthy.

The addition of the attributes to the member's profile is done by simply looping through the attributes that are required to be migrated, and saving each attribute individually:

```
If ( NULL != varValueIndex->parray && varValueIndex->vt != VT_EMPTY)
{
    For ( i = 0; i < m_pprwProfiles[dwIdIndex].plPGcount[0]; i++)
    {
        int attIndex = m_pprwProfiles[dwIdIndex].plShuffledPGIndex[0][i];
        COMCALL(IsValidIndexInSafeArray(varValueIndex->parray,_
                                        attIndex, &fValidIndex));
        If ( FALSE == fValidIndex)
        {
            // this use has no value for this attribute
            continue;
        }
        COMCALL(pFields->get_Item (CComVariant(pwszAttrNames[attIndex]),_
                                                        &pField));
        ATLASSERT(V_VT(&pvarAttrValues[attIndex]) == VT_BSTR);
        If (attIndex == m_pprwProfiles[dwIdIndex].lSamAccountIndex &&
            m_pprwProfiles[dwIdIndex].bGenerateSAMAccount &&
                SysStringLen(pvarAttrValues[attIndex].bstrVal)
                >MAXSAMACCOUNT) //attindex != -1
        {
            CComBSTR pVal;
            // we will not try to generate sam account more than once
            // here as if the generated sam account is the same as some
            // existing user, then update will fail and when retry we
            // will generate a new one.
            COMCALL(get_SAMAccountName(&pVal));
            COMCALL(pField->put_Value (CComVariant(pVal)));
        }
        Else
        {
            // put values
            COMCALL(pField->put_Value (pvarAttrValues[attIndex]));
        }
    pField = NULL;
    }
}
```

MigrationModifyObj

The MigrationModifyObj has two methods:

❑ **Initialize** – this will initialize the modify object

❑ **ModifyAttributes** – this takes the profile key, profile ID and an array of values as input. It uses the profile ID to determine the modification to perform on the array structure

ModifyAttributes does not make many modifications, except to change the data type. The code it uses to modify the data type is shown:

```
If ( 0 == wcscmp(bstrAttribute, L"c") && targetType == VT_BSTR)
{
   CComVariant varMid;
   COMCALL(VariantChangeType(&varMid, varTarg, 0, VT_BSTR));
   COMCALL(VariantCopy(varTarg, &varMid));
}
```

Both the source and target data type are inputs to the method.

MigrationLogObj

This object has three methods:

- ❏ **Initialize** – this will initialize the object and should be called before calling the other object methods.

- ❏ **RecordInfo** – this method writes meaningful information to the log file. The input of this method is the text that will be logged to the log file.

- ❏ **LogSuccess** – this method logs the successful migration to the log file. The input is the profile key and the profile ID.

The `MigrationLogObj` methods are very straightforward and simply write to log files with either the successes or, the errors, of the calling functions.

MigUtil

The `MigUtil` object contains the global settings and methods, which includes the following:

- ❏ **Global variable g_pwszUserObject** – a default setting in Commerce Server corresponding to the UserObject profile. If you wish to change the profile for the migration, then this variable must reflect this change.

- ❏ **Global variable g_searchOrder** – holds all the possible symbols that could appear in the common name of the objects being migrated.

- ❏ **Global variable g_numSymbols** – contains the number of symbols you wish to store in the array of `g_searchOrder`.

This utility object becomes very important if you modify the current objects and then wish to recompile them, as all the other objects depend on this one for their global settings.

Recompiling the Objects

To recompile the objects, you will have to do so in the following order, due to interdependencies:

1. `MigUtil`

2. `MigrationModifyObj` and `MigrationLogObj` (both depend on `MigUtil`)

3. `MigrationReadObj` (depends on `MigUtil` and `MigrationModifyObj`)

4. `MigrationWriteObj` (depends on `MigUtil` and `MigrationLogObj`)

5. MigrationMainObj (depends on MigrationReadObj, MigrationWriteObj, MigrationLogObj and MigrationModifyObj)

Both the MigrationMainObj and the MigrationWriteObj use the MigrationLogObj; therefore it must be compiled before the other two objects. In most cases, the MigrationMainObj will log errors. However, if errors are encountered during the MigrationWriteObj roll back process, MigrationWriteObj will log those errors directly through the MigrationLogObj.

> *To recompile the objects, ensure that you are using Visual C++ with Service Pack 3 or above. You must also set the* **Active Project** *to* **Release, Unicode, Minsize** *for the five main migration objects and for* MigUtil, *set the* **Active Project** *configuration to* **Release**.

Verification of the Membership Directory Migration

The one sure way to ensure that your objects have all been successfully migrated is to query the Site Server 3.0 Membership Directory for a migration attribute with a value of False, or for all accounts that have no migration attribute. When these queries return nothing at all, then you can be certain that the migration has been completed. Once this is the case, remember to remove the migration code from the login page (if the real-time mode was activated), unregister all objects from the servers from which migration was activated, and backup the migration log files.

Summary

This chapter has outlined the steps involved in migrating the membership directory. Three tools are provided with the Commerce Server SDK to help with the migration process:

❑ Profile Builder Tool

❑ Group Pre-Population Tool

❑ Directory Migration Tool

Aside from migrating the data, you must also migrate the ASP code that you use to retrieve the membership data from the data store. Some of the drawbacks that were outlined in the chapter, include:

❑ Active Directory Group Structure is limited to 5000 Members per group

❑ Migration process involves several steps

❑ Out of the Box Business Desk has a poor performance

Some of the benefits associated with the migration to Commerce Server 2000 include:

❑ Easier management of your member base through the Business Desk

❑ Ability to use different types of datastore aside from SQL Server

Even with the help of these tools, the directory migration process can be quite involved and the code migration laborious. Unless you believe you're are ready to take advantage of the new features in Commerce Server 2000, it may not be worth your while to migrate at this time.

The next chapter now moves on to address the issues of migrating your e-commerce store.

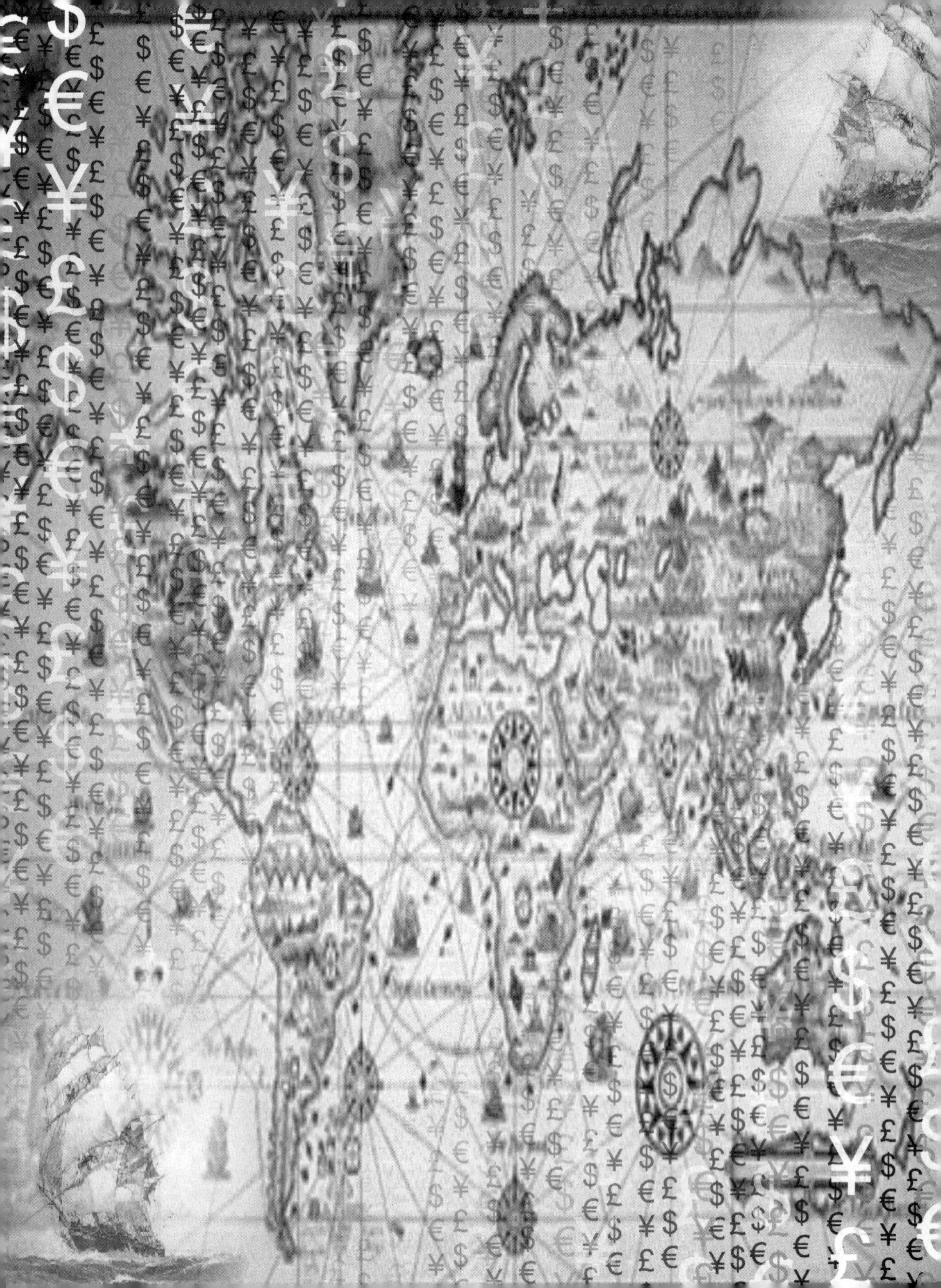

18

Migrating Your Store

The previous chapter dealt with membership directory migration. This chapter will concentrate on migrating the rest of your Site Server 3.0 features, such as your catalog, ad store, analysis reports, etc. We will assume that you have a basic understanding of Commerce Server 2000 functionality, including the Business Desk (especially its catalog features). We'll also assume that you have a good understanding of Site Server 3.0 Commerce Edition, and how to implement a site under Site Server 3.0.

This chapter will first cover the catalog migration that, along with the membership directory migration, is the biggest task in migrating to Commerce Server 2000. Then, we will discuss how to convert your code, by looking at the necessary modifications to your pipeline components, following that we will discuss migrating the AdServer feature, then the Rules, and finally your site vocabulary. A study of the analysis reports and data conversion to the CS2K platform will be performed. The last discussion will be centered on migration planning, logical step order, and testing of your migrated site.

The migration of your store from Site Server 3.0 Commerce Edition to CS2K is no easy task; it will need careful planning and implementation. This discussion will guide you through an element-by-element conversion/migration of your Site Server 3.0 features. It will also give you a better understanding of the differences between the features offered on both platforms.

Migrating the Product Catalog

Unfortunately there is no automated way to migrate your catalog schema. Because CS2K has such a different structure to Site Server 3.0, the catalog schema must be recreated in CS2K. On the up side, the catalog function in the Business Desk has a feature that will let you import and export the catalog data. This feature will speed up the conversion especially if you have access to an XML format of your existing catalog.

Migrating the Catalog Schema

Migrating the catalog schema involves recreating the structure of the catalog on the Commerce Server platform. This includes recreating the property definitions and reconstructing the category and product information using the Business Desk. The following steps will guide you through migrating your catalog schema.

The first step in the migration of the catalog schema will be to identify the properties, products and categories that are currently being used within the Site Server 3.0 catalog schema. These property definitions must be created for each of the custom properties identified. This is performed through Business Desk | Catalogs | Catalog Designer. The View icon will allow you to rotate through three different views of the catalog elements. Select the Properties View Definitions. If your properties do not appear in the view pages, you will need to add them to the property definitions of your Commerce Server Data Store.

The next step is to create the category definitions. This is done in the same manner as the properties but by selecting the Category Definitions view. If your categories do not exist in the list, you will have to add them. Once the categories are created, you will need to assign properties to each. The same steps will have to be performed for the products.

The next step is to create the catalog. This will be performed through the Catalog Editor. There are a few ways to accomplish this task.

❑ The first is to manually convert the catalog, by recreating the catalog, and manually re-entering the products. This option would be logical if the structure of the catalog is in need of revamping – otherwise, it is not advisable.

❑ A second method would be to use the Import feature of the catalog and import the data using a comma-delimited file. This method is an improvement on the first, since the product data is migrated for you, but will not migrate the catalog schema. In this method, all products are mapped to one product definition and are not separated into categories. The catalog name will be used as the name of the product definition in which all migrated products will reside.

❑ The last, and most recommended, method is the XML import method. This allows you to migrate both the catalog schema and the catalog data. Once imported, you will have the ability to modify the catalog as you see fit.

Be advised that you cannot import a product which contains a product definition with a different set of properties to an existing product definition of the same name.

Since the most logical method to import your Site Server 3.0 catalog would be using the XML import function, we will describe the necessary requirements for this method.

XML Requirements:

OK, so you have just found out that you can import your existing catalog into CS2K with fairly limited manual reconfiguration. Of course, all of the properties and product definitions, etc. have to be manually recreated but this is an acceptable compromise, if you don't have to re-enter your entire product base into the database. However, the XML file that you produce will have to conform to the XML Schema dictated by CS2K.

The **XML Structure** has the following design. The non-italicized terms refer to the elements of the XML structure while the italicized terms represent the attributes associated with each element. The elements and their attributes will not be fully discussed here since complete definitions are available in the Commerce Server help file.

```
<MSCommerceCatalogCollection>
    <CatalogSchema>
       <AttributeDefinition name DataType Id />
       <Definition Name DefinitionType properties variantProperties />
       <PropertiesDefinition>
          <Property name DataType MinValue MaxValue DisplayName id
                    AssignAll DefaultValue DisplayInProductsList
                    DisplayOnSite ExportToDW IncludeInSpecSearch
                    IsFreeTextSearchable />
             <PropertyValue DisplayName />
          </Property>
       </PropertiesDefinition>
    </CatalogSchema>
    <Catalog catalogName description locale startDate endDate
             productIdentifier productVariantIdentifier currency>
       <Category name Definition isSearchable id parentCategories
                 listprice>
          <Field fieldID fieldValue />
          <Relationship name description relation />
       </Category>
       <Product definition listprice id parentCategories pricingCategory>
          <Field fieldID fieldValue />
          <ProductVariant Id>
             <Field fieldID fieldValue />
          </ProductVariant>
          <Relationship name description relation />
       </Product>
    </Catalog>
</MSCommerceCatalogCollection>
```

The interesting thing to note from the XML structure is that it is separated into two sections. The first half describes the catalog schema and the second imports the product data. The XML import must follow some basic rules. For example, the catalog schema must not conflict with any elements already existing in the catalog database, such as properties, categories or product definitions. You cannot delete schema elements during an XML import but only add new elements to the schema. Some rules for the Catalog data import exist. One of those rules is that you can only add a new a catalog, or update an existing one, by merging the two catalogs (the existing one and the imported one) or the imported catalog can totally overwrite the existing catalog. If a catalog is merged: you can only add or modify product data, no deletion is allowed. The same is true for product variants and categories.

The Commerce Server help file also presents the XDR, the XML-Data Reduced schema that defines the individual elements of the XML file, their attributes and also the relations used.

Since this import feature is not directly geared for importation from the Site Server 3.0 platform, Microsoft does not provide a tool with the SDK for the extraction of your site catalog into an XML format. You can either create your own XML Conversion program using hierarchical recordsets or you can use the export tool from Microsoft provided on the CS2K Resource Kit CD.

Migrating Your Code

In this section, we will look at the coding modifications required to migrate your e-commerce store from Site Server 3.0 to CS2K. We must consider converting Site Server's pipeline components, AdServer functionality and data, site rules, site vocabulary, and analysis data and reports into their counterpart forms as defined under Commerce Server 2000.

Migrating Your Pipeline Components

Although the migration of your pipeline, or pipelines, is not necessary, it is certainly recommended. There have been significant upgrades to the pipeline process in CS2K and it is in your best interest to migrate your components to the new platform to take advantage of all of these benefits. Some of the more significant upgrades, which were incorporated in the CS2K Pipelines, are:

- Different orderform structure
- Support for multiple 'ship to's
- Support for 64-Bit currency

Since the structure of the orderform has changed, the pipeline components in CS2K are significantly different from those in Site Server 3.0. Therefore, pipeline components that were written for Site Server 3.0 cannot be used in conjunction with pipeline components in CS2K. However, all APIs are backward compatible, which means that you can still use your pipeline and its components in the Commerce Server platform depending on how the pipeline component has been implemented. For example, if your component interacts with pipeline data at the dictionary level then you will be able to use that component in the Commerce Server platform. However, if your component interacts with data at the database level, you will have to redesign your component since the database will have changed in CS2K. Also be aware that you cannot mix components within the pipeline, they must either all be Site Server components or all be Commerce Server components.

Also keep in mind that CS2K has also introduced a new series of components to help you with some of the other processes encountered in an online store. Among these pipelines, you will find:

- Order Processing Pipelines
- Basket Pipeline
- Total Pipeline
- Checkout Pipeline
- Direct Mail Pipeline
- Content Selection Pipeline
- Discounts Pipeline
- Advertising Pipeline
- Related Sell Pipeline

To migrate your pipeline components, you essentially need to rewrite your component, changing the data type format for both the currency and the addresses. Also you will have to modify your access to the database to account for the database structure changes.

Migrating Your AdServer Functionality and data

The Site Server AdServer feature is replaced by the Campaign Manager in CS2K. You can access the Campaign Manager through the Management Desk. The existing functionality will remain but the store schema has changed significantly. Source code is provided for data transformation to populate the CS2K Schema with the Site Server Commerce Ad Schema. All of the Site Server Commerce `GetAd` calls are backward compatible, so minimum modification of your web pages should be required. But, it is certainly recommended to modify their function calls due to the significant performance impact of keyword conversion at the time of the implementation. Commerce Server Campaign Manager will convert the keywords by mapping all keyword parameters to a `CSO.GetContent` property so that the new 'expressions' can be properly evaluated.

However, you will be required to convert any store schema configurations in your `global.asa`. The AdServer Migration tool will not do the conversion for you. These modifications will include the re-coding of any site-specific procedure references to take account of the new platform.

Migrating Your AdServer Data

Microsoft has provided a tool you will be able to use to migrate your AdServer data. This tool is located in `C:/Program Files/Microsoft Commerce Server/SDK/Tools/Migration/Ad Server` and is called `AdServerMigration.exe`.

The tool requires three input parameters:

- ❏ Site Server 3.0 Connection String
- ❏ Commerce Server 2000 Marketing System Connection String
- ❏ Commerce Server 2000 Expression Store Connection String

The connection string will therefore look similar to the following:

```
Adservermigration.exe /CS30:"dsn=SSAdServer;uid=sa;pwd=;"
/CS2000:"dsn=BizDataStore;uid=sa;pwd=;" /exprstore:"dsn=BizDataStore;uid=sa;pwd=;"
[/silent]
```

The tool will create a log file in the same directory as itself and logs the progress of the migration. Once complete, most of the ad campaign and ad campaign items configuration can be found in three tables: `Campaign` (for the campaign configuration), `Campaign_Item` (for all items under that campaign), `Campaign_Item_Types` (for the campaign item type). However, in total, the whole campaign management system uses 24 tables in your e-commerce database.

Migrating Your AdServer Code

As we have mentioned before, you will have to make some code modifications to convert your AdServer site to CS2K. But before we dive into the code conversion, let's establish some terminology and base knowledge of the Campaign System in CS2K.

The whole advertising process falls into the Content Selection Framework in CS2K. The AdServer object in Site Server 3.0 makes way to the `ContentSelector` (CSO) object in CS2K. The CSO object will instantiate the Advertising pipeline called `Advertising.pcf`. Upon successful completion of the pipeline process, the CSO object will return a `SimpleList` object of the available formatted advertisements, which can then be rendered on the ASP page. If the user clicks on an ad, they will be redirected to an ASP page called `Redir.asp` that invokes a `RecordEvent` and `IISAppendToLog` component to log the advertisement click-through and the content of the advertisement is rendered on the page.

The necessary coding change will be in the `global.asa` file in order to replace the old AdServer instantiation with the new CSO object instantiation The code in need of replacing is located in the `Application_OnStart` subroutine and should look similar to the following:

```
Set Ad = Server.CreateObject("Commerce.AdServer")

'  Set the connection string to the AdServer Database
Ad.ConnectionString = "DSN=AdServer;UID=SA;PWD=;"

'  Set a default ad to be shown when no other ads are eligible for
'  selection
Ad.DefaultAd = "&lt;B&gt;&lt;FONT SIZE=+4 COLOR=BLUE&gt;&lt;MARQUEE
WIDTH=468&gt;Default Ad&lt;/MARQUEE&gt;&lt;/FONT&gt;&lt;/B&gt;"

'  Specify the URL of the adredir.asp script.
Ad.RedirectURL = "/adsamples/adredir.asp"

'  Set the error handling mode.
Ad.DesignMode = TRUE

'  Set the Application property.
Ad.Application = "/adsamples"

'  Store a reference to the object for later use
Set Application("Ad")  = Ad
```

The new code will also reside in the `Application_OnStart` subroutine. An example of the code is shown below:

```
' Modify sConnStr to point to a valid Campaigns database.
' The Campaigns database can be created either by unpacking a site,
' such as blank.pup, or by running the campaign database creation
' scripts in the C:/Program Files/Microsoft Commerce Server/Site
' Create diretory.
const sConnStr = "provider=SQLOLEDB;Data Source=(local);Initial
catalog=Retail_commerce;User ID=sa;Password=;"

Dim oPipe, dCSFAdsContext
Dim oExpressionEval, oCacheManager, dCacheConfig

' Set up CacheManager object.
Set dCacheConfig = CreateObject("Commerce.Dictionary")
dCacheConfig.ConnectionString = sConnStr
Set oCacheManager = CreateObject("Commerce.CacheManager")
oCacheManager.LoaderProgId("Ads") = "Commerce.CSFLoadAdvertisements"
Set oCacheManager.LoaderConfig("Ads") = dCacheConfig
oCacheManager.RefreshInterval("Ads") = 15 * 60 ' 15 minutes

' Create the Expression Evaluator and connect it to the database.
Set oExpressionEval = CreateObject("Commerce.ExpressionEvaluator")
Call oExpressionEval.Connect(sConnStr)

' Create CSF advertising context, a dictionary.
Set dCSFAdsContext = CreateObject("Commerce.Dictionary")
```

```
' Create an advertising pipeline and add it to the context.
Set oPipe = CreateObject("Commerce.OrderPipeline")
' Load the pipeline configuration
oPipe.LoadPipe(Server.MapPath("Advertising.pcf"))
' Store a reference to the pipeline object in the Context
' dictionary.
Set dCSFAdsContext("pipeline") = oPipe

' Other context configuration for CSF ads.
dCSFAdsContext("RedirectUrl") = ".\redir.asp"
' Add a reference to an expression evaluator to the Context
Set dCSFAdsContext("Evaluator") = oExpressionEval
' InitCacheManager, a routine that would appear elsewhere in the
' global.asa, returns a reference to a CacheManager object.
Set dCSFAdsContext("CacheManager") = oCacheManager
dCSFAdsContext("CacheName") = "Ads"

' Store a reference to the dCSFAdsContext dictionary in the
' Application collection.
Set Application("Ad") = dCSFAdsContext
```

While it is not compulsory to change the GetAd call in your ASP code, it is certainly recommended due to the large performance impact of converting the GetAd call to a CSO.keyword. The GetAd call to replace is as follows:

```
<% Set Ad = Application("Ad") %><% = Ad.GetAd(Response) %>
```

Here is an example of how to implement the CSO.keyword, as a replacement:

```
' Create a ContentSelector object.
Set CSO = Server.CreateObject("Commerce.ContentSelector")

' Use the GetContent method to get some content. Use the dictionary
' previously created in the Global.asa file and referenced through the
' Application collection.
Set Ads = CSO.GetContent(Application("Ad"))
' Ads is a SimpleList containing the selected content.
' Write the content to the page, if any.
For Each Ad in Ads
    Response.Write(Ad)
Next
```

Converting Rules into Expressions

In Site Server 3.0, we had the concept of rules that could be used to display advertisements, content, etc. This concept of rules has remained; however their structure has changed drastically. The rules are now called expressions and these expressions are based more on a neat If...Then...Else... structure than the cumbersome rule format of Site Server 3.0. Expressions will make it much easier to convert business rules than the rules in SS3.0.

However, because of these structural changes, there is no easy way to migrate the rules from your SS3.0 platform to CS2K. All rules will need to be manually re-entered in the new format. This can be done via the business desk – and since it has been covered previously in this book, it will not be addressed here.

Converting the Site Vocabulary to Site Terms

The Site Vocabulary has also changed in CS2K. Instead of the hierarchical list, the Site Vocabulary is now simply an enumerated list called Site Terms. The terms themselves can be migrated programmatically if the hierarchical structure is dismantled prior to the migration. The Site Terms can be accessed through the Business Desk, via the Users Menu.

Even though the site terms do not contain a hierarchical structure, they do allow you to create groups in order to manage your site terms more efficiently. The default Site Term contains two main groups: user and calendar. As an example, the calendar group contains a site term called Days that has the 7 days of the week as possible values. You have the option of adding more groups and/or site terms to any groups.

You have two options for the conversion of your Site Vocabulary, you can either re-enter the terms manually or you can create a DTS job that will export the terms from Site Server Membership Directory Database into the Commerce Server Database. Since the hierarchy must be flattened before exporting to Commerce Server, if you don't have a lot of terms in your Site Vocabulary, it may be faster for you to simply re-enter the terms manually.

Migrating Your Analysis Data and Analysis Reports

The analysis feature in Site Server 3.0 was a nice option to have. Especially as it provided out of the box reports that were easy to implement. However, the feature was not scalable and its performance deteriorated rapidly as the size of the database, and the complexity of the report, increased. In order to fix these problems, Microsoft has totally restructured the data store to support the feature and improve its performance. Therefore, the structure of the analysis process is no longer recursive but instead it is a 3-tiered structure that is based on the CS2K data warehouse calculations. The data warehouse has an extensible and versatile structure with several aggregations built in to facilitate the custom import of data. The Commerce Server Data Warehouse and Business Analytics System features are not compatible with the Analysis Feature of Site Server.

This new structure will force you to re-import all your site web logs. You will also have to recreate any custom reports to the new Business Analytics System. The old report writer has been replaced with the Business Desk Report Feature.

Migrating Your Data

You will need to migrate both your web logs and your custom data. To import your web logs, you only need to re-import enough data to satisfy your trending reports. For example, if you are currently trending two months of data, that is, 60 days, you will need to re-import the web logs for the past 60 days.

Both Site Server and Commerce Server recommend that you use the extended W3C log file format for your web logs. They both require that you log the following:

❑ Time
❑ Client IP address
❑ User name
❑ URI stem
❑ URI query
❑ HTTP status

- ❏ Bytes sent
- ❏ User agent
- ❏ Cookie
- ❏ Referrer

Commerce Server also recommends the following to be logged:

- ❏ Date
- ❏ Server IP Address
- ❏ Server Port
- ❏ Method
- ❏ Win32 Status
- ❏ Bytes Received

The extra items that Commerce Server requests aren't critical; for example, the date is included to ensure accuracy in the data. If your historical log files do not include the items, you will still be able to import the logs as long as you are at least logging the following: Client IP Address, URI Stem and Time.

Importing to the data warehouse is done through a scheduled DTS job. This is quite different from the import tool in Site Server, which was scheduled through the NT task scheduler. The DTS tasks are already created, so you will have to configure the task for your server,(that is, make sure that path to the log files is correct, etc.) The DTS import is much more efficient than the Import Usage that Site Server offered. All custom imports must be done through DTS Tasks.

Migrating Your Reports

There are two different types of reports offered in Commerce Server: Static Reports and Dynamic Reports. The Dynamic Reports are created at runtime and they are based on an XML framework that is, in turn, based on a SQL query to the Data Warehouse or on a reference to a data cube. The report gathers the most recent data in the Data Warehouse at run time. Only the report definition is stored, the report results are not. This type of report is used for calculations that you would want to perform on the current statistics in the database where the calculations are very specific.

The Static Reports are run upon request and the results are stored in the Complete Report module. The Static Reports are based on either a SQL Query to the data warehouse or on a multidimensional expression of a SQL or online analytical processing (OLAP) database. Another improvement in the Commerce Server platform is that the Static Reports are run asynchronously, allowing you to continue working without having to wait for the report to finish. Only Static multidimensional expressions are run synchronously. This type of report is used for reports that aren't as time sensitive and that are broader in scope. You may also want to create static reports if the reports are fairly resource intensive to run, or if they are going to be accessed by several individuals.

The reports which are available in Site Server range from Advertising, to Inventory, to Intranet, to Site Server Feature Specific and of course, a whole range of detail and summary reports. The list below illustrates the reports available in Site Server 3.0.

Site Server 3.0 Reports	
Category	Report
Advertising	Advertisement Detail
	Advertisement Placement
	Advertiser Detail
	Advertising Overview
	Audit Report (ABVS compliant)
	Audit Report (BPA compliant)
Detail	Bandwidth Detail
	Browser Detail
	Comprehensive Report
	Content Detail
	Geography Detail
	Hit Detail
	Organization Detail
	Path Detail
	Referrer Detail
	Request Detail
	User Detail
	Visit Detail
Intranet	Intranet Content
	Intranet Users
	MS Proxy
Inventory	Advertising
	Browser
	Geography
	Organization
	Referrer
	Request
	User
	Visit

Site Server 3.0 Reports	
Site Server	AdServer
	AdTags
	Commerce
	Content Analysis
	Netshow
	Rules
	Search Queries
	Search Trends
	Top Users
	User List
	User by Area
Summary	Bandwidth Summary
	Browser Summary
	Content Summary
	Executive Summary (extended Logs)
	Executive Summary
	Geography Summary
	Hits Summary
	Organization Summary
	Path Summary
	Referrer Summary
	Request Summary
	User Summary
	Visit Summary

The following is the list of the out of the box reports available in Commerce Server. The report categories are different and so are the reports themselves. There is no straight one-to-one relationship between the Site Server and Commerce Server Reports.

Commerce Server 2000		
Category	Report	Static (S) or Dynamic (D)
Advertising	Ad Placement	D
	Ad Reach and Frequency per Campaign	D
	Ad Reach and Frequency per Campaign Item	D
	Ad Reach and Frequency per Day	D
	Campaign Even Summary	D
	Campaign Item Summary	D
Diagnostic	Bandwidth Summary	D
	Bandwidth Trends	D
	Hits by HTTP Status	D
	Hits by Win32 Status	D
Query String	Query Strings (Multi Value)	S
	Query Strings (Single Value)	S
Sales	Buyer Browse to Purchase	D
	Customer Sales	S
	Customer Spend Summary	D
	Order Events	D
	Product Sales	D
	Shopping Basket Events	D
User	Distinct Users and Visits by Week	D
	Distinct Users by Day	D
	New Registered Users	S
	Registered User Properties	S
	Registered Users by Date Registered	D
	User Days to Register	D
	User Registration Rate	D
	User Trends	D

Commerce Server 2000		
Visit	Entry Pages	D
	Exit Pages	D
	General Activity Statistics	D
	User Visit Trend	D
Web Usage	Entry Path Analysis	S
	Top Referring Domains by Requests	S
	Top Requested Pages	S
	Usage Summary by Day of Week	D
	Usage Summary by Hour of Day	D
	Usage by Week of Year	D
	Usage Trends	D
	Visits by Browser, Version, and OS	D

In Commerce Server the reports are structured differently since some reports may be saved as completed reports and other must be run to get the results. Because of the dynamic nature of most of the Commerce Server reports, several must be viewed in order to get the same information available in one Site Server report. This new structure is great if you want up to the minute facts and numbers for a very specific purpose, for example calculating the Ad Frequency per Campaign Item. However, if you want a global report on your ad campaigns, which does not need to be calculated to be viewed, you will have to custom create a report with that functionality.

Commerce Server also includes some reporting on the Commerce aspects of your site, such as Customer Sales and Order Events. Such reports are an improvement on Site Server, where this type of information used to be custom imported and a report definition created manually.

On the down side, with Commerce Server, the report writing tool is much more complex than Site Server's. This helps you to get more valuable information out of your data warehouse but if your knowledge of SQL or the Transact-SQL language is not top-notch, it may take some time to get to grips with.

Migrating Your Site

In this final section, we are going to consider the three main stages of site migration. To help ensure that the process runs smoothly, you should always begin with a clear **plan**, stick to that plan while **performing** the migration, and follow up by thoroughly **testing** the new deployment.

Planning for the Migration

Planning the migration of your site is the most important task that you will have to undertake in the migration process. Planning not only includes the planning for additional hardware and software that you may require, but also planning and scheduling the tasks during the migration from the development to the deployment. For example, during the migration, you may want to consider implementing some of the upgrades that you have been putting off.

When planning the migration, you should consider which tasks can be done in parallel to improve efficiency, and reduce the overall time of migration. Some of the items, you should be including in your migration plan are:

❑ The features that you are currently using in your e-commerce site and whether or not the features will be migrated

❑ Any upgrades that you will want to include under the new platform

❑ Timing for the migration, both length of time and date

❑ Resources: how many people, how long will they be working on the migration project, the skills required of the people

❑ Deployment: will you require additional hardware for the deployment of the new site, who will be supporting the new site on the new platform and do they have the knowledge/information to provide adequate support

❑ Testing: do your testing resource have enough information to develop a proper test plan with thorough test cases

❑ Fallback plan: how long will you test the site into production, what will be your fallback plan if the migration fails

The fallback plan is very important since it should outline issues such as: determining factors of success and failure, recovery if the migration is not successful, and a plan for data integrity. We would suggest that you log the data that is critical to your business, that is, orders, transactions, etc. and possibly develop a tool during the development phase which would allow you to migrate these critical items back to the Site Server 3.0 platform if the migration is not successful.

During the development phase of the migration, make sure you have planned the migration of all elements of your site from data (Catalog, transactions, users, ads, etc.) to code (custom components, static HTML pages, and asp pages) to software (include third-party software), thoroughly.

Development: Performing the Migration

The development phase will not only include the migration from Site Server 3.0 to CS2K but for some of you it may also include the migration from Windows NT 4.0 to Windows 2000. This also includes the migration from one ADO version to another. Which means that if you have any custom components that are registered in MTS, they will have to be migrated over to the COM+ platform. This type of migration is more involved than just converting the site to CS2K, and all of these conversions and upgrades increase the impact of the modification on your site.

Even if a section of your code does not need to be modified or converted, the simple act of moving to the new Operating System platform will require you to perform testing in order to verify that the new Operating System is compatible with your code. An example of this is the poor performing LDAP instantiation under Windows 2000 if the name of the server is not given as a fully qualified domain name. For example under Windows NT 4.0, the LDAP call would look like so:

```
Dim oLDAP
Dim oMember
Set oLDAP = GetObject("LDAP:")
Set oMember =
oLDAP.OpenDSObject("LDAP://laptop:1003/o=WroxConference/ou=Members/cn=jdoe,
sAdmin, sPassword, 0)
```

However, this must be converted to the following in Windows 2000 due to performance issues:

```
Dim oLDAP
Dim oMember
Set oLDAP = GetObject("LDAP:")
Set oMember =
oLDAP.OpenDSObject("LDAP://laptop.craigmcqueen.com:1003/o=WroxConference/ou=Member
s/cn=jdoe, sAdmin, sPassword, 0)
```

1. The first step in the migration would be to implement a development, testing or production environment with the same configuration (that is, Windows 2000). The ideal would be to have a separate server for each of these environments; however, if this is not feasible, you could combine the testing and development environment in one server. Production really requires its own server for both stability and performance.

2. Next, migrate your current Site Server Commerce site to the Windows 2000 development environment. This will help you migrate to Commerce Server 2000 and will minimize the risks and impact on the users and help isolate issues. This would be a good point to test your current site for the issues that were mentioned above, that is, ADO, LDAP, etc.

3. The next step would be for you to install and familiarize yourself with the Commerce Server 2000, its features and its management tools, like the Commerce Server MMC and the Biz Desk. We also highly recommend that you unpack one of the solution sites (the retail site is an excellent example) and play around with it. This will help you get an understanding of the features that Commerce Server has to offer.

4. To create your own site under the CS2K platform, we recommend that you start with the Blank Solution Site. It will be available to you for unpacking upon installation of CS2K.

5. This step involves migrating your membership directory to the User Profile System. As seen in the previous chapter, this step can be quite a lengthy exercise, and is comprised of the sub-tasks below:

    a. Identify all custom attributes and site vocabulary that you are currently using

    b. Determine whether ot not your site will be employing Active Directory as a Data Store or simply using SQL Server

    c. Migrate your membership directory data

    d. Modify your code to use the User Profile System instead of the Active User Object

6. Similar to Step 5, migrating your Ad Server requires several tasks to be performed in order to ensure successful migration:

    e. Migrate your Ad Server Data

    f. Modify your `global.asa` to use the CSO pipeline to instantiate the your ads

    g. (Optional) Convert your `GetAd` calls to `CSO.GetContent` to improve performance

7. Migrate your catalog:

    a. Identify all properties, categories and products currently used in your site and recreate all of these in the CS2K

b. If you are not using the XML import tool, you will have to first recreate the catalog Schema in your Commerce Server Platform

c. If you are using the XML import tool, export your Site Server 3.0 catalog to an XML file using the XML Structure described earlier

d. Import the Catalog Data either via the XML import, CSV import or by manually recreating every product

8. Once the catalog is migrated, you must migrate the transactions to provide some history to your customer and provide a smooth transition. You must also ensure that there are no transactions that get lost between the transition periods. Depending on how long and how many transactions you have accumulated, you may only want to migrate the most recent transactions or for the past *x* number of months. You can migrate your Transactions from the Receipts table by using the Transaction Migration Tool located on the CS2K Resource Kit CD.

9. Migrate your Analysis Feature:

a. Import your historical logs to the Commerce Server Data Warehouse

b. Recreate your usage analysis reports through the Business Desk

10. You will also need to convert all of your Site Server 3.0 Rules to Expressions for your content selection and targeting system.

11. Along with the conversion of your rules, you will also need to convert your Site Vocabulary to Site Terms.

12. One of the final steps involves converting all of your ASP scripts from using the catalog system to the Commerce Server Catalog Object.

These steps give only an outline of what is required to migrate your existing site and do not include information on adding new functionality, or touch upon any of the new features offered by Commerce Server. It would be a nice touch to add in a new feature, or some new functionality for your users, as a payoff for the inconvenience that you may have caused by migrating your site to the new platform. But, we caution you not to undertake too much at this stage as it may introduce more risk than benefit for you. Also, the Commerce Server features can be added in once the site has stabilized.

Testing and Deploying Your Migration

This phase is probably as important as the development phase. In fact, the testing will introduce a cycle that will take the code back to development for fixing – and then back to testing again. It will also mean that the users have the least amount of disruption possible by ensuring that all the existing features work as intended. The person in charge of the testing, would also be an excellent choice to take care of documenting the migration and site functionality. This documentation will be crucial as the testing team gets ready for the testing cycle and prepares their test cases. The team should also test the performance of the site to ensure that it will be able to handle the anticipated site traffic.

The following testing steps should be included:

1. The first step for the testing team will be to locate some functionality documentation for your current site. If no documentation is available, they will have to draft some of their own.

2. The next step will be to create test cases that will fully test all the features and scenarios encountered in your site.

3. Once some of the features have been migrated, these can be deployed to the testing environment using the PUP tool. The testing team can then start to test the migrated features as the development team finishes the migration of the remaining features.

4. Once the whole site is finished, it should be deployed as a whole to the testing environment. This is done to test the Package that has been created and will also give the testing team a chance to test the whole site as an entity including all third-party work under the new platform.

5. Once the functionality has passed all the tests, the testing team will test the performance of the site.

6. You should create a backup of your site and perform a final migration of all users and transactions.

7. Deploy your site to the production environment using the PUP and change your DNS to point to the new site. Monitor your site for any problems.

8. You should create a backup of the site under the new platform and the testing team should update the documentation to reflect the modifications that were performed during the migration/conversion.

We recommend a short trial window for the production implementation. If the site is still working satisfactorily after 24 hours then the migration was successful, otherwise you have to resort to your fallback plan.

We recommend you limit the time window to 24 hours since the migration is unidirectional, which means that the transaction made to the CS2K platform cannot be migrated back to the Site Server platform.

Summary

This chapter has dealt with the issues surrounding the migration of all elements of an e-commerce site. We have covered such topics as the migration of your catalog, migration of your AdServer, conversion of your Site Vocabulary, Rules and Pipelines and finally the migration of the Analysis Feature. As you have just witnessed, migration is a long arduous process, ranging from migrating your user base to re-coding your ASP pages. If you have committed yourself to migrating to the CS2K, do not underestimate the effort and risks that the migration involves. That said, once the migration is completed you stand to reap many rewards from CS2K in terms of ease of use and greater scalability and control.

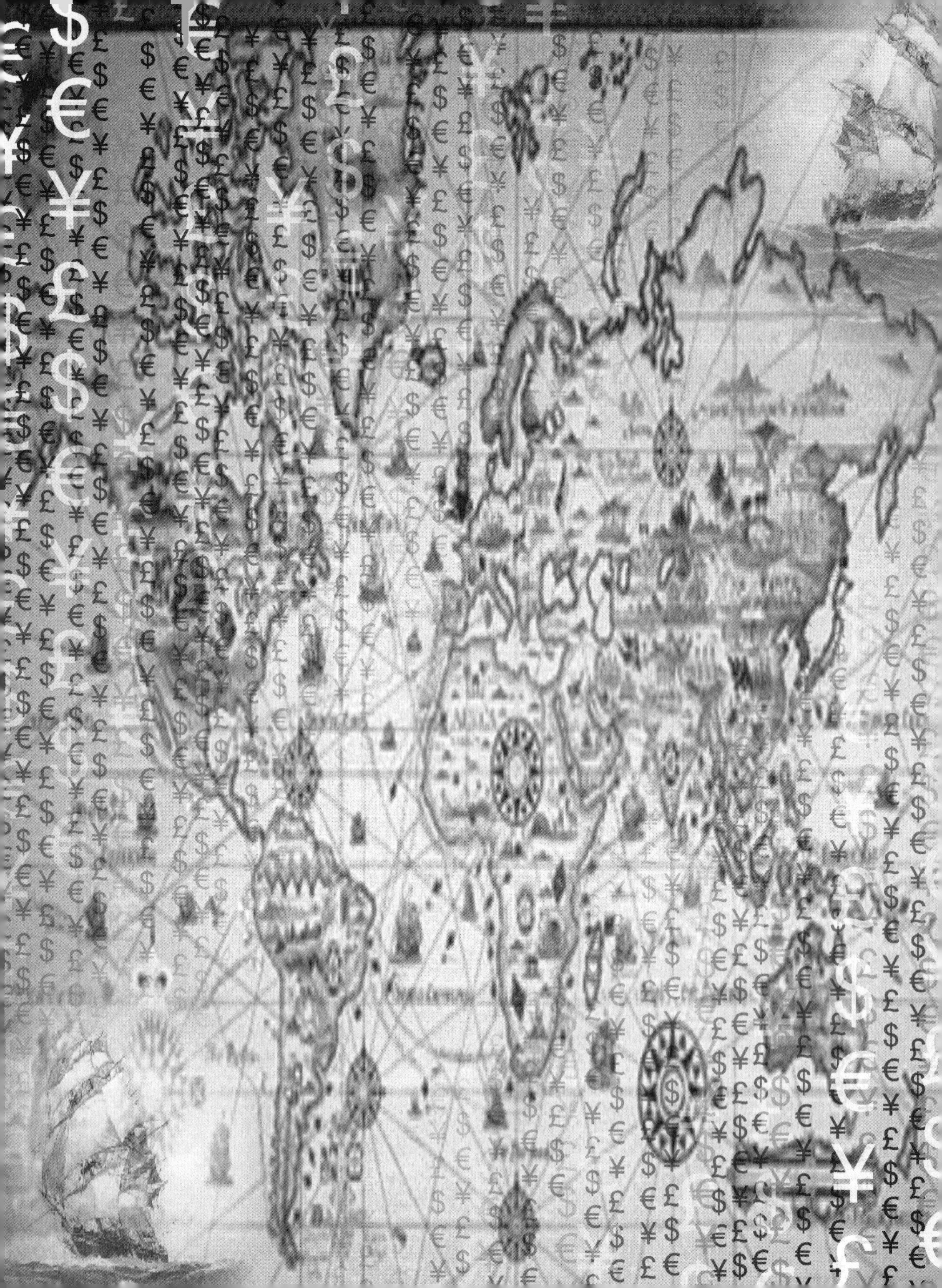

Commerce Server 2000 Installation

Many people that used Site Server Commerce Edition found that its installation was a frustrating and painful experience. Fortunately, installing Commerce Server 2000 is far more straightforward. In the course of this appendix, we will look in detail at the installation process, and take the opportunity to describe how to adjust the installation to meet your specific requirements.

Hardware Requirements

This section details minimum suggested hardware requirements for installation of Commerce Server, its associated Administration Tools and the Business Desk Client. Keep in mind that an e-commerce site may need to provide high availability and support a high volume of users across multiple servers. These issues require a detailed discussion of web server tuning which could be its own chapter – if not its own book – and is beyond the scope of this appendix.

Commerce Server 2000 Server

These are the minimum hardware requirements to have a machine up and running as a web server with Commerce Server 2000 installed:

- ❑ 400 MHz or faster Pentium-compatible CPU
- ❑ 256 MB of RAM *
- ❑ 100 MB of hard disk space

128MB of Ram is adequate for evaluation and development environments

Administration Tools

These specifications are adequate for Commerce Server 2000 Administration Tools only:

❑ 266 MHz or faster Pentium-compatible CPU

❑ 128 MB of RAM

❑ 20 MB of hard disk space

Business Desk Client

These specifications are adequate for a client machine running one or more website Business Desks:

❑ 266 MHz or faster Pentium-compatible CPU

❑ 5 MB of hard disk space

Software Requirements

Commerce Server 2000

These are the software prerequisites necessary before you can install Commerce Server 2000 on a web server machine:

❑ Microsoft Windows 2000 Server or Advanced Server

❑ Windows 2000 Server Service Pack 1

❑ Microsoft Windows 2000 Hotfix Q275455 and Hotfix Q271976

❑ SQL Server 2000 or SQL Server 7.0 (see specific database requirements listed below)

SQL Server 2000 Software Requirements

❑ SQL Server 2000 Client Tools

❑ SQL Server 2000 Analysis Services

❑ SQL Server 2000 Analysis Services Client Tools

SQL Server 2000 Evaluation edition is available for download from the Microsoft website, at: http://www.microsoft.com/sql/productinfo/evaluate.htm.

> **Note that Commerce Server 2000 requires that SQL Server 2000 be installed in Mixed Authentication Mode.**

SQL Server 7.0 Software Requirements

- ❑ Microsoft SQL Server 7.0 Client Tools
- ❑ Microsoft SQL Server 7.0, Service Pack 2
- ❑ Microsoft SQL Server 7.0 OLAP Services
- ❑ Microsoft SQL Server 7.0 OLAP Services, Service Pack 2
- ❑ OLAP Add-in Manager
- ❑ OLAP Server Client Tools
- ❑ MDAC 2.6

> Note that Commerce Server 2000 does *not* support a mixed SQL Server 7.0 and SQL Server 2000 configuration for the Data Warehouse and online analytical processing (OLAP) server databases.

Business Desk Client

These software prerequisites are required to install Business Desk software on a client machine:

- ❑ Microsoft Windows 98, Microsoft Windows Millennium Edition, Microsoft Windows NT 4.0, Windows 2000 Professional, Windows 2000 Server, or Windows 2000 Advanced Server
- ❑ Internet Explorer 5.5 – download this from http://www.microsoft.com/windows/IE/
- ❑ Microsoft Office Web components or SQL Server 2000 Client Tools

Installing SQL Server 2000

Run the SQL Server 2000 setup program and you will be presented with a screen similar to the one pictured below on the left-hand side:

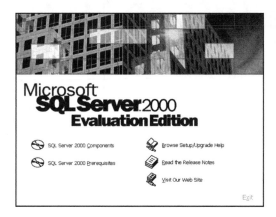

You should select SQL Server 2000 Components, followed by Install Database Server from the next window (shown above on the right). This will start the InstallShield Wizard – select Next to begin the installation.

1. First, you must enter the details of the server on which you want to install SQL Server, or select Local Computer to install it to the local machine:

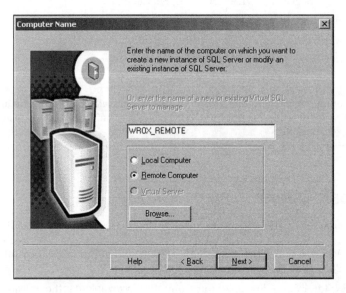

2. The next screen shows options to install a new instance of SQL Server, upgrade an existing version, or set advanced options. If this is the first time you have run SQL Server, then the upgrade option will be deactivated. Select Create a new instance of SQL, or install Client Tools, and click Next.

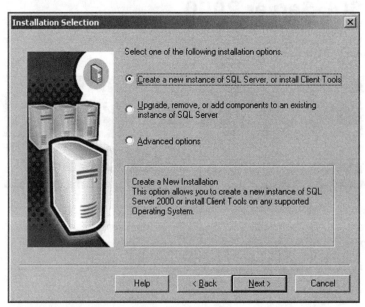

3. You will now get a dialog asking for your user name and company information, which you should enter before clicking **Next** again.

4. Microsoft's standard Software License agreement is now shown, which you should read. Assuming the conditions are acceptable, click **Yes** to continue.

5. There are three possible types of installation. We need to select the middle **Server and Client Tools** option, which will allow us to set up a server with administration capabilities.

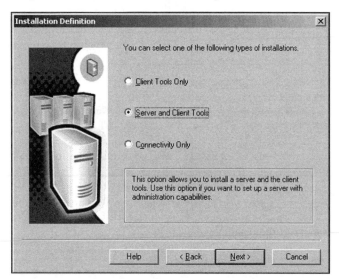

6. On your first installation of SQL Server to a server you will be given the option of making a **Default** installation, which does not require an instance name. Every installation of SQL after this will require you to specify an instance so the installations can be told apart. You can specify an instance name for this first installation as well, should you so wish.

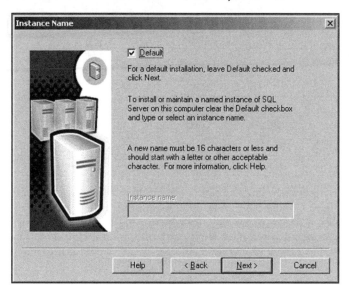

7. You are now prompted to specify the type of Setup you prefer. For present purposes, the Typical installation should suffice.

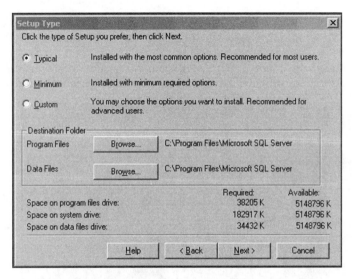

8. You are prompted to enter user name and password authority for the SQL Server Service, on either the Local System account, or the network Domain. You should select and enter these details according to your own system.

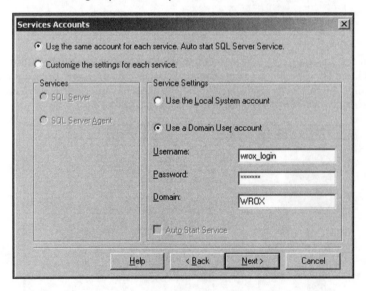

9. Next, you must change the authentication mode to Mixed Mode – note that without this setting in place, Commerce Server 2000 will not be able to use the database server. You can also select a password for the sa (System Administrator) account on this page. Click Next to continue, and then click Next again on the following screen to begin copying the SQL Server files onto your server.

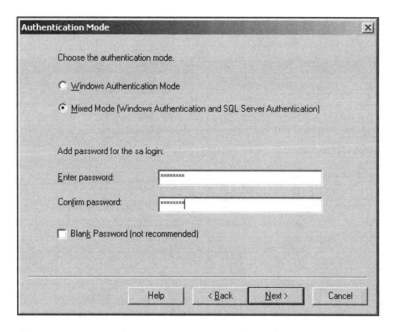

10. Select Finish to complete the Setup.

It is recommended that you now reboot your server.

Installing SQL Server 2000 Analysis Services

SQL Server 2000 Analysis Services allow you to perform complex analyses on large volumes of data, and are used to support much of the Data Warehousing functionality behind Commerce Server's Analytics system. Starting from the same screens as the database installation, select SQL Server 2000 Components, followed by Install Analysis Services.

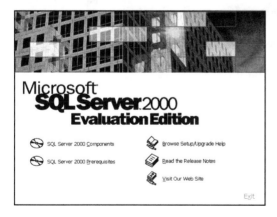

1. Click Next on the Welcome screen – then read the Software License Agreement and accept by clicking Yes.

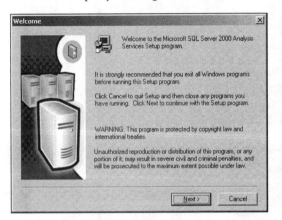 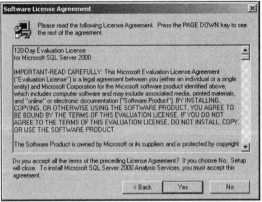

2. The next screen gives you a list of six sets of components to be installed: Commerce Server will require both the Analysis server and Analysis Manager components; Decision Support Objects and Client components are both integral to Analysis Services, and therefore cannot be unchecked; Sample applications and Books Online are both useful but non-essential. We will proceed with all of these options checked.

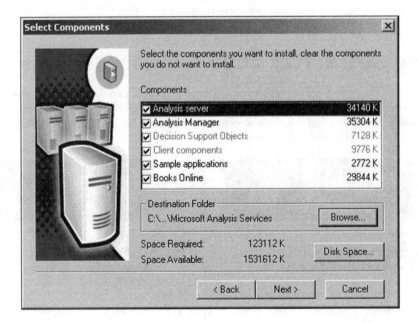

3. The final pair of screens simply let you specify a shortcut folder, and confirm that installation is complete.

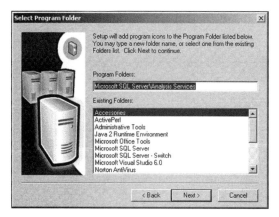 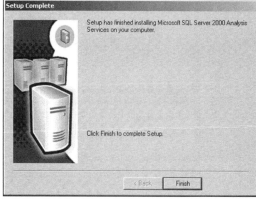

Installing Commerce Server 2000

Commerce Server 2000 has very strict hardware and software requirements. Before continuing, make sure you have thoroughly reviewed the requirement sections at the beginning of this appendix. Your system should at least meet the minimum specified recommendations before proceeding with setup.

> *Please, bear in mind that in a production environment it is strongly advised that Commerce Server 2000 should **not** be installed onto a web server that also contains a Data Warehouse.*

Now let's proceed with the installation:

4. Run the setup program from the Commerce Server 2000 CD. You will receive the startup screen as pictured below. Click Next to continue.

5. If you are unsure whether your system will be able to run Commerce Server 2000, you should click the button labeled Visit the Commerce Server 2000 Support Site, which will give up to date information on the product's installation requirements. Otherwise, click Next to continue.

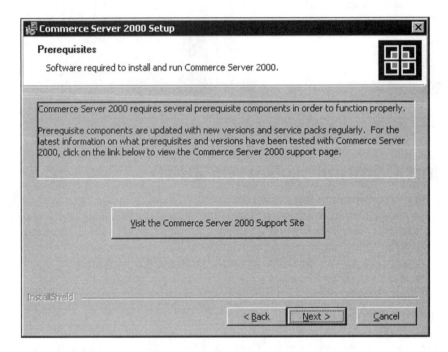

6. Read and accept the standard Microsoft License Agreement, then click Next.

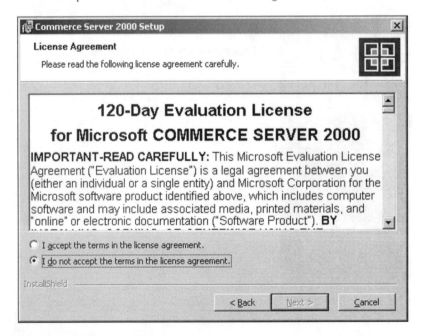

7. Enter your user information and click Next.

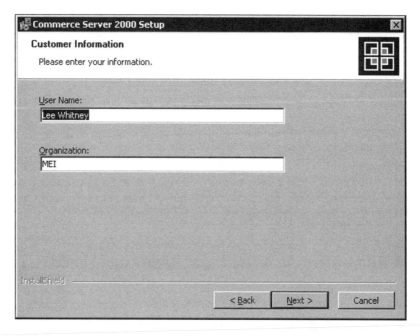

8. Specify the folder in which Commerce Server is to be installed, then Click Next to continue.

While you can select the default installation path, as shown below, it is recommended that you do not do this on a production server. Instead you should install the files onto a separate NTFS partition from your system files because this will yield additional security.

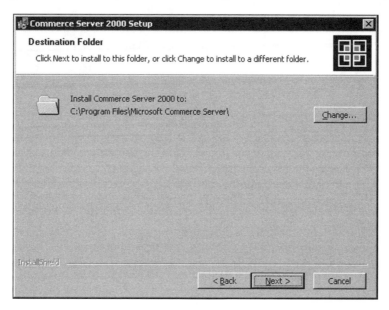

9. The next screen provides three installation options.

❏ Web Server – this installs the components necessary to operate a Commerce Server 2000 web server. These include Commerce Server and Data Warehouse components, the Microsoft Management Console (MMC), the Commerce Manager and Data Warehouse snap-ins, the Pipeline Editor and the Commerce Server 2000 help files.

Note that components for the Predictor resource and Direct Mailer Service are omitted in the standard web server installation.

❏ Complete – this installs all the Commerce Server components. Including all the components listed in the Typical installation as well as those necessary for the Predictor Resource, Direct Mailer Service and the Software Development Kit (SDK).

❏ Custom – allows you to select any of the components mentioned in the Web Server and Complete installation options. We will briefly examine each feature in the next step.

❏ Choose Custom and click Next to continue.

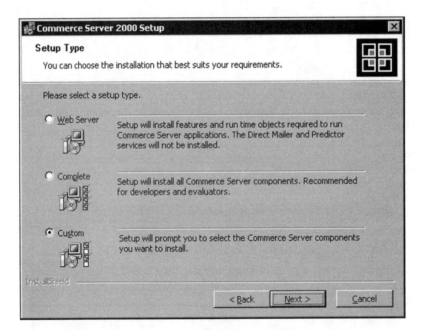

The Custom setup allows you to choose exactly what options you want to install. Let's review the install options:

❏ Runtime Objects – The full complement of COM objects used by Commerce Server 2000. These are a necessary component of any Commerce Server installation.

❏ Commerce Site Packages – The blank.pup solution site package. We discuss the use of this file in the *Installing Solution Sites* section of this appendix.

❏ Analysis and Data Warehouse – This installs tools that store data about your sites. The data can be used for analysis and reporting.

❑ **Predictor Service** – This feature tracks user behavior and purchase trends so that the website can tailor its content to a user's specific preferences based on the previous actions of that user, or others like them. Amazon.com is well known for this type of dynamic website content. For example if a user buys a book it will recommend several other titles based on the purchases of others who bought similar books. It is this kind of functionality that the Predictor Service supplies.

❑ **Direct Mailer Service** – This service does exactly what the name implies. It creates and sends e-mails to targeted users.

❑ **SDK** – The Software Development Kit, a set of tools and code libraries for use by e-commerce web application developers.

❑ **Administration Tools** – MMC Snap-ins that allow system administrators to manage e-commerce sites and global resources remotely.

❑ **On-line Documentation** – This gives you access to the Commerce Server help files.

In our custom setup example we will select all of the available features. This will produce the same results as a Complete installation would have achieved, but allows us to view the feature options. Click Next to continue.

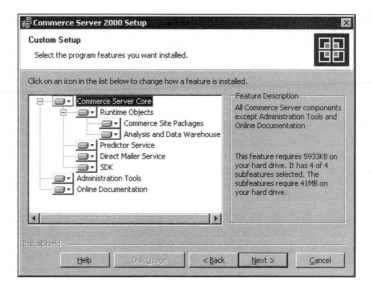

10. The Commerce Server 2000 installation will create an Administration database for us. The Administration database will track global Commerce Server information such as Commerce Server sites installed and both global and site specific resources (we'll discuss Commerce Server resources briefly in the next step).

11. Supply the SQL Server computer name where the administration database is to be installed. Keep in mind that if the computer for SQL Server 2000 is running multiple instances of SQL Server, then both the computer name and the instance will have to be specified (for example, LEEW\LEEW). Include the user account and password of your SQL server in the appropriate boxes. Note that Commerce Server 2000 does not allow you to use only Integrated NT Security, but requires that a SQL Server username and password be specified.

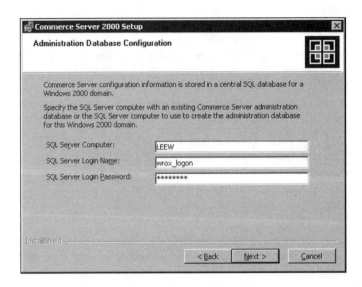

Do not use the SQL Server Login name of **sa** in a production environment. This login name is a default and could present a security threat.

Login information can be modified after installation by using the SQL Server Enterprise Manager.

12. Direct Mailer requires a local SQL Server – in other words, an instance of SQL Server that is running on the local machine. Direct Mailer will use the local computer's name as the **SQL Server Computer** name. You should type in the user account name for the Direct Mailer database in the **SQL Server Login Name** field. Type the login password in the **SQL Server Login Password** field. Click **Next** to continue.

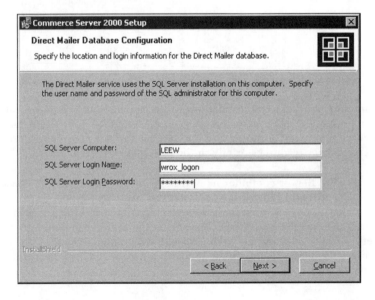

13. We can specify a separate SQL Server Service Logon account for Direct Mailer, List Manager and Predictor services, or use the same one by checking the corresponding check box. Click Next to continue.

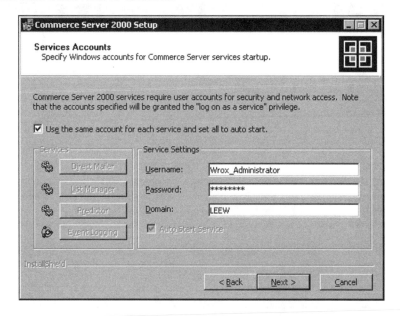

You should use a permanent logon account, as if the account name is disabled, or the password changed, Commerce Server 2000 will cease to function.

14. Click Install to begin copying files to your system.

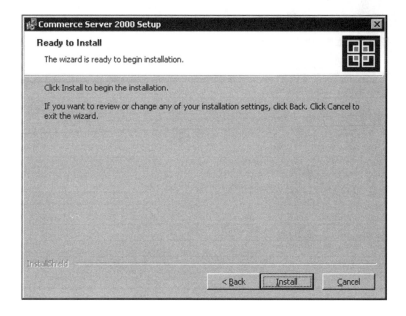

Commerce Server 2000 Installation will update you with the progress of your installation using the status screen shown below.

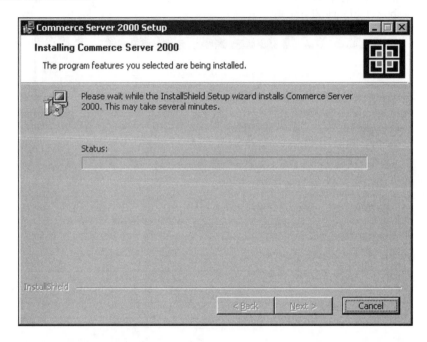

15. When the installation completes click Finish to exit the Setup program. Microsoft recommends that you restart your computer after installing Commerce Server 2000.

For up to the minute information on changes to the Commerce Server installation, see: http://support.microsoft.com/support/commerceserver/2000/install/default.asp.

You can find plenty of additional information and updates at Microsoft's main Commerce Server 2000 web page at: http://www.microsoft.com/commerceserver/.

Troubleshooting Commerce Server

This section will look at some of the more common errors that have been known to occur during Commerce Server 2000 installation, together with their potential solutions. The best resource for troubleshooting issues within Commerce Server 2000 (as with all Microsoft products) is the MS Knowledge Base, which can be found at http://search.support.microsoft.com/kb/c.asp. At time of writing, there are some issues regarding searches on the Knowledge Base for Commerce Server 2000, as articles regarding Site Server are often included in the returned results. To get round this, simply append 'CS2K' to your search string.

Note that if you install CS2K on top of SSCE3.0, the current SSCE stores will continue to work, but you will be unable to create any new ones.

SQL Error Encountered

The error message shown below may appear during the Administration Database Configuration step of Commerce Server installation:

This will happen if Commerce Server isn't able to log on to the specified SQL Server account. Here is a list of items to check to resolve this issue. This often happens when the specified SQL Server instance has been installed in Windows Authentication mode (rather than Mixed mode). Other things to check SQL Server for include the following:

- ❑ Verify that it is running.
- ❑ Verify that it is running SQL Server Agent Service.
- ❑ Verify that no `CommerceServer_Admin` database already exists on it.
- ❑ Verify that no `DirectMailer` database already exists on it.
- ❑ Verify that its data directory does not contain any of the following files:

- ❏ mscs_admin.mdf
- ❏ mscs_admin.ldf
- ❏ directmailer.mdf

❏ If you are using a remote SQL Server instance, ensure that both the machine name and instance name are specified (for example **LEEW/LEEW**).

❏ Verify that you have an adequate number of licenses for your SQL Server installation.

❏ Verify that you are not using an expired pre-release or evaluation copy.

Mscspagen.dll... failed to register

The following error message may be shown during the Commerce Server installation process:

Error 1904.Module C:\Program Files\Commerce Server\mscspagen.dll failed to register.

After clicking OK it may be followed by a similar error, this time specifying the following files:

- ❏ commerce.dll
- ❏ pipeconfig.dll
- ❏ pipeline.dll
- ❏ mscssnapin.dll.

Installation then fails. In this case, you should ensure that you aren't attempting to install an outdated beta or evaluation copy of Commerce Server 2000.

Error... MSCSResource.DLL not found

The following error message may appear after installing Commerce Server 2000:

The dynamic-link library mscsresource.DLL could not be found in the specified path.

If this happens, try rebooting the Commerce Server 2000 machine.

Application Failed Error when Installing Predictor Resource

The following error message may be generated when attempting to install the Predictor resource:

The application failed to initialize properly (0xc0000022). Click on OK to terminate.

The logon account for the Predictor resource needs to have the proper rights in order to logon as a service. Verify that you are *not* using a GUEST account.

Msmdarch.exe not found

The following error may be encountered when attempting to install the Data Warehouse:

Msmdarch.exe not found

Click the Skip button to continue without installing Data Warehousing. After completing installation of Commerce Server 2000, go back to SQL Server and verify that OLAP services have been installed correctly. Refer to the *Software Requirements* section at the beginning of this appendix for the SQL Server prerequisites necessary to install Commerce Server 2000. Once the OLAP Service has been installed correctly, run the Commerce Server 2000 setup again to add Data Warehousing.

Message... OLAP database may be in use

The following message may be encountered when reinstalling Commerce Server 2000:

The OLAP database <database name> may be in use by some other site, using this database might potentially break the reports for that site. Do you want to continue?

When Commerce Server is reinstalled it will overwrite all the existing Commerce Server Analysis Server Databases. If you are happy for this to occur, simply select OK.

Installing Solution Sites

Commerce Server 2000 provides a framework for building e-commerce solutions. The Solution Sites are ASP-based code templates that serve as working examples of how you can use that framework. (Note that Commerce Server sites do not *have* to use ASP – they can also make use of ISAPI and any other COM-compliant technologies.)

These templates are packaged into files with the extension .PUP so they can be simply transported. Once the Solution Site package is on your server the code-templates can be unpacked. You can use the Site Packager to package your own commerce sites into .PUP files, for transport, and then deploy them on other web servers.

.PUP files can also contain any custom scripts and COM components that have been created for your site. The Blank Solution Site comes as part of the standard Commerce Server 2000 installation. Two additional Solution Sites, a Retail Solution and a Supplier Solution, are available for download as a single file at http://www.microsoft.com/commerceserver/solutionsites.

Once you have downloaded the executable file `commerceserversolution.exe` from the solution site page, double-click on it to start the InstallShield Wizard and installation of the Solution Sites. There are no options to select in the course of this process, so we're not going to detail every click of the Next button. Suffice to say it's a very simple process, and once it's complete, you can find the two PUP files under Programs | Microsoft Commerce Server 2000 | Solution Sites in the Windows Start menu.

The following section gives step–by–step instructions on installing the Blank Solution Site. The installation process for each of the other Solution Sites is essentially the same, although a few minor differences are detailed in Chapter 10, where we study these sites in detail.

Unpacking the Blank Solution Site

You can start the unpacking process in two ways:

❑   Run the Packager tool from Start | Programs | Microsoft Commerce Server 2000 | Commerce Site Packager. Choose to Unpack from a package file (.pup), click Next and specify the name and location of the .pup file you wish to unpack.

❏   Alternatively, navigate to the location of the .pup file in Explorer, and double-click on it.

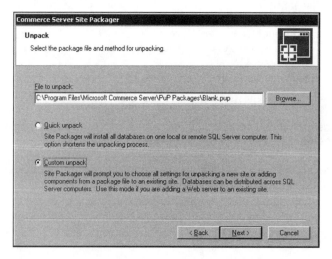

To install the Blank Solution Site you must specify the location of Blank.pup. You then have two more options:

❏   Quick unpack – this option automatically creates the appropriate databases and ASP files for a new Solution Site. The configuration settings used are identical to the defaults used by the Custom unpack process.

❏   Custom unpack – this option will likewise create a new site, but can also be used to add components to an existing site. Either way, it allows you to exercise a greater degree of control over the processes involved in setting up the site.

As we are creating the Blank Solution Site from scratch, and want to create all new components, we could choose either option. In order to follow the separate stages of the process, select the Custom unpack option and click Next to continue.

1.   Custom unpack gives you four options to choose from – since you are creating a new site, choose the first: Create a new site. This will create the appropriate components in your new site based on information contained in Blank.pup. Click Next to continue.

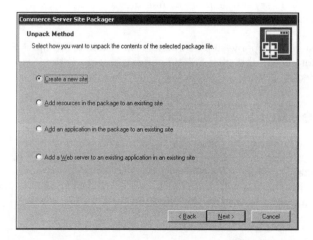

2. Type a name for your site in the Site Name text box. Click Next to continue.

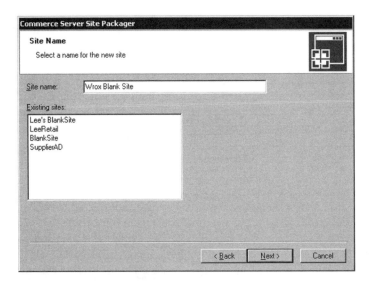

3. The next screen allows you to select which resources to unpack into the new site. All resources contained in the .pup file being unpacked are displayed in the list box on the right; any resources your site will not require can be deselected here. For demonstration purposes, we accept the default, and install all of the resources. Click Next to continue.

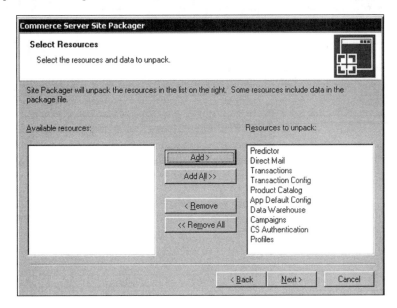

4. You may want your new website to share an existing resource's data store – if so, you can specify this resource in the Existing global resources drop-down list. In this case, there are no existing global resources we wish to access, so we select Add new global resource.

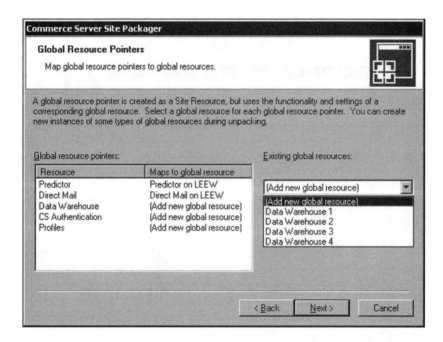

5. You can now specify connection strings for the SQL database resources that your site will be using. Click Next to continue.

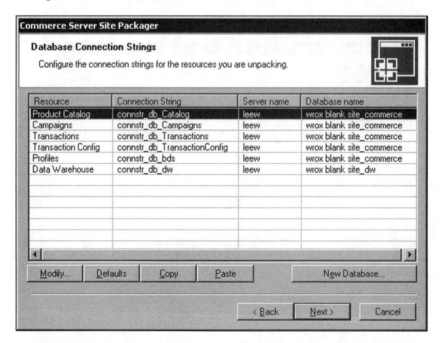

6. The database resources specified in the previous step will be created as new resources on the **master database** located on the specified server, in this case LEEW. Enter the correct username and password for the master database and click OK to continue.

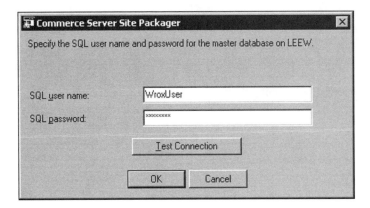

7. You can now select the applications contained in `Blank.pup` that you want to install to your new website. Select both the **BlankSite** and **BlankBizDesk** applications and click **Next** to continue.

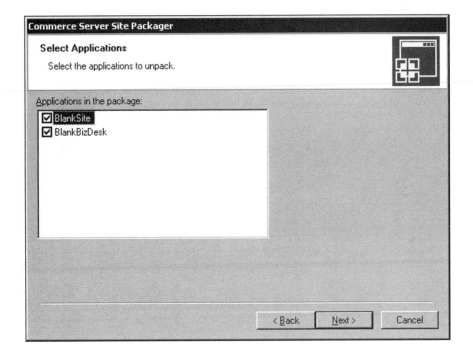

8. You can now select the **IIS Websites and Virtual Directories** in which the new website and Business Desk will be created. Click **Next** to continue.

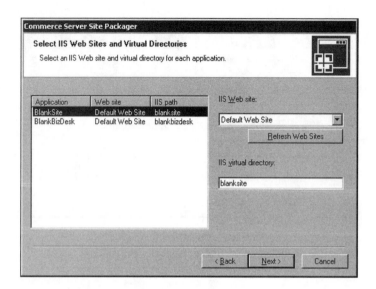

9. Commerce Server Site Packager now has the information it needs to unpack the `.pup` file and create your new web applications. The following status screen will inform you of the Site Packager's progress.

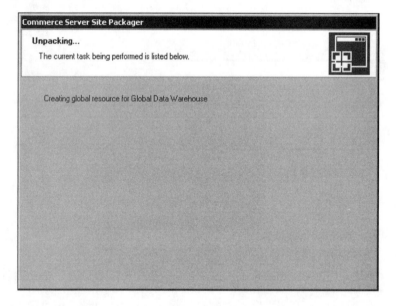

10. When the main installation completes you will be prompted to enter Data Warehouse information. Specify a name for the Data Warehouse, the name of the SQL Server machine it resides on, and the database name.

Bear in mind that while for evaluation purposes your Data Warehouse can reside on the same server as your website, in a production environment your Data Warehouse should reside on its own server.

If you are not planning to use Data Warehousing on your site select Skip Resource, otherwise click OK.

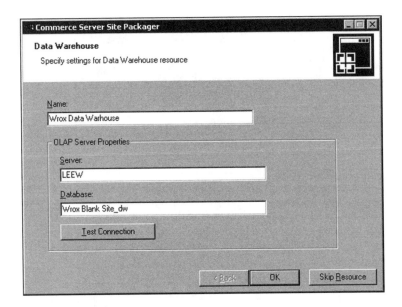

11. If you intend to use Profiling on your site (and you really should on an e-commerce site, as it allows you to track users) specify the locations where the XML initialization files can be located and click Next to continue. Alternatively, click the Skip Resource button to bypass the Profiling option.

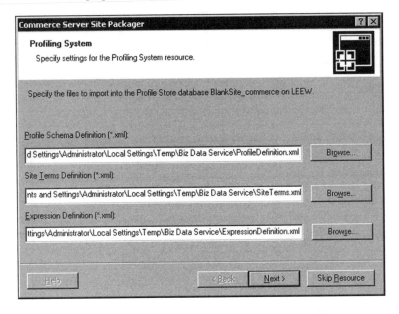

12. Since we have chosen to install the Profiling System we must now verify the connection string and the location of the data definition and population scripts. Enter the names of the server and database together with the appropriate username and password. The Site Packager will default the Server and Database names to those that you specified in step 10 above. Click OK to continue.

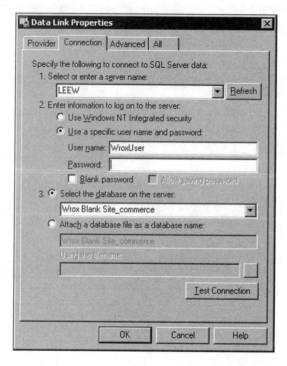

13. After installation is complete we are presented with a results screen showing the database and IIS applications that were created from the package file. If any errors occurred during installation the log file could be instrumental in helping you trouble shoot, click View Log File to access it.

To see the finished work of the Site Packager click View Selected Application and it will open a browser window to the default start page of your blanksite or blankbizdesk (depending on which was highlighted). Click Finish to complete the setup program.

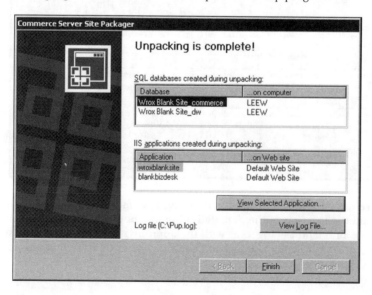

Installing the Business Desk Client

The Business Desk (BizDesk) Client is an administration tool that allows managers to remotely monitor the site and also configure the site's content and business logic. It allows remote management of campaigns, user profiles, catalog maintenance, and the fine-tuning of order processes.

The following steps show how the BizDesk Client is installed.

1. Start up IE5.5 and enter the URL of the relevant BizDesk – for the blank site, the default will be http://*<hostname>*/blankdesk.

2. If the Business Desk client hasn't been previously installed on the local machine, the installation will begin by prompting us for a location in which to store required files:

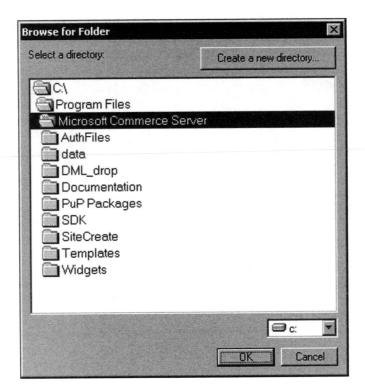

3. BizDesk installation now proceeds with the browser displaying information on its progress. Once the installation is complete the progress box will display a link to the Business Desk, as shown below. Shortcuts will also be placed on the client desktop as well as in the Start menu.

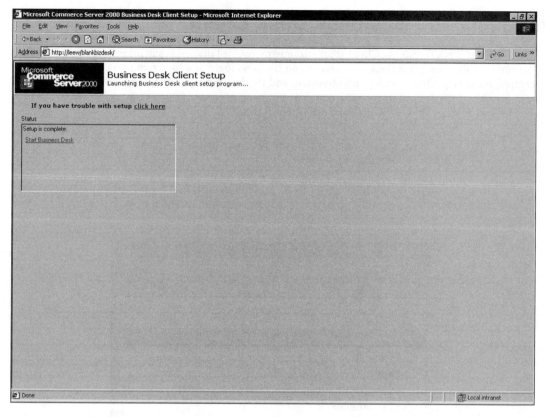

The BizDesk client must be installed on every machine that needs access to the business desk interface. A single computer can run multiple clients simultaneously, as long as they administer different websites.

Using the BizDesk Client over Wide Area Network (WAN) links can consume a lot of bandwidth and significantly degrade system performance. A better alternative is to use Windows 2000 Terminal Services to access a Business Desk Client located on the server. Terminal Services can also overcome reported conflicts caused by using the BizDesk Client across some firewalls.

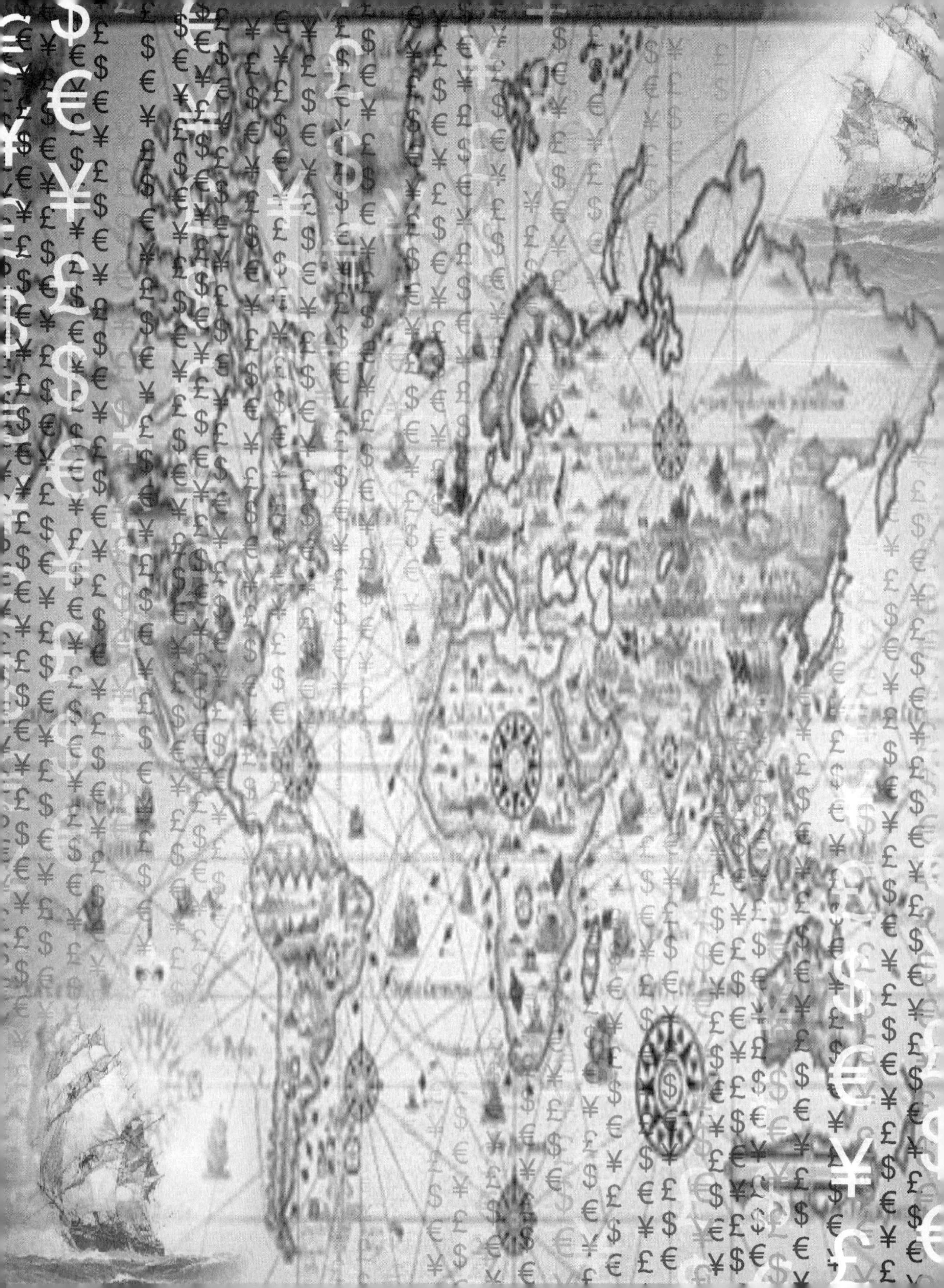

CS2K: COM Quick Reference

If you haven't already figured out how big this product is, then dig into this reference. Compared to the object model of Site Server 3.0 Commerce Edition, this reference morphs its size weighing in at 60+ pages compared to the 9 pages of the SSCE 3.0 COM reference. Yes, with power comes complexity, but we all know how hard it was trying to develop our own objects to accomplish what was necessary to compete with the other commerce sites out there. CS2K has given us the power and the ammo to destroy the competition. The objects below are briefly outlined and will not contain exhaustive information; however, this tool, I am sure, will be invaluable to you as you embark on building the next generation of Microsoft Commerce sites. This reference is dedicated to your success.

Objects Covered in this Reference:

- ❏ Backward Compatibility Objects
- ❏ General Purpose Objects
- ❏ Business Process Objects
- ❏ Configuration Objects
- ❏ Content Selection Objects
- ❏ Display Objects
- ❏ Expression Objects
- ❏ List Management Objects
- ❏ Pipeline Objects
- ❏ Prediction Objects
- ❏ Product Catalog Objects

- ❏ Profile Objects
- ❏ Reporting Objects
- ❏ Site Security Objects

Backward Compatibility Objects

These objects enable backwards compatibility with Site Server 3.0 Commerce Edition. The objects are not to be used with Commerce Server 2000 (CS2K). These objects are useful if you are still supporting SSCE sites that need to migrate to Commerce Server 2000. The objects listed under this category are for that purpose only and this section was not written to exemplify CS2K matching objects. The reason for this is that in most cases there are no direct equivalents due to the increase in extensibility, flexibility and functionality of CS2K.

Please note that these objects will not be supported in future releases of Commerce Server 2000.

AdminSite

This object allows centralized access to Site Server 3.0 Commerce Edition (SSCE 3.0) for the purpose of maintaining and configuring the site. It can be found in the **AdminLib** type library (`mscsadmin.dll`).

Member	Method/Property	Type	Description
Directory	Property	STRING	Read/write – Contains the Location of the SSCE 3.0 physical directory
Status	Property	VARIANT	Read/write – Contains the open/closed status of SSCE 3.0
Version	Property	LONG	Read Only – Contains the SSCE 3.0 version number
Create	Method	-	Creates a new SSCE 3.0 Site
Delete	Method	-	Deletes an SSCE 3.0 Site
Initialize	Method	-	Initializes an instance of the AdminSite object to load SSCE 3.0 related information
InitializeFromMDPath	Method	-	Initializes an instance of the AdminSite object using an IIS metabase path

Member	Method/Property	Type	Description
ISValidName	Method	-	Determines whether a given text string is a valid short name for an SSCE 3.0 site. Returns True or False.
ReadDefaultProperties	Method	-	Returns a Dictionary object containing properties from the Site.csc file.
ReadManagerProperties	Method	-	Returns a Dictionary object containing properties from the Site\Manager\Config\Site.csc file.
Reload	Method	-	Resets all session and application objects for a SSCE 3.0 site.
WriteDefaultProperties	Method	-	Writes properties from the chosen site Dictionary to the Site.csc file.
WriteManagerProperties	Method	-	Same as WriteManagerProperties, but writes properties from the chosen site Dictionary to the Site\Manager\Config\Site.csc file.

Example:

```
AdminSite.Create ("1", szSite, NULL, szSiteRoot, true, true)
```

StandardSManager

This object allows the run time creation and retrieval of user (shopper) IDs. The new AuthManager object has replaced this object. It can be found in the **COMMERCELib** type library (Commerce.dll).

Member	Method/Property	Type	Description
Mode	Property	INTEGER	Determines how the GetShopperID and PutShopperID methods of the Page object retrieve and store user/shopper IDs
CreateShopperID	Method	-	Creates a unique Shopper ID

Table continued on following page

Member	Method/Property	Type	Description
GetShopperID	Method	-	Retrieves the unique Shopper ID for the current user
InitManager	Method	-	Initializes the StandardSManager object
PutShopperID	Method	-	Saves the Shopper ID to maintain session state for the current user

Example:

```
oStdSManager.InitManager("mySiteName", "Cookie")
```

Page

This object provides validation and formatting methods that make forms processing easier using Active Server Pages. The formatting methods include Encode, Option and Check. The validation methods begin with Request. These methods retrieve values from a URL query string, then convert the values to given data types based on an application local value, and then validate these against a specified range. The AuthManager and AppFramework object are new objects that replace similar functionality. See these objects for more details under *Display Objects* and *Site Security Objects* later in this reference..

Member	Method/Property	Type	Description
Context	Property	IDispatch	Read Only – a value that contains the IIS scripting Context.
Check	Method	-	Creates an HTML check box Control.
Encode	Method	-	Encodes (ASCII) text in HTML.
GetShopperID	Method	-	Retrieves the unique Shopper ID for the current shopper.
HTMLEncode	Method	-	Encodes (ASCII) text in HTML. This member performs the same function as Encode, but is included for backwards compatibility with SSCE code.
Option	Method	-	Creates an option item in HTML.

Member	Method/Property	Type	Description
ProcessVerifyWith	Method	-	Posts contents of hidden fields from a shopping cart order and writes the values into a `Dictionary` object called _verify_with which is stored in the `Orderform` object.
PutShopperID	Method	-	Saves the shopper ID in a cookie or a URL to maintain session for the user.
RequestDate	Method	-	Retrieves a variable from a URL query string or FORM POST variable that will convert it to a date value (Date Variant) based on the specified date range or default values.
RequestDateTime	Method	-	Same as `RequestDate` except it will convert it to a date/time value.
RequestDefault	Method	-	Retrieves a value from a URL query string or FORM POST variable and returns the value as a string.
RequestFloat	Method	-	Retrieves a value from a URL query string or FORM POST variable and returns the value as a floating-point value. It also checks the number against a specified range.
RequestMoneyAsNumber	Method	-	Retrieves a value from a URL query string or FORM POST variable and returns the value as a money value.
RequestNumber	Method	-	Retrieves a value from a URL query string or FORM POST variable and returns the value as a number value.

Table continued on following page

Member	Method/Property	Type	Description
RequestString	Method	-	Retrieves a value from a URL query string or FORM POST variable and returns the value as a string value.
RequestTime	Method	-	Same as RequestDate except it will convert it to a time value.
SiteRoot	Method	-	Retrieves the Commerce Server 2000 physical site directory.
SURL	Method	-	Constructs a secure URL which will sometimes include the Shopper ID.
SURLPrefix	Method	-	Retrieves a secure root domain.
URL	Method	-	Constructs a URL which can include arguments.
URLArgs	Method	-	Generates query string Arguments for passing in a URL.
URLEncode	Method	-	Encodes (ASCII) text to be suitable for query string usage.
URLPrefix	Method	-	Retrieves the (non-secure root domain) prefix to build a URL.
URLShopperArgs	Method	-	Returns a URL with the Shopper ID for the current user in the query parameter.
VerifyWith	Method	-	Sends outputs that contain verification values to the page's hidden fields.
VirtualDirectory	Method	-	Returns the name of the virtual directory for the site.

Example:

```
<INPUT TYPE="RADIO" NAME="CONTROL1" VALUE="0"<% = _
    oPage.Check(my_color="Red")%>>Red
```

General Purpose Objects

These objects are commonly used for general uses throughout Commerce Server 2000. It will be important to get familiar with these objects.

AdminEventLog

Use this object to write error, informational, and warning messages to the event log. It can be found in the AdminLib type library (mscsadmin.dll).

Member	Method/Property	Description
Initialize	Method	Initializes the site, the source, and the event server for writing events.
WriteErrorEvent	Method	Writes error messages (such as resource problems, missing files, and so on) to the Commerce Server event log.
WriteInformationalEvent	Method	Writes informational messages (such as names of logged-on users) to the Commerce Server event log.
WriteWarningEvent	Method	Writes warning messages (such as low memory levels) to the Commerce Server event log.

Example:

```
oAdminEventLog.WriteWarningEvent("MySite", "Low Disk Space")
```

AdminFiles

This object is used for read-only access to server-side files. Different methods are provided to access binary and text files, respectively. It can be found in the **AdminLib** type library (`mscsadmin.dll`).

Member	Method/Property	Description
ReadFromBinaryFile	Method	Reads the content of the specified binary file.
ReadFromFile	Method	Reads the content of the specified text file.

Example:

```
sFileContents = oFile.ReadFromFile("c:\temp\newfile.asp")
```

CacheManager

This object is used to establish and use a collection of data caches. Each data cache is either a `Dictionary` object or an `LRUCache` object. You can specify which one you would like to use by setting the `CacheObjectProgID` property. It can be found in the **CacheCompLib** type library (`mscscache.dll`).

Member	Method/Property	Type	Description
AppUrl	Property	STRING	Read/Write – Stores the full Uniform Resource Locator (URL) of the application.
CacheObjectProgId	Property	STRING	Read/Write – Stores the Programmatic Identifier (ProgID) for the object that is to be used for cache functions internally within the `CacheManager` object. Determines the type of object returned by the `GetCache` method.
LoaderConfig	Property	IDispatch	Read/Write – Stores the configuration `Dictionary` object that should be passed to the Loader component.
LoaderProgId	Property	STRING	Read/Write – Stores the ProgID of the component used to create and populate a data cache.
RefreshInterval	Property	LONG	Read/Write – Stores the number of seconds between automatic cache refresh operations.
RetryInterval	Property	LONG	Read/Write – Stores the number of seconds to wait before retrying after a cache load has failed.
WriterConfig	Property	IDispatch	Read/Write – Stores the configuration `Dictionary` object that should be passed to the Writer component.
WriterProgId	Property	STRING	Read/Write – Stores the ProgID of the component used to write out some type of data that has been accumulated since the last refresh. Advertising event data is one example of the type of data that might be accumulated.
GetCache	Method	-	Retrieves the data cache `Dictionary` object associated with a specified data cache name.
RefreshCache	Method	-	Forces an immediate, synchronous refresh of the cache.

Example:

```
Set oMyCache = myCacheManager.GetCache(strMyCacheName)
```

DBStorage

This object is used to map `Dictionary` and `SimpleList` objects to and from the database, primarily for the storage of receipt and order information. The `DBStorage` object is created as needed on each page. It can be found in the **COMMERCELib** type library (`Commerce.dll`).

Member	Method/Property	Type	Description
Mapping	Property	OBJECT	Read/Write – Use this method to map `Dictionary` and `SimpleList` objects to and from the database, primarily for the storage of receipt and order information. The `DBStorage` object is created as needed on each page.
CommitData	Method	-	Updates one or more records in the database storage.
DeleteData	Method	-	Deletes a row from the database storage, based on the data stored in a `Dictionary` or `OrderForm` object.
DeleteDataKey	Method	-	Deletes a row of data from the database storage, based on the specified key.
GetData	Method	-	Retrieves a row of data from the database storage, based on a specified key value.
InitStorage	Method	-	Initializes the object. This method must be called prior to calling any other `DBStorage` method.
InsertData	Method	-	Inserts the specified data into the database storage.
LookupData	Method	-	Retrieves a single row from the database storage, based on the specified column names and values.
LookupMultipleData	Method	-	Retrieves multiple results from the database storage.
ProcessData	Method	-	Unpacks the data stored in the MarshalColumn column for a given row, and returns the resulting row in a `Dictionary` object.

Example:

```
Order.order_id = "Order_tmp"
VtVar = OrderFormStorage.GetData(Null, Order.order_id)
```

Dictionary

This object is used to support the creation, storage, and retrieval of name/value pairs in memory. Every value in a Dictionary object is a Variant, which means you can create a Dictionary object that consists of almost any kind of value (including other Dictionary objects), and that you can store any combination of Variant types in the same Dictionary object.

Member	Method/ Property	Type	Description
Count	Property	LONG	Read Only – Returns the number of elements in the Dictionary object.
Prefix	Property	STRING	Read/Write – Stores the string that acts as a filter when the contents of the Dictionary object are saved (usually to a database). When the name of a name/value pair begins with the specified prefix, that name/value pair is not saved.
Value	Property	VARIANT	Read/Write – Stores the value of a given Dictionary key.

Example:

```
Set dictUser = Server.CreateObject("Commerce.Dictionary")
dictUser.first_name = "Joey"
my_first_name = dictUser.first_name
my_first_name = dictUser.Value("first_name")

' Get the key names
For Each element In dictUser
    Response.Write element
Next

' Get the values
For Each element In dictUser
    Response.Write dictUser.Value(element)
Next
```

DictionaryXMLTransforms

Use this object to transform data from a Dictionary object into Extensible Markup Language (XML) and vice-versa, using a specified XML Data Reduced (XDR) schema. It can be found in the CS_DictXMLXfrmsLib type library (DictionaryXMLTransforms.dll).

Member	Method/ Property	Description
GenerateSampleXMLInstanceFromDictionary	Method	Produces an XML instance based on the specified Dictionary object.
GenerateXMLForDictionaryUsingSchema	Method	Extracts an XML instance from the specified Dictionary object that conforms to the specified schema.
GetXMLFromFile	Method	Generates an XML Document Object Model (DOM) document from the specified file.
ReconstructDictionaryFromXML	Method	Transforms the specified XML instance (which must comply with the specified schema) into a Dictionary object.

Example:

```
' oXMLDOMDocument is a XMLDOMDocument object
oXMLDOMDocument = oDictionaryXMLTransforms.GetXMLFromFile("sMyFileName.txt")
```

GenID

Use this object to generate globally unique identifiers (GUID), or to create and maintain multiple, global sequential counters that are persisted in a database. A global counter is one that can work across multiple computers. It can be found in the **GENIDLib** type library (GenID.dll).

Member	Method/Property	Description
GenBase5GUIDString	Method	Generates a base5 GUID string.
GenGUIDString	Method	Generates a GUID string.
GetCounterValue	Method	Retrieves the value of the specified counter and then increments the counter.
Initialize	Method	Connects the GenID object to the database that stores the table of counters.
InitializeCounter	Method	Initializes a new counter or resets an existing counter.

Note: A base5 GUID is used to store a slightly more compact version of the traditional GUID. The 128 binary digits are divided into groups of 5 instead of 4 with each group represented by the characters 0-9, and 22 characters of the alphabet. This results in a 26-digit representation for the GUID rather than the customary 32-digit representation.

Example:

```
sCounterValue = oGenID.GetCounterValue("OrderIDCounter", 4)
```

LRUCache

This object is used to support the creation, storage, and retrieval of name/value pairs, referred to as elements, from a cache in memory. The LRUCache object functions similarly to the Dictionary object, except that it only stores a limited number of elements, and internally ranks them according to use. When the cache is full and a new element needs to be added, the least recently used element is removed from the cache to make room for the new element. It can be found in the **CacheCompLib** type library (mscscache.dll).

Member	Method/Property	Description
Flush	Method	Removes an element from the cache.
FlushAll	Method	Removes all elements from the cache.
Insert	Method	Inserts an element into the cache.
Lookup	Method	Returns the value of an element in the cache when given the name of the element.
LookupObject	Method	Returns an object in the cache when given the name of the object.
SetSize	Method	Sets the maximum size of the cache.

Example:

```
oLRUCache.Insert("ManufacturerAd", vManAd)
```

SimpleList

Use this object to create an array of variants that supports enumeration. It can be found in the MSCSCoreLib type library.

Member	Method/Property	Type	Description
Count	Property	LONG	Read Only – Stores the number of elements in the SimpleList object.
Item	Property	VARIANT	Read/Write – Stores an element of the SimpleList object.

Member	Method/Property	Type	Description
Add	Method	-	Adds the specified item to a `SimpleList` object.
Delete	Method	-	Deletes a specified item from the `SimpleList` object.

Example:

```
oSimpleList.Add("Hello Universe")
```

Business Process Objects

These objects are used for standard business processing including orders, shipping and auctions. These objects are centered on the management of baskets, templates and submitted orders. You will mainly use them for order creation, order storage and order searches on the database.

Auction

This great new object allows for the creation of an eBay-style site. With this object, you can auction products, accept bids, qualify winners and set up rules of engagement, to name a few. It can be found in the CS_Auction type library (`auction.dll`).

Member	Method/Property	Type	Description
AuctionID	Property	STRING	Read Only – Stores the Auction ID (GUID) Globally Unique Identifier
dtAMT	Property	DATE	Read/Write – Stores date/time by the auction engine
objMessageManager	Property	OBJECT	Read/Write – Stores the `MessageManager` object that is used in generating error messages
szBidOrderBy	Property	STRING	Read/Write – Stores the sort string that is used in resolving ties (Bidders of the same amount)
szBidTableName	Property	STRING	Read/Write – Stores the name of the Bid table in the database

Table continued on following page

Member	Method/Property	Type	Description
szDSN	Property	STRING	Read/Write – Stores the DSN connection string for the database
szItemTableName	Property	STRING	Read/Write – Stores the name of the Item table in the database
szLanguage	Property	STRING	Read/Write – Stores the language used by the MessageManager object when generating error messages to the client
AuctionAddBid	Method	-	Adds or updates a bid
AuctionAddItem	Method	-	Adds a new item to the auction
AuctionBidNormalize	Method	-	Normalizes a bid to the bid increment amount
AuctionDeleteBid	Method	-	Deletes a bid
AuctionDeleteBids	Method	-	Deletes all bids
AuctionDeleteItem	Method	-	Deletes items and all bids on the item
AuctionGetBid	Method	-	Returns a rowset of data containing a bid from a specified user for a specified auction
AuctionGetBids	Method	-	Returns a rowset containing all bids
AuctionGetItem	Method	-	Returns a rowset for the item up for bid
AuctionGetStatus	Method	-	Returns a Dictionary object for the item up for bid
AuctionInit	Method	-	Initializes the Auction object
AuctionRandomBids	Method	-	Adds random bids for testing purposes
AuctionResolve	Method	-	Based on current rules and settings, this object resolves the outcome of the auction
AuctionUpdateItem	Method	-	Updates an auction item

Example:

```
lNumErrStrings = oAuction.AuctionAddBid(szAuctionID, _
   "Bidder65432", szBidName, "JayH123456@injoy.com", 25.00, _
   5, FALSE, 19.99, oErrorList, TRUE)
```

OrderForm

This object provides the in-memory storage of the user and his/her purchase information. The object will store, using SimpleList and Dictionary objects, items the user has chosen to purchase as well as purchase history. It can be found in the **MSCSCoreLib** type library.

Member	Method/Property	Description
AddItem	Method	Adds items to the items collection
ClearItems	Method	Clears the items collection
ClearOrderFrom	Method	Clears the OrderForm object

Example:

```
Order.AddItem("SKUnumber", 5,0)
```

OrderGroup

This object is used to access, capture, and compute shopping basket information. This object works in conjunction with OrderGroupManager as shown below. It can be found in the **CS_Req** type library (requisition.dll).

Member	Method/Property	Type	Description
LogFile	Property	STRING	Read/Write – Log file name for pipeline runs
SavePrefix	Property	STRING	Specifies a prefix for the prevention of an entry being saved to the database
Value	Property	VARIANT	Read Only – Returns OrderGroup object attributes
AddItem	Method	-	Adds item to the Orderform Object
AddItemsFromTemplate	Method	-	Adds line items associated with an on-disk OrderGroup to the current OrderGroup object

Table continued on following page

Member	Method/ Property	Type	Description
AddOrderForm	Method	-	Adds an Orderform object and contents to the OrderGroup object.
AddXMLAsOrderForm	Method	-	Converts XML to an Orderform object and adds it to the OrderGroup object.
AggregrateOrderFormValues	Method	-	Iterates across all OrderForm objects, computes a total of the specified key, then stores the total at the OrderGroup level.
Clear	Method	-	Clears the OrderGroup object of all OrderForm objects.
GetAddress	Method	-	Gets the specified address dictionary object.
GetItemInfo	Method	-	Gets a reference to the line item dictionary from the specified OrderForm at the specified index.
GetOrderFormAsXML	Method	-	Converts an OrderForm object into an XML string.
GetOrderFormValue	Method	-	Gets the OrderForm value specified by the supplied OrderForm key.
Initialize	Method	-	Initializes the OrderGroup object.
LoadOrder	Method	-	Loads the specified OrderGroup from the database.
LoadTemplate	Method	-	Loads the specified template from the database.
LoadBasket	Method	-	Loads the basket for the current user from the database.

Member	Method/ Property	Type	Description
PurgeUnreferencedAddresses	Method	-	Removes all addresses in the OrderGroup object that are not being referenced by any line item shipping address.
PutItemValue	Method	-	Puts the specified values into the specified keys of the line item.
PutOrderFormValue	Method	-	Puts the specified values into the specified keys of the OrderForm object.
RemoveItem	Method	-	Removes a line item from the specified OrderForm object. The item index specified indicates which line item to remove.
RemoveOrderForm	Method	-	Removes the specified OrderForm object from the OrderGroup object.
RunPipe	Method	-	Runs the Pipeline Component File on each OrderForm object in the OrderGroup object.
SaveAsBasket	Method	-	Saves the OrderGroup object to the database with a basket status.
SaveAsOrder	Method	-	Saves the OrderGroup object to the database with an order status.
SaveAsTemplate	Method	-	Saves the OrderGroup object to the database with a template status.
SetAddress	Method	-	Sets the OrderGroup object address dictionary values as specified by the address dictionary object supplied.
SetAddressFromFields	Method	-	Sets the OrderGroup object address dictionary values as specified by the fields object supplied.

Table continued on following page

Member	Method/ Property	Type	Description
SetShippingAddress	Method	-	Sets the shipping address to that referenced by the database address ID supplied.

Example:

```
lLineItemIndex = oOrderGroup.AddItem(dDict, sMyOrder)
```

OrderGroupManager

This object is used to mange the OrderGroups object. The great thing about this object is that it allows you to search orders, and/or baskets without SQL queries. It can be found in the CS_Req type library (requisition.dll).

Member	Method/ Property	Type	Description
OrderFormHeaderColumns	Property	STRING	Read Only – Returns a string of comma-separated OrderFormHeader table column names.
OrderFormLineItemsColumns	Property	STRING	Read Only – Returns a string of comma-separated OrderFormLineItems table column names.
OrderGroupColumns	Property	STRING	Read Only – Returns a string of comma-separated OrderGroup table column names.
DeleteOrderGroupFromDisk	Method	-	Checks whether a connection to the database has been established for the specified OrderGroup then deletes the OrderGroup and all objects contained within it from the database.
Find	Method	-	Performs a SQL search based on the specified SQL clause fragments.
FindTemplatesForUser	Method	-	Finds an ADO recordset of OrderGroup templates for the specified user. Returns an ADO recordset of the search results.

Member	Method/Property	Type	Description
Initialize	Method	-	Creates a connection to the specified database.
SimpleDelete	Method	-	Deletes all entries that meet the search criteria as specified by the supplied SimpleFindSearchInfo and SimpleFindResultInfo objects.
SimpleFind	Method	-	Returns an ADO recordset (ADODB.Recordset) of OrderGroup items based on the specified SimpleFindSearchInfo values and SimpleFindResultInfo values. These object values contain the search criteria.

Example:

```
vRecordset = oOrderGroupManager.Find(vOrderGroupCriteriaArray, _
    vOrderFormCriteriaArray, vLineItemCriteriaArray)
```

Shipping

This object with only one method allows you to preview a cost of shipping for each method and shipment. It can be found in the **CS_ShipMgr** type library (shipmgr.dll).

Member	Method/Property	Description
PreviewShipments	Method	Provides a shipping cost preview for each shipment and method

Example:

```
slShipments = oShip.PreviewShipments(dOrder, dContext, Distinguishers)
```

ShippingMethodManager

This object is the master shipment methods tool. It allows you to configure various aspects of shipping including description, availability and configuration. It can be found in the **CS_ShipMgr** type library (shipmgr.dll).

Member	Method/Property	Description
CreateMethodInstance	Method	Creates an empty instance of a shipping method.
DeleteMethodInstance	Method	Deletes the current shipping method instance.

Table continued on following page

Member	Method/Property	Description
GetComponentConfig	Method	Retrieves the `Configuration` dictionary for the shipping component, which implements the current shipping method.
GetInstalledMethodList	Method	Returns a recordset containing the current shipping methods.
GetMethodInfo	Method	Returns a recordset containing information about the loaded shipping method.
Initialize	Method	Initializes the `ShippingMethodManager` object and connects it to a database.
LoadMethodInstance	Method	Loads a given shipping method to be manipulated by other methods.
SaveMethodConfig	Method	Saves information about the current method.
SetCachableComponentConfig	Method	Saves configuration and other component information for a component.
SetMethodConfig	Method	Sets pairs of names and values for the current method.

Example:

```
Set rsResult = oSMM.GetMethodInfo(Array("shipping_method_name", _ "description",
"enabled"))
```

SimpleFindResultInfo

This object is used to define search criteria when using the `SimpleFind` and `SimpleDelete` methods of the `OrderGroupManager` object. It can be found in the **CS_Req** type library (`requisition.dll`).

Member	Method/Property	Type	Description
Columns	Property	VARIANT	Specifies a custom set of columns to be returned by the `OrderGroupManager` `SimpleFind` method.
JoinLineItemInfo	Property	BOOLEAN	Specifies whether to join the OrderFormLineItems table with the results.

Member	Method/ Property	Type	Description
JoinOrderFormInfo	Property	BOOLEAN	Specifies whether the OrderFormHeader table is joined in the results.
OrderGroupSortColumn	Property	VARIANT	Specifies the column name to sort on.
PageNumber	Property	LONG	Specifies the page number of the resultset to show if the resultset exceeds the PageSize.
PageSize	Property	LONG	Specifies the page size.
SortDirection	Property	VARIANT	Specifies the sort direction.

Example:

```
Dim oSFResult
Set osfResult =Server.CreateObject("Commerce.SimpleFindResultInfo")
oSFResult.JoinLineItemInfo = True
oSFResult.JoinOrderFormInfo = True
```

SimpleFindSearchInfo

This object is used to specify search criteria when conducting searching and deleting operations using the SimpleFind and SimpleDelete methods of the OrderGroupManager object. It can be found in the **CS_Req** type library (requisition.dll).

Member	Method/ Property	Type	Description
Description	Property	VARIANT	Read/Write – Specifies the product description to search for; if left null, the product description does not become part of the search criteria.
Order_number	Property	VARIANT	Read/Write – Specifies the order number to search for; if left null, the order number does not become part of the search criteria.
Ordergroup_id	Property	VARIANT	Read/Write – Specifies the OrderGroup ID to search for; if left null, the OrderGroup ID does not become part of the search criteria.

Table continued on following page

Member	Method/ Property	Type	Description
Po_number	Property	VARIANT	Read/Write – Specifies the OrderForm ID to search for; if left null, the OrderForm ID does not become part of the search criteria.
Product_id	Property	VARIANT	Read/Write – Specifies the product ID to search for; if left null, the product ID does not become part of the search criteria.
SearchDateTimeColumn	Property	VARIANT	Read/Write – Specifies the DateTime column name to search for; if left null, the DateTime column name does not become part of the search criteria.
SearchDateTimeEnd	Property	VARIANT	Read/Write – Specifies the DateTime end value to search for; if left null, the DateTime end value does not become part of the search criteria.
SearchDateTimeStart	Property	VARIANT	Read/Write – Specifies the DateTime start value to search for; if left null, the DateTime start value does not become part of the search criteria.
StatusFilter	Property	LONG	Read/Write – Specifies the OrderGroup status. This property allows the user to filter the status (ie basket, template or new order).
User_firstname	Property	VARIANT	Read/Write – Specifies the first name of the user to search for; if left null, the first name of the user does not become part of the search criteria.
User_id	Property	VARIANT	Read/Write – Specifies the user ID to search for; if left null, the user ID does not become part of the search criteria.
User_lastname	Property	VARIANT	Read/Write – Specifies the last name of the user to search for; if left null, the last name of the user does not become part of the search criteria.

Member	Method/ Property	Type	Description
User_org_id	Property	VARIANT	Read/Write – Specifies the user organization ID to search for; if left null, the user organization ID does not become part of the search criteria.
User_org_name	Property	VARIANT	Read/Write – Specifies the user organization to search for; if left null, the user organization does not become part of the search criteria.

Example:

```
Dim oSFSearch, sReqID
Set oSFSearch = Server.CreateObject("Commerce.SimpleFindSearchInfo")
sReqID ="754C40C6-EAA9-454C-A8AB-02789FBE0FB9"
oSFSearch.ordergroup_id = sReqID
```

Configuration Objects

These objects are for the configuration management of Commerce Server 2000 websites.

AdminWebServer

This object will retrieve all websites and Commerce sites for any specified web server. It can be found in the AdminLib type library (mscsadmin.dll).

Member	Method/Property	Description
GetCommerceSites	Method	Based on an instance of a Website, this will gather all SSCE 3.0 sites.
GetWebSiteProperties	Method	Based on an instance of a Website, this will return properties of the site.
GetWebSites	Method	This will enumerate ALL Websites.

Example:

```
Set objWebServer = CreateObject("Commerce.AdminWebserver")
' Get Web sites
WebSites = objWebServer.GetWebSites
```

AppCfg

This object is used to retrieve settings from the configuration store including the names and codes of various countries and regions. It can be found in the **APPHELPERLib** type library (`AppHelper.dll`).

Member	Method/ Property	Description
DecodeStatusCode	Method	Decodes the specified status code.
GetCountryCodeFromCountryName	Method	Returns the country code for the specified country name.
GetCountryNameFromCountryCode	Method	Returns the country name for the specified country code.
GetCountryNamesList	Method	Returns an alphabetical list of country names.
GetOptionsDictionary	Method	Returns a `Dictionary` object that maps site configuration keys to site configuration values.
GetRegionCodeFromCountryCodeAndRegionName	Method	Returns the region code for the specified country code and region name.
GetRegionNameFromCountryCodeAndRegionCode	Method	Returns the region name for the specified country code and region code.
GetRegionNamesListFromCountryCode	Method	Returns an alphabetical list of region names for the specified country code.
Initialize	Method	Initializes the `AppConfig` object.
RefreshCache	Method	Refreshes the `AppConfig` object cache.

Example:

```
Set dictConfig = oAppConfig.GetOptionsDictionary("")
For Each sKey In dictConfig
   Response.Write sKey & "=" & dictConfig.Value(sKey)
Next
```

GlobalConfig

This object is used to create or delete resource configuration information as well as to save any updated global configuration information to the administration database. You can also use this object to add a site. It can be found in the **CS_MSCSCfg** type library (MSCSCfg.dll).

Member	Method/ Property	Type	Description
Fields	Property	FIELDS	Read Only – Returns group-level configuration data.
CreateServiceConfig	Method	-	Creates and writes configuration information for the specified resource to the Administration database.
CreateSiteConfig	Method	-	Creates a site and returns a SiteConfig object that contains the new site's settings.
DeleteServiceConfig	Method	-	Deletes configuration information for the specified resource.
DeleteSiteConfig	Method	-	Deletes the specified configuration for the site and all configurations for the associated resources.
GetIfCollection	Method	-	Converts values read from the Fields property into appropriate objects such as a SimpleList object or a Variant Array.
GetResourcePropAttrib	Method	-	Gets a dictionary of key/value pairs that denote the attributes of the specified property of the specified resource.
Initialize	Method	-	Loads the global configuration data from the Administration database.

Table continued on following page

Member	Method/ Property	Type	Description
MakeArrayFromSimpleList	Method	-	Converts the specified SimpleList object into an Array.
MakeArrayFromString	Method	-	Converts values read from the Fields property into an Array.
MakeSimpleListFromArray	Method	-	Converts an Array into a SimpleList object.
MakeStringFromArray	Method	-	Converts an Array into an encoded string, which can be written to the Fields property.
MakeStringFromSimpleList	Method	-	Converts a SimpleList object into an encoded string, which can be written to the Fields property.
SaveConfig	Method	-	Saves the global configuration settings to the Administration database.
Sites	Method	-	Returns a list of all of the sites available in the administration data store.

Example:

```
vVariant = oGlobalConfig.GetIfCollection(vEncodedString)
```

SiteConfig

There are several uses for this object. You can use it to create or delete site configuration information, save any updated site configuration information to the Administration database, load site configuration information from the Administration database, and to import resource configuration data to a site and export resource configuration data from a site. It can be found in the **CS_MSCSCfg** type library (MSCSCfg.dll).

Member	Method/ Property	Type	Description
Fields	Property	FIELDS	Read/Write – Returns configuration fields, some of which hold configuration settings of resources.
AddRefToGroupComponent	Method	-	Adds a reference to a global resource so that a site can access that resource.

Member	Method/ Property	Type	Description
CreateComponentConfig	Method	-	Creates and writes configuration information for the specified resource to the Administration database.
DeleteComponentConfig	Method	-	Deletes configuration information for the specified resource.
DeleteSQLScript	Method	-	Deletes the specified SQL script file from the Administration database.
ExportResource	Method	-	Writes the specified resource, resource properties, and attributes to the specified file.
GetAppsInSite	Method	-	Gets a list of Commerce Server 2000 applications for the specified site.
GetResourcePropAttrib	Method	-	Gets a dictionary of key/value pairs that denote the attributes of the specified property of the specified resource.
GetSQLScript	Method	-	Gets the specified SQL script file from the Administration database.
ImportResource	Method	-	Reads the specified resource, resource properties, and attributes from the specified file, and writes them to the Commerce Server 2000 database.
Initialize	Method	-	Loads the site configuration data from the Administration database.
MakeArrayFromSimpleList	Method	-	Converts the specified SimpleList object into an Array.
MakeArrayFromString	Method	-	Converts values read from the Fields property into an Array.
MakeSimpleListFromArray	Method	-	Converts an Array into a SimpleList object.
MakeStringFromArray	Method	-	Converts an Array into an encoded string that can be written to the Fields property.

Table continued on following page

Member	Method/Property	Type	Description
MakeStringFromSimpleList	Method	-	Converts a SimpleList object into an encoded string that can be written to the Fields property.
PutSQLScript	Method	-	Puts the specified SQL script file into the Administration database.
SaveConfig	Method	-	Saves the site configuration settings to the Administration database.

Example:

```
sContents = oSiteConfig.GetSQLScript(sMyCatalog, sMySQLFileName.sql)
```

SiteConfigReadOnly

Use this object to load site configuration information from the Administration database. It can be found in the CS_MSCSCfg type library (MSCSCfg.dll).

Member	Method/Property	Type	Description
Fields	Property	FIELDS	Read Only – Returns configuration settings of the site and the site resources.
GetAppsInSite	Method	-	Gets a list of Commerce Server 2000 applications for the specified site.
GetIfCollection	Method	-	Use this method to convert values read from the Fields property, if appropriate, into either a SimpleList object or a Variant Array.
Initialize	Method	-	Loads the site configuration data from the Administration database.
MakeArrayFromSimpleList	Method	-	Converts the specified SimpleList object into an Array.
MakeArrayFromString	Method	-	Converts values read from Fields property into an Array.

Member	Method/Property	Type	Description
MakeSimpleListFromArray	Method	-	Converts an Array into a SimpleList object.
MakeStringFromArray	Method	-	Converts an Array into an encoded string, which can be written to the Fields property.
MakeStringFromSimpleList	Method	-	Converts a SimpleList object into an encoded string, which can be written to the Fields property.

Example:

```
vVariant = SiteConfigReadOnly.GetAppsInSite(sMySiteName)
```

Content Selection Objects

These objects are used to select dynamic content for page display.

ContentList

This object is used to access a particular collection of content items. The ContentList object provides combined access to the private data that it stores and to the shared data stored in the ContentListFactory object that created it. This object also flows through the Content Selection Framework (CSF) pipeline for the purpose of scoring content items. See Chapter 8 for more details and the CSP model later in this section. It can be found in the **CacheCompLib** type library (mscscache.dll).

Member	Method/ Property	Type	Description
ActiveRows	Property	IRowCollection	Read Only – The collection of rows that meet the current Threshold and RowLimit properties and that have not been filtered out of the ContentList object.
AllRows	Property	IRowCollection	Read Only – The collection of all rows in the ContentList object.
Count	Property	LONG	Read/Write – Stores the number of rows in the ContentList object.

Table continued on following page

Member	Method/ Property	Type	Description
Factory	Property	IContentListFactory	Read Only – Stores a reference to the `ContentListFactory` object that created this `ContentList` object.
Fields	Property	FIELD	Read Only – The `Fields` collection for a particular row in the `ContentList` object.
RowLimit	Property	LONG	Read/Write – Stores the maximum number of rows that can exist in the `ActiveRows` collection property.
Sorted	Property	BOOLEAN	Read/Write – Stores a flag that controls whether or not the rows in the `ActiveRows` collection property are returned sorted by score.
Threshold	Property	FLOAT	Read/Write – Stores the `Threshold` score that items must meet to be included in the `ActiveRows` collection property.
TraceMessages	Property	ISimpleList	Read Only – Stores the list of `TraceMessage` strings accumulated for a particular row in the `ContentList` object.
TraceMode	Property	BOOLEAN	Read/Write – Stores the `TraceMode` value. A value of `True` enables score tracing, a value of `False` disables it.
AdjustScore	Method	-	Adjusts the score associated with an item in the `ContentList` object by applying a multiplier.
BuildIndex	Method	-	Builds an index on all rows based on the specified column.
Filter	Method	-	Filters items in a `ContentList` object based on the specified criteria.
GetData	Method	-	Gets data from a specified row and column in a `ContentList` object in a high-performance, non-scriptable manner. *Note: This method is not usable from Microsoft Visual Basic or Microsoft Visual Basic Scripting Edition (VBScript).*

Member	Method/ Property	Type	Description
GetScore	Method	-	Gets the score of an item in a ContentList object.
Search	Method	-	Returns a collection of content items that match the search criteria.
SetData	Method	-	Sets data at a specified row and column in a ContentList object in a high-performance, non-scriptable manner. *Note: This method is not usable from Microsoft Visual Basic or Microsoft Visual Basic Scripting Edition (VBScript).*
SetScore	Method	-	Sets the score of an item in a ContentList object.

Example:

```
'myCol is a RowCollection object
Set myCol = myContentList.Search(10, "BookAds")
```

ContentListFactory

This object is used to efficiently maintain lists of content items that compete with each other to be selected for display on a Web page by a Content Selection pipeline (CSP). See Chapter 8 for more details and the CSP model later in this section. It can be found in the CacheCompLib type library (mscscache.dll).

Member	Method/ Property	Type	Description
AllRows	Property	IRowCollection	Read Only – The collection of all rows in the ContentListFactory object.
Count	Property	LONG	Read/Write – Stores the number of rows in the ContentListFactory object.
Fields	Property	FIELDS	Read Only – The Fields collection for a particular row in the ContentListFactory object.

Member	Method/Property	Type	Description
Schema	Property	IContentListSchema	Read/Write – Stores a reference to the `ContentListSchema` object used by this `ContentListFactory` object.
BuildIndex	Method	-	Builds an index on the specified column.
ConstructFromRecordSet	Method	-	Initializes a `ContentListFactory` object, and creates and initializes a new `ContentListSchema` object, from an ADO `Recordset` object. The `ContentListFactory` object is populated with the data from the `Recordset` object.
CreatNewContentList	Method	-	Creates a new `ContentList` object based on the schema in use by this `ContentListFactory` object. The new `ContentList` object has access to the shared data in the `ContentListFactory` object that created it.
GetData	Method	-	Gets data from a specified row and column in a `ContentList` object in a high-performance, non-scriptable manner. *Note: This method is not usable from Visual Basic or VBScript.*
Search	Method	-	Returns a `RowCollection` object containing the collection of content items that match the search criteria.

Member	Method/ Property	Type	Description
SetData	Method	-	Sets data at a specified row and column in a ContentListFactory object in a high-performance, non-scriptable manner. *Note: This method is not usable from Visual Basic or VBScript.*

Example:

```
Call myContentListFactory.BuildIndex("AdType")
```

ContentListSchema

This object is used to manipulate the schema for a ContentListFactory object. It can be found in the CacheCompLib type library (mscscache.dll).

Member	Method/ Property	Type	Description
ColumnFlags	Property	LONG	Read/Write – Stores the column flags, represented as a bit field.
ColumnName	Property	STRING	Read/Write – Stores the column name.
ColumnType	Property	ColumnTypeEnum	Read/Write – Stores the data type of the column.
Count	Property	LONG	Read Only – Stores the number of columns defined by the schema.
Locked	Property	BOOLEAN	Read/Write – Indicates whether this schema can be modified. It is initially set to False. Once set to True, it can never be set back to False.
Add	Method	-	Adds a new column to the schema.

Table continued on following page

Member	Method/ Property	Type	Description
FindColumn	Method	-	Returns the position of a named column. Column positions are counted starting from zero (0), not one (1). This position index may be used as the *Column* index parameter for the GetData, SetData, Filter, and Search methods of the ContentList object.
GetSchema	Method	-	Returns the entire schema in a high-performance, non-scriptable manner.
SetSchema	Method	-	Sets the entire schema in a high-performance, non-scriptable manner.

Example:

```
Dim iColumnNum As Long
iColumnNum = myContentListSchema.Add("Color", CLCOL_STRING,_ 0)
```

ContentSelector

This object is used to select one or more items of content for display on a web page. The content may come from customer campaigns (ads, discounts), or from custom applications built on the Content Selection Framework (CSF). See Chapter 8 for more details and the CSP model later in this section. It can be found in the **CSFCompLib** type library (CSFComp.dll).

Member	Method/Property	Description
GetContent	Method	Will execute a pipeline that will select content items to be stored in a SimpleList object as strings in XML or HTML format

Example:
```
<%
    Set CSO = Server.CreateObject("Commerce.ContentSelector")
    Set Ads = CSO.GetContent(Application("CSFAdsContext"))
    For Each Ad in Ads
        Response.Write(Ad)
    Next
%>
```

RowCollection

This object is used to access data contained in a ContentList object and its corresponding ContentListFactory object. Some RowCollection objects allow access to all of the rows in these objects. Other RowCollection objects allow access to a calculated subset of the rows in these objects. It can be found in the **CacheCompLib** type library (mscscache.dll).

Member	Method/Property	Type	Description
_NewEnum	Property	IUnknown	Read Only – Allows iteration through the rows in the RowCollection object using the Microsoft Visual Basic "for each *Row* in *Collection*" syntax.
Count	Property	LONG	Read Only – Stores the number of rows in the RowCollection object.
EOF	Property	VARIANT_ BOOL	Read Only – Tracks whether the *current row* is beyond the actual number of rows in the RowCollection object.
Fields	Property	FIELDS	Read Only – Contains the Fields collection object for the *current row*.
RowNum	Property	LONG	Read Only – Stores the position of the *current row*, starting from zero (0).
MoveFirst	Method	-	Sets the first row in the RowCollection object to be the *current row*.
MoveNext	Method	-	Sets the row after the *current row* in the RowCollection object to be the new *current row*.

Example:

```
'myRowCollection is a RowCollection object.
myRowCollection.MoveFirst
```

Side Reference: Content Selection Pipeline (CSP)

This pipeline is used mainly for the selection of ads and or discounts. The components in this pipeline are used to gather, filter, score, and select content.

There are seven stages to this pipeline. These stages consist of the following:

❑ Load Content Stage – Prepares for the execution of the rest of the stages in the pipeline

❑ Filter Stage – Contains components that filter or trim the content list

- ❏ Initial Score Stage – Sets an initial score for each item
- ❏ Scoring Stage – Contains components that adjust the score of each content item
- ❏ Select Stage – Contains a component to select one or more content items for return
- ❏ Record Stage – Contains components that record the selection made to the database, server logfile or history
- ❏ Format Stage – Contains components that format the selected items as HTML or XML for return to the page that executed the pipeline

Content Selection Components

It can be found in the **CSFCompLib** type library (CSFComp.dll).

Component	Stage	Description
InitCSFPipeline	Load Content	Initializes values needed in the remainder of the pipeline.
LoadHistory	Load Content	Retrieves a history string from a user profile, an item in the Active Server Pages (ASP) session collection, or a cookie.
FilterContent	Filter	Applies provided filters to the content list.
AdvertisingNeedOfDelivery	Initial Score	Scores ads so that they are selected often enough to meet business commitments.
EvalTargetGroups	Scoring	Targets particular groups for advertising, content, or discounts by evaluating a list of expressions for each item in a list and adjusting item selection.
HistoryPenalty	Scoring	Applies penalties to content items based on how recently they have been selected.
ScoreDiscounts	Scoring	Adjusts scores of discount items to promote discounts most relevant to the current user.
SelectWinners	Select	Selects items based on their final scores.
IISAppendToLog	Record	Records information about content selection, results in the QueryString field of the Internet Information Services (IIS) log file.
RecordEvent	Record	Records event delta counts for the selected content items (the winners) in the Performance dictionary. The values are used to calculate the need of delivery of an item.

Component	Stage	Description
RecordHistory	Record	Records the identifiers of the winning content items in the history list string.
SaveHistory	Record	Saves the history string in one of three locations: the user profile object, the ASP session collection, or the HTTP cookie.
FormatTemplate	Format	Merges data from selected items with their associated templates to form formatted strings. These are usually HTML strings ready for display on the page.

Example:

Since these objects are edited through the pipeline editor, no script is provided. To manipulate these objects, open the Commerce Server Pipeline editor and select the Advertising.PCF *file.*

Display Objects

These objects are used to format data for web page display. These objects are intended to simplify programming efforts for various useful functions.

AppFrameWork

This object is used to simplify forms processing using Active Server Pages. It can be found in the ASPLIBLib type library (asplib.dll).

Member	Method/Property	Description
Option	Method	Generates an option tag on a page.
RequestDate	Method	Retrieves a value from a URL query string or FORM POST variable and converts it to a Date value (Date Variant).
RequestDateTime	Method	Retrieves a value from a URL query string or FORM POST variable and converts it to a DateTime value (Date Variant).
RequestFloat	Method	Retrieves a value from a URL query string or FORM POST variable and converts it to a floating-point value.
RequestMoneyAsNumber	Method	Retrieves a value from a URL query string or FORM POST variable and converts it as money, based on the specified locale.

Table continued on following page

Member	Method/Property	Description
RequestNumber	Method	Retrieves a value from a URL query string or FORM POST variable and converts it to a number.
RequestString	Method	Retrieves a value from a URL query string or FORM POST variable and performs string processing on it.
RequestTime	Method	Retrieves a value from a URL query string or FORM POST variable and converts it to a Time value (Date Variant).
VerifyWith	Method	Generates hidden input fields that contain verification values.
VirtualDirectory	Method	Returns the name of the virtual directory for the site.

Example:

```
vString = oAppFrameWork.RequestString("String", "Default String", _
   1, 100, True, True, 0, 1033)
```

DataFunctions

This object is used to perform locale-based formatting, parsing, and value range checking in a site. This object also has a variety of methods and properties useful for site development.

Member	Method/Property	Type	Description
Locale	Property	LONG	Read/Write – Stores a number that represents the default locale to be used to format date, time, money, and number values.
CurrencySymbol	Property	VARIANT	Read/Write – Stores the currency symbol to use if no currency symbol is specified in the ConvertStringToCurrency and LocalizeCurrency methods. The default value is the system default currency symbol.

Member	Method/Property	Type	Description
CleanString	Method	-	Processes the specified string. This processing can include stripping out white spaces, modifying the case of the string, and validating that the length of the string falls within a specified range.
ConvertDateString	Method	-	Converts the specified string representation of the date to a date Variant, based on the default or specified locale.
ConvertDateTimeString	Method	-	Converts the specified string representation of the date and time to a date Variant, based on the default or specified locale.
ConvertFloatString	Method	-	Converts the specified string representation of a floating-point number to a double Variant, based on the default or specified locale.
ConvertMoneyStringToNumber	Method	-	Converts the specified string representation of a currency value to a long Variant, based on the default or specified locale.
ConvertNumberString	Method	-	Converts the specified string representation of a number to an integer Variant, based on the default or specified locale.
ConvertTimeString	Method	-	Converts the specified string representation of a time value to a date Variant, based on the default or specified locale.
Date	Method	-	Returns a string representation of a date stored in a date Variant, based on the default or specified locale.

Table continued on following page

927

Member	Method/ Property	Type	Description
DateTime	Method	-	Returns a string representation of a date and time stored in a date `Variant`, based on the default or specified locale.
Float	Method	-	Returns a string representation of a floating-point number, based on the default or specified locale.
GetLocaleInfo	Method	-	Retrieves information about the specified locale.
GetLocaleList	Method	-	Retrieves a list of installed locales.
Money	Method	-	Returns a formatted currency string, based on the default or specified locale.
Number	Method	-	Returns a string representation of a number, based on the default or specified locale.
Time	Method	-	Returns a string representation of a time stored in a date `Variant`, based on the default or specified locale.
ValidateDateTime	Method	-	Checks whether the specified string contains a valid date and/or time, and optionally checks against a specified range.
ValidateFloat	Method	-	Checks whether the specified string contains a valid floating-point number, and optionally checks the value of the number against a specified range.

Member	Method/Property	Type	Description
ValidateNumber	Method	-	Checks whether the specified string contains a valid number, and optionally checks the value of the number against a specified range.
CloneObject	Method	-	Clones a SimpleList or Dictionary object.
ConvertStringToCurrency	Method	-	Converts the specified string representation of currency value into a currency Variant.
LocalizeCurrency	Method	-	Creates a string representation of a currency value formatted to a specified locale and currency symbol.

Example:

```
strData = " Wrox Press     "
Result = MSCSDataFunctions.CleanString(strData, 1, 20, True, True, 1)
Response.Write Result
' " WROX PRESS    " will be written to the page
```

EuroDisplay

This object is used to convert and format currency amounts where multiple currencies must be displayed. It can be found in the EURODISPLib type library (EuroDisp.dll).

Member	Method/Property	Description
ConvertAltStringToCurr	Method	Converts a string representation of a monetary value in the currency specified by the alternate locale identifier to a currency Variant.
ConvertBaseStringToCurr	Method	Converts a string representation of a monetary value in the currency specified by the base locale identifier to a currency Variant.

Table continued on following page

Member	Method/Property	Description
ConvertMoney	Method	Converts the specified currency Variant (representing a monetary value in the base currency) to a currency Variant representing a monetary value in the alternate currency, using the initialized conversion rate.
FormatAltMoney	Method	Creates a string representation of a currency Variant, based on the alternate locale identifier and the alternate currency symbol string.
FormatBaseMoney	Method	Creates a string representation of a currency Variant, based on the base locale identifier and the base currency symbol string.
Initialize	Method	Initializes the object with the specified alternate currency symbol, base currency symbol, alternate locale identifier, base locale identifier, and conversion rate.

Example:

```
Set MSCSEuroDisplay=Server.CreateObject("Commerce.EuroDisplay")
MSCSEuroDisplay.Initialize "$$",1033,"FF",1036, 2
Result = MSCSEuroDisplay.ConvertMoney(100)
Response.Write "Converted $100 from $ to F ($1 = 2F) : " & _ Result & "<P>"
```

MessageManager

This object is used to store error messages in multiple languages that the Order Processing pipeline (OPP) components use to describe error conditions generated during order processing.

Member	Method/Property	Type	Description
defaultLanguage	Property	STRING	Read/Write – Specifies the default message set for the MessageManager object.
AddLanguage	Method	-	Adds a new message set to the MessageManager object and associates that message set with a locale.
AddMessage	Method	-	Adds a new message to the MessageManager object.

Member	Method/Property	Type	Description
GetLocale	Method	-	Returns the locale for the specified message set.
GetMessage	Method	-	Returns the message associated with the specified message name constant.

Example:

```
Sub Application_OnStart
    ' Set up the MessageManager and messages.
    Set oMessageManager = _
       Server.CreateObject("Commerce.MessageManager")
    Call oMessageManager.AddLanguage("usa",&h0409)
    oMessageManager.defaultLanguage = "usa"
    Call oMessageManager.AddMessage("pur_cc_expired", _
       "Credit card has expired.")
    Call oMessageManager.AddMessage("pur_badcc", _
       "The credit-card number is not valid.")
    ' Set up the data functions.
    Set oDataFunctions = Server.CreateObject("Commerce.DataFunctions")
    oDataFunctions.Locale = &H0409
    Application.Lock
       Set Application("MSCSMessageManager") = oMessageManager
       Set Application("MSCSDataFunctions") = oDataFunctions
    Application.UnLock
End Sub
```

Expression Objects

These objects are used to create, store and evaluate expressions.

ExpressionEval

This object is used to evaluate one or more expressions against a specified context. In addition, use this object to parse and evaluate user-defined expressions written as Extensible Markup Language (XML) fragments. It can be found in the EXPRARCHLib type library (exprarch.dll).

Member	Method/Property	Type	Description
ExprCount	Property	LONG	Read Only – Retrieves the number of expressions loaded into the expression cache.
Connect	Method	-	Establishes communication between the ExpressionEval object and an expression store.

Table continued on following page

Member	Method/Property	Type	Description
CreateEvalContext	Method	-	Creates a new ExprEvalContext object in the context cache.
Eval	Method	-	Evaluates an expression.
EvalInContext	Method	-	Evaluates an expression in a context previously loaded into the context cache.
EvalXML	Method	-	Evaluates the specified XML text as an expression.
FlushAll	Method	-	Removes all expressions from the expression cache.
FlushExpr	Method	-	Removes the specified expression from the expression cache.
LoadAll	Method	-	Reads all expressions from the expression store and loads them into the expression cache.
LoadExpr	Method	-	Reads the specified expression from the expression store and loads it into the expression cache.
ParseXML	Method	-	Parses the specified XML text to determine if it represents a valid expression.

Example:

```
strXMLExpr = "<CLAUSE OPER=""equal"">" & _
    "<PROPERTY" & _
        "ID=""User.firstName""" & _
            "TYPE=""string/>" & _
        "<IMMED-VAL TYPE=""string"">Jay</IMMED-VAL>" & _
    "</CLAUSE>"
' vResult is a Variant
' dictProfiles is a Dictionary object containing a set of _ profiles

vResult = oExpressionEval.EvalXML(sXMLExpr, dictProfiles)
```

ExpressionStore

This object is used to manipulate expressions contained in an expression store. An expression store is a database of expressions along with information about the expressions. There is one expression store for each commerce site. It can be found in the **EXPRARCHLib** type library (exprarch.dll).

Member	Method/Property	Description
Connect	Method	Validates and stores the connection string to the specified expression store.
DeleteExpression	Method	Deletes an expression from the expression store.
Disconnect	Method	Sets the connection string to an empty string.
Export	Method	Exports expressions from the expression store to a file (.txt or .xml).
GetAllExprs	Method	Retrieves all expressions from the expression store.
GetExpression	Method	Retrieves an expression from the expression store.
GetExprID	Method	Translates an expression name into its corresponding expression ID.
GetExprName	Method	Translates an expression ID into its corresponding expression name.
Import	Method	Imports a set of expressions to the expression store from a file.
NewExpression	Method	Creates a new ADO Recordset object that contains an empty expression.
Query	Method	Queries for a list of expressions based on one or more criteria.
RenameExpression	Method	Renames an existing expression.
SaveExpression	Method	Saves a new or changed expression to the expression store.

Example:

```
' oExpressionStore is an ExpressionStore object connected to
' a valid expression store.
' 48577 is a valid expression ID retrieved from the GetExprIdMethod.

oExpressionStore.RenameExpression(48577, "MyNewName")
```

ExprEvalContext

> WARNING: Do not change the properties of this object: doing so will corrupt it. If you
> need to edit or change values associated with this object, use **ExpressionEval** to create,
> access or delete the **ExprEvalContext** object.

ExprFltrQueryBldr

This object is used to translate an expression in Extensible Markup Language (XML) form into a SQL filter query string. A filter query returns a subset of items from a database based on a combination of attribute values. It can be found in the **EXPRFLTRBLDRLib** type library (`exprfltrbldr.dll`).

Member	Method/Property	Description
`ConvertExprToSqlFltrStr`	Method	Converts an expression in XML form to a SQL filter string.
`ConvertExprUsingDict`	Method	Converts an expression in XML form that references a `Dictionary` object into a SQL filter string.

Example:

```
strXMLExpr2 = "<CLAUSE OPER=""at-least"">" & _
    "<PROPERTY" & _
        "ID=""user.age""" & _
          "TYPE=""number/>" & _
        "<IMMED-VAL TYPE=""number"">31</IMMED-VAL>" & _
    "</CLAUSE>"
```

```
sSqlFilter = oExprFltrQueryBldr.ConvertExprToSqlFltrStr(strXMLExpr2)
```

List Management Objects

The objects contain methods and properties behind the Master list capabilities of CS2K.

ListManager

This object is used to create and manage lists of users for the User Profile Management system, lists of e-mail addresses for the Direct Mailer, lists of segment members for the Predictor resource, lists generated from Analysis reports, and lists created from files and SQL queries. It can be found in the **LISTMANAGERLib** type library (`listmanager.exe`).

Member	Method/ Property	Type	Description
ConnectionString	Property	STRING	Read Only – Stores the connection string to the database used by the ListManager object to store lists. This value is set when passing the *ConnectionString* parameter to the Initialize method.
Status	Property	LONG	Read Only – Stores the current status of the ListManager object.
AddUserToMailingList	Method	-	Adds a user to a mailing list.
CancelOperation	Method	-	Cancels a currently running asynchronous operation.
Copy	Method	-	Makes a copy of a list.
CreateEmpty	Method	-	Creates an empty list for subsequent operations.
CreateFromDWCalc	Method	-	Creates a list from an Analysis report.
CreateFromFile	Method	-	Creates a list from a file.
CreateFromSegment	Method	-	Creates a list from a Predictor Resource segment.
CreateFromSQL	Method	-	Creates a list from an SQL query.
Delete	Method	-	Deletes a list.
ExportToFile	Method	-	Exports a list to a file.
ExportToSql	Method	-	Exports a list to a database table.
ExtractMailingList	Method	-	Creates a new mailing list from a generic list that contains an rcp_e-mail column.
GetListFlags	Method	-	Retrieves the Flags bitmask for a list.

Table continued on following page

Member	Method/ Property	Type	Description
GetListId	Method	-	Retrieves the list ID.
GetListName	Method	-	Retrieves the list name.
GetListProperty	Method	-	Retrieves a list property.
GetLists	Method	-	Enumerates all known lists at the time of the call.
GetListUserFlags	Method	-	Retrieves the UserFlags bitmask for a list.
GetOperationInfo	Method	-	Retrieves information on a list operation.
GetOperations	Method	-	Enumerates all operations running at the time of the call.
Initialize	Method	-	Initializes the ListManager object.
RemoveUserFromMailingList	Method	-	Removes a user from a mailing list.
Rename	Method	-	Renames a list.
SetDesc	Method	-	Assigns a description to a list.
SetListProperty	Method	-	Sets a list property.
Subtract	Method	-	Subtracts one list from another list, and stores the results in a third list.
Union	Method	-	Produces a union of two lists (combines the lists and eliminates duplicates), and stores the results in a third list.
WaitOnOperation	Method	-	Waits for an operation to complete or a timeout to occur, then returns.

Example:

```
oListManager.AddUserToMailingList _
    "{2B544800-4169-4C49-8713-_1B794078B4C9}", _
    "JoeySmith@somewhere.com", "{454799A2-312B-4F5F-90A0-514FBA0EC5A}", _
    2, 1033, VT_NULL
```

Pipeline Objects

These objects are used in conjunction with pipeline processing within a Commerce Server Pipeline.

MicroPipe

This object is used to run a single pipeline component from an Active Server Page file without using a pipeline configuration file (`.pcf`). It can be found in the **UPIPELINELib** type library (`micropipe.dll`).

Member	Method/Property	Description
Execute	Method	Runs the component indicated in the `SetComponent` method.
SetComponent	Method	Indicates the pipeline component to load and execute.
SetLogFile	Method	Identifies the file in which to log pipeline events.

Example:

```
errVal = pMicropipeline.Execute(dOrder, dContext, 0)
```

MtsPipeline

Use this object to execute a non-transacted Microsoft Commerce Server 2000 pipeline. The pipeline may be an Order Processing Pipeline (OPP). It can be found in the **PIPELINELib** type library (`pipeline.dll`).

Member	Method/Property	Description
Execute	Method	Runs the components in the pipeline.
LoadPipe	Method	Loads a pipeline configuration file (.pcf) into the pipeline.
SetLogFile	Method	Identifies the file in which to log pipeline events.

Example:

```
errVal = pMtsPipeline.Loadpipe("CustomShip.pcf")
```

MtsTxPipeline

Use this object to execute a transacted Microsoft Commerce Server 2000 pipeline configuration. The pipeline may be an Order Processing Pipeline (OPP). It can be found in the **PIPELINELib** type library as **TxPipeline** (`pipeline.dll`).

Member	Method/Property	Description
Execute	Method	Runs the components in the pipeline.
LoadPipe	Method	Loads a pipeline configuration file (.pcf) into the pipeline.
SetLogFile	Method	Identifies the file in which to log pipeline events.

Example:

```
errVal = pMtsTxPipeline.SetLogFile("CustomShipping.log")
```

OrderPipeline

This object is used to execute a Microsoft Commerce Server 2000 Content Selection pipeline. Order Processing Pipelines (OPP) should generally use a PooledPipeline, PooledTxPipeline, MtxPipeline, or MtsTxPipeline object. It can be found in the PIPELINELib type library (pipeline.dll).

Member	Method/Property	Description
LoadPipe	Method	Loads a pipeline configuration file (.pcf) into the pipeline.
OrderExecute	Method	Runs the components in the pipeline.
SetLogFile	Method	Identifies the file in which to log pipeline events.

Example:

```
errVal = pOrdPipeline.OrderExecute (1, dOrder, dContext, 0)
```

PooledPipeline

Use this object to execute a Microsoft Commerce Server 2000 pipeline configuration file. The pipeline may be an Order Processing Pipeline (OPP). It can be found in the PIPELINELib type library (pipeline.dll).

Member	Method/Property	Description
Execute	Method	Runs the components in the pipeline.
LoadPipe	Method	Loads a pipeline configuration file (.pcf) into the pipeline.
SetLogFile	Method	Identifies the file in which to log pipeline events.

Example:

```
errVal = pPooledPipeline.LoadPipe("CustomShip.pcf")
```

PooledTxPipeline

Use this object to execute a Microsoft Commerce Server 2000 pipeline. The pipeline may be an Order Processing Pipeline (OPP). Use in place of the `PooledPipeline` object where you need transactions. It can be found in the **PIPELINELib** type library (`pipeline.dll`).

Member	Method/Property	Description
Execute	Method	Runs the components in the pipeline as configured by the `LoadPipe` method.
LoadPipe	Method	Loads a pipeline configuration file (.pcf) into the pipeline.
SetLogFile	Method	Identifies the file in which to log pipeline events.

Example:

```
errVal = pPooledTxPipeline.Execute(1, dOrder, dContext, 0)
```

Prediction Objects

These objects are used for the Commerce Server predictor tool.

PredictorClient

This object is used to load an analysis model, set properties controlling the prediction context, and execute the prediction algorithm. Two types of models are supported: prediction models, and segment models. Results of a prediction model are used to recommend products, and supply missing profile data. Results of a segment model are used to categorize a user. Prediction models provide more accurate recommendations than segment models and the use of segment models for predictions is discouraged. It can be found in the **PREDICTORCLIENTLib** type library (`PredictorClient.dll`).

Member	Method/Property	Type	Description
fpDataFitScore	Property	SINGLE	Read Only – Stores the Data Fit Score.
fpDefaultConfidence	Property	SINGLE	Read/Write – Stores the threshold for confidence in a prediction.
bFailOnUnknownInputAttributes	Property	BOOLEAN	Read/Write – Controls the behavior of the `Predict` method when input attributes are unknown.

Table continued on following page

Member	Method/ Property	Type	Description
fpPopularityPenalty	Property	SINGLE	Read/Write – Stores the penalty applied when selecting popular items to recommend.
fpRecommendScore	Property	SINGLE	Read Only – Stores the Recommend Score.
sSiteName	Property	SINGLE	Read/Write – Stores the site name in which the PredictorClient object is running.
Explain	Method	-	Explains the prediction of a property in terms of the relevant property/value pairs used as input to the prediction model.
LoadModelFromDB	Method	-	Loads a model from a database.
LoadModelFromFile	Method	-	Loads a model from the specified file.
Predict	Method	-	Predicts recommend products or missing profile data.
PredictAllSegments	Method	-	Calculates the probabilities that the user belongs to each segment of a population of past users.
PredictMostLikelySegment	Method	-	Calculates the segment to which the user most likely belongs.
SaveModelToFile	Method	-	Saves a model to the specified file.

Example:

```
Dim oPredictorClient
Set oPredictorClient = Server.CreateObject("Commerce.PredictorClient")

oPredictorClient.LoadModelFromDB "Purchase1", sDWConnect

oPredictorClient.bFailOnUnknownInputAttributes = True
oPredictorClient.fpDefaultConfidence = 95
oPredictorClient.fpPopularityPenalty = 0.2
```

```
oPredictorClient.sSiteName = "Retail"

Set oPredictorClient = Nothing
```

PredictorServiceAdmin

This object is used to retrieve a list of the available analysis models, a list of the available model configurations, and the date the Predictor resource was last started. It can be found in the PREDICTORSERVICELib type library (PredServ.exe).

Member	Method/Property	Type	Description
dateLastStarted	Property	DATE	Read Only – Retrieves the date the Predictor resource was last started.
slModelConfigs	Property	OBJECT	Read Only – Retrieves a list of currently available model configurations.
slModels	Property	OBJECT	Read Only – Retrieves a list of currently available models.

Example:

```
Dim oPredictorServiceAdmin
Set oPredictorServiceAdmin = _
  Server.CreateObject("Commerce.PredictorServiceAdmin")

Response.Write "The date the Predictor Service was last started = " _
  & oPredictorServiceAdmin.dateLastStarted & "<P>"

Response.Write "The number of model configurations = " & _
  oPredictorServiceAdmin.slModelConfigs.Count & "<BR>"

Dim oDict
For Each oDict In oPredictorServiceAdmin.slModelConfigs
Response.Write oDict("ModelCfgName") & "<BR>"
Next

Response.Write "The number of models = " & _
  oPredictorServiceAdmin.slModels.Count & "<BR>"

For Each oDict In oPredictorServiceAdmin.slModels
Response.Write oDict("ModelName") & "<BR>"
Next

Set oPredictorServiceSiteAdmin = Nothing
```

PredictorServiceSiteAdmin

This object is used to manage analysis models and model configurations. It can be found in the PREDICTORSERVICELib type library (PredServ.exe).

Member	Method/Property	Type	Description
lCaseCount	Property	LONG	Read Only – Retrieves the number of cases used by a model configuration.
dModelInfo	Property	OBJECT	Read Only – Retrieves information on the specified model.
SegmentLabels	Property	VARIANT	Read/Write – Stores the segment labels for a segment model.
DeleteModel	Method	-	Deletes the specified predictor model.
DeleteModelConfig	Method	-	Deletes the specified model configuration.
GenerateSegmentList	Method	-	Generates a list of members of a segment.
Init	Method	-	Initializes the server.
RenameModel	Method	-	Renames a predictor model.
RenameModelConfig	Method	-	Renames a model configuration.

Example:

```
oPredictorServiceSiteAdmin.GenerateSegmentList _
   "Provider=SQLOLEDB;Data Source=servername;" & _
   "Initial Catalog=Retail_commerce;User ID=sa;Password=;", _
   "Developers", "Demog1", "Developers", .5
```

PredModelBuilder

This object is used to control the creation of analysis models using multiple prioritized build threads. It can be found in the PREDICTORSERVICELib type library (PredServ.exe).

Member	Method/Property	Type	Description
dModelInfo	Property	OBJECT	Read Only – Retrieves information on the specified running model.
Priority	Property	ENUM	Read/Write – Stores the build thread priority.
slRunningModels	Property	OBJECT	Read Only – Retrieves a list of running models.
Status	Property	ENUM	Read Only – Indicates the build thread status.
Pause	Method	-	Pauses a running build thread.
Resume	Method	-	Resumes a paused build thread.
Start	Method	-	Sets the thread identifier for a build and starts a new build thread.
Stop	Method	-	Stops a running build thread.
StopAllBuilds	Method	-	Stops all currently running build threads.

Example:

```
lBuildID = oPredModelBuilder.Start _
("Provider=SQLOLEDB;Data Source=servername;" & _
 "Initial Catalog=Retail_dw;User ID=sa;Password=;", _
 "", "PurchaseCfg1", "Demog1", sXMLBuildParams, False)
```

Product Catalog Objects

These objects are used to manage the Commerce Server 2000 product catalogs.

CatalogManager

This object is used to work with the entire Product Catalog System. The methods and properties of this object effect all catalogs contained in the Product Catalog System. It can be found in the CATALOGLib type library (Catalog.dll).

Member	Method/ Property	Type	Description
Catalogs	Property	_Recordset	Read Only – Returns a recordset containing a record for each catalog contained in the Product Catalog System, including their properties.
CategoryDefinitions	Property	_Recordset	Read Only – Returns a recordset containing the names of all of the category definitions that currently exist in the Product Catalog System.
CustomCatalogs	Property	_Recordset	Read Only – Returns a recordset containing a record for each custom catalog. These records include the custom catalog names and the names of the catalogs they are based on.
ProductDefinitions	Property	_Recordset	Read Only – Returns a recordset containing the names of all the product definitions that currently exist in the Product Catalog System.
Properties	Property	_Recordset	Read Only – Returns a recordset containing the name of each property that currently exists in the Product Catalog System.
AddDefinitionProperty	Method	-	Adds a property to a definition.
AddDefinitionVariantProperty	Method	-	Adds a variant property to a definition.
AddPropertyValue	Method	-	Adds a value to the list of defined values for this property. Only applies to enumerations.
CreateCatalog	Method	-	Creates a new catalog.

Member	Method/Property	Type	Description
CreateCategoryDefinition	Method	-	Creates a new category definition.
CreateProductDefinition	Method	-	Creates a new product definition.
CreateProperty	Method	-	Creates a new property.
DeleteCatalog	Method	-	Deletes a catalog.
DeleteDefinition	Method	-	Deletes a product or category definition
DeleteProperty	Method	-	Deletes a property.
ExportCSV	Method	-	Exports catalog data as a comma-separated value format file.
ExportXML	Method	-	Exports catalog data as an Extensible Markup Language (XML) format file.
FreeTextSearch	Method	-	Performs a free-text search of catalogs.
GetCatalog	Method	-	Returns the specified catalog object.
GetDefinitionProperties	Method	-	Returns the properties of a specified product or category definition
GetPropertyAttributes	Method	-	Returns all the attributes of a specified property.
GetPropertyValues	Method	-	Returns a list of appropriate values for an enumeration property.
ImportCSV	Method	-	Imports a comma-separated value format file as catalog data.
ImportXML	Method	-	Imports an XML format file as catalog data.
Initialize	Method	-	Initializes the CatalogManager object.

Table continued on following page

Member	Method/ Property	Type	Description
Query	Method	-	Performs queries against product, variant, and category data in one or more catalogs.
RemoveDefinitionProperty	Method	-	Removes the specified property or variant property from a definition.
RemovePropertyValue	Method	-	Removes a defined value from an enumeration property.
RenameDefinition	Method	-	Renames a definition.
RenameProperty	Method	-	Renames a property.
SetDefinitionProperties	Method	-	Use this method to change the properties of a category or product definition.
SetPropertyAttributes	Method	-	Changes the attributes of a property.

Example:

```
Set oNewCatalog = myCatalogManager.CreateCatalog _
    ("NewCatalog", "ItemNum", "SKU")
```

CatalogSets

This object is used to work with catalog sets in the catalog management system. Catalog sets allow you to present different collections of catalogs to different users and organizations. It can be found in the CS_CtlgSetsLib type library (CatalogSets.exe).

Member	Method/ Property	Description
CreateCatalogSet	Method	Creates a new catalog set.
DeleteCatalogSet	Method	Deletes the specified catalog set.
GetCatalogs	Method	Returns a list of all catalogs.
GetCatalogSetIDForUser	Method	Returns the catalog set ID for a user.
GetCatalogSetInfo	Method	Returns information about the specified catalog set.

Member	Method/ Property	Description
GetCatalogSets	Method	Returns a list of all catalog sets.
GetCatalogsForUser	Method	Returns a list of catalogs associated with the specified user.
GetCatalogsInCatalogSet	Method	Returns a list of catalogs associated with the specified catalog set.
GetCatalogsNotInCatalogSet	Method	Returns a list of all catalogs not associated with the specified catalog set.
Initialize	Method	Initializes the CatalogSets object.
RemoveCatalogFromCatalogSet	Method	Removes a catalog from all catalog sets.
UpdateCatalogSet	Method	Allows modification of an existing catalog set.

Example:

```
Set rsMyCatalogs = myCatalogSets.GetCatalogs()
```

CatalogToVendorAssociation

This object is used to associate catalogs with vendors. It can be found in the CS_CtlgVndrLib type library (CatalogVendorAssociation.exe).

Member	Method/ Property	Description
GetVendorInfoForCatalog	Method	Returns information about the vendor associated with the specified catalog.
GetVendorList	Method	Returns a list of vendors available for association with catalogs.
Initialize	Method	Initializes a CatalogToVendorAssociation object by connecting to the appropriate database.
SpecifyVendorForCatalog	Method	Associates the specified vendor and catalog.
UnspecifyVendorForCatalog	Method	Disassociates the specified vendor and catalog.

Example:

```
Set rsVendorList = myCatalogToVendorAssociation _
    GetVendorList (szSourceAliasQualifier, _
    szSourceAliasValue, szInputDocumentName)
```

Category

This object is used to work with relationships between categories and products. You can also use this object to manipulate parent/child relationships for a category. It can be found in the CATALOGLib type library (Catalog.exe).

Member	Method/ Property	Type	Description
AncestorCategories	Property	RECORDSET	Read Only – Contains a recordset of category names that exist anywhere above this category, and that directly or indirectly contain this category, in the hierarchy.
CatalogName	Property	STRING	Read Only – Contains the name of the catalog of which this Category object is a member.
CategoryName	Property	BSTR	Read Only – Contains the name of this category.
ChildCategories	Property	RECORDSET	Read Only – Contains a recordset containing the child Category objects for this category.
DescendantProducts	Property	RECORDSET	Read Only – Contains all products that exist anywhere below this category. Accessing this property on the root category returns every product in the entire catalog.
GetCategoryProperties	Property	RECORDSET	Read Only – Contains a recordset containing the property values for this category.
ParentCategories	Property	RECORDSET	Read Only – Contains a recordset containing the names of the Category objects that are parent categories to this category.

Member	Method/ Property	Type	Description
Products	Property	RECORDSET	Read Only – Contains the products that exist within this category, but not within descendant categories.
RelatedCategories	Property	RECORDSET	Read Only – Contains a recordset that describes all of the categories and product families that have relationships to this category.
RelatedProducts	Property	RECORDSET	Read Only – Contains a recordset that describes all the product variants and product families that have relationships to this category.
AddChildCategory	Method	-	Adds another specified category as a child of this category.
AddParentCategory	Method	-	Adds another specified category as a parent of this category.
AddProduct	Method	-	Adds another specified product variant as a child of this category.
AddRelationshipTo Category	Method	-	Adds a relationship from another category to this category.
AddRelationshipTo Product	Method	-	Adds a relationship from this category to a specified product.
RemoveChildCategory	Method	-	Removes the specified category as a child of this category.
RemoveParentCategory	Method	-	Removes the specified category as a parent of this category.

Table continued on following page

Member	Method/ Property	Type	Description
RemoveProduct	Method	-	Removes a product from this category.
RemoveRelationshipTo Category	Method	-	Removes the relationship between this category and a specified category.
RemoveRelationshipTo Product	Method	-	Removes the relationship between this category and a specified product.
SetCategoryProperties	Method	-	Assigns new properties to a category.

Example:

```
myCategory.SetCategoryProperties pRSCategory, "TRUE"
```

Product

This object is used to work with products and variants in a catalog. It can be found in the **CATALOGLib** type library (`Catalog.exe`).

Member	Method/ Property	Type	Description
AncestorCategories	Property	RECORDSET	Read Only – Contains a recordset of category names that exist anywhere above this product, and that directly or indirectly contain this product in the hierarchy.
CatalogName	Property	STRING	Read Only – Contains the name of the catalog of which this `Product` object is a member.
GetProductProperties	Property	RECORDSET	Read Only – Contains a recordset containing the property values for this product.

Member	Method/Property	Type	Description
ParentCategories	Property	RECORDSET	Read Only – Contains a recordset of categories that directly contain this product.
PricingCategory	Property	STRING	Read/Write – Contains the name of the pricing category for this product.
ProductID	Property	BSTR	Read Only – Contains the unique identifier for this product.
RelatedCategories	Property	RECORDSET	Read Only – Contains a recordset that describes all of the categories that are related to this product.
RelatedProducts	Property	RECORDSET	Read Only – Contains a recordset that describes all of the products that are related to this product.
Variants	Property	RECORDSET	Read Only – Contains a recordset that describes all of the variants of this product, if any.
AddRelationshipToCategory	Method	-	Adds a relationship to a specified category from this product.
AddRelatioshipToProduct	Method	-	Adds a relationship to another specified product from this product.
CreateVariant	Method	-	Creates a new product variant.

Table continued on following page

Member	Method/Property	Type	Description
DeleteVariant	Method	-	Deletes a product variant.
GetVariantProperties	Method	-	Returns the properties of a specified product variant.
RemoveRelationshipToCategory	Method	-	Removes the specified relationship between this product and the specified category.
RemoveRelationshipToProduct	Method	-	Removes the specified relationship between this product and the specified product.
SetProductProperties	Method	-	Sets the properties for this product and all its variants.
SetVariantProperties	Method	-	Sets the properties for variants of this product.

Example:

```
set rsProductProps = myProduct.GetProductProperties
rsProductProps.fields("cy_list_price").value = CCur(1.278)
myProduct.SetProductProperties rsProductProps, TRUE
```

ProductCatalog

This object is used to alter catalogs and to modify catalog contents. The ProductCatalog object is the primary object for working with catalogs in the Product Catalog System. It can be found in the CATALOGLib type library (Catalog.exe).

Member	Method/Property	Type	Description
BaseCatalogName	Property	BSTR	Read Only – Contains the name of a base catalog for the custom catalog.

Member	Method/ Property	Type	Description
CatalogName	Property	BSTR	Read Only – Contains the name of a base catalog for the custom catalog.
IdentifyingProductProperty	Property	STRING	Read Only – Contains the name of the column used to uniquely identify products and product families.
IdentifyingVariantProperty	Property	STRING	Read Only – Contains the name of the column used to uniquely identify product variants.
RootCategories	Property	_Recordset	Read Only – Returns a recordset containing the names of categories that are the root categories for this catalog.
RootProducts	Property	_Recordset	Read Only – Returns a recordset containing the products that are part of this catalog, but are not contained in any category.
SearchableCategories	Property	_Recordset	Read Only – Returns a recordset with a single field that contains the names of the categories that are defined as searchable.
AddSpecificationSearchClause	Method	-	Adds a search constraint to the search context when performing a specification search of this catalog.
BeginSpecificationSearch	Method	-	Initiates a specification search of this catalog.

Table continued on following page

Member	Method/ Property	Type	Description
CreateCategory	Method	-	Creates a new category based on the specified category definition.
CreateCustomCatalog	Method	-	Creates a new custom catalog template. The returned recordset is disconnected and updateable.
CreateProduct	Method	-	Creates a new product based on the specified product definition.
DeleteCategory	Method	-	Deletes a category from this catalog.
DeleteCustomCatalog	Method	-	Deletes a custom catalog from this catalog.
DeleteProduct	Method	-	Deletes a product from this catalog.
GenerateCustomCatalog	Method	-	Populates the specified custom catalog template with data derived from this catalog.
GetCatalogAttributes	Method	-	Returns the attributes of this catalog. The returned recordset is disconnected and updateable.
GetCategory	Method	-	Returns the specified category.
GetCategoryCustomPrice	Method	-	Returns the custom price of the specified category.
GetCustomCatalogAttributes	Method	-	Returns the attributes of the specified custom catalog. The returned recordset is disconnected and updateable.
GetProduct	Method	-	Returns the specified product.

Member	Method/ Property	Type	Description
GetProductVariant	Method	-	Returns a recordset with a single row containing all of the properties for the specified product variant.
GetSpecificationSearchClauses	Method	-	Returns a recordset with a single field containing all of the search clauses for a specification search.
GuaranteedSpecificationSearch	Method	-	Performs a specification search in which search constraints are removed until a match is found.
PerformSpecificationSearch	Method	-	Performs a specification search of this catalog using the specified search context.
RegenerateFreeTextSearch Index	Method	-	Updates the free text search index for this catalog.
RemoveSpecificationSearch Clause	Method	-	Removes the last search constraint from the specified search context.
SetCatalogAttributes	Method	-	Sets attributes for this catalog.
SetCategoryCustomPrice	Method	-	Defines a custom price for the specified category.
SetCustomCatalogAttributes	Method	-	Sets attributes for the specified custom catalog.

Example:

```
Set rsMyCustomCat = myProductCatalog.CreateCustomCatalog("SeniorDiscountCatalog")
```

Profile Objects

These objects are used to manage profiles.

ProfileObject

This object is used to retrieve the data in specific profile object instances and modify the property values for that profile object. In addition, use the `ProfileObject` object to examine and navigate the property attributes of a profile object. It can be found in the **MSCSUPSLib** type library (`mscsups.exe`).

Member	Method/Property	Type	Description
Fields	Property	OBJECT	Read Only – Stores the profile property collection.
GetProfileXML	Method	-	Retrieves an XML fragment representing the data structure of the profile object.
Update	Method	-	Saves the profile data to the underlying data store.

Example:

```
sXMLProfile = oProfileObject.GetProfileXML(psRetrieveDataOnly, True)
```

ProfileService

This object is used to create, delete, and retrieve `ProfileObject` objects. It can be found in the **MSCSUPSLib** type library (`mscsups.exe`).

Member	Method/Property	Type	Description
Errors	Property	OBJECT	Read Only – Stores the collection of errors encountered in the last Profiles resource operation.
BindAs	Method	-	Sets the user credentials for accessing the underlying Profiles store.
CreateProfile	Method	-	Creates the specified `ProfileObject` object.
DeleteProfile	Method	-	Deletes a `ProfileObject` object specified by a primary key value from the Profiling System.

Member	Method/Property	Type	Description
DeleteProfileByKey	Method	-	Deletes a `ProfileObject` object specified by a key member/value pair from the Profiling System.
GetProfile	Method	-	Retrieves a `ProfileObject` object specified by a primary key value from the Profiling System.
GetProfileByKey	Method	-	Retrieves a `ProfileObject` object specified by a key member/value pair from the Profiling System.
GetProfileDefXML	Method	-	Retrieves the XML description of the specified profile definition.
Initialize	Method	-	Establishes connection to the specified Profiles store and populates the schema cache.
UnBind	Method	-	Clears the user credentials for accessing the underlying Profiles store.

Example:

```
oProfileObject1 = oProfileService.CreateProfile _
    ("{75A4C9C1-D38D-13D0-68BF-00A0C90DC8DF}", "Address")

oProfileObject2 = oProfileService.CreateProfile _
    ("JulieDree@somewhere.com", "UserObject")
```

Reporting Objects

These objects are used in the creation of site reporting.

AsyncRpt

This object is used to render (display) or export a static report asynchronously. It can be found in the ASYNCREPORTLib type library (`AsyncReport.exe`).

Member	Method/Property	Description
RunReport	Method	Runs or exports reports

Example:

```
Set objReport = CreateObject("Commerce.AsyncReportMgr")
bResponse = objReport.RunReport(iReportStatusID & "|" & _
g_MSCSDataWarehouseSQLConnStr & "|" & g_MSCSDataWarehouseOLAPConnStr & _
"|||" & sRunDateTime)

Set objReport = nothing
```

ReportRenderer

This object is used to render (display) or export a static report synchronously. It can be found in the
CS_RptRndrerLib type library (ReportRenderer.exe).

Member	Method/Property	Description
Init	Method	Initializes the ReportRenderer object

Example:

```
oReportRenderer.Init("7|DRIVER={SQL Server};SERVER=MyServer;" _
& "DATABASE=Retail_dw;UID=sa;PWD=;||Provider=SQLOLEDB;" _
& "Persist Security Info=False;User ID=sa;Password=;" _
& "Initial Catalog=Retail_commerce;Data Source=MyServer;|" _
& "OutPutTableName|5/01/2001 5:01:01 pm")
```

Site Security Objects

These objects are used to secure a Commerce Server website.

BizDeskSecurity

This object is used to determine whether to display a module in the navigation pane of Commerce Server
Business Desk. It can be found in the **BDSECURITYLib** type library (BDSecurity.exe).

Member	Method/Property	Description
CanUserAccess	Method	Checks for UAR (User's Access Rights) to read a specified file

Example:

```
bAccess = oBizDeskSecurity.CanUserAccess ("CatalogEditor.asp")
```

AuthManager

This object is used to perform user identification and authentication and to manage user security information. This object also contains methods for cookie and cookie-less browsing. It can be found in the MSCSAUTHLib type library (mscsauth.exe).

Member	Method/Property	Description
GenerateEncryptionKey	Method	Generates an encryption key for the administration of cookie data. Use this method in administration or setup components only.
GetProperty	Method	Retrieves the specified custom property stored in a cookie or query string.
GetURL	Method	Generates a Uniform Resource Locator (URL) containing optional name/value pairs.
GetUserID	Method	Retrieves the unique ID for the current user.
GetUserIDFromCookie	Method	Retrieves a user ID from a cookie.
Initialize	Method	Initializes the AuthManager object by caching all the required site configuration resource properties.
IsAuthenticated	Method	Indicates whether or not a user is currently authenticated.
Refresh	Method	Updates the cached site configuration resource properties after any of the properties have been changed.
SetAuthTicket	Method	Generates an encrypted MSCSAuth ticket for a registered user.
SetProfileTicket	Method	Generates an encrypted MSCSProfile ticket for an anonymous user.
SetProperty	Method	Adds a property/value pair to a cookie or query string containing a ticket.
SetUserID	Method	Sets the user ID property on a ticket.
UnInitialize	Method	Removes the site-specific configuration resource properties from the cache.
URLArgs	Method	Generates a URL-encoded query string from arrays of parameter names and values.
URLShopperArgs	Method	Generates a URL-encoded query string from arrays of parameter names and values and appends the ticket of the user to the string.

Example:

```
' vUserID is a Variant
' oAuthManager is a Commerce AuthManager object

vUserID = oAuthManager.GetUserID(enumMSCS_ProfileTicketType)
```

For more detailed information on these objects, you can refer to the Microsoft Commerce Server 2000 (Commerce_Server.chm) documentation for ProgIDs, Type Library Names, DLL Names, Definitions and Threading models. The intent of this reference is for quick Object guidance where granular detail is *not* needed.

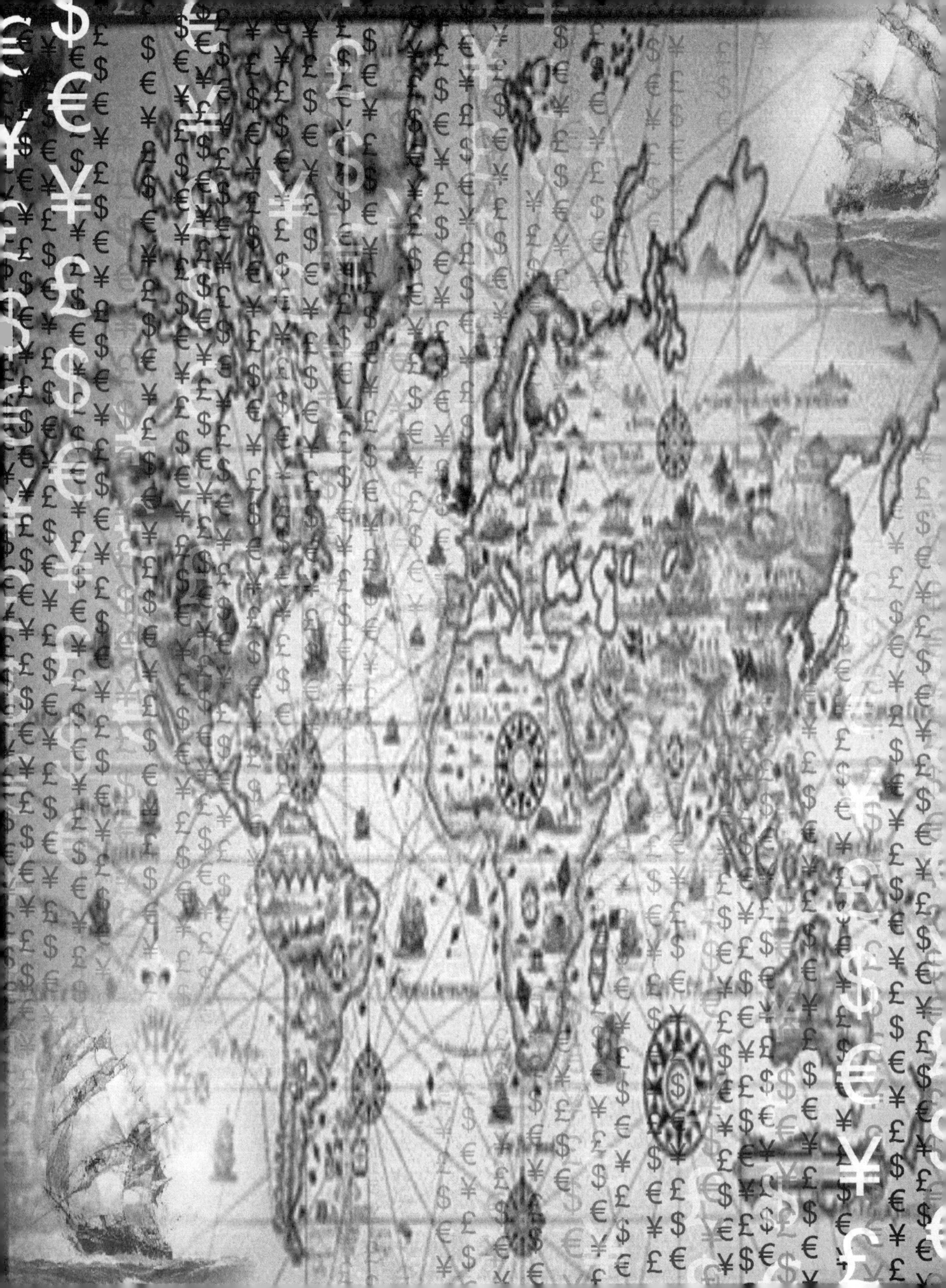

CS2K: Schemas Quick Reference

What is a schema? Let's first begin by defining the term: schema refers to an outline of business processes or models that is used in programming to direct and control functions. What does this mean in relation to Microsoft Commerce Server 2000? This term has many uses: it is sometimes used to define an XML model, and it can also be used to describe a physical layout of data. A great majority of web developers uses this term to describe the layout or model of their usability, for example, a UI (user interface) schema. In any case, the following pages are going to document the various XML Schemas that Microsoft has identified to be important to the developer, at least from a framework point of view.

The scope of building a reference section on schemas is a task that is daunting in nature; there are over one hundred XML pages and well over thousands of properties, most of which are not included in Microsoft documentation. This side of the Commerce Server equation has a new name in my book, the black hole. Like the Active Directory structure, the XML structure is far reaching. The good news is that most of this code will never have to be touched by the developer. Perfect XML is code that doesn't have to be interacted with by a human. Machines are much better at interacting with XML than we are, hence the reason for a product like BizTalk. A great deal of the XML content is used in the creation of new sites and for sending and receiving data through the various tools to gain resource efficiencies.

Below are a few of the important XML structures that Microsoft has identified for you to be familiar with; for more detailed information, I would recommend the Microsoft Commerce Server Help document.

The following XML Structures will be referenced:

❑　Analysis/Reporting

❑　Business Desk

❑　Catalog

❑　Expression

❑　Profile

Commerce Server XML Jumpstart

What is XML?

XML (Extensible Markup Language) in its purest form was created to delimit text data over Internet technologies. XML is a subset of SGML (Standard Generalized Markup Language) to be served, received and processed over the web-using internet technologies. SGML is a meta-language, containing a set of rules for constructing other markup languages. As you know, HTML is also a markup language, but the main difference is that HTML contains limitations in its delivery of structure and output. In other words, HTML has clear-cut semantics which results in limitations in marking up documents. Another key difference is that HTML presents data whereas XML can store data. XML gives you the ability to define your own way to organize and markup documents.

This is the quick and dirty explanation – for further information, look at http://www.oasis-open.org/cover. This appendix assumes common knowledge in XML and will focus on Microsoft's Commerce Server implementation of XML. For more information on XML, see the following books from Wrox Press:

❑   *XML Applications,* ISBN 1-861001-52-5

❑   *Professional XML,* ISBN 1-861003-11-0

❑   *Professional XML Design and Implementation,* ISBN 1-861002-28-9

XML Structures

Microsoft uses XML in many different scenarios with this new implementation of Commerce Server; you could say that CS2K is their first product along with SQL 2000 that embraces this technology to a large degree. When .NET was released and new technologies were adopted, XML was embraced and leveraged by the Commerce team to make CS2K a viable product for the .NET future. As you may know, this product is leaning towards .NET, but the development methodology is still very much 2000. Future releases of Commerce Server will include the use of web services, ASP.NET and ADO.NET to name a few. The good news is that XML will still be the cornerstone markup language for the future of Commerce Server and any time invested in learning it is time well spent.

> **Note: It is important to remember that unlike HTML, XML is case sensitive, so be careful when constructing or modifying these document types.**

Analysis/Reporting

This structure is used in the creation of dynamic site reports. If you need to report using online analytic processing (OLAP), you must supply the name of the cube. If you are making reports against a SQL database, a query needs to be provided. Please note that the XML structure shouldn't be edited after the initial report creation. You will need to make modifications to the report using the pivot control found in the Business Desk suite of tools.

Dynamic reports are stored in SQL Server queries. As you can see below, the pivot table view is stored in XML in the Data Warehouse. Query results are displayed in the OWC (Outlook Web Component) Pivot Table component.

Analysis XML Structure

```
<xml xmlns:x='urn:schemas-microsoft-com:office:excel'>
<x:PivotTable>
   <x:OWCVersion>9.0.0.3821</x:OWCVersion>
   <x:DisplayFieldList/>
      <x:FieldListTop>300</x:FieldListTop>
      <x:FieldListLeft>800</x:FieldListLeft>
      <x:FieldListBottom>700</x:FieldListBottom>
      <x:FieldListRight>1000</x:FieldListRight>
   <x:CacheDetails/>
   <x:ConnectionString>ConnectionString</x:ConnectionString>
   [<x:CommandText>QueryString</x:CommandText>]
   [<x:DataMember>CubeName</x:DataMember>]
</x:PivotTable>
</xml>
```

Notice that the <xml xmlns:x='urn:schemas-microsoft-com:office:excel'> tag is using excel in the tag. This is a control used by Microsoft Office to manage the pivot table output.

The <x:CommandText>QueryString</x:CommandText> represents an element that is used for SQL only reports as described above. This element will contain the SQL query. The <x:DataMember>CubeName</x:DataMember> represents the element for specifying on OLAP cube.

Business Desk

Business Desk utilizes XML in three key areas. These areas are:

❏   **Module Configuration** – These files are modified when a new module is added to Business Desk, or if existing modules are removed or restructured.

❏   **HTML (HTC) Component Data** – This represents data that is displayed within a number of HTCs that are a part of Business Desk. An HTC is a DHTML control that is used to manipulate the presentation of the data.

❏   **HTC Configuration** – These are XML structures that basically provide meta-data about the data being displayed. This meta-data gives detail about the dimensions of the display to the output.

Module Configuration

Master Configuration XML

This master file ties all other configuration files together. The related Schema file can be found in the Business Desk config folder: Bdmodule-schema.xml.

```
<?xml version = '1.0' encoding='windows-1252' ?>
<Schema xmlns="urn:schemas-microsoft-com:xml-data" name="config"_
xmlns:d="urn:schemas-microsoft-com:datatypes"><ElementType name="tooltip">
```

965

```
<AttributeType name="localize"/>
<attribute type="localize"/>
</ElementType><ElementType name="tasks">
<element type="task" maxOccurs="*" minOccurs="0"/>
</ElementType><ElementType name="task">
<AttributeType name="type"/>
<AttributeType name="id"/>
<AttributeType name="icon"/>
<element type="goto" maxOccurs="*" minOccurs="1"/>
<element type="postto" maxOccurs="*" minOccurs="1"/>
<element type="name" maxOccurs="1" minOccurs="1"/>
<element type="key" maxOccurs="1" minOccurs="1"/>
<element type="tooltip" maxOccurs="1" minOccurs="1"/>
<attribute type="icon"/>
<attribute type="id" required="yes"/>
<attribute type="type"/>
</ElementType><ElementType name="postto">
<AttributeType name="localize"/>
<AttributeType name="formname"/>
<AttributeType name="action"/>
<attribute type="action" required="yes"/>
<attribute type="formname"/>
<attribute type="localize"/>
</ElementType><ElementType name="name">
<AttributeType name="localize"/>
<attribute type="localize"/>
</ElementType><ElementType name="modules">
<element type="module" maxOccurs="*" minOccurs="0"/>
</ElementType><ElementType name="module">
<AttributeType name="id"/>
<element type="name" maxOccurs="1" minOccurs="1"/>
<element type="tooltip" maxOccurs="1" minOccurs="1"/>
<attribute type="id" required="yes"/>
</ElementType><ElementType name="key">
<AttributeType name="localize"/>
<attribute type="localize"/>
</ElementType><ElementType name="goto">
<AttributeType name="localize"/>
<AttributeType name="action"/>
<attribute type="action" required="yes"/>
<attribute type="localize"/>
</ElementType><ElementType name="config">
<element type="actions" maxOccurs="1" minOccurs="1"/>
<element type="modules" maxOccurs="1" minOccurs="1"/>
</ElementType><ElementType name="actions">
<element type="action" maxOccurs="*" minOccurs="1"/>
</ElementType><ElementType name="action">
<AttributeType name="id"/>
<AttributeType name="helptopic"/>
<element type="name" maxOccurs="1" minOccurs="1"/>
<element type="tooltip" maxOccurs="1" minOccurs="1"/>
<element type="tasks" maxOccurs="1" minOccurs="1"/>
<attribute type="id" required="yes"/>
<attribute type="helptopic"/>
</ElementType></Schema>
```

Module Configuration XML

These files specify configuration information for the Business Desk at the module level. As you can see below, each module configuration file is referenced by a `moduleconfig` element:

```
<moduleconfig id="analysis.xml" category="analysis"/>
```

in the master configuration file, together making up the overall configuration of categories and modules for a particular instance of Business Desk. A good analogy of this concept is comparing this procedure to how developers use include files. As you can see below, the XML is documented in the code in simple form.

```xml
<?xml version = '1.0' encoding='windows-1252' ?>
<config xmlns="x-schema:bdconfig-schema.xml">
   <categories>
      <category id="analysis">
         <name>Anal&lt;U&gt;y&lt;/U&gt;sis</name>
         <key>y</key>
         <tooltip>Design, Run, and View Analysis Reports</tooltip>
      </category>
      <category id="campaigns">
         <name>&lt;U&gt;C&lt;/U&gt;ampaigns</name>
         <key>c</key>
         <tooltip>Manage Campaigns</tooltip>
      </category>
      <category id="catalogs">
         <name>Ca&lt;U&gt;t&lt;/U&gt;alogs</name>
         <key>t</key>
         <tooltip>Design and Edit Your Catalogs</tooltip>
      </category>
      <category id="orders">
         <name>&lt;U&gt;O&lt;/U&gt;rders</name>
         <key>o</key>
         <tooltip>Manage Orders</tooltip>
      </category>
      <category id="users">
         <name>&lt;U&gt;U&lt;/U&gt;sers</name>
         <key>u</key>
         <tooltip>Manage Users and Organizations</tooltip>
      </category>
      <category id="framework">
         <name>do not delete</name>
         <key>|</key>
         <tooltip>do not delete - used by framework</tooltip>
      </category>
   </categories>
   <moduleconfigs>
      <moduleconfig id="analysis.xml" category="analysis"/>
      <moduleconfig id="marketing_cmanager.xml" category="campaigns"/>
      <moduleconfig id="catalogs_designer.xml" category="catalogs"/>
      <moduleconfig id="catalogs_editor.xml" category="catalogs"/>
      <moduleconfig id="catalog_sets.xml" category="catalogs"/>
      <moduleconfig id="baskets.xml" category="orders"/>
      <moduleconfig id="application.xml" category="orders"/>
      <moduleconfig id="orders.xml" category="orders"/>
```

```
        <moduleconfig id="shipping_methods.xml" category="orders"/>
        <moduleconfig id="tax.xml" category="orders"/>
        <moduleconfig id="refreshcache.xml" category="orders"/>
        <moduleconfig id="users.xml" category="users"/>
        <moduleconfig id="organizations.xml" category="users"/>
        <moduleconfig id="profiles.xml" category="users"/>
        <moduleconfig id="bdmaster.xml" category="framework"/>
    </moduleconfigs>
</config>
```

HTML (HTC) Component Data

Introduced in Microsoft Internet Explorer 5, HTML Components (HTC) provide a mechanism to implement components in script as Dynamic HTML (DHTML) behaviors. Saved with a `.htc` extension, an HTC is an HTML file that contains script and a set of HTC-specific elements that define the component.

Here are some sample ways that XML is used to structure Record Data in CS2K.

Standard Data Record Schema

In the standard data record structure, there are three different tier models. Each one is shown below:

One Tier Model

In this mode, any extra tiers are ignored and presented as a single table with no collapsing.

```
<?xml version = '1.0' encoding='windows-1252' ?>
<document id = 'recordcount'>
   <record>
       <dataid1>Value</dataid1>
       <dataid2>Value</dataid2>
       <dataid3>Enumeration value</dataid3>
       <dataid3_displayname>Display name for value</dataid3_displayname>

       <dataidN>Value</dataidN>
   </record>

   <record>
       <dataid1>Value</dataid1>
       <dataid2>Value</dataid2>
       <dataid3>Enumeration value</dataid3>
       <dataid3_displayname>Display name for value</dataid3_displayname>

       <dataidN>Value</dataidN>
   </record>
</document>
```

Two Tier Model

This model is appropriate when there are two or three levels of data to be displayed.

```
<?xml version = '1.0' encoding='windows-1252' ?>
<document id  = 'recordcount'>
   <record>
      <dataid1>Value</dataid1>
      <dataid2>Value</dataid2>
      <record>
         <dataid21>Value</dataid21>
         <dataid22>Value</dataid22>
      </record>
   </record>
</document>
```

Three Tier Model

This model is used when three levels of data are to be displayed. This is the greatest number of tiers that are supported.

```
<?xml version = '1.0' encoding='windows-1252' ?>
<document id =  'recordcount'>
   <record>
      <dataid1>Value</dataid1>
      <dataid2>Value</dataid2>
      <record>
         <dataid21>Value</dataid21>
         <dataid22>Value</dataid22>
         <record>
            <dataid31>Value</dataid31>
            <dataid32>Value</dataid32>
         </record>
      </record>
   </record>
</document>
```

HTC Configuration

This XML configuration is used to provide additional metadata about the data being displayed. What this means is that the data being displayed contains metadata that communicates what this data looks like and feels like. If the data were a table cell, the metadata would tell us what type of information the table cell could hold, how large it is, and so on. This also is an XML data island that is one of two data islands that must exist for a particular HTC to operate correctly.

> *Microsoft describes an XML data island as data, described in XML, which is accessed through an id attribute associated with one of two different elements (XML and script) that might be contained in the ASP page. The data often exists in the page but is not required.*

An XML data-island can exist in an ASP page, either hard-coded or generated programmatically using ASP script, using one of the following three tagging mechanisms:

Within an XML tag

```
<xml id='DataIslandID'>
   data-island XML can go here
</xml>
```

Within a Script tag

```
<script type='text/xml' id='DataIslandID'>
   data-island XML can go here
</script>
```

Or within a Script tag that uses the language attribute set to xml

```
<script language='xml' id='DataIslandID'>
   data-island XML can go here
</script>
```

The XML data comprising the data-island does not need to be specified on the ASP page itself. Any of the above mechanisms for embedding an XML data-island on an ASP page can use the src attribute to specify the URL of another file from which the contents of the data-island will be retrieved. This is actually quite cool and flexible. You can use any of the following three single lines of code, in conjunction with the data-island XML contained in the specified source file:

```
<xml id='DataIslandID' src='XMLDataFileURL' />
```

or

```
<script id='DataIslandID' src='XMLDataFileURL' language='xml' />
```

or

```
<script id='DataIslandID' src='XMLDataFileURL' type='text/xml' />
```

Please note: the XML elements and attributes in the MetaXML data-island for the previous examples must be expressed in lowercase letters.

Dynamic Table Configuration

The structure below is a data island found in the DTschema.xml file that is used to dynamically build report tables used by the (HTC) HTML component.

```
<Schema xmlns="urn:schemas-microsoft-com:xml-data" xmlns:dt="urn:_
    schemas-microsoft-com:datatypes">
  <AttributeType name="required" dt:type="enumeration" dt:values="yes no"_
    default="no" required="no" />
  <ElementType name="global" content="empty">
    <AttributeType name="keycol" required="yes" />
    <AttributeType name="uniquekey" dt:type="enumeration" dt:values=_
      "yes no" default="no" required="no" />
    <AttributeType name="sortbykey" dt:type="enumeration" dt:values=_
      "yes no" default="no" required="no" />
    <AttributeType name="overx" dt:type="enumeration" dt:values="yes no"_
      default="no" required="no" />
    <AttributeType name="newbutton" dt:type="enumeration" dt:values=_
      "yes no" default="yes" required="no" />
    <AttributeType name="deletebutton" dt:type="enumeration"_
```

```
        dt:values="yes no" default="yes" required="no" />
    <attribute type="required" />
    <attribute type="keycol" />
    <attribute type="uniquekey" />
    <attribute type="sortbykey" />
    <attribute type="overx" />
    <attribute type="newbutton" />
    <attribute type="deletebutton" />
</ElementType>

<AttributeType name="id" required="yes" />
<AttributeType name="width" dt:type="int" required="no" />
<AttributeType name="disabled" dt:type="enumeration" dt:values="yes no"_
    default="no" required="no" />
<AttributeType name="readonly" dt:type="enumeration" dt:values="yes no"_
    default="no" required="no" />
<AttributeType name="min" required="no" />
<AttributeType name="max" required="no" />
<AttributeType name="maxlen" required="no" />
<AttributeType name="browsereadonly" dt:type="enumeration" dt:values=_
    "yes no" default="no" required="no" />
<AttributeType name="browse" dt:type="enumeration" dt:values="yes no"_
    default="no" required="no" />
<AttributeType name="onbrowse" required="no" />
<AttributeType name="onchange" required="no" />
<AttributeType name="onrequire" required="no" />
<AttributeType name="onvalid" required="no" />
<AttributeType name="onerror" required="no" />
<AttributeType name="hide" dt:type="enumeration" dt:values="yes no"_
    default="no" required="no" />

<ElementType name="browsetooltip" content="textOnly" model="closed" />
<ElementType name="prompt" content="textOnly" model="closed" />
<ElementType name="format" content="textOnly" model="closed" />
<ElementType name="charmask" content="textOnly" model="closed" />
<ElementType name="name" content="textOnly" model="closed" />
<ElementType name="error" content="textOnly" model="closed" />

<ElementType name="label" content="textOnly" model="closed" />
<ElementType name="boolean" content="eltOnly" model="closed"_
    order="many">
    <attribute type="id" />
    <attribute type="width" />
    <attribute type="disabled" />
    <attribute type="readonly" />
    <attribute type="browsereadonly" />
    <attribute type="browse" />
    <attribute type="onbrowse" />
    <attribute type="onchange" />
    <attribute type="onerror" />
    <attribute type="hide" />
    <element type="label" />
    <element type="browsetooltip" minOccurs="0" />
    <element type="name" minOccurs="0" />
</ElementType>
```

```
<ElementType name="date" content="eltOnly" model="closed" order="many">
    <attribute type="id" />
    <attribute type="width" />
    <attribute type="disabled" />
    <attribute type="readonly" />
    <attribute type="required" />
    <attribute type="min" />
    <attribute type="max" />
    <attribute type="browsereadonly" />
    <attribute type="browse" />
    <attribute type="onbrowse" />
    <attribute type="onchange" />
    <attribute type="onrequire" />
    <attribute type="onvalid" />
    <attribute type="onerror" />
    <attribute type="hide" />
    <element type="browsetooltip" minOccurs="0" />
    <element type="name" minOccurs="0" />
    <element type="format" minOccurs="0" />
    <element type="prompt" minOccurs="0" />
    <element type="error" minOccurs="0" />
</ElementType>
<ElementType name="numeric" content="eltOnly" model="closed"_
    order="many">
    <AttributeType name="subtype" dt:type="enumeration" dt:values=_
        "integer float currency" default="integer" required="no" />
    <attribute type="id" />
    <attribute type="subtype" />
    <attribute type="width" />
    <attribute type="disabled" />
    <attribute type="readonly" />
    <attribute type="required" />
    <attribute type="min" />
    <attribute type="max" />
    <attribute type="browsereadonly" />
    <attribute type="browse" />
    <attribute type="onbrowse" />
    <attribute type="onchange" />
    <attribute type="onrequire" />
    <attribute type="onvalid" />
    <attribute type="onerror" />
    <attribute type="hide" />
    <element type="browsetooltip" minOccurs="0" />
    <element type="name" minOccurs="0" />
    <element type="format" minOccurs="0" />
    <element type="prompt" minOccurs="0" />
    <element type="error" minOccurs="0" />
    <element type="name" />
</ElementType>
<ElementType name="text" content="eltOnly" model="closed" order="many">
    <AttributeType name="subtype" dt:type="enumeration" dt:values=_
        "short long password" default="short" required="no" />
    <attribute type="id" />
    <attribute type="subtype" />
    <attribute type="width" />
```

```
         <attribute type="disabled" />
         <attribute type="readonly" />
         <attribute type="required" />
         <attribute type="maxlen" />
         <attribute type="browsereadonly" />
         <attribute type="browse" />
         <attribute type="onbrowse" />
         <attribute type="onchange" />
         <attribute type="onrequire" />
         <attribute type="onvalid" />
         <attribute type="onerror" />
         <attribute type="hide" />
         <element type="browsetooltip" minOccurs="0" />
         <element type="name" minOccurs="0" />
         <element type="charmask" minOccurs="0" />
         <element type="prompt" minOccurs="0" />
         <element type="error" minOccurs="0" />
      </ElementType>
      <ElementType name="time" content="eltOnly" model="closed" order="many">
         <attribute type="id" />
         <attribute type="width" />
         <attribute type="disabled" />
         <attribute type="readonly" />
         <attribute type="required" />
         <attribute type="min" />
         <attribute type="max" />
         <attribute type="browsereadonly" />
         <attribute type="browse" />
         <attribute type="onbrowse" />
         <attribute type="onchange" />
         <attribute type="onrequire" />
         <attribute type="onvalid" />
         <attribute type="onerror" />
         <attribute type="hide" />
         <element type="browsetooltip" minOccurs="0" />
         <element type="name" minOccurs="0" />
         <element type="prompt" minOccurs="0" />
         <element type="error" minOccurs="0" />
      </ElementType>
      <ElementType name="option" content="textOnly" model="closed">
         <AttributeType name="value" />
         <attribute type="value" />
      </ElementType>
      <ElementType name="select" content="eltOnly" model="closed" order="many">
         <attribute type="id" />
         <attribute type="width" />
         <attribute type="disabled" />
         <attribute type="readonly" />
         <attribute type="browsereadonly" />
         <attribute type="browse" />
         <attribute type="onbrowse" />
         <attribute type="onchange" />
         <attribute type="onrequire" />
         <attribute type="onvalid" />
         <attribute type="onerror" />
```

```
        <attribute type="hide" />
        <AttributeType name="value" required="yes" />
        <group order="one">
            <group order="many">
                <element type="option" maxOccurs="*" />
                <element type="browsetooltip" minOccurs="0" />
                <element type="name" minOccurs="0" />
                <element type="prompt" minOccurs="0" />
            </group>
            <element type="select" maxOccurs="*" />
        </group>
    </ElementType>

    <ElementType name="fields" content="eltOnly" model="closed" order="many">
        <element type="boolean" minOccurs="0" maxOccurs="*" />
        <element type="date" minOccurs="0" maxOccurs="*" />
        <element type="numeric" minOccurs="0" maxOccurs="*" />
        <element type="select" minOccurs="0" maxOccurs="*" />
        <element type="text" minOccurs="0" maxOccurs="*" />
        <element type="time" minOccurs="0" maxOccurs="*" />
    </ElementType>

    <ElementType name="dynamictable" content="eltOnly" model="closed"_
        order="seq">
        <element type="global" />
        <element type="fields" />
    </ElementType>
</Schema>
```

EditField Configuration

The structure below is a data island found in the EFschema.xml file that is used to dynamically edit report fields used by the (HTC) HTML component.

```
<Schema xmlns="urn:schemas-microsoft-com:xml-data" xmlns:dt="urn:schemas-
microsoft-com:datatypes">
    <AttributeType name="id" required="yes" />
    <AttributeType name="width" dt:type="int" required="no" />
    <AttributeType name="disabled" dt:type="enumeration" dt:values="yes no"_
        default="no" required="no" />
    <AttributeType name="readonly" dt:type="enumeration" dt:values="yes no"_
        default="no" required="no" />
    <AttributeType name="required" dt:type="enumeration" dt:values="yes no"_
        default="no" required="no" />
    <AttributeType name="min" required="no" />
    <AttributeType name="max" required="no" />
    <AttributeType name="maxlen" required="no" />
    <AttributeType name="browsereadonly" dt:type="enumeration" dt:values=_
        "yes no" default="no" required="no" />
    <AttributeType name="browse" dt:type="enumeration" dt:values="yes no"_
        default="no" required="no" />
    <AttributeType name="onbrowse" required="no" />
    <AttributeType name="onchange" required="no" />
    <AttributeType name="onrequire" required="no" />
    <AttributeType name="onvalid" required="no" />
```

```
<AttributeType name="onerror" required="no" />
<AttributeType name="hide" dt:type="enumeration" dt:values="yes no"_
   default="no" required="no" />

<ElementType name="browsetooltip" content="textOnly" model="closed" />
<ElementType name="prompt" content="textOnly" model="closed" />
<ElementType name="format" content="textOnly" model="closed" />
<ElementType name="charmask" content="textOnly" model="closed" />
<ElementType name="name" content="textOnly" model="closed" />
<ElementType name="error" content="textOnly" model="closed" />

<ElementType name="label" content="textOnly" model="closed" />
<ElementType name="boolean" content="eltOnly" model="closed"_
   order="many">
   <attribute type="id" />
   <attribute type="width" />
   <attribute type="disabled" />
   <attribute type="readonly" />
   <attribute type="browsereadonly" />
   <attribute type="browse" />
   <attribute type="onbrowse" />
   <attribute type="onchange" />
   <attribute type="onerror" />
   <attribute type="hide" />
   <element type="label" />
   <element type="browsetooltip" minOccurs="0" />
</ElementType>
<ElementType name="date" content="eltOnly" model="closed" order="many">
   <attribute type="id" />
   <attribute type="width" />
   <attribute type="disabled" />
   <attribute type="readonly" />
   <attribute type="required" />
   <attribute type="min" />
   <attribute type="max" />
   <attribute type="browsereadonly" />
   <attribute type="browse" />
   <attribute type="onbrowse" />
   <attribute type="onchange" />
   <attribute type="onrequire" />
   <attribute type="onvalid" />
   <attribute type="onerror" />
   <attribute type="hide" />
   <element type="browsetooltip" minOccurs="0" />
   <element type="format" minOccurs="0" />
   <element type="prompt" minOccurs="0" />
   <element type="error" minOccurs="0" />
</ElementType>
<ElementType name="numeric" content="eltOnly" model="closed"_
   order="many">
   <AttributeType name="subtype" dt:type="enumeration" dt:values=_
      "integer float currency" default="integer" required="no" />
   <attribute type="id" />
   <attribute type="subtype" />
   <attribute type="width" />
```

```
            <attribute type="disabled" />
            <attribute type="readonly" />
            <attribute type="required" />
            <attribute type="min" />
            <attribute type="max" />
            <attribute type="browsereadonly" />
            <attribute type="browse" />
            <attribute type="onbrowse" />
            <attribute type="onchange" />
            <attribute type="onrequire" />
            <attribute type="onvalid" />
            <attribute type="onerror" />
            <attribute type="hide" />
            <element type="browsetooltip" minOccurs="0" />
            <element type="format" minOccurs="0" />
            <element type="prompt" minOccurs="0" />
            <element type="error" minOccurs="0" />
            <element type="name" />
        </ElementType>
        <ElementType name="text" content="eltOnly" model="closed" order="many">
            <AttributeType name="subtype" dt:type="enumeration" dt:values=_
                "short long password" default="short" required="no" />
            <attribute type="id" />
            <attribute type="subtype" />
            <attribute type="width" />
            <attribute type="disabled" />
            <attribute type="readonly" />
            <attribute type="required" />
            <attribute type="maxlen" />
            <attribute type="browsereadonly" />
            <attribute type="browse" />
            <attribute type="onbrowse" />
            <attribute type="onchange" />
            <attribute type="onrequire" />
            <attribute type="onvalid" />
            <attribute type="onerror" />
            <attribute type="hide" />
            <element type="browsetooltip" minOccurs="0" />
            <element type="charmask" minOccurs="0" />
            <element type="prompt" minOccurs="0" />
            <element type="error" minOccurs="0" />
        </ElementType>
        <ElementType name="time" content="eltOnly" model="closed" order="many">
            <attribute type="id" />
            <attribute type="width" />
            <attribute type="disabled" />
            <attribute type="readonly" />
            <attribute type="required" />
            <attribute type="min" />
            <attribute type="max" />
            <attribute type="browsereadonly" />
            <attribute type="browse" />
            <attribute type="onbrowse" />
            <attribute type="onchange" />
            <attribute type="onrequire" />
```

```
            <attribute type="onvalid" />
            <attribute type="onerror" />
            <attribute type="hide" />
            <element type="browsetooltip" minOccurs="0" />
            <element type="prompt" minOccurs="0" />
            <element type="error" minOccurs="0" />
        </ElementType>
        <ElementType name="option" content="textOnly" model="closed">
            <AttributeType name="value" />
            <attribute type="value" />
        </ElementType>
        <ElementType name="select" content="eltOnly" model="closed" order="many">
            <attribute type="id" />
            <attribute type="width" />
            <attribute type="disabled" />
            <attribute type="readonly" />
            <attribute type="browsereadonly" />
            <attribute type="browse" />
            <attribute type="onbrowse" />
            <attribute type="onchange" />
            <attribute type="onrequire" />
            <attribute type="onvalid" />
            <attribute type="onerror" />
            <attribute type="hide" />
            <AttributeType name="value" required="yes" />
            <group order="one">
                <group order="many">
                    <element type="option" maxOccurs="*" />
                    <element type="browsetooltip" minOccurs="0" />
                    <element type="prompt" minOccurs="0" />
                </group>
                <element type="select" maxOccurs="*" />
            </group>
        </ElementType>

        <ElementType name="editfields" content="eltOnly" model="closed"_
            order="many">
            <element type="boolean" minOccurs="0" maxOccurs="*" />
            <element type="date" minOccurs="0" maxOccurs="*" />
            <element type="numeric" minOccurs="0" maxOccurs="*" />
            <element type="select" minOccurs="0" maxOccurs="*" />
            <element type="text" minOccurs="0" maxOccurs="*" />
            <element type="time" minOccurs="0" maxOccurs="*" />
        </ElementType>
    </Schema>
```

EditSheet Configuration

The structure below is a data island found in the ESschema.xml file that is used to dynamically configure the editsheet used by the (HTC) HTML component.

```
<Schema xmlns="urn:schemas-microsoft-com:xml-data" xmlns:dt="urn:_
    schemas-microsoft-com:datatypes">
    <ElementType name="name" content="textOnly" model="closed" />
    <ElementType name="key" content="textOnly" model="closed" />
```

977

```
<ElementType name="global" content="eltOnly" model="closed" order="many">
  <AttributeType name="expanded" dt:type="enumeration" dt:values=_
    "yes no" default="no" required="no" />
  <AttributeType name="title" dt:type="enumeration" dt:values=_
    "yes no" default="yes" required="no" />
  <attribute type="expanded" />
  <attribute type="title" />
  <element type="name" minOccurs="0" />
  <element type="key" minOccurs="0" />
</ElementType>

<AttributeType name="id" required="yes" />
<AttributeType name="width" dt:type="int" required="no" />
<AttributeType name="disabled" dt:type="enumeration" dt:values=_
  "yes no" default="no" required="no" />
<AttributeType name="readonly" dt:type="enumeration" dt:values=_
  "yes no" default="no" required="no" />
<AttributeType name="required" dt:type="enumeration" dt:values=_
  "yes no" default="no" required="no" />
<AttributeType name="min" required="no" />
<AttributeType name="max" required="no" />
<AttributeType name="maxlen" required="no" />
<AttributeType name="browsereadonly" dt:type="enumeration" dt:values=_
  "yes no" default="no" required="no" />
<AttributeType name="browse" dt:type="enumeration" dt:values=_
  "yes no" default="no" required="no" />
<AttributeType name="onbrowse" required="no" />
<AttributeType name="onchange" required="no" />
<AttributeType name="onrequire" required="no" />
<AttributeType name="onvalid" required="no" />
<AttributeType name="onerror" required="no" />
<AttributeType name="hide" dt:type="enumeration" dt:values="yes no"_
  default="no" required="no" />

<ElementType name="browsetooltip" content="textOnly" model="closed" />
<ElementType name="tooltip" content="textOnly" model="closed" />
<ElementType name="prompt" content="textOnly" model="closed" />
<ElementType name="format" content="textOnly" model="closed" />
<ElementType name="charmask" content="textOnly" model="closed" />
<ElementType name="error" content="textOnly" model="closed" />

<ElementType name="label" content="textOnly" model="closed" />
<ElementType name="boolean" content="eltOnly" model="closed"_
  order="many">
  <attribute type="id" />
  <attribute type="width" />
  <attribute type="disabled" />
  <attribute type="readonly" />
  <attribute type="browsereadonly" />
  <attribute type="browse" />
  <attribute type="onbrowse" />
  <attribute type="onchange" />
  <attribute type="onerror" />
  <attribute type="hide" />
  <element type="name" minOccurs="0" />
```

```
        <element type="tooltip" minOccurs="0" />
        <element type="label" />
        <element type="browsetooltip" minOccurs="0" />
    </ElementType>
    <ElementType name="date" content="eltOnly" model="closed" order="many">
        <attribute type="id" />
        <attribute type="width" />
        <attribute type="disabled" />
        <attribute type="readonly" />
        <attribute type="required" />
        <attribute type="min" />
        <attribute type="max" />
        <attribute type="browsereadonly" />
        <attribute type="browse" />
        <attribute type="onbrowse" />
        <attribute type="onchange" />
        <attribute type="onrequire" />
        <attribute type="onvalid" />
        <attribute type="onerror" />
        <attribute type="hide" />
        <element type="browsetooltip" minOccurs="0" />
        <element type="name" minOccurs="0" />
        <element type="tooltip" minOccurs="0" />
        <element type="format" minOccurs="0" />
        <element type="prompt" minOccurs="0" />
        <element type="error" minOccurs="0" />
    </ElementType>
    <ElementType name="numeric" content="eltOnly" model="closed"_
        order="many">
        <AttributeType name="subtype" dt:type="enumeration" dt:values=_
            "integer float currency" default="integer" required="no" />
        <attribute type="id" />
        <attribute type="subtype" />
        <attribute type="width" />
        <attribute type="disabled" />
        <attribute type="readonly" />
        <attribute type="required" />
        <attribute type="min" />
        <attribute type="max" />
        <attribute type="browsereadonly" />
        <attribute type="browse" />
        <attribute type="onbrowse" />
        <attribute type="onchange" />
        <attribute type="onrequire" />
        <attribute type="onvalid" />
        <attribute type="onerror" />
        <attribute type="hide" />
        <element type="browsetooltip" minOccurs="0" />
        <element type="name" minOccurs="0" />
        <element type="tooltip" minOccurs="0" />
        <element type="format" minOccurs="0" />
        <element type="prompt" minOccurs="0" />
        <element type="error" minOccurs="0" />
        <element type="name" />
    </ElementType>
```

979

```
    <ElementType name="text" content="eltOnly" model="closed" order="many">
        <AttributeType name="subtype" dt:type="enumeration" dt:values=_
            "short long password" default="short" required="no" />
        <attribute type="id" />
        <attribute type="subtype" />
        <attribute type="width" />
        <attribute type="disabled" />
        <attribute type="readonly" />
        <attribute type="required" />
        <attribute type="maxlen" />
        <attribute type="browsereadonly" />
        <attribute type="browse" />
        <attribute type="onbrowse" />
        <attribute type="onchange" />
        <attribute type="onrequire" />
        <attribute type="onvalid" />
        <attribute type="onerror" />
        <attribute type="hide" />
        <element type="browsetooltip" minOccurs="0" />
        <element type="name" minOccurs="0" />
        <element type="tooltip" minOccurs="0" />
        <element type="charmask" minOccurs="0" />
        <element type="prompt" minOccurs="0" />
        <element type="error" minOccurs="0" />
    </ElementType>
    <ElementType name="time" content="eltOnly" model="closed" order="many">
        <attribute type="id" />
        <attribute type="width" />
        <attribute type="disabled" />
        <attribute type="readonly" />
        <attribute type="required" />
        <attribute type="min" />
        <attribute type="max" />
        <attribute type="browsereadonly" />
        <attribute type="browse" />
        <attribute type="onbrowse" />
        <attribute type="onchange" />
        <attribute type="onrequire" />
        <attribute type="onvalid" />
        <attribute type="onerror" />
        <attribute type="hide" />
        <element type="browsetooltip" minOccurs="0" />
        <element type="name" minOccurs="0" />
        <element type="tooltip" minOccurs="0" />
        <element type="prompt" minOccurs="0" />
        <element type="error" minOccurs="0" />
    </ElementType>
    <ElementType name="option" content="textOnly" model="closed">
        <AttributeType name="value" />
        <attribute type="value" />
    </ElementType>
    <ElementType name="select" content="eltOnly" model="closed" order="many">
        <attribute type="id" />
        <attribute type="width" />
        <attribute type="disabled" />
```

```
            <attribute type="readonly" />
            <attribute type="browsereadonly" />
            <attribute type="browse" />
            <attribute type="onbrowse" />
            <attribute type="onchange" />
            <attribute type="onrequire" />
            <attribute type="onvalid" />
            <attribute type="onerror" />
            <attribute type="hide" />
            <AttributeType name="value" required="yes" />
            <group order="one">
               <group order="many">
                  <element type="option" maxOccurs="*" />
                  <element type="browsetooltip" minOccurs="0" />
                  <element type="name" minOccurs="0" />
                  <element type="tooltip" minOccurs="0" />
                  <element type="prompt" minOccurs="0" />
               </group>
               <element type="select" maxOccurs="*" />
            </group>
         </ElementType>

         <ElementType name="fields" content="eltOnly" model="closed" order="many">
            <element type="boolean" minOccurs="0" maxOccurs="*" />
            <element type="date" minOccurs="0" maxOccurs="*" />
            <element type="numeric" minOccurs="0" maxOccurs="*" />
            <element type="select" minOccurs="0" maxOccurs="*" />
            <element type="text" minOccurs="0" maxOccurs="*" />
            <element type="time" minOccurs="0" maxOccurs="*" />
         </ElementType>

         <ElementType name="template" content="textOnly" model="closed">
            <AttributeType name="register" required="no" />
            <attribute type="register" />
         </ElementType>

         <ElementType name="editsheet" content="eltOnly" model="closed"_
            order="seq">
            <element type="global" />
            <group order="one">
               <element type="fields" minOccurs="0" />
               <element type="template" minOccurs="0" />
               <group order="seq">
                  <element type="fields" minOccurs="0" />
                  <element type="template" minOccurs="0" />
               </group>
            </group>
         </ElementType>

         <ElementType name="editsheets" content="eltOnly" model="closed" order="seq">
            <element type="editsheet" maxOccurs="*" />
         </ElementType>
      </Schema>
```

Expression Builder Configuration

See the `ExprBldr.htc` file under the `Commerce Server Install Directory\widgets\exprbldrHTC\` for more information and in-code documentation.

List Editor Configuration

The structure below is a data island found in the `LEschema.xml` file that is used to dynamically configure lists used by the (HTC) HTML component.

```
<Schema xmlns="urn:schemas-microsoft-com:xml-data" xmlns:dt="urn:_
   schemas-microsoft-com:datatypes">
   <AttributeType name="id" required="yes" />
   <AttributeType name="width" dt:type="int" required="no" />
   <AttributeType name="disabled" dt:type="enumeration" dt:values=_
      "yes no" default="no" required="no" />
   <AttributeType name="readonly" dt:type="enumeration" dt:values=_
      "yes no" default="no" required="no" />
   <AttributeType name="required" dt:type="enumeration" dt:values=_
      "yes no" default="no" required="no" />
   <AttributeType name="min" required="no" />
   <AttributeType name="max" required="no" />
   <AttributeType name="maxlen" required="no" />
   <AttributeType name="browsereadonly" dt:type="enumeration" dt:values=_
      "yes no" default="no" required="no" />
   <AttributeType name="browse" dt:type="enumeration" dt:values="yes no"_
      default="no" required="no" />
   <AttributeType name="onbrowse" required="no" />
   <AttributeType name="onchange" required="no" />
   <AttributeType name="onrequire" required="no" />
   <AttributeType name="onvalid" required="no" />
   <AttributeType name="onerror" required="no" />
   <AttributeType name="hide" dt:type="enumeration" dt:values="yes no"_
      default="no" required="no" />

   <ElementType name="browsetooltip" content="textOnly" model="closed" />
   <ElementType name="prompt" content="textOnly" model="closed" />
   <ElementType name="format" content="textOnly" model="closed" />
   <ElementType name="charmask" content="textOnly" model="closed" />
   <ElementType name="name" content="textOnly" model="closed" />
   <ElementType name="tooltip" content="textOnly" model="closed" />
   <ElementType name="error" content="textOnly" model="closed" />

   <ElementType name="label" content="textOnly" model="closed" />
   <ElementType name="boolean" content="eltOnly" model="closed"_
      order="many">
      <attribute type="id" />
      <attribute type="width" />
      <attribute type="disabled" />
      <attribute type="readonly" />
      <attribute type="browsereadonly" />
      <attribute type="browse" />
      <attribute type="onbrowse" />
      <attribute type="onchange" />
      <attribute type="onerror" />
      <attribute type="hide" />
```

```
            <element type="label" />
            <element type="browsetooltip" minOccurs="0" />
            <element type="name" minOccurs="0" />
            <element type="tooltip" minOccurs="0" />
        </ElementType>
        <ElementType name="date" content="eltOnly" model="closed" order="many">
            <attribute type="id" />
            <attribute type="width" />
            <attribute type="disabled" />
            <attribute type="readonly" />
            <attribute type="required" />
            <attribute type="min" />
            <attribute type="max" />
            <attribute type="browsereadonly" />
            <attribute type="browse" />
            <attribute type="onbrowse" />
            <attribute type="onchange" />
            <attribute type="onrequire" />
            <attribute type="onvalid" />
            <attribute type="onerror" />
            <attribute type="hide" />
            <element type="browsetooltip" minOccurs="0" />
            <element type="name" minOccurs="0" />
            <element type="tooltip" minOccurs="0" />
            <element type="format" minOccurs="0" />
            <element type="prompt" minOccurs="0" />
            <element type="error" minOccurs="0" />
        </ElementType>
        <ElementType name="numeric" content="eltOnly" model="closed"_
            order="many">
            <AttributeType name="subtype" dt:type="enumeration" dt:values=_
                "integer float currency" default="integer" required="no" />
            <attribute type="id" />
            <attribute type="subtype" />
            <attribute type="width" />
            <attribute type="disabled" />
            <attribute type="readonly" />
            <attribute type="required" />
            <attribute type="min" />
            <attribute type="max" />
            <attribute type="browsereadonly" />
            <attribute type="browse" />
            <attribute type="onbrowse" />
            <attribute type="onchange" />
            <attribute type="onrequire" />
            <attribute type="onvalid" />
            <attribute type="onerror" />
            <attribute type="hide" />
            <element type="browsetooltip" minOccurs="0" />
            <element type="name" minOccurs="0" />
            <element type="tooltip" minOccurs="0" />
            <element type="format" minOccurs="0" />
            <element type="prompt" minOccurs="0" />
            <element type="error" minOccurs="0" />
            <element type="name" />
```

```
    </ElementType>
    <ElementType name="text" content="eltOnly" model="closed" order="many">
       <AttributeType name="subtype" dt:type="enumeration" dt:values=_
          "short long password" default="short" required="no" />
       <attribute type="id" />
       <attribute type="subtype" />
       <attribute type="width" />
       <attribute type="disabled" />
       <attribute type="readonly" />
       <attribute type="required" />
       <attribute type="maxlen" />
       <attribute type="browsereadonly" />
       <attribute type="browse" />
       <attribute type="onbrowse" />
       <attribute type="onchange" />
       <attribute type="onrequire" />
       <attribute type="onvalid" />
       <attribute type="onerror" />
       <attribute type="hide" />
       <element type="browsetooltip" minOccurs="0" />
       <element type="name" minOccurs="0" />
       <element type="tooltip" minOccurs="0" />
       <element type="charmask" minOccurs="0" />
       <element type="prompt" minOccurs="0" />
       <element type="error" minOccurs="0" />
    </ElementType>
    <ElementType name="time" content="eltOnly" model="closed" order="many">
       <attribute type="id" />
       <attribute type="width" />
       <attribute type="disabled" />
       <attribute type="readonly" />
       <attribute type="required" />
       <attribute type="min" />
       <attribute type="max" />
       <attribute type="browsereadonly" />
       <attribute type="browse" />
       <attribute type="onbrowse" />
       <attribute type="onchange" />
       <attribute type="onrequire" />
       <attribute type="onvalid" />
       <attribute type="onerror" />
       <attribute type="hide" />
       <element type="browsetooltip" minOccurs="0" />
       <element type="name" minOccurs="0" />
       <element type="tooltip" minOccurs="0" />
       <element type="prompt" minOccurs="0" />
       <element type="error" minOccurs="0" />
    </ElementType>
    <ElementType name="option" content="textOnly" model="closed">
       <AttributeType name="value" />
       <attribute type="value" />
    </ElementType>
    <ElementType name="select" content="eltOnly" model="closed" order="many">
       <attribute type="id" />
       <attribute type="width" />
```

```
                <attribute type="disabled" />
                <attribute type="readonly" />
                <attribute type="browsereadonly" />
                <attribute type="browse" />
                <attribute type="onbrowse" />
                <attribute type="onchange" />
                <attribute type="onrequire" />
                <attribute type="onvalid" />
                <attribute type="onerror" />
                <attribute type="hide" />
                <AttributeType name="value" required="yes" />
                <group order="one">
                    <group order="many">
                        <element type="option" maxOccurs="*" />
                        <element type="browsetooltip" minOccurs="0" />
                        <element type="name" minOccurs="0" />
                        <element type="tooltip" minOccurs="0" />
                        <element type="prompt" minOccurs="0" />
                    </group>
                    <element type="select" maxOccurs="*" />
                </group>
            </ElementType>

            <ElementType name="fields" content="eltOnly" model="closed" order="many">
                <element type="boolean" minOccurs="0" maxOccurs="*" />
                <element type="date" minOccurs="0" maxOccurs="*" />
                <element type="numeric" minOccurs="0" maxOccurs="*" />
                <element type="select" minOccurs="0" maxOccurs="*" />
                <element type="text" minOccurs="0" maxOccurs="*" />
                <element type="time" minOccurs="0" maxOccurs="*" />
            </ElementType>

            <ElementType name="column" content="textOnly" model="closed">
                <AttributeType name="format" dt:type="enumeration" dt:values=_
                    "select float none" default="none" required="no" />
                <attribute type="format" />
                <attribute type="id" />
                <attribute type="width" />
                <attribute type="hide" />
            </ElementType>

            <ElementType name="columns" content="eltOnly" model="closed">
                <element type="column" maxOccurs="*" />
            </ElementType>

            <ElementType name="listeditor" content="eltOnly" model="closed"_
                order="seq">
                <element type="columns" />
                <element type="fields" />
            </ElementType>
        </Schema>
```

ListSheet Configuration

The structure below is a data island found in the LSschema.xml file that is used to dynamically configure the listsheet used by the (HTC) HTML component.

```
<Schema xmlns="urn:schemas-microsoft-com:xml-data" xmlns:dt="urn:_
    schemas-microsoft-com:datatypes">
    <ElementType name="global" content="empty">
        <AttributeType name="selectall" dt:type="enumeration" dt:values=_
            "yes no" default="no" required="no" />
        <AttributeType name="curpage" dt:type="int" required="no" />
        <AttributeType name="pagesize" dt:type="int" required="no" />
        <AttributeType name="recordcount" dt:type="int" required="no" />
        <AttributeType name="selection" dt:type="enumeration"_
            dt:values="single multi" default="single" required="no" />
        <AttributeType name="headers" dt:type="enumeration" dt:values=_
            "yes no" default="yes" required="no" />
        <AttributeType name="scroll" dt:type="enumeration" dt:values=_
            "yes no" default="yes" required="no" />
        <AttributeType name="pagecontrols" dt:type="enumeration"_
            dt:values="yes no" default="yes" required="no" />
        <AttributeType name="selectionbuttons" dt:type="enumeration"_
            dt:values="yes no" default="yes" required="no" />
        <AttributeType name="sort" dt:type="enumeration" dt:values="yes no"_
            default="yes" required="no" />
        <attribute type="selectall" />
        <attribute type="curpage" />
        <attribute type="pagesize" />
        <attribute type="recordcount" />
        <attribute type="selection" />
        <attribute type="headers" />
        <attribute type="scroll" />
        <attribute type="pagecontrols" />
        <attribute type="selectionbuttons" />
        <attribute type="sort" />
    </ElementType>

    <AttributeType name="id" required="yes" />
    <AttributeType name="id2" required="no" />
    <AttributeType name="id3" required="no" />
    <AttributeType name="sortdir" dt:type="enumeration" dt:values=_
        "asc desc" default="asc" required="no" />
    <AttributeType name="width" dt:type="int" required="no" />
    <AttributeType name="format" dt:type="enumeration" dt:values=_
        "select float none" default="none" required="no" />
    <AttributeType name="hide" dt:type="enumeration" dt:values="yes no"_
        default="no" required="no" />

    <ElementType name="column" content="textOnly" model="closed">
        <attribute type="format" />
        <attribute type="id" />
        <attribute type="id2" />
        <attribute type="id3" />
        <attribute type="width" />
        <attribute type="sortdir" />
        <attribute type="hide" />
    </ElementType>

    <ElementType name="subobject" content="eltOnly" model="closed">
        <AttributeType name="type" dt:type="enumeration" dt:values=_
            "list properties" required="yes" />
```

```xml
            <AttributeType name="labelwidth" dt:type="int" required="no" />
            <AttributeType name="datawidth" dt:type="int" required="no" />
            <attribute type="type" />
            <attribute type="labelwidth" />
            <attribute type="datawidth" />
            <element type="column" maxOccurs="*" />
    </ElementType>

    <ElementType name="columns" content="eltOnly" model="closed">
            <element type="column" maxOccurs="*" />
            <element type="subobject" minOccurs="0" />
    </ElementType>

    <AttributeType name="formid" required="yes" />
    <ElementType name="newpage" content="empty" model="closed">
            <attribute type="formid" />
    </ElementType>
    <ElementType name="sort" content="empty" model="closed">
            <attribute type="formid" />
    </ElementType>
    <ElementType name="sublist" content="empty" model="closed">
            <attribute type="formid" />
    </ElementType>
    <ElementType name="operations" content="eltOnly" model="open"_
            order="many">
            <element type="newpage" minOccurs="0" />
            <element type="sort" minOccurs="0" />
            <element type="sublist" minOccurs="0" />
    </ElementType>

    <ElementType name="listsheet" content="eltOnly" model="closed"_
            order="seq">
            <element type="global" />
            <element type="columns" />
            <element type="operations" minOccurs="0" />
    </ElementType>
</Schema>
```

QueryBuilder Configuration

See the `QueryBuilder.htc` file under the `Commerce Server Install Directory\widgets\exprbldrHTC\` for more information and in-code documentation.

Catalog

There are three groups of elements associated with the catalog structure that will be referenced below. They are the root node element `MSCommerceCatalogCollection` (which will not be described in detail because of its simplicity) the Schema Elements and the Data Elements. We will first start with the Catalog Schema Elements.

Catalog Schema Elements

These elements are used to extend the catalog.

CatalogSchema – Contains the schema definition elements for the Catalog collection.

Parent Elements	Child Elements	Attributes
MSCommerceCatalogCollection	AttributeDefinition Definition PropertiesDefinition	None

AttributeDefinition – Defines an attribute that can be used to describe an aspect of a property.

Parent Elements	Child Elements	Attributes
CatalogSchema	None	DataType – values are datetime money number string bignumber real float currency Boolean Id – a unique ID for each node in the document. May not contain spaces (an XML requirement) Name – the name of the attribute definition

Definition – Defines a type of product or category.

Parent Elements	Child Elements	Attributes
CatalogSchema	None	DefinitionType – the type of the definition, either product or category Name – the name of the property. This name must be unique within the XML document Properties – the XML node IDs of the properties that are to be included in this product or category definition VariantProperties – the XML node IDs of the properties that are to be included as variant properties for this product definition. Use this attribute only for definitions of type product

PropertiesDefinition – Container for the individual property definitions.

Parent Elements	Child Elements	Attributes
CatalogSchema	Property	None

Property – Defines a property that can be used to describe an aspect of a product or category.

Parent Elements	Child Elements	Attributes
PropertiesDefinition	PropertyVale	AssignAll – indicates whether this property should automatically be assigned to product definitions as they are created through Commerce Server Business Desk. The values are: 1 (True) or 0 (False).
		DataType – legal values are: datetime enumeration filename float money number string bignumber currency Boolean real
		DefaultValue – the default value for instances of the property. This value will be interpreted according to the datatype specified for this property. Datetime values must be specified in XML Date format.
		DisplayInProductsList – indicates whether this property is to be displayed in summary lists of products in the Business Desk Catalog Editor, or in other areas where product lists are displayed. The values are: 1 (True) or 0 (False).
		DisplayName – the display name for the property, for example, the label that will be shown next to the values for this property to site users.
		DisplayOnSite – indicates whether this property should be shown to users visiting the website. The values are: 1 (True) or 0 (False).

Table continued on following page

Parent Elements	Child Elements	Attributes
		ExportToDW – indicates whether the Catalog DTS task should export this property into the Data Warehouse. Properties with this attribute set to True will be available for use in reports and data analysis. The values are: 1 (True) or 0 (False).
		Id – a unique ID for each node in the document. May not contain spaces (an XML requirement).
		IncludeInSpecSearch – indicates whether this property should be exposed to specification searches. The values are: 1 (True) or 0 (False).
		IsFreeTextSearchable – indicates whether this property should be included in the full-text index, and therefore, be free text searchable. The values are: 1 (True) or 0 (False).
		MaxValue – the maximum legal value for number data types, and the maximum length for string data types.
		MinValue – the minimum legal value for number data types, and the minimum length for string data types.
		Name – the unique name of the property.

PropertyValue – Defines a legal value for a property.

Parent Elements	Child Elements	Attributes
Property	None	DisplayName – a legal value for the containing property

Catalog Data Elements

These elements are used for the actual catalog and its members.

Catalog – Defines an individual catalog.

Parent Elements	Child Elements	Attributes
`MSCommerceCatalogCollection`	`Category`	`CatalogName` – the name of the catalog.
	`Product`	`currency` – the currency used in the catalog, expressed as a three letter ISO 4217 currency code; for example `USD`, `AUD`, `CDN`, `GBP`, `DEM`, `JPY`.
		`description` – a description of the catalog.
		`endDate` – the date the catalog validity expires. Used for documentation purposes only – Commerce Server does not apply any logic to this value.
		`locale` – the locale of the catalog, specified using a Windows Locale ID (LCID). Used for documentation purposes to indicate which locale the catalog is intended for.
		`productIdentifier` – the name of the property that uniquely identifies products (or product families) in the catalog.
		`productVariantIdentifier` – the name of the property that uniquely identifies product variants in the catalog. If the catalog does not contain products with variants, set this attribute to the same value as the value in the `productIdentifier` attribute.
		`startDate` – the date the catalog becomes valid. Used for documentation purposes only – Commerce Server does not apply any logic to this value.

Category – Defines an instance of a type of category.

Parent Elements	Child Elements	Attributes
Catalog	Field	Definition – the name of the category definition that the category is based on.
	Relationship	Id – the XML ID for the category element.
		isSearchable – indicates whether this category is to be used as a starting point for specification searches. True indicates this category will be included in the record set returned by calls to the ProductCatalog.GetSearchableCategories object. The values are 0 for False; 1 for True.
		name – the name of the category. This name must be unique for all categories in the same catalog.
		parentCategories – the XML IDs of the categories that are immediate parents of this category.
		listprice – the price that should be applied to any products that reference this category as their pricing category. Units for this value are determined by the currency attribute of the containing catalog.

Field – Defines a name and value pair for a field.

Parent Elements	Child Elements	Attributes
Category	None	FieldID – the name of the property a value is being supplied for
Product		FieldValue – the value for the property
ProductVariant		

Product – Defines an instance of a type of product.

Parent Elements	Child Elements	Attributes
Catalog	Field	Definition – the name of the product definition that the product is based on.
	ProductVariant	Id – the XML ID for the product element.
	Relationship	Listprice – the price for this product. Units for this value are determined by the currency attribute of the containing catalog.

Parent Elements	Child Elements	Attributes
		ParentCategories – the XML IDs of the categories that the product belongs to.
		PricingCategory – The XML ID of the category that the product inherits pricing from. *Use of this attribute is optional.*

ProductVariant – Defines an instance of a variant of a product.

Parent Elements	Child Elements	Attributes
Product	Field	Id – the XML ID for the variant element

Relationship – Defines a relationship between one product or category and another product or category.

Parent Elements	Child Elements	Attributes
Category	None	Description – the description of the relationship
Product		Name – the name of the relationship
		Relation – the XML ID of a product or category in the same catalog in which to relate the containing product or category

Catalog XML Schema Document Example

Below is the XML schema document `CatalogXMLSchema.xml` found on the root of the Commerce Server install folder.

```
<?xml version="1.0"?>
<Schema name="MSCommerceCatalogCollection" xmlns="urn:schemas_
    -microsoft-com:xml-data"
    xmlns:dt="urn:schemas-microsoft-com:datatypes" >
    <!--Model is open (default)-->
    <AttributeType name="name" dt:type="string" required='yes'/>
    <AttributeType name="id" dt:type="id" required='yes'/>
    <AttributeType name="dataType" dt:type="enumeration" dt:values=_
        "string number bignumber datetime money real float currency _
        boolean enumeration filename " required='yes'/>
    <AttributeType name="value"/>
    <AttributeType name="parentCategories" dt:type="idrefs"/>
    <AttributeType name="Definition" dt:type="string" required='yes'/>


    <ElementType name="MSCommerceCatalogCollection">
        <element type="CatalogSchema" minOccurs="1" maxOccurs="1"/>
        <element type="Catalog" minOccurs="0" maxOccurs="*"/>
    </ElementType>


    <ElementType name="PropertiesDefinition">
```

993

```
      <element type="Property" minOccurs="0" maxOccurs="*"/>
   </ElementType>

   <ElementType name="CatalogSchema">
      <element type="PropertiesDefinition" minOccurs="0" maxOccurs="1"/>
      <element type="Definition" minOccurs="0" maxOccurs="*"/>
      <element type="AttributeDefinition" minOccurs="0" maxOccurs="*"/>
   </ElementType>

   <ElementType name="AttributeDefinition">
      <attribute type="name"/>
      <attribute type="dataType"/>
   </ElementType>

   <ElementType name="PropertyValue">
      <AttributeType name="displayName" dt:type="string" required='yes'/>

      <attribute type="displayName"/>
   </ElementType>


   <ElementType name="Property" model="open">
      <AttributeType name="DefaultValue"  dt:type="string"/>
      <AttributeType name="MinValue"  dt:type="string"/>
      <AttributeType name="MaxValue"  dt:type="string"/>
      <AttributeType name="IsFreeTextSearchable"  dt:type="boolean"/>
      <AttributeType name="IncludeInSpecSearch"  dt:type="boolean"/>
      <AttributeType name="DisplayOnSite" dt:type="boolean"/>
      <AttributeType name="DisplayName"  dt:type="string"/>
      <AttributeType name="AssignAll"  dt:type="boolean"/>
      <AttributeType name="ExportToDW"  dt:type="boolean"/>
      <AttributeType name="DisplayInProductsList"  dt:type="boolean"/>


      <attribute type="DefaultValue"/>
      <attribute type="MinValue"/>
      <attribute type="MaxValue"/>
      <attribute type="IsFreeTextSearchable"/>
      <attribute type="IncludeInSpecSearch"/>
      <attribute type="DisplayOnSite" />
      <attribute type="DisplayName" />
      <attribute type="AssignAll"/>
      <attribute type="ExportToDW"/>
      <attribute type="DisplayInProductsList"/>
      <attribute type="name"/>
      <attribute type="dataType"/>
      <attribute type="id"/>

      <element type="PropertyValue" minOccurs="0" maxOccurs="*"/>
   </ElementType>

   <ElementType name="Definition">
      <AttributeType name="properties"  dt:type="idrefs"/>
      <AttributeType name="variantProperties"  dt:type="idrefs"/>
      <AttributeType name="DefinitionType"  required= "yes"_
```

```
                dt:type="enumeration" dt:values="product category "/>

    <attribute type="name"/>
    <attribute type="DefinitionType"/>
    <attribute type="properties"/>
    <attribute type="variantProperties"/>
</ElementType>

<ElementType name="Catalog">
    <AttributeType name="currency" required='yes'/>
    <AttributeType name="locale" dt:type="string"/>
    <AttributeType name="startDate" dt:type="string"/>
    <AttributeType name="endDate" dt:type="string"/>
    <AttributeType name="productUID"  required= "yes" dt:type="string"/>
    <AttributeType name="variantUID"  required= "yes" dt:type="string"/>
    <AttributeType name="weight_measuring_unit" dt:type="string"/>

    <element type="Category" minOccurs="0" maxOccurs="*"/>
    <element type="Product" minOccurs="0" maxOccurs="*"/>
    <attribute type="name"/>
    <attribute type="currency"/>
    <attribute type="locale"/>
    <attribute type="startDate"/>
    <attribute type="endDate"/>
    <attribute type="productUID"/>
    <attribute type="variantUID"/>
    <attribute type="weight_measuring_unit"/>
</ElementType>

<ElementType name="Field">
    <AttributeType name="fieldID" dt:type="idref"  />
    <AttributeType name="fieldValue" dt:type="string" required='yes'/>

    <attribute type="fieldID"/>
    <attribute type="fieldValue"/>
</ElementType>


<ElementType name="Category">

    <AttributeType name="isSearchable" dt:type="string"/>
    <AttributeType name="listprice" dt:type="string"/>


    <attribute type="listprice"/>
    <attribute type="id"/>
    <attribute type="name"/>
    <attribute type="parentCategories"/>
    <attribute type="Definition"/>
    <attribute type ="isSearchable" />
    <element type="Field" minOccurs="1" maxOccurs="*"/>
    <element type="Relationship" minOccurs="0" maxOccurs="*"/>
</ElementType>

<ElementType name="Product">
```

```
            <AttributeType name="pricingCategory" />
            <AttributeType name="listprice" dt:type="string" required="yes"/>

            <attribute type="listprice"/>
            <attribute type="id"/>
            <attribute type="Definition"/>
            <attribute type="pricingCategory"/>
            <attribute type="parentCategories"/>
            <element type="Field" minOccurs="1" maxOccurs="*"/>
            <element type="Relationship" minOccurs="0" maxOccurs="*"/>
            <element type="ProductVariant" minOccurs="0" maxOccurs="*"/>
    </ElementType>


    <ElementType name="ProductVariant">
            <AttributeType name="listprice" dt:type="string" required="yes"/>

            <attribute type="listprice"/>
            <element type="Field" minOccurs="1" maxOccurs="*"/>
    </ElementType>


    <ElementType name="Relationship">
            <AttributeType name="description" dt:type="string" />
            <AttributeType name="relation" required ="yes" dt:type="idref"/>

            <attribute type="name"/>
            <attribute type="description"/>
            <attribute type="relation"/>
    </ElementType>

</Schema>
```

XDR Schema

The XML-Data Reduced (XDR) schema defines the individual elements, attributes, and relations used in the XML structure of the catalog.

```
<Schema name="MSCommerceCatalogCollection" xmlns="urn:schemas-_
    microsoft-com:xml-data" xmlns:dt="urn:schemas-microsoft-com:datatypes">
    <AttributeType name="name" dt:type="string" required="yes" />
    <AttributeType name="id" dt:type="id" required="yes" />
    <AttributeType name="dataType" dt:type="enumeration" dt:values="string_
                    number bignumber datetime money real float currency_
                    boolean enumeration filename" required="yes" />
    <AttributeType name="value" />
    <AttributeType name="parentCategories" dt:type="idrefs" />
    <AttributeType name="Definition" dt:type="string" required="yes" />
    <ElementType name="MSCommerceCatalogCollection">
        <element type="CatalogSchema" minOccurs="1" maxOccurs="1" />
        <element type="Catalog" minOccurs="0" maxOccurs="*" />
    </ElementType>
    <ElementType name="PropertiesDefinition">
        <element type="Property" minOccurs="0" maxOccurs="*" />
    </ElementType>
```

```
<ElementType name="CatalogSchema">
   <element type="PropertiesDefinition" minOccurs="0" maxOccurs="1" />
   <element type="Definition" minOccurs="0" maxOccurs="*" />
   <element type="AttributeDefinition" minOccurs="0" maxOccurs="*" />
</ElementType>
<ElementType name="AttributeDefinition">
   <attribute type="name" />
   <attribute type="id" />
   <attribute type="dataType" />
</ElementType>
<ElementType name="PropertyValue">
   <AttributeType name="displayName" dt:type="string" required="yes" />
   <attribute type="displayName" />
</ElementType>
<ElementType name="Property" model="open">
   <AttributeType name="DefaultValue" dt:type="string" />
   <AttributeType name="MinValue" dt:type="string" />
   <AttributeType name="MaxValue" dt:type="string" />
   <AttributeType name="IsFreeTextSearchable" dt:type="boolean" />
   <AttributeType name="IncludeInSpecSearch" dt:type="boolean" />
   <AttributeType name="DisplayOnSite" dt:type="boolean" />
   <AttributeType name="DisplayName" dt:type="string" />
   <AttributeType name="AssignAll" dt:type="boolean" />
   <AttributeType name="ExportToDW" dt:type="boolean" />
   <AttributeType name="DisplayInProductsList" dt:type="boolean" />
   <attribute type="DefaultValue" />
   <attribute type="MinValue" />
   <attribute type="MaxValue" />
   <attribute type="IsFreeTextSearchable" />
   <attribute type="IncludeInSpecSearch" />
   <attribute type="DisplayOnSite" />
   <attribute type="DisplayName" />
   <attribute type="AssignAll" />
   <attribute type="ExportToDW" />
   <attribute type="DisplayInProductsList" />
   <attribute type="name" />
   <attribute type="DataType" />
   <attribute type="id" />
   <element type="PropertyValue" minOccurs="0" maxOccurs="*" />
</ElementType>
<ElementType name="Definition">
   <AttributeType name="properties" dt:type="idrefs" />
   <AttributeType name="variantProperties" dt:type="idrefs" />
   <AttributeType name="DefinitionType" required="yes" dt:type=
                   "enumeration" values="product category" />
   <attribute type="name" />
   <attribute type="DefinitionType" />
   <attribute type="properties" />
   <attribute type="variantProperties" />
</ElementType>
<ElementType name="Catalog">
   <AttributeType name="currency" required="yes" />
   <AttributeType name="locale" dt:type="string" />
   <AttributeType name="startDate" dt:type="string" />
   <AttributeType name="endDate" dt:type="string" />
```

```
        <AttributeType name="productIdentifier" required="yes"_
           dt:type="string" />
        <AttributeType name="productVariantIdentifier" required="yes"_
           dt:type="string" />
        <AttributeType name="weight_measuring_unit" dt:type="string" />
        <element type="Category" minOccurs="0" maxOccurs="*" />
        <element type="Product" minOccurs="0" maxOccurs="*" />
        <attribute type="catalogName" />
        <attribute type="description" />
        <attribute type="currency" />
        <attribute type="locale" />
        <attribute type="startDate" />
        <attribute type="endDate" />
        <attribute type="productIdentifier" />
        <attribute type="productVariantIdentifier" />
</ElementType>
<ElementType name="Field">
        <AttributeType name="fieldID" dt:type="idref" />
        <AttributeType name="fieldValue" dt:type="string" required="yes" />
        <attribute type="fieldID" />
        <attribute type="fieldValue" />
</ElementType>
<ElementType name="Category">
        <AttributeType name="isSearchable" dt:type="string" />
        <AttributeType name="listprice" dt:type="string" />
        <AttributeType name="image" dt:type="string" />
        <AttributeType name="description" dt:type="string" />
        <attribute type="listprice" />
        <attribute type="id" />
        <attribute type="name" />
        <attribute type="parentCategories" />
        <attribute type="Definition" />
        <attribute type="isSearchable" />
        <element type="Field" minOccurs="1" maxOccurs="*" />
        <element type="Relationship" minOccurs="0" maxOccurs="*" />
</ElementType>
<ElementType name="Product">
        <AttributeType name="pricingCategory" />
        <AttributeType name="listprice" dt:type="string" required="yes" />
        <attribute type="listprice" />
        <attribute type="id" />
        <attribute type="definition" />
        <attribute type="pricingCategory" />
        <attribute type="parentCategories" />
        <element type="Field" minOccurs="1" maxOccurs="*" />
        <element type="Relationship" minOccurs="1" maxOccurs="*" />
        <element type="ProductVariant" minOccurs="0" maxOccurs="*" />
</ElementType>
<ElementType name="ProductVariant">
        <attribute type="Id" />
        <element type="Field" minOccurs="1" maxOccurs="*" />
</ElementType>
<ElementType name="Relationship">
        <AttributeType name="description" dt:type="string" />
        <AttributeType name="relation" required="yes" dt:type="idref" />
```

```
        <attribute type="name" />
        <attribute type="description" />
        <attribute type="relation" />
    </ElementType>
</Schema>
```

Expression

This schema is output when exporting expressions from the Expression Store and is required for importing expressions into the Expression Store from a file. The file will be called ExpressionDefinition.xml.

```
<xml xmlns:s='uuid:BDC6E3F0-6DA3-11d1-A2A3-00AA00C14882'
    xmlns:dt='uuid:C2F41010-65B3-11d1-A29F-00AA00C14882'
    xmlns:rs='urn:schemas-microsoft-com:rowset' xmlns:z='#RowsetSchema'>
<s:Schema id='RowsetSchema'>
    <s:ElementType name='row' content='eltOnly' rs:CommandTimeout='300'
        rs:ReshapeName='DSRowset1'>
        <s:AttributeType name='ExprID' rs:number='1'>
            <s:datatype dt:type='int' dt:maxLength='4' rs:precision='10'
                rs:fixedlength='true' rs:maybenull='false'/>
        </s:AttributeType>
        <s:AttributeType name='ExprName' rs:number='2'
            rs:writeunknown='true'>
            <s:datatype dt:type='string' dt:maxLength='30'
                rs:maybenull='false'/>
        </s:AttributeType>
        <s:AttributeType name='Category' rs:number='3' rs:nullable='true'
            rs:writeunknown='true'>
            <s:datatype dt:type='string' dt:maxLength='30'/>
        </s:AttributeType>
        <s:AttributeType name='ExprDesc' rs:number='4' rs:nullable='true'
            rs:writeunknown='true'>
            <s:datatype dt:type='string' dt:maxLength='200'/>
        </s:AttributeType>
        <s:AttributeType name='ExprBody' rs:number='5'
            rs:writeunknown='true'>
            <s:datatype dt:type='string' dt:maxLength='3400'
                rs:maybenull='false'/>
        </s:AttributeType>
        <s:AttributeType name='DateCreated' rs:number='6'
            rs:writeunknown='true'>
            <s:datatype dt:type='dateTime' rs:dbtype='timestamp'
                dt:maxLength='16' rs:scale='3' rs:precision='23'
                rs:fixedlength='true' rs:maybenull='false'/>
        </s:AttributeType>
        <s:AttributeType name='DateModified' rs:number='7'
            rs:writeunknown='true'>
            <s:datatype dt:type='dateTime' rs:dbtype='timestamp'
                dt:maxLength='16' rs:scale='3' rs:precision='23'
                rs:fixedlength='true' rs:maybenull='false'/>
        </s:AttributeType>
        <s:ElementType name='rsExprDeps' content='eltOnly'
            rs:CommandTimeout='300' rs:ReshapeName='DSRowset2'
            rs:relation='0100000001000000000000000'>
```

```
               <s:AttributeType name='ExprID' rs:number='1'
                  rs:writeunknown='true'>
                  <s:datatype dt:type='int' dt:maxLength='4' rs:precision='10'
                     rs:fixedlength='true' rs:maybenull='false'/>
               </s:AttributeType>
               <s:AttributeType name='ExprDep' rs:number='2'
                  rs:writeunknown='true'>
                  <s:datatype dt:type='int' dt:maxLength='4' rs:precision='10'
                     rs:fixedlength='true' rs:maybenull='false'/>
               </s:AttributeType>
               <s:extends type='rs:rowbase'/>
            </s:ElementType>
            <s:ElementType name='rsProfDeps' content='eltOnly'
               rs:CommandTimeout='300' rs:ReshapeName='DSRowset3'
               rs:relation='0100000001000000000000000'>
               <s:AttributeType name='ExprID' rs:number='1'
                  rs:writeunknown='true'>
                  <s:datatype dt:type='int' dt:maxLength='4' rs:precision='10'
                     rs:fixedlength='true' rs:maybenull='false'/>
               </s:AttributeType>
               <s:AttributeType name='ProfDep' rs:number='2'
                  rs:writeunknown='true'>
                  <s:datatype dt:type='string' dt:maxLength='128'
                     rs:maybenull='false'/>
               </s:AttributeType>
               <s:extends type='rs:rowbase'/>
            </s:ElementType>
            <s:extends type='rs:rowbase'/>
         </s:ElementType>
      </s:Schema>
```

Profile

There are three XML schema definitions for Profiles in CS2K: these are the Address, Organization, and UserObject schemas. The definitions are what is returned by the `GetProfileDefXML` method of the `ProfileService` object. See `ProfileService` in Appendix B.

Address Schema

This shows the attribute-centric schema for the Address profile. This profile stores both user and organization addresses.

```
<?xml version="1.0"?>
<ProfileDocument>
<Schema xmlns="urn:schemas-microsoft-com:xml-data"
   xmlns:dt="urn:schemas-microsoft-com:datatypes">
<ElementType name="Address">
   <attributeType name="address_id" dt:type="string" required="yes"/>
   <attributeType name="id" dt:type="string"/>
   <attributeType name="last_name" dt:type="string"/>
   <attributeType name="first_name" dt:type="string"/>
   <attributeType name="address_name" dt:type="string"/>
   <attributeType name="address_type" dt:type="int"/>
   <attributeType name="description" dt:type="string"/>
```

```
            <attributeType name="address_line1" dt:type="string" required="yes"/>
            <attributeType name="address_line2" dt:type="string"/>
            <attributeType name="city" dt:type="string"/>
            <attributeType name="region_code" dt:type="string" required="yes"/>
            <attributeType name="region_name" dt:type="string"/>
            <attributeType name="postal_code" dt:type="string" required="yes"/>
            <attributeType name="country_code" dt:type="string" required="yes"/>
            <attributeType name="country_name" dt:type="string"/>
            <attributeType name="tel_number" dt:type="string"/>
            <attributeType name="tel_extension" dt:type="string"/>
            <attributeType name="locale" dt:type="int"/>
            <attributeType name="user_id_changed_by" dt:type="string"/>
            <attributeType name="date_last_changed" dt:type="datetime"/>
            <attributeType name="date_created" dt:type="datetime"/>
    <ElementType name="GeneralInfo" content="eltOnly">
        <attribute type="address_id"/>
        <attribute type="id"/>
        <attribute type="last_name"/>
        <attribute type="first_name"/>
        <attribute type="address_name"/>
        <attribute type="address_type"/>
        <attribute type="description"/>
        <attribute type="address_line1"/>
        <attribute type="address_line2"/>
        <attribute type="city"/>
        <attribute type="region_code"/>
        <attribute type="region_name"/>
        <attribute type="postal_code"/>
        <attribute type="country_code"/>
        <attribute type="country_name"/>
        <attribute type="tel_number"/>
        <attribute type="tel_extension"/>
        <attribute type="locale"/>
        <attribute type="user_id_changed_by"/>
    </ElementType>
    <ElementType name="ProfileSystem" content="eltOnly">
        <attribute type="date_last_changed"/>
        <attribute type="date_created"/>
    </ElementType>
        <element type="GeneralInfo"/>
        <element type="ProfileSystem"/>
    </ElementType>
    </Schema>
    </ProfileDocument>
```

Runtime Rep – This contains the runtime representation of the above profile.

```
    <?xml version="1.0"?>
    <ProfileDocument>
    <Address>
        <GeneralInfo address_id id last_name first_name address_name
            address_type description address_line1 address_line2 city
            region_code region_name postal_code country_code country_name
            tel_number tel_extension locale />
        <ProfileSystem date_last_changed date_created>
```

1001

```
        </ProfileSystem>
    </Address>
    </ProfileDocument>
```

Organization Schema

This shows the attribute-centric schema for the Organization profile. This profile stores information about organizations including home companies, partners, etc.

```
<?xml version="1.0"?>
<ProfileDocument>
<Schema xmlns="urn:schemas-microsoft-com:xml-data"
    xmlns:dt="urn:schemas-microsoft-com:datatypes">
<ElementType name="Organization">
    <attributeType name="org_id" dt:type="string" required="yes"/>
    <attributeType name="name" dt:type="string" required="yes"/>
    <attributeType name="trading_partner_number" dt:type="string"/>
    <attributeType name="user_id_admin_contact" dt:type="string"/>
    <attributeType name="user_id_receiver" dt:type="string"/>
    <attributeType name="org_catalog_set" dt:type="string"/>
    <attributeType name="user_id_changed_by" dt:type="string"/>
    <attributeType name="date_last_changed" dt:type="datetime"/>
    <attributeType name="date_created" dt:type="datetime"/>
    <attributeType name="user_id_purchasing_manager" dt:type="string"/>
<ElementType name="GeneralInfo" content="eltOnly">
    <attribute type="org_id"/>
    <attribute type="name"/>
    <attribute type="trading_partner_number"/>
    <attribute type="user_id_admin_contact"/>
    <attribute type="user_id_receiver"/>
    <attribute type="org_catalog_set"/>
    <attribute type="user_id_changed_by"/>
</ElementType>
<ElementType name="ProfileSystem" content="eltOnly">
    <attribute type="date_last_changed"/>
    <attribute type="date_created"/>
</ElementType>
<ElementType name="Purchasing" content="eltOnly">
    <attribute type="user_id_purchasing_manager"/>
</ElementType>
    <element type="GeneralInfo"/>
    <element type="ProfileSystem"/>
    <element type="Purchasing"/>
</ElementType>
</Schema>
</ProfileDocument>
```

Runtime Rep – This contains the runtime representation of the above profile.

```
<?xml version="1.0"?>
<ProfileDocument>
<Address>
    <GeneralInfo address_id id last_name first_name address_name
        address_type description address_line1 address_line2 city
```

```
          region_code region_name postal_code country_code country_name
          tel_number tel_extension locale />
          <ProfileSystem date_last_changed date_created>
          </ProfileSystem>
      </Address>
    </ProfileDocument>
```

UserObject Schema

This shows the attribute-centric schema for the UserObject profile. This profile stores information about registered and anonymous users such as the logon_name and the email_address to name a few.

```xml
<?xml version="1.0"?>
<ProfileDocument>
<Schema xmlns="urn:schemas-microsoft-com:xml-data"
    xmlns:dt="urn:schemas-microsoft-com:datatypes">
<ElementType name="UserObject">
    <attributeType name="org_id" dt:type="string"/>
    <attributeType name="account_status" dt:type="int" required="yes"/>
    <attributeType name="user_catalog_set" dt:type="string"/>
    <attributeType name="date_registered" dt:type="datetime"/>
    <attributeType name="campaign_history" dt:type="string"/>
    <attributeType name="partner_desk_role" dt:type="int"/>
    <attributeType name="user_id" dt:type="string" required="yes"/>
    <attributeType name="logon_name" dt:type="string" required="yes"/>
    <attributeType name="user_security_password" dt:type="string"_
        required="yes"/>
    <attributeType name="email_address" dt:type="string"/>
    <attributeType name="user_type" dt:type="int"/>
    <attributeType name="user_title" dt:type="string"/>
    <attributeType name="last_name" dt:type="string"/>
    <attributeType name="first_name" dt:type="string"/>
    <attributeType name="tel_number" dt:type="string"/>
    <attributeType name="tel_extension" dt:type="string"/>
    <attributeType name="fax_number" dt:type="string"/>
    <attributeType name="fax_extension" dt:type="string"/>
    <attributeType name="user_id_changed_by" dt:type="string"/>
    <attributeType name="date_last_changed" dt:type="datetime"/>
    <attributeType name="date_created" dt:type="datetime"/>
<ElementType name="AccountInfo" content="eltOnly">
    <attribute type="org_id"/>
    <attribute type="account_status"/>
    <attribute type="user_catalog_set"/>
    <attribute type="date_registered"/>
</ElementType>
<ElementType name="Advertising" content="eltOnly">
    <attribute type="campaign_history"/>
</ElementType>
<ElementType name="BusinessDesk" content="eltOnly">
    <attribute type="partner_desk_role"/>
</ElementType>
<ElementType name="GeneralInfo" content="eltOnly">
    <attribute type="user_id"/>
    <attribute type="logon_name"/>
    <attribute type="user_security_password"/>
```

```
      <attribute type="email_address"/>
      <attribute type="user_type"/>
      <attribute type="user_title"/>
      <attribute type="last_name"/>
      <attribute type="first_name"/>
      <attribute type="tel_number"/>
      <attribute type="tel_extension"/>
      <attribute type="fax_number"/>
      <attribute type="fax_extension"/>
      <attribute type="user_id_changed_by"/>
  </ElementType>
  <ElementType name="ProfileSystem" content="eltOnly">
      <attribute type="date_last_changed"/>
      <attribute type="date_created"/>
  </ElementType>
      <element type="AccountInfo"/>
      <element type="Advertising"/>
      <element type="BusinessDesk"/>
      <element type="GeneralInfo"/>
      <element type="ProfileSystem"/>
  </ElementType>
  </Schema>
  </ProfileDocument>
```

Runtime Rep – This contains the runtime representation of the above profile.

```
  <?xml version="1.0"?>
  <ProfileDocument>
  <Address>
      <GeneralInfo address_id id last_name first_name address_name
          address_type description address_line1 address_line2 city
          region_code region_name postal_code country_code country_name
          tel_number tel_extension locale />
      <ProfileSystem date_last_changed date_created>
      </ProfileSystem>
  </Address>
  </ProfileDocument>
```

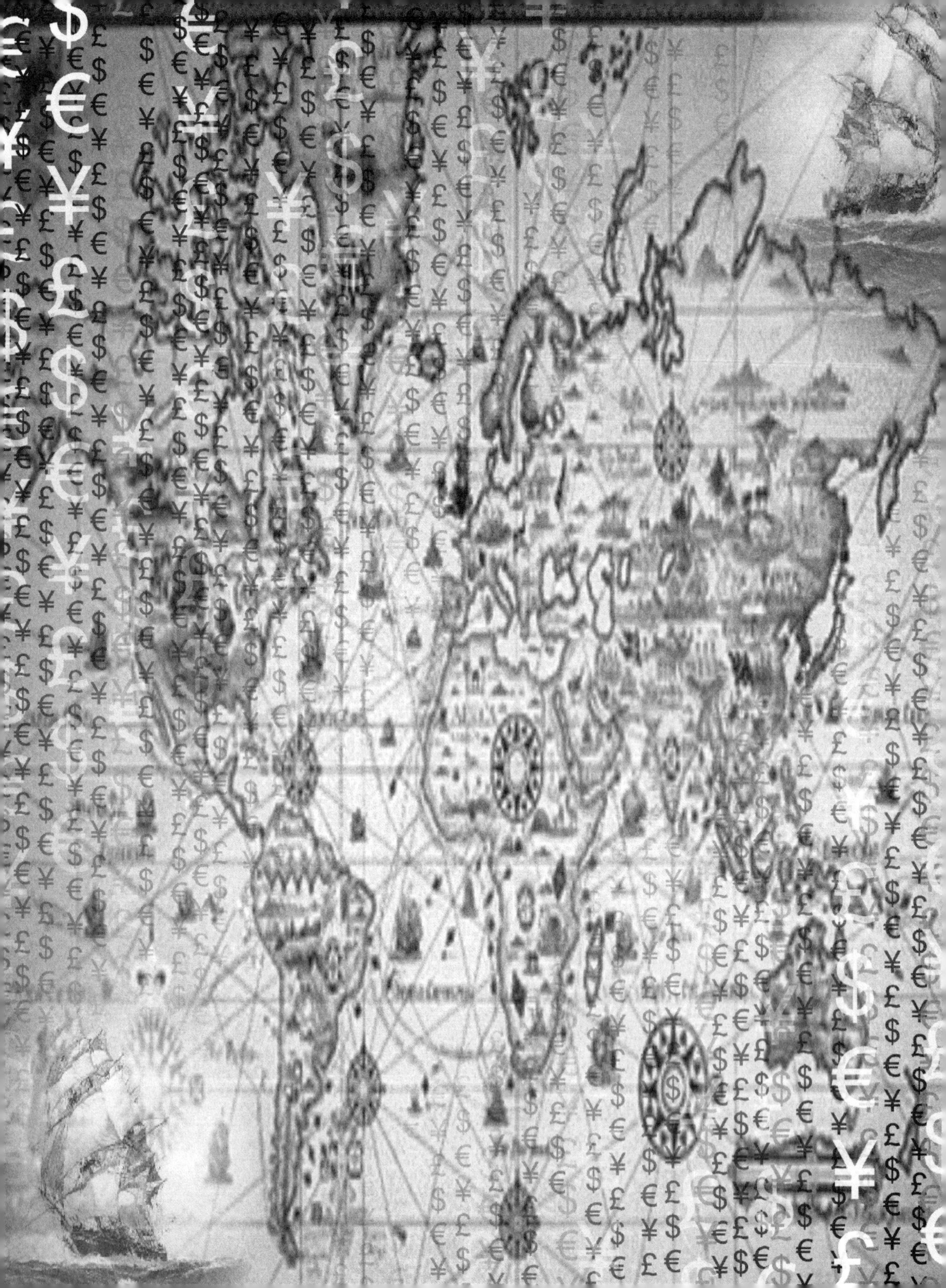

D

E-Commerce System Deployment

A successful deployment of Commerce Server 2000 (CS2K) requires more than a server or two; a highly-available, reliable and scalable network and systems environment must be designed to ensure your transaction environment is available to your customers 24 hours a day, seven days a week. Unlike brick-and-mortar commerce environments, your digital customers demand access at all hours from wherever they may be. Your transaction engine and website must be available through peak transaction periods, scheduled maintenance, and unscheduled network and systems outages. Additionally, your site must load quickly and be streamlined or your potential customer will leave your site for the next one on the list.

This appendix will discuss in detail the infrastructure required to support this successful deployment. It specifically discusses the needs of the entire environment, not just the servers and Commerce Server 2000 software configuration. We will discuss network and systems architecture as well as Windows 2000 and Active Directory deployment and configuration. In addition, we will cover security issues, content and systems management, backup and disaster recovery. As we work through the requirements, we will discuss Commerce Server 2000 deployment scenarios for small, medium and enterprise environments. Whether your revenue is based entirely on digital commerce or as a supplement to a current brick-and-mortar commerce environment, the name of the game is to please prospective customers and convince them to purchase your goods and/or services, return for later purchases, and tell their friends about your commerce site.

The focus of this appendix is on providing the framework for the entire network and systems environment. It will give you an understanding of what is required to successfully deploy CS2K in your environment, and the blueprints you need to design and deploy a stable, reliable and scalable digital commerce environment. We will look at design considerations and deployment options to tailor the CS2K deployment to your unique environment and transaction needs (with a little of the author's bias on design philosophy and hardware/network recommendations thrown in).

This appendix is written for developers with little infrastructure experience and little or no network and systems engineering resources available. It is also designed to help you understand the requirements for a successful Commerce Server 2000 deployment. Many small organizations do not have the resources available for network and systems engineering and require their development team to take on these duties. This appendix will help these developers understand the environmental requirements for a successful Commerce Server 2000 implementation. This appendix is not written by a developer and does not include any code, but if you need help designing and deploying an infrastructure to support your Commerce Server 2000 deployment, then read on!

The Five E-Commerce Commandments

The primary goal of any e-commerce site is to attract new customers and convince them to return for additional purchases. There are five E-Commerce Commandments that must be followed to afford the greatest chance of success for your CS2Kdeployment.

- ❑ **Thy Site Shall Be Reliable**. The commerce site must be available any time a potential customer wants to use your site. This is even more important as Internet usage and digital commerce is growing around the world. Unavailable pages and services will drive customers away and to your competitor's site.

- ❑ **Thy Site Shall Be Secure**. The customer wants to be assured that his transaction and personal information is secure from prying eyes. This means tightening security on your public Internet connections as well as securing your web servers, database and transaction engine.

- ❑ **Thou Shall Not Wait Long For Page Load**. The average customer will not wait more than 5-10 seconds for a page to load, database to respond or transaction to complete. If your site responds slowly to a customer's request, you can be assured that they will leave your site for one that can provide a quicker shopping experience.

- ❑ **Thy Site Shall Be User Friendly**. The site must be intuitive for the average Internet user to use. The navigation and search engine should require little effort to quickly and reliably find the product the customer is looking for. Also, the checkout experience should be quick, requiring few keystrokes and page loads.

- ❑ **Thy Products or Services Shall Be Competitively Priced**. The last requirement, and the one reason most people flock to digital commerce sites, is to get a good deal. Your site must be price competitive. You may have the greatest site since the invention of the Internet, but if you are selling your widget for 20% more than anyone else, you will be hard pressed to attract new customers and retain old ones.

This list is applicable to all facets of design, deployment and management of your digital commerce initiative, from technology design to merchandising price changes. We will be covering the first three bullet points as we design the network and systems infrastructure for your Commerce Server 2000 environment. The other two are design considerations while developing the site and are discussed elsewhere in the book. The most important thing to remember as you design and rollout your CS2K environment is that each of these five considerations must be evaluated and implemented for your digital commerce initiative to be a success.

As we discuss the deployment of CS2K in your environment, we will touch on all design considerations to provide a highly available, secure and scalable infrastructure, as every environment is different and reliability requirements vary from site to site, and your requirements may vary. This appendix is written with the goal of high availability, high security and the ability to scale easily in mind. Some of these design options may be cost-prohibitive or excessive for your environment; the goal of this appendix is to give you all of the options available to design and deploy a highly available, secure environment, leaving you to determine which design options are best for your business.

Infrastructure Design

The design of your infrastructure is the basis for any digital environment and care must be taken to ensure that the foundation is laid correctly to support the Commerce Server 2000 environment that will be built on top of it. No part of the infrastructure design can be left to chance as any weakness at this level will bring compounded problems to your commerce environment. Close consideration must be given to redundancy, reliability and security of your network. Think of your network stability as a chain, with redundancy, reliability and security as links in that chain. Your network's ability to perform efficiently and reliably is only as strong as the weakest link. It is this appendix's goal to help you create a network and systems infrastructure for your Commerce Server 2000 environment, maximizing the strength of each link based on resources available for this implementation. We will discuss data center, network and systems design with the premise that we are building a digital commerce environment that must be available to your customers at any time with a minimum of delay.

Data Center Requirements and Hosting/Co-location Facilities

The first consideration before designing your network and systems infrastructure, is deciding where your environment is going to be hosted. If you currently operate your own data center, you need to ensure it is capable of providing highly available services to your network and systems infrastructure. The primary considerations for your data center are power availability, HVAC (High Volume Air Conditioning), and local loop redundancy (the connection from your data center to your telephone company's Central Office).

Power Availability

The lifeblood of your commerce environment is electricity and steps must be taken to ensure that the power flows under any circumstance. The golden rule in power availability is the more you have control, the more you control the ability of your environment to function despite service provider failures. In order to control your destiny, you need to provide electricity even if your power company has an interruption of service. If you are unable to command the electricity gods to do your bidding, you will have to rely on more terrestrial devices, such as redundant UPSs (Uninterruptible Power Supplies), PDUs (Power Distribution Units), ATSs (Automatic Transfer Switches) and Generators. The following figure shows a power distribution infrastructure for a typical enterprise data center.

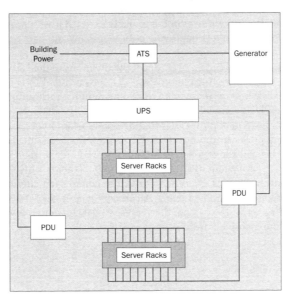

Uninterruptible power supplies provide two important services:

- ❑ Continued power delivery during an interruption of service
- ❑ Line conditioning

Line conditioning ensures that the same level of power is provided at all times, eliminating power surges and brownouts. UPSs come in many varieties and there is one to fit every data center. Larger organizations supporting an enterprise data center will probably opt for a single large UPS unit that will support the entire environment. Smaller organizations without the resources available for this type of unit can still protect their systems with rack-mounted UPS units that will power your servers or network equipment in that rack. When deciding which type of UPS unit to deploy in your data center, it is important to understand your servers' power requirements and how many units will be required to provide power to your rack. If resources allow and you are supporting an enterprise environment with multiple racks of servers, an enterprise UPS system is usually your best bet.

There are three types of UPSs available: offline, line interactive and online. The offline UPS provides power directly from the wall and cuts over to battery when primary power is lost. This is less expensive because of the switching employed within the UPS. Offline UPSs do little, if any, line conditioning and the switch from primary power to battery may be enough of a disruption of service to cause a systems outage. At a minimum there will be a momentary decrease in power service usually followed by a momentary spike as battery power is applied. This type of UPS should only be used for non-critical systems.

A more reliable type of UPS is line interactive. A line interactive UPS provides additional line conditioning, specifically voltage regulation and noise filtering. This UPS system provides a greater quality of power delivery, but still suffers from the effects of power switchover from your primary power source to battery. This is a cost effective solution that provides power backup as well as line conditioning, critical for any highly available systems and network infrastructure.

The last, and most reliable type of UPS is the online UPS. Like a line interactive UPS, the online UPS provides additional power conditioning. The primary difference is the online UPS uses a power inverter to ensure a clean power transfer from primary power to battery. This means a transfer time of zero when switching to and from battery. Additionally, most UPS systems of this type employ an internal bypass switch, which will provide continual primary power in the unlikely event of inverter failure. This is the recommended UPS type for data centers deploying critical systems and network infrastructure.

Now that you have decided on a UPS, you need to get the power from the UPS to your servers and network equipment. This is where the Power Distribution Unit (PDU) comes in. PDUs are exactly what their name implies, centers of power distribution. If you plan to deploy multiple rack-mounted or stand-alone UPSs you will not require a separate PDU; you will utilize the existing building PDU. If you plan on deploying a site-wide UPS system, you will need to deploy PDUs to distribute power to your racks. The author recommends two PDU systems receiving power from your room UPS. A minimum of one circuit per PDU will be delivered to every rack. This will allow you maximum power redundancy and ensure that a PDU failure will not result in power loss to every system in a rack. To go a step further in power redundancy, if you deploy servers with redundant power supplies, every server will remain up even after a complete PDU failure. As PDU failures are rare, a budget-constrained business can deploy a single PDU system without sacrificing reliability. UPS and PDU sizing will vary from data center to data center and will require a power audit. This can be done quickly and inexpensively from your electrician.

Now we have a power infrastructure that is providing electricity to our systems even if someone drives into a power pole, but what do we do when the batteries run out in the UPS? A UPS is designed to support power continuity until a new power source is brought online, not for continued power delivery from its own store. This is where the generator and ATS come in. At this point you have two choices: a generator that is onsite and connected at all times or the ability to deploy a rental generator on an as-needed basis. An on-site generator is the best bet as far as reliability and efficiency are concerned, but many office locations will not allow a generator to be permanently deployed. On the other hand, a rental generator requires manual intervention for deployment and power switchover as well as a much larger UPS battery-life (which can be a very expensive proposition as the capital outlay for large battery caches and the UPS(s) to support them is substantial). The automatic transfer switch will be used between the UPS and the generator to facilitate automatic cutover to generator power once an outage in standard power delivery occurs.

Now that we have reliable power to the tens, or even hundreds, of heat-emitting systems how do we maintain a computer-friendly environment?

Environment Conditioning

It is important to condition the environment to ensure that the systems are operating within normal physical parameters; this is performed using High Volume Air Conditioning (HVAC) units. HVACs are a requirement for any server room or data center and are sized according to the volume of air and number of systems in the room. These units must operate separately from the building HVAC; this ensures that someone doesn't turn up the thermostat because their office is too cold, and turn the data center into the sauna the CEO always wanted. In an enterprise data center, air conditioning redundancy is as much a requirement as power redundancy. Usually, two HVAC units are deployed, one on either side of the room, to provide uniform air conditioning and redundancy in case of failure of one of the units. These systems will also supply humidity monitoring and conditioning to ensure that your systems run in their optimal environment.

Hosting/Co-Location Facilities

Now that you are on information overload and are reconsidering the offer from your uncle to manage his mattress superstore, WAIT...there is an easy way out. Hosting and Co-Location facilities, like Exodus and Level(3) and many others, have put this power and environment infrastructure in place. All you have to do is send them a check every month and they will lease you a cage and supply you with the environment that you were just trying to figure out how to pitch to your boss.

Exodus and Level(3)'s core competency is data center and environment support. More and more businesses are moving their entire data center to these facilities and utilizing their expertise in data center management. This allows the business to provide their Internet customers a high level of availability without incurring the cost of building out a reliable, redundant data center environment.

Their cage lease will provide you with redundant power and ISP connectivity. If you have special needs, such as specific service providers or power needs, the larger data center and co-location facilities can customize a solution for your environment. Most of these facilities also provide in-house network and systems consulting to ensure that you design the most reliable infrastructure your budget and resources will allow. The only downfall to these environments is that you will rely on them to ensure that your environment is stable. A connectivity change for one customer may cause an outage for you. The more you outsource your core infrastructure, the less control you have to ensure that your systems will be available to your customer any time of the day with little delay.

Network Design

Now that your data center is set up to ensure a reliable computing environment, it is time to design your data backbone, the network infrastructure. The goal of network design is to create a scalable environment that will withstand multiple outages without your site being down to your customers. This includes redundancy planning for unscheduled outages (equipment and service failures) as well as planned equipment maintenance and upgrade. If you thought data center redundancy could be complex, hold on to your hats! In this section we will be looking at Internet path redundancy, bandwidth needs, core routing and switching design, traffic shaping and QoS (Quality of Service), server farm layouts and VPNs (Virtual Private Networks).

This network design discussion will be centered on a typical network infrastructure for an enterprise digital commerce environment. The following figure depicts this environment and will be used throughout this appendix. This design assumes local connectivity to the corporate network.

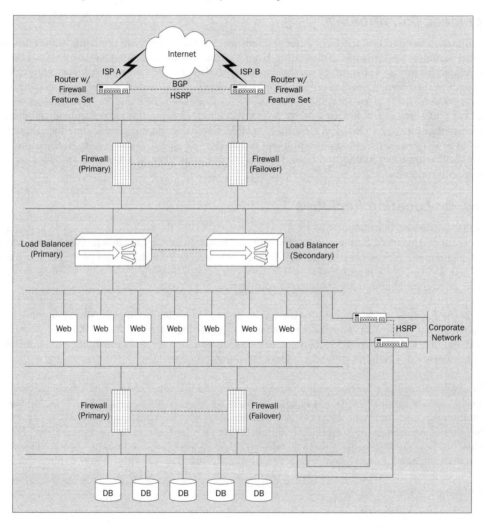

The design for a production environment with remote connectivity to the corporate network is almost identical to the design above; the only change is that the connection from the routers to the corporate network will be wide-area links and not direct connections. Point-to-point and frame-relay are the most common links for this type of deployment.

Path Redundancy

Due to the highly available nature of digital commerce, path redundancy to the Internet is a requirement regardless of the size of your network. To minimize the effects of outages within your carrier's environment or failures within the Telco equipment (located in Telco's Central Office) itself, a minimum of two separate Internet connections should be deployed. Each of these connections should use unique ISPs or at a minimum a single ISP should terminate at separate POPs (Points of Presence) - a POP is where your circuit terminates at your ISP's data center or switching environment. Before you can utilize your two unique paths to the Internet, you must obtain an ASN (Autonomous System Number) and deploy BGP (Border Gateway Protocol) on your gateway routers.

ASNs are unique network identifiers (much like an IP address, but for entire networks). When you subscribe to an ISP, your network becomes a subset of their network and you do not need your own ASN. When you wish to deploy multiple distinct paths to the net, you must obtain your own ASN. This allows your ISPs to route traffic correctly to your environment. An ASN is obtained through the American Registry for Internet Numbers (ARIN – http://www.arin.net). ARIN will only provide you with an ASN after proof that you require a unique routing policy and that your network is already multi-homed or is soon to be multi-homed. A multi-homed network is simply a network that has path connectivity to two or more ISPs. The registration cost (as of early 2001) is $500US and the annual renewal fee is $30US. The RIPE Network Coordination Centre takes care of these services in Europe and can be found at http://www.ripe.net. The registry for Asia Pacific is aptly named the Asia Pacific Registry and can be found at http://www.apnic.net. Additionally, ARIN has delegated the Brazilian and Mexican registries to RNP (http://www.registro.br) and NIC-Mexico (http://www.nic.mx), respectively.

Now that your network is multi-homed to two or more ISPs, you must configure your border routers to take advantage of the redundancy. Implementing BGP on your border routers performs this. The Border Gateway Protocol is an exterior gateway protocol that performs routing between multiple Autonomous Systems (AS). BGP exchanges routing information and path availability with other exterior gateway routers to ensure that nodes across the Internet have updated routing information to exchange data with your network. Use of this protocol ensures that even if one of the paths (or equipment) connecting your network to your ISP goes down, customers across the network will still be able to exchange data with the path(s) that are still up.

When deploying BGP you have the choice of receiving full Internet routes or just your ISPs' customer routes. It is preferable to receive full BGP routes on your routers, but it will require more CPU cycles and memory resources. Currently, the full BGP route table is just over 40MB, all of which is stored in your router's memory. This makes your memory requirements for each router at least 64MB but for safety's sake should be 128MB. Other router configurations, like security access lists and firewall support require additional resources and will be discussed in more detail later in this section.

Choosing to receive customer routes from your ISPs requires less router resources, but you are relying on your ISPs' routers to accurately provide path determination for your network. As was mentioned before, the more you outsource your core infrastructure, the less control you have over its reliability.

Bandwidth Needs

To determine the amount of bandwidth needed for your environment, you must understand what your bandwidth will be used for. Larger organizations will utilize redundant Internet connectivity for their production Commerce Server 2000 environment and another set of Internet connections to support their internal corporate network(s). VPNs (Virtual Private Networks) are a very popular way to provide secure connectivity between company sites and require allocated bandwidth.

To support the highly available environment that your digital commerce environment will require, it is recommended that redundant Internet connectivity be used exclusively for your data center. Additional links can then be implemented to support your internal corporate network.

Most initial environments will be best served by deploying T1 connections to their ISP (E1 in Europe and some of Asia). The T1 is a copper circuit and will provide 1.54Mbit/sec data transfer rates (2Mbit/sec for the E1). T1 circuits are relatively inexpensive and require less network equipment resources than a T3 circuit (which we will discuss shortly). As your traffic grows, careful attention must be paid to ensure that the connection paths do not get saturated. A good rule of thumb is to add an additional T1 or larger circuit after 50% continued use is seen on the circuit. Continued utilization over 50% will introduce latency into your data transmissions.

Larger organizations or those with a rapid growth plan may wish to employ T3 or fractional T3 circuits within their environment. T3 circuits, unlike T1/E1 circuits, run over fiber. T3s allow for data transfer rates up to 45Mbit/second, and come in many different flavors. You can purchase a full T3, fractional T3 (3Mbit/sec, 6, 9 12, etc.) or a Burstable T3. The Burstable T3 provides bandwidth on demand; you use as much of the 45Mbit pipe as is needed and you are charged on a baseline of utilization for that month (usually a baseline of 90-95%). Burstable T3s are more expensive than fractional T3 circuits, but there is no provisioning delay when adding additional bandwidth.

Core Routing Design

So now you have designed your redundant connectivity to the Internet (and your customers). Let us now discuss the equipment that will perform this data routing and switching. Routers provide connectivity between two or more distinct network segments. These segments can include your network and your ISP's network or just unique segments within your LAN. Switches provide the node-to-node connectivity within a network segment. Redundancy, reliability and scalability are very important in deciding what class and manufacture of network equipment to deploy.

Ensure that you pick a network equipment manufacturer that provides quality goods and 24 hours technical support and component exchange. This is very important when handling equipment failures within your commerce environment. The author's recommendation when purchasing network equipment is using a reputable manufacture like Cisco Systems or Nortel. Their equipment is rock-solid and their support and component exchange is available around the globe. Regardless of which network equipment manufacturer you choose, be sure that you purchase the warranty that will best support your environment's needs. There are many types of warranty options including on-site support of equipment for remote sites where internal engineering support is not available.

There are many styles and class of routers available. To ensure reliability within your network, redundancy is key. As is seen in the figure, above, each path to the Internet should be homed to a unique router. This ensures that one router failure will not take down your entire network. To increase reliability in your routing architecture, you can implement failover protocols, like Cisco's proprietary HSRP (Hot Standby Router Protocol). This type of protocol groups two or more routers together to form a virtual router. This ensures that if a router failed or is taken down for maintenance the other router(s) will assume the downed router's duties. This, like any protocol, takes up resources and your routers must be chosen to provide enough resources for the services you wish to run.

Mid-range and high-end routers have been manufactured with additional redundancy features. Many routers provide redundant power supplies, dual bus architecture, redundant management units and hot-swappable card chassis. These provide additional single-unit reliability and maintenance ease. When choosing routers, pick a class that will provide you with room to grow. Purchasing a 2-slot chassis with no redundancy may be cheaper now, but it will have to be discarded as your environment grows. On the other hand, purchasing an 8-slot hot-swap chassis may be more expensive, but as your infrastructure needs grow, you will only be purchasing additional cards, not entire units. A good router chassis class for mid-sized environments is the Cisco 7200 series. These routers provide the additional reliability and scalability needed in your digital commerce enterprise without breaking the bank. Nortel also has similar product lines available.

Another set of redundant routers must be deployed to provide corporate network connectivity to the production environment. This is a requirement regardless of whether the corporate environment is local to the production network or not. The only thing that changes is the type of connectivity deployed and interface cards used within the routers. One important thing to take into consideration is that these routers should be the default gateway for all nodes within the corporate network. If the firewall was the default gateway, and since most firewalls do not perform routing services, manual route entries would have to be added to all nodes within the corporate network (a network management nightmare of the fourth degree).

Switching Design

We have discussed network segment connectivity; let us now look at data switching design. Switches, not hubs, should be used in your environment. For example, a 100Mbit hub shares 100Mbit with all ports in the hub, while a 100Mbit switch provides 100Mbit of bandwidth to each port. Switches provide 10Mbit, 100Mbit and even 1Gbit speeds. These port speeds can be quadrupled using technologies like Cisco's Fast EtherChannel that will channel up to four ports, giving the connected device up to 4GB of bandwidth.

Mid- and high-level switches even allow segmenting of ports into unique network segments, allowing one larger switch to do the job of multiple smaller switches. These segmented switch ports are known as VLANs (or virtual LANs). All network segments of our production network reside within two trunked switches. A trunk is a physical connection (usually Gigabit fiber connection(s)) between the two switches. This trunk allows every VLAN to be spanned across both switches, providing data switching reliability in the event of a hardware failure or maintenance outage. Each switch has been designed with redundancy in mind. As is seen, each switch has redundant power supplies and supervisor engines. The switch chassis itself provides redundant bus architecture. The switch design and deployment maximizes redundancy and reliability of the data-switching infrastructure.

Each unique segment of your production network environment is encapsulated in its own VLAN. In the earlier figure, there are five separate VLANs needed to support this environment. These VLANs are used to eliminate multiple round-trip packet switching on any segment. For example, if VLANs 101 and 102 were combined into a single VLAN, a single segment would be used to transfer an incoming data packet from the firewall to the load balancer and again from the load balancer to the web farm. This doubles the load on a given VLAN for any packet transfer. To eliminate this possible bottleneck, multiple VLANs are employed.

Each switch also has a layer 3 routing card installed. This provides additional reliability and enhanced path determination from the switch to the requesting host. A routing protocol, such as OSPF or Cisco's proprietary EIGRP (Enhanced Interior Gateway Routing Protocol), is used to provide the routing tables and traffic balancing from your production environment to your customers.

Traffic Shaping and QoS

Traffic shaping and quality of service become a concern when utilizing your production ISP connectivity to support corporate network and VPN connectivity. Whenever you decide to utilize your production Internet connectivity to support these types of services, you run the risk of introducing latency into your customer's data requests. To minimize this, businesses can deploy QoS (Quality of Service) found in most router operating systems, firewalls and third party traffic shaping solutions, such as Checkpoint Firewall's FloodGate (www.checkpoint.com) and Packeteer's TrafficShaper (www.packeteer.com).

These solutions provide policy-based traffic shaping, filtering and queuing to ensure that your business-critical data is provided with the bandwidth it requires. This ensures that high-volume file transfers, e-mail, streaming media or other corporate network-based data does not become a bottleneck for your production environment. These services help cut the cost of bandwidth by prioritizing traffic.

With traffic shaping services in place, a business no longer has to purchase bandwidth based on corporate Internet traffic combined with production traffic. A business can now prioritize traffic to ensure that the critical systems have the bandwidth required to service customers while throttling back corporate bandwidth hogs, like large multi-threaded file transfers and streaming media.

QoS services are deployed within your routers and are standard within Cisco and other router manufacturers. QoS can either be configured manually through the command line interface or through policy administration software. This, like any other router service, requires additional router CPU cycles and memory allocation and should be taken into consideration when purchasing your gateway routers.

The third party traffic shaping appliances sit just inside your gateway routers and also provide policy-based traffic shaping, filtering and queuing. In addition, these solutions provide traffic reporting, including: response times, packet transit times, server and client response times and many other useful reports. This allows the administrator to ensure whether his or her traffic policies are effective or detrimental to the enterprise. The only downfall to these solutions (besides additional cost) is the introduction of additional hops and failure points to your network. The best solution to traffic shaping is to provide dedicated connectivity for your production environment, but if this is not possible, QoS mechanisms and traffic shaping appliances will help ensure your critical systems receive the bandwidth they require.

Administrators need continuous feedback. PacketShaper tracks and reports a network's ongoing results including: application response times, divided into time spent in transit and time spent on the server; comparisons between actual performance and service-level goals; clients and servers with the worst performance records; and over thirty other per-application statistics with corresponding graphs.

Server Farm Layout

As we can see in the following figure, the two primary server farms (web and database) are deployed on two separate VLANs. This serves two purposes: additional security for your database environment and traffic segmentation to minimize data flooding of the segments. With the farm layout as such, you will notice that your web and database servers are multi-homed to two network segments. This facilitates connectivity between your web farm and database farm without overloading the segments with traffic. It also facilitates the additional security of the firewall deployed between the two server farms. Security, which plays a large part in the design of commerce environments, will be discussed next in this appendix.

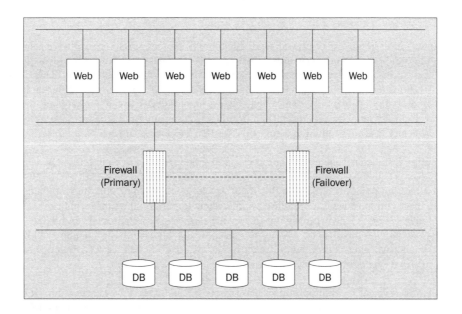

Network Security

We have discussed the design of your network infrastructure; now let us talk about how to protect it. Security systems should be deployed throughout your entire digital commerce environment. These security systems include: routers, firewalls, VPNs, IDS (Intrusion Detection Systems) and virus protection software. Security, like network and systems design, is only as strong and stable as your weakest link. It is not enough to deploy 80% of the appropriate security measures; care must be taken to secure all borders within your environment and ensure security policies are not bypassed by hardware or software installed by users within the network.

A security fallacy that many engineers accept is 'now that I have deployed my security measures, my network is secure'. Security is not obtained by deploying some hardware and software. Security is a process, which must be continually modified and molded to ensure your data is safe. There is no software in the world that cannot be cracked given the appropriate time and resources; you just want to secure your environment to deter would-be hackers from your site. Ensure that your security is strong enough so that those hackers pass your environment up for one that is easier to crack.

Routers Revisited

Your border gateway routers are your first possible line of defense for your environment, so use them. Most router manufactures have available firewall software that will run on your routers. For example, you can purchase IPFW (IP Firewall) feature set for Cisco routers. This is a subset of features from a firewall appliance and should only be used in conjunction with a dedicated firewall solution in an enterprise digital commerce environment. The firewall feature set will provide traffic filtering; allowing clients access only to authorized systems and ports. Using your router as a preliminary traffic filtering firewall, helps offload some responsibility from your primary firewalls, allowing them to perform more elaborate security duties.

Firewalls

There are many different flavors of firewall available today. You can purchase a software solution, (like Microsoft's Internet Security and Acceleration Server 2000 or Checkpoint Firewall) which will run on non-proprietary hardware or an integrated hardware/software firewall solution (like Cisco PIX). Choosing a firewall is like choosing a car: they all get you where you want to go, but they have different handling characteristics and options. It is important to take factors like longevity in the marketplace, operating system security, and reliability into consideration when deciding on the solution that is right for you. This author shies away from any firewall solution that runs on a non-proprietary security operating system.

If your firewall is installed as a layer on your OS, you open yourself up to a plethora of attacks that firewalls don't cover. This is true for Unix as well as Microsoft. The design of a good security system is like that of a castle: the farthest out point from the core (the moat) is where you want to stop the vast majority of unwanted traffic. From there you have walls, portcullises, and soldiers to pare off the more stubborn attackers. Ergo, a firewall is of more value the farther away it is from your company's assets (servers and data). Given that almost every machine on the planet is a Windows machine, hackers will have a tendency to be very familiar with all of the inner workings; NOT every hacker has access to a $30,000 CISCO router running firewall support or an actual security-only network device.

The firewall is one of your most important security assets, but in order to be effective it must be deployed correctly. Care has to be taken that other hardware and software within the environment do not bypass security policies configured within your firewall. This includes modems, remote control software (PCAnywhere and NetMeeting), VPNs, and point-to-point links. While some of these are standard in most environments, they must be deployed using the same security policies as the firewall. A firewall only protects the network segment gateways directly attached, it cannot protect against an administrator running NetMeeting or PCAnywhere on the database server so he or she can work from home.

As shown earlier, there are two separate firewalls deployed within the production environment and a third protecting the connection between the production environment and the corporate network. The first firewall sits between the gateway routers and the load balancing devices (which we will discuss later in the appendix). This device is your primary firewall and your last security checkpoint before your web servers. As mentioned in the above section on routers, your first defense is the firewall feature set running on your border routers. This takes processing of your primary security policies off the firewall, leaving more resources to provide packet filtering and address translation security. In most organizations, this firewall will also provide NAT (Network Address Translation) for your production environment. NAT provides additional security by shielding internal IP addresses from direct connectivity and allows the administrator to effectively distribute the finite number of public IP addresses within the environment.

Now is the time to turn our attention to our corporate network. The majority of security breaches come from within the corporate environment. This can be because of disgruntled or 'curious' employees, or from outside entities exploiting a security hole in the corporate network. The production environment must be protected from all possible threats, either external or internal. The most efficient way to do this is to deploy a firewall between the two networks. The typical network deployment in the earlier figure shows the use of a router running the firewall feature set. This gives you firewall services without deploying another firewall and burning through your budget faster than a dot com company. It is shortsighted to believe that your corporate network will not be used as a forward base for attacks on your production environment; when deploying this environment you should ensure that this connection is secured.

The configuration that we have been discussing assumes that Internet connectivity is not a shared resource between the production environment and the corporate network. But how do we secure the environment if it is? The following figure shows the production and corporate networks sharing Internet connectivity. This solution requires a third network interface on the primary and failover firewalls and provides cost-effective resource sharing by reducing the amount of hardware and service cost incurred. As discussed earlier, this solution can introduce latency issues if bandwidth utilization is not managed appropriately.

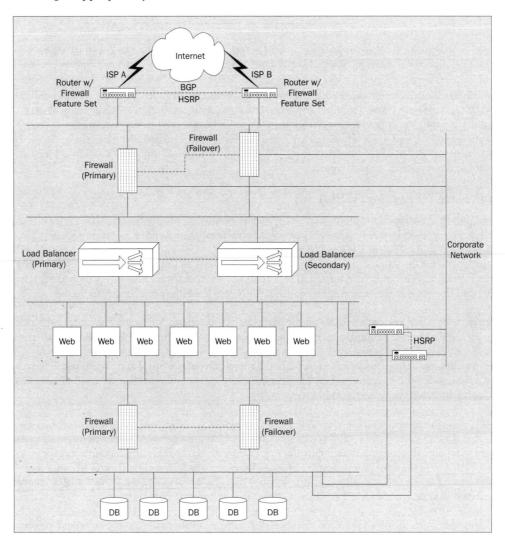

Sample Firewall Configuration

When securing your firewall it is important to minimize traffic accepted into your network; specifying which addresses and ports the firewall will let through does this. The following table shows the common ports utilized within a production network. Initial firewall configuration takes some time, but a reliable firewall configuration helps ensure your essential and private data is not compromised.

Port	Protocol	Service
80	TCP	HTTP
443	TCP	HTTPS
21	TCP	FTP
25	TCP	SMTP

For more information on port assignments, see RFC 1700. A copy of this request for comments can be found at http://info.internet.isi.edu/in-notes/rfc/files/rfc1700.txt.

The configurations of the database and corporate firewalls are even more granular. These configurations restrict access to a very limited number of nodes and ports. Port security configurations will vary depending on your network architecture and how your corporate environment connects to your production network and what services are utilized (for example, terminal services, telnet, Active Directory management and other RPC connections, etc). The appropriate ports and their configurations can usually be found in the service documentation.

Virtual Private Networks (VPNs)

Providing secure remote administration to your production site has always been troublesome: it is inefficient to completely close off remote connectivity to your developers, but you have to ensure security. The solution to this problem is the VPN. A VPN is a secure connection from one client or network to another network over the Internet. This solution is incredibly valuable but it must be implemented correctly to ensure security and not overtax the enterprise's resources. It is very important that secure access is provided for remote administration, configuration and troubleshooting; VPNs are the most popular way to do this.

There are many VPN devices available on the market, such as Cisco's VPN concentrators and Nortel's Contivity VPN switches. Redundancy options are also available with these VPN appliances. Microsoft has direct support for VPN connectivity through Windows 2000's Routing and Remote access. They also provide VPN configuration wizards and support through their new Internet Security and Acceleration Server. This server is a firewall, VPN solution and caching engine all rolled into one product. We will discuss ISA when we discuss network security later in this appendix.

Enabling secure connectivity to your production environment is not enough; user authentication must also be performed. Cisco's and Nortel's VPN appliances provide local user authentication but do not, by default, authenticate a user through the Active Directory. To perform Active Directory authentication a Radius/TACAS server must also be implemented. This requires additional hardware, software and configuration. These solutions will not only cost more initially, but also additional time will be needed for system maintenance.

Another option is Microsoft's Windows 2000 Server Routing and Remote Access Services. This provides VPN connectivity and direct Active Directory authentication. The most challenging aspect of deploying Microsoft's VPN services is the hardening of the OS to ensure the server is as secure as possible. Microsoft's Internet Security and Acceleration Server is an easy solution to providing easy VPN configuration, administration and security. ISA includes wizards for simple VPN configuration in operating system hardening, easing administrative burden on ensuring a secure, reliable VPN solution for client-to-site and site-to-site remote connectivity. It also supports high-availability by allowing multiple ISA servers to be grouped for load balancing and redundancy.

The following diagram shows the VPN device deployed within the corporate environment utilizing a high-availability corporate network configuration. Other opportunities to minimize network cost include, dedicated Internet connectivity and dedicated Internet connectivity using the production connectivity as a backup. Use of VPN services allows remote connectivity into your corporate network, utilizing Active Directory authentication (in the case of ISA). If a VPN product like Cisco's VPN Concentrator or Nortel's Contivity switch are used, you will require an additional authentication server (RADIUS/TACACS) to provide authentication through the Active Directory.

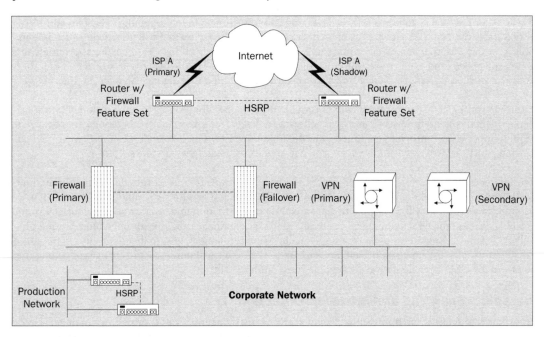

Remote administration of the production environment will take place through the same network path as users within the corporate network. This is the most secure solution for remote administration. Users should not be allowed to bypass this security environment by installing local modems and remote access software, such as PCAnywhere or Terminal Services. These types of solutions bypass network security perimeters and invalidate your security infrastructure. They should only be allowed through a VPN connection.

Virus Protection

Inadequate virus protection and quickly spreading viruses have caused millions of dollars in damage and lost revenue. Some viruses utilize bugs and insecure design of operating systems and/or installed applications, but most new viruses utilize features within these products that are supposed to make the user's life easier. The current virus trends are VBS worms like VBS.LoveLetter, which was unleashed on May 4th, 2000. This worm originated in the Philippines and spread rapidly throughout the world. Once opened, it sent a friendly message to all of your contacts in Outlook, which in turn duped your contacts to open the file and repeat the process exponentially. This in itself caused Internet congestion and mail server clogging, but that was not all. The script replaced media, script and system files with copies of itself, and did this on all local and network-mapped drives. This wreaked havoc on many production environments, bringing entire sites down and causing many e-commerce sites to lose revenue.

This virus was the first recognized worm that took advantage of Microsoft's scripting abilities. It also woke many people up to the idea that security is a chain that is only as strong as the weakest link. VBS.LoveLetter traveled so fast that most damage was done before the antivirus software manufacturers could provide updated virus definition files. IT personnel were collectively pulling their hair out getting their sites back up, restoring lost files (if they were backed up correctly) and cleaning the damage on all of the systems the virus touched.

This virus spread so quickly that the antivirus software could not be updated in time to combat the initial threat. After this attack, antivirus software was updated to warn you before opening .vbs files and Microsoft added a security patch disallowing .vbs and .exe files from being opened when receiving attachments. Still, after this was done, many environments succumbed to variants of this virus because appropriate updates were not applied (and even worse, antivirus software was still not deployed). This lack of action did not only apply to small organizations. Today .vbs worm variants are still doing damage all over the Internet.

Your enterprise CS2K environment cannot provide high-availability services to your customers without deployment of an enterprise-class antivirus software package. It is important to pick a software package that is highly supported and provides continual virus definition updates. The two leaders in this field are Symantec's Norton AntiVirus (www.symantec.com) and McAfee's VirusScan (www.mcafee.com).

The author has had great success deploying Symantec's Norton AntiVirus Corporate Edition throughout the world and would recommend it in any environment. The greatest feature is the ability to implement a centralized server that will deploy client software and virus definition updates throughout your environment. It will allow customized scheduling and centralized file quarantine, easing the administrative burden of antivirus support. Regardless of the solution you choose to implement, ensure that your virus definitions (and the antivirus software application itself) are kept up-to-date. This will minimize the chances of getting the 3am call from the CEO because he can't access the site from his yacht!

Vulnerability Scanning and Intrusion Detection

Now that your security environment is deployed and your engineering staff is providing continual security updates (service packs, hot fixes, virus definition updates, etc.), how do you ensure that your security policies are implemented properly and any change to the environment doesn't introduce new security holes? The answers are continual vulnerability scanning and intrusion detection services.

Frequently running vulnerability scanning software will help you discover and correct any security holes or incorrect policy configurations before they are exploited. These scanners look for ports and services on the subnet with low security, testing a continually updated list of system vulnerabilities against them. They then provide reporting of vulnerabilities found and usually offer suggestions on how to secure against them. The reporting and scheduling features allow you to continually monitor your network's security while providing you with a security baseline on which to measure future vulnerability checks. There are many software vendors that provide vulnerability checking software, including Cisco's Secure Scanner and Symantec's NetRecon.

This software's strength lies in the availability of continued vulnerability signature updates. A vulnerability scanner is much like an antivirus program: both are only as effective as the consistency with which the company provides updates. The weakness in these products, and the reason additional security measures must be taken, is that they can only find vulnerabilities that the signature updates include. It is very important to ensure that the vulnerability signatures are kept up-to-date. But what if you want to provide active monitoring and catch security breaches as they happen?

IDS (Intrusion Detection Systems) provide this real-time eye into your production network. IDS systems actively monitor network and/or system traffic to determine probable attack signatures. To do this, most systems incorporate a management console and multiple sensor devices. One sensor is deployed on each network segment you wish to monitor. The following diagram shows an IDS deployment within our enterprise digital commerce environment.

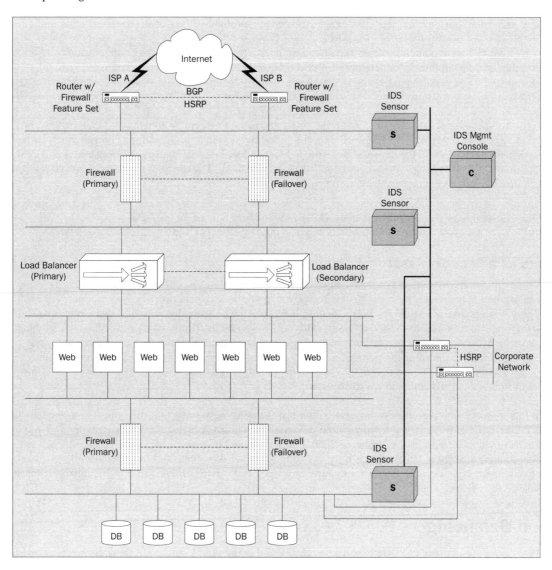

This deployment shows three sensors and one management console. A sensor is deployed behind each firewall device: gateway routers, web segment firewalls and database segment firewalls. This allows us to verify that our firewall configurations are providing the appropriate level of security. The sensor attached to the database segment will monitor access from the web and corporate network segments. The management console and sensors are deployed on a separate network segment to ensure security of the devices. They are accessed for management through a fourth interface on one of the internal routers, allowing you to secure access to the IDS segment through ACLs.

Cisco's IDS offering is their Cisco Secure Intrusion Detection System. This is the leading IDS system deployed today. Their sensor offerings include dedicated sensor devices, Catalyst Switch line cards and IOS-based IDS functionality (much like the firewall feature set option deployed in the gateway routers). This system detects probable attacks and actively responds by terminating the session and sending an administrative alert to the management console. Additionally, and the reason this IDS is so popular in Cisco networks, is that access lists can be applied dynamically to routers within your environment to further secure your environment. In this scenario, once a probable attack is discovered the session is terminated, an administrative alert is sent and an access list is added to the gateway router to deny continued connection attempts from the offending host. This access control list configuration can be maintained permanently or on a temporary basis. Alarms can also be fed into a database to provide customized trend reporting, allowing the engineer to apply security policies based on historical data. More information about this product can be found on Cisco's website.

Intrusion detection is as much art as it is science. To maximize the security benefits of IDS, time must be taken to continually review the historical data and refine the system's configuration. This requires a network or systems engineer with the time and expertise to create a baseline and manage trending and report analysis. This may be a tall order for many overextended IT organizations. Luckily, there are service providers that can provide remote maintenance and trending of your IDS.

> *A great resource for more information on IDS and Vulnerability Scanners can be found at* www.icsa.net/html/communities/ids/buyers_guide/guide/Technology/technology.shtml.

Users as a Security Asset

When one brings up users to a security engineer, they all roll their eyes and spout off daily transgressions against their holy security policies. Most will give you 'the most secure network is one without users' routine. This is because users are thought of as a security liability. An uninformed user is your worst nightmare and it is up to you to turn users into security assets. This is achieved by the continual training of users, including: new-hire network and systems orientation, weekly e-mail announcements on ways to increase security, security articles in the company newsletter, etc. Most employees want to conform to your requests and policies and many don't even realize they are creating security risks. Empower your employees; transform them from a security liability to a security asset.

While this section on security covers more than just securing the servers that run your Commerce 2000 services, none of it is any less important. As discussed previously, unless your entire network and systems environment is secure, your Commerce 2000 deployment will be susceptible to malicious attacks. Remember, security is a chain and is only as strong as the weakest link. Make sure your entire environment is as secure as possible so your Commerce 2000 environment will provide reliable, secure service to your customers.

Load Balancing

Web farms are deployed for two reasons: reliability and scalability. Using multiple web servers allows for availability even if systems failure occurs, but more importantly, it ensures that many customers can be serviced utilizing the resources of a cluster of servers. To provide this type of environment, you must deploy a load balancing solution. There are many hardware and software load-balancing solutions available on the market today.

Hardware Solutions

In an enterprise environment, the author recommends a hardware load balancing solution. This allows load balancing to be provided from a dedicated box without taking away server resources that can be used to service customer requests. Cisco, Nortel and F5 manufacture the leading load balancing solutions. The two top-end products are Cisco's Content Service Switch (www.cisco.com) and Nortel's Alteon ACEdirector (www.alteonwebsystems.com). Both of these are content switches that provide Layer 2, 3 and 7 (switching, routing and application-aware) support. Some of the features of these content switches include:

❑ Global server farm load balancing and site redirects

❑ Content-aware switching (using HTTP headers, cookies and host tags)

❑ Denial of Service (DoS) attack security (integrated firewall support)

❑ Wire-speed switching

❑ Dynamic server farm expansion/contraction

❑ 'Sorry' server redirection (the ability to redirect to an alternate web farm if transaction services are unavailable)

❑ Failover support

❑ Load weight configurations

As these solutions are enterprise content switches, they are more expensive than the traditional load balancing devices. Smaller organizations may choose to deploy a less expensive solution, like Cisco's LocalDirector (www.cisco.com) or F5's BigIP (www.f5.com). These are basic load balancing bridges that redirect requests based on an assigned matrix. Redirection is based solely on the IP address and port the request is received on. They do not provide additional security, wire-speed switching or many other advanced features of a content delivery switch. Additionally, these products are a network bridge and require additional switch hardware to support the network segments they are attached to. However, these products do support failover, so a highly available environment can be built around them. These devices are still a cost-effective and viable alternative to the more expensive content delivery switches.

Software Solutions

There are many third party software solutions available on the market today, such as Resonate's Commander solution (www.resonate.com). This type of solution provides load balancing by distributing code across all of the servers in your environment. They provide some of the advanced functionality that a content switch does, but it requires additional server resources that could be used for customer request servicing. The advantage of this type of architecture is that redundancy is inherent; a single system is not responsible for the load balancing service.

A more cost effective software load balancing solution is Microsoft's Network Load Balancing within Windows 2000 Advanced Server and Data center Server. It provides basic network load balancing based on IP address and port number(s). Network Load Balancing can be installed either during initial operating system install, or afterwards through network properties.

NLB is more cost effective than Resonate's solution, but is a more basic load balancer. Resonate's Commander provides multi-site, multi-cluster support, rules-based redirection, real-time performance management and reporting, enhanced server resource management and more efficient resource-based redirection. If basic load balancing is all your environment requires, NLB is probably the way to go. If you need a more advanced load balancing solution, the author highly recommends a dedicated hardware solution.

The following figure shows the NLB Cluster Parameters configuration page. This page configures the global cluster settings, including: cluster IP address and subnet mask, FQDN (Fully Qualified Domain Name), multicast support, etc.

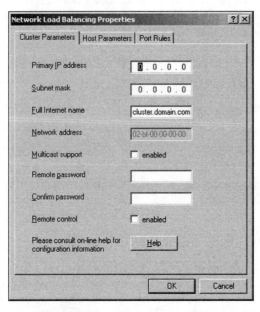

The next screenshot shows the Host Parameters configuration page. This page is used to configure the local network settings, including the unique host ID, host IP address and subnet mask.

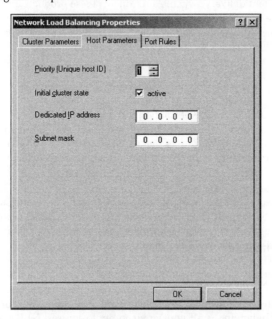

And below, we can see the Port Rules configuration page. This is used to configure the following: port range the system will accept service requests from, load weight and handling priority. NLB provides a lot of functionality in a load balancing solution that ships with the OS. However, its server limitation of 32 nodes per cluster causes NLB not to be widely utilized in large environments.

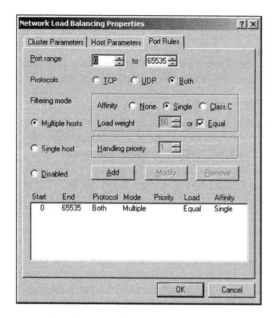

This configuration should utilize two network adapters. While NLB with one network adapter will work, it will not provide network communication between servers and traffic intended for one server will generate additional overhead for the other servers in the cluster. Additionally, if utilizing one network adapter with Application Center 2000, request forwarding will not be available.

Microsoft has expanded on NLB with Application Center 2000. Application Center 2000 is a site and system management server for enterprise environments. One of the features of this product is request forwarding. Request forwarding utilizes NLB to provide stateful failover in case of primary network adapter (or port) failure. It does this through the secondary network adapter. There are two issues with the deployment of Application Center 2000 for request forwarding:

❑   it requires an additional network adapter for inter-cluster communications
❑   request forwarding only protects against a small percentage of failures

For more information on Request Forwarding, see the February 2001 issue of IIS Administrator article 'Managing a Web Farm with Application Center 2000' by Tim Huckaby and Christopher George (http://www.iisadministrator.com/Articles/Index.cfm?ArticleID=16468).

Application Center 2000 as a management resource will be discussed later in this appendix.

State Management

Hardware failures within the environment (for example firewall failure) initiate an immediate failover to the secondary device. By default, when this failure occurs, all sessions are dropped and your customers will have to initiate a new connection to your site. They will have to start their transaction over, reducing their confidence in your site. To overcome this, stateful failover should be configured wherever possible in your environment.

Many of the firewalls and load balancers available today, such as Cisco's PIX and LocalDirector, allow stateful failover configuration. State is maintained through secondary dedicated interfaces on each device. Through these interfaces, state is transferred packet by packet in case of failover. When failure occurs, the secondary device will be able to continue supporting the customer's session, without loss. However, latency sensitive applications may timeout before the failover is complete and the user will then have to establish a new connection.

As we discussed earlier, software applications, like Application Center 2000, can also provide stateful failover. However, as seen with Application Center's request forwarder, most of these products can successfully support stateful failover only in a small number of failure scenarios.

There are still many failures within the enterprise that will result in session termination. The point is to minimize this and ensure reliable customer sessions wherever possible. Most enterprise devices will inherently support stateful failure but it is usually not a default configuration. Make sure you take the time to configure stateful failover wherever possible.

Development Network Needs

Now on to the holy grail of developers: development and staging networks. The word 'networks' is underlined because most companies deploy development and staging servers, but not dedicated networks. It is important to provide dedicated development and staging networks that are similar to the production environment. There are two main reasons for this:

❑ A security boundary that will minimize changes to production that were meant for the development or staging servers

❑ An environment that simulates the production environment

Development Networks

A development network is usually one with less control and security in place to facilitate development without slowdown. Usually they are no more than a single network segment on which many development web, database, and application servers reside. This allows developers full access to the segment and the servers, allowing them to change, test and run new code without concern about congestion within the corporate or production networks. It also allows security administrators the ability to give development staff complete access to the systems without compromising security policies within the production or corporate networks. The following figure shows the development network placement within the corporate environment.

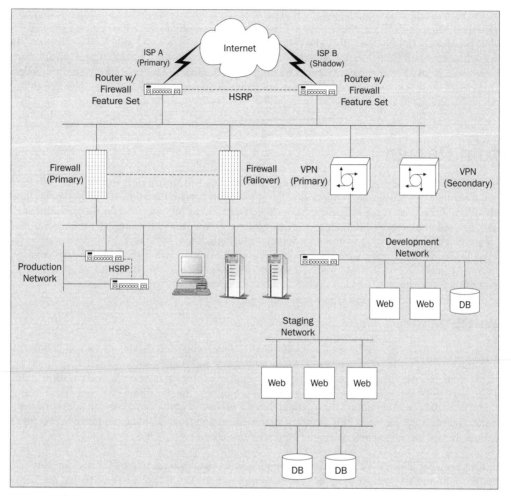

Staging Networks

A more structured environment is needed to support your staging environment. This environment should closely mimic your production environment to ensure that any possible changes are stable prior to pushing them to the production environment. It is also important to minimize your costs when designing this environment (or chances are you will not get the funding for this network). You could also have a staging environment that simulates the production environment without purchase of additional hardware, other than an additional network adapter for each staging web server. This environment utilizes VLANs within your corporate switch, employs Network Load Balancing and forgoes the database firewalls to minimize costs.

Code Safes

With all these different versions of code flying around the enterprise and multiple developers working on them, it is important to put in place a code safe that supports versioning and checkout. A code safe is nothing more than a centralized data repository for developers. Utilization of a code safe allows a central repository that can be backed up nightly, a versioning and check-in/check-out system, and authenticated security. This way, we minimize lost code, version mismatches between developers and erroneous code pushes to the production environment.

There are many code safes available on the market today, but the most popular with Microsoft-platform developers is Microsoft's Visual SourceSafe. This product is currently in its sixth revision and is available as a stand-alone product or bundled with Visual Studio. Additional products available include Vertical Sky's Software Manager and Collaboration Manager (www.verticalsky.com), Rational's ClearQuest (www.rational.com), Perforce (www.perforce.com) and NCompass Labs (http://www.ncompasslabs.com). The important thing is not whose code safe you are going to deploy, but the understanding that this type of product is invaluable to your business.

System Design

In this section we will discuss the systems and applications that will run on our network infrastructure. As before, we will design our systems with redundancy, reliability, scalability and security in the forefront of our minds. We will first discuss the role of Windows 2000 Active Directory in your CS2K environment and how to use it as a reliable, scalable addition to your environment. After that we will discuss the recommendations and requirements for deploying Commerce Server 2000, including web servers, SQL database servers, Business Desk and Commerce Server Administration Tools. Within each we will also discuss security recommendations to ensure a healthy production environment. Let us now start with a look at Microsoft's greatest unified authorization and administration tool, Windows 2000 Active Directory.

Active Directory

Before you can deploy Active Directory in your environment, you must decide on the role it is to play in your Commerce Server 2000 environment. Many companies will require some form of user authentication when providing services to customers, from account logon for retrieval of saved user data (for example, credit card numbers and delivery addresses) to pay services requiring authentication before service delivery (for example, financial reporting information). If you have a need to provide authenticated access anywhere in your site, you must decide where this authentication information resides. In a Commerce Server 2000 environment, you have two choices: Active Directory or SQL Server 2000.

If your site requires file access control then authenticated access through Active Directory is most likely the way to go, but there are limitations and considerations that must be discussed to ensure that this use of AD is right for your environment. First, you need to have an idea of how many users will need to be supported within your environment. Active Directory has a user limitation of approximately one million users in a single domain before directory services become impacted. Additionally there is an approximate limit of five domains, each with one million user objects, before global catalog replication severely hampers directory services. So Active Directory is limited to five million users in a forest. These numbers are approximate and are impacted by hardware performance and tuning as well as Active Directory design and deployment, but as a baseline are valid when determining the use of AD within your environment.

When utilizing AD within a CS2K environment, Microsoft recommends only non-volatile data within the AD (for example, username and password objects). All other profile attributes (for example, credit card numbers, addresses, phone numbers, etc.) are stored on a SQL Server 2000 instance. This streamlines directory access by only storing stable data in the Directory, utilizing SQL Server to store the more volatile data. Commerce Server 2000's Profiling System would then merge data from these two sources to create a single profile for targeting and analysis. Microsoft's directory is an expensive data repository and should be used to provide authentication and authorization to objects within. Customer profile data is best stored within your SQL Server environment to minimize cost of data storage and provide greater scalability.

Even if you don't utilize Active Directory for user authentication, you will most likely still deploy it to simplify management and security of the production environment. When deploying Active Directory within the production environment, it is important to spend an appropriate amount of time designing your AD. Most of your development time will be spent designing your AD Forest(s) and Domain(s). These layers of the AD are relatively fixed and require a lot of engineering time to change a deployed environment. On the other hand, Organizational Units (OUs) are easy to reconfigure and should not take up much of your design cycle. Now let us start our discussion of Active Directory design with Forests and Domains.

This section will discuss the overall requirements when deploying Active Directory within your production environment. It will also discuss the interoperability between your production and corporate network environments. It will give you the insight needed to deploy a reliable, secure Active Directory foundation on which your Commerce 2000 deployment will reside. Let us now take a look at Active Directory Forest and Domain designs.

Forest and Domain Design

An Active Directory Forest is nothing more than a boundary in which your enterprise's domain(s) reside. All domains within the forest share the same schema and Global Catalog and are interconnected with transitive trusts. The Global Catalog contains a partial replica of all domains within the Forest to provide administrative control and user/object access across domains. Assuming that you have already deployed Active Directory within your corporate environment, the question is do you deploy your production environment within the current AD Forest, or do you deploy a separate Forest?

Single versus Multiple Forest Deployment

Before deciding on deploying a second forest, be sure it is necessary. Most implementation concerns can be addressed by deploying multiple domains. Remember, multiple forests are going to greatly increase your administrative overhead (something you are hoping to minimize by deploying AD). You will now have two schemas and configurations to manage as well as manual non-transitive trust relationships to maintain. Maintenance of these cross-forest domain trusts increase exponentially with each domain deployed within the forests. Additionally, authorization across these trusts only use NTLM (and not the more secure Kerberos) authentication. Using UPN (User Principal Name) suffixes (for example, chrisg@interknowlogy.com) during login will not work across forests.

The use of Exchange 2000 within this environment complicates matters further if address list and public folder (including free/busy scheduling) synchronization is necessary. Exchange 2000 now uses AD for its directory structure rather than its own directory (as in past versions of Exchange). To provide synchronized address lists and scheduling data the users and groups must be synchronized across the forests. This can be performed as a workaround utilizing Microsoft's Metadirectory Service (MMS).

Some of the above concerns may not be valid for your environment; in fact, you may benefit from multiple forests. Multiple forests provide a border between schemas so you can customize one schema without affecting the other. It also provides a secure boundary that doesn't require great competence or experience with group policies to maintain secure interconnectivity. Also, there may be no need to maintain synchronicity between users, groups or Exchange organizations. You may even want a distributed IT authority, allowing multiple administrative groups to work independently of one another. Let's look at some of the differences between single- and multiple-forest Active Directory designs. The following table explains some of the major differences between a single- and multiple-forest Active Directory implementation. It will also help you to understand the additional administrative and security overhead required when implementing a multiple-forest AD.

	Single-Forest	Multiple-Forest
Schema	Shared, schema changes affect all Domains	Shared only by Domains within the same Forest, schemas can be modified for one Forest without affecting the other
Trusts	Automatic Two-way transitive	Manual One-way non-transitive
Administrative Authority	Authority for entire Forest, can be delegated	Separate Authorities for each Forest, delegation performed only within the domain
Global Catalog	Provides authorization for all domains	Must be synchronized to provide authorization across Forests
Domain Authentication	Kerberos authentication throughout Forest	NTLM authentication across Forests, Kerberos within Forests
Border Security	Default security border between domains is relatively weak, requires manual policy configuration to strengthen, chance of security failure through incorrect configuration	Default strong security border between Forests, less chance of incorrect border security configuration
UPN Login	Supported throughout the Forest	UPN Login will not work across Forests
Exchange 2000	Default synchronization of address list and scheduling data throughout Forest	Manual synchronization required to provide enterprise-wide address list and scheduling information
Forest Change Control	Change control resides within one authority group	Multiple authority groups provide change control

Domain Design

Regardless of whether you choose to implement a single- or multiple-forest Active Directory, your entire production environment should be housed within a single domain. In AD, a domain is a group of users and computers that share the same domain schema and security policy. It is recommended that all of your domains (corporate and production) utilize valid domain names owned by your company. A good example would be interknowlogy.org for the corporate domain and interknowlogy.com for the production domain.

If you are using a single forest with multiple domains, it is important to deploy a strong security policy between the production and corporate domains. While cross-forest domain security is very strong out of the box, intra-forest domain security requires security policies to be deployed. Group policies can be deployed from the domain level down to the individual organizational unit. Group policies are cumulative and build upon each other from the domain to the OU. It is good practice to layer no more than 2-3 group policies for any object within the directory to minimize CPU cycles and latency. Group policies can be created through the Group Policy MMC snap-in or through the properties of the domain or OU to which you want to assign it.

When deploying a single-forest AD, consider creating the production environment as a stand-alone domain rather than a child of your corporate domain. This allows you to securely separate domain resources between the two environments. Additionally, this allows you to use second-level domain names (for example, interknowlogy.com) in each environment.

If you are using multiple forests, you must manually create the trusts between your corporate domain and your production domain. Manual trusts are created using the **Active Directory Domains and Trusts** MMC snap-in. From there, right-click on the domain you wish to add the trust to and choose Properties. From there, go to the **Trusts** tab to create your domain trusts. This configuration must be performed on both domains to complete the trust. The following figure shows the **Active Directory Domains and Trusts** properties page. It shows two external, non-transitive domain trusts created across multiple forests.

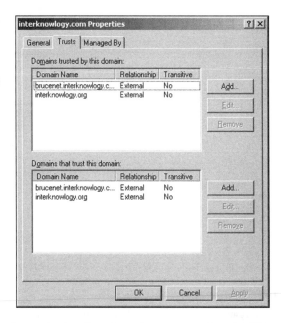

You may consider only creating a one-way trust from the production domain to the corporate domain. This allows additional security by allowing resources in the production environment to be accessed by the corporate environment, but not vice versa. In the event of a security breach within the production environment, the corporate domain is still secure. Utilizing a two-way trust provides the opportunity for your corporate network to be compromised if a breach in the production domain occurs. When creating inter-forest trust, limit them to only the domains needed. In the figure below there are multiple domains within the corporate environment, but only the domain where the development and administrative staff reside is trusted. The golden rule of security is to give access only where it is required.

The figure overleaf shows an example of the two Active Directory designs discussed above: one utilizing two forests for the corporate and production networks and the other utilizing a single forest with separate domains for the networks.

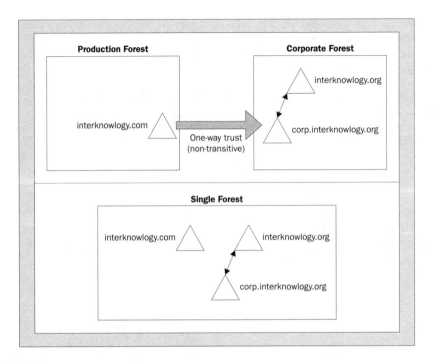

Organizational Units

Organizational Units are nothing more than a way to group objects for easy administration. Some of the default OUs include: Users and Groups, Computers and Built-in. These object containers provide easy administrative and security handling. OUs are easily added, removed and changed and should not take up much of your planning time. It is best to group OUs based on group policy or administrative delegation needs. Refrain from creating extraneous organizational units, as they will only increase administrative burden. It is good practice not to nest OUs more than three levels deep and minimize the use of group policies at these levels. The deeper the OU levels and the more nested the group policies, the more CPU cycles used and less resources available to respond to authentication and authorization requests. This becomes increasingly important as the enterprise grows. Multiple nested OUs and group policies aren't much of a concern when handling 100 simultaneous requests, but as they creep into the thousands, a sloppy AD implementation can cause severe latency. If customer authentication is required on your commerce site and severe latency is encountered, your customers will become someone else's customers.

Active Directory Limitations

Microsoft has been very bearish on providing numbers on how many users Active Directory supports: they say that AD will currently support around 5 million users in one forest. They spread the users over five domains within the forest (with approximately 1 million users per domain). These numbers assume 1% of users are actively using the AD at any one time (10,000 simultaneous users). Additionally, only 5,000 users are allowed in any one group (whether they are Security or Distribution groups). However, there is a workaround in the Commerce Server 2000 SDK: the SubGroupManager is a helper object within the SDK that creates virtual groups that are then added to the Active Directory group. This object allows you a workaround for the 5,000-user limitation inherent in AD groups.

These numbers are very conservative and a properly designed AD environment can support twice that number. It is important to design a streamlined Active Directory environment by minimizing the use of nested organizational units and group policies. Hardware implementation (which we will discuss later) also plays a large role in the number of active requests that can be supported.

Active Directory Database Sizing

Another concern is ensuring that you plan for the size of the AD database. The database is a file named `ntds.dit` and its default location is in the `WINNT\NTDS` directory. Database sizing is very predictable as all objects in AD have a set size. The following table shows common Active Directory objects and their size.

Active Directory Object	Size (in bytes)
User Object (standard attributes)	4,366
Additional Object Attributes	100
Group Object	2,097
Organizational Unit	1,992
Computers	4,086
Printers	2,412
Certificates	2,181
Access Control Entry	60

As you can see, it is simple to size your disk to ensure your database has the resources you need, but space requirements are not small. For example, a database with 1 million user objects is over 4GB alone.

If you have a database that supports frequent object adds and deletes, your disk size requirements are going to be much larger. When an object is deleted within Active Directory, it is not deleted but held as a tombstone – an object marked for deletion. This tombstone is held by default for 60 days to ensure synchronization with other domain controllers and global catalogs within the forest. The deleted objects are still taking up space two months after you issued the delete command. This can significantly increase your database size if frequent, large-scale adds and deletes are necessary. Make sure you plan accordingly.

Hardware Requirements and Recommendations

As with the network design, redundancy, reliability and scalability are the name of the game. When deploying servers the author recommends 'redundancy in threes'. 'Redundancy in threes' is the rule that you deploy a minimum of three servers to support a given application or service. Take a domain controller for example: the deployment of three domain controllers provides the environment with stability in the event that one is lost to catastrophic hardware. Even with this failure you are able to perform routine maintenance on the other two without affecting service to the network. This ensures the uptime required to support an enterprise commerce environment. This said, your production Active Directory environment should have a minimum of three Domain Controllers, two of which also host the Global Catalog. Obviously, smaller organizations may not be able to afford the hardware required for 'redundancy in threes', but no matter how small your organization is, a minimum of two servers for each service is strongly recommended.

The redundancy discussed above maximizes your directory availability but does not take into consideration the number of servers needed to provide simultaneous directory access for a large number of users and computers. A conservative estimate of simultaneous user connections for logon and network authentication is 17,000 requests. This estimate assumes the following server configuration:

❑ Quad processor – 600MHz or faster
❑ 1GB Memory

- ❑ 100Mbit full-duplex network connection (or dual channeled 100Mbit connections – for example, Cisco's Fast EtherChannel)
- ❑ 3 Disk Volumes
  - ❑ Operating System Volume (RAID 1)
  - ❑ AD Database Volume (RAID 5)
  - ❑ AD Logging Volume (RAID 1)

Active Directory requires disk architecture much like Exchange for maximum efficiency. The O/S and Logging volumes should exist in a hardware-mirrored set to provide quick writes. The database volume is configured using a stripe-set with parity to provide high-speed reads. Combining these volume sets in any way will decrease the efficiency of your Domain Controller and reduce the number of simultaneous requests it is able to support.

Active Directory utilizes DNS services to provide service announcement and computer mapping throughout the forest. It is important to provide the same level of hardware redundancy as seen in the domain controllers discussed above.

The following figure shows a possible server farm supporting the production active directory environment. These servers will exist on the same network segment as your database servers. This example will support approximately 50,000 simultaneous directory requests (assuming the hardware configuration as described above).

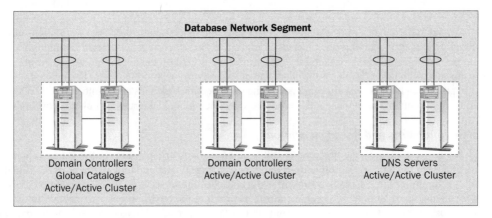

This example uses active/active clustering to provide additional redundancy and reliability. There are many clustering options like Microsoft's clustering service (Advanced and Data center Server only) and Legato's Co-standby server. If you are deploying these clusters in a large enterprise environment, you may consider deploying an active/standby cluster solution but this will require twice the hardware of an active/active solution to support the same number of directory and DNS requests. The advantage of using an active/ passive cluster solution is that on failure an already active server will not have to take on additional load.

Systems and Application Deployment

As you undoubtedly know, Microsoft's hardware recommendations and real-world requirements differ slightly. This is compounded by other factors, such as efficient ASP coding, number of database requests per session, and security and encryption settings (for example, SSL). In this section we will take a look at Microsoft hardware recommendations and real-world hardware requirements. We will discuss the requirements for the database servers, web servers and the Business Desk servers.

SQL Server

Software Requirements and Recommendations

Commerce Server 2000 can utilize either SQL Server 2000 or SQL Server 7. However, it is recommended that you utilize SQL Server 2000 within the production environment due to the enhancements in transaction speed, reliability and synchronization. Regardless of the version you choose to deploy, you must stick with it for all SQL Server databases within your environment. Commerce Server 2000 will not support a multi-version SQL environment for the Data Warehouse and OLAP (On-Line Analytical Processing)/Analysis Services server databases.

Commerce Server 2000 requires additional software to be installed on the SQL Server and it varies from SQL Server 2000 to SQL Server 7.0. The additional software required for SQL Server 2000 is as follows:

- ❑ SQL Server 2000 Client Tools
- ❑ SQL Server 2000 Analysis Service
- ❑ SQL Server 2000 Analysis Services Client Tools

SQL Server 7.0 has a longer list of required software. The list is as follows:

- ❑ SQL Server 7.0 Client Tools
- ❑ SQL Server 7.0, Service Pack 2
- ❑ SQL Server 7.0 OLAP Services
- ❑ SQL Server 7.0 OLAP Services, Service Pack 2
- ❑ OLAP Add-in Manager
- ❑ OLAP Server Client Tools
- ❑ MDAC 2.6

Additionally, if the SQL Server is not installed locally on the Commerce Server 2000 computer you must install **MSXML2.DLL** on each server. This file can be installed through the SQL Server 2000 Client Tools or MDAC 2.6. Additionally, the newest version of this file, **MSXML3.DLL** is available through Microsoft's XML parser and tools installation.

Like Windows 2000 Server there are two versions of SQL Server 2000 available, Enterprise Edition and Standard Edition. The table below shows the primary differences between the two SQL Server 2000 editions currently available.

	SQL 2000 Standard Edition	SQL 2000 Enterprise Edition
Maximum Processors Supported	4 (all W2K Versions)	32 (W2K Data center Server)
		8 (W2K Advanced Server)
		4 (W2K Server)
Maximum Memory Supported	2 GB (all W2K Versions)	64 GB (W2K Data center Server)
		8 GB (W2K Advanced Server)
		4 GB (W2K Server)

Table continued on following page

1037

	SQL 2000 Standard Edition	SQL 2000 Enterprise Edition
Additional Features		Online Backups
		Log Shipping
		Failover Clustering
		Enhanced Analysis Support
List Price	$4,999 per processor	$19,999 per processor

Given the processor and memory limitations alone, most organizations will opt for SQL Server 2000 Enterprise Edition. When all things are even though, the deciding factor is usually the high-availability features bundled with the Enterprise Edition. These features include the following:

❑ **Online Backups** – allows data to be backed-up while online and accessible by users (including differential backups and server-less backups using third party VDI (virtual device interfaces)

❑ **Log Shipping** – synchronizes transaction logs providing the ability to deploy 'warm standby' database servers

❑ **Failover Clustering** – allows active/passive and active/active clustering of up to four nodes

A complete comparison of the features available within each SQL Server 2000 version is available on Microsoft's MSDN site at http://msdn.microsoft.com/library/psdk/sql/8_ar_ts_1cdv.htm.

Hardware Requirements and Recommendations

Unlike web servers, database servers scale vertically, by adding additional resources (for example CPUs, memory, disk space) within the server. This type of scaling requires more thought when designing the hardware requirements for your environment. It is important to purchase servers that scale beyond your current resource needs. For example, if your environment currently requires a dual processor database server, deploy a server that can scale to four processors. If you do not deploy systems with the ability to be upgraded, you will be forced to throw out your existing hardware and purchase new systems when your resource needs grow.

There are three main database stores required in Commerce Server 2000: the Data Warehouse, Analysis Services (OLAP) and profile data. The Data Warehouse database stores all data for your website and is the main store from which analysis reports are run. The Analysis Services (OLAP) installation is where all reports are run from. Profile data is where all user information (such as name, address, credit card information, preferences, etc) is stored. Additionally, if you wish to utilize Commerce Server 2000's Direct Mailing application, you must install the Direct Mailer on SQL Server. This application will utilize a SQL Server database to perform direct mailing campaigns for your site. Depending on how small or large your environment is you can choose to install all the database stores on a single SQL Server cluster or spread them out to three SQL Server clusters.

Most environments will want to split out the stores on three separate SQL Server clusters: one for the data warehouse, one for the profile database and the last for OLAP reporting and the direct mail database. The following figure shows this configuration, which will sit alongside the Active Directory resource servers within the database network segment.

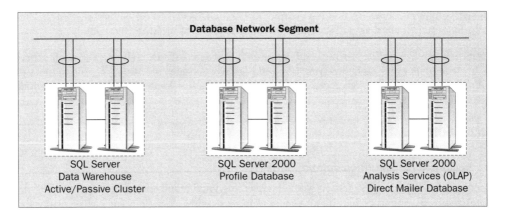

For most environments the question is not how many SQL Server clusters to deploy, but what type of server hardware and system software to deploy. The first question is what type of storage solution do you wish to deploy. Clustered servers require an external storage solution that the clustered servers are directly attached to. There are many storage options, from a simple SCSI array to a SAN (Storage Area Network). The deciding factors are the amount of storage needed and the pain threshold of capital expenditures. Most small and medium-sized organizations will opt for an external drive array connected via SCSI or Fibre Channel. Larger organizations with a healthy budget will more than likely opt for a SAN solution. SANs provide many high-availability enhancements, such as redundant array controllers, multiple path access to the drive array and triple-mirrored arrays for increased reliability and snapshot backups.

Now let us take a look at SQL Server deployment recommendations for small, medium and large enterprise environments. Estimated concurrent database transactions for the environments are 200, 1000, and 10,000 respectively. You can download a SQL Server 2000 hardware-sizing tool from Compaq at http://activeanswers.compaq.com/ActiveAnswers/Render/1,1027,536-6-100-225-1,00.htm, after registering as a user. No matter what size your organization is, it is very important to design a database environment that can scale vertically without having to throw out hardware and replace it with larger systems. The following table highlights generic recommendations for these three business types.

	Small Environment	**Medium Environment**	**Large Environment**
Processor	Dual processor (expandable to Quad)	Quad Processor (expandable to 8-way)	8-way (expandable up to 32-way)
RAM	2 GB	4GB	8GB +
Storage Array	SCSI Array	SCSI or Fibre Channel Array	Storage Area Network
Operating System	W2K Advanced Server	W2K Advanced Server	W2K Data center Server

SQL Server 2000 is much like Active Directory Domain Controllers and Exchange servers, requiring three separate disk volumes to optimize server resources. The volumes should be configured as follows:

- ❑   Operating System – RAID 1
- ❑   SQL Transaction Logs – RAID 1
- ❑   SQL Database Store

The operating system and transaction log volumes are unique to each server within the cluster. The SQL Database Store is the only shared disk volume (connected via SCSI or Fibre Channel).

Your Analysis Services (OLAP) server need not be as robust as the data warehouse and profile servers. However, redundancy and even clustering is still important as business decisions rely on up-to-date reporting data. A standard OLAP server design would be on par with the small-enterprise SQL recommendation discussed above.

Commerce Server

Hardware Requirements and Recommendations

Commerce Server 2000 installs on each web server serving your digital commerce site. This will obviously take more hardware resources than IIS alone and must be designed to scale accordingly. Most web farms are designed to scale horizontally; this means that scalability is achieved by introducing additional web servers into the farm. In contrast, database servers (which we will discuss later in this section) scale vertically by adding additional resources (CPUs, memory, drive space) to the existing servers. The table below shows Microsoft's requirements for Commerce Server 2000 and the author's recommendations based on real-world e-commerce environments.

	Microsoft's Minimum Requirements	Author Recommendations
CPU	Single (400 MHz or faster)	Dual (500 MHz or faster)
RAM	256 MB	512 MB – 1 GB (100 MHz or faster)
Hard Disk Space	100 MB	9 GB Total Usable (for O/S, Commerce Server and Website Code)
Network adapter card	100 MB (recommended)	100 MB Full-Duplex (two required)
CD-ROM Drive	Required	Required
VGA Monitor	Required	Not Required if running headless web server (using Terminal Services or Compaq's Remote Insight Board)
Mouse or pointing device	Required	Not Required if headless
Operating Systems	Windows 2000 Server or greater	

These recommendations are made based on experience with several e-commerce environments. There is now a wide array of server offerings available for deployment as a web server. It is important to understand the unique needs of a web server as opposed to a database or application server. Since scalability and reliability of a web farm depends upon multiple servers within the farm, high intra-server redundancy is not necessary. Since the web farm is going to be your largest collection of servers within your production environment, space is the greatest concern. Servers such as the Compaq DL360 provide dual CPUs, dual network adapters, and RAID 1 capability in a very small footprint. You can deploy up to 42 of these servers within one standard computer rack (if utilizing remote management services like Terminal Services and/or Compaq's Remote Insight Board and a non-racked UPS). This minimizes the space requirements within your data center or leased cage.

The standard recommended web server would include the following:

- Compaq DL360 (or comparable 1U server)
- Dual Pentium III 500 MHz (or greater) processors
- 512 MB (or greater) RAM
- Two 9 GB (10,000 rpm) Wide Ultra2 SCSI hard drives in a RAID 1 configuration
- Dual 10/100 network adapters
- If Headless: Compaq Remote Insight Board – Lights-Out Edition board (or comparable)

These are guidelines and are subject to refinement based upon your production environment's unique needs. Before deploying your web farm, it is important to test your web servers with a load balancing tool to obtain a baseline for how many concurrent users a single web server will handle efficiently. This will give you the knowledge to determine how many production web servers should be deployed to handle your expected customer volume. We will discuss load testing of your production environment later in this appendix.

Some of the smallest Commerce Server environments may initially only need one web server to provide the resources needed to support your estimated customer load. However, the web farm still should include a minimum of three web servers to ensure availability in the event of systems failure. A minimum of three production web servers provides availability using the 'redundancy of three' rule discussed earlier in the appendix.

Software Requirements and Recommendations

You have two operating system options for your web farm, Window 2000 Server and Windows 2000 Advanced Server; the following table shows the main differences between them.

	Windows 2000 Server	**Windows 2000 Advanced Server**
Maximum Processors	4	8
Maximum Memory	4 GB	8 GB
Additional Features		Network Load Balancing
		Cluster Service
List Price	$1,199 (with 10 CALs) + [$199 per 5 additional CALs]	$3,999 (with 25 CALs)

Given the processor and memory requirements discussed above, either Windows 2000 version will do nicely; the question is whether or not you will be utilizing the additional features of Windows 2000 Advanced Server. It is doubtful that you would utilize Cluster Service within your web farm as it only allows clusters of two servers. However, smaller organizations may wish to utilize NLB (Network Load Balancing) to load balance customer traffic to your web farm. NLB is limited to a cluster of 32 servers; after that you will have to split the farm into multiple NLB clusters or upgrade to a more robust load balancing solution. Even small organizations may think twice if considering NLB as a cost-effective solution over a hardware load balancer. If you are deploying more than 14 web servers, consider deploying Windows 2000 Server and purchasing an entry- or mid-level hardware load balancing solution, such as the Cisco LocalDirector 416 or 430, in a failover configuration. For approximately the same capital outlay, you are able to deploy a much more robust and secure web farm and load balancing environment.

Now for a quick word on Windows 2000 licensing. The Windows 2000 Server software is bundled with a small number of client access licenses (CALs). It is important to purchase enough licenses to support your maximum number of secure concurrent connections. The IIS SSL session counter is set to the number of CALs installed on the server and one session is used with every HTTPS connection to your site. If the SSL session counter is exceeded, your customers will receive the HTTP 403.15 error, Client Access Licenses Exceeded. Standard HTTP requests do not require a client access license.

Business Desk

The Business Desk is the software tool you use to configure and manage your Commerce Server 2000 site. This includes: catalog management, advertising campaigns, payment and shipping options, report analysis, and user management. This is your most important tool within Commerce Server 2000 and it should be deployed with a high level of availability and security. The BizDesk for your production environment should be deployed within your corporate network to maximize security and provide local access to the tool. As it is an integral component of your Commerce Server 2000 environment, it is recommended to install BizDesk on a clustered server. Many organizations will opt for an active/active cluster solution that will provide resources for the corporate intranet as well as BizDesk. The following figure shows the deployment of this type of cluster within the corporate network.

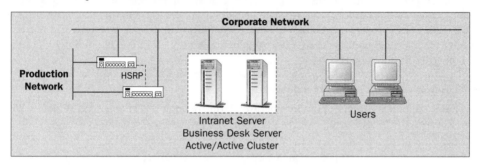

The recommended hardware requirements for this type of Business Server deployment is as follows:

❑   Single processor minimum (dual recommended)

❑   512 MB – 1 GB RAM

❑   Drive Volumes

❑   O/S Partition – RAID 1 (9 GB Usable)

❑   Cluster Partition – RAID 5 (18 GB + Usable)

The software requirements for Business Desk is as follows:

❑   Windows 2000 Server, Advanced Server or Data center Server

❑   Windows 2000, Service Pack 1 (or greater)

❑   Commerce Server 2000

❑   MSXML2.DLL (this file is required to access a remote SQL server and can be installed through SQL Server 2000 Client Tools or MDAC 2.6)

The Business Desk is installed when you unpack a Commerce Server 2000 site. By default it will install BizDesk on each and every server on which you install Commerce Server 2000. This default deployment is inherently insecure and a waste of server resources. To this end, you must install your packaged site using the **Custom Unpack** option in the Commerce Server Site Packager. The following figure shows the point in the Custom Unpack where you choose the applications to be installed. In this example we uncheck the Retail site and only install the RetailBizDesk to our Business Desk server.

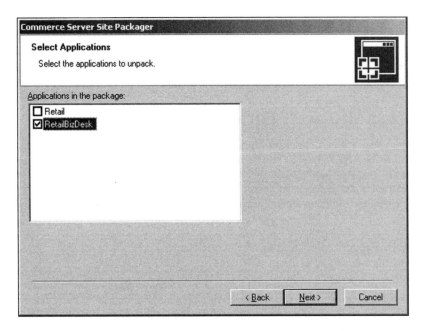

If your Commerce 2000 environment is deployed within an ISP's hosting environment, you will not be able to install the Business Desk within your corporate environment (unless you spend a bit of cash for a high-speed direct connection). In this case, it is recommended that Terminal Services be deployed within the hosted production environment. This gives you the ability to administer your site without having to be local to the production environment. Unless you do have a secure direct connection between your corporate network and your hosted production network, it is recommended that a VPN connection be used.

Business Desk Client

After the BizDesk application installation is complete, the Business Desk client must be installed; this takes place by opening the BizDesk website, usually found at its default location of http://localhost/retailbizdesk. However, before we install the BizDesk client, let's take a look at the software requirements:

- ❑ Windows 98 to Windows 2000 Server (all versions)
- ❑ Internet Explorer 5.5
- ❑ Microsoft Office 2000 or SQL Server 2000 Client Tools
- ❑ SQL Server 7.0 Client tools and the OLAP Server Client Tools (if you are utilizing a SQL 7.0 database)

Once the required software has been installed on the BizDesk client machine, you can connect to the BizDesk website to complete the installation. You will be prompted as to where you would like the application files to be installed; once chosen, the installation completes and installs the Business Desk shortcut on your desktop and Start Menu.

Commerce Server Administration Tools

You may wish to install the Commerce Server Administration Tools on an administration-only machine (such as an operations machine) or a remote machine to allow you to administer Commerce Server 2000 from multiple locations. The only requirement is that the remote machine must reside in a trusted domain or the same domain in which Commerce Server 2000 resides.

You install the Commerce Server Administration Tools from the Commerce Server 2000 install disk. Run the setup and choose Custom Installation. From here, select Administration Tools and unselect all other options. This will install just the Commerce Server Manager without the need to install the complete application and will connect to the existing Administration database deployed during your first full Commerce Server 2000 install.

Securing Your Microsoft Environment

As we discussed towards the beginning of this appendix, security is a chain and is only as strong as its weakest link. We have discussed how to secure the network infrastructure, now is the time to discuss security within the servers themselves. We will discuss securing your production web and database servers as well as ongoing security administration duties, but keep in mind that security is a process and doesn't end when the last current Hotfix is applied: ongoing security maintenance is required to ensure that your environment risk of intrusion is minimized.

Knowledge is the Key

Ignorance of new vulnerabilities and security enhancements are the reason most environments are compromised. It is of the utmost importance to ensure that you are equipped with the knowledge to maintain a high level of understanding of current trends, vulnerabilities, and enhancements to maintain your ever-evolving security infrastructure. As Confucius once said; 'A network without continual security maintenance will soon not be your network at all'.

But how do you keep up with the current security events? There are so many changes in this field every day that no one person can keep track of them all. Luckily, Microsoft and other security sites/agencies do this for you. They will provide you with continual security bulletins and security updates for free. The following are resources to help you keep up-to-date with current security news and events:

- ❑ **Microsoft's Security Notification Service.** This service is free and keeps you up-to-date on Microsoft platform security news, alerts and updates. This service is the best way to keep track of new post-Service Pack hotfixes released. You can sign up for this service at: http://www.microsoft.com/technet/security/notify.asp.

- ❑ **Microsoft's TechNet Security Website.** This website is full of whitepapers, checklists, tools and security patches and is one of the best Microsoft-platform security websites available. It can be found at http://www.microsoft.com/technet/security.

- ❑ **SANS Institute.** The System Administration, Network, and Security Institute is a valuable resource for security information regardless of platform. They provide security bulletins and free electronic newsletters. Their Security Alert Consensus (SAC) is a weekly e-mail newsletter that combines security alerts and bulletins from many security agencies, including: SANS, CERT, DoD, Security Portal and NTBugTraq. They also provide a monthly Windows Security Newsletter that not only discusses new threats and bugs, but also service packs and security fixes and whether or not they should be implemented. You can access their site at http://www.sans.org.

- ❑ **CERT Coordination Center.** The Carnegie Mellon CERT Coordination Center is a reporting center for Internet-based security problems and software bugs. They are also an excellent reference for multi-platform security alerts and information. CERT also provides a series of free electronic newsletters. These newsletters include: CERT/CC Current Activity (current security incidents and vulnerabilities), CERT Advisories (notification on current vulnerabilities and fixes or workarounds) and CERT Summaries (quarterly summaries of all incidents and vulnerabilities reported). You can search their archives and sign up for their newsletters at http://www.cert.org.

❑ **Internet Security Systems**. ISS is another resource on security threats and vulnerabilities. They offer news and alerts and a myriad of electronic security newsletters, as well as links to additional resources. You can visit them and sign-up for their newsletters at http://xforce.iss.net.

❑ **Windows IT Security.** This site is part of the Windows 2000 Magazine network and reports on Microsoft-platform security issues. They can be reached at http://www.ntsecurity.net.

There are many other security sites available, but the sites listed above give you a well-rounded look at what is currently going on with computer security throughout the world. Take time to look through the offerings every site has and pick two or three sites and electronic newsletters that best fit you and your environment. Be selective; don't sign up for every newsletter you find, as you will not have time to review them and put their recommendations into practice. These resources are designed to ease your administrative burden, not overwhelm you with information. Remember to always test any security change, hotfix or service pack within your staging environment before deploying it throughout your production Commerce Server 2000 environment.

Securing Windows 2000

Microsoft has made securing your Windows 2000 machine fairly easy compared to NT. They have provided administrators with security policies and templates, IPSec and Kerberos integration, and continual security updates and patches. Microsoft's guiding principle when deploying security is 'if it isn't easy to secure, it won't be'. To this end they have automated security updates and created wizard security policies to make deployment as painless as possible. There are also some common sense recommendations that we will discuss to ensure your Windows 2000 environment is as secure as possible.

Security Recommendations

Here are a few recommendations to secure your Windows 2000 environment:

1. **Limit logon access to the box**. Limit the number of users that have administrative access to the server and remove shares accessible by everyone.

2. **Rename the Administrator account**. For a malicious user to gain access to your system, they need two pieces of information, a username and password. Many organizations help these users along by continuing to use the Administrator account within their production environment. Rename the Administrator account; make the hacker's job as hard as possible.

3. **Remove unnecessary services and applications**. Make sure that you have only deployed services and applications that are required for your production environment. Do not utilize security-compromising services/applications (like Telnet, NetMeeting Desktop Sharing and PCAnywhere). While they may ease remote administrative burden, they are detrimental to the security of your servers.

4. **Utilize NTFS**. NTFS is the most secure file system available within Windows 2000. Use it to control directory and file access through users and groups. Remove NTFS permissions to the Everyone group. If you have already deployed FAT partitions on your servers, you can convert the file system by running the Convert utility from the command line (type `convert /?` for syntax). Additionally, files can be encrypted by utilizing EFS (Encrypting File System), minimizing the ability of third party tools to bypass NTFS access checks.

5. **Utilize security templates**. Microsoft has provided administrators with pre-built security templates within AD. These can be found within the Group Policy MMC snap-in and can be configured to fit your environment's needs. The following figure shows the Group Policy snap-in and the Computer and Users settings available. Additionally, Microsoft has developed a free high security template specific to web server deployments. This template can be customized to support your unique environment and is available for download at http://download.microsoft.com/download/win2000srv/SCM/1.0/NT5/EN-US/hisecweb.exe. This template makes configuration changes to the password policy, audit policy, system privilege rights and security registry values. Microsoft also has a web-based template wizard to build security templates for web servers, which is discussed later in this section.

6. **Consider deploying IPSec policies.** An IPSec policy deployed on every web server will provide another level of packet filtering behind your firewall. This will allow you to further block port access and minimize security breaches. This is not a mandatory step as this additional packet filtering requires additional CPU cycles and will utilize resources that could otherwise be used to service customer requests.

7. **Use Windows Update**. Windows Update provides you with instant access to all relevant security updates. The Windows update bundles updates for Internet delivery to your systems and you can even download a notifier to let you know when a new update is available. You can access the Windows update site by clicking on Windows Update in your Start Menu, through Internet Explorer under Tools | Windows Update, or directly at http://windowsupdate.microsoft.com.

8. **Deploy Active Directory In Native Mode**. In Native Mode, Active Directory only supports Kerberos authentication. In Mixed Mode, authentication is available via Kerberos and NTLM. NTLM is a less secure authentication and should be removed from your production environment.

Security is as much art as science and will take trial and error to ensure the security enhancements are correctly applied and valid for your environment. Make sure that all security configuration changes are fully tested before deployment to your production environment. There is nothing like a call at 3 o'clock in the morning from the operations staff saying that they installed a new security patch to the web servers and now no one can access the site. Also, the best defense against security failures is knowledge: the entire administration and operations team should be kept up-to-date on security fixes and service pack updates. Organizations may choose to distribute security tasks among the team members. For example, one staff member may be responsible for OS security updates, another for IIS security updates and yet another for database security updates. This distribution of security roles allows a greater chance that security updates are discovered and deployed efficiently. An organization with an overextended and understaffed administration team will be hard pressed to keep up with the necessary security alerts and fixes and is a common reason why many large sites are so vulnerable to attack.

Securing Internet Information Services 5.0

Now that you have secured the operating system, let us look at IIS. As with Windows 2000, Microsoft has whitepapers, checklists and tools available to secure your Internet Information Services. They can be found on Microsoft's Security website at http://www.microsoft.com/technet/security. Just as with securing the operating system, securing IIS requires trial and error to ensure security enhancements are compatible with your environment. Be sure to test all changes within your staging environment before deploying them within your production environment.

Securing the Application

The following is a list of security recommendations for IIS 5.0:

1. **Remove unnecessary IIS services**. Minimize the applications and ports available to the public by removing unnecessary services. Most Commerce Server 2000 web servers do not require NNTP (Network News Transfer Protocol) and FTP (File Transfer Protocol); these services should be removed from the web server. Additionally, if there is a need for these services within your production environment, it is more secure to relegate them to their own servers.

2. **Reset Access Control Lists on Virtual Directories**. By default, virtual directories created initially have Full Control. It is important to reset this to allow only the minimum access to support your customer's needs. Static content (for example, HTML and graphic files) should be restricted to everyone only having read (R) permission. Script, CGI and include files require that everyone have Execute (X) access. Administrators and System should have Full Control on all website files and directories.

    If these various files reside in one directory, you will have to manually change the ACL on each and every file. To minimize administrative effort to secure these files, Microsoft recommends creating a directory for each file type and then setting the ACL at the directory level. This allows files to be added or changed without having to continually apply security permissions

3. **Utilize IIS Logging**. Without logging enabled, you are blind to the daily operations of your web servers. Most organizations employ some form of website analysis software (like HitList or WebTrends) and utilize logging for these applications. If you are not utilizing this type of application, it is important to utilize IIS logging to have a view into server requests and responses.

1047

4. **Remove Sample Applications and Web Administration**. IIS 5.0 deploys samples and web administration that can compromise security on a production web server and should be removed. The `IISSamples`, `IISAdmin` and `MSDAC` virtual directories should be removed and associated files deleted. The Administration Website allows remote IIS administration from a browser and should also be deleted and all associated files removed.

5. **Remove unneeded Application Mappings and disable parent paths**. The following figure shows the Application Mapping properties page. This is accessed by right clicking on the server within Internet Services Manager, choosing Properties | Master Properties, Edit | Home Directory, Configuration | App Mappings. Some of the mappings to consider removing are: password reset (`.htr`), Internet Database Connector (`.idc`), Server-side includes (`.stm`, `.shtm`, `.shtml`), and Internet printing (`.printer`).

Parent paths provide a tool to traverse parent directories using the relative '..' syntax; this can allow malicious users access to the parent directory structure. However, if you do utilize parent paths, be sure that execute access is not allowed within the parent directory. This option resides in the same properties page as the App Mappings, in the App Options tab. The second figure below shows the App Options tab where you can disable the use of parent paths.

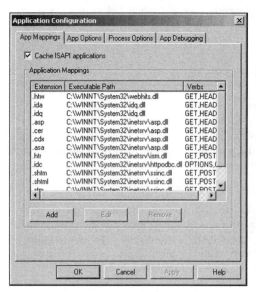 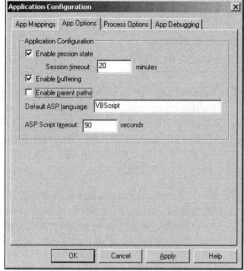

Microsoft's Security Tools

Microsoft has IIS 5.0 security tools available for free. You can download them from Microsoft's Security Website at http://www.microsoft.com/technet/security. The author highly recommends the use of the Hotfix Checking Tool for IIS 5.0 and the Windows 2000 Internet Server Security Configuration Tool.

The Hotfix Checking Tool for IIS 5.0 is a script written by a member of the Microsoft Security Team. The downloaded executable has a Windows and Java Script version of the tool. It queries the local box for installed hotfixes and checks it against Microsoft's released hotfixes (http://www.microsoft.com/technet/security/search/bulletins.xml). The tool will then write a Warning error to the local Application Event Log. This warning event includes a hyperlink to the Microsoft Security Bulletin where you can obtain more information about the vulnerability and download the hotfix. The screenshot below shows the warning event within the application event log.

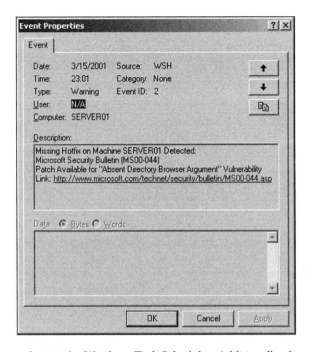

This tool can be automated using the Windows Task Scheduler. Additionally, there are command-line parameters that allow you to search multiple machines rather than having to run it locally on every machine. As this is a script it is highly customizable and can be tweaked to fit your environment. The documentation for this tool is great and will give you additional information on the parameters and customization possible. The only limitation is that this tool currently only supports IIS 5.0 related hotfixes. This tool is one of the best defenses against minimizing vulnerabilities within your production environment while minimizing resources needed to keep up to date on patches available.

The Windows 2000 Internet Server Security Configuration Tool is a web-based application that will help you to create a security template to be deployed within your web farm. It further refines the high security web server security template (available at http://download.microsoft.com/download/win2000srv/SCM/1.0/NT5/EN-US/hisecweb.exe by asking a series of questions about services to be deployed on your web server. It takes your answers, updates the high security template and writes the new template to a text file (named `IISTemplate.txt` by default). The following figure shows the questions used to create your security template. You then can deploy the template to your web servers using the `IISConfig.cmd` script that is included in the download. This template can be further modified manually before deploying it to your web farm, just as you could with the `hisecweb` template. This template allows administrators a head start in creating security policies without having to directly configure registry settings, IIS property settings, IPSec properties and service manager configurations. This tool also automates some of the IIS security recommendations discussed above, greatly reducing administrative overhead to secure your Internet Information Services.

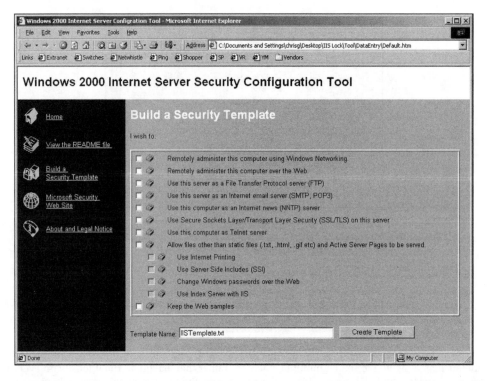

These tools greatly reduce the administrative burden of securing your web servers and keeping them up-to-date. They allow you to efficiently deploy strong security templates and keep up-to-date on the latest security vulnerabilities and hotfixes. The greatest thing about these tools (and the others available on Microsoft's Security website) is that they are free, Free, FREE! Work smarter, not harder: deploy these tools within your production environment, but make sure you test any changes and updates before releasing them to your production servers.

Securing the Data Transmission

Securing the web server is not enough. You must also secure the transmission of critical data to and from your customer's computer. In order to provide secure data transfer you will utilize Secure Sockets Layer (SSL) 3.0 connections between you and your customers. Before you can utilize SSL on your Commerce Server 2000 web servers, you must obtain and install an SSL certificate from a Certification Authority (CA). A Certification Authority is a trusted third party organization that can vouch for the authenticity of your organization. This gives your customers some level of assurance that you are who you say you are and can be trusted to perform a monetary transaction with.

There are many Certification Authorities that would gladly issue you an SSL certificate, but it is important to choose a security that is well known and widely used. Verisign (www.verisign.com) is the most widely used CA throughout Internet commerce sites and is a safe bet when choosing an authority. It is important to utilize a CA that is widely accepted by the most popular browsers: you would not want to lose a sale to a potential customer because their browser doesn't trust the CA by default. Verisign offer 40-bit and 128-bit server IDs and pricing currently starts at around $350 for the 40-bit key and $900 for the 128-bit key. It is important to note that you will need a certificate for each fully qualified domain name (FQDN) you wish to secure. For example, if your entire site runs under the FQDN www.retailstore.com you only need one certificate, but if you separate into multiple FQDNs (like sports.retailstore.com and electronics.retailstore.com) you will need a certificate for each one. Remember this when designing your website/directory structure; it is much more cost effective to separate your site via directories than FQDNs and is simpler to administer as well.

Before you can purchase an SSL certificate from a Certificate Authority, you must create a Certificate Signing Request (CSR) from your web server. A CSR is created from within the Internet Services Manager by right clicking on the site you wish to secure and choosing **Properties**. Choose the **Directory Security** tab and click the **Server Certificate** button (in the **Secure Communications** section). The following figure shows this properties page. This will start the Server Certificate Wizard, which will create the CSR for your Certificate Authority. Once the CSR is created it is saved in the file `C:\certreq.txt` (by default, but can be customized when creating the CSR). You will then send this to your CA for certificate creation.

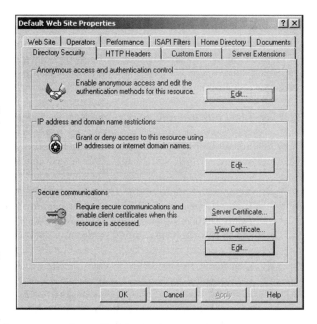

Depending on the service level you paid for, the request will usually take 2-5 business days to complete. Once you have received your certificate from the CA, you will use the Server Certificate Wizard to complete the certificate installation.

Once the certificate installation is complete, you have to enable SSL security on either the website or virtual directories with which you need secure connectivity. This is done within the same **Directory Security** properties page from which you installed your SSL certificate. From here you click on the **Edit** button; this will bring up the Secure Communications property page, in which you can enable secure channel (SSL) connections. Here you can see this Secure Communications property page.

You should not attempt to transact business over the web without the use of secure channels for transmission of personal data. Internet-savvy users will not even utilize a site that doesn't offer secure checkout. You would also be doing a great disservice to those users that are not as knowledgeable about Internet security. These certificates are relatively inexpensive to purchase and easy to deploy, so there is no reason why you should forgo this security measure. Additionally, you may wish to secure FTP and Extranet connections in the same manner. Remember, all of the security that you have implemented counts for nothing if you are sending volatile data in clear text.

Securing SQL 2000

Your databases hold the key to your production environment. They hold the data that makes you money and should be guarded by all means possible. By deploying a firewall solution between your web farm and database clusters, you have greatly secured your database environment. However, there are a few additional security enhancements you should deploy before taking your site live. Some recommendations are as follows:

1. **Limit Administrative Access and Require Unique Accounts**. There should only be a handful of staff that has administrative access to the SQL servers. Additionally, require use of unique accounts for each administrator. This allows auditing and tracking of changes to the SQL server. Do not allow user accounts and passwords to be shared among multiple users.

2. **Remove the SA Account**. The SA account is the administration account for the SQL server. It should be removed and another account given administrative control. As was discussed in the section on securing Windows 2000, don't help the attacker out by giving them 50% of the information needed to administratively access your SQL servers.

3. **Consider Utilizing IPSec Policies**. Utilizing IPSec policies helps to further secure data transmission between your web servers and database servers. You can create virtual tunnels between the SQL servers and web servers, explicitly securing connectivity parameters. Remember that simplicity is the key. Keep away from deploying highly complex policies that will take valuable server resources that can be used to service customer requests.

4. **Stay Up-to-Date**. Ensure that you stay current of the vulnerabilities found and the fixes available. Ensure that you deploy all critical service packs and hotfixes that are valid for your environment.

5. **Use Microsoft's Resources**. Microsoft's Database security website is a wealth of knowledge and will help you to further secure your database environment as well as keep you current on new security threats, fixes and workarounds. It can be accessed at http://www.microsoft.com/technet/security/database.asp.

Production Server Performance and Load Testing

So, you have deployed your web and database farms and installed all necessary code and applications, but you aren't ready to go live yet. Many hundreds of e-commerce sites in the past few years with a highly robust and reliable production environment only grind to a halt during peak usage times due to inadequate performance and load testing. This hit many of the dot com companies during the Christmas seasons. Companies like Toys R Us had to limit connections and turn away paying customers because they were unable to handle the loads. Don't be caught with a great production deployment that cannot service peak customer loads. End-to-end test your production systems before you launch your Commerce Server 2000 environment.

There are many third party performance and load balancing testing solutions available on the market today. This software simulates customer load by utilizing customized scripts that you write. They also provide integrated performance monitoring statistics and reporting. Segue's SilkPerformer (http://www.segue.com/html/s_solutions/s_performer/s_performer.htm) is one of the leading performance and load testing suites on the market. This type of solution tests end-to-end connectivity and speed as seen from the customer's viewpoint. You can simulate a variety of tasks, including: site browsing, searching, cart loading, and checkout and order verification. You can also simulate customer connection speeds, such as dialup, DSL, cable modems and wireless.

These types of software solutions are high-end and do not come cheap: you can easily spend $10,000 - $50,000 on a testing suite depending on the number of concurrent simulated connections required and add-on packages purchased. In addition, most of these software applications require a significant amount of engineering resources to create and refine the scripts and evaluate the reports.

Microsoft's Web Application Stress Tool

Performance and load testing is a requirement to deploy a Commerce Server 2000 environment, so what do you do if you can't afford the price tag of a solution like Segue's SilkPerformer? Well, budget constrained organizations (and who isn't) take heart. Microsoft offers their Web Application Stress (WAS) Tool (code-named Homer) for free. The only catch is that there is no support available for the product. This is a small price to pay to save tens of thousands of dollars. You can download this free tool from http://webtool.rte.microsoft.com.

Like the other load testing software available, this tool allows you to create scripts from which to test. You can create scripts manually through the scripting tool, automatically through browser recording, from existing IIS logs or from your website content tree. This feature also allows you to introduce a link delay to simulate a users delay in choosing a new page (this link delay can also be randomized). Here you can see a script that was created through browser recording.

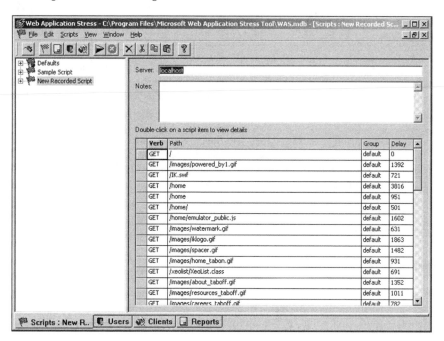

You can add numerous simulated clients and can distribute the tool across multiple machines to increase the number of simulated users that the tool can support. It will also simulate multiple browser types and bandwidth connections. The only limitation is that this tool can only support one bandwidth throttle at a time. The throttling options include: 14.4 modem, 28.8 modem, 56 modem (44k), ISDN Single Channel (64k), ISDN Dual Channel (128k) and T1.

One of the best features of this load-testing tool is its integration with performance monitor counters. From within the script you can choose which counters should be reported when running the load simulation. The following figure shows the adding of performance counters within WAS. This allows you full view into your systems while running the simulation.

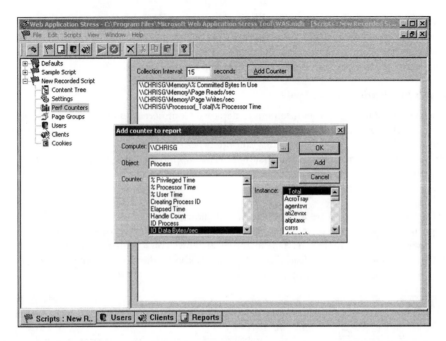

While this tool isn't as feature-rich as the other third party applications available, it is simple to use and very cost effective. Even though Microsoft won't directly support this tool, the documentation is well done and easy to understand; you will not have any problem getting this application configured and working in very little time.

This application is a Microsoft work in progress and they are eager for your feedback and recommendations on feature enhancements. There is also an online knowledge base specifically for the WAS tool. You can suggest new features, get online help and search the dedicated knowledge base at http://homer.rte.microsoft.com. Microsoft also has a great whitepaper on the WAS tool, discussing its use, limitations configuration and recommendations, available at http://msdn.microsoft.com/library/techart/d5wast_2.htm.

Management

We are now on to our last subject in the deployment of a Commerce Server 2000 environment. You have now deployed a stable, reliable, secure and scalable network and systems infrastructure. Now is the time to deploy management policies and applications to ease administrative burden. In this section we will discuss backup and disaster recovery as well as content and systems management. There are many backup and management solutions available but in this section we will discuss only the most common and widely used solutions.

Backup and Disaster Recovery

Your most valuable resource is the data that resides within your production environment. Without it you will not be able to conduct business. It is important to ensure this data is available to you even if the unthinkable (like a fat-fingered delete command or building fire) occurs. To facilitate disaster recovery you need to deploy a robust system and data backup policy. This policy will include online data backup, nightly backup rotations, and offsite media storage.

Online SQL Backups

SQL Server allows you to automate online backups of your data store, minimizing the risk of data corruption when someone decides it will be much faster to cycle the database server by turning the power button off instead of shutting down gracefully. At least in this case you will have scheduled online SQL backups and can roll back to a data store that is only a few hours old.

You should consider scheduling online backups three or four times a day (resources allowing). This ensures that in the event of data corruption within the store, you can roll back to a clean data store that is only out of date by a couple of hours. Online backups allow you to quickly bring your database store online without the time-consuming process of restoring from tape.

Enterprise Backup

Your production environment requires an enterprise-class backup solution. The Travan 4GB tape drive attached to the 486 in the lab will not cut it. Companies like Compaq have many solutions available, one of which is bound to fit your environment. When choosing a device, take into consideration not only your backup needs now, but also a year from now. Look for a solution that will grow with your business, not one that will have to be thrown out in nine months so a larger system can be purchased.

Large enterprise data centers with large data stores should consider a cabinet solution. These cabinets are customizable and provide multiple DLT tape drives integrated with a tape storage unit and robotic controls. This type of system is very self-reliant and requires tape changes every two weeks to a month. Additionally, they provide SCSI and Fibre Channel support for SAN and NAS storage deployments. A good example of this type of backup system is Compaq's ESL9326D automated backup cabinet. This unit at its maximum configuration can store 11.5 terabytes of data with data transfer rates of up to 288 GB per hour. It can support between 6 and 16 35/70 DLT tape drives. Additional reliability is built into the cabinet by utilizing redundant power supplies and hot swappable drives, fans and power units. These units can easily cost $20,000 – $50,000.

Smaller organizations with neither the capacity requirements nor the budget for the enterprise cabinet systems can opt for a DLT or AIT tape array system that will allow scalable growth. Compaq solutions in this range include the TL881 DLT Library and the SSL2020 AIT Library. They offer dual tape drive configurations and can be stacked up to five high to grow with your backup and data storage needs. These units are small (5U) and can be mounted within a server rack. These units are more reasonably priced and start around $7,500.

These units require a separate server to control them. It is important to deploy a server dedicated to backup rather than utilize one of your servers deployed to process customer requests. When the backup is running, it will consume the majority of the resources of the box. A dual processor box is recommended with 1GB of memory and no more than 9GB of usable drive space. Your backups are important, so your server should be built with the appropriate amount of redundancy: redundant power supplies, hot-swappable hard drives, RAID, etc.

Rotation Schemes

Now you need to decide on what gets backed up. You should perform a full backup of all database and application servers. When it comes to web servers it is a waste of processing time and tape media to backup every web server in your farm. Since your web servers are identical to one another, only backup two or three during a backup. This will ensure that you have a good backup even if one or two of the systems fail.

When backing up the production environment you should use the GFS (Grandfather-Father-Son) rotation scheme. This rotation requires 21 tape sets and daily rotation. The tapes should be labeled as follows:

❑   Weekday Rotation: Monday, Tuesday, Wednesday, Thursday

❑   Friday Rotation: Friday1, Friday2, Friday3, Friday4, Friday5

❑   Month-end Rotation: January, February, March, April, May, June, July, August, September, October, November, December

If possible, all of your rotations should be full backups. At the point that your data store has grown too large for full backups nightly, you should schedule differential backups Monday – Thursday and run full backups only on the Friday and Month-end backups. The Friday full backup is not set in stone: you should run this full backup on the day you receive the least customer activity, usually Friday evening through Sunday.

Your backups should run in the non-peak hours and can vary depending on where your customer base is located in relation to your data center. If the majority of your customers are within a few time zones of your data center, consider starting your nightly backups between 10pm and 1am.

Media Storage

Many organizations put a lot of time and resources into designing and deploying a highly reliable backup solution only to lose their tape media due to improper or insecure storage of the media. At a minimum, all backup media should be stored in a locked cabinet or closet. The better storage solution is to use a fire safe; this way you can store tape media, licensing information and financial records in a safe, secure environment.

However, onsite security is not enough. You should strongly consider utilizing an offsite media storage company like Arcus Data Security (w3.arcusds.com). They provide offsite vaulting of your backup media on a daily or weekly rotation schedule; they also provide online backup and recovery utilizing their data center facilities and data transfer over the net. It is not as important how your data gets offsite, as long as it is offsite and readily available for disaster recovery.

Content and Systems Management

Your production enterprise Commerce Server 2000 environment is now quite a feat of engineering prowess and there is no way you can efficiently manage the systems given the limited staff available. And after spending all this money on hardware and software, there is no way your boss will let you purchase a pencil, much less hire additional staff. Luckily, there is a plethora of applications to help automate much of your content and systems management. In this section we will talk about management solutions available from Microsoft, Cisco, and NetIQ. We will also briefly cover website reporting and traffic analysis.

Content Deployment

Managing content on a web server or two is not very difficult to do manually, but add ten or twenty servers to that equation and you have a lot of room for error and inefficient updating. You need an application that can automate this management. Administrators have been screaming at Microsoft for years to provide a robust, reliable content deployment solution. They tried with Site Server 3.0, but it just wasn't ready for prime time. Well, Microsoft has finally answered our prayers with one of the newest servers in its Windows 2000 suite, Application Center 2000.

Application Center 2000 creates a cluster of managed servers, designates a server master and deploys any code, COM and configuration changes to the other servers. It is one of the best products that they have ever released. After the cluster is configured (via a simple-to-use wizard), the application automatically pushed changes on the master to the other servers in the cluster. It will even push and install COM objects and other applications. You can even utilize Application Center to push code, application and system changes directly from your staging servers to your production web farm.

While this is a great product, it doesn't come free. The estimated list price is $2,999 per CPU and licensing will be required for each web server in your farm. Before your jaw drops all the way to the floor, it also provides some impressive enterprise management features, much in the way of a NetIQ or Tivoli. We will discuss these features in greater detail in the next section.

You can read more about Microsoft's Application Center 2000 and download a trial version at http://www.microsoft.com/applicationcenter/. Also, for an in-depth look at Application Center, check out *Professional Application Center 2000* by Wrox Press.

Enterprise Management Tools

We discussed automating code and content management of your web farm but what about the servers themselves? Microsoft has included within Application Center 2000 enterprise management features to automate much of the administration process. The software allows you to remotely manage servers throughout your production environment and push configuration changes to many servers at once. However, the most valuable feature is the integrated system monitoring and alerting. You can monitor all processes and resources of every server in the Application Center cluster. Additionally you can script actions to be performed (for example, restarting of a service, rebooting of a box, removal of a server from an NLB cluster) and alerts to be sent when problems occur or thresholds are reached.

This product offers a lot of functionality and is quite extensible. However, much of the monitoring and alerting has to be configured manually; not much is available out of the box. However, this is true of most of the monitoring and management applications available today as every environment is unique and the software must be highly customizable. You can obtain more detailed information from the Application Center 2000 website at http://www.microsoft.com/applicationcenter.

Another great monitoring and alerting application comes from NetIQ (www.netiq.com). Their AppManager Suite provides monitoring and management software for many of Microsoft's products, including: Windows 2000, Active Directory, Terminal Services, NLB, Cluster Service, Exchange, IIS, Proxy, SQL, and many backup solutions. Much like Application Center 2000, the AppManager Suite provides monitoring, alerting and action response for your production environment. The difference lies in the maturity of NetIQ's product: AppManager is currently in release 3.4 and its maturity shows through in the stability of the product and number of applications it supports. Additionally, it has an extensive array of prepackaged business rules to allow you to be up and monitoring quickly. It is also highly customizable, allowing you to configure thresholds and action scripts that best support your environment.

AppManager, unlike Application Center 2000, is not a distributed application and requires its own hardware. It requires a minimum of two additional servers, one Windows 2000 Server for the AppManager management server and one SQL server for the AppManager data repository. You may also wish to deploy the optional AppManager web management server, which will also require another Windows 2000 server. The web management server allows you to run the AppManager console through an Internet Explorer or Netscape Navigator browser. Additionally, you will have to deploy agents on each of the servers you wish to monitor. You can obtain more information and request an evaluation package from NetIQ at http://www.netiq.com.

Monitoring and configuration of your network infrastructure is important and should not be overlooked. There are many applications available, but if your network environment is Cisco-based, you should consider the CiscoWorks2000 Suite of tools. Their tools include monitoring, alerting and configuration of their network hardware (including LAN/WAN switching, routing, VPN, security and content delivery hardware) as well as configuration of Quality of Service (QoS), Access Control, SLA metrics, IDS (Intrusion Detection Systems) and other networking services.

No matter the size or complexity of your Cisco environment, they have a CiscoWorks2000 package that will fit you. You can get more information about CiscoWorks2000 from their website at http://www.cisco.com/warp/public/44/jump/ciscoworks.shtml.

Nortel also has similar offerings available for their network hardware. You can get more information from their website at http://www.nortelnetworks.com/products/netmgmt.

Website Reporting and Traffic Analysis

Now that you have deployed this rocking Commerce Server 2000 production environment and are transacting business, people are going to start screaming for reports. The two most widely deployed products on the market today are WebTrends (www.webtrends.com) and Accrue's Hit List (www.accrue.com). Both of these products provide real-time reporting and traffic analysis of your site. Quest Software (www.quest.com) also has a very popular web reporting tool called Funnel Web.

WebTrends Live provides real-time traffic analysis without need for additional hardware or software. It is an ASP service offered via the web. This is highly attractive for companies, as they do not have to incur additional cost purchasing, deploying and maintaining additional hardware. This also provides up to the minute analytical reporting. Pricing depends on maximum page views per month and ranges from $25 to $6000 per month. You can obtain more information from their website at http://www.webtrendslive.com.

You can also purchase their reporting software that will run within your environment. The software starts at $6000 for one server with unlimited access. They also offer high-end software solutions that not only provide reporting and traffic analysis, but business logic to help you market effectively and retain customers. More information can be found on their site at http://www.webtrends.com.

Accrue Hit List provides the same functionality as WebTrends and is purchased in modules. The pricing starts at $15,000 and goes up from there. This product used to be owned by MarketWave and was once an off-the-shelf reporting and traffic analysis product. Accrue has since broadened its scope to include marketing analysis and customer loyalty statistics. You can obtain more information from their site at http://www.accrue.com.

Another reporting and analysis product that has gained popularity due to its ease of use and quick reporting is Quest Software's Web Funnel. This product was purchased from ActiveConcepts to be added into their WebQA suite. While it doesn't supply real-time analysis reporting, it crunches logs faster than the other two products discussed, reducing the necessity for a real-time solution. The software starts at $500 for the standard version and $1200 for the enterprise version. This product is aimed at the small- to medium-size e-commerce companies looking for a reliable cost-effective reporting and analysis solution. More information can be found at http://www.quest.com.

The above products are just examples of the many that are available on the market today. In the end it doesn't matter what solution you choose as long as you can provide daily trend and analysis reporting to the executive management. Without these reports, the executive management is blind to market changes that could make or break your company.

When deploying a reporting and analysis solution, consider posting the reports to your organization's intranet website. This allows quick dissemination of valuable data throughout your company with little administrative overhead.

Additionally, Commerce Server 2000 provides a lot of the same information as the above products through the data warehouse. It provides reporting on basic website performance, advertising efficiency, customer profile (average number of products bought, average total, etc.) most popular products, etc. These reports are run through the Business Desk Analysis modules and this is discussed in detail in Chapter 5. While the Biz Desk analytics may not give you as comprehensive a reporting structure for website performance, it may satisfy your organization's needs without the additional cost of these third party solutions.

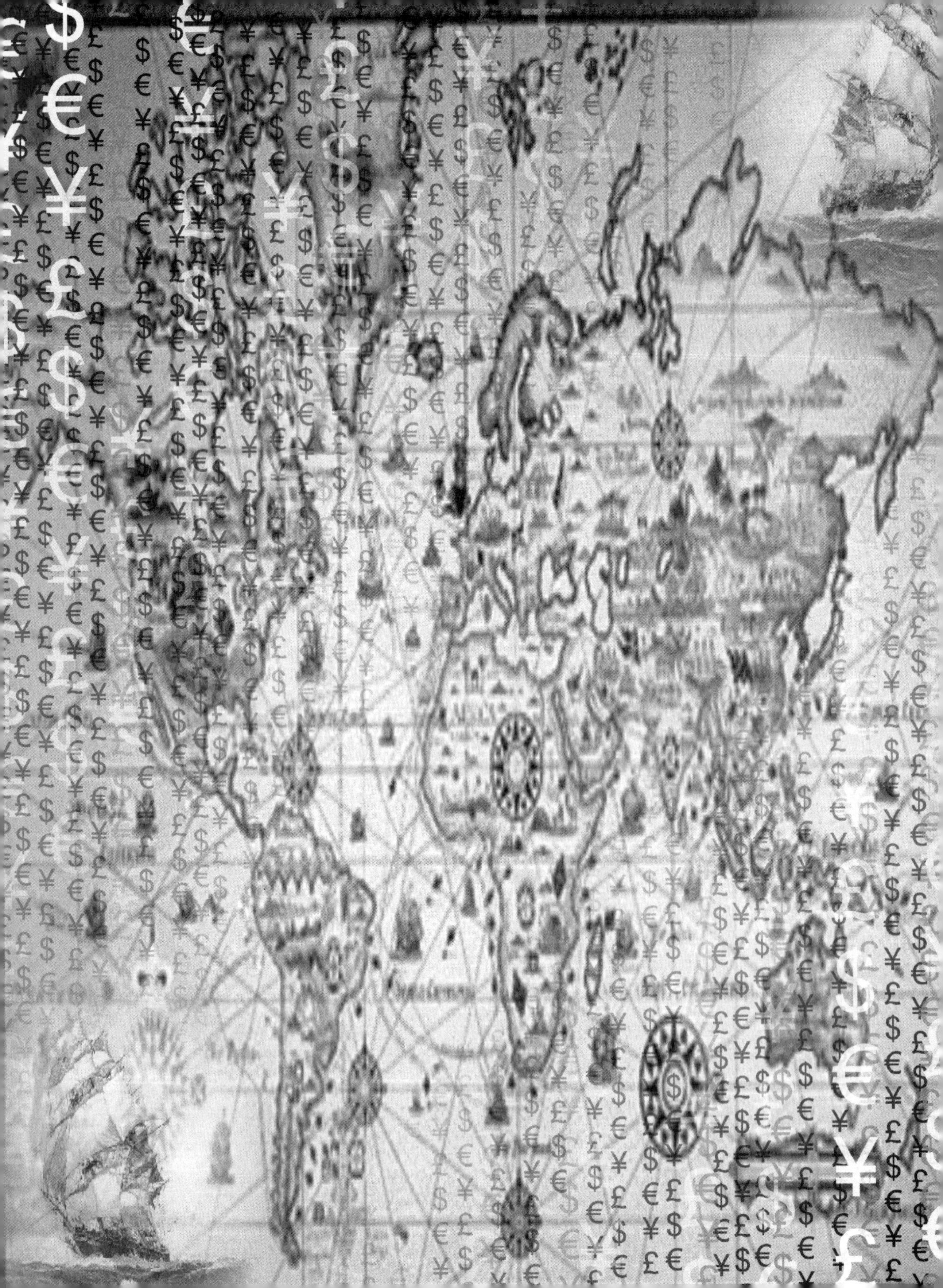

Index

A Guide to the Index

The index is arranged hierarchically, in alphabetical order, with symbols preceding the letter A. Most second-level entries and many third-level entries also occur as first-level entries. This is to ensure that users will find the information they require however they choose to search for it.

E

O

retail_commerce database, 57
iOrderGroupID, 370
retail_dw database, 57
RetailBizDesk
create VID project for, 685
Retained in Memory checkbox
pipeline wizard, 346
Retry Queue, 742
robots
see crawlers.
RootCategories method
ProductCatalog object, 181
RootObject, 284
routers revisited, 1017
RowCollection object
methods and properties, 923
RUCache object
least used cache, 411
Lookup method, 411
LookupObject method, 411

S

SANS Institute
securing the environment, 1044
Save method
ExpressionBuilder HTC, 676
SaveReceipt, 310
DBStorage object used to save orders, 310
Scheduled Queue, 742
Scheduler Engine
XLANG Schedules, invoked through, 748
Schema Extender sample application, 233
creating classes, 236
creating data members, 244
creating keys, 250
creating relations, 255
data source, selecting, 235
extending RegisteredUser class, 259
schema of data warehouse, 220, 231
adding data members to existing classes, 244
creating classes, 236
data source, selecting, 235
turning edit mode on, 241
schemas
Active Directory, 496
data warehouse, 220, 231
extending data warehouse schema, 232
turning edit mode on, 241
XML, 325
schemas quick reference, 963
XML introduction, 964
XML structures, 964
analysis XML structure, 965
analysis/reporting, 964
SCMP
used by CyberSource, 607
ScoreDiscounts component
Content Selection pipeline, 401
scores, 312
scripted pipeline components, 340
Scriptor, 293, 332
AIC, create, 756
example, 334
filesystemobject object, 757

internal and external components, 332
OrderForm object, 757
standards, 332
Search
carried forward in SharePoint, 810
search support
free-text search, 201
query, 205
specification search, 205
SearchableCategories property
ProductCatalog object
specification searches example, 209
Secure Intrusion Detection System, 1024
Secure Scanner, 1022
securing the environment
CERT Coordination Center, 1044
IIS, 1047
Internet Security Systems, 1045
SANS Institute, 1044
Security Notification Service, 1044
SQL Server, 1052
TechNet Security Website, 1044
Windows 2000
security recommendations, 1045
Windows IT Security, 1045
security
see also network security.
Active Directory, 494
authentication, 109
setting access permissions, 725
security descriptors, 494
Security Notification Service
securing the environment, 1044
segment analysis, 220
Segment Model
analyzing, 454
creating, 453
Segment Viewer tool
analyzing, 454
create lists of user records, 459
Property/Value pairs, 454
segmentation, 264
Select method
ListSheet HTC, 674
SelectAll method
ListSheet HTC, 674
SelectAllRows method
ListSheet HTC, 659
Selected property
EditField HTC, 650
ListSheet HTC, 674
Send E-mail stage, 480
serializer
creates file format, 734
Server Administration
Console is visual representation of BizTalk Server
components, 741
MMC snap-in, 741
Server Groups, 741
expand groups, 743
server farm layout, 1016
Server Groups
features held in common, 742
Server object
CreateObject calls, 813

1089

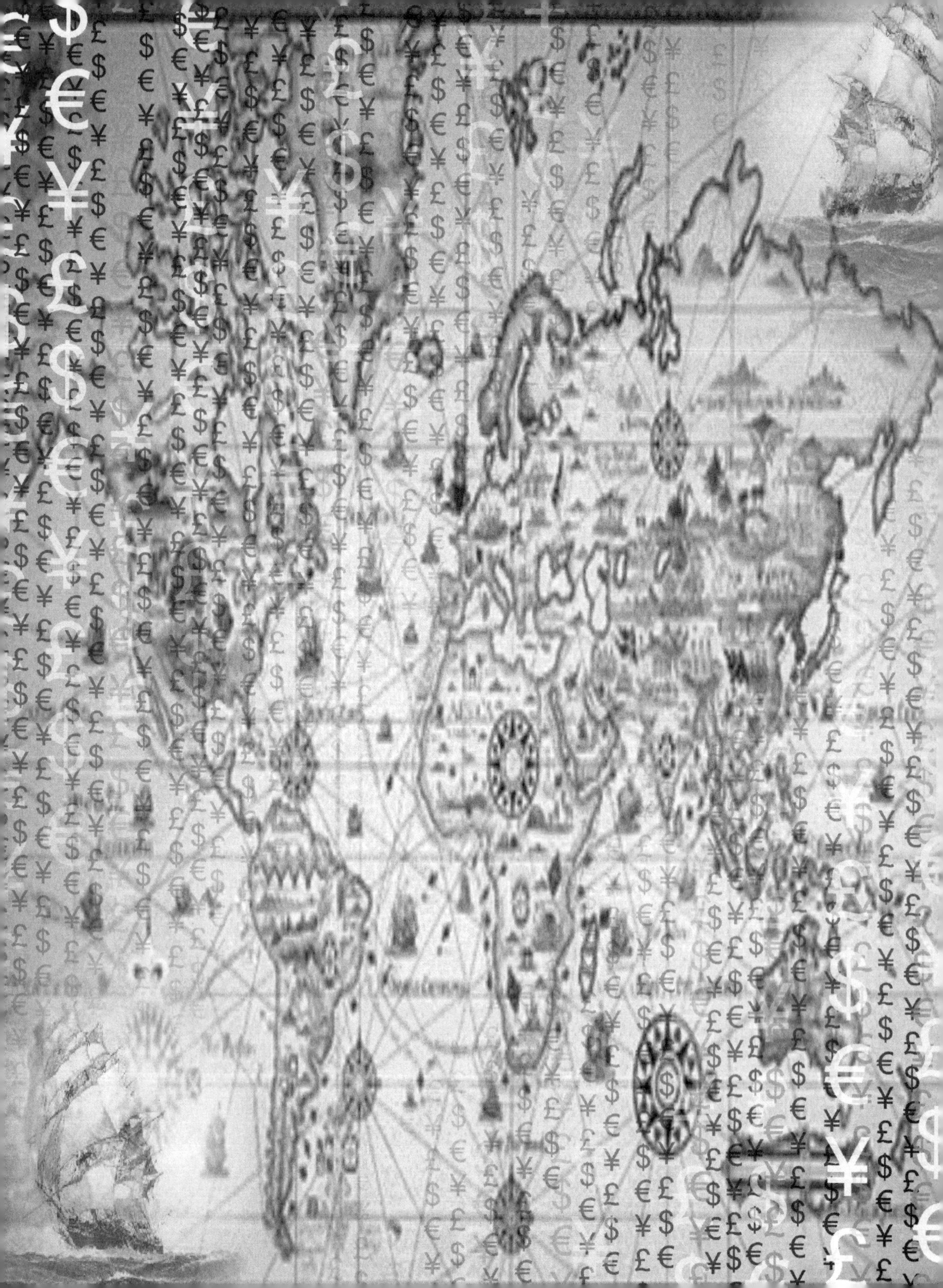

p2p.wrox.com
The programmer's resource centre

A unique free service from Wrox Press
with the aim of helping programmers to help each other

Wrox Press aims to provide timely and practical information to today's programmer. P2P is a list server offering a host of targeted mailing lists where you can share knowledge with your fellow programmers and find solutions to your problems. Whatever the level of your programming knowledge, and whatever technology you use, P2P can provide you with the information you need.

ASP
Support for beginners and professionals, including a resource page with hundreds of links, and a popular ASP+ mailing list.

DATABASES
For database programmers, offering support on SQL Server, mySQL, and Oracle.

MOBILE
Software development for the mobile market is growing rapidly. We provide lists for the several current standards, including WAP, WindowsCE, and Symbian.

JAVA
A complete set of Java lists, covering beginners, professionals,and server-side programmers (including JSP, servlets and EJBs)

.NET
Microsoft's new OS platform, covering topics such as ASP+, C#, and general .Net discussion.

VISUAL BASIC
Covers all aspects of VB programming, from programming Office macros to creating components for the .Net platform.

WEB DESIGN
As web page requirements become more complex, programmer sare taking a more important role in creating web sites. For these programmers, we offer lists covering technologies such as Flash, Coldfusion, and JavaScript.

XML
Covering all aspects of XML, including XSLT and schemas.

OPEN SOURCE
Many Open Source topics covered including PHP, Apache, Perl, Linux, Python and more.

FOREIGN LANGUAGE
Several lists dedicated to Spanish and German speaking programmers, categories include .Net, Java, XML, PHP and XML.

How To Subscribe

Simply visit the P2P site, at **http://p2p.wrox.com/**

Select the 'FAQ' option on the side menu bar for more information about the subscription process and our service.

wrox

PROGRAMMER TO PROGRAMMER™

Wrox writes books for you. Any suggestions, or ideas about how you want information given in your ideal book will be studied by our team. Your comments are always valued at Wrox.

Free phone in USA 800-USE-WROX
Fax (312) 893 8001

UK Tel. (0121) 687 4100   Fax (0121) 687 4101

Professional Commerce Server 2000 - Registration Card

Name _____

Address _____

_____

_____

_____

City_____ State/Region _____

Country_____ Postcode/Zip_____

E-mail _____

Occupation _____

How did you hear about this book?_____

☐ Book review (name) _____

☐ Advertisement (name) _____

☐ Recommendation _____

☐ Catalog_____

☐ Other _____

Where did you buy this book? _____

☐ Bookstore (name)_____ City _____

☐ Computer Store (name)_____

☐ Mail Order _____

☐ Other _____

What influenced you in the purchase of this book?

☐ Cover Design

☐ Contents

☐ Other (please specify) _____

How did you rate the overall contents of this book?

☐ Excellent   ☐ Good

☐ Average   ☐ Poor

_____

What did you find most useful about this book? _____

_____

What did you find least useful about this book? _____

_____

Please add any additional comments. _____

_____

What other subjects will you buy a computer book on soon? _____

_____

What is the best computer book you have used this year?

_____

Note: This information will only be used to keep you updated about new Wrox Press titles and will not be used for any other purpose or passed to any other third party.

wrox
PROGRAMMER TO PROGRAMMER™

NB. If you post the bounce back card below in the UK, please send it to:

Wrox Press Ltd., Arden House, 1102 Warwick Road,
Acocks Green, Birmingham B27 6BH. UK.

———— *Computer Book Publishers* ————

NO POSTAGE
NECESSARY
IF MAILED
IN THE
UNITED STATES

BUSINESS REPLY MAIL
FIRST CLASS MAIL   PERMIT#64   CHICAGO, IL

POSTAGE WILL BE PAID BY ADDRESSEE

WROX PRESS INC.,
29 S. LA SALLE ST.,
SUITE 520
CHICAGO IL 60603-USA